A Tale of Two Prime Ministers

Who Won The Legal Battle But Lost The Regime

First Edition 2015

A Tale of Two Prime Ministers

Who Won The Legal Battle But Lost The Regime

Justice S.N. Aggarwal
Former Judge, Punjab & Haryana High Court

Foreword by
Justice R.M. Lodha
Former Chief Justice of India

Two Words by
Justice Ashok Bhan
Former Judge Supreme Court of India

Universal Law Publishing
an imprint of LexisNexis

LexisNexis®

This book is a publication of **LexisNexis®**
(A Division of Reed Elsevier India (Pvt) Ltd)
14th floor, Building No 10, Tower–B, DLF Cyber City, Phase-II,
Gurgaon–122002, Haryana, India.
Tel : + 91 124 4774444 Fax: + 91 124 4774100

Website : www.lexisnexis.co.in / E-mail : help.in@lexisnexis.com

---

Justice S.N. Aggarwal, *A Tale of Two Prime Ministers,* First Edition, 2015

ISBN: 978-93-5035-610-4

Printed by: Sanat Printers (Haryana)

Printed and bound in India.

DEDICATED TO

MY REVERED PARENTS WHO LIVED A SIMPLE LIFE BUT RICH WITH MORAL, ETHICAL, SPIRITUAL AND PATRIOTIC VALUES

JUSTICE S.N. AGGARWAL

R.M. Lodha
Former Chief Justice of India

C-61, First Floor
Soami Nagar
(Near Panchsheel Enclave, 'A' Block)
New Delhi-110017
Tel: 011-26493040

FOREWORD

"Be you never so high, the Law is above you" stated Dr. Thomas Fuller way back in 1733 (Gnomologia: Adageis and Proverbs). In a country governed by the rule of law, no one is above law. All are subject to the same law; there is no special law which deals with Prime Ministers. Our Constitution requires that laws be equal in operation for all including the government.

S.N. Aggarwal, a former High Court judge, in his latest book, *'A Tale of Two Prime Ministers Who Won The Legal Battle But Lost The Regime'* has put together two judgments, one delivered by the Supreme Court of India in an election appeal arising from the judgment of Allahabad High Court unseating a Prime Minister of her parliamentary election on the ground of corrupt practices and the other by the Delhi High Court in a criminal appeal arising from the judgment of a special court convicting a former Prime Minister of criminal conspiracy and bribery. Both of them were successful in their appeals albeit on different grounds but lost in people's court.

Proclamation of Emergency was felt by the people of India as utter disregard for democracy. They were hugely shocked by its ugly manifestations and their discontentment was reflected in the ballot boxes. In the words of Jayaprakash Narayan, '...........freedom is indivisible and dictatorship anywhere is a threat to freedom everywhere.' In a democracy of the people, for the people and by the people, the constitutional fundamentals, ethos and values must be respected by the political class at all times.

General erosion of moral values and adoption of unethical means in achieving the political goals have robbed the country of its legitimate benefits. Corruption is the worst enemy of the country. The biggest loss that may occur due to corruption is loss of our confidence in democracy. India being the largest democracy of over 1.25 billion people cannot afford corruption because we cannot allow democracy to be weakened and fail our great Constitution.

The events immediately preceding and following the two judgments clearly tell us one thing: Don't take people of India for granted. They know who to elect and when to throw a government out.

Justice Aggarwal's work may be of interest to those who want to understand a few important events which took place after independence of the country.

R.M. LODHA
Former Chief Justice of India

Justice Ashok Bhan
Former Judge
Supreme Court of India

TWO WORDS

JUSTICE, SOCIAL, ECONOMIC AND POLITICAL was the spirit and vision of our CONSTITUTION which "WE, THE PEOPLE OF INDIA" gave "TO OURSELVES" on "twenty-sixth day of November 1949".

JUSTICE, Social, Economic and Political were to be achieved by democratic process based on Universal Franchise. Foundations of democracy were dug deep by Shri Jawaharlal Nehru, first Prime Minister of India and during his tenure for long 17 years, it got cemented and strengthened.

The foundations of our democratic set-up were jolted and shaken by his daughter Mrs. Indira Gandhi who assumed the office as third Prime Minister of our country in 1966 by imposing Emergency on the night intervening 25th and 26th June, 1975. As the foundations of democracy were strong and deep, she could not sustain the emergency for long and declared elections in the beginning of 1977 in which she suffered an ignoble defeat first ever in her political career.

Though we have given political justice, we have not been able to give social and economic justice to our people because of all-pervading corruption in all walks of life. Even two Prime Ministers of our country could not escape the allegations of misuse of official position/corruption. They were tried in the Court of Law; they were found guilty by the lower Courts but were acquitted of all such charges by the higher Courts either because of the amendment of law with retrospective effect or on technical grounds.

Justice S.N. Aggarwal has compiled the judgments of these two events of historical value in proper perspective for the use of posterity. Justice Aggarwal is democrat at heart and deeply feels hurt about the frittering away of the gains of democracy by petty-minded people. He has a patriotic fervour and gets emotionally upset for the sufferings of those who languished for long periods in the British jails or gave their lives under the British rule for the freedom of our country. This is evident from the book titled THE HEROES OF CELLULAR JAIL written by him about the revolutionary patriots who suffered innumerous cruelties in the Cellular Jail during the independence struggle.

I hope this book will be well received by the readers.

I wish him all success. I am sure he will keep up his passion in the future also.

JUSTICE ASHOK BHAN

1st May, 2015
Chandigarh

Res.: 302, Sector 10-B Chandigarh - 160011
Tel.: +91-172-2742084 Mobile: +91-9868219003, +91-8968962737 E-mail: justicebhan@yahoo.co.in

JUSTICE S.N. AGGARWAL
Former Judge
Punjab & Haryana High Court
Former President
Punjab State Consumer Disputes
Redressal Commission

House No. 1458, Sector 40-B
Chandigarh-160036
Phone : 0172-2626800
Mobile : 09876716983

PREFACE

This book contains the judgments and news reports which show that two Prime Ministers, Mrs. Indira Gandhi and P.V. Narasimha Rao won the legal battle but lost the regime.

The only difference is that the Prime Minister Indira Gandhi had won the legal battle first on 7-11-1975 when her appeal was accepted by the Supreme Court and the judgment of the Allahabad High Court setting aside her election as Member, Lok Sabha from Raebareli for adopting *'Corrupt Practices'*, was set aside. However, she had lost the Lok Sabha elections and also the regime in March, 1977.

Converse is the case of Prime Minister P.V. Narasimha Rao as he had lost the regime first in 1996, (although he himself was elected as Member, Lok Sabha) but won the legal battle later on 15 March, 2002 when his appeal was accepted by the Delhi High Court and the judgment of the Special Court, New Delhi, convicting and sentencing him in a case of conspiracy and bribery relating to the No Trust Motion in July, 1993 when he was the Prime Minister, was set aside.

What drived me to collect these judgments and place them in the form of this book is that, not ordinary mortals, but two Prime Ministers of our country were locked in the litigation. In one case Prime Minister of the country was the party. In the other case Prime Minister was the party when the case started but after the regime was lost, the legal battle was won. The facts and circumstances of these cases and the judgments were of great significance which changed the course of history of our country. There is no parallel to these cases of any other Prime Minister.

The question that begs an answer is that when these two Prime Ministers won in the Law Courts, how was it that they lost their regime. Most humbly, I leave it open to the readers and the future generation to assess the reasons; whether it was the maturity of voters of our largest democracy that they can seat and unseat even the established regimes and even the Prime Ministers if they choose to do so or whether these facts reveal something much more?

Chandigarh
August 2015

JUSTICE S.N. AGGARWAL

JUSTICE S.N. AGGARWAL
Former Judge
Punjab & Haryana High Court
Former President
Punjab State Consumer Disputes
Redressal Commission

House No. 1458, Sector 40-B
Chandigarh-160036
Phone : 0172-2626800
Mobile : 09876716983

ACKNOWLEDGMENTS

I will be failing in my duty if I do not acknowledge the help and guidance I received from various sources while writing this book.

First and foremost my thoughts go to Param Pujya Sudhanshu Ji Maharaj who has always showered his blessings on me in abundance. His inspiring words always keep me in high spirits and impel me to do something which may be of some use to the society. This book is also a result of motivation from His Holiness.

I shall ever remain indebted to Hon'ble Mr. Justice R.M. Lodha former Chief Justice of India who has very kindly contributed the FOREWORD to this book. The thoughts penned in the FOREWORD by a jurist of his eminence, are a significant contribution and a valuable addition to this book which I certainly consider is a matter of great honour for me. I express my gratitude to Hon'ble Mr. Justice R.M. Lodha.

I also feel obliged to Hon'ble Mr. Justice D.K. Jain, President, National Consumer Disputes Redressal Commission, New Delhi (former Judge, Supreme Court of India). Hon'ble Mr. Justice D.K. Jain has always been benevolent to me and a guiding force since the days he was Chief Justice of Punjab and Haryana High Court and I was a Judge in that High Court. In this book also the help rendered to me by Hon'ble Mr. Justice D.K. Jain is very significant.

I also express my gratitude to Hon'ble Mr. Justice Ashok Bhan, former Judge, Supreme Court of India. His doors are always open for me and the warmth I enjoy while conversing with him, cannot be explained in words. Hon'ble Mr. Justice Ashok Bhan has very kindly contributed 'TWO WORDS' to this book which has added to its worth and which is matter of great honour to me.

My dear friend Mr. T.C. Gupta, former IAS officer is always ready for rendering any help to me by sparing his valuable time from his busy schedule. I just take the raw material to him and he presses into service his wisdom and craftsmanship of words to convert it into a presentable item. He is so humble that he never claims credit for it, although from the core of my heart I always feel indebted to him.

My friend Iqbal Singh Sidhu, former IAS Officer, now Member, Right to Service Commission, Punjab encouraged me while I was in the process of preparing the manuscript of this book. His encouragement means a lot to me as he has stood with me for the last more than three decades.

My son Harsh Aggarwal, Advocate, Punjab and Haryana High Court, though remains extremely busy in his professional commitments, has helped me in tracing out the reported judgments and transferring the same on to my laptop. He always spares time for me almost every day for exchange of views and shares thoughts on the subject in hand. This process not only takes away my weariness but also moulds my thought process for the better. He has played a big role in giving final shape to the book.

I express my thanks to the Protocol branch of Punjab and Haryana High Court which facilitated me to get copies of some of the Judgments, from the proper sources. I am also thankful to the staff of the Judges' Library of this High Court for tracing out some of the judgments for me. I also availed the help from Dwarka Dass Library Sector 15 Chandigarh for which I am thankful to Ms. Alka, Assistant Librarian.

Last of all but not the least, I express my deep gratitude to Shri Manish Arora, Director, Universal Law Publishing, New Delhi who while accepting the book for publication made valuable suggestions and improved the quality of the book. It is my third book being published by this well-known Publishing Company. I am thankful also to his editorial staff especially to Shri Hasan Imam who did his job very well and devotedly, in spite of last stage changes made by me.

Chandigarh
August 2015

JUSTICE S.N. AGGARWAL

CONTENTS

TABLE OF CASES

D

E

F

G

M

N

S

T

U

V

W

Y

INTRODUCTION

The theory of *'DHARMA'* has come to us from our *Rishis and Munis* of yore. It is a term of wider import which takes in its sweep both legal duty and ethical values. Some acts may be legally right but may fail the test of moral values. The legal rights can be enforced in law Courts but the moral values rest with the Conscience of a human being. Our sages have taught us since ages that conscience guides the human beings to walk on the right path. Any person, especially the one, while holding public office, does not follow the dictates of conscience and departs from moral and ethical values, falls in the eyes of the public.

Mahatma Gandhi in his political life followed the principles of 'Truth' and 'Non-violence'. He also believed in self-sacrifice and not in selfish interest. These are the basics of moral and ethical values. Mahatma Gandhi made these principles the *mool mantra* of his fight against the mighty British Empire for the freedom of our country.

In the independent India, right from the very beginning, certain things did not happen the way Gandhiji desired or even revolutionary patriots thought. Even during the life time of Mahatma Gandhi, the news about moral degradation of Congressmen and resort to corruption among some of them in power had started trickling in. Mahatma Gandhi had himself mentioned about it in his post-prayer speech. **This was highlighted in a front-page report by 'The Tribune' dated 14 January 1948 in the following words:—**

'Political Power has turned Their Heads'

"Moral Degradation of Congressmen"

> *"NEW DELHI. Jan. 13.- Gandhiji in his post-prayer speech yesterday read extracts from two letters complaining of the moral degradation into which the men in Congress circles have fallen. The letter said that the taste of political power had turned their heads and that some of the Congress M.L.As and M.L.Cs. were following the policy of "make hey while the sun shines"*
>
> *Gandhiji said:*
>
> *"I had told you yesterday of two letters from Andhra. One was from the aged friend, no other than Deshbakta Konda Venkatappayya Garu. I give here extracts from it:*
>
> *"The one great problem, apart from many other political and economical issues of very complicated nature, is the moral degradation into which the men in Congress circles have fallen. I cannot say much about other provinces. But in my province, the conditions are very deplorable. The taste of political power has turned their heads. Several of the M.L.As and M.L.Cs. are following the policy of make hey while the sun shines and making money by the use of influence, even to the extent of obstructing the administration of justice in criminal courts presided over by the magistrates. Even the district collectors and other revenue officials do not feel free in the discharge of their duties on account of the frequent interference by the M.L.As. and M.L.Cs. on behalf of their partisans. A strict and honest officer cannot hold his position, for false reports are carried against him to the ministers who easily lend their ears to these unprincipled self-seekers.*

'Political Power Has Turned Their Heads'

"Moral Degradation Of Congressmen"

NEW DELHI, Jan. 13.—Gandhiji in his post prayer speech yesterday read extracts from two letters complaining of the moral degradation into which the men in Congress circles had fallen. The letter said that the taste of political power had turned their heads and that some of the Congress M. L. As. and M L.Cs. were following the policy of "make hay while the sun shines."

Gandhiji said:

"I told you yesterday of two letters from Andhra. One was from the aged friend, no other than Deshabakta Konda Venkatappayya Garu. I give here extracts from it:

'The one great problem, apart from many other political and economic issues of very complicated nature, is the moral degradation into which the men in Congress circles have fallen. I cannot say much about other provinces. But in my province, the conditions are very deplorable. The taste of political power has turned their heads. Several of the M.L.As. and M.L.Cs. are following the policy of make hay while the sun shines and making money by the use of influence, even to the extent of obstructing the administration of justice in the criminal courts presided over by magistrates. Even the district collectors and other revenue officials do not feel free in the discharge of their duties on account of the frequent interference by the M.L.As. and M.L.Cs. on behalf of their partisans. A strict and honest officer cannot hold his position, for false reports are carried against him to the ministers who easily lend their ears to these unprincipled self-seekers.

All Moral Restrictions Gone

'Swaraj was the only all absorbing passion which goaded men and women to follow your leadership. But now that the goal had been reached, all moral restrictions have lost their power on most of the fighters in the great struggle who are joining hands even with those who were sworn opponents of the national movement and who, now, for their personal ends enlist themselves as Congress members.

'The situation is growing intolerable every day with the result that the Congress as well as the Congress Government have come into desrepute.

'The recent municipal elections in Andhra had proved how far and how fast the Congress is loosing its hold upon the people.

Elections Stopped

"The municipal elections in the town of Guntur were suddenly ordered to be stopped by an urgent message from the Minister for Local Bodies (Madras) after every preparation was made for carrying on elections. Only a nominated council was in power for, I believe the last ten years or more, and for nearly a year now the municipal administration has been in the hands of a Commissioner.

'Now the talk prevails that the Government would soon nominate councillors to take charge of the municipal affairs of this town. I, old, decrepit, and with a broken leg, slowly limping on the crutches within the walls of my house have no axe to grind. I no doubt entertain certain strong views against some of the leading Congressmen in the two parties into which the members of the provincial and district Congress committees now stand divided. And I have made no secret of my views.

Factions in Congress

'The factions in the Congress circles, the money making activities of several of the M.L.As.

He could only give first hand evidence about Andhra. Let us beware.

"My Bahawalpur friends, I have to ask to be patient. Sardar Sahib saw me only at noon. Being silent and preoccupied I could say or write nothing. Shri Shanker from his office was too busy to come so that I could not place your case before him and possibly save the Sardar's precious time"

—A.P.I.

"All Moral Restrictions Gone

"Swaraj was the only all absorbing passion which goaded men and women to follow your leadership. But now that the goal had been reached, all moral restrictions have lost their power on most of the fighters in the great struggle who are joining hands even with those who were sworn opponent of the national movement and who, now, for their personal ends enlist themselves as Congress members.

"The situation is growing intolerable every day with the result that the Congress as well as the Congress Government have come into disrepute.

"The recent municipal elections in Andhra had proved how far and how fast the Congress is loosing its hold on the people.

"Elections Stopped

"The municipal elections in the town of Guntur were suddenly ordered to be stopped by an urgent message from the Minister for Local Bodies (Madras) after every preparation was made for carrying on elections. Only a nominated council was in power for, I believe, the last ten years or more, and for nearly a year now the municipal administration has been in the hands of a Commissioner.

"Now the talk prevails that the Government would soon nominate councillors to take charge of the municipal affairs of this town. I, old, decrepit, and with a broken leg, slowly limping on the crutches within the walls of my house have no axe to grind. I, no doubt, entertain certain strong views against some of the leading Congressmen in the two parties into which the members of the provincial and district Congress committees now stand divided. And I have made no secret of my views.

"Factions in Congress

"The factions in the Congress circles, the money-making activities of several M.L.As. and M.L.Cs. and the weakness of the Ministers has been creating rebellious spirit amongst the people at large. The people have begun to say that the British Government was much better and they are even cursing the Congress.'

"Let the people of Andhra and the other provinces measure the words of this self-sacrificing-servant of India. As he rightly says- the corruption described by him is no monopoly of Andhra. He could only give first hand evidence about Andhra. Let us beware."

"My Bahawalpur friends, I have to ask to be patient. Sardar Sahib saw me only at noon. Being silent and pre-occupied, I could say or write nothing. Shri Shankar from his office was too busy to come so that I could not place your case before him and possibly save the Sardar's precious time".-A.P.I.

Before his assassination**, Mahatma Gandhi left a Commandment** of great resonance for the national leaders that in Free India they would work to **'wipe every tear from every eye'.**

Sardar Patel also addressed '**a word to the Congressmen**' as to how they should conduct themselves in public life. He said:

'For long years I have worked as a soldier of the Congress. I still consider myself a soldier though many call me a Sardar. To my fellow-soldiers, I respectfully submit that our only aim to power and authority springs from our having followed Mahatma Gandhi in the fight for India's freedom. Any further and future claim or honour that we find shall also be through sacrifice for the poor and the downtrodden. Humility is a Congressman's first requisite because that is the badge of service. Our proper place is not at the vantage points of power but at vantage points of service. Who shall be Ministers, and where shall state capitals and other things be located are matters

> *for small people to talk or write about. Congressmen will be forced and pushed into seats of power if they are true Congressmen.*
>
> *"For years I never spoke from a Congress platform. Even now I fear to make a speech, lest some unguarded word of mine should hurt somebody's feelings or interests. It would be unbefitting a servant. A soldier keeps his feet firmly on the soil. He is not afraid to fall. But those who have risen high, risk a fall if they are not careful. Hence those in positions of authority should be watchful day and night. Let Congressmen eschew desire for power. Let able workers be brought forward. If it becomes necessary for us to sit in seats of authority, let our hands be clean, our tongues mild, our hearts sound and our vision clear."* (*see* the FOREWORD at page XII by Durga Das Editor-in-Chief 'SARDAR PATEL'S CORRESPONDENCE 1945-50 Volume X').

From the narration given above, one thing is clear that the leading figures of those times, who fought for the independence of the country, attached utmost importance to moral and ethical values. The wording of the Oath as prescribed by the Founding Fathers in the Constitution also imposed upon the high office holders to swear or solemnly affirm that *'....I will faithfully and conscientiously discharge my duties as a Minister for the Union and that I will do right to all manner of people in accordance with the Constitution and the law, without fear or favour, affection or ill-will'*. It was all the more necessary for the Prime Minister who is to decide the destiny of the country and the countrymen, to follow the moral and ethical values *i.e.,* DHARMA. They were to develop the spirit of self-sacrifice and not of selfish-interest.

There are many shining examples before the Nation. Lal Bahadur Shastri was the Railway Minister in Jawaharlal Nehru's Government. A railway accident took place for which he was not liable personally but owning moral responsibility, he resigned from his office. Three Hon'ble Judges of the Supreme Court resigned after a Judge junior to them was elevated as Chief Justice in 1975 by the Indira Gandhi Government. A few months later another Supreme Court Judge resigned after a Judge junior to him was elevated as Chief Justice again by the Indira Gandhi Government. Similarly Bharat Ratna Atal Bihari Vajpayee took no time to resign as PM, when he lost the trust motion just by one vote in the Lok Sabha. He was guided by his moral principles and values. In the fresh elections that followed, the people of India rewarded him, by giving the NDA absolute majority in the Lok Sabha. The recent example is of Naval Chief of India, Admiral D.K. Joshi who resigned as Naval Chief following mishaps involving naval ships on moral ground only. Those are the sterling examples of moral courage and rectitude which should guide the actions of the people holding high public offices.

It appears that the message of Mahatma Gandhi, the patriarch of Congress Party which was binding on all the Indian Prime Ministers especially on the Congress leaders and Prime Ministers to wipe out '**every tear from every eye**' and of Sardar Patel as to how Congressmen should conduct themselves in public life while in power or even without it, just remained on the pages of history without being followed with seriousness and concerted efforts.

The facts as to how these two Prime Ministers were arraigned in litigation are that in the case of Indira Gandhi, she was declared successful in the Parliamentary elections held in March, 1971 and was sworn-in as the Prime Minister. Her election was challenged by her opponent Raj Narain by filing an election petition in the Allahabad High Court. To make infructuous a plea taken by the petitioner in the election petition which was supported by an earlier Supreme Court Judgment, Indira Gandhi got amended the provisions of The Representation of the People Act on 19 October, 1974 by Act 58 of 1974 with retrospective effect. The amendment proved inconsequential, as her election was set aside by the Allahabad High Court by holding her **guilty of 'corrupt practices'** under section 123(7) of Representation of People Act, 1951 on two other grounds *vide* judgment dated 12-6-1975.

Indira Gandhi filed an appeal before the Apex Court. Raj Narain also filed counter-appeal. During the pendency of these cross-appeals, Indira Gandhi got amended the Representation of People Act again on August 6, 1975 when the Parliament passed the Election Laws (Amendment) Act, 1975 (Act 40 of 1975) with retrospective effect to nullify both the grounds on which the decision of the Allahabad High Court was based.

What was far more significant was, Indira Gandhi succeeded in pushing through Parliament, Constitution (39th Amendment) Act, 1975 on 10 August, 1975 with retrospective effect which was of far-reaching consequences. By this Constitutional amendment not only review jurisdiction of the Supreme Court was taken away by placing both the amendments (Act 40 of 1975 and Act 58 of 1974) in 9th Schedule of the Constitution but also added Article 329A. Clause (4) of Article 329A freed the disputed election of the Prime Minister from the restraints of all election laws. It declared such election as valid notwithstanding any judgment. Clause (5) ordained that any appeal or cross appeal pending before the Supreme Court shall be disposed of in conformity with the provisions of clause (4). Although clause (4) of Article 329A of the Constitution was set aside, but her appeal was accepted by the Supreme Court in view of the amended Representation of People Act *vide* judgment dated 7-11-1975.

After the election of Indira Gandhi was set aside by the Allahabad High Court on 12 June, 1975, she imposed internal Emergency on the night intervening 25 and 26 June, 1975 under the cover of darkness on an unsuspecting nation, put thousands of public-spirited Indians including Jayaprakash Narayan and the main opposition leaders in the jails, suspended the fundamental rights of the citizens, gagged the Press, reduced the important institutions to one-man show, were among some of the black deeds perpetrated during the Emergency days. These actions of Indira Gandhi were totally bereft of moral values and were intended to stay in power.

It was reported in the newspapers that during the Emergency days, not only Indira Gandhi herself committed excesses, even some of the Ministers were in some way or the other linked with abhorable measures like coercive sterilisation, imposition of an extra-constitutional authority, stifling of the mass media and devaluing the Judiciary. They had been responsible for manipulation of news, and other distortions of the mass media. To the dismay of seasoned journalists, they were told to 'behave' as if the Fourth Estate in the country was on probation. Some distinguished editors refused to acquiesce in the 'diktat' of the concerned minister at the cost of the publication of their journals. For most people, especially in the countryside, the issue was doubtlessly not joined till the police force was extensively used to drag thousands and thousands to hastily set up and ill-equipped vasectomy camps for sterilization. But these often illiterate and desperately poor people were quick to realize that their dignity as human beings could not have been trampled upon so brazenly, arbitrarily and dictatorially unless the Press had been completely muffled, the Courts deprived of their authority and Parliament reduced to a rubber stamp and Cabinet Ministers to the status of hapless spectators or court jesters.

Mrs. Indira Gandhi interfered, by way of Forty-second Amendment in the Constitution of India, with the normal duration of 5 years term of the Parliament as laid down in Article 83 of the Constitution and it was made 6 years term.

Sometimes one is misguided, by the coterie around him or her for their selfish ends. It so happened in the case of Indira Gandhi that she convinced herself that she alone could save India from a looming doom. 'India was Indira' 'Indira was India' was the popular refrain of those days. It has also been enunciated by Hon'ble Pranab Mukherjee, who was in June, 1975, Minister of State in the Indira Gandhi Cabinet and now the President of India, in his latest book titled, "**The Dramatic Decade: The Indira Gandhi Years**" which hit the stands recently, that *"Once the Emergency was declared, many people claimed credit for the idea behind it. But these very people took a sharp about-turn when the Shah Commission was set up to look into the 'Excesses'. Not only did they disown their involvement, they pinned all the blame on Indira Gandhi"*.

Emergency was disliked by many well-meaning people in authority. Scores of High Court Judges refused to be intimidated and gave judgments on merits, at considerable risk to themselves, as these were inconvenient to the ruling clique. A large number of senior civil servants made no secret of their abhorrence of what was going on in the name of discipline.

In the normal course the next elections were due in 1976 after the 1971 elections, but because its tenure was extended by another one year, the next elections were announced in January, 1977. It appears that before announcing the elections, Mrs. Indira Gandhi was convinced, though mistakenly, that she had everything sewed up neatly for her. The opposition, she calculated, would remain splintered, would be in no position to raise the necessary resources by way of men or money, indeed, might not be able even to field a sufficient number of candidates. The press was too terrorized to raise its voice; the mass media were firmly under her control. The people could be managed with the help of an 'obliging' bureaucracy. In the process, she thought, she would not only regain her legitimacy but also pave the way for the 'son' by choosing 150 to 200 candidates from among the youth Congress.

During the elections the loud claims the 'dynamic' decade under Mrs. Gandhi's leadership, 'Gains' of the emergency in terms of stable prices, the record rise in exports and the highest ever foreign exchange reserves were propagated. Finding things re-bouncing, Mrs. Gandhi and her colleagues spoke more loudly about their innocence. The more, they made claims of gains or pleaded innocence of excesses, the more the public realised the sins of the last 19 months. Indira Gandhi camp then compaigned that the alleged excesses committed during the sterilization camps have been grossly exaggerated by the Press and the opposition. Although the Chief Ministers of the States tried to excel each other in giving utmost importance to Sanjay Gandhi but Indira Gandhi camp denied if extra-constitutional centre of power ever existed or exercised any executive authority.

The Indian people practised non-violent non-cooperation, in the emergency dark days, with the government on a far bigger scale than during the freedom struggle itself when Gandhiji himself was in command. The resistance was not active in most cases and therefore not visible. On a surface view, the Indian nation lay prostrate for 19 long months at the feet of the all powerful Prime Minister and the small coterie around her from 26 June, 1975, when the emergency was imposed. From that time onward, they were waiting for an opportunity when they could sweep away the oppressors. When on 18 January, 1977, the sixth general election to the Lok Sabha were announced, they seized the opportunity with an enthusiasm that has never been witnessed in this country before. It was neither a general election nor a referendum in the general terms. For a vast majority of the people from metropolitan cities to the tiny villages in almost all, except few, parts of the country, it was like a second liberation struggle.

The 90-year-old congress party, which had provided coherence to Indian Polity in the 30 years of independence, with Indira Gandhi, once a great and popular leader in power for 11 years, has, in terms of seats, been reduced to a party confined to the southern States. The complete rout of the Congress in the entire Hindi-belt was the result of emergency excesses. The Congress Party could not win even a single seat out of the 57 constituencies which Indira Gandhi had visited in Uttar Pradesh during her hectic election campaign. What had caused this unimaginable defeat? And how it happened that the leader who was generally known to have a finger on the pulse of the people knew nothing about it? It was a political earthquake but "a triumph for the common man in India".

The popular verdict was certainly a total rejection of the emergency and of the men who, in the eyes of the people, were mainly responsible for creating the climate of fear. That was why none of the voters cared to ask what the Janata Party would do to hold the price line or meet the demands of the workers. They refused to be beguiled by the swelling foreign exchange reserves or the bulging stocks of rice or wheat in the godowns. They were clear only on one point. They wanted to have nothing to do with a regime that made a virtue of forcible sterilization, arbitrary arrests, choking up the channels of communication, nurturing a whole new breed of sycophants. India once again demonstrated that in a choice between democratic freedom and trains running on time, it will instinctively go for democracy.

Certain fundamental rights of the citizen suspended by a Presidential order under Article 359 of the Constitution following the proclamation of emergency in June, 1975 were restored after the trend of the election result was becoming clear in 1977 elections. These related to the rights conferred by Articles 14, 19, 21 and 22 of the Constitution of India. An official release from the Ministry of Home Affairs said that the earlier Presidential order had automatically lapsed, with the revocation of emergency.

The press release said: "Similarly, sections 15(A) of MISA and section 12 of COFEPOSA have also lapsed with the revocation of emergency on March 21. No separate action is required in this regard. The State Governments have already been advised to release all detenus held under the aforesaid provisions."

Parliamentary elections held in March, 1977 gave a thumping majority to Janata Party and Congress for Democracy combine. Shri Morarji Desai was elected as leader and was sworn-in as Prime Minister on 24 March, 1977. For Jayaprakash Narayan, it was the happiest day of his life. About Indira Gandhi he said: "She had got her deserts. She deserved it." Even the foreign press admired the love of Indians for democratic values.

So far as the second Prime Minister is concerned, P.V. Narasimha Rao was sworn-in as Prime Minister in 1991. No-Trust-Motion was moved against the Rao Government on 26 July, 1993 by CPI (M) Party MP and the voting had taken place on 28 July, 1993. Congress Party was 14 votes short from absolute majority but still the no-trust-motion was defeated. A complaint was filed on 1 February, 1996 with the CBI against Prime Minister P.V. Narasimha Rao and other Congressmen for criminal conspiracy and bribing of JMM MPs who had voted for defeating the No-Trust-Motion. No legal action was taken by the CBI. The complainant then filed writ petition in Delhi High Court. Notice was issued to the CBI as also to the Union of India. Additional Solicitor-General appeared and the Union of India had taken an objection on the maintainability of the Writ Petition which was rejected by the Delhi High Court. The Additional Solicitor-General told the Court that no Preliminay Enquiry has been held by the CBI, only complaint has been registered in the Complaint Register. On 20 March, 1996 the High Court directed the CBI to complete the investigation within a week. On 27 March the Additional Solicitor General told that FIR has been registered against the JMM MPs. On 12 April, 1996 the High Court directed the CBI to give a copy of the FIR to the complainant.

On 22 April the complainant filed the affidavit in the High Court that material facts stated in the complaint have not been incorporated in the FIR and it was a mockery of justice. The CBI could not explain the reasons for not doing so. In para 16 of the judgment it was observed by the High Court as under:—

> *"At this stage it deserves to be noticed that for existence of democracy and rule of law, which is life and blood of Constitution of India, probity in public life has to be maintained at every cost, whosoever may be the casualty and irrespective of height and might of person or his office. We may also notice that exercise of registration of a regular case/First Information Report under section 154 Criminal Procedure Code is not an idle formality".*

The CBI did not register the FIR on the basis of the complaint even after the passing of various interim orders by the Delhi High Court. The High Court quoted from a Supreme Court judgment that *"The quality of a nation's civilisation can be largely measured by the methods it uses in the enforcement of criminal law."* The High Court then directed the CBI *vide* detailed judgment dated 24 May, 1996 to register the FIR on the basis of the complaint and then investigate the case as per law.

A criminal case of conspiracy and bribery was registered against P.V. Narasimha Rao and some other Congressmen with the CBI on the direction of the Delhi High Court. After the completion of the trial, P.V. Narasimha Rao and Buta Singh were convicted *vide* judgment dated 29 September, 2000 and sentenced *vide* judgment dated 12 October, 2000. An appeal was filed by Shri Rao. It was accepted and Shri P.V. Narasimha Rao was acquitted by the Delhi High Court *vide* Judgment dated 15 March, 2002. The fact remains that CBI did not register the case on the basis of the facts stated in the complaint during the tenure of Shri Rao as Prime Minister. But it is also a fact that when the case was registered, Shri Rao faced trial for serious offences, relating to an occurrence of July, 1993 when he was the Prime Minister of the Country, for about 6 long years till his acquittal on 15 March, 2002.

Moreover when the elections took place in 1996 the writ petition filed by the complainant for registration of the criminal case against P.V. Narasimha Rao and other Congressmen was pending in the Delhi High Court. In the elections to the Lok Sabha held in 1996, BJP emerged as the single largest Party and with allies single largest group, Bharat Ratna Shri Atal Bihari Vajpayee was elected as leader of the House and he was sworn-in as Prime Minister on 16 May, 1996.

The proverb goes, 'Janata sab dekhti hai' or 'Janata sab janati hai'. (Public watches everything, Public knows everything). The public expects that the persons in public life must perform their legal duties coupled with ethical and moral values.

Shakespeare was right when he famously said that '**Caesar's wife must be above suspicion**'.

The spirit of renunciation is well known to Hindu philosophy of life. Mahatma Gandhi preferred to remain away from power after winning the freedom of the country even when nobody could have opposed him. Even Sardar Vallabhbai Patel, as a disciplined soldier of Gandhiji, respected his wishes and sacrificed the high office of Prime Ministership, although majority of Congressmen wanted Sardar to be the first Prime Minister of Independent India. It is clear from the article 'Sardar Vallabhbhai Patel-As I knew him' written by Morarji Desai (later on remained Prime Minister of India from 24 March, 1977 to 28 July, 1979) in the book 'THIS WAS SARDAR-THE COMMEMORATIVE VOLUME, VOL. I'. So also Jayaparkash Narayan could have become the Prime Minister in 1977 after he had led the opposition to defeat the Congress Party and their regime. These instances amply prove that the great people in India who feel bound by moral and ethical values do not care for power even when it comes their way of its own.

Every Constitutional functionary is supposed to work in accordance with the Constitution to meet the dreams of Mahatma Gandhi and to fulfil the aspirations of thousands of revolutionary patriots who had made supreme sacrifices for the independence of our country with a view to provide comfortable living to our countrymen.

I have reproduced the judgments of national importance in this book by collecting the same from different sources as also the news reports of the relevant period. I have also most humbly expressed my views, as above, having a bearing on the subjects of law, morality and ethics in the fond hope that the National leadership, State leadership, within power or without it, of all political parties, all public servants and the countrymen will always follow the rules of moral and ethical value, in the build up of our Nation, and will be guided by the noble principle handed down to us by the holy Scripture '**Mundaka Upanishad**' and which we have adopted as a **National Motto** on the independence of our country encapsuled in two words: '**SATYAMEVA JAYATE**'.

JUSTICE S.N. AGGARWAL

INDIRA NEHRU GANDHI

Equality is the faith and creed of our Democratic Republic and without it, neither the Constitution nor the laws made under it could reflect the common conscience of those who owe allegiance to them. And if they did not, they would fail to command respect and obedience without which any Constitution would be doomed to founder on the rocks of revolution.

Justice Y.V. Chandrachud

Para 678

SUPREME COURT OF INDIA

Raj Narain
v.
Smt. Indira Nehru Gandhi

AIR 1972 SC 1302: (1972) 3 SCR 841: (1972) 3 SCC 850

Before: K.S. Hegde, P. Jaganmohan Reddy and K.K. Mathew, JJ.

Civil Appeals Nos. 108 and 109 of 1972.

Dated 15.3.1972.

Judgment

Hegde, J.—1. These appeals by special leave arise from the election petition filed by the appellant challenging the validity of the election of respondent No. 1 (who will hereinafter be referred to as the respondent) to the Lok Sabha, from Raebareli constituency, in the General Election held in March, 1971.

APPLICATION FOR LEAVE TO SERVE INTERROGATORIES – OBJECTED BY RESPONDENT – ALLOWED BY HIGH COURT

2. After the pleadings of the parties were completed and the issues framed, the appellant applied to the Court under Order XI of the Civil Procedure Code for leave to deliver interrogatories in writing for the examination of the respondent. The respondent object to the same on the ground that the provisions of Order XI, Civil Procedure Code cannot be applied to election petitions. In her objection-statement, the respondent reserved her right to object to the interrogatories sought to be served at a later stage. The application filed by the appellant for leave to serve interrogatories on the respondent was heard by Broome J. The learned Judge by his order dated September 14, 1971 overruled the objections of the respondent and directed as follows:

> "Accordingly I allow the application A-29 and grant leave to the petitioner to deliver the accompanying interrogatories for the examination of respondent No. 1. The affidavit in reply shall be filed by 4-10-1971."

APPEAL FILED BY RESPONDENT – WITHDRAWN

3. The respondent appealed against the order to this Court after obtaining special leave. The appeal was withdrawn during the course of the hearing.

APPLICATION BY RESPONDENT – QUESTIONING SERVED INTERROGATORIES – APPLICATION ALLOWED – APPLICATION BY APPELLANT FOR AMENDING PETITION – DISMISSED – HENCE, TWO APPEALS BY APPELLANT

4. During the pendency of the appeal, the respondent filed an application before the High Court under rule 7, Order XI, Civil Procedure Code praying that the interrogatories served on her may be set aside as they were 'unreasonable, vexatious, oppressive, unnecessary and irrelevant." As many as 31 interrogatories had been served on the respondent. All these interrogatories object to each one of them. At the hearing of the petition, it appears it was contended on behalf of the respondent that the allegations in the election petition did not afford any basis for issues 1 to 3. Consequently the interrogatories served were irrelevant as well as unnecessary. The entire argument before the trial Judge proceeded on the basis that the facts stated in the petition did not disclose the corrupt practices which were the subject-matter of issues 1 to 3. The learned Judge accepted the contention and set aside some of the interrogatories served on the respondent. Proceeding further, he struck out issues 1 to 3. Thereafter the appellant applied to that Court for amendment of paragraphs 2 and 5 of the election petition by giving better particulars. The learned Judge rejected the application on the sole ground that by the amendment in question, the appellant was seeking to add to material facts and hence they cannot be accepted after the period of limitation for filing the election petition. Civil Appeal No. 108 of 1972 is directed against the Order setting aside the interrogatories served and the striking out of issues 1 to 3 and Civil Appeal No. 109 of 1972 arises from the order rejecting the application seeking permission to amend the election petition.

ISSUE NO. 2 NOT PRESSED – ISSUE NO. 3 LEFT OUT – ISSUE NO. 1 RECAST – SUPREME COURT HELD

5. Issue No. 2 had not been pressed before the trial court nor was it pressed before us. Therefore we need not consider whether that issue should be restored. Issue No. 3 is largely consequential to Issue No. 2 though a portion of that issue bears on issue No. 1. Hence, at present we are only concerned with Issue No. 1 and that portion of the third issue which has a bearing on Issue No. 1. Both those aspects will be covered if issue No. 1 is recast thus:

> "Whether respondent No. 1 obtained and procured the assistance of Yashpal Kapur in furtherance of the prospects of her election while he was still a Gazetted Officer in the service of Government of India. If so from what date?"

6. We can now leave out of consideration issue No. 3.

WHETHER ELECTION PETITION DISCLOSES 'CORRUPT PRACTICE' – QUESTION NEEDS CONSIDERATION – OBSERVED SUPREME COURT

7. The main question to be decided in these appeals is whether the allegations made in the election petition can be said to disclose the corrupt practice which is the subject matter of issue No. 1.

SECTION 123(7) OF THE REPRESENTATION OF THE PEOPLE ACT DEFINES 'CORRUPT PRACTICES' – REPRODUCED

8. Section 123 of the Representation of the People Act, 1951 (to be hereinafter referred to as the 'Act') begins by saying that "The following shall be deemed to be corrupt practices for the purposes of this Act."

9. Sub-section (7) of section 123 to the extent material for our present purpose reads:

> "The obtaining or procuring or abetting or attempting or obtain or procure by a candidate or his agent or, by any other person with the consent of a candidate or his election agent, any assistance (other than the giving of vote) for the furtherance of the prospects of that candidate's election, from any person in the service of the Government and belonging to any of the following classes, namely:
>
> (a) Gazetted Officers:
>
> x x x"

WHAT NEEDS BE PLEADED AND PROVED BY APPELLANT – OBSERVED SUPREME COURT

10. The appellant's contention is that the respondent after she became a candidate in the election in question obtained the services of Yashpal Kapur when he was still a gazetted officer in the Government of India for the furtherance of the prospects of her election. In order to establish that plea he must plead and prove:

(1) That the respondent obtained the assistance of Yashpal Kapur when he was a Gazetted Officer;

(2) That the assistance obtained by her was for the furtherance of the prospects of her election and

(3) That she obtained that assistance after she became a candidate.

'CANDIDATE' DEFINED IN SECTION 79(b) OF THE ACT – REPRODUCED – ITS EFFECT – SUPREME COURT

11. A 'candidate' is defined in section 79(b) of the Act. That section says:

> " 'candidate' means a person who has been or claims to have been duly nominated as a candidate at any election and any such person shall be deemed to have been a candidate as from the time when, with the election in prospect, he began to hold himself out as a prospective candidate."

12. The respondent became a candidate within the first part of section 79(b) when she was nominated on February 1, 1971. But if she had held herself out as a prospective candidate with the election in prospect before her nomination, she must be deemed to have become a candidate from the date she so held out.

13. In order to establish his plea the appellant has to establish that the assistance of Yashpal Kapur was obtained when he still was a Government servant and at the time such an assistance was obtained, the respondent had become a "candidate."

14. Now let us turn to the averments in the Election Petition which alone is relevant for finding out whether the corrupt practice referred to in issue No. 1 is made out. Relevant averments are said to be in paragraphs 2, 5 and 6. They read as follows:

> "2. That the respondent No. 1 Shrimati Indira Nehru Gandhi and the respondent No. 2 Swami Advaita Nand were also candidates in the said election from the 22 – Raebareli Parliamentary constituency for the Lok Sabha.
>
> 5. That the said Shri Yashpal Kapur was Gazetted Officer in the Government of India, holding the post of an officer on Special Duty. The respondent No. 1 Shrimati Indira Nehru Gandhi obtained and procured the assistance of the said Shri Yashpal Kapur for the furtherance of the prospects of her election from the constituency aforesaid in as much as the said Shri Yashpal Kapur was a Gazetted Officer in the service of the Government of India when his assistance was obtained and procured (a corrupt practice under section 123(7) of the R.P. Act, 1951 was committed by the respondent No. 1. Shrimati Indira Nehru Gandhi). The said Shri Yashpal Kapur on the directions of Shrimati Indira Nehru Gandhi organised the electioneering work for her in the constituency as her election agent during the entire period even before the filing of the nomination paper, the counting and the declaration of the result of the election. The election of the respondent No. 1 is liable to be declared void on the ground of the commission of this corrupt practice under section 100(1)(b) of the Representation of the People Act, 1951.

6. That as the petitioner's candidature was being supported not only by Samyukta Socialist Party to which the petitioner belonged but also by the Jan Sangh, the Indian National Congress (Organization), Bhartiya Kranti Dal and the Swatantra Parties and since the candidature of respondent No. 1, Shrimati Indira Nehru Gandhi was being supported by the Muslim Majlis, Muslim League and the Communist Party of India, it was apprehended by Shrimati Indira Nehru Gandhi and her election agent Shri Yashpal Kapur that an overwhelming majority of Hindu voters might cast their votes for the petitioner against Shrimati Indira Nehru Gandhi. It was accordingly decided by them to induce the respondent No. 2 Swami Advaita Nand to also stand as a candidate in the election. The said Shri Yashpal Kapur, the election agent of Shrimati Indira Nehru Gandhi offered and paid a sum of Rupees 50,000 to the respondent No. 2 Swami Advaita Nand as a gift with the object of directly inducing him to stand as a candidate at the said election. The offer and payment of the amount of Rupees 50,000 was made by the said Shri Yashpal Kapur to Swami Advaita Nand on the 28th January, 1971 in the town of Raebareli. A corrupt practice of 'bribery' under section 123(1)(A)(a) was thus committed by Shri Yashpal Kapur, election agent of Smt. Indira Nehru Gandhi and her election is therefore liable to be declared void under section 100(1) of the R.P. Act."

APPELLANT PLEADED RESPONDENT WAS 'A CANDIDATE' EVEN BEFORE FILING NOMINATION PAPERS—KAPUR GAZETTED OFFICER WHEN ELECTIONEERED FOR HER – OBSERVED SUPREME COURT

15. It is true that the election petition no where specifically says as to when the appellant became a "candidate". But it is clear from a reading of paragraphs 5 and 6 that according to the appellant, the respondent became a "candidate" even before she was nominated on February 1, 1971. The petition proceeds on that basis. It is not clear from the petition that how long before her nomination the respondent held herself out as a prospective candidate. But all the same, it is obvious from those averments that the respondent is alleged to have obtained the assistance of Yashpal Kapur when he continued to be a Gazetted Officer for organising her electioneering, work. The expression "electioneering" is explained in Universal English Dictionary as "act of canvassing for votes, speaking in public and otherwise promoting the election of a particular candidate for Parliament."

16. Reference to Yashpal Kapur as an election agent on a date prior to the date when he was appointed as such – his nomination as an election agent could not have been done before February 1, 1971 – is clearly a misnomer but that is irrelevant. The mention in Paragraph 5 of the election petition that Yashpal Kapur organised the electioneering work in the constituency at the direction of the respondent even before her nomination and again the reference to her candidature in January in paragraph 6 shows that according to the petitioner the respondent was a "candidate" even before her nomination and further that she obtained the assistance of Yashpal Kapur when he was still a Gazetted Officer. There is no gainsaying the fact that the election petition was not artistically drawn up. That unfortunately is the case with most of our pleadings. But if the petition is read reasonably, as it should be, it is clear that the allegation of the petitioner is that the services of Yashpal Kapur were obtained by the respondent when she had already become a candidate and when she so obtained his assistance, Yashpal Kapur was still a Gazetted Officer. It is true that one of the ingredients of the corrupt practice alleged *i.e.* that when the respondent obtained the assistance of Kapur, she was a candidate is not specifically set out in the petition but from the allegations made, it flows as a necessary implication. While a corrupt practice has got to be strictly proved but from that it does not follow that a pleading in an election proceeding should receive a strict construction.

'CORRUPT PRACTICE' – A SERIOUS CHARGE – SHOULD NOT BE DEFEATED ON TECHNICALITIES – OBSERVED SUPREME COURT

This Court has held that even a defective charge does not vitiate a criminal trial unless it is proved that the same has prejudiced the accused. If a pleading on a reasonable construction could sustain the action, the court should accept that construction. The courts are reluctant to frustrate an action on technical grounds. The charge of corrupt practice in an election is a very serious charge. Purity of election is the very essence of real democracy. The charge in question has been denied by the respondent. It has yet to be proved. It may or may not be proved. The allegations made by the appellant may ultimately be proved to be wholly devoid of truth. But the question is whether the appellant should be refused an opportunity to prove his allegations? Should the court refuse to enquire into those allegations merely because the appellant or someone who prepared his brief did not know the language of the law. We have no hesitation in answering those questions in the negative. The implications of the rule of law are manifold.

SECTIONS 83(1)(a)(b) AND SECTION 86(5) OF THE ACT – RELIED UPON BY RESPONDENT – REPRODUCED BY SUPREME COURT

17. It was contended on behalf of the respondent that the relevant provisions of the Act precluded the appellant from proving his allegations. Therefore, let us look at those provisions in the Act *i.e.* Clauses (a) and (b) of section 83(1) and clause (5) of section 86 for finding out whether the charge has to be rejected *in limine.*

Section 83(1)(a) and (b) read:

"(1) An election petition—

(a) shall contain a concise statement of the material facts on which the petitioner relies;

(b) shall set forth full particulars of any corrupt practice that the petitioner alleges, including as full a statement as possible of the names of the parties alleged to have committed such corrupt practice and the date and place of the commission of each such practice. xxx"

18. Sub-section (5) of section 86 prescribes:

> "The High Court may upon such terms as to costs and otherwise as it may deem fit, allow the particulars of any corrupt practice alleged in the petition to be amended or amplified in such manner as may in its opinion be necessary for ensuring a fair and effective trial of the petition but shall not allow any amendment of the petition which will have the effect of introducing particulars of a corrupt practice not previously alleged in the petition."

SECTIONS 83(1)(a)(b) AND 86(5) OF THE ACT—REQUIRE THAT FACTS PLEADED, MUST MAKE OUT 'CORRUPT PRACTICE' – OBSERVED SUPREME COURT

19. From these two provisions, it follows that if the allegations made regarding a corrupt practice do not disclose the constituent parts of the corrupt practice alleged, the same will not be allowed to be proved and further those allegations cannot be amended after the period of limitation for filing an election petition; but the court may allow particulars of any corrupt practice alleged in the petition to be amended or amplified. The scope of these provisions has been considered in several decisions of this Court. The leading decision on this point is **Harish Chandra Bajpai v. Triloki Singh, 1957 SCR 370.** It is not necessary to go to that decision as the ratio of that decision has been elaborately explained by this Court in **Samant N. Balakrishna v. George Fernandez, (1969) 3 SCR 603.** Dealing with the scope of sections 83 and 86 (5). This Court observed that section 83 requires that the petition must contain a concise statement of the material facts on which the petitioner relies and the fullest possible particulars of the corrupt practice alleged. 'Material facts' and 'particulars' may overlap but the word 'material' shows that the ground of corrupt practice and the facts necessary to formulate a complete cause of action must be stated. The function of the particulars is to present as full a picture of the cause of action as to make the opposite party understand the case he will have to meet. Under section 86(5), if corrupt practice is alleged in the petition, the particulars of such corrupt practice may be amended or amplified for ensuring a fair and effective trial, that is, more and better particulars of the charge may be given later, even after the period of limitation : but if a corrupt practice is not previously alleged in the petition, an amendment which will have the effect of introducing particulars of such a corrupt practice will not be permitted after the period of limitation, because, it would tantamount to making a fresh petition. The same view was taken by this Court in **Hardwari Lal v. Kanwal Singh, (1972) 1 SCC 214.** From these decisions, it follows that facts stated in the petition relating to any corrupt practice must be sufficient to constitute a cause of action. In other words, the facts must bring out all the ingredients of the corrupt practice alleged. If the facts stated fail to satisfy that requirement then they do not give rise to a triable issue. Such a defect cannot be cured by any amendment after the period of limitation for filing the election petition.

ELECTION PETITION DISCLOSES CAUSE OF ACTION – AMENDMENT FOR BETTER PARTICULARS CAN BE ALLOWED – OBSERVED SUPREME COURT

But even if all the material facts are stated in the election petition, for a proper trial better particulars may still be required. If those particulars are not set out in the election petition, they may be incorporated into the election petition with the permission of the court even after the period of limitation. The controversy in this case is whether the election petition discloses a cause of action for trying Issues No. 1. We think it does. The allegation made in paragraphs 2, 5 and 6 of the petition, if read together do show that the allegation against the respondent is that she obtained the assistance of Yashpal Kapur, a Gazetted Officer, to support her candidature by organising her electioneering work. These allegations bring out all the ingredients of the corrupt practice alleged though they are lacking in better particulars such as the date on which the respondent became a candidate and the date on which Yashpal Kapur was entrusted with the responsibility of organising the electioneering work of the respondent. The absence of those particulars do not *per se* invalidate the charge. They can be supplied even now with the permission of the Court. In this connection it is necessary to mention that the respondent in her written statement did not say that the allegations in question did not raise a triable issue. No such objection appears to have been taken at the time of the framing of the issues or in any of her pleadings. It seems that the objection was taken up for the first time when the petition to set aside the interrogatories was heard. We are saying all these only to show as to how the parties understood the allegations at the earlier stages, of the proceedings.

RULES OF PLEADINGS INTENDED AS AID TO FAIR TRIAL – OBSERVED SUPREME COURT

20. Rules of pleadings are intended as aids for a fair trial and for reaching a just decision. An action at law should not be equated to a game of chess. Provisions of law are not mere formulae to be observed as rituals. Beneath the words of a provision of law, generally speaking, there lies a juristic principle. It is the duty of the Court to ascertain that principle and implement it. What then is the principle underlying section 86(5)? In our opinion the aim of the section is to see that a person accused of a corrupt practice must know precisely what he is accused of so that he may have the opportunity to meet the allegations made against him. If the accusation made is nebulous and is capable of being made use of for establishing more than one charge or if it does not make out a corrupt practice at all then the charge fails at the very threshold. So long as the charge levelled is beyond doubt, section 86(5) is satisfied; rest is mere refinement. They either pertain to the region of particulars or evidence. That section is not designed to interdict a mere clumsy pleading like the petition before us. The purpose of the section is to see that every charge of corrupt practice should be brought before the court before the prescribed period of limitation and none thereafter so that the trial of the case may not be converted into a persecution by adding more and more charges or by converting one charge into another as the trial proceeds.

VAGUE PLEADINGS IN *HARDWARI LAL'S* CASE – SECTION 86(5) WAS APPLIED – HELD SUPREME COURT

The best illustration of the problem that section 86(5) tries to meet is found in *Hardwari Lal's* case, (supra). The allegations made in paragraph 16 of the petition therein were as follows:

> "That the respondent committed the corrupt practice of obtaining and procuring or attempting to obtain and procure the assistance for the furtherance of the prospects of his election from the following persons who are in the service of the Government and belonging to the prohibited classes within the meaning of section 123(7) of the Act:
>
> 1. Shri Chand Ram Rathi, Lecturer in Political Science, Government College, Gurgaon.
> 2. Shri Gulab Singh, B.A., B.Ed., Government High School Jharsa (Gurgaon).
> 3. Pt. Bhim Singh, Asstt. Sub-Inspector, Police-Security Lines, Lytton Road, New Delhi.
> 4. Ch. Chhatar Singh, M.A. B.T., Teacher, V. and P.O. Bharai via Bahadurgarh, District Rohtak.
> 5. Ch. Mukhtiar Singh, Inspector of Police, Delhi.
> 6. Ch. Raghbir Singh, M.A., B.T. Bahadurgarh.
>
> The respondent has written letters under his own signatures to the above Government servants soliciting their help and assistance in furtherance of the prospects of his election."

21. These were all the material facts stated in the petition. From those averments, it was not possible to make out from whom among the government servants mentioned, the returned candidate alleged to have obtained or procured assistance for the furtherance of the prospects of his election and who are those from whom he is alleged to have attempted to obtain and procure the assistance for the said purpose. That petition was also silent as regards the type of assistance obtained or procured or attempted to be obtained or procured. In that case, it was necessary to state the type of assistance obtained or procured or attempted to be obtained or procured because a candidate can take the assistance of government servants in certain respects. The allegations made in the petition were so elastic that it could have been used for establishing multitude of charges, leaving it free to the petitioner to pick and choose the charge he is in a position to establish. That was an intolerable position for his opponent. In substance, the petitioner therein had merely quoted the relevant provisions of law; he had failed to state the material facts to bring out the charge sought to be levelled. He had cast a wide net.

SECTION 86(5) OF THE ACT NOT APPLICABLE TO THIS CASE – HIGH COURT ORDER UNJUSTIFIED – HELD SUPREME COURT

This is not so in the case before us. Herein all the ingredients of the corrupt practice *viz.* (1) that the respondent obtained the assistance of Kapur; (2) Kapur was a government servant and (3) his services were obtained in support of the candidature of the respondent by organising her election campaign, are mentioned in the petition. The question when the respondent became a candidate is merely a matter of evidence.

22. For the reasons mentioned above, we think that the learned Judge was not justified in striking out issue No 1. On the other hand, he should have re-framed that issue, as mentioned earlier.

RESIGNATION OF KAPUR DATED 13.1.1971 – ACCEPTED BY PRESIDENT ON 25.1.1971 WITH EFFECT FROM 14.1.1971 – NOTIFIED ON 6.2.1971 – NEEDS RE-EXAMINATION – HELD SUPREME COURT

Before leaving this question, it is necessary to mention one other fact. Yashpal Kapur appears to have tendered his resignation to the office he was holding on January 13, 1971. The certified copy of the notification produced shows that the President accepted his resignation on the 25th of January, 1971 and the same was gazetted on February 6, 1971. The order of the President shows that he accepted Yashpal Kapur's resignation with effect from January 14, 1971. The learned trial Judge without examining the true effect of the President's order has abruptly come to the conclusion that Yashpal Kapur's resignation became effective as from January 14, 1971. This conclusion, in our opinion, requires re-examination. It is necessary to examine whether a government servant's resignation can be accepted with effect from an earlier date. At any rate whether such an acceptance has any validity in considering a corrupt practice under section 123(7). If such a course is permissible, it might enable the government to defeat the mandate of section 123(7).

DATE OF ACCEPTANCE NORMALLY MATTERS – HELD IN *RAJ KUMAR'S* CASE – OBSERVED SUPREME COURT

The question as to when a government servant's resignation becomes effective came up for consideration by this Court in **Raj Kumar v. Union of India, (1968) 3 SCR 857.** Therein this Court ruled that when a public servant has invited by his letter of resignation the determination of his employment, his service normally stands terminated from the date on which the letter of resignation is accepted by the appropriate authority and, in the absence of any law or statutory rule governing the conditions of his service, to the contrary, it will not be open to the public servant to withdraw his resignation after it is accepted by the appropriate authority. Hence, the question as to when Yashpal Kapur's resignation became effective will have to be examined with reference to his conditions of service. This examination having not been done, the conclusion of the learned trial Judge that it became effective on January 14, 1971, has to be ignored.

AMENDMENT SOUGHT ONLY CLARIFICATORY – DOES NOT CAUSE PREJUDICE – ORDER OF HIGH COURT SET ASIDE – ISSUE NO. 1 RECAST– SUPREME COURT HELD

23. For the foregoing reasons, we set aside the order of the trial judge striking out issue No. 1 and the last part of issue No. 3 and restore issue No. 1 as amended by us.

24. Now coming to the appeal against the order on the amendment application, the learned trial judge disallowed the amendments sought on the sole ground that if those amendments are allowed it will amount to amending the statement of material facts and the same is not permissible in view of section 86(5). We have already found that the conclusion of the learned trial judge is not correct. The amendment application was moved even before the trial of the case commenced. It is not shown how the amendments sought in respect of paragraphs 2 and 5 of the petition can prejudice the case of the respondent. They are merely clarificatory in character. This Court ruled in **Balwan Singh v. Lakshmi Narain, (1960) 3 SCR 91**, that an election petition was not liable to be dismissed *in limine* because full particulars of corrupt practice alleged were not set out. It further observed that if an objection was taken and the tribunal was of the view that the full particulars have not been set out, the petitioner had to be given an opportunity to amend or amplify the particulars. It was only in the event of non-compliance with the order to supply the particulars that the charge which remained vague could be struck out. In that case the amendment was sought after the evidence was closed in the cases. This Court allowed the same. Courts are ordinarily liberal in allowing amendment of pleadings unless it results in prejudicing the case of the opposite party. Any inconvenience caused by an amendment can always be compensated by costs. We think that the amendments asked for, should have been allowed and we allow the same. The election petition will be accordingly amended and the respondent will be afforded an opportunity to file any additional written statement, if she so desires.

INTERROGATORIES – RIGHTLY DISALLOWED – SUPREME COURT HELD

25. This leaves us with the question of interrogatories. As many as 31 interrogatories have been served on the respondent as mentioned earlier. Out of them Nos. 24 of 30 have been allowed. Hence we need not consider them. Interrogatories Nos. 19 to 23 relate to Issue No. 2. Therefore, they are rightly struck out. We now come to interrogatories Nos. 1 to 18 and 31. We have carefully examined those interrogatories. None of them touch the core of the allegations relating to commission of the corrupt practice which is the subject matter of Issue No. 1. They merely touch the fringe of the matter.

26. Order XI, rule 1, C.P.C. provides:

> "In any suit the plaintiff or defendant by leave of the court may deliver interrogatories in writing for the examination of the opposite parties or any one or more of such parties and such interrogatories when delivered shall have a note at the foot thereof stating which of such interrogatories each of such person is required to answer : Provided that no party shall deliver more than one set of interrogatories to the same party without an order for that purpose.

Provided also that interrogatories which do not relate to any matters in question in the suit shall be deemed irrelevant, notwithstanding that they might be admissible on the oral cross-examination of a witness."

27. Questions that may be relevant during cross-examination are not necessarily relevant as interrogatories. The only questions that are relevant as interrogatories are those relating to "any matters in question" The interrogatories served must have reasonably close connection with "matters in question". Viewed thus, interrogatories 1 to 18 as well as 31 must be held to be irrelevant.

APPEAL 108 PARTLY ALLOWED – APPEAL 109 ALLOWED IN FULL SUPREME COURT

28. In the result Civil Appeal No. 108 of 1972 is allowed to the extent mentioned above. In other respects the same is dismissed. Civil Appeal No. 109 of 1972 is allowed in full. In the circumstances of these cases, we make no order as to costs.

Order accordingly.

ALLAHABAD HIGH COURT

Raj Narain
v.
Smt. Indira Nehru Gandhi

AIR 1974 All 324

Before:—K.N. Srivastava, J.

Election Petition No. 5 of 1971.
Dated 20 March, 1974

Order

In this election petition privilege has been claimed regarding three sets of documents. Sri S.S. Saxena is alleged to have claimed privilege regarding four papers, including copy of a blue book with the title as "Rules and Instructions for the Protection of Prime Minister when on Tour or in Travel". Privilege was claimed by the Superintendent of Police, Raebareli, regarding two papers which relate to the Tour Programme of Smt. Indira Nehru Gandhi at Raebareli during the election period. Sri K.P. Sood claimed privilege regarding two documents. Sri Sood is an officer of the Accountant General's Office, Central Revenue, New Delhi. Sri Saxena is alleged to have claimed privilege orally as an agent and representative of Sri R.K. Kaul, Home Secretary, Uttar Pradesh Government. This privilege was claimed by Sri Saxena on 10-9-1973, but an affidavit was filed by Sri Kaul claiming that privilege on 20-9-1973. Much stress was laid by the parties' counsel in support of their respective contentions regarding the production of the blue book with the title "Rules and Instructions for the Protection of Prime Minister when on Tour or in Travel". It shall hereinafter be called as the 'blue book'.

CONDITIONS FOR CLAIMING 'PRIVILEGE' NOT MET OUT-CLAIMS PETITIONER

2. According to the petitioner, *firstly*, privilege under section 123 of the Evidence Act could not be claimed orally. *Secondly*, Sri Saxena did not claim privilege. The third contention of the petitioner's counsel was that after a lapse of ten days the affidavit of Sri Kaul should not be considered as Sri Kaul knew fully well that Sri Saxena was bringing that book to Court for production and, as such, if he had to claim any privilege he should have armed Sri Saxena with the necessary affidavit. The fourth contention was that requisite conditions of section 123, Evidence Act, were not fulfilled.

SECTIONS 123 AND 162 EVIDENCE ACT DEAL WITH CLAIMING PRIVILEGE – REPRODUCED

3. Section 123 of the Evidence Act reads as below:

> "Section 123. No one shall be permitted to give any evidence derived from unpublished official records relating to any affairs of State, except with the

permission of the officer at the head of the department concerned, who shall give or withhold such permission as he thinks fit."

4. In this connection, reference to section 162 will also be relevant because it lays down the procedure which should be adopted while deciding the question of privilege. Section 162 of the Evidence Act reads as below:

> "Section 162. A witness summoned to produce a document shall, if it is in his possession or power, bring it to Court, notwithstanding any objection which there may be to its production or to its admissibility. The validity of any such objection shall be decided on by' the Court.
>
> The Court, if it sees fit, may inspect the document, unless it refers to matters of State, or take other evidence to enable it to determine on its admissibility.
>
> If for such a purpose it is necessary to cause any document to be translated, the Court may, if it thinks fit, direct the translator to keep the contents secret, unless the document is to be given in evidence; and if the interpreter disobeys such direction, he shall be held to have committed an offence under section 166 of the Indian Penal Code."

WHAT ARE 'UNPUBLISHED OFFICIAL RECORD' OR 'AFFAIRS OF THE STATE' AND WHETHER 'PRIVILEGE' CAN BE CLAIMED – DISCUSSED

5. A bare reading of section 123 of the Evidence Act clearly indicates that in order to claim privilege there must be certain prerequisite conditions; (1) the document must be an unpublished official record, (2) it should relate to the affairs of State, and (3) it can be admitted in evidence with the permission of the head of the department concerned who shall give or withhold such a permission.

6. Under section 162 of the Evidence Act, the Court has power to inspect the document for the purpose of deciding the question of its admissibility or to get it translated if such a course be required. But, the words "Unless it refers to matters of State" clearly indicate that documents relating to matters of State cannot even be inspected by the Court for determining the question of its admissibility.

7. Before taking up the Question involved in this case, we have to see as to whether the evidence derived from the blue book is from unpublished official records and, secondly, if they relate to the affairs of State, and also as to whether the Court would *suo motu* refuse permission for the production of the documents or it can do so only when privilege is claimed by the head of the department concerned. No doubt, even if the document fulfills the first two conditions, the head of the department can permit its production if he so decides, but he has power to withhold it if the two conditions, mentioned above, are satisfied and it is not in public interest to disclose its contents.

RELEVANT SECTIONS 122 TO 127 EVIDENCE ACT DISCUSSED – ITS EFFECT

8. The question, therefore, would arise as to what would be the stage for deciding this question and by whom. Learned Counsel for the respondent as well as the State Counsel and the Advocate-General contended that the Court shall refuse permission for production of document even if the head of the department did not withhold permission or permitted its production because according to them it was the primary duty of the Court to do so in view of the word "permitted" which has been used in this section. They contended that different languages have been used in different sections of the Evidence Act such as in section 123 the word used is "permitted", in sections 124 and 125 the words used are "shall be compelled", while in section 126 the word used is "permitted". I shall therefore, examine all these four sections separately. It is no doubt correct that the witness must be competent to make the statement, and that his statement should be relevant. If these conditions are fulfilled, a statement would be admitted.

9. Sections 122 to 127 of the Evidence Act are exceptions to the general rule. These sections do not allow a certain evidence to be brought in unless the conditions laid down in these sections are fulfilled. Under section 124, no public officer can be compelled to disclose communications made to him in official confidence, when by that disclosure public interest is likely to suffer. Similarly, under section 125, no Magistrate or Police Officer can be compelled to tell the source of his information about the commission of an offence. Under section 126, no Barrister, attorney, pleader or Vakil, can be compelled to disclose any communication made to him in the course of his employment, unless the client consents for that disclosure. In my opinion, the words "permitted" and "compelled" have been used in different contexts in the aforesaid sections. A public officer and a Magistrate or a police officer have been empowered to withhold information relating to the matters referred to in sections 124 and 125 of the Evidence Act. Similarly, a Barrister, an attorney, a pleader or Vakil also has a right to withhold information received by him from the client in the course of his employment. Sections 124, 125 and 126 of the Evidence Act clearly give power of withholding information by certain set of persons and the law protects them from making disclosure of the same. In this regard, these sections lay down that the persons mentioned in these sections cannot be compelled by any law court to make the disclosure.

10. In section 123, there is a comma, before the words "except with the permission of the officer at the head of the department concerned" and, therefore, to my mind, the word "permitted" governs the aforesaid expression. A reading of this section clearly indicates that the Court shall permit the disclosure of evidence regarding unpublished documents relating to the affairs of State if the officer at the head of the department so permits. The words "shall not be permitted" would, therefore have to be read with the last line which reads, "shall give or withhold such permission as he thinks fit."

COURT'S ROLE COMES IN ONLY WHEN 'PRIVILEGE' IS CLAIMED – HOLDS HIGH COURT

11. From the above discussion it, therefore, becomes clear that even if the information is based on unpublished official records relating to the affairs of State, the same could be given in evidence in law courts, provided the head of the department has no objection and he so permits. Therefore, the question about permitting any evidence to be led could only arise when the permission had been withheld by the head of the department concerned. In my opinion, therefore, the Court will not come into picture unless the permission has been withheld. It is then and then alone that the Court would step in and find out whether the document sought to be adduced in evidence relates to the unpublished official records relating to the affairs of the State, and hold an enquiry as to whether the privilege has been rightly claimed and the claim is justified.

AT WHAT STAGE AND BY WHAT PROCEDURE 'PRIVILEGE' CAN BE CLAIMED – HIGH COURT

12. Before proceeding further, I would like to discuss various (sic) to find out at what stage and in what manner such a claim can be made. But, before deciding this question it appears necessary to decide as to whether any procedure is provided by the law or not because the contention of the learned Counsel for the other side was that every procedure should not be taken as prohibitory unless it is laid down by law. In this connection, reliance was placed on certain decisions of different High Courts and the Supreme Court.

13. The first case relied upon was Full Bench decision of this Court in **Narsingh Das v. Mangal Dubey, (1883) ILR 5 All 163 (KB)**. This case has absolutely no bearing with the present case. The question in this case was about joining of different causes of action against different sets of persons.

14. The other case is **Jai Jai Ram Manohar Lal v. National Building Material Supply, Gurgaon, AIR 1969 SC 1267.** In this case the question arose as to whether an amendment should be allowed or disallowed. It was held as below:

> "The order passed by the High Court cannot be sustained. Rules of procedure are intended to be a handmaid to the administration of justice. A party cannot be refused just relief merely because of some mistake, negligence, inadvertence or even infraction of the rules of procedure."

15. So far as the principle laid down in this case is concerned, there is no doubt about it. But, in the instant case, the question about the evidence to be allowed or not to be allowed depends upon certain prerequisite conditions mentioned in section 123 of the Evidence Act, and, therefore, no question of any technicality arises.

MINISTER CONCERNED OR HEAD OF DEPARTMENT TO FILE AFFIDAVIT AT THE FIRST INSTANCE CLAIMING 'PRIVILEGE' – HIGH COURT HOLDS

16. Reverting to the main point, there can be no doubt that privilege can be claimed by the Minister or head of the department through the person who is sent to the Court with the records summoned. But, the question will arise whether such a claim can be made by him orally or under affidavit signed by the officer concerned. In this connection, reliance was placed on a decision of the Supreme Court in **State of Punjab v. Sodhi Sukhdeo Singh, AIR 1961 SC 493.** In this case, K. Subba Rao, J., observed as below:

> "The next point is, what is the procedure to be allowed by a Judge for deciding on the said objection? When an officer of the State is summoned as a witness to produce a document, if the State seeks to take a plea of privilege then it is the duty of the minister in charge of the department concerned to file an affidavit at the first instance. The affidavit so filed shall ex facie show that the minister concerned has read and considered each of the documents in respect of which the privilege is claimed. It shall also contain the general nature of the document and the particular danger to which the State would be exposed by its production".

17. This was the view expressed in some earlier cases, and it is a well settled principle of law that privilege must be claimed by the Minister or head of the department concerned, who has to file an affidavit at the very first instance. In the instant case, no such affidavit was filed at the first instance.

OFFICIAL DEPUTED WITH RECORD – PLEADS NO INSTRUCTIONS TO PRODUCE IT IN COURT – NOR INSTRUCTIONS TO CLAIM PRIVILEGE – HIGH COURT

All that was done, according to the contentions of the learned Counsel for the respondent and the State Counsel, was that Sri Saxena was deputed by the Home Secretary to produce this document and claim such a privilege.

18. I shall, therefore, examine the statement of Sri Saxena to see as to what he has stated regarding this matter. When a question was asked about the blue book, he replied:—

"I have brought it. I cannot file it unless permitted by the head of the department." This statement does not go to show that he was claiming privilege or that he had been directed by the head of the department to claim such a privilege and to withhold the production of the document. To a Court question, the witness made the following statement:

"My head of department has not permitted me to file the booklet whose title is "Rules and Instructions for the Protection of Prime Minister when on Tour or in Travel". This booklet has been marked "SECRET" at the top of the first page."

THE WORD 'SECRET' ON IT DOES NOT MAKE IT A 'PRIVILEGED' DOCUMENT – HIGH COURT

19. Simply because it is marked 'secret', it will not be a privileged document.

20. Further on, in examination-in-chief, this witness stated:—

> "I have come to attend this Court under the order of the Home Secretary, Uttar Pradesh Secretariat. He directed me to attend this Court with the papers mentioned in the summons."

He further stated:

> "The Home Secretary did not instruct me not to bring to this Court any paper summoned by the Court. He had directed me to show all the papers I have brought to the Court. .... In obedience to the Home Secretary's order and direction, I have brought this printed booklet which is marked 'SECRET' for being shown to this court. I have no instructions to produce this printed booklet in this Court."

A question was asked in his examination-in-chief as to whether the Home Secretary had given any affidavit to this witness to claim privilege under section 123 of the Evidence Act. The witness replied in the negative. In cross-examination, this witness stated:

> "I was authorised by the Home Secretary to bring these papers to this court. Except this, he did not give me any additional authority." To another question, this witness replied:
>
> > "No orders were received. The L.R. gave opinion that the circulars and programmes regarding tour of the Prime Minister were secret documents and privilege should be claimed."

Yet, to another question, if he had any specific instructions from anybody about bringing the secret documents relating to the security arrangements of the Prime Minister's tour to this Court, this witness replied in the negative.

LAW DEPARTMENT ADVISED TO CLAIM 'PRIVILEGE' BUT NO STEP TAKEN – HIGH COURT

21. A reading of the entire statement of Sri Saxena, therefore, clearly indicates that at no stage he claimed any privilege under section 123 of the Evidence Act. He stated that the Law Department had advised the Home Department to claim privilege and yet no formality was observed, nor any step was taken by the Home Minister to claim such a privilege. Therefore, it is abundantly clear that at the first instance no privilege was claimed.

22. According to Sri Saxena, this document was brought for being shown to the Court. As shown above, if it was a document relating to the affairs of the State, in accordance with section 162 of the Evidence Act, it could not be seen by the Court as well. I am conscious of the fact that later on the law on the subject has been changed and the Court can see such a document for a limited purpose, that is, to decide.

Whether the privilege has been properly and rightly claimed. But, all the same, the law does not permit that, except for the above purpose, even the Court can see it. When this document was brought to be shown in Court, there was no reason as to why the party should not be allowed to see or use it, specially when no such claim of privilege, as required by law, was claimed at the first instance.

'PRIVILEGE' CAN BE CLAIMED SUBSEQUENTLY – SUBMITS ADVOCATE-GENERAL – NOT ACCEPTED – HIGH COURT

23. It was contended by the learned Advocate-General that the paper had not yet been admitted in evidence and, therefore, Sri Kaul could file an affidavit claiming such a privilege even on 20-9-1973. This argument has no force in it for the simple reason that it was produced without such a claim being made at the first instance. It is evident from the statement of Sri Saxena that the head of the department had not withheld the permission. He was not filing the paper simply because he had not been specifically asked by the head of the department to file it and because at the top of the booklet the word 'Secret' was printed.

24. Certain decisions were cited at the Bar about the stage when a claim for privilege could be made even at a later stage. A reference was made to **Henry Greer Robinson v. State of South Australia, AIR 1931 PC 254.** In this case it was held as below:

> "But the privilege has not, in their Lordships' judgement, been lost merely by the insufficiency of the form in which it has been claimed. It is quite possible that there may be amongst the scheduled documents some, at least, to which the privilege genuinely attaches, and to throw open these documents to the inspection of the plaintiff, without more, would destroy the protection of the privilege. Therefore, it would or might be contrary to the public interest to deprive the respondent State of a further opportunity of regularising its claim to protection, by producing as its next step, an affidavit of the description already indicated."

25. Even in this case at the very first instance the claim of privilege was made, although, the affidavit sworn was defective. In these circumstances, an opportunity was given to the State to file a detailed affidavit with full reasons.

26. In **Sujit Kantha v. Union of India, AIR 1970 Assam and Nagaland 131**, in a petition certified copies of certain documents were annexed. After notice had been served, claim for privilege was made. In this case it was observed as below:

> "The statute has clearly proscribed inspection of documents relating to the affairs of the State. The rule of conduct which is prescribed by this law is that no person should pry into confidences of Governmental affairs. But the conduct of the petitioner clearly runs counter to the rule for conduct laid down by the statute. It is significant, as Cohen has neatly observed in his Ethical Systems – "Words are frail packages for legislative hopes. The voyage to the realm of law observance is long and dangerous." It is a question of serious import whether a person should be allowed to take advantage of his illegitimate action in securing by any means whatsoever secret and' confidential documents of the Government. It is not possible to show any leniency in a matter of this description and we cannot too strongly condemn this unlawful practice and would be loath to give the erring party any advantage of his wrong action. It should be a warning to those who want to thrive from such unethical disclosures which are clearly opposed to the provisions of law."

27. In this case also privilege was claimed as soon as the matter came to the notice of the department concerned. The facts of this case are altogether different from the instant case.

28. In **S.B. Chaudhury v. I.P. Changkakati, AIR 1960 Assam 210,** it was held as below:

> "No particular form is prescribed for claiming any such privilege and if the Sessions Judge acted on the said affidavit and considered it sufficient, it cannot be said that the order of the Sessions Judge is vitiated even if the contention of the petitioners is accepted that the affidavit was not in proper form.
>
> The claim of privilege can be raised in any manner as the head of the department desires. It is for the court to decide whether it will insist upon the examination on oath of the head of the department to ascertain if the documents relate to the affairs of the State or not. It is for the court to determine as I have already pointed out earlier, from the circumstances and from the nature of the documents, as to whether the documents relate to the affairs of the State or not. No particular mode of proof is prescribed in the Act."

COURT CANNOT GRANT 'PRIVILEGE' UNLESS CLAIMED BY DEPARTMENT BY FILING AFFIDAVIT OF MINISTER OR HEAD OF DEPARTMENT – HIGH COURT

29. This too does not lay down that even where no privilege is claimed, the Court will *suo motu* decide the question of privilege without being raised.

30. The Court's function begins only after a proper privilege has been claimed. A law court is not supposed to be an agent of any party. If an act has to be done by any party, it must be done by that party and then only the legal formalities following from that act would be taken up by the Court. It is thus clear that the Court's function is only to find from evidence or from the inspection of the documents if the privilege bas been properly claimed and whether the information is relating to the affairs of the State and about the unpublished records.

31. A duty under section 123 of the Evidence Act is cast on the Minister or the head of the department to claim privilege or to permit the production of the document in Court. This duty, which under the law is cast on those persons, cannot be exercised by a court nor a court would be justified in *suo motu* ordering that the document be not produced. The Minister or the head of the department concerned has to apply his mind to decide whether the document should be produced or not. The Court's duty is only to see if that discretion has been applied in proper manner and in good faith. In this view of the matter, it cannot be argued that it is the court's duty, even without privilege being claimed, not to permit the production of a document.

32. It has next to be seen as to what is the power of the court for making enquiries under section 123 of the Evidence Act. Would it not permit the production of a document the moment a claim is made or proceed further to enquire into the matter. This question came up for discussion in the case of **State of Punjab, AIR 1961 SC 493,** (*supra*) and their Lordships considered three views possible. The first view, which was considered by their Lordships of the Supreme Court, was that it was for the head of the department to decide whether the document was innocuous or noxious and when it comes to the conclusion that it was innocuous the head of the department will give the necessary permission, but if he comes to the conclusion that it is noxious, the permission will be withheld. The second view was that the courts should decide and determine after enquiry as to whether the disclosure be made or not. And, the third view was that the court could determine the question relating to the character of the document and if the court comes to the conclusion that the document is noxious it may leave it to the head of the department to decide whether it should be produced or not in this connection, the following observation was made in the case of State of Punjab (supra):

> "The last decision on which considerable reliance has been placed by Mr. Seervai is the case of **Beatson v. Skene, (1860) 5 H and N 838**. It may incidentally be pointed out that Chief Baron Pollock's observations in this judgement are frequently cited in judicial decisions where the question of privilege falls to be considered. In that case the plaintiff had been a general who commanded a corps of irregular troops during the war in Crimea. Compliant having been made about the insubordination of troops the corps was placed under the superior command of *V*. Thereupon the plaintiff resigned his command. *V* directed S to inspect and report upon the state of the corps and referred *S* for information to the defendant who was a Civil Commissioner. The defendant in a conversation with *S*, made a defamatory statement respecting the conduct of the plaintiff. The plaintiff brought an action against the defendant for slander. The defence set up against the plaintiff's claim was that what had passed between the defendant and *S* was a privileged communication. The jury had found a verdict for the defendant. A new trial was claimed by the plaintiff, inter alia, on the ground that the learned Judge had declined to compel the production of certain documents. It appeared that the Secretary for War had been subpoenaed to produce certain letters written by the plaintiff to him and also the minutes of the Court of enquiry as to the conduct of S in writing the letter to V. The plea for a new trial was rejected on the ground that the Court was of the opinion that the non-production of the said documents furnished no ground for a new trial. There was a difference of opinion among the members of the Court on the question as to whether Bramwell, J., was justified in upholding the claim of privilege; Pollock, C.B. Bramwell, B. and Wilde, *B.*, held that the claim for privilege was properly upheld, whereas Martin, *B.*, took a contrary view."

Further on, it was observed:

> "Reading this clause on this assumption what is its effect? It empowers the Court to inspect the document while dealing with the objection; but this power cannot be exercised where the objection relates to a document having reference to matters of State and it is raised under section 123. In such a case the Court is empowered to take other evidence to enable it to determine the validity of the objection."

33. In this case the third view was accepted, and it was held as below:

> "Thus our conclusion is that reading sections 123 and 162 together the Court cannot hold an enquiry into the possible injury to public interest which may result from the disclosure of the document in question. That is a matter for the authority concerned to decide; but the Court is competent, and indeed is bound, to hold a preliminary enquiry and determine the validity of the objections to its production, and that necessarily involves an enquiry into the question as to whether the evidence relates to an affair of State under section 123 or not."

34. In this case, the Supreme Court held that the court had no power to look into the document itself while dealing with the objection under section 123 of the Evidence Act.

COURT HAS THE RIGHT TO PERUSE THE DOCUMENT TO CONSIDER VALIDITY OF CLAIM OF 'PRIVILEGE' – HOLDS HIGH COURT

35. The question whether the court is empowered to peruse the document Itself was again considered in **Amar Chand Butail v. Union of India, AIR 1964 SC 1658.** In this case it was observed as below:

> "But on the merits also we feel no doubt in rejecting the said claim. The statement made by the Home Minister does not show that he seriously applied his mind to the contents of the documents and examined the question as to whether their disclosure would injure public interest. We are constrained to observe that this case illustrates how a claim for privilege can be and is sometimes made in a causal manner without realising the solemnity and significance attached to the exercise of the power conferred on the head of the department to make that claim. As we will presently point out, one of the documents which were produced before us under our directions would tend to show that the sole reason for claiming privilege in respect of that document was the fear rightly entertained that the disclosure of the said document would entirely defeat the whole of the defence made by respondents 1 and 2. Since it was necessary for us to consider whether the claim had been rightly upheld by the courts below, we directed respondents 1 and 2 to produce the said documents before us for our inspection. Accordingly such of the documents as were available have been produced before us and it is to one of them that we propose to refer. Having seen all the documents produced before us we were satisfied that the claim for privilege made by respondent No. 2 was not justified at all and may even be characterised as not *bona fide.*"

36. The question as to whether a Court is empowered to look into the documents was considered in this case and, as observed above, it was held that in cases where the claim for privilege is made in a causal manner without reaslising the solemnity and significance attached to the exercise of the power, the court is entitled to consider the document itself. In this case it was held that the documents produced should be inspected by the court itself for deciding the question as to whether the claim for privilege had been properly exercised.

37. On behalf of the respondent reliance was placed on the following paragraph of the judgement of the Supreme Court in **Amar Chand Butail's case, AIR 1964 SC 1658:**

> "The position in law about the liability of respondents 1 and 2 to meet the appellant's claim in regard to the dealings between the appellant and the State of Jubbal is not in doubt or dispute. If it can be shown that respondents 1 and 2 had recognised the appellant's claim against the State of Jubbal, that would give him a valid cause of action against both of them. It is hardly necessary to deal with this point elaborately because the position under Article 295 of the Constitution is fairly clear in respect of this point. Recognition of the claim made by the appellant can be proved by the appellant either by express acknowledgement or recognition or may even be established on relevant facts and circumstances which may lead to the inference of such recognition. In other words, recognition of such a claim can be either express or implied and in the latter class of cases the inference as to recognition may be drawn legitimately from facts and circumstances which reasonably support such an inference."

38. This paragraph has nothing to do with the interpretation of section 123 or section 162 of the Evidence Act. This discussion relates to recognition by Government, which may be express or implied. Therefore, this would not help the respondent.

39. In this connection reference was made to certain English decisions. One of the cases referred at the Bar is **Conway v. Rimmer, (1967) 2 All ER 1260**. The Bench was constituted of Lord Denning, Davies and Russell, L.JJ. Lord Denning gave a dissenting judgement that the reasons of the Home Secretary were not conclusive and the document to be produced should be inspected by the court itself, although the majority took a contrary view. The same case came before the House of Lords in **Conway v. Rimmer, (1968) 1 All ER 874**. The opinion given by Lord Denning was upheld and it was held that the court had the power to examine the document. In this case the law on the subject was revised and it was held as below:

> "The courts have and are entitled to exercise a power and duty to hold a balance between the public interest, as expressed by a Minister, to withhold certain documents or other evidence and the public interest in ensuring the proper administration of justice. That does not mean that a court would reject a Minister's view; full weight must be given to it in every case, and if the Minister's reasons are of a character which judicial experience is not competent to weigh then the Minister's view must prevail; but experience has shown that reasons given for withholding whole classes of documents are often not of that character."

40. Lord Morris in the concluding portion of his judgement observed as below:

> "I have come to the conclusion that the appeal should be allowed, and that the best procedure to follow for weighing the public and private interests which are involved in this case will be to have an inspection of the five documents which are in question."

41. These two decisions coupled with the Supreme Court's decision in **Amar Chand Butail's case, AIR 1964 SC 1658** leave no room for doubt that in appropriate cases the court has the power to inspect the document to keep the balance between the State and the subject even.

42. Learned Counsel for the respondent contended that in India the law was codified while in England the position was otherwise, and, therefore, these English decisions were of no help for deciding the question in issue. No doubt, our Evidence Act is a codified law, but all the same reference can be made to the English Law for appreciating the general principles of law. Lord Denning, who gave the dissenting judgement in **Conway's** case, referred to a number of cases from all the dominion countries for holding the view that the documents could be inspected by the Court for keeping the balance between the parties even. The following observation of Lord Denning in **Conway's** case can be read with advantage:

> "I know that in **Duncon v. Cammell, Laird and Co. Ltd., (1942) 1 All ER 587: (1942) AC 624**, the House of Lords dissented from **Robinson's case, (1931) All ER 333: (1931) AC 704;** but the courts of the Commonwealth being free to choose have unanimously followed **Robinson's** case and have endorsed the views of this court in the **Grosvenor Hotel case (1964) 3 All ER 354: (1965) Ch 1210;** or in other cases have acted on like principles. Let me recite the cases. They are a veritable roll call. The Supreme Court of Canada in **R. v. Snider, 1954 SLR 479**, and **Gagnon v. Quebec Securities Commission, 1964 SCR 329.** The Supreme Court of Victoria in **Bruce v. Waldron, 1963 VLR 3.** The Court of Appeal of New South Wales **In re: Tunstall, Ex. P. Brown, (1966) 84 WN (Ft. 2) (N.S.W.) 13.** The Court of Appeal of **New Zealand in Corbett v. Social Security Commission, (1962) NZ IR 878.** The Supreme Court of India in **Amar Chand v. Union of India, AIR 1964 SC 1658**. The Supreme Court of Ceylon in **Apponhamy v. Illangaratue, (1964) 66 CLW 17.** The Court of Appeal of Jamaica in **Alien v. Byfield (No. 2), (1964) 7 WIR 69 (71).** To say nothing of the Court of Session in Scotland backed in this respect by the House of Lords itself in **Glassgow Corpn. v. Central Land Board, 1966 SC (HL) 1.**" Further on, he went on to observe:
>
> "Despite this impressive array, my brethren today feel that we are still bound by the observations of the House of Lords in **Duncan v. Cammell**

Laird and Co. Ltd., (1942) 1 All ER 587: (1942) AC 624, and by the decision of this Court in **Auten v. Rayner, (1966) 3 All ER 77.** I do not agree."

43. The general trend of opinion even in countries where the law on the subject is codified appears to be that in appropriate cases the court has the power to inspect the document, and the reasoning given by Lord Denning appears to be very sound and correct because instances might not be wanting where an authority might claim privilege *mala fide* or without exercising proper care or in a cursory manner. Therefore, in this view of the matter, there is consensus of opinion in this country as well as in other countries that the document can be inspected in appropriate cases.

PART OF BLUE BOOK HAS BECOME PUBLIC – NO LONGER UNPUBLISHED RECORD – HOLDS HIGH COURT

44. The next question to be decided is whether the blue book is an unpublished record, as defined in section 123 of the Evidence Act. There is evidence on the record to prove and show that a portion of this book was quoted in the Lok Sabha Debate on Wednesday, April 18, 1973. On 7-3-1973 Sri Jyotirmoy Bosu, M.P., had put the following question as a supplementary:

> "If it is or it is not a fact that before November, 1969, the tours undertaken by the Prime Minister for election and other party purposes used to be paid by the party, but since November, 1969, the procedure has been changed and the expenses are now debited to the Exchequer."

45. The reply was that it was not a fact. Then, section 71(6) of the blue book was quoted by the Hon'ble Member and the amendment made in that section on 19-11-1969. As given in this proceeding, section 71(6) runs as below:

> "It has been noticed that the rostrum arrangements are not always properly made because the hosts are sometimes unable to bear the cost. As the Prime Minister's security is the concern of the State, all arrangements for putting up the rostrum and the barriers at the meeting place will be borne by the State whatever may be the occasion for which the public meeting is called, except election meetings."

46. After amendment, as shown in the Lok Sabha debates, the section now reads as below:

> "It has been noticed that the rostrum arrangements are not always properly made because the hosts are sometimes unable to bear the cost. As the security of the Prime Minister is the concern of the State, all arrangements for putting up the rostrum, the barriers etc., at the meeting place including that of an election meeting will have to be made by the State Government concerned."

47. It is not denied that this quotation from the blue book is correct nor any objection was made in the Lok Sabha that it being a privileged document its contents could not be disclosed. The Minister concerned also did not deny this fact. A perusal of the proceeding would show that without denying the correctness of this quotation, an explanation was tried to be given.

48. Not only this, on behalf of the respondent a document, Paper No. A-75/1, was filed. This is the reproduction of section 71(6) as it now stands after the amendment. Learned Counsel for the respondent contended that this paper was obtained from the record, of writ proceedings in which the Union Government had filed the extracts of the amended section 71(6) and from that case the petitioner had obtained the copy.

49. This clearly goes to show that the Union Government itself disclosed a part of this blue book, on the top of which the word 'Secret' is printed. It cannot be imagined for a minute that some portion of the blue book which relates to the security of the Prime Minister when on tour or in travel is secret and other parts of it are not so. Had it been so, the entire blue book would not have been marked 'Secret'. If a portion of this secret book is disclosed, there is no sanctity left behind its secrecy. If any other exigency arises, as it arose in the above writ petition, the other parts of the book could also be divulged. It might be that this booklet was intended to be an unpublished record, but due publicity was given to some parts of it and, therefore, it cannot be said that it is an unpublished record.

50. Paper No. A-75/1 reads as below:

> "Rule 71(6) of the Rules and Instructions for the protection of the Prime Minister when on tour and travel is amended to read as follows:—
>
> "It has been noticed that the rostrum arrangements are not always properly made because the hosts are sometimes unable to bear the cost. As the security of the Prime Minister is the concern of the State, all arrangements for putting up the rostrum, the barriers etc., at the meeting place, including that of an election meeting will have to be made by the State Government concerned.
>
> In the case of public meetings, other than election Meetings, all expenditure on the arrangements including provision of rostrum, the setting up of barricades, making lighting arrangements, public address system, etc., will be borne by the State Government.
>
> In the case of election meetings, all expenditure on police, setting up of barricades and making lighting arrangements will be borne by the State Government, while expenditure on the public address system and any decorative arrangements will be the responsibility of the political party concerned. (The expenditure on all these items may, in the first instance be borne by the State Government and recovered from the political party concerned). In regard to the rostrum, only 25% of the cost of the rostrum or Rs. 2500.00 whichever is less, shall be contributed by the party as the rostrum has to be of certain specifications because of security considerations."

51. The following shall be added as a new sub-rule after rule 71(6):—

> "71 (6). Any extravagance in expenditure should be avoided."

52. Thus, it is clear that in the writ petition from where the respondent has obtained the copy, Paper No. A-75/1, something more was disclosed than what had been disclosed in the Lok Sabha debate, referred to above.

'PUBLISHED' DOES NOT MEAN PRINTING PUBLICALY – IF KNOWN TO PARTIES IT AMOUNTS TO 'PUBLISH' – HOLDS HIGH COURT

53. It was argued by the learned Counsel for the respondent that the word 'published' means printed in large number for use of the public in general. In *Law Lexicon of British India,* 'publish' is defined as below:—

> "publish" primarily means to make known, so that where a notice is required to be published in a newspaper, printed in German, the notice must also be in German. When printed in English, it would be merely printed, not published."

Further on, *Law Lexicon* says:

> "To publish is the most general of these terms, conveying in its extended sense the idea of making known; but it is in many respects indefinite; we may make known to many or few; but to promulgate is always to make known to many. We may publish that which is a domestic or a national concern; we promulgate properly only that which is of general interest; the affairs of a

family or of a nation are published in the newspapers; doctrines, principles, precepts and the like are promulgated. To publish is said of that which was never before known or never before existed; to reveal and disclose are said of that which has been only concealed or lay hidden; we publish the events of the day; we reveal the secret or the mystery or a transaction; we disclose the whole affair from beginning to end which has never been properly known or accounted for."

CLAIM OF 'PRIVILEGE' SHOULD BE MADE AT THE FIRST OPPORTUNITY BY SENDING THE DOCUMENT IN SEALED COVER ALONGWITH AFFIDAVIT OF COMPETENT AUTHORITY – HOLDS HIGH COURT

54. In **Bhalchandra Dattatraya v. Chanbasappa Mallappa, AIR 1939 Bom 237,** copies of the documents were allowed to be taken and then privilege was claimed. The claim was rejected on three grounds. Firstly, that it was not the document of a confidential nature, secondly, that the claim was not based on the ground that the disclosure would adversely affect public interest, and, thirdly that no claim was made when the document was produced and had been inspected by the parties. The following observation was made in this case.

"They would not come within the category of official documents of a confidential nature as was the case in ILR 44 All 360: AIR 1922 All 37; secondly, because the public officer, the Collector in this-case, did not base his claim on the ground that public interest would suffer by the disclosure of the record; and thirdly, because no privilege was claimed when the documents were produced and inspected by the parties. It was claimed so late that the object could not be served even by admitting the claim."

55. On this case reliance can be placed about the stage also when this claim should be made, and the following observations can be read with advantage:

"It seems obvious that at the time he produces it according to the exigency of the summons, it is for the witness to claim the privilege. It is the duty of the Court then to determine whether the document shall be admitted and exhibited."

Further on, it was observed:

"As to when and how the privilege should be claimed, there is no clear-cut rule of procedure. But, it seems sufficiently clear that it should be claimed at the earliest opportunity by the public officer concerned when in reply to the summons be produces the document in his control or charge. It is futile to claim the privilege at a very late stage when there has already been a disclosure of the document given in charge of the Court."

56. In this connection, it should also be noted that when privilege is to be claimed, the document must be sent in a sealed, cover accompanied by an affidavit. For this reference be made to **Narayanaswami v. State of Madras, AIR 1953 Mad 228**. In the instant case, the document was not sent in a sealed cover. It was sealed by Sri Saxena a day after it was produced in Court and it had not been brought in a sealed cover as it should have been done.

57. In this connection, reference be made to **Chandra Dhar v. Deputy Commr., Lucknow, AIR 1939 Oudh 65**, wherein the following observation was made:

"It has been urged by Counsel supporting this application for privilege that section 124, Evidence Act, applies to disclosure in Courts and therefore privilege can be claimed even if there has been disclosure outside the Court I am not able to attach this restricted meaning to the section, for I hold that the object is to prevent the disclosure of things not known outside that circle which is in confidence and this section has no application when once there has been disclosure to what I might call a member of the public to whom the contents of such papers have not been made known in confidence. To hold otherwise would be to place Courts in an unfavourable position, while actually the Courts are favoured in the sense that they have the power to order the production of documents which an ordinary individual has not even if the propagation of this knowledge is contrary to the public interest, the person who has been allowed to obtain knowledge of the contents of such documents can make known to any person what he himself has come to know, and the mischief therefore is done. I do not see that the public Interests in the contemplation of the framers of the Evidence Act would suffer by promulgation in a Court of law and not by promulgation outside it."

NOTES ARE TAKEN FROM DOCUMENT – SANCTITY OF UNPUBLISHED DOCUMENT IS LOST – HOLDS HIGH COURT

58. Disclosure should not be taken in a narrow sense. If one is able to lay his hands on a confidential document and even if he takes notes of a part of the document disclosure is already made and, therefore, that document loses the sanctity of being an unpublished record.

59. In **Union of India v. T. Sudhir Kumar Roy, AIR 1963 Ori 111,** the following observations can be read with advantage:

> "I am, therefore, of the view that the word 'unpublished' in section 123 of the Evidence Act and the disclosure contemplated in section 124 of that Act relates primarily to the person against whom privilege is claimed under those sections and if he has been permitted lawfully to see those papers and also to take copies of the same it will be futile for the authorities to claim privilege under either of those sections."

60. Thus, there is not the least doubt that 'published' is not to mean only those documents or papers which are printed for general circulation. Even if a secret document or a part of it is revealed, the document will lose the sanctity as an unpublished record because there cannot be any guarantee as to when and in what contingency the other parts may also be made known. In this view of the matter, the document in question cannot be called an unpublished record.

61. The following observations in (1968) 1 All ER 874, decided by the House of Lords, at page 882 can be read with advantage:

> "The Attorney-General did not deny that, even where the full contents of a report have already been made public in a criminal case, Crown privilege is still claimed for that report in a later civil case; and he was quite candid about the reason for that Crown privilege is claimed in the civil case not to protect the document – its contents are already public property – but to protect the writer from civil liability should he be sued for libel or other tort."

62. Though in **Conway's case, (1966) 1 All ER 874** the entire document had been published in a criminal case, but all the same it does not make any difference If part of the document, which as a whole is claimed to be unpublished record is revealed and published.

63. The contention of the learned Counsel for the petitioner in this connection was that according to the statement of Sri Saxena this book passed from, table to table, from official to official, and, therefore, it was not a document which had been kept secret under lock and key by the Home Secretary or other Head of the Department entitled to keep it. It is a matter of common experience that even a most secret document in the course of daily dealings passes from one table to another in an office. But, that does not mean that the contents are divulged or published because the officers or officials concerned are duty bound to maintain its secrecy and they become liable for criminal prosecution in case the contents are leaked. The above argument has, therefore, no force in it.

64. When a part of the document has already been divulged in the Lok Sabha debates, no secrecy can be maintained, and it cannot be said that the other parts or portions of the blue book remained secret and the disclosure of the same would be protected by calling the other part an unpublished official record. In this view of the matter, this document cannot be termed as an unpublished record, as laid down in section 123 of the Evidence Act.

NO INSTRUCTIONS TO PRODUCE IT – DOES NOT AMOUNT TO CLAIM OF PRIVILEGE – SUBSEQUENT CLAIM OF PRIVILEGE MEANINGLESS – HOLDS HIGH COURT

65. It should be noted here, as stated by Sri Saxena, that there was some noting by the Law Department of the Government of Uttar Pradesh that the blue book was an unpublished record and privilege should be claimed. Even after this opinion of the Legal Remembrancer, Sri Saxena, was permitted to bring the blue book without being sealed in a cover and to keep it in his possession till a day or two after his examination started. When there was such a note by the Law Department, the head of the department should have sent this document in a sealed cover along with an application and affidavit that privilege was being claimed about the production of the document, by giving grounds for the same. For the reason best known to the authorities concerned, this was not done. On the other hand, a suggestion was thrown to Sri Saxena in his cross-examination that he brought the blue book without authority and only to help the petitioner. We are not aware if this suggestion has any force what action can be taken against Sri Saxena. On the other hand, I find from the perusal of the affidavit sworn by Sri Kaul that it does not bear out the above suggestion made in the cross-examination. The application was made by Sri Saxena on 20-9-1973 stating that he had brought the blue book as directed by the Home Secretary. He further stated in this application that he had been clearly instructed to claim privilege under section 123 of the Evidence Act. But, his statement recorded ten days earlier, referred to above does not show that at the very first instance he claimed any privilege under section 123 of the Evidence Act.

66. It was contended that when Sri Saxena stated that he had no instructions to file the blue book, it meant that he was claiming the privilege. When a document is summoned, a party or a witness cannot refuse to produce it in court. He can be forced to produce the same. Unless the production of the document is covered under any of the sections under Chapter IX of the Evidence Act, a witness cannot say that he has no authority to produce it, and such a statement will not amount to claim of privilege. In order to claim privilege, as shown above, the document must be produced in obedience to the summons in a sealed cover and along with it the privilege under section 123 of the Evidence Act should be claimed. If the privilege is claimed by an affidavit and the reasons are not fully detailed, therein, the Court may call for a fresh affidavit and even examine witnesses as required under section 162 of the Evidence Act. But, in no circumstance, a witness can say that he has no permission to produce the document. He has to produce it and then claim privilege. Mere saying that he has no permission to file the document would not amount to a claim of privilege.

COURT TO DECIDE IF DISCLOSURE WOULD BE AGAINST PUBLIC INTEREST – HOLDS HIGH COURT

67. In this connection it has also to be seen as to whether the claim for privilege can be scrutinised by a law court or the claim of privilege has to be accepted without such a scrutiny. The law on the point is now very clear. It is for the court to decide whether the document is noxious document and its disclosure would be against public interest. As shown above, the law right upto 1961 was that if the document was a noxious one then it was for the head of the department or the Minister concerned to produce it or not to produce it. But from 1961 onwards there was change in the interpretation of law on this point and now the court will look into the fact even if the document is noxious to see that privilege has been claimed judiciously and on valid grounds. It means that genuineness of the claim and the good faith has to be looked into by the court, as has been held by the Supreme Court in **Amar Chand Butail's** case as well as in the latest English decisions referred to above.

SUPREME COURT IN AMAR CHAND BUTAIL'S CASE IS COMPLETE ANSWER – HOLDS HIGH COURT

68. Thus, I am of the opinion that what has been said in **Amar Chand Butail's case, AIR 1964 SC 1658** (supra) and **(1967) 2 All ER 1260** (supra) coupled with section 162 of the Evidence Act is a complete answer to the above question. I have already discussed the evidence regarding the stage at which the aforesaid privilege could be claimed.

69. I would like to refer here at this stage to certain observations made in **Rambhotla Ramanna v. Government of Andhra Pradesh, AIR 1971 AP 196**; in this case it was observed:

> "Under section 162, when a public servant is summoned to produce the document in respect of which he wishes to claim privilege, he has first to produce the document summoned and then raise the objection claiming privilege by filing an affidavit in that behalf and if the Court comes to the conclusion that the document does not relate to any affairs of the State the claim must be negatived and the document must be received in evidence".

'AFFAIRS OF STATE' DEPENDS ON FACTS OF EACH CASE – HIGH COURT

70. Coming to the question as to whether the document relates to the affairs of the State the expression 'affairs of State' has not been defined by the legislature. Attempts have been made in a number of decisions to show what the expression 'affairs of state' means. The term affairs of State' is of very wide amplitude and it will cover every business activity of the State in even day to day routine administration as also highly confidential matters pertaining to defence, foreign affairs, Cabinet minutes, and advice or notes exchanged between Ministers and other heads of departments of the Government. The State activities now cover many other fields of trade, commerce etc., which would also be covered in the definition of the expression 'affairs of State'. But, simply because the matter relates to affairs of the State it would not be protected under section 123 of the Evidence Act unless evidence is derived from the unpublished record. In **Rambhotla Ramanna's case, AIR 1971 AP 196** (*supra*) the principle laid down by the Supreme Court in the case of **State of Punjab** (*supra*) was followed. It was held in this case that as to what would be the affairs of the State has to be determined in each case on the relevant facts and circumstances adduced before the Court. In **Amar Chand Butail's case, AIR 1964 SC 1658** (*supra*) the Supreme Court held that in exercising right under section 123 of the Evidence Act, heads of department should act with scrupulous care and the privilege should not only be claimed on the ground that it will defeat the defence of the State, but it should be on the ground that the disclosure would be prejudicial to public interest.

AFFIDAVIT FILED LATER ON – DOCUMENT ALREADY MADE PUBLIC – NO PRIVILEGE FOR WHOLE OR OF PART – HOLDS HIGH COURT

71. Even if it be assumed that the blue book had not been admitted in evidence and that the affidavit filed by Sri Kaul after a lapse of ten days be taken into consideration, even then the privilege in this case cannot be claimed for the simple reason that the Central Government had allowed this book to be within the reach of individuals who have taken notes from the book of those parts which served their purpose in a debate in the Lok Sabha. Not only this, Paper No. A-75/1, which is a portion of this Book, has been filed by the respondent and has been perused by the parties as well as their lawyers. It cannot be said that this part was so innocent that its disclosure would not be prejudicial to public interest.

72. If privilege is claimed regarding the entire document, it would not lie in the mouth of the person claiming the privilege to say that the portion of the document so published was of innocent nature and the other part of it if divulged would be prejudicial to public interest. This matter is not to rest with the authorities concerned, and they cannot be allowed to say that privilege should have been claimed only regarding that part or portion of the blue book, disclosure of which they thought to be prejudicial in public interest. In the instant case, the privilege has been claimed about the entire blue book, which includes that portion also which has already been published. In this view of the matter, even if this document relates to the affairs of the State, it is not an unpublished record, and, as such, it is not covered within the four corners of section 123 of the Evidence Act.

ELECTION PETITION UNDER CONSTITUTIONAL PROVISION – PRIVILEGE CLAIMED UNDER LEGISLATIVE ENACTMENT – CONTENTION OF RESPONDENT REJECTED – HIGH COURT

73. On behalf of the petitioner it was argued that the matter related to election petition, which arises out of the constitutional provisions, the legislative enactment cannot override the constitutional authority. Reliance was placed on Article 329 of the Constitution, which reads as below:

"Notwithstanding anything in this Constitution—

(a) the validity of any law relating to the delimitation of constituencies or the allotment of seats to such constituencies, made or purporting to be made under Article 327 or Article 328, shall not be called in question in any Court;

(b) no election to either House of Parliament or to the House or either House of the Legislature of a State shall be called in question except by an election petition presented to such authority and in such manner as may be provided for by or under any Legislature."

74. On the basis of this Article, it was argued that legislative bar cannot undo a constitutional right and power, and when a right is given under the Constitution the same cannot be curtailed or modified by any legislative enactment Chapter XV, which deals with Articles 324 to 329, relates to elections. Articles 245 and 246 of the Constitution provide that the Parliament may make laws for the whole or any part of the territory of India, and the Legislature of a State may make laws for the whole or any part of the State. Article 328 deals with the power of State to make legislation for the purposes of election. Election petitions are decided in accordance with the procedure laid down in the Representation of the People Act. Section 87 of the Representation of the people Act lays down that the provisions of the Indian Evidence Act, 1872, shall apply in all respects to the trial of an election petition, subject to the provisions of this Act. The Representation of the People Act was passed under constitutional authority and, therefore, the above argument has no force in it.

PART OF DOCUMENT FILED BY RESPONDENT IN DEFENCE – CLAIM OF PRIVILEGE NOT VALID – HOLDS HIGH COURT

75. I have already held that the Court has power to inspect the document. But, as I have held that the blue book is not an unpublished official record, therefore, I do not feel any necessity to inspect this document regarding which the privilege has been claimed.

Smt. Indira Nehru Gandhi as Prime Minister is fully entitled to know the contents of the blue book and to possess it but certainly in her individual capacity, in which she is placed in this case, she has no right to file even a portion of the blue book in support of her defence. When a part of the blue book, that is section 71(6) has been used by the respondent in support of her defence it cannot be said that the blue book has not been admitted in evidence. No privilege has been claimed by the State regarding use of the above portion of the blue book. The State cannot be permitted to have two yardsticks for two different individuals. Even when paper No. A-75/1 was referred by the learned Counsel for the petitioner in the course of his argument, no attempt was made by the State to claim such a privilege, even if it be assumed that till then the State had no knowledge of such use of a portion of the blue book.

76. Besides this, the petitioner has no occasion to show to the Court about the correctness or otherwise of paper No. A-75/1 unless the blue book is made available to him. Nor he can be in a position to efficiently cross-examine the respondent's witnesses regarding paper No. A-75/1 in the absence of the blue book. The Court has to keep the balance even and it cannot tilt it in favour of one party or the other. It is, therefore, just, equitable and in accordance with the principle of natural justice that the claim of privilege regarding the blue book and other papers which are correlated with the blue book be rejected.

OTHER PART OF BLUEBOOK STANDS ON THE SAME FOOTING – HOLDS HIGH COURT

77. So far as the other two documents are concerned, they do not stand on a different footing. As far as the documents summoned from the Superintendent of Police, Raebareli, are concerned, they were sent under a sealed cover along with an affidavit that these documents related to the affairs of the State and being unpublished records, privilege was claimed as the Superintendent of Police came to the conclusion that their disclosure was prejudicial to public interest. In the affidavit he stated that the documents related to the security arrangements for the Prime Minister of India. All the instructions relating to the security arrangements, which were issued to the District Officers and Superintendent of Police etc., are contained in the blue book. If that very blue book cannot be called a privileged document then it cannot be said that the papers, which have been filed by the Superintendent of Police, Raebareli, which owe their existence to the blue book, relating to the security arrangements of the Prime Minister, can be called privileged documents, in accordance with section 123 of the Evidence Act. All that the Superintendent of Police stated was that it was 'Top secret security arrangements in connection with the visit of the Prime Minister of India.' He did not give any reason which led him to the conclusion' that the disclosure of the documents would be against public interest. As stated above, top security arrangements are derived from the blue book, and as the blue book itself cannot be said to be a privileged document, therefore, these documents also cannot be called privileged documents as provided under section 123 of the Evidence Act. Since I have held that privilege cannot be claimed regarding these documents, I do not feel any necessity to inspect these documents.

NO PRIVILEGE CLAIMED FOR DOCUMENTS FROM ACCOUNTANT – GENERAL OFFICE – NO AFFIDAVIT FILED – HIGH COURT

78. Sri K.P. Sood, who is an officer of the Accountant General's office, Central Revenue, New Delhi, filed three documents which relate to the pay and emoluments paid to Sri Y.P.R. Kapoor. No privilege under section 123 has been claimed regarding these papers. These papers were brought in a sealed cover. As the application or affidavit has also been placed in the file of the case, I got the said sealed cover opened to find out as to whether any application or affidavit under section 123 of the Evidence Act has been filed. The seal was opened only with this limited purpose, but the documents were not inspected. I find that only one application is attached with these papers, relevant portion of which runs as below:

> "I am further to state that under I.R. L.A. System of payment, officer is not required to submit monthly salary bill. Salary is paid on the basis of register maintained at (b) above.
>
> These documents after perusal may kindly be returned. In case they are required by the Court, their photostat copies will be produced, provided appropriate time is allowed."

79. In view of this, it cannot be said that any privilege in respect of these documents was claimed. These papers are allowed to be produced.

NOT ENTITLED TO ANY PRIVILEGE – PETITION ALLOWED – HIGH COURT

80. For the reasons given above, I hold that no privilege can be claimed in respect of any of the three sets of papers and they are allowed to be produced.

Order accordingly.

ALLAHABAD HIGH COURT

Sri Raj Narain, Son of Sri Anant Prasad Singh, Resident of Village Gaujari, Post Gangapur, District Varanasi

v.

1. Smt. Indira Nehru Gandhi, daughter of Pt. Jawaharlal Nehru, resident of 1, Motilal Nehru Road, (Purbi Bhag) Allahabad (at present resident at No. 1 Safdarjang Road, New Delhi).
2. Swami Advaita Nand, son of Sri Brahma Nand, resident of 13 North Avenue, M.P's. Flat, New Delhi

Before Hon'ble J.M.L. Sinha, J.

Civil Side Original Jurisdiction

Election Petition No. 5 of 1975 Connected With Writ Petition No. 3761 of 1975

Dated" 12 June, 1975

Judgment by the Court

Hon'ble J.M.L. Sinha, J.—

VERSION OF THE PETITIONER IN THE ELECTION PETITION

In the elections that took place for the Lok Sabha in 1971, Sri Raj Narain (hereafter to be called the petitioner) and Shrimati Indira Nehru Gandhi (here after to be called the respondent No. 1) were the principal contenders from 22 Raebareli parliamentary constituency. The other two candidates in the field were Rameshwar Dutta Mandoy and Swami Advaitanand. The respondent No. 1 obtained 1,83,309 votes. The petitioner got 71,499 votes. Rameshwar Dutta Mandoy and Swami Advaitanand got 4,839 and 16,627 votes respectively. The respondent No. 1 was accordingly declared elected. The petitioner has filled the present petition, challenging the election of respondent No. 1. Shorn of the grounds not pressed or adhered to, the rest of the grounds on which the election has been challenged are as follows:

(1) That the respondent No. 1 held herself out as a prospective candidate from 22 Raebareli constituency immediately after the dissolution of the Lok Sabha on 27th November, 1970 and that, for the furtherance of her election prospects, she obtained and procured the assistance of Sri Yashpal Kapur, a Gazetted Officer in the Government of India holding the post of Officer on Special Duty, and thereby the respondent No. 1 committed a corrupt practice under section 123(7) of the Representation of the People Act, 1951.

(2) That the respondent No. 1 and her election agent procured the assistance of members of the Armed Forces of the Union for furtherance of her election prospects, in as much as the members of the Armed Forces arranged planes

and helicopters of the Air Force at her instance for her flights to enable her to address meetings in her constituency, and thereby the respondent No. 1 committed another corrupt practice under section 123(7) of the Representation of the People Act.

(3) That the respondent No. 1 and her election agent also obtained and procured the assistance of a number of Gazetted officers and members of the Police Force for the furtherance of her election prospects, in as much as the services of the District Magistrate, Raebareli, the Superintendent of Police Raebareli and the Home Secretary, U.P. Government were utilised for the purpose of

(a) construction of rostrums and installation of loudspeakers at various places within the constituency where the respondent No. 1 addressed her election meeting

And

(b) making arrangements of barricading and posting of police personnel on the routes by which the respondent No. 1 was to travel in her constituency and at the places where she was to address meetings, in visits and to attract larger crowds,

and thereby the respondent No. 1 committed another corrupt practice under section 127(7) of the Representation of the People Act.

(4) That Sri Yashpal Kapur, the election agent of respondent No. 1, and her other agents with the consent of Sri Yashpal Kapur, freely distributed quilts, blankets, dhotis and liquor among the voters to induce them to vote for her and thereby the respondent No. 1 committed the corrupt practice of bribery under section 123(1)(A)(b)(ii) of Representation of the People Act.

(5) That the respondent No. 1 and her election agent made extensive appeals to the religious symbol of cow and calf and thereby committed a corrupt practice under section 123(3) of the Representation of the People Act.

(6) That Sri Yashpal Kapur, the election agent of respondent No. 1 and some other agents or persons with his consent hired and produced a number of vehicles for the free conveyance of electors to the polling stations and thereby committed a corrupt practice under section 123(5) of the Representation of the People Act.

(7) That the respondent No. 1 and her election agent incurred or authorized expenditure in contravention of the section 77 of the Representation of the People Act and thereby committed a corrupt practice under section 123(6) of the Representation of the People Act.

VERSION OF RESPONDENT NO. 1 (SMT. INDIRA NEHRU GANDHI)

The respondent No 1, denying the aforesaid allegations made against her, pleaded:

(i) That Sri Yashpal Kapur resigned from his post on 13th January 1971 and the resignation was accepted with effect from 14th January 1971, in regard to which a notification dated 25th January 1971 was issued by the Prime Minister's Secretariat. In the Additional Written statement it was added that Sri P.N. Haksar, the then Secretary to the Prime Minister told Sri Yashpal Kapur on the same date, on which the resignation was tendered, that it was accepted and that formal orders would follow.

(ii) That Sri Yashpal Kapur became her election agent on 4th of February, 1971, and that during the period he was Gazetted Officer in the Government of India he did not do any work in furtherance of her election prospects.

(iii) Referring to the use of planes and helicopters of the Air Force, the respondent No. 1 admitted that on 1st of February, 1971 she went by a plane of the Air Force from Delhi to Lucknow, from where she went by car to Raebareli, addressing meetings enroute. She further admitted that on 24th of February, 1971 she went by a helicopter of the Air Force to Gonda on regular party work and that from there she went by car to Lucknow, Unnao and Raebareli, addressing public meetings in several constituencies besides her own. She referred to the Pillai Committee Report and the Office Memorandums issued by the Government of India to plead that the aforesaid flights were made by her in compliance thereof. It was further pleaded by her that, under the rules, bills for those flights were to be paid by the A.I.C.C. and most of them had already been paid. According to her, neither did she nor her election agent solicit, require or order the use of Air Force planes, and that the Government of India provided the planes as part of their normal duty,

(iv) That the respondent or her election agent did not obtain the assistance of the District Magistrate, Raebareli and the Superintendent of Police, Raebareli not that of the Home Secretary, U.P. Government for any of the purpose alleged in the petition. She then referred to the instructions issued by the Comptroller & Auditor General of India dated 29th November, 1958 the Accountant Generals of all the States, as also to the letter dated 12th January, 1959 issued by the Government of India. She then pleaded that the arrangements for posting of police on the routes which she followed and the arrangements of rostrums were made by the State Government itself in compliance of those instructions. In regard to the loudspeakers, she pleaded that they were arranged by the District Congress Committee and not by the officers of the State Government. Respondent No. 1 denied that any directions or instructions in that regard were issued by her or her election agent.

(v) That allegations regarding distribution of blankets, dhotis and liquor were absolutely false.

(vi) Referring to the symbol of cow and calf, the respondent No. 1 pleaded that

(a) it was not a religious symbol and that it was wrong that extensive appeals were made by her or her election agent to that symbol. She added that she and her election agent merely informed the voters that the symbol of Congress (R) was cow and calf and that the voting mark should be put against that symbol,

And

(b) the decision of the Election Commission allotting the symbol of cow and calf to her party was final and could not be made a ground of attack, nor can the Court go into that question, in the present proceedings.

(vii) That the allegations regarding hiring and procuring of vehicles and the use thereof for conveyance of the voters to the polling stations were false.

(viii) That the allegation that the respondent No. 1 or her election agent incurred expenditure in excess of the prescribed limit was also wrong.

ISSUES AND ADDITIONAL ISSUES FRAMED

On the pleadings of the parties one set of issues was framed by the Court on 19th of August, 1971. Three additional issues were framed on 27th April, 1973. These issues are as follows:

ISSUES

(1) Whether respondent No. 1 obtained and procured the assistance of Yashpal Kapur in furtherance of the prospects of her election while he was still a Gazetted Officer in the service of Government of India. If so, from what date?

(2) Whether at the instance of respondent No. 1 members of the Armed Forces of the Union arranged Air Force planes and helicopters for her, flown by members of the Armed Forces, to enable her to address election meetings on 1.2.1971 and 25.2.1971; and if so, whether this constituted a corrupt practice under section 123 (7) of the Representation of the People Act?

(3) Whether at the instance of respondent No. 1 and her election agent Yashpal Kapur, the District Magistrate of Raebareli, and the Home Secretary of U.P. Government arranged for rostrums, loudspeakers and barricades to be set-up and for members of the Police Force to be posted in connection with her election tour on 1.2.1971 and 25.2.1971; and if so, whether this amounts to a corrupt practice under section 123(7) of the Representation of the People Act?

(4) Whether quilts, blankets, dhotis and liquor was distributed by agents and workers of respondent No. 1, with the consent of her election agent Yashpal Kapur, at the places and on the dates mentioned in Schedule A of the petition in order to induce electors to vote for her?

(5) Whether the particulars given in paragraph 10 and Schedule A of the petition are too vague and general to afford a basis for allegations of bribery under section 123(1) of the Representation of the People Act?

(6) Whether by using the symbol of cow and calf, which had been allotted to her party by the Election Commission, in her election campaign the respondent No. 1 was guilty of making an appeal to a religious symbol and committed a corrupt practice as defined in section 123(3) of the Representation of the People Act?

(7) Whether on the dates fixed for the poll voters were conveyed to the polling stations free of charge on vehicles hired and procured for the purpose by respondent No. 1's election agent Yashpal Kapur, or other persons with his consent, as detailed in Schedule *B* to the petition?

(8) Whether the particulars given in paragraph 12 and Schedule *B* of the petition are too vague and general to form a basis for allegations regarding a corrupt practice under section 123(5) of the Representation of the People Act?

(9) Whether respondent No. 1 and her election agent Yashpal Kapur incurred or authorized expenditure in excess of the amount prescribed by section 77 of the Representation of the People Act, read with rule 90, as detailed in Para 13 of the petition?

(10) Whether the petitioner had made a security deposit in accordance with the rules of the High Court as required by section 117 of the Representation of the People Act?

(11) To what relief, if any, is the petitioner entitled?

ADDITIONAL ISSUES

(1) Whether respondent No.1 obtained and procured the assistance of Yashpal Kapur in furtherance of the prospects of her election while he was still a Gazetted Officer in the service of the Government of India. If so, from what date?

(2) Whether respondent No. 1 held herself out as a candidate from any date prior to 1.2.1971 and if so; from what date?

(3) Whether Yashpal Kapur continued to be in the service of Government of India from and after 14.1.1971 or till which date?

DURING THE PENDENCY OF THE ELECTION PETITION AMENDMENT MADE IN SECTION 77 OF THE REPRESENTATION OF THE PEOPLE ACT – CHALLENGED IN CWP – TO BE HEARD WITH ELECTION PETITION – HIGH COURT

During the pendency of the election petition in this Court, the Parliament amended section 77 of the Representation of the People Act by Ordinance No. XIII of 1974, which has now been replaced by Act No. 58 of 1974. The petitioner has filed Writ Petition No. 3761 of 1975, challenging the vires of the Amending Act; and that writ petition has been connected with the present election petition. The writ petition can have a bearing only on issue no.9 I shall, therefore, address myself on the contentions raised on either side in the writ petition while dealing with issue no.9 The respondents impleaded in the writ petition are the Union of India and Smt. Indira Nehru Gandhi (respondent No. 1 in the election petition).

FINDINGS

ISSUES NO. 2

SUBMISSION OF PETITIONER THAT RESPONDENT NO. 1 USED MILITARY AIRCRAFT FOR TRAVELLING AND TOOK THE ASSISTANCE OF ARMED FORCES FOR ELECTION PURPOSE – REJECTED – HIGH COURT

It is the admitted case of the parties that on 1st of February, 1971 the respondent No. 1 travelled by an I.A.F. plane from Delhi to Lucknow, from where she went by car to Raebareli and that, besides filing her nomination paper at Raebareli, she also made election speeches at various places in her constituency. It is also not disputed that on 24th of February, 1971 the respondent No. 1 went by an I.A.F. helicopter from Delhi to Gonda, from where she went by car to Raebareli (*via* Unnao and Lucknow), reaching Raebareli on 25th February, 1971; and that on the said date she also delivered election speeches at various places in her constituency. According to the allegations contained in the petition, the respondent No. 1 thereby procured the assistance of members of the Armed Forces of the Union for furthering the prospects of her election, which is a corrupt practice under section 123(7) of the Representation of the People Act.

At the time of argument learned counsel for the petitioner stated that since on 24th February, 1971 the respondent No. 1 travelled by an I.A.F. helicopter to Gonda, it is possible to contend that the said journey was made by the respondent for party work and not to further her own election prospects and, consequently, the fact of the respondent No. 1 using an I.A.F. helicopter on 24th February, 1971 can be excluded from consideration under this issue. Learned counsel however, stressed that the journey made by the respondent No. 1 on 1st of February, 1971 by an I.A.F. plane from Delhi to Lucknow was to enable her to file her nomination paper at Raebareli and to deliver election speeches in her constituency and, consequently that should constitute a corrupt practice under section 123(7) of the Act. The contention of the respondent No. 1 in reply thereto is two-fold:

(a) that the respondent No. 1 or her election agent did not solicit, require or order the use of the Air-Force plane (para 12(d) of the written statement), and

(b) that in view of the Pillai Committee Report, and the Office Memorandums issued on its basis from time to time, the government provided an aeroplane for her journey as part of their normal duty and, consequently, the fact of the respondent having travelled by an I.A.F. plane from Delhi to Lucknow on 1.2.1971 cannot constitute a corrupt practice.

Now, so far as the first part of the contention is concerned, it is not possible to accept it. The Office Memorandum was also operative on 1st of February,

1971 when the impugned flight was made by the respondent No. 1 Under this office Memorandum, read along with the previous Memorandums, and the Pillai Committee Report, the respondent No. 1, as Prime Minister of the country, was entitled to make use of an I.A.F. aircraft while travelling for non- official purposes as well. In answer to interrogatory no. 24 it was admitted on behalf of the respondent No. 1 that she was aware of the existence of the Government Order and the substance thereof. Even during her deposition in Court the respondent No. 1 admitted that when the Prime Minister goes on an election tour, a plane of the Indian Air Force is put at her disposal and that such plane is flown by members of the Indian Air Force. The respondent No. 1 further admitted during her deposition that though the tour programmes concerning the party work are sent by the All India Congress Committee, they are finalized after her approval is obtained. According to Sri Seshan (PW. 53), Private Secretary to the respondent No. 1, instructions are sent from the Prime Minister's Secretariat to the Air Headquarters for arranging for an I.A.F. aeroplane for the tour of the Prime Minister, even when the tour is non-official, and it is then the duty of the Air Headquarters to arrange for the same. Wing Commander K.G. Mohan Chand (P.W. 49) , Deputy Director, Air Traffic Control & Co-ordinating Officer, V.I.P.'s, Air Headquarters stated during his cross-examination made on behalf of respondent No. 1:

> "It is correct that on receipt of the tour programme of the Prime Minister it is my duty to arrange for the aircraft according to her programme on the basis of the Standing Order of the Government of India"

Since the tour programme is sent from the Secretariat of respondent No. 1, after her approval is obtained, since the respondent No. 1 as Prime Minister fully well knew that thereafter it was the duty of the Air Headquarters to place a plane at her disposal, there is no escape from the conclusion that, by sending the tour programmes to the Air Headquarters, the respondent No. 1 required an I.A.F. plane being placed at her disposal. The fact that the respondent No. 1 did not require any particular plane being placed at her disposal is not material. It may not be out of place to add here that in answer to interrogatory No. 27 the respondent No. 1 admitted that the aircraft and helicopter used by her on 1st February, 1971 and 24th and 25th February, 1971 were flown by members of the Air Force. During her deposition in Court also she stated that when she boarded that plane on 1st of February, 1971 in order to make her journey from Delhi to Lucknow, she was aware that the plane was to be flown by the members of the Indian Air Force.

It should, therefore, be accepted that a plane of the Indian Air Force, manned by Armed Forces of the Union, was placed at the disposal of the respondent No. 1 on 1st of February, 1971 at her instance for her flight from Delhi to Lucknow and the respondent No. 1 thus did obtain the assistance of the members of the Armed Forces of the Union, who constituted the crew on the I.A.F. plane.

This takes me to the second limb of the contention raised on behalf of the respondent No. 1 namely, Whether the aforesaid assistance of the Armed Forces of the Union was obtained by the respondent No. 1 in furtherance of her election prospects, or the Government placed the plane at her disposal as part of their normal duty, in view of the Pillai Committee Report and the Office Memorandums issued on the basis thereof.

It will be convenient first to refer to the Pillai Committee Report and the Office Memorandums issued on the basis thereof.

A copy of the Pillai Committee Report has been filed by Sri V. Srikantan (R.W.4) Deputy Secretary, Ministry of Defence, Government of India. It is Exh. A-22 on record and is dated 17th October, 1971. In Para 12 thereof it is stated:

> "The position of the Prime Minister is for a different reason also special. Whether at headquarters or away from it in camp or in transit, the disposal of public business must have first claim on his time and attention. It is, therefore, clearly in the public interest to ensure that when he goes on tour the arrangements for his travel are such as would eliminate the long irritating delays which, depended on normal modes of public transport, inevitably entails. It is equally necessary to ensure that during the journey adequate facilities are provided for him for the transaction of official business. For these as well as security reasons which are no less important, we consider that the Prime Minister should use the I.A.F. aircraft for all journeys by air."

In Para 13 of the interim report it is said that there may be occasions 'when the object of a journey undertaken by the Prime Minister may be prominently connected with the work relating to the party of which he is a leader.'

In Para 14 of the interim report the Committee examined as to on what terms the I.A.F. aircraft may be employed on journeys undertaken by the Prime Minister otherwise on official duty.

It will thus transpire on a perusal of the interim report of the Pillai Committee that, while referring to the unofficial tours to be made by the Prime Minister by the I.A.F. Aircraft, the Committee had in mind, in all probability, the work relating to the party of which the Prime Minister happens to be the leader, and not the work exclusively and personally relating to the Prime Minister.

On 20th October, 1951 the Ministry of Defence issued a press note (Exh. A-23) on the basis of the interim report of the Pillai Committee. After highlighting what was stated in the interim report of the Pillai Committee about the desirability of the Prime Minister travelling by an I.A.F. aircraft, it stated:

> "The Prime Minister, in his capacity as the leader of his political party, recently had, and will in future continue to have, occasion to undertake journeys by air for other than official purposes. The nature of the journey on such occasions is different from normal official tours, but the Prime Minister cannot on this account divest himself, for the period of the journey, of his position and responsibility as head of the Government. The business of the Government never comes to stand still and the Prime Minister is never off duty. Whatever the character of the journey performed by him, the need for eliminating delays in travel, for providing facilities for the transaction of official business during the journey and for making suitable security arrangements remains unchanged. It is, therefore, desirable that, even for journeys by air for other than official purposes, the Prime Minister should, as for as possible, travel by I.A.F. Aircraft."

From the underlined portion occurring in the aforesaid press note it will appear that even in this press note, while referring to the non-official tours, what the Ministry of Defence had in its mind were the tours made by the Prime Minister in his capacity as the leader of his party.

Exh. A-24 is the final report of the Pillai Committee and is dated 20th May, 1953. It only refers to its interim report, so far as the use of the I.A.F. Aircraft by the Prime Minister is concerned. Exh.126 is the Office Memorandum dated 17th August, 1968, which was issued in supersession of the previous Memorandums, (which it is not necessary to refer). Para II(d) thereof reads as follows:—

> "The aircraft of the V.I.P. flight are to be used on official duty only. In the case of the Prime Minister, it is necessary that, even on occasions when he/she has to undertake journeys mainly for reasons other than official duties, he or she would be able to travel by I.A.F. Aircraft for the due performance

of his/her duties as the head of the Government as well as for reasons of security."

A cumulative reading of all the aforesaid papers gives an impression that, while referring to non-official purposes, what was conceived was the work of the party to which the Prime Minister belonged and not the work relating exclusively to the Prime Minister.

Assuming, however, that the flights for non-official purposes, referred to in the interim report of the Pillai Committee and the Office Memorandums also included flights made by the Prime minister for works exclusively relating to him, it cannot be ignored that the interim report of the Pillai Committee had an advisory nature and the Press Note and Office Memorandums relied upon by the respondent are mere administrative orders. Nothing contained therein can render the provisions contained in the Representation of the People Act nugatory. If a Prime Minister used the I.A.F. Aircraft for official purposes, obviously such use cannot be in conflict with section 123(7) of the Representation of the People Act. Similarly, if a Prime Minister used the I.A.F. Aircraft for the political work of the party, that too will not be in conflict with the aforesaid provision contained in the Representation of the People Act. If, however, the Prime Minister uses an aircraft exclusively for the purposes of frequently flying to his/her constituency during the period of his/her election with the sole purpose of doing election propaganda, it has the potentiality of violating the provision contained in section 123(7) of the Representation of the People Act, for, by making use of the I.A.F. Aircraft for frequently flying into his/her constituency as a candidate he/she avails of the means for quick and speedy movement in his/her election campaign. The aircraft being manned by the Armed Force of the Union, the use thereof under such circumstances can fall within the mischief of section 123(7) of the Act. Neither the interim Pillai Committee Report nor the Office Memorandums referred to by respondent No. 1 can under such circumstances salvage the position.

Learned counsel for respondent No. 1 referred me to Article 298 of the Constitution and urged that it was within the executive power of the Union to establish a commercial wing of the I.A.F. Aircraft for the exclusive use of the Prime Minister and a couple of other dignitaries of the Government. Learned counsel pointed out that according to Office Memorandum dated 3rd December 1951 (Exh. 125) as well as Office Memorandum dated 17th August 1968 (Exh.126) fare for the air journeys made by the Prime Minister for other than official purpose was recoverable at the rate specified in the said Memorandum, and it should, therefore, be accepted that, while permitting the use of the I.A.F. planes by the Prime Minister for other than official purposes, the union in exercise of its executive power established a commercial wing of the I.A.F. Aircraft for the use of the Prime Minister. Learned counsel for respondent No. 1 urged that, in that view of the matter, the use of the I.A.F. Aircraft by the Prime Minister for any purpose whatsoever cannot be violative of section 123(7) of the Representation of the People Act. I have given my careful thought to the argument raised, but I am unable to accept it. It is true that under Article 298 of the Constitution the Union can, in exercise of its executive power, indulge in commercial activities and it can while doing so also establish air service. That should, however, be an independent service open to all and sundry. Permitting the use of the I.A.F. aircraft to the Prime Minister only for non-official purpose on payment of certain fare cannot be construed as establishing a commercial wing of the Air Force by the Union in exercise of its executive power under Article 298 of the Constitution. It only means extending a special privilege to the Prime Minister. Article 298 of the Constitution can have no application to it.

Learned counsel for respondent No. 1 then referred me to the Full Bench decision of the Delhi High Court in the case **Prakashvir Shastri v. Union of India, AIR 1974 Del 1** and urged that the validity of the Office Memorandum dated 17th of August, 1968 has been upheld in that case. The validity of the said memorandum in that case, however, was examined *vis-à-vis* Article 14 of the Constitution and not vis-à-vis any provision contained in the Representation of the People Act. The case referred to by learned counsel for the respondent No. 1 has, therefore, no bearing on the point in issue before me and, consequently, no reliance can be placed by the respondent No. 1 on that decision.

The question that, however, still remains to be considered is whether on the facts of this case it can be said that, in obtaining the services of the Armed Forces of the Union, who manned the Aircraft by which the respondent No. 1 travelled on 1st of February, 1971 from Delhi to Lucknow, she obtained their assistance for the furtherance of her prospects in the election.

The petitioner filed copies of some tour programmes of the respondent No. 1, besides examining Wing Commander K.G. Mohan Chand (P.W. 49), who filed office copy of the bill relating to the flight made by respondent No. 1 on 1st of February 1971 from Delhi to Lucknow. On the basis thereof the petitioner sought to make out that the said flight was made by respondent No. 1 only to reach Raebareli to file her nomination paper and do her election propaganda. A perusal of the record, however, reveals that factually it was not so. The petitioner himself filed copy of a letter dated 27th January, 1971 (Exh.27) from the Under Secretary, U.P. Government to the District Magistrate, Lucknow, the District Magistrate, Raebareli, the Estates Officer, Lucknow, the Commissioner, Lucknow and the Inspector-General of Police, Lucknow. Along with this letter is annexed a copy of the tour programme of the respondent No. 1. A perusal of this tour programme shows that on the 2nd of February 1971, on her return from Raebareli to Lucknow, the respondent No. 1. was to fly by the I.A.F. Aircraft to Panagarh. Sri N.K. Seshan (P.W. 53), Private Secretary to the Prime Minister, produced in Court a file which, *inter alia*, contained the bill for the non-official journeys made by the respondent No. 1 in the I.A.F. Aircraft from 1st of February, 1971 to 7th of February, 1971. Sri Seshan stated that this bill was prepared by his office on the basis of the bill received from the Air Headquarters. These bills were flagged by Sri Seshan as 'B' and 'X' respectively. It is true that these bills were not got marked as exhibits. The fact, however, remains that the file was produced in Court in the presence of counsel for the petitioner and counsel for the respondent No. 1 and Sri Seshan made the required statement in regard to those bills. Consequently there can be no valid objection to reference being made to those bills. That apart, Raj Kumar Singh (P.W. 56), In-Charge Legal Affairs Department and Assistant Secretary, Parliamentary Affairs of All India Congress Committee, also produced in Court a file containing the tour programme of the respondent No. 1 for the period from 1st of February, 1971 to 7th of February, 1971. That tour programme was admitted by the respondent No. 1 and got formally exhibited in the case. (Exh. A-64). The aforesaid documents clearly revealed that on 1st of February, 1971 the respondent No. 1 set out from Delhi on an extensive election tour of the country, visiting a number of places, including Lucknow, Panagarh, Shantiniketan, Serampur, Kaikunda, Calcutta, Bahrampur, Krishna Nagar, Teetagarh, Gauhati, Agartala, Kgram, Silchar, Mohanbari, Rawriah, Roopsi, Kooch Behar, Purnea, Raiganj and Malda. Since the respondent No. 1 had to file her nomination paper at Raebareli during the same period, she landed at Lucknow and drove from there to Raebareli for that Purpose. After filing her nomination paper and delivering a few speeches, both inside and outside her constituency, she came back to Lucknow to resume her flight onwards on her election tour.

In the context of the aforesaid facts, it cannot be held that by flying in the I.A.F. Aircraft on 1st of February, 1971 the respondent No. 1 obtained the assistance of the Armed Forces of the Union for furtherance of her prospects at the election.

Learned counsel for the petitioner urged that *mens rea* is not a necessary ingredient of the corrupt practice under section 123(7) of the Representation of the People Act. It was stressed by him that the flight made by the respondent No. 1 in so far as it extended between Delhi and Lucknow, was connected with the respondent No. 1 filing her nomination paper at Raebareli and doing election propaganda. Learned counsel further urged that it is immaterial whether the respondent No. 1, while travelling by the I.A.F. Aircraft from Delhi to Lucknow, did or did not intend to further her election prospects thereby. According to learned counsel, once it is shown that the flight had facilitated the filing of the nomination paper by the respondent No. 1 at Raebareli and doing of election propaganda, she must be held guilty of corrupt practice under section 123(7) of the Act. In support of his argument regarding *mens rea*, learned counsel referred me to the decision of the Supreme Court in the case **Dr. Y.S. Parmar v. Hira Singh, AIR 1959 SC 244.**

I have, however, already stated that the flight made by the respondent No. 1 from Delhi to Lucknow was not connected with her filing of nomination paper or with her doing election propaganda in her constituency. As already stated earlier, on 1st of February, 1971 the respondent No. 1 had set out on a general election tour of the country. Since, however, she had also to file her nomination paper at Raebareli during the same period, she landed on way at Lucknow and then drove to Raebareli for that purpose. Having reached there she also delivered a few speeches. It cannot, therefore, reasonably be said that the use of the I.A.F. Aircraft was directly connected with her election work. As for the case referred to by learned counsel for the petition No. 1, it cannot be ignored that it related to utilizing the services of a personnel of the Armed Forces as polling agent. Clause (2) of Explanation 1, appended to section 123(7) of the Representation of the People Act, as it then existed, stated that for the purposes for sub-clause (7) a person shall be deemed to assist in the furtherance of the prospects of a candidate's election, if he, *inter alia,* acts as a polling agent of that candidate. It was in that context that the Supreme Court said that the question of *mens rea* was not relevant. That observation cannot have an universal application. It was so pointed out in the case **Babu Bhai Vallabh Das Gandhi v. Pilloo Homi Mody, 36 Election LR Guj 108 on pp Election LR 409 (432) (Alld.).**

For the reasons stated above, I find that, on the basis of the respondent No. 1 having flown in an I.A.F. Aircraft from Delhi to Lucknow on 1st of February 1971, she cannot be held guilty of having obtained the assistance of the Armed Forces of the Union for furtherance of her election prospects and thereby of having committed a corrupt practice under section 123(7) of the Representation of the People Act. Issue No. 2 is accordingly answered against the petitioner and in favour of respondent No. 1.

ISSUE NO. 3

In para 9 of the petition it is alleged that the respondent No. 1 and her election agent obtained and procured the assistance of the Gazetted Officers and members of the Police Force in the service of the Government for furthering the prospects of her election. Further clarifying the allegation, it is stated that the services of the District Magistrate of Raebareli, the Superintendent of Police, Raebareli and the Home Secretary, U.P. Government were utilized by the respondent No. 1 on 1st of February, 1971 and 25th of February 1971 for the construction of rostrums, for erection of barricades, for making arrangements of loudspeakers at the places of the meetings, and for posting police along the route by which the respondent No. 1 was to travel. According to learned counsel for the petitioner, this amounted to a corrupt practice under section 123(7) of the Representation of the People Act.

The respondent No. 1 in her written statement denied that either she or her election agent obtained the aforesaid assistance of the District Magistrate, Raebareli, the Superintendent of Police, Raebareli and the Home Secretary, U.P. Government. She admitted that rostrums were constructed at some places where she addressed the meetings. She, however, added (in paras 13(k) and 13(1) of the written statement) that the rostrums were constructed by private contractors under the direction issued by the State Government and that none of the Gazetted Officers of the State Government, mentioned in para 9 of the petition, were in any manner connected with the construction thereof. Erection of barricades and posting of police was not denied by the respondent. With regard to the loudspeakers, the respondent pleaded that they were arranged by the District Congress Committee. The respondent then referred to the instructions issued by the Comptroller and Auditor General of India on 29th November, 1958 (Exh. 123) and to the letter of the Government of India dated 12th of January, 1959 (Exh. 124) and pleaded that the aforesaid arrangements were made by the Government on its own initiative in the discharge of their Governmental duties and by the officers of the Government in the discharge of their duty.

BUILDING OF ROSTRUMS FOR RESPONDENT NO. 1 BY GOVERNMENT OFFICERS – AMOUNTS TO CORRUPT PRACTICE – CONTENTION OF PETITIONER

The fact that rostrums were got constructed and barricading was got done by the Superintendent of Police, Raebareli, is supported by a mass of documentary evidence, besides oral evidence. Exh. 148 is the letter dated 31st March, 1973 from the U.P. Police Headquarters, Allahabad, to the Deputy Secretary, Home Department. It clearly states that five rostrums were constructed for the meetings addressed by the respondent No. 1 on 1st of February 1971, and one prefab rostrum and barricade were transported by truck from Allahabad to Raebareli for another meeting addressed by the respondent No. 1 on the same date. According to this letter, a cost of Rs. 8,000 was incurred on the construction of five rostrums and a cost of Rs. 490 was incurred in transporting the prefab rostrum from Allahabad to Raebareli. Exh. 149 is the letter dated 2nd February, 1973 from the Superintendent of Police, Raebareli, to the U.P. Police Headquarters, Allahabad, containing the same information. Exh. 154 is a letter dated 1st of February, 1972 sent by the Superintendent of police, Raebareli to the U.P. Police Headquarters, Allahabad, containing the details of the expenditure incurred in connection with the arrangements made on 1st of February, 1971. This also shows that a sum of Rs. 8,000 was incurred in the construction of rostrums and a sum of Rs. 490 was incurred in connection with the transporting of the prefab. rostrum and barricade. It is not necessary to mention here other details of expenditure contained in this letter. Exh.185 is a radiogram dated 26th January, 1971 sent by the Superintendent of Police, Raebareli to the U.P. Police Headquarters, Allahabad soliciting sanction for the construction of rostrums and barricades through the P.W.D. Exh. 184 is the radiogram dated 28th January, 1971 according sanction for incurring expenditure on barricading and construction of rostrums through the P.W.D. Exh.186 is the copy of a letter dated January 26, 1971 sent by the Superintendent of Police, Raebareli to the Executive Engineer, P.W.D., Raebareli apprising him that the respondent No. 1 would be addressing meetings at seven places specified in the letter and that all the meetings, except one, shall require construction of rostrums and barricades. Exh. 158 is the letter dated 4th January 1972 sent by the Superintendent of Police, Raebareli, to the Officiating Executive Engineer, P.W.D., Raebareli, acknowledging receipt of bills for construction of barricades and rostrums at the seven places specified therein and requesting the Executive Engineer to submit separate bills for barricading and construction of rostrums. Exh. 155 is the letter dated 1st of February, 1972 from the Executive Engineer, P.W.D., Raebareli, enclosing therewith separate bills of expenditure incurred in erection of barricades and rostrums on the occasion of the visit of respondent No. 1 on 1st of February, 1971.

It is not necessary to refer to the other papers. The aforesaid documents over whelmingly show that rostrums were got constructed through Government agency for the purposes of the meetings addressed by the respondent No. 1 in Raebareli on 1st of February, 1971.

CONCLUSIVELY PROVED THAT ROSTRUMS WERE CONSTRUCTED BY GOVERNMENT OFFICERS FOR SPEECHES OF RESPONDENT NO. 1 – HIGH COURT HOLDS

Exh. 199 is a radiogram dated 17th of February, 1972 from the Superintendent of Police, Raebareli, to the U.P. Police Headquarters, Allahabad, soliciting sanction for construction of rostrum and barricades for six meetings to be addressed by the respondent No. 1 on 25th of February, 1971. Exh. 201 is the letter dated 17th February, 1971 from the Superintendent of Police, Raebareli, to the Executive Engineer, P.W.D., Raebareli, apprising him of the places where the respondent No. 1 was to address meetings on the 25th February, 1971. And requesting him to take up the construction of rostrums and barricades on top priority basis, to be completed by 22nd of February, 1971. Exh. 193 is a letter dated 23rd June, 1971 sent by the Superintendent of Police, Raebareli to the U.P. Police Headquarters, Allahabad, apprising him, inter alia, of the cost incurred in the construction of barricades and rostrums in connection with the meetings addressed by the respondent No. 1 on 25th of February, 1971. Exh. 190 is the letter dated 27th September, 1972 sent by the U.P. Police Headquarters to the Deputy Secretary, U.P. Government, Home and Police Department, apprising the Government of the cost incurred over the construction of rostrums and barricades in connection with the meetings addressed by respondent No. 1 in Raebareli, on 25th of February, 1971. It is conclusively proved by these documents that rostrums were constructed through Government agency for the meetings addressed by the respondent No. 1 in her constituency on 25th of February, 1971 also.

Learned counsel for the petitioner also referred me to the evidence of Sri E. Lawrenece, the then S.D.M. Dalmau (district Raebareli) (R.W. 10) and to the evidence of Sri Mohinder Singh, District Magistrate, Raebareli (R.W. 36) in order to show that rostrums for the purposes of the meetings of the respondent No. 1 were always got constructed through officers. Sri E. Lawrenece (R.W.10) stated during his deposition that barricading and construction of rostrum are done by the P.W.D. and payment for the same is made by the Superintendent of Police of the district concerned, though the actual work of putting up of barricades and construction of rostrums is done by the contractors. Further on, he stated in cross-examination that it was the duty of the Sub-Divisional Officer to make sure that a rostrum was constructed at the place in his sub-division where the Prime Minister proposed to address the meeting. He also stated that the Superintendent of Police and the District Magistrate ask the Public Works Department to get the rostrum constructed at the place where the meeting is proposed to be addressed by the Prime Minister and that the S.D.O. personally goes to that place to supervise the construction of rostrums. During his re-examination by learned counsel for the respondent No. 1 he affirmed that he had personal knowledge regarding the rostrum and barricade constructed in connection with the meeting addressed by the respondent No. 1 at Raebareli on 1st of February, 1971 because he knew the Assistant Engineer who got it done and because he had himself seen the rostrum being constructed and the barricade being put up. Sri Mohinder Singh

(R.W. 36) was the District Magistrate at Raebareli during the election that took place in 1971. He stated, "whenever the tour programme of the Prime Minister is received, whether the visit is official or unofficial, they inspect the site of the meeting to be addressed by the Prime Minister and the Superintendent of Police then, besides making other security arrangements, sends a letter to the Executive Engineer, Public Works Department, to invite tenders for construction of rostrums and barricades." He further stated that if a rostrum is constructed, barricading is also done because it is a part of that work.

There is thus not an *iota* of doubt that it were the Gazetted Officers of the State, particularly the Superintendent of Police, Raebareli and the Executive Engineer, P.W.D. Raebareli, who got the rostrums constructed for the purposes of the meetings addressed by the respondent no.1 in her constituency on 1st of February, 1971 and 25th of February, 1971.

LOUDSPEAKERS ARRANGED BY THE PARTY AT ITS OWN EXPENSES – HOLDS HIGH COURT

As for the arrangement of loudspeakers, no evidence, oral or documentary, has been led by the petitioner in order to prove that arrangement for loudspeakers was done by or through the Government officers. On the contrary, there are some papers which lend support to the contention raised on behalf of respondent No. 1 that the arrangement of loudspeakers was done by the District Congress. Exh.177 is a letter dated 29th January, 1971 sent by the Superintendent of Police, Raebareli, to Sri Gaya Prasad Shukla of the Central Congress Office, Raebareli. It states that, according to the verbal decision reached between them, Sri Gaya Prasad Shukla was to make arrangements of loudspeakers for the meetings of the respondent No. 1. The letter being dated January 29, 1971, it obviously refers to the meetings addressed by the respondent No. 1 on 1st of February, 1971. Exh.193 is a letter dated June 23, 1971, from the Superintendent of Police, Raebareli, to the U.P. Police Headquarters, Allahabad, containing details of the expenditure incurred in connection with the visit of respondent No. 1 to Raebareli on 25th of February, 1971. It explicitly states that no expenditure was incurred in connection with the arrangement of loudspeakers for the meetings addressed by the respondent No. 1 as the same was arranged by the party concerned.

POWER SUPPLY FOR LOUDSPEAKERS ARRANGED BY GOVERNMENT OFFICERS – AMOUNTED TO CORRUPT PRACTICE – CONTENTION OF PETITIONER

Learned counsel for the petitioner, however, contended that even though the loudspeakers were not arranged by the Government officers for the purposes of the meetings addressed by the respondent No. 1 in her constituency, there is unimpeachable evidence on record to show that the Government officers arranged for supply of power for the functioning of the loudspeakers at some places where the respondent No. 1 addressed her election meetings. This appears to be correct. Exh. 147 is copy of a letter dated 24th July, 1973 sent by the Superintendent of Police, Raebareli to the President, U.P.C.C., Lucknow, stating that the respondent No. 1 had addressed meetings at Harchandpur, Jagatpur, Parewa and Reohara (besides Bachrawan, which was not in Raebareli constituency), in connection with the election, on 1st of February, 1971, that power had been supplied for functioning of loudspeakers in those meetings, and that five bills for total amount of Rs. 1151 were sent for payment in that connection to the U.P.C.C. Office. It was requested that the payment may be expedited. Exh.146 is the letter dated 1st September, 1973 from the President. U.P.C.C. to the Superintendent of Police, Raebareli, which indicated that a cheque for Rs. 1151 was forwarded by the U.P.C.C. in payment of the aforesaid bills for supply of power. Exh.154 is a copy of the letter dated 1st of February, 1972 from the Superintendent of Police, Raebareli to the Police Headquarters, Allahabad, containing a break-up of the expenditure incurred in connection with the visit of respondent No. 1 to Raebareli on 1st of February, 1971. This also lends support to the fact that arrangement for supply of power for functioning of the loudspeakers at some meetings addressed by the respondent No. 1 was made through the Government officers. Exh. 178 is a letter dated January 29, 1971, from the Superintendent of Police, Raebareli, to the Assistant Engineer, Hydel, asking him to make available power at Harchandpur and Jagatpur for installation of public address system for the meeting of the respondent No. 1 on 1st of February, 1971.

The above-mentioned papers conclusively prove that arrangements had been made by the Government officers for supply of power for the functioning of the loudspeakers at some of the election meetings addressed by the respondent No. 1. But for the same. It would not have been possible for the respondent No. 1 to effectively address these meetings.

BARRICADING, POSTING OF POLICE ALONG THE ROUTE AND AT THE PLACE OF SPEECH TO MAINTAIN LAW AND ORDER – NO CORRUPT PRACTICE – HOLDS HIGH COURT

The fact that police had been posted along the routes by which the respondent No. 1 had to travel and that the police was also posted at the places where the respondent No. 1 addressed election meetings has not been controverted by her. As also stated earlier, the erection of barricades along the routes and erection of barricades at the places of meetings was also not denied by her. According to respondent No. 1, the aforesaid arrangements were made by the State Government in discharge of its Governmental duties.

It is a matter of common knowledge that on the occasion of the visit of the Prime Minister of the country vast crowds gather in order to see and hear him/her. People also swarm along the routes by which he/she travels in order to have a glimpse of him/her. It is the first duty on every Government to maintain law and order in the State. If the police were not posted and barricades were not put up along with routes by which the respondent No. 1 travelled as also at the places where she addressed the meetings, It may not be possible for the Government to control the crowd. Failure in that regard could lead to a law and order situation and no Government worth the name can take any risk in that regard. Needless to say that neither the posting of the police along the routes and at the places of the meetings, not the erection of the barricades at the two places could contribute to the furtherance of the prospects of the respondent No. 1 in the election. Exception cannot therefore validly be taken by the petitioner in regard to the said arrangements made by the Government. I am accordingly in agreement with the plea put forward by the respondent No. 1 that the posting of police along the routes and at the place of the meetings as well as the setting up of barricades at the two places was done by the Government in discharge of its Governmental duties.

CONSTRUCTION OF ROSTRUMS – SUPPLY OF POWER FOR LOUDSPEAKERS – STATE GOVERNMENT DUTY – UNDER ADMINISTRATIVE INSTRUCTIONS – CONTENDS RESPONDENT NO. 1

The construction of rostrums and the supply of power by or through the officers of the State Government, however, stand at a different footing. The rostrums constructed by the officers of the State Government enabled the respondent No. 1 to address her meetings from a dominating position. The resources of the Government having been employed, the rostrums were got constructed in the shortest possible time so that they were ready by the time the respondent No. 1 reached the places where she had to address the meetings. Further, even though the loudspeakers had been arranged by the District Congress Committee, supply of power for the same was arranged by the officers of the State Government. But for it the loudspeakers would have been ineffective and it would not have been possible for the respondent No. 1 to make her speech audible to the entire audience. The construction of the rostrums and the arrangement of the supply of power for the functioning of the loudspeakers, therefore, amounted to assisting the respondent No. 1 in her election campaign which put her in a clearly advantageous position over her opponents. I do not think it was indispensable for the State Government for maintenance of law and order, or security, that its officers should have taken upon themselves to get rostrums constructed for the meetings of the respondent No. 1 and to make arrangements for the supply of power for the functioning of the loudspeakers at her meetings. Both the things could be left to be arranged by the political party concerned.

Reliance has been placed by learned counsel for the respondent No. 1 on the Instructions (Exh. 123) dated 29th November, 1958 issued by the Comptroller and Auditor General of India to the Accountant Generals of the State, the letter dated 12th of January, 1959 (Exh. 124) issued by the Government of India to the Chief Secretaries of all State Governments, enclosing therewith copy of the Instructions issued by the Comptroller and Auditor General and the letter dated 19th November, 1969 (Exh. 121) issued by the Government of India, Ministry of Home Affairs, to all State Governments, in order to contend that it was the duty of the State Government and its officers to arrange, inter alia, for the construction of rostrums and for putting up of public address system in the meetings addressed by the Prime Minister. Now, so far as the secret instructions (enclosed with Exh.124) issued by the Comptroller and Auditor General of India are concerned, it is not explicitly stated therein that these instructions will also apply on the occasion of the election meetings addressed by the Prime Minister as a candidate within her own constituency. It is worthy of notice that in the Blue Book (which contains detailed instructions regarding security arrangements of the Prime Minister) election meetings were specifically excluded. This is apparent from the first paragraph of the letter (Exh. 121) issued by the Ministry of Home Affairs, Government of India, on 19th November, 1969. Learned counsel for the petitioner also produced before me Lok Sabha debates dated April 10, 1973. Rule 71(6) of the Blue Book, as it originally existed, has been reproduced in Column 241 of these debates as follows:

> "It has been noticed that the rostrum arrangements are not always properly made because the hosts are sometimes unable to bear the cost. As the Prime Minister's security is the concern of the State, all arrangements for putting up the rostrum and the barriers at the meeting place will be borne by the State, whatever may be the occasion for which the public meetings are called, except election meetings".

Now, if the instructions issued by the Comptroller and Auditor General of India in 1958 are read with rule 71(6) of the Blue Book, as it originally existed, it becomes abundantly clear that the instructions contained therein did not apply to election meetings, much less to the meetings addressed by the Prime Minister as a candidate in her own constituency.

Rule 71(6) of the Blue Book was amended in 1969, as is apparent from the letter Exh. A.21 dated 19th November, 1969 issued by the Government of India to all State Governments. The relevant part of amended rule 71(6) reads as follows:

> "It has been noticed that the rostrum arrangements are not always properly made because the hosts are sometimes unable to bear the cost. As the security of the Prime Minister is the concern of the State, all arrangements for putting

up the rostrum, the barricades etc. at the meeting place, including that of an election meeting, have to be made by the State Government concerned."

ADMINISTRATIVE INSTRUCTIONS CANNOT OVERRIDE STATUTORY PROVISIONS – CONSTRUCTION OF ROSTRUMS OR TO PROVIDE POWER FOR LOUDSPEAKERS BY STATE GOVERNMENT OFFICERS – VIOLATE SECTION 123(7) OF THE ACT – HOLDS HIGH COURT

It was thus for the first time in 1969 that arrangements pertaining to election meetings were also made the responsibility of the State Government. It is, however, extremely doubtful whether even the amendment of rule 71(6) of the Blue Book in 1969 required that State Government and its officers to make arrangements for rostrums and loudspeakers at the meetings which the Prime Minister was to address in his/her own constituency as a candidate. Assuming, however, that it did, it cannot be ignored that the instructions issued by the Comptroller and Auditor- General of India (enclosed with Exh. 124) are the instructions of administrative nature and they cannot override the provisions contained in section 123 of the Representation of the People Act. Consequently, if it is shown that the construction of rostrum and arrangement for supply of power for the functioning of the loudspeakers at the meetings addressed by the respondent No. 1 falls within the mischief of section 123(7) of the Representation of the People Act, neither the instructions issued by the Comptroller and Auditor-General of India nor the instructions issued by the Government of India through its letters dated 12th of January, 1959 (Exh. 124) and 19th November, 1969 (Exh. 121) can come to the rescue of the respondent No. 1

The question that, therefore, ultimately falls for consideration is whether the fact that rostrums had been got constructed and supply of power for the functioning of the loudspeakers was arranged by the Gazetted officers of the State Government, particularly the Superintendent of Police, the Executive Engineer, P.W.D. and the Engineer, Hydel Department, for the meetings addressed by the respondent No. 1 as a candidate in her constituency, brings the matter within the mischief of section 123(7) of the Act.

Sub-section (7) section 123 of the Representation of the People Act reads as follows:

> "The obtaining or procuring or abetting or attempting to obtain or procure by a candidate or his agent, or, by any other person with the consent of a candidate or his election agent, any assistance other than the giving of vote for the furtherance of the prospects of that candidates' election, from any person in the service of the Government and belonging to any of the following classes, namely—
>
> (a) Gazetted Officers;
>
> (b) .....
>
> (c) ....
>
> (d) ......
>
> (e) .....
>
> (f) ......

MEANING OF WORDS 'OBTAINED' – 'PROCURED' USED IN SECTION 123(7) OF THE REPRESENTATION OF THE PEOPLE ACT – HOLDS HIGH COURT

In the light of the above provision, the first question that arises for consideration is whether on the facts found proved it can be said that the assistance of the gazetted officer of the State was obtained or procured by the respondent No. 1

The words 'obtain' and 'procure' imply some initiative or effort on the part of the returned candidate. According to *Webster's New International Dictionary,* the word 'obtain' means to take hold of, to gain or attain possession or disposal by some planned action or method. The meaning assigned to the word 'procure' in the same dictionary, *inter alia,* are to bring about, obtain, to get possession of by care or effort. In **Moti Lal v. Mangla Prasad, AIR 1958 All 794 (797)** it was observed:—

> "We think that the word 'obtain' in section 123(7) has been used in the essence of the meaning which connotes purpose behind the action of the candidate. The word has not been used in the sub-section in the sense of a mere passive receipt of assistance without the candidate being even conscious of the fact that the assistance has been rendered. In order to bring the case under sub-section (7), it must be shown that the candidate did make some effort or perform some purposeful act in order to get the assistance." (under lining is by me).

In case **Biresh Misra v. Ram Nath Sharma, 17 Election LR 243 (253)** a Division Bench of the Assam High Court observed:—

> "The words 'obtain' or 'procure' or 'abetting or attempting to obtain or procure' any assistance necessarily imply some effort on the part of the candidate or his agent. Mere passive receipt of assistance is not contemplated by the section."

Similar view has been expressed in the case **Babu Bhai Vallabh Das Gandhi v. Piloo Homi Mody, 36 Election LR 108 (126 and 127)** and **C. Chiranjeevulu Naidu v. E.S. Thyagarajan, 25 Election LR 201 (217).**

In Para 13(c) of the written statement the respondent No. 1 admitted that rostrums were constructed at Harchandpur, Raebareli, Jagatpur, Paterwa and Reuhara. In Para 13 (d) of the written statement the respondent No. 1 quoted extensively from the instructions dated 29th November, 1958 issued by the Comptroller & Auditor–General of India, copy whereof was sent by the Government of India to the Chief Secretaries of all the States under their letter dated 12th January, 1959 (Exh. 124). It may be recalled that under the aforesaid instructions it is the duty of the State Government, inter alia, to make loudspeaker arrangements and to provide for rostrums for non-official meetings of the Prime Minister also. In Para 13(e) the respondent No. 1 made reference to the letter of the Government of India dated 19th November, 1969 (Exh. A-21), which amended rule 71(6) of the Blue Book to bring the election meetings also within the ambit of the instructions issued by the Comptroller & Auditor- General. In answer to interrogatory No. 28 the special attorney of the respondent No. 1 admitted that the respondent No. 1 was generally aware of the substance of the rules and instructions. (the words "such use of Indian Air Force planes by the P.M." appear to have been inserted in the reply by inadvertence). In reply to interrogatory No. 29 it was admitted that the respondent No. 1 was a party to the decision of the Union Government on the basis of which the letter dated 19th November, 1969 (Exh. A-21) was issued. During her deposition in Court the respondent No. 1 again said that, according to the standing instructions from the Government of India, whenever the Prime Minister visits any State and addresses meetings, including election meetings, necessary arrangements in connection with it, have to be made by the officers of the State Government. She added that she was aware of those instructions even prior to 1st of February, 1971. From all these facts it is apparent that, with the issue of letter from the Government of India dated 19th November, 1969 (Exh. A-21), the respondent No. 1 held that it was also the duty of the State Government to arrange for construction of rostrums and installation of public address system for her meetings, regardless of the fact whether those meetings were to be addressed by her as a candidate in her own constituency or otherwise.

Sri Yashpal Kapur (R.W.32), earlier Private Secretary and O.S.D. in the respondent's secretariat, deposed that when a regular tour programme of the Prime Minister is prepared, the Private Secretary to the Prime Minister issues it to the authorities concerned after it is approved by the Prime Minister. The respondent No. 1 also conceded in her deposition that the tour programmes concerned with the political work are prepared by the A.I.C.C. and are finalised after her approval is obtained. In answer to interrogatory No. 3 of the second set, it was admitted that the tour programmes are issued, among others, to the State Government.

SINCE ARRANGEMENTS FOR ROSTRUM/SUPPLY OF POWER FOR LOUDSPEAKERS WERE MADE BY STATE GOVERNMENT OFFICERS WITH IMPLIED CONSENT OF RESPONDENT No. 1 – SECTION 123(7) OF THE ACT APPLIES – AMOUNTED TO CORRUPT PRACTICE – HOLDS HIGH COURT

Now, since the instructions issued by the Comptroller & Auditor-General read with the letter of the Government of India dated 12th January, 1959 (Exh.124) and the letter of the Government of India dated 19th of November, 1969 (Exh. A -21) required the State Government to construct rostrums and to arrange for the public address system for the meetings of the respondent No. 1, besides making other arrangements, and since the respondent No. 1 believed that it also applied to the election meetings to be addressed by her in her constituency, it should be presumed that the purpose behind sending those tour programmes to the State Government was that the State Government should make all those arrangements for the meetings of the respondent No. 1. In other words, the tour programmes carried an implied direction that the State Government should also get constructed rostrums and arrange for public address system for the election meetings to be addressed by her on 1st February, 1971 and 25th of February, 1971. It should be presumed that the respondent No. 1, as Prime Minister of this country, and with five years experience of that office behind her in 1971, also knew that the said work was to be done by the officers of the State Government. In fact respondent No. 1 stated in her cross-examination that she was aware that, according to the Standing Orders, necessary arrangements in connection with the meetings, including election meetings, had to be made by the officers of the State Government.

As already stated earlier, the word 'obtain' occurring in section 123(7) only implies some effort or initiative on the part of the returned candidate. Since the tour programmes were sent from the office of the respondent No. 1 with her approval and they contained an implied direction that the State Government may, *inter alia,* arrange for construction of rostrums and for loudspeakers for the meetings of the respondent No. 1, the needed initiative had thereby emanated from her. Further, on her own admission, respondent No. 1 knew that the aforesaid arrangement shall be made by the officers of the State Government. The arrangements having been made the respondent No. 1 availed of the same in all the meetings on 1st of February, 1971 and again in the meetings addressed on 25th of February, 1971. She did not do anything in between the two dates to disavow those arrangements or to prevent the officers of the State Government again undertaking them on 25.2.1971. The only reasonable conclusion that can under the circumstances be reached is that the respondent No. 1 obtained the assistance of the officers of the State Government, within the meaning of that expression used in section 123(7) of the Act.

The question that next falls for consideration is whether the assistance had been obtained for the furtherance of the prospects of the election of respondent No. 1.

The position of the respondent No. 1 in her constituency first of all was that of a candidate. Her position as Prime Minister came thereafter. What she could not do as a candidate, she could as well not do as Prime Minister. She could not therefore obtain the assistance of the Government Officers in her election campaign. Yet we find that it was done. The services of the officers of the State Government were obtained for construction of rostrums. The resources of the State Government were utilized for that purpose. At some of the meetings the officers of the State Government also arranged for supply of power for the functioning of the loudspeakers, as shown earlier. The assistance of the State Government was thus obtained so that the respondent No. 1 could effectively address the meetings for the furtherance of her prospects in the election. It may not be out of place to add that the association of the senior officers of the State Government with the arrangements of rostrums and loudspeakers in the meetings of the respondent No. 1 was also likely to create an impression on the mind of the electors within the constituency that the Government was assisting the respondent No. 1. It can, therefore, be safely said that the assistance of the officers of the State Government was obtained for the furtherance of the prospects of election of respondent No. 1.

JUDGMENTS RELIED UPON BY RESPONDENT No. 1 – NOT APPLICABLE TO THE FACTS OF THIS CASE – HOLDS HIGH COURT

Learned counsel for the respondent No. 1. urged that the construction of rostrums and arrangements of loudspeakers could not in any way further the prospects of the respondent No. 1's election and, consequently, even if it be held that the assistance of the officers of the State Government had been obtained by the respondent No. 1 for the said purpose, it cannot constitute a corrupt practice. In support of his arguments learned counsel referred me to the cases: (1) **Raj Krushna Bose v. Binod Kanungo, 9 Election LR 295 SC;** (2) **Satya Dev Bushahri v. Padam Dev, 10 Election LR 193 (112 and 117)** (3) **Chandrashekhar Singh v. Sarjoo Prasad Singh, 22 Election LR 206 (217)** Pat. On a perusal of these cases, however, I find that they are distinguishable. In the first case the Court said that section 33(2) of the Act, as it then existed, conferred a right on every person to subscribe as proposer or seconder as many nomination papers as there were vacancies to be filled. It was further held that section 123(8) {which now corresponds to section 123(7)} was to be interpreted in harmony with section 33(2) and, interpreting in that manner, the act of a Government servant subscribing any nomination paper as a proposer or seconder did not fall within the mischief of section 123(8). In the second case the Court held that in view of the duties that a polling agent has to perform, it cannot be said that the fact of a Government servant acting as a polling agent for any candidate can constitute a corrupt practice. In reaching this conclusion it was also taken into consideration that, while the relevant section contained a prohibition against the appointment of certain persons as election agent, there was no such reference to the appointment of polling agents. The Court proceeded to say on page 120—

> "To hold that Government servants are, as such and as a class, disqualified to act as polling agents would be to engraft an exception to the statue, which is not there."

In the third case the son of the returned candidate, who was a Sub-Inspector of Police under suspension, had driven the jeep of Sarvasri S.K. Sinha and Morarji Desai when they came into the constituency for election campaign and the Court observed:

> "Mere driving of the jeep of Dr. S.K. Sinha and Sri Morarji Desai, even if proved cannot be said to be any assistance in the furtherance of the prospects of the respondent's election from a person in the service of the Government. Mere driving of the jeep is an act of carrying the leaders who were important members of either State Government or Central Government and the Sub- Inspector of Police, even if he was on leave could be expected, if required,

to show this much of courtesy to the important leaders who were members of the Government too".

It is worthy of notice that in this case the Sub-Inspector of Police had not rendered any service directly to the candidate but had rendered some service by way of courtesy to two leaders of outstanding importance who were also members of the Government. Thus, on facts none of the three cases referred to by learned counsel for the respondent No. 1 is analogous to the case before me.

ARTICLES 256 AND 257 OF THE CONSTITUTION DO NOT HELP RESPONDENT No. 1 – NO PROVISION IN SECTION 123(7) OF THE ACT TO DEAL DIFFERENTLY IF PM IS THE CANDIDATE – HOLDS HIGH COURT

Learned counsel for the respondent No. 1 also referred me to Articles 256 and 257 of the Constitution and urged that the earlier mentioned instructions were issued by the Government of India in exercise of its executive power under those Articles. The Representation of the people Act was, however, enacted by the Parliament in exercise of its constitutional power. Therefore, whether or not the earlier mentioned instructions were issued by the Government of India under Articles 256 and 257 of the Constitution they cannot override the mandate of the Parliament contained in the Act.

Learned counsel for the respondent No. 1 stressed that the Prime Minister of a country commands special position and that it is mandatory that arrangements for her security are made even when he/she visits a particular constituency as a candidate seeking election from there. Learned counsel urged that the provisions contained in the Representation of the People Act should not be interpreted in a rigid manner and that allowance should be given to that position while interpreting them. I, have, however, already said earlier that the construction of rostrums and arrangements of public address system are not intimately connected with security and could be conveniently allowed to be arranged by the party concerned. But assuming that security was involved in the construction of rostrums, the fact remains that the Representation of the People Act makes no concession in favour of the Prime Minister or any other office-bearer of the Government. According to law, as it stands, obtaining assistance of the officers specified in section 123(7) of the Act by a candidate for furtherance of her election prospects is a corrupt practice, regardless of the fact whether the candidate is an ordinary person or a person holding high office in the Government. If it were felt that the position of the Prime Minister required some concession being made in the matter, the Legislature could be moved to make necessary provision in that regard in section 123(7) of the Act. In the absence of any such provision, the mere fact that the respondent No. 1 happened to be the Prime Minister cannot undo the effect of her obtaining assistance of the officers of the State Government for furtherance of her election prospects.

RESPONDENT NO. 1 DID NOT CANVAS FOR HER – CONTENDS RESPONDENT – REJECTED BY HIGH COURT

Learned counsel for the respondent No. 1 also urged that, according to the evidence on record, respondent No. 1 did not make any canvassing for herself while addressing meetings on 1st of February, 1971 and 25th February, 1971 and that she only did propaganda for the party. On this basis it was urged that any assistance given to the respondent No. 1 in those meetings could not be held to be assistance for furtherance of the election prospects of the respondent No. 1. This argument cannot be accepted for any moment. The respondent No. 1 was the only congress candidate from Raebareli parliamentary constituency. The respondent No. 1 pleaded in Para 15(a) of the written statement that she has requested the voters to put the prescribed mark on the symbol of cow and calf. As a congress candidate that was her symbol also. Therefore, when she asked the electors within the constituency of Raebareli to put their mark against the symbol of cow and calf, she clearly canvassed for herself.

ISSUE NO. 3 DECIDED AGAINST RESPONDENT NO. 1 – HIGH COURT

In view of all that has been said above, I hold that the respondent No. 1 obtained the assistance of the officers of the State Government, particularly the District Magistrate, the Superintendent of Police, the Executive Engineer, P.W.D. and the Engineer, Hydel Department for construction of rostrums and arrangement of supply of power for loudspeakers in the meetings addressed by her on 1st of February, 1971 and 25th of February, 1971 and further that the said assistance was for the furtherance of the prospects of the respondent No. 1 in her election. The respondent No. 1 was thus guilty of a corrupt practice under section 123(7) of the Act.

Issue No. 3 is accordingly answered against the respondent No. 1 and in favour of the petitioner.

ISSUE NOS. 4 & 7

NO PROOF IF QUILTS, BLANKETS OR DHOTIS DISTRIBUTED OR FREE CONVEYANCE PROVIDED BY ELECTION AGENTS OF RESPONDENT No. 1 TO THE ELECTORS – HOLDS HIGH COURT

These issues arise out of the allegations contained in Para 10 and Para 12 of the petition. In para 10 it is alleged that Sri Yashpal Kapur, the election agent of respondent No. 1, and her other agents with the consent of the said Sri Kapur, distributed a large number of quilts, blankets and dhotis as well as liquor among the electors of the constituency with the object of inducing them to vote for the respondent No. 1. According to Schedule A-1, which contains the details of this corrupt practice, distribution of blankets, dhotis, quilts and liquor was done in Salon, Bhaon, Dalmau, Harchandpur, Sareni and Lalganj. In Para 12 of the petition it is alleged that Sri Yashpal Kapur, the election agent of the respondent No. 1, and some other agents and persons with his consent, hired and procured a number of vehicles for the free conveyance of electors to various polling stations in the said constituency on 1st March, 3rd March and 5th March, 1971. The details of this corrupt practice are mentioned in Schedule B-1 and, according to that schedule, this corrupt practice was committed at polling stations Rahi, Bhaon, Salon, Sareni, Harchandpur and at six polling stations situate in Raebareli proper and three polling stations situate in Bawan Buzurf.

The respondent No. 1 in her written statement stoutly denied the commission of both the alleged corrupt practices.

The petitioner in order to prove the aforesaid allegations examined Sri A.C. Mathur (P.W. 19) and Budhu (P.W.24) only.

Sri A.C. Mathur (P.W.19) was Presiding Officer at Rahi polling station on 1st of March 1971. He said that on that date some person, whose name he did not remember, handed over to him an application (Paper No. A-295) and that he made an endorsement on that application. Application (Paper No. A-295) purports to have been given by Sarat Kumar Singh, Polling Agent of the petitioner at Rahi polling station, alleging that the workers of the respondent No. 1 were transporting voters by bus UPF 214. The endorsement made by Sri Mathur on this application is Exhibit 55 and it reads as follows:

> "Received with the remark that the vehicle under reference has not been seen by me personally. However, the application is being forwarded to the section Magistrate".

The petitioner did not examine Sarat Kumar Singh, the purported author of the complaint (Paper No. A-295); and Sri A.C. Mathur , the Presiding Officer has not said anything , either in his deposition or in the endorsement made by him on that complaint, lending support to it. The evidence of Sri A.C. Mathur thus fails to prove that any voters were transported by or on behalf of the respondent No. 1 free of cost to Rahipur polling station.

This takes me to the other witness, namely Budhu (P.W.24). He is a resident of village Bhaon. He deposed that on the date of polling a big jeep came to the village; that the people were saying that the jeep belonged to Smt. Premwati; that the jeep carried the flag and posters of the Congress Party; and that it made 8 or 10 trips for carrying the voters. He said that Smt. Premwati remained present in the village till about 3 p.m.

Now, if it were true that voters had been transported in the manner alleged by Budhu P.W., some complaints about the same should have been made by the polling agent of the petitioner at the relevant polling stations and evidence about the same could be adduced. No such evidence has, however, been adduced. The oral testimony of Budhu alone cannot, therefore, be given much credence. That apart, the respondent examined a number of witnesses to rebut the evidence of Budhu (P.W. 24). Smt. Premwati (R.W. 21) herself entered the witness-box and made a statement on oath to the effect that she did not come to Raebareli constituency during the period of election and that she remained busy in connection with the election of Smt. Shiela Kaul in Lucknow City constituency. It is true that Smt. Shiela Kaul was also a candidate of Congress (R) and is an aunt of respondent No. 1. However, the mere fact that Smt. Premwati (R.W. 21) was working for the aunt of respondent No. 1 cannot constitute a sufficient ground for discarding her testimony.

Other witnesses examined by the respondent No. 1 in this connection are Gajraj Singh (R.W. 19), a resident of village Sarai Damu, Lalu (R.W. 20), also a resident of village Sarai Damu, Ganga (R.W. 22), Pradhan of village Jamalpur Nankari, Kuir (R.W. 23), another resident of village Jamalpur Nankari and Thakur Ambika Singh (R.W. 24). Gajraj Singh and Lalu R.Ws. said that they had gone to give their votes at the polling station situate in Mohanmmadpur Kuchari. They further said that they and other people of their village had gone on foot to cast their votes and that it was wrong that any jeep or tractor was utilized to transport any voters from their village to the polling stations. Ganga and Kuir R.Ws. deposed that they went to Bhaon polling station to cast their votes. They further said that they and other people of their village went to the polling station on foot and that it was wrong that any vehicle has been used for transporting them to the polling station. It may be mentioned here that according to the statement made by Budhu in cross-examination, Kuir and Gajraj Singh were among the persons who had been transported by jeep. Thakur Ambika Singh (R.W.24) was named in Schedule B-1 as one of those persons who transported voters. He stated on oath that he never transported any voters from any place in the constituency to any polling station. The above being the state of evidence, I find that the petitioner failed to prove that the election agent of the respondent No. 1, or any other person with his consent, transported voters free of cost to any polling station.

In support of the allegation that blankets, dhotis or quilts were distributed, it is Budhu (P.W. 24) only who has made a statement. According to him, Madan Mohan Misra and some other persons visited his village on the date preceding the election for distributing the aforesaid articles to the voters in village Bhaon. He also claimed to have received one dhoti. He further named Kuir and said that, among the residents of Jamalpur Nankari, he was one of those who had been distributed cloth.

The respondent examined Shitla Bux Singh (R.W. 15), Kuir (R.W. 23) and Thakur Ambika Singh (R.W. 24). According to the Schedule A-1 appended to the petition, Shitla Bux Singh was one of those persons who got blankets etc. distributed. Shitla Bux Singh entered the witness-box to deny it on oath. Kuir (R.W. 23) contradicted that part of the statement of Budhu (P.W. 24) wherein he said that cloth had also been distributed to him. Thakur Ambika Singh (R.W. 24) is Pramukh of the Kshettra Samiti. He also denied having participated in connection with the distribution of quilts, kambals, dhotis etc. in any part of the constituency.

In the aforesaid circumstances, reliance cannot be placed on the solitary testimony of Budhu in order to accept that any quilts, blankets, dhotis etc. were at all distributed on behalf of respondent No. 1 in the constituency.

Issue Nos. 4 and 7 are accordingly decided against the petitioner and in favour respondent No. 1.

ISSUE NO. 1

SECURITY DEPOSIT MADE WAS IN ORDER – HOLDS HIGH COURT

In Para 22 of the written statement the respondent No. 1 pleaded that the security deposit was not made according to rules and hence this issue. This question, however, stands concluded with the decision of this Court in case, Election Petition No. 1 1971 **Brahma Datta v. Paripurna Nand,** decided on 9th November, 1971. The objection taken in this case is precisely the same as was raised in Election Petition No. 1 of 1971. Learned counsel for respondent No. 1 has failed to show any reason for which the present case may be held to be distinguishable on facts from the case of **Brahma Datta** v. **Paripurna Nand**, (supra). In view of the decision of this Court in that case, I find that the security deposit made by the petitioner was in order.

The issue is accordingly answered in favour of the petitioner and against the respondent No. 1.

ISSUE NOS. 5 and 8

In the written statement filed by respondent No. 1 it was pleaded that Para 10 read with Schedule *A* and Para 12 read with Schedule *B* of the petition furnished no particulars of corrupt practice and were, therefore, liable to be struck off.

The allegation contained in Para 10 of the petition, briefly stated, is that the election agent of the respondent No. 1 and her other agents with the consent of the election agent, freely distributed quilts, blankets, dhotis and liquor among the electorate to induce them to vote for respondent No. 1. Schedule A contained the names of the persons who distributed the aforesaid articles, the names of the places where they were distributed. The allegation contained in Para 12 of the petition is that on 1st March, 1971, 3rd March, 1971 and 15th March, 1971 the election agent of the respondent No. 1 and some other persons with his consent, hired or procured a number of vehicles for free conveyance of electors to various polling stations. Schedule *B*, accompanying the petition, disclosed the names of the persons who transported the voters, the registration number of the vehicles used by them for transporting voters, the names of the polling stations to which the voters were transported, and the dates on which they were transported.

From the order dated 20th September, 1971, passed by K.N. Srivastava, J., it appears that after the statements of 15 witnesses on the side of the petitioner had been recorded, it was pressed on behalf of the respondent No. 1 that issues Nos. 5 and 8 be decided as preliminary issues. After hearing learned counsel for the parties, it was held by K.N. Srivastave, J. that allegations contained in Paras 10 and 12 were vague in some respects. In regard to para No. 10 and Schedule *A*, he pointed out that it did not disclose—

(i) whether the liquor, blankets, quilts and dhotis were distributed at the same time and place or separately; and

(ii) so far as big places like Salon and others mentioned in Schedule A are concerned, the places where the alleged corrupt practice was committed should have been specifically mentioned.

In regard to Para 12 and Schedule *B*, it was pointed out by K.N. Srivastave, J. that the allegations contained there in were vague in following manner:—

(1) The petitioner should have given the details as to which vehicle mentioned in Schedule *B* was procured or hired by which worker or agent of respondent No. 1

(2) The names of polling stations from or to which the voters were carried required to be disclosed:

(3) It was also required to be disclosed

Whether the vehicles mentioned in Schedule *B* were tractors, taxies, buses or motorcars.

Other objections raised on behalf of the respondent were rejected with the following observations:—

> "The other objections are of a technical nature about the vagueness and they have no force in them."

In consequence of the above order passed by K.N. Srivastava J. the petitioner furnished better particulars.

Counsel for both the parties were again heard and thereafter a detailed order was passed by me on 29th of August, 1974. By that order the particulars furnished by the petitioner in regard to distribution of blankets, quilts and dhotis were accepted as sufficient and those particulars were allowed to be incorporated. With regard to the other allegation about the distribution of liquor, it was held that it continued to remain vague and consequently, that part of Para 10 of the petition which related to distribution of liquor, was ordered to be deleted.

In regard to particulars furnished to clarify the allegation contained in para 12, the only objection raised before me was that the description of Amresh Prasad Srivastave, Zulfiqar Khan and Anad Kumar, mentioned in column 1 of Schedule B-1 (sought to be substituted for Schedule *B* was not sufficient to enable the respondent to fix their identity. That objection was upheld and it was directed that while Schedule *B* may be substituted with Schedule B-1, as prayed, the aforesaid names shall be deleted therefrom.

ISSUE NOS. 5 AND 8 ARE NOT VAGUE – DECIDED IN FAVOUR OF PETITIONER – HOLDS HIGH COURT

The result of the order dated 29th August, 1974 is that thereafter the allegations contained in paras 10 and 12 of the petition, coupled with Schedule A-1 and Schedule B-1 do not suffer from any vagueness. Needless to say that learned counsel for the petitioner also failed to point out at the time of the final arguments in the case that Paras 10 and 12, coupled with Schedule A-1 and Schedule B-1, still suffer from any vagueness:

Issues 5 and 8 are accordingly answered in favour of the petitioner and against the respondent No. 1.

ISSUE NO. 6

COW AND CALF WAS NOT A RELIGIOUS SYMBOL – RESPONDENT NO. 1 COMMITTED NO CORRUPT PRACTICE BY TELLING VOTERS TO PUT VOTING MARK ON COW AND CALF SYMBOL – HOLDS HIGH COURT

In para 11 of the petition it is alleged that the symbol of cow and calf is a religions symbol; that the party to which the respondent No. 1 belongs induced the Election Commission of India to allot to the party the symbol of cow and calf; that the respondent No. 1 made use of and appealed to that religious symbol in each of her election meetings addressed by her in the constituency meetings addressed by her in the constituency on 25th of February, 1971. It is further alleged that the respondent No. 1 exhorted the voters to cast their votes by putting the prescribed seal mark on the symbol of cow and calf in the meetings addressed by her on 25th of February, 1971 at Bhojpur, Murai – ka – bagh, Lalganj, Sothi and other places.

In reply to the above allegation, the respondent No. 1 pleaded that the symbol of cow and calf was not a religious symbol nor was it so regarded by the Hindu community; that it was wrong that her political party induced the Election Commission of India to allot that symbol to her party; that it was also wrong that extensive use of and appeal to the religious symbol of cow and calf was made by her in any of the meetings addressed on 25th of February, 1971. She added that during her speeches she merely informed the voters that the cow and calf was the election symbol of Congress (R) and that voting mark should be put on that symbol. Another plea raised on behalf of the respondent No. 1 in this connection was that the decision of the Election Commission in the matter of reservation of symbols was final and the symbol of cow and calf having been allotted to the Congress (R), to which party the respondent No. 1. belonged, it could not be made a ground for her election being avoided under section 100 of the Representation of the People Act.

The evidence adduced by the petitioner under this issue can be classified under two heads:

(1) Raghubar Mithu Lal Shastri (P.W. 16) and Surya Bali Shukla (P.W. 34) were examined in order to depose about the position of the cow and calf in the Hindu religion. Sant Saran Vedanti (P.W. 33) deposed that he was a member of the Akhil Bhartiya Ram Rajya Parishad. He was examined to prove that in 1952 the Akhil Bhartiya Ram Rajya Parishad applied for the symbol of cow and calf being allotted to it but it was refused on the ground that it was a religious symbol. A.N. Sen (P.W. 54), Secretary, Election Commission of India, was examined to prove that Akhil Bhartiya Ram Rajya Parishad applied for the allotment of the symbol of cow and calf for the general election of 1952 and the same was refused.

(2) Ram Nihore (P.W. 25), Raj Kishore Singh (P.W. 26), Ram Kumar (P.W. 46) are witnesses under the second head. They were examined to prove that during her speeches the respondent No. 1 said that cow and calf was a religious symbol and that people should therefore put their mark on that symbol while casting their votes.

So far as the evidence of the witnesses mentioned under the second head above is concerned, learned counsel for the respondent No. 1 urged that since there was no pleading in the petition that the respondent No. 1 made an appeal in any of her election meetings that the symbol of cow and calf was a *'dharmik prateek'*, the evidence was not in conformity with the pleadings and cannot be looked into. I have already referred to what has been alleged in the petition. As mentioned earlier, all that is stated therein that in the meetings addressed by the respondent No. 1 on

25th February, 1971 she made use of and appealed to the religious symbol of cow and calf. It has not been clarified as to what words were used by the respondent No. 1 while making that appeal. In other words, the pleadings on the point have been left vague in the petition. Learned counsel for the respondent No. 1 urged that the evidence adduced by the petitioner in order to prove that, in the meetings addressed by her, the respondent No. 1 said that cow and calf was a religious symbol and consequently people should put their mark on that symbol, is not strictly in conformity with the pleadings. Learned counsel pointed out that no amount of evidence can be looked into upon a plea which has not been put forth in the pleadings. In view of the objection raised on behalf of the respondent, learned counsel for the petitioner said at the time of argument that he confined his case only to the use of the symbol of cow and calf. He gave up that part of the case wherein it was alleged that appeals were made to the religious symbol of cow and calf by the respondent No. 1. It is accordingly not necessary to refer to the evidence of Ram Nihore (P.W. 25), Raj Kishore Singh (P.W. 26) and Ram Kumar (P.W. 46), nor is it necessary to refer to the evidence adduced by the respondent to rebut the evidence of the aforesaid P.Ws.

The question that, therefore, remains for consideration is whether the symbol of cow and calf was a religious symbol and the mere use of that symbol as an election symbol constituted a corrupt practice under section 123(3) of the Representation of the People Act.

It will first be convenient to dispose of the evidence of Sant Saran Vedanti (P.W. 33) and A.N. Sen (P.W. 34). Sant Saran Vedanti merely stated that the Akhil Bhartiya Ram Rajya Parishad applied for the election symbol of cow and calf in 1952 and that the Election Commission refused to grant that symbol to the Akhil Bhartiya Ram Rajya Parishad on the ground that it was a religious symbol.

The statement of Sri Sant Saran Vedanti that Akhil Bhartiya Ram Rajya Parishad, inter alia, applied for the symbol of cow and calf for the election of 1952 finds some support from the statement of Sri A.N. Sen (P.W. 54), Secretary to the Election Commission of India, who stated that it was apparent from the report of the First General Elections in India in 1951-52 that Akhil Bhartiya Ram Rajya Parishad asked for allotment of symbol of "milch cow with calf and milkmaid". A copy of that report was placed by Sri A.N. Sen on the record of this case and a perusal thereof does show that for the elections of 1952 Akhil Bhartiya Ram Rajya Parishad had applied for the aforesaid symbol. Sri Sant Saren Vedanti, however, failed to place on record any copy of the order passed on the application of Akhil Bhartiya Ram Rajya Parishad for the allotment of the said symbol. He said that a reply had been received from the Election Commission but it was not traceable. In cross-examination he conceded that the reply received from the Election Commission was in English and that he could neither read nor understand English. The Statement made by Sri Sant Saran Vedanti does not, therefore, constitute a sufficient proof of the fact that the Election Commission of India refused to allot the symbol of "milch cow with calf and milkmaid" because it treated that symbol to be a religious symbol. My attention was invited to the views expressed by the Election Commission in their report in the First General Elections in India (1951-52), wherein they said:

> "The Commission decided that the symbols should be familiar to, and easily recognizable by, illiterate and ignorant voters and readily distinguishable by them from each other and that no object having any religious or sentimental association, *e.g.* a cow, a temple, the national flag, a spinning wheel and the like should find a place in the list of approved symbols."

I do not think that on the basis of the above view held by the Election Commission it can be inferred that the symbol of "milch cow with calf and milkmaid" was really treated by the Election Commission as a religious symbol and was refused on that ground. Assuming, however, that the Election Commission had a feeling that the symbol of cow with calf and milkmaid, applied for by the Akhil Bhartiya Ram Rajya Parishad, was a religious symbol, that view is not binding on this Court. The court has to come to its own conclusion on the basis of the material placed before it and not to adopt the view expressed by the Election Commission.

Therefore, looked at from any angle, the evidence of Sri Sant Saran Vedanti (P.W. 33) fails to prove that the cow and calf is a religious symbol.

Coming to the evidence of Sri A.N. Sen (P.W. 54), as already stated, he merely said that it appeared from the report of the Election Commission for the year 1951-52 that Akhil Bhartiya Ram Rajya Parishad had applied for the symbol of milch cow with calf and milkmaid. The report filed by Sri Sen further shows that Akhil Bhartiya Ram Rajya Parishad was allotted the symbol of 'Rising Sun', which was their second preference. Nothing further is proved either by the statement of Sri A.N. Sen or by the report of the Election Commission for the year 1951-52. I accordingly hold that the evidence of Sri A.N. Sen (P.W. 54) can also have no bearing on the point whether the symbol of cow and calf allotted to the Congress (R) for the elections of 1971 was a religious symbol. In fact Sri A.N. Sen stated that the Election Commission did not consider the symbol of cow and calf to be a religious symbol within the meaning of section 123(3) of the Representation of the People Act and it was for that reason that the said symbol was allotted by the Commission to the Congress (R).

This takes me to the other two witnesses examined on this point by the petitioner, *i.e.* Raghubar Mithu Lal Shastri (P.W. 16) and Surya Bali Shukla (P.W. 34).

Raghubar Mithu Shastri claimed to be a scholar of Hindu scriptures. After making a reference to the Vedas, Nirukti, the Bhagwat Puran, the Mahabharat etc., he deposed:

> "The cow and even the image of cow or any portrait and even things closely associated with cow are sacred, have always been treated as God and worshipped by Hindus."

Now, it is a matter of common knowledge that in all scriptures of the yore resort has been made to similes, metaphors, allegories and hyperboles. Scholars in mythology give allowance to it while understanding the same. A reading of the statement made by Sri Raghubar Mithu Lal Shastri as a whole does not show that cow has been held to be one of the recognized Gods in the Hindu mythology, though she has been held sacred and worthy of great veneration. After making a reference to the 47th and 48th Verse of Chapter XXIII of Yajurveda, the witness said that according to said Verses, Vedas were light like Surya, lake equal to the Ocean is sky, Indra is greater than earth, but there is no measure for cow. The statement that there was no measure for cow does not in my opinion, leads to the conclusion that the cow was a God. It can very well mean that cow had no measure for its utility and usefulness in the Hindu society. Again after referring to the 10th Kanda of the Yatherveda, the witness said that according to the First, Second and Third Mantras thereof anybody who worships cow when it is born and worships it in its entirety, namely its hair, its hoofs, its colour and its appearance, alone is fit for being given the cow as a gift. Now, this again does not show that cow was equated with God. It only states that no person should be given a cow in gift unless he adores her, for, if he is not an adorer of a cow, he may maltreat her. Then the witness referred to Verse 101 in Chapter X, Mandal 8 and Mantra 151 of the Rigveda and said that the sense of that Mantra is that cow is the mother of 11 Rudra Gods, daughter of 8 Vasus, sister of 12 Adityas and centre of immortality or nectar. According to the witness, the Mantra carries a mandate that a cow which is without any defect or default and at the same time most humble should never be killed. Now, the mere fact that cow has been described in the aforesaid part of Rigveda as mother of some Gods and sister of others cannot in my opinion lead to the conclusion that cow was given the status of God. It is well known that the cow's milk has been held to be extremely useful and it is said that it carries medicinal properties. It is also said that one who lives on cow's milk enjoys a long life. It was, therefore, said in this Mantra that cow was the centre of immortality or of nectar. It appears that it was also for this reason that cow has been associated with Rudra Gods and Vasus in the aforesaid Mantra. After making a reference to Sloka 10 of Chapter XVI, third Askandh of the Bhagwat the witness said:

> "Those people who treat the highly spiritual Brahmins, cows and living beings having no shelter, who are the very physical body of mine, thinking them to be different from me will have trouble by the vulture like messengers of Yama representating me."

COW IS NOT EQUATED WITH GOD BY ANY HINDU SCRIPTURE – HOLDS HIGH COURT

The Hindu belief is that God resides within every living being and more so within those who are holy and live a sacred life. It is also one of the beliefs that God looks after those who are not looked after by anybody. It is in that sense that it has been stated in the Bhagwat that God resides within spiritual Brahmins, cows, and living beings having no shelter. To enjoin that they are treated with respect, it is further stated therein that if anybody treats them to be different from God he will have to suffer consequences for the same. I do not think it can be inferred on the basis thereof that cow was herself a God. In fact Sri Raghubar Mithu Lal Shastri himself made significant concessions during his cross-examination to dispel the theory sought to be enunciated by him during his examination-in-chief that cow is God in Hindu mythology. He said that if by seeing the picture of a calf, one's pity is aroused then that calf will be religious symbol. In answer to a further question he said that not only a bullock but any living creature that evoked pity is a religious symbol. In answer to the question as to what was the quality, besides being fit for worship, which makes an article a religious symbol, the witness said that if anything or object serves the purpose of coming in great use in life *e.g.* to preserve human life, it becomes a thing of worship, and that economics also plays a part in the matter. It is needless to dilate any further on the statement made by Sri Raghubar Mithu Lal Shastri (P.W. 16). I would state at the cost of repetition that his evidence in my opinion does not lead to the conclusion that cow is God and, therefore, a religious symbol.

Learned counsel for the petitioner also referred me to the evidence of Dr. Pattabhi Ram Shastri (P.W. 34) and urged that the statement made by him also leads to the conclusion that cow has been held to be a God in Hindu mythology. I have, therefore, perused the statement of Dr. Pattabhi Ram Shastri (P.W. 34) as well and I am unable to agree with learned counsel for the petitioner. Dr. Pattabhi Ram Shastri clearly stated in the examination-in-chief that the picture or portrait of a cow and calf is not a religious symbol. He further stated that in Shastras cow has been mentioned only as one of the dravyas (articles) and in Vedas it has been considered to be the national wealth. He was then confronted with some scriptures in order to elicit from him that cow was God. Most of the scriptures were the same as have been referred to by Dr. Raghubar Mithu Lal Shastri (P.W. 16) and it would be useless to refer to them in detail again. The statement made by Dr. Pattabhi Ram Shastri in cross-examination also leads to the same conclusion, namely that cow has been mentioned with reverence and adoration in the holy scriptures. That certainly does not mean that cow is God or one of the Gods.

Learned counsel for the petitioner then referred to the book 'Gosewa' written by Mahatma Gandhi (Translated by Ram Narain Chaudhary). The portion relied upon by the learned counsel for the petitioner occurs on page 12 of the Book and reads as follows:

> "Phirbhi samanya Hinduon ke liye to goraksha ka prem hi Hindu tatva ka mukhya lakchanya thahraya hai".

Learned counsel stressed that Mahatma Gandhi was a great scholar and the aforesaid view expressed by him in his book should also lead to the conclusion that cow has been held to be a God in Hindu mythology. I cannot ascribe that meaning to the aforesaid words occurring in the Book 'Gosewa'. To my mind that does not mean anything beyond this that to carry love for cow is one of the tenets of Hindu religion. That obviously is based on the fact that since a long time, rather since the times of the holy scriptures, cow has been treated sacred in Hindu religion. Everything that is sacred does not become God.

BABUR IN HIS FARMAN PROHIBITED THE MUSLIMS FROM SLAUGHTERING COWS – EVEN IT DOES NOT EQUATE COW WITH GOD – HOLD HIGH COURT

Reference was also made by learned counsel for the petitioner to a Book "*Gae ki jan bachane ka bayan*" by Khwaja Hasan Nizami. Particular stress was laid by learned counsel for the petitioner on the contents of pages 35 and 46-47 of this Book. Page 35 reproduces a Fatwa by one Maulana Abdul Hai. All that has been stressed in it is that cow slaughter was not one of the essentials of Islam, that since cow slaughter offends against Hindu religion and causes pain to the Hindu neighbour, it was necessary for the Muslims to refrain from indulging in cow slaughter. I fail to understand how anything contained in this Fatwa can go to prove that cow is God. It only mentions a humane principle that nothing should be done which offends the followers of another religion. Coming to pages 46 and 47, they purport to carry the translation of the *farman* of the Emperor Babar. The advice given in this Farman by Emperor Babar to his son was that he should refrain from cow slaughter, so that he could capture the love and respect of the Hindu population of the country. Again, it was a lesson in politics that was given by Emperor Babar through this Farman. That certainly does not prove that cow is God.

IN HINDU SCRIPTURES COW IS HELD SACRED AND ITS KILLING PROHIBITED BUT NOT EQUATED WITH GOD – HOLDS HIGH COURT

Reference was also made by learned counsel for the petitioner during his arguments to a Book "Hindu Pantheon" by Edward Moor (pages 78 and 79), On page 79 it is stated that images of cow and of her calf are worshipped in India. In paragraph 3 on page 78 it is said "A cow, the reader will perceive, is no unimportant mythological personage, nor is the bull, the latter has been spoken of, in another place, as the nandi of Mahadeva, and the symbol of divine justice." In the third paragraph on page 79 it is said, "A cow sucking a calf is a very favourite subject of Hindu artists, in paint, ivory, brass, mortar etc." It is not stated either on page 78 or on page 79 of this Book that cow is held to be a God in the Hindu religion.

Learned counsel for the petitioner then referred me to *Enclyclopedia Britania,* 1962 Edition, Vol. II, wherein describing Hinduism, It is stated:—

> "Many animals, plants, and natural objects are sacred in varying degree, the most noteworthy being the cow, The bull is specially sacred because of his connection with God Shiva, <u>But the cow is divine in her own right</u> and is generally revered as the representative of mother earth."

In the *Webster's New International Dictionary* the word 'divine' has been assigned the meaning of "God or pertaining to God, proceeding from God; appropriated to God; pertaining to or proceeding from a deity; God like and heavenly. "Now, everything that pertains to God or proceeds from God or is appropriated to God or is God like or heavenly is not necessarily itself a God. While saying that the cow is divine in her own right, the sense conveyed is that though bulls and other animals are held sacred because of their association with some God, cow is held sacred without any such association. Reliance was also placed by learned counsel for the petitioner on some observations made by the Supreme Court in the case **Mohammad Hanif Qurreshi v. State of Bihar, AIR 1958 SC 731 (744 and 755) para 22.** Learned counsel particularly invited my attention to the sentence occurring on page 75, which states that cow was gradually raised to the status of divinity. That sentence is, however, to be read in the context in which it is mentioned and not removed from it. In the opening part of paragraph 22 it is stated that in the vedic times animal flesh the staple food of the people, and that goats, sheep, cows, buffaloes and even horses were slaughtered for food and for religious sacrifices and that their flesh used to be offered to the Gods. Thereafter reference has been made to some authorities of Hindu mythology and it is stated:

> "Though the custom of slaughtering of cows and bulls prevailed during the Vedic period, nevertheless, even in the Rigveda times there seems to have grown up a revulsion of feeling against the custom. The cow gradually came to acquire a special sanctity and was called 'Aghnya' (not to be slain). There was a school of thinkers amongst the Rishis, who set their face against the custom of killing such useful animals as the cow and the bull. High praise was bestowed on the cows as will appear from the following verses from Rg. Veda, Book VI, Hymn XXVIII (Cows) attributed to the worship of sage Bhardvaja..."

A reading of para 20 as a whole thus makes it appear that in the early Vedic times cow and bull were slaughtered for food as well as for religious sacrifice. Gradually the Aryans realized the usefulness of the cow and the bull which led to the cow and bull being praised in the Hindu mythology in high terms. It appears that in order to prevent the slaughter of the bull and cow, particularly in realization of the great utility of the cow, this course was adopted in the Hindu scriptures. I do not agree that anything said by the Supreme Court in the decision **M.H. Qurreshi v. State of Bihar**, (supra) and contained in Para 22 of the report thereof, amounts to saying that cow is treated to be a God in the Hindu religion.

WHETHER COW AND CALF ARE A RELIGIOUS SYMBOL SHOULD BE SEEN FROM THE ANGLE OF A COMMON MAN – HOLDS HIGH COURT

Whether the cow and calf is a religious symbol, should in fact be understood in the sense common man understands it. The common man in our country does not delve deep into the Vedas, Purans and Smritis in order to know the identity and status of deities in the Hindu mythology. No one can deny that cow, like other cattle, are bought and sold all over the world since times immemorial. It also cannot be denied that cows are so often shabbily treated by an ordinary man. It is beyond the understanding of a common man professing Hindu religion that the Hindu Gods and deities should be so humble and weak and any person may buy and sell them at his pleasure and any person can maltreat them. Again, if cow is a deity, the entire race thereof in this universe should be held deities which is not very much understandable. The rational view, therefore, is that, in view of her high utility, cow is treated with great reverence. It cannot, however, be equated with God or deity.

MEANING OF A SYMBOL – PICTURE OF COW AND CALF – NOT A RELIGIOUS SYMBOL – HOLDS HIGH COURT

Another aspect of the matter is that section 123(3) makes the use of a religious symbol to be a corrupt practice. According to learned counsel for the petitioner, cow is a deity and the picture of the cow should, therefore, be a religious symbol. The question, however, is what is the meaning of the word 'symbol'? According to *Webster's New International Dictionary* 'symbol' can signify in common, a visible thing that stands for or suggests something invisible or intangible; it can apply to anything that serves as an outward sign of something else. According to *Corpus Juris Secundum,* 'symbol' means an object chosen to typify or represent some idea or quality in something else because of a resemblance in one or more of their characteristics or association.

In view of the aforesaid meaning of the word 'symbol' the picture of cow and calf cannot be held to be the symbol of cow herself. On this reasoning also it cannot be held to be a religious symbol.

The point whether the cow and calf is a religious symbol or not came up for consideration directly in the cases **Bhanwar Lal v. Ram Sahai Pandey, AIR 1972 MP 176 (179)**, Election Petition No. 2 of 1971 (**Shital Prasad Misra v. Nitiraj Singh Chaudhary**), decided by the High Court of Madhya Pradesh on 21st July, 1971 and published in Madhya Pradesh Gazette, dated 23rd June, 1971, Pt. I.P. 809 paras 18 to 23 and **Sri Prasanna Das Damodar Das Palwar v. Indu Lal Kanhaiya Lal Yajnik,** decided by the High Court of Gujarat on 27th August, 1971, published in Gujarat Gazette dated 20th July, 1972, Pt IV C, p. 1342 (1355 to 1362). It was uniformly held in all the three cases that the cow and calf is not a religious symbol. The point whether cow is a religious symbol or not also came up for consideration in one context or the other in the cases **Shah Jayanthi Lal Amba Lal v. Kasturi Lal Nagin Das Doshi, 36 Election LR 189; Baijnath Singh Vaidya v. Ravendra Pratap Singh, 36 Election LR 327; Bishambhar Dayal v. Raj Rajeshwar, 39 Election LR 363 (376); Dinesh Dangi v. Daulat Ram, 39 Election LR 465 (476); Shyam Lal v. Mausa Din, 37 Election LR 67 (89); B.P. Maurya v. Prakashvir Shastri, 37 Election LR 137 (147); Sohadar Rai v. Ram Singh Aharwar, 37 Election LR 176 (188); Vishwanath Prasad v. Salamat Ullah, 27 Election LR 145 (186 bottom) and Lachchi Ram v. Jamuna Prasad Mukhariya, 9 Election LR 149 (157).** It was held in all these cases that cow in not a religious symbol.

It will thus appear that the consensus of authorities overwhelmingly supports the view that the picture of cow and calf is not a religious symbol. Learned counsel for the petitioner could not cite any case in which a contrary view may have been expressed.

RESPONDENT NO. 1 NOT GUILTY UNDER SECTION 123(3) OF THE ACT – ISSUE NO. 6 DECIDED IN FAVOUR OF RESPONDENT NO. 1 – HOLDS HIGH COURT

I accordingly find that the respondent No. 1 cannot be held guilty of having committed a corrupt practice under section 123(3) of the Representation of the People Act merely because of the user of the symbol of cow and calf as her election symbol or because of her having said to the electors, during the speeches addressed by her within the constituency, that cow and calf was the symbol of the Congress Party and that they should put the voting mark against that symbol.

Issue No. 6 is, therefore answered against the petitioner and in favour of respondent No. 1.

ISSUE NO. 9 AND WRIT PETITION NO. 3761 of 1975 – VERSION OF PETITIONER ON THE AMOUNT OF EXPENDITURE INCURRED BY RESPONDENT NO. 1 – HIGH COURT

In para 13 of the election petition it is alleged that the respondent No. 1 and her election agent incurred an expenditure much beyond the prescribed limit of Rs. 35,000 and thereby committed a corrupt practice under section 123(6) of the Representation of the People Act. The petitioner has also given some items of expenditure alleged to have been incurred by the respondent No. 1 and her election agent but not shown in the return of election expenses. They are as follows:—

(1)	The hiring charges of vehicles specified in para 13(1) ..	Over Rs. 1,28,700
(2)	Cost of petrol & diesel for the vehicles specified in Para 13(1)………	Over Rs. 43,230
(3)	Payments made to the drivers of the vehicles specified in para 13(1)....	Over Rs. 9,900
(4)	Repairing & servicing charges of the vehicles specified in Para 13(1) of the petition........	Over Rs. 5,000
(5)	Payments made to the workers engaged for the purpose of election propaganda.........	Over Rs 6,600
(6)	Expenses on the erection of polling camps near the polling stations on the polling days.........	Rs. 10,000
(7)	Expenses on the erection of rostrums for the public meetings addressed by the respondent No. 1 in the constituency on 1st February and 25th February, 1971...........	Rs. 1,32,000
(8)	Expenses on arrangement of loudspeakers for the various election meetings of respondents No. 1 addressed on 1st of February and 25th of February, 1971..........	Rs. 7,000
(9)	Expenses on respondent No. 1's transport by Air Force planes and helicopters for addressing election meetings on 1st of February, 1971 and 25th of February, 1971..........	Rs. 1,68,000
(10)	Expenses on barricading of the routes to the places of the election meetings addressed by the respondent No. 1 on 1st of February, 1971 & 25th February by. 1971...........	Rs. 2,00,000
(11)	Expenses on T.A. & D.A. paid to the members of the Police Force posted along the route up the place of election meetings of respondent No. 1 on 1.2.1971 and 25.2.1971.........	Rs. 1,40,000
(12)	Expenses on motor transport for the conveyance of respondent No. 1 and her party to the place of her election meetings on 1st of February, 1971 and 25th of February, 1971.........	Over Rs. 2,000

REPLY OF RESPONDENT NO. 1 – HIGH COURT

The reply of the respondent No. 1 to the above allegation is contained in para 17 of her written statement, wherein she denied that any of the alleged expenditure was incurred by her or her election agent. In regard to the item mentioned at Serial No. 1 above, she said that some vehicles were used by the District Congress Committee for doing work of the Indian National Congress (R) in the three parliamentary constituencies, and that hiring charges thereof, if any, were also paid by the District Congress Committee, out of its own party funds. The registration nos. of vehicles alleged to have been so used by the District Congress Committee are mentioned in Para 17(b) of the written statement. In regard to the items of expenditure mentioned at serial Nos. 2, 3 and 4 above, the respondent pleaded that the expenditure in that connection, if any, must have been incurred by the District Congress Committee and that, in any case, she or her election agent did not incur any expenditure in that connection. With regard to the item of expenditure mentioned at Serial No. 5, the respondent No. 1 pleaded that all the workers who participated in the election were members and office bearers of the party and that they did the work voluntarily and not for any remuneration. With regard to the item of expenditure mentioned at serial No. 6, the respondent No. 1 said that the polling camps, where ever they were established, were arranged by the District Congress Committee or the Mandal Congress Committee, and that at most of the places local workers brought daris, jajims etc. to spread them under some shady tree near the polling stations. The respondent added that no expenditure was incurred by her, or by her election agent in that connection and that the expenditure, wherever it was necessary was incurred by the District Congress Committee. Referring to the item of expenditure mentioned at Serial No. 7, she pleaded that the rostrums were constructed under the direction of the State Government and that the bills for the same, in accordance with Government notifications, were either paid or shall be paid by the Pradesh Congress Committee. She added that no expenditure in that connection was incurred by her or by her election agent. Referring to the expenses mentioned at serial No. 8, the respondent No. 1 pleaded that the arrangement of loudspeakers was made by the District Congress Committee of Raebareli and that the bills were paid by them out of their own funds. She denied any amount having been paid by her or by her election agent in that connection. Referring to the item of expenditure mentioned at serial No. 9, the respondent No. 1 pleaded that the charges for the air journeys made by her had either been paid or shall be paid by the All India Congress Committee. In regard to the item of expenditure mentioned at Serial No. 10, the respondent No. 1 pleaded that the entire arrangements in that connection were made voluntarily by the State Government at their own initiative as a part of their duty and the expenses were also borne by them. It was added that in any event she or her election agent did not incur any expenditure in that connection.

EXPENDITURE MADE BY THE PARTY SHOULD BE INCLUDED IN THE EXPENDITURE OF RESPONDENT NO. 1 – CONTEND PETITIONER

The petitioner did not adduce any evidence in order to prove that any of the expenditures alleged by him in Para 13 and its sub-paras were actually incurred by the respondent No. 1 or her election agent. The petitioner's stand was that, on the own admission of respondent No. 1, expenditure on most of the items alleged by him was incurred by the political party to which she belonged, and that those expenses are liable to be added to the election expenses of the respondent No. 1, in view of the decision of the Supreme Court in the case **Kanwar Lal Gupta v. Amar Nath Chawla, AIR 1975 SC 308**. After taking into consideration various aspects of the matter, the Supreme Court in the aforesaid case summed up its conclusion thus (on page 316 Col. 1):

> "When the political party sponsoring a candidate incurs expenditure in connection with his election, as distinguished from expenditure on general party propaganda, and the candidate not only takes advantage of it or participates in the programme or activity or fails to disavow the expenditure or consents to it or acquiesces in it, it would be reasonable to infer, save in special circumstances, that he impliedly authorised the political party to incur

such expenditure and he cannot escape the rigor of the ceiling by saying that he has not incurred the expenditure, but his political party has done so."

Further on (at 316, Col. 2) it was again said:—

> "In the first place, a political party is free to incur any expenditure it likes on its general party propaganda though, of course, in this area also some imitative ceiling is eminently desirable coupled with filing of return of expenses and an independent machinery to investigate and take action. It is only where expenditure is incurred which can be identified with the election of a candidate that it would be liable to be added to the expenditure of that candidate as being impliedly authorised by him."

Relying on the above case, learned counsel for the petitioner urged that such items of expenditure as may, in the present case, be found to have been incurred by the Congress (R), either through the D.C.C. or the P.C.C. or the A.I.C.C., must be added to the election expenses of the respondent No. 1 as shown in the return (Exh. 5). Learned counsel further urged that if it is found that the total exceeds the prescribed limit of Rs. 35,000, the election of the respondent No. 1 should be set aside.

SECTION 77 OF THE ACT AMENDED BY AN ORDINANCE BY GOVERNMENT OF INDIA – REPLACED BY THE AMENDING ACT, 1974 TO UNDO THE EFFECT OF SUPREME COURT JUDGMENT – PETITIONER FILED CWP TO CHALLENGE AMENDMENT – HIGH COURT

In order to undo the effect of the decision of the Supreme Court in the case **Kanwar Lal Gupta v. Amar Nath Chawla,** (supra) the Representation of the People (Amendment) Ordinance, 1974 was promulgated by the President, which was later replaced by the Representation of the People (Amendment) Act, 1974, hereinafter to be called the Amending Act. Two Explanations have been added to section 77 of the Representation of the People Act. Explanation I reads as follows:

> "Notwithstanding any judgment, order or decision of any Court to the contrary, any expenditure incurred or authorized in connection with the election of a candidate by a political party or by any other association or body of persons or by any individual (other than the candidate or his election agent) shall not be deemed to be and shall not ever be deemed to have been, expenditure in connection with the election incurred or authorised by the candidate or by his election agent, for the purposes of this sub-section:
>
> Provided that nothing contained in this Explanation shall affect:—
>
> (a) Any judgment, order or decision of the Supreme Court whereby the election of a candidate to the House of the People or to the Legislative Assembly of a State has been declared void or set aside before the commencement of the Representation of the People (Amendment) Ordinance, 1974 (13 of 1974).
>
> (b) Any judgment, order or decision of a High Court whereby the election of any such candidate has been declared void or set aside before the commencement of the said Ordinance if no appeal has been preferred to the Supreme Court against such judgment, order or decision of the High Court before such commencement and the period of limitation for filing such appeal has expired before such commencement."

The Petitioner felt that the Amending Act was constitutionally void. Entertaining some doubt on the point whether the constitutionality of the Amending Act could be challenged in the proceedings under the election petition, the petitioner filed Writ Petition No. 3761 of 1975, impleading the Union of India and Smt. Indira Nehru

Gandhi (respondent No. 1 of the election petition) as the respondents. In the writ petition, the petitioner first reproduced para 13 of the election petition which contained allegations regarding the undisclosed expenditure incurred by the respondent No. 1. The petitioner then reproduced Para 17 of the written statement of the respondent No. 1 in extenso, which contained a reply to the allegations contained in para 13 of the election petition. The petitioner then proceeded to give a brief resume of the proceedings in the election petition and then said in para 16 that from the admissions made by the respondent No. 1 (of the election petition) and the documentary evidence it was apparent that the respondent No. 1, the State Government and the ruling Congress Party together incurred an expenditure well beyond the permissible limit of Rs. 35,000 and that the entire expenditure was incurred in connection with the election of respondent No. 1. Reference has thereafter been made to the decision of the Supreme Court in the case of **Kanwar Lal Gupta v. Amar Nath Chawla,** (supra) to the Amending Ordinance and to the Amending Act. The relevant provision of the Amending Act has been reproduced in the petition. Thereafter the petitioner has alleged the grounds on which he challenged the constitutional validity of the Amending Act and prayed for the following reliefs:

(i) That the Representation of the People (Amending) Ordinance, 1974 (No. 13 of 1974) and the Representation of the People (Amending) Act, 1974 (No. 58 of 1974) be declared unconstitutional and void.

(ii) That a writ, direction or order be issued restraining the respondent No. 1 from placing any reliance on the alleged Ordinance and the Act aforesaid.

Counter affidavits have been filed on behalf of both the respondents in the writ petition maintaining that the Amendment Act was constitutionally valid. The Learned Attorney-General appeared on behalf of The Union of India to support the constitutional validity thereof.

CONSTITUTIONALITY OF THE AMENDMENT COMES LATER – MERITS TO BE CONSIDERED FIRST – HOLDS HIGH COURT

In case **State of Bihar v. Hardutta Mills, AIR 1960 SC 378,** it was observed:

> "In case where the vires of the statutory provisions are challenged on constitutional grounds, it is essential that the material facts should first be clarified and ascertained with a view to determine whether the impugned provisions are attracted, if they are, the constitutional challenge to its validity must be examined and decided.
>
> If, however, the facts admitted or proved do not occasion to decide the issue about the vires of the said provisions, there is no occasion to decide the issue about the vires of the said provisions. Any decisions on the said question would in such a case be purely academic. Courts are and should be reluctant to decide constitutional points merely as matters of academic importance."

In the case **Barsi Municipality v. Lokmanya Mills, AIR 1973 SC 1021** the Supreme Court observed:—

> "It is a wise tradition with courts not to decide a constitutional question if the case can be disposed of on other grounds."

IF THE EXPENSES OF THE PARTY AND OF THE CANDIDATE DO NOT EXCEED THE LIMIT – NO NEED FOR CONSIDERING LEGALITY OF THE AMENDMENT – HIGH COURT

In the above view of the matter, it will be desirable first to consider the petitioner's case on the point of expenses, assuming that the Amendment Act does not exist and accepting the interpretation of section 77 of the Representation of the People Act as made by the Supreme Court in the case of **Kanwar Lal Gupta v. Amar Nath Chawla,** (supra). In case it is found, after examining the petitioner's case in that manner, that the expenses incurred by the Congress (R) in connection with the election of the respondent No. 1, together with the expenses shown by the respondent No. 1 in her return (Exh. 5), exceed the prescribed limit of Rs. 35,000 it will be further necessary to examine the contentions raised on either side about the constitutional validity of the Amending Act. The point whether the expenditure incurred by the State Government, independently of the respondent and the Congress (R), should or should not be added to the expenses of the candidate shall also have to be considered at the same time. If it is found that the expenditure incurred by the Congress Party in connection with the election of the respondent No. 1, together with the election expenses of the respondent No. 1, together with the election expenses shown by her in the return (Exh. 5) do not exceed the prescribed limit, there will be no occasion to consider the constitutional validity of the Amendment Act.

Before I proceed to examine each item of expenditure alleged by the petitioner, it will be necessary to take notice of the legal position regarding the burden of proof. It has been consistently held that a charge of corrupt practice is substantially akin to a criminal charge and the standard of proof therefore is the same as in a criminal trial. A grave and heavy onus, therefore, rests on the accused to establish each and every ingredient of the charge by clear, unequivocal and unimpeachable evidence beyond reasonable doubt. A charge of corrupt practice cannot be established by a mere balance of probabilities and, if, after giving due consideration to the totality of the evidence and circumstances of the case, the mind of the Court suffers with reasonable doubt, it must be held that that charge is not proved. See **Razik Ram v. J.S. Chauhan, AIR 1975 SC 667, paras 15 and 16; Rahim Khan v. Khurshid Ahmad, AIR 1975 SC 290; Maghraj Patodia v. R.K. Birla, AIR 1971 SC 1295; Mohan Singh v. Dhanwari Lal, AIR 1964 SC 1366, para 12 and Jagdish Singh v. Pratap Singh, AIR 1965 SC 183.**

Having thus noticed the legal position about the burden of proof, I now proceed to consider each item of expenditure, which according to the stand now taken by the petitioner was incurred either by Congress Party or the Government in connection with election of respondent No. 1.

PETITIONER FAILED TO PROVE IF ANY AMOUNT WAS SPENT BY RESPONDENT NO. 1 OR THE PARTY ON HIRING VEHICLES FOR ELECTIONEERING OF RESPONDENT NO. 1 – HOLDS HIGH COURT

According to the petitioner, 32 vehicles, registration nos. whereof have been specified, had been hired and used for the purpose of election propaganda for the respondent No. 1 and an expenditure of over Rs. 1,28,700 was incurred in that connection. As already stated earlier, the respondent No. 1 denied this allegation but added that 23 vehicles (registration nos. whereof are specified in Para 17 (b) of the written statement) were so used by the District Congress Committee, Raebareli, for election work of the Indian National Congress (R) in the three Parliamentary constituencies *viz.* Raebareli, Amethi (situate in district Sultanpur and partly in district Raebareli) and Ram Sanehi Ghat (situate in district Barabanki and partly in the district of Raebareli). It was further pleaded by the respondent No. 1 that the hiring charges of those vehicles, if any, were paid by the District Congress Committee out of its own party fund as they were engaged for the party work by the District Congress Committee.

The petitioner did not lead any evidence to prove that the 32 vehicles specified in the election petition were either hired or engaged by or on behalf of the respondent No. 1 for election work. The petitioner has relied on the admission made by the respondent No. 1 in the written statement and it was urged on his behalf that the expenses incurred over hiring the 23 vehicles mentioned in the written statement of the respondent No. 1 are liable to be added to the election expenses of the respondent No. 1. Before however, it is done the petitioner must prove two things:

(i) That the 23 vehicles referred to in Para 17(b) of the written statement had been taken on hire; and

(ii) That those 23 vehicles had been used in connection with the election of the respondent No. 1 and not for the general party propaganda.

Taking up point No. (1) above, it cannot be ignored that in view of the position held by the respondent No. 1, there could be no dearth of people who could offer their vehicles, without charging anything, for election work within the constituency of respondent No. 1. It has not been admitted by the respondent No. 1 in the written statement that the 23 vehicles referred to by her had been obtained by the District Congress Committee on hire. All that has been pleaded is that they had been engaged or used by the District Congress Committee for the purposes of the election. While referring to the hire charges, the respondent No. 1 qualified her statement in the written statement by saying that such charges. If any, were paid by the District Congress Committee. There is thus nothing in the written statement of the respondent No. 1 on which the petitioner may rely in order to contend that all the 23 vehicles referred to in the written statement had been obtained on hire, and that no vehicle was obtained gratis. The respondent No. 1 had disclosed the registration numbers of the vehicles in the written statement and, consequently, it cannot be successfully contended that it was impossible for him to adduce any evidence on the point whether the vehicles were obtained on hire or they, or any of them, were obtained gratis. Once the petitioner was in possession of the registration numbers of the vehicles, he could find out the names of the owners thereof from the Regional Transport Office concerned and he could examine at least some of them in order to prove weather the vehicles had been obtained on hire or gratis. The petitioner has not done so nor has he offered any explanation for that omission.

The petitioner had also to prove as to what was the rate of the hire charges for which the vehicles had been obtained and for what period they had been obtained. The petitioner could conveniently prove that fact also by examining the owners of the vehicles referred to by the respondent No. 1 in her written statement. The petitioner could even examine some other persons before whom the settlement between the owners of the vehicles and the representative of the District Congress Committee may have been reached regarding the rate of hire and the period for which the vehicles were obtained. Needless to say that no evidence has been adduced by the petitioner to prove the aforesaid fact.

Taking up the second point, it has been observed in the case of **Kanwar Lal Gupta v. Amar Nath Chawla,** (supra) that expenditure incurred by the political party sponsoring a candidate shall be liable to be added to the expenses of the candidate only if it is incurred in connection with the election of the candidate as distinguished from the expenditure on general party propaganda. It was clearly stated that a political party is free to incur any expenditure it likes on its general party propaganda. It was, therefore, necessary for the petitioner to prove that the 23 vehicles referred to in Para 17(b) of the written statement were used in connection with the election of the respondent and not on general party propaganda. It is admitted on both hands that part of Amethi constituency and part of Ram Sanehi Ghat constituency also fall within the district of Raebareli. It is, therefore, not impossible that the vehicles were used for the general party propaganda for the benefit of the three candidates, without the propaganda being particularly connected with the respondent No. 1 Obviously, a number of persons within the constituency would have seen the vehicles operating during the period of election. It was, therefore, not impossible for the petitioner to examine a couple of witnesses to indicate to the Court as to whether the vehicles were used only for party propaganda or they, or any of them, were used in connection with the election of the respondent No. 1. The petitioner, however, did not examine any witness to throw any light on that point, nor has he offered any explanation in that connection.

Learned counsel for the petitioner referred me to the documents (Exhs. A-10, A-42 and A-43) in order to contend on the basis thereof that the 23 vehicles referred by the respondent No. 1 in her written statement were actually engaged and used in connection with her election. Exh. A-10 is the copy of the letter dated 23rd February, 1971 sent by Dal Bahadur Singh, President, District Congress Committee, Raebareli, to the District Election Officer, Raebareli, intimating that the 23 vehicles specified in that letter had been engaged by the District Congress Committee for election work in Raebareli, Amethi and Ram Sanehi Ghat constituencies. It was prayed that the vehicles may be derequisitioned. It appears that this letter failed to achieve its purpose. Sri Dal Bahadur Singh, therefore, scribbled out a note for Sri Yashpal Kapur (R.W. 32), on the original letter. This note is Exh. A-43. Through this note Sri Dal Bahadur Singh requested Sri Yashpal Kapur to send a letter to the District Election Officer on the lines of his letter (Exh. A-10), requesting him that, since the vehicles specified in his letter had been engaged by the District Congress Committee, the same may be derequisitioned. It was also mentioned in this note that Sri Dal Bahadur Singh had tried to contact the candidates from the other two constituencies, namely Amethi and Ram Sanehi Ghat, but they were not available. Exh. A-42 is the letter sent by Sri Yashpal Kapur to the District Election Officer, repeating the prayer that was contained in the letter dated 23rd February, 1971 (Exh. A-10) sent by Sri Dal Bahadur Singh. The registration numbers of the vehicles were specified in the letter and it was urged that since the vehicles had been engaged by the District Congress Committee for election work in Raebareli, Amethi and Ram Sanehi Ghat constituencies, they may be derequisitioned. Learned counsel then referred me to section 160 of the Representation of the People Act. Clause (b) of sub-section (1) thereof confers power on the State Government to requisition any vehicle, vessel etc. needed in the election for the purposes specified therein. The proviso appended to sub-sec. (1) states that no vehicle, vessel or animal which is being lawfully used by a candidate or his agent for any purpose connected with the election of such candidate shall be requisitioned under this sub-section until the completion of the poll at such election. Learned counsel for the petitioner stressed that in view of the provision contained in section 160 of the Representation of the People Act vehicles derequisitioned by the Government under sub-section (1) of section 160 could be released only on the ground that they were engaged and were being used by a particular candidate. It was urged that since Sri Yashpal Kapur, election agent of respondent No. 1, moved the District Election Officer for the release of the vehicles, it should be inferred that the vehicles were engaged and were being used in connection with the election of respondent No. 1. The argument superficially looking appears to be quite attractive, but it does not bear out a careful scrutiny. As already stated, Sri Dal Bahadur Singh first wrote a letter to the District Election Officer for the release of the vehicles. It was expressly stated in that letter that the vehicles had been engaged by the District Congress Committee for the election work in the three parliamentary constituencies falling within the district of Raebareli and consequently they may be released. The implied mandate in section 160, however, was that the vehicles requisitioned by the State Government under sub-section (1) thereof could not be de-requisitioned unless it was shown that they had been engaged or were being used by any candidate. Sri Dal Bahadur Singh had, therefore, no option but to request Sri Yashpal Kapur to send a letter to the District Election Officer in his name for the release of the vehicles. It cannot be lost sight of that even in his note (Exh. A-43) to Sri Yashpal Kapur, Sri Dal Bahadur Singh expressly stated that the vehicles had been engaged by the District Congress Committee. Towards the end of the letter it is mentioned:

> *"Aap se nivedan hai ki zila nirvachan adhikari ko ukta patra avashya likh dewen taaki teeno Lok Sabha kshettra ka karya chunao jo ki zila congress committee ki ore se chal raha hai thap na ho jave."*

As to why this request was made to Sri Yashpal Kapur only is also explained by the note (Exh. A-43), for, it states that efforts had been made to contact the candidates of the other two constituencies but it could not be possible and hence the request was made to Sri Yashpal Kapur. A perusal of the letter (Exh. A-42) sent by Sri Yashpal Kapur to the District Election Officer would reveal that it was explicitly stated in that letter as well that the 23 vehicles mentioned in that letter had been engaged by the District Congress Committee for election work in Raebareli, Amethi and Ram Sanehi Ghat constituencies. It was not mentioned even by implication that the vehicles had been engaged in connection with the election of the respondent No. 1. Sri Yashpal Kapur (R.W. 32) was cross-examined on this point and he said that the vehicles specified in the list accompanying Exh. A-42 were used in the three parliamentary constituencies by the District Congress Committee. He was not confronted by the provision contained in section 160 of the Representation of the People Act and was not questioned specifically as to why did he write a letter to the District Election Officer for release of vehicles if they had not been engaged and were not being used in connection with the election work of the respondent No. 1. I do not think the documents Exhs. A-10, A-42 and A-43 can constitute a safe basis for concluding that the 23 vehicles had been engaged or used in connection with the election of the respondent No. 1. I concede that the letter Exh. A-42, sent by Sri Yashpal Kapur to the District Election Officer for release of vehicles, raises a suspicion that those vehicles or most of them were possibly used in connection with the election of the respondent No. 1. This is all the more so because according to Sri Yashpal Kapur, he had only one vehicle for his exclusive use. No other vehicle, according to him, was exclusively used in connection with the election of respondent No. 1. It indeed does not appear very credible that, for a candidate like the respondent No. 1, only one vehicle would have been used exclusively for her election work. All the same the fact remains that suspicion, howsoever strong it may be, cannot take the place of proof. I accordingly refuse to infer on the basis of the aforesaid three documents that the 23 vehicles mentioned in the letters (Exh. A-10 and Exh. A-42) were used in connection with the election work of the respondent No. 1.

Learned counsel for the petitioner next urged that the best way for the petitioner to prove as to how many vehicles were hired by the District Congress Committee in connection with the election work and for what amount, was to summon the election expenses of the District Congress Committee. Learned counsel pointed out that, with that end in view, the petitioner summoned Mohan Lal Tripathi (P.W. 59) along with the election expenses and Sri Tripathi has filed a register (marked as No. 1) containing a statement of expenses. Learned counsel for the petitioner urged that help can be obtained from the entries contained in that register about the amount spent by the District Congress Committee over the vehicles used for election work. It will, therefore, be necessary to refer to the evidence of Sri Mohan Lal Tripathi (P.W. 59).

Sri Mohan Lal Tripathi (P.W. 59) is the existing General Secretary of the District Cogress Committee, Raebareli. He filed two registers and, for the sake of easy reference only, they were marked as Register No. 1 and Register No. 2. The Register No. 1 , according to Sri Mohan Lal Tripathi contains entries relating to the expenditure incurred in connection with the election in all the three parliamentary constituencies within the district of Raebareli. Sri Mohan Lal Tripathi, however, further on showed a negative attitude in the witness box in order to prevent the entries contained in the register being proved according to law. He said that since the register was five years' old, he could not say who had made the entries. It was then put to him whether the entries were in the hand of Sri Gaya Prasad Shukla and he said that even though he had seen Gaya Prasad Shukla writing, he could not say whether the entries in the register were in his hand. The Register No. 1 contains initials of some person at two different places in lieu of the entries having been checked. The witness was, therefore, asked whether he could identify those initials and he said that he could not. Sri Mohan Lal Tripathi thus neither himself proved the entries in the register nor did he provide any information to enable the petitioner or the Court to summon some other person for proving those entries.

At the time of argument learned counsel for the respondent No. 1 moved an application admitting four of the credit entries in the Register No. 1 and for getting them marked as exhibits. Learned counsel for the petitioner urged that since four of the entries have already been admitted by the respondent No. 1, it should be assumed that the respondent No. 1 has accepted the correctness of the entries and, consequently, there should be no hurdle in the way of the entries being taken into consideration. I am unable to accept this argument. Register No. 1, technically speaking, is not the document of respondent No. 1. It was produced in Court at the instance of the petitioner as petitioner's document. It was open to the respondent No. 1 to admit it in part, and that is what the respondent No. 1 has done by getting four of the entries therein exhibited. On that account it cannot be said that all the entries in the register stand proved.

Since the register containing the four entries admitted by the respondent No. 1 is not proved, no help can be taken by the petitioner from that register in order to prove the expenditure incurred by the District Congress Committee on the hiring of the vehicles in question.

Learned counsel for the petitioner also urged that the respondent No. 1 did not file in Court the original account of election expenses. It was further urged that on the own admission of Sri Yashpal Kapur the account was maintained by Sri Gaya Prasad Shukla, and Sri Dal Bahadur Singh was overall in charge of election work, but the respondent No. 1 withheld those witnesses, even though they had been summoned to give evidence. According to learned counsel for the petitioner, this circumstance should lead to an inference being drawn against the respondent No. 1, and the inference would be that the vehicles specified in Para 17(b) of the written statement, as also in the letters Exh. A-10 and A-42, had been obtained on hire in connection with the election of the respondent No. 1. I am afraid I cannot agree with this contention. It was necessary for the petitioner first to discharge the primary burden that lay on him. He should have adduced evidence by examining the owners or the drivers of some of the vehicles alleged to have been obtained on hire and should have further adduced evidence to show that the vehicles were used in connection with the election of the respondent No. 1 and not for party propaganda. Without discharging that initial burden of proof, the petitioner cannot ask the Court to draw an inference against the respondent No. 1 on the ground that the expenses contained in register No. 1 were not admitted by her and that Gaya Prasad Shukla and Dal Bahadur Singh, who played prominent role in the election, were summoned and yet not examined.

I, therefore, conclude that the petitioner has failed to prove that any expenditure was incurred either by the respondent No. 1 or by the District Congress Committee in obtaining any vehicles for doing work in connection with the respondent No. 1's election.

2. SINCE USE OF VEHICLES IS NOT PROVED – COST OF PETROL AND DIESEL USED BY SAID VEHICLES CANNOT BE ADDED IN THE EXPENSES OF RESPONDENT NO. 1 – HOLDS HIGH COURT

According to the petition, petrol and diesel costing Rs. 43,230 was used by those vehicles. I have, however, already held that the petitioner has failed to prove that the vehicles in question were used in connection with the election of the respondent No. 1 and that the possibility of the vehicles having been used only for party propaganda in all the three constituencies cannot be excluded.

According to the observations made by the Supreme Court in the case of **Kanwar Lal Gupta v. Amar Nath Chawla, AIR 1975 SC 308,** on which reliance is placed by the petitioner, a political party can incur any expenditure on the party work and that expenditure cannot be added to the election expenses of the candidate sponsored by that party, unless it is shown that the expenditure had been incurred in connection with the election of the candidate in as much as the candidate took advantage of it or participated therein. As also stated earlier, not an iota of evidence has been led by the petitioner in order to show that propaganda was being done from those vehicles or for what purpose those vehicles were used. The respondent No. 1 personally participated in the propaganda that was being done from those vehicles or that the respondent No. 1 of course did not visit the constituency except twice. It is not even suggested that the respondent No. 1 personally participated in the propaganda that was being done from those vehicles or that the respondent No. 1 utilised those vehicles in any other manner. Sri Yashpal Kapur was the election agent of the respondent No. 1 and there is no evidence even to show that Sri Yashpal Kapur in any manner participated in the propaganda that was being done from those vehicles or that he made use of any of those vehicles in any other manner for the purposes of the election. The election campaign continued for a fairly long time and people must have seen how and in what manner those vehicles were being used. Even if it was not possible for the petitioner to give evidence in regard to each of the 23 vehicles, evidence could be given at least in regard to some of them. This has not been done. Nor is there any explanation for that omission. There can be no presumption in the circumstances of the case to the effect that the vehicles were actually used in connection with the election of the respondent No. 1. Consequently any expenditure incurred over purchase of petrol for those vehicles cannot be added to the election expenses of the respondent No. 1.

3. FOR THE ABOVE REASON PAYMENTS MADE TO THE DRIVERS OF THE VEHICLES CANNOT BE ADDED IN THE EXPENSES OF RESPONDENT NO. 1 – HOLDS HIGH COURT

As already stated earlier, the petitioner alleged in the election petition that 32 vehicles had been hired and engaged by the respondent No. 1 but he adduced no evidence to prove it. The stand taken by him was that the expenditure incurred by the District Congress Committee on the vehicles hired by it should be added to the election expenses of the respondent No. 1. According to the respondent No. 1, only 23 vehicles had been hired by the District Congress Committee and, according to the stand taken by the petitioner at the time of arguments , the expenditure incurred in making payments to the drivers of the said 23 vehicles is in any case liable to be added to the election expenses of the respondent No. 1.

While considering the first item of expenditure, I have already held that it is not proved that the said vehicles were in any manner used in connection with the election of the respondent No. 1 and that the possibility of those vehicles having been used solely for party work during the election cannot be excluded. In that view of the matter, any expenditure incurred in making payments to the drivers of those vehicles can by no means be added to the election expenses of the respondent No. 1.

4. FOR THE ABOVE REASON REPAIRING AND SERVICING CHARGES OF THE VEHICLES CANNOT BE ADDED INTO THE EXPENSES OF RESPONDENT NO. 1 – HOLDS HIGH COURT

In view of my conclusion earlier that there is no evidence to prove that the said vehicles were used in connection with the election of the respondent No. 1, any amount spent over the repairing and servicing of those vehicles cannot be added to the election expenses of the respondent No. 1. It is needless to dilate any further on this point.

5. NO PROOF IF ANY WORKER ENGAGED FOR THE PURPOSE OF ELECTION PROPAGANDA BY RESPONDENT NO. 1 OR HER AGENT – HENCE NO EXPENSES – HOLDS HIGH COURT

According to the allegations contained in the petition, a sum of Rs. 6,600 was spent in making payments to the workers engaged for the purpose of election propaganda. The allegation is of a bald nature. It does not disclose as to what was the approximate number of workers engaged and at what rate they had been engaged. If the petitioner knew that a large number of persons were engaged by the respondent No. 1 or his election agent on payment for doing election work, it should not have been impossible for the petitioner to disclose a few names out of those workers or to give some idea about the number of workers. This has not been done. When Sri Yashpal Kapur (R.W. 32) was cross-examined on this point, he denied that any workers had been engaged on payment for doing election work. According to him, people worked voluntarily for the respondent No. 1. There being no evidence to the contrary, the statement made by Sri Yashpal Kapur cannot reasonably be discarded.

I accordingly find that the petitioner has failed to prove this item of expenditure as well.

6. NO ERECTION OF POLLING CAMPS FOR RESPONDENT NO. 1 PROVED – HENCE NO EXPENSES CAN BE ADDED IN THE EXPENSES OF RESPONDENT NO. 1 – HOLDS HIGH COURT

According to the allegations in the petition, a sum of Rs 10,000 had been spent in erection of polling camps. It is, however, not alleged in the petition as to at what polling stations the respondent No. I had erected polling camps of the nature which could cost any substantial expenditure. The allegation is, therefore, of a wholly bald nature. The workers of the petitioner must have been present at all the polling stations and there appears no reason why the petitioner could not furnish some evidence to indicate as to what was the nature of the polling camps erected on behalf of the respondent No. 1 at those polling stations so that the Court could make any assessment of the expenditure incurred in that connection, if at all. Sri Yashpal Kapur, cross-examined on that point, said that he took round of quite a large number of polling stations on the polling days and at many of the polling stations there were no *Shamiyanas* or *kanatas* but *duries* and *jajims* alone had been spread, which had been brought by the local people. He further said that at some polling station *shamiyanas* and *kanatas* were there, but they too were arranged by the local people. Questioned further, he said that he could not say if the District Congress Committees arranged for the *shamiyanas* and *kanats* in the city , but so far as rural area was concerned, the arrangement was made by the local people only.

The result, therefore, is that on the evidence, as it exists on record, it is impossible to cull out as to what was the nature of the polling camps erected on behalf of the respondent No. 1 at the various polling stations. If Shamiyanas and Kanats had actually been used in erecting the polling camps at any polling station, at how many of the polling stations such arrangement was done. Assuming for a moment that even if the District Congress Committee spent any money over the erection of polling camps, that expenditure is liable to be added to the election expenses of the respondent No. 1, being in a way connected with her election, there should be some evidence to show the nature thereof and further the fact as to at how many polling stations it was done. Unless this information is provided it would be pure speculation to form any idea about the number of the polling camps, the nature thereof and the expenditure incurred on the erection thereof. Such speculation to my mind is not permissible. I accordingly hold that the petitioner has failed to prove the expenditure alleged to have been incurred over erection of polling camps.

7. BARRICADING IS NORMAL DUTY OF STATE GOVERNMENT – HOLDS HIGH COURT

According to the allegation in the petition, a sum of Rs. 1,30,000 was spent on this head. Learned counsel for the petitioner urged that since barricading in the meeting forms part of the rostrum, as deposed to by Sri Mohinder Singh (R.W. 30), the cost of barricading has also been included under this head.

Now, so far as the barricading constructed at the place of the meeting is concerned, it is done by the State Government for the purposes of maintenance of law and order, apart from the purpose of security. It is the first duty of any Government established by law to maintain law and order. It is a matter of common knowledge that a very large number of people collect in order to see and hear the speeches of their Prime Minister, whoever he or she may be. If proper arrangements for controlling of the crowds at such meetings are not made, there can be stampeding in the event of any disturbance, and this can lead to greater trouble. It is, therefore, for controlling the crowds that the Government breaks up the place of the meetings into segments by putting up barricades. Setting up of barricades does not facilitate in the Prime Minister delivering a speech. The Prime Minister can do so even without it.

It is thus apparent that the barricades had been set up by the Government at its own expense in discharge of its normal duty. Consequently that expenditure cannot be added to the election expenses of the respondent No. 1

8. EXPENSES OF THE ERECTION OF ROSTRUMS FOR THE PUBLIC MEETINGS OF THE RESPONDENT No. 1 WITHIN THE CONSTITUENCY TO THE TUNE OF RS. 16,000 CAN BE ADDED IN THE EXPENSES OF RESPONDENT NO. 1 – HOLDS HIGH COURT

This takes me to the expenditure over construction of rostrums. It cannot be denied that the rostrums had been constructed by the Government for the use of the respondent so that she could deliver speeches to the audiences in her meetings from a commanding position and in an effective manner. The question, however, is whether the expenditure incurred by the State Government would fall under section 77, even according to the interpretation put on that section in the case of **Kanwar Lal Gupta v. Amar Nath Chawla,** (supra). After the decision in that case, there is no doubt that expenditure incurred by a political party in connection with the election of a candidate sponsored by it, as well as the expenditure incurred by friends and admirers of that candidate should be added to the election expenses of that candidate. This is so in order that a candidate may not circumvent the ceiling imposed by section 77 of the Act, by asking his political party or his friends and admirers to do what he himself cannot do. The Government seldom incurs any expenditure in connection with the election of any candidate. It does not, therefore, appear that the Legislature, while enacting section 77 of the Act, intended to include therein expenses incurred by the Government as well. Assuming, however, that the expenditure incurred by the State Government in connection with the construction of rostrums is liable to be added to the expenses of the respondent No. 1, in view of the fact that the rostrums were constructed as a result of the tour programmes sent from the office of the respondent No. 1 and she latter made use of those rostrums and did not disavow them, the total expenditure incurred by the State Government in that connection comes to Rs. 16,000. It may be appropriate to clarify the position further in this connection. The respondent No. 1 attended meetings on the occasion of her visit on 1st of February, 1971. One of those meetings was addressed at Bachchrawan, which does not fall within the constituency of Raebareli. Thus, only four meetings at which rostrums were constructed, were addressed by the respondent No. 1 in her constituency on 1st of February, 1971. According to letter (Exh. 158) a sum of Rs. 1600 was spent on construction of each of those rostrums. The total costs of the four rostrums thus comes to Rs. 6400. According to letter Exh. 201, rostrums had been constructed for 6 meetings addressed by the respondent No. 1 on 25th of February, 1971. According to letter Exh. 190, a total amount of 9,600 was spent on the construction of those rostrums. The total amount spent on the 10 rostrums comes to Rs. 16,000. This amount will include the money paid by the District Congress Committee as their share of the cost of rostrums.

I, therefore, conclude that at best a sum of Rs. 16,000 can be added to the election expenses of the respondent No. 1 as expenditure incurred on the construction of rostrums.

9. EXPENSES OF LOUDSPEAKER ARRANGEMENTS RS. 800 AND FOR ELECTRIC POWER RS. 1,151 CAN BE ADDED IN THE EXPENSES OF RESPONDENT NO. 1 – HOLDS HIGH COURT

According to the election petition, a sum of Rs. 7,200 was spent on the expenses of loudspeakers in the meeting addressed by the respondent No. 1 on the 1st of February, 1971 and 25th of February, 1971. The letter (Exh. 177) sent by the Superintendent of Police, Raebareli to Sri Gaya Prasad Shukla shows that arrangements for loudspeakers for the meetings addressed by the respondent No. 1 on 1st of February, 1971 was done by him. Presumably, he did so on behalf of the District Congress Committee. The letter (Exh. 193) shows that on the occasion of the visit of the respondent No. 1 to Raebareli on 25th of February, 1971 as well no expenditure had been incurred by the Government. Learned counsel for the petitioner, however, urged that even though the expenditure on arrangement of loudspeakers had been done by the District Congress Committee, or by Sri Gaya Prasad Shukla personally, the fact remains that the expenditure was directly connected with the election of respondent No. 1 and the latter participated therein by making use of those loudspeakers. Learned counsel stressed that the expenditure incurred over arrangement of loudspeakers should therefore be added to the election expenses of the respondent No. 1. There can be no denying the fact that the loudspeakers had been installed for the use of the respondent No. 1 and, consequently, I agree that, even though the expenditure was incurred in that connection by the District Congress Committee, it must be added to the expenses of the respondent No. 1. The petitioner has not led any evidence to show as to what was the number of loudspeakers used at every meeting. On 1st of February, 1971 the respondent No. 1 addressed meetings in the rural part of the constituency except one which appears to have been addressed by her in Raebareli city (*vide* tour programmes Exh. 26 and 42). In view of the fact that a large number of people should have gathered in the meetings of the respondent No. 1 because she happened to be the Prime Minister of the country. It should be presumed that at least 3 loudspeakers should have been used at each of the meetings. It would therefore follow that at the four meetings addressed on 1st of February, 1971 the total number of loudspeakers installed would have been approximately 32. According to exhibit 193, loudspeakers were hired for the police lines at the rate of Rs. 10 per loudspeaker per day on the aforesaid occasions.

Expenditure over installation of loudspeakers in the meetings of the respondent No. 1 can also be calculated on the same rate, and, thus calculated, the total cost of 32 loudspeakers would come to Rs. 320. On 25th of February, 1971 the respondent No. 1 addressed 6 meetings within the constituency. If 8 loudspeakers were installed at each of these meetings, the total number of loudspeakers for all the six meetings would come to 48. Calculating the expenditure incurred thereon at the rate of Rs 10 per loudspeaker the total comes to Rs. 480.

Therefore, the total amount incurred on installation of loudspeakers in the meetings addressed by the respondent No. 1 on 1st of February, 1971 and 25th of February, 1971 comes to Rs. 800.

Apart from it, electricity had also been provided for functioning of the loudspeakers at some meetings, as is apparent from the letter (Exh.147). Through this letter the Superintendent of Police, Raebareli asked the President of the Pradesh Congress Committee to pay a sum of Rs. 1151 as cost of energy supplied for the functioning of the loudspeakers. From the letter (Exh. 146) it appears that this amount was remitted by the Pradesh Congress Committee. This amount should be treated as amount spent in the installation of the loudspeakers.

Adding the amount of Rs. 1151 to the aforesaid amount of Rs. 800, the total comes to Rs. 1951.

Learned counsel for the petitioner also urged that some poles had been erected to carry the line to the place of the meetings and the expenditure incurred in that connection should also be added. It is, however, a matter of common knowledge that in the matter of temporary connection the poles etc. that are utilized for providing the temporary connection are taken away by the department after the energy is disconnected. In that view of the matter, the amount spent over putting any poles for carrying the line to the places of the meetings cannot be held to be expenditure within the meaning of that word.

In the result, therefore, a sum of Rs. 1951 only should be added to the election expenses of the respondent No. 1, being the expenditure incurred in connection with the arrangement of loudspeakers in the meetings addressed by the respondent No. 1.

10. EXPENSES OF RESPONDENT No. 1'S TRANSPORT BY AIR FORCE PLANES WERE NOT HER ELECTION EXPENSES – HOLDS HIGH COURT

According to the allegations in the petition, a sum of Rs. 1,68,000 was spent in this connection. In answer to issue No. 2, however, I have held that none of the two flights were made by the respondent No. 1 in connection with her election and that, on the contrary, the flights on both occasions were parts of the general election tour of the country made by the respondent No. 1. For the same reason I find that any expenditure incurred in the flights made by the respondent No. 1 on 1st of February, 1971 and 25th of February, 1972 should not be added to the election expenses of the respondent No. 1.

11. BARRICADING OF ROUTES TO PLACES OF ELECTION MEETINGS WAS NORMAL DUTY OF STATE GOVERNMENT – HOLDS HIGH COURT

While answering Issue No. 3, I have held that barricading along the routes had been done by the State Government as part of its own duty for controlling the crowd and maintaining law and order. That expenditure cannot in any way he held to be connected with the election of the respondent No. 1. The expenditure incurred by the State Government in setting up barricades along the routes by which the Prime Minister travelled on 1st of February, 1971 and 25th of February, 1971 cannot therefore be added to her election expenses.

12. EXPENSES ON T.A. & D.A. PAID TO THE MEMBERS OF THE POLICE FORCE ARE NOT ELECTIONS EXPENSES OF RESPONDENT NO. 1 – HOLDS HIGH COURT

Once I have concluded that barricading along the routes was done by the Government in discharge of its own duties to control the crowd and to maintain law and order, it is obvious that the members of the Police Force were also posted along the routes for the same purpose. Any amount paid to the members of the Police Force for lining the routes on the aforesaid dates cannot be held to be expenditure incurred in connection with the election of the respondent No. 1.

Consequently, any amount spent by the State Government in paying T.A. and D.A. to the members of the Police Force for their remaining on duty on 1 st of February, 1971 and 25th of February, 1971 cannot be added to the election expenses of the respondent No. 1.

13. EXPENSES OF MOTOR TRANSPORT FOR THE CONVEYANCE OF RESPONDENT No. 1 to THE PLACES OF ELECTION MEETINGS ARE THE ELECTION EXPENSES OF RESPONDENT NO. 1 – HOLDS HIGH COURT

According to the allegation in the petition, a sum of Rs. 2,000 was spent under that head. According to the letter (Exh. 136), the charge payable for the car journey made by the respondent No. 1 was 75 paise per kilometer. Learned counsel for the respondent No. 1 worked out the distance covered by the respondent No. 1 on 1st of February, 1971 and 25th of February, 1971 within her constituency and, calculating the charges payable at the rate 75 paise per kilometer, the figure arrived at by him comes to Rs. 232-50 paise only. So Rs. 232-50 paise was payable in that connection. A copy of the chart prepared by learned counsel for the respondent No. 1 was handed over by him to the learned counsel for the petitioner and the latter has not refuted the correctness thereof.

It should, therefore be accepted that the expenditure of Rs. 232-50 p. only was incurred in providing transport to the respondent No. 1 on 1st of February, 1971 and 25th of February, 1971.

TELEPHONE EXPENSES WERE NOT PLEADED BY THE PETITIONER CANNOT BE ADDED – HOLDS HIGH COURT

Learned counsel for the petitioner urged that from the evidence on record it transpired that expenditure was also incurred on the telephone connection and telephone charges; on the meetings addressed by Sri Yaspal Kapur within the constituency during the period of election; on the election material *viz.* pamphlets, posters etc. and on the lighting arrangements made for some meetings addressed by the respondent No. 1. According to learned counsel, these expenses are also liable to be added to the election expenses of the respondent No. 1. None of these expenses were, however, pleaded in the petition. In fact, till the commencement of the arguments in the case the respondent No. 1 could not even anticipate that the petitioner shall rely on these expenses for the purpose of his case. It will, therefore, be prejudicial to the interest of the respondent No. 1 if the aforesaid expenses are taken into consideration. The submission made by learned counsel for the petitioner is accordingly negative.

EVEN IF ALLEGED EXPENSES ARE INCLUDED IN THE EXPENSES OF RESPONDENT NO. 1 – REMAIN WITHIN PRESCRIBED LIMIT – NO CORRUPT PRACTICE – HOLDS HIGH COURT

To sum up the only expenses that can possibly be added to the election expenses of the respondent No. 1 are:—

1. Cost of construction of Rostrums	Rs.	16,000
2. Cost incurred in installation of loudspeakers	Rs.	1,951
3. Cost in providing car transport to the Respondent No. 1	Rs.	232.50
		Rs. 18,183-50p

According to the return of election expenses of the respondent No. 1 (Exh. 5), an amount of Rs. 12,892/97 p was incurred over her election expenses. Adding the aforesaid amount of Rs. 18,183-50 to this figure of Rs. 12,892-97 the total comes to Rs. 31,976-47 p; *i.e.* sufficiently below the prescribed limit of Rs. 35,000

My conclusion, therefore, on issue No. 9 is that the total amount of expenditure incurred or authorised by the respondent No. 1 or her election agent, together with the amount proved to have been incurred by the party or by the State Government in connection with her election, does not exceed the prescribed limit, and, therefore, the respondent No. 1 has not committed any corrupt practice under section 123(6) of the Act.

Coming to the writ petition, since the petitioner has failed to prove that the expenses incurred by the respondent No. 1 or her election agent, together with the expenses found to have been incurred by the political party *viz.* Congress (R) or the State Government, in connection with her election exceed the prescribed limit, no ground is made out for inquiring into the vires of the Amending Act and the writ petition should accordingly fail.

ISSUE NO. 2 OF THE ADDITIONAL ISSUES—RESPONDENT NO. 1 HAD HELD HER OUT AS A CANDIDATE FROM RAEBARELI PRIOR TO 25.1.1971 – CONTENDS PETITIONER LETTERS WERE RECEIVED—IN LUCKNOW ON 25 JANUARY, 1971 THAT SHE WOULD FILE HER NOMINATION PAPERS FROM RAEBARELI ON 1 FEBRUARY, 1971

In Para 2 of the petition it is alleged that the respondent No. 1 held herself out as a prospective candidate from 22 Raebareli parliamentary constituency, with the election in prospect, immediately after the dissolution of the Lok Sabha on 27th December, 1970, and as such she was a candidate from the said constituency on and from 27th December, 1970. The plea of the respondent on that point is contained in Para 1 and Para 1(a) of the additional written statement. She denied therein that she held herself out as a candidate from Raebareli parliamentary constituency and was a candidate from that constituency from 27th December, 1970 onwards. It was further pleaded by her that she held herself out as a candidate on filing her nomination paper in Raebareli on 1st of February, 1971.

The question for consideration, therefore, is as to whether the respondent No. 1 held herself out as a candidate only on 1st of February, 1971, or she had held herself out as a candidate on any date earlier than that. If so, from what date?

The plea of the respondent No. 1 that she held herself out as a candidate from 22 Raebareli parliamentary constituency on 1st of February, 1971, on filing her nomination paper at Raebareli, has no legs to stand. There is over-whelming documentary evidence which points to the conclusion that the respondent No. 1 had positively held herself out as a candidate before that day.

Exh. 26 is the copy of a radiogram dated 25th of January, 1971 sent by the Private Secretary of the respondent No. 1 to the Chief Secretary, U.P. Government Lucknow, apprising him of the tour programme of respondent No. 1. According to this tour programme the respondent No. 1 had to file her nomination at Raebareli on 1st of February, 1971 at 12 o'clock noon. Exh. 27 is a letter dated 27th January, 1971 sent by the Assistant Secretary, U.P. Government to the various authorities, enclosing therewith a copy of this tour programme. According to that copy as well, the respondent No. 1 was to file her nomination paper at Raebareli at 12.15 o' clock noon. Exh. 188 is copy of a letter sent by the Superintendent of Police, Training and Security Branch, Intelligence Department, U.P., dated 25th January, 1971, enclosing therewith a copy of the D.O. letter of the same date sent by him to D.I.G. Police, Lucknow, asking for police force. In the copy of that D.O. letter it is stated that the Congress Office at Raebareli had indicated to him (Superintendent of Police, Raebareli) the tour programme of the respondent No. 1 as specified therein. According to that tour programme, the respondent No. 1 was to file her nomination paper at Collectorate, Raebareli between 12 and 12.15 o'clock noon. Raj Kumar Singh (P.W. 58) is Secretary Parliamentary Affairs of All India Congress Committee. According to him, the tour programme of the Prime Minister as leader of the party is prepared in the office of the All India Congress Committee. It is then sent to the Prime Minister's secretariat and it is only after the tour programme is approved by the respondent No. 1 that it is issued from there. The respondent No. 1 also, during her cross- examination, conceded that the tour programme concerning the political work is sent by the All India Congress Committee and that they are finalized after her approval is obtained. She further conceded that the tour programme (Exh. 26) must have been issued after she had approved of it.

Since a tour programme was received from the office of the respondent No. 1 by the State Government at Lucknow on 25th of January, 1971, and since a tour programme was also received in the Congress office at Raebareli on the same day, as is apparent from Exhibit 188, and further since it was explicity stated in those tour programme that the respondent No. 1 would file her nomination paper at Raebareli on 1st of February, 1971 at or about 12 o'clock noon, there appears no escape from the conclusion that the respondent No. 1 had held herself out as a candidate from Raebareli constituency at least some time before 25th of January, 1971.

SHE TOOK FINAL DECISION OF FILING NOMINATION FROM RAEBARELI ON 1.2.1971 – CONTENDS RESPONDENT NO. 1 CANNOT BE BELIEVED MERELY BECAUSE SHE HOLDS HIGH OFFICE WHEN STRONG EVIDENCE SAYS OTHERWISE – HOLDS HIGH COURT

A reference may also be made at this stage to the statement on oath made by Smt. Gandhi, respondent No. 1 (R.W.37). She deposed that final decision for contesting election to the Lok Sabha from the Raebareli parliamentary constituency was taken by her on 1st of February, 1971 and that she did not make any announcement or declaration before 1st of February, 1971 in that regard. Learned counsel for the respondent No. 1 stressed that the statement made by the respondent No. 1 could not be disbelieved. In fact he even suggested that while assessing the weight of the evidence of the respondent No. 1, the fact of the high office held by her should not be ignored. It should be conceded that when a person appears in Court as a witness and his evidence appears to be natural and probable, the status and respectability attaching to him is also taken into consideration to lend further assurance to his testimony. The status and respectability of the witness alone cannot, however, induce the Court to accept his/her testimony, more so when he or she is himself/herself a party to the proceedings and interested in the result of the case. In such cases the evidence of that person has to be assessed without in any manner being obsessed by the high office that he or she may hold. The evidence of the respondent No. 1 should therefore be assessed according to the established principles, like the evidence of any other witness without in any manner being influenced by her high office.

The respondent No. 1 stated in cross-examination that she took decision to contest election from Raebareli after her arrival there and after she had talked to the President of the P.C.C. and the workers of the area. Her attention was then invited to the tour programme (Exh. 26) dated 25th of January, 1971, which *inter alia,* mentioned that the respondent No. 1 was to file her nomination paper at Raebareli on 1st of February, 1971. She then said that the words "file nomination" appeared to have been added in ink and, consequently, she could not say whether those words existed originally or not. Her attention was then invited to the tour programme (Exh. 43) and she then conceded that she could recollect that the tour programme approved by her included the filing of nomination paper by her at Raebareli at 11.50 a.m. She, however, still asserted that no decision had been taken by her on or about 25th of January, 1971 to file the nomination paper for contesting election from Raebareli constituency. She said that it was tentatively mentioned in the tour programme, so that if she decided to contest election from Raebareli the nomination paper could be filed there on 1st of February, 1971 at 11.50 a.m. Now, this statement does not appear to me to be natural or probable. If no such decision had really been taken, there is no reason why it should have been explicitly mentioned in the tour programme that she would file her nomination paper at Raebareli on 1st of February, 1971. If she were eventually to take a decision on her arrival at Raebareli on 1st of February, 1971, she could file the nomination paper there without that fact being even tentatively mentioned in the tour programme, which was officially communicated to the State Government. It is also worthy of notice that this fact was also mentioned in the copy of the tour programme received in the Congress Office at Raebareli. It can safely be inferred from the letter (Exh. 188) that the tour programme was received in the Congress Office at Raebareli on or before 25th of January, 1971. If the respondent No. 1 had not decided till 25th January, 1971 to contest election from Raebareli, why it was so mentioned in the tour programme sent to the State Government and to the Congress Office at Raebareli that the respondent No. 1 shall file her nomination paper there on 1st of February, 1971.

RESPONDENT NO. 1 DID NOT HAVE ANY OTHER CONSTITUENCY IN HER MIND ON 1.2.1971 – SHE HAD MADE UP MIND FOR RAEBARELI PRIOR TO 25-1-1971 – HOLDS HIGH COURT

The respondent No. 1 said that she had several places in her mind and it was for this reason that she did not take a decision in the matter till 1st of February, 1971, on which date she went to the Raebareli and had a talk with the Congress workers there. It was, therefore, put to her whether in the tour programme relating to any other district or place, issued from her office, there was a mention of her filing the nomination paper from there, and she had to concede that no tour programme was issued from her office indicating that she would file her nomination paper from any place other than Raebareli. The nomination paper could be filed only between 1st of February and 3rd of February, 1971. If it were true that the respondent No. 1 had other places in her mind till 1st of February, 1971, from where she contemplated to contest election, the tour programmes covering those places would also normally have been issued, and it should have been tentatively mentioned in the tour programme as well, as was mentioned in the tour programme (Exh. 26), that she would file her nomination paper there. The fact that in the tour programme (Exh. 26), issued from the office of respondent No. 1, was to file her nomination paper at Raebareli, together with the fact that no tour programme was issued indicating that she would file her nomination paper from any place other than Raebareli, leaves no room for doubt that the respondent No. 1 had decided before 25th of January, 1971 to contest election from Raebareli. The fact that a copy of the tour programme indicating that fact was also received in the Congress Office at Raebareli on or about

25th January, 1971, further shows that the respondent No. 1 not only had formed a decision to contest election from Raebareli, but that she has also conveyed that decision to the constituency. In fact even the tour programme (Exh. 26) received by the State Government was not to be kept secret. It was conveyed to the relevant authorities and copies of that tour programme (Exh. 43) were, inter alia, forwarded to the President, District Congress Committee and Sri Gaya Prasad Shukla of the Kendriya Congress Karyalaya, Raebareli. The explanation given by the respondent No. 1 in regard to the mention in the tour programme (Exh. 26) about her filing nomination paper thus does not bear any scrutiny.

EVEN AS PER HER ADDITIONAL W.S. AICC ANNOUNCED HER CANDIDATURE FROM RAEBARELI ON 29.1.1971 – HIGH COURT

It may not be out of place to add that the statement made by the respondent No. 1 that she had decided to contest election from Raebareli only after her arrival there on 1st of February, 1971 and after her having talked to the President of the P.C.C. and local Congress workers is also inconsistent with her own pleadings. Para 1(a) of her additional written statement reads as follows:

> "That in fact there were offers, from other parliamentary constituencies in India, requesting this respondent to stand as a candidate for the Lok Sabha from those constituencies and <u>a final decision in regard to the constituency was announced by the All India Congress Committee only on January 29, 1971</u>, and she only held herself out as a candidate on filing her nomination at Raebareli on 1st of February, 1971 (underlining is by me)."

The contents of para 1(a) from beginning up to the words 'only on January 29, 1971' were verified by the respondent No. 1 to be true on information received from Sri K.N. Joshi, Parlimentary Secretary of the All India Congress Committee, New Delhi. Further a final decision about the candidature of respondent No. 1 to contest election from Raebareli parliamentary constituency could not have been taken by the All India Congress Committee without the respondent No. 1 herself arriving at a decision in that regard. The respondent No. 1 was, therefore, questioned on that point in cross-examination. She first said that the Congress Party did not take any decision about the constituency from which she was to contest the election. Her attention was then invited to Para 1(a) of the Additional Written Statement and she said:

> "There appears to be some mistake in the averment contained in this paragraph of the Additional Written Statement. As I know, the All India Congress Committee did not take any decision or make any announcement regarding my candidature on January 29, 1971. Sri K.N. Joshi, Parliamentary Secretary of the All India Congress Committee did not, within my knowledge, make any announcement regarding my candidature on 29th of January, 1971."

She was then asked whether she received any information from Sri K.N. Joshi, Parliamentary Secretary of the All India Congress Committee, New Delhi, to the effect that the final decision in regard to her constituency was announced by the All India Congress Committee on January 29, 1971. After going through the Additional Written Statement the respondent No. 1 replied that even though it was so stated therein, she did not recollect about it. She was then asked whether she could say with certainty that no announcement was made by the All India Congress Committee on January 29, 1971 about her constituency and she only replied that she did not know whether any such announcement was or was not made. Pressed further, she said that she had read the Additional Written Statement before signing it and that, to the best of her ability, she took care that whatever was contained in the Additional

Written Statement was true. She, however, added that the language contained in the Additional Written Statement was legal language which she found difficult to clearly understand. All that I would say is that the statement made by the respondent No. 1 fails to satisfactorily explain the inconsistency.

Learned counsel for the respondent No. 1, in a bid to explain the inconsistency, urged at the time of argument that the pleading contained in Para 1(a) of the Additional Written Statement only mean that the final decision taken by the All India Congress Committee was to leave the matter to the respondent No. 1 for a decision being taken by her. The argument is stated only to be rejected. If all that the All India Congress Committee had done was to have left the matter to be decided by the respondent No. 1, it could not be said that the All India Congress Committee had taken any decision, much less a final decision, about the constituency. The explanation offered by learned counsel for the respondent No. 1 can also, therefore, be not accepted.

Reference may also be made here to interrogatory No. 5 of the second set of interrogatories and the answer thereto given by Sri Jagpat Dubey, the Attorney of the respondent. Interrogatory No. 5 reads as follows:

> "Whether the All India Congress Committee decided your candidature without having your approval? (If the answer is in the negative, on what date did you give your approval for being a candidate from 22 Raebareli Parliamentary Constituency)".

The answer to this interrogatory is as follows:—

> "The decision of the All India Congress Committee was a tentative one. It was open to respondent No. 1 to stand from any constituency, whether it was 22 Raebareli Parliamentary Constituency or any other, and the All India Congress Committee would not have objected to any decision by her. The question, therefore, of respondent No. 1 giving any formal approval to any decision did not arise."

From the above it would appear that, till the stage of filing reply to the interrogatories, the respondent No. 1 did not deny that a decision had been taken by the All India Congress Committee about her candidature. All that she said was that the decision was tentative and could be changed by her. When the respondent No. 1, however, entered the witness box she took a different stand and said that so far as she knew no decision about her candidature was taken by the All India Congress Committee. When the attention of the respondent No. 1 was invited to the aforesaid reply given on her behalf, she again said that she had no knowledge if the All India Congress Committee took even a tentative decision about her constituency, Now, if she had no knowledge about any such decision, how and under what circumstances it was admitted in reply to the interrogatories served on her, remains unexplained.

In view of the pleadings contained in Para 1(a) of the Additional Written Statement and in view of the reply to interrogatory No. 5, I have no doubt that the All India Congress Committee did take a formal decision about the candidature of respondent No. 1, namely that she would contest election from Raebareli.

SHE TOOK THE DECISION ABOUT RAEBARELI ON 1.2.1971 – PLEADS RESPONDENT NO. 1 – IS UNBELIEVABLE – HIGH COURT

The respondent No. 1 was the unquestioned leader of the Congress (R). The A.I.C.C. could not, therefore, have taken a decision about the constituency of respondent No. 1 without the respondent No. 1 having given out her own mind. This circumstance, together with the fact that the tour programme issued from the office of the respondent No. 1 on 25th January, 1971, copies whereof had been sent not only to the Government but also to the Congress Office at Raebareli, intimating that the respondent No. 1 shall file her nomination paper at Raebareli on 1st of February, 1971, leaves no room for doubt that the respondent No. 1 held herself out as a candidate before 25th of January, 1971. The plea of the respondent No. 1 that she held herself out as a candidate for the first time on the 1st of February, 1971 is not established to be true.

YASHPAL KAPUR CANNOT BE BELIEVED THAT RESPONDENT NO. 1 CONSULTED KAMALAPATI TRIPATHI AND HIM ON 1.2.1971 AT RAEBARELI – THEN SHE MADE UP HER MIND FOR RAEBARELI – HOLD HIGH COURT

Reference was also made by learned counsel for respondent No. 1 in this connection to the statement on oath made by Sri Yashpal Kapur (R.W.32). I shall deal with the evidence of Sri Yashpal Kapur exhaustively when I record my finding on Issue No. 1 (first set) and on Additional Issue No. 1. It should be sufficient at this stage to consider only that part of the testimony of Sri Yashpal Kapur which relates to the point under consideration. Sri Yaspal Kapur stated that on the arrival of the respondent No. 1 at Raebareli Inspection House, the members of the District Congress Committee, Raebareli, had an interview with her in which they requested her to contest election to the Lok Sabha from Raebareli. He further said that after having heard the members of the District Congress Committee, the respondent No. 1 took Sri Kamlapati Tripathi aside and talked to him. He further said that the respondent No. 1 also talked to him, after having talked to Sri Kamlapati Tripathi, and it was thereafter that she announced that she had decided to contest election to the Lok Sabha from Raebareli. The statement appears to be too artificial to carry credence. In the first instance, in view of the fact that the tour programme had already been sent by the respondent No. 1 to the State Government as well as to the Congress Office at Raebareli, intimating that she would file her nomination paper at Raebareli on 1st of February, 1971, it is not understandable why the members of the District Congress Committee should have waited upon the respondent No. 1 in order to request her to contest election from Raebareli. Again, on the own admission of Sri Yashpal Kapur, Sri Kamlapati Tripathi and respondent No. 1 had travelled together in the same plane from Delhi to Amausi. It is not disputed by the respondent No. 1 that Raebareli was one of three places from where she intended to contest election. Sri Kamlapati Tripathi was the President of the U.P. Congress Committee. Therefore, if respondent No. 1 had to talk to Sri Kamlapati Tripathi about the propriety of her contesting election from Raebareli, or anything connected with it, she could conveniently talk to him in the plane during the journey between Delhi and Amausi. Further, it was also admitted by Sri Yashpal Kapur that the respondent No. 1 and Sri Kamlapati Tripathi travelled in the same car from Lucknow to Raebareli. Therefore, even if the respondent No. 1 had not talked to Sri Kamlapati Tripathi about any matter connected with her election when she travelled in the plane with him, she could have done so when she travelled with Sri Tripathi from Lucknow to Raebareli in the same car. In the face of these circumstances, it is not at all understandable why it should have become necessary for the respondent No. 1 to take Sri Kamlapati Tripathi aside and talk to him after she had talked to the members of the District Congress Committee at the Inspection House, Raebareli, before announcing her decision to contest the election from Raebareli. I have no doubt in my mind that Sri Yashpal Kapur states so to fortify the plea set up by the respondent No. 1 that she had decided to contest election from Raebareli only on 1st of February, 1971 and not earlier than that.

Sri Yashpal Kapur was also confronted with the tour programme (Exh. 26 and Exh. 43), wherein it was explicitly stated that the respondent No. 1 was to file her nomination paper at Raebareli on 1st of February, 1971. He, however, said that he still maintained that the respondent No. 1 had not taken any decision before 1st of February, 1971 to contest election from Raebareli. He was then questioned as to what was the basis of that statement made by him, and to that the witness replied:

> "My reply that the respondent No. 1 had taken a decision to contest election from Raebareli constituency on 1st of February, 1971 is based on what happened in the Inspection House that day within my view."

I have, however, already said that the statement made by Sri Yashpal Kapur about what happened at the Inspection House, Raebareli, on 1st February, 1971 is not at all probable.

IT WAS PUBLISHED IN THE NAVJEEWAN ON 15.1.1971 THAT RESPONDENT NO. 1 WILL CONTEST FROM RAEBARELI – YASHPAL KAPUR FAILS TO EXPLAIN IT PROPERLY – HOLDS HIGH COURT

Sri Yashpal Kapur was also confronted with the news item (Exh. 84 A) published in the issue of 'Navjeewan' dated 15th of January, 1971, wherein, quoting the decision of the Congress Parliamentary Board, it was said that the respondent No. 1 would contest election from Raebareli and that sitting members of Parliament U.P. shall contest election from the same constituency from which they had been elected to the dissolved Parliament. The witness replied that he was not aware whether any such decision had been taken by the Central Congress Parliamentary Board, nor could he vouch whether the news item had been rightly published. Sri Yashpal Kapur was examined as a witness in the case long after the election was over and it does not appear probable that, till the date of his examination, he did not even know whether the Congress Parliamentary Board had or had not taken any decision of the nature reported in the news item (Exh. 84-A). It is also worthy of notice in this connection that, on his own admission, the respondent No. 1 was at Delhi between 21st January, 1971 and 26th January, 1971. He was not a stranger to the respondent No. 1's secretariat and, on his own admission, the respondent No. 1 had such confidence in him that when he resigned in 1971, the respondent No. 1 insisted on his rejoining her secretariat. In the context of that association between him and the respondent No. 1, the natural course of conduct on his part was to have apprised the respondent No. 1, when he met her at Delhi during the period between 21st January and 26th January, 1971, of the alleged decision of the Congress Parliamentary Board published in the 'Navjeewan' dated 15th of January, 1971, and to have enquired from her whether it was true. Sri Yashpal Kapur conceded that during the period between 21st January and 26th January, 1971 he met respondent No. 1 twice but did not ask her anything about it. On the contrary, he stated that the respondent No. 1 told him that leaders of several other States had asked her to contest election from their States. The witness said that even then he did not enquire from the respondent No. 1 as to what had been decided by her. Now it is not at all probable that having come across the news item (Exh. 84A) at Raebareli and despite having met the respondent No. 1 at Delhi twice thereafter, he would neither have apprised the respondent No. 1 about the news item nor would have cared to know from her whether it was true or not.

For all the aforesaid reasons, no reliance can be placed on the statement of Sri Yashpal Kapur to conclude that the respondent No. 1 held herself out as a candidate from Raebareli constituency for the first time on 1st of February, 1971.

VERSION OF RESPONDENT No. 1 THAT SHE HELD HERSELF OUT AS A CANDIDATE FROM RAEBARELI ON 1 FEBRUARY, 1971 – REJECTED BY HIGH COURT

The result, therefore, is that the plea set up by the respondent No. 1 that she held herself out as a candidate for the first time on 1st of February, 1971 as a candidate from Raebareli Parliamentary Constituency has to be discarded. It is then to be considered as to when did the respondent No. 1 really hold herself out as a candidate.

The expression 'candidate' has been defined in section 79(b) of the Act as follows:—

> " 'candidate' means a person who has been or claims to have been duly nominated as a candidate at any election, and any such person shall be deemed to have been a candidate as from the time when, with the election in prospect, he began to hold himself out as a prospective candidate."

(underlining by me)

The question as to when a person becomes a candidate within the meaning of section 79(b) of the Representation of the People Act came in for consideration in the case **S. Khader Sheriff v. Munnuswami, AIR 1955 SC 775 (777),** and it was observed:—

> "When, therefore, a question arises under section 79(b) whether a person had become a candidate by a given point of time, what has to be seen is whether at that time he had clearly and unambiguously declared his intention to stand as a candidate, so that it could be said of him that he had held himself out as a prospective candidate. That he has merely formed an intention to stand for an election is not sufficient to make him a prospective candidate. That can only be if he communicates that intention to the outside world by declaration or conduct from which it could be inferred that he intends to stand as a candidate."

RESPONDENT No. 1 IN HER PRESS STATEMENT HELD ON 29th DECEMBER, 1970 CLEARLY AND UNAMBIGUOUSLY HELD HERSELF AS A PROSPECTIVE CANDIDATE FROM RAEBARELI – HOLDS HIGH COURT

The petitioner summoned from the All India Radio the tapes (Exh. 129 to 131) of the Press Conference addressed by the respondent No. 1 on 29th December, 1970. Sri P. Mathur (P.W. 60), Station Director, All India Radio, Lucknow, produced the tapes before this Court. He also filed the transcript (Exh. 132) of the Press Conference which he claimed to have prepared with the assistance of the tape recorded in his presence. The tape was, however, played in Court in the presence of counsel for the parties, when Sri P. Mathur was still in the witness – box, to check whether the relevant portion of the transcript (sidelined by me) tallied with the tape, and it was found to tally. Sri P. Mathur (P.W. 60) also stated in cross-examination that he indentified the voice on the tape to be that of the respondent No. 1. The sidelined portion of the transcript of the tape record (Exh. 132) was read over to the respondent No. 1 when she entered the witness-box and she too admitted it to be correct. The relevant question put to the respondent No. 1 and the answer given by her in the press conference, according to the transcript, (Exh. 132) are as follows:

> **"Q. A** short while ago there was a meeting of the opposition leaders and there they said that the Prime Minister is changing her constituency from Raebareli to Gurgaon?
>
> P.M.: No, I am not."

It is worthy of notice that in December 1970, a Government formed by the opposition parties, popularly known as S.V.D. Government, was in the saddle in U.P. It was in that context that question was put to the respondent No. 1 that the opposition leaders were saying that she would not contest election from Raebareli and that she would change her constituency to Gurgaon. The answer made by the respondent No. 1 to my mind, therefore, did not mean anything except that she was not going to change her constituency and that she would contest the election from Raebareli.

When the respondent No. 1 entered the witness-box and the aforesaid question and answer were put to her by her own counsel in the examination-in-chief with a view to bring on record her explanation to it, she stated that her reply did not 'necessarily' mean that she would not change her constituency and that she only meant that she would not contest from Gurgaon constituency. She was again questioned on that point in cross-examination and she then stated:

> "It is wrong to assume that while giving the reply marked B in the transcript (Exh. 132) I conveyed that I was not changing my constituency from Raebareli at all and emphatically held out that I would contest election again from Raebareli. In my opinion there is no basis for this assumption."

I have given my very careful and dispassionate consideration to the aforesaid reply given by respondent No. 1 during her cross-examination and I regret my inability to accept it. As I have already stated earlier, the question was put to the respondent No. 1 in a particular setting, namely that the opposition Government was in power in the State of U.P. and the leaders of that Government were saying that, presumably because of their being in power in U.P., the respondent No. 1 was changing her constituency from Raebareli. It was a sort of challenge and was conveyed to the respondent No. 1 in the Press Conference in the same form by a question put by some press correspondent. The emphatic manner in which the respondent No. 1 replied to that question, saying 'No, I am not' cannot under the circumstances be interpreted to mean anything except that she conveyed that whatever the opposition leaders were saying was not correct and that she was not changing her constituency. It also deserves consideration in this connection that at the Press Conferene mention was made only of two places *viz.* Raebareli (the original constituency) and Gurgaon (as prospective constituency). No other constituency was either named or suggested. In that context the answer given by the respondent No. 1 could mean and convey nothing except that she was not changing her constituency and that she would contest election from Raebareli. If there was a mention of some other constituency as well besides Gurgaon, there could be some substance in the explanation sought to be given by the respondent No. 1 in Court that, while saying "No, I am not", she only meant to convey that she would not change her constituency from Raebareli to Gurgaon and that she could yet change her constituency to some other place.

To my mind, therefore, by making the aforesaid statement at the Press Conference on 29th December, 1970 the respondent No. 1 clearly and unambiguously indicated to the outside world her declaration to contest election from Raebareli and she should therefore be deemed to have been a candidate from that very date.

ON THE DISSOLUTION OF LOK SABHA ON 27.12.1970 – THE ELECTIONS WERE IN PROSPECT WITHIN MEANING OF SECTION 79(B) OF THE ACT – HOLDS HIGH COURT

It may be appropriate at this stage to dispose of some technical pleas raised by learned counsel for the respondent No. 1, before proceeding further with this point. Learned counsel for respondent No. 1 urged that the election should be in prospect when any person holds himself/herself out as a prospective candidate, so as to fall within the definition of the word 'candidate' as contained in section 79(b) of the Act. Learned counsel then urged that the expression 'with the election in prospect' occurring in section 79(b) should be construed to mean the commencement of the election, *i.e.,* when a writ is issued in that connection. Reference was made by learned counsel for the respondent No. 1 to several cases in this connection: **The**

Counties of Elgin and Nairn Case (V.O.M & H-p.1); The Lichfield Case (V.O.M & H p. 27); The Borough of Great Yarmouth Case (V.O.M. & Hp.176); The Bodmin Division of the Country of Cornwall Case (IV OM & Hp. 123) and The Borrough of Walsall Case (IV OM & Hp. 123) and The Berwick-Upon – Tweed Division of the Country of Northumberland Case (VII OM & Hp.1).

In the first instance, it cannot be culled cut from these cases that, according to rule laid down therein, the expression 'election in prospect' should be interpreted to mean that the election commences with the issue of a writ . The consensus as expressed in these cases appears to be that election commences when it is reasonably imminent In the Countries of **Elgin and Nairm** case it was observed at page 10:—

> "For some reason, good or bad, the Legislature has confined the enactment to expenses which can be attributed to the 'conduct and management of the election'; and these words, as it seems to me, at least suggest and contemplate an election, which is not in nubibus, but is reasonably imminent."

And again on page:

> ". . . . . the period of election which was to be conducted and managed – was a period not at least much anterior, I will not say to the date of nomination, but to the group or series of events which immediately precede the nomination, and which, as we know, begin in the case of a general election with the announcement of the Dissolution, and in the case of a bye-election with the announcement of the vacancy."

In the Lichfield Division of the Country of **Stafford** case, Baron Pollock J. posed the following question:

> "The question no doubt turns on when the election may be said to have commenced."

After referring to **Elgin's** case, he said:

> "I will not refer to the facts of it because it would only complicate the matter, but I entirely agree with Lord M'Laren when he said that what is meant by 'an election' is a definite election within the knowledge and contemplation of parties."

In the Borough of **Great Yarmouth** case, Justice Channel said at page 188:—

> "I quite adopt the view which has been put forward by other Judges that the time when the election is supposed to commence may for several purposes, be an important matter, and that it certainly is not limited to the commencement of the active part of the election by the occurrence of a vacancy or by the issue of the writ."

In the Bodmin Division of the Country of **Cornwall** case Lawrence J. said at page 228:

> "In view of our findings upon other changes it becomes unnecessary to discuss this point at length, but I wish to say a few words, since, if it had been necessary to determine the point, which it is not I should have felt bound to come to the conclusion that this election began months before the issue of the writ, and that the expenses of all these meetings ought to have been returned."

In Borough of **Wal Sali** case it was said at page 125:

> "I cannot think that the period of candidature or the period of agency is to be limited, either by the date of the issuing of the writ, or by the day of nomination; but I think that when an election is contemplated as probable in the course of a few months and it is well recognized that to secure the election

of a particular candidate active steps must be taken and every exertion made at once to secure that object, it cannot be reasonably said that there can be no agency to take such steps, or to take such exertions, until the immediate approach of the election by the issuing of the writ."

In the **Berwick – UPON- Tweed** case it was said on page 30:

"Mr. Philipson was nominated candidate upon the 4th of November. It is unnecessary to decide the exact day upon which the election began, but having regard to the facts and to Mr. Philipson's own admission when he said, 'On October 19th, we knew there was going to be an election' it is sufficient to decide that the election certainly began not later than October 19th, the day after the Coalition Party meeting at the Carlton Club in London."

Apart from the fact that in none of the aforesaid cases it has been said that election shall be deemed to commence or be in prospect with the issue of the notification, there is also the fact that the law in this country is not precisely the same as in England. Election Tribunal Vellore, while deciding **Munnuswami Gounder v. Khader Sheriff, 4 Election LR 283 (292),** said:—

"In this respect the law in this country makes a significant departure and that departure, in our opinion, again emphasizes the application of a vital democratic principle, in the light of differing conditions. We may here note, briefly, a feature of the political practice in the United Kingdom, which repeatedly colours and influences the English Cases, *viz.*, the fact that there a person is often adopted as a candidate by a political association, without any move on his behalf, until a particular stage when the adoption is formalized by his consent."

Be it as it may, in the case before us, the election became in prospect immediately after the dissolution of the Lok Sabha on 27th December, 1970. I do not think this view is inconsistent either with the observations made in any of the English decision cited by learned counsel for the respondent No. 1 or any of the Indian decisions. In the case **Krishna Kant v. Banmali, AIR 1968 Ori 200** a declaration was made by the Home Minister, Government of India on 10th of December, 1965 postponing general election of Orissa Legislative Assembly till the general elections to be held early in 1967. On 20th December, 1965 the Election Commission communicated the aforesaid decision of the Government of India to the Chief Electoral Officer, Orissa. The life of the Orissa Assembly was thereafter extended till 1st of March, 1967. It was observed that the election was in prospect by 18th of June, 1967, that is long before the extended term of the Assembly came to an end.

The contention raised by learned counsel for the respondent that the election was not in prospect when the respondent No. 1 made the earlier mentioned statement in her press conference on 29th December, 1970 cannot therefore be accepted. As stated earlier, the statement made by the respondent No. 1 at her press conference on 29th December, 1970 by itself constitutes sufficient proof of the fact that she held herself out as a candidate from Raebareli constituency with effect from that date.

ALMOST ALL THE IMPORTANT NATIONAL NEWSPAPERS REPORTED ON 30 DECEMBER, 1970 THAT RESPONDENT No. 1 WOULD CONTEST ELECTIONS FROM RAEBARELI – NO CONTRADICTION FROM RESPONDENT No. 1 OR FROM THE CONGRESS PARTY – HOLDS HIGH COURT

It will, however, not be futile to refer to a few more circumstances which fortify this conclusion.

In order to find what did the respondent No. 1 convey by making the aforesaid statement, it will be of some relevance to know as to how that statement was commonly understood. Exh. A-17 is the issue of the 'National Herald ' dated 30th

December, 1970. The news item relating to the press conference addressed by the respondent No. 1 on 29th December, 1970 was published in this newspaper with the HEADLINE "Prime Minister not changing her constituency". Further on the news item contains the synopsis of the question put to the respondent No. 1 and the reply given by her. Exh. 81 is the issue of the 'Statesman' dated December 30,1970. The Headlined news item in this news paper is "No Change in Constituency". Further on the news item said:

> "The Prime Minister denied at the outset whether she intended to contest the coming election for the Lok Sabha from Gurgaon and not Raebareli."

Exh. 85 is the issue of the 'Indian Express' dated 30th December, 1970. The headline of the news item in this news paper was:

> "Raebareli is constituency."

Exh. 92 is the issue of the *'Hindustan Times'* dated December 13, 1970.(It appears that the Newspaper must be of 31 December, 1970). The headline of this newspaper also was:

> "No shifting of seat."

Thereafter the relevant portion of the news item reads as follows:—

> "The Prime Minister denied that she was thinking of shifting her constituency from Raebareli to Gurgaon.
>
> 'No I am not', she said when correspondent asked whether it was true as some opposition leaders were saying that she contemplated a change in her present constituency."

It will thus appear that almost every important newspaper in the country understood the statement made by the respondent No. 1 at her press conference to mean that she was not changing her constituency. It may also not be out of place to add that no contradiction to any aforesaid news items was issued either from the secretariat of the Prime Minister or from the A.I.C.C.

IMPORTANT LEADERS OF MANY POLITICAL PARTIES UNDERSTOOD FROM HER PRESS STATEMENT GIVEN ON 29th DECEMBER, 1970 THAT RESPONDENT NO. 1 WOULD BE CONTESTING ELECTIONS FROM RAEBARELI – OBSERVES HIGH COURT

There is then the evidence of S. Nijilingappa (P.W. 14), Sri Arjun Singh Bhadoria (P.W. 15), Sri S.P. Lalaviya (P.W. 36), Sri Karpoori Thakur (P.W. 37), Ram Saran Das (P.W. 38), Sri Banarsi Das (P.W. 40) and Sri L.K. Advani (P.W. 44). Though they belong to opposition parties, the fact remains that all of them are public workers of some reputation. Each one of them stated on oath that the statement made by the respondent No. 1 at the press conference on 29th December, 1970 was construed by them to mean that the respondent No. 1 was not changing her constituency.

IMMEDIATELY IMPORTANT LEADERS OF CONGRESS(R)/ MINISTERS OF CENTRAL GOVERNMENT STARTED VISITING RAEBARELI FROM 5 JANUARY, 1971 – A CLEAR INDICATOR THAT RESPONDENT NO. 1 WAS CONTESTING FROM RAEBARELI – OBSERVES HIGH COURT

Yet another thing which is worthy of notice is that right after the press conference, held by the respondent No. 1 on 29th December, 1970, important leaders of the Congress (R) started pouring into the constituency. Ram Kumar Singh (P.W. 42) stated that Raja Dinesh Singh, then a Minister in the Central Government, visited Raebareli on 5th of January, 1971. The fact that Raja Dinesh Singh did visit Raebareli on 5th January, 1971, as deposed by Ram Kumar Singh, was not denied on behalf of respondent No. 1, as would appear from the following question put to Ram Kumar Singh in cross-examination:

Q. I suggest to you that Raja Dinesh Singh was only investigating the possibility whether the respondent No. 1 should or should not fight election."

On 7th January, 1971 Sri Gulzari Lal Nanda and Sri Yashpal Kapur came to Raebareli, a fact which is admitted by the respondent No. 1. On 17th of January, 1971 Sri Chandra Shekhar, another important leader of Congress (R), visited Raebareli, as deposed by Ram Kumar Singh (P.W. 42). It is worthy of notice that it was not suggested to Ram Kumar Singh in his cross- examination that Chandra Shekhar did not visit Raebareli and that he was making a wrong statement in that connection. On the contrary, the suggestion made to him was that it was wrong that Sri Chandra Shekhar in his speech said anything about the candidature of respondent No. 1. Ram Kumar Singh denied that suggestion. It was then suggested to him that Chandra Shekhar had only stated that Congress (R) as a party should be successful in the election. It should, therefore, be accepted that Chandra Shekhar also visited Raebareli on 17th January, 1971. On 18th and 19th January, 1971 Professor Sher Singh, another Minister of the Government of India, visited Raebareli. It cannot be accepted that all these leaders of Congress (R) were visiting Rar Bareli for nothing. To my mind that circumstance, together with the other circumstances already mentioned earlier, is also a pointer to the conclusion that the respondent No. 1 had held herself out as a candidate from Raebareli constituency on 29th December, 1970 and the leaders of the Congress (R) were visiting Raebareli as part of the election campaign of the respondent No. 1.

STATEMENT MADE BY RESPONDENT No. 1 FROM COIMBATORE WAS REPORTED IN THE NEWSPAPERS DATED 11 JANUARY, 1971 THAT RAJ NARAIN HAS BEEN SPONSORED AGAINST HER FROM RAEBARELI FOR MUD-SLINGING – OBSERVES HIGH COURT

Learned counsel for the petitioner also urged that the fact that the petitioner was set up as a candidate to contest election against the respondent No. 1 in the early part of January 1971; and the fact that the respondent No. 1 while delivering a speech at Coimbatore criticized Raj Narain and said that the candidature of Raj Narain had been sponsored for mud slinging against her, also lends support to the fact that the respondent No. 1 had declared herself as a candidate on 29th of January, 1971. In regard to the first circumstance, learned counsel referred me inter alia to the evidence of Ram Saran Das (P.W. 38), Sri Karpoori Thakur (P.W. 37) and Banarsi Das (P.W. 40). Ram Saran Dass said that he issued a statement on 20th of January, 1970 that the petitioner shall contest election to the parliament from Raebareli. He filed the issue of the 'Pioneer' dated 11th January, 1971 (Exh. 78) and the issue of the '*National Herald*' of the same date (Exh. 80) in which that statement was published. Sri Banarsi Das (P.W. 40) said that the leaders of the opposition parties met at the residence of Sri C.B. Gupta at Lucknow in 1st or 2nd week of January, 1971, and a decision was then taken to set up the petitioner as a candidate against the respondent No. 1. Sri Karpoori Thakur (P.W. 37) deposed that in 1970-71 he was Chairman of All India Sanyukta Socialist Party. He further said that on 18th of January, 1970, in a meeting attended by several parties, he gave his concurrence to the decision that the petitioner may contest election from Raebareli against the respondent No. 1 In regard to the second circumstance, learned counsel referred me to the issue of the 'National Herald' dated 20th January, 1971 (Exh. 82). This newspaper was put to the respondent No. 1 during her cross-examination and she admitted that she could have said all the things mentioned in this news item. The news item (Exh.82) in the 'National Herald' dated January 20, 1971 was thus proved. Learned counsel stressed that unless the petitioner had held herself out as a candidate from Raebareli constituency there was hardly any occasion for her to have said at Coimbatore (as reported In Exh. 82) that the candidature of Raj Narain from Raebareli had been sponsored by the front parties for maximum mud-slinging against her. The least that can be said on the basis of the two circumstances is that the respondent No. 1 held herself out as a candidate sometime before 10th January, 1971, otherwise there was no occasion for Ram Saran Das having issued a statement that the petitioner shall contest election from Raebareli against the respondent, and for the respondent No. 1 having said at Coimbatore that Raj Narain had been chosen as a candidate from Raebareli for mud-slinging against her.

RESPONDENT NO. 1 HAD HELD HERSELF AS A PROSPECTIVE CANDIDATE FROM RAEBARELI AS PER HER PRESS STATEMENT ON 29 DECEMBER, 1970 – ISSUE NO. 2 DECIDED ACCORDINGLY – HIGH COURT

Therefore, without dilating any further, I conclude that it has been proved beyond doubt that the respondent No. 1 held herself out as a candidate from Raebareli Parliamentary constituency on 29th December, 1970. Issue No. 2 of the additional issues is answered accordingly.

ISSUE NO. 3 OF ADDITIONAL ISSUES

YASHPAL KAPUR DID SUBMIT HIS RESIGNATION ON 13 JANUARY, 1971 – HOLDS HIGH COURT

In Para 5 of the petition it is alleged that Sri Yaspal Kapur was a Gazetted Officer in the Government of India holding the post of an Officer on Special Duty; that the respondent No. 1 obtained/procured the assistance of Sri Yashpal Kapur for the furtherance of her election prospects; and that Sri Yashpal Kapur organised the election work of the respondent No. 1 in her constituency during the entire period commencing from 27th December, 1970 till the declaration of the result.

In Para 5 of the written statement the respondent No. 1 admitted that Sri Yashpal Kapur was a Gazetted Officer in the Government of India holding the post of Officer on Special Duty in the Prime Minister's Secretariat. She, however, pleaded that the said Sri Yashpal Kapur submitted his resignation from the aforesaid post by a letter dated 13th January, 1971, that the President was pleased to accept his resignation with effect from 14th January, 1971, and that Sri Yashpal Kapur ceased to be in the service of the Government of India from that date. Respondent No. 1 denied that she procured or obtained the assistance of Sri Yashpal Kapur for the furtherance of her election prospects while he was in the service of the Government of India.

In Para 2(a) of the Additional Written Statement the respondent No. 1 further pleaded that Sri P.N. Haksar, the then Secretary to the Prime Minister, who had the authority to relieve Sri Yashpal Kapur, informed him on 13th January, 1971 on receipt of the resignation, that the resignation was accepted and that formal orders will be issued in due course. According to the plea set up in the Additional Written Statement, the services of Sri Yashpal Kapur stood terminated as a result of his resignation with effect from time and date mentioned in the letter of resignation and that the subsequent notification issued in the name of the President of India was a mere formality.

In view of the aforesaid pleadings, the question formulated for consideration is whether Sri Yashpal Kapur continued to be in the service of the Government of India after 14th of January, 1971, and if so, till what date.

Sri Yashpal Kapur (R.W. 32) made a statement on oath that, after having a talk with the respondent No. 1, he submitted his letter of resignation to Sri P.N. Haksar on 13th of January, 1971. The respondent No. 1 (R.W. 37) also deposed that in the second week of January 1971 Sri Yashpal Kapur one day expressed a desire to resign from his post and she then asked him to consider over the matter again. She said that on 13th of January, 1971 Sri Yashpal Kapur again visited her and said that he had reconsidered the matter and was clear in his mind that he must resign from the post to which she agreed. She then asked Sri Yashpal Kapur to go to Sri P.N. Haksar in order to complete the formalities. Sri P.N. Haksar (R.W. 1) deposed that on 13th of January, 1971 Sri Yashpal Kapur telephoned to him near about 10 or 11 a.m. that he wanted to resign from his post and he then directed Sri Yashpal Kapur to send his letter of resignation in writing to him and also to meet him. Sri Haksar further said that within an hour Sri Yashpal Kapur came to his office with a letter of resignation duly signed by him and submitted the same. Learned counsel for the petitioner urged that no document has been produced by the respondent No. 1, in which the resignation letter submitted by Sri Yashpal Kapur may have been entered, to show that it was actually presented on 13th of January, 1971. On this basis learned counsel urged that it should not be accepted that the resignation letter was actually presented on 13th of January, 1971. According to him, the resignation was presumably prepared and submitted at some later stage and was antedated in order to make it appear that it was presented on 13th January, 1971. I do not think that, merely for the reason that no register etc. has been brought on record to indicate that the resignation letter was presented by Sri Yashpal Kapur on 13th January, 1971, the statement on oath made by the respondent No. 1 (R.W. 37), the statement of Sri Yashpal Kapur (R.W. 32) and the statement of Sri P.N.Haksar (R.W.1) can be discarded as untrue. Learned counsel for the petitioner could not point out any infirmity in the evidence of the aforesaid witnesses, so far as it relates to the presentation of the resignation letter on 13th of January, 1971. Therefore, relying on the evidence of the respondent No. 1 (R.W. 37), Sri Yashpal Kapur (R.W. 32) and Sri P.N. Haksar, I accept that Sri Yashpal Kapur had submitted his letter of resignation in the office of Sri P.N. Haksar on 13th of January, 1971.

The question, however, is when did the resignation submitted by Sri Yashpal Kapur take effect.

RESIGNATION OF YASHPAL KAPUR WAS ACCEPTED ON 25 JANUARY, 1971 – IT WOULD BE THE DATE OF HIS RESIGNATION – HOLDS HIGH COURT

The fact that Sri Yashpal Kapur was a Gazetted Officer in the Government of India holding the post of Officer on Special Duty in the written statement filed by respondent No. 1. is conceded in the written statement filed by respondent No. 1. Sri N.K. Seshan (P.W. 53), Private Secretary to the Prime Minister, also stated that the designation of Sri Yashpal Kapur, before he tendered his resignation, was 'Officer on Special Duty' and that it was a Gazetted post equivalent in rank to that of an Under Secretary drawing the maximum pay. It was admitted before me on both hands that the Central Civil Services (Temporary Service) Rules, 1949 were applicable to him. Rule 5 of the said Rules, insofar as it is relevant for our purposes, reads as follows:

> "5 (a). The service of a temporary government servant who is not in *quasi*-permanent service shall be liable to termination at any time by notice in writing given either by the government servant to the appointing authority, or by the appointing authority to the government servant.
>
> (b). The period of such notice shall be one month, unless otherwise agreed to by the Government and by the government servant:
>
> Provided that the service of any such government servant may be terminated forthwith by payment to him of a sum equivalent to the amount of his pay plus allowances for the period of the notice or as the case may be,

for the period by which such notice falls short of one month or any agreed longer period."

Sri S.K. Krishnan (R.W. 5), Director, Department of Personnel Administrative Reforms, filed O.M. dated 6th May, 1958 (Exh. A-25) containing instructions regarding resignations and acceptance thereof. It is *inter alia* stated therein that a resignation becomes effective when it is accepted and the officer is relieved of his duties.

It further states that 'where a resignation has not become effective and the officer wishes to withdraw it, it is open to the authority, which accepted the resignation, to accept or to refuse the request for such withdrawal.'

In view of the fact the Sri Yashpal Kapur held a Gazetted post in the Government of India; and further in view of the Central Civil Services (Temporary Sercive) Rules, 1949, and the instructions (Exh. A-25), it is apparent that Sri Yashpal Kapur could not cease to be a Government servant unless an order had been passed accepting the letter of resignation submitted by him. So far as the statement of the respondent No. 1 (R.W. 37) is concerned, she only deposed that after Sri Yashpal Kapur had expressed a desire to her that he wanted to resign from his post, she directed him to go to Sri P.N. Haksar to complete the formalities. No doubt, she also stated that Sri P.N. Haksar later told her that the resignation of Sri Yashpal Kapur had been accepted. That is, however, evidence in the nature of hearsay which should not be attached much importance. Sri Yashpal Kapur (R.W. 32) did not state that any order was passed in his presence accepting his letter of resignation. The evidence of Sri P.N. Haksar on this point is rather interesting. In the examination-in-chief he stated that when Sri Yashpal Kapur met him in his office on 13th of January, 1971 and submitted his resignation, he said to Sri Yashpal Kapur that he was a free man straight away that his resignation was accepted. He was then questioned in cross-examination whether it is permissible to appoint a government servant by word of mouth and to dispense with his services by word of mouth, and to that he replied:

> "I am not aware of any rule under which it is permissible to make appointments by word of mouth. In my opinion, the services of a temporary Government servant can also be terminated by word of mouth, to be later followed by an order in writing."

It was then put to him whether it was the practice prevalent in the offices of the Government of India and he replied:

> "I have held charge of large and important offices both inside the country and abroad and this is the practice I have followed and that practice has never been questioned so far."

The aforesaid statement made by Sri P.N. Haksar is not at all understandable to me. Appointment of persons in Government offices, more so to Gazetted posts, as well as termination of their services, is now governed by statutory rules, and the appointing authorities have to act under those rules in order to appoint a Government servant and in order to dispense with the services of a Government servant. It is the implied mandate of the rules that there should be an order in writing terminating his services. In the absence of any rules, appointing and removing of government servants by word of mouth cannot be imagined. Needless to say that Sri Haksar expressed his inability to mention any rule under which it was permissible to appoint people and to remove them by word of mouth. The statement appears to have been made only to fortify the plea set-up by the respondent No. 1 in the additional written statement regarding oral acceptance of the letter of resignation. It will not be out of place to mention in that connection that the respondent No. 1 filed her written statement on or about 2nd August, 1971 (the written statement was verified on 2nd August, 1971). The additional written statement was filed on or about 27th August, 1972 (it was verified on that day). The plea of oral acceptance of resignation was not set up in the original written statement. It was for the first time set-up in the additional written statement which was filed after a lapse of one year from the date on which the original statement was filed. The plea, therefore, appears to be an after thought.

Since Sri P.N. Haksar stated that verbal orders had to be followed by orders in writing, he was questioned whether any order in writing was passed on the letter of resignation submitted by Sri Yashpal Kapur on 13th January, 1971 and he said that he was not aware of it. He was then questioned whether he ever sent for the letter of resignation in order to see if any order in writing had been passed thereon or not, and to that he also replied that he did not remember. The point was pressed further in cross-examination as would appear from the following question and answer:

> **"Q:** You said that a verbal order is always followed by an order in writing. You were the appointing authority of the O.S.D. Did you at any stage, as Secretary and appointing authority of the O.S.D., make sure after 13th of January, 1971 that an order in writing had been passed in confirmation of the order that had been passed by you verbally?
>
> **"A:** I do not recollect at the moment whether the letter of resignation was at any stage recalled by me to make sure whether any order in writing had been passed."

Further on Sri P.N. Haksar said:

> "I must have passed some order in writing on the letter of resignation of Sri Yashpal Kapur, <u>but I do not today remember as a matter of fact whether I did or did not pass the order</u>." (underlining by me.) The aforesaid statement made by Sri P.N. Haksar speaks for itself and hardly calls for any comment. Needless to say that it cannot be held for any moment on the basis of the statement made by Sri P.N. Haksar that any order in writing was passed on the letter of resignation of Sri Yashpal Kapur till the date on which an order accepting the resignation was sent for being notified in the Gazette. In other words, the only order on record which can be said to have been passed on the letter of resignation of Sri Yashpal Kapur is that which is contained in the notification (Exh. A-8) dated 25th of January, 1971. The letter of resignation of Sri Yashpal Kapur was in the custody of the respondent No. 1, and Sri P.N. Haksar was the best person to know if any order accepting the resignation had been passed prior to 25th of January, 1971. Since no evidence, oral or documentary, has been brought on record in order to show that any order in writing had been passed on the letter of resignation of Sri Yashpal Kapur prior to 25th of January, 1971, it should be held that an order was passed on the letter of resignation only on 25th of January, 1971 accepting the same.

RETROSPECTIVE EFFECT GIVEN TO THE ACCEPTANCE OF RESIGNATION IS OF NO CONSEQUENCE – HOLDS HIGH COURT

It is true that, according to the Gazette notification (Exh. A-8), the resignation of Sri Yashpal Kapur had been accepted with effect from 14h January, 1971. It cannot, however, be ignored that the order accepting the resignation was passed on 25th of January, 1971. Till that order was passed the status of Sri Yashpal Kapur continued to remain that of a Government servant despite the fact that when that order was passed it was given retrospective effect so as to be valid from 14th of January, 1971.

The question as to when does a resignation take effect has come in for consideration in quite a few cases. In case **Ram Murthi v. Sumba Sardar, 2 Election**

LR 331, one of the respondents was a teacher in a school and therefore held an office of profit. He tendered an unqualified resignation of his office on 19th of October, 1951. He was intimated that the could not be relieved until a substitute was available. He then applied for one month's leave on medical certificate on 6th November, 1951 and ceased to work. On 10th November, 1951 he filed his nomination paper. His resignation was accepted on 14th January, 1952. It was held that the respondent did not cease to hold his office by tendering his resignation or by ceasing to work and was unqualified to stand for election on 10th of November, 1951. The following observation contained in that case at page 336 appears to be material;

> "The point material for consideration now is if the submission of resignation by the respondent even without its acceptance by the authorities tantamounts to cessation of service. Article 310 of the Indian Constitution is that except as expressly provided by the Constitution, every person who is a member of a civil service of a State or holds any civil post under a State holds office during the pleasure of the Governor. If a person is to hold office during the pleasure of the Governor or the Union as the case may be, it is impossible to think that the person holding the office shall hold it at his pleasure. The respondent No. 1 as the holder of a post under the State was therefore not free to cease the service at his pleasure so long as he held the post under the State."

In case **Bahori Lal Paliwal v. District Magistrate, Bulandshahr, AIR 1956 All 511 (FB)** the same question arose for consideration *qua* the Chairman, Town Area Committee and it was observed:

> "In certain cases a resignation may be effective as soon as it is delivered to the proper authority. In other cases it may not be effective till it is accepted by that authority. In voluntarily organisations like Clubs a person is free to be a member and, unless the contrary is laid down in the rules of the association, he is free to resign at any time he likes."

Thereafter reference was to *Halsbury's Laws of England,* Simond's Edition, Vol. V 61 and the Court proceeded to say:—

> "But in corporation created by Statute for the discharge of public functions a member may not have an absolute right to resign at will, because the law may cast a duty upon the person elected to a public office to act in that office in the public interest."

The Court cited with approval the following observation from the decision of the Supreme Court of the United States in **Edwards M. Edwards v. United States, (1880) 26 LE 314 (C):**

> "In England a person elected to the Municipal office was obliged to accept it and perform its duties and subject himself to a penalty by refusal. An office was regarded as a burden which the appointee was bound, in the interest of the community and good Government, to bear. And from this it followed of course that, after an office was conferred and assumed, it could not be laid down without the consent of the appointing power.

This was required in order that the public interests might suffer no inconvenience for the want of public servants to execute the laws....To complete a resignation it is necessary that the corporation manifest their acceptance of the offer to resign, which may be done by an entry in the public books, or electing another person to fill the place, treating it as vacant."

It was held in the case that since the Chairman had withdrawn the resignation before its acceptance by the District Magistrate, there was no right left in the District Magistrate, to accept the resignation even though it was unconditional.

In the case **Rai Kumar v. Union of India, AIR 1969 SC 180** it was observed:

> "Termination of an employment by order passed by the Government does not become effective until the order is intimated to the employee. But where a public servant has invited by his letter of resignation determination of his employment, his services normally stand terminated from the date on which the letter of resignation is accepted by the appropriate authority and, in the absence of any law or rule governing the conditions of his service to the contrary, it will not be open to the public servant to withdraw his resignation after it is accepted by the appropriate authority. Till the resignation is accepted by the appropriate authority in consonance with the rules governing the acceptance, the public servant concerned has *locus paenitentiae* but not thereafter."

The view expressed by the Supreme Court in the aforesaid case **Raj Kumar v. Union of India,** was reiterated when the present case went up before the Supreme Court **Raj Narain v. Smt Indira Nehru Gandhi, AIR 1972 SC 1302.**

On the basis of the declaration of law in the aforesaid decisions it can be said that Sri Yashpal Kapur continued to remain in the service of the Government of India till 25th of January, 1971, on which date the order accepting his resignation was passed. According to the dicta laid down in those cases, till 25th of January, 1971 Sri Yashpal Kapur could even ask for the withdrawal of his resignation. The fact that by the order dated 25th of January, 1971, the order accepting resignation was given effect from 14th of January, 1971 cannot lead to the conclusion that Sri Yashpal Kapur ceased to be a Government servant with effect from 14th of January, 1971.

Learned counsel for the respondent No. 1 then referred me to the part of the statement made by the respondent No. 1 (R.W. 37) wherein she stated that on 13th January, 1971 Sri Yashpal Kapur visited her and said that he had reconsidered the matter and was clear in his mind that he must resign, whereupon the respondent No. 1 said to Sri Yashpal Kapur that he should go to Sri P.N. Haksar to complete the formalities. Learned counsel urged that this virtually amounts to tendering of resignation by Sri Yashpal Kapur orally to respondent No. 1. Learned counsel referred me to the meaning of the expressions 'Mode of resignation' and 'Mode of acceptance' from *Corpus Juris Secondum* in order to contend that a resignation can be tendered orally and can be accepted orally. I do not think the argument carries any force. While defining 'Mode of resignation' it is also mentioned in the *Corpus Juris Secondum*:

> "Where no particular mode of resigning an office is provided by constitutional or statutory requirements, no formal method is necessary; it may be by parole or it may be implied. <u>A mode of resignation prescribed by statute generally is exclusive.</u>" (Underlining is by me)

Similarly while defining the expression 'Mode of acceptance' it is also mentioned in the *Corpus Juris Secondum*:

> <u>"Where no particular mode of accepting a resignation is provided by constitution or statue, no formal mode of acceptance is necessary</u>, and it may be by parole, or it may be shown by performance of an official act which could not be legally performed unless the resignation was accepted ."
>
> (Underlining is by me)

SERVICES OF YASHPAL KAPUR WERE GOVERNED BY STATUTORY RULES – HOLDS HIGH COURT

I have already pointed out earlier that in the matter of resignation and termination of service, the parties *viz.* the Government of India and Sri Yashpal Kapur were governed by the Central Civil Services (Temporary Service) Rules, 1949 which were statutory rules. It cannot, therefore, be accepted on the basis of the meaning assigned to the aforesaid expressions in Corpus Juris Secondum that the resignation could be tendered by Sri Yashpal Kapur orally or could be accepted orally.

Learned counsel then urged that in any case a resignation, in order to be effective, does not call for a formal order of acceptance and that it becomes effective as soon as it is tendered. In support of this contention, learned counsel referred me to Articles 56, 67, 90(b), 101 (3)(b), 124(2) C1. (a) of the proviso, 156, 190(3), 217(1)(a) and 316 C1. (a) of the proviso. I have looked into all these Articles. Option has been given to the persons mentioned in these Articles, to resign from their seat or office by writing under their hand addressed to the relevant authority. Thus, by letter of law, the matter of resignation in regards to the persons specified in the aforesaid Articles of the Constitution has been made an unilateral act. These Articles could have no application to Sri Yashpal Kapur, who was governed by separate set of rules, already mentioned above.

Learned counsel for the respondent No. 1 then referred me to a few English cases in support of his contention that resignation, in order to be effective, begs no formal order for its acceptance. The cases are:-

(a) In the Matter of The Gloucester, Aberystwith and South wales Railways Company and of the Joint Stock Companies Winding – up Acts Maitlands' Case **(English Reports 43 Chancery 708);**

(b) **Latchford Premier Cinema, Limited v. Ennion (Chancery Division, Vol. 2 1931):**

(c) **Merris v. Baron and Company (1918 AC 1);**

(d) **Attorney-General for New South Wales v. Perpetual Trustee Co. Ltd., (1965 1 All Election LR 846)**; and

(e) **Glossop v. Glossop, 1907 Vol. 2, Chancery Division.**

Learned counsel also referred to the Queen's Bench decision in the case:

Inland Revenue Commissioners v. Hambrook, 1956 (1) All Election LR 807)

as also to the decision of the Court of Appeal in the same case reported in **1956 (3) All England Law Reports 338.**

All these cases are clearly distinguishable. *Maitlands'* case relates to the resignation by the director of a company. It does not relate to the resignation by a public servant. It does not appear from the report of the case that the Articles of Association of the Company prescribed any mode for tendering a resignation or accepting it. In the case **Latchford Premier Cinema Ltd. v. Ennion,** again the matter did not relate to the resignation of a public servant but resignation by director of a company. The resignation having been tendered and accepted at the annual general meeting, it was said that it was a case of mutual agreement. **Morris v. Baron And Company,** case relates to a contract of sale of goods and not to any resignation whatsoever. In the case **Glossop v. Glossop,** again the matter in issue was the resignation of a director of a limited liability company on the basis of the Articles of Association of the Company it was held that the resignation became effective as soon as it was tendered. The remaining three cases only deal with the relations between the Crown and its servants.

It cannot, therefore, be accepted on the basis of anything said in the aforesaid cases that the resignation tendered by Sri Yashpal Kapur, who was governed by statutory rules, became effective immediately after it was tendered.

Learned counsel for the respondent No. 1 then referred me to 'Rodgers on Election,' 20th Edition, Vol. 2, page 21, mentioned the cases of **Abrobrothock** and

Lanarkshire, in order to support his argument. The first case is of the year 1748 and the other of the year 1774 and they relate to Scotland. It will thus appear that these cases are two centuries old. We do not know what were the rules governing the matter of resignation in Scotland during that time. That apart, both these cases have been considered and distinguished in the case **Sudarsana Rao v. Christian Pillai, AIR 1924 Mad 306;** and again in the case **Ram Murti v. Sumha Sadar, 2 Election LR 331 (337).** No reliance can consequently be placed on the aforesaid two cases mentioned in the Book 'Rodgers on Election'.

Coming to the Indian decisions, learned counsel for the respondent No. 1 first referred me to the case **P.R.N. Abdul Haq v. Catpadi Industries Limited, AIR 1960 Mad 482.** This case again relates to the director of a company. It does not appear that there was anything in the Articles of Association of the Company relevant on the subject. Therefore, relying on the English cases, it was held that a director, who has resigned, will be deemed to have resigned from the date of his resignation. This case can have no application to the case before me.

Learned counsel next referred me to the case **A.H. Rangrez v. M.N. Koul, 40 Election LR 130.** In this case an orderly-peon of Public Health Engineering Department tendered resignation on 3rd August, 1966. It kept moving between a couple of offices and was accepted on 27th of February, 1967 with effect from 3rd August, 1966. The orderly – peon had filed his nomination paper some time before 23rd January, 1967. The scrutiny of the nomination papers took place on 23rd January, 1967. The question arose whether the petitioner, namely the orderly – peon held any office of profit on the date of scrutiny of the nomination papers and was disqualified to be chosen. It was held that since the resignation had been accepted with effect from a date prior to the date of scrutiny it could not be held that the petitioner held any office of profit on that date. There are two things worthy of notice about this case. In the first instance, we do not know what were the rules governing the service conditions of orderly-peon in Jammu & Kashmir (to which place this case relates). Further, there is no discussion in the case on the point as to what was the status of the petitioner between the date on which the resignation was tendered and the date on which the order accepting the resignation was passed. In the present case **Raj Narain v. Smt. Indira Nehru Gandhi** also similar situation had arisen earlier when the case went up before the Supreme Court and the Supreme Court observed **(Raj Narain v. Smt. Indira Nehru Gandhi, AIR 1972 SC 1302 (1308):—**

> "Yashpal Kapur appears to have tendered his resignation to the office he was holding on January 13, 1971. The certified copy of the notification produced shows that the President accepted his resignation on the 25th of January, 1971 and the same was Gazetted on February 6, 1971. The order of the President shows that he accepted Yashpal Kapur's resignation with effect from January 14, 1971. The learned Trial Judge without examining the true effect of the President's order has abruptly come to the conclusion that Yashpal Kapur's resignation became effective as from January 14, 1971. This conclusion, in our opinion, requires re-examination."

As already stated, there is no detailed examination of that point in the case, **A.H. Rangrez** v. **M.N. Kaul.** It is, therefore, difficult for me to hold on the basis of the aforesaid decision that the resignation of Yashpal Kapur took effect on 14th of January, 1971, merely because the order dated 25th of January, 1971, by which the resignation was accepted , has been made effective from that date.

Learned counsel then referred me to the case **V.P. Gindroniya v. State of Madhya Pradesh, AIR 1970 SC 1494).** In this case the appellant gave a notice to the Government on June 6, 1964 terminating his service. The Government, however, issued him a show-cause notice for departmental inquiry. A question arose whether the appellant continued to remain in service after June 6, 1964. The rules governing the service of the appellant in that case were akin to the Central Civil Services (Temporary Service) Rules. Rule 12 of those rules corresponded to rule 5 of the Central Civil Services (Temporary Service) Rules. After taking those rules into consideration, the Court observed:

> "There is hardly any room for dispute that the notice contemplated by the main clause (a) of rule 12 can be given either by the Government or its temporary servant. The rule in question specifically says so. It is not necessary for us in the present case to decide whether the two provisions to that rule or clause (b) thereof apply to a notice given by a Government servant. The appellant has assumed that those provisions also apply to a notice given under that rule. We shall for the purpose of this case proceed on the basis of that assumption and see whether the appellant has satisfied that part of the rule also."

Thereafter, accepting that the appellant had satisfied that part of the rule, the Court held that the appellant was not in service after he had tendered his resignation on June 6, 1964.

From the above it will appear that the case **V.P. Gindroniya v. State of Madhya Pradesh** (supra) is distinguishable from the case **Raj Kumar v. Union of India** (supra), in as much as in the former case the Court proceeded on the assumption that under the rules the Government servant had a right to terminate his services forthwith by submitting his resignation and by tendering one month's pay in lieu of the period of notice. On the language contained in rule 5 of the Central Civil Services (Temporary Service) Rules, 1949, it does not appear that a Government servant also has the right to terminate his services forthwith by a notice in writing, also tendering therewith one month's pay and the allowances. That apart, it is not the respondent No. 1's plea in this case that, while tendering his resignation, Sri Yashpal Kapur also tendered or offered to tender one month's pay or emoluments. This case is also therefore of no help to the respondent.

Reference has also been made by learned counsel for respondent No. 1 to an unreported decision of the High Court of Punjab & Haryana, dated April 29, 1975 in Civil Writ No. 2083 of 1975: **Smt. Satwant Kaur v. State of Punjab,** I have carefully gone through this decision and I find that instead of supporting the contention raised by learned counsel for the respondent, it contradicts it. In this case the petitioner was a teacher in the Education Department of the State of Punjab and was on deputation in the Union territory of Chandigarh with effect from November 1, 1966. On 22nd April, 1975 the petitioner submitted her resignation along with one month's salary as she wanted to contest election to the legislative assembly of the State. The last date for filing nomination paper was April 30, 1975. Since the acceptance of the petitioner's resignation was being delayed she filed a writ petition asking for a writ of *mandanus* directing the respondents to accept the resignation and further to declare that the petitioner was no longer in the service of the State of Punjab or the Union territory with effect from the date of her resignation. It was observed:

> "Right to enter into a contract implies a right to get out of it. The petitioner while accepting service in the State of Punjab had obviously entered into a contract of service. Such a contract can be terminated by making an offer to the appointing authority which is to be accepted by it within a reasonable time. What is a reasonable time for the acceptance of an offer of this type depends upon the circumstances of each case. In a situation like this when a public servant tenders resignation in order to contest an election, the resignation tendered by him should be accepted as early as possible and under all circumstances prior to the date on which the nomination papers can be filed for the last time."

With the above observation the Court directed the respondents 'to accept the resignation of the petitioner from the post of teacher held by her by today".

From the above it will appear that the Court considered the acceptance of the resignation to be essential for the termination of the service of the petitioner. Otherwise the Court could very well declare that, since the resignation had been tendered on 22nd April, 1975 alongwith one month's salary, it became effective that very day and the petitioner ceased to be in the employment of the Government from that day. Needless to say that a declaration to that effect had actually been asked for by the petitioner in the writ petition and yet it was not granted. Instead the Court directed the respondents to accept the resignation. Therefore, as already stated, this argument more supports the stand taken by the petitioner than the contention raised on behalf of the respondents.

MERELY BECAUSE YASHPAL KAPUR CEASED TO WORK FROM 14.1.1971 – DOES NOT MEAN ACCEPTANCE OF HIS RESIGNATION – IN LAW YASHPAL KAPUR REMAINED IN SERVICE TILL 25 JANUARY, 1971 – HOLDS HIGH COURT

Learned counsel for the respondent lastly urged that, according to the evidence on record, Sri Yashpal Kapur had ceased to work with effect from the afternoon of 13th of January, 1971 and had also submitted a charge report on the same date, though it was dated as 14th January, 1971. On this basis learned counsel urged that Sri Yashpal Kapur was relieved of his work and consequently it be held that his resignation became effective from 14th of January, 1971.

Now so far as the cessation of the work is concerned, I do not think that by itself it can bring about termination of employment, for, such cessation of work and absence from duty can always be regularized later by applying for leave with or without pay. As for the charge report, It may be mentioned that neither the charge report nor any copy thereof has been got exhibited in the case. The respondent no doubt examined Sri K.P. Sood (R.W.8), section Officer of the Office of the Accountant General (Central Revenues), New Delhi, to prove that Sri Yashpal Kapur was paid his salary only for the period ending on 13th of January, 1971. Sri Sood, however, conceded in cross-examination that the salary for the period ending on 13th January, 1971 was passed for payment as late as 28th August, 1972. The evidence of Sri K.P. Sood cannot, therefore , be proof of the fact that a charge report had actually been submitted by Sri Yashpal Kapur on 13th of January, 1971. But assuming that a charge report had been submitted by Sri Yashpal Kapur when he submitted his resignation on 13th January, 1971, I do not think mere submission of a charge report along with the letter of resignation, by the appointing authority, can bring about the termination of the service, regardless of the fact whether the resignation is accepted or not. This argument also therefore fails to convince me.

No other argument having been raised, my finding on Issue No. 3 of the additional issues is that Sri Yashpal Kapur continued to be in the service of the Government of India till 25th of January, 1971.

ISSUE No. 1 (first set)

And

ISSUE No. 1 (of the additional issues)

Both these issues are repetition of each other word for word and are therefore being taken up at one place. The question for consideration under this issue is:—

> Whether respondent No. 1 obtained and procured the assistance of Sri Yashpal Kapur in furtherance of the prospects of her election while he was still a Gazetted Officer in the service of the Government of India.

Learned counsel for both the parties argued the matter by splitting the entire period from 29th of December, 1970 onwards into three sub-periods, *viz*—

(1) the period ending on 13th January, 1971;

(2) the period from 14th to 25th January, 1971;
And

(3) the period from 26th January to 6th February, 1971.

I would consider the evidence and the arguments advanced on either side in the same arrangement.

1. Period ending on 7.1.1971.

The petitioner's case is that the respondent No. 1 had held herself out as a candidate from Raebareli parliamentary constituency on 29th of December, 1970, when she held the press conference at Delhi, and that Sri Yashpal Kapur (R.W.32) started doing election work for her with effect from the same date. It is further the petitioner's case that on 7th of January, 1971 Sri Yashpal Kapur accompanied Sri Gulzari Lal Nanda to Raebareli where they first held a meeting with public representatives at Raebareli and then delivered speeches in the Shaheed Mela held in Munshiganj, seeking support for the candidature of respondent. No. 1

The respondent No. 1 denied that she held herself out as a candidate on any date prior to 1st of February, 1971. According to her, it was for the first time on 1st of February, 1971 at Raebareli that she held herself out as a candidate from that constituency. It has also been denied by the respondent No. 1 that Sri Yashpal Kapur did any electioneering work for her till that date.

Now, while recording my finding on Addl. Issue No. 2 I have already discarded the respondent No. 1's plea that she held herself out as a candidate for the first time on 1st of February, 1971. I have further recorded a positive finding that the respondent No. 1 held herself out as a candidate with effect from 29th December, 1970. The whole matter has to be considered in that background.

It shall first be necessary to notice a few circumstances which have a material bearing on the point under consideration.

On the own admission of Sri Yashpal Kapur (R.W. 32) he had been working in the Prime Minister's secretariat since 1951. He further conceded that during the years 1956 and 1964 he was working at the Prime Minister's secretariat at his residence and, since the respondent No. 1 was hostess, she occasionally called for his assistance for certain function which she had to perform, with the result that the respondent No. 1 had come to know about his work fairly well. He also stated that when the respondent No. 1 was appointed as Minister for Information & Broadcasting, he was transferred to the Ministry of Information & Broadcasting at the instance of the respondent No. 1, and that when the respondent No. 1 became Prime Minister he was again transferred back to the Prime Minister's secretariat and was appointed as Private Secretary to her. In 1967, when the respondent No. 1 was to contest election from Raebareli Parliamentary constituency, he resigned his post in the respondent's secretariat and worked for respondent No. 1 in Raebareli constituency. After the 1967 elections were over he rejoined the respondent's secretariat, and according to him, he did so on the insistence of the respondent No. 1 herself. The relevant portion of the statement of Sri Yashpal Kapur in this connection reads as follows:

> "I left public life in 1967 and joined the Prime Minister's secretariat because the respondent No. 1 asked me to help her in the discharge of her duties. It was thus on her request that I rejoined the Prime Minister's secretariat as Officer on Special Duty. I did not make any formal application while joining

the Prime Minister's secretariat in April 1967. If the respondent No. 1 had not requested me I would not have joined the Government service in April 1967. I agreed to join because I found that the Prime Minister was keen on that point."

It will thus appear that, in view of the fact that Sri Yashpal Kapur had been working either with the father of the respondent No. 1 or with the respondent No. 1 herself since quite a long time, Sri Yashpal Kapur had obtained complete confidence of the respondent No. 1, so much so that he even resigned from his post in order to do electioneering work for the respondent, when the latter contested election for the Lok Sabha in 1967. After Sri Yashpal Kapur had done that job for the respondent No. 1, he was reappointed in the Prime Minister's secretariat. If the statement made by Sri Yashpal Kapur is correct, the respondent No. 1 almost considered his services indispensable and insisted on him to join her secretariat to assist her in the discharge of her official duties.

YASHPAL KAPUR HAD CONVASSED THE GATHERING ON 7-1-1971 AT SHAHEED MELA MUNSHIGANJ FOR SUPPORTING RESPONDENT NO. 1 –HOLDS HIGH COURT

In the above background, once it has been accepted that the respondent No. 1 had held herself out as a candidate from Raebareli constituency from 29th December, 1970, the fact that Sri Yashpal Kapur visited Raebareli on 7th of January, 1971 could well be associated with the election work of the respondent No. 1. In this connection it is also worthy of notice that on 5th of January, 1971 Raja Dinesh Singh, who was then a Minister in the Government of India, had visited Raebareli and, according to the suggestion made to Ram Kumar Singh (P.W. 42), he held a meeting in the Central Election Office at Raebareli and told the workers that the respondent No. 1 was to contest election from Raebareli. According to Ram Kumar Singh, Raja Dinesh Singh even asked him to help the respondent No. 1. The suggestion made to Ram Kumar Singh itself shows that the visit of Raja Dinesh Singh was connected with the election of the respondent No. 1. It would so appear from the following question put to Ram Kumar Singh in cross-examination:

> "I suggest to you that Raja Dinesh Singh was only investigating the possibility whether respondent No. 1 should or should not fight election."

Having thus stated the surrounding circumstances of the case, I now proceed to consider the evidence adduced by the parties in support of their respective contentions.

The petitioner examined Nankau (P.W. 28), R.K. Dixit *alias* Phakkar (P.W. 31) and Sri Vidya Shankar Yadav (P.W. 43) in order to prove that in the speech delivered by Sri Yashpal Kapur on 7th January, 1971 in the Shaheed Mela at Munshiganj he canvassed support for the respondent No. 1. The petitioner also relied on an issue of the newspaper 'Beer Vaishwara' (Exh. 67) for this purpose.

Nankau (P.W. 28) is Pradhan of the Gaon Sabha Jhakrasi. He said that his village was about half a mile away only from Munshiganj, that he attended the Shaheed Mela at Munshiganj and further that Sri Gulzari Lal Nanda, the then Railway Minister, Government of India, said in the meeting that the respondent No. 1 wanted to contest election from Raebareli constituency and that the people should give her their vote in order to enable her to win the election. Nankau further said that Sri Yashpal Kapur said the same thing at the meeting.

The fact that Sarvsri Gulzari Lal Nanda and Yashpal Kapur attended the Shaheed Mela at Munshiganj on 7th of January, 1971 has not been controverted on behalf of the respondent No. 1. The contention raised on behalf of the respondent, however, is two-fold:

(1) that the evidence adduced by Nankau, and for that matter by other witnesses, with regard to the alleged speeches delivered in the Shaheed Mela at Munshiganj on 7th January, 1971 is not admissible because no such meeting was pleaded by the petitioner; and

(2) that in any case even though Sri Yashpal Kapur, accompanied by Sri Gulzari Lal Nanda, attended the Shaheed Mela at Munshiganj on the aforesaid date and also delivered speeches there, they did not say anything pertaining to the candidature of respondent No. 1 in the election but only paid tributes to the martyrs.

Now, so far as the first contention is concerned, it is explicitly alleged in para 5 of the petition that the election work done by Sri Yashpal Kapur, *inter alia,* included 'making speeches in support of the candidature of respondent No. 1 Smt. Indira Nehru Gandhi on 7th of January, 1971 as well as on other dates canvassing for votes'. It is true that it is not mentioned in the petition that Sri Yashpal Kapur made any speech in the Shaheed Mela at Munshiganj. Since, however, it was clearly alleged that a speech was delivered by Sri Yashpal Kapur canvassing support for respondent No. 1 on 7th January, 1971, the mere fact that the place of the meeting was not alleged cannot be said to be a material omission. It is also worthy of notice that no objection in writing was filed on behalf of the respondent No. 1 urging that the aforesaid part of the pleadings contained in para 5 of the petition were vague and that better particulars should be furnished. An oral objection was raised at the time the statement of Nankau was being recorded, namely that it was not alleged in the petition that any meeting was held at Munshiganj on 7th of January, 1971. I have, however, already stated that the fact of a meeting having been held on 7th January, 1971 and speech having been delivered by Sri Yashpal Kapur in that meeting does find place in the petition. If the respondent felt that it was necessary to know the place of the meeting, an objection could be filed on her behalf in that regard at the proper stage and the petitioner could then be called upon to furnish the particulars. The respondent No. 1 had every opportunity to cross-examine Nankau and the other witnesses who deposed about the meeting held at Munshiganj on 7th of January, 1971. It was also open to the respondent No. 1 to adduce any amount of evidence in rebuttal. In fact the respondent No. 1 has adduced that evidence. Once the parties have joined issue on that point and have led evidence, the objection raised by learned counsel for the respondent No. 1 cannot be countenanced, more particularly because learned counsel for the respondent No. 1 has failed to show that any prejudice has been caused to the respondent No. 1 for the reason of the place of the meeting not having been disclosed in the petition.

P.W. NANKAU IS A RELIABLE WITNESS – HOLDS HIGH COURT

Coming to the merits of the evidence of P.W. Nankau, learned counsel for the respondent urged that Nankau could not tell the dates on which he had visited his relations; that he could not tell the date on which his marriage took place; that he could not tell the date of birth of his first child not could he tell the date of birth of his youngest child. It was urged that if Nankau could not remember any of the aforesaid dates, it did not appear probable that he could remember about the date of the alleged meeting held at Munshiganj. The argument fails to convince me. It is admitted on both hands that during the non-cooperation movement shooting had taken place at Munshiganj resulting in loss of life of some people, who were fighting for the freedom of the country. It is again admitted on both hands that in the memory of these persons who lost their lives in that incident a 'Shaheed Mela' is held on 7th of January every year at Munshiganj. The Shaheed Mela has thus a special significance for those residing near about Munshiganj, and since the mela takes place every year on the same date, there was absolutely no improbability in Nankau having remembered the date even though he could not recollect the dates of other events in his life.

Learned counsel next contended that, on the own admission of Nankau P.W., Uma Shanker Yadav contested election from Raebareli constituency as a B.K.D. candidate in the election that took place in 1974 and that he was a worker for Uma Shanker Yadav. On this basis it was stressed that Nankau belongs to a hostile party and it should therefore be inferred that he came forward to give evidence about the alleged speech delivered by Sri Yashpal Kapur on account of his political association with the hostile party. I am afraid, the mere fact that in the year 1974 Nankau worked for a B.K.D. candidate cannot constitute a sufficient ground for discarding his testimony. So many persons, who do not have any association with a political party, sometimes come forward to serve a candidate sponsored by that party, not because of their association with the party but on the ground of their association with the candidate himself in one way or the other. That by itself does not make them unreliable witnesses. In the case of **Ambika Saran Singh v. Mahant Mahadeo Nand Giri, 41 Election LR 183 (193)** the Supreme Court said:—

> "We do not in the present case have to decide whether a person acting as a polling agent or a counting agent or a person wishing the success of a particular candidate is necessarily an interested witness. Assuming that he is, his evidence cannot be rejected only for that reason. At the most the Court in such a case should scrutinize his testimony closely and demand corroboration before acting upon it."

It could not be shown in the instant case that the evidence of Nankau is otherwise inconsistent or infirm. I have already stated earlier that looking to the setting in which Sri Yashpal Kapur came to Raebareli on 7th of January, 1971, it is not improbable that, while delivering speech in the Shaheed Mela at Munshiganj, he exploited the occasion also to canvass support for the respondent No. 1 in the election. The statement made by Nankau thus is therefore amply supported by the surrounding circumstances.

Some stress was also laid by learned counsel for the respondent No. 1 on the admission made by Nankau in cross-examination that it was for the first time in Court that he made a statement about the meeting held on 7th of January, 1971 and that he never told about that meeting to any person prior to it. It was argued that if Nankau did not make a statement about his visit to the Shaheed Mela at Munshiganj to any person, it is not understandable as to how he could be cited as a witness in the case, and this impairs the value of his testimony. I am once again unable to agree. In the first instance, while saying that he did not make a statement about the meeting prior to his being examined in the case, he presumably meant a formal statement, But, even if he did not mention about it to any person even in mutual conversation prior to his being examined in Court, he was after all not the only person to have attended the meeting. There should have been quite a big gathering and any person who would have seen Nankau in the meeting could furnish information to the petitioner to enable him to examine Nankau as a witness in the case.

Learned counsel then said that according to the statement made by Nankau in cross-examination two other persons, namely Sarju Prasad and Ram Pal of village Jhakrasi attended the meeting and that all three of them had gone to the meeting and that all three of them had gone to the meeting together. Sarju Prasad and Ram Pal were examined as R.W. 12 and R.W. 13 respectively. It was stressed by learned counsel for the respondent that, according to the submissions on oath made by Sarju Prasad and Ram Pal R.Ws., they never went to Saheed Mela at Munshiganj and this establishes that the statement made by Nankau is wholly false. In view of this contention raised on behalf of the respondent, it will be appropriate to consider the evidence of Sarju Prasad (R.W. 12) and Ram Pal (R.W.13) at this very stage.

Sarju Prasad (R.W.12) and Ram Pal (R.W. 13) are residents of village Jhakrasi and both of them said that they did not go to attend the Saheed Mela in January, 1971. I do not, however, feel impressed with their evidence. Sarju Prasad was a teacher in a Primary Pathshala during the year 1971. He conceded in cross-examination that Gaya Prasad Shukla was the Adhyksha of the Zila Parishad and that his Pathshala was run by the Zila Parishad. It may be recalled that Gaya Prasad Shukla was doing important work in the election. The copies of the tour programmes of the respondent No. 1 used to be issued to him. It was he who issued a general appeal in support of the candidature of the respondent No. 1 (Exh. 24), and it was he who, according to Sri Yashpal Kapur, was maintaining the accounts pertaining to the election of the respondent No. 1. It is quite likely that once Nankau had conceded in cross-examination that Sarju Prasad had accompanied him to the Shaheed Mela, pressure was brought to bear on Sarju Prasad (R.W. 12) by Gaya Prasad Shukla in order to make him appear as a witness in the case and give evidence to contradict the testimony of Nankau. It is true that in his re-examination Sarju Prasad admitted that on the date on which he was examined as a witness in the case the school was being run by the Government under the control of the District Basic Education Officer. However, the association that Gaya Prasad Shukla had with the Pathshala in his capacity as Adhyaksha, and consequently with Sarju Prasad, who was a teacher in that Pathshala, could not have been wiped off overnight merely because the school was taken over by the Government to be run under its own officers. Material was also elicited in the cross-examination of Sarju Prasad to show that he did not exhibit a straightforward conduct while in the witness box. I have already said earlier that the Shaheed Mela at Munshiganj carried some importance in the locality. Sarju Prasad himself admitted that on 7th January, 1971 the Pathshala was closed because of the Shaheed Mela. It is then not improbable that Sarju Prasad R.W. would also have gone to the Saheed Mela, which was only one and half miles away from his village, particularly when a leader of all India importance, namely Sri Gulzari Lal Nanda had came to pay tributes to the martyrs. Sarju Prasad, however, stated that he had not even seen that site in Munshiganj on which the Shaheed Mela takes place, and that he has never been to the Shaheed Mela. Now, this is a statement which cannot be accepted for any moment.

Sarju Prasad (R.W. 12) is, therefore, not a reliable witness in my opinion and the evidence of Nankau cannot be discarded on the basis of his evidence.

Ram Pal (R.W. 13) also stated in cross-examination that he had not been to the Shaheed Mela since he had attained discretion. I have already said that Shaheed Mela carried some importance in the locality and, consequently, it cannot be accepted that he would not have gone to the Shaheed Mela during his life time. That alone shows that he was not making a true statement while in the witness - box. He admitted in cross-examination that Sri R.C. Shukla Advocate belongs to his village. This R.C. Shukla was at one stage doing pairvi on behalf of the respondent in this case and a complaint was lodged in the court on behalf of the petitioner that one of his witnesses was taken away by him to prevent the witness from giving evidence in the case. Notice for contempt was therefore issued against him, which has since been discharged. The fact that Sri R.C. Shukla was working for the respondent No. 1 during the election, was elicited in the cross- examination of Sri Yashpal Kapur (R.W. 32). Sri Mohan Lal Tripathi (P.W. 59), General Secretary, District Congress Committee (R), Raebareli, stated that Sri Ramesh Chand Shukla was one of the general secretaries of the District Congress Committee (R) in 1970-1971. Now, since Ramesh Chand Shukla Advocate is a resident of the same village where Ram Pal resided, and since he was an important worker for the respondent No. 1 during the election and was also her pairokar at some stage, the possibility of Ram Pal having been pressurized by Sri Ramesh Chand Shukla cannot be excluded. Together with it there is also the fact that Sri Gaya Prasad Shukla, another important worker of the respondent No. 1, happened to be the Adhyaksha of the Zila Parishad during the period the witness was examined in the case. It is a matter of common knowledge that the Adhyaksha of the Zila Parishad always wields influence in the rural areas. It will not be out of place to add that when it was put to Ram Pal in cross-examination as to which party did Sri Ramesh Chand Shukla belong, he pleaded ignorance about it. It cannot be accepted for any moment that even though Sri Shukla resided in the village in which this witness resided, and even though Sri Shukla was such a prominent worker of the Congress Party, Ram Pal would not have known about it.

All the above reasons make it abundantly clear that Ram Pal (R.W. 13) is also not a truthful witness. The evidence of Nankau cannot, therefore, be discarded on the basis of anything stated by him.

No other criticism having been made against the evidence of Nankau (P.W. 8), I find that he is quite reliable witness and there is no risk in acting on his testimony.

R.K. DIXIT JOINT EDITOR OF BEER BAISHWARA WEEKLY STATED YASH PAL KAPUR HAD CONVASSED THE GATHERING ON 7.1.1971 AT SHAHEED MELA FOR RESPONDENT NO. 1 – IS A RELIABLE WITNESS – ALSO PUBLISHED IN THE WEEKLY – HOLDS HIGH COURT

R.K. Dixit *alias* Phakkar (P.W. 31), during January to March, 1971, was Joint Editor of 'Beer Baishwara', a weekly paper printed and published from Raebareli. He deposed that he also served that paper as a reporter, that he had himself attended the meeting that took place at Shaheed Smarak, Munshiganj, on 7th January, 1971, and that Sri Gulzari Lal Nanda and Sri Yashpal Kapur, besides others, delivered speeches in that meeting. Referring to the speech said to have been made by Sri Yashpal Kapur, the witness deposed:—

> "Sri Yashpal Kapur in his speech said that respondent No. 1 shall contest election to the Parliament from Raebareli constituency and, like the previous occasion, we should again make her successful."

The witness then referred to the news item relating to that meeting published in Beer Baishare dated 9th January, 1971 (p. 1 columns 1 & 2) and said that this report was sent by him. The report has been marked (Exh. 67).

It was not even suggested to Sri R.K. Dixit alias P.W. that he had any affiliation with any political party, or with any candidate hostile to the respondent No. 1. It could also not be shown that he had any other reason in order to make a false statement affecting Sri Yashpal Kapur and the respondent No. 1. Learned counsel for the respondent No. 1, however, pointed out that in the news item (Exh. 67) it is not explicitly stated as to what had been said by Sri Yashpal Kapur in the speech delivered by him in the Shaheed Mela. Learned counsel urged that on that ground that statement of Sri R.K. Dixit in Court should not be accepted. It is a matter of common knowledge that it is only the purport of the speeches, that is sometimes published in the papers. In the first part of exhibit 67 it is stated:—

> Pradhan Mantri ke chunao prachar abhiyan ka Shri Ganesh dinank 5 January ko kendriya Udyog Mantri dwara Congress Karyalaya men karya kartaon ko sambodhan se shuru hua jiska vidhivat udghatan 7 January ko Munshiganj Shaheed Ashthal par kendriya rail Mantri Shri Gulzari Lal Nanda dwara aek bhaari Jansabha ke sambodhan se hua."

In the other part of the issue of 'Beer Baiswara' dated 9th January, 1971 (Exh. 67) it is first stated that the Railway Minister Shri Gulzari Lal Nanda and Shri Yashpal Kapur, Private Secretary of the respondent No. 1 reached Raebareli station on 7.1.1971 at 11.0 a.m. It is further stated that in the Shaheed Mela held at Munshiganj, Sri Gulzari Lal Nanda delivered a speech and said that the respondent No. 1 stood for removing poverty, starvation and unemployment from the country and that her hands should be strengthened by making her successful in the election. In the next paragraph it is said that the leaders of the District Congress Committee, including Dal Bahadur Singh, Devi Charan Pandey, Ram Shankar Tripathi, Amresh Advocate, Ramesh Chand Shukla Advocate and Dr. P.N. Mehrotra, also delivered speeches, throwing light on the policies of the respondent No. 1 and doing mud-slinging on the opposition parties. In the paragraph following it, there is mention of the fact that Sri Yashpal Kapur, Sri Madan Mohan Misra, Sri Shiv Shankar Singh and Sri Parmanand also delivered speeches in that meetings. Since Sri Gulzari Lal Nanda was the leading speaker, his speech was reported at length. Thereafter the names of other speakers were disclosed. Since the substance of their speeches was also the same as that of Sri Gulzari Lal Nanda, It was presumably considered futile to repeat it over again. Reading the news item as a whole, it is clear that all those persons who delivered speeches at the Shaheed Mela solicited support for the respondent No. 1 as a candidate seeking election from Raebareli constituency. At one place in the news item, while referring to the substance of the speech delivered by Sri Gulzari Lal Nanda, it is mentioned:

> "Vashtava men chunao prachar sabha thi."

The contention raised by learned counsel for the respondent that, while sending report about the speeches delivered at the Shaheed Mela (Munshiganj) on 7.1.1971, Sri R.K. Dixit *alias* Phakkar did not report the substance of the speech of Sri Yashpal Kapur and, consequently, the statement made by him in Court about the contents of the speech delivered by Sri Yashpal Kapur at the said Shaheed Mela should not be held to be true, is not justified and cannot be accepted.

In my opinion, therefore, Sri R.K. Dixit *alias* Phakkar (P.W. 31) is quite an independent and reliable witness and there is no risk in acting on his testimony.

VIDYA SHANKAR YADAV ADVOCATE ALSO STATES ABOUT YASHPAL KAPUR CONVASSING FOR RESPONDENT NO. 1 ON 7.1.1971 SHAHEED MELA MUNSHIGANJ – AT A SMALL DISTANCE FROM RAEBARELI – A RELIABLE WITNESS – HOLDS HIGH COURT

Vidya Shankar Yadav (P.W. 43) is a practicing Advocate. He deposed that he had also gone to the Shaheed Mela in order to attend the meeting that took place there. He further on stated that Sarvasri Gulzari Lal Nanda and Yashpal Kapur also delivered speeches in that meeting besides other persons and that Sri Yashpal Kapur, after paying tributes to the martyrs, said in his speech:

> 'Respondent No. 1 had successfully contested election earlier from Raebareli constituency and that she would contest election from the same constituency and we should make her successful.'

In cross-examination he said that in 1921 firing had taken place at Munshiganj in which a number of persons had lost their lives and that a meeting is held every year there in order to pay tributes to the martyrs. According to him, members of all political parties had attended that meeting and it was for that reason that he had gone to attend it.

It was elicited in the cross-examination of Sarju Prasad (R.W. 12) that a distance of two miles intervened between Munshiganj and Raebareli. Looking to the very small distance that intervenes between Raebareli and Munshianj, and further looking to the fact that a meeting was to take place at Munshiganj for paying tributes to the martyrs and a leader of all India importance *viz.* Sri Gulzari Lal Nanda had come for the purpose, there is absolutely no improbability in Sri Vidya Shankar Yadav Advocate having gone to Munshiganj to attend the meeting.

Learned counsel for the respondent No. 1 pointed out that, on his own admission, Sri Vidya Shankar Yadav was polling agent for the petitioner and also looked after his election work, It was also pointed out that, according to the admissions elicited in cross-examination, he belonged to Bhartiya Kranti Dal and, during the year 1974, he was a proposer of Uma Shankar Yadav who contested election as a candidate of the Sanyukt Socialist Party. Learned counsel stressed that partly for the reason that this witness had worked for the petitioner in the election and partly for the reason that he belongs to the opposition party, it would be fraught with risk to rely on his testimony. True, Vidya Shankar Yadav frankly admitted that he had worked for the respondent in the election and that he was also a member of opposition party, namely Bhartiya Kranti Dal. The fact, however, remains that he is a practicing Advocate and further that his evidence is supported by the evidence of two other witnesses, whom I have already held to be reliable witnesses.

Learned counsel for the respondent No. 1 also urged that Sri Vidya Shankar Yadav was an educated person, being an Advocate, and further he also belonged to an opposition political party. It was stressed that if it were a fact that any electioneering was done at the meeting held at Shaheed Mela (Munshiganj), complaints about it would have been sent by Sri Vidya Shankar Yadav to some authorities. Learned counsel pointed out that, on the own admission of Sri Vidya Shankar Yadav, he did not send any complaint about it anywhere and, consequently, the statement made by Sri Vidya Shankar Yadav that any electioneering was done by any person in the meeting at Munshiganj should be discarded as untrue. I am once again unable to agree. Sri Vidya Shankar Yadav, on being questioned on that point, clearly stated that he had raised a protest at the meeting about its being converted into an election meeting. He, however, said that since there were 3 or 4 persons only who raised the protest, they were not heeded. Further on, he said that he did not send any complaint about it because the meeting was organised by the people residing at Raebareli and most of them belonged to Congress (R). There is thus some explanation as to why no complaint was sent by Sri Vidya Shankar Yadav. Together with it, there is also the fact that no notification in regard to the election had till then been issued by the Election Commission of India. This could have dissuaded Sri Vidya Shankar Yadav from sending any complaint to the Election Commission, and there could be hardly any logic in sending complaints about it to any other authority. As for Sri Vidya Shankar Yadav P.W. not having issued any statement to the press, it could be due to the fact that the matter had already otherwise obtained publicity in Raebareli.

Since Sri Vidya Shankar Yadav is a respectable witness and since his evidence is corroborated by the evidence of two independent persons, I see no risk in relying on his testimony as well.

R.D. TRIVEDI EDITOR OF BEER BAISWARA ALSO STATES SAME THING – ALSO PROVES NEWS-ITEM – RELIABLE EVIDENCE – HOLDS HIGH COURT

Lastly, there is the issue of 'Beer Baiswara' dated 9th January, 1971. The paper was filed in Court by Sri Ram Dev Trivedi (P.W. 23), Editor thereof. He stated that the news item (Exh. 67) in that paper was based on the information received from Sri R.K. Dixit, who was then the City Reporter for the paper. Sri R.K. Dixit (P.W. 31), as also mentioned earlier, having entered the witness-box, has proved that news item. He has also given direct evidence about the speech delivered by Sri Yashpal Kapur at that meeting. The news item (Exh. 67) published in Beer Baiswara dated 9th January, 1967 therefore stands proved. A reading of that news item as a whole shows that in the election speech delivered by Sri Yashpal Kapur, canvassing was done for respondent No. 1. It cannot be accepted that this news item was published on 9th January, 1971 by way of any peshbandi. No foundation could be laid by learned counsel for the respondent No. 1 in order to contend that this issue of 'Beer Baiswara' was got printed some time after the election for the purpose of this petition. I accordingly hold that the news item (Exh. 67) contained in the issue of 'Beer Baiswara' dated 9th January, 1971 can also be utilized to corroborate the evidence of Nankau (P.W. 28), R.K. Dixit alias Phakkar (P.W. 31) and Vidya Shankar Yadav (P.W. 33). I must, however, make it clear that even if this issue of Beer Baiswara were not there, I would not have felt any hesitation in relying on the evidence of the aforesaid witnesses.

The aforementioned evidence adduced by the petitioner thus does show that Sri Yashpal Kapur delivered a speech in the Shaheed Mela at Munishiganj on 7th January, 1971 and in that speech he did canvassing for the candidature of the respondent No. 1.

NOT PROVED CONCLUSIVELY IF YASHPAL KAPUR HAD PURCHASED VOTERS' LIST ON 11.1.1971 FOR RESPONDENT NO. 1 – HOLDS HIGH COURT

The second item of evidence relied upon by the petitioner for the period ending on 13.1.1971 is the entry at serial No. 1. of the return of election expenses (Exh.5) filled by the respondent. According to this entry, a sum of Rs. 657/90 was paid on 11.1.1971 to the District Election Officer, Raebareli, on account of payment of cost of voters' list. Learned counsel pointed out that the first column in the return is meant to carry the date of expenditure and sixth column thereof is meant to carry the name of the person to whom payment is made. Learned counsel urged that since the entry in the first column shows that the amount was paid on 11.1.1971, and since the entry in the sixth column indicates that it was paid to the District Election Officer, it should be held that on 11.1.1971 Sri Yashpal Kapur purchased voters' list for the respondent and thus rendered assistance to her.

According to Sri Yashpal Kapur, after he had started serving as election agent, he wanted to obtain a list of voters and, since he came to know that the District Congress Committee had already obtained the voters' list, he obtained the same from the D.C.C. and paid the sum of Rs. 657.92 to them.

I am not fully convinced with the statement of Sri Yashpal Kapur, for, if it were the whole truth, the expenditure should have been entered in the return (Exh. 5) in the date in which the money was actually paid by Sri Kapur, and in column six of the return there should have been the name of the District Congress Committee instead of the name of the District Election Officer.

All the same, since there is no positive evidence of the fact that Sri Yashpal Kapur was present at Raebareli on 11th of January, 1971, it will not be very safe to conclude on the basis of the aforesaid entry that Sri Yashpal Kapur himself purchased the voters' list for respondent No. 1 on 11.1.1971. Sri Gaya Prasad Shukla was a prominent worker for the respondent No. 1. According to Sri Yashpal Kapur, he was in charge of maintaining accounts. It is quite likely that, under some instructions, he purchased the voters' list for the respondent No. 1 and hence the entry.

I would, therefore, place no reliance on Entry 1 of the return of election expenses (Exh.5) while considering the services rendered by Sri Yashpal Kapur to the respondent No. 1 during the period ending on 13.01.1971.

The respondent No. 1 examined four witnesses in rebuttal. Out of them, I have considered the evidence of Sarju Prasad (R.W. 12) and Ram Pal (R.W. 13) while assessing the evidence of Nankau (P.W. 28) and have found both of them to be unworthy of reliance. The third witness examined by the respondent is Thakur Ambika Singh (R.W. 24). He deposed that he too attended the Shaheed Mela that took place in Munshi Gunj on 7th January, 1971, and that , while Sarvasri Gulzari Lal Nanda, Yashpal Kapur and some local leaders paid tributes to the martyrs in that Shaheed Mela, it was not said by any of them that the respondent No. 1 shall contest election to the Lok Sabha from Raebareli constituency. It was, however, elicited in his cross-examination that he was a member of the Congress Party since 14 or 15 years and that in the election that took place in 1971 he had worked for the respondent No. 1 as a member of that party. It was also elicited in his cross-examination that about six years ago he was prosecuted on a charge of dacoity. The trial court held him guilty, but he was acquitted in appeal. He is thus in the first instance an interested witness and, further, his antecedents were also not wholly above-board. Material was also elicited in his cross-examination to show that he tried to suppress facts. He said that it was wrong that Gaya Prasad Shukla was in-charge of the election office in 1971. It has, however, already been mentioned earlier that copies of the tour programmes were forwarded, among others, to Sri Gaya Prasad Shukla, and that his address is mentioned therein as 'Kendriya Congress Karyalaya, Raebareli' (Exh. 43). Again on 1st of February, 1971 he had issued a general appeal in the constituency in support of the candidature of the respondent No. 1, copy whereof is Exhibit 24 on record. Sri Yashpal Kapur conceded in cross-examination that Sri Gaya Prasad Shukla was in charge of maintaining election accounts on behalf of the respondent No. 1. The statement made by Thakur Ambika Singh about Sri Gaya Prasad Shukla is thus not the whole truth.

For all the aforesaid reasons, implicit reliance cannot be placed on testimony of Thakur Ambika Singh.

YASHPAL KAPUR ADMITS TO BE PRESENT ON 7.1.1971 AT SHAHEED MELA MUNSHIGANJ BUT DENIES CONVASSING FOR RESPONDENT NO. 1 – SECOND PART UNRELIABLE – HOLDS HIGH COURT

Lastly, there is the evidence of Sri Yashpal Kapur (R.W. 32). He admitted having attended the meeting in Shaheed Mela at Munshiganj on 7.1.1971 and also having delivered a speech there. He, however, said that he only paid tributes to the martyrs in the brief speech given by him, and that he did not say anything about the candidature of the respondent No. 1 or about the election in that meeting. It will be appropriate here to make an overall estimate of the evidence of Sri Yashpal Kapur in order to find out as to what extent reliance, if any, can be placed on his testimony.

While recording my finding on issue No. 1 of the additional issues, I have already held that the statement made by Sri Yashpal Kapur to the effect that the respondent No. 1 had held herself out as candidate for the first time on 1st of February, 1971 after having a talk with Sri Kamlapati Tripathi and the members of the District Congress Committee, Raebareli, was untrue and had been made with a view to fortify the plea that had been set up by the respondent No. 1.

YASHPAL KAPUR WAS LOYAL TO THE CORE FOR RESPONDENT NO. 1 AS HIS CONDUCT CLEARLY PROVED – WAS TELLING LIES TO SUPPORT HER – AND TO CONCEAL HIS ROLE – HOLDS HIGH COURT

Sri Yashpal Kapur also stated that in 1967 be resigned from his post because he wanted to do public service. It is, however, strange that his zeal for public service was very short lived, for, very shortly after the election was over, he again joined service in the secretariat of the respondent No. 1. In that context it should be held that the statement made by Sri Yashpal Kapur that he resigned in 1967 with a view to do public service was untrue, and the fact is that he did so only with a view to work for the respondent No. 1 in the election. Again, he stated that having attended the Shaheed Mela at Munshiganj on 7.1.1971, he returned to Delhi next day, and that on 9th or 10th January, 1971 he again expressed a desire to the respondent No. 1. to resign so that he could enter public life. Now, it is not understandable as to why, having peacefully worked as Officer on Special Duty in the respondent No. 1's Secretariat till 7th of January, 1971, he was again seized of a desire to do public service. The desire was so intense that within a couple of days he took decision, despite the warning said to have been given by the respondent No. 1, and actually tendered his resignation on 13th of January, 1971. The fact that he was seized of a desire once again on the eve of parliamentary elections after the respondent No. 1 had expressed her intention to contest election from Raebareli, only shows that it was not the desire to do public service, but the desire or behest to do election work for the respondent No. 1 that induced him to resign.

Testing the statement of Sri Yashpal Kapur regarding the motive of his resignation a little further, we find that having submitted his resignation on 13th of January, 1971 he met the same evening Sri Kamlapati Tripathi, the then President of the U.P.C.C., who was camping at Delhi. Sri Yashpal Kapur said that he told Sri Kamlapati Tripathi that he was a free man and could do any work assigned to him, whereupon Sri Kamlapati Tripathi asked him to go to the districts east of Lucknow. Now, it is worthy of notice that general election to the Lok Sabha had taken place in the country in 1971. Sri Yashpal Kapur claims to have resigned on the eve of those elections. It may be assumed that he did so at that time because there was opportunity to do greater and more hectic service during that period. It is, however, strange that once again he was asked to go in the direction of Raebareli. Proceeding further, Sri Yashpal Kapur said that having reached Lucknow in the morning of 14th January, 1971 he obtained a car from the U.P.C.C. and went to Raebareli the same day. Why to Raebareli? According to him, Sri Kamlapati Tripathi had asked him to go to the districts east of Lucknow. Raebareli was not the only district east of Lucknow. Why should he then have gone to Raebareli unless the reason underlying his resignation was to do election work for the respondent No. 1 in the constituency.

Sri Yashpal Kapur said that having stayed at Raebareli till the noon of 17th January, 1971 he left for Sultanpur and Barabanki. He, however, said in cross-examination that he did not stay at Barabanki for more than one day because Barabanki was very near to Lucknow and staying at Lucknow was more comfortable. About Sultanpur, he said that he stayed only for one day, but he did not remember the place of his stay there. Asked about the work done by him at Sultanpur and Barabanki, he said that he just talked to the local people there about the organizational work. This does not appear to be convincing. As I will show a little later, there is evidence on record to indicate that he stayed on at Raebareli till 19th of January, 1971. It appears that he made the aforesaid statement to avoid admitting his presence in the meeting that took place at the Clock Tower, Raebareli, on 17th January, 1971, and in the meetings and functions of Professor Sher Singh that took place on 18th and 19th January, 1971.

It was put to Sri Yashpal Kapur that in 1967 he resigned on the eve of election and worked in the constituency of the respondent No. 1; that in the year 1971 he again worked in the constituency of the respondent No. 1; and whether there was any particular reason behind this coincidence. He replied that he did so because everyone wants to get into the work which may push him into the Parliament or the Legislature of some State. He conceded that he had that ambition in 1967 as well as in 1971. In fact the respondent No. 1 (R.W. 37) also said during her cross- examination that in 1967 Sri Yashpal Kapur was looking for some opportunities which were not available at that time. That being so, it is obvious that Sri Yashpal Kapur did not resign in 1967, nor in 1971, for the sake of any public service but only to work for the respondent No. 1 in her constituency and thereby obtain her help in the fulfilment of his ambition.

YASHPAL KAPUR GOT ENTERED HIMSELF AS RESIDENT OF RAEBARELI FALSELY FOR BECOMING MEMBER OF RAJYA SABHA FROM U.P. – DID BECOME MP IN 1972 – OBSERVES HIGH COURT

According to Sri Yashpal Kapur, his ambition was fulfilled in 1972 when he was elected to Rajya Sabha from the Uttar Pradesh. The statement made by Sri Yashpal Kapur in that connection also deserves some notice. He conceded that a person who is not a resident of a particular State cannot be elected a member of Rajya Sabha from that State. In the electoral roll of the year 1970 (Exh. 17) he is entered as a resident of House No. 968, Kutchery Road, Raebareli. He, however, conceded that neither in 1968-69 nor in 1970-71 he ever resided in Raebareli. It was obviously so because he was then employed in the Prime Minister's Secretariat at Delhi. It was, thereafter put to him whether his residence shown in the electoral roll (Exh. 17) was incorrectly mentioned as House No. 968, Kutchery Road, Bareilly. He first said:

> "I would not call it wrong. I remember when the revision of the electoral roll was taking place I was at Raebareli and I was told that my name has been entered in the electoral roll of Raebareli."

The question that was next put to the witness and the answer given by him are as follows:—

> **"Q:** The answer given by you does not answer the question that was precisely put to you. You have still to answer as to how the description of your residence in Exh. 17 is correct when you concede that during the year 1970 you were not residing in any town or district in U.P.?
>
> **A:** I am not able to answer the question."

It will thus appear that Sri Yashpal Kapur has not been able to give any explanation whatsoever as to how he was recorded as an elector in the State of Uttar Pradesh during the year 1970.

YASHPAL KAPUR ALSO OPENED BANK ACCOUNT IN BANK OF BARODA SHOWING THAT ADDRESS – OBSERVES HIGH COURT

It was further elicited in his cross-examination that on 14th November, 1970 a branch of the Baroda Bank was opened at Raebareli, and Sri Jagannath Paharia, the then Deputy Minister, Finance, had inaugurated it. He said that he had then opened a symbolic account of Rs. 101 in the above branch of the Baroda Bank. He was confronted with the letter (Exh. 54) sent by the Agent, Bank of Baroda, Raebareli branch to the Deputy Registrar, High Court, which, inter alia, states that the Bank had 'a Saving Bank Account No. 26 in the name of Sri Yashpal Kapur, address: Kutchery Road, Raebareli'. Sri Yashpal Kapur stated that while opening the account he did not furnish any address for being entered in the record of the Bank of Baroda. He conceded that he was aware of the fact that while opening an account in any bank a person has to furnish his address. He, however, said that he did not furnish any address because he had opened a symbolic account only. Sri Ashok Kumar Dhupar (P.W. 11) an officer of the Bank of Baroda, was examined by the petitioner and he deposed:

> "Sri Yashpal Kapur, who opened the account, gave his name as Yashpal Kapur and address as Kutchery Road, Raebareli."

He further on said that any person opening an account in the Bank of Baroda has to present himself personally in the Bank for opening the account and his specimen signatures are obtained and kept. In view of the letter (Exh. 54), the aforesaid admission made by Sri Yashpal Kapur and the statement of Sri Ashok Kumar Dhupar (P.W. 11), it is difficult to accept that the address of Sri Yashpal Kapur was recorded in the Bank as Kutchery Road, Raebareli, without his telling so. It was put to him that since he conceded that during the year 1970 he resided at Delhi and went to Raebareli occasionally, and since he further conceded that he did not furnish any address while opening the account with the Bank of Baroda, could he tell at whose instance his address was recorded in the Bank papers as is contained in the letter (Exh. 54). The witness expressed his inability to say as to at whose instance his address came to be recorded like that in the records of the Baroda Bank.

Learned counsel for the petitioner vehemently argued that Sri Yashpal Kapur manipulated to get his name entered in the electoral roll (Exh. 17) as resident of House No. 968, Kutchery Road, Raebareli, and that he again made a wrong representation in that connection while opening his account in the Bank of Baroda in the year 1970, in order that he could be elected to the Parliament as an elector from this State. Since Sri Yashpal Kapur failed to offer any explanation whatsoever as to under what circumstances his name came to be entered in the electoral roll (Exh. 17) and under what circumstances his address was entered in the Bank papers, as Kutchery Road, Raebareli, the contention raised on behalf of the petitioner cannot be rejected as devoid of substance. According to learned counsel for the petitioner, this exposes Sri Yashpal Kapur to the charge that he could make any statement in order to achieve his purpose. The criticism cannot be said to be uncalled for, in view of the own statement of Sri Yashpal Kapur.

Learned counsel for the respondent No. 1 objected that anything pertaining to the entries in the electoral roll could not be questioned as there are exhaustive provisions pertaining to that matter in the Representation of the People Act, 1950 and the rules framed thereunder. I agree that the finality of an electoral roll cannot be questioned in an election petition assailing the election of a particular elector. It does not, however, mean that the statement of a witness on the point as to how he came to be recorded as an elector in any State cannot be considered even for assessing the worth of his testimony in any other case too. The objection raised by learned counsel for the respondent No. 1 cannot, therefore, be accepted.

YASHPAL KAPUR TOLD LIES THAT HE HAD MADE NO ELECTION EXPENSES IN RAEBARELI PRIOR TO 1.2.1971 – HOLDS HIGH COURT

The statement made by Sri Yashpal Kapur on the point of expenditure incurred by him on behalf of the respondent No. 1 also appears to be dubious. He said that he did not incur any expenditure on behalf of the respondent before 1st of February, 1971. Exh. 22/9 is, however, the copy of the receipt obtained by him for the remuneration paid to Siraj Ahmad, driver. This receipt is annexed to the return of election expenses. According to Sri Yashpal Kapur, he obtained the jeep after 1st of February, 1971 and the driver had been engaged by him (This would mean that the driver had been engaged on or after 1st February, 1971) A perusal of the aforesaid receipt, however, shows that the driver was paid salary for the period from 15th Jan., 1971 to 10th of March, 1971. It, therefore, follows that Sri Yashpal Kapur had started incurring election expenses with effect from 15th January, 1971. Confronted with the receipt (Exh. 22/9), Sri Yashpal Kapur tried to modify his statement and said that the jeep was already at Raebareli when it was given to him and he was told that Siraj Ahmad was the driver on the jeep. Now, this statement is inconsistent with his previous statement that the driver had been engaged by him. Further, even that statement made by him fails to explain as to why remuneration for the period prior to 1st of February, 1971 was paid by him, if he had obtained the jeep for election work on or after 1st of February, 1971. On being specifically questioned with regard to it, Sri Yashpal Kapur said that he paid the salary to the driver for the period commencing from 15th January, 1971, because Sri Gaya Prasad Shukla told him that the driver was on the jeep with effect from that date. As already stated, this statement again contradicts his previous statement that the driver had been engaged by him. However, he was questioned that, if he was aware that in the return of election expenses only the amounts spent in connection with the election had to be shown, why that part of the remuneration which related to the period prior to 1st of February, 1971 and was not election expenditure, was included by him in the receipt (Exh. 22/9) and in the return of election expenses. To that the witness replied:

> "I may have erred but I erred on the right side. There was a big margin available. I, therefore, saw no harm in including the whole amount specified in the receipt (Exh. 22/9) in the election return."

The reply is not at all convincing.

Again, according to the return of election expenses (Exh.5), he incurred an expenditure of Rs. 657.90 on 11.1.1971 on account of cost of voters' list. The next six entries in the return relate to the expenditure incurred on 28th January, 1971. The seventh and eighth entries relate to the expenditure incurred on 29th January, 1971 and the entry following it relates to the expenditure incurred on 30th January, 1971. If it was true that Sri Yashpal Kapur did not incur any expenditure before 1.2.1971, as stated by him, how do all these entries exist in the return (Exh.5). That apart, vouchers Nos. 54, 53, 52, 51 and 50, accompanying the return of election expenses (Exh. 5) show that Nanhey Dhobi, Smt. Rawa Ram Pyari, Smt. Dayya Dulari, Ram Pal and Ram Sagar had been paid wages for the period with effect from 28th January, 1971. What is the explanation thereof if the petitioner did not incur any election expenditure before 1st of February, 1971. Sri Yashpal Kapur tried to explain the earlier mentioned entries in the return of election expenses by saying that since the District Congress Committee had put it to him that the aforesaid expenditure had been incurred by them for organizing the election of any person who may later hold himself/herself out to be a candidate, he considered it appropriate to repay that amount as well to the D.C.C. This explanation again is not convincing. Needless to say that Sri Yashpal Kapur offered no explanation whatsoever about the vouchers. It is, therefore, difficult to accept that part of the statement of Sri Yashpal Kapur wherein he said that he incurred no expenditure in connection with the election of the respondent No. 1 prior to 1st of February, 1971.

It appears that when the return of election expenses was filed, it was not realized that the fact of respondent No. 1 having held herself out as a candidate on 29.12.1970 and the fact of Sri Yashpal Kapur having started doing election work for her shortly thereafter could create any complications. It was for this reason that the expenditure was entered in the dates in which it was incurred. When, however, the present petition was filed, it was presumably realized that any admission to the effect that the respondent No. 1 held herself out as a candidate on 29th December, 1970 or that Sri Yashpal Kapur started working for her shortly thereafter could create complications. The respondent No. 1, therefore, took the stand that she held herself out as a candidate for the first time on 1st of February, 1971, and that she did not ask Sri Yashpal Kapur or any other person to do any work for her till then. Sri Yashpal Kapur tried to make a statement in conformity with the stand taken by the respondent No. 1 and that has given rise to the aforesaid inconsistencies.

WIFE OF YASHPAL KAPUR HAD PURCHASED PROPERTY WITH FINANCIAL HELP FROM HIM ALSO – BUT HE PLEADED IGNORANCE ABOUT DOCUMENTS EXECUTED BY HIS WIFE FOR LOANS TAKEN FROM OTHERS – HOLDS HIGH COURT

Cross-examination was also done with Sri Yashpal Kapur regarding some property, said to have been acquired by him in the name of his wife. He admitted that a property had been purchased by his wife in Golf Link area for which she had paid something above Rs four lacs. According to him, he contributed a sum of Rs. 50,000 to his wife for that purpose, a sum of Rs. 1,00,000 was advanced to her by his mother-in-law, a little more than Rs. 1,00,000 was advanced to his wife by Narang Bank and a sum of a little more than Rs. 1,00,000 was given on loan by a family friend. He was, therefore, questioned as to on what conditions the loans were obtained by his wife, and to that he replied that he was not aware as to on what conditions the loans had been taken. He also pleaded ignorance if the building purchased by his wife or part thereof had been mortgaged in favour of any of those persons from whom loans were taken, or if any pronote or bonds had been executed in that connection. He also pleaded ignorance about the covered accommodation in the building purchased by his wife. Now, it cannot be ignored that the building had been purchased by a person no other than the wife of Sri Yashpal Kapur. It is not his case that the relations between him and his wife are strained. On the other hand, on his own admission, he contributed Rs. 50,000 towards the purchase of the building. In that background, it is difficult to accept that Sri Yashpal Kapur did not know whether any bonds, pronotes or mortgage deeds had been executed in respect of the loans taken, and about the covered accommodation in the house. Again, a perusal of the written statement and Addl. Written statement filed by the respondent No. 1 shows that a number of the paragraphs thereof have been verified by the respondent No. 1 on the basis of the information received from her election agent, namely Sri Yashpal Kapur. The respondent No. 1 during her deposition also stated that after she had received copy of the election petition she had talked to Sri Yashpal Kapur on the subject. The statement made by Sri Yashpal Kapur on that point is inconsistent with that made by the respondent No. 1, for, he stated that he did not discuss the election petition with the respondent No. 1 any time before appearing in Court to give his evidence. His attention was then invited to the verification clause contained in the written statement and he said: "I still maintain that I did not have any talk with the respondent No. 1 about the election petition."

STATEMENT OF YASHPAL KAPUR IS A MIXTURE OF HALF TRUTHS AND UNTRUTHS – HOLDS HIGH COURT

From the above discussion of the statement made by Sri Yashpal Kapur it would appear that it is not a statement of straightforward nature and on several points it is an admixture of half truths and untruths. Consequently, no reliance can be placed on that part of his statement wherein he denied to have said anything in his speech on 7th January, 1971, pertaining to the candidature of the respondent No. 1 It may also not be out of place to add that since it is Sri Yashpal Kapur himself who was charged with having rendered the assistance to the respondent No. 1 in his capacity as a Gazette Officer of Government of India, he could not be expected to admit it.

CONDUCT OF YASHPAL KAPUR – SURROUNDING CIRCUMSTANCES REVEALED – YASHPAL KAPUR WENT TO RAEBARELI ON 7 JANUARY, 1971 FOR ELECTIONEERING OF RESPONDENT NO. 1 AT HER INSTANCE AS SHE HAD HELD HERSELF AS A CANDIDATE FROM RAEBARELI IN HER PRESS STATEMENT DATED 29 DECEMBER, 1970 – HOLDS HIGH COURT

Learned counsel for the respondent then urged that even accepting that Sri Yashpal Kapur delivered a speech at Munshiganj on 7th January, 1971 and that he canvassed support for the respondent in that speech, he was not an election agent on that date, and there is no evidence of the fact that he had been instructed to do so by the respondent No. 1. Learned counsel stressed that, consequently, it should not be held on that basis that the respondent No. 1 obtained or procured the assistance of Sri Yashpal Kapur for the furtherance of her election prospects.

I have given my careful consideration to this argument as well, but I regret my inability to accept the same. As also stated earlier, Sri Yashpal Kapur was occupying a position of trust and confidence with the respondent No. 1 since quite a long time. During the period in question he was Officer on Special Duty in the respondent No. 1's Secretariat. In 1967, he had resigned from his post for the sake of respondent No. 1 to be able to do her election work in the constituency. After that was done, he was taken back in the respondent's secretariat as Officer on Special Duty. Respondent No. 1 held herself out as a candidate on 29th December, 1970. On 5th of January, 1971 Raja Dinesh Singh was sent to the constituency . On 7th of January, 1971 Sri Yashpal Kapur visited Raebareli and, on the own admission of respondent No. 1, he did so with previous notice to the respondent No. 1. The subsequent events also appear to be material, for according to Sri Yashpal Kapur, immediately on return from Raebareli he held a talk with the respondent No. 1 on 9th or 10th of January, 1971; on 13th January he again resigned from the post and the same day set out once again for the constituency of the respondent No. 1. It was again he who was ultimately appointed election agent for the respondent No. 1. It may be added that it was not possible to adduce any direct evidence on the point whether the respondent No. 1 instructed Sri Yashpal Kapur to go to Raebareli on 7th January, 1971 for any election work. That can be inferred only on the basis of the surrounding circumstances. I have already mentioned those circumstances above and to my mind the only inference that can be drawn on the basis of those circumstances is that the respondent No. 1 (Yashpal Kapur?) went to Raebareli on the aforesaid date under instructions of the respondent No. 1 for doing preliminary work pertaining to her election.

To sum up, therefore, it is satisfactorily proved that the respondent No. 1, during the period ending on 13th January, 1971, obtained/procured the assistance of Sri Yashpal Kapur, A Gazetted Officer in the Government on India for the furtherance of her election prospects, in as much as Sri Yashpal Kapur was made to go to Raebareli on 7.1.1971 and deliver a speech at Saheed Mela in Munshiganj canvassing support for her candidature.

The period from 14.1.1971 to 25.1.1971.

RESPONDENT No. 1 HAVING HELD HER A CANDIDATE FROM RAEBARELI ON 29.12.1970 – OBTAINED AND PROCURED ASSISTANCE OF YASHPAL KAPUR WHEN HE WAS STILL A GAZETTED OFFICER IN GOVERNMENT OF INDIA DURING PERIOD FROM 7 JANUARY TO 24 JANUARY, 1971 IN FURTHERANCE OF HER ELECTION PROSPECTS – GUILTY OF COMMITTING CORRUPT PRACTICE – HOLDS HIGH COURT

There is no controversy about the fact that Sri Yashpal Kapur tendered his resignation from the post of Officer on Special Duty on 13th of January, 1971 and the same day he left for Lucknow. Further, on the own admission of Sri Yashpal Kapur, he reached Raebareli on 14th of January, 1971. I have already held earlier that on 7th of January, 1971 he had gone to Raebareli in order to start election work for the respondent No. 1 and, while delivering speech in the Saheed Mela in Munshiganj, he solicited support for the respondent No. 1 He returned to Delhi on 8th January, 1971, and on 9th or 10th January, 1971 he held talks with the respondent No. 1. In the context of my finding that he had gone to Raebareli on 7th of January, 1971 for doing election work it should be inferred presumeable that he talked about the same during the conversation that he had with the respondent No. 1 on 9th or 10th of January, 1971. The fact that he resigned on 13th of January, 1971 with a view to do political work and directly came to Raebareli, in that background, is a strong pointer to the conclusion that he did with a view to do election work for the respondent No. 1. It is also worthy of notice in this connection that voucher No. 49 accompanying the return of election expenses (Exh. 5) of the respondent, related to the salary paid to Siraj Ahmad as driver of the jeep that was admittedly used by Sri Yashpal Kapur for doing election work for the respondent No. 1. A perusal of this receipt shows that Siraj Ahmad was paid his salary for the period commencing from 15th of January, 1971. This voucher also, therefore, proves that at least with effect from 15th of January, 1971 Sri Yashpal Kapur started doing election work for the respondent No. 1. It may be mentioned at this place that the explanation given by Sri Yashpal Kapur about the aforesaid voucher has already been held by me earlier to be unworthy of acceptance.

The statement of Sri Mohan Lal Tirpathi (P.W. 59), General Secretary, District Congress Committee (R), Raebareli, also lends support to the fact that during the period commencing from 14th of January, 1971 Sri Yashpal Kapur was doing election work at Raebareli. He said that till 1st of February, 1971 they were making propaganda for votes being cast in favour of the congress candidate. He, however, added that they were not canvassing for any particular candidate. He further said that Sri Yashpal Kapur also did canvassing in a similar manner.

The fact that Sri Yashpal Kapur did work pertaining to election during his stay at Raebareli with effect from 14th of January, 1971 also finds some support from the additional written statement filed by the respondent No. 1. In Para 2(b) the respondent No. 1, *inter alia,* pleaded:

> "The statement in the amended paragraph 5 of the petition that Sri Yashpal Kapur, at the direction of this respondent, organised the electioneering work for her during the entire period commencing from 27th December, 1970 is denied, except that, Sri Yashpal Kapur did some work in the constituency, though there was no electioneering work done by him for this respondent till a few days before his appointment as election agent." (Underlining is by me)

By the aforesaid pleading the respondent No. 1 appears to have admitted that Sri Yashpal Kapur did some work in the constituency prior to his being appointed as election agent and that a few days before his appointment as election agent he also did some electioneering work for the respondent. In Para 2(c) the respondent No. 1, *inter alia*, pleaded:

> "It is also denied that Sri Yashpal Kapur made any speech on 7.1.1971 in support of her candidature. Though a few days even before his appointment as election agent he did make speeches appealing to the voters for the Indian National Congress but not particularly for any candidate or canvassing for this respondent." (Underlining is by me).

This part of the pleading appears to be inconsistent with the above-quoted pleading contained in Para 2(b) of the petition, in as much as while the pleading contained in Para 2(b) of the additional written statement concedes that some electioneering work was also done by Sri Yashpal Kapur for the respondent No. 1 a few days before his appointment as election agent, it is denied in the above-quoted part of the pleading contained in Para 2(c) of the Additional written statement. A cumulative reading of Para 2(b) and Para 2(c) of the additional written statement, however, shows a clear concession on the part of the respondent No. 1 that Sri Yashpal Kapur was doing some election work at Raebareli before his appointment as election agent, though that work was not particularly for any candidate. Now, once it is accepted that, during the period before his appointment as election within the constituency, it should be inferred that the work related to the candidature of the respondent No. 1, in view of my finding recorded earlier that the respondent No. 1 had held herself out as a candidate on 29th of December, 1970. The fact that the respondent No. 1 was a candidate from Raebareli constituency with effect from 29th December, 1970 and the fact that Sri Yashpal Kapur had also gone to Raebareli on 7th January, 1971 and had then delivered a speech in support of her candidature, rather make it obvious that during the period between 14th of January, 1971 and 25th of January, 1971 also the work done by Sri Yashpal Kapur at Raebareli pertained to the election of the respondent No. 1.

Therefore, the circumstances emanating from the additional written statement of the respondent No. 1, from the statement on oath made by Sri Yashpal Kapur (R.W. 32) and from the statement made by Sri Mohan, Sri Yashpal Kapur was doing election work for the respondent No. 1.

YASHPAL KAPUR WAS ONE OF THOSE WHO LED A FLEET OF CARS, JEEPS ON 14.1.1971 IN RAEBARELI WITH BANNER-POSTER AND LOUD SPEAKERS FITTED – APPEALING TO PUBLIC FOR VOTING FOR RESPONDENT NO. 1 – HOLDS HIGH COURT

Coming to the specific instances, it is first alleged that on 14th of January, 1971 Sri Yashpal Kapur led a fleet of cars through the town of Raebareli as part of the election propaganda for the respondent No. 1. The oral evidence relied upon by the petitioner in this connection consists of the statements of Uma Shanker Yadav (P.W. 41) and Ram Kumar Singh (P.W. 42).

Sri Uma Shankar Yadav is a practicing Advocate. He stated that on 14th of January, 1971 a number of vehicles started in procession from the Central Election Office, Raebareli, carrying posters and banners in favour of the candidature of respondent No. 1. He added that loudspeakers were fitted on the vehicles; and the people on the vehicles appealed to the public through the loudspeakers that they should give votes to the respondent No. 1 and should make her successful. He, however, did not claim to have seen Sri Yashpal Kapur in that procession, though he added that he had seen him round about 15th of January, 1971 doing election propaganda. Learned counsel for the petitioner urged that Uma Shankar Yadav (P.W. 41), according to an admission elicited in his cross-examination, was a staunch worker of the S.S.P., and that during the election of 1971 he worked as counting agent for the petitioner besides working for him in connection with his election campaign. Learned counsel stressed that Uma Shankar Yadav is, therefore, a strongly partisan witness and consequently no reliance can safely be placed on his testimony.

There is more than one reason, however, for which I am unable to accept the criticism levelled by learned counsel for the petitioner. Sri Uma Shankar Yadav is a practicing Advocate and therefore a respectable person. It was not put to him in cross-examination that no procession of vehicles was taken out by the Congress Party in Raebareli on 14th of January, 1971 and that the statement made by the witness was an outright lie. On the contrary the following question was put to him:

> "**Q:** Is it not correct that the propaganda that was started on 14th January, 1971 by the congress men was for the success of the Congress Party in the election and not for a particular candidate?"

This question contains a clear suggestion to the effect that even though the election propaganda had started on 14th of January, 1971, as deposed by this witness, it was for the success of the Congress Party and not for any particular candidate. Further, the statement of this witness is corroborated by the evidence of Ram Kumar

Singh (P.W. 31). In the context of these circumstances, there does not appear any risk in relying on the testimony of Sri Uma Shankar Yadav Advocate, even though he is a partisan witness.

Sri Ram Kumar Singh (P.W. 42) deposed that on 14th of January, 1971 a fleet of cars started under the leadership of Sri Yashpal Kapur, that the procession moved throughout the town and publicity was made that respondent No. 1 was contesting election, as she did on the previous occasion, and further that she should be made successful. In cross-examination a suggestion was made to him that there were no banners on the vehicles, showing " Indira Ji ko vote do" and that the only propaganda being made was "Indira Congress Ko Jitao" The relevant portion of the statement reads as follows:

> "It is wrong to say that there was no banner on any of those vehicles, saying "Indira Ji Ko vote do" It is also wrong to say that the only (propaganda) being made was "Indira Congress ko Jitao"."

It will thus appear that in the cross-examination of Ram Kumar Singh as well, it was not put that the statement made by him regarding a fleet of cars having been taken out on 14th of January, 1971 was *falso ab initio*. The trend of the cross-examination, on the contrary, was that even though a fleet of cars or jeeps was taken out, the only propaganda done from those cars and jeeps was that "Indira Congress" should be made successful and not that 'Indira Ji' herself should be made successful. That being the shape of cross-examination, there does not appear any good justification for refusing to accept the statement on oath made by Ram Kumar Singh.

Learned counsel for the respondent No. 1 no doubt urged that Ram Kumar Singh is a member of the Organisation Congress and that he worked for the respondent No. 1 in the election. True, it is so. The fact, however, remains that, with the shape of cross-examination done with Ram Kumar Singh, that circumstance is not sufficient to lead to the conclusion that the statement made by Ram Kumar Singh about the fleet of cars having been taken out in the town on 14th January, 1971 under the leadership of Yashpal Kapur is a lie.

The petitioner also relied on the news item published in the issue dated 22.1.1971 of 'Swantra Bharat' (Exh. 39) in support of the fact that a fleet of cars had been taken out by Sri Yashpal Kapur on 14th of January, 1971. Since, however, the person who reported the relevant news item has not been examined, it may not be very safe to act thereon even as a piece of corroborative evidence. I would accordingly not take that news item into consideration.

On the side of the respondent, there is the sole testimony of Sri Yashpal Kapur (R.W. 32), who said that he did not take out any fleet of cars in the town on the 14th January, 1971. I have, however, already discussed the evidence of Sri Yashpal Kapur in detail earlier and have concluded that he is not a reliable witness. I accordingly find that the evidence of Sri Yashpal Kapur fails to rebut the evidence of Sri Uma Shankar Yadav (P.W. 41) and Ram Kumar Singh (P.W. 42).

On the evidence of Sri Uma Shankar Yadav (P.W. 41) and Ram Kumar Singh (P.W. 42), it is borne out that a fleet of cars and jeeps was taken out in procession on 14th of January, 1971 doing propaganda for the respondent No. 1 and Sri Yashpal Kapur was associated with it.

ON 17.1.1971 AN ELECTION MEETING HELD AT CLOCK TOWER RAEBARELI BY YASHPAL KAPUR – OTHER LEADERS – CONVASSING SUPPORT FOR RESPONDENT NO. 1 – HOLDS HIGH COURT

It is next alleged that on 17th of January, 1971 an election meeting was held at the Clock Tower, Raebareli, in which Sri Chandra Shekhar and Sri Yashpal Kapur

(R.W. 32) participated in that connection consists of the statements of Sri Ram Kumar Dixit alias Phakkar (P.W. 31) and Ram Kumar Singh (P.W. 42).

Ram Kumar Dixit *alias* Phakkar (P.W. 31), speaking on the point, deposed that Sri Yashpal Kapur was also present in the meeting, though he did not remember whether he delivered any speech in that meeting or not. The witness further said that some excitement and shouting of slogans took place at the meeting and displeasure was expressed against Sri Yashpal Kapur in the slogans. He proved the news item (Exh. 69) contained in the issue of 'Beer Baiswara' dated 23rd January, 1971 pertaining to that meeting. He deposed that as a reporter 'Beer Baiswara' he had himself sent the report about that news item. In the news item (Exh. 69) it is stated that disturbance was created in the election meeting of the respondent No. 1, held on 17th January, 1971 at the crossing of the Clock Tower, Raebareli, which was addressed by Sri Chandra Shekhar, when some young persons made some accusations against Sri Yashpal Kapur and shouted slogans against him. It is further reported in the news item that some counter slogans were also shouted thereafter. I have considered the statement made by Sri Ram Kumar Dixit earlier in connection with the speech delivered by Sri Yashpal Kapur at Munshiganj on 7.1.1971 and have come to the conclusion that he is a reliable witness. Further, the statement made by Sri Ram Kumar Dixit regarding the meeting that took place on 17th January, 1971 is supported by the news item (Exh. 69), which was published in 'Beer Baiswara' on 23rd January, 1969. Indeed, it cannot be said that this issue of 'Beer Baiswara' was prepared later on for the purposes of the election meeting. It may also be added at this place that the factum of an election meeting having taken place as deposed by Sri Ram Kumar Dixit was not seriously challenged on behalf of the respondent, as would appear from the following question that was put to Ram Kumar Dixit in cross-examination:

> "I put it to you that this meeting was convened for the purpose of making a propaganda in favour of the Congress as a party."

This question contains a clear admission of the fact that a meeting did take place as alleged by the petitioner.

For all these reasons, I see absolutely no justification for refusing to act on the testimony of Ram Kumar Dixit alias Phakkar (P.W. 31).

Coming to the evidence of Ram Kumar Singh (P.W. 42), he deposed that an election meeting was convened at the Clock Tower in Raebareli on 17th of January, 1971 and that, when Sri Yashpal Kapur wanted to deliver a speech in that meeting, some disturbance was created by the students, as a result of which he could not do so and the meeting was then controlled by Sri Chandra Shekhar. Referring to the speech of Sri Chandra Shekhar, the witness said that he canvassed support for the respondent No. 1 in his speech. It is true that Ram Kumar Singh is a staunch worker of the Congress (0) Party and had also worked for the petitioner in the election that took place in 1971. In view, however, of the fact that the factum of the meeting is not seriously challenged on behalf of the respondent No. 1, as is apparent from the earlier-mentioned question put to R.K. Dixit (P.W. 31), and further in view of the fact that the evidence of Ram Kumar Singh is amply supported by the evidence of R.K. Dixit and the news item (Exh. 69) published in the issue of 'Beer Baiswara' dated 23rd January, 1971, I see no risk in acting on the evidence of Ram Kumar Singh as well.

The respondent examined Sri Vimal Chand Dwivedi (R.W. 18) and Sri Yashpal Kapur (R.W. 32) in rebuttal. Sri Vimal Chand Dwivedi accepted that a meeting had taken place at the Clock Tower, Raebareli, which was addressed by Sri Chandra Shekhar. He, however, added that Sri Yashpal Kapur was not present in that meeting. A perusal of his cross-examination, however, shows that he is not at all a truthful witness. He said that the meeting addressed by Sri Chandra Shekhar was not an election meeting. I have already shown earlier that the case put to Sri R.K. Dixit (P.W. 31) in cross-examination was that the meeting was being done for the Congress as a party and not for any candidate. The statement to the contrary made by Sri Vimal Chand Dwivedi must, therefore, be rejected as incorrect. Again, Sri Dwivedi went to the extent of saying that Sri Yashpal Kapur did not visit Raebareli on 7th January, 1971, a fact admitted by Sri Yashpal Kapur himself. It was also elicited in his cross-examination that the brother of this witness is a lecturer in Feroz Gandhi College and Sri Yashpal Kapur is the Vice-President of the Managing Committee of that College. It appears that he gave statement under that influence. The influence was so great that he went to the extent of denying even admitted facts, namely that Sri Yashpal Kapur visited Raebareli on 7th of January, 1971 with Sri Gulzari Lal Nanda. Obviously no reliance can be placed on the evidence of such a witness.

As for Sri Yashpal Kapur, I have already considered his evidence elaborately earlier and have not found him to be reliable witness.

There being no other evidence on the side of the respondent, the evidence of Sri R.K. Dixit (P.W. 31) and Ram Kumar Singh (P.W. 42) remains unrebutted. On the basis of that evidence I conclude that an election meeting of the respondent No. 1 was convened on 17th of January, 1971 at the Clock Tower, Raebareli, and that Sri Yashpal Kapur participated in that meeting.

YASHPAL KAPUR SOUGHT VOTES FOR RESPONDENT NO. 1 IN VILLAGE NIHASTA WHERE PROFESSOR SHER SINGH, MINISTER ADDRESSED PEOPLE – INAUGURATED TELEPHONE EXCHANGE ON 19.1.1971 – HOLDS HIGH COURT

It is next alleged that on 19th of January, 1971 Professor Sher Singh, a Minister of State in the Government of India, and Sri Yashpal Kapur addressed a meeting in village Nihasta and in those speeches they, *inter alia*, canvassed support for the candidature of the respondent No. 1. It is true that Raj Kishore Singh belongs to Jan Sangh Pary and looked after the election work of the petitioner at Nihasta polling station. It is, however, significant to find that in the cross-examination of Raj Kishore Singh a question was put to him, which is as follows:

> "I suggest to you that Sri Yashpal Kapur only said that we should support the leadership of the respondent No. 1 and the Congress."

The above question implies a clear admission that Sri Yashpal Kapur was not only present with Professor Sher Singh when the latter addressed the meeting at Nihasta on 19th January, 1971, but further that he also delivered a speech. All that was sought to be contended was that in the speech canvassing was done not for the respondent No. 1 but for the leadership of the respondent No. 1 and for the party. Now, once it is accepted that respondent No. 1 had given herself out as a candidate from Raebareli on 29th December, 1970, even seeking support from the electorate for the leadership of the respondent or for the Congress as a party meant nothing except soliciting support for the respondent No. 1 in the constituency. Learned counsel for the respondent No. 1 argued that the above question does not contain any admission to the effect that Sri Yashpal Kapur was present at Nihasta on 19th January, 1971 or that he delivered any speech whatsoever, Learned counsel submitted that the above-quoted question was put because there was no means to know till that stage whether Sri Yashpal Kapur was actually present in the meeting or not. In other words, it was just a probing question. The explanation offered by learned counsel for the respondent No. 1 is not acceptable to me. Learned counsel for the respondent No. 1 had the advantage of being instructed by more than one pairokar. One of them, namely Sri Jagpat Dubey was always present by the side of the learned counsel. Further, Sri Yashpal Kapur was no other than the election agent of respondent No. 1. In the circumstances, the explanation sought to be given by learned counsel for the respondent appears to be mere afterthought.

The only infirmity in the evidence of Raj Kishore Singh P.W. is that according to him Professor Sher Singh visited village Nihasta on 19th January, 1971, while according to the tour programme (Exh. 47) he should have visited that village on 18th January, 1971. I cannot, however, ignore the fact that Raj Kishore Singh P.W. was examined as a witness in the case after a lapse of more that three years. Further, Professor Sher Singh was present within the district on both the dates. The mistake about the date in the statement of Raj Kishore Singh P.W. can therefore be due to lapse of time and consequent confusion in his mind. The evidence of Raj Kishore Singh cannot be discarded on that account.

I thus see no justification for refusing to act on the testimony of Raj Kishore Singh (P.W. 26).

In order to rebut the evidence of Raj Kishore Singh, the respondent No. 1 examined Jagannath Prasad (R.W. 16) and Krishna Dutta Pandey (R.W. 17).

Jagannath Prasad (R.W. 16) is a resident of village Nihasta. Krishna Dutta Pandey (R.W. 17) was Sub Postmaster in the Sub Post Office, Nihasta during the year 1971. Both of them deposed that Professor Sher Singh visited village Nihasta on 18th January, 1971 to inaugurate the Telephone Exchange section in the Sub Post Office. It was further stated by them that Sri Yashpal Kapur was not present at the said inaugural function. Their evidence cannot be accepted for the simple reason that it is inconsistent with the respondent No. 1's case, as was clearly put to Raj Kishore Singh (P.W. 26) in cross-examination. It appears that till quite a late stage the respondent No. 1 did not intend to deny the presence of Sri Yashpal Kapur in the function that took place at Nihasta in connection with the inauguration of the Telephone Exchange section in the Sub Post Office, and that it was only when the respondent entered on her defence that it was decided to deny that fact. Indeed, it is never difficult for any party to find one or two witnesses to bolster up his case, whether it is true or false.

Therefore, placing reliance on the evidence of Raj Kishore Singh in preference to the evidence of Jagannath Prasad (R.W. 16) and Krishna Dutta Pandey (R.W. 17), I hold that Sri Yashpal Kapur was present at Nihasta when Professor Sher Singh inaugurated the Telephone Exchange section in the Sub Post Office there and that Sri Yashpal Kapur on that occasion delivered a speech, saying that the respondent No. 1 was to contest election from Raebareli and that people should support her.

It is next alleged that on 19th of January, 1971 Professor Sher Singh and Sri Yashpal Kapur attended a meeting held in Lalganj and that at the said meeting Sri Yashpal Kapur said that respondent No. 1 would contest election from Raebareli constituency and that people should make her successful. The only evidence adduced by the petitioner in proof of the above fact is that of Sri Girish Narain Pandey (P.W. 30). Sri Girish Narain Pandey, however, conceded in cross-examination that during the year 1971 he was a worker of the Jan Sangha Party and that during the year he was examined in Court he was a member of the Rashtriya Swayam Sewak. He further conceded that he actively supported the petitioner in the election and had worked for him as a counting agent as well as polling agent. He is, therefore, a partisan witness. There being no evidence to corroborate the evidence of Girish Narain Pandey, it will not be safe to place reliance on his testimony.

The respondent examined Abdul Jabbar (R.W. 25), Fateh Bahadur Singh (R.W. 26), Ishwar Chand (R.W. 27) and Ranjit Singh (R.W. 28) to rebut the evidence of Girish Narain Pandey. In view, however, of the fact that I have not considered it safe to place reliance on the solitary evidence of Girish Narain Pandey, it is needless to refer to the evidence of the aforesaid witnesses of the respondent No. 1 in any detail.

I accordingly find that the petitioner failed to prove that Sri Yashpal Kapur delivered any speech of the nature alleged at Lalganj on 19th of January, 1971.

ON 19.1.1971 YASHPAL KAPUR ALSO SOUGHT VOTES FROM PUBLIC FOR RESPONDENT NO. 1 – IN VILLAGE BEHTA KALAN WHERE PROF. SHER SINGH INAUGURATED TELEPHONE EXCHANGE AND ADDRESSED PUBLIC – HOLDS HIGH COURT

It is next alleged that on 19th of January, 1971 inaugural function of the Telephone Exchange section took place at Behta Kalan and in that connection Professor Sher Singh, accompanied by Sri Yashpal Kapur visited village Behta Kalan. It is also alleged that on that occasion Sri Yashpal Kapur delivered speech saying that the respondent No. 1 would contest election from Raebareli and that people should make her successful. The petitioner examined Pandit Sheshank Misra (P.W. 32), who made a statement in support of the above said allegation.

Learned counsel for the respondent No. 1 pointed out that the father of Pt. Sheshank Misra P.W. is a member of the Jan Sangh Working Committee, and that during the year 1971 he himself was polling agent for the petitioner. It is true that Pt. Sheshank Misra himself candidly accepted both the aforesaid facts during his cross-examination. It is, however, once again worthy of notice that in the case that was put to Pt. Sheshank Misra (P.W. 32) it appears to have been clearly conceded that Sri Yashpal Kapur was not only present at the inaugural function that took place at Behta Kalan on 19th January, 1971 but that he also delivered some speech. This is apparent from the following questions put to him:—

> "**Q:** I put it to you that the moment Sri Yashpal Kapur started speaking there was an excitement and uproar as a result of which no person in the meeting could hear what was being said by Sri Yashpal Kapur.?
>
> **A:** It is wrong.
>
> **Q:** I put it to you that Sri Yashpal Kapur did not say anything regarding the candidature of respondent No. 1. from Raebareli parliamentary constituency and that he made an appeal only for the help to be given to the Congress in general.
>
> **A:** This is wrong."

Learned counsel for respondent No. 1 once again offered the same explanation for having put these questions as were given in connection with the suggestion that was made to Raj Kishore Singh (P.W. 26) in cross-examination. I have already said at that stage that the explanation is not at all well founded. I have the same reply to give to the explanation sought to be given by learned counsel for the respondent No. 1 in regard to the above-quoted questions put to Pt. Sheshank Misra. In that view of the matter, it has to be accepted that Sri Yashpal Kapur was present at Behta Kalan on 19th of January, 1971 when Professor Sher Singh inaugurated the Telephone Exchange section there, and that he delivered an election speech on that occasion. In view of my finding earlier that by that time the respondent No. 1 had held herself out as a candidate from Raebareli parliamentary constituency, it follows that in the election speech delivered by Sri Yashpal Kapur he should have solicited support for the respondent No. 1 as deposed by Pt. Sheshank Misra.

The respondent No. 1 examined Shitla Bux Singh (R.W. 14) and Raghubans Bahadur Singh (R.W. 15) in order to rebut the evidence of Sheshank Misra. One of the reasons why the respondent No. 1 chose to examine these persons in his defence, presumably was that Sheshank Misra P.W. had filed a notice (Exh. 74) said to have been issued to the public in regard to .... that took place at Behta Kalan on 19th January ...... notice, *inter alia*, mentioned that Sri Yashpal Kapur, Private Secretary of the Prime Minister, shall also be present on the occasion. The notice was issued under the signatures of Shitla Bux Singh and Raghubans Bahadur Singh R.Ws. besides Gupta Singh, M.L.A. Both these witnesses deposed that Professor Sher Singh inaugurated Telephone Exchange at Behta Kalan on 19th January, 1971. They, however, denied the presence of Sri Yashpal Kapur on that occasion. In view, however, of the clear case that was put to Sheshank Misra in cross-examination admitting the presence of Sri Yashpal Kapur in the function that took place at Behta Kalan on 19th January, 1971, no reliance can be placed on the statement of Shitla Bux Singh and Raghubans Bahadur Singh R.Ws. denying his presence in that function.

I accordingly find that Sri Yashpal Kapur did deliver a speech at Behta Kalan on 19th January, 1971 wherein he solicited support for the candidature of the respondent No. 1 in the election.

The last allegation is that on 18th of January, 1971 Professor Sher Singh laid the foundation stone of the new building of the Post Office at Raebareli and in the function held there Sri Yashpal Kapur delivered a speech canvassing support for the respondent No. 1. The only evidence relied upon by the petitioner in that connection is that of Uma Shanker Yadav (P.W. 41). A perusal of this statement would show that while he deposed about the foundation-stone laying ceremony of the Post Office building at Raebareli by Professor Sher Singh, he did not depose either about the presence of Sri Yashpal Kapur at that function or about any speech having been delivered by him. It will thus follow that there is evidence on the side of the petitioner in support of that allegation and that allegation is accordingly not proved.

The period from 25th of January to 6th of February, 1971.

RESIGNATION OF YASHPAL KAPUR ACCEPTED ON 25 JANUARY – BUT GAZETTED ON 6 FEBRUARY – SHOULD BE DEEMED IN SERVICE TILL 6 FEBRUARY – SUBMITTED PETITIONER – CONTENTION REJECTED – HIGH COURT

Learned counsel for the petitioner urged that unless an order accepting the resignation is communicated to the Government servant concerned the resignation does not take effect. Learned counsel further urged that it is not disputed even to the respondent that Sri Yashpal Kapur had started doing election work for her with effect from 1st of February, 1971. It was urged that the resignation of Sri Yashpal Kapur having been Gazetted on 6th of February, 1971, it should be inferred that it was communicated to Sri Yashpal Kapur on that date and it was on the same date that it took effect. On this reasoning, learned counsel urged that the act of the respondent No. 1 in obtaining the assistance of Sri Yashpal Kapur between 1st of February, 1971 and 6th of Feburary, 1971 shall also constitute a corrupt practice under section 123(7) on the Representation of the People Act.

I have, however, already held on the basis of the decision of the Supreme Court in case **Raj Kumar v. Union of India, AIR 1969 SC 180,** that a resignation takes effect on the date it is accepted and that its formal communication to the Government servant concerned is not necessary. As also stated earlier, the order accepting the resignation of Sri Yashpal Kapur was passed on 25th of January, 1971, as is apparent from the Gazette notification. Sri Yashpal Kapur, therefore, ceased to be a Government servant with effect from that date. Consequently, on the basis of anything done by Sri Yashpal Kapur for the respondent No. 1 during the period between 25th of January, 1971 and 6th of February, 1971, the respondent No. 1 cannot be held guilty of having committed corrupt practice.

RESPONDENT NO. 1 OBTAINED ASSISTANCE OF YASHPAL KAPUR – A GAZETTED OFFICER GOVERNMENT OF INDIA – FROM 7 JANUARY TO 24 JANUARY, 1971 IN FURTHERANCE OF HER ELECTION PROSPECTS – GUILTY OF CORRUPT PRACTICE UNDER SECTION 123(7) OF RP ACT, 1951 – HOLDS HIGH COURT

My conclusion, therefore, on Issue No. 1 (first set) read with Issue No. 1 (of the additional issues) is that the respondent No. 1 obtained and procured the assistance of Sri Yashpal Kapur during the period from 7th of January, 1971 to 24th of January, 1971 in furtherance of her election prospects, when Sri Yashpal Kapur was still a Gazetted Officer in the service of the Government of India holding the post of Officer on Special Duty in the Prime Minister's secretariat; and the respondent No. 1 is hereby guilty of the commission of a corrupt practice under section 123(7) of the Act.

ELECTION OF INDIRA NEHRU GANDHI TO LOK SABHA SET ASIDE – HIGH COURT

In view of my findings on Issue No. 3 (first set) Issue No. 1 (first set) read with additional Issue No. 1, Additional Issue No. 2 and Additional Issue No. 3, this petition is allowed and the election of Smt. Indira Nehru Gandhi respondent No. 1, to the Lok Sabha is declared void.

ELECTION OF INDIRA NEHRU GANDHI TO LOK SABHA SET ASIDE – HIGH COURT RESPONDENT NO. 1 ALSO OBTAINED SERVICES OF GAZETTED OFFICERS – U.P. GOVERNMENT – FOR HER ELECTIONEERING – GUILTY OF CORRUPT PRACTICE UNDER SECTION 123(7) OF RP ACT – DISQUALIFIED FOR 6 YEARS UNDER SECTION 80A OF RP ACT – HIGH COURT

The respondent No. 1 has been found guilty of having committed a corrupt practice under section 123(7) of the Representation of the People Act by having obtained the assistance of the Gazetted Officers of the State Government of U.P. *viz.* the District Magistrate, Raebareli, the Superintendent of Police, Raebareli, the Executive Engineer, P.W.D., Raebareli, Engineer, Hydel Department, Raebareli, in furtherance of her election prospects in the manner indicated in my finding on Issue No. 2. She has further been found guilty of having committed another corrupt practice under section 123(7) of the Representation of the People Act by having obtained the assistance of Sri Yashpal Kapur, a Gazetted Officer in the Government of India, holding the post of Officer on Special Duty in the Prime Minister's Secretariat, for the furtherance of her election prospects in the manner indicated in my finding on Issue No. 1 read with Additional Issue No. 1. The respondent No. 1 accordingly stands disqualified for a period of six years from the date of this order, as provided in section 8A of the Representation of the People Act.

ELECTION PETITION ACCEPTED WITH COSTS – WRIT PETITION DISMISSED – HIGH COURT

The petitioner shall get his costs of the election petition from the respondent No. 1. A table of costs shall be prepared by the office in accordance with rule 30 Chapter XV of the Rules of Court.

As already pointed out while recording my finding on issue No. 9, the petitioner has not been able to lay any foundation on facts to compel an inquiry into the constitutionality of the Representation of the People (Amendment) Ordinance, 1974 (No. XIII of 1974) or that of the Representation of the People (Amendment) Act, 1974 (Act No. 58 of 1974). The writ petition No. 3761 of 1975 is accordingly rejected. The Parties shall bear their own costs in the writ petition.

Dated 12.6.1975
TYPED BY
(R.S. PANDEY)
Examined by
TRUE COPY

Sd/ Jagmohan L. Sinha

SECTION OFFICER (GRADE II)
COPYING DEPARTMENT,
HIGH COURT, ALLAHABAD

STAY ORDER AGAINST THE OPERATION OF THE ORDER DATED 12 JUNE, 1975 FOR A PERIOD OF 20 DAYS BY THE HIGH COURT

ALLAHABAD HIGH COURT

Smt. Indira Gandhi
In re: Shri Raj Narain v. *Smt. Indira Gandhi*

Before: J.M.L. Sinha, J.

Civil Side Appellate Jurisdiction
Dated The 12th June, 1975
Civil Misc. Application No. Nil, 1975
In Election Petition No. 5 of 1971

BY THE COURT

Having heard learned counsel for the Respondent No. 1, I am satisfied that there are sufficient reasons for the stay of the operation of the judgment and order delivered in Election Petition No. 5 of 1971 connected with Writ Petition No. 3761 of 1975. The operation of the said order is, accordingly stayed for a period of 20 days. On the expiry of the said period of 20 days or as soon as an appeal is filed in the Supreme Court, whichever takes place earlier, this order shall cease to carry effect.

Dated 12.6.1975 **Sd/ Justice J.M.L. Sinha**

SUPREME COURT OF INDIA

Indira Nehru Gandhi
v.
Raj Narain

AIR 1975 SC 1590: (1975) 2 SCC 159

Coram: 1 V.R. Krishna Iyer, J.

Civil Misc. Petition No. 887 of 1975, Civil Misc. Petn. No. 3557 of 1975 decided on June 24, 1975

The Order was delivered by

Judgment

V.R. KRISHNA IYER, J.:—1. Right at the beginning, I must record appreciation of the valuable assistance given by counsel on both sides to the Court in clarifying the twilt aspects and unravelling the latent facets of what, viewed in typically isolated legal perspective, untuned to the national wave-length and unclouded by the dust -storms of politics is a humdrum case. Having regard to the obstreperous environs and mounting tensions surrounding the events following upon the judgment of the Allahabad High Court, it must be stated to the credit of Shri Palkhivala and Shri Shanti Bhushan that in their suave submissions they have shown how sound and fury only help thwart the thought-ways of law and extra-legal tumults can be walled off from the Court hall.

ARGUMENTS RAISED WERE NOT CONFINED TO STAY APPLICATION – SUPREME COURT

The arguments have been largely legal and their merits have to be weighed in judicial scales. What, perhaps in a certain view, are not strictly pertinent to the stay proceedings have, however, been adverted to at the bar, inevitably and understandably, but within marginal limits, if I may say so, because the proceedings in the Halls of Justice must be informed, to some extent, by the great verity that the broad sweep of human history is guided by sociological forces beyond the ken of the noisy hour or the quirk of legal nicety. Life is larger than Law. Now I proceed to discuss the merits of the matter.

APPELLANT CHALLENGED THE 'UNSEATING' ORDER AND SEEKS 'ABSOLUTE STAY' – SUPREME COURT

2. The appellant has moved this Court challenging the 'unseating' verdict against her by the High Court. She has also sought 'absolute stay' of the judgment and order under appeal. Entering a caveat, the respondent has also appeared through counsel and opposed the grant of stay.

JUSTICE IS THE GOAL FOR COURTS – WHILE EXERCISING POWER – SUPREME COURT

3. While the right to appeal is statutory, the power to stay is discretionary. But judicial discretion-indeed, even executive discretion - cannot run riot. The former, though plenary, is governed in its exercise by sound guidelines, and courts look for light, *inter alia*, from practice and precedent, without however being hide-bound mechanically by the past alone. After all, judicial power is dynamic, forward-looking and socially lucent and aware. I mention this dimension of 'judge-power' because the industry and ingenuity of both lawyers have unearthed prior instances zig zagging now and then but substantially striking the same note. A few orders from the debris of old records have been brought up which seem to suggest variations in the type of stay granted by the higher courts. I shall have occasion to dilate on them a little later, Suffice it to note that the power of the court must rise to the occasion, if justice, in its larger connotation, is the goal-and it is.

COURT IS GUIDED BY HIGH JUDICIAL PRINCIPLES IN DECIDING STAY APPLICATIONS – SUPREME COURT

4. Having regard to the historic power-stakes involved in this election appeal and stay proceeding, vigorous arguments, marked by strokes of heat and flashes of light, have been heard in this application for stay and the time consumed at the bar has been considerably more than, when like matters have been routinely dealt with by this Court. Let it be plainly understood that the Court decides forensic questions without getting embroiled in non-legal disputes working as it does in a sound-proof system of sorts. Moreover, notwithstanding the unusual, though natural, excitement and importance surrounding the case, the Court is the quiet of the storm center and views, with an equal eye, the claims on each side, taking judicial note of the high issues and balance of convenience in the wider context. Arguments about public sentiment, political propriety and moral compulsion though touched upon at the bar and relevant at other levels, fall beyond the conventional judicial orbit and have to be discriminatingly sifted.

URGENCY AND NATIONAL SITUATION – PLEADS APPELLANT'S COUNSEL – SUPREME COURT

Nevertheless, Shri Palkhivala has pressed before me the propriety and urgency of the Court taking into consideration the national situation even while exercising its discretionary power.

DEMOCRATIC DESTINY SHOULD NOT BE SURRENDERED FOR A SINGLE SOUL – PLEADS RESPONDENT'S COUNSEL – SUPREME COURT

As a counter- weight to this submission, Shri Shanti Bhushan has claimed that no republic can surrender its democratic destiny to a single soul without being guilty of overpowering the parliamentary process by a personality cult.

BALANCE OF CONVENIENCE AND INTEREST OF JUSTICE AS SANCTIFIED BY USAGE OF SUPREME COURT ARE THE GUIDING PRINCIPLES – SUPREME COURT

This brings to the fore an activist interrogation about the cognisibility of such considerations by a court. Do the judicial process and its traditional methodology sometimes make the Judicature look archaic, with eyes open on law and closed on society, forgetting the integral yoga of law and society? If national crises and democratic considerations, and not mere balance of convenience and interests of 'justice', were to be major inputs in the Judge's exercise of discretion, systemic changes and shifts in judicial attitudes may perhaps be needed. Sitting in time-honoured forensic surroundings I am constrained to judge the issues before me by the canons sanctified by the usage of this Court.

APPELLANT GOT STAY ORDER FROM HIGH COURT BY MIS-STATEMENT – PLEADS RESPONDENT – SUPREME COURT

5. Now to the points urged before me. More or less by way of preliminary objection, Shri Shanti Bhushan asserted that the petitioner, having come with unclean hands, was not entitled to seek the equitable relief of stay. How were her hands unclean? Because, the argument runs, her advocate induced the High Court into granting a stay by misrepresenting that if the judgment came into immediate effect, the national government would be paralysed for want of a Prime Minister and so time was needed for the ruling Party to elect a new leader to head the Government. Taken in by this alleged critical need of the democratic process, the learned Judge granted 20 days stay. This spell, ingeniously secured, was perverted to consolidate her leadership, not to find a successor. If the version of the respondent were veracious, the petitioner's conduct were dubious and this Court would not condone such 'solemn mockery.'

LEADER WAS TO BE ELECT – NOT ANOTHER LEADER – NO MISSTATEMENT – SUBMITS PETITIONER – SUPREME COURT

But Shri Shanti Bhushan's submission loses its sting if Shri Palkhivala were to be heeded. For, according to the latter, all in a hurry a stay was moved by the Allahabad advocate praying for stay stating both the need to elect a leader (not, another leader) and to enable filing of an appeal. The Congress Parliamentary Party was since convoked but there was a thunderously unanimous vote reaffirming faith in the petitioner as leader and Prime Minister. If her Party so full boldly plumped in favour of her remaining in office as Prime Minister and guiding the Party as its one and only leader, the petitioner could not be faulted as having prayed false to the Court. She could only call a meeting of the Party but not coerce the members to elect anyone other than the one they had set their hearts upon. Whether that Party's leadership resources were too inadequate to secure an alternative chief may be an interesting a question but the Court does not peep into that penumbral area.

PRELIMINARY OBJECTION OF RESPONDENT OVER-RULED – SUPREME COURT

Moreover, the stay order does not state that it was to enable the election of a different leader that time was granted. I have no good reason to reject the petitioner's plea that the choice of an alternative leader was left to her party that she did what she could in the spirit of the representation to Court and did not what she could not *viz.*, to force her partymen to push her aside for the nonce for the Court's satisfaction. In these matters one has to go by Prima facie materials and probabilities. I overrule the unclean hands' objection.

APPELLANT'S COUNSEL PLEADS FOR 'ABSOLUTE STAY' IN NATIONAL INTEREST – SUPREME COURT

6. Shri Palkhivala, for the petitioner, contended that an unconditional stay was appropriate and essential because (a) it was sanctioned by some precedent: (b) there were momentous consequences disastrous to the country if anything less than the total suspension of the order under appeal were made; (c) the adverse holding of the High Court on two counts hardly exceeded, even on its face, technical violations unworthy of being visited with an interim embargo on Parliament Membership during the pendency of the appeal apart from being palpably perverse and (d) the nation was solidly behind the petitioner as Prime Minister. Minimal justice, public interest and balance of convenience concurred in his favour.

APPELLANT TO BE TREATED AS AN ORDINARY APPELLANT – PLEADS RESPONDENT – SUPREME COURT

Shri Shanti Bhushan, on the contrary joined issue on these pleas and asserted that (a) the appellant must be treated like any other party: (b) that an absolute stay was unprecedented; (c) that the democratic process would take care of itself even if the petitioner stepped aside for a while; (d) the corrupt practices were corrupt in law and fact, fully proved and could not be glossed over by a court of law as technical and (e) the alleged solid support by party minion meant little since similar phenomena could be organized by any strategist in top office and the rule of law cannot be drowned by the drums and shouts of numbers. In his submission, public interest and balance of convenience as also justice to the High Court judgment demanded that an illegally elected Member did not continue longer as Prime Minister under the umbrella of a stay order from this Court, without jeopardizing the credibility of the country abroad.

MERITS OF APPEAL CANNOT BE ASSESSED FOR DECIDING STAY APPLICATION – SUPREME COURT

7. Shri Palkhivala assailed, in his opening submissions, the two findings recorded against the appellant holding her guilty of corrupt practice. Indeed, he was at pains to convince me that his client had strong *prima facie* case on the merits, in the sense that the judgment, on its face, was perverse and legally untenable. Although I listened at some length to these arguments and, to an extent, to the counter-submissions made, by Shri Shanti Bhushan in his endeavour to establish that the holdings were sound. I made it fairly clear in the course of the hearing that at this stage when I was considering whether a stay should be granted or not, it was premature and perhaps unwise to pronounce on the merits of the appeal itself except where the judgment contained grotesque errors, absurd conclusions or grossly erroneous propositions of law. Having considered the submissions on this basis. I do not think I should express any opinion one way or the other on the merits of the findings. Nor do I regard it just for counsel for the respondent to say that every discrepancy in the petitioner's evidence or other incorrectness in testimony can be called false. Not to accept a witness's evidence may be due to many grounds of probability not always because of unveracity or unreliability. These aspects will surely be examined at the hearing of the appeal, not now.

ORDER OF *STATUS QUO* – PLEADS APPELLANT'S COUNSEL – SUPREME COURT

8. Counsel for the petitioner, after dealing with the *ex facie* untenability of the Judgment under appeal which I have just disposed of, moved on to what he called justice between the parties. This is not an ordinary list, where even after stepping down from office, the petitioner can, if and after she wins the appeal, step back into office. In politics, 'red in tooth and claw', power lost is not necessarily followed, after legal victory, by power regained. The Court cannot, in that sense, restore the parties to their original position as in ordinary cases. Moreover, the respondent suffers no prejudice by the continuance of the petitioner as Parliament Member and Prime Minister. To cap it all, there is hardly a run of a little over half-a-year for two full term of this Parliament to expire. So, he pressed for continuance of the status quo which had gone on for a few years now during the pendency of the Election Petition.

PURITY OF POLLS MATERIAL – PLEADS RESPONDENT'S COUNSEL – SUPREME COURT

9. The respondent's counsel retorted that the question of justice between two private persons was alien to election litigation and cited a ruling to emphasize what is obvious. In an election case, the whole constituency is, in an invisible but real sense, before the court and justice to the electoral system which is the paramount consideration is best done by safeguarding the purity of the polls regardless of the little rights of individual combatants.

JUDGMENT IS VALID TILL SET ASIDE – SUPREME COURT

10. At the first flush I was disposed to prolong the 'absolute stay' granted by the High Court, moved not only by what Shri Palkhivala had urged but by another weighty time factor that the appeal itself, in the light of the directions I have already given yesterday, may well be decided in two or three months. But on fuller reflection I have hesitated to take that course. After all, the High Court's finding, until upset, holds good, however weak it may ultimately prove. The nature of the invalidatory grounds upheld by the High Court, I agree, does not involve the petitioner in any of the graver electoral vices set out in section 123 of the Act. May be they are only venial deviations but the law, as it stands, visits a returned candidate with the same consequence of invalidation. Supposing a candidate has transported one voter contrary to the legal prohibition and even though he has won by a huge plurality of votes his election is set aside. Draconian laws do not cease to be law in court but must alert a wakeful and quick acting legislature. So it follows that I cannot, at this preliminary stage, lightly dismiss the illegality of the election as field by the High Court. But more importantly. I am disinclined to set store by Shri Palkhivala's 'private Justice' submission (to borrow his own phrase) because the ultimate order I propose to make, if I may even here anticipate, substantially preserves the position of the petitioner as Member of Parliament and does not adversely affect her legal status as Prime Minister.

VIOLATION OF ELECTORAL LAW – OFFENCE MAY BE GRAVE OR MINOR – IS VIOLATION – SUPREME COURT

11. In another facet of the same argument Shri Palkhivala urged that, after all, the petitioner had been held 'technically' guilty of 'corrupt practice' and that the grounds set out by the learned Judge were too flimsy to stand scrutiny at the appellate level. Therefore, the 'justice' of the case demanded continuance of the 'absolute stay' granted by the trial Judge himself. Shri Shanti Bhushan, on the other side, refuted this submission as specious. His argument is this. 'Corrupt practice' could not be dismissed as 'technical' if one had any respect for the law of the land as laid down by Parliament. Once the law has defined 'corrupt practice', commission' thereof cannot be condoned as 'technical'. That is defiance of the law and challenge to the wisdom of Parliament. It is one thing to amend the law, but it is another to disregard it on a ground unknown to law that it is only a nominal deviance, I am afraid it is premature and presumptuous for me, at this stage, to pronounce upon the relative worth of the findings of the High Court. The offence may be light or grave. But that is for the Bench which hears the appeal *in extenso* to hold, one way or the other. Before me are findings of contravention of the election law and I cannot take the prima facie view that the justice of the case justifies indifference to those findings. In short, I am not influenced by this aspect of Shri Palkhivala's argument.

CUSTOMARY FACTORS FOR DECIDING STAY APPLICATION MAY BE NOTICED – SUPREME COURT

12. Leaving aside the injury to private rights as of lesser consequence in election disputes, let me look at the customary factors courts are prone to probe in stay matters where the discretion vests court.

GRANT OF 'ABSOLUTE STAY' IS NOT THE PRACTICE – SUPREME COURT

13. What has been the prior practice of this Court in such cases ? What, if any are the special circumstances compelling departure in favour of the petitioner? What is the balance of convenience? What does the public justice of the case dictate? Which way does public interest lie? These are the socio-legal considerations which are relevant to the grant or refusal of stay and the terms to be imposed on the petitioner in the event of grant. Stay pending appeal has been usually granted but hemmed in by conditions. The respondent himself has filed a sheaf of orders of conditional stay granted by this Court, suggesting by implication that those conditions should be attached to any stay the Court may be inclined to issue. The terms in which such limited stay orders have been couched, the legal implications thereof, the right surviving under them and the impact thereof on the office of Prime Minister of the petitioner will be scanned more closely later in this order. Suffice is to say for the present that for around two decades there has rarely been what Shri Palkhivala calls an 'absolute stay' issued by this Court in election cases where a Member as been unseated by the High Court for corrupt practice.

POLITICAL COMPULSIONS OF A PARTY DO NOT AFFECT THE LEGAL BARRIERS – SUPREME COURT

14. There was reference at the bar to political compulsions like the swell of the tidal wave in favour of the petitioner which, even if true (though controverted by the other side), cannot breach the legal dykes to force a stay where presidentially it has not been granted. Nor can the national crisis, conjured up by counsel for the petitioner, in the event of her exit from office, be a valid legal consideration, even it may perhaps have weight in other spheres. Shri Shanti Bhushan urges that moreover one cannot readily accept that the nation will come to a grinding halt if one person is not available to fill the office of Prime Minister, I make no comment on these rival presentations for it is difficult for the Judge to guage with his traditional court room apparatus the reality and extent of the circumstances of national magnitude the parties have dwelt upon.

BALANCE OF CONVENIENCE IS TAKEN CARE OF IN THE SHAPE OF CONDITIONAL STAY – SUPREME COURT

15. So we come to the next criterion which is common place, in this jurisdiction *viz.*:—the balance of convenience. Here, counsel for the petitioner has addressed an attractive argument (repeating in some measure what, under a different head, he had urged) that if the appeal itself were disposed of early, the continuance of the status quo would go a long way to preserve and promote administrative stability and policy continuity having regard to the fact that the petitioner in this case was more than a Member of Parliament but was the Prime Minister and leader of the ruling Party. In a democracy the Prime Minister is the central figure who decides crucial internal and international policy, directs measures of great economic moment and is responsible and accountable to the Parliament and the nation for the performance of the Administration. Of course, collective Cabinet responsibility is of the essence of the democratic process, but the Council of Ministers is virtually chosen by the President in accordance with the wishes of the Prime Minister. The broad guidance of the Party in power notwithstanding, the personality of a Prime Minister has a telling effect on democratic government. If, therefore, the appeal itself will be disposed of in some months, as it is likely to be, the balance of convenience will be in favour of continuance of the same team which is animated by the presence of the key -personality within the Council of Ministers. Again, the short spell of the pendency of the appeal – a case of this climactic pitch deserves to be disposed of with quick dispatch and I have already given some directions to facilitate it – is a strong factor for non disturbance of the petitioner's position, having regard to the traumatic effect on and grievous consequences to the petitioner. Of course, these are components of a wider concept of balance of convenience and not altogether forbidden ground in dealing with discretionary exercise. May be there is some force in the plea that there should be a stay of operation of the judgment and order in such manner that upsetting the Ministry in office should be obviated. Ordinarily, even with the same

Party ruling, when a Prime Minister resigns, the whole team is ushered out leaving it free for the new leader to choose his new set.

16. Shri Shanti Bhushan has countered this argument by reliance on the practice in the Parliamentary system where within the ruling Party a leader is changed or ceases to be available and a new leader is elected, so that the democratic process finds smooth expression. This, he said, has happened in India, as elsewhere and no plea of balance of convenience can be built on what in fact is a desire to remain in office. The judicial approach as already pointed out by me, is to shy away from political thickets and view problems with institutionalised blinkers on, so long as the court methodology remains what it is. So no comments again. But the balance of convenience, widely or limitedly connoted, is reasonably taken care of in the shape of the conditional stay granted at the conclusion of this judgment.

LAW PRE 1966 WAS DIFFERENT – CANNOT BE APPLIED IN CHANGED LAW SITUATION – SUPREME COURT

17. Shri Palkhivala drew my attention to a few vintage instances of what he calls absolute stay having been granted in election matters by higher Courts. These are cases of long ago and the argument based on them stems from an insufficient comprehension about the anatomy of the pre-1956 Representation of the People Act, 1951 (Act XLIII of 1951). The Court speaks for today, based on current practice and present law.

18. In this context, it is necessary to remember that in the Act as it originally stood, Election Tribunals tried election disputes and section 107 provided:

> "107. Orders to take effect only on publication- An order of the Tribunal under section 98 or section 99 shall not take effect until it is, published in the Gazette of India under section 106."

Indeed, there was no right of appeal provided in the Act, and the aggrieved parties had to approach the High Court or the Supreme Court under the provisions of the Constitution. The higher Courts in such situations merely stayed the publication in the Gazette, the consequence being that the order of the Tribunal did not come into effect at all. The question, therefore, of an absolute stay or a qualified stay of the unseating verdict did not and could not arise. To rely upon orders passed under the then law merely staying publication of the order of the Tribunal in the Gazette as tantamount to absolute stay of an order which took effect would be untenable.

19. In 1956 a major change in the law was made whereby the order of the Election Tribunal appointed under section 86 shall take effect as soon as it is pronounced by the Tribunal (*vide* section 107, as amended by Act XXVII of 1956) By the same amending Act, an appeal was provided from orders of Election Tribunals to the High Court of the State and section 116A(4) clothed the High Courts with power to stay operation of the order appealed from and if stay was granted the order shall be deemed never to have taken effect'. Of course, against appellate orders of the High Court the disappointed party could come to this Court under the provisions of the Constitution (Article 133 or 136).

20. Still later, by amending Act No. LXVII of 1966, the High Court was conferred original jurisdiction to try election petitions and it was provided in section 107 that the order of the High Court shall take effect as soon as it is pronounced......'. While a limited power to stay operation of the order of the High Court' was conferred by section 116B(1) on the High Court itself, the statutory right of appeal to the Supreme Court was provided for by section 116A. However, by virtue of section 116B(2) it was enacted:

"116B(2). Where an appeal has been preferred against an order made under section 98 or section 99, the Supreme Court may, on sufficient cause being shown and on such terms and conditions as it may think fit, stay the operation of the order appealed from."

Thus, for the first time, it was in 1966 that a statutory right of appeal to this Court was created, and a plenary power to grant stay, conditional or otherwise, was vested in this Court, independently of constitutional remedies.

21. This narration of the historical background regarding the pre-1966 statutory position is sufficient to distinguish old examples of the pattern of stay granted by this Court. Today there is no case of prohibition of publication in the Gazette. Above-all, the type-design, if I may use such an expression, of stay orders made by this Court under the present law has, with marginal variations, acquired a standardized form. Naturally, this *cursus curiae* is mere persuasive for adoption, unless exceptional legal or other grounds for deviation are made out for grant of absolute stay.

EVEN UNDER POST-1966 LAW – APPELLANT SEEKS 'ABSOLUTE STAY' – SUPREME COURT

22. Even on the basis of the post 1966 law, Shri Palkhivala has argued that taking legitimate cognizance of the peerless position of the appellant as Prime Minister of the country, judicial discretion must least disturb not merely her seat in Parliament but her office in Government.

OLD ORDERS – JUDGMENTS – CONSIDERED – SUPREME COURT

23. I proceed to take a close-up of the 'sample orders' made by this Court during the last many years, dissect them in the background of the judgments under appeal where such orders were passed and mould my order deriving support therefrom. So I turn the focus on the implications and effect of the stay orders in the cases covered by Annexure A filed by the respondent which are in consonance with the usual orders passed by this Court in election appeals.

IF OPERATION OF THE ORDER STAYED – DISQUALIFICATION ALSO STANDS STAYED TILL DISPOSAL OF APPEAL – SUPREME COURT

24. It is evident on its face that the orders are dichotomous in character. The two limbs stand out clearly and they are (a) that 'the operation of the Judgment and Order of the High Court be and is hereby stayed' and (b) the petitioner shall abide by certain enumerated terms *viz.*, (i) he will be entitled to attend the Sessions of the Legislature and sign the Register: (ii) he shall not take part in the proceedings of the House or vote or draw any remuneration as such Member. In the instances I have examined, the appeals are against orders 'unseating the returned candidate on the ground of corrupt practice and disqualifying him for the statutory six-year period prescribed in section 8A. If corrupt practice is found, disqualification follows, although sometimes the trial Court expressly writes it into the order itself, as in the present case, If the finding of corrupt practice does not come into effect, the sequel of disqualification also does not come into effect. If the biopsy of the stay order inevitably shows that the finding of corrupt practice is suspended and is not operative, the electoral disqualification automatically stands eclipsed. Section 8A being the necessary follow up of the judgment under section 100, what is the legal effect of an order by this Court suspending the operation of the judgment and order of the High Court? By sheer force of the first limb of this Court's stay order, the judgment and order of the High Court is nullified for the nonce *i.e.*, till the appeal is disposed of. Consequentially the disqualification also *ipso jure* remains in abeyance.

GRANT OF STAY ECLIPSES HIGH COURT JUDGMENT – CERTAIN CONDITIONS CAN BE IMPOSED – SUPREME COURT

25. What then is the import of the conditions imposed in the stay order? They inhibit the elected member, who otherwise by virtue of the stay of the judgment, will be entitled to exercise all his rights and privileges as Member, from doing certain things expressly tabooed, *viz.*, (a) participating in the proceedings; (b) voting or drawing remuneration. For all other purposes, the voiding judgment being suspended, he continues as Member. Indeed, the very direction that he attend the House and sign in the Register as Member to avoid disqualification under Art. 101 of the Constitution postulates that he is a Member and is not disqualified under section 8A of the Act, For, if the disqualification under section 8A operates and he ceases to be a Member, there is no need to veto his drawing remuneration, voting or participating in the proceedings. It would be a curious contradiction to say that a person is disqualified to be chosen as or being a Member and yet be allowed to sign the Register as Member. Can the Court, without stultifying itself and usurping power, permit a non-Member to sit in the House instead of or even in the Visitor's gallery, unless it necessarily reads into the order of stay of judgment a suspension of the disqualification also? There are a number of other privileges for a Member of Parliament which are left untouched by this Court's prior stay orders. Moreover, the specific direction suspending the judgment and order under appeal, read in its plenitude, also suspends the finding of corrupt practice. So much so the disqualification also shares the fate. I have no doubt that the reasonable effect of a stay order is that there is a plenary eclipse of the High Court's judgment and order during the pendency of the appeal, subject to the few restraints clamped down on an appellant. Those restraints are the second limb of the stay order and are explicit enough.

NORMALLY 'CONDITIONAL STAY' RESTORES FULL STATUS EXCEPT DEBATES – VOTING AND REMUNERATION – SUPREME COURT

26. The essential point to note is that by necessary implication the disqualification imposed on every appellant also, stands suspended in all cases of conditional stay. The stay is complete, but carved out of it are but three limitations. For all other purposes, the appellant, in all such cases, continues a Member. For instance, if he is prevented from entering the Legislature, a breach of privilege arises. I have gone at length into these ramifications to remove recondite doubts. The typical stay restores to the appellant, during its operation, the full status of a Member of a Legislature minus the right to participate in debates, including voting and drawing of remuneration as a legislator.

27. For these reasons I propose to direct a stay, substantially on the same lines as have been made in earlier similar cases, modified by the compulsive necessities of this case.

LOK SABHA SEAT OF APPELLANT UNDER LITIGATION – NOT PM'S OFFICE – NO EMBARGO ON HER DUTIES AS PRIME MINISTER – SUPREME COURT

28. What would be the legal impact of an order of this type on the Prime Ministership of the petitioner? The question canvassed about the office of the Prime Minister and its involvement in the present case has exercised counsel on both sides and it is but proper to dissolve the mists of possible misunderstanding by an explicit statement. This appeal, it is plain, relates solely to the Lok Sabha Membership of the appellant and the subject-matter of her office *qua* Prime Minister is not directly before this Court in this litigation. Indeed, that office and its functions are regulated carefully by a separate fasciculur of Articles in the Constitution. There is some link between Membership of one of the two Houses of Parliament and Ministership (Art. 75) but once the stay order is made, as has been indicated above, the disqualification regarding Membership is in suspended animation and does not operate. Likewise, the appellant's Membership of the Lok Sabha remains in force so long as the stay lasts. However, there will be a limitation regarding the appellant's participation in the proceedings of the Lok Sabha in her capacity as Member thereof but, independently of the Membership, a Minister and, a fortiori, the Prime Minister, has the right to address both Houses of Parliament (without right to vote, though) and has other functions to fulfil (Arts. 74, 75, 78 and 88 are illustrative). In short, the restrictions set out in the usual stay order cannot and will detract from the appellant being entitled to exercise such rights as she has, including addressing Parliament and drawing salary, in her capacity as Prime Minister. There will thus, be no legal embargo on her holding the office of Prime Minister. However, this legal sequitur of the situation arising from the stay of the judgment and order of the High Court, including the suspension of the disqualification under section 8A, has nothing to do with extra-legal considerations. Legality is within the Court's province to pronounce upon, but canons of political propriety and democratic dharma are polemical issues on which judicial silence is the golden rule.

VIRTUALLY NO DIFFERENCE BETWEEN 'ABSOLUTE STAY' PRAYED – STAY GRANTED – SUPREME COURT

29. It is true that between an absolute stay as sought and the stay as granted there is practically little difference when the petitioner is a Minister. Moreover when the House is not in session, as now, even the restrictions set out in sub-para III of para 31 of this order hardly have any operation. In this view, the dispute between the parties one asking for an absolute stay (as if it were a magic formula) and the other citing heaps of orders of conditional stay for adoption (as if much difference would be made in practical effect) appears to be shadow-boxing, as pointed out by me even during the arguments.

NO AMBIGUITY SHOULD BE LEFT – SUPREME COURT

30. May be, brevity which is usual in this Court in orders of stay of this sort might well have sufficed here also but, the over-all desirability to dispel possible ambiguity warrants a hopefully longer speaking order.

TERMS AND CONDITIONS OF THE OPERATIVE ORDER PASSED – SUPREME COURT

31. Let me sum up the terms of the operative order I hereby pass:

I. Subject to Para III below, there will be a stay of the operation of the judgment and order of the High Court under appeal.

II. Consequentially, the disqualification imposed upon the appellant as a statutory sequel under section 8A of the Act and as forming part of the judgment and order impugned will also stand suspended. That is to say, the petitioner will remain a Member of the Lok Sabha for all purposes except to the extent restricted by Para III so long as the stay order lasts.

III. The appellant-petitioner, qua Lok Sabha Member, will be entitled to sign the Register kept in the House for that purpose and attend the Sessions of the Lok Sabha, but she will neither participate in the proceedings in the Lok Sabha nor vote nor draw remuneration in her capacity as Member of the Lok Sabha.

IV. Independently of the restrictions under Para III on her Membership of the Lok Sabha, her rights as Prime Minister or Minister, so long as she fills that office, to speak in and otherwise to take part in the proceedings of either House of Parliament or a joint sitting of the Houses (without right to vote) and to discharge other functions such as are laid down in Articles 74, 75, 78, 88 etc., or under any other law, and to draw her salary as Prime Minister, shall not be affected or detracted from on account of the conditions contained in this stay order.

ORDER IS PROVISIONAL – CAN BE RECONSIDERED – SUPREME COURT

32. This order, by me sitting single as Vacation Judge, is being delivered with a sense of hurry, although after careful consideration of arguments heard till last evening. Now the Parliament is not in session and the veto on the right to vote is currently academic. Situations may develop, circumstances may change and this order itself, like any interlocutory order, is provisional. If new events like the convening of Parliament take place or fresh considerations crop up warranting the review of the restrictions in this stay order, the petitioner appellant will be at liberty to move a Division Bench of this Court again to modify the restrictions or pray for an unconditional stay. Likewise, the respondent may also if justifying considerations appear a new, move for variation of the conditions in this stay order.

Order accordingly.

SUPREME COURT OF INDIA

Smt. Indira Nehru Gandhi
v.
Shri Raj Narain

AIR 1975 SC 2299: (1976) 2 SCR 347: 1975 (Supp) SCC 1

Before: A.N. Ray, C.J.I., H.R. Khanna, K.K. Mathew, M.H. Beg and Y.V. Chandrachud, JJ.

Civil Appeal Nos. 887 and 909 of 1975, D/d. 7.11.1975.

C.A. No. 909 of 1975

Raj Narain
v.
Smt. Indira Nehru Gandhi

For the Appellant:—M/s. A.K. Sen, J.N. Kaushal, D.P. Singh Sr. Advocates, M/s. J.B. Dadachanji, R.H. Debar, Madun Gujadhur, S.C. Agarwal, Yogeshwar Prasad, H.K.L. Bhagat, Sudhir Bera and K.P. Bhandari and Mrs. Anjali K. Verma Advocates.

For the Respondent No. 1:—Mr. Shanti Bhushan, Sr. Advocate, M/s. J.P. Goyal, R.C. Dvivedi, R.C. Srivastava, Pranab Chatterjee, S.S. Khanduja, E.C. Agarwala, C.K. Ratnaparkhi, M.C. Gupta, T.N. Porwar, U.N.R. Rao, S.K. Garg, B. Soloman, K.C. Dua Raghunath Singh and Sripal Singh, Advocates.

For the Attorney-General for India.—Mr. Niren De. Attorney General for India, Mr. Lal Narain Sinha, Solicitor General for India and Dr. V.A. Seyid Muhammad. Senior Advocates, M/s. R.N. Sachthey, P.P. Rao, Miss Sumitra Chakravarty and Mr. S.P. Nayar Advocates.

Judgment

A.N. RAY, C.J.—1. In Civil Appeal No. 887 of 1975 the appellant is Indira Nehru Gandhi and the respondent is Raj Narain. Civil Appeal No. 909 of 1975 is the cross objection of the respondent. On 14 July, 1975 it was directed that both the appeals would be heard together. The appeals arise out of the judgment of the High Court of Allahabad dated 12 June, 1975. The High Court held that the appellant held herself out as a candidate from 29 December, 1970 and was guilty of having committed corrupt practice by having obtained the assistance of Gazetted Officers in furtherance of her election prospects. The High Court further found the appellant guilty of corrupt practice committed under section 123(7) of the Representation of the People Act, 1951 hereinafter referred to as the 1951 Act by having obtained the assistance of Yashpal Kapur a Gazetted Officer for the furtherance of her election prospects. The High Court held the appellant to be disqualified for a period of six years from the date of the order as provided in section 8(a) of the 1951 Act. The High Court awarded costs of the election petition to the respondent.

2. It should be stated here that this judgment disposes of both the appeals. Under directions of this Court the original record of the High court was called for. The appeal filed by the respondent with regard to Issue Nos. 2, 4, 6, 7 and 9 formed the subject-matter of cross objections in Civil Appeal No. 909 of 1975. The cross-objections are the same which form grounds of appeal filed by the respondent in the High Court at Allahabad, against an order of dismissal of Civil Misc. Writ No. 3761 of 1975 filed in the High Court at Allahabad.

ARTICLE 71 OF THE CONSTITUTION REPLACED BY NEW ARTICLE *VIDE* 39TH AMENDMENT OF THE CONSTITUTION – CJI

3. The Constitution (Thirty-ninth Amendment) Act, 1975 contains three principal features. First, Article 71 has been substituted by a new Article 71. The new by law regulate any matter relating to or connected with the election of a President or Vice-President including the grounds on which such election may be questioned.

ARTICLE 329A HAVING 6 CLAUSES ALSO ADDED BY THIS AMENDMENT IN THE CONSTITUTION – CJI

4. The second feature is insertion of Article 329A in the Constitution. Clause 4 of Article 329A is challenged in the present appeals. There are six clauses in Article 329A.

AS PER CLAUSE (1) ELECTION OF PM OR SPEAKER CAN BE CHALLENGED BEFORE AUTHORITY AND IN MANNER PRESCRIBED BY PARLIAMENT – CJI

5. The first clause states that subject to the provisions of Chapter II of Part V (except sub-clause (e) of clause (1) of Article 102) no election to either House of Parliament of a person who holds the office of Prime Minister at the time of such election or is appointed as Prime Minister after such election, and to the House of the People of a person who holds the office of Speaker of that House at the time of such election or who is chosen as the Speaker for that House after such election, shall be called in question, except before such authority (not being any such authority as is referred to in clause (b) of Article 329) or body and in such manner as may be provided for by or under any law made by Parliament and any such law may provide for all other matters relating to doubts and dispute in relation to such election including the grounds on which such election may be questioned.

AS PER CLAUSE (2) VALIDITY OF CLAUSE (1) CANNOT BE CALLED IN QUESTION IN ANY COURT – CJI

6. Under the second clause the validity of any such law as is referred to in clause (1) and the decision of any authority or body under such law shall not be called in question in any court.

AS PER CLAUSE (3) IF ANY SUCH ELECTION PETITION/APPEAL IS PENDING – IT SHALL STAND ABATED – ELECTION CAN BE CHALLENGED UNDER LAW MADE UNDER CLAUSE (1) – CJI

7. The third clause states that where any person is appointed as Prime Minister or, as the case may be, chosen to the office of the Speaker of the House of the People, while an election petition referred to in Article 329(b) in respect of his election to either House of Parliament or, as the case may be, to the House of the People is pending, such election petition shall abate upon such person being appointed as Prime Minister or, as the case may be, being chosen to the office of the Speaker of the House of the People, but such election may be called in question under any such law as is referred to in clause (1).

AS PER CLAUSE (4) ANY LAW PRE 39TH AMENDMENT OF THE CONSTITUTION OF INDIA SHALL NOT APPLY OR EVER HAVE APPLIED TO THE ELECTION OF PM OR SPEAKER – ANY ORDER PASSED IN ELECTION PETITION UNDER THE OLD LAW SHALL BE VOID – CJI

8. The fourth clause which directly concerns the present appeals states that no law made by Parliament before the commencement of the Constitution (Thirty-ninth Amendment) Act, 1975, in so far as it relates to election petitions and matters connected therewith, shall apply or shall be deemed ever to have applied to or in relation to the election of any such person as is referred to in clause (1) to either House of Parliament and such election shall not be deemed to be void or ever to have become void on any ground on which such election could be declared to be void under any such law and notwithstanding any order made by any court, before such commencement, declaring such election to be void, such election shall continue to be valid in all respects and any such order and any finding on which such order is based shall be deemed always to have been void and of no effect.

AS PER CLAUSE (5) ANY APPEAL OR CROSS APPEAL PENDING AGAINST ANY SUCH ORDER PASSED BEFORE 39TH AMENDMENT SHALL BE DISPOSED OF IN TERMS OF CLAUSE (4) – CJI

9. The fifth clause states that any appeal or cross appeal against any such order of any court as is referred to in clause (4) pending immediately before the commencement of the Constitution (Thirty-ninth Amendment) Act, 1975, before the Supreme Court shall be disposed of in conformity with the provisions of clause (4).

AS PER CLAUSE (6) PROVISIONS OF ARTICLE 329A SHALL PREVAIL OVER EVERYTHING ELSE CONTAINED IN THE CONSTITUTION – CJI

10. The sixth clause states that the provisions of this Article shall have effect notwithstanding anything contained in the Constitution.

ENTRY NO. 87 TO 124 ADDED IN THE NINTH SCHEDULE BY 39TH AMENDMENT OF THE CONSTITUTION – CJI

11. The third feature in the Constitution (Thirty-ninth Amendment) Act is that in the Ninth Schedule to the Constitution after Entry 86 and before the Explanation several enteries Nos. 87 to 124 inclusive are inserted. The Representation of the People Act, 1951, the Representation of the People (Amendment) Act, 1974 and the Election Laws (Amendment) Act, 1975 are mentioned in Entry 87.

1974 AND 1975 AMENDMENT ACTS DESTROY BASIC STRUCTURE OF THE CONSTITUTION – CONTENDS RESPONDENT – CJI

12. The respondent contends that the Representation of the People (Amendment) Act, 1974 and the Election Laws (Amendment) Act, 1975 referred to as the Amendment Acts, 1974 and 1975 do not enjoy constitutional immunity because these Acts destroy or damage basic structure or basic features.

NOTICE WAS GIVEN TO THE ATTORNEY GENERAL – CJI

13. In view of the challenge by the respondent to the constitutional validity of the Amendment Acts, 1974 and 1975 notice was given to the Attorney-General.

39TH AMENDMENT CAME INTO FORCE ON 10.8.1975 – CJI

14. The appeals were to be heard on 11 August, 1975. In view of the Constitution (Thirty-ninth Amendment) Act, 1975 which came into existence on 10 August, 1975 the hearing was adjourned till 25 August, 1975.

CLAUSE (4) OF ARTICLE 329A UNCONSTITUTIONAL IN VIEW OF KESAVANANDA BHARATI'S CASE – CONTENDS RESPONDENT – CJI

15. The constitutional validity of clause (4) of Article 329A falls for consideration. Clause (4) of Article 329-A is challenged on two grounds. First, it destroys or damages the basic features or basic structure of the Constitution. Reliance is placed in support of the contention on the majority view of 7 learned Judges in **Keshavananda Bharti Sripadanagalavaru v. State of Kerala, 1973 Sup SCR 1.**

16. It should be stated here that the hearing has proceeded on the assumption that it is not necessary to challenge the majority view in **Keshvananda Bharati's** case. The contentions of the respondent are these: *First*, under Article 368 only general principles governing the organs of the State and the basic principles can be laid down. An amendment of the Constitution does not contemplate any decision in respect of individual cases. Clause (4) of Article 329A is said to be in exercise of a purely judicial power, which is not included in the constituent power conferred by Article 368.

17. *Second*, the control over the result of the elections and on the question whether the election of any person is valid or invalid is vested in the judiciary under the provisions of Article 329 and Article 136. The jurisdiction of judicial determination is taken away, and, therefore, the democratic character of the Constitution is destroyed.

18. *Third*, the Amendment destroys and abrogates the principle of equality. It is said that there is no rational basis for differentiation between persons holding high offices and other persons elected to Parliament.

19. *Fourth*, the rule of law is the basis for democracy and judicial review. The fourth clause makes the provisions of Part VI of the Representation of the People Act inapplicable to the election of the Prime Minister and the Speaker.

20. *Fifth*, clause (4) destroys not only judicial review but also separation of power. The order of the High Court declaring the election to be void is declared valid. The cancellation of the judgment is denial of political justice which is the basic structure of the Constitution.

SOME MPs KEPT UNDER ILLEGAL DETENTION BY GOVERNMENT AT THE TIME OF THIS AMENDMENT – HENCE THIS AMENDMENT WAS UNCONSTITUTIONAL – CONTENDS RESPONDENT – CJI

21. The second ground is that the constitution of the House which passed the Constitution (Thirty-ninth Amendment) Act is illegal. It is said that a number of members of Parliament of the two Houses were detained by executive order after 26 June, 1975. These persons were not supplied any grounds of detention or given any opportunity of making a representation against their detention. Unless the President convenes a session of the full Parliament by giving to all members thereof an opportunity to attend the session and exercise their right of speech and vote, the convening of the session will suffer from illegality and unconstitutionality and cannot be regarded as a session of the two Houses of Parliament. The mere fact that a person may be deprived of his right to move any court to secure his release from such illegal detention by means of a presidential order under Article 359 does not render the detention itself either legal or constitutional. The important leaders of the House have been prevented from participation. Holding of the session and transacting business are unconstitutional.

BASIC STRUCTURE OF EQUALITY VIOLATED BY KEEPING PM OR SPEAKER ABOVE THE LAW – CONTENDS RESPONDENT – CJI

22. Under the first ground these are the contentions. The Constitution Amendment affects the basic structure of institutional pattern adopted by the Constitution. The basic feature of separation of powers with the role of independence of judiciary is changed by denying jurisdiction of this Court to test the validity of the election. The essential feature of democracy will be destroyed if power is conceded to Parliament to declare the elections void according to law under which it has been held to be valid. This is illustrated by saying that Parliament can by law declare the election of persons against the predominant ruling party to be void. If the majority party controls the legislature and the executive, the legislature could not have any say as to whether the executive was properly elected. Free and fair elections are part of democratic structure and an election, which has been held to be invalid for violation of the principles of free and fair elections and by commission of corrupt practices is validated. The basic structure of equality is violated by providing that those who hold office of Prime Minister and Speaker are above law although election laws were there. The persons who will hold the office of Prime Minister and Speaker have been free from those laws and they are not under rule of law and there is no judicial review with regard to their elections.

CONSTITUENT POWER CANNOT TAKE OVER JUDICIAL POWER – CONTENDS RESPONDENT – CJI

23. The nature of the constituent power is legislative. The constituent power cannot exercise judicial power. Exercise of judicial power or of a purely executive power is not power of amendment of the Constitution. The Constitution may be amended to change constitutional provisions but the constituent power cannot enact that a person is declared to be elected. The consequence of change of law may be that the decision given by a court under the law as it stood will not stand.

JUDICIAL REVIEW IS ESSENTIAL FEATURE OF BASIC STRUCTURE – TAKEN AWAY BY CLAUSE (4) – CONTENDS RESPONDENT – CJI

24. The respondent contends that judicial review is an essential feature of basic structure because of the doctrine of separation of powers for these reasons: Judicial review is basic structure in the matter of election to ensure free, fair and pure election. In the American and the Australian Constitutions the judicial power of the State is located in the judiciary. There is no such provision in our Constitution. The Executive, the Legislature and the Judiciary are all treated under our Constitution with respective spheres. The jurisdiction of this Court and of High Courts under our Constitution is dealt with by Articles under the Heads of the Union Judiciary and the State Judiciary. Under Article 136 any Tribunal or Court is amenable to the jurisdiction of this Court. The corollary drawn from this is that if under clause (4) of the Thirty-ninth Amendment the power of judicial review is taken away it amounts to destruction of basic structure.

* * * * *

AS PER *CORPUS JURIS* – ELECTIONS ARE POLITICAL QUESTIONS – NOT IN JUDICIAL DOMAIN – CONTESTED ELECTIONS ARE LEGISLATIVE PARAMOUNT CONCERN – CJI

27. In *Corpus Juris* Vol. 16 (1956) it is said that the judiciary cannot exercise powers which are to be found in the other two departments of Government which are normally legislative or powers which are generally executive in their nature. All matters relating to or affecting elections are political questions and as such, are not questions for the Judiciary. All matters relating to or affecting elections are in the absence of controlling constitutional or statutory provisions to the contrary, political questions and, as such, are not questions for the Judiciary. So, subject to express constitutional restrictions, all matters relating to the holding of elections and determining their results, including contests are political questions (pp. 691, 692, 710).

28. In *Corpus Juris* Vol. 29 (1965) it is stated that under constitutional provision as to conferring on the legislature the power to determine by law, before what authority, and in what manner the trial or contested elections shall be conducted, the legislature is given broad power. A constitutional provision authorising the legislature to provide for the mode of contesting elections in all cases not otherwise specifically provided for in the Constitution itself confers on the legislature adequate authority to provide for all election contests and to determine where and by what means election contests shall be conducted. The right to contest an election is not a common law right. Elections belong to the political branch of the Government, and, in the absence of the special constitutional or statutory provisions, are beyond the control of the judicial power. (Sections 245, 246), A contested election case is a proceeding in which the public is interested, since it is for the public good. An election contest is not merely a proceeding for the adjudication and settlement of the private rights of rival claimants to an office. It is the public interest, not the parties' claims, which is the paramount legislative concern (Section 247).

* * * * *

JUDICIAL REVIEW CAN BE EXCLUDED IN MANY MATTERS – DETERMINING DISPUTED ELECTION CAN ALSO BE LEGISLATIVE POWER – HELD CJI

32. Judicial review in many matters under statute may be excluded. In many cases special jurisdiction is created to deal with matters assigned to such authorities. A special forum is even created to hear election disputes. A right of appeal may be conferred against such decision, if Parliament acts as the forum for determination of election disputes; it may be a question of parliamentary privilege and the courts may not entertain any review from such decisions. That is because the exercise of power by the Legislature in determining disputed elections may he called legislative power. A distinction arises between what can be called the traditional judicial determination by courts and tribunals on the one hand and the peculiar jurisdiction by the legislature in determining controverted elections on the other.

33. The legal order is a system of general and individual norms connected with each other according to the principle that law regulates its own creation. Each norm of this order is created according to the provisions of another norm and ultimately according to the provisions of the basic norm constituting the unity of this system, the legal order. A norm belongs to a certain legal order, because it is created by an organ of the legal community constituted by this order. Creation of law is application of law. The creation of a legal norm is normally an application of the higher norm, regulating its creation. The application of higher norm is the creation of a lower norm determined by the higher norm. A judicial decision is an act by which a general norm, a statute, is applied but at the same time an individual norm is created binding one on both parties to the conflict. Legislation is creation of law. Taking it into account is application of law. The higher norm may determine the organ and the procedure by which a lower norm and the contents of the lower norm are created. For a norm the creation of which is not determined at all by another norm cannot belong to another legal order. The individual creating a norm cannot be considered the organ of the legal community, his norm-creating function cannot be imputed to the community, unless in performing the function he applies a norm of the legal order constituting the community. Every law-creating act must be a law-applying act. It must apply a norm preceding the act in order to be an act of the legal order or the community constituted by it. When settling a dispute between two parties a court applies a general norm or statutory or customary law. Simultaneously, the court creates an individual norm providing that a definite sanction shall be executed against a definite individual. The individual norm is related to the general norm as the statute is related to the constitution. The judicial function is thus like legislation, both creation and application of law. The judicial function is ordinarily determined by the general norms both as to procedure and as to the contents of the norm to be created, whereas legislation is usually determined by the constitution only in the former respect.

34. The general norm, which attaches abstractly determined consequences, has to be applied to concrete cases in order that the sanction determined in abstract may be ordered and executed in concrete. The two essential elements of judicial functions are to apply a pre-existing general norm in which a certain consequence is attached to certain conditions. The existence of the concrete conditions in connection with the concrete consequence are what may be called individualization of the general and abstract norm to the individual norm of the judicial decision.

CONSTITUENT POWER CAN EXERCISE LEGISLATIVE JUDICIAL AND EXECUTIVE POWERS – HOLDS CJI

35. The contention is that the constituent power is an exercise in legislative process. The constituent power, it is said, can exercise legislative as well as judicial and executive powers. It is said that if a legislation can validate a matter declared invalid by a judgment the constituent power may equally do so. Special emphasis is laid on Article 105 of the Constitution which is amended by the Constitution (Thirty-ninth Amendment) Act. Article 105(e) speaks of disqualification by certain laws. The constitutional amendment seeks to amend Article 105 and remove the disqualification in the case of the Prime Minister and the Speaker. Reliance was placed on the decisions in **Abeyesekara v. Jayatilake, 1932 AC 260** and **Piare Dusadh v. The King Emperor, 1944 FCR 61** that an amendment is supportable to invalidate a judgment.

36. Abeyesekera's case (supra) is an authority for the proposition that the legal infirmity can be removed and active indemnity can be passed to relieve from penalties incurred.

LEGISLATURE CHANGES THE LAW FOR UNDOING A JUDGMENT – BY DOING SO IT EXERCISES LEGISLATIVE POWER – NOT JUDICIAL – DOES NOT ENCROACH UPON JUDICIAL POWER – HELD CJI

37. In **Piare Dusadh's** case (supra) the Special Criminal Courts (Repeal) Ordinance, 1943 which conferred validity and full effectiveness on sentences passed by special courts which functioned under the Special Criminal Courts Ordinance, 1942 was challenged. It was argued in **Piare Dusadh's** case (supra) that the 1943 Ordinance attempted to exercise judicial power. The Federal Court did not accept the contention on the ground that in India the legislature has enacted laws providing that suits which had been dismissed on a particular view of the law must be restored and retried. Our Federal Court said that Parliament simply takes up certain determinations which exist in fact, though made without authority, and prescribes not that they shall be acts done by a Board of Review, but that they shall be treated as they would be treated if they were such acts. The sections do not constitute an exercise of the judicial power. The legislature had not attempted to decide the question of the guilt or innocence of any of the accused. That question had as a matter of fact been decided by Tribunals which were directed to follow a certain judicial procedure. Our Federal Court held that once the decisions of the special courts were held void for want of jurisdiction the legislature created those special courts and authorised them to try cases and pass sentences. The legislature gave jurisdiction to the courts to pass the sentences. The Ordinance did not exercise any judicial power because the sentences in due course were subject to an appeal and review by the regular courts of the land.

38. The power of the legislature to validate matters which have been found by judgments or orders of competent courts and Tribunals to be invalid or illegal is a well-known pattern. The legislature validates acts and things done by which the basis of judgments or orders of competent courts and Tribunal is changed and the judgments and orders are made ineffective. All the Sales Tax Validation cases, the election validation cases are illustrations of that proposition. The present appeals are not of the type of providing indemnity against penalties or determining existing facts to be treated in accordance with change of law.

39. The effect of validation is to change the law so as to alter the basis of any judgment, which might have been given on the basis of old law and thus make the judgment ineffective. A formal declaration that the judgment rendered under the old Act is void, is not necessary. If the matter is pending in appeal, the appellate court has to give effect to the altered law and reverse the judgment. The rendering of a judgment ineffective by changing its basis by legislative enactment is not an encroachment on judicial power but a legislation within the competence of the Legislature rendering the basis of the judgment non est. If a competent court has found that a particular tax or levy has been imposed by a law, which is void because the legislature passing the law was not competent to pass the law, then the competent legislature has validated the tax or levy by a validation Act involving a re-enactment of the invalid law. Where the competent legislature has passed a law which is contrary to any of the Fundamental Rights in Part III of the Constitution and the law has been declared void by a competent court, the appropriate legislature has passed a retrospective law validating the actions taken under the old invalid law by curing the defects in the old law so as to make the new law consistent with Part III of the Constitution.

WHERE ELECTIONS ARE DECLARED INVALID BY REASON OF 'CORRUPT PRACTICES' – ARE VALIDATED BY CHANGING THE DEFINITION OF 'CORRUPT PRACTICES' – HOLDS CJI

40. Where invalid elections declared by reason of corrupt practices have been validated by changing the definition of corrupt practices in the Representation of the People Act, 1951 retrospectively the original judgment is rendered ineffective; See **Kanta Kathuria v. Manak Chand Surana, (1970) 2 SCR 835.**

A DIRECTION BY LEGISLATURE THAT A PROCEEDING PENDING IN COURT IS DISCHARGED IS A JUDICIAL ACT – AS NOTHING IS LEFT FOR THE COURT TO DECIDE WAS THE RATIO OF LAW IN BASANTA CHANDRA GHOSE'S CASE – HELD CJI

41. Our Federal Court in **Basanta Chandra Ghose v. The King Emperor, 1944 FCR 295** dealt with the validity and effect of Ordinance No. 3 of 1944. One of the objects of that Ordinance was to enact a presumption in the Ordinance itself in favour of detention orders to preclude their being questioned in courts of law and to take away or limit the power of the High Court to make orders under section 491 of the Cr.P.C. The third object of the Ordinance was challenged on the ground that section 10(2) of the Ordinance which provided that if at the commencement there is pending in any Court any proceeding by which the validity of an order having effect by virtue of section 6 as if it had been made under this Ordinance is called in question, that proceeding is hereby discharged. Section 10(2) of the Ordinance was challenged on the ground that this was in abrogation of judicial power by legislative authority. It was said that the legislative authority only passed the law and the disposal of the particular case could remain the function of the court. Section 10(2) of the Ordinance was said not to leave it to the court to apply the rule of law to the decision of cases but to discharge all pending proceedings. Our Federal Court noticed the distinction between a legislative act and the judicial act, and said "a direction such a proceeding is discharged is clearly a judicial act and not an enactment of law". In **Piare Dusadh's** case (supra) the latter Ordinance provided that the decisions of the earlier Tribunals which were negatived by a decision of the Federal Court should be treated as decisions of duly constituted Tribunals. That was held not to constitute a judicial power by the Ordinance making authority. In **Basanta Chandra Ghose's** case (supra) the Federal Court held section 10(2) of the Ordinance to be a direct disposal of cases by the legislature itself. **Basanta Chandra Ghose's** case (supra) was decided on the ground that the section in the Ordinance discharged the proceedings. There was nothing left to the Court.

CONSTITUENT POWER CAN MODIFY THE CONSTITUTION BUT CANNOT VALIDATE A VOID ELECTION – SUBMITS RESPONDENT

42. Counsel on behalf of the respondent contended that the constituent power could deal with amendments of the Constitution, but could not exercise constituent power in relation to validating an election.

In para 43 American Constitutional Law on Judicial Review was discussed, in para 44 Jullian Bond's case, in para 45 Adam Clayton Powell's case referred in para 29 were discussed.

JUDICIAL REVIEW IS NOT FOUNDED IN THE CONSTITUTION – THERE IS NO SEPARATION OF POWER IN THE CONSTITUENT POWER – HELD CJI

46. Judicial review is not to be founded on any Article similar to the American Constitution. In the Australian Constitution also the judicial power is located in the court. The doctrine of separation of powers is carded into effect in countries like America, Australia. In our Constitution there is separation of powers in a broad sense. But the larger question is whether there is any doctrine of separation of powers when it comes to exercise of constituent power. The doctrine of separation of powers as recognised in America is not applicable to our country. (See **Delhi Laws Act, 1951 SCR 747 at pp. 965-66; Jayantilal Sodhan v. F.N. Rana, (1964) 5 SCR 294; Chandra Mohan v. State of Uttar Pradesh, (1967) 1 SCR 77 (87)** and **Udai Ram Sharma v. Union of India, (1968) 3 SCR 41 at p. 67.**

PROCEDURE OF ELECTION LAW IS GIVEN BY PARLIAMENT – IT CAN CHANGE ALSO – IT CAN TAKE OVER TO ITSELF – HELD CJI

47. The rigid separation of powers as under the American Constitution or under the Australian Constitution does not apply to our country. Many powers which are strictly judicial have been excluded from the purview of the courts. The whole subject of election has been left to courts traditionally under the common Law and election disputes and matters are governed by the Legislature. The question of the determination of election disputes has particularly been regarded as a special privilege of Parliament in England. It is a Political question in the United States. Under our Constitution Parliament has inherited all the privileges, powers and immunities of the British House of Commons. In the case of election disputes Parliament has defined the procedure by law. It can at any time change that procedure and take over itself the whole question. There is, therefore, no question of any separation of powers being involved in matters concerning elections and election petitions.

CONSTITUENT POWER IS SOVEREIGN – COVERS LEGISLATIVE, JUDICIAL AND EXECUTIVE POWERS – HELD CJI

48. When the constituent power exercises powers the constituent power comprises legislative, executive and judicial powers. All powers flow from the constituent power through the Constitution to the various departments or heads. In the hands of the constituent authority there is no demarcation of powers. It is only when the constituent authority defines the authorities or demarcates the areas that separation of power is discussed. The constituent power is independent of the doctrine of separation of powers. The constituent power is sovereign. It is the power which creates the organs and distributes the powers.

49. The constituent power is *sui generis*. It is different from legislative power. The position of unlimited law making power is the criterion of legal sovereignty. The constituent power is sovereign because the Constitution flows from the constituent power.

50. In Article 329A an exercise of judicial power is the question for determination. In regulative processes there may be judicial process. If the legislature has to fix the amount or lay down the principle for fixation of amount the question will arise as to whether this is exercise of judicial power. The determination of the amount will involve judicial procedure. When the legislature determines the amount the fixation of amount is purely by legislative process. But in doing so the legislature takes into account factors relevant to individual properties.

CONSTITUENT POWER IS HIGHER THAN LEGISLATIVE POWER – HELD CJI

51. Every organ of the State has to ascertain facts which make the foundation of its own decision. The executive usually collects its materials through its departments. The judiciary acts in a field where there are two or more parties before it and upon evidence placed before it pronounces its verdict according to principles of natural justice. The legislature is entitled to obtain information from any source. The legislature may call witnesses. The rule of *Audi Alterm Partem* is not applicable in a legislative process. Legislation is usually general. It may sometimes be for special reasons an individual case. There is no doubt that the constituent power is not the same as legislative power. The distinction between constituent power and legislative power is always to be borne in mind because the constituent power is higher in norm.

JUDICIAL REVIEW CAN BE ELIMINATED EVEN BY LEGISLATIVE MEASURES – DOES NOT MEAN EQUALITY IS VIOLATED – HELD CJI

52. Judicial review in election disputes is not a compulsion. Judicial review of decisions in election disputes may be entrusted by law to a Judicial Tribunal. If it is to a Tribunal or to the High Court the judicial review will be attracted either under the relevant law providing for appeal to this Court or Article 136 may be attracted. Under Article 329(b) the contemplated law may vest the power to entertain election petitions in the House itself which may determine the dispute by a resolution after receiving a report from a special Committee, in such judicial review may be eliminated without involving amendment of the Constitution. The Constitution permits by amendment exclusion of judicial review of a matter if it is necessary to give effect to the Directive Principles of State Policy. A similar power may be available when such exclusion is needed in the larger interest of the security of the State. In either case the exclusion of judicial review does not mean that principles of equality are violated. It only means that the appropriate body making the law satisfied itself and determines conclusively that principles of equality have not been violated. That body conclusively makes classification for the purpose of applying the principles of equality. It is said that in this class of cases the answer to the question of the validity of the classification rests on factors to which the court has no access and the materials may be of highly confidential nature and the decision has to be on a matter of political necessity. If judicial review is excluded the court is not in a position to conclude that principles of equality have been violated.

EQUALITY CAN BE CLASSIFIED BY LEGISLATION IN PUBLIC INTEREST – HELD CJI

53. Equality of status as well as equality of opportunity is a fundamental right in Articles 14 and 16 of the Constitution. It also means equality before law and equal protection of the laws. Equality is spoken in the Preamble. There is liberty to legislature to classify to establish equality. When Articles 31A and 31B eliminated judicial review the meaning was not that the legislature would go on discriminating. The task of classification can be left to the legislature. It is the very nature of legislation that classification must be in public interest. The amending body has excluded judicial review in Articles 31A, 31B and 31C.

54. Exclusion of the operation of the equality principle from some fields is constitutionally possible, Article 33 excludes judicial review in matters relating to the Armed Forces. Article 262(2) excludes jurisdiction of courts in water disputes.

CONCEPT OF FREE AND FAIR ELECTIONS – IS NOT A BASIC STRUCTURE – HELD CJI

55. Decisions in election disputes may be made by the legislature itself or may be made by courts or tribunals on behalf of the legislature or may be made by courts and tribunals on their own exercising judicial functions. The concept of free and fair election is worked out by the Representation of the People Act. The Act provides a definition of "corrupt practice" for the guidance of the court. In making the law the legislature acts on the concept of free and fair election. In any legislation relating to the validity of elections the concept of free and fair elections is an important consideration. In the process of election the concept of free and fair election is worked out by formulating the principles of franchise, and the free exercise of franchise. In cases of disputes as to election, the concept of free and fair election means that disputes are fairly and justly decided. Electoral offences are statutory ones. It is not possible to hold that the concept of free and fair election is a basic structure, as contended for by the respondent. Some people may advocate universal franchise. Some people may advocate proportional representation. Some people may advocate educational qualifications for voters. Some people may advocate property qualifications for voters. Instances can be multiplied on divergence of views in regard to qualifications for voters qualifications of members, forms of corrupt practices. That is why there is law relating to and regulating elections.

IMPLICATIONS OF CLAUSE (4) OF ARTICLE 329A – CJI

56. Clause (4) in Article 329A has done four things. *First*, it has wiped out not merely the judgment but also the election petition and the law relating thereto. *Secondly*, if has deprived the right to raise a dispute about the validity of the election by not having provided another forum. *Third* there is no judgment to deal with and no right or dispute to adjudicate upon. *Fourth,* the constituent power of its own legislative judgment has validated the election.

57. At the outset it has to be noticed that constituent power is not the same as ordinary law making power. On behalf of the appellant it was rightly contended that if any amendment of Article 105 of the Constitution had to be made, it had to be made by amendment of the Constitution. The matter does not rest there.

CLAUSE (4) OF ARTICLE 329A ELIMINATES LAW PRIOR TO 39TH AMENDMENT – OFFENDS THE RULE OF LAW – IT MEANS NO ELECTION PETITION – NO ELECTION DISPUTE – NO NORMS TO BE APPLIED – NO DECISION – HOLDS CJI

58. If no law prior to the Constitution (Thirty-ninth Amendment) Act will apply to election petitions or matters connected therewith the result is that there is not only no forum for adjudication of election disputes but that there is also no election petition in the eye of law. The insurmountable difficulty is in regard to the process and result of validating the election by clause (4). Two answers were given on behalf of the appellant. One was that the validation of the election is itself the law. The other was that the constituent power applied its own norms to the election petition. Both the answers are unacceptable. If the election petition itself did not have any existence in law there was no petition which could be looked into by the constituent power. If there was no petition to look into it is difficult to comprehend as to what norms were applied to the election dispute. The dispute has to be seen. The dispute has to be adjudicated upon

59. Clause (4) suffers from these infirmities. *First,* the forum might be changed but another forum has to be created. If the constituent power became itself the forum to decide the disputes the constituent power by repealing the law in relation to election petitions and matters connected therewith did not have any petition to seize upon to deal with the same. *Secondly* any decision is to be made in accordance with law. Parliament has power to create law and apply the same. In the present case, the constituent power did not have any law to apply to the case, because the previous law did not apply and no other law was applied by clause (4). The validation of the election in the present case is, therefore, not by applying any law and it, therefore, offends Rule of Law.

THERE IS SEPARATION OF POWER BETWEEN JUDICIARY, EXECUTIVE AND LEGISLATURE UNDER OUR CONSTITUTION – HOLDS CJI

60. It is true that no express mention is made in our Constitution of vesting in the judiciary the judicial power as is to be found in the American Constitution. But a division of the three main functions of Government is recognised in our Constitution. Judicial power in the sense of the judicial power of the State is vested in the Judiciary. Similarly, the Executive and the Legislature are vested with powers in their spheres, Judicial power has lain in the hands of the Judiciary prior to the Constitution and also since the Constitution. It is not the intention that the powers of the Judiciary should be named to or be shared by the Executive or the Legislature or that the powers of the Legislature or the Executive should pass to or be shared by the Judiciary.

CHANGES MADE BY AMENDMENT ACTS 1974 AND 1975 ARE APPLICABLE TO ALL – RETROSPECTIVE LEGISLATION IS NOT BAD IN LAW – HELD CJI

61. The constituent power is sovereign. Law making power is subject to the Constitution. Parliament may create forum to hear election disputes. Parliament may itself hear election disputes. Whichever body will hear election disputes will have to apply norms. Norms are legal standards. There is no discrimination if classification on national basis is made for determination of disputes relating to persons holding the office of Prime Minister or the Speaker. The changes effected by the Amendment Acts 1974 and 1975 apply to all and there is no discrimination. Retrospective legislation is not by itself discrimination. The changes introduced to the 1951 Act apply to all.

CLAUSE (4) HAS PASSED A DECLARATORY JUDGMENT NOT LAW – HELD CJI

62. Clause 4 of Article 329A in the present case invalidating the election has passed a declaratory judgment and not a law. The legislative judgment in clause 4 is an exercise of judicial power. The constituent power can exercise judicial power but it has to apply law.

63. The validation of the election is not by applying legal norms. Nor can it be said that the validation of election in clause 4 is by norms set up by the constituent power.

APPEAL CANNOT BE DISPOSED OF IN CONFORMITY WITH CLAUSE (4) – IT HAS TO BE HEARD – HELD CJI

64. Clause 5 in Article 329-A states that an appeal against any order of any court referred to in clause 4 pending, before the commencement of the Constitution (Thirty-ninth Amendment) Act, 1975, before the Supreme Court, shall be disposed of in conformity with the provisions of Clause 4. The appeal cannot be disposed of in conformity with the provisions of Clause 4 in as much as the validation of the election cannot rest on clause 4.

65. In view of the conclusion that the appeal cannot be disposed of in conformity with clause 4, it is necessary to hear the appeals on other grounds in accordance with the provisions of the 1951 Act and the Amendment Acts, 1974 and 1975.

PROCEEDINGS OF LOK SABHA AND RAJYA SABHA WERE INVALID AS SOME MPs WERE UNDER DETENTION BY EXECUTIVE ORDER – SO AMENDMENTS WERE ALSO INVALID – CONTENDS RESPONDENT

66. The second contention of the respondent is that the session of the Lok Sabha and the Rajya Sabha is invalid for these reasons. If the Executive illegally and unconstitutionally detains any person the detention affects the validity of the proceedings. A number of members of Parliament of the two Houses, namely, the Lok Sabha and the Rajya Sabha were detained by executive orders after 26th June, 1975 and before the summoning of a session of the two Houses of Parliament. Parliament commenced the sessions on 21st July, 1975. None of the members of Parliament were either supplied any grounds of detention or given any opportunity to make any representation against their detention. The President who was the authority to summon a session of Parliament issued the Presidential Order under Article 359 of the Constitution on 27th June, 1975. The right of the detained members of Parliament to move any court for the enforcement of their fundamental right under Article 22 of the Constitution was taken away by the executive order of the President who became a party to the unconstitutional and illegal detention of the members of Parliament by preventing them from securing their release.

67. The constitutional position of the two Houses of Parliament is governed by the provisions of Articles 79 and 81 of the Constitution. The respondent contends that unless the President convenes a session of the Full Parliament by giving to all members thereof an opportunity to attend the session and exercise their right to speech and vote, the convening of the session will suffer from illegality and unconstitutionality and cannot be regarded as a session of the two Houses of

Parliament. Any business transacted in a session of such truncated House cannot, therefore, be regarded in law as a session of a House.

68. The mere fact that a person who is under unconstitutional and illegal detention may be deprived of his right to move a court to secure his release from such illegal detention by means of a Presidential Order under Article 359 is said by the respondent not to render the detention of a person either legal or constitutional, and, therefore, such a detenu must be provided an opportunity to participate in the proceedings of the House. It is emphasised by the respondent that when important leaders of different parties are unconstitutionally prevented from participating in the session of the House, a session cannot be held for deliberations in which different members influence the views of others by their own participation. If in the holding of a session and in transacting business therein, the provisions of the Constitution are not complied with, this is said to amount to illegality or unconstitutionality and not a mere procedural irregularity within the meaning of Article 122(1) of the Constitution.

69. The essence of the respondent's contention is that the right of participation of some members of the House of Parliament in the proceedings of Parliament under Article 105(3) of the Constitution has been interfered with. When a member is excluded from participating in the proceedings of the House, that is a matter concerning Parliament and the grievance of exclusion is in regard to proceedings within the walls of Parliament. In regard to rights to be exercised within the walls of the House the House itself is the judge; See *May's Parliamentary Practice,* 18th Ed. pp. 82-83, (1884) 12 QBD 271 at pp. 285-286.

* * * * *

74. The composition of Parliament is not dependent on inability of a member to attend for whatsoever reason. The purpose of Article 85 is to give effect to the collective right of the House which represents the nation to be called as often as the situation demands, and in any case the interval between two sessions must not exceed six months. Assuming a conflict were to arise between the privileges of member under Article 105(3) and the functions of the House to assemble under Article 85 the privilege of the member will not prevail. The detention of members of Parliament is by a statutory authority in the exercise of his statutory powers.

75. The suspension under Article 359 of the remedy for the enforcement of fundamental rights is dependent on a Proclamation of Emergency under Article 352. Parliament has the power not to approve of the Proclamation and, thereafter the emergency shall cease to operate. The contention of the respondent means that Parliament cannot meet even so as to withhold approval of the emergency and thus terminate the suspension of the members right of moving the Court. The Constitution provides for proclamation of emergency, the suspension of the remedy under Article 359 for enforcement of fundamental rights enabling even detention of members of Parliament when necessary. Article 85 is not suspended. The six months rule is obligatory. It follows that the members' rights under Article 105 are not available under a detention in these circumstances. For the purposes of Article 105(3) a conviction under Penal laws or detention under Emergency laws must be deemed to be valid till it is set aside.

DURING EMERGENCY RIGHTS CONFERRED BY PART III REMAIN SUSPENDED – HELD CJI

76. When under Article 359 the President during the operation of a Proclamation of Emergency by order declares that the right to move any Court for the enforcement of rights conferred by Part III shall remain suspended and persons who are members of House of Parliament are in detention under orders made under the Maintenance of Internal Security Act, the detention cannot be challenged by collateral attack on the ground of deprivation of their participation in the Parliamentary proceedings. The challenge will be questioning the detention on the ground that the detention is in violation of Articles 19, 21 and 22.

ARTICLE 85 MANDATES THAT PARLIAMENT HAS TO MEET WITHIN 6 MONTHS – HELD CJI

77. Article 85 provides that not more than six months shall intervene between the two Sessions of Parliament. Article 85 is not a provision regarding the constitution of Parliament but of holding of Sessions. The powers, privileges and immunities of Parliament and its members as provided in Article 105 are that they shall be such as may be defined by Parliament by law, and, until so, defined, shall be those of the House of Commons of the Parliament of the United Kingdom.

PARLIAMENTARY PRIVILEGE OF MPs OF FREEDOM FROM ARREST IS LIMITED – HELD CJI

78. In **Special Reference No. 1 of 1964 (1965) 1 SCR 413** it was held that the court could entertain a petition under Article 226 on the ground that the imposition of penalty by the legislature on a person who is not a member of the legislature or issuing process against such person for its contempt committed outside the four walls of the House.

79. The scope of the parliamentary privilege of freedom from arrest has been defined positively and negatively. The positive aspect of the privilege is expressed in the claim of the Commons to freedom from arrest in all civil actions or suits during the time of Parliament and during the period when a member was journeying or returning from Parliament. The privilege has been defined negatively in the claim of the Commons which specifically excepted treason, felony and breach of surety of the peace.

80. The privilege of freedom from arrest is limited to civil cases, and has not been allowed to interfere with the administration of criminal justice or emergency legislation. (See *May's Parliamentary Practice,* 18th Edn. at p. 100). In early times the distinction between "civil" and "criminal" was not clearly expressed. The development of the privilege has shown a tendency to confine it more, narrowly to cases of a civil character and to exclude not only every kind of criminal case, but also cases which, while not strictly criminal partake more of a criminal than of a civil character. This development is in conformity with the principle laid down by the Commons in a conference with the Lords in 1641: "Privilege of Parliament is granted in regard of service of the Commonwealth and is not to be used to the danger of the Commonwealth".

* * * * *

82. These being the general declarations of the law of Parliament, the House will not allow even the sanctuary of its walls to protect a Member from the process of criminal law, although a service of a criminal process on a Member within the precincts of Parliament, whilst the House is sitting without obtaining the leave of the House, would be a breach of privilege.

* * * * *

ORDER OF DETENTION PASSED UNDER STATUTORY POWER – FUNDAMENTAL RIGHTS SUSPENDED BY PROPER AUTHORITY – ARTICLE 105 IS NOT VIOLATED BY DETENTION – NOR IT GIVES RIGHT TO CHALLENGE DETENTION – HELD CJI

84. In **K. Anandan Nambiar v. Chief Secretary Government of Madras, (1966) 2 SCR 406** the petitioners who were members of Parliament and detained by orders passed by the State Government under rule 30(1)(b) of the Defence of India Rules, 1962 challenged the validity of the orders of detention on the ground that rule 30(1) (b) was not valid because "a legislator cannot be detained so as to prevent him from exercising his constitutional rights as such legislator while the legislative chamber to which he belongs is in session." The State raised a preliminary objection that the petitions were incompetent in view of the order issued by the President under article 359(1) suspending the rights of any person to move any Court for the enforcement of rights conferred by articles 14, 21 and 22. This Court held that the validity of the Act, Rule or order made under the Presidential Order could not be questioned on the ground that they contravene articles 14, 21 and 22.

85. The petitioners also contended in **Nambiar's** case (supra) that rule 30(1) (b) under which the orders of detention had been passed was invalid on grounds other than those based on articles 14, 19, 21 and 22. The Court held that if that plea was well founded, the last clause of the Presidential Order was not satisfied, and, therefore could, the bar created by it suspending the citizens' fundamental rights under articles 14, 21 and 22 not be pressed into service by the respondent.

86. Articles 79, 85, 86, 100(1) and 105(3) were considered in **Nambiar's** case (supra) in relation to rights of Members of Parliament, and it was held that the totality of rights cannot claim the status of fundamental rights and freedom of speech on which reliance was placed is a part of the privileges falling under Article 105. The reason is that freedom from arrest under a detention order is not recognised as a privilege which can be claimed by members of House of Commons in England. This Court then posed the question that if a claim for freedom from arrest by a detention order could not be sustained under the privileges of the Members of Parliament whether it could be sustained on the ground that it is a constitutional right which could not be contravened. The statement in *May's Parliamentary Practice,* 7th Edn. at p. 78 which is to be found in the 18th Edition at p. 100 that the privilege of freedom from arrest is limited to civil causes, and has not been allowed to interfere with the administration of criminal justice or emergency legislation was accepted as the basis of two propositions laid down in **Nambiar's** case (supra), First, articles 79, 85, 86, 100 and 105 cannot be construed to confer any right as such on individual Members or impose any obligation on them. It is not as if a Member of Parliament is bound to attend the session, or is under an obligation to be present in the House when the President addresses it. The context in which these articles appear shows that the subject-matter of these Articles is not the individual rights of the Members of Parliament, but they refer to the right of the President to issue a summons for the ensuing session of Parliament or to address the House or Houses. Second, the freedom of speech to which article 105 refers would be available to a Member of Parliament when he attends the session of the Parliament. If the order of detention validly prevents him from attending a session of Parliament, no occasion arises for the exercise of the right of freedom of speech and no complaint can be made that the said right has been invalidly invaded.

THERE WAS NO VALID SESSION OF PARLIAMENT – PROCEEDING ILLEGAL – CONTENTION OF RESPONDENT – REJECTED – CJI

87. The second ground of challenge that there was no valid session of the House cannot be accepted for the reasons given above. It has also to be stated that it is not open to the respondent to challenge the orders of detention collaterally. The principle is that what is directly forbidden cannot be indirectly achieved.

FINDING OF HIGH COURT AND THE FINAL ORDER PASSED – DISCUSSED – HELD CJI

88. The High Court found first that the appellant has to be regarded as a candidate from 29th December, 1970 as she held herself out on that date as a candidate.

The second finding is that the appellant obtained and procured the assistance of Yashpal Kapur for the furtherance of her election prospects when Yashpal Kapur was serving as a Gazetted Officer within the Government of India. The High Court found that Yashpal Kapur's resignation from his service though submitted on 13th January, 1971 did not become effective until 25th January, 1971 when it was notified. The further finding by the High Court is that Yashpal Kapur under the instructions of the appellant delivered election speech on 7th January, 1971 at Munshi Gani and another speech at Kalan on 19th January, 1971. The third finding by the High Court is that the appellant and her election agent Yashpal Kapur procured and obtained the assistance of the officers of the State Government, particularly, the District Magistrate, the Superintendent of Police, the Executive Engineer. P.W.D. and the Engineer to Hydel Department for the construction of rostrums and arrangement for supply of power for loudspeakers at meetings addressed by the appellant on 1st February, 1971 and 25th February, 1971 and further that the said assistance was for furtherance of the prospects of election of the appellant. The High Court found the appellant guilty of corrupt practice under section 123(7) of the 1951 Act. The High Court declared the election of the appellant to be void. The High Court also held the appellant to be disqualified for a period of six years from the date of the order.

DEFINITION OF 'CANDIDATE' AS PER THE AMENDED LAW CHANGED RETROSPECTIVELY – HELD CJI

89. The definition of "candidate" in section 79(b) of the 1951 Act until the amendment thereof by the Election Laws (Amendment) Act, 1975 was as follows:—

> 'Candidate' means a person who has been or claims to have been duly nominated as a candidate at any election and any such person shall be deemed to have been a candidate as from the time when, with the election in prospect, he began to hold himself out as a prospective candidate. "

90. This definition has now been substituted by section 7 of the Amendment Act, 1975, as follows:

> "'Candidate' means a person who has been or claims to have been duly nominated as a candidate at any election."

91. Section 10 of the Amendment Act, 1975 further enacted that the amendments shall have retrospective operation so as to apply to and in relation to any election held before the commencement of the Amendment Act, 1975 on 6th August, 1975 to either House of Parliament or to either House or the House of the Legislature of a State, *inter alia,* (iv) in respect of which appeal from any order of any High Court made in any election petition under section 98 or section 99 of the 1951 Act is pending before the Supreme Court immediately before such commencement.

92. Section 9 of the Amendment Act, 1975 has substituted clause (a) in section 171A of the Indian Penal Code and a "candidate" means for the purpose of section 171A of the Indian Penal Code a person who has been nominated as a candidate at any election. Previously the definition of "candidate" in section 171A of the Indian Penal Code was the same as in section 79(b) of the 1951 Act prior to the amendment thereof by the Amendment Act, 1975. In section 171A of the Indian Penal Code there was a proviso to the effect that candidate would mean a person who holds himself out as a prospective candidate provided he is subsequently nominated as a candidate.

APPELLANT WAS A CANDIDATE ON THE DATE OF NOMINATION FILED ON 1.2.1971 UNDER THE LAW AMENDED RETROSPECTIVELY – CONTENDS APPELLANT

93. Relying on the provisions introduced by the Amendment Act, 1975, it is contended on behalf of the appellant that she will be regarded as a candidate only from 1st February, 1971, namely, the date when she has been duly nominated as a candidate at her election, and, therefore, the finding of the High Court cannot be sustained. It is also contended by the appellant that the finding of the High Court that Yashpal Kapur delivered election speeches on 7th January, 1971 and 19th January, 1971 under instructions of the appellant cannot be supported because the appellant was not a candidate either on 7th January, 1971 or on 19th January, 1971.

RESIGNATION OF YASHPAL KAPUR STOOD ACCEPTED ON 14.1.1971 AS PER LAW AMENDED RETROSPECTIVELY – CONTENDS APPELLANT

94. The second finding by the High Court with regard to the resignation of Yashpal Kapur not to be effective until 25th January, 1971 is contended to be displaced by legislative change by the Amendment Act 1975. Section 8(b) of the Amendment Act, 1975 has introduced Explanation (3) at the end of section 123(7) of the 1951 Act.

This Amendment has retrospective operation.

95. The Explanation is as follows:

> "(3) For the purposes of clause (7), notwithstanding anything contained in any other law, the publication in the Official Gazette of the appointment, resignation, termination of service, dismissal or removal from service of a person in the service of the Central Government (including a person serving in connection with the administration of a Union territory) or of a State Government shall be conclusive proof—
>
> (i) of such appointment, resignation, termination of service, dismissal or removal from service, as the case may be, and
>
> (ii) where the date of taking effect of such appointment, resignation, termination of service, dismissal or removal from service, as the case may be, is stated in such publication, also of the fact that such person was appointed with effect from the said date, or in the case of resignation, termination of service, dismissal or removal from service, such person ceased to be in such service with effect from the said date. "

96. The effect of Explanation (3) at the end of section 123(7) of the 1951 Act incorporated by the notification dated 25th January, 1971 in the Gazette dated 6th February, 1971 makes the fact of the resignation of Yashpal Kapur from his service fully effective from 14th January, 1971. It is, therefore, contended that from 14th January, 1971 Yashpal Kapur was not a Government servant.

UNDER THE LAW AMENDED RETROSPECTIVELY APPELLANT HAS NOT COMMITTED ANY 'CORRUPT PRACTICE' – CONTENDS APPELLANT

97. To constitute a corrupt practice within the meaning of section 123(7) of the 1951 Act, the act complained of must be an act of obtaining or procuring of assistance of the categories of Government servants mentioned therein by the candidate or his election agent or by any other person with the consent of the candidate or his election agent. Section 100(1)(b) of the 1951 Act enacts that if the High Court is of opinion that any corrupt practice has been committed by a returned candidate or his election agent or by any other person with the consent of a returned candidate or his election agent, the High Court shall declare the election of the returned candidate to be void. A returned candidate is defined in section 79(f) of the 1951 Act to mean a candidate whose name has been published under section 67 of the 1951 Act as duly elected. A returned candidate in order to be guilty of a corrupt practice within the meaning of section 123(7) of the 1951 Act must be guilty of any of the acts mentioned in the different sub-sections of section 123 as a candidate. The appellant contends that the appellant was not a candidate on 7th January, 1971 or 19th January, 1971 and there could not be any procuring or obtaining of any assistance by the appellant as a candidate or by anybody else with the consent of the appellant. All the sub-sections of section 123 of the 1951 Act refer to the acts of a candidate or his election agent or any other person with the consent of the candidate or his election agent. The present definition of "candidate" which has retrospective effect is contended to exclude completely acts by candidate prior to the date he is nominated as a candidate.

UNDER THE LAW AMENDED RETROSPECTIVELY ARRANGEMENT MADE OR FACILITY RENDERED BY GAZETTED OFFICERS – U.P. GOVERNMENT – IN DISCHARGE OF OFFICIAL DUTY, DID NOT AMOUNT TO RENDERING ASSISTANCE, FOR THE FURTHERANCE OF ELECTION PROSPECTS – CONTENDS APPELLANT

98. The third finding by the High Court that the appellant and her election agent Yashpal Kapur procured and obtained the assistance of the officers of the State Government, particularly, the District Magistrate, the Superintendent of Police, the Executive Engineer, P.W.D. and the Engineer to Hydel Department for construction of rostrums and arrangement for supply of power for loudspeakers and for their assistance for furtherance of the prospects of the election of the appellant has to be tested in the light of the provisions contained in section 123(7) of the 1951 Act. Under the said provision obtaining or procuring by candidate or his agent any assistance for the furtherance of the prospect of that candidate from Gazetted Officers is corrupt practice. The Amendment Act, 1975 by section 8 thereof has added a proviso to section 123(7) of the 1951 Act. The proviso is as follows:

> "Provided that where any person, in the service of the Government and belonging to any of the classes aforesaid, in the discharge or purported discharge of his official duty makes any arrangements or provides any facility or does any other act or thing for, to, or in relation to any candidate or his agent or any other person acting with the consent of the candidate or his election agent, (whether by reason of the office held by the candidate or for any other reason), such arrangement, facility or act or thing shall not be deemed to be assistance for the furtherance of the prospects of that candidate's election".

99. The proviso aforesaid shows that where persons in the service of the Government in the discharge of official duty make any arrangement or provide any facility or do any act or thing in relation to a candidate, such arrangement and facility shall not be deemed to be assistance for furtherance of the prospect of the candidate's election. Therefore, the service rendered by Government servants for construction of rostrums and arrangement for supply of power for loudspeakers according to the contention of the appellant could not be considered as assistance for the furtherance of the prospects of the election of the appellant.

IF AMENDMENT ACTS 1974 AND 1975 ARE HELD VALID, APPELLANT SUCCEEDS – HELD CJI

100. The contentions of the appellant can succeed if the Amendment Acts of 1974 and 1975 are valid. The respondent has challenged the constitutional validity of these Acts. Therefore, that question has to be examined before the appellant's contentions can be answered.

IN CROSS-APPEAL, RESPONDENT CHALLENGES FINDING OF HIGH COURT ON ISSUE NOS. 9 AND 6 – HELD CJI

101. The respondent in cross-appeal challenged the findings of the High Court on issue No. 9 and contended that the High Court should have held that the election expenses of the appellant exceeded the limit. The respondent also challenged the finding of the High Court with regard to issue No. 6 and contended that the High Court should have held that the symbol of cow and calf was a religious symbol and the appellant committed corrupt practice as defined in section 123(3) of the 1951 Act. The respondent did not press issue Nos. 4 and 5 which related to distribution of quilts, blankets, dhoties and liquor. The respondent also abandoned Issue No. 7 which related to voters being conveyed to the polling stations free of charge on vehicles hired and procured by Yashpal Kapur.

102. The issue pressed by the respondent was that the appellant and her election agent Yashpal Kapur incurred or authorised expenditure in excess of the amount prescribed by section 77 of the 1951 Act read with rule 90. The respondent alleged that the election expenses of the appellant, inter alia, were Rs. 1,28,700 on account of hiring charges of vehicles, Rs. 43,230 on account of cost of petrol and diesel; Rs. 9,900 on account of payment made to the drivers of the vehicles. The respondent further alleged that the appellant spent Rs. 1,32,000 on account of construction of rostrums for public meetings on 1st February, 1971 and 25th February, 1971. The respondent contended that the findings of the High Court should be reversed.

ELECTION EXPENSES OF APPELLANT WERE WITHIN LIMITS – HIGH COURT HELD – HOLDS CJI

103. The High Court found that the election expenses furnished by the appellant were Rs. 12,892.97. The High Court added another sum of Rs. 18,183.50. The three items which were added by the High Court were cost of erection of rostrums amounting to Rs. 16,000, cost incurred in installation of loudspeakers amounting to Rs. 1,951 and cost for providing car transport to respondent No. 1 amounting to Rs. 232. 50. The total election expenses found by the High Court came to Rs. 31,976.47 which was below the prescribed limit of Rs. 35,000.

HIRING CHARGES OF CARS BY APPELLANT – NOT PROVED – HIGH COURT HELD

104. With regard to hiring charges of vehicles the High Court found that the respondent did not examine any witness to indicate as to whether the vehicles were used only for party propaganda or they were used in connection with the election of the appellant. The High Court further found that the documents which were relied on by the respondent did not establish that the vehicles had been engaged or used in connection with the election work of the appellant.

FINDING OF HIGH COURT REGARDING HIRING CHARGES OF CARS UPHELD – CJI

105. The respondent repeated the following contentions which had been advanced before the High Court. Dal Bahadur Singh, President, District Congress Committee wrote a letter to the District Election Officer intimating that 23 vehicles had been engaged by the District Congress Committee for election work in Raebareli, Amethi and Ram Sanehi Ghat constituencies, and, therefore, the vehicles should be derequisitioned. Dal Bahadur Singh thereafter wrote a note to Yashpal Kapur and requested that the letter be sent to the District Election Officer to that effect. Yashpal Kapur wrote a letter to the District Election Officer and repeated the prayer contained in Dal Bahadur Singh's letter. It was, therefore, contended that because Yashpal

Kapur was the election agent of the appellant and he moved for the derequisition of the vehicles it should be inferred that the vehicles were engaged for the election of the appellant. Yashpal Kapur said that the vehicles were used in the three Parliamentary constituencies. The High Court rightly held that the evidence did not establish that the vehicles had been used for the election work of the appellant. The High Court also correctly found that there was no evidence to show that Yashpal Kapur made any propaganda from the vehicles in any manner for the purpose of the election.

HIGH COURT PARTLY ACCEPTED PLEA OF RESPONDENT ON ROSTRUMS EXPENSES – HELD CJI

106. With regard to the expenses for the erection of rostrums the respondent contended that the appellant's election expenses should include Rs. 1,32,000 as the costs for erection of rostrums for the meetings on 1st February, 1971 and the meeting on 25th February, 1971. The High Court held that Rs. 16,000 could only be added to the election expenses of the appellant consisting of Rs. 6,400 for four rostrums and Rs. 9,600 for six rostrums.

UNDER AMENDED LAW EVEN ROSTRUM EXPENSES COULD NOT BE ADDED IN ELECTION EXPENSES OF THE APPELLANT – HELD CJI

107. The amount of Rs. 16,000 which was added by the High Court on account of cost of erection of rostrums cannot be included in the election expenses of the appellant by reason of amendment to section 77 of the 1951 Act by the Amendment Act, 1975, Explanation 3 has been added as follows:

> "For the removal of doubt, it is hereby declared that any expenditure incurred in respect of any arrangements made, facilities provided or any other act or thing done by any person in the service of the Government and belonging to any of the classes mentioned in clause (7) of section 123 in the discharge or purported discharge of the official duty as mentioned in the proviso to that clause shall not be deemed to be expenditure in connection with the election incurred or authorised by a candidate or by his election agent for the purposes of this sub-section".

108. By the Amendment Act, 1975 a proviso has been added to section 123(7) of the 1951 Act to the effect that arrangements made or facilities provided or any act done by a Government servant belonging to the class mentioned there in the discharge of official duty shall not be deemed to be assistance for furtherance of the prospects of that candidate's election. All these amendments have retrospective operation. Therefore, the cost of rostrums cannot be added to the election expenses of the appellant. Services rendered by Government servants for the erection of rostrums and for supply of power for loudspeakers cannot be deemed to be assistance for the furtherance of the prospects of that candidate's election.

NO PLEADINGS FOR OTHER ALLEGED EXPENSES – NOT ACCEPTABLE – CJI

109. The respondent contended that Exhibit 118 which was the Bank account of the District Congress Committee showed on the one hand that there was deposit of Rs. 69,930 on 4th March, 1971 and on the other there was a withdrawal of Rs. 40,000 on 4th March, 1971 and of Rs. 25,000 on 6th March, 1971, and, therefore, the sum of Rs. 65,000 should be added to the election expenses of the appellant. When it was put to Yashpal Kapur that the sums of Rs. 40,000 and Rs. 25,000 were withdrawn by Dal Bahadur Singh. Yashpal Kapur said that he was not aware of it. There is no pleading in the election petition that the appellant authorised incurring expenditure by a political party. There is no pleading that any amount has been paid by the political party. There is no complaint in the petition about the sum of

Rs. 65,000 or the sum of Rs. 69,930 Yashpal Kapur denied knowledge of Rs. 70,000. The appellant was not asked a single question. There is no evidence to identify any of these payments with the election of the appellant.

MOREOVER AMENDING ACT, 1974 EXCLUDES CERTAIN EXPENSES – HELD CJI

110. It is appropriate at this stage to refer to the amendment which was introduced by the Amendment Act, 1974. The appellant relies on the provision to show that expenses incurred or authorised by a political party cannot be included in election expenses. *Explanation I* which was inserted at the end of section 77 of the 1951 Act by Amendment Act, 1974 is that any expenditure incurred or authorised in connection with the election of a candidate by a political party or by any other association or body of persons or by an individual other than the candidate or his election agent shall not be deemed to be and shall not ever be deemed to have been expenditure in connection with the election incurred or authorised by the candidate or by his election agent.

PROVISO TO *EXPLANATION I* BY AMENDING ACT 1974 – IS THE LAW – HELD CJI

111. A proviso was also added to the aforesaid *Explanation I* by the Amendment Act, 1974. The proviso stated that nothing contained in the *Explanation* shall affect (a) any judgment, order or decision of the Supreme Court whereby the election of a candidate to the House of the People or to the Legislative Assembly of a State has been declared void or set aside before the commencement of the Representation of the People (Amendment) Ordinance, 1974; (b) any judgment, order or decision of a High Court whereby the election of any such candidate has been declared void or set aside before the commencement of the said Ordinance if no appeal has been preferred to the Supreme Court against such judgment, order or decision of the High Court before such commencement and the period of limitation for filing such appeal has expired before such commencement.

EXPLANATION 2 ADDED TO SECTION 77 BY AMENDING ACT 1974 CHANGES THE PRE-AMENDMENT LAW – HELD CJI

112. *Explanation* 2 which was added to section 77 of the 1951 Act by the Amendment Act, 1974 is as follows:

> "For the purposes of Explanation I "political party" shall have the same meaning as in the Election Symbols (Reservation and Allotment) Order, 1968, as for the time being in force".

LAW LAID DOWN IN KANWAR LAL GUPTA'S CASE – RELIED UPON BY RESPONDENT – AMENDED LAW OVER RULES THE JUDGMENT – HELD CJI

113. Counsel for the respondent relied on the recent decision of this Court in **Kanwar Lal Gupta v. Amarnath Chawla, AIR 1975 SC 308** in support of the proposition that there has been no change in law and if expenses incurred by a political party can be identified with the election of a candidate then that expenditure is to be added to the election expenses of a candidate as being authorised by him. There are no findings by the High Court in the present appeals that any expenses by a political party were authorised by the appellant. There is also no finding in the present appeals that any expenses incurred by a political party can be identified with the election of the appellant. The changes in law effected by the Amendment Acts, 1974 and 1975 totally repel the submissions on behalf of the respondent. Expenses incurred or authorised in connection with the election of a candidate by a political party shall not be deemed to be and shall not ever be deemed to have been expenditure in connection with the election incurred or authorised by the candidate. Furthermore, the ruling in **Kanwar Lal Gupta's** case (supra) is no longer good law because of the legislative changes.

FINDING OF HIGH COURT ON EXPENSES BE REVERSED – PLEADS RESPONDENT

114. Counsel for the respondent contended that the judgment of the High Court should be reversed with regard to election expenses of the appellant on three counts. *First,* Exhibit 118 shows that the sum of Rs. 65,000 which was drawn by the Congress Committee should have been held by the High Court on a reasonable inference to have been spent by the District Congress Committee as having been authorised by the election agent of the appellant. *Second,* the High Court has not taken into account expenses of the election agent at 12 meetings other than the meetings addressed by the appellant and has also not taken into account the telephone expenses of the election agent. The telephone expenses amounted to Rs. 836.85 between 11th January, 1971 and 10th February, 1971 and a further sum of Rs. 2,514 for the period 11th February, 1971 to 15th March, 1971. *Third,* it is said that there were 5000 polling booths and if 20 workers were required per booth then 10,000 workers would be required and the only inference is that an amount in excess was spent for workers with the authority of the election agent.

HIGH COURT FINDING ON TELEPHONE EXPENSES UPHELD – CJI

115. In Issue No. 9 there was no amount alleged with regard to telephone bills or election meetings under the heading of alleged election expenses. There was no allegation to that effect in the petition. With regard to expenses for the alleged 12 meetings addressed by the election agent the evidence of Yashpal Kapur is that he addressed about a dozen meetings and he did not include in the election return the expenses incurred for installation of loudspeakers because the expenditure was not incurred by him. He also said that he did not include in the election return the expenses incurred over the construction of platforms because the meetings were arranged by the District Congress Committee. No allegations were made in the petition with regard to any alleged sum of money on account of election meetings where the election agent spoke. The High Court rightly said that the telephone expenses and expenses for meetings could not be taken into consideration because no suggestion of the case was made until the stage of arguments.

116. The respondent's submission is that the appellant was the Prime Minister at the time of the election, and, therefore, there was a big campaign and the expenses were enormous. That will mean little. Expenses incurred or authorised by a political party are under the Amendment Act, 1974 not to be deemed to be expenditure in connection with the election incurred or authorised by the candidate or by his election agent for the purposes of section 77 of the 1951 Act. The part played by a political party in connection with candidates of the party at the election particularly in relation to expenditure incurred by the political party with regard to candidates of the party has been the subject of some decisions of this Court: This Court has observed that expenditure must be by the candidate himself and any expenditure in his interest by others (not his agent within the meaning of the term of the Election Laws) is not to be taken note of. Where vehicles were engaged by the Congress Committee and used by the candidate, the amount spent by the Congress Committee could not be taken to be included in the expenditure of the candidate's election expenses; *See* **Hans Raj v. Pt. Hari Ram, (1968) 40 Ele LR 125 (SC)**.

EXPENSES BY POLITICAL PARTY OR VOLUNTARILY MADE BY OTHERS – WITHOUT AUTHORISATION BY CANDIDATE OR AGENT – ARE NOT EXPENSES OF CANDIDATE – AMENDED LAW MAKES THE THINGS CLEAR – CONTENTION OF RESPONDENT REJECTED – HELD CJI

116. The respondent's submission is that the appellant was the Prime Minister at the time of the election, and, therefore, there was a big campaign and the expenses were enormous. That will mean little. Expenses incurred or authorised by a political party are under the Amendment Act, 1974 not to be deemed to be expenditure in connection with the election incurred or authorised by the candidate or by his election agent for the purposes of section 77 of the 1951 Act. The part played by a political party in connection with candidates of the party at the election particularly in relation to expenditure incurred by the political party with regard to candidates of the party has been the subject of some decisions of this Court: This Court has observed that expenditure must be by the candidate himself and any expenditure in his interest by others (not his agent within the meaning of the term of the Election Laws) is not to be taken note of. Where vehicles were engaged by the Congress Committee and used by the candidate, the amount spent by the Congress Committee could not be taken to be included in the expenditure of the candidate's election expenses; *See* **Hans Raj v. Pt. Hari Ram, (1968) 40 Ele LR 125 (SC)**.

117. Expenses incurred by a political party in support of its candidates have been held by this Court not to fall within the mischief of section 123(6) of the 1951 Act (*See* **Shah Jayantilal Ambalal v. Kasturilal Nagindas Doshi, (1969) 42 Ele LR 307 (SC)**). In **Rananjaye Singh v. Baijnath Singh, (1955) 1 SCR 671** this Court pointed out that expenses must be incurred or authorised by the candidate or his agent. In that case the Manager, the Assistant Manager, 20 Ziladars and their peons were alleged to have worked for the election of the appellant. This Court held that the employment of extra persons and the incurring or authorising of extra expenditure was not by the candidate or his election agent. The extra men employed and paid were in the employment of the father of the appellant. This Court said that the position in law could not be at all different if the father had given those employees a holiday on full pay and they voluntarily worked in connection with the election of the appellant. Persons who volunteer to work cannot be said to be employed or paid by the candidate or by his election agent.

118. In **Ram Dayal v. Brijraj Singh, (1970) 1 SCR 530** the appellant challenged the election of the respondent on the ground that the Maharaja and the Rajmata of Gwalior had helped the respondent's election in a number of ways and acted as his agents and the respondent incurred considerable expenditure, which exceeded the limit. This Court found that assuming the expenditure was incurred by the Maharaja and the Rajmata of Gwalior for the purpose of canvassing votes, in the absence of any evidence to show that the Maharaja and the Rajmata acted as election agents or that the expenditure was authorised by the respondent, it was not liable to be included in the election expenses.

119. On behalf of the respondent it was said relying on the decision of this Court in **Kanwar Lal Gupta's** case, (supra) that if the candidate takes advantage of expenditure incurred by the political party in connection with the election of the candidate or participates in the programme of activity or fails to disavow the expenditure the candidate cannot escape the rigour of the ceiling by saying that he has not incurred the expenditure but his political party has done so. Expenditure incurred by a political party in connection with the election of the candidates of the party is not a part of the election expenses of the candidate. Similarly, participation in the programme of activity organised by a political party will not fall within the election expenses of the candidate of the party. A candidate is not required to disavow or denounce the expenditure incurred or authorised by the political party because the expenditure is neither incurred nor authorised by the candidate. One can disavow what would be ascribed to be incurred or authorised by one. In the case of expenses of a political party there is no question of disavowing expenditure incurred or authorised by the political party.

120. The decision in **Kanwar Lal Gupta's** case, (supra) was based on an observation extracted from the decision of this Court in **Megh Raj Patodia v. R.K. Birla, (1971) 2 SCR 118**. In **Megh Raj Patodia's** case (supra) the allegations were that the respondent had been put up by one of the wealthiest business houses in the country which owned or controlled a large number of companies and during the election campaign vast material and human resources of these companies were drawn upon by the respondent. This Court dismissed the appeal on the ground that the appellant had failed to establish that expenditure in excess of the prescribed limit was incurred by the respondent. In **Megh Raj Patodia's** case (supra) there is an observation that expenses incurred by a political party to advance the prospects of the candidates put up by it without more do not fall within section 77 of the 1951 Act. The words "something more" were construed by counsel for the respondent to mean that if a candidate takes advantage of expenditure incurred or authorised by a political party such expenses could be attributed to a candidate. The Amendment Act, 1974 has added *Explanation 1* to section 77 of the 1951 Act which shows that expenditure incurred or authorised in connection with the election of a candidate by the political party shall not be deemed to be expenditure incurred or authorised by the candidate or his election agent.

121. Allegations that election expenses are incurred or authorised by a candidate or his agent will have to be proved. Authorisation means acceptance of the responsibility. Authorisation must precede the expenditure. Authorisation means reimbursement by the candidate or election agent of the person who has been authorised by the candidate or by the election agent of the candidate to spend or incur. In order to constitute authorisation the effect must be that the authority must carry with it the right of re-imbursement.

122. For the foregoing reasons the contentions of the respondent that the appellant exceeded the limit of election expenses fail.

1974 AND 1975 AMENDMENTS BAR FREE AND FAIR ELECTIONS – DESTROY BASIC STRUCTURE OF THE CONSTITUTION-HENCE INVALID – CONTENDS RESPONDENT

123. The respondent contended that the amendments by the Amendment Acts of 1974 and 1975 are constitutionally invalid. It may be stated here that the Constitution (Thirty-ninth Amendment) Act, 1975 in section 5 thereof enacts that in the Ninth Schedule to the Constitution after entry 86, *inter alia,* the following Entries shall be inserted, namely:

> "87. The Representation of the People Act, 1951 (Central Act 43 of 1951); the Representation of the People (Amendment) Act, 1974 (Central Act 58 of 1974); and the Election Laws (Amendment) Act, 1975 (Central Act 40 of 1975)."

124. The contention of the respondent is that when the power of amending the Constitution cannot be exercised to damage or destroy the basic features of the Constitution or the essential elements of the basic structure or framework thereof the limitations on the exercise of legislative power will arise not only from the express limitations contained in the Constitution, but also from necessary implication either under Articles or even in the Preamble of the Constitution. This contention on behalf of the respondent is expanded to mean that if the democratic way of life through Parliamentary institutions based on free and fair elections is a basic feature which cannot be destroyed or damaged by amendment of the Constitution, it cannot similarly be destroyed or damaged by any legislative measure.

125. These reasons were submitted by the respondent. *First,* the power to resolve doubts and disputes about the validity of elections of Parliament and State Legislatures has been vested by the Constitution in the judicial organ competent to decide election petitions and, therefore, it is not open to the Legislature to take away and interfere with these exclusive functions of the judiciary by any legislation amending the law governing the election adjudicated by the judiciary. *Second,* the insertion of these Acts in the Ninth Schedule will not confer any immunity on the legislative measure if basic features of the Constitution are damaged or destroyed on the ground that the provisions contravene Part III of the Constitution. *Third,* any provision in the legislative measures which has the effect of bringing about unfairness between different rival candidates in the matter of election is discriminatory and it not only contravenes Article 14 but also violates the implied limitation on legislative power relating to free and fair elections. *Fourth,* any amendment of the law with retrospective operation governing an election which has already been held necessarily introduces an element of unfairness and brings about a denial of equality among rival candidates. *Fifth,* the deeming clause introduced in the 1951 Act by sections 6(b) and 8(a) and (b) of the Amendment Act, 1975 and the device of conclusive proof adopted by section 8(c) in the Amendment Act, 1975 are unconstitutional encroachments on judicial power. Sixth, power conferred by an enactment including a constitutional enactment has to be so exercised as to give effect to the guiding principles of the basic norms of that legislation and not so as to militate against those guiding principles or basic norms.

126. The definition of "candidate" is amended by the Amendment Act, 1975. The contentions of the respondent on the amendment of the definition of "candidate" are these. The expression "returned candidate" is descriptive of the person and the corrupt practices mentioned in section 123 of the 1951 Act in relation to a candidate will not be confined to corrupt practices committed with reference to the definition of "candidate". Corrupt practices alleged in relation to candidates will be relatable to any period and will not be confined to corrupt practices alleged between the date of nomination and the date of election. If corrupt practices are committed by candidates who eventually become returned candidates such corrupt practices will be offences within the meaning of section 123 of the 1951 Act without any reference to the time of commission.

127. Counsel on behalf of the respondent also contended as follows. The basis of fair and free elections is that the election of a candidate will be avoided if any corrupt practice has been committed by the candidate by or with the knowledge and consent of that candidate. The acts of a candidate may be either anterior to the date of nomination or it may be subsequent to the date of nomination. Therefore, the Amendment Act, 1975 destroys and damages free and fair election by allowing candidates to commit corrupt practices prior to the date of nomination.

128. The Amendment Act, 1975 is also challenged as falling within the vice of delegated legislation by the amendments inserted as *Explanation* 3 to section 77 of the 1951 Act and the insertion of the proviso to section 123(7) of the 1951 Act. These provisions have already been noticed. Broadly stated expenditure, incurred by persons in Government service will not be deemed to be for furtherance of the candidate's election. The contention are these. No guidelines have been laid down as to what expenditure can be incurred or what facilities can be made, what acts or things can be done. Delegation cannot include the change of policy. Policy must be clearly laid down in the Act for carrying into effect the objectives of the legislation.

The legislature must declare the policy. Any duty can be assigned. Any facility in connection with the election can be asked for by the party in power to be done for the candidate. The official duty opens a wide power of instructions to Government servants who may be asked to assist candidates by canvassing, influencing which will damage fair elections.

129. The device of conclusive proof which is introduced to add *Explanation* 3 to section 123(7) of the 1951 Act with regard to the date with effect from which the person ceased to be in service is said to be an encroachment on judicial power.

130. Section 8(a) of the Amendment Act, 1975 which adds a proviso to section 123 of the 1951 Act to the effect that no symbol allotted under this Act to a candidate shall be deemed to be a religious symbol or a national symbol for the purposes of this clause is attacked as legalising religious symbols and thus offending secularism.

131. Section 10 of the Amendment Act, 1975 which enacts that the amendments shall have retrospective effect is challenged as retrospectively legalising a void election. These submissions are made. If this power is upheld there can be a legislative measure to avoid valid elections. The distinction between law abiding persons and lawless persons is eliminated. One person has not been given the opportunity of spending money at the time of election but the other is retrospectively given the advantage of spending in excess and thereafter of avoiding the effect of excess expenses by validation.

CONSTITUTION IS SUPREME – ARTICLES 245 AND 246 GIVE PLENARY POWERS TO LEGISLATURE TO LEGISLATE CAN CHANGE THE LAW – HELD CJI

132. The contentions on behalf of the respondent that ordinary legislative measures are subject like Constitution amendments to the restrictions of not damaging or destroying basic structure, or basic features are utterly unsound. It has to be appreciated at the threshold that the contention that legislative measures are subject to restrictions of the theory of basic structure or basic feature is to equate legislative measures with Constitution amendment. The hierarchical structure of the legal order of a State is that the Constitution is the highest level within national law. The Constitution in the formal sense is a solemn document containing a set of legal norms which may be changed only when special prescriptions are observed. The purpose of special prescriptions is to render the change of these norms more difficult by regulating the manner and form of these amendments. The Constitution consists of those rules which regulate the creation of the general legal norms, in particular, the creation of statutes. It is because of the material Constitution that there is a special form for constitutional law. If there is a constitutional form then constitution laws must be distinguished front ordinary laws. The material Constitution may determine not only the organs and procedure of legislation, but also, to some degree the contents of future laws. The Constitution can negatively determine that the laws must not have a certain content *e.g.,* that the Parliament may not pass any statute which restricts religious freedom. In this negative way not only contents of statutes but of the other norms of legal order, judicial and administrative decisions likewise, may be determined by the Constitution. The Constitution can also positively prescribe certain contents of future statutes. This may be illustrated with reference to the provisions in Article 22 that no person who is arrested shall be detained in custody without being informed, as soon as may be of the grounds for such arrest nor shall he be denied the right to consult, and to be defended by, a legal practitioner of his choice.

133. Articles 245 and 246 give plenary powers to legislature to legislate. The only question is whether any provision of the Constitution is violated. The power of plenary body is not to be construed like the power of a delegate. The largest kind of power will be attributed to legislature. The only prohibition is with reference to the provisions of the Constitution. The Constitution is the conclusive instrument by which powers are affirmatively created or negatively restricted. The only relevant test for the validity of a statute made under Article 245 is whether the legislation is within the scope of the affirmative grant of power or is forbidden by some provision of the Constitution.

PLENARY POWER OF LEGISLATURE CANNOT BE DEFEATED BY BASIC STRUCTURE THEORY – AMOUNTS TO RE-WRITING CONSTITUTION – HELD CJI

134. To accept the basic feature or basic structure theory with regard to ordinary legislation would mean that there would be two kinds of limitations for legislative measures. One will pertain to legislative power under Articles 245 and 246 and the legislative entries and the provision in Article 13. The other would be that no legislation can be made as to damage or destroy basic feature or basic structure. This will mean rewriting the Constitution and robbing the legislature of acting within the framework of the Constitution. No legislation can be free from challenge on this ground even though the legislative measure is within the plenary powers of the legislature.

LEGISLATURE CAN AMEND CONSTITUTION – THEORY OF BASIC STRUCTURE OF CONSTITUTION IS VAGUE AND INDEFINABLE – HELD CJI

135. The theory of implied limitations on the power of amendment of the Constitution has been rejected by seven Judges in **Keshvananda Bharati's** case (supra). Our Constitution has not adopted the due process clause of the American Constitution. Reasonableness of legislative measures is unknown to our Constitution. The crucial point is that unlike the American Constitution where rights are couched in wide general terms leaving it to the Courts to evolve necessary limitations, our Constitution has denied due process as a test of invalidity of law. In **A.K. Gopalan v. State of Madras, 1950 SCR 88** due process was rejected by clearly limiting the rights acquired and by eliminating the indefinite due process. Our Constitution contemplates that considerations of justice or general welfare might require restriction on enjoyment of fundamental rights.

136. The theory of basic structure or basic feature is an exercise in imponderables. Basic structure or basic feature are indefinable. The legislative entries are the fields of legislation. The pith and substance doctrine has been applied in order to find out legislative competency, and eliminate encroachment on legislative entries. If the theory of basic structure or basic feature will be applied to legislative measures it will denude Parliament and State legislatures of the power of legislation and deprive them of laying down legislative policies. This will be encroachment on the separation of powers.

ARTICLE 13 GIVES SUFFICIENT POWER TO PARLIAMENT TO LEGISLATE ANY LAW – 1974 AND 1975 AMENDMENTS ARE ONLY EXPLANATORY – HELD CJI

137. The Constitutional validity of a statute depends entirely on the existence of the legislative power and the express provision in Article 13. Apart from the limitation the legislature is not subject to any other prohibition. The amendments made to the 1951 Act by the Amendment Acts, 1974 and 1975 are to give effect to certain views expressed by this Court in preference to certain views departed from or otherwise to clarify the original intention. It is within the powers of Parliament to frame laws with regard to elections. Parliament has power to enumerate and define election expenses Parliament has power to lay down limits on election expenses. Parliament has power to state whether certain expenses can be included or may be excluded from election expenses. Parliament has power to adopt conclusive proof with regard to matters of appointment resignation or termination of service. Parliament has power to state what can be considered to be office of profit. Parliament has power to state as to what will and what will not constitute corrupt practice. Parliament has power to enact what will be the ground for disqualification. Parliament has power to define "candidate". Parliament has power to state what symbols will be allotted to candidates at election. These are all legislative policies.

PARLIAMENT HAS POWER TO GIVE 'RETROSPECTIVE EFFECT' - HELD CJI

138. The conclusive evidence or conclusive proof clause is an accepted legislative measure. Similarly, giving retrospective effect to legislative amendment is accepted to be valid exercise of legislative power. The well-known pattern of all Validation Acts by which the basis of judgments or orders of competent Courts and Tribunals is changed and the judgments and orders are made ineffective is to be found in **M.P.V. Sundaramier and Co. v. The State of Andhra Pradesh, 1958 SCR 1422.** The power of the legislature to pass a law includes a power to pass it retrospectively. An important illustration with reference to retrospective legislation in regard to election is the decision of this Court in **Kanta Kathuria's** case (supra). Kanta Kathuria was disqualified by reason of holding an office of profit. First the Ordinance and later the Act was passed to nullify the decision of the High Court. The Ordinance as well as the Act stated that notwithstanding any judgment or order of any Court or Tribunal, the officer shall not be disqualified or shall be deemed never to have disqualified the holders thereof as a member of the Legislative Assembly. The rendering of a judgment ineffective by changing the basis by legislative enactment is not encroachment on judicial power because the legislation is within the competence of the legislature.

139. A contention was advanced that the legislative measure could not remove the disqualification retrospectively because the Constitution contemplates disqualification existing at certain time in accordance with law existing at that time. One of the views expressed in that case is that Article 191 recognises the power of the Legislature of the State to declare by law that the holder of the office shall not be disqualified for being chosen as a Member. Power is reserved to the Legislature of the State to make the declaration. There is nothing in the Article to indicate that this declaration cannot be made with retrospective effect. The Act was held not to be ineffective in its retrospective operation on the ground that it is well-recognised that Parliament and State Legislatures can make their laws operate retrospectively. Any law that can be made prospectively can be made with retrospective operation. It is said that certain kinds of laws cannot operate retrospectively. That is *ex-post facto* legislation. The present case does not fall within that category. Reference may be made to *May's Parliamentary Practice,* 17th Edn., p. 515 where, instances are given of validation of election by the British Parliament.

140. This Court in **Jumuna Prasad Mukhariya v. Lachhi Ram, (1955) 1 SCR 608** rejected the contention advanced there that sections 123(5) and 124(5) of the 1951 Act interfered with a citizen's fundamental right to freedom of speech. This Court said that these laws do not stop a man from speaking. They merely prescribe conditions which must be observed if one wants to enter Parliament. The right to stand as a candidate and to contest an election is not a common law right. It is a special right created by statute which can only be exercised on the conditions laid down by the statute. The Fundamental Rights Chapter has no bearing on a right like this created by a statute relating to election.

CHANGE IN DEFINITION OF 'CANDIDATE' RETROSPECTIVELY DESTROYS BASIC STRUCTURE – CONTENTION REJECTED – CJI

141. The contention on behalf of the respondent that the amendment of the definition of "candidate" has damaged or destroyed basic structure is untenable. There is no basic structure or basic feature or basic framework with regard to the time when under the Election Laws a person is a candidate at the election. The contention of the respondent that the expression "returned candidate" is descriptive of the expression "candidate" will rob section 100 of its content. The word "candidate" in relation to various electoral offences shows that he must be a candidate at the time of the offence. Time is necessary for fixing the offences. A significant distinction arises between the electoral offences under the 1951 Act and the offences under sections 171-A to 171-I of the Indian Penal Code namely that the 1951 Act uses the word "candidate" or his election agent with reference to various offences, whereas the Indian Penal Code does not use the word "candidate" in relation to commission of any offence. Any person may fall within the offences of bribery, undue influence, personation at elections within the provisions of the Indian Penal Code or for false statement or illegal payments in connection with any election or failure to keep election accounts.

* * * * *

SECTIONS 171A AND 171-I, IPC – SECTIONS 125 TO 136 OF 1951 ACT DEAL WITH 'CANDIDATE' AT ANY TIME EITHER BEFORE, DURING AND AFTER ANY ELECTION – HELD CJI

145. Sections 171A to 171-I of the Indian Penal Code and the provisions contained in sections 125 to 136 of the 1951 Act follow the pattern of English Acts, namely, Statutes 17 and 18 Victoria. Chapter CII (1853-54); Statutes 21 and 22 Victoria, Chapter LXXXVII (1858) and Statutes 46 and 47 Victoria Chapter LI (1882). These English Statutes make certain acts punishable as corrupt practice when they relate to persons other than candidates or voters. Section II of 17 and 18 Victoria Chapter CI enacts that the persons mentioned therein shall be deemed guilty of bribery and punishable in accordance with the provisions of the Act. The words used there are "every person" who shall do the acts mentioned therein shall be punishable. In these sections dealing with the acts of persons other than candidates and voters no time is mentioned. On the other hand, section IV of Statutes 17 and 18 Victoria Chapter CII makes certain acts of voters and candidates corrupt practice. Section IV of the aforesaid English Statute enacts that every candidate at an election who shall corruptly by himself, or by or with any person or by any other ways or means on his behalf, at any time, either before, during, or after any election, directly or indirectly give or provide, or cause to be given or provided any expenses incurred for any meat, drink, entertainment, etc. shall be deemed guilty of an offence of treating. In these sections when the acts of voters and candidates are made punishable the words used are "before or during any election directly or indirectly or at any time either before, during or after any election" in Section IV of the Act. These words make acts of voters or candidates committed before or during an election also corrupt practice. Without these words acts of the candidate made punishable under the English Statutes would only be the acts committed by the candidate after he becomes a candidate.

THE 1951 ACT USES WORD 'CANDIDATE' FOR PURPOSE OF SEVERAL OFFENCES – HELD CJI

146. The 1951 Act uses the expression "candidate" in relation to several offences for the purpose of affixing liability with reference to a person being a candidate. If no time be fixed with regard to a person being a candidate it can be said that from the moment a person is elected he can be said to hold himself out as a candidate for the next election. The definition in the English Act cannot be of any aid to the construction of the 1951 Act.

LEGISLATURE HAS SET AT REST MEANING OF WORD 'EXPENSES' BY AMENDMENT – HELD CJI

147. The contention of the respondent is that if a candidate is free to spend as much as a candidate likes before the date of nomination a great premium would be placed on free use of money before the date of nomination. The 1951 Act specifies what election expenses are of a candidate. The statute specifies time in regard to a candidate. That time cannot be enlarged or reduced. The holding out by a person of candidature was a flexible and elastic idea. The date of nomination is definite and doubtless. Different views may be taken as to the time of holding out. The legislature has now set the matter at rest.

148. The word "incur" according to the dictionary meaning means to become liable to. The word "incur" means undertake the liability even if the actual payment may not be made immediately. The undertaking of the responsibility for the expenditure concerned may be either by the candidate or his election agent. Again, a candidate is also to be deemed responsible for the expenditure if he has authorised a particular expenditure to be made by someone else on his behalf.

1974 AND 1975 AMENDMENTS SUFFER FROM VICE OF 'DELEGATED LEGISLATION' – CONTENDS RESPONDENT – REJECTED – CJI

149. The contention on behalf of the respondent is that the Amendment Acts of 1974 and 1975 fall within the vice of delegated legislation because there are no guiding principles with regard to official duty or nature of expenditure in *Explanation* 3 to section 77 of the 1951 Act and in the proviso to section 123(7) of the 1951 Act. Official duty will be a duty in law. Official duty will be duty under administrative directions of the Executive. Official duty will be for security, law and order, and matters in aid of public purpose. These duties will be in connection with election. To illustrate, section 197 of the Criminal Procedure Code speaks of official duty.

150. This Court in **Matajog Dobey v. H.C. Bhari, (1955) 2 SCR 925** interpreted the words "official duty" to have reasonable connection between the act and the discharge of duty. The act must bear such relation to the duty that the person could lay a reasonable claim, but not a pretended fanciful claim, that he did it in the course of the performance of his duty. Where a power is conferred or a duty imposed by statute or otherwise, and there is nothing said expressly inhibiting the exercise of the power or the performance of the duty by any limitations or restrictions, it is reasonable to hold that it carries with it the power of doing all such acts or employing such means as are reasonably necessary for such execution, because it is a rule that when the law commands a thing to be done, it authorises the performance of whatever may be necessary for executing its command.

151. There is no vice of delegation in the Statutes. "Delegation is not the complete handing over or transference of a power from one person or body of persons to another. Delegation may be defined as the entrusting by a person or body of persons, of the exercise of a power residing in that person or body of persons to another person or body of persons. With complete power of revocation or amendment remaining in the grantor or delegator. It is important to grasp the implications of this, for, much confusion of thought has unfortunately resulted from assuming that delegation involves or may involve, the complete abdication or abrogation of a power. This is precluded by the definition. Delegation often involves the granting of discretionary authority to another, but such authority is purely derivative. The ultimate power always remains in the delegator and is never renounced"; *See* **Gwalior Rayon Silk Mfg. (Wvg.) Co. Ltd. v. The Asstt. Commr. of Sales Tax, (1974) 4 SCC 98 (116)**.

29th CONSTITUTIONAL AMENDMENT CONSIDERED IN KESAVANANDA BHARATI'S CASE – CJI

152. The Constitution 29th Amendment Act was considered by this Court in **Keshavananda Bharati's case** (supra). The 29th Amendment Act inserted in the Ninth Schedule to the Constitution Entries 65 and 66 being the Kerala Land Reforms Act, 1969 and the Kerala Land Reforms Act, 1971. This Court unanimously upheld the validity of the 29th Amendment Act. The unanimous view of this Court in **Keshavananda Bharati's** case (supra) is that Article 31B is not open to challenge. Six Judges held that the 29th Amendment Act would be ineffective to protect the impugned Act if they took away the fundamental rights. Six Judges took the view that the 29th Amendment Act is valid and further that Article 31B has been held by this Court to be independent of Article 23A and that Article 31B protects Scheduled Acts and Regulations and none of the Scheduled Acts and Regulations is deemed to be void or ever to have become void on the ground of contravention of any fundamental rights. Article 31B gives a mandate and complete protection from the challenge of fundamental rights to the Scheduled Acts and Regulations. The view of seven Judges in **Keshavananda Bharati's** case is that Article 31B is a constitutional device to place the specified statutes in the Schedule beyond any attack that these infringe Part III of the Constitution. The 29th Amendment is affirmed in **Keshavananda Bharti's** case (supra) by majority of seven against six Judges.

LEGISLATIVE MEASURES ARE NOT SUBJECT TO BASIC STRUCTURE – AMENDMENTS OF 1974 AND 1975 UPHELD – CJI

153. The contentions of the respondent that the Amendment Acts of 1974 and 1975 are subject to basic feature or basic structure or basic framework fails on two grounds. *First*, legislative measures are not subject to the theory of basic feature or basic structure or basic framework. *Second*, the majority view in **Keshavananda Bharati's** case (supra) is that the 29th Amendment which put the two statutes in the Ninth Schedule and Article 31B is not open to challenge on the ground of either damage to or destruction of basic feature, basic structure or basic framework or on the ground of violation of fundamental rights.

RELIGIOUS SYMBOL – SUBMISSION OF RESPONDENT REJECTED BY HIGH COURT RIGHTLY – CJI

154. The symbol allotted to the party of the appellant was characterised by the respondent as a religious symbol. Under Article 324 the superintendence, direction and control of elections to Parliament, is vested in the Election Commission. Rule 5 of the Conduct of Elections Rules, 1961 states that the Election Commission shall by notification in the Gazette of India and in the Official Gazette of each State, specify the symbols that may be chosen by candidates at elections in Parliamentary or Assembly constituencies and the restrictions to which their choice shall be subject. Rule 10(4) of the 1961 Rules aforesaid states that at an election in a Parliamentary or Assembly constituency, where a poll becomes necessary, the returning officer shall consider the choice of symbols, expressed by the contesting candidates in their nomination papers and shall, subject to any general or special direction issued in this behalf by the Election Commission allot a different symbol to each contesting candidate in conformity, as far as practicable with his choice. It is, therefore, apparent that the power to specify permissible symbols is vested by rule 5 in the Election Commission. The choice of candidates is limited to the symbol specified by the Election Commission. The Election Symbols (Reservation and Allotment) Order, 1968 was made in exercise of the powers conferred by Article 328 of the Constitution read with rule 5 and rule 10 of the Conduct of Election Rules and all other powers enabling in this behalf.

155. Clause 17 of the Election Symbols (Reservation and Allotment) Order, 1968 provides that the Commission shall by notification in the Gazette of India publish lists specifying national parties and the symbols respectively reserved for them etc. There can, therefore, be no doubt that the power of evolving permissible symbols is exclusively vested in the Election Commission. It is under their direction that the Returning Officer has to make allotments and allotments are made in terms of Clauses 5, 6 and 8. Therefore, in the matter of evolving of the permissible symbols, the jurisdiction is vested in the Election Commission. If a candidate displays in addition to the allotted symbol an additional symbol which may have a special appeal on grounds of religion to a particular community, then the Court will be entitled to go into this question.

156. With regard to the symbol of cow and calf being a religious symbol it was said on behalf of the respondent that the Akhil Bhartiya Ram Rajya Parishad asked for cow, calf and milkmaid symbol and were refused. They were given the symbol of a "Rising sun". It is impossible to hold that because one party has not been given the symbol of cow, calf and milkmaid, therefore, the symbol of cow and calf becomes a religious symbol. The High Court on the evidence adduced by the respondent, rightly came to the conclusion that there was no evidence to prove that the cow and calf is a religious symbol. The High Court rightly held that cow and calf is not a religious symbol.

FINDING OF HIGH COURT ON 'CORRUPT PRACTICE' BY APPELLANT – SET ASIDE – CJI

157. The finding of the High Court that the appellant held herself out to be a candidate from 29th December, 1970 is set aside because the law is that the appellant became a candidate only with effect from the date of nomination which was 1st February, 1971. The finding of the High Court that the resignation of Yashpal Kapur did not become effective until it was notified in the Gazette is also set aside because under the law the resignation became effective from 14th January, 1971. The finding of the High Court that the appellant committed corrupt practice in breach of section 123(7) of the 1951 Act is also repelled by the legislative changes and is, therefore, set aside. The order of disqualification of the appellant is also set aside.

APPEAL OF APPELLANT ACCEPTED – COUNTER APPEAL OF RESPONDENT REJECTED – CJI

158. For the foregoing reasons the contentions of the appellant succeed and the contentions of the respondent fail. The appeal is accepted. The judgment of the High Court appealed against is set aside. The cross-objection of the respondent is dismissed. There will be no order as to costs.

Khanna, J.—Civil Appeal No. 887 of 1975 has been filed by Smt. Indira Nehru Gandhi (hereinafter referred to as the appellant) against the judgment of the Allahabad High Court whereby election petition filed by Shri Raj Narain respondent No. 1 (hereinafter referred to as the respondent) to question the election of the appellant to the Lok Sabha from Raebareli Parliamentary constituency was allowed and the election of the appellant was declared void. The appellant was found guilty of having committed corrupt practices under section 123(7) of the Representation of the People Act, 1951 (hereinafter referred to as the RP Act) and as such was stated to be disqualified for a period of six years in accordance with section 8A of the RP Act. Cross Appeal No. 909 of 1975 has been filed by Shri Raj Narain against the judgment of the High Court insofar as it decided certain issues against the respondent.

NOTIFICATION FOR ELECTIONS TO LOK SABHA ISSUED ON 27 JANUARY, 1971 – APPELLANT FILED NOMINATION PAPERS FROM RAEBARELI ON 1 FEBRUARY, 1971 – KHANNA, J.

160. The President of India called upon different constituencies in the country to elect members to the Lok Sabha by notification dated January 27, 1971 under section 14(2) of the RP Act. Last date for filing nomination papers was fixed as February 3, 1971 for Raebareli constituency by the Election Commission. The appellant filed her nomination paper on February 1, 1971. The appellant was for a number of years before the election Prime Minister of India and is since then continuing to hold that office. Yashpal Kapur, who was previously a gazetted officer in the Government of India holding the post of Officer on Special Duty in the Prime Minister's Secretariat and who subsequently submitted his resignation, was appointed the election agent of the appellant.

APPOINTED YASHPAL KAPUR AS ELECTION AGENT ON 4 FEBRUARY, 1971 – KHANNA, J.

The signed form about the appointment of Yashpal Kapur as election agent was submitted to the Returning Officer of February 4, 1971, the date of scrutiny. The date on which Yashpal Kapur submitted his resignation and the same became effective is, however, a matter of controversy between the parties. The appellant, who was a candidate of the Indian National Congress (R), was allotted the party symbol of cow and calf.

POLLING TOOK PLACE ON 1, 3, 5 MARCH – RESULT DECLARED ON 10 MARCH, 1971 – APPELLANT WON ELECTIONS BY MORE THAN 1 LAKH VOTES – KHANNA, J.

Polling took place in the first week of March on March 1, March 3 and March 5, 1971. The appellant and the respondent were the principal contestants. There were two other candidates but we are not concerned with them. The result of the election was declared on March 10, 1971. The appellant got 1,83,309 votes, while the respondent secured 71,499 votes and the former was declared elected.

RESPONDENT FILED ELECTION PETITION ON 24 APRIL, 1971 AGAINST APPELLANT – KHANNA, J.

The respondent thereafter filed election petition on April 24, 1971 to challenge the election of the appellant. Apart from some grounds which were not pressed, the election of the appellant was assailed on the following grounds:

(1) The appellant held herself out as a prospective candidate from the Raebareli constituency immediately after the dissolution of the Lok Sabha on December 27, 1970 and for furtherance of her election prospects, she obtained and procured the assistance of Yashpal Kapur who was at that time holding the post of Officer on Special Duty. The appellant thus committed corrupt practice under section 123(7) of the RP Act.

(2) The appellant and her election agent procured the assistance of members of armed forces of the union for furtherance of her election prospects in as much as the members of the armed forces arranged planes and helicopters of the Air Force at her instance for her flights to enable her to address meetings

in her constituency. The appellant thereby committed corrupt practice under section 123(7) of the RP Act.

(3) The appellant and her election agent obtained the assistance of a number of gazetted officers and members of the police force for the furtherance of her election prospects in as much as the services of the District Magistrate, Superintendent of Police Raebareli and the Home Secretary, Uttar Pradesh Government were utilised for the purposes of the construction of rostrums and installation of loudspeakers at various places within the constituency where the appellant addressed her election meetings as also for the purpose of making arrangements of barricading and posting of police personnel on the routes by which the appellant was to travel in her constituency and at the places where she was to address meetings, in order to give publicity to her visits and thus attract large crowds. The appellant was thereby stated to have committed corrupt practice under section 123(7) of the RP Act.

(4) Yashpal Kapur, election agent of the appellant and her other agents with the consent of Yashpal Kapur, freely distributed quilts, blankets, photos and liquor among the voters to induce them to vote for her and thereby the appellant committed corrupt practice of bribery under section 123(1) of the RP Act.

(5) The appellant and her election agent made extensive appeals to the religious symbol of cow and calf and thereby committed corrupt practice under section 123(3) of the RP Act.

(6) Yashpal Kapur and some other persons with his consent hired and procured a number of vehicles for the free conveyance of electors to the polling stations and thereby committed corrupt practice under section 123(5) of the RP Act.

(7) The appellant and her election agent incurred or authorised expenditure in contravention of section 77 of the RP Act and thereby committed corrupt practice under section 123(6) of the RP Act.

IN WRITTEN STATEMENT APPELLANT PLEADED – RESIGNATION OF YASHPAL KAPUR ACCEPTED WITH EFFECT FROM 14 JANUARY, 1971 – APPOINTED AS AN ELECTION AGENT ON 4 FEBRUARY, 1971 – KHANNA, J.

161. The appellant in her written statement denied the various allegations levelled against her and pleaded that Yashpal Kapur resigned from his post on January 13, 1971 and his resignation was accepted with effect from January 14, 1971. Notification dated January 25, 1971 was issued by the Prime Minister's Secretariat in that connection. It was added that P.N. Haksar, then Secretary to the Prime Minister, told Yashpal Kapur on the same day on which the resignation was tendered that it was accepted and that formal orders would follow. Yashpal Kapur became the election agent of the appellant on February 4, 1971. During the period he was a gazetted officer in the Government of India, he did not do any work in furtherance of the appellant's election prospects.

ADMITTED TRAVELLED BY INDIAN AIR FORCE PLANE/CAR AND HELICOPTER/CAR – PLANE/HELICOPTER WERE PROVIDED TO HER AS PART OF THEIR DUTY – KHANNA, J.

Regarding the use of planes and helicopters of the Air Force, the appellant admitted that on February 1, 1971 she went by an Indian Air Force plane from Delhi to Lucknow from where she went by car to Raebareli, addressing meetings enroute. It was further admitted that on February 24, 1971 the appellant went by helicopter of the Indian Air Force to Gonda on regular party work and that from there she went by car to Lucknow, Unnao and Raebareli addressing public meetings in several constituencies besides her own. The appellant referred to the Pillai Committee Report and the Office Memoranda issued by the Government of India and asserted that the aforesaid flights were made by her in accordance with them. It was added that under the rules, bills for those flights were to be paid by the All India Congress Committee and most of them had already been paid. According to the appellant, neither she nor did her election agent solicit, require or order the use of Air Force planes and the Government of India provided the planes as part of their normal duty.

SERVICES OF DISTRICT MAGISTRATE, SUPERINTENDENT OF POLICE OR HOME SECRETARY WERE PROVIDED TO HER – POLICE POSTING OR ROSTRUMS BY STATE GOVERNMENT AS PER CAG INSTRUCTIONS – KHANNA, J.

The appellant denied having obtained the assistance of the District Magistrate and the Superintendent of Police Raebareli as also that of the Home Secretary, U.P. Government for any of the purposes mentioned in the petition. The appellant in this context referred to the instructions issued by the Comptroller and Auditor-General of India. She pleaded that arrangements for posting of police on the routes which she followed and the arrangements of rostrums were made by the State Government itself in compliance with those instructions. In regard to the loudspeakers, she pleaded that those were arranged by the District Congress Committee and not by the officers of the State Government. It was denied that any directions or instructions in that regard were issued by the appellant or her election agent.

DISTRIBUTION OF BLANKETS/DHOTIS/LIQUOR WERE DENIED – SYMBOL OF COW AND CALF WAS NOT RELIGIOUS – ALLOCATED BY ELECTION COMMISSION – KHANNA, J.

The allegations regarding the distribution of blankets, dhotis and liquor were stated to be absolutely false. As regards the Symbol of cow and calf, the appellant stated that it was not a religious symbol and that it was wrong that extensive appeals were made by her or her election agent to that symbol. The appellant added that she and her election agent merely informed the voters that the symbol of the Indian National Congress (R) was cow and calf and that the voting mark should be put against that symbol. The decision of the Election Commission allotting the symbol of cow and calf to her party was final and the same could not, according to the appellant, be made a ground of attack nor could the Court go into that question.

HIRING OF CARS/BRINGING VOTERS TO POLLING STATION WAS DENIED – KHANNA, J.

The allegation regarding hiring and procuring of vehicles and the use thereof for conveyance of the voters to the polling stations was described by the appellant as false. Likewise, she denied the allegation that she or her election agent incurred expenditure in excess of the prescribed limit.

ISSUES – ADDITIONAL ISSUES WERE FRAMED – KHANNA, J.

162. Following issues were framed in the case:

"(1) Whether respondent No. 1 obtained and procured the assistance of Yashpal Kapur in furtherance of the prospects of her election while he was still a Gazetted Officer in the service of Government of India ? If so, from what date?

(2) Whether at the instance of respondent No. 1 members of the Armed Forces of the Union arranged Air Force planes and helicopters for her, flown by

members of the Armed Forces, to enable her to address election meetings on 1-2-1971 and 25-2-1971, and if so, whether this constituted a corrupt practice under section 123(7) of the Representation of the People Act?

(3) Whether at the instance of respondent No. 1 and her election agent Yashpal Kapur, the District Magistrate of Raebareli, the Superintendent of Police of Raebareli and the Home Secretary of U.P. Government arranged for rostrums, loudspeakers and barricades to be set up and for members of the Police Force to be posted in connection with her election tour on 1-2-1971 and 25-2-1971; and if so, whether this amounts to a corrupt practice under section 123(7) of the Representation of the People Act?

(4) Whether quilts, blankets, dhotis and liquor were distributed by agents and workers of respondent No. 1, with the consent of her election agent Yashpal Kapur, at the places and on the dates mentioned in Schedule *A* of the Petition in order to induce electors to vote for her?

(5) Whether the particulars given in paragraph 10 and Schedule *A* of the Petition are too vague and general to afford a basis for allegations of bribery under section 123(1) of the Representation of the People Act?

(6) Whether by using the symbol cow and calf, which had been allotted to her party by the Election Commission in her election campaign the respondent No. 1 was guilty of making an appeal to religious symbol and committed a corrupt practice as defined in section 123(3) of the Representation of the People Act?

(7) Whether on the dates fixed for the poll voters were conveyed to the polling stations free of charge on vehicles hired and procured for the purpose by respondent No. 1's election agent Yashpal Kapur, or other persons with his consent, as detailed in Schedule *B* to the Petition?

(8) Whether the particulars given in paragraph 12 and Schedule *B* of the Petition are too vague and general to form a basis for allegations regarding a corrupt practice under section 123(5) of the Representation of the People Act?

(9) Whether respondent No. 1 and her election agent Yashpal Kapur incurred or authorised expenditure in excess of the amount prescribed by section 77 of the Representation of the People Act, read with rule 90, as detailed in Para 13 of the Petition?

(10) Whether the petitioner had made a security deposit in accordance with the rules of the High Court as required by section 117 of the Representation of the People Act?

(11) To what relief, if any, is the petitioner entitled?"

Subsequent to the framing of the above issues, the following three additional issues were framed in pursuance of the judgment of this Court in an appeal against an interlocutory order of the High Court:

"(1) Whether respondent No. 1 obtained and procured the assistant of Yashpal Kapur in furtherance of the prospects of her election while he was still a Gazetted Officer in the service of the Government of India? If so, from what date?

(2) Whether respondent No, 1 held herself out as a candidate from any date prior to 1-2-1971 and, if so, from what date?

(3) Whether Yashpal Kapur continued to be in the service of Government of India from and after 14-1-1971 or till which date?"

DURING PENDENCY OF ELECTION PETITION SECTION 77 REPRESENTATION OF PEOPLE ACT WAS AMENDED – HAD BEARING ON ISSUE NO. 9 – KHANNA, J.

163. During the pendency of the election petition in the High Court, section 77 of the Representation of People Act was amended by an Ordinance which was subsequently replaced by Act 58 of 1974 (hereinafter referred to as the 1974 amending Act or Act 58 of 1974). The said amending Act inserted two explanations at the end of sub-section (1) of section 77 of the Representation of People Act. The material part of the explanations reads as under:

> "*Explanation 1.*—Notwithstanding any judgment, order or decision of any Court to the contrary, any expenditure incurred or authorised in connection with the election of a candidate by a political party or by any other association or body of persons or by any individual (other than the candidate or his election agent) shall not be deemed to be, and shall not ever be deemed to have been, expenditure in connection with the election incurred or authorised by the candidate or by his election agent for the purposes of this sub-section:
>
> Provided... ....
>
> *Explanation 2.*—For the purposes of explanation 1, 'political party' shall have the same meaning as in the Election Symbols (Reservation and Allotment) Order, 1968, as for the time being in force."

The above amendment in section 77 had a bearing on the allegation, which was the subject matter of Issue No. 9. The respondent filed writ petition challenging the validity of the amending Act.

HIGH COURT FINDINGS ON VARIOUS ISSUES – VALIDITY OF 1974 AMENDMENT NOT EXAMINED – KHANNA, J.

164. The High Court decided Issues 4, 6 and 7 in favour of the appellant and against the respondent. Issues 5, 8 and 10 were found in favour of the respondent and against the appellant. On Issue No. 9 the finding of the High Court was that the total amount of expenditure incurred or authorised by the appellant or her election agent, together with the expenditure proved to have been incurred by the party or by the State Government in connection with the appellant's election amounted to Rs. 31,976.47 which was sufficiently below the prescribed limit of Rs. 35,000. The appellant as such was held not guilty of any corrupt practice under section 123(6) of the Representation of People Act. As the respondent was found to have failed to prove that the expenses of the appellant or her election agent, together with the expenses found to have been incurred by the political party and the State Government in connection with the appellant's election exceeded the prescribed limit, the High Court held that no ground had been made out for inquiring into the validity of the 1974 amending Act. The writ petition filed by the respondent was accordingly dismissed.

ADDITIONAL ISSUES 1, 2 AND 3 DECIDED BY HIGH COURT IN FAVOUR OF RESPONDENT – KHANNA, J.

165. On additional issue No. 2, the finding of the High Court that the appellant held herself out as a candidate from the Raebareli Parliamentary constituency on December 29, 1970. Issue No. 3 was decided by the High Court against the appellant. It was held that the appellant obtained the assistance of the officers of the U.P. Government, particularly the District Magistrate, Superintendent of Police, the Executive Engineer PWD and the Engineer Hydel Department for construction of rostrums and arrangement of supply of power for loudspeakers in the meetings addressed by her on February 1, 1971 and February 25, 1971 in furtherance of her election prospects. The appellant, as such, was found guilty of corrupt practice under section 123(7) of the RP Act. On additional Issue No. 3, the High Court found that Yashpal Kapur continued to be in the service of the Government of India till January 25, 1971, which was the date of the notification regarding the acceptance of Yashpal Kapur's resignation. The High Court referred to the fact that according to the notification resignation of Yashpal Kapur had been accepted with effect from January 14, 1971 and observed that the order accepting the resignation was passed on January 25, 1971 and till that order was passed, the status of Yashpal Kapur continued to remain that of a Government servant despite the fact that when that order was passed it was given retrospective effect so as to be valid from January 14, 1971. As regards Issue No. 1 and additional issue No. 1, the High Court held that the appellant obtained and procured the assistance of Yashpal Kapur during the period from January 7 to 24, 1971 when Yashpal Kapur was still a gazetted officer in the service of the Government of India in the furtherance of her election prospects.

IN VIEW OF FINDINGS – PETITION ALLOWED – ELECTION OF APPELLANT SET ASIDE BY HIGH COURT – KHANNA, J.

166. As a result of its findings on Issues No. 3, Issue No. 1 read with additional Issue No. 1, additional issue No. 2 and additional issue No. 3, the High Court allowed the petition and declared the election of the appellant to the Lok Sabha to be void. The appellant was found guilty of having committed corrupt practice under section 123(7) of the RP Act by having obtained the assistance of Gazetted Officers of the U.P. Government, *viz.*, the District Magistrate and the Superintendent of Police Raebareli, the Executive Engineer PWD Raebareli and Engineer Hydel Department Raebareli in furtherance of her election prospects. The appellant was further found guilty of having committed another corrupt practice under section 123(7) of the RP Act by having obtained the assistance of Yashpal Kapur, a Gazetted Officer in the Government of India holding the post of Officer on Special Duty in Prime Minister's Secretariat, for the furtherance of her election prospects. The appellant, it was accordingly observed, stands disqualified for a period of six years from the date of the order in accordance with section 8A of the RP Act. The writ petition as mentioned earlier, was dismissed.

RESPONDENT FILED APPEAL AGAINST FINDING OF SOME ISSUES AGAINST HIM – KHANNA, J.

167. An appeal against the judgment of the learned single Judge of the High Court dismissing the writ petition is pending before the High Court.

168. During the pendency of these appeals, Parliament passed the Election Laws (Amendment) Act, 1975 (Act 40 of 1975) (hereinafter referred to as 1975 amending Act or Act 40 of 1975) and the same was published in the Gazette of India Extraordinary dated August 6, 1975. Section 2 of the 1975 amending Act substituted a new section for section 8-A in the Act. According to the new section the case of every person found guilty of a corrupt practice by an order under section 99 shall be submitted as soon as may be, after such order takes effect to the President for determination of the question as to whether such person shall be disqualified and if so, for what period not exceeding six years. It is also provided that the person who stands disqualified may before the expiry of the period of disqualification submit a petition to the President for the removal of such disqualification for the unexpired portion of the said period. The President shall then give his decision on such petition after obtaining the opinion of the Election Commission and in accordance with such opinion. Sections 3, 4 and 5 of the 1975-amending Act deal with other consequential matters relating to disqualification, and it is not necessary for the purpose of the present case to go into them.

DURING PENDENCY OF APPEAL – PARLIAMENT PASSED ELECTION LAWS (AMENDMENT) ACT, 1975 – WAS PUBLISHED ON 6 AUGUST, 1975 – MATERIAL CHANGES WERE BROUGHT IN REPRESENTATION OF PEOPLE ACT, 1951 – INDIAN PENAL CODE – WITH RETROSPECTIVE EFFECT – KHANNA, J.

* * * * *

Sections 6 and 7 amended sections 77 and 79 of the RP Act and we shall refer to them presently. Same is the position of section 8 of the amending Act which introduced changes in section 123 of the RP Act. Section 9 amended section 171-A of the Indian Penal. Code. Section 10 gives retrospective effect to sections 6, 7 and 8. Sections 6, 7, 8, 9 and 10 of Act 40 of 1975 read as under:

"6. In section 77 of the principal Act, in sub-section (1),

(a) for the words the date of publication of the notification calling the election', the words 'the date on which he has been nominated' shall be substituted;

(b) after *Explanation* 2, the following *Explanation* shall be inserted, namely:

'*Explanation* 3.—For the removal of doubt, it is hereby declared that any expenditure in respect of any arrangements made, facilities provided or any other act or thing done by any person in the service of the Government and belonging to any of the classes mentioned in clause (7) of section 123 in the discharge or purported discharge of his official duty as mentioned in the proviso to that clause shall not be deemed to be expenditure in connection with the election incurred or authorized by a candidate or by his election agent for the purposes of this sub-section.'

7. In section 79 of the principal Act, for clause (b), the following clause shall be substituted, namely:

'(b) 'candidate' means a person who has been or claims to have been duly nominated as a candidate at any election.'

8. In section 123 of the principal Act,

(a) in clause (3), the following proviso shall be inserted at the end, namely:

Provided that no symbol allotted under this Act to a candidate shall be deemed to be a religious symbol or a national symbol for the purposes of this clause.'

(b) in clause (7), the following proviso shall be inserted at the end, namely:'

Provided that where any person, in the service of the Government and belonging to any of the classes aforesaid, in the discharge or purported discharge of his official duty, makes any arrangements or provides any facilities or does any other act or thing, for, to, or in relation to, any candidate or his agent or any other person acting with the consent of the candidate or his election agent, (whether by reason of the office held by the candidate or for any other reason), such arrangements, facilities or act or thing shall not be deemed to be assistance for the furtherance of the prospects of that candidate's election.'

(c) in the *Explanation* at the end, the following shall be added, namely:'

(3) For the purposes of clause (7), notwithstanding anything contained in any other law, the publication in the Official Gazette of the appointment, resignation, termination of service, dismissal or removal from service of

a person in the service of the Central Government (including a person serving in connection with the administration of a Union territory) or of a State Government shall be conclusive proof

(i) of such appointment, resignation, termination of service, dismissal or removal from service, as the case may be, and

(ii) where the date of taking effect of such appointment, resignation, termination of service, as the case may be, is stated in such publication, also of the fact that such person was appointed with effect from the said date, or in the case of resignation, termination of service, dismissal or removal from service, such person ceased to be in such service with effect from the said date.'

'9. In the Indian Penal Code, in section 171A, for clause (a), the following clause shall be substituted, namely:

'(a) 'candidate' means a person, who has been nominated as a candidate at any election,'

"10. The amendments made by sections 6, 7 and 8 of this Act in the principal Act shall also have retrospective operation so as to apply to and in relation to any election held before the commencement of this Act to either House of Parliament or to either House or the House of the Legislature of a State—

(i) in respect of which any election petition may be presented after the commencement of this Act; or

(ii) in respect of which any election petition is pending in any High Court immediately before such commencement; or

(iii) in respect of which any election petition has been decided by any High Court before such commencement but no appeal has been preferred to the Supreme Court against the decision of the High Court before such commencement and the period of limitation for filing such appeal has not expired before such commencement; or

(iv) in respect of which appeal from any order of any High Court made in any election petition under section 98 or section 99 of the principal Act is pending before the Supreme Court immediately before such commencement."

AMENDMENTS MATERIALLY CHANGE THE RESULT – CONTENDS RESPONDENT

169. It is submitted by Mr. Shanti Bhushan on behalf of the respondent that the amendments made in the RP Act have an impact upon five out of the seven grounds which were set up by the respondent to assail the election of the appellant.

ON 10 AUGUST, 1975 CONSTITUTION (39TH AMENDMENT) ACT, 1975 PUBLISHED – ARTICLE 329A WAS ADDED – KHANNA, J.

170. On August 10, 1975 the Constitution (Thirty-ninth Amendment) Act, 1975 was published. A number of constitutional changes were made by the Constitution Amendment Act. We are, however, concerned with section 4 of the Constitutional Amendment Act which inserted Article "329A in the Constitution after Article 329. Article 329A reads as under:

"*329A. Special provision as to elections to Parliament in the case of Prime Minister and Speaker.*—(1) Subject to the provisions of Chapter II of Part V (Except sub-clause (e) of clause (1) of Article 102), no election

(a) to either House of Parliament of a person who holds the office of Prime Minister at the time of such election or is appointed as ' Prime Minister after such election;

(b) to the House of the People of a person who holds the office of Speaker of that House at the time of such election or who is chosen as the Speaker for that House after such election;

shall be called in question, except before such authority (not being any such authority as is referred to in clause (b) of Article 329) or body and in such manner as may be provided for by or under any law made by Parliament and any such law may provide for all other matters relating to doubts and disputes in relation to such election including the grounds on which such election may be questioned.

(2) The validity of any such law as is referred to in clause (1) and the decision of any authority or body under such law shall not be called in question in any court.

(3) Where any person is appointed as Prime Minister or, as the case may be, chosen to the office of the Speaker of the House of the People, while an election petition referred to in clause (b) of Article 329 in respect of his election to either House of Parliament or, as the case may be, to the House of the People is pending, such election petition shall abate upon such person being appointed as Prime Minister or, as the case may be, being chosen to the office of the Speaker of the House of the People, but such election may be called in question under any such law as is referred to in clause (1).

(4) No law made by Parliament before the commencement of the Constitution (Thirty-ninth Amendment) Act, 1975, in so far as it relates to election petitions and matters connected therewith, shall apply or shall be deemed ever to have applied to or in relation to the election of any such person as is referred to in clause (1) to either House of Parliament and such election shall not be deemed to be void or ever to have become void on any ground on which such election could be declared to be void or has, before such commencement, been declared to be void under any such law and notwithstanding any order made by any court, before such commencement, declaring such election to be void, such election shall continue to be valid in all respects and any such order and any finding on which such order is based shall be and shall be deemed always to have been void and of no effect.

(5) Any appeal or cross appeal against any such order of any court as is referred to in clause (4) pending immediately before the commencement of the Constitution (Thirty-ninth Amendment) Act, 1975, before the Supreme Court shall be disposed of in conformity with the provisions of clause (4),

(6) The provisions of this article shall have effect notwithstanding anything contained in this Constitution."

CONSTITUTIONAL AMENDMENT AND AMENDMENT IN RP ACT INSERTED IN 9TH SCHEDULE – KHANNA, J.

171. Section 5 of the above Constitution Amendment Act inserted in the Ninth Schedule to the Constitution a number of enactment's including the RP Act as also Acts 58 of 1974 and 40 of 1975.

LAW PRIOR TO AMENDMENT SHALL NOT APPLY IN VIEW OF CLAUSE (4) OF ARTICLE 329A – APPELLANT'S ELECTION WAS NOT VOID – CONTEND APPELLANT

172. At the hearing of the appeal Mr. Sen on behalf of the appellant has relied upon clause (4) of the new Article 329A and has contended that that clause clearly applies to the present case. It is urged that in view of that clause no law made by Parliament before the coming into force of the Constitution (Thirty-ninth Amendment) Act, 1975, *i.e.*, before August 10, 1975, in so far as it relates to the election petitions and matters connected therewith shall apply or shall be deemed ever to have applied to or in relation to the election to the Lok Sabha of the appellant who being Prime Minister is one of the persons referred to in clause (1) of that article. It is further submitted that in view of that clause, the election of the appellant shall not be deemed to be void or ever to have become void on any ground on which such election could be declared to be void or has before such commencement been declared to be void under any such law. Mr. Sen also adds that notwithstanding the order made by the High Court before such commencement declaring the election of the appellant to be void, her election shall continue to be valid in all respects and any such order and any finding on which such order is based shall be and shall be deemed always to have been void and of no effect. Submission is consequently made that in view of the mandate contained in clause (5) of the article, the appeal filed by the appellant and the cross appeal filed by the respondent should be disposed of in conformity with the provisions of clause (4).

CLAUSE (4) OF ARTICLE 329A WAS INVALID – CONTENDS RESPONDENT

173. In reply Mr. Shanti Bhushan on behalf of the respondent has not controverted, and in our opinion rightly, the stand taken by Mr. Sen that clause (4) of the article applies to the facts of the present case. He, however, contends that section 4 of the Constitution Amendment Act which has inserted Article 329A in the Constitution is invalid. The validity of the above constitutional amendment has been challenged by Mr. Shanti Bhushan on the following two grounds:

(1) The above constitutional amendment affects the basic structure or framework of the Constitution and is, therefore, beyond the amending power under Article 368.

(2) The Constitution Amendment Act was passed in a session of Parliament after some members of Parliament had been unconstitutionally detained and thus illegally prevented from influencing the views of other members present at the time the above Act was passed. This ground, it is urged, also affects the validity of the amending Act 40 of 1975.

IMPLICATION OF ALL THE 6 CLAUSES OF ARTICLE 329A ANALYSED – KHANNA, J.

174. Article 329A deals with election to either House of Parliament of a person who holds the office of Prime Minister at the time of such election or is appointed as Prime Minister after such election and to the House of the People of a person who holds the office of Speaker of that House at the time of such election or who is chosen as the Speaker for that House after such election. According to clause (I) of Article 329A, no election of persons mentioned above shall be called in question, except before such authority or body and in such manner as may be provided for by or under any law made by Parliament. It is made clear that the authority before which such election shall be called in question would not be the one as is referred to in clause (b) of Article 329. The law to be made by Parliament under clause (1) may provide for all other matters relating to doubts and disputes in relation to such election including the grounds on which such election may be questioned. The above law shall be subject to the provisions of clause (1) of Article 102 except sub-clause (e). The law made under clause (1) cannot, therefore, remove the disqualification for being chosen a member of either House of Parliament because of that person holding an office of profit or because of his unsoundness of mind or because of his being an undischarged insolvent or because of his being not a citizen of India, or because of his having voluntarily acquired the citizenship of a foreign State, or because of his being under any acknowledgment of allegiance or adherence to a foreign State, as contemplated by sub-clauses (a) to (d) of clause (1) of Article 102 of the Constitution.

The law made under clause (1) of Article 329A would not, however, be subject to clause (e) of clause (1) of Article 102, according to which a person shall be disqualified for being chosen as and for being, a member of either House of Parliament if he is so disqualified by or under any law made by Parliament, According to clause (2) of Article 329A, the validity of a law referred to in clause (1) and the decision of any authority or body under such law shall not be called in question in any court.

Clause (3) provides for the abatement of an election petition which is pending in respect of the election of any person who is appointed as Prime Minister or chosen as Speaker of the House of the People during the pendency of the petition. It is further provided that the election of such person can be called in question under any such law as is referred to in clause (1) of Article 329A.

Clause (4) is the crucial clause for the present case. According to this clause, no law made by Parliament before the commencement of the Constitution (Thirty-ninth Amendment) Act in so far as it relates to election petitions and matters connected therewith, shall apply or shall be deemed ever to have applied to or in relation to the election of any of the persons mentioned above to either House of Parliament. The remaining part of the clause deals with some further matters. It is provided in clause (4) that the election of the aforesaid person shall not be deemed to be void or ever to have become void on any ground on which such election could be declared to be void or has, before such commencement, been declared to be void under any such law.

It is further provided that notwithstanding any order made by any court before the commencement of the Constitution (Thirty-ninth Amendment) Act declaring such election to be void, such election shall continue to be valid in all respects and any such order and any finding on which such order is based shall be and shall be deemed always to have been void and of no effect.

According to clause (5), any appeal or cross appeal against any such order as is referred to in clause (4) pending immediately before the commencement of the Constitution (Thirty-ninth Amendment) Act, before the Supreme Court shall be disposed of in conformity with the provisions of clause (4).

Clause (6) states that the provisions of Article 329A shall take effect notwithstanding anything contained in the Constitution.

ARTICLE 368 DOES NOT ALLOW CONSTITUENT POWER TO AMEND BASIC STRUCTURE OF THE CONSTITUTION – KHANNA, J.

175. The proposition that the power of amendment under Article 368 does not enable Parliament to alter the basic structure or framework of the Constitution was laid down by this Court by a majority of 7 to 6 in the case of **His Holiness Keshavananda Bharathi v. State of Kerala, (1973) Supp SCR 1.** Apart from other reasons which were given in some of the judgments of the learned Judges who constituted the majority, the majority dealt with the connotation of the word "amendment." It was held that the words "amendment of the Constitution" in Article 368 could not have the effect of destroying or abrogating the basic structure of the Constitution. Some of us who were parties to that case took a different view and came to the conclusion that the words "amendment of the Constitution" in Article 368 did not admit of any limitation. Those of us who were in the minority in **Kesavananda's** case (supra) may still hold the same view as was given expression to in that case. For the purpose of the present case, we shall have to proceed in accordance with the law as laid down by the majority in that case.

COURT DOES NOT EXAMINE THE WISDOM OF THE AMENDMENT - ONLY VALIDITY - KHANNA, J.

176. Before dealing with the question as to whether the impugned amendment affects the basic structure of the Constitution, I may make it clear that this Court is not concerned with the wisdom behind or the propriety of the impugned constitutional amendment. These are matters essentially for those who are vested with the authority to make the constitutional amendment. All that this Court is concerned with is the constitutional validity of the impugned amendment.

SOME MEMBERS OF PARLIAMENT WERE UNDER DETENTION - COULD NOT ATTEND SESSION - AMENDMENTS WERE NOT VALID - CONTENDS RESPONDENT

177. I may first deal with the second contention advanced by Mr. Shanti Bhushan. According to him, the impugned constitutional amendment and the amending Act of 1975 were passed in sessions of Parliament wherein some members, including the respondent, could not be present because they had been illegally detained. The fact that those measures were passed by the requisite majority has not been questioned by the learned counsel but he submits that if the above mentioned members had not been detained and had not been prevented from attending the sittings of Parliament, they could have influenced the other members and as such it is possible that the impugned Constitution Amendment Act and the 1975 RP amending Act might not have been passed. Mr. Shanti Bhushan accordingly asserts that the sittings of the Houses of Parliament in which the above mentioned two measures were passed were not legal sittings. Any measure passed in such sittings, according to the learned counsel, cannot be considered to be a valid piece of constitutional amendment or statutory amendment.

DETENTION COLLATERAL ISSUE - SUBMISSION REJECTED - KHANNA, J.

178. There, is in my opinion, no force in the above submission. The proposition that a member of Parliament cannot claim immunity from being detained under a law relating to preventive detention does not now admit of much doubt. The privileges, powers and the immunities of the members of the two Houses of Indian Parliament as well as of the Indian legislatures are the same as those of the members of the House of Commons as they existed at the time of the commencement of the Constitution. The position about the privileges of the members of the House of Commons as it obtained in the United Kingdom to the relevant time has been stated in *Erskine May's Parliamentary Practice*, 18th Edn. (p. 100) as under:

> "The privilege of freedom from arrest is limited to civil causes, and has not been allowed to interfere with the administration of criminal justice or emergency legislation. "

The above observations were relied upon by this Court in the case of **K. Anandan Nambiar v. Chief Secretary Government of Madras, (1966) 2 SCR 406.** The petitioners in that case were members of Parliament. They were detained by orders passed by the State Government under rule 30(1)(b) of the Defence of India Rules, 1962. They challenged the validity of the orders of detention, *inter alia*, on the ground that rule 30(1)(b) was invalid because a legislator cannot be detained so as to prevent him from exercising his constitutional rights as legislator while the legislative chamber to which he belongs is in session. This Court rejected that contention and held that the true constitutional position is that so far as a valid order of detention is concerned, a member of Parliament can claim no special status higher than that of an ordinary citizen and that he is as much liable to be arrested and detained under it as any other citizen. It was also held that if an order of detention validly prevents a member from attending a session of Parliament no occasion would arise for the exercise by him of the right of freedom of speech.

179. Question as to whether a member of Parliament has been validly detained under a law relating to preventive detention can, in my opinion, be appropriately gone into in proceedings for a writ of habeas corpus. Such question cannot be collaterally raised in proceedings like the present wherein the court is concerned with the validity of a Constitution Amendment Act and an Act to amend the Representation of the People Act. In deciding a case before it the court should decide matters which arise directly in the case. A court should resist the attempt of a party to induce it to decide a matter which though canvassed during arguments is only incidental and collateral and can appropriately be dealt with in separate proceedings.

PROCEEDINGS OF TWO HOUSES – PASSING AMENDMENTS – INVALID CONTENTION REJECTED – KHANNA, J.

180. The contention advanced by Mr. Shanti Bhushan that the sittings of the two Houses of Parliament in which the impugned Acts were passed were not valid essentially relates to the validity of the proceedings of the two Houses of Parliament. These are matters, which are not justifiable and pertain to the internal domain of the two Houses. Of course, the courts can go into the question as to whether the measures passed by Parliament are constitutionally valid. The court cannot, however, go into the question as to whether the sittings of the Houses of Parliament were not constitutionally valid because some members of those Houses were prevented from attending and participating in the discussions in those Houses. It has not been disputed before us, as already mentioned, that the impugned Constitution Amendment Act and the statutory amendment Act were passed by the requisite majority.

It is not the case of the respondent that the number of the detained members of Parliament was so large, that if they had voted against the impugned measures, the measures would not have been passed. Indeed, according to the affidavit filed during the course of arguments, the number of members of the Lok Sabha who were detained was 21 and of the Rajya Sabha the number was 10.

An amendment of the Constitution under Article 368, it is noteworthy, has apart from the requirement in certain cases of ratification by the State legislatures, to be passed in each House of Parliament by majority of the total membership of that House and by a majority of two-thirds of the members of that House present and voting.

According to clause (1) of Article 100 of the Constitution, save as otherwise provided in this Constitution, all questions at any sitting of either House or joint sitting of the Houses shall be determined by a majority of votes of the members present and voting, other than the Speaker or person acting as Chairman or Speaker. The Chairman or Speaker, or person acting as such, shall not vote in the first instance, but shall have and exercise a casting vote in the case of an equality of votes. Clause (2) of that article provides that either House of Parliament shall have power to act notwithstanding any vacancy in the membership thereof, and any proceedings in Parliament shall be valid notwithstanding that it is discovered subsequently that some person who was not entitled so to do sat or voted or otherwise took part in the proceedings.

Further, it is provided in clause (1) of Article 122 that the validity of any proceedings of Parliament shall not be called in question on the ground of any alleged irregularity of procedure. All this would show that the framers of the Constitution were anxious to ensure that the procedural irregularities and other grounds like those mentioned in clause (2) of Article 100 should not vitiate the validity of proceedings of Parliament and that it would not be permissible to call in question those proceedings on such grounds.

The observations on page 456 in the case of **Special Reference No. 1 of 1964 (1965) 1 SCR 413: AIR 1965 SC 745** that if the impugned proceedings of a legislature are illegal and unconstitutional and not merely irregular, the same can be scrutinised in a court of law do not, in my opinion, warrant the inference that a court can hold the proceedings of a legislature to be not valid and constitutional by going into the question as to whether the detention of any member who was prevented from being present in the sitting of the legislature on account of his detention was or was not in accordance with law.

The acceptance of the above submission of Mr. Shanti Bhushan would necessarily result in a situation that whenever a law is made by Parliament, it would be open to a person affected by that law to question the validity of that law by asking the court to examine the validity of detention of each of the members of Parliament who were under detention at the time the said law was passed even though those members do not themselves assail the validity of their detention.

It is plain that it would not be possible for the court in such collateral proceedings to record a finding about the validity of the detention of the members because the full material having a bearing on the validity of the detention would normally be, apart from the authority passing the order for detention, only with the person ordered to be detained or his friends and relatives. It would plainly be hazardous to record a finding without such material and a court of law, in my opinion, should decline to record such a finding in collateral proceedings.

Till such time as a finding is recorded in appropriate proceedings about the validity of the detention of the members of Parliament, the court would have to proceed upon the assumption that the detention has not been shown to be invalid.

181. According to clause (3) of article 105 of the Constitution, to which a short reference has been made earlier, the powers, privileges and immunities of each House of Parliament, and of the members and the committees of each House, shall be such as may from time-to-time be defined by Parliament by law, and, until so defined, shall be those of the House of Commons of the Parliament of the United Kingdom, and of its members and committees, at the commencement of this Constitution. No law contemplated by clause (3) has been made by the Parliament in India and as such we have to find out the powers, privileges and immunities of the House of Commons in the United Kingdom at the relevant time. In the case of **Bradlaugh v. Gossett, (1884) 12 QBD 271** the plaintiff, having been returned as member for the borough of Northampton, required the Speaker of the House of Commons to call him to the table for the purpose of taking oath. In consequence of something which had transpired on a former occasion the Speaker declined to do so. The House of Commons then upon motion resolved "that the Sergeant-at-Arms do exclude Mr. Bradlaugh (the plaintiff) from the House until he shall engage not further to disturb the proceedings of the House. "In an action against the Sergeant-at-Arms praying for an injunction to restrain him from carrying out the resolution, the court held that this being a matter relating to the internal management of the procedure of the House of Commons, the court had no power to interfere. Dealing with the fights to be exercised within the walls of the House, Stephen J., observed that those rights must be dependent upon the resolution of the House. He also added that there was no appeal from the decision of the House of Commons. Stephen J. in the course of the judgement also observed:

> ".......for the purpose of determining on a right to be exercised within the House itself, and in particular the right of sitting and voting, the House and the House alone could interpret the statute but.... as regarded rights to be exercised out of and independently of the House, such as the right of suing for a penalty for having sat and voted, the statute must be interpreted by this Court independently of the House. "

The above passage has been cited on page 83 in *Erskine May's Parliamentary Practice*, 18th Ed. with a view to show that it is a right of each House of Parliament to be the sole judge of the lawfulness of its own proceedings. It would follow from the above that the courts cannot go into the lawfulness of the proceedings of the Houses of Parliament.

182. The act of detaining a person is normally that of an outside agency and not that of the House of Parliament. It would certainly look anomalous if the act of an outside agency which might ultimately turn out to be not legal could affect the validity of the proceedings of the House of Parliament or could prevent that House from assembling and functioning.

PUBLICATION IN THE GAZETTE OF THESE TWO ACTS – COURTS ARE TO ASSUME THAT THESE ACTS WERE VALIDLY PASSED – KHANNA J.

183. The matter can also be looked at from another angle. Gazette copies of the Election Laws Amendment Act, 1975 (Act 40 of 1975) and the Constitution (Thirty-ninth Amendment) Act, 1975 have been produced before us. In the face of the publication in the Gazette of the above mentioned two Acts this Court must assume that those two Acts were duly passed. It may be pertinent in this context to refer to the position in the United States where it was laid down in the case of **Marshall Field and Co. v. John M. Clark, (1892) 143 US 649** as under:

> "The signing by the Speaker of the House of Representatives, and by the President of the Senate in open session, of an enrolled bill, is an official attestation by the two houses that such bill has passed Congress; and when the bill, thus attested receives the approval of the President, and is deposited in the public archives, its authentication as a bill, that has passed Congress is complete and unimpeachable. An enrolled Act thus authenticated is sufficient evidence of itself that it passed Congress."

In the case of a constitutional amendment which requires ratification by the States, the position was stated by Brandeis J. in the case of **Oscar Leser v. J. Mercer Garnett, (1921) 66 L Ed 505** as follows:

> "The proclamation by the Secretary certified that, from official documents on file in the Department of State, it appeared that the proposed Amendment was ratified by the legislatures of thirty-six states, and that it 'has become valid to all intents and purposes as a part of the Constitution of the United States'. As the legislatures of Tennessee and of West Virginia had power to adopt the resolutions of ratification, official notice to the Secretary duly authenticated, that they had done so, was conclusive upon him, and, being certified to by his proclamation is conclusive upon the courts."

184. I am, therefore, of the view that the constitutional validity of the Constitution Amendment Act and the 1975 Act amending the Representation of the People Act cannot be assailed on the ground that some members of Parliament were prevented because of their detention from attending and participating in the proceedings of the respective Houses of Parliament.

CLAUSE (4) OF ARTICLE 329A ADDED ON 10.8.1975 ANALYSED – KHANNA, J.

185. We may now deal with clause (4) of Article 329A which has been added by the Constitution (Thirty-ninth Amendment) Act, 1975. It is necessary to clarify at the outset that we are concerned in the present case only with the constitutional validity of clause (4) and not with that of the other clauses of that article. I, therefore, express no opinion about the validity of the other clauses of Article 329A. Clause (4) consists of four parts:

(i) No law made by Parliament before the commencement of the Constitution (Thirty-ninth Amendment) Act, 1975 in so far as it relates to the election petitions and matters connected therewith shall apply or shall be deemed even to have applied to or in relation to the election of any such person as is referred to in clause (1) to either House of Parliament;

(ii) and such election shall not be deemed to be void or ever to have become void on any ground on which such election could be declared to be void or has before such commencement been declared to be void under any such law :

(iii) and notwithstanding any order made by any court before such commencement declaring such election to be void, such election shall continue to be valid in all respects;

(iv) and any such order and any finding on which such order is based shall be and shall be deemed always to have been void and of no effect.

PART (i) OF CLAUSE (4) WITH RETROSPECTIVE EFFECT CAN BE LEGISLATED – HELD KHANNA, J.

186. Insofar as Part (i) is concerned, I find that it relates to a matter, which can be the subject of an ordinary legislation or a constitutional amendment. According to this part, no law made by Parliament before the commencement of the Constitution (39th Amendment) Act, 1975 insofar as it relates to the election petitions and matters connected therewith shall apply and shall be deemed ever to have applied to or in relation to the election of any such person as is referred to in clause (1) to either House of Parliament. A law in the above terms can validly be made by a legislature as well as by a constituent authority. The fact that the above law would have retrospective effect would not detract from the competence of the legislature or constituent authority to make such a law. It is well-settled that it is permissible for a legislature to make a law with retrospective effect. The power of a legislature to make a law with retrospective effect is not curtailed or circumscribed by the fact that the subject matter of such retrospective law is a matter relating to an election dispute (see **State of Orissa v. Bhupendra Kumar Bose, (1962) Supp 2 SCR 380** and **Kanta Kathuria v. Manak Chand Surana, (1970) 2 SCR 835.** Detailed reference to these cases would be made at the appropriate stage subsequently. If a legislature can pass legislation in respect of matters relating to an election dispute with a retrospective effect, the constituent authority, which is a kind of super legislature, would a fortiori be entitled to do so.

PART (ii) AND ONE PART (iv) OF CLAUSE (4) ARE CONSEQUENTIAL TO PART (i) – HELD KHANNA, J.

187. Part (ii) of clause (4) spells out the consequence which flows from Part (i) of the clause. If the previous law in so far as it relates to the election petitions and matters connected therewith was not to apply to the election of the Prime Minister and the Speaker, it would necessarily follow that the election of the appellant who was the Prime Minister would not be deemed to be void or ever to have become void on the ground on which such election could be declared to be void or has before such commencement been declared to be void under any such law.

188. The same, to some extent, appears to be true of Part (iv) of clause (4). If the previous law in so far as it relates to the election petitions and matters connected therewith was not to apply to the election of the appellant, the High Court shall be deemed to have had no jurisdiction to decide the election petition challenging the election of the appellant. The effect of Part (i) of clause (4) is that the High Court was divested of the jurisdiction to decide the dispute relating to the election of the appellant with a retrospective effect. The law under which the election of the appellant was declared to be void as a result of the amendment was also made inapplicable with retrospective effect to the dispute relating to the election of the appellant. The resultant effect of the amendment thus was that the order by which the election of the appellant was declared to be void and the findings on which such order was based were rendered to be void and of no effect.

ANOTHER ASPECT OF PART (iv) CLAUSE (4) ANALYSED – CAN A DECLARATION OF AN ORDER BEING VOID BE MADE BY LEGISLATIVE FUNCTION OR BY CONSTITUENT AUTHORITY OR BY NONE – DISCUSSED – NO OPINION EXPRESSED – KHANNA, J.

189. Another aspect of Part (iv) of clause (4) relates to the question as to whether it is open to the constituent authority to declare an order and a finding of the High Court to be void and of no effect or whether such a declaration can be made only either in separate judicial proceedings or in proceedings before a higher court.

190. A declaration that an order made by a court of law is void is normally part of the judicial function and is not a legislative function. Although there is in the Constitution of India no rigid separation of powers, by and large the spheres of judicial function and legislative function have been demarcated and it is not permissible for the legislature to encroach upon the judicial sphere. It has accordingly been held that a legislature while it is entitled to change with retrospective effect the law which formed the basis of the judicial decision, it is not permissible to the legislature to declare the judgment of the court to be void or not binding (see **Shri Prithvi Cotton Mills Ltd. v. Broach Borough Municipality, (1970) 1 SCR 388 (392); Janapada Sabha, Chhindwara v. The Central Provinces Syndicate Ltd., (1970) 3 SCR 745 (751);** ***Municipal Corporation of the City of Ahmedabad*** **v.** ***New Shorock Spg. and Wvg. Co. Ltd.,*** **(1970) 1 SCR 288** and **State of Tamil Nadu v. M. Rayappa Gounder, AIR 1971 SC 231.**

* * * * *

192. Question arises whether the above limitation imposed upon the legislature about its competence to declare a judgment of the court to be void would also operate upon the constituent authority?

193. View has been canvassed before us that the answer to the above question should be in the negative. Although normally a declaration that the judgment of a court is, void can be made either in separate proceedings or in proceedings before the higher court, there is, according to this view, no bar to the constituent authority making a declaration in the constitutional law that such an order would be void especially when it relates to a matter of public importance like the dispute relating to the election of a person holding the office of Prime Minister. The declaration of the voidness of the High Court judgment is something which can ultimately be traced to Part (i). Whether such a declaration should be made by the court or by the constituent authority is more, it is urged, a matter of the mechanics of making the declaration and would not ultimately affect the substance of the matter that the judgment is declared void.

According to Article 31B, without prejudice to the generality of the provisions contained in Article 31A, none of the Acts and Regulations specified in the Ninth

Schedule nor any of the provisions thereof shall be deemed to be void, or ever to have become void, on the ground that such Act, Regulation or provision is inconsistent with, or takes away or abridges any of the rights conferred by, any provisions of this Part, and notwithstanding any judgment, decree or order of any court or tribunal to the contrary, each of the said Acts and Regulations shall, subject to the power of any competent Legislature to repeal or amend it, continue in force. The effect of the above article, it is pointed out, is that even if a statute has been declared to be void on the ground of contravention of fundamental rights by a court of law, the moment that statute is specified by the constituent authority in the Ninth Schedule to the Constitution, it shall be deemed to have got rid of that voidness and the order of the court declaring that statute to be void is rendered to be of no effect. It is not necessary in such an event to make even the slightest change in the statute to rid it of its voidness. The stigma of voidness attaching to the statute because of contravention of fundamental rights found by the Court is deemed to be washed away as soon as the statute is specified by the constituent authority in the Ninth Schedule and the judgment of the Court in this respect is rendered to be inoperative and of no effect.

In the case of **Don John Douglas Liyange v. The Queen, 1967 AC 259** the Judicial Committee struck down as ultra vires and void the provisions of the Criminal Law (Special Provisions) Act, 1962 on the ground that they involved the usurpation and infringement by the legislature of the judicial powers inconsistent with the written constitution of Ceylon. Their Lordships, however, expressly referred on page 287 to the fact that the impugned legislation had not been passed by two-third majority in the manner required for an amendment of the Constitution contained in section 29(4) of the Constitution. It was observed:

> "There was speculation during the argument as to what the position would be if Parliament sought to procure such a result by first amending the Constitution by a two-third majority. But such a situation does not arise here. In so far as any Act passed without recourse to section 29(4) of the Constitution purports to usurp or infringe the judicial power it is *ultra vires*".

The above observations, it is urged, show that the restriction upon the legislature in encroaching upon judicial sphere may not necessarily hold good in the case of constituent authority.

194. The above contention has been controverted by Mr. Shanti Bhushan and he submits that the limitation on the power of the legislature that it cannot declare void a judgment of the Court equally operates upon the constituent authority. It is urged that the constituent authority can only enact a law in general terms, even though it is a constitutional law. The constituent authority may also, if it so deems proper change the law which is the basis of a decision and make such change with retrospective effect, but it cannot, according to the learned counsel, declare void the judgment of the Court. Declaration of voidness of a judgment, it is stated, is a judicial act and cannot be taken over by the constituent authority. Although legislatures or the constituent authority can make laws including those for creation of courts, they cannot, according to the submission, exercise judicial functions by assuming the powers of a super court in the same way as the Courts cannot act as a super legislature. It is in my opinion, not necessary to dilate upon this aspect and express a final opinion upon the rival contentions, because of the view I am taking of Part (iii) of clause (4).

NO BASIS GIVEN IN PART (iii) OF CLAUSE 4 OF ARTICLE 329A FOR DECLARING ELECTION OF APPELLANT VALID – KHANNA, J.

195. We may now come to Part (iii) of clause (4). By Part (iii) it is declared that the election of the appellant shall continue to be valid in all respects. Such a declaration would not follow from part (i) of the clause. It would not also follow from Part (ii) and Part (iv) of the clause which, as mentioned earlier, in effect represented the consequences flowing from Part (i). The election to the Lok Sabha of the appellant, who was the Prime Minister, was challenged on the ground that she or her election agents had been guilty of some malpractices. The declaration that her election was to be valid in all respects necessarily involved the process of going into the grounds on which her election had been assailed and holding those grounds to be either factually incorrect or to be of such a nature as in law did not warrant the declaration of her election to be void. The case of the appellant is that some of the grounds mentioned against her were factually incorrect and in respect of those grounds the findings of the High Court is against the respondent and in her favour. In respect of some other grounds, except in one or two matters there is not much divergence between the appellant and the respondent on the question of facts. The point of controversy between the parties mainly is that, according to the respondent, those facts constituted corrupt practice as defined in section 123 of the RP Act, while according to the appellant those facts did not constitute corrupt practice. In any, case, according to the appellant, in view of the amendment made in the RP Act by amending Acts 58 of 1974 and 40 of 1975, these facts did not constitute corrupt practice.

The declaration made in Part (iii) of clause (4) that the election of the appellant was to be valid in all respects was tantamount in the very nature of things to the repelling of the grounds advanced by the respondent to challenge the election of the appellant. Question, therefore, arises as to what, if any, was the law which was applied in repelling the grounds advanced by the respondent to challenge the election of the appellant. So far as the existing law relating to election disputes was concerned, Part (i) of clause (4) expressly stated that such a law would not apply to the petition filed by the respondent to challenge the election of the appellant. This means that the provisions of the Representation of the People Act were not to apply to the petition filed by the respondent against the appellant. This also means that the amending Acts 58 of 1974 and 40 of 1975 were not to apply to the dispute relating to election of the appellant.

196. The dispute relating to the election of the appellant is also not to be governed by law which is to be enacted under clause (1) of Article 329 A. Such a law would apply only to future elections. The result is that so far as the dispute relating to the election of the appellant is concerned, a legal vacuum came into existence. It was open to the constituent authority to fill that vacuum by prescribing a law which was to govern the dispute arising out of the petition filed by the respondent to challenge the election of the appellant. The constituent authority, however, did not to do so and straightway proceeded to declare the election of the appellant to be valid. There is nothing in clause (4) to indicate that the constituent authority applied any law in declaring the election of the appellant to be valid and if so, what was that law.

LAW PRIOR TO AMENDMENT INCLUDING 1974, 1975 AMENDMENTS BARRED BY FIRST PART OF CLAUSE (4) OF ARTICLE 329A – BY WHAT LAW ELECTION OF APPELLANT HAS BEEN HELD VALID UNDER PART (iii)? – HELD KHANNA, J.

197. I am unable to accede to the argument that the constituent authority kept in view the provisions of the RP Act as amended by Acts 58 of 1974 and 40 of 1975 and their impact on the challenge to the election of the appellant in declaring the election of the appellant to be valid. The difficulty in accepting this argument is that in Part (i) of clause (4) the constituent authority expressly stated that the previous law, namely, the RP Act as amended in so far as it related to election petitions and matters connected therewith was not to apply so far as the challenge to the election of the appellant was concerned. It is also difficult to agree that the constituent authority took into account some other unspecified law or norm in declaring the election of the appellant to be valid.

As mentioned earlier, there is nothing in clause (4) to indicate that the constituent authority took into account some other law or norm and if so, what that law or norm was. The position which thus emerges is that according to clause (4) no law was to apply for adjudicating upon the challenge to the election of the appellant and the same was in terms of Part (iii) to be valid in all respects. The question with which we are concerned is whether the provisions of clause (4) of Article 329 A by which the constituent authority in effect prescribed that no election law was to govern the challenge to the election of the appellant and that the same in any case was to be valid in all respects is a permissible piece of constitutional amendment or whether it is void on the ground that it affects the basic structure of the Constitution.

FREE AND FAIR ELECTIONS CONSTITUTE DEMOCRACY – ARE A BASIC STRUCTURE OF CONSTITUTION – WHEN MALPRACTICE IN ELECTIONS IS ALLEGED – THERE MUST BE SOME FORUM TO DECIDE – ELECTION DISPUTES CANNOT BE DECIDED BY WISHFUL THINKING – HELD KHANNA, J.

198. This Court in the case of **Kesavananda Bharati**, (supra) held by majority that the power of amendment of the Constitution contained in Article 368 does not permit altering the basic structure of the Constitution. All the seven Judges who constituted the majority were also agreed that democratic set up was part of the basic structure of the Constitution. Democracy postulates that there should be periodical elections, so that people may be in a position either to re-elect the old representatives or, if they so choose, to change the representatives and elect in their place other representatives. Democracy further contemplates that the elections should be free and fair, so that the voters may be in a position to vote for candidates of their choice. Democracy can indeed function only upon the faith that elections are free and fair and not rigged and manipulated, that they are effective instruments of ascertaining popular will both in reality and form and are not mere rituals calculated to generate illusion of deference to mass opinion. Free and fair elections require that the candidates and their agents should not resort to unfair means or malpractices as may impinge upon the process of free and fair elections. Even in the absence of unfair means and malpractices, sometimes the result of an election is materially affected because of the improper rejection of ballot papers. Likewise, the result of an election may be materially affected on account of the improper rejection of a nomination paper. Disputes, therefore, arise with regard to the validity of elections. For the resolving of those disputes, the different democratic countries of the world have made provisions prescribing the law and the forum for resolving of those disputes. To give a few examples, we may refer to the United Kingdom where a parliamentary election petition is tried by two judges on the rota for the trial of parliamentary election petitions in accordance with the Representation of the People Act, 1949. Section 5 of Article 1 of the US Constitution provides that each House (Senate and the House of Representatives) shall be judge of the elections, returns and qualifications of its own members. Section 47 of the Australian Constitution provides that until the Parliament otherwise provides, any question respecting the qualification of a senator or of a member of the House of Representatives, or respecting a vacancy in either House of Parliament, and any question of a disputed election to either House, shall be determined by the House in which the question arises. Article 55 of the Japanese Constitution states that each House shall judge disputes related to qualifications of its members. However, in order to deny a seat to any member, it is necessary to pass a resolution by a majority of two-thirds or more of the members present. Article 46 of the Iceland Constitution provides that the Althing itself decides whether its members are legally elected and whether a member is disqualified. Article 64 of the Norwegian Constitution states that the representatives elected shall be furnished with certificates, the validity of which shall be submitted to the judgment of the Starting. Article 59 of the French Constitution provides that the Constitutional Council shall rule, in the case of disagreement, on the regularity of the election of deputies and senators. Article 41 of the German Federal Republic Constitution states that the scrutiny of elections shall be the responsibility of the Bundestag. It shall also decide whether a deputy has lost his seat in the Bundestag. Against the decision of the Bundestag an appeal shall lie to the Federal Constitutional Court. Details shall be regulated by a federal law. According to Article 66 of the Italian Constitution, each Chamber decides as to the validity of the admission of its own Members and as to cases subsequently arising concerning ineligibility and incompatibility. In Turkey Article 75 provides *inter alia* that it shall be the function of Supreme Election Board to review and pass final judgment on all irregularities, complaints and objections regarding election matters during and after elections.

The function and powers of the Supreme Election Board shall be regulated by law. Article 53 of the Malaysian Constitution provides that if any question arises whether a member of a House of Parliament has become disqualified for membership, the decision of that House shall be taken and shall be final.

199. Not much argument is needed to show that unless there be a machinery for resolving an election dispute and for going into the allegations that elections were not free and fair being vitiated by malpractices the provision that a candidate should not resort to malpractices would be in the nature of a mere pious wish without any legal sanction. It is further plain that if the validity of the election of a candidate is challenged on some grounds, the said election can be declared to be valid only if we provide a forum for going into those grounds and prescribe a law for adjudicating upon those grounds. If the said forum finds that the grounds advanced to challenge the election are not well-founded or are not sufficient to invalidate the election in accordance with the prescribed law or dismisses the petition to challenge the election on some other ground, in such an event it can be said that the election of the returned candidate is valid.

ELECTION LAWS LAY DOWN CERTAIN CODE OF CONDUCT – RULES OF ELECTORAL MORALITY – LACK OF POWER TO PUNISH THE VIOLATION IS MOCKERY – HELD KHANNA, J.

200. Besides other things, election laws lay down a code of conduct in election matters and prescribe, what may be called, rules of electoral morality. Election laws also contain a provision for resolving disputes and determination of controversies which must inevitably arise in election matters as they arise in other spheres of human activity. The object of such a provision is to enforce rules of electoral morality and to punish deviance from the prescribed code of conduct in election matters. It is manifest that but for such a provision, there would be no sanction for the above code of conduct and rules of electoral morality. It is also plain that nothing would bring the code of conduct into greater contempt and make a greater mockery of it than the absence of a provision to punish its violation. The position would become all the more glaring that even though a provision exists on the statute book for punishing violation of the code of conduct in election matters, a particular election is made immune and granted exemption from the operation of such a provision.

PRIOR LAW WITH AMENDMENTS OVERRULED – NEW LAW OR FORUM – NOT PROVIDED – TO DECIDE ELECTION DISPUTE – VIOLATIVE OF FREE AND FAIR ELECTIONS – CLAUSE (4) OF ARTICLE 329A SIMPLY DECLARES THE ELECTIONS OF THE PM VALID – NO MAN IS ABOVE THE LAW – HELD KHANNA, J.

201. The vice of clause (4) of Article 329A is not merely that it makes the previous law contained in the RP Act as amended by Act 58 of 1974 and 40 of 1975 inapplicable to the challenge to the election of the appellant it also makes no other election law applicable for resolving that dispute. The further vice from which the said clause suffers is that it not merely divests the previous authority, namely, the High Court of its jurisdiction to decide the dispute relating to the election of the appellant, it confers no jurisdiction on some other authority to decide that dispute. Without even prescribing a law and providing a forum for adjudicating upon the grounds advanced by the respondent to challenge the election of the appellant, the constituent authority has declared the election of the appellant to be valid.

202. To confer an absolute validity upon the election of one particular candidate and to prescribe that the validity of that election shall not be questioned before any forum or under any law would necessarily have the effect of saying that howsoever gross may be the improprieties which might have vitiated that election, howsoever flagrant may be the malpractices which might have been committed on behalf of the returned candidate during the course of the election and howsoever foul and violative of the principles of free and fair elections may be the means which might have been employed for securing success in that election, the said election would be nonetheless valid and it would not be permissible to complain of those improprieties, malpractices and unfair means before any forum or under any law with a view to assail the validity of that election.

Not much argument is needed to show that any provision which brings about that result is subversive of the principle of free and fair election in a democracy. The fact that the candidate concerned is the Prime Minister of the country or the Speaker of the lower House of Parliament would, if anything, add force to the above conclusion because both these offices represent the acme of the democratic process in a country. That in fact the elections of the incumbents of the two offices were not vitiated by any impropriety, malpractice or unfair means is not relevant or germane to the question with which we are concerned, namely, as to what is the effect of clause (4) of Article 329A.

203. The vice of declaration contained in Part (iii) of clause (4) regarding the validity of the election of the appellant is aggravated by the fact that such a declaration is made after the High Court which was then seized of jurisdiction had found substance in some of the grounds advanced by the respondent and had consequently declared the election of the appellant to be void. To put a stamp of validity on the election of a candidate by saying that the challenge to such an election would not be governed by any election law and that the said election in any case would be valid and immune from any challenge runs counter to accepted norms of free and fair elections in all democratic countries. In the case of **Marbury v. Madison, (1803) 1 Cranch 137 (163)** Marshall, C.J., said that "the government of the United States has been emphatically termed a government of laws and not of men". In **United States v. Lee, (1883) 106 US 196 (220)** Samuel Miller, J. observed that "no man is so high that he is above the law.... All...., officers are creatures of the law and are bound to obey it". Although the above observations were made in the context of the US Constitution, they, in my opinion, hold equally good in the context of our Constitution.

ELECTION HELD VOID ON TECHNICALITIES – CONTENDS APPELLANT – CLAUSE (4) OF ARTICLE 329A MAKES ELECTION OF PM VALID HOWSOEVER GRAVE MALPRACTICES COULD BE – HELD KHANNA, J.

204. It has been argued on behalf of the appellant that the grounds on account of which the election of the appellant had been held to be void by the High Court were of a technical nature. I need not express any opinion about this aspect of the matter at this stage but, assuming it to be so, I find that clause (4) of Article 329A is so worded that however serious may be the malpractices vitiating the election of the Speaker or the Prime Minister, the effect of clause (4) is that the said election would have to be treated as valid. I cannot accede to the submission that in construing clause (4) we should take into account the facts of the appellant's case. This is contrary to all accepted norms of construction. If a clause of a constitution or statutory provision is widely worded, the width of its ambit cannot be circumscribed by taking into account the facts of an individual case to which it applies. As already mentioned, clause (4) deals with the past election not merely of the Prime Minister but also of the Speaker. So far as the election of the Speaker is concerned, we do not know as to whether the same was ever challenged and, if so, on what grounds, and whether such a dispute is still pending.

CONSTITUENT AUTHORITY ITSELF DECIDED ON THE FACTS OF THE CASE – CONTENDS APPELLANT CLAUSE (4) OF ARTICLE 329A DECLARES THE ELECTIONS VALID WITH APPLICATION OF NO LAW – HENCE BAD – HELD KHANNA, J.

205. Another argument advanced in support of the validity of the amendment is that we should take it that the constituent authority constituted itself to be the forum for deciding the dispute relating to the validity of the election of the appellant, and after considering the facts of the case, declared the election of the appellant to be valid. There is, however, nothing before us to indicate that the constituent authority went into the material which had been adduced before the High Court relating to the validity of the election of the appellant and after considering that material held the election of the appellant to be valid.

Indeed, the statement of Objects and Reasons appended to the Constitution (Thirty-ninth Amendment) Bill makes no mention of this thing. In any case, the vice of clause (4) would still lie in the fact that the election of the appellant was declared to be valid on the basis that it was not to be governed by any law for settlement of election disputes. Although the provisions of a constitutional amendment should be construed in a fair and liberal spirit, such liberal spirit should not be carried by the court to the extent of discovering the application of a dormant and latent law in the declaration of the validity of an election even though there is not even a remote indication of such a law in the impugned provision. Rule of law postulates that the decisions should be made by the application of known principles and rules and in general such decisions should be predictable and the citizen should know where he is. If a decision is taken without any principle or without any rule, it is not predictable and such decision is the antithesis of a decision taken in accordance with the rule of law.

CLAUSE (4) HAS TAKEN AWAY THE RIGHT AND REMEDY – HENCE VOID – HELD KHANNA, J.

206. The matter can also be looked at from another angle. The effect of impugned clause (4) is to take away both the right and the remedy to challenge the election of the appellant. Such extinguishment of the right and remedy to challenge the validity of the election, in my opinion, is incompatible with the process of free and fair elections. Free and fair elections necessarily postulate that if the success of a candidate is secured in elections by means which violate the principle of free and fair elections, the election should on that account be liable to be set aside and be declared to be void. To extinguish the right and the remedy to challenge the validity of an election would necessarily be tantamount to laying down that even if the election of a candidate is vitiated by the fact that it was secured by flagrant violation of the principles of free and fair election, the same would still enjoy immunity from challenge and would be nonetheless valid. Clause (4) of Article 329A can, therefore, be held to strike at the basis of free and fair elections.

IN SOME COUNTRIES ELECTION DISPUTES ARE DECIDED BY FORUMS OTHER THAN JUDICIARY – CLAUSE (4) DECLARES THE ELECTION VALID – NO FORUM – NO LAW – NOT PERMISSIBLE IN DEMOCRACY – HELD KHANNA, J.

207. I agree that it is not necessary in a democratic set up that disputes relating to the validity of the elections must be settled by courts of law. There are many countries like France, Japan, and the United States of America where consistently with the democratic set up the determination of such controversies is by legislatures or by authorities other than the courts. The question with which we are concerned, however, is whether it is permissible in a democratic set-up that a dispute with regard to the validity of a particular election shall not be raised before any forum and shall not be governed by law and whether such an election can be declared, despite the existence of a dispute relating to its validity to be valid by making the existing law relating to election disputes not applicable to it and also by not applying any other election law in such a dispute. The answer to such a question, for the reasons given earlier by me, should be in the negative.

*   *   *   *   *

PM OR SPEAKER MAY BE SEPARATE CLASS – BUT LAW HAS TO APPLY– SOME FORUM HAS TO ADJUDICATE – HELD KHANNA, J.

209. Argument has also been advanced that the offices of the Prime Minister and Speaker are of great importance and as such they constitute a class by themselves. This argument, in my opinion, would have relevance if instead of the law governing disputes relating to the election of other persons, another law had been prescribed to govern the dispute relating to the election of a person who holds the office of the Prime Minister or Speaker. As it is, what we find is that so far as the dispute relating to the election of the appellant is concerned, neither the previous law governing the election of persons holding the office of the Prime Minister is to apply to it nor the future law to be framed under clause (1) of Article 329A governing the election of persons holding the office of Prime Minister is to apply to this dispute. Likewise, the previous forum for adjudicating upon the election dispute, which went into the matter, has been divested of its, jurisdiction with retrospective effect and, at the same time, no jurisdiction has been vested in any other forum to go into the matter. The present is not a case of change of forum. It is, on the contrary, one of the abolition of forum. As such, the question as to whether the office of Prime Minister constitutes a class by itself loses much of its, significance in the context of the controversy with which we are concerned.

CLAUSE (4) PRESERVES VALIDITY OF ONE ELECTION – STRIKES AT THE BASIC STRUCTURE OF THE CONSTITUTION – HELD KHANNA, J.

210. It has been argued in support of the constitutional validity of clause (4) that as a result of this amendment, the validity of one election has been preserved. Since the basic structure of the Constitution, according to the submission, continues to be the same, clause (4) cannot be said to be an impermissible piece of constitutional amendment. The argument has a seeming plausibility about it, but a deeper reflection would show that it is vitiated by a basic fallacy. Law normally connotes a rule or norm which is of general application. It may apply to all the persons or class of persons or even individuals of a particular description. Law prescribes the abstract principles by the application of which individual cases are decided. Law, however, is not what Blackstone called "a sentence". According to Roscoe Pound, law, as distinguished from laws, is the system of authoritative materials for grounding or guiding judicial and administrative action recognised or established in a politically organised society (*see* page 106. Jurisprudence, Vol. III).

Law is not the same as judgment. Law lays down the norm in abstract terms with a coercive power and sanction against those guilty of violating the norm, while judgment represents the decision arrived at by the application of law to the concrete facts of a case. Constitutional law relates to the various organs of a State; it deals with the structure of the government, the extent of distribution of its powers and the modes and principles at its operation. The Constitution of India is so detailed that some of the matters which in a brief constitution like that of the United States of America are dealt with by statutes form the subject-matter of various Articles of our Constitution. There is, however, in a constitutional law, as in them is the very idea of law, some element of generality or general application. It also carries with it a concept of its applicability in future to situations which may arise in that context. If there is amendment of some provision of the Constitution and the amendment deals with matters which constitute constitutional law in the normally accepted sense, the court while deciding the question of the validity of the amendment would have to find out, in view of the majority opinion in **Kesavananda Bharati's** case (supra), as to whether the amendment affects the basic structure of the Constitution.

The constitutional amendment contained in clause (4) with which we are concerned in the present case is, however, of an altogether different nature. Its avowed object is to confer validity on the election of the appellant to the Lok Sabha in 1971 after that election had been declared to be void by the High Court and an appeal against the judgment of the High Court was pending in this Court. In spite of our query, we were not referred to any precedent of a similar amendment of any Constitution of the world. The Uniqueness of the impugned constitutional amendment would not, however, affect its validity. If the constituent authority in its wisdom has chosen the validity of a disputed election as the subject-matter of a constitutional amendment, this Court cannot go behind that wisdom. All that this Court is concerned with is the validity of the amendment. I need not go into the question as to whether such a matter, in view of the normal concept of constitutional law, can strictly be the subject of a constitutional amendment. I shall for the purpose of this case assume that such a matter can validly be the subject matter of a constitutional amendment.

The question to be decided is that if the impugned amendment of the Constitution violates a principle which is part of the basic structure of the Constitution, can it enjoy immunity from an attack on its validity because of the fact that for the future, the basic structure of the Constitution remains unaffected. The answer to the above question, in my opinion, should be in the negative.

What has to be seen in such a matter is whether the amendment contravenes or runs counter to an imperative rule or postulate which is an integral part of the basic structure of the Constitution. If so, it would be an impermissible amendment and it would make no difference whether it relates to one case or a large number of cases. If an amendment striking at the basic structure of the Constitution is not permissible, it would not acquire validity by being related only to one case. To accede to the argument advanced in support of the validity of the amendment would be tantamount to holding that even though it is not premise the constitution, whenever the authority concerned deems it proper to make such an amendment, it can do so and circumvent the bar to the making of such an amendment by confining it to one case. What is prohibited cannot become permissible because of its being confined to one matter.

DIFFERENT PARTS OF CLAUSE (4) ARE INTEGRAL TO EACH OTHER – HENCE CLAUSE (4) IS STRUCK DOWN IN ITS ENTIRETY AS VIOLATIVE OF FREE AND FAIR ELECTIONS – BASIC STRUCTURE OF THE CONSTITUTION – HELD KHANNA, J.

211. Lastly, question arises whether we should strike down clause (4) in its entirety or in part. So far as this aspect is concerned, I am of the view that the different parts of clause (4) are so integrally connected and linked with each other that it is not possible to sever them and uphold the validity of part of it after striking down the rest of it. It would indeed be unfair to the appellant if we were to uphold the first part of clause (4) and strike down other parts or even Part (iii). As would be apparent from what follows hereafter, the election of the appellant is being upheld by applying the provisions of the RP Act as amended by Act 40 of 1975. Such a course would not be permissible if we were to uphold the validity of the first part of clause (4) and strike down the other parts. We would also in that event be creating a vacuum which is the very vice for which we are striking down clause (4). I am therefore, of the view that clause (4) should be struck down in its entirety.

212. In view of my finding that clause (4) strikes at the basic structure of the Constitution, it is not necessary to go into the question as whether, assuming that the constituent authority took it upon itself to decide the dispute relating to the validity of the election of the appellant, it was necessary for the constitution of the authority to hear the parties concerned before it declared the election of the appellant to be valid and thus in effect repelled the challenge of the respondent to the validity of the appellant's election.

213. As a result of the above, strike down clause (4) of Article 329A on the ground that it violates the principle of free and fair elections which is an essential postulate of democracy and which in its turn is a part of the basic structure of the Constitution in as much as (1) it abolishes the forum without providing for another forum for going into the dispute relating to the validity of the election of the appellant and further prescribes that the said dispute shall not be governed by any election law and that the validity of the said election shall be absolute and not consequently be liable to be assailed, and (2) it extinguishes both the right and the remedy to challenge the validity of the aforesaid election.

AMENDED LAW SAVES VALIDITY OF ELECTION – PLEADS APPELLANT – AMENDED LAW INVALID – PLEADS RESPONDENT

214. We may now deal with Appeal No. 887 of 1975 filed by the appellant So far as this appeal is concerned, it has been argued by Mr. Sen on behalf of the appellant that the grounds on which the election of the appellant has been declared by the High Court to be void no longer hold good in view of the amendment in the RP Act by Act 40 of 1975. As against that, Mr. Shanti Bhushan on behalf of the respondent has assailed the validity of Act 40 of 1975. In the alternative, Mr. Shanti Bhushan contends that even if the validity of Act 40 of 1975 were to be upheld, the grounds on which the election of the appellant has been declared to be void would still hold good.

COURT PROCEEDS ON THE ASSUMPTION THAT ACT 40 OF 1975 VALID – KHANNA, J.

215. The question as to whether Act 40 of 1975 is not vitiated by any constitutional infirmity would be dealt with by me subsequently. For the time being I would proceed upon the basis that the statutory amendment in the RP Act by Act 40 of 1975 is constitutionally valid.

BY AMENDED LAW APPELLANT BECAME 'CANDIDATE' ON 1.2.1975 – KHANNA, J.

216. Section 10 of Act 40 of 1975, which has been reproduced earlier, makes it clear, *inter alia,* that the provisions of sections 6, 7 and 8 of that Act shall have retrospective operation, so as to apply to or in relation to any election held before the commencement of this Act, to either House of Parliament in respect of which appeal from any order of any High Court made in any election petition under the RP Act is pending before the Supreme Court immediately before such commencement. It is, therefore, obvious that the provisions of sections 6, 7 and 8 of Act 40 of 1975 would be attracted to this case. One of the questions which actually arose for determination before the High Court was as to what was the date on which the appellant held herself out as a candidate. According to the written statement filed on behalf of the appellant, she held herself out as a candidate from the Raebareli constituency on February 1, 1971. When she filed her nomination paper. As against that, the case of the respondent was that the appellant held herself out as a candidate from that constituency on December 27, 1970 when the Lok sabha was dissolved.

The finding of the High Court is that the appellant held herself out as a candidate from the Raebareli constituency on December 29, 1970 when she addressed a Press conference. The question as to when the appellant held herself out as a candidate from the Raebareli constituency has now become purely academic in view of the change in the definition of the word "candidate" as given in clause (b) of section 79 of the RP (Act by Act 40 of 1975). According to the original definition, "unless the context otherwise requires, 'candidate" means a person who has been or claims to have been duly nominated as a candidate at any election and any such person shall be deemed to have been a candidate as from the time when, with the election in prospect, he began to hold himself out as a prospective candidate." The new definition states that "unless the context other requires, 'candidate' means a person who has been or claims to have been duly nominated as a candidate, at any election." The question as to when a person holds himself out as candidate, therefore, loses its importance in the context of the new definition.

APPELLANT OBTAINED ASSISTANCE OF YASHPAL KAPUR BETWEEN 7-24 JANUARY IN FURTHERANCE OF ELECTION PROSPECTS – APPELLANT BECAME 'CANDIDATE' ON 1.2.1975 AS PER AMENDED LAW – HELD KHANNA, J.

217. One of the grounds which weighed with the High Court in declaring the election of the appellant to be void was that the appellant committed corrupt practice under section 123(7) of the RP Act in as much as she obtained and procured the assistance, for the furtherance of her election prospects, of Yashpal Kapur during the period from January 7 to 24, 1971 when Yashpal Kapur was still a gazetted officer in the service of the Government of India.

218. According to clause (7) of section 123 of the RP Act, the following act shall constitute corrupt practice under that clause :

> "The obtaining or procuring or abetting or attempting to obtain or procure by a candidate or his agent or, by any other person with the consent of a

candidate or his election agent, any assistance (other than the giving of vote) for the furtherance of the prospects of that candidate's election, from any person in the service of the Government and belonging to any of the following classes, namely:—

(a) Gazetted Officers;

(b) stipendiary Judges and Magistrates;

(c) members of the armed forces of the Union;

(d) members of the police forces;

(e) Excise Officers;

(f) revenue officers other than village revenue officers known as lambardars, malguzars, deshmukhs or by any other name, whose duty is to collect land revenue and who are remunerated by a share of, or commission, on, the amount of land revenue collected by them but who do not discharge any police function; and

(g) Such other class of persons in the service of the Government as may be prescribed.

Explanation.—(1) In this section the expression 'agent' includes an election agent, or polling agent and any person who is held to have acted as an agent in connection with the consent of the candidate.

(2) For the purposes of clause (7), a person shall be deemed to assist in the furtherance of the prospects of a candidate's election if he acts as an election agent."

Perusal of the above clause shows that what constitutes corrupt practice under the above clause is the obtaining or procuring or abetting or attempting to obtain or procure by a candidate or his agent or by any person with the consent of a candidate or his election agent any assistance (other than the giving of vote) for the furtherance of the prospects of the candidate's election from any person in the service of the Government and belonging to any of the classes specified therein. It is, in my opinion, essential that at the time the impugned act namely, the obtaining or procuring or abetting or attempting to obtain or procure the assistance of a Government servant is done, the person doing the act must be a candidate or his agent or any other person with the consent of a candidate or his election agent. Candidate in this clause would mean a person who has been or who claims to have been duly nominated as a candidate at the election.

I am unable to accede to the submission of Mr. Shanti Bhushan that the word "candidate" has been used merely to identify the person who is duly nominated as a candidate at an election and that the word "candidate", as mentioned in clause (7), would also include a person who, after the commission of the corrupt practice specified in that clause, is subsequently nominated as a candidate. The amended definition reproduced above shows that unless context otherwise requires, candidate means a person who has been or claims to have been duly nominated as a candidate at an election. To accede to the submission of Mr. Shanti Bhushan would be tantamount to read "has been or claims to have been duly nominated" also the words "who is subsequently nominated as a candidate". There is nothing to indicate that the word "candidate" in clause (7) of section 123 has been used merely to identify the person who has been or would be subsequently nominated as a candidate.

A definition clause in a statute is a legislative device with a view to avoid making different provisions of the statute to be cumbersome. Where a word is defined in the statute and that word is used in a provision to which that definition is applicable, the effect is that wherever the word defined is used in that provision, the definition of the word gets substituted. Reading the word "candidate" in section 123(7) of the RP Act in the sense in which it has been defined as a result of the amendment made by Act 40 of 1975. I find that the only reasonable inference is that the person referred to as a candidate in that clause should be a person who has been or claims to have been duly nominated as a candidate at an election and not one who is yet to be nominated.

219. Mr. Shanti Bhushan has invited our attention to clause (b) of section 100(1) of the RP Act wherein it is stated that subject to the provisions of sub-section (2) of the section if the High Court is of the opinion that any corrupt practice has been committed by a returned candidate or his election agent or by any other person with the consent of a returned candidate or his election agent, the High Court shall declare the election of the returned candidate to be void. "Returned candidate" has been defined in clause, (f) of section 79 to mean, unless the context otherwise requires, a candidate whose name has been published under section 67 as duly elected. It is urged that as the corrupt practice referred to in clause (b) of section 100(1) of the RP Act would in the very nature of things have to be committed by the returned candidate before his name was published under section 67 as duly elected, the words "returned candidate" in clause (b) of section 100(1) must be taken to have been used with a view to identify the person who subsequently became a returned candidate.

It is urged that if while dealing with corrupt practice committed by a candidate before he became a returned candidate in the context of section 100(1) (b), it is permissible to hold that the words "returned candidate" are intended to identify the person who subsequently became a returned candidate, the same criterion should apply when construing the word "candidate" in section 123 of the RP Act. This contention, in my opinion, is devoid of force. The definition of the words "returned candidate" and "candidate" given in section 79 of the RP Act are preceded by the words "unless the context otherwise requires." The connotation of the above words is that normally it is the definition given in the section which should be applied and given effect to. This normal rule may, however, be departed from if those be something in the context to show that the definition should not be applied. So far as clause (b) of section 100(1) is concerned, the context plainly requires that the corrupt practice referred to in that clause should have been committed by the candidate before he became a returned candidate, or by his agent or by any other person with his consent or that of his election agent. The compulsion arising from the context which is there in clause (b) of section 100(1) of the RP Act is singularly absent in section 123(7) of the RP Act. There is nothing in the context of the latter provision which requires that we should not give full effect to the new definition of the word "candidate."

In para 220 laws of England have been discussed.

RESIGNATION OF YASHPAL KAPUR SANCTIONED ON 14.1.1975 AS PER AMENDED LAW – APPELLANT BECAME A CANDIDATE ON 1.2.1971 AS PER AMENDED LAW – ANY ASSISTANCE – BETWEEN 7-24 JANUARY, 1971 – IS NO 'CORRUPT PRACTICE' – HELD KHANNA, J.

221. As the appellant filed her nomination paper on February 1, 1971, in view of the amended definition of the word- "candidate", it would have to be taken that the appellant became a candidate only on February 1, 1971. The result is that even if the finding of the High Court that the appellant obtained and procured the assistance of Yashpal Kapur during the period from January 7 to 24, 1971 were assumed to be correct, the appellant shall not be deemed to have committed corrupt practice under section 123(7) of the RP Act. As regards the assistance of Yashpal Kapur which the appellant is alleged to have obtained and procured after January 14, 1971, the controversy stands resolved also by another amendment. According to the case of the appellant, Yashpal Kapur tendered his resignation by letter dated January 13, 1971 with effect from January 14, 1971. The High Court found that Yashpal Kapur continued to be in the service of the Government of India till January 25, 1971 which was the date of the notification regarding the acceptance of Yashpal Kapur's resignation. According to the said notification, the President was pleased "to accept the resignation of Shri Y.P.R. Kapur, Officer on Special Duty in the Prime Minister's Secretariat, with effect from the forenoon of the 14th January, 1971".

The explanation which has been added to section 123 of the RP Act makes it clear, *inter alia,* that for the purpose of clause (7), notwithstanding anything contained in any other law, the publication in the Official Gazette of the resignation and termination of service of a person in the service of the Central Government shall be conclusive proof of his resignation and termination of service and where the date of taking effect of his resignation or termination of service is stated in such publication, also of the fact that such person ceased to be in such service with effect from the said date: Yashpal Kapur in view of the newly added explanation, shall be taken to have ceased to be in Government service with effect from January 14, 1971. Any assistance of Yashpal Kapur which the appellant was alleged to have obtained or procured on or after January 14, 1971 would not therefore, make her guilty of corrupt practice under section 123(7) of the RP Act.

ASSISTANCE OF GAZETTED OFFICERS – U.P. GOVERNMENT – WAS OFFICIAL DUTY AS PER AMENDED LAW – NO CORRUPT PRACTICE – KHANNA, J.

222. Another ground on which the High Court declared the election of the appellant to be void was that she committed corrupt practice under section 123(7) of the RP Act in as much as she obtained the assistance of the officers of the UP Government, particularly the District Magistrate, Superintendent of Police, the Executive Engineer PWD and the Engineer Hydel Department for construction of rostrums and arrangement of supply of power for loudspeakers in the meetings addressed by her on February 1, 1971 and February 25, 1971 in furtherance of her election prospects. It is not disputed that what was done by the above-mentioned officers was in pursuance of official directions and in the discharge or purported discharge of the official duties. This is indeed clear from letter dated November 19, 1969 from the Government of India, Ministry of Home Affairs to State Governments wherein there is reference to rule (6) of the Rules and Instructions for the protection of the Prime Minister and it is stated:

> "As the security of the Prime Minister is the concern of the State all arrangements for putting up the rostrum, the barricades etc. at the meeting place, including that of an election meeting will have to be made by the State Government concerned...
>
> ....
>
> In the case of election meetings, all expenditure on police, setting up of barricades and taking lighting arrangements will be borne by the State Government while expenditure on the public address system and any decorative arrangements will be the responsibility of the political party concerned. (The expenditure on all these items may in the first instance be borne by the State Government and then recovered from the political parties concerned). In regard to the rostrum only 25 per cent of the cost of the rostrum or Rs. 2500.00 whichever is less, shall be contributed by the

party as the rostrum has to be of certain specifications because of security considerations."

Assuming that the finding of fact recorded by the High Court in this respect is correct, the appellant can still be not guilty of the commission of corrupt practice under section 123(7) of the RP Act in view of the new proviso which has been inserted at the end of clause (7) of section 123 and which reads as under:

> "Provided that where any person, in the service of the Government and belonging to any of the classes aforesaid, in the discharge or purported discharge of his official duty, makes any arrangements or provides any facilities or does any other act or thing, for, to or in relation to any candidate or his agent or any other person acting with the consent of the candidate or his election agent, (whether by reason of the office held by the candidate or for any other reason), such arrangements; facilities or act or thing shall not be deemed to be assistance for the furtherance of the prospects of that candidate's election." The above proviso has also a direct bearing on the allegation of the respondent that the appellant committed corrupt practice under section 123(7) of the RP Act in as much as she or her election agent procured the assistance of members of armed forces of the Union for furtherance of her election prospects because of the fact that the members of the armed forces arranged planes and helicopters of the Air Force for her flights to enable her to address meetings in her constituency.

ONLY STATUTORY DUTY IS 'OFFICIAL DUTY' – NO DUTY UNDER ADMINISTRATIVE INSTRUCTIONS – CONTENDS RESPONDENT – REJECTED – KHANNA, J.

223. It has been argued by Mr. Shanti Bhushan that the words "in the discharge or purported discharge of his official duty" in the above mentioned proviso have reference only to statutory duty and to no other duty performance of which takes place in pursuance of administrative instructions. I find it difficult to accede to the above submission as there is nothing in the above proviso to confine the words "official duty" to duty imposed by statute. Official duty would include not merely duties imposed by statutes but also, those which have to be carried out in pursuance of administrative instructions.

SUBJECT TO VALIDITY OF ACT 40 OF 1975 – NO VALID GROUNDS FOR DECLARING ELECTION OF APPELLANT VOID – KHANNA, J.

224. Mr. Shanti Bhushan during the course of arguments made it plain that apart from his submission with regard to the validity of Act 40 of 1975, his objection relating to the applicability of Act 40 of 1975 was confined to two matters, namely the connotation of the word "candidate" and the meaning to be attached to official duty. Both these objections have been found by me to be not tenable. I would, therefore, hold that subject to the question as to whether the provisions of Act 40 of 1975 are valid the grounds on which the High Court has declared the election of the appellant to be void no longer hold good for declaring the said election to be void.

SYMBOL OF COW AND CALF ALLOTTED BY ELECTION COMMISSION – AMENDED LAW MAKES IT LEGAL – NO CORRUPT PRACTICE – KHANNA, J.

225. We may also before dealing with the validity of Act 40 of 1975 refer to one other change brought about by that Act which has a bearing upon the present case. It was the case of the respondent that the appellant and her election agent made extensive appeals to the religious symbol of cow and calf and thereby committed corrupt practice under section 123(3) of the RP Act. Corrupt practice has been defined in that provision as under:

> "(3) The appeal by a candidate or his agent or by any other person with the consent of a candidate or his election agent to vote or refrain from voting for any person on the ground of his religion, race, caste, community or language or the use of or appeal to religious symbols or the use of, or appeal to, national symbols, such as the national flag or the national emblem, for the furtherance of the prospects of the election of that candidate or for prejudicially affecting the election of any candidate."

It is the common case of the parties that the symbol of cow and calf was allotted to the Congress party by the Election Commission. The learned counsel for the respondent stated during the course of arguments in the High Court that he confined his case only to the use of the symbol of cow and calf. The learned counsel gave up that part of the case of the respondent wherein it had been alleged that appeals were made to the religious symbol of cow and calf by the appellant. The following proviso has now been inserted in clause (3) of section 123 by section 8 of Act 40 of 1975:

> 'Provided that no symbol allotted under this Act to a candidate shall be deemed to be a religious symbol or a national symbol for the purpose of this clause."

It is, therefore, apparent in view of the above proviso that the symbol of cow and calf which was allotted to the appellant shall not be deemed to be a religious symbol or a national symbol for the purpose of section 123(3) of the RP Act. The appellant as such cannot be deemed to have committed a corrupt practice under section 123(2) of the RP Act by use of the symbol of cow and calf.

ACT 40 OF 1975 – MADE RETROSPECTIVE – ILLEGAL – SUBMITS RESPONDENT – CONTENTION REJECTED – RETROSPECTIVE ELECTION LEGISLATION PERMISSIBLE – HELD KHANNA, J.

226. In assailing the validity of Act 40 of 1975 Mr. Shanti Bhushan has referred to section 10 of that Act, according to which the amendments made by sections 6, 7 and 8 of the Act in the RP Act shall have retrospective operation, so as to apply to any election held before the commencement of the Act in respect of which an election petition is pending or in respect of which appeal from any order of the High Court is pending immediately before the commencement of Act 40 of 1975. It is urged that a change in the election law with retrospective effect strikes at the principle of free and fair elections. Retrospective operation of the amending Act, according to the learned counsel, has the effect of condoning what was at the time it was committed a corrupt practice.

227. I have given the matter my earnest consideration, and am of the opinion that there is no substance in the above contention. A legislature has, except in a matter for which there is prohibition like the one contained in Article 20(1) of the Constitution, the power to make laws which are prospective in operation as well as laws which have retrospective operation. There is no limitation on the power of the legislature in this respect. Essentially it is a matter relating to the capacity and competence of the legislature. Although most of the laws made by the legislature have a prospective operation, occasions arise quite often when necessity is felt of giving retrospective effect to a law. This holds good both in respect of a principal Act as well as in respect of an amending Act. If the provisions of an Act passed by the legislature are not violative of the provisions of the Constitution, those provisions shall have to be given effect to and the fact that the operation of the Act is prospective or retrospective would make no difference. It is also permissible to amend a law which is basis of the decision of a court with retrospective effect and rely upon the provisions of the amended law in appeal, against the above decision of the court. The court of appeal in such an event gives full effect to the amended law even though such amendment has been made after the decision of the original court.

The one field in which it is not permissible to make a law with retrospective effect is contained in clause (1) of Article 20, according to which no person shall be convicted of any offence except for violation of a law in force at the time of the commission of the act charged as an offence, nor be subjected to a penalty greater than that which might have been inflicted under the law in force at the time of the commission of the offence. Apart from the field in which there is a constitutional prohibition for giving retrospective effect to a law, power of making amendment in law with retrospective effect has now become a part of normal legislative process. Question then arises as to whether in spite of the general competence of the legislature to make a law with retrospective effect, is the legislature rendered incompetent to make a law with retrospective effect in election matters? The answer to this question, in opinion, should plainly be in the negative.

Election laws are a part of the normal legislative process and what is permitted in the matter of ordinary legislation would also be permissible in the matter of legislation relating to elections unless there be some provision in the Constitution which forbids such a course. We have not been referred to any provision in the Constitution which has the effect of creating a bar in the way of the legislature making a law relating to elections with retrospective operation. If a party seeks to carve out an exception to the normal rule, it can do so only on the basis of some cogent ground. No such ground has been brought to our notice. The matter indeed is not *res integra* because there have been two cases wherein this Court has upheld the validity of the law making amendments in election laws with retrospective effect.

228. The first such case was **State of Orissa v. Bhopendra Kumar Bose,** (supra). It arose out of elections to the Cuttack Municipality held in December 1957 to March 1958 as a result of which 27 appellants were declared elected as Councillors. The respondent, who was defeated at the elections, filed a writ petition before the High Court, challenging the elections. The High Court held that the electoral rolls had not been prepared in accordance with the provisions of the Orissa Municipalities Act, 1950, as the age, qualification had been published too late thereby curtailing the period of claims and objections to the preliminary roll to 2 days from 21 days as prescribed. The High Court consequently set aside the elections. The State took the view that the judgment affected not merely the Cuttack Municipality but other municipalities also. Accordingly, the Governor promulgated an Ordinance validating the elections to the Cuttack Municipality and validating the electoral rolls prepared in respect of various municipalities. The respondent thereupon filed a writ petition before the High Court contending that the Ordinance was unconstitutional. High Court struck down the Ordinance. One of the grounds which weighed with the High Court in striking down the Ordinance was that it contravened Article 14 of the Constitution. The State and the Councillors came up in appeal to this Court. It was held by this Court that the Ordinance was valid and that it successfully cured the invalidity of the electoral rolls and of elections to the Cuttack Municipality. The Ordinance was further held not to offend Article 14 of the Constitution as its object was not only to save the election to the Cuttack Municipality but also to other municipalities whose validity might be challenged on similar ground. The Ordinance, in the opinion of the Court, did not single out the respondent for discriminatory treatment. Gajendragadkar, J. (as he then was) speaking for the Constitution Bench of this Court observed:

> "'The Cuttack Municipal Elections had been set aside by the High Court and if the Governor thought that in the public interest, having regard to the factors enumerated in the Preamble to the Ordinance, it was necessary to validate the said elections, it would not necessarily follow that the Ordinance suffers from the vice of contravening Article 14."
>
> It was further observed:
>
> "Therefore, if the infirmity in the electoral rolls on which the decision of the High Court in the earlier writ petition was based, had not been applicable to the electoral rolls in regard to other Municipalities in the State of Orissa, then it may have been open to the Governor to issue an Ordinance only in respect of the Cuttack Municipal Elections, and if, on account of special circumstances or reasons applicable to the Cuttack Municipal Elections, a law was passed in respect of the said elections alone, it could not have been challenged as unconstitutional under Article 14. Similarly, if Mr. Bose was the only litigant affected by the decision and as such formed a class by himself, it would have been open to the Legislature to make a law only in respect of his case. But as we have already pointed out, the Ordinance does not purport to limit its operation only to the Cuttack Municipality, it purports to validate the Cuttack Municipal Elections and the electoral rolls in respect of other Municipalities as well. Therefore, We are satisfied that the High Court was in error in coming to the conclusion that section 4 contravenes Article 14 of the Constitution."

229. In **Kanta Kathuria v. Manak Chand Surana**, (supra) the dispute related to the election of the appellant to the Rajasthan Legislative Assembly. The appellant in that case had been appointed as a Special Government Pleader to represent the State of Rajasthan in an arbitration case. The appellant then stood for election to the State Legislative Assembly and was declared elected. The election of the appellant was challenged *inter alia* on the ground that the appellant held an office of profit within the meaning of Article 191(1) of the Constitution. The High Court set aside the election of the appellant. The appellant then came up in appeal to this Court. During the pendency of the appeal, Rajasthan Act 5 of 1969 was passed declaring among other that the holder of the office of Special Government Pleader was not disqualified from being chosen or for being a member of the State Legislative Assembly. The Act was made retrospective and removed the appellant's disqualification retrospectively. On the question as to whether the appellant was holding an office of profit and hence was disqualified, Sikri, Ray and Reddy, JJ. held that the appellant was not holding an office of profit. Hidayatullah, C.J. and Mitter, J., however, held that the High Court was right in holding that the appellant held an office of profit. All the five Judges constituting the Constitution Bench were, however, unanimous on the point that the Act of 1969 had removed the disqualification of the appellant retrospectively. Hidayatullah, C.J. speaking for himself and Mitter, J. observed:

> "It is also well recognised that Parliament and Legislatures of the States can make their laws operate retrospectively. Any law that can be made

prospectively may be made with retrospective operation except that certain kinds of law cannot operate retroactively. This is not one of them.

This position being firmly grounded we have to look for limitations, if any, in the Constitutions. Article 191 (which has been quoted earlier) itself recognises the power of the Legislature of the State to declare by law that the holder of an office shall not be disqualified for being chosen as a member. The Article says that a person shall be disqualified if he holds an office of profit under the Government of India or the Government of any State unless that office is declared by the Legislature not to disqualify the holder. Power is thus reserved to the Legislature of the State, to make the declaration. There is nothing in the words of the article to indicate that this declaration cannot be made with retrospective effect."

It was further observed:

"Regard being had to the legislative practice in this country and in the absence of a clear prohibition either express or implied we are satisfied that the Act cannot be declared ineffective in its retrospective operation."

Sikri J. (as he then was) speaking for himself, Ray, J. (as he then was) and Reddy, J. dealt with the matter in the following words:

"Mr. Chagla, learned counsel for the respondent, contends that the Rajasthan State Legislature was not competent, to declare retrospectively under Article 191(1)(a) of the Constitution. It seems to us that there is no force in this contention. It has been held in numerous cases by this Court that the State Legislatures and Parliament can legislate retrospectively subject to the provisions of the Constitution. Apart from the question of fundamental rights, no express restriction has been placed on the power of the Legislature of the State, and we are unable to imply, in the context, any restriction. Practice of the British Parliament does not "oblige us to place any implied restriction. We notice that the British Parliament in one case validated the election: (*Erskine May's Treatise on the Law Privileges Proceedings and Usage of Parliament* – Seventeenth (1964) Edition)—

"After the general election of 1945 it was found that the persons elected for the Coatbridge Division of Lanark and the Springbourn Division of Glassgow were disqualified at the time of their election because they were members of Tribunals appointed by the Minister under the Rent of Furnished Houses Control (Scotland) – Act, 1943, which entitled them to a small fee in respect of attendance at a Tribunal. A Select Committee reported that the disqualification was incurred inadvertently, and in accordance with their recommendation the Coatbridge and Springbourn Elections (Validation) Bill was introduced to validate the irregular elections (H.C. Deb. (1945-46) 414, c. 564-6). (*See* also H.C. 3 (1945-46); *ibid.*, 71 (1945-46) and *ibid.* 92 (1945-46)):

We have also noticed two earlier instances of retrospective legislation, *e.g.*, the House of Commons (Disqualification) Act, 1813 (*Halsbury Statutes of England*, p. 467) and section 2 of the Re-election of Ministers Act, 1919 (*ibid.* p. 515.)

Great stress was laid on the word 'declare', in Article 191(1)(a), but we are unable to imply any limitation on the powers of the Legislature from this word. Declaration can be made effective as from an earlier date."

230. The above two authorities of this Court clearly lend support for the view that it is permissible to amend a law relating to elections with retrospective operation. Mr. Shanti Bhushan has criticised the observations of Sikri, J. reproduced above on the score that in the United Kingdom amendments, in election law have not been made to affect pending proceedings in courts. This is essentially a matter for the legislature to decide, this does not affect the competence of the legislature to make a change in election law with retrospective effect. In any case, the proposition of law laid down in the case of Kanta Kathuria, is binding upon us and I do not find any reason, to detract either from the soundness of the view expressed therein or its binding effect.

* * * * *

RETROSPECTIVE EFFECT TO ACT 40 OF 1975 DOES NOT AFFECT FREE AND FAIR ELECTION – IT ONLY REMOVES UNCERTAINTIES AS TO WHEN A PERSON BECOMES A CANDIDATE – WHEN THE RESIGNATION BECOMES EFFECTIVE – HELD KHANNA, J.

232. I am not impressed by the argument that retrospective operation of the relevant provisions of Act 40 of 1975 affects free and fair elections. The said provisions or Act 40 of 1975 are general in terms and would apply to all election disputes which may be either in the High Court or in appeal in the Supreme Court or which may arise in future. It is no doubt true that the reapportion of an amending Act has effect of placing one of the parties to the case in a more advantageous position compared to others but that is inevitable in most of the amendments with retrospective operation. This Court in the case of **Harbhajan Singh v. Mohan Singh, (1974) 2 SCC 363 (364)** dealt with the provisions of section 3 of the Punjab Pre-emption (Repeal). Act, 1973, according to which on and from the date of commencement of that Act, no court shall pass a decree in any suit for pre-emption. This Court held that the above provision was also applicable to appeals which were pending at the commencement of that Act as an appeal was in the nature of a re-hearing, and as such even if the suit had been decreed by the trial court, the suit was liable to be dismissed because of the coming into force of the Punjab Pre-emption (Repeal) Act during the pendency of the appeal. It is plain that only those vendees obtained the benefit of the above Act who had filed appeals against the decree awarded against them in pre-emption suit. Vendees in other cases who did not file appeal against the decrees awarded against them in view of the then existing law had to lose the purchased property and thus be at a disadvantage. That fact, however, did not prevent this Court from giving effect to the amendment.

Whenever a legislature makes a law or amends a law, it has to indicate the time from which it would come into effect. This is essentially a matter for the legislature and the court cannot substitute its own opinion for that of the legislature. The fact that the change in law is made applicable to pending cases and the classification treats the decided cases as belonging to one category and pending cases as belonging to another category is not offensive to Article 14 (*see* **Anant Mills v. State of Gujarat, (1975) 2 SCC 175**). Nor can the court interfere on the score of the propriety of giving retrospective effect to an amendment made in an election law. Indeed, the question of propriety is a matter which is entirely for the legislature to think of and decide. It cannot affect the validity of the law. This Court in the case of **Kanta Kathuria** (supra) expressly rejected the contention that amendment in election law was void because it gave advantage to a party. Hidayatullah, C.I. observed in this context:

> "It is true that it gave an advantage to those who stand when the disqualification was not so removed as against those who may have kept themselves back because the disability was not removed. That might raise questions of the propriety of such retrospective legislation but not of the capacity to make such laws."

Likewise, Sikri, J. expressly rejected the contention that retrospective amendment in election law was bad because it was not a healthy practice and because such a course was liable to be abused in the following words :

> "The apprehension that it may not be a healthy practice and this power might be abused in a particular case are again no grounds for limiting the powers of the State Legislature."

233. The above observations also provide an answer to the contention of Mr. Shanti Bhushan that the provisions of the amendment made by Act 40 of 1975 can be abused. I may state that in case the provisions of the amended law are abused, and some of the instances of abuse were visualized by Mr. Shanti Bhushan during the course of arguments, this Court would not be helpless in the matter. The proper course in such an event would be to strike down the action taken under the amended law and not the law itself.

234. Reference was also made by Mr. Shanti Bhushan to the effect of retrospective amendment in cases which may arise under section 123(1) of the R.P. Act, we are in the present case not concerned with section 123(1) of the R.P. Act and consequently it is not necessary to express any opinion with regard to the impact of the amendment upon section 123(1) of the R.P Act. Nor is it necessary to express opinion on the point as to whether it is permissible to make a law which has the effect of creating a corrupt practice or disqualification retrospectively and thus unseating a returned candidate as such a question does not arise in this case.

235. The change in the definition of the word "candidate" to which our attention has been invited by Mr. Shanti Bhushan does not impinge upon the process of free and fair elections. The fact that as a result of the above change, we have to take into account only the prejudicial activity of the candidate or his election agent from the date of the nomination of the candidate and not from the date he holds himself out as a candidate does not affect the process of free and fair elections. It is necessary while dealing with corrupt practice relating to elections to specify the period within which the impugned act, alleged to constitute corrupt practice should have been done. As a result of the amendment, the legislature has fixed the said period to be as from the date of nomination instead of the period as from the date on which the candidate with the election in prospect began to hold himself out as a prospective candidate. It is common experience that the date from which a candidate hold himself out as a prospective candidate is often a matter of controversy between the parties. The result is that an element of indefiniteness and uncertainty creeps in finding the date from which a person can be said to be candidate. As a result of the change in the definition of candidate, the legislature has fixed a definite date, *viz.*, that of nomination, instead of the earlier time which had an element of indefiniteness and uncertainty about it for finding as to when a person became a candidate.

Certainty is an essential desideratum in law and any amendment of law to achieve that object is manifestly a permissible piece of legislation. The choice of date was a matter for the legislature to decide and the court cannot substitute its own opinion for that of the legislature in this respect, more so, when whatever be the choice of date, has aspects of both pros and cons. The date of nomination is normally, as in the present case, about a month before the date of polling and it is plain that most of the acts of corrupt practice are committed during this period. In any case, as mentioned above, the court cannot substitute its own opinion for that of the legislature in the choice of date. The choice of date, as observed in the case of **Union of India v. M/s. Parameshwaran Match Works, AIR 1974 SC 2349** as a basis for classification cannot always be dubbed as arbitrary even if no particular reason is forthcoming for the choice unless it is shown to be capricious or whimsical in the circumstances. When it is seen that a line or a point there must be and there is no mathematical or logical way of finding it precisely, the decision of the legislature or its delegate must be accepted unless we can say that it is very wide of any reasonable mark.

236. One of the objects of the change effected by Act 40 of 1975 is to remove the uncertainty and set at rest the controversy as to what would be the precise date of a person in the service of the Central Government ceasing to be in such service in case he tenders his resignation. The amended law makes it clear that where the date of taking effect of the resignation is stated in the publication in the Official Gazette, it shall be that date. Similarly, in the case of appointment of a person, the date of taking effect of such appointment shall be the date mentioned in the publication in the Official Gazette in case such a date is stated in such publication. The fact that the new provision creates a conclusive presumption with regard to the date of taking effect of appointment or resignation does not mean, as is sought to be argued on behalf of the respondent, that there has been an encroachment by the legislature upon the judicial sphere. Laying down a rule of conclusive presumption in a statute with a view to remove uncertainty with regard to the date of the taking effect of appointment or resignation of a Government employee cannot be characterised as an assumption of judicial power by the legislature.

Another object of the change effected by Act 40 of 1975 is that a candidate who is bound, in view of Para 8 of the Election Symbols (Reservation and Allotment) Order, 1968 to use the party symbol allotted by the Election Commission and who cannot use any other symbol, shall not suffer and be guilty of corrupt practice under section 123(3) of the RP Act because of the use of that symbol. It is to be assumed that Election Commission, which is an independent body, would act fairly and properly and would not allot a symbol, which is a religious symbol, to a party or a candidate. The fact that the allotted symbol was one of those suggested by the party concerned would not relieve the Election Commission of its duty to see that it does not allot a religious symbol to that party. Assuming that the Election Commission makes an error of judgment in this respect and allots a symbol which, in fact, is a religious symbol, the object of the new provision is that a candidate should not be penalised because of such an error on the part of the Election Commission. The third object of the change effected by Act 40 of 1975 is that a candidate should not suffer or be held guilty of corrupt practice because of any act done by any person in the service of the Government and belonging to any of the classes mentioned in section 123(7) of the RP Act in the discharge or purported discharge of his official duty. None of the three objects mentioned above has any taint of unconstitutionality and I find it difficult to hold that the impugned provisions impinge upon the principle of free and fair elections.

237. So far as the newly added proviso to section 123(7) is concerned, it may be stated that the act in the discharge or purported discharge of official duty of the Government employees referred to above would in the very nature of things have to be of a kind which is germane to their official duties. It may include steps taken by the Government employees for maintenance of law and order or in connection with the security of a candidate or other persons. It would not, however, include canvassing or doing such acts which may properly be considered to be part of the election propaganda for furtherance of the prospects of a candidate's election. In taking action under the above provision, it must be borne in mind as stated on page 152 of Free Elections by W.J. Mackenzie that in the last resort "the system of free elections depends on a certain separation of power between administrators (or policemen) and politicians: "there must be some public sense that police and administration serve the public, not the party leaders." What would be permissible under the above provision would be that which is conceived to be done in public interest and not something conceived to be done in the personal interest of a candidate.

In spite of some difficulty, which may arise in borderline cases, this distinction must be borne in mind. If, however, because of doing something conceived in public interest, *e.g.*, as in the present case the security arrangement for the person holding the office of the Prime Minister, some advantage may also possibly accrue to a candidate, it will have to be regarded as incidental and would not detract from action taken under the above provision being in public interest. As against that any action taken with a view to further the personal interest of a candidate should not be allowed to be camouflaged as an action taken in public interest. Care must be taken to ensure that public interest is not allowed to degenerate into a cloak for furtherance of the personal interests of a candidate in an election. The discharge or purported discharge of official duty must necessarily have public interest and not the personal interest of a candidate as its basis. The courts while dealing with the newly added proviso to section 123(7) should construe it, if reasonably possible, in such a manner as would sustain the validity of that proviso. In case there is abuse of the above provision, the proper course, as already mentioned, would be to strick down the action taken under the proviso and not the proviso itself.

238. One other change brought about by Act 40 of 1975 is the addition of an explanation in section 77 of the RP Act. According to the new explanation any expenditure incurred in respect of any arrangements made, facilities, provided or any other act or thing done by any person in the service of the Government and belonging to any of the classes mentioned in clause (7) of section 123 in the discharge or purported discharge of his official duty as mentioned in the proviso to that clause shall not be deemed to be expenditure in connection with the election incurred or authorized by a candidate or by his election agent for the purposes of section 77(1). The validity of the above explanation in a great measure is linked with the validity of the new proviso to section 123(7) of the RP Act, and for the reasons stated for upholding the proviso to section 123(7), the new explanation to section 77, it seems, may have also to be upheld. It is not necessary to dilate upon this aspect because even without invoking the aid of the new explanation to section 77, the High Court has found and I see no reason to disturb that finding that the total expenses incurred by the appellant were less the prescribed limit.

ACT 40 OF 1975 DOES NOT SUFFER FROM ANY CONSTITUTIONAL INFIRMITY – HELD KHANNA, J.

239. Argument has also been advanced that validity of Act 40 of 1975 cannot be assailed on the ground that it strikes at the basic structure of the Constitution. Such a limitation, it is submitted, operates upon an amendment of the Constitution under Article 368 but it does not hold good when Parliament enacts a statute in exercise of powers under Article 245 of the Constitution. In view of my finding that the provisions of Act 40 of 1975 with which we are concerned have not been shown to impinge upon the process of free and fair elections and thereby to strike at the basic structure of the Constitution, it is not necessary to deal with the above argument. I would, therefore, hold that the provisions of Act 40 of 1975 with which we are concerned are valid and do not suffer from any constitutional infirmity.

CROSS-APPEAL 909 OF 1975 FILED BY RESPONDENT – FINDINGS OF HIGH COURT ON ISSUE NO.9 ASSAILED – FINDING OF HIGH COURT UPHELD – KHANNA, J.

240. We may now deal with cross appeal No. 909 of 1975. Mr. Shanti Bhushan has not pressed the challenge to the finding of the High Court on issues 4 and 7. He has, however, assailed the finding of the High Court on issue No. 9 whereby the High Court held that the appellant incurred an expenditure of Rs. 31,976.47 on her election as against the prescribed limit of Rs. 35,000. In Ex. 5, Return of her election expenses, the appellant showed her total election expenses to be Rs. 12,892,97. The respondent in para 13 of the election petition alleged that the appellant and her election agent had incurred expenditure much beyond the prescribed limit of Rs. 35,000 and thereby committed corrupt practice under section 123(6) of the RP Act. The respondent gave some items of the expenditure, which were alleged to have been incurred by the appellant and her election agent but were not shown in the return of the election expenses. The material items with which we are now concerned were as under:

(i) The hiring charges of the vehicles specified in para 13(1) ... Over Rs. 1,28,700

(ii) Cost of petrol and diesel for the vehicles specified in para 13(1) ... Over Rs. 43,230

(iii) Payments made to the drivers of vehicles specified in para 13(1) ... Over Rs. 9,900

(iv) Repairing and servicing charges of vehicles specified in para 13(1) ... Over Rs. 5,000

(v) Payments made to the workers engaged for the purpose of election propaganda ... Over Rs. 6,600

(vi) Expenses on the erection of rostrums for the public meeting addressed by the appellant in the constituency on February 1 and 25, 1971 ... Over Rs. 1,32,000

(vii) Expenses on arrangement of loudspeakers for the various election meetings of the appellant addressed on February 1 and 25, 1971... Over Rs. 7,000

(viii) Expenses on motor transport for the conveyance of the appellant and her party to the place of her election meetings on February 1 and 25, 1971 ... Over Rs. 2,000

The High Court held that the respondent had failed to prove the first five items. As regards the expenses for the erection of rostrums for the public Meetings addressed by the appellant on February 1 and 25, 1971, the High Court found that four meetings were addressed by the appellant in the constituency on February 1 and six meetings on February 25, 1971. The cost of a rostrum in each meeting came to Rs. 1,600 The total expenses of the ten rostrums thus came to Rs. 16,000 and the same, it was held, was liable to be added to the amount shown in the return of election expenses of the appellant. The amount of Rs. 16,000 included the money paid by the District Congress Committee as its share of the cost of rostrums. Regarding the expenses of loudspeakers, the High Court found that the total expenses of Rs. 800 had been incurred on the installation of loudspeakers in the meetings addressed by the appellant on February 1 and 25, 1971. In addition to that, the High Court added Rs. 1,151 as cost of energy supplied for the functioning of the loudspeakers. The total amount which was added to the election expenses of the appellant on account of the loudspeakers thus came to Rs. 1,951. An amount of Rs. 232.50 was found by the High Court to have been incurred by the appellant for her transport on February 1 and 25, 1971. Adding the aggregate of Rs. 16,000, Rs. 1,951 and Rs. 232.50, in all Rs. 18,183.50, to the figure of Rupees 12,892.97 which had been shown by the appellant in her return, the total expense incurred by the appellant in her election was found by the High Court to be Rs. 31,976.47.

241. In appeal before us Mr. Shanti Bhushan has assailed the finding of the High Court insofar as the High Court has not accepted the case of the respondent that the appellant incurred expenses on the cost of hiring, petrol and the salary of the drivers for 23 vehicles. It may be mentioned that the respondent in para 13 of the election petition referred to 32 vehicles which were alleged to have been hired by the appellant, but both before the High Court and in appeal before us, learned counsel for the respondent has confined his argument to 23 vehicles.

242. To appreciate the point of controversy between the parties, it may be necessary to set out some material facts. Section 160 of the RP Act provides for *inter alia* that if it appears to the State Government that in connection with an election held within the State, any vehicle is needed or is likely to be needed for the purpose of transport of ballot boxes to or from any polling station, or transport of members of the police force for maintaining order during the conduct of such election, or transport of any officer or other person for performance of any duties in connection with such election, the Government may by order in writing requisition such vehicle, provided that no vehicle which is being lawfully used by a candidate or his agent for any purpose connected with the election of such candidate shall be requisitioned until the completion of the poll at such election. It appears that 23 vehicles, described at some places as cars and at other places as jeeps, were requisitioned by the district authorities Raebareli for election purposes under the above provision on February 23, 1971. Dal Bahadur Singh, who was the President of the District Congress Committee Raebareli, addressed a letter to the District officer Raebareli praying that the above mentioned 23 vehicles, of which the numbers were given, had been taken by the District Congress Committee Raebareli for the Parliamentary constituencies of Raebareli, Amethi and Ram Sanehi Ghat. There are, it may be stated, seven Assembly constituencies in Raebareli district. Out of them, five Assembly constituencies constitute Raebareli Parliamentary constituency. One of the Assembly constituencies in Raebareli district is part of Ram Sanehi Ghat Parliamentary constituency, while the seventh Assembly constituency is part of Amethi Parliamentary constituency. On February 24, 1971 a reply was sent on behalf of the District Election Officer to Dal Bahadur Singh regarding the latter's request for release of 23 vehicles. It was pointed out in the reply that it was not possible to release the vehicles in favour of any party for election purposes. At the same time, it was mentioned that the question of releasing of the vehicles could be considered at the request of a candidate or his election agent. On receipt of the above reply, Dal Bahadur Singh sent the same to Yashpal Kapur on February 24, 1971 alongwith note A43, the material part of which reads as under:

> "You are requested to kindly write a letter with your recommendation to the Election Officer so that the cars taken by the District Congress Committee may be released. I have tried to find out Shri Vidyadhar Vajpayee who is contesting the election (from Amethi Parliamentary Constituency and Shri Baiznath Kureel who is contesting the election from Ram Sanehi Parliamentary Constituency, but they are not available. You are, therefore, requested to write the above letter to the District Election Officer positively so that the election work of all the three Parliamentary Constituencies which is going on, on behalf of District Congress Committee, may not suffer."

On February 25, 1971 Yashpal Kapur addressed a letter to the District Officer Raebareli stating that the 23 vehicles in question had been taken by the District Congress Committee Raebareli for the three Parliamentary constituencies of Raebareli, Amethi and Ram Sanehi Ghat. The District Office was requested to release the 23 vehicles without delay. Yashpal Kapur also enclosed with that letter the note of Dal Bahadur Singh. The 23 vehicles, it would appear, were thereafter released by the District Election Officer. The appellant, in para 17(b) of her written statement, admitted that those 23 vehicles were used by the District Congress Committee Raebareli for election work in the three Parliamentary constituencies of Raebareli, Amethi and Ram Sanehi Ghat. The High Court, in not accepting the case of the respondent in respect of the 23 vehicles, observed that there was nothing to show that the above mentioned vehicles had been obtained on hire or were obtained gratis. There was also, according to the High Court, no cogent material to show that the said vehicles had been engaged and used in connection with election work of the appellant.

243. Mr. Shanti Bhushan, while assailing the finding of the High Court, has submitted that, as five out of the seven Assembly constituencies in Raebareli district were in Raebareli Parliamentary constituency, five-seventh of the expenses incurred on the said 23 vehicles should be added to the election expenses of the appellant. I find it difficult to accede to the above submission because of the paucity of the material on record. There is no cogent evidence to show that the 23 vehicles in question were used for the election of the appellant. It is no doubt true that the said 23 vehicles were used by the District Congress Committee Raebareli for election work in the three Parliamentary constituencies, *viz.*, Raebareli, Amethi and Ram Sanehi Ghat. The record is, however, silent on the point as to what extent they were used in Raebareli Parliamentary constituency. One can in the above context visualise three possibilities:

(i) As the appellant, who was the Prime Minister of the country, was contesting from Raebareli constituency, the District Congress Committee concentrated its attention on that constituency and used the 23 vehicles mostly for the election work in that constituency.

(ii) As the appellant had a mass appeal the District Congress Committee office-bearers thought that the Raebareli constituency was very safe and, therefore, concentrated attention on the other two Parliamentary constituencies and used the 23 vehicles mostly for those two constituencies.

(iii) Equal attention was paid to all the three constituencies and there was proportionate use of the vehicles for the three constituencies.

Mr. Shanti Bhushan would have us to accept the first or the third possibility and would rule out the second. If so, it was, in my opinion, essential for the respondent to lead some evidence regarding the use of the 23 vehicles. He did nothing of the kind. Neither the owners nor the drivers of those vehicles were examined as witnesses. There was also, as mentioned earlier, no other cogent evidence to show that those vehicles or any of them were used for the appellant's election in the Raebareli constituency, and if so, to what extent. The respondent himself did not come into the witness box to substantiate the charge against the appellant regarding the use of the 23 vehicles. The fact that Dal Bahadur Singh was not examined as a witness on behalf of the appellant would not warrant the filling in of the gaps and lacunae in the evidence adduced by the respondent by a process akin to guess work. It is no doubt true that by using a vehicle for the furtherance of the prospects of candidates in more than one constituency one should not be allowed to circumvent the salutary provisions of the RP Act in this respect. To prevent such circumvention, it is essential that evidence should be led to show as to what was the extent of the user of the vehicle in the constituency concerned. In **Hans Raj v. Pt. Hari Ram, (1968) 40 Ele LR 125 (SC)** a jeep hired by the Congress Committee during elections was used in more than one constituency, including that of the returned candidate who was a Congress nominee. Question arose as to whether the expense incurred in connection with that jeep could be included in the election expenses of the returned candidate. While answering the question in the negative, Hidayatullah, C.J. observed:

> "The bill stands in the name of the Congress Committee and was presumably paid by the Congress Committee also. The evidence, however, is that this

jeep was used on behalf of the returned candidate and to that extent we subscribe to the finding given by the learned judge. Even if it be held that the candidate was at bottom the hirer of the jeep and the expenditure on it must be included in his account, the difficulty is that this jeep was used also for the general Congress propaganda in other constituencies. As we stated, the jeep remained in Chalet and at Mubarakpur. No doubt Chalet is the home town of the returned candidate and his office was situated at Mubarakpur but that does not indicate that the jeep was used exclusively on his account. The petrol chart shows that petrol was bought at several pumps, both inside the constituency and outside. This shows, as does the evidence, that the jeep was used not only in this constituency but also in the other constituencies. If this be true, the it is almost impossible on the evidence as it exists in this case to decide how much of the use went for the benefit of the returned candidate and how much for the use of candidates in the other constituencies also put up by the Congress Committee. In this situation it is difficult to say that the whole of the benefit of the jeep went to the returned candidate and once we hold that the entire benefit did not go to him, we are not in a position to allocate the expenses between him and the other candidates in the other constituencies."

244. Reference has also been made during the course of arguments by Mr. Shanti Bhushan to some entries in a register of the Congress Committee. The High Court declined to place any reliance on those entries as those entries had not been proved. I see no cogent ground to take a different view. Our attention has been invited by Mr. Shanti Bhushan in to a report in issue dated January 22, 1971 of Swantantra Bharat wherein there was a reference to the Personal Secretary of the Prime Minister having reached Raebareli with a caravan of 70 motor vehicles. No reliance can be placed upon that report as the correspondent who sent that report was not examined as a witness.

245. The other difficulty which I find in accepting the submission of Mr. Shanti Bhushan in respect of 23 vehicles is that there is no evidence to show that any payment was made for the use of the above mentioned vehicles. There is also nothing to show that those vehicles were engaged on hire. As mentioned earlier, the owners and drivers of those vehicles were not examined as witnesses. I, therefore, find no sufficient ground to interfere with the finding of the High Court in respect of the above mentioned 23 vehicles.

NO EVIDENCE TO PROVE IF Rs. 6,600 WERE SPENT BY APPELLANT FOR ENGAGING WORKERS – HIGH COURT FINDING CORRECT – UPHELD – KHANNA, J.

246. Mr. Shanti Bhushan has next assailed the finding of the High Court in so far has it has held that the respondent has failed to prove that the appellant incurred an expense of Rs. 6,600 on workers engaged for the purposes of election propaganda. I, however, find no infirmity in the finding of the High Court in this respect as there is no cogent evidence whatsoever that any expense was incurred for engaging workers for the election work of the appellant. The case of the appellant is that her workers did the work voluntarily and without receipt of any remuneration.

EXPENDITURE OF RS. 70,000 NOT PLEADED IN THE ELECTION PETITION – TELEPHONE EXPENSES NOT PROVED – HIGH COURT FINDING UPHELD – KHANNA, J.

247. Apart from challenging the findings of the High Court in respect of 23 vehicles and the alleged payment to workers, Mr. Shanti Bhushan has also referred to some other circumstances with a view to show that, the election, expenses of the appellant exceeded the prescribed amount of Rs. 35,000. It has been pointed out that a cheque for Rs, 70,000 was sent by the Provincial Congress Committee to Dal Bahadur Singh, President of the District Congress Committee Raebareli, and the same was credited in Dal Bahadur Singh's account after deducting the bank charges on March 4, 1971. Dal Bahadur Singh withdrew out of that amount Rs. 40,000 and Rs. 25,000 on March 4 and 6, 1971 respectively nearabout the days of polling. It is urged that the said amount must have been spent for the purpose of the elections. There was no reference to the said amount of Rs. 70,000 in the petition. There is also no reference to the amount of Rs. 70,000 in the judgment of the High Court or in the grounds of appeal. As such, I am of the view that the respondent should not be allowed to set up a case against the appellant on the basis of the bank entries in the account of Dal Bahadur Singh. Reference has further been made by Mr. Shanti Bhushan to the expenses which are alleged to have been incurred on the telephone charges on the meetings addressed by Yashpal Kapur. The High Court rejected the submission in this respect on behalf of the respondent in the following words:

> "Learned counsel for the petitioner urged that from the evidence on record, it transpires that expenditure was also incurred on the telephone connection and telephone charges, on the meetings addressed by Sri Yashpal Kapur within the Constituency during the period of election, on the election material *viz.* pamphlets, posters, etc. and on the lighting arrangements made for some meetings addressed by the respondent No. 1. According to learned counsel, these expenses are also liable to be added to the election expenses of the respondent No. 1. None of these expenses were, however, pleaded in the petition. In fact, till the commencement of the arguments in the case, the respondent No.1 could not even anticipate that the petitioner shall rely on these expenses for the purpose of his case. It will, therefore, be prejudicial to the interest of respondent No.1 if the aforesaid expenses are taken in consideration. The submission made by learned counsel for the petitioner is accordingly negatived."

I am in full agreement with the above observations of the High Court and find no cogent ground to take a different view.

EXPENSES ON THE CONSTRUCTION OF ROSTRUMS – ELECTION EXPENSES REMAINING IN PRESCRIBED LIMIT – HIGH COURT FINDING UPHELD – KHANNA, J.

248. It may be stated that in view of the new explanation added to section 77 of the RP Act by Act 40 of 1975, the amount of Rs. 12,000 which represented 75 per cent of the expenditure incurred on the construction of 10 rostrums borne by the Government cannot be included in the total election expenses of the appellant. The High Court was also inclined to hold that the said amount of Rs. 12000 could not be included in the appellant's expenses. The High Court, however, included the total amount of Rs. 16,000 in the election expenses of the appellant upon the assumption that the appellant had not disavowed that expenditure. Be that as it may, the fact remains that the High Court has found on issue No. 9 that the total expenses incurred by the appellant on her election have I find no cogent reason to interfere with that finding.

249. I also agree with the High Court that as the election expenses of the appellant have not been shown to exceed the prescribed limit of Rs. 35,000, the question of invoking and going into the validity of Act 58 of 1974 does not arise. Nor is it necessary to express an opinion about the view taken in **Kanwarlal v. Amarnath Chawla, AIR 1975 SC 308** in expense of the appellant has not been shown to exceed the prescribed limit.

FINDING OF HIGH COURT ON ISSUE NO. 6 UPHELD – KHANNA, J.

250. So far as the finding of the High Court on issue No. 6 regarding the use of the symbol of cow and calf is concerned, the matter as already discussed earlier, is now covered by the amendment made in section 123(3) of the RP Act by section 8 of Act 40 of 1975.

JUSTICE KHANNA HAD HELD IN KESAVANANDA BHARATI'S CASE THAT FUNDAMENTAL RIGHTS WERE NOT A PART OF BASIC STRUCTURE OF THE CONSTITUTION – CONTENDS SOLICITOR GENERAL – CLARIFIED – IT WAS NOT SAID SO – PARTS OF VIEW EXPRESSED IN THAT CASE REPRODUCED – KHANNA, J.

251. There was a controversy during the course of arguments on the point as to whether I have laid down in my judgment in **Kesavananda Bharati's** case (supra) that fundamental rights are not a part of the basic structure of the Constitution.

As this controversy cropped up a number of times, it seems apposite that before I conclude I should deal with the contention advanced by learned Solicitor General that according to my judgment in that case no fundamental right is part of the basic structure of the Constitution. I find it difficult to read anything in that judgment to justify such a conclusion. What has been laid down in that judgment is that no article of the Constitution is immune from the a mandatory process because of the fact that it relates to a fundamental right and is contained in Part III of the Constitution. It was also held that a Constitutional Amendment under Article 368 does not constitute "law" as mentioned in Article 13.

I also did not agree with the view taken in the case of **Golaknath, (1967) 2 SCR 672** that there was a limitation on the power of Parliament to amend the provisions of Part III of the Constitution so as to abridge or take away the fundamental rights. I thereafter dealt with the scope of the power of amendment under Article 368 and the connotation of the word "amendment" and said in this context:

> "I am further of the opinion that amendment of the Constitution necessarily contemplates that the Constitution has not to be abrogated, but only changes have to be made in it. The word 'amendment' postulates that the old Constitution survives without loss of identity despite the change and continues even though it has been subjected to alterations. As a result of the amendment, the old Constitution cannot be destroyed and done away with, it is retained though in the amended form. What then is meant by the retention of the old Constitution? It means the retention of the basic structure or framework of the old Constitution. A mere retention of some provisions of the old Constitution even though the basic structure or framework of the Constitution has been destroyed would not amount to the retention of the old Constitution. Although it is permissible under the power of amendment to effect changes, however important, and to adopt the system to the requirements of changing conditions, it is not permissible to touch the foundation or to alter the basic institutional pattern. The words 'amendment of the Constitution' with all their wide sweep and amplitude cannot have the effect of destroying or abrogating the basic structure or framework of the Constitution. It would not be competent under the garb of amendment, for instance, to change the democratic Government into dictatorship or hereditary monarchy nor would it be permissible to abolish the Lok Sabha and the Rajya Sabha. The secular character of the State according to which the State shall not discriminate against any citizen on the ground of religion only cannot likewise be done away with. Provision regarding the amendment of

the Constitution does not furnish a pretence for subverting the structure of the Constitution nor can Article 368 be so construed as to embody the death wish of the Constitution or provide sanction for what may perhaps be called its lawful harakiri. Such subversion or destruction cannot be described to be amendment of the Constitution as contemplated by Article 368."

It was further observed by me:

> "The word 'amendment' in Article 368 must carry the same meaning whether the amendment relates to taking away or abridging fundamental rights in Part III of the Constitution or whether it pertains to some other provision outside Part III of the Constitution. No serious objection is taken to repeal, addition or alteration of provisions of the Constitution other than those in Part III under the power of amendment conferred by Article 368. The same approach, in my opinion, should hold good when we deal with amendment relating to fundamental rights contained in Part III of the Constitution. It would be impermissible to differentiate between scope and width of power of amendment when it deals with fundamental rights and the scope and width of that power when it deals with provisions not concerned with fundamental rights."

It would appear from the above that no distinction was made by me so far as the ambit and scope of the power of amendment is concerned between a provision relating to fundamental rights and provisions dealing with matters other than fundamental rights. The limitation inherent in the word "amendment" according to which it is not permissible by amendment of the Constitution to change the basic structure of the Constitution was to operate equally on articles pertaining to fundamental rights as on other articles not pertaining to those rights. This was further made clear by the following observations on page 688:

IN THAT CASE IT WAS HELD BY KHANNA, J. THAT SUBJECT TO THE RETENTION OF BASIC STRUCTURE AND FRAMEWORK OF THE CONSTITUTION, THE CONSTITUENT AUTHORITY CAN AMEND ANY PART OF THE CONSTITUTION – SUBMISSION OF AG WAS REJECTED – KHANNA, J.

"Subject to the retention of the basic structure or framework of the Constitution I have no doubt that the power of amendment is plenary and would include within itself the power to add, alter or repeal the various articles including those relating to fundamental rights."

Proposition (vii) of the summary of my conclusions on page 758 of the judgment also bears it out and the same reads as under:

> "(vii) The power of amendment under Article 368 does not include power to abrogate the Constitution nor does it include the power to alter the basic structure or framework of the Constitution. Subject to the retention of the basic structure or framework of the Constitution, the power of amendment is plenary and includes within itself the power to amend the various articles of the Constitution, including those relating to fundamental rights as well as those which may be said to relate to essential features. No part of a fundamental right can claim immunity from amendatory process by being described as the essence or core of that right. The power of amendment would also include within itself the power to add, alter or repeal the various articles."

SUBMISSION OF THE SOLICITOR GENERAL WAS REJECTED THAT HAD HELD IN KESHAVANANDA BHARATI'S CASE THAT FUNDAMENTAL RIGHTS WERE NOT A PART OF THE BASIC STRUCTURE OF THE CONSTITUTION – KHANNA, J.

252. It has been stated by me on page 685 of the judgment (already reproduced above) that the secular character of the State according to which the State shall not discriminate against any citizen on the ground of religion only cannot likewise be done away with. The above observations show that the secular character of the Constitution and the rights guaranteed by Article 15 pertain to the basic structure of the Constitution. The above observations clearly militate against the contention that according to my judgment fundamental rights are not a part of the basic structure of the Constitution. I also dealt with the matter at length to show that the right to property was not a part of the basic structure of the Constitution. This would have been wholly unnecessary if none of the fundamental rights was a part of the basic structure of the Constitution.

ASSISTANCE RENDERED BY THE COUNSEL IN THIS CASE APPRECIATED – KHANNA, J.

253. Before parting with this case I must acknowledge the assistance we received from the learned counsel for the parties as also from learned Attorney General and Solicitor General in resolving the points of controversy. In spite of the political overtones, the case was argued forcefully yet without generating any heat and in an atmosphere of befitting calmness. It has been said by Holmes, J. that great cases like hard cases make bad law. For great cases are called great not by reason of their real importance in shaping the law of the future, but because of some accident of immediate overwhelming interest, which appeals to the feelings and distorts the judgment. These immediate interests exercise a kind of hydraulic pressure (**Northern Securities Co. v. U.S.), (1903) 193 US 197 (400-1).** It, therefore, became essential to rid the case of all the embellishments resulting from the political overtones and to bring it to a level which is strictly judicial, so that the various constitutional and legal aspects of the matter may be examined in a dispassionate atmosphere. Learned counsel for the parties made a significant contribution towards the attainment of this objective. It may not be inappropriate in the above context to reproduce what was said by one of us (Khanna, J.) in **Keshvananda Bharti's** case (supra) at p. 755 (of SCR) (at p, 1902 of AIR):

> "That all constitutional interpretations have political consequences should not obliterate the fact that the decision has to be arrived at in the calm and dispassionate atmosphere of the court room, that judges in order to give legitimacy to their decision have to keep aloof from the din and controversy of politics and that the fluctuating fortunes of rival political parties can have for them only academic interest. Their primary duty is to uphold the Constitution and the laws without fear or favour and in doing so, they cannot allow any political ideology or economic theory, which may have caught their fancy, to colour the decision."

APPEAL FILED BY APPELLANT ACCEPTED – FILED BY RESPONDENT DISMISSED – KHANNA, J.

254. As a result of the above, I accept Appeal No. 887 of 1975 filed by Shrimati Indira Nehru Gandhi, set aside the judgment of the High Court in so far as it has found the appellant guilty of corrupt practice under section 123(7) of the RP Act and has declared her election to the Lok Sabha to be void. The order that the appellant shall accordingly stand disqualified for a period of six years as provided in section 8A would also consequently be set aside. The election petition filed by the respondent shall stand dismissed. Appeal No. 909 of 1975 filed by Shri Raj Narain is dismissed. Looking to all the circumstances, more particularly the fact that the election petition filed by the respondent is being dismissed because of changes made in law during the pendency of the appeal, the parties are directed to bear their own costs throughout.

K.K. Mathew, J.—In the election petition filed by the respondent in Civil Appeal No. 887 of 1975 (hereinafter referred to as 'respondent') seven charges of corrupt practice were made against the appellant therein (hereinafter called the 'appellant') and it was prayed that the election of the appellant be set aside. The learned Judge who tried the petition found that two of the charges had been made out but that the rest of the charges were not substantiated. He set aside the election of the appellant with the result that the appellant incurred the disqualification for a period of six years as visualized in section 8A of the Representation of the People Act, 1951. It is against this judgment that Civil Appeal No. 887 of1975 has been filed.

256. The respondent has filed a cross appeal (Civil Appeal No. 909 of 1975) challenging the findings of the High Court in respect of the other charges of corrupt practice.

ELECTION LAW WAS AMENDED ON 6.8.1975 DURING PENDENCY OF THIS APPEAL – MATHEW, J.

257. During the pendency of these appeals, the Parliament passed the Election Laws (Amendment) Act, 1975 on 6-8-1975 by which certain amendments were made in the provisions of the Representation of the People Act, 1951, and the Indian Penal Code.

CONSTITUTION WAS AMENDED ON 10.8.1975 DURING PENDENCY OF APPEAL – ARTICLE 71 OF THE CONSTITUTION WAS REPLACED – MATHEW, J.

258. On 10-8-1975 the Parliament in the exercise of its constituent power passed the Constitution (Thirty-ninth Amendment) Act, 1975 (hereinafter referred to as the 'Amendment'). By the Amendment, Article 71 of the Constitution was substituted by a new Article and that Article provided by clause (1) that, subject to the provisions of the Constitution, Parliament may, by law, regulate any matter relating to or connected with the election of a President or Vice-President, including the grounds on which such election may be questioned. By clause (2) of the Article it was provided that all doubts and disputes arising out of or in connection with the election of a President or Vice-President shall be inquired into and decided by such authority or body in such manner as may be provided for by or under any law referred to in clause (1). Clause (3) stated that the validity of any such law referred to in clause (1) and the decision of any authority or body under such law shall not be called in question in any court.

BY THIS AMENDMENT ARTICLE 329A WAS ADDED – REPRODUCED – MATHEW, J.

259. By clause 4 of the amended Article 329A was inserted reading as follows:

"329A. Special provision as to elections to Parliament in the case of Prime Minister and Speaker:

(1) subject to the provisions of Chapter II of Part V (except sub-clause (e) of clause (1) of Article 102), no election

  (a) to either House of Parliament of a person who holds the office of the Prime Minister at the time of such election or is appointed as Prime Minister after such election;

(b) to the House of the People of a person who holds the office of a Speaker of that House at the time of such election or who is chosen as the Speaker for that House after such election: shall be called in question except before such authority (not being any such authority as is referred to in clause (b) of Article 329) or body and in such manner as may be provided for by or under any law made by Parliament and any such law may provide for all other matters relating to doubts and disputes in relation to such election including the grounds on which such election may be questioned.

(2) The validity of any such law as is referred to in clause (1) and the decision of any authority or body under such law shall not be called in question in any court.

(3) Where any person is appointed as Prime Minister or, as the case may be, chosen to the office of the Speaker of the House of the People, while an election petition referred to in clause (b) of Article 329 in respect of his election to either House of Parliament or as the case may be, to the House of the People is pending, such election petition shall abate upon such person being appointed as Prime Minister or, as the case may be being chosen to the office of the Speaker of the House of the People, but such election may be called in question under any such law as is referred to in clause (1).

(4) No law made by Parliament before the commencement of the Constitution (Thirty-ninth Amendment) Act, 1975, in so far as it relates to election petitions and matters connected therewith shall apply or shall be deemed ever to have applied to or in relation to the election of any such person as is referred to in clause (1) to either House of Parliament and such election shall not be deemed to be void or ever to have become void on any ground on which such election could be declared to be void or has, before such commencement, been declared to be void under any such law and notwithstanding any order made by any court, before such commencement, declaring such election to be void, such election shall continue to be valid in all respects and any such order and any finding on which such order is based shall be and shall be deemed always to have been void and of no effect.

(5) Any appeal or cross appeal against any such order of any court as is referred to in clause (4) pending immediately before the commencement of the Constitution (Thirty-ninth Amendment) Act, 1975 before the Supreme Court shall be disposed of in conformity with the provisions of clause (4).

(6) The provisions of this Article shall have effect notwithstanding anything contained in this Constitution."

CLAUSE (4) INVALID AS IT DAMAGED BASIC STRUCTURE OF CONSTITUTION – ELECTION OF APPELLANT HAS BEEN DECLARED VALID – WITHOUT ASCERTAINING WITHOUT APPLYING LAW – CONTENDED RESPONDENT

260. The respondent contended that clause (4) of Article 329A (hereinafter referred to as clause (4) is invalid for the reason that some of the basic structures of the Constitution have been damaged by its enactment.

261. The argument was that although the amending body could declare that the election of the appellant shall not be deemed to be void and the judgment of the High Court to be void on the basis that no law relating to election petition and matters connected therewith would apply to the election, yet the amending body could not have held the election to be valid as it did not ascertain the facts relating to the election and apply the relevant law to them. Counsel submitted that by its very nature, an election dispute in a democratic system of Government raises questions which can be decided only by the exercise of judicial power, that by retrospectively rendering the forum for investigation into the complaints regarding the validity of the election of the appellant *coram non judice*, and by the amending body judging its validity without ascertaining the facts and applying the relevant law, the Amendment has fundamentally damaged an essential feature of the democratic structure of the Constitution, namely, free and fair election.

EQUALITY AND RULE OF LAW ARE DESTROYED BY THIS AMENDMENT – HENCE ILLEGAL – CONTENDS RESPONDENT

262. Counsel also submitted that equality and rule of law are essential features of democracy; that clause (4) by dispensing with the application of the law relating to election petition and matters connected therewith to the appellant, made an unreasonable classification among persons similarly situated with reference to the purpose of the law.

BY DECLARING ELECTION OF APPELLANT VALID – JUDICIAL POWER HAS BEEN ENCROACHED – SEPARATION OF POWER RULE VIOLATED – CONTENDS RESPONDENT

263. The further submission was that separation of powers is a basic structure of the Constitution and that if it be supposed that the amending body ascertained the facts regarding the election of the appellant and applied the relevant law, the exercise of that power by the amending body would offend the doctrine of separation of powers and that, at any rate, this process would not result in an amendment of the Constitution by enacting a law, but only in the passing of a judgment or sentence which can never be characterized as a law, let alone a law relating to the Constitution of India.

KESAVANANDA BHARATI'S CASE RELIED UPON BY RESPONDENT WHICH LAID DOWN THAT CONSTITUENT POWER CANNOT DAMAGE BASIC STRUCTURE OF CONSTITUTION – MATHEW, J.

264. In **His Holiness Kesavanada Bharati Sripadagalvaru v. State of Kerala, (1973) Supp SCR 1** (hereinafter referred to as **'Bharati's** case'), a majority of seven Judges held that the power conferred under Article 368 of the Constitution was not absolute. They took the view that by an amendment, the basic structure of the Constitution cannot be damaged or destroyed. And, as to what are the basic structures of the Constitution, illustrations have been given by each of these Judges. They include supremacy of the Constitution democratic republic form of Government, secular character of the Constitution, separation of powers among the legislature, executive and judiciary, the federal character of the Constitution, Rule of Law, equality of status and of opportunity; justice, social, economic and political; unity and integrity of the nation and the dignity of the individual secured by the various provisions of the Constitution. There was consensus among these Judges that democracy is a basic structure of the Constitution. I proceed on the assumption that the law as laid down by the majority in that case should govern the decision here, although I did not share the view of the majority.

CLAUSE (4) IS BAD IF IT DAMAGES BASIC STRUCTURE OF CONSTITUTION – HELD MATHEW, J.

265. Therefore, if by clause (4), any essential features of the democratic republication structure of our polity as visualised by the Constitution has been damaged or destroyed, the clause would be *ultra vires* the Constitution.

BY DECLARING JUDGMENT OF HIGH COURT VOID SIMPLICITER THE AMENDING POWER HAS ASSUMED JUDICIAL FUNCTION – HELD MATHEW, J.

266. One way of looking at the first part of clause (4) is that the amending body has, with retrospective effect, repealed the law relating to election petition in respect of the persons specified in clause (1) and hence the judgment rendered on the basis of the previous law relating to election petition became automatically void, and the amending body was merely stating the consequence of the retrospective repeal of the law and, therefore, the declaration that the judgment was void was not an exercise of judicial function. On the other hand, it might be possible to view the first part of clause (4) as an exercise of judicial power for the reason that, even assuming that by virtue of the retrospective repeal of the law relating to election petition, there was no jurisdiction in the High Court to entertain or try the election petition and pass the judgment, a repeal simpliciter did not render the judgment *ipso facto* void and, therefore, in making the declaration that the judgment was void, the amending body was performing a function which has traditionally been in the province of court.

AMENDING BODY HAS DECLARED ELECTION OF THE APPELLANT VALID WITHOUT ADJUDICATING FACTS – HELD MATHEW, J.

267. Be that as it may, I feel no doubt that the amending body, when it declared the election of the appellant to be valid, had to ascertain the adjudicative facts* and apply the relevant norm for adjudging its validity. If, however, the amending body did not ascertain the facts relating to the election and apply the relevant norm, the declaration of the validity of the election was a flat of a *sui generis* character of the amending body.

> *"Adjudicative facts are facts about the parties or their activities, business and properties usually answering the question of who did what, where when, how, why, with what motive or intent; adjudicative facts are roughly the kind offices that go to a jury in a jury case. Legislative facts do not usually concern the immediate parties but are general facts which help the tribunal decide questions of law, policy and discretion.
>
> "Facts pertaining to the parties and their activities that is, adjudicative facts, are intrinsically the kind of the facts that ordinarily ought not to be determined without giving the parties a chance to know and to meet any evidence that may be unfavourable to them, that is, without providing the parties an opportunity for trial." (*See* K.C. Davis: "The Requirement of a Trial-type Hearing", 70 Harv L. Rev, 193 at 191).

DEMOCRATIC SET-UP NEEDS THREE ORGANS – LEGISLATURE, EXECUTIVE, JUDICIARY – HELD MATHEW, J.

268. The concept of democracy as visualised by the Constitution presupposes the representation of the people in Parliament and State Legislatures by the method of election. And, before an election machinery can be brought into operation, there are three requisites which require to be attended to, namely, (1) there should be a set of laws and rules making provisions with respect to all matters relating to or in connection with, elections, and it should be decided as to how these laws and rules are to be made; (2) there should be an executive charged with the duty of securing the due conduct of elections; and (3) there should be a judicial tribunal to deal with disputes arising out of or in connection with elections. Articles 327 and 328 deal with the first of these requisites, Article 324 with the second and Article 329 with the third requisite; *see* **N.P. Ponnuswami v. Returning Officer, Namakkal Constituency, (1952) 3 SCR 218 (229).**

ARTICLE 329(B) PROVIDES ALL REQUISITES OF ELECTIONS INCLUDING AUTHORITY BEFORE WHOM THE VALIDITY OF ELECTION RESULT CAN BE CHALLENGED – HELD MATHEW, J.

269. Article 329(b) envisages the challenge to an election by a petition to be presented to such authority as the Parliament may, by law prescribe. A law relating to election should contain the requisite qualification for candidates, the method of voting, definition of corrupt practices by the candidates and their election agents, the forum for adjudication of election disputes and other cognate matters. It is on the basis of this law that the question whether there has been a valid election has to be determined by the authority to which the petition is presented. And, when a dispute is raised as regards the validity of the election of a particular candidate the authority entrusted with the task of resolving the dispute must necessarily exercise a judicial function, for the process consists of ascertaining the facts relating to the election and applying the law to the facts so ascertained. In other words, it is obvious that a power must be lodged somewhere to judge the validity of the election, for, otherwise, there would be no certainty as to who were legitimately chosen as members, and any intruder or usurper might claim a seat and thus trample upon the privileges and liberties of the people. Indeed, elections would become under such circumstances, a mockery. In whichever authority the power is lodged, the nature of the function is such that it requires a judicial approach. It cannot be resolved on considerations of political expediency.

* * * * *

WHICHEVER AUTHORITY MAY DECIDE – IT EXERCISES JUDICIAL FUNCTION – BY ASCERTAINING FACTS – BY APPLYING LAW – HELD MATHEW, J.

273. In whichever body or authority, the jurisdiction is vested, the exercise of the jurisdiction must be judicial in character. This Court has held that in adjudicating an election dispute an authority is performing a judicial function and a petition for leave to appeal under Article 136 of the Constitution would lie to this Court against the decision notwithstanding the provisions of Article 329(b) (*see* **Durga Shankar Mehta v. Thakur Rathuraj Singh, (1955) 1 SCR 267**).

* * * * *

275. It might be that if the adjudication of election disputes in respect of its members had been vested in each of the Houses of Parliament by the Constitution, the decision of the House would have been final. That would have been on the basis of the doctrine of the political question, namely, that the function has been exclusively committed textually to another agency, I am aware that the doctrine of political question has no hospitable quarter in this Court since the decision in **Madhav Rao Scindia v. Union of India, AIR 1971 SC 530.** But I venture to think that the doctrine alone can explain why the courts abstain from interfering with a verdict on an impeachment of the President for violation of the Constitution, a function essentially judicial.[1]

1. *See* Wechsler: Toward Neutral Principles of Constitutional Law, 73 Harv L Rev 1 (7-9)

276. An election dispute has a public aspect in that it is concerned more with the right of a constituency to be represented by a particular candidate. But it does not follow from the public character of the controversy that there is no *lis* between the parties to the election contest, and that the *lis* can be resolved otherwise than by ascertaining the facts relating to the election, and applying the relevant law:

> "A judicial inquiry investigates, declares and enforces liabilities as they stand on present or past facts and under laws supposed already to exist. This is its purpose and end. Legislation, on the other hand, looks to the future and changes existing conditions by making a new rule, to be applied thereafter to all or some part of some subject to its power."[2]

2. *Justice Holmes in Pretis* v. *Atlantic Coast Line Co.*, (1908) 211 US 210 (226).

* * * * *

IF BY AMENDMENT AN ELECTION IS DECLARED VALID – IS IT AN AMENDMENT OF THE CONSTITUTION? – MATHEW, J.

279. If, therefore, the decision of the amending body that the election of the appellant was valid was the result of the exercise of judicial power or of despotic discretion governed society by considerations of political expediency, the question is whether that decision, though couched in the form of an enactment, can be characterized as an amendment of the Constitution.

CONSTITUENT POWER IS TO FRAME A CONSTITUTION OR TO AMEND IT – MATHEW, J.

280. The constituent power is the power to frame a constitution. The people of India, in the exercise of that power, framed the Constitution and it enacts the basic norms. By that instrument, the people conferred on the amending body the power to amend by way of addition, variation or repeal any of its provisions (Article 368). It is not necessary to go in detail into the question whether the power to amend is coextensive which the constituent power of the people to frame a constitution. In **Bharati's** case I said:

> ".....", under the Indian Constitution, the original sovereign – the people – created, by the amending clause of the Constitution, a lesser sovereign, almost coextensive in power with itself. This sovereign, the one established by the revolutionary act of the full or complete sovereign has been called by Max Radin, the "pro-sovereign", the holder of the amending power under the Constitution."

SOVEREIGN AND "LEGAL SOVEREIGNTY" EXPLAINED – MATHEW, J.

281. I fully appreciate that 'sovereign', if conceived of as an omnipotent being, has no existence in the real world. Several thoughtful writers have deprecated the use of the expression in legal discussion as it has theological and religious overtones. Nevertheless, as the practice has become inveterate it will only create confusion if any departure is made in this case from the practice. If it is made clear that sovereign is not a 'mortal God' and can express himself or itself only in the manner and form prescribed by law and can be sovereign only when he or it acts in a certain way also prescribed by law, then perhaps the use of the expression will have no harmful consequence.

282. "Legal sovereignty' is a capacity 'to determine the actions of persons in certain intended ways by means of a law..... were the actions of those who exercise the authority, in those respects in which they do exercise it, are not subject to any exercise by other persons of the kind of authority which they are exercising;' *See* W.J. Rees *"The Theory of Sovereignty Re-started"* in Mind. Vol. 1ix (1950) quoted (68) of *'In Defence of Sovereignty'*, ed. W.J. Stankiewicz.

283. The point to be kept in mind is that the amending body which exercises the constituent power of the legal sovereign, though limited by virtue of the decision in **Bharati's case,** can express itself only by making laws.

EXERCISE OF DESPOTIC DISCRETION – IS NOT A LAW – CAN BE A LEGISLATIVE JUDGMENT – MATHEW, J.

284. The distinction between constitutional law and ordinary law in a rigid constitution like ours is that the validity of the constitutional law cannot be challenged whereas that of ordinary law can be challenged on the touchstone of constitution. But constitutional law is as much law as ordinary law. A Constitution cannot consist of a string of isolated dooms. A judgment or sentence which is the result of the exercise of judicial power or of despotic discretion is not a law as it has not got the generality which is an essential characteristic of law. A despotic decision without ascertaining the facts of a case and applying the law to them, though dressed in the garb of law, is like a bill of attainder. It is a legislative judgment.

LAW-CENTRIC VIEWS OF VARIOUS JURISTS DISCUSSED – THERE WAS A CLEAR DISTINCTION AS THE LAW IS MADE BY LEGISLATURE AND JUDGMENT IS GIVEN ON THE BASIS OF THAT LAW – MATHEW, J.

285. According to Blackstone, a law and a particular command are distinguished in the following manner: a law obliges generally the members of a given community, or a law obliges generally persons of a given class. A particular command obliges a single person or persons, whom it determines individually. Most of the laws established by political superiors are, therefore, general in a twofold manner: as enjoining or forbidding generally acts of kinds or sorts; and as binding the whole community, or, at least whole classes of its members. He then said: See *Blackstone: Commentaries*, Vol. 1, p. 44.

> "Therefore, a particular act of the legislature to confiscate the goods of Titus, "or to attaint him of high treason, does not enter into the idea of a municipal law: for the operation of this act is spent upon Titus only and has no relation to the community in general: it is rather a sentence than a law."

This passage was cited with approval by the Privy Council in **Liyanage v. The Queen, (1967) 1 AC 259 (291)** to show that the end product of the exercise of judicial power is a judgment or sentence and not a law.

286. St. Thomas Aquinas (after considering the views of Aristotle, St. Augustine and the opinions of jurists in pandects) has said that since the end of law is common good the law should be framed not for private benefit but for the common good of all citizens, *see "The Treatise on Law"* Gateway Ed, (1970) p. 87.

287. Rousseau wrote: *Contract Social*, Bk II, Chap. VI.

> "When I say that the object of laws is always general, I mean that the law considers subjects collectively and actions as abstract; never a man as an individual, nor an action as particular.....neither is what the sovereign himself orders about a particular object a law but a decree; not an act of sovereignty, but of magistracy."

288. Austin draws an explicit distinction between 'laws' and 'particular commands'. Where a command, he says, obliges generally to acts or forbearances of a class, a command is a law of rule. But where it obliges to a specific act or forbearance, a command is occasional or particular. See Austin's *Jurisprudence*, 2nd Ed. Vol. I, p. 18.

289. Kelsen, after noting the distinction made by Austin has observed:

> "We can of course recognize as law only general norms. But there is no doubt that law does not consist of general norms only. Law includes individual norms, *i.e.*, norms which determine the behaviour of one individual in one non-recurring situation and which, therefore, are valid only for one particular case and may be obeyed or applied only once. "

According to him, such norms are valid law because they are parts of the legal order as a whole in exactly the same sense as those general norms on the basis of which they have been created. He said that particular norms are the decisions of courts as far as their binding force is limited to the particular case at hand and that a Judge who orders a debtor A to return $ 1000 to his creditor B was passing a law: Kelsen: *General Theory of Law and State*, 1961, p. 38.

290. It may be noted that Kelsen made no distinction between law-creation and law-application. According to him, every act of applying the law involved the creation of norms. In his view, there was no distinction between creation and application of law, a view I find difficult to accept in the light of clear distinction made by the decisions of this Court between legislative and judicial functions.

291. A statute is a general rule. A resolution by the legislature that a town shall pay one hundred dollars to Timothy Coggan is not a statute, John Chipman Gray : Nature and Source of Law, p. 161.

* * * * *

293. J.C. Carter has said that statute books contain vast masses of matter which, though in the form of laws, are not laws in the proper sense, that these consist in the making of provisions for the maintenance of public works of the State, for the building of asylums, hospitals, school buses, and a great variety of similar matters, and that this is but the record of actions of the State in relation to the business in which it is engaged. According to him, the State is a great public corporation which conducts a vast mass of business, and the written provisions for this, though in the form of laws are not essentially different from the minutes of ordinary corporate bodies recording their actions.*

294. Walter Bagehot has said:

> "An immense mass, indeed of the legislation is not, in the proper language of jurisprudence legislation at all. A law is a general command applicable to many cases. The 'special acts' which crowd the statute book and weary parliamentary committees are applicable to one case only. They do not lay down rules according to which railways shall be made, but enact that such and such a railway shall be made from this place to that place and they have no bearing on any other transaction."**

295. "When the authors of books on jurisprudence write about law, when professional lawyers talk about law, the kind of law about which they are mainly thinking is that which is found in Justinian's Institutes, or in the Nepoleonic Codes, or in the New Civil Code of the German Empire, that is to say, the legal rules which relate to contracts and torts, to property, to family relations and inheritance, or else to law of crimes as is to be found in a Penal Code."***

296. John Locke was of the view that 'legislative authority is to act in a particular way....... (and) those who wield this authority should make only general rules. They are to govern by promulgated established laws not to be varied in particular cases.****

297. Perhaps the most exhaustive treatment of the question of the necessity for generality in law is to be found in "*Jurisprudence, Men and Ideas of the Law*" by

---

* Law, Its Origin, Growth and Function (New York and London, 1907), p. 116.

** "The English Constitution" (1967), World's Classics Edition (Oxford 1928), p. 119.

*** *See* Courtnancy Ilbert. Legislative Methods and Forms, (Oxford, 1901), p. 209.

**** *See* the passage quoted at p. 129 of Hayek: Law, Legislation and Liberty.

Patterson (see Chapter V). According to him, the generality of a law depends upon its being applicable to an indefinite number of human beings and that is the most significant aspect of law. He said that an ordinary judgment of a court is not law as a judgment applies only to a limited number of individuals, the parties to the case. He disagreed with Dr. Kelsen's statement that the judicial decision is an individual legal norm' as the expression 'individual' legal norm is a self contradiction.

298. To Freedman the most essential element in the concept of law is a degree of generality:

> "The first desideratum of a system for subjecting human conduct to the governance of rules is an obvious one: there must be rules. This may be stated as a requirement of generality. Here as in so many other fields, John Austin's distinction was basically fight, but too rigidly drawn."

Friedman was of the view that a community which had no general prescription at all but only an infinite multitude of individual commands, would not be regarded as having a legal order. It would dissolve into millions of individual relationships.*

* * * * *

302. In *Liyanage* v. *The Queen*, (1967) 1 AC 259 the appellants had been charged with offences arising out of an abortive *coup d'etat* on January 27, 1962. The story of the *coup d'etat* was set out in a White Paper issued by the Ceylon Government. On March 16, 1972 the Criminal Law (Special Provisions) Act was passed and it was given retrospective effect from January 1, 1962. The Act was limited in operation to those who were accused to offences against the State in or about January 27, 1962. The Act legalised the imprisonment of the appellants while they were awaiting trial and modified a section of the Penal Code so as to enact *ex post facto* a new offence to meet the circumstances of the abortive coup. The Act empowered the Minister of Justice to nominate the three Judges to try the appellants without a jury. The validity of the Act was challenged as well as the nomination which had been made by the Minister of Justice of the three Judges. The Ceylon Supreme Court upheld the objection about the vires of some of the provisions of the Act as well as the nomination of the Judges. Subsequently the Act was amended and the power of nomination of the Judges was conferred on the Chief Justice. The appellants having been convicted at the trial before a Court of three Judges nominated under the amended Act, went up in appeal before the Judicial Committee. It was contended that the Acts of 1962 offended against the Constitution in that they, amounted to a direction to convict the appellants or to a legislative plan to secure the conviction and severe punishment of the appellants and thus constituted an unjustifiable assumption of judicial power by the legislature, or an interference with judicial power which was outside the legislature's competence.

PRIVY COUNCIL LAID DOWN THAT ALTHOUGH THE LAW ENACTMENT WAS A LEGISLATIVE FUNCTION – BUT WHEN ULTIMATE OBJECT OF THE ENACTMENT IS TO AFFECT A JUDGMENT – IT AMOUNTS TO INTERFERENCE AND IT IS FATAL TO ITS VALIDITY – THESE OBSERVATIONS HAVE GREAT RELEVANCE TO THE CASE IN HAND – MATHEW, J.

303. The Privy Council said in the course of their judgment that the *pith* and *substance* of the law enactments was a legislative plan *ex post facto* to secure the conviction, that although legislation *ad hominem* which is directed to the course of particular proceedings may not always amount to an interference with the functions

* Friedmann: "Legal Theory" 5th Edn., pp. 15-16. *See* also: Lon L. Fuller: "The Morality of Law" pp. 46-49.

of the Judiciary, but in the present case they had no doubt that there was such interference: that it was not only the likely but the intended effect of the impugned enactment's and that it was fatal to their validity. They further said that the true nature and purpose of these enactments were revealed by their conjoint impact on the specific proceedings in respect of which they were designed and they took their colour, in particular from the alterations they purported to make as to their ultimate objective the punishment of those convicted - and that these alterations constituted a grave and deliberate incursion into the judicial sphere and then they quoted with approval the observations of Blackstone already referred to: *See Blackstone*: Commentaries, Vol. I, p. 44. These observations have great relevance to the cease in hand. True it is that their Lordships did not decide the question whether by a constitutional amendment the result could have been achieved or not.

AMENDMENTS DURING PENDENCY OF APPEAL AND CROSS APPEAL BEFORE THE SUPREME COURT – DIRECT INTERFERENCE IN JUDICIAL DECISION – MATHEW, J.

304. At the time when the Amendment was passed, the appeal filed by the appellant and the cross appeal of the respondent were pending before the Supreme Court. Clause (4) was legislation *ad hominem* directed against the course of the hearing of the appeals on merits as the appeal and the cross appeal were to be disposed of in accordance with that clause and not by applying the law to the facts as ascertained by the Court. This was a direct interference with the decision of these appeals by the Supreme Court on their merits by a legislative judgment.

IF THE AMENDING BODY EXERCISED JUDICIAL POWER WITHOUT HEARING – IT WAS IN VIOLATION OF THE PRINCIPLES OF NATURAL JUSTICE – MATHEW, J.

305. If the amending body really exercised judicial power, that power was exercised in violation of the principles of natural justice of *audi alteram partem*. Even if a power is given to a body without specifying that the rules of natural justice should be observed in exercising it, the nature of the power would call for its observance.

AMENDING BODY WAS EXERCISING ITS CONSTITUENT LEGISLATIVE POWER IN DECLARING THE ELECTION VALID – SUBMITS SOLICITOR GENERAL – REJECTED – WHEN AMENDING BODY EXCLUDED PRIOR LAW – IT COULD NOT HAVE FREE AND FAIR ELECTIONS IN MIND – MATHEW, J.

306. The Solicitor General contended that the amending body, in declaring that the election was valid, was exercising its constituent legislative power; that legislative power does not adjudicate but only creates validity, even retrospectively, by enacting a law with the effect; that validation is law-making; that it alters the legal position by making new law and that validation may take place before or after a judgment. He said that by the repeal of the provisions of the Representation of the People Act, 1951, the amending body had wiped out not only the election petition but also the judgment of the High Court and has deprived the respondent of the right to raise any dispute as regards the validity of the election of the appellant and, therefore, there was no dispute to be adjudicated upon by the amending body. He also said – I think, in the alternative – that although the law relating to election petitions and other matters connected therewith was dispensed with in respect of the appellant, the amending body had the ideal norms of fair and free election in its view for adjudging the validity of the election. He submitted that it was open to the amending body to gather facts from any source and as the facts collected by the High Court were there factually the amending body looked into them and applied the ideal norms of election for adjudging its validity.

307. It is difficult to understand, when the amending body expressly excluded the operation of all laws relating to election petition and matters connected therewith by the first part of Clause (4), what ideal norms of free and fair election it had in view in adjudging the validity of the election of the appellant. I cannot conceive of any pre-existing ideal norms of election apart from the law enacted by the appropriate legislatures. If the amending body evolved new norms for adjudging the validity of the particular election, it was the exercise of a despotic power and that would damage the democratic structure of the Constitution.

THERE IS NOTHING TO SHOW IF THE AMENDING BODY HAD ASCERTAINED FACTS OR APPLIED ANY LAW OR EVEN CHANGED LAW TO DETERMINE VALIDITY OF THE ELECTION – NO ELECTION CAN BE DECLARED VALID WITHOUT APPLYING THE LAW – MATHEW, J.

308. Quite apart from it, there is nothing on the face of the amendment to show that the amending body ascertained the facts of the case or applied any norms for determining the validity of the election. I do not think that under Article 368 the amending body was competent to pass an ordinary law with retrospective effect to validate the election. It can only amend the Constitution by passing a law of the rank of which the Constitution is made of.

309. There is also nothing to show that the amending body validated the election with reference to any change of the law which formed the foundation of the judgment. The cases cited by the Solicitor General to show that a competent legislature has power to validate an invalid election do not indicate that there can be a validation without changing the law which invalidated the election. Nor do I think that a contested election can be validated without an authority applying the new law to the facts as ascertained by judicial process. If the Court which ascertained the facts and applied the law was rendered *coram non judice*, the facts ascertained by it have ceased to be facts. There are no absolute or immediately evident facts. Only by being first ascertained through legal procedure are facts brought into the sphere of law or, we may say, though it may sound paradoxical, that the competent organ legally creates facts. The Courts perform a constitutive function in ascertaining facts. There is no fact in itself that *A* has killed *B*. There is only somebody's belief or knowledge. They are all private opinion without relevance. Only establishment by a competent organ has legal relevance. *See* Kelsen: *General Theory of Law and State*, p. 136. And, when that organ was rendered *coram non judice*, and its judgment declared void, the facts created by it perished. They ceased to be facts. Adjudicative facts of an election dispute cannot be gathered by legislative process behind the back of the parties; they can be gathered only by judicial process. The amending body did not ascertain the facts by resorting to judicial process.

CLAUSE (4) IS LEGISLATIVE VALIDATION OF AN ELECTION WITHOUT GOING INTO FACTS ETC. – IT DAMAGES DEMOCRATIC STRUCTURE OF THE CONSTITUTION – MATHEW, J.

310. If Clause (4) was an exercise in legislative validation without changing the law which made the election invalid, when there ought to have been an exercise of judicial power of ascertaining the adjudicative facts and applying the law, the clause would damage the democratic structure of the Constitution, as the Constitution visualizes the resolution of an election dispute by a petition presented to an authority exercising judicial power. The contention that there was no election dispute as clause (4) by repealing the law relating to election petition had rendered the petition filed by the respondent *non est*, if allowed, will toll the death knell of the democratic structure of the Constitution. If Article 329(b) envisages the resolution of an election dispute by judicial process by a petition presented to an authority as the appropriate legislature may by law provide, a constitutional amendment cannot dispense with that requirement without damaging an essential feature of democracy, *viz.*, the mechanism for determining the real representative of the people in an election as contemplated by the Constitution.

CASES CITED BY SOLICITOR GENERAL WERE THOSE WHERE LEGISLATIVE VALIDATION WAS MADE BY APPLYING NEW LAW

311. All the cases cited by the Solicitor General pertain either to legislative validation of a void election by applying a new law to undisputed facts or to the removal of an admitted disqualification by a law with retrospective effect.

* * * * *

IN PIARE DUSADH'S CASE, LEGISLATURE HAD CONFERRED JURISDICTION ON A COURT WHICH HAD CONVICTED AND SENTENCED WITHOUT JURISDICTION – MATHEW, J.

313. The decision in **Piare Dusadh v. King Emperor, (1944) 6 FCR 61** concerned the validation of a sentence imposed by a special Criminal Court which was held to have no jurisdiction to try the case by an order of a Court. By a validation Act, the jurisdiction was conferred with retrospective effect on the special Criminal Court and the sentence imposed by it was made lawful. It was held that there was no exercise of any judicial power by the legislating authority.

IN KANTA KATHURIA'S CASE, DISQUALIFICATION TO CONTEST WAS REMOVED BY LEGISLATIVE ENACTMENT – MATHEW, J.

314. In **Kanta Kathuria v. Manak Chand Surana, (1970) 2 SCR 835**, the appellant, a Government advocate stood for election to the State Legislative Assembly of Rajasthan and was declared elected. The election was challenged and the ground of challenge was that the appellant held an office of profit within the meaning of Article 191 of the Constitution. The High Court set aside the election for that reason. While the appeal was pending in this Court, Rajasthan Act 5 of 1969 was passed declaring among others that the holder of the office of a Special Government Pleader was not disqualified from being chosen or for being a member of the State Legislative Assembly : and, by section 2(2), the Act was made retrospective removing the appellant's disqualification retrospectively. It was held that Act 5 of 1969 had removed the disqualification retrospectively, that Parliament and the State legislatures can legislate retrospectively subject to the provisions of the Constitution, that no limitation on the powers of the legislature, to make a declaration validating an election could be put, and that, by enacting the impugned Act, the disqualification if any which existed in the 1951 Act had been removed.

IN STATE OF ORISSA CASE DEFECT IN THE ELECTORAL ROLLS AND DELAY IN PUBLISHING IT – WERE REGULATED BY STATE ORDINANCE – MATHEW, J.

315. In **State of Orissa v. Bhupendra Kumar Bose, 1962 Supp (2) SCR 380,** the facts were as follows: Elections were held for the Cuttack Municipality and 27 persons were declared elected as councillors. One B, who was defeated at the elections, filed a writ petition before the High Court challenging the elections. The High Court held that the electoral rolls had not been prepared in accordance with the provisions of the Orissa Municipalities Act, 1950, as the age qualification had been published too late thereby curtailing the period of claims and objections to the preliminary roll to 2 days from 21 days as prescribed; consequently, the High Court set aside the elections. The State took the view that the judgment affected not merely the Cuttack Municipality but other municipalities also. Accordingly, the Governor promulgated an ordinance validating the elections to the Cuttack Municipality and validating the electoral rolls prepared in respect of other municipalities. Thereupon, B filed a writ petition before the High Court contending that the Ordinance was unconstitutional. The High Court found that the Ordinance contravened Art, 14 of the Constitution, that it did not successfully cure the invalidity and that it offended Article 254(1) of the Constitution as it was inconsistent with many Central Acts falling in the concurrent list and was unconstitutional. The State and the Councillors appealed and challenged the findings of the High Court.

316. This Court held that section 3(1) of the Ordinance effectively removed the defects in the electoral rolls found by the High Court by its judgment and that it successfully cured the invalidity of the electoral roll and of the elections to the Cuttack Municipality.

IN OTHER JUDGMENTS RELIED UPON BY SOLICITOR GENERAL – NEW SET OF LAWS WITH RETROSPECTIVE EFFECT WERE MADE APPLICABLE – MATHEW, J.

317. The Solicitor General also cited other decisions to show that a legislature can validate proceedings rendered invalid by judgment of Court. As I said, they all involved substitution of new law with retrospective effect for the old one and the basic facts were all taken to have been admitted or not controverted. If the facts are not admitted, the legislature cannot determine them except by employing judicial process. Besides, those cases being cases of legislative validation, need not pass the test of the theory of basic structure which, I think, will apply only to constitutional amendment.

NO ELECTION BEING CONTESTED WAS VALIDATED BY HOUSE OF COMMONS IN ENGLAND IN THE CASES RELIED UPON BY THE APPELLANT – MATHEW, J.

318. Counsel for the appellant also brought to the notice of the Court certain election validation Acts passed by the House of Commons in England. These Acts removed with retrospective effect disqualifications of members of Parliament. In none of these cases was an election which was being contested validated by Parliament. Nor can these instances of legislative removal of disqualification furnish any assistance to this Court for the reason that in England there is no theory of basic structure operating as a fetter on the power of Parliament.

EXERCISE OF JUDICIAL POWER BY AMENDING BODY WAS UNCONSTITUTIONAL – CONTENDS RESPONDENT

319. It was argued for the respondent that if the amending body exercised judicial power and held the election of the appellant valid, its act was unconstitutional also on the ground that it damaged another basic structure of the Constitution, namely, the doctrine of separation of powers.

SEPARATION OF POWER INTO THREE ORGANS – LEGISLATIVE JUDICIAL AND EXECUTIVE IS TO ENSURE JUSTICE – POWERS IN ONE HAND IS A DICTATOR – MATHEW, J.

320. The major problem of human society is to combine that degree of liberty without which law is tyranny with that degree of law without which liberty becomes licence; and, the difficulty has been to discover the practical means of achieving this grand objective and to find the opportunity for applying these means in the ever shifting tangle of human affairs. A large part of the effort of man over centuries has been expended in seeking a solution of this great problem. A reign of law, in contrast to the tyranny of power, can be achieved only through separating appropriately the several powers of Government. If the law-makers should also be the constant administrators and dispensers of law and justice, then, the people would be left without a remedy in case of injustice since no appeal can lie under the fiat against such a supremacy.

And, in this age-old search of political philosophers for the secret of sound Government, combined with individual liberty, it was Montesquieu who first saw the light. He was the first among the political philosophers who saw the necessity of separating judicial power from the executive and legislative branches of Government. Montesquieu was the first to conceive of the three functions of Government as exercised by three organs, each juxtaposed against others. He realised that the efficient operation of Government involved a certain degree of overlapping and that the theory of checks and balances required each organ to impede too great an aggrandizement of authority by the other two powers. As Holdsworth says, Montesquieu convinced the world that he had discovered a new constitutional principle which was universally valid. The doctrine of separation of Governmental powers is not a mere theoretical, philosophical concept. It is a practical, work-a-day principle. The division of Government into three branches does not imply, as its critics would have made us think, three water-tight compartments. Thus, legislative impeachment of executive officers of judges, executive veto over legislation, judicial review of administrative or legislative actions are treated as partial exceptions which need explanation.*

321. There can be no liberty where the legislative and executive powers are united in the same person or body of magistrates, or, if the power of judging be not separated from the legislative and executive powers. Jefferson said: All powers of Government – legislative, executive and judicial – result in the legislative body. The concentration of these powers in the same hands is precisely the definition of despotic Government. It will be no alleviation than these powers will be exercised by a plurality of hands and not by a single person. One hundred and seventy three despots would surely be as oppressive as one. See Jefferson Works : 3 : 223. And, Montesquieu's own words would show that where the whole power of one department is exercised by the same hands which possess the whole power of another department, the fundamental principles of a free constitution are subverted. In Federalist No. 47, James Madison suggests that Montesquieu's doctrine did not mean that separate departments might have "no partial agency in or no control over the acts of each other." His meaning was, according to Madison, no more than that one department should not possess the whole power of another.

JUDICIARY IS THE WEAKEST OF THE THREE ORGANS – IT HAS NO INFLUENCE OVER THE SWORD OR THE PURSE – MATHEW, J.

322. The Judiciary, said the Federalist, is beyond comparison the weakest of the three departments of power. It has no influence over either the sword or the purse; no direction either of the strength or of the wealth of the society and can take no active resolution whatever. It may truly be said to have neither force nor will, but merely judgment. Of the three powers Montesquieu said, the judiciary is in some measure next to nothing. If he realised the relative weakness of the judiciary at the time he wrote, it is evidence of his vision that he appreciated the supreme importance of its independence. There is no liberty, he said, if the judicial power be not separated from the legislative and executive.

323. But this doctrine which is directed against the concentration of these powers in the same hand has no application as such when the question is whether

* *See* generally: "The Doctrine of Separation of Powers and its present day significance" by T. Vanderbilt.

an amending body can exercise judicial power. In other words, the doctrine is directed against the concentration of these sovereign powers in one or other organ of Government. It was not designed to limit the power of a constituent body.

* * * * *

POSSESSION OF POWER IS DISTINCT FROM ITS EXERCISE – MATHEW, J.

325. The possession of power is distinct from its exercise.* The possession of legislative power by the amending body would not entitle it to pass an ordinary law, unless the Constitution is first amended by passing a constitutional law authorizing it to do so. In the same way, the possession of judicial power by the amending body would not warrant the exercise of the power, unless a constitutional law is passed by the amending body enabling it to do so. Until that is done, its potential judicial power would not become actual. Nobody can deny that by passing a law within its competence, Parliament can vest judicial power in any authority for deciding a dispute or vest a part of that power in itself for resolving a controversy, as there is no exclusive vesting of judicial power in Courts by the Constitution. The doctrine of separation of powers which is directed against the concentration of the whole or substantial part of the judicial power in the legislature or the executive would not be a bar to the vesting of such a power in itself. But, until a law is passed enabling it to do so, its potential judicial power would not become actual.

* * * * *

A SOVEREIGN IN CIVILISED JURISPRUDENCE IS NOT LIKE AN ORIENTAL DESPOT WHO CAN DO ANYTHING HE LIKES, IN ANY MANNER HE LIKES AND AT ANY TIME HE LIKES – A SOVEREIGN CAN ACT ONLY BY ENACTING LAWS – MATHEW, J.

327. A sovereign in any system of civilized jurisprudence is not like an oriental despot who can do anything he likes, in any manner he likes and at any time he likes. That the Nizam of Hyderabad had legislative, judicial and executive powers and could exercise any one of them by a firman has no relevance when we are considering how a pro-sovereign – the holder of the amending power – in a country governed by a constitution should function. Such a sovereign can express 'himself' only by passing a particular kind of law; and not through sporadic acts. 'He cannot pick and choose cases; according to his whim and dispose them of by administering 'cadi-justice': nor can the amending body, as already noticed, pass an ordinary law, as Article 368 speaks of the constituent power of amending by way of addition, variation or repeal, any provision of the Constitution in accordance with the procedure laid down in that Article. An ordinary law can be passed by it only after amending the provisions of the Constitution authorising it to do so.

328. If the basic postulate that a sovereign can act only by enacting laws is correct, then that is a limitation upon his power to do anything he likes. If I may re-phrase the classical statement of Sir Owen Dixon: the law that a sovereign can act only by law is supreme but as to what may be done by a law so made, the sovereign is supreme over that law.** Of course, this is subject to the theory of basic structure. In other words, even though a sovereign can act only by making law, the law he so makes may vest the authority to exercise judicial power in himself; without such law he cannot exercise judicial power.

---

* *See* Jacques Maritain: "Man and State". pp. 101-102; also the judgment of Hidayatullah, J. in **Golaknath v. State of Punjab, (1967) 2 SCR 762.**

** *See* "Law and the Constitution". 50 Law Quarterly Rev., 590, 604.

BY ARTICLE 329A ELECTION OF APPELLANT HAS BEEN HELD TO BE VALID – IT COULD NOT DO SO WITHOUT ASCERTAINING FACT AND WITHOUT APPLYING LAW – HAS GIVEN A JUDGMENT – MATHEW, J.

329. The result of the discussion can be summed up as follows: Our Constitution by Article 329(b) visualizes the resolution of an election dispute on the basis of a petition presented to such authority and in such manner as the appropriate legislature may, by law, provide. The nature of the dispute raised in an election petition is such that it cannot be resolved except by judicial process, namely, by ascertaining the facts relating to the election and applying the pre-existing law; when the amending body held that the election of the appellant was valid, it could not have done so except by ascertaining the facts by judicial process and by applying the law. The result of this process would not be the enactment of constitutional law but the passing of a judgment or sentence.

The amending body, though possessed of judicial power, had no competence to exercise it, unless it passed a constitutional law enabling it to do so. If, however, the decision of the amending body to hold the election of the appellant valid was the result of the exercise of an 'irresponsible despotic discretion' governed solely by what it deemed political necessity or expediency, then, like a bill of attainder, it was a legislative judgment disposing of a particular election dispute and not the enactment of a law resulting in an amendment of the Constitution.

And, even if the latter process (the exercise of despotic discretion) could be regarded as an amendment of the Constitution, the amendment would damage or destroy an essential feature of democracy as established by the Constitution, namely, the resolution of election dispute by an authority by the exercise of judicial power by ascertaining the adjudicative facts and applying the relevant law for determining the real representative of the people. The decision of the amending body cannot be regarded as an exercise in constituent legislative validation of an election for these reasons: *firstly*, there can be no legislative validation of an election when there is dispute between the parties as regards the adjudicative facts; the amending body cannot gather these facts by employing legislative process; they can be gathered only by judicial process.

Secondly, the amending body must change the law retrospectively so as to make the election valid, if the election was rendered invalid by virtue of any provision of the law actually existing at the time of election; Article 368 does not confer on the amending body the competence to pass any ordinary law whether with or without retrospective effect. Clause (4) expressly excluded the operation of all laws relating to election petition to the election in question. Therefore, the election was held to be valid not by changing the law which rendered it invalid.

Thirdly, the cases cited for the appellant are cases relating to legislative validation of invalid elections or removal of disqualification with retrospective effect. Being cases of legislative validation, or removal of disqualifications by legislature, they are not liable to be tested on the basis of the theory of basic structure, which, I think, is applicable only to constitutional amendments.

Fourthly, there was no controversy in those cases with regard to adjudicative facts: if there was controversy with regard to these facts, it is very doubtful whether there could be legislative validation of an election by changing the law alone without ascertaining the adjudicative facts by judicial process.

EVEN IF ARTICLE 14 IS NOT BASIC STRUCTURE OF THE CONSTITUTION – INEQUALITY IS UNFAIR – MATHEW, J.

330. Then I come to the argument of counsel that equality is a basic structure of the Constitution and that that has been damaged or destroyed by clause (4).

331. The Solicitor General submitted that the majority in *Bharati's* case did not hold that Article 14 pertains to the basic structure, that apart from Article 14, there is no principle of equality which is a basic structure of the Constitution and that it is not a chameleon like concept which changes its colour With the nature of the subject-matter to which it is applied.

332. The majority in *Bharati's* case did not hold that Article 14 pertains to the basic structure of the Constitution. The majority upheld the validity of the first part of Article 31C; this would show that a constitutional amendment which takes away or abridges the fight to challenge the validity of an ordinary law for violating the fundamental right under that Article would not destroy or damage the basic structure. The only logical basis for supporting the validity of Articles 31A, 31B and the first part of 31C is that Article 14 is not a basic structure.

333. Counsel for the respondent, however, submitted that even if Article 14 does not pertain to basic structure, equality is an essential feature of democracy and rule of law and that clause (4), by dispensing with the application of the law relating to election petition and matters connected therewith to the appellant and another has made an unreasonable distinction between persons similarly situated and has thereby damaged or destroyed that essential feature, and therefore, the clause is bad. He said that in so far as laws are general instructions to act or refrain from acting in certain ways in specified circumstances enjoined upon persons of a specified kind, they enjoin uniform behaviour in identical cases; that to fall under a law is *pro-tanto* to be assimilated to a single pattern; and that a plea for rule of law in this sense is, in essence, a plea for life in accordance with laws as opposed to other standards, namely, the ad hoc dispensation from its operation. He argued that if some persons, for no stated reason, and in accordance with no rule, obtain exemption from the operation of law, while persons who are sufficiently similar in relevant characteristics are governed by it, that is manifestly unfair, for, to allow some persons to do that which is forbidden to all others is irrational.

DEMOCRACY PROCEEDS ON TWO BASIC ASSUMPTIONS – POPULAR SOVEREIGNTY AND EQUALITY AMONG CITIZENS – MATHEW, J.

334. Democracy proceeds on two basic assumptions: (1) popular sovereignty in the sense that the country should be governed by the representatives of the people; that all power came from them; at their pleasure and under their watchful supervision it must be held; and (2) that there should be equality among the citizens in arriving at the decisions affecting them.*

335. Today, it is impossible to conceive of a democratic republican form of Government without equality of citizens. It is true that in the republics of Athens and Rome there were slaves who were regarded as chattels. And, even in the United States of America, there was a republic even before the Negroes were enfranchised. Our Constitution envisages the establishment of a democratic republican form of Government based on adult suffrage.

EQUALITY IS MULTI-COLOURED CONCEPT – HAS MANY SHADES AND CONNOTATIONS – MATHEW, J.

336. Equality is a multi-coloured concept incapable of a single definition. It is a notion of many shades and connotations. The preamble of the Constitution guarantees equality of status and of opportunity. They are nebulous concepts. And I am not sure whether they can provide a solid foundation to rear a basic

* *See* Robert A. Dahl: "A Preface to Democratic Theory", pp. 4-33: and Bryce: Modern Democracies, Vol. II, p. 9.

structure. I think the types of equality which our democratic republic guarantees are all subsumed under specific articles of the Constitution like Articles 14, 15, 16, 17, 25, etc., and there is no other principle of equality which is an essential feature of our democratic policy.

MAJORITY IN BHARATI'S CASE HELD 'RULE OF LAW' AS BASIC STRUCTURE APART FROM 'DEMOCRACY' – MATHEW, J.

337. In the opinion of some of the judges constituting the majority in Bharati's case Rule of Law is a basic structure of the Constitution apart from democracy.

338. The rule of law postulates the pervasiveness of the spirit of law throughout the whole range of Government in the sense of excluding arbitrary official action in any sphere. 'Rule of law' is an expression to give reality to something which is not readily expressible. That is why Sir Ivor Jennings said that it is an unruly horse. Rule of law is based upon the liberty of the individual and has as its object, the harmonizing of the opposing notions of individual liberty and public order. The notion of justice maintains the balance between the two; and justice has a variable content. Dicey's formulation of the rule of law, namely, "the absolute supremacy or predominance of regular law, as opposed to the influence of arbitrary power, excluding the existence of arbitrariness, of prerogative, even of wide discretionary authority on the part of the Government" has been discarded in the later editions of his book. That is because it was realized that it is not necessary that where law ends, tyranny should begin. As Culp Davis said, where the law ends, discretion begins and the exercise of discretion may mean either beneficence or tyranny; either justice or injustice, either reasonableness or arbitrariness. There has been no Government or legal system in world history which did not involve both rules and discretion. It is impossible to find a Government of laws alone and not of men in the sense of eliminating all discretionary powers. All Governments are Governments of laws and of men. Jerome Frank has said:

> "This much we can surely say: For Aristotle, from whom Harrington derived the notion of a Government of laws and not of men, that notion was not expressive of hostility to what today we call administrative discretion. Nor did it have such a meaning for Harrington."*

339. Another definition of rule of law has been given by Friedrich A. Hayek in his books: "Road to Serfdom" and "Constitution of Liberty". It is much the same as that propounded by the Franks Committee in England, Report (1957) p. 6:

> "The rule of law stands for the view that decisions should be made by the application of known principles or laws. In general such decisions will be predictable, and the citizen will know where he is. On the other hand there is what is arbitrary. A decision may be made without principle, without any rules. It is, therefore, unpredictable, the antithesis of a decision taken in accordance with the rule of law."

RULE OF LAW ALSO MEANS DECISIONS BE BASED ON KNOWN PRINCIPLES – APPLICATION OF RULES ALSO MEANS EQUALITY BEFORE LAW – MATHEW, J.

340. This Court said in **Jaisinghani v. Union of India (1967) 2 SCR 703 (718)** that the rule of law from one point of view means that decisions should be made by the application of known principles and rules, and, in general, such decisions should be predictable and the citizen should know where he is.

---

* *See* "If Men were Angels", (1942), p. 203.

341. This exposition of the rule of law is only the aspiration for an ideal and it is not based on any down-to-earth analysis of practical problems with which a modern government is confronted. In the world of action, this ideal cannot be worked out and that is the reason why this exposition has been rejected by all practical men.

342. If it is contrary to the rule of law that discretionary authority should be given to government departments or public officers, then there is no rule of law in any modern State. A judge who passes a sentence has no other guidance except a statute which says that the person may be sentenced to imprisonment for a term which may extend to, say, a period of ten years. He must exercise considerable discretion. The High Courts and the Supreme Court overrule their precedents. What previously announced rules guide them in laying down the new precedents? A court of law decides a case of first impression; no statute governs, no precedent is applicable. It is precisely because a judge cannot find a previously announced rule that he becomes a legislator to a limited extent. All these would show that it is impossible to enunciate the rule of law which has as its basis that no decision can be made unless there is a certain rule to govern the decision. See "*Discretionary Justice*" by K.C. Davis.

343. Leaving aside these extravagant versions of rule of law there is a genuine concept of rule of law and that concept implies equality before the law or equal subjection of all classes to the ordinary law. But, if rule of law is to be a basic structure of the Constitution, one must find specific provisions in the Constitution embodying the constituent elements of the concept. I cannot conceive of rule of law as a twinkling star up above the Constitution. To be a basic structure, it must be a terrestrial concept having its habitat within the four corners of the Constitution. The provision of the Constitution were enacted with a view to ensure the rule of law. Even if I assume that rule of law is a basic structure, it seems to me that the meaning and the constituent elements of the concept must be gathered from the enacting provisions of the Constitution. The equality aspect of the rule of law and of democratic republicanism is provided in Article 14. May be, the other articles referred to do the same duty.

ENGLISH DOCTRINE 'RULE OF LAW' AND AMERICAN CLAUSE 'EQUAL PROTECTION' COLLECTIVELY CONSTITUTE ARTICLE 14 – QUOTES DAS C.J. – MATHEW, J.

344. Das, C.J. said that Article 14 combines the English doctrine of the rule of law and the equal protection clause of the 14th Amendment to the American Federal Constitution. **Basheshar Nath v. The Commr. of I.T., 1959 Supp (1) SCR 528 (550, 551).** In **State of Bengal v. Anwar Ali Sarkar, (1952) 3 SCR 284 (293)**, Patanjali Sastri, C.J. observed that the first part of the Article which has been adopted from the Irish Constitution, is a declaration of equality of the civil rights of all persons within the territories of India and thus enshrines what American judges regard as the "basic principle of republicanism" **C.F. Ward v. Flood, (1874) 17 Am Rep 405** and that the second part which is a corollary of the first is based on the last clause of the first section of the Fourteenth Amendment of the American Constitution. So, the concept of equality which is basic to rule of law and that which is regarded as the most fundamental postulate of republicanism are both embodied in Article 14. If, according to the majority in **Bharati's** case, Article 14 does not pertain to basic structure of the Constitution which is the other principle of equality incorporated in the Constitution which can be a basic structure of the Constitution or an essential feature of democracy or rule of law? However, it is unnecessary to pursue this aspect of the question as I have already given reasons to show clause (4) to be bad.

CLAUSE (4) OF ARTICLE 329A IS BAD IN LAW– CLAUSES (1) TO (3) ARE SEVERABLE BUT NO OPINION ON LEGALITY – MATHEW, J.

345. I think clause (4) is bad for the reasons which I have already summarized. Clauses (1) to (3) of Article 329-A are severable but I express no opinion on their validity as it is not necessary for deciding this case.

AMENDMENT ACTS 1974 – 1975 – DAMAGE FREE AND FAIR ELECTIONS – HENCE BAD – PLEADS RESPONDENT – REJECTED – MATHEW, J.

346. Then the question is, whether the Representation of the People (Amendment) Act, 1974, and the Election Laws (Amendment) Act 1975, are liable to be challenged for the reason that they damage or destroy a basic structure of the Constitution. Counsel for the respondent submitted that, if, by a constitutional amendment, the basic structure of the Constitution cannot be destroyed or damaged, it would be illogical to assume that an ordinary law passed under a power conferred by that instrument can do so and since these Acts damage the concept of free and fair election the Acts were bad.

347. I think the inhibition to destroy or damage the basic structure by an amendment of the Constitution flows from the limitation on the power of amendment under Article 368 read into it by the majority in **Bharati's** case because of their assumption that there are certain fundamental features in the Constitution which its makers intended to remain there in perpetuity. But I do not find any such inhibition so far as the power of parliament or state legislatures to pass laws is concerned.

Articles 245 and 246 give the power and also provide the limitation upon the power of these organs to pass laws. It is only the specific provisions enacted in the Constitution which could operate as limitation upon that power. The preamble, though a part of the Constitution, is neither a source of power nor a limitation upon that power. The preamble sets out the ideological aspirations of the people. The essential features of the great concepts set out in the preamble are delineated in the various provisions of the Constitution. It is these specific provisions in the body of the Constitution which determine the type of democracy which the founders of that instrument established, the quality and nature of justice, political, social and economic which was their desideratum, the content of liberty of thought and expression which they entrenched in that document, the scope of equality of status and of opportunity which they enshrined in it.

These specific provisions enacted in the constitution alone can determine the basic structure of the Constitution as established. These specific provisions either separately or in combination determine the content of the great concepts set out in the preamble. It is impossible to spin out any concrete concept of basic structure out of the gossamer concepts set out in the preamble. The specific provisions of the Constitution are the stuff from which the basic structure has to be woven.

CONSTITUTION AMENDMENT CAN BE EXAMINED ON THE TOUCH STONE OF BASIC STRUCTURE – NOT ORDINARY LAWS – MATHEW, J.

The argument of counsel for the respondent proceeded on the assumption that there are certain norms for free and fair election in an ideal democracy and the law laid down by Parliament or State legislatures must be tested on those norms and, if found wanting, must be struck down. The norms of election set out by Parliament or State Legislatures tested in the light of the provisions of the Constitution or necessary implications therefrom constitute the law of the land. That law cannot be subject to any other test, like the test of free and fair election in an ideal democracy.

348. I do not think that an ordinary law can be declared invalid for the reason that it goes against the vague concepts of democracy; justice, political, economic and social; liberty of thought, belief and expression; or equality of status and opportunity, or some invisible radiation from them.

".......(N)o political terms have, been so subjected to contradictory definitions as 'democracy' and 'democratic' since it has become fashionable and profitable for every and any state to style itself in this way. The Soviet Union and communist states of Eastern Europe, the Chinese People's Republic, North Korea and North Vietnam all call themselves democracies. So does Nasser's Egypt; so does General Stoessner's Paraguay; so did Sukarno's Indonesia. Yet, if anything is clear, it is that these states do not all meet the same definition of democracy".*

THE WORD 'DEMOCRACY' AND THE WORD 'JUSTICE' HAVE MULTIPLE DEFINITIONS – MEANINGS – MATHEW, J.

Definitions are important, for, they are responsible in the last analysis for our image of democracy. The question is not only what does the word 'democracy' mean but also what is the thing. And, when we try to answer this latter query, we discover that the thing does not correspond to the word. So, although 'democracy' has a precise literal meaning, that does not really help us to understand what an actual democracy is. In the real world, R.A. Dahl has pointed out that, democracies are 'polyarchies". The term democracy has not only a descriptive or denotative-function but also a normative and persuasive function. Therefore, the problem of defining democracy is two-fold, requiring both a descriptive and prescriptive function. To avoid pitfalls, it is necessary to keep in mind two things-first, that a firm distinction should be made between the is and the ought of democracy, and, second, that the prescriptive and the descriptive definitions of democracy must not be confused, because the democratic ideal does not define the democratic reality and vice versa; the real democracy is not and cannot be the same as the ideal one.** One cannot test the validity of an ordinary law with reference to the essential elements of an ideal democracy. It can be tested only with reference to the Principles of democracy actually incorporated in the Constitution.

349. Nor can it be tested on the touchstone of justice. The modern Pilate asks. What is justice? and stays not for an answer. To Hans Kelsen, justice is an irrational ideal, and regarded from the point of rational cognition, he thinks there are only interests and hence conflict of interests. Their solution, according to him, can be brought about by an order that satisfies one interest at the expense of the other or seeks to achieve a compromise between opposing interests. *"General Theory of Law and State"* 1946, p. 13. Mr. Allen has said that the concept of social justice is vague and indefinite. *"Aspects of Justice"* p. 31. Liberty of thought expression, belief, faith and worship are not absolute concepts. They are emotive words. They mean different things to different people. Equality of status and of opportunity are concepts laden with emotional overtones. In their absoluteness they are incapable of actual realisation. The enacting provisions in the body of the Constitution alone give concrete shape to these ideas and it is on the basis of these provisions that the validity of ordinary law should be tested.

OUR CONSTITUTION-MAKERS ESTABLISHED DEMOCRACY BY MAKING PROVISIONS – TASK OF MAKING ELECTION LAWS IS ENTRUSTED TO PARLIAMENT AND LEGISLATURES – NOT COURTS – MATHEW, J.

350. The democracy which our Constitution-makers established is based on the representation of the people in the law-making organs. The method by which this

* *See* Finer: Comparative Government (1970) pp. 62-63.

** *See* "Democratic Theory" by Giovanni Sartori, Chapter I.

representation has to be effectuated has been provided in the Constitution. Part XV of the Constitution deals with the topic of elections. Article 326 provides that elections to the House of the people and to the legislative assemblies of States should be on the basis of adult suffrage. Articles 327 and 328 provide for making of laws with respect to all matters relating to, or in connection with, elections to either House of Parliament or to the House or either House of the Legislature of a State including the preparation of electoral rolls, the delimitation of constituencies and all other matters necessary for securing the due constitution of such House or Houses. The validity of any law relating to the delimitation of constituencies or the allotment of seats to the constituencies, made or purporting to be made under Article 317 or Article 328 shall not be called in question in any court (*See* Article 329(a)).

351. This would indicate that the Constitution has entrusted the task of framing the law relating to election to Parliament, and, subject to the law made by Parliament to the State legislatures. An important branch of the law which sounds in the area of free and fair election, namely, delimitation of constituencies and allotment of seats to such constituencies is put beyond the cognizance of court. When it is found that the task of writing the legislation on the subject has been committed to parliament and state legislatures by the Constitution, is it competent for a court to test its validity on the basis of some vague norms of free and fair election? I think not. As I said, like other laws made by parliament or state legislatures, the laws made under Articles 327 and 328 are liable to be tested by Part III of the Constitution or any other provision of the Constitution; but it is difficult to see how these laws could be challenged on the ground that they do not conform to some ideal notions of free and fair election to be evolved by the court from out of airy nothing.

SPIRIT OF CONSTITUTION IS A SLIPPERY SLOPE – MATHEW, J.

352. The doctrine of the 'spirit' of the Constitution is a slippery slope. The courts are not at liberty to declare an act void, because, in their opinion, it is opposed to the spirit of democracy or republicanism supposed to pervade the Constitution but not expressed in words. When the fundamental law has not limited, either in terms or by necessary implication, the general powers conferred upon the legislature, we cannot declare a limitation under the notion of having discovered some ideal norm: of free and fair election.

353. Cooley has observed that courts are not at liberty to declare statutes void because they appear to the minds of the judges to violate fundamental principles of republican government, unless it shall be found that those principles are placed beyond legislative encroachment by the Constitution. The principles of democratic republican government are not a set of inflexible rules: and unless they are specifically incorporated in the Constitution, no law can be declared bad merely because the Court thinks that it is opposed to some implication drawn from the concept.*

AN ACT THOUGH KEPT IN NINTH SCHEDULE BY A CONSTITUTIONAL AMENDMENT BECOMES VULNERABLE – IF DAMAGES BASIC STRUCTURE – KESAVANANDA BHARTI'S CASE – MATHEW, J.

354. Counsel for the respondent relied upon the observations of Sikri, C.J. at p. 216, Shelat and Grover JJ. at p. 292, Hegde and Mukherjea, JJ., at p. 355 and Reddy, J. at p. 556 in their judgments in **Bharati's** case in support of his contention that when these Acts were put in the Ninth Schedule by the constitutional amendment, their provisions became vulnerable to attack if they or any one of them damaged or destroyed the basic features of democracy or republicanism.

* *See* Constitutional Limitations, 8th Edn., Vol. 1, pp. 349-352.

355. Sikri, C.J. has said that the Constitution 29th Amendment Act, 1971, is ineffective to protect the impugned Acts there if they abrogate or take away fundamental rights. This would not show that the learned Chief Justice countenanced any challenge to an Act on the ground that the basic structure of the Constitution has been damaged or destroyed by its provisions not constituted by the fundamental rights abrogated or taken away. In other words, if by taking away or abridging the fundamental rights, the basic structure of the Constitution is damaged or destroyed, then according to the learned Chief Justice, the legislation would be vulnerable on that score, even though it is put in the Ninth Schedule by a constitutional amendment. But it would not follow that an Act so put can be challenged for a reason not resulting from the taking away or abrogation of the fundamental right. To put it differently, even though an Act is put in the Ninth schedule by a constitutional amendment, its provisions would be open to attack on the ground that they destroy or damage the basic structure if the fundamental right or rights taken away or abrogated pertains or pertain to basic structure. But the Act cannot be attacked, if I may say so, for a collateral reason, namely, that the provisions of the Act have destroyed or damaged some other basic structure, say, for instance, democracy or separation of powers.

356. Shelat and Grover, JJ. have said in their judgment that the 29th Amendment is valid, but the question whether the Acts included in the Ninth Schedule by that Amendment or any provision of those Acts abrogates any of the basic elements of the constitutional structure or denudes them of their identity will have to be examined when the validity of those Acts comes up for consideration. Similar observations have been made by Hegde and Mukherjea, JJ. and by Reddy, J. Khanna, J. only said that the 29th Amendment was valid.

357. It is rather strange that an Act which is put in the Ninth Schedule with a view to obtain immunity from attack on the ground that the provisions thereof violate the fundamental rights should suddenly become vulnerable on the score that they damage or destroy a basic structure of the Constitution resulting not from the taking away or abridgment of the fundamental rights but for some other reason.

358. There is no support from the majority in **Bharati's** case for the proposition advanced by counsel that an ordinary law, if it damages or destroys basic structure should be held bad or for the proposition that a constitutional amendment putting an Act in the Ninth Schedule would make the provisions of the Act vulnerable for the reason that they damage or destroy a basic structure constituted not by the fundamental rights taken away or abridged but some other basic structure. And, in principle, I see no reason for accepting the correctness of the proposition.

'DUE PROCESS' INTENTIONALLY NOT INCLUDED IN THE CONSTITUTION BY ITS MAKERS – AS IT WAS A VAGUE TERM OPEN TO DIFFERENT INTERPRETATIONS – MATHEW, J.

359. The Constitution-makers eschewed to incorporate the 'due process' clause in that instrument apprehending that the vague contours of that concept will make the court a third chamber. The concept of a basic structure as brooding omnipresence in the sky apart from the specific provisions of the Constitution constituting it is too vague and indefinite to provide a yardstick to determine the validity of an ordinary law.

ORDINARY LAWS EVEN IF KEPT IN NINTH SCHEDULE BY CONSTITUTIONAL AMENDMENT REMAIN ORDINARY LAWS – MATHEW, J.

360. So if it be assumed that these election laws amendment Acts, even after they were put in the Ninth Schedule by constitutional amendment remained open to attack for contravention, if any, of the fundamental rights, these Acts would not be open to attack on the ground that their provision destroyed or damaged an essential feature of democracy, namely, free and fair election. The Acts remain part of the ordinary law of the land. They did not attain the status of constitutional law merely because they were put in the Ninth Schedule. The utmost that can be said is, as I indicated, that even after putting them in the Ninth Schedule, their provisions would be open to challenge on the ground that they took away or abrogated all or any of the fundamental rights and, therefore, damaged or destroyed a basic structure if the fundamental rights or right taken away or abrogated constitute or constitutes a basic structure.

RETROSPECTIVITY GIVEN TO AMENDMENT LAWS – DENY FREE AND FAIR ELECTIONS – DESTROYS BASIC STRUCTURE OF THE CONSTITUTION – SUBMITS RESPONDENT – SUBMISSION REJECTED – MATHEW, J.

361. Counsel for the respondent then contended that retrospective operation has been given to the provisions of these Acts and that that would destroy or damage an essential feature of democracy *viz.*, free and fair elections. The argument was that if one set of laws existed when an election was held and the result announced, you cannot thereafter substitute another set of laws and say that those laws must be deemed to have been in operation at the time when the election was held and the result announced, as that would lead to inequality, injustice and unfairness.

362. Retrospective operation of law in the field of election has been upheld by this Court (*See* **Kanta Kathuria v. Manak Chand.** Retrospective operation of any law would cause hardship to some persons or other. This is inevitable; but that is no reason to deny to the legislature the power to enact retrospective law. In the case of a law which has retrospective effect, the theory is that the law was actually in operation in the past and if the provisions of the Acts are general in their operation; there can be no challenge to them on the ground of discrimination or unfairness merely because of their retrospective effect. In other words, if an Act cannot be challenged on the ground that its provisions are discriminatory or unreasonable if it is prospective in operation, those provisions cannot be attacked on these grounds merely because the provisions were given retrospective effect, unless there are special circumstances. I see no such special circumstances here.

363. I, therefore, hold that these Acts are not liable to be challenged on any of the grounds argued by counsel.

MANY OPPOSITION MPs UNDER DETENTION – CONSTITUTIONAL AMENDMENT AND ELECTION LAW AMENDMENT PASSED – BAD IN LAW – CONTENDS RESPONDENT – OPPOSED BY APPELLANT – MATHEW, J.

364. Counsel for the respondent submitted that the session of Parliament in which the Election Laws Amendment Act, 1975 and the 39th Amendment to the Constitution were passed was not properly convened and, therefore, the amendments were invalid.

365. The argument was that a number of members of the two Houses of Parliament, were illegally detained by executive orders before the summoning of the two Houses and that was made possible by the President – the authority to summon the two Houses – making an order under Article 359 of the Constitution on 27-6-1975, which precluded these members from moving the court and obtaining release from illegal detention and attending the session. In effect, the contention of counsel was that the authority to summon Parliament effectually prevented by its order made under Article 359, those members who were illegally detained from attending the session and, as the composition of the session was unconstitutional, any measure passed in the session would be bad. Reliance was placed by counsel upon the decision in **K.A. Nambiar v. Chief Secretary, (1966) 2 SCR 406** in support of this proposition.

366. The question which fell for consideration in that case was whether, when a member of Parliament was convicted for a criminal offence and was undergoing a sentence in pursuance thereof, he has an unconditional right to attend a session of parliament. This Court held that he had no privilege which obliged the court to release him from custody in order to enable him to attend the session. This decision has no relevance to the point in controversy here.

* * * * *

369. It has since been said that Parliamentary Roll is not conclusive, that when the jurisdiction of a court is invoked, it has power to determine whether everything necessary has been done for the production of a valid statute, that rule of law requires that the court should determine legal questions raised before it and if its jurisdiction is properly invoked, it has to answer the question whether the document is a statute duly enacted by a parliament. The view as propounded has been summarised as follows:

> "(1) Sovereignty is a legal concept: the rules which identify the sovereign and prescribe its composition and functions are logically prior to it.
>
> (2) There is a distinction between rules which govern, on the one hand, (a) the composition, and (b) the procedure, and on the other hand (c) the area of power, of a sovereign legislature.
>
> (3) The courts have jurisdiction to question the validity of an alleged Act of Parliament on grounds 2(a) and 2(b), but not on ground 2(c)."*

The reasons for the view are these: When the purported sovereign is anyone but a single actual person, the designation of him must include the statement of rules for the ascertainment of his will, and these rules, since their observance is a Condition of the validity of his legislation, are rules of law logically prior to him. *See* Latham: *"The Law and the Commonwealth"* (O.U.P. 1949) p. 523. The extraction of a precise expression of will from a multiplicity of human beings is, despite all the realists say, an artificial process and one which cannot be accomplished without arbitrary rules. It is, therefore, an incomplete statement to say that in a State such and such an assembly of human being is sovereign. It can only be sovereign when acting in a certain way prescribed by law. At least some rudimentary manner and form is demanded of it: the simultaneous incoherent cry of a rabble, small or large, cannot be law, for it is unintelligible. *See* Latham: *"What is an Act of Parliament"*? 1939 Kings Counsel, p. 152.

370. Sir Frederick Pollock has said that supreme legal power is in one sense limited by the rules which prescribe how it shall be exercised.

Even if no constitutional rule places a limit or boundary to what can be done by sovereign legal authority, the organs which are to exercise it must be delimited and defined by rules. *See* Geoffrey Marshall: *Constitutional Theory*. P. 40-41.

371. So, the questions to be asked are: how is Parliament composed ? How does Parliament express its will?

372. The rules which identify the sovereign are as important as the institution so identified. If this is so, it is open to the court to see whether a Parliament has been properly summoned in order to decide the question whether a measure passed by it answers the description of a Statute or an Act and that Parliamentary roll, if such a thing exists, is not conclusive.

---

* *See* R.F.V. Heuston : Essays in Constitutional Law, Second edition, pp. 6-7.

373. As to Parliamentary Roll, Heuston has said:

> "The 'Parliamentary Roll', whatever exactly it may have been, disappeared in England a century ago, though even good authors sometimes write as if it still exists. Since 1849 there has been no 'Roll', simply two prints of the Bill on durable vellum by Her Majesty's Stationery Office, which are signed by the Clerk of the Parliament and regarded as the final official copies. One is preserved in the Public Record Office and one in the library of the House of Lords".*

374. Article 122(1) provides that the validity of any proceedings in Parliament shall not be called in question on the ground of any alleged irregularity of procedure. So, even if there is any irregularity in the procedure in the passing of the statute, it is not open to a court to question its validity. But this is distinct from the question whether the two Houses have been properly summoned and the composition of the Session was proper.

375. The Solicitor General said that if a member is excluded from participating in the proceedings of a House, that is a matter concerning the privilege of that House as the grievance is one of exclusion from the proceedings within the walls of the House, And, in regard to the right to be exercised within the walls of the House, the House itself is the judge. He referred to May's Parliamentary Practice (18th Edn. pp, 82-83) and also to **Bradlaugh v. Gossett, (1884) 12 QBD 271, 285-286** in this connection. He further said that if an outside agency illegally prevents a member from participating in the proceedings of the House, the House has power to secure his presence in the House and cited May's Parliamentary Practice (18th Edn. pp. 92-95) to support the proposition.

376. These passages throw no light on the question in issue here. Ever since the decision of Holt C.J. in **Ashby v. White, (1703) 14 St Tr 695** it has been settled that privilege is part of the common law and cannot affect rights to be exercised outside or independently of the House. Regularity of internal proceedings is one thing; the constitutional rights of the subject are another; and it is the latter which are in issue in a case where the question is whether the document is a statute; *See* Heuston: *Essays in Constitutional Law*, 2nd Edn., p. 22.

FUNDAMENTAL RIGHT SUSPENDED DURING EMERGENCY DETENTION ORDER BY COMPETENT AUTHORITY OF SOME MPs – AMENDMENTS ARE NOT ILLEGAL – MATHEW, J.

377. Article 85(1) provides that the President shall from time to time summon each House of Parliament to meet at such time and place as he thinks fit, but six months shall not intervene between its last sitting in one session and the date appointed for its first sitting in the next session.

378. The detention of these members of parliament was by statutory authorities in the purported exercise of their statutory power. It would be strange if a statutory authority, by an order which turns out to be illegal, could prevent the Houses of Parliament from meeting as enjoined by Article 85. If a statutory authority passes an illegal order of detention and thus prevents a member of parliament from attending the House, how can the proceedings of parliament become illegal for that reason? It is the privilege of parliament to secure the attendance of persons illegally detained. But what would happen if the privilege is not exercised by parliament? I do not think that the proceedings of parliament would become illegal for that reason.

---

* Essays in Constitutional Law, p. 18 (2nd ed.)

379. The suspension of the remedy for the enforcement of fundamental rights by the order of the President under Article 359 is dependent upon a valid proclamation of emergency under Article 352. If a situation arose which authorised the President to issue a proclamation under Article 352, he could also suspend, under Article 359, the remedy to move the court to enforce the fundamental rights. These are the constitutional functions of the President and unless it is established that the proclamation made by the President under Article 352 or the suspension under Article 359 of the remedy for enforcement of fundamental rights is unconstitutional, it is impossible to hold that the President has, in any way, illegally prevented the release of these members from the supposed illegal detention so as to make a session of parliament unconstitutional, in consequence of the inability of those members to attend the session. In other words, the President, in performing his constitutional function under these articles has not authorised the illegal detention of any person let alone any member of parliament or unconstitutionally prevented the release from custody of any member. He has only discharged his constitutional functions. If this be so, it is difficult to hold that the session in which the amendments were passed was illegally convened. The challenge to the validity of the amendments on this score must be overruled.

APPELLANT BECAME A CANDIDATE ON 1.2.1971 WHEN SHE FILED NOMINATION PAPERS – YASHPAL KAPUR WORKED FOR HER PRIOR THERETO – NO CORRUPT PRACTICE – AGREED WITH CJI – MATHEW, J.

380. Counsel for the respondent submitted that it is immaterial when a candidate committed a corrupt practice whether it was before or after he became a candidate and that an election would be set aside even if a person committed the corrupt practice before he became a candidate. Section 79(b) of the Representation of the People Act, 1951, defined the word 'candidate' as follows:

> " 'candidate' means a person who has been or claims to have been duly nominated as a candidate at any election, and any such person shall be deemed to have been a candidate as from the time when, with the election in prospect, he began to hold himself out as a prospective candidate."

Clause 7 of the Election Laws (Amendment) Act, 1915, substituted the present definition in section 79(b) which reads:

> " 'candidate' means a person who has been or claims to have been duly nominated as a candidate at an election."

381. In support of the proposition that an election can be set aside even if a person has committed corrupt practice of bribery before he became a candidate, counsel cited *Halsbury's Laws of England,* 3rd Edn., Volume 14, Pages 222 (Para. 386) and 218 (para 380).

382. These paragraphs state that in order to constitute the offence of bribery, it does not matter how long before an election a bribe is given, provided that the bribe is operative at the time of the election, and that, time is material only when considering the question of evidence.

383. Counsel further said that Under section 100 of the Representation of the People Act, 1951, an election is liable to be set aside if it is found under clause (b) of sub-section (1) of that section that a returned candidate has committed corrupt practice; that ex hypothesis, a returned candidate cannot commit a corrupt practice, and therefore, it is not the description of a person as a returned candidate that is material. He argued that if in section 100(1)(b) the word 'returned candidate' is used not with the idea of indicating that a person should have committed corrupt practice after he became a returned candidate, there is no reason to think that the word 'candidate' in section 123(7) has been used to show that the corrupt practice therein mentioned should have been committed after a person has become a 'candidate' in order that the election of the candidate might be set aside.

384. There can be no doubt that section 100(1)(b), when it speaks of commission of corrupt practice by a returned candidate, it can only mean commission of corrupt practice by a candidate before he became a returned candidate. Any other reading of the sub-section would be absurd. But there is no such compulsion to read the word 'candidate' in section 123(7) in the same manner. It is the context that gives colour to a word. A word is not crystal clear. Section 79 of the Act indicates that the definitions therein have to be read subject to the context.

385. The legislature must fix some point of time before which a person cannot be a 'candidate' in an election, and, a wide latitude must be given to the legislature in fixing that point. In **Union of India v. Parameswaran Match Works, Civil Appeal Nos. 262-273. 587-591 and 1351-1402 of 1971 and 1883-1921 of 1972, decided on 4-11-1974. (reported in AIR 1974 SC 2349)** this Court observed:

> "The choice of a date as a basis for classification cannot always be dubbed as arbitrary even if no particular reason is forthcoming for the choice unless it is shown to be capricious or whimsical in the circumstances. When it is seen that a line or point there must be, and there is no mathematical or logical way of fixing it precisely, the decision of the legislature or its delegate must be accented unless we can say that it is very wide of the reasonable mark. See **Louisville Gas Co. v. Alabama Power Co., 240 US 30 (32)** per Justice Holmes."

386. The learned Chief Justice has, in his judgment, referred to the relevant English statutes and the decisions of the English Courts bearing on this point and has pointed out the difference between the English Law and the Indian Law. I do not consider it necessary to cover the same ground. I agree with his conclusion on the point.

387. I would, therefore, hold that even if it be assumed that the finding of the High Court that the appellant obtained or procured the assistance of Shri Yashpal Kapur during the period from January 7 to 24, 1971, is correct, the appellant shall not be deemed to have committed corrupt practice under section 123(7) of the Representation of the People Act, 1951, as she became a candidate only on February 1, 1971. The learned Chief Justice has also dealt with the contention urged by counsel for respondent that Clause 8(b) of the Election Laws Amendment Act, 1975 suffers from the vice of excessive delegation and is arbitrary. I agree with his reasoning for repelling the same.

IN VIEW OF THE AMENDED LAW – APPEAL ACCEPTED – IN VIEW OF THE FINDINGS OF KHANNA, J; CROSS-APPEAL DISMISSED – MATHEW, J.

388. There can be no dispute that if the Election Laws Amendment Act, 1975, is valid, the appeal has to be allowed. I would, therefore, set aside the findings of the High Court against the appellant and allow the appeal without any order as to costs. In the cross appeal, the only question raised, was about the correctness of the finding of the High Court that the appellant has not exceeded the prescribed limit of election expense. For the reasons given by Khanna, J. in his judgment, I hold that the finding of the High Court on this issue was correct. In this view, I have no occasion to reach the other questions argued. I would dismiss the cross appeal without any order as to costs.

389. Beg, J.:—There are two Election Appeal Nos. 887 and 909 of 1975, before us under section 116-A of the Representation of the People Act of 1951 (hereinafter referred to as 'the Act'). They are directed against decision on different issues contained in the same judgment of a learned Judge of the Allahabad. High Court allowing an election petition filed by Shri Raj Narain (hereafter referred to as the 'Election Petitioner'), defeated candidate at the election held in February 1971, for, the membership of the Lok Sabha or the House of the People, against Shrimati Indira Nehru Gandhi, the Prime Minister of India (hereinafter referred to as 'the Original Respondent'). The election petitioner is the respondent in Appeal No. 887 of 1975 filed by the original respondent. He is the appellant in Appeal No, 909 of 1975 where the original respondent is the contesting respondent.

ELECTION PETITION FILED ON 24.4.1971 – RP ACT, 1951 AMENDED DURING ITS PENDENCY – BEG, J.

390. Before the election case, instituted on 24-4-1971, could be decided by the trial Court, an explanation was added to section 77(1) of the Act. It had some bearing on questions relating to the expenses incurred on the original respondent's election, sought to be raised by the election petitioner, but, on findings of fact recorded by the trial Court, it became immaterial for the merits of the case and would continue to be that so long as the election petitioner is unable to dislodge the trial Court's findings on election expenses.

ELECTION LAW AMENDMENT MADE ON 6-8-1975 – CONSTITUTIONAL AMENDMENT MADE ON 10-8-1975 – DURING PENDENCY OF APPEAL IN SUPREME COURT AFFECTING MERITS OF THE CASE – BEG, J.

Other amendments were made by the Election Laws (Amendment) Act No. 40 of 1975, (hereinafter referred to as the 'Act of 1975'), notified on 6-8-1975, after the decision of the case by the learned Judge of the Allahabad High Court on 12-6-1975 and after the filing of the appeals before us. These amendments deal directly with several questions decided by the Allahabad High Court which were pending consideration before this Court. Finally, came the Constitution (Thirty-ninth) Amendment Act of 1975, (hereinafter referred to as the 39th Amendment'), gazetted on 10-8-1975, just before the commencement of the hearing of the appeals by this Court.

CLAUSE (4) ARTICLE 329A OUSTED JURISDICTION OF SUPREME COURT – DECLARED THE ELECTION OF APPELLANT VALID – SUBMITS APPELLANT

391. It was submitted by the learned counsel for the original respondent, in his opening address, that section 4 of the 39th Amendment, adding clause (4) to Article 329A of the Constitution, meant that Parliament itself, acting in its constituent capacity, had taken the case in hand and had, after applying its own standards decided it in favour of the original respondent so that the jurisdiction of this Court to go into the merits of the case was ousted by clause (4), read with clauses (5) and (6), sought to be added to Article 329A of the Constitution. It was submitted by him that each one of the amendments of the Act was aimed at removing genuine uncertainties or doubts about what the law was so that it may be brought into the line with what it had been previously understood to be as declared by this Court, or, in any case, with what Parliament, correctly exercising it unquestionable law making powers, thought that it should be.

AMENDMENTS OF 1974 AND 1975 – CONSTITUTION AMENDMENTS ARE MISUSE – INTENDED TO – TO UNDO HIGH COURT JUDGMENT – SUBMITS RESPONDENT

392. The constantly requiring and vehemently pressed theme of the arguments of the learned counsel for the election petitioner was that the context and the contents of the Acts of 1974 and 1975, and, after that, of section 4 of the 39th Amendment, clearly indicated that the whole object of the Acts of 1974 and 1975 and of the Constitutional amendment was an oblique one: to deprive the election petitioner of the remedies he had under the law against an election vitiated by corrupt practices, and of the benefits of a decision of the High Court in his favour by taking away its grounds and then the jurisdiction of Courts, which existed at the time of the 39th Amendment, to deal with the case so that this case may not in any event, terminate in favour of the election petitioner. It was repeatedly suggested by the learned counsel for the election petitioner, throughout his arguments, that the law making powers had been really abused by a majority in Parliament for the purposes of sending majority party and personal ends which were constitutionally unauthorised. It was even alleged that the President of India had also become a party to the misuse of Constitutional powers by passing an ordinance depriving Court of jurisdiction to entertain *Habeas Corpus* petitions so that members of Parliament belonging to opposition parties, detained under preventive detention laws, may not secure release and oppose proposals which became embodied in the 1975 Act and the 39th Amendment. It is when the country is faced with issues of this nature that the constitutionally vital role of the judicature as a co-ordinate and independent organ of a democratic system of Government, comes into prominence and has to be performed without fear or favour, affection or ill will as the custodian of constitutionality.

393. In the circumstances indicated above, it seemed to me to be absolutely essential for us to call upon the parties defending or assailing the 39th Amendment and the Acts of 1974 and 1975, to take us, *inter alia*, into the merits of the cases of the two sides and the findings given by the trying Judge so as to enable us to see how far these findings were justifiable under the law as it stood even before the amendment by the Acts of 1974 and 1975, how they were affected by these amendments, and how they were related to the validity of section 4 of the 39th Amendment. Speaking for myself, I clearly indicated to learned counsel for the parties that I regard the nature and merits of the case decided to be of crucial importance not only in considering the validity of the 39th Amendment and of the Acts of 1974 And 1975 but also in the wider interests of justice which are bound to be served by the vindication of the case of the party which should, on merits, win. Elementary considerations of justice required that the party with a better case should not be deprived of an opportunity of justifying its position, on facts and law touching the merits of the case, in the highest Court of the land, particularly when the original respondent, who happens to be the Prime Minister of this country, was accused of corrupt practices to secure her election and then of abuse of constitutional power and position to shield them. The high office of the original respondent, far from disabling this Court from investigating such allegations, ought to provide a good ground for this Court to go into the merits of the case if we are not really deprived of our jurisdiction to do that by section 4 of the 39th Amendment. This follows from the Rule of law, as I understand it, embodied in our Constitution. National interests cannot, or, at least, should not, I believe suffer if justice and right, as determined by the highest Court in the country, prevail.

VALIDITY OF A STATUTE OR CONSTITUTIONAL AMENDMENT IS TO BE TESTED ON "REAL WILL" OF THE PEOPLE CONTAINED IN THE CONSTITUTION – HELD BEG, J.

394. Citizens of our country take considerable pride in being able to challenge before superior Courts even an exercise of constituent power resting on the combined strength and authority of Parliament and the State legislatures. This Court when properly called upon by the humblest citizen, in a proceeding before it, to test the Constitutional validity of either an ordinary statute or of a Constitutional amendment, has to do so by applying the criteria of basic constitutional purpose and constitutionally prescribed procedure. The assumption underlying the theory of judicial review of all law making, including fundamental law making is that Courts, acting as interpreters of what has been described by some political philosophers (*See*: Bosanquet's *"Philosophical theory of the State"* Chap. V. p. 96-115) as the "Real Will" of the people embodied in their Constitution and assumed to be more lasting and just and rational and less liable to err than their "General Will" reflected by the opinions of the majorities in Parliament and the State Legislatures for the time being, can discover for the people the not always easily perceived purpose of their Constitution. The Courts thus act as agents and mouth pieces of the "Real Will" of the people themselves. Although, Judges, in discharging their onerous constitutional duties, cannot afford to ignore the limitations of the judicial technique and their own possibly greater liability to err than legislators could on socio-economic issues and matters of either social philosophy or practical policy, or political opinion only, yet they cannot, without violating their oaths of office fail to elucidate and uphold a basic constitutional principle or norm unless compelled by the law of the Constitution to abstain from doing so.

JUDICIARY CANNOT LEGISLATE BY NAMING IT INTERPRETATION – PARLIAMENT CANNOT ASSUME POWER TO DECIDE BY NAMING IT LAW-MAKING – HELD BEG, J.

One of these basic principles seems to me to be that, just as Courts are not constitutionally competent to legislate under the guise of interpretation so also neither our Parliament nor any State Legislature, in the purported exercise of any kind of law-making power perform an essentially judicial function by virtually withdrawing a particular case, pending in any Court, and taking upon itself the duty to decide it by an application of law or its own standards to the facts of that case. This power must at least be first constitutionally taken away from the Court concerned and vested in another authority before it can be lawfully exercised by that other authority. It is not a necessary or even a natural incident of a "Constituent power". As Hens Kelsen points out, in his *"General Theory of Law and the State"*, (*See*: p. 143), "while creation and annulment of all general norms, whether basic or not so basic, is essentially a legislative function, their interpretation and application to findings reached, after a correct ascertainment of facts involved in an individual case, by employing the judicial technique, is really a judicial function. Neither of the three constitutionally separate organs of State can, according to the basic scheme of our Constitution today, leap outside the boundaries of its own constitutionally assigned sphere or orbit of authority into that of the other. This is the logical and natural meaning of the principle of Supremacy of the Constitution."

WHAT IS THE EXTENT OF CONSTITUENT POWER UNDER ARTICLE 368 – VALIDITY OF 39th AMENDMENT – 1974-1975 AMENDMENTS – BASIC STRUCTURE – WILL BE CONSIDERED IF FACTS OF THE CASE WILL DEMAND – BEG, J.

395. Issues raised before us relating to the validity of the 39th Amendment and the Acts of 1974 and 1975 were: What are the Constitutional purposes and ambit of the 'Constituent power" found in Article 368 of our Constitution? Were they, in any way exceeded by the constituent authorities in making the 39th Amendment in an unauthorised manner, or, for objects which, however, laudable, were outside the scope of Article 368? Was there any procedural irregularity in the composition of Parliament which could enable this Court to hold that there was a basic defect in the enactment of either the 1975 Act or of the 39th Amendment? Whether provisions of the Acts of 1974 and 1975 are immune from attack even on the ground that they resulted in a departure from the "basic structure" of our Constitution as explained by this Court in **Keshvananda Bharti v. State of Kerala, 1973 (1) Supp SCR 1** by having been included in the 9th Schedule of our Constitution which does protect them from a challenge on the ground of any contravention of Part III guaranteeing fundamental rights to citizens and other persons, or, in other words, were the limits of the basic structure only operative against Constitutional amendments or apply to ordinary statutes as well? Are any of the provisions of the Acts of 1974 end 1975 void for departures from or damage to any part of the "basic structure" of our Constitution or for any other excess or misuse of law making powers?

396. We do not, when such a case comes up before us, concern ourselves with the validity of provisions other than those which affect the case before us. Nor do we consider the objects of any provision, in vacuum, divorced from the facts of the case to be decided. Therefore, parties had to and did address us on the broad features of the findings given by the learned trial Judge and the nature of the evidence given to support them so that we may be able to decide, inter alia, whether any "validation" of the original respondent's election, which was the evident purpose of clause (4) of Article 329A, sought to be added by section 4 of the 39th Amendment, was at all necessary. If that election was not really 'void' and had been wrongly held by the trial Court to be vitiated, it did not need to be validated at all. In that event, a purported validation would be an exercise in futility before this Court had decided these appeals. Could it not be said that the intended validation was premature in as much as it proceeded on a basically erroneous premise that the original respondent's election was invalid when the question of its validity was sub-judice in this Court? How could such a premise be assumed to be correct before this Court had gone into merits and decided the appeals pending before it? Such an inquiry is not irrelevant if the very nature and purpose of the exercise of a power are put in issue by both sides.

ALLAHABAD HIGH COURT JUDGMENT – HAS ERRONEOUS CONCLUSIONS – HELD BEG, J.

397. If the existence of the judgment of the Allahabad High Court created the impression that it must be assumed to be correct even before this Court had pronounced upon the correctness of the judgment, the stay order given by this Court should have removed it. The legal effect of that stay order was that the trial Court's order to use the language of sections 116A(4) (sic) 116B (3) (?)) of the Act, "shall be deemed never to have taken effect." It did not matter if the stay order, out of deference for existing precedents, had been framed in the form of a "conditioned" stay, that is to say, a stay in law and effect with certain conditions annexed. It was not a 'conditional' stay. Indeed, having regard to the nature of the order the operation of which was to be stayed, there could be no 'conditional' stay here. As to the legal effect of such a stay order there is no doubt in my mind that considering the clear words of sections 116A(4) (sic) 116B(3) (?) of the Act it deprived the order of the High Court of any operative force whatsoever during the pendency of these appeals. There could be really no binding precedent in discretionary matters depending on the facts and circumstances of each case. The operation of the judgment of the trial Court and the consequential orders are stayed only on "sufficient cause" shown on the facts of that case. In the case before us, the sufficient cause seems to me to be apparent from a bare perusal of the judgment of the trial court.

As I have pointed out below, the judgment under appeal contains glaringly erroneous conclusions reached by ignoring what has been repeatedly laid down in election cases by this Court even if one were to assume, for the sake of argument, that all the findings of fact recorded by the trial Court, including some very questionable ones, on which its conclusions rest, were correct.

398. In a case where the *bona fides* of legislation and even of a Constitutional amendment, is questioned on the ground of a suggested frightfulness in the facts of the case which Parliament and the ratifying State Legislatures are to be supposed, if we are to accept the suggestion, to have been acting in concert to prevent this Court from examining on merits. It was, I think, the duty of counsel making any such suggestion to invite our attention to any fact not fully disclosed or discussed in the judgment under appeal at least when he was asked, as I repeatedly asked him in the course of his arguments extending over a period of about fifteen days out of a total period of hearing of the case for thirty-two days, how the trial Court's conclusions on the two matters, forming the subject-matter of Appeal No. 887 of 1975 of the original respondent, could possibly be justified. However, I have also satisfied myself, by going through the whole evidence on record on these two matters, which I shall presently deal with that learned counsel for the election petitioner could not possibly usefully add anything to the replies he actually gave on the questions put to him on these matters and to the discussion of the whole evidence on these questions by the trial Court. I have taken pains to clarify this position as the learned counsel for the election petitioner at the end of arguments of both sides, extending over thirty-two days of actual hearing, stated that he had argued on the assumption that we will be concerned only with the validity of the 39th Amendment and the validity and correct interpretation of the Acts of 1974 and 1975. I think that it was made clear to him that we will have to enter into the merits if that was necessary, as I think it is, for judging whether amendments in law were either necessary or justified. Learned counsel for the election petitioner was not prevented from dealing with any question, whether of fact or law, which he may have wanted to raise. Learned counsel for both sides had fully argued at least the election Petitioner's Appeal No. 909 of 1975 on facts and law. They had taken us sufficiently into facts and findings involved in the original respondent's Appeal No. 887 of 1975 to justify our dealing with all questions necessary to decide this appeal on merits also. Indeed, it is not necessary for us to go beyond findings of fact recorded by the learned Judge, as distinct from conclusions based upon them which are questions of law, to demonstrate the very palpable errors committed by the learned Judge on the two questions which are the subject-matter of Appeal No. 887 of 1975.

399. Shrimati Indira Nehru Gandhi was elected to the House of the People from the Raebareli constituency in Uttar Pradesh by an overwhelming majority of 1,11,800 votes against Shri Raj Narain.

ISSUES – ADDITIONAL ISSUES FRAMED IN THE ELECTION PETITION – BEG, J.

As is not unusual, the defeated candidate filed an election petition under the Act making all kinds of allegations, including some quite extravagant ones, which formed the subject-matter of the first set of eleven issues framed on 19-8-1971. Thereafter, three additional issues were framed on 27-4-1973 when the question whether an amendment of the petition, sought after the period of limitation for filing petition to challenge the election had expired should be permitted, had been finally decided by this Court in favour of Shri Raj Narain.

400. The issues framed give an idea of the cases set-up on behalf of the two sides. They were:

ISSUES

"1. Whether respondent No. 1 obtained and procured the assistance of Yashpal Kapur in furtherance of the prospects of her election while he was still a Gazetted Officer in the service of Government of India. If so, from what date?

2. Whether at the instance of respondent No. 1 members of the Armed Forces of the Union arranged Air Force Planes and helicopters for her, flown by members of the Armed Forces to enable her to address election meetings on 1-2-1971 and 25-2-1971, and if so, whether this constituted a corrupt practice under section 123(7) of the Representation of the People Act?
3. Whether at the instance of respondent No. 1 and her election agent Yashpal Kapur, the District Magistrate of Raebareli, the Superintendent of police of Raebareli and the Home Secretary of U.P. Government arranged for rostrums, loudspeakers and barricades to be set-up and for members of the Police Force to be posted in connection with her election tour on 1-2-1971 and 25-2-1971; and, if so, whether this amounts to a corrupt practice under section 123(7) of the Representation of the People Act?
4. Whether quilts, blankets, dhotis and liquor were distributed by agents and workers of respondent No. 1 with the consent of her election agent Yashpal Kapur, at the places and on the dates mentioned in Schedule A of the petition in order to induce electors to vote for her?
5. Whether the particulars given in paragraph 10 and Schedule *A* of the petition are too vague and general to afford a basis for allegations of bribery under section 123(1) of the Representation of the People Act?
6. Whether by using the symbol cow and calf which had been allotted to her party by the Election Commission in her election campaign the respondent No. 1 was guilty of making an appeal to a religious symbol and committed a corrupt practice as defined in section 123(3) of the Representation of the People Act?
7. Whether on the dates fixed for the poll voters were conveyed to the polling stations free of charge on vehicles hired and procured for the purpose by respondent No. 1's election agent Yashpal Kapur, or other persons with his consent, as detailed in Schedule *B* to the petition?
8. Whether the particulars given in paragraph 12 and Schedule *B* of the petition are too vague and general to form a basis for allegations regarding a corrupt practice under section 123(5) of the Representation of the People Act?
9. Whether respondent No. 1 and her election agent Yashpal Kapur incurred or authorised expenditure in excess of the amount prescribed by section 77 of the Representation of the People Act, read with Rule 90 as detailed in para 13 of the petition?
10. Whether the petitioner had made a security deposit in accordance with the rules of the High Court as required by section 117 of the Representation of the People Act?
11. To what relief, if any, is the petitioner entitled?

ADDITIONAL ISSUES

1. Whether respondent No. 1, obtained and procured the assistance of Yashpal Kapur in furtherance of the prospects of her election while he was still a Gazetted Officer in the service of the Government of India. If so, from what date?
2. Whether respondent No. 1 held herself out as a candidate from any date prior to 1-2-1971 and if so, from what date?
3. Whether Yashpal Kapur continued to be in the service of Government of India from and after 14-1-1971 or till which date?"

FINDINGS OF HIGH COURT ISSUE-WISE – ELECTION PETITION ACCEPTED – APPEAL – CROSS-APPEAL – BEG, J.

401. The High Court trying the case had, in the course of a lengthy judgment, rejected the election petitioner's case on issue Nos. 2, 4, 6, 7, and 9 of the first set of issues, after minutely and meticulously scrutinizing every material allegation of the election petitioner and the evidence given in support of it on each of these issues. Out of these the election petitioner in his cross appeal No. 909 of 1975, has questioned the findings of the High Court only on issue Nos. 2, 4, 6, 7 and 9 set out above. Issue Nos. 5 and 8 and 10, decided in favour of the election petitioner, were technical and are immaterial now. It will be noticed that the additional issue No. 1, due to some error or oversight, is an exact and unnecessary repetition of the initial issue No. 1. Additional issues numbered 2 and 3 are connected with and subsidiaries of the initially framed issues numbered 1 and 3.

402. The learned trial Judge had accepted the election petitioner's case on the material issues numbered 1 and 3 of the initially framed issues, and on the overlapping and subsidiary additional issues 1, 2 and 3. He was of opinion that Shri Yashpal Kapur, a Central Government servant and a Gazetted Officer of the rank of an Under-Secretary, deputed to serve in the Prime Minister's Secretariat as an Officer on Special. Duty had held his post until 25-1-1971, when his resignation, tendered on 13-1-1971, was accepted by the President of India with effect from 14-1-1971, by means of a notification published on 6-2-1971. Consequently, the learned Judge set aside the election of the original respondent after holding that she was guilty of a "corrupt practice", as defined by section 123(7) of the Act on each of two grounds: firstly, that she must be deemed to have obtained the help of Shri Yashpal Kapur in the furtherance of her election, before he had ceased to be a Gazetted Officer in Government service, and after the original respondent had first held herself out, on 29-12-1970, as candidate at the forthcoming election from the Raebareli constituency by answering in the negative a question put to her at a Press Conference in New Delhi inquiring whether she had decided to change her constituency from Raebareli in U.P. to Gurgaon in Haryana; and, secondly, that she must be deemed to have obtained the help of officials of the State of U.P. who got rostrums constructed for her election speeches and electricity provided and arrangements made for loudspeakers. The learned Judge declared her to be disqualified under section 8A of the Act from holding her office for a period of six years from the date of his order dated 12-6-1975. I deliberately employ the word "deemed" to describe the nature of the findings of the trial Judge on both these questions because the learned judge had himself indicated, that they were inferences based entirely on circumstantial and not any direct evidence whatsoever of any instructions issued either by the original respondent or by her election agent during the period following 29-12-1970. Election Appeal No. 887 of 1975 was filed against decisions on these two questions and consequential orders of the learned trial Judge.

'CORRUPT PRACTICE' WITHIN THE MEANING OF SECTION 123(7) RP ACT, 1951 – EXPLAINED – BEG, J.

403. The law as found in the Act of 1951 did not unlike the English Act of 1949, make a distinction between corrupt practices and illegal practices. Section 123(7) as it has stood unamended, enumerates, as the last of the 7 classes of corrupt practice, as follows:

> "Section 123(7) The obtaining or procuring or abetting or attempting to obtain or procure by a candidate or his agent or, by any other person with the consent of a candidate or his election agent any assistance other than the

giving of vote for the furtherance of the prospects of that candidate's election from any person in the service of the Government and belonging to any of the following classes, namely:

(a) Gazetted Officers;

(b) stipendiary Judges and Magistrates;

(c) members of the Armed Forces of the Union;

(d) members of the Police Forces;

(e) Excise Officers:

(f) and (g) xx xx xx

Explanation.—(1) In this section the expression 'agent' includes an election agent, a polling agent and any person who is held to have acted as an agent in connection with the election with the consent of the candidate."

(2) For the purposes of clause (7), a person shall be deemed to assist in the furtherance of the prospects of a candidate's election if he acts as an election agent of that candidate."

404. It is clear that "the obtaining or procuring or abetting or attempting to obtain or procure" had to take place either by a candidate or by his agent or by somebody "with the consent of the candidate or his election agent". Until the candidate had appointed an election agent, the action of any other person could not constitute him automatically an agent so that he may be doing something voluntarily, succeed in making the candidate vicariously liable for his own actions whether he was or was not a gazetted officer at the time when he committed the act complained of. The question of obtaining assistance through "an agent" or "other person with the consent of a candidate or his election agent" could only arise where such a case of obtaining assistance indirectly through others is set up but not otherwise.

CASE SET-UP BY RESPONDENT IN PARA 5 OF ELECTION PETITION – BASIS OF ISSUE NO. 1 – PARA 9 BASIS OF ISSUE NO. 3 – BUT HIGH COURT MADE OUT A NEW CASE IN DISCUSSION – HELD BEG, J.

405. On issue No. 1 the case set-up in paragraph 5 of the petition is:

"Smt. Indira Nehru Gandhi obtained and procured the assistance of the said Shri Yashpal Kapur for the furtherance of the prospects of her election from the constituency aforesaid in as much as the said Shri Yashpal Kapur was a Gazetted Officer in the service of Government of India when his assistance was obtained and procured....... The said Shri Yashpal Kapur on the direction of Smt. Indira Nehru Gandhi organised the electioneering work for her in the constituency during the period commencing from 27-12-1970.

It is a case of liability resulting from an alleged "direction" given by Smt. Indira Nehru Gandhi herself to Shri Kapur. No case of procurement of assistance of Shri Kapur through a third person is set up although the word "procured" is mechanically lifted from section 123(7) and used. On issue No. 3 the case set up in para. 9 of the petition is that both Smt. Indira Gandhi and her election agent, Shri Kapur. "Obtained and procured" the assistance of Government Officers, but no directions or orders given by anyone are mentioned there. Issue No. 1 shows that the case which was put in issue and went on trial was whether the original respondent had herself issued some direction to Shri Kapur. Issue No. 3 shows that what was in issue here was whether the Government officers mentioned there rendered the assistance indicated there "at the instance" of the original respondent or her election agent. The discussion of evidence and finding of the learned Judge, particularly on issue No. 1 show that the learned Judge had almost made out a new case for the election petitioner and accepted it. This was, on issue No. 1 whether Shri Kapur had done some acts in circumstances which justify the inference that he was constituted a de facto agent of the Prime Minister even before he was appointed her election agent on 1-2-1971, and on issue No. 3 whether sending round of certain tour programmes with the approval of the Prime Minister, in the background of certain long standing instructions of the Comptroller and Auditor-General, read with letters sent by the Government of India, as long ago as 12-1-1959, and 19-11-1969, amounted to "implied" directions by the Prime Minister or her election agent to the State Government to provide the facilities the Government officials gave. Now, whenever a case of a liability by "implication", where there is such a species of liability in law comparable to a criminal liability, is to be fastened upon an individual, the prosecutor is to be expected, as a part of an elementary duty to give fair notice and a fair opportunity to meet what the individual has really to be made liable for, either because of some act or omission of the individual concerned, or, even more so, for that of an agent or another person for which there may be some sort of vicarious liability from facts showing consent or agency, to give full particulars of circumstances from which such implications or vicarious liabilities may arise. I do not find that this was done here.

406. The law must lay down a duty to prevent, by taking some steps which are not taken, before person is held liable for an omission. And, there is a difference between omission to prevent the doing of something and actual consent to the doing of it. I do not find, in the petition, any case of a liability from omissions to do something set up, obviously because the law does not impose upon the candidate the duty to prevent the giving of voluntary assistance by others whether officials or not, nor is there anywhere in the petition a case of procurement by consenting to aid obtained through others. It was to be remembered that on the language of section 123(7) a liability is not created by merely not rejecting voluntarily given aid. The candidate may not often be aware of the voluntarily given assistance as to be able to reject it. A case of consent which can be legally set up is only one of consenting to active obtaining or procurement by an agent or by some other person who becomes, for the purposes of the specific aid given and consented to, ordinarily prior to obtaining it as good as an agent employed by the candidate.

OBTAINING OR PROCURING ASSISTANCE IN SECTION 123(7) – THREE KINDS – RESPONDENT PLEADED ONLY FIRST KIND OF ASSISTANCE – FINDINGS RECORDED DIFFERENT – HELD BEG, J.

407. On the terms of section 123(7) the following three types of cases of actual obtaining of assistance, as distinguished from abetment or attempting to obtain. It, can be legally set up either exclusively or alternatively, against a candidate; firstly, a direct obtaining of it by the act of the candidate himself: secondly, an indirect or vicarious procurement of it by the acts of a duly constituted agent; and, thirdly, an indirect or vicarious procurement of it by the acts of a person who, though not a duly constituted agent, becomes constructively an agent, for the purpose of some particular aid obtained, because it was assented to by the candidate at a time which must, ordinarily be before the aid is given, so that the person through whom assistance is obtained is a constructive agent for this particular aid at the time when it is given. The term procurement should, strictly speaking, apply only in the last two types of cases. A reference to section 100(1)(b) further emphasises the position that a corrupt practice for which the High Court is to declare an election void must have been committed either "by a returned candidate or his election agent or by any other person with the consent of the returned candidate or his election agent." A case falling under section 100(1)(d)(ii) of "a corrupt practice committed in the interests of a candidate by an agent other than his election agent" is very different and postulates: *firstly*, a corrupt practice which can be committed only by an agent; and *secondly*, the existence of such an agent. A case falling under section 100(1) (d) requires also proof of the further fact that the result of the election was materially affected by the corrupt practice.

408. As I read the petition. I find only the first of the three types of cases mentioned above set up exclusively on Issue No. 1 because there are no particulars there which could apply to the other two types of cases. Obviously, the case set-up was not of a corrupt practice by some act of person to which the candidate became a party by merely giving consent in which case the circumstances from which the consent was to be inferred had to be indicated. It was a case of a direction given by the Prime Minister herself to Shri Kapur who, it had to be presumed for the purposes of such a case, would not have given the aid if the direction or order was not there. This deliberately given "direction" had to be proved on the case set up. On Issue No. 3 the petition mentions, only what was obtained, that is to say, the aid of particular officers and the form it took, but, what caused that aid to be given or the means adopted to get it were not set up there. I think these distinctions should have been borne in mind. I shall indicate below how the learned Judge, in dealing with a case of the first type only falling under section 100(1)(b) of the Act, found in Issue No. 1, mixed up facts which could, strictly speaking, be relevant only in considering a case of one of the other two types. And, in deciding Issue No. 3 what really and quite naturally flowed from and was the well understood appurtenant of the office of a Prime Minister, and, indeed, absolutely necessary for the due protection of the life and freedom of movement of the holder of that high office was mistaken by the learned Judge to be the result of some kind of assumed solicitation for aid. What the learned Judge entirely missed was that it is the act of solicitation for the aid of the officials mentioned in section 123(7), whether successful or not, and not the mere fact that certain advantages flow quite naturally and conventionally from the occupation of an office, without any solicitation, or the mere fact that some assistance is voluntarily given by someone to an election campaign which is penalized by the provision.

'CORRUPT PRACTICE' ARISES IF THERE IS A 'CANDIDATE' – BEG, J.

409. The definition given above in section 123(7) meant, on an ordinary and natural interpretation of words used, that the corrupt practice defined there could not be committed by any person before there was a "candidate" for an election. "Hence, it became necessary to examine the definition of a "candidate" found in section 79(b) which laid down:

> "79. In this part and in Parts VII and VIII, unless the context otherwise requires,—
>
> * * * * *
>
> (b) 'candidate' means a person who has been or claims to have been duly nominated as a candidate at any election, and any such person shall be deemed to have been a candidate as from the time when, with the election in prospect he began to hold himself out as a prospective candidate."

410. Section 123, defining corrupt practices, is found in Part VII of the Act. Therefore, the definition of candidate in section 79, as it originally stood, was sought to be applied by the Trial Court to determine whether the original respondent could have committed a corrupt practice at the time of the alleged commission of it. Before, however, I deal with that question, it is necessary to examine what "obtaining, or procuring or abetting or attempting" meant in the light of the law laid down repeatedly by this Court in cases of alleged corrupt practices.

CHARGE OF 'CORRUPT PRACTICE' AS SERIOUS AS 'CRIMINAL CHARGE' – *MENS REA* IS TO BE PROVED – HIGH COURT CONSIDERED IT A CASE OF 'ABSOLUTE STATUTORY LIABILITY' – HELD BEG, J.

411. The logical consequence of placing a charge of corrupt practice on the same footing as a criminal charge is obligation to interpret the words which define it strictly and narrowly. Indeed, any natural and ordinary interpretation on the words "obtaining or procuring or abetting or attempting" must carry with it the imperative requirement that the candidate concerned or his agent must have intentionally done an act which has the effect contemplated by section 123(7). In other words a "*mens rea*" or a guilty mind as well as an "*actus reus*" or a wrongful act must concur to produce the result, contemplated by law. So far as election expenses are concerned, it is possible to conceive that even an unintentional result (*i.e.*, expenses "incurred" exceeding the prescribed limit) may be enough so that a duty to prevent this result may be there in law. But, section 123(7) requires actual intended acts of "obtaining" or "procuring" or attempting or abetting. For section 123(7) results are immaterial.

412. In the case before us, the petition contains, as I have indicated above, the necessary averment of a deliberate direction by the original respondent herself, so far as Issue No. 1 is concerned and of "obtaining" and "procuring" as regards issue No. 3. These are enough to denote the ingredients of a *mens rea*. But one will search the evidence in vain for any indication of a *mens rea* or guilty intent on the part of the original respondent or of her election agent when she had appointed one. As regards both Issues 1 and 3, the learned Judge seemed to think that section 123(7) creates what is called an "absolute statutory liability," which does not require a *mens rea* although, in dealing with Issue No. 2, he had himself, after citing the necessary authorities, taken the view that a *mens rea* was also essential. He had himself in dealing with Issue No. 2, distinguished **Dr. Y.S. Paramour v. Hira Singh, AIR 1959 SC 244** a decision with whose ratio *decidendi* I have never, with due respect, felt happy in so far as it meant that a charge of corrupt practice under section 123(7) does not require proof of *mens rea*. It was decided on the strength of a statutory presumption. There were other decisions of the Supreme Court under earlier law showing that mere appointment of a Government servant as a polling agent could not be corrupt practice (*See*: **Satya Dev v. Padam Dev, 10 Ele LR 103, Mahendra Kumar v. Vidyavati, 10 Ele LR 214. Dr. Parmar's** case (supra) had necessitated an amendment in clause (2) of *Explanation* 1 of section 123(7) of the Act so that a Government servant, by merely acting as a polling agent, could not be "deemed" to have so acted as to further the prospects of a candidate's election. The learned judge had relied in his findings on Issue No. 2 on **Babu Bhai Vallabh Das Gandhi v. Pilloo Homi Mody, (1971) 36 Ele LR 108 (123-124) (Guj)** and **Haji Abdul Wahid v. B.V. Keskar, (1960) 21 Ele LR 409 (432) (All).** But, when he came to Issue No. 3 and, right at the end of his judgment to Issue No. 1, he appears to have overlooked the basic requirements of a *mens rea* and an *actus reus*, or in any case, if he had these requirements in view, he erred in assuming that they existed here. I think he gravely erred in holding that some "*actus reus*" of the original respondent lay buried beneath circumstances which seem to me to really point in the opposite direction. Sometimes, even if direct evidence is lacking, circumstantial evidence, which inescapably points to a particular conclusion, may be even better. But, where is that evidence here? I fail to see it and none was pointed out to us.

413. Let me here quote the exact language used by the Trial Judge himself in giving his findings on the first part (relating to 27-12-1970 to 13-1-1971) of Issue No. 1 of the "first set" of issues combined with the issue No. 1 of the additional issues, both issues, for some inexplicable reason, being identically worded. The learned Judge said:

> "Learned counsel for the respondent then urged that even accepting that Shri Yashpal Kapur delivered a speech at Munshiganj on 7th January, 1971

and that he canvassed support for the respondent in that speech, he was not an election agent on that date, and there is no evidence of the fact that he had been instructed to do so by the respondent No. 1. Learned counsel stressed that, consequently it should not be held on that basis that the respondent No. 1 obtained or procured the assistance of Shri Yashpal Kapur for the furtherance of her election prospects.

I have given my careful consideration to this argument as well, but I regret my inability to accept the same. As also stated earlier, Shri Yashpal Kapur was occupying a position of trust and confidence with the respondent No. 1 since quite a long time. During the period in question he was officer on Special Duty in the respondent No. 1's Secretariat. In 1967 he had resigned from his post for the sake of respondent No. 1 to be able to do her election work in the constituency. After that was done, he was taken back in the respondent's Secretariat as Officer on Special Duty. Respondent No. 1 held herself out as a candidate on 29th December, 1970. On 5th of January, 1971 Raja Dinesh Singh was sent to the constituency. On 7th of January. 1971 Shri Yashpal Kapur visited Raebareli and on the own admission of respondent No. 1 he did so with previous notice to the respondent No. 1. The subsequent events also appear to be material, for, according to Shri Yashpal Kapur, immediately on return from Raebareli he held a talk with the respondent No. 1 on 9th or 10th of January, 1971, on 13th January he again resigned from the post and the same day set out once again for the constituency of the respondent No. 1. It was again he who was ultimately appointed election agent for the respondent No. 1. It may be added that it was not possible to adduce any direct evidence on the point whether the respondent No. 1 instructed Shri Yashpal Kapur to go to Raebareli on 7th January, 1971 for any election work. That can be inferred only on the basis of the surrounding circumstances. I have already mentioned those circumstances above and to my mind the only inference that can be drawn on the basis of those circumstances is that Yashpal Kapur went to Raebareli on the aforesaid date under instruction of the respondent No. 1 for doing preliminary work pertaining to her election.

To sum, therefore, it is satisfactorily proved that the respondent No. 1 during the period ending on 13th January, 1971 obtained/procured the assistance of Shri Yashpal Kapur, a Gazetted Officer in the Government of India for the furtherance of her election prospects, inasmuch as Shri Yashpal Kapur was made to go to Raebareli on 7-1-1971 and deliver a speech at Shaheed Mela in Munshiganj canvassing support for her candidature."

414. Now, it is a well-settled rule repeatedly laid down by this Court that allegations of corrupt practice in the course of an election must be judged by the same standards of a criminal charge. And, no rule of evidence, in judging guilt on a criminal charge, is more firmly rooted than that no charge, resting on circumstantial evidence could be held to be proved beyond reasonable doubt unless the chain of circumstances is so complete and so connected with the charge that it leaves no other reasonable hypothesis open for the Court to adopt except that the offender had committed the offence alleged (See : *e.g.* **Smt. Om Prabha Jain v. Charan Das, AIR 1975 SC 1417 (1426).)**

HIGH COURT DIVIDED ACTIVITIES OF YASHPAL KAPUR INTO 3 PARTS – NO CONSENT OF THE APPELLANT DIRECT OR INDIRECT FOR THE FIRST PERIOD PROVED – UNRELIABLE EVIDENCE CONSIDERED AS PROOF – HELD BEG, J.

415. The learned Judge dealt with evidence on Issue No. 1 relating to the activities of Shri Yashpal Kapur by dividing it into three periods (1) from 27-12-1970 to

13-1-1971 when Shri Kapur had not resigned from Government service: (2) from 14-1-1971 to 25-1-1971, the period after Shri Kapur's resignation upto its acceptance by the President of India evidenced by a notification dated 25-1-1971; (3) from 26-1-1971 to 6-2-1971, the period after the acceptance of Shri Kapur's resignation and upto the date of the publication of it in the Official Gazette. The learned judge considered only the first two periods material as he held the activities in the third period to be above board because Shri Kapur was free to do what he liked in this period. Hence, the fact that the original respondent appointed Shri Kapur her election agent on 1-2-1971 made no difference to the result in the third period. But, we will find that a very glaring feature of the findings relating to the first two periods is that the original respondent is held vicariously responsible without anything beyond the activities of Shri Yashpal Kapur and his position as an Officer on Special Duty in the Prime Minister's Secretariat to justify the inference that he had an express or implied authorisation or direction from the Prime Minister to do anything in general or in particular on her behalf for her election.

416. Let us take the first period. What was required to be approved beyond all reasonable doubt from the evidence on record on this part of the case, was that Shri Yashpal Kapur had been instructed or directed by the original respondent to render the help if any, that he did give by the speech he was alleged to have made at a fair at Shaheed Mela (Martyrs' fair) at Munshiganj in Raebareli on 7-1-1971, canvassing support for the original respondent's election- an allegation which Shri Yashpal Kapur had denied in so far as any mention of the original respondent's candidature is concerned. Shri Kapur admitted that he had gone there with Shri Gulzarilal Nanda, a former Minister of the Central Government, but said that he had only, when called upon to do so, paid his tribute to the memory of the martyrs.

417. The learned Judge held that the recollection of Shri Yashpal Kapur about what he said at the Shaheed Mela on 7-1-1971 was less reliable than the statement of Shri Vidya Shankar Yadav (P.W. 43) an Advocate belonging to an opposition party, supported by his political co-worker Nankau Yadav (P.W.28) a witness who, in his transparent anxiety to appear truthful, went so far as to make the absurd assertion that he had not told anyone, before he appeared in the witness box, that he had attended the Shaheed Mela on 7-1-1971, and who could not remember either the date of his marriage or the date of birth of his children but asserted that he had noted 7-1-1971 without even having ever talked on any previous occasion to anyone about this date if he is to be believed – and, by Shri R.K. Dixit (P.W. 31), a joint editor of a newspaper who claimed to be present on the occasion and who, while reporting other facts and reasons in his newspaper for believing that the original respondent will stand from the Raebareli constituency, had not mentioned what he claimed, in the witness box, to have heard Shri Yashpal Kapur himself say at the Mela. Obviously, both these witnesses, if they were not committing perjury did not have good memories on their own admissions. But, the learned Judge had believed them quite unhesitatingly although the meeting at Shaheed Mela, addressed by Shri Yashpal Kapur, had not even been given any prominence in the pleadings by being at least specifically mentioned in the petition.

418. The learned Judge disbelieved the evidence of the original respondent's witness Shri Sarju Prasad (R.W. 12), the Headmaster of a School, who had denied that he ever accompanied Shri Nankau (P.W. 28) to the Shaheed Mela as claimed by Nankau. The ground for holding that Shri Sarju Prasad must be deposing falsely appears to me to be very unfair both to Shri Sarju Prasad and Shri Gaya Prasad Shukla, a Congressman, who was suspected, without the slightest foundation in evidence, of having induced Shri Sarju Prasad to give perjured evidence simply because Shri Gaya Prasad, who did not even appear as a witness, was a member of the Congress (R) party and was once connected with the School in which Shri Sarju Prasad served. The learned Judge said:

> "It is quite likely that once Nankau had conceded in cross-examination that Sarju Prasad had accompanied him to the Shaheed Mela, pressure was brought to bear on Sarju Prasad (P.W. 12) by Gaya Prasad Shukla in order to make him appear as a witness in the case and give evidence to contradict the testimony of Nankau. It is true that in his re-examination Sarju Prasad (R.W. 12) admitted that on the date on which he was examined as a witness in the case the school was being run by the Government under the control of the District Basic Education Officer, However, the association that Gaya Prasad Shukla had with the Pathshala in his capacity as Adhyaksha, and consequently with Sarju Prasad, who was a teacher in that pathshala could not have been wiped off overnight merely because the school was taken over by the Government to be run under its own officers."

419. The reasons given by the learned judge for holding that it was "abundantly clear" that Shri Ram Pal (R.W. 13) another witness of Smt. Gandhi was "also not a truthful witness", were:

> "Now, since Ramesh Chand Shukla Advocate is a resident of the same village where Ram Pal resided, and since he was an important worker for the respondent No. 1 during the election and was also her Pairokar at some stage, the possibility of Ram Pal having been pressurised by Shri Ramesh Chand Shukla cannot be excluded. Together with it there is also the fact that Shri Gaya Prasad Shukla, another important worker of the respondent No. 1, happened to be the Adhyaksha of the Zila Parishad during the period the witness was examined in the case. It is a matter of common knowledge that the Adhyaksha of the Zila Parishad always wields influence in the rural areas. It will not be out of place to add that when it was put to Ram Pal in cross-examination as to which party did Sri Ramesh Chand Shukla belong he pleaded ignorance about it. It cannot be accepted for any moment that even though Shri Shukla resided in the village in which this witness resided, and even though Shri Shukla was such a prominent worker of the Congress party, Ram Pal would not have known about it."

420. I do not know how, when workers of the Congress party were divided into two camps and had been changing sides, from time to time, ignorance of a worker's precise party loyalties meant that Ram Pal was untruthful. If mere possibilities of being "pressurised" or biased were enough to tar a witness as untruthful, it is difficult to see how or why the witnesses of the election petitioner on whom lay the primary burden of proof, could escape similar treatment. V.S. Yadav, was, no doubt, an Advocate. But, he was not even paying Income Tax. He felt free, on a working day in Courts, to go to the Mela. He was enthusiastic enough as a member of an opposition party to object, according to himself, to Shri Yashpal Kapur bringing in the candidature of the original respondent even at a meeting which, according to him, consisted mostly of Congress (R) sympathisers. Shri Yashpal Kapur was not so ignorant or inexperienced in election matters and could not be assumed, without any evidence to support the assumption, to be so imprudent as to make a speech when he would know that as he was still a Government servant, this would be misinterpreted.

421. Let us, for the sake of argument, assume that Shri Yashpal Kapur had been over-powered by such a desire to exhibit an excessive zeal, which got the better of his prudence that he, believing that a publicly made gesture of his loyalty was needed on this particular occasion cast all caution to the winds and, while paying the tribute he was called upon to pay to the memory of the martyrs, suddenly decided to jump into the electoral fray by making an appeal at the martyrs' mela to support Smt. Indira Gandhi, as though the speeches of all those local leaders who in addition to Shri Gulzarilal Nanda, a former Minister are said to have spoken there to the same effect, were not enough. What follows? It is here that we find the weakest link in the misty and fanciful chain of the learned Judge's logic. Where was the evidence that whatever else Shri. Yashpal Kapur may or may not have been supposed to do on his visit to Raebareli, this particular piece of "frolic", a term used by law relating to scope of authority, carried the "direction" of Smt. Indira Gandhi herself behind it? Indeed, there is not only not a jot of evidence to suggest that Shri Yashpal Kapur was actually asked by Smt. Gandhi to go to Raebareli to do anything for her election on this visit, but there is ample absolutely unshaken evidence of Shri Yashpal Kapur to the contrary, supported by the evidence of the Prime Minister herself which the learned trial Judge had, for some reason, entirely ignored. In any case, it is utterly unthinkable that the Prime Minister herself could have conceivably authorised Shri Kapur to go to Munshiganj and make a public speech, while he was still a Government servant, to support her candidature. And, if he had no authority from her either to act generally or to do any particular act on her behalf how could each and every action of Shri Kapur possibly make the Prime Minister legally liable vicariously for it?

422. The learned Judge, as is evident, from his summary of evidence and conclusions, relied on circumstantial evidence only. But, in order that the circumstances should have a conclusive effect, so as to exclude any reasonable hypothesis except that of guilt, they had to point in one direction only and in no other. What is the position that emerges from a consideration of the circumstances found and detailed by the learned Judge himself? It was held that Shri Yashpal Kapur was occupying a position of trust and confidence with the original respondent for quite a long time. Indeed, his evidence shows that he was so attached to the family of the original respondent and the political and national causes its members had represented that he was just the type of person who could, even without the slightest suggestion on the part of the original respondent voluntarily taken upon himself the duty to do whatever he could do in his private capacity, to help her return at the election. Indeed, his private capacity, as a person attached to the family of the original respondent and to the causes espoused by its members, could very well be considered more important by him than his Government service. And, this is exactly what the findings given by the learned Judge relating to services rendered by Shri Yashpal Kapur at the previous elections of the original respondent, showing how he had resigned his post on a previous occasion, to help in her election, indicated.

423. In the passage from the judgment, quoted above, the learned Judge draws an inference of a previous instruction, from the Prime Minister to Shri Kapur, to say what he is alleged to have said in a speech, because, *inter alia*, Shri Kapur met the Prime Minister on his return from Raebareli; Again, the necessary inference of a previous intimation by Shri Kapur to the Prime Minister of his intention to visit Raebareli, could not be that there was any authority or direction given by the Prime Minister to Shri Kapur to do or to say anything on her behalf. All this would lie in the realm of pure conjecture and suspicion. It left other possible and more reasonable inferences wide open.

424. The learned Judge had himself held, so far as use of rostrums is concerned, that the Prime Minister sheds her personality, as the holder of her office, and assumes the role of a mere candidate as soon as she ascends a platform to make an election speech. But, when the learned Judge deals with the action of Shri Kapur, in making a speech from a platform at a martyrs' mela, because Shri Kapur is called upon to pay his tribute to the martyrs, he holds that not only must the capacity of a Government servant unshakably stick to him, but that Shri Kapur must have been authorised by the Prime Minister herself knowing, as she did, that he was a Government servant to go and make a public speech at the Mela and canvass for votes for her. I do not think that we can indulge in a flight of fancy which could be described as "flamboyant."

425. The uncontroverted evidence of Shri Kapur which had been ignored by the trial Judge was that it was the special business of this witness, as an officer on Special Duty in the Prime Minister's Secretariat, in his own words. "To deal with the representations received from public and other works of semi-political nature." It is difficult to understand how the occupant of such a difficult and responsible office as that of the Prime Minister of the numerically largest democracy in the world can possibly discharge his or her duties towards the public satisfactorily without the aid of such officers. Naturally, as the Prime Minister was contemplating standing for election from the Raebareli constituency, it would not be outside the scope of the duties of such an officer to attend especially to the complaints and representations from Raebareli. He stated that Shri Gulzarilal Nanda, who was then the Railway Minister, had received some representations from the Raebareli. He also said that he had from time to time, forwarded some representations to Shri Gulzarilal Nanda who had asked him to accompany him to Raebareli. Therefore, apparently without being asked by the Prime Minister, but, after informing her of his intention to go with Shri Gulzarilal Nanda, the witness had, in the course of the performance of duties especially assigned to him since his appointment, visited Raebareli in the company of Shri Gulzarilal Nanda. This could not be outside the scope of his duties.

426. Again, without any contradiction from any evidence whatsoever, his statement, unquestioned also in cross-examination, was that the Prime Minister did not, at any time, ask him, in his own words "either directly or indirectly to do anything pertaining to her election". The Prime Minister's replies to interrogatories served upon her show that she had no personal knowledge of what Shri Kapur did at Raebareli before he was appointed her election agent. It is also apparent from the evidence of this witness and of the Prime Minister herself that, when he expressed his desire on 9th or 10th January, 1971, to the Prime Minister to resign from his post as Officer on Special Duty, she asked him to think over the matter as this would mean that he could not return to his post. He had earlier said that this decision was taken with a view to do work for the public in general and the congress party in particular as he wanted to enter public life.

YASHPAL KAPUR RESIGNED ON 13.1.1971 – HAKSAR TOLD HIM HE WAS A FREE MAN – ACCEPTED BY PRESIDENT ON 25.1.1971 – NOTIFIED ON 6.2.1971 WITH EFFECT FROM 14.1.1971 – EVIDENCE IGNORED – MISINTERPRETED BY HIGH COURT – HELD BEG, J.

It is clear that the Prime Minister had left the decision entirely to the free will and option of Shri Kapur who had been asked to ponder over it carefully. When Shri Kapur had informed the Prime Minister again on 13-1-1971 that he had reached his, final decision, after due consideration, to resign from his post so as to be able to do public work as he had political ambitions she had agreed to it and had asked him to see Shri P.N. Haksar, who was Incharge of the Prime Minister's Secretariat. He informed Shri P.N. Haksar about this decision on the telephone and then met him an hour later on 13-1-1971 to submit his letter of resignation. Shri Haksar, relying upon rule 3 of the Government of India Transaction of Business Rules had orally accepted his resignation, as the head of the Prime Minister's Secretariat. He told Shri Kapur that he was a free man. Naturally, the necessary notification, showing that Shri Kapur was relieved of his office with effect from 14-1-1971, was to follow.

427. The statement of Shri Kapur, supported by those of the Prime Minister and Shri P.N. Haksar, had been accepted by the trial Court as correct so far as tender of his resignation and its acceptance, in all the stages, followed by the notification in the Gazette went. The learned Judge held that the President gave his assent on 25-1-1971. Shri Kapur's letter of resignation must have been duly forwarded and was acted upon. This was the learned Judge's finding. Shri Kapur did not work in the Prime Minister's Secretariat after 13-1-1971 and he drew no salary as a Government servant after that date. The notification in the Gazette could not, according to rules, take place until Shri Kapur had handed over charge. He signed and completed the necessary papers relating to relinquishment of the charge of his office on 13-1-1971, but he put the date 14-1-1971 under his signature on the document evidencing a formal handing over of charge as it was to take effect from that date. The trial Court held that the resignation of Shri Kapur would be effective from 25-1-1971 notwithstanding the fact that his request to be relieved from office, with effect from 14-1-1971, had been accepted and acted upon immediately by Shri P.N. Haksar as the official head of the Prime Minister's Secretariat. The papers were sent to the Secretariat of the President of India for completion of formalities. The formal Presidential sanction having been obtained, the notification dated 25-1-1971, declaring the resignation of Shri Kapur to be effective from 14-1-1971, was published on 6-2-1971.

428. On the facts stated above there could be no doubt whatsoever that Shri Kapur was not asked to do anything at all in connection with her election by the Prime Minister herself, but he had decided to take interest in it voluntarily as he had some political ambition: and, therefore, he had asked the Prime Minister to be relieved of his office in her Secretariat with effect from 14-1-1971. It is unfortunate that the learned Judge thought that there was something almost sinister in Shri Kapur taking such interest in the election or in hoping to enter political life through absolutely legitimate means. There is not the slightest reason for anyone who fairly examines the evidence of Shri Kapur, supported by that of the Prime Minister and Shri P.N. Haksar, to doubt the motives or the veracity of Shri Kapur on this point. He frankly stated that his ambition was to enter political life. In any case, the motives of Shri Kapur were not on trial, If such assistance as he may have rendered was entirely voluntary, without any request or solicitation from the Prime Minister, I do not see how, on the view of the correct legal position stated above, it made any difference to the result even if Shri Kapur had continued to be a Government servant upto 25-1-1971.

429. Shri P.N. Haksar was aware of and cited the applicable rule for a resignation by a temporary Government servant, as Shri Kapur was and stated also the practice followed, in his experience, in such cases. He presumably thought that the resignation was effective from 14-1-1971. Shri Kapur also acted upon that assumption and in that belief. The Prime Minister, who could not be expected to examine *suo motu* the question whether Shri P.N. Haksar and Shri Kapur were right in their beliefs about the effectiveness of the resignation, assumed that everything was alright. In any case, there could not possibly, on these facts, be any *mens rea* on her part.

430. The learned Judge having accepted, on the unimpeachable evidence of the date of notification of 25-1-1971 published in the Official Gazette on 6-2-1971, that Shri Kapur must have handed in his resignation in a letter of 13-1-1971, it is very difficult to see how one could possibly doubt the correctness of the statement of Shri P.N. Haksar that, as the Head of the Prime Minister's Secretariat he had accepted the resignation orally and forwarded it on for necessary action. The resignation had taken place with the consent of the Prime Minister. It is inconceivable, in the circumstances, that Shri P.N. Haksar would not have, as the Head of the Department in which Shri Kapur was working agreed to relieve him of his duties by telling him that he was a free man, and, thereby accepted his resignation. He very honestly stated that he does not remember whether he wrote anything on the margin of that letter. He must have made so many endorsements on so many letters and documents that it was expecting the impossible to hold that he must remember what he wrote on every one of them. The only other ground given by the learned Judge for doubting the correctness of this version, which completely accords with the natural and ordinary course of official business, was that the additional written statement filed a year after the original written statement, mentions this fact for the first time. It seems to me that the learned Judge was carrying his suspicions to excessive lengths. The real question involved was the legal effect of the facts accepted by the learned Judge to be correct. These were: firstly, that such a letter of resignation was handed in on 13-1-1971 by Shri Kapur to Shri Haksar asking to be allowed to resign with effect from 14-1-1971; and, secondly, this very request was accepted by the President of India and incorporated in a notification dated 25-1-1971.

431. The learned Judge had found Shri P.N. Haksar's statement, that such an oral acceptance followed by the necessary notification afterwards, was "rather interesting", and, that the resignation could not be effective until 25-1-1971 the date of drafting the notification. But, what the learned Judge completely overlooked was that the notification itself made the resignation effective from 14-1-1971, the date from which Shri Kapur had neither worked in the Prime Minister's Secretariat nor drawn any salary. There was no plea anywhere, and there is no express finding on it, that the President's notification itself, which made the resignation effective from 14-1-1971, was invalid to the extent that it purported to give any retrospective effect to the resignation, in the sense that it made it effective from a date prior to its actual acceptance. The fact that it is made effective from 14-1-1971 shows that the letter must have reached the President's Secretariat with the request that this should be done. And, in the ordinary course of business, the head of the office concerned makes his endorsment on such letters.

432. The learned Judge had relied on rule 5 of the Central Civil Services (Temporary Service) Rules, 1949, which runs as follows:

> "5 (a) The service of a temporary Government servant who is not in quasi-permanent service shall be liable to termination at any time by notice in writing given either by the Government servant to the appointing authority, or by the appointing authority to the Government servant.
>
> (b) The period of such notice shall be one month, unless otherwise agreed to by the Government and by the Government servant:
>
> Provided that the service of any such Government servant may be terminated forthwith by payment to him of a sum equivalent to the amount of his pay plus allowances for the period of the notice or as the case may be for the period by which such notice falls short of one month or any agreed longer period."

433. The learned Judge had referred to Halsbury's Laws of England Vol. V (S'mond's Edn.) p. 61. where it was laid down that in a "corporation created by Statute for the discharge of public functions a member may not have an absolute right to resign at Will, because the law may cast a duty upon the person elected to a public office to act in that office in public interest." He also referred to an American case. **Edwards M. Edwards v. United States, (1880) 26 Law Ed 314** to the effect that only the appointing authority could have accepted the resignation of an occupant of a public office, and that under the special provisions of the law, the holder of such an office could be subjected to a penalty for a wrongful refusal to perform the duties of his office. The desire or wish of the holder of the office had to give place to public interest in such special cases. It is clear that the cases cited could have no relevance whatsoever for an interpretation of rule 5 set out above.

AMENDED LAW MAKES IT MORE CLEAR – RETROSPECTIVITY DOES NOT MAKE AMENDED LAW INVALID – HELD BEG, J.

434. The learned Judge had then relied upon **Raj Kumar v. Union of India, AIR 1969 SC 180: (1968) 3 SCR 857** where this Court held that "normally, and, in the absence of any law or rule governing the conditions of his service to the contrary it will not be open to the public servant to withdraw his resignation after it is accepted by the appropriate authority." In that case, there was a dispute between the Government servant and the Union of India on the question whether the Government servant concerned would withdraw his resignation after it was accepted. It was held that he could not. It was not a case of an agreement between the parties at all as to the date from which the resignation could effectively terminate service.

SUPREME COURT IN AN EARLIER JUDGMENT BETWEEN PARTIES LEFT IT TO HIGH COURT FOR FRAMING ISSUE ON DATE OF ACCEPTANCE OF KAPUR'S RESIGNATION – HIGH COURT MISINTERPRETED THE RULES APPLICABLE – HELD BEG, J.

It is true that in **Raj Narain v. Smt. Indira Nehru Gandhi, AIR 1972 SC 1302: (1972) 3 SCR 841** when this very matter came up to this Court to decide whether an issue should be struck on it, this Court had sent back the matter to the High Court after holding that an issue should be framed to decide when Shri Kapur's resignation became effective and that this question "will have to be examined with reference to his conditions of service." Now it is clear, from the rule itself that a condition of Shri Kapur's service was that the Government and the Government servant could dispense with the period of notice if it was mutually agreed upon to do that. Rule 5(b) makes that abundantly clear. The learned Judge for some reason, completely overlooked this aspect.

435. Neither the Government nor the Government servant is in a worse position than an ordinary master or servant on a matter governed by contract. In fact, Article 310 makes it clear that in such a case the tenure of office of a Central Government servant is "during the pleasure of the President". In the instant case the President's pleasure was contained in the notification dated 25-1-1971 showing that the President had accepted the resignation of Shri Kapur with effect from the forenoon of 14-1-1971. And, this is what Shri Kapur himself wanted. Hence, there is no difficulty at all in accepting the correctness of a resignation effective from the date which both parties to the contract, on patent facts, had agreed to. No rights of an innocent 3rd party were either involved or affected by such an acceptance of the resignation from the date immediately after the date on which Shri Kapur had tendered his resignation. That as already pointed out was also the date after which he had ceased to work or draw his salary. It is inconceivable that the law should thrust the status of a Government servant upon one who does not want it particularly when the Government also does not, in public interest, refuse to relieve him by making him stick to any terms to the contrary in his contract. Our law, on this point, is not so monstrous. The position accepted by the learned Judge appears to me to be quite indefensible.

However there was an amendment also in the law by section 7 of Act 40 of 1975, adding the following at the end of the Explanation to section 123(7) of the Act:

> "(3) For the purposes of clause (7), notwithstanding anything contained in any other law the publication in the Official Gazette of the appointment, resignation, termination of service, dismissal or removal from service of a person in the service of the Central Government including a person serving

in connection with the administration of a Union Territory or of a State Government shall be conclusive proof.

(i) of such appointment, resignation, termination of service, dismissal or removal from service, as the case may be, and

(ii) where the date of taking effect of such appointment, resignation, termination of service, dismissal or removal from service, as the case may be, is stated in such publication, also of the fact that such person was appointed with effect from the said date, or in the case of resignation, termination of service, dismissal or removal from service, such person ceased to be in such service with effect from the said date."

436. I find that this amendment, which was made retrospective, by section 10 of Act 40 of 1975, makes the legal position still clearer. The learned Counsel for the election-petitioner had assailed the validity of this amendment on the ground that powers conferred by it upon the Government are bound to be abused by those who hold the reins of Government. I am afraid I am unable to see any force in this contention. The presumption is that a bona fide use will be made of this power lodged in such responsible hands. If such powers are ever exercised in a *mala fide* manner, it is the particular exercise of the power that can be questioned and struck down. The provision does not become invalid merely because it could be abused as practically any provision of law can be by those who may want to do so.

FINDINGS OF HIGH COURT ON KAPUR FOR PERIOD 14.1.1971 TO 25.1.1971 – HE HAD NO AUTHORITY FROM APPELLANT TO SEEK SUPPORT OF VOTERS FOR HER – HELD BEG, J.

437. I will next take up the period from 14-1-1971 upto 25-1-1971, when Shri Kapur is said to have gone and voluntarily worked at Raebareli and to have done whatever he could to organise the conduct of the Prime Minister's election after his talks with the Prime Minister. The position, with regard to allegations in this period is summarised as follows:

1. He is said to have either led or to have joined a procession of cars taken out on 14-1-1971 in the town of Raebareli as a part of the election campaign for the original respondent although Shri U.S. Yadav (P.W. 41), an Advocate, who was a staunch S.S.P. worker, produced on behalf of the election-petitioner, clearly stated that he had not seen Shri Kapur in that procession which he watched but he had seen him only on 15-1-1971. The learned Judge, however, not only relied on the evidence of Shri R.K. Singh (P.W. 42) but also on that of Shri U.S. Yadav to hold that Shri Kapur must have been "associated with" the procession of people seen in cars and jeeps taken out on 14-1-1971 shouting Congress (R) party slogans to start off the election campaign.
2. On 17-1-1971, Shri Kapur is said to have participated in an election meeting held at the Clock Tower. On this allegation, the learned Judge accepted the evidence of Shri R.K. Dixit (P.W. 31), and Shri R.K. Singh. (P.W. 42). Although both these witnesses only stated that some confusion took place at the meeting and Shri R.K. Dixit did not even remember whether any speech was made at all by Shri Kapur. Shri R.K. Singh also did not state that Shri Kapur actually made a speech but had said that "a disturbance took place when Shri Kapur wanted to deliver a speech as a result of which he could not do so." The learned Judge rejected the evidence of Shri V.L. Dwivedi (R.W. 18) supported by Shri Kapur (R.W. 32) himself, that Shri Kapur was not present at all at this meeting. However, on the evidence of the election petitioner's witnesses themselves, Shri Kapur could do nothing whatsoever in furtherance of the election of the original respondent at this meeting.

3. On 19-1-1971, Shri Kapur is said to have addressed a meeting at village Nihasta where he is said to have gone in the company of Prof. Sher Singh a Minister of State in the Government of India. Although, the tour programme of the Minister concerned showed that the Minister went to that village to inaugurate a Telephone Exchange on 18-1-1971, supported by the evidence of Jagannath Prasad (R.W. 16), a resident of village Nihasta, and K.D. Pandey (R.W. 17) Post Master, Sub-Post Office yet, the learned Judge preferred the evidence at Shri R.K. Singh (P.W. 42) for the election-petitioner despite the infirmity in this evidence that it was neither consistent with the tour programme of the Central Government Minister sent in advance for this function nor with the unshaken evidence of those who organised the function.
4. It was alleged that Shri Kapur on 19-1-1971, again in the company of Prof. Sher Singh, the Central Government Minister, mentioned above attended a meeting held in Lalganj. So far as this particular allegation is concerned, the learned Judge thought that it could not be accepted because it was supported only by one highly partisan witness. Shri G.N. Pandey, against 4 faultless witnesses: Abdul Jabbar (R.W. 25). Fateh Bahadur Singh (R.W. 26), Ishwar Chand (R.W. 27). and Ranjit Singh (R.W. 28).
5. On 19-1-1971, Shri Kapur was said to be present at the inaugural function of the Telephone Exchange at Behta Kalan and is said to have delivered a speech there. The learned trial Judge accepted the evidence of Pt. Shashank Misra. (P.W. 32) admittedly a highly partisan witness, who was believed because of a question put to him in cross-examination suggesting that there was uproar when Shri Kapur started speaking so that nobody could hear what he said. The learned Judge held that this amounted to an admission of Shri Kapur's presence and participation in this meeting.
6. Shri Kapur was alleged to have delivered a speech on 18-1-1971 at the foundation laying ceremony of a new post Office building at Raebareli in the company of Prof. Sher Singh the Central Government Minister, mentioned above. This allegation was not accepted on the ground that it was not supported by any evidence whatsoever.

438. All that the witnesses could remember of Shri Kapur's speech, on each occasion, was that he supported the original respondent's candidature. Out of allegations of acts said to have been committed on 6 occasions by Shri Kapur in this period, the learned Judge found only 4 instances proved. Out of these, it was clear that Shri Kapur could not have done anything in furtherance of the original respondent's election on 17-1-1971 when, according to the election-petitioner's witnesses, he was not even allowed to speak. Even if all the election petitioner's witnesses accepted by the learned Judge are to be implicitly believed for this period the position is:

(a) On three occasions in this period from 14-1-1971 to 25-1-1971, Shri Kapur is shown to have made a speech supporting the original respondent's candidature.

(b) There is no evidence whatsoever from any source that Shri Kapur did so on any of these three occasions either after having been requested by the original respondent to do so or with her knowledge or consent or approval.

(c) The only evidence in the case, on the decisive question, coming from the side of the original respondent is that Shri Kapur did, whatever he did, entirely on his own initiative and in his private and individual capacity without the slightest solicitation, request, or suggestion from the original respondent who did not even know what he was doing at Raebareli. And, this evidence, being uncontroverted, could not be rejected. In fact, it was not rejected by the trial

Court. It was ignored by it presumably under an erroneous belief that it was not material.

439. There is no evidence whatsoever that Shri Kapur was constituted a sort of general de facto agent of the Prime Minister even before he became her election agent on 1-2-I971. Indeed, such a case, that Shri Kapur was constituted a *de facto* agent of the Prime Minister, and, if so, what was the scope of his authority, was not set up in the petition and was not put in issue. Therefore, there is no finding on it by the learned Judge. Could the Court then, without any proof of any specific request or solicitation or even knowledge of or consent to the doing of any particular acts Shri Kapur may have done in this period make the Prime Minister liable for them in any way? I think not. The election petitioner had to be confined to the case he had set up. This, as already pointed out, could only be on a fair reading of the petition on issue No. 1, one of specific authorisation of particular individual acts of Shri Kapur. Of this, there is not only no evidence whatsoever on record but the evidence is to the contrary.

440. Issue No. 1, as framed, and the form of findings given on it indicate that the learned Judge realized that the election petitioner's case must be confined to proof of specific acts or statements of the original respondent herself which induced Shri Kapur, as a Government servant, to give some assistance in furtherance of her election, but the discussion of evidence and the inferences which the learned Judge reached upon the circumstances found, indicated that the learned Judge thought that Shri Kapur was constituted a sort of de facto agent even before Shri Kapur was clothed with legal authority on 1-2-1971. This appears to me to be the underlying current of thought and reasoning of the learned Judge. Thus, the result was that what was really decided was the case of a de facto agency which was neither set up nor was the subject-matter of an issue. I, therefore, think that the principle that no amount of evidence could be looked into on a case not really set up was applicable here. It was quite unfair to expect the original respondent to meet a case not set-up at all. Furthermore, the case of *de facto* agency was, in the circumstances of the particular case, only possible to set up if the Prime Minister had made some request to Shri Kapur to go and conduct the election campaign even before he was appointed her election agent on 1-2-1971. If this was not established by evidence on record, it could be said that the bottom was knocked out of even such a hypothetical case. Had a case of *de facto* agency been even argued, it is not conceivable that certain cases of Division Benches of the Allahabad High Court itself would not have been cited to show on what kind of evidence it could succeed.

441. In **Rustom Satin v. Dr. Sampoornanand, (1959) 20 Ele LR 221 (243) (All)** it had been held by a Division Bench of the Allahabad High Court (V. Bhargava and J.N. Takru. JJ.), *inter alia* (243):

> "So far as the election law in this country is concerned it is a creation of statute and as such has to be interpreted in accordance with the provisions of that statute. Section 100 of the Act clearly refers to corrupt practices committed by four classes of persons only, *viz.*, the candidate, his election agent, persons acting with the consent of the candidate or his election agent, and those acting without such consent. The corrupt practices committed by the first three classes of persons are covered by section 100(1)(b). while those committed by persons falling in the fourth class are provided against in section 100(1)(d)(ii)."

The same Bench of the Allahabad High Court in **J.P. Rawat v. K.D Paliwal, (1959) 20 Ele LR 443 (All)** had held (456):

> "............ :. even in the case of admitted workers in whose case also general consent to work for the candidate may be implied, the consent of the returned candidate to corrupt practice or practices complained against have to be

separately proved, and reliance upon general consent, express or implied to work legitimately for the candidate is not deemed sufficient"

442. After 14-1-1971, the Prime Minister, like everyone else concerned obviously believed that Shri Kapur was no longer a Government servant. As I have already pointed out, this was the legally correct assumption. Even if one were to assume, for the sake of argument that this was not so and that the learned Judge had correctly held that Shri Kapur's resignation became effective from 25-1-1971, there could be no liability for a corrupt practice by merely permitting Shri Kapur to resign. The uncontroverted evidence is that, after resigning Shri Kapur went to Raebareli voluntarily without any request or suggestion made to him by the original respondent or by anybody else to go to Raebareli and work for her election. Even his appointment as the original respondent's election agent on 1-2-1971, according to Shri Kapur's evidence, was the result of a suggestion of Shri Dal Bahadur Singh at Raebareli, apparently during the Prime Minister's visit to her constituency.

VOLUNTARY ACTS DO NOT CONSTITUTE 'CORRUPT PRACTICE' – OVERLOOKED BY HIGH COURT – HELD BEG, J.

443. Cases in which help rendered voluntarily by a Government servant without any attempt by the candidate concerned to "obtain" or "procure" it were held not to constitute a "corrupt practice" of the candidate, whatever be the impropriety of it for the Government servant himself, were completely overlooked by the learned Judge. In **Hafiz Mohd. Ibrahim v. Election Tribunal, (1957) 13 Ele LR 262 (All)** a Division Bench of Allahabad (Mootham C.J. and Mukerji, J.) had pointed out that a Government servant has a "private personality" too. Similar observations of Dua J. are found in a Division Bench decision of the Punjab High Court; *See*; **Ram Phal v. Braham Parkash, 23 Ele LR 92.**

444. On the conclusions reached by the learned Judge himself the acts of Shri Kapur between the period 25-1-1971 and 6-2-1971, the date of the publication of the notification, could not be taken into account as no corrupt practice could possibly exist in that period, due to the participation of Shri Kapur in any election work. And, with regard to the two earlier periods beginning with 7-1-1971, I am unable to see, for the reasons given above, how, any corrupt practice could be committed by the original respondent vicariously due to any thing done by Shri Kapur, even if one were to apply the law as it existed before the amendments of the Act.

WHEN APPELLANT BECAME A 'CANDIDATE' FROM RAEBARELI – HIGH COURT FINDING BASED ON PRESS CONFERENCE OF 29.12.1970 OR PRESS REPORTS OR STATEMENTS OF OPPOSITION – BASED COMPLETELY ON GUESS WORK – NO DECISIVE AND CONCLUSIVE EVIDENCE – HELD BEG, J.

445. Another question, which I may now briefly consider, is the date from which the original respondent could be said to have held herself out as a candidate. If she was not a "candidate", upto 25-1-1971, as defined by law, that would, in itself, be a sufficient ground for wiping out the effect of findings of the learned Judge on the two periods dealt with above.

446. The learned Judge had inferred that the Prime Minister was a "candidate" from 29-12-1970 as she had held herself out as a candidate when she answered a question put to her on 29-12-1970 at a Press Conference at New Delhi. The question and answer were as follows:

> "**Q.** A short while ago there was a meeting of the opposition leaders and there they said that the Prime Minister is changing her constituency from Raebareli to Gurgaon?
>
> P.M. No. I am not."

In the witness box, the Prime Minister disclosed that what she meant by the answer was that she would not contest from the Gurgaon constituency. On further cross-examination, she stated:

> "It is wrong to assume that while giving the reply marked 'B' in the transcript (Ext. 132) I conveyed that I was not changing my constituency from Raebareli at all and emphatically held out that I would contest election again from Raebareli. In my opinion there is no basis for this assumption."

447. The learned Judge had, in preference to the statement of the Prime Minister herself as to what she meant, together with the evidence given by her Secretariat that there were entreaties or offers to her from other constituencies that she should be their representative, relied on Press reports and what members of other parties thought and did as a result of the above-mentioned statement of the Prime Minister on 29-12-1970. The learned Judge also referred to paragraph 1(A) of the additional written statement which runs as follows:

> "That in fact, there were offers, from other Parliamentary Constituencies in India, requesting this respondent to stand as a candidate for the Lok Sabha from those Constituencies and a final decision in regard to the Constituency was announced by the All India Congress Committee only on January, 29 1971, and she only held herself out as a candidate on filing her nomination at Raebareli on 1st of February, 1971 (underlining is by me.)" He had also referred to the visits made by Congress (R) leaders to Raebareli, particularly, Shri Dinesh Singh, and Shri Gulzarilal Nanda and by Prof. Sher Singh. He had not accepted the explanation that they had gone there of their own accord."

448. The learned Judge had also considered several English authorities but had noted that the law here was not the same as in England. It had been laid in **Munniswami Gounder v. Khader Sheriff, (1953) 4 Ele LR 283 (292)** (Ele. Tri., Vellore) where it was said:

> "In this respect the law in this country makes a significant departure and that departure, in our opinion, again emphasises the application of vital democratic principle, in the light of differing conditions. We may here note, briefly, a feature of the political practice in the United Kingdom, which repeatedly, colours and influences the English Cases. *viz.*, the fact that there a person is often adopted as a candidate by a political association without any move on his behalf, until a particular stage when the adoption is formalised by his consent."

449. I am unable to see what bearing the activities of opposition leaders and statements issued by them or Press Reports, with regard to the candidature of the original respondent No. 1 from the Raebareli constituency, had upon either an interpretation of her own statement of 29.12.1970 or the date on which she made a final decision to stand as a candidate from the Raebareli constituency or the communication of that decision by her to her constituency. The material relied upon by the learned Judge consisted of speculation and hearsay coming from persons who were certainly interested in finding out which constituency the Prime Minister, who had a choice of Gurgaon, a constituency much nearer to New Delhi, and, possibly of other constituencies as well if she only wanted to change it. Absence of proof of a desire to change the constituency is not proof of a positive "holding out". It has been repeatedly laid down in decided cases on the point that what is relevant is not what other people think or say about what a possible candidate would do but what the candidate concerned himself has said or done, so as to amount to "a holding out" as a candidate by the candidate from a particular constituency. Mere speculation or rumour circulated by other persons interested in finding out the Prime Minister's constituency could only prove what their own expectations or beliefs were. This type of "evidence", strictly speaking could not even be admissible unless it could be related to something actually said or done by the candidate. All that such "evidence" could prove was that people interested were speculating or indulging in guesswork. It seems to me that the learned Judge did not take into consideration the tactics in the political game which, to some extent, every party participating in such a game adopts. Some of those tactics are quite legitimate and honourable, but others are not.

450. The learned Judge referred to the contents of a speech made by the Prime Minister at Coimbatore in South India, in the early part of January, 1971, castigating one of the tactics of the opposition parties in choosing Shri Raj Narain to oppose her, for purposes of maximum "mud slinging". The learned Judge pointed out that the Prime Minister admitted in her evidence, that she could have said this in her speech at Coimbatore, She was not asked whether this amounted to holding herself out as a candidate from Raebareli constituency. If such a question had been asked, there is little doubt that she could have explained the statement by the context in which it was made, just as she had given the precise meaning of her statement of 29-12-1970, in the context in which it was made. Apparently, the context of the statement made in early January in Coimbatore was that the opposition parties had chosen a candidate, who, in the opinion of Prime Minister, possessed certain capacity for "mud slinging" which others did not have. The apparent object of what she mentioned in the speech was to expose tactics of opposition parties in choosing such a candidate from a constituency from which they thought the Prime Minister must be standing. It was obviously meant to disparage such tactics and not to disclose her own intentions or future course of action.

A healthy democratic practice or convention certainly is that the election of some candidates, of certain stature and standing or position in public life, is not contested. To point out that the opposition parties, far from intending to adopt such an attitude towards her, were busy devising methods of maligning her, could not reasonably be construed as a holding out of herself as a candidate from a particular constituency unless one was predisposed to put such a construction on every ambiguous statement of the Prime Minister, made anywhere after the dissolution of Parliament in December, 1970, until the election in the first week of March, 1971. Similarly, the context of the question of 29-12-1970, put to the Prime Minister at a conference at New Delhi, was that members of the opposition parties thought that she may be contesting from Gurgaon. In the light of the opposition tactics, which the Prime Minister herself had referred to in her speech at Coimbatore, it was not unlikely that the Prime Minister would have preferred to keep her own interventions about the constituency, from which she would ultimately stand, either a closely guarded secret or, at least, in a fluid State. In any case it was not likely that she would announce her own intention very clearly to stand from any particular constituency until it was considered by her or by her political advisers to be politically expedient to do so.

Again, it may be that the prospect of such a leader standing from a particular constituency was likely to have a politically exhilarating effect upon the workers or on party activities in that constituency. From such a point of view also the Congress Party (R) of the Prime Minister may also have preferred that the Prime Minister should not announce her decision until the last moment. A disputed question of fact on such a matter could not possibly be determined by a court on evidence of guess-work or speculations of others which are, strictly speaking, not relevant. I have indicated here that if some guess-work were permissible, as it is to give its benefit to the person against whom circumstantial evidence is to be used, other possible explanations and interpretations were not excluded. The question had to be decided on proof of the actual statements and actions of the candidate herself which could amount to clear and unequivocal expressions of intention, showing a decision to stand from a particular constituency, meant primarily for the benefit of the voters of the particular constituency so chosen by a candidate. Where was that evidence here?

451. It seems to me that the learned Judge had given an exaggerated importance to what were either not strictly relevant or insignificant matters in preference to what could be and was decisive and unequivocal. I do not think that the answer of the Prime Minister at the Press Conference on 29-12-1970 or the contents of her speech in Coimbatore, in early January, 1971, or even a declaration or announcement of the All India Congress Committee on 29-1-1971, assuming that there was such an announcement, could mean that the Prime Minister had herself finally decided to contest from the Raebareli constituency and had held herself out as a candidate for this constituency. This holding out had to take place by the Prime Minister herself and not by the Congress Committee. Even if the fact of a declaration made by the Congress Committee, on 29-1-1971, which is all that the written statement admits, proves that the Prime Minister was chosen by her party for this particular constituency on this date, her own decision on the matter could only come and was proved by her to have actually come later than that.

This admission was, in my opinion misconstrued by the learned Judge as a contradiction. In the absence of any evidence whatsoever which could conflict with the Prime Minister's statement about the actual date of her final decision to stand from this Constituency, it seems to me, that the learned Judge had no option reasonably open to him except to accept the correctness of the only and the best evidence on this question available in the case. The learned Judge in observing quite unnecessarily that his finding on this question was not going to be affected by the importance of the office held by Prime Minister seems subconsciously to have been so affected by it that he did not act on the normal rule that the best evidence of a person's state of mind is his or her own statements and actions and not of others. He seems to have felt that judicial independence consists in inverting this rule and judging the matter primarily from the evidence of the states of minds and opinions and actions of other individuals in the case of a Prime Minister of this country. I do not consider this to be a Judicially correct approach.

452. The fact that the tour programmes were circulated in advance for the Raebareli District, in which the Prime Minister made electioneering speeches, could also not determine what the final declaration of intention by the Prime Minister was going to be in regard to the Raebareli constituency. It is not enough that the candidate should have by then formed an intention to stand from a particular constituency. There is a gap between intent and action which has to be filled by proof of either statements or of conduct which amount to unequivocal declarations made to voters in the constituency in order to amount to a "holding out" to them. This seems to me to be the clear position in the law as laid down by Courts in this country on the meaning of section 79(b) of the Act.

453. It is significant that despite the large number of speeches and statements the Prime Minister must have made throughout the country, in this period, not a single statement made by her could even be cited in which she had said before 1-2-1971, that she was standing as a candidate from the Raebareli constituency. It is possible, as I have indicated above, that this may be a part of the political game or permissible party tactics so as to keep opposition parties guessing.

It seems to me that the learned Judge was overlooking the context, the probabilities, the natural course of events in such a case, the legal and logical relevance and effect of what he thought was decisive, and, finally, the importance of the statement of the Prime Minister herself on this question, supported by complete absence of any evidence to show that she had herself made any clear and decisive statement in any speech or conversation which could shake her stand, that her final decision and unequivocal act was the filing of a nomination paper as a candidate on 1-2-1971 at Raebareli. I may mention here that, according to the findings of the learned Judge himself, the question of the Prime Minister holding herself out as a candidate for the Raebareli constituency became quite immaterial after 25-1-1971, and, on the findings I have reached above the whole question becomes unimportant. However, I will indicate some authorities which the learned Judge himself had noticed.'

454. In **S. Khader Sheriff v. Munnuswami Gounder, (1955) 2 SCR 469 (473),** this Court said (473 of SCR): (777 of AIR):

> "When, therefore, a question arises under section 79(b) whether a person had become a candidate at a given point of time, what has to be seen is whether at that time he had clearly and unambiguously declared his intention to stand as a candidate, so that it could be said of him that he held himself out as a prospective candidate. That he has merely formed an intention to stand for election is not sufficient to make him a prospective candidate, because it is of the essence of the matter that he should hold himself out as a prospective candidate."

455. In **J.P. Rawat v. Krishna Dutt Paliwal, (1959) 20 Ele LR 443 (463) (All)** a Division Bench of the Allahabad High Court (V. Bhargava and J.N. Takru, JJ.). Following the decision of this Court in **S. Khader Sheriff's** case (supra) said (at p. 463):

> "The determining factor, therefore, is the decision of the candidate himself not the act of other persons or bodies adopting him as their candidate."

456. In **Haji Abdul Wahid v. B.V. Keskar, (1960) 21 Ele LR 409 (All)** it was held by a Division Bench of the Allahabad High Court (R.N. Gurtu and S.N. Dwivedi, JJ.):

> "(i) that the purchase of the nomination forms and voters lists, could not amount to holding out as a candidate: (ii) the arranging of public meetings by the officials and the respondent's moving about in the constituency on the 15th and 16th could not by themselves amount to a holding out by the respondent as a prospective candidate on those days in the absence of evidence to show that the respondent had utilised those meetings and tours for the purpose of making utterances of an electioneering character."

457. In **K.K. Mishra v. Banamali Babu, 38 Ele LR 451 at D. 475** the Orissa High Court, relying upon the following observations of this Court in S. Khader Sheriff's case (supra), held that a holding out within the meaning of section 79(b) must be by declaration of the candidate to an elector or to the electorate in a particular constituency and not to others:

> "It may be that the holding out which is contemplated by that section is to the Constituency: but if it is the Central Committee that has to decide who shall be adopted for election from the concerned constituency, any declaration made to the Committee is, in effect, addressed to the constituency through its accredited representative."

IF EARLIER LAW WAS UNCERTAIN – WAS MADE CERTAIN BY AMENDED LAW ACT 40 OF 1975 – AS TO WHEN A PERSON BECOMES A 'CANDIDATE' – RETROSPECTIVITY DOES NOT AFFECT FREE AND FAIR ELECTION – DOES NOT DESTROY BASIC STRUCTURE OF THE CONSTITUTION – HELD BEG, J.

458. The view of the learned Judge appears to me to run counter to the weight of authorities cited above. In any case, if there was any uncertainty at all, in the law, it has been removed by an amendment by section 7 of Act No. 40 of 1975 so that section 79(b) reads as follows:

> "'Candidate' means a person who has been or claims to have been duly nominated as a candidate at any election."

459. Learned Counsel for the election petitioner contended that this amendment, read with section 10 of the Act 40 of 1975, would retrospectively alter the "rules of the game" and would be destructive of the concept of free and fair elections, if it means that a person is only a candidate after he has been duly nominated and that he can indulge in any amount of corrupt practices until the day previous to his nomination.

460. Even if the present definition is a new one, it cannot be said to be arbitrary. The concept contained in it is found in the English definition which lays down: (*See*: *Halsbury's Laws of England* – 3rd Edn. Vol. 14 p. 162):

> "........... a candidate in relation to a Parliamentary election means a person who is elected to serve in Parliament at the election or a person who is nominated as a candidate at the election, or is declared by himself or by others to be a candidate on or after the day of the issue of the writ for the election..............."

The English definition is wider but contains, as its first part, the very concept found in our new definition of a "candidate."

461. Corrupt practices of a candidate cannot go unpunished, whether they are committed before or after he becomes a candidate when they amount to acts which come within the purview of electoral offences dealt with by Chapter 3. Sections 125, 126, 127, 127(A) or Chapter 9-A of the Indian Penal Code, offences, such as bribery for purposes of either inducing persons to vote or not to vote or to stand or not to stand as candidates, undue influence, and personation, are all dealt with here. These should be sufficient deterrents against perversion of the electoral process by a prospective candidate, who wants to adopt corrupt and objectionable means for gaining success at the polls.

462. The amendment appears to me to be within the unquestionable powers of Parliament to legislate, either prospectively or retrospectively with regard to election matters. I am unable to see how it is capable of being interpreted as an attack on free and fair elections, which, according to the reared Counsel for the election-petitioner, is part of the basic structure of the Constitution. I think it is important to bear in mind that Courts cannot take upon themselves the task of laying down what electoral laws should be. The law makers, assembled in Parliament, are presumed to know and understand their business of making laws for the welfare and well-being of the mass of people of this country for the protection of democracy and of free and fair elections, in accordance with the needs of the democratic process, better than Courts know and understand these. It is only where a piece of legislation clearly infringes a constitutional provision or indubitably overrides a constitutional purpose or mandate or prohibition that Courts can interfere. After having listened to the lengthy and vehement arguments of the election petitioner, I fail to see any invalidity in this provision.

RAISING OF ROSTRUMS – SUPPLY OF POWER FOR LOUDSPEAKERS – AMOUNTS TO TAKING ASSISTANCE OF DM, SP, XEN PWD, XEN HYDEL – AMOUNTED TO CORRUPT PRACTICE UNDER ISSUE NO. 3 – THIS FINDING OF HIGH COURT – CLEARLY ERRONEOUS – BEG, J.

463. I will now take up Issue No. 3 of the 1st set of issues on which after rejecting the contention that the erection of barricades and the provision of the police force for security purposes by the Government of U.P. during the election tours of the Prime Minister on 1-2-1971 and 25-2-1971 in the Raebareli constituency contravened section 123(7) the learned Judge held that nevertheless the arrangements made by the District Magistrate of Raebareli, the Superintendent of Police, Raebareli, the Executive Engineer. P.W.D. and the Engineer, Hydel Department for constructing rostrums and the supply of power for loud speakers, on the instructions given by the State Government, was a corrupt practice struck by the provisions of section 123(7) of the Act. As I have already indicated, the only evidence relied upon by the learned Judge for this extraordinary finding, after having rejected a similar allegation of a corrupt practice under Issue No. 2, on account of provision of the Air Force planes and helicopters flown by members of the Air Force, on necessary official instructions, to enable the Prime Minister to go to places where she could address election meetings on 1-2-1971 and 25-2-1971, was that the visits of the Prime Minister to her constituency on these occasions were preceded by the issue from the Prime Minister's Office of the tour programmes to the officials of the District through the State Government with the knowledge and consent of the Prime Minister. The State Government had acted in compliance with the instructions issued by the Comptroller and Auditor-General of India in 1958 read with rule 71(6) of what is known as the Blue Book.

The relevant part of this rule reads as follows:

> "It has been noticed that the rostrum arrangements are not always properly made because the hosts are sometimes unable to bear the cost. As the security of the Prime Minister is the concern of the State, all arrangements for putting up the rostrum, the barricades etc. at the meeting place, including that of an election meeting, will have to be made by the State Government concerned."

464. The Government of India had also issued a letter (Ex. A 21) dated 19-11-1969 inviting the attention of the State Governments to rule 71(6), mentioned above, and directing them to ensure that, whenever rostrums are constructed on such occasions, they should conform to certain specifications laid down with due regard to security considerations. The letter also directed the State Governments to bill the political party concerned with expenses upto 25% of the cost of the rostrums or Rs. 25,000, whichever is less. The letter also directed that extravagance in expenditure should be avoided.

465. It was proved by the evidence of Shri R.K. Kaul (P.W. 58) the Home Secretary in the Government of U.P., that rostrums and arrangements for barricading are made by the local officials employing contractors for the purpose, under instructions issued by the State Government. The reasoning adopted by the learned Judge, however was that as the Prime Minister's Office had issued her tour programmes, with the approval of the Prime Minister, the result must be, in the language of the learned Judge himself:

> "......... the tour programmes carried on an implied direction that the State Government should also get constructed rostrums and arrange for public address system for the election meetings to be addressed by her on 1st of February 1971 and 25th of February, 1971. It should be presumed that the respondent No. 1, as Prime Minister, of this country, and with five years experience of that office behind her in 1971, also knew that the said work was to be done by the officers of the State Government."

466. This meant that the learned Judge was holding the Prime Minister herself responsible for instructing the State Government knowing that it will make the necessary arrangements through its servants. The case thus accepted, that the Prime Minister was employing the State Government as her agency in procuring the aid of the officers concerned, was neither set up nor put in issue. Apart from this objection, the learned Judge overlooked that the provisions of section 123(7) were intended to prevent solicitation for aid and not sending of information to the State Government in the course of ordinary official business even if the candidate concerned knows that the State Government is bound, under the rules, to make the necessary arrangements dictated by the needs of security of the Prime Minister and convenience of the Public.

467. The view of the learned Judge involves holding that the "persona" (a term derived from the concept of the mask worn by Greek actors on the stage in a drama) of a candidate during an election must not only be different from that of the Prime Minister, but also that, when the two capacities are held by the same person, what is due to the occupant of the office of the Prime Minister must be withdrawn when the same person acts as a candidate. On a similar argument, with regard to use of helicopters and aeroplanes, the learned Judge himself had refused to acknowledge what amounts to a separable legal personality of a candidate in the eyes of law. The ground given for this difference between the use of aeroplanes and helicopters by the Prime Minister and the use of rostrums by her was that the former was more connected with the office or capacity of the Prime Minister and that the latter was exclusively meant for her use in the capacity of a candidate. Even if we were to recognise this distinction between the "persona" of the Prime Minister and that of a candidate, it is impossible to separate the special arrangements made for the security of the person of the Prime Minister from those to which she may be entitled as a candidate only. It is impossible to deny at any time the facilities and precautions meant for the person who holds the office of the Prime Minister to the person just because she also figures as a candidate at an election. So long as the person is the same what is meant for the person must be attributed to the person or capacity of the Prime Minister and not to that of a candidate only. The learned Judge however, thought that a candidate, who happens to hold the office of the Prime Minister of the country, is not entitled to the facilities or precautionary measures taken to protect the person of the holder of the office when electioneering as though the Prime Minister and the candidate were two different persons. He was unable to see that, so long as the person was the same, the distinction between the two capacities or personal, for the purposes for which facilities were given and protection provided, was both factually as well as legally impossible and quite immaterial.

468. I also think that the learned Judge erred in holding that such a case could be one of solicitation of official aid and assistance at all. It is a case in which certain precautions are taken and arrangements made almost "automatically", if one may use this word here, by officers of the State as a matter of duty towards the office held by a candidate who undoubtedly enjoys certain advantages which an ordinary candidate cannot have. It is as futile to complain of such a distinction made as it is to complain that a candidate possesses certain advantages at an election because of the personal services rendered to the country or distinctions achieved by the candidate. Again there are advantages which attach themselves to a candidate because of that candidate's personal qualities qualifications, capacities or background. The appurtenances of office or distinctions achieved are, in my opinion, comparable to such personal advantages insofar as they are not enjoyed because they are "obtained" or "procured". If such a result in law is unfair, it is not for Courts to find a remedy by accepting the argument advanced before us also: that those who enjoy the benefits of office must be made to realize and suffer some of its handicaps. This clearly means the benefit which law gives, without solicitation by the candidate must be converted by a judicial flat, into a disadvantage and a handicap. It is for Parliament to step in and change the law if an alteration of it is considered necessary by it. The only change that need be made in the law, if that could be the legislative intent is to provide that the holder of any office for the time being would not be qualified to stand at an election. In that event, holders of all Ministerial Offices will have to resign before they offer themselves as candidates. But, such is not our law found in the 1951 Act or anywhere else, I think that it would be extending the scope of section 123(7) too wide to hold that the facilities, automatically provided by the State to the Prime Minister, by virtue of his or her office, are also struck by a provision directed against solicitation of official aid and assistance by candidates.

469. The learned Judge had mentioned a Division Bench decision of the Allahabad High Court in **Motilal v. Mangla Prasad, AIR 1958 All 794 (797)** where it was laid down:

> "We think that the word 'obtain' in section 123(7) has been used in the essence of the meaning which connotes purpose behind the action of the candidate. The word has not been used in the sub-section in the sense of a mere passive receipt of assistance without the candidate even being conscious of the fact that the assistance has been rendered. In order to bring the case under sub-section (7) it must be shown that the candidate did make some effort or perform some purposeful act in order to get the assistance."

470. He had also cited another Division Bench decision of the Assam High Court in **Biresh Mishra v. Ram Nath Sharma, 17 Ele LR 243 (253)** that:

> "The words 'obtain' or 'procure or 'abetting or attempting to obtain or procure' any assistance necessarily imply some effort on the part of candidate or his agent. Mere passive receipt of assistance is not contemplated by the section."

471. I think that the import of such observations was clearly what has been laid down repeatedly by this Court and emphasized by me already – that a *mens rea* as well as an *actus reus* must be shown, on the evidence on record, before a candidate can be held guilty of a corrupt practice. In **Sheopal Singh v. Ram Pratap, (1965) 1 SCR 175** this Court held, in dealing with the allegation of corrupt practice under section 121(4) of the Act, that *mens rea* was a necessary ingredient of the corrupt practice and that the doctrine of constructive knowledge was not applicable here.

'MENS REA' AS WELL AS *'ACTUS REUS'* ON PART OF APPELLANT OR HER AGENT NOT PROVED BY RESPONDENT – DESERVED DISMISSAL ON THIS GROUND ALONE – BEG, J.

472. In the case before us, the election petitioner alleged a wrongfully "obtained and procured" assistance due to acts of the original respondent as well as her election agent Shri Yashpal Kapur. Hence, proof of actual *mens rea* as well as *actus reus* on the part of either the candidate herself or her election agent had to be given. This was not done. The election petition was, therefore, liable to be rejected on this ground alone.

BY AMENDMENT ACT 40 OF 1975 PARLIAMENT MADE THE LAW MORE CLEAR – RETROSPECTIVE – AMENDMENT IS VALID – HELD BEG, J.

473. If, however, there was any doubt or uncertainty on the matter, the view taken by the learned Judge had, at any rate, directed the attention of Parliament to the need for a clarification of the law which became necessary. It is not possible to object to the motives behind the legislation on this ground. Parliament could certainly set right a defect in law which may have come to its notice as a result of the learned Judge's interpretation of section 123(7). The defect may be due to a possible ambiguity. In order to clarify the law section 7 of the Act 40 of 1975 inserted a proviso at the end of section 123(7), which runs as follows:

> "Provided that where any person, in the service of the Government and belonging to any of the classes aforesaid, in the discharge or purported discharge of his official duty makes any arrangements or provides any

facilities or does any other act or thing for, to or in relation to, any candidate or his agent or any other person acting with the consent of the candidate or his election agent, (whether by reason of the office held by the candidate or for any other reason), such arrangements, facilities or act or thing shall not be deemed to be assistance for the furtherance of the prospects of that candidate's election."

474. The learned Counsel for the election petitioner has very fairly, conceded that, if this amendment, which is retrospective by reason of the operation of section 10 of Act 40 of 1975, is valid, the decision of the learned Judge on the above mentioned issue No. 3 would not be sustainable. Such a concession incidentally means that whatever facilities were given to the Prime Minister by the construction of rostrums or provision of power for the loud-speakers for which the party was also billed, at least to the extent of 1/4th of the expenses of the rostrums and wholly as regards the expenses of loud-speakers, were given by the officers concerned in the performance of their official duties. This is not the same thing as "obtaining" or "procuring" by solicitation.

475. Learned Counsel for the election petitioner has, however, put forward the same objection to this retrospective amendment as the one against a change in the definition of "candidate". It appears to me that this amendment is merely clarificatory of the state of law as it really was even before the amendment. On the view I take, there is no question here of altering the "rules of the game" to the disadvantage of the election petitioner. The disadvantage, if any, was there already because of the consequences which I think, legally and naturally flow from the occupation of the high office of the Prime Minister of this country.

476. There is no attack on the validity of section 123(7) of the Act as it existed before the amendment. Hence, there could be no challenge to the validity of the amendment if it does not, as I think it does not, change the law but merely clarifies it.

AMENDMENT ACT 40 OF 1975 KEPT IN 9TH SCHEDULE BY 39TH AMENDMENT – AMENDMENTS ACTS – CONSTITUTIONAL AMENDMENT ARE *BONA FIDE* – CANNOT BE ASSAILED ON GROUND OF BASIC STRUCTURE – BEG, J.

477. Learned Counsel for the election petitioner contended that, as a candidate at an election the Prime Minister and an ordinary candidate should enjoy equal protection of the laws and should be afforded equal facilities irrespective of the office occupied by one of two or more candidates. Such an attack upon the validity of this amendment seems to me to be possible only under the provisions of Article 14 of the Constitution. But, as Act 40 of 1975, has been placed by section 5 of the 39th Amendment in the protected 9th Schedule of the Constitution, it becomes immune from such an attack. After the practically unanimous opinion of this Court in **Kesavananda Bharati's** case (supra), that such an immunisation of an enactment from an attack based upon an alleged violation of the chapter on fundamental rights is constitutionally valid, I do not think that a similar attack can be brought in through the back door of a "basic structure" of the Constitution. Moreover. I am unable to see how this particular amendment has anything to do with damage to any part of the "basic structure" of the Constitution. Even if an attack on the ground of a violation of Article 14 were open today. I think that the occupation of such a high and important office as that of the Prime Minister of this country, with all its great hazards and trials, would provide a rational basis for reasonable classification in respect of advantages possessed by a Prime Minister as a candidate at an election due to arrangements made necessary by considerations of safety and protection of the life and person of the Prime Minister. Hence, I am unable to see any sustainable ground of attack at all on the validity of this provision.

HIGH COURT FINDING HAD MANIFEST ERRORS – OBSERVES BEG, J.

478. Before I proceed further, I may mention that I have dealt with the findings of the learned Judge, assailed by the original respondent's appeal No. 887 of 1975, perhaps in greater length and depth, after going through the evidence in the case, than I had set out to do. I have done so for several reasons. *Firstly*, I think that the nature of the attack upon the bona fides of the amendments made, although ordinarily not even entertainable, having been permitted due to the constitutional importance and gravity of the allegations made, this question could not, in my opinion, be satisfactorily dealt with without considering the nature of the findings and the evidence at some length so as to satisfy myself that no such question could possibly arise here. *Secondly*, if the amendments were made necessary for reasons brought out fully only by dealing with facts and finding in this case, they could not give rise to any grounds to suggest that there was anything wrong in making amendments to remove such reasons. Therefore, I think, it was necessary to go into these for determining whether the amendments are good. *Thirdly*, even if the amendments are valid, we had to be satisfied that the tests of corrupt practices alleged are not fulfilled despite the concession of the election petitioner's learned Counsel that this would be the position. *Fourthly*, I find that the learned Judge has made certain manifest errors in appraising the evidence and interpreting the law which call for rectification by this Court as no other authority can properly do this.

479. It appears to me, as already indicated by me, that the learned Judge was perhaps unduly conscious of the fact that he was dealing with the case of the Prime Minister of this country. He, therefore, as he indicated in his judgments, seemed anxious not to allow this fact to affect his judgment. Nevertheless, when it came to appraising evidence, it seems to me that, as I have already pointed out, he applied unequal standards in assessing its worth so as to largely relieve the election petitioner of the very heavy onus of proof that lies on a party which challenges the verdict of the electors by allegations of corrupt practices. He also appeared to be attempting to achieve by means of judicial interpretation, an equalisation of conditions under which, in his opinion candidates should contest elections. I think it is not the function of Courts to embark on attempts to achieve what is only in the power of Parliament to accomplish, that is to say, to bring about equality of conditions where the law permits justifiable discrimination. As this Court has repeatedly pointed out, to treat unequally situated and circumstanced person as though they were equals in the eye of law for all purposes is not really to satisfy the requirements of the equality contemplated by the Constitution.

480. As regards appraisal of evidence in such a case. I may point out that, in **Rahim Khan v. Khurshid Ahmed, (1974) 2 SCC 660 (666, 672)** Krishna Iyer, J. speaking for this Court, said:

> "An election once held is not to be treated in a light-hearted manner and defeated candidates or disgruntled electors should not get away with it by filing election petitions on unsubstantial grounds and irresponsible evidence, thereby introducing a serious element of uncertainty in the verdict already rendered by the electorates. An election is a politically sacred public act, not of one person or of one official, but of the collective will of the whole constituency. Courts naturally must respect this public expression secretly written and show extreme reluctance to set aside or declare void an election which has already been held unless clear and cogent testimony compelling the Court to uphold the corrupt practice alleged against the returned candidate is adduced. Indeed, election petitions where corrupt practices are imputed must be regarded as proceedings of a quasi-criminal nature wherein strict proof

is necessary. The burden is, therefore, heavy on him who assails an election which has been concluded."

This Court also said there (672) (of SCC) = (at p. 299 of AIR):

> "We regard it as extremely unsafe, in the present climate of kilkenny-cat election competition and partisan witnesses wearing robes of veracity, to upturn a hard won electoral victory merely because lip service to a corrupt practice has been rendered by some sanctimonious witnesses. The Court must look for serious assurance, unlying circumstances or unimpeachable documents to uphold grave charges of corrupt practices which might not merely cancel the election result, but extinguish many a man's public life."

CROSS-APPEAL NO. 909 OF 1975 FILED BY RESPONDENT – ISSUE NOS. 2-4-7 NOT ASSAILED – OBSERVES BEG, J.

481. I will now take up the election petitioner's Cross Appeal No. 909/75. Learned Counsel for the election petitioner, very properly and frankly, conceded that he could not successfully assail the findings of the learned Judge on issue Nos. 4 and 7 relating to alleged distribution of quilts, blankets, dhotis, and liquor by workers of the original respondent or the alleged provision of free conveyance by vehicles said to have been hired by Shri Kapur. The evidence on these questions given by the election petitioner was too flimsy and extravagant and was met by overwhelming evidence to the contrary given by respectable residents of localities in which the alleged corrupt practices are said to have taken place. No driver of any conveyance was produced. Nor was any person produced who had actually received any alleged gift or had consumed anything provided on behalf of the successful candidate.

482. As regards Issue No. 2, relating to the use of airplanes and helicopters by the original respondent which was not separately pressed evidently because it was covered by the amendment which was assailed by the election petitioner, the reasons I have given on issue No. 3 for upholding the validity of the amendment relating to the services rendered by Government Officials and members of defence forces in due discharge of their duties are enough to cover the points raised.

HIGH COURT RIGHTLY HELD SYMBOL OF COW AND CALF NOT RELIGIOUS – AMENDED LAW MAKES THE THINGS MORE CLEAR – OBSERVES BEG, J.

483. As regards Issue No. 6, relating to the adoption of the drawing of a cow and a calf as the symbol of the Congress: (R) Party of the original respondent, the finding of the Trial Court, based on a large number of authorities, was that this is not a religious symbol. This question was directly decided in **Bhartendra Singh v. Ram Sahai Pandey, AIR 1972 MP 167 (179); Shital Prasad Misra v. Nitiraj Singh Chaudhary,*** decided by M.P. High Court on 21-7-1971; and **Sri Prasanna Das Damodar Das Palwar v. Indu Lal Kanhaiya Lal Yajnik,**** decided on 27-8-1971 by the High Court of Gujarat. The learned Judge also cited the following cases where it was decided that a cow is not a religious symbol:

> **Shah Jayanthi Lal Amba Lal v. Kasturi Lal Nagin Das Dosi, (1968) 36 ELR 188 (Guj); Baijnath Singh Vaidya v. R.P. Singh, (1968) 36 ELR 327 (All) Bishambhar Dayal v. Raj Rajeshwar, (1968) 39 ELR 363 (376) (All); Dinesh Dang v. Daulat Ram, (1968) 39 ELR 463 (476) (Raj); Shyamlal v. Mansa Din, (1968) 37 ELR 67 (All); B.P. Maurya v. Prakashvir Shastri, (1968) 37 ELR 137 (147) (All); Sohadar Rai v. Ram Singh Aharwar, (1968) 37 ELR 176 (188) (MP); Vishwanath Pd. v. Salamat Ullah, (1965) 27 ELR 145 (186) (All)** and **Lachchi Ram v. J.P. Mukhariya, (1953) 9 ELR 149 (157 (Ele. Tri. Gwalior).**

* M.P. Gazette, 23-6-1971, Pt. I. P. 809 paras 18 to 23.

** Gujarat Gazette decided on 20-7-1972, Pt. 4C, p. 1042 (1355 to 1362).

484. In addition, section 8 of the Act 40 of 1975 has made the position on this point also very clear by providing that, in section 123 of the Act in clause (3), the following proviso shall be inserted at the end:

> "Provided that no symbol allotted under this Act to a candidate shall be deemed to be a religious symbol or a national symbol for the purposes of this clause."

AMENDMENTS WERE CHALLENGED ON THEIR LIKELY MISUSE – SUCH GROUNDS CANNOT SUCCEED – OBSERVES BEG, J.

485. As in the case of other amendments, this amendment was also challenged on behalf of the election petitioner on the ground that it could be misused. I am afraid that attacks made on such sweeping suggestions of likelihood of misuse, in future, cannot possibly succeed. It has been repeatedly laid down by this Court that the possibility of misuse of a power given by a statute cannot invalidate the provision conferring the power. (*See*: **Dr. N.B. Khare v. State of Delhi, (1950) SCR 519 (526); State of West Bengal v. A.A., (1952) SCR 284 at D. 301; R.K. Dalmia v. Justice Tendolkar, (1959) SCR 279 (306); T.K. Mudaliar v. Venkatachalam, (1955) 2 SCR 1196 (1239); Chitralekha v. State of Mysore, (1964) 6 SCR 368 (382-383); M.R. Deka v. N.E.F. Rly., (1964) 5 SCR 683**). The occasion to complain can only arise when there is such alleged misuse. Even the possibility of such misuse of this power by so responsible an official as the Election Commissioner cannot be easily conceived of.

486. It was submitted that the Election Commissioner's decision on this question was unreasonable. The best class of evidence as to what is and what is not to be reasonably regarded as a religious symbol, according to the customs, mores, traditions, and outlook of the people of a country at a certain time consists of contemporaneous decisions of Courts. It is useless to quote passages from -ancient texts about the sacredness of the cow in support of the use of the cow as a religious symbol today. The use of pictures of this excellent and useful animal is so frequently made today for commercial purposes or purposes other then religious that the representation of a cow and a calf cannot, except in some special and purely religious contexts, be held to have a religious significance. I therefore, see no force at all in this submission of the election petitioner.

ISSUE NO. 9. – HIGH COURT RIGHTLY HELD EXPENSES WITHIN LIMITS – KANWARLAL GUPTA'S CASE ALSO DISCUSSED – HELD BEG, J.

487. The only question argued with some seriousness in the election petitioner's appeal was that the election expenses, which form the subject-matter of Issue No. 9, had exceeded the limit of authorised expenditure imposed by section 77 of the Act read with Rule 90. On this issue, the learned Judge had considered every allegedly omitted item of expense very thoroughly and had reached the conclusion that the following 3 items, totalling upto Rs. 18,183.50 had to be added to the return of election expenses of the original respondent which mentioned items totaling upto Rs. 12,892.97. These were: (1) Cost of rostrums Rs. 16,000: (2) Cost of installation of loud-speakers Rs. 1,951: (3) Cost of providing transport for one journey by car Rs. 232.50.

488. On this issue, the learned Judge's appreciation of evidence was not only very thorough and correct but the application of the governing law on the subject also appears to me to be faultless. Ordinarily, we do not, sitting even in first appeals on questions of law as well as of fact in election cases, go into findings of fact arrived at without misapplication of law or errors of approach to evidence. In the case before us, two main questions and one subsidiary question, each of which is a mixed question of fact and law, which deserve consideration by this Court on this issue, have been raised before us. I will deal with these questions briefly seriatim.

489. The first question is: If the party, which a candidate represents, spends or others also spend some money on his or her election, is this expenditure one which can be or should be properly included in the statement of election expenses submitted by the candidate? Arguments before us have proceeded on the assumption made by both sides that some expenditure was incurred by the Congress (R) Party and some expenditure must also have been incurred by those who either voluntarily helped or even thrust their supposed assistance, whether it was helpful or not, upon those managing the original respondent's election, which was not shown as part of her election expenses. Is the successful candidate bound, under the law, to show this also as part of election expenses?

490. This question assumed special importance after the decision of this Court in **Kanwarlal Gupta v. Amarnath Chawla, AIR 1975 SC 308 (315-316)**, where a Division Bench of this Court observed:

> "Now, if a candidate were to be subject to the limitation of the ceiling, but the political party sponsoring him or his friends and supporters were to be free to spend as much as they like in connection with his election, the object of imposing the ceiling would be completely frustrated and the beneficent provision enacted in the interest of purity and genuineness of the democratic process would be wholly emasculated. The mischief sought to be remedied and the evil sought to be suppressed would enter the political arena with redoubled force and vitiate the political life of the country. The great democratic ideal of social, economic and political justice and equality of status and opportunity enshrined in the Preamble of our Constitution would remain merely a distant dream eluding our grasp. The legislators could never have intended that what the individual candidate cannot do, the political party sponsoring him or his friends and supporters should be free to do. That is why the legislators wisely interdicted not only the incurring but also the authorising of excessive expenditure by a candidate. When the political party sponsoring a candidate incurs expenditure in connection with his election, as distinguished from expenditure on general party propaganda, and the candidate knowingly takes advantage of it or participates in the programme or activity or fails to disavow the expenditure or consents to it or acquiesces in it, it would be reasonable to infer, save in special circumstances, that he impliedly authorised the political party to incur such expenditure and he cannot escape the rigour of the ceiling by saying that he has not incurred the expenditure, but his political party has done so. A party candidate does not stand apart from his political party and if the political party does not want the candidate to incur the disqualification, it must exercise control over the expenditure which may be incurred by it directly to promote the poll prospects of the candidate. The same proposition must also hold good in case of expenditure incurred by friends and supporters directly in connection with the election of the candidate."

491. After making the above-mentioned observations, the apparently broad sweep of the observation was limited as follow:

> "It may be contended that this would considerably inhibit the electoral campaign of political parties but we do not think so. In the *first* place, a political party is free to incur any expenditure it likes on its general party propaganda though, of course, in this area also some limitative ceiling is eminently desirable coupled with filing of return of expenses and an independent machinery to investigate and take action. It is only where expenditure is incurred which can be identified with the election of a given candidate that it would be liable to be added to the expenditure of that candidate as being impliedly authorised

by him. *Secondly,* if there is continuous community involvement in political administration punctuated by activated phases of well-discussed choice of candidates by popular participation in the process of nomination, much of unnecessary expenditure which is incurred today could be avoided."

492. It is not necessary to quote further from the judgment which suggests taking of steps for reform of electoral machinery so as to ensure "choice of candidates by popular participation in the process of nomination," because that would take us into a territory beyond mere interpretation of the law as it exists. It is clear from the passages cited and later parts of the judgment that the earlier decisions of this Court, requiring proof of authorisation by the candidate of the election expenditure for which he could be held responsible, and, in particular **Rananjaya Singh v. Baijnath Singh, (1955) 1 SCR 671** which I shall refer to again a little later, are considered. It is enough to observe that the passages quoted above rest on the assumption that, where there are special circumstances in a case which constitute a political party an implied agent of the candidate himself, the candidate will be responsible. It was also suggested there that a political party itself must exercise some control over the expenses of the candidate it sets-up. The objection was to a candidate merely using the political party as a channel or cover for expenses incurred by the candidate himself. This explains the exclusion of expenses for "general party propaganda" from those for which, the candidate is accountable and liable. Such expenses could be, it was held, properly incurred by the party itself, irrespective of the source from which the party obtained funds for carrying it on. What is declared to be expense incurred by the candidate is that expense which his party may incur either as an express or implied agent of the candidate and that only.

493. The difficulty which faces the election petitioner at the outset in taking up a case of implied authorisation, on the strength of anything observed or decided by this Court in **Kanwarlal Gupta's** case (supra), is that no such case was set-up here. The petition does not say that the local Congress (R) Party was really an express or implied agent of the original respondent or that it had acted in a manner from which it could be inferred that the funds were really being supplied by the original respondent and were merely being spent by the party or its workers for the election under consideration. No facts or circumstances were at all indicated either in the petition or in evidence from which such inferences were possible. On the other hand, what is sought to be pointed out now in the case before us is that a sum of Rs. 70,000 was shown to have been received from some undisclosed sources by Shri Dal Bahadur Singh, the President of the District Congress Committee at Raebareli, and that a large part of it was shown, from entries in the bank account of the President of this Committee, to have been disbursed during or soon after the election. The responsibility of the District Congress Committee was, however, to carry on propaganda and supply information in 3 Parliamentary Constituencies. Neither party summoned Shri Dal Bahadur Singh to give evidence so that it could not be proved what proportion of any of this sum of Rs. 70,000 was spent and in what work and for which of the 3 Parliamentary constituencies. All that was alleged, in paragraph 13 of the petition, is that the "expenditure incurred by the respondent No. 1, Smt. Indira Nehru Gandhi and/or her election agent Shri Yashpal Kapur was much more then Rs. 35,000 which was the permissible amount." After that particulars of 11 items were given out of which the first was hiring of 32 vehicles whose numbers are mentioned. There is no mention whatsoever in this list of any sum paid either by the original respondent or by anyone else on her behalf to Shri Dal Bahadur Singh or of any expense incurred on behalf of the original respondent by this gentleman. The principle that no amount of evidence can be looked into on a case not set-up is sufficient to dispose of this evidence of a cheque of Rs. 70,000 received by Shri Dal Bahadur Singh.

494. It is true that the case set up is that the prescribed limit of expenditure was exceeded and the case is so stated that items beyond the list could conceivably be added. Nevertheless, unless and until there is a plea that whatever was spent by the Congress (R) Party, either as an express or implied agent of the original respondent, this loop-hole left in the petition, would not suffice. Section 83(1)(b) of the Act contains the mandatory provisions that the petition "shall set forth full particulars of any corrupt practice that the petitioner alleges, including as full a statement as possible of the name of the parties alleged to have committed such corrupt practice and the date and place of the commission of each such practice."

KANWARLAL GUPTA'S CASE TOOK CONTRARY VIEW – AMENDMENT 58 OF 1974 CORRECTED IT – OBSERVES BEG, J.

495. The judgment of this Court, in **Kanwarlal Gupta's** case (supra) discusses a number of cases decided by this Court which shows that it is not enough to prove expenditure of money by a candidate's party or friends or relations. It must be also proved that this was expenditure authorised by the candidate and incurred as the candidate's express or implied agent. These cases were:

Rananjaya Singh v. Baijnath Singh, (1955) 1 SCR 671; Ram Dayal v. Brijraj Singh, (1970) 1 SCR 530; Magraj Patodia v. R.K. Birla, (1971) 2 SCR 118 and B. Rajagopala Rao v. N.G. Ranga, AIR 1971 SC 267.

496. After examining this catena of cases, I think, with great respect, that the decision of this Court in **Kanwarlal Gupta's** case (supra) could be understood to point in a direction contrary to that in which the previous cases were decided. Hence, it appears to me that the amendment made by Act 58 of 1974, by adding the explanation (1) to section 77(1) of the Act, could be justified as merely an attempt to restore the law as it had been understood to be previous to decision of this Court in **Kanwarlal Gupta's** case (supra):

> "*Explanation 1.*—Notwithstanding any judgment, order or decision of any court to the contrary any expenditure incurred or authorised in connection with the election of a candidate by a political party or by any other association or body of persons or by any individual (other than the candidate or his election agent) shall not be deemed to be, and shall not ever be deemed to have been, expenditure in connection with the election incurred or authorised by the candidate or by his election agent for the purposes of this sub-section:
>
> Provided that nothing contained in this *Explanation* shall effect:
>
> (a) any judgment, order or decision of the Supreme Court whereby the election of a candidate to the House of the People or to the Legislative Assembly of a State has been declared void or set aside before the commencement of the Representation of the People (Amendment) Ordinance, 1974.
>
> (b) any judgment, order or decision of a High Court whereby the election of any such candidate has been declared void or set aside before the commencement of the said Ordinance if no appeal has been preferred to the Supreme Court against such judgment, order or decision of the High Court before such commencement and the period of limitation for filing such appeal has expired before such commencement."

497. It appears to me that both parties to the case now before us were under the impression that the expenses incurred by a political party over its candidate's election was outside the prescribed limit which operated only against expenditure by a candidate himself. Hence, the petitioner had not pleaded expenses incurred by the party of the original respondent as expenses authorised by the original respondent. The test of authorisation would naturally be the creation of a liability to reimburse whoever spends the money and not necessarily the provision of money before-hand by the candidate on whose behalf it is spent. Nevertheless, the authorisation has to be set up and proved. In the written statement filed on behalf of he original respondent, it was very frankly admitted that some expenditure, incurred by the local Congress Party itself, had not been shown as election expenses of the candidate herself. This was the position because, on the side of the original respondent also, the law was understood to be as it is found now clarified by the addition of an explanation to section 77(1) of the Act.

498. The second question which arises for consideration is: if some expenses are shown or admitted to have been incurred by the candidate's party or third persons over the election of the successful candidate, is it possible to separate it from a total expenditure on more than one constituency by some process of estimation and apportionment? Of course, this question can only arise if it is first proved that whatever expenditure was incurred by candidate's party or by some other person, who may be a friend a relation or a sympathiser was incurred in circumstances from which it can be inferred that the successful candidate would reimburse the party or person who incurred it. As I have already held, it is only then that expenditure could be held to be authorised by the candidate. It is not enough that some advantage accrued or expenditure was incurred within the knowledge of the candidate. This was very clearly brought out in **Rananjaya Singh v. Baijnath Singh, (1955) 1 SCR 671.** In this case, the Manager, Assistant Manager, 20 Ziladars, and peons of the proprietor of an estate in Uttar Pradesh had carried on election work, after having been given a holiday on full pay by the proprietor of the estate who was the father of the successful candidate. It was contended that in as much as these persons were virtually employees of the candidate himself, their salary for the day must be added to the list of election expenses. This Court repelled this contention on the ground that this extra expenditure had not been authorised by the candidate or his agent. Hence, it need not be shown as an item of election expense. Voluntary expenditure by friends relations, or sympathisers and expenditure incurred by a candidate's party, without any request or authorisation by the candidate, has never been deemed to be expenditure by the candidate himself; *See*: **Ram Dayal v. Brijraj Singh, (1970) 1 SCR 530; Magraj Petodia v. R.K. Birla, (1971) 2 SCR 118.**

VEHICLES NOT REQUIRED FOR APPELLANT – HIGH COURT FINDING CORRECT – OBSERVES BEG, J.

499. An attempt was then made to pass the responsibility on to the original respondent for the expenses of at least 23 vehicles whose numbers are mentioned in a letter dated 25th February, 1971, written by Shri Kapur, who then (was) the original respondent's election agent, and sent to the District Officer, Raebareli stating as follows:

> "Sir, I beg to say that the District Congress Committee, Raebareli has taken the following cars for election purposes in the three Parliamentary Constituencies, Raebareli. Amethi and Ram Sanehi Ghat. You may, therefore, kindly release them."

After giving numbers of the vehicles the letter proceeds:

> "It is, therefore, requested that the abovesaid cars may kindly be released without delay. The letter of the President of District Congress Committee about the abovesaid cars is enclosed herewith."

The letter of the President of the Committee, mentioned by Shri Kapur, was a rather urgent request made to him by Shri Dal Bahadur Singh, on 24-2-1971. (Ex. A-43), after informing him that he is in difficulties as he had tried to find out unsuccessfully the whereabouts of Shri. V. Vajpayee, who was contesting election from Amethi Parliamentary Constituency, and of Shri Baiznath Kureel, who was contesting the election from Ram Sanehi Parliamentary Constituency. He, therefore, asked Shri Kapur, the election agent of the original respondent to send a letter to the District Officer, who had refused to release the vehicles without the endorsement of the candidate concerned or his or her election agent.

500. It is clear from the above-mentioned correspondence that Shri Kapur was not speaking on behalf of the other two candidates of adjoining Parliamentary Constituencies. He was not even undertaking to pay anything for the use of the vehicles on behalf of the original respondent. Shri Kapur also did not state that these vehicles were needed for work in the original respondent's constituency. He merely forwarded the letter with a request for compliance with what Shri D.B. Singh wanted. Shri Dal Bahadur Singh was concerned and entrusted with conducting electioneering work in three adjoining Parliamentary Constituencies successfully. He had, therefore, made a frantic appeal to Shri Kapur to come to his help. Shri Kapur, without concealing any fact, had sent this very letter with a request for the release of the vehicles to the District Officer concerned. On this evidence, the learned Judge came to the conclusion that it was not possible to say which vehicles, said to be jeeps, had been utilized for election work and in which constituency. The learned Judge after considering the evidence recorded the finding that it was not possible to hold that the 23 vehicles in question had been used exclusively for the purposes of the election of the original respondent and not for "general party propaganda purposes" for which the original respondent was not liable to pay.

501. In **Hans Raj v. Hari Ram, (1972) 40 Ele LR 125 (128-129) (SC)** this Court in a similar situation said:

> "Whichever way one looks at the matter it is quite clear in view of the decision of this Court reported in **Rananjaya Singh v. Baijnath Singh, (1955) 1 SCR 671** that the expenditure must be by the candidate himself and any expenditure in his interest by others (not his agents within the meaning of the term in the election law) is not to be taken note of. Here the hiring was by the Congress Committee which was not such an agent and, therefore, the amount spent by the Congress Committee cannot be taken as an amount which must compulsorily be included in the expenditure over the election by a candidate. If this be the position, we have to decide whether this amount spent on the jeeps must be taken to be an expenditure made by the candidate himself. Of that there is no evidence. The bill stands in the name of the Congress Committee and was presumably paid by the Congress Committee also. The evidence, however, is that this jeep was used on behalf of the returned candidate and to that extent we subscribe to the finding given by the learned judge. Even if it be held that the candidate was at bottom the hirer of the jeep and the expenditure on it must be included in his account, the difficulty is that this jeep was used also for the general Congress propaganda in other constituencies."

502. In **Shah Jayantilal Ambalal v. Kasturilal Nagindas Doshi, (1972) 42 Ele LR 307 (311)**, this Court held:

> "It is now well-settled that expenses incurred by a political party in support of its candidates do not come within the mischief of section 123(6) read with section 77 of the Act."

503. In **Samant N. Balakrishna v. George Fernandez, (1969) 3 SCR 603 (637)** this Court pointed out:

> "In India all corrupt practices stand on the same footing. The only difference made is that when consent is proved on the part of the candidate or his election agent to the commission of corrupt practice, that itself is

sufficient. When a corrupt practice is committed by an agent and there is no such consent then the petitioner must go further and prove that the result of the election insofar as the returned candidate is concerned was materially affected."

504. However, as I have already held, there is no case or evidence before us that the Congress Party was the agent, express or implied of the original respondent or acting as the channel through which any money whatsoever was spent by the original respondent. The petition could not possibly succeed on the ground of exceeding election expenses. On the other hand, on the findings given by me above, the expenses on the construction of rostrums were also erroneously added by the learned Judge. In fact, it seems that other two items mentioned there were also wrongly added. Expenses of the installation and use of loud-speakers and the power supplied were certainly shown to have been borne by the Congress Party itself. It is true that when elections of persons in the position of the Prime Minister or even of Ministers, whether in the Central Government or a State Government, take place, a number of people come forward to either give or thrust their supposed aid in the election. It may be impossible for the candidate to refuse it without offending them. But it is also impossible for the Courts to make the candidate himself or herself responsible so as to impose an obligation upon the candidate to find out what expenses incurred by them were and then to add these on to the candidate's account of expenses. That would be, obviously a most unfair result. And, this is not what the law requires in this Country. The law requires proof of circumstances from which at least implied authorisation can be inferred.

505. The third and the last and a subsidiary submission on behalf of the election petitioner, on election expenses, was that, Shri Dal Bahadur Singh not having been produced by the original respondent, some sort of presumption arises against the original respondent. I do not think that it is possible to shift a burden of the petitioner on to the original respondent whose case never was that Shri Dal Bahadur Singh spent any money on her behalf. The case of **M. Chenna Reddy v. Ramchandra Rao, (1972) 40 Ele LR 390 (415) (SC)** was relied upon to submit that a presumption may arise against a successful candidate from the non-production of available evidence to support his version. Such a presumption, under section 114 Evidence Act, it has to be remembered, is always optional and one of fact depending upon the whole set of facts. It is not obligatory.

506. In **Chenna Reddy's** case (supra) the evidence seemed to have resulted in a prima facie case whose effect the respondent had to get rid of. In the case before us, the election petitioner had summoned Shri M.L. Tripathi (P.W. 59), the Secretary of the District Congress Committee, who appeared with account books of the Party at Raebareli. The election petitioner could get nothing useful out of his evidence. Even if the election petitioner did not, for some reason, desire to summon Shri Dal Bahadur Singh, similarly his counsel could have requested the Court to exercise its discretionary powers under Order XVI, rule 14 C.P.C., but this was never done. A presumption could not arise on the facts and circumstances of a case in which it could not be said that Shri Dal Bahadur Singh's evidence was necessary to discharge some burden of the original respondent. The original respondent had discharged whatever onus lay upon her by producing her own election agent Shri Kapur, who had kept her accounts. And, she had herself appeared in the witness-box and faced a cross-examination which could not be held up as an example of complete fairness and propriety. I do not quite understand what presumption could possibly arise, due to non-production of Shri Dal Bahadur Singh, against what part of her case, and to what effect. It could certainly not be suggested that there was any duty on her part to repeal some case never set up against her. It was nobody's case that the local Congress Party was her agent.

SOME MEMBERS COULD NOT ATTEND PARLIAMENT BECAUSE OF THEIR ILLEGAL DETENTION – AMENDMENTS BY PARLIAMENT INVALID – SUBMITS RESPONDENT – REJECTED – BEG, J.

507. I may now very shortly deal with the objection that, as a number of Members of Parliament belonging to the opposition parties were in detention, under the preventive detention laws, which could not be questioned before the Courts of law; because of the declaration of the emergency by the President, there was a procedural defect in making the amendments of the Act of 1951 and the 39th Constitutional Amendment.

508. Article 122 of the Constitution prevents this Court from going into any question relating to irregularity of proceedings "in Parliament." It reads as follows:

> "122. (1) The validity of any proceedings in Parliament shall not be called in question on the ground of any alleged irregularity of procedure.
>
> (2) No officer or member of Parliament in whom powers are vested by or under this Constitution for regulating procedure or the conduct of business, or for maintaining order, in Parliament shall be subject to the jurisdiction of any Court in respect of the exercise by him of those powers."

509. What is alleged by the election petitioner is that the opposition Members of Parliament, who had been detained under the preventive detention laws, were entitled to get notice of the proposed enactments and the 39th Amendment, so as to be present "in Parliament", to oppose these changes in the law. I am afraid, such an objection is directly covered by the terms of Article 122 which debars every Court from examining the propriety of proceedings "in Parliament." If any privileges of Members of Parliament were involved, it was open to them to have the question raised "in Parliament". There is no provision of the Constitution which has been pointed out to us providing for any notice to each Member of Parliament. That, I think, is also a matter completely covered by Article 122 of the Constitution. All that this Court can look into in appropriate cases is whether the procedure which amounts to legislation or, in the case of a constitutional amendment, which is prescribed by Article 368 of the Constitution, was gone through at all. As a proof of that, however, it will accept, as conclusive evidence, a certificate of the Speaker that a Bill has been duly passed, *See*: **State of Bihar v. Kameshwer, AIR 1952 SC 252 (266).**

510. Again, this Court has held, in **Sharma v. Sri Krishna, AIR 1960 SC 1186 (1189)**, that a notice issued by the Speaker of a Legislature for the breach of its privilege cannot be questioned on the ground that the rules of procedure relating to proceedings for breach of privilege have not been observed. All these are internal matters of procedure which the Houses of Parliament themselves regulate.

511. As regards the validity of the detentions of the Members of Parliament, that cannot be questioned automatically or on the bare statement by counsel that certain Members of Parliament are illegally detained with some ulterior object. The enforcement of fundamental rights is regulated by Articles 32 and 226 of the Constitution and the suspension of remedies under these Articles is also governed by appropriate constitutional provisions. Their legality and regularity cannot be collaterally assailed by mere assertions made by Counsel before us. I therefore, overrule these objections to the validity of the amendments and the 39th Amendment as we cannot even entertain them in this manner in these proceedings.

ARTICLE 329A BY 39TH CONSTITUTIONAL AMENDMENT – REPRODUCED – BEG, J.

512. I will now turn to the validity of clause (4) of Article 329A sought to be added by section 4 of the 39th Amendment. I will quote the whole of section 4 as some argument was advanced on the context in which clause (4) of Article 329A occurs. Section 4 reads as follows:

"4. In Part XV of the Constitution. After Article 329, the following article shall be inserted, namely:—

"329-A. (1) Subject to the provisions of Chapter II of Part V (except sub-clause (e) of clause (1) of Article 102), no election—

(a) to either House of Parliament of a person who holds the office of Prime Minister at the time of such election or is appointed as Prime Minister after such election :

(b) to the House of the People of a person who holds the office of Speaker of that House at the time of such election or who is chosen as the Speaker for that House after such election:

shall be called in question, except before such authority (not being any such authority as is referred to in clause (b) of Article 329) or body and in such manner as may be provided for by or under any law made by Parliament and any such law may provide for all other matters relating to doubts and disputes in relation to such election including the grounds on which such election may be questioned.

(2) The validity of any such law as is referred to in clause (1) and the decision of any authority or body under such law shall not be called in question in any court.

(3) Where any person is appointed as Prime Minister or, as the case may be, chosen to the office of the Speaker of the House of the People, while an election petition referred to in clause (b) of Article 329 in respect of his election to either House of Parliament or, as the case may be, to the House of the People is pending, such election petition shall abate upon such person being appointed as Prime Minister or, as the case may be, being chosen to the office of the Speaker of the House of the People, but such election may be called in question under any such law as is referred to in clause (1).

(4) No law made by Parliament before the commencement of the Constitution (Thirty-ninth Amendment) Act, 1975, in so far as it relates to election petitions and matters connected therewith, shall apply or shall be deemed ever to have applied to or in relation to the election of any such person as is referred to in clause (1) to either House of Parliament and such election shall not be deemed to be void or ever to have become void on any around on which such election could be declared to be void or has, before such commencement, been declared to be void under any such law and notwithstanding any order made by any Court, before such commencement, declaring such election to be void, such election shall continue to be valid in all respects and any such order and any finding on which such order is, based shall be and shall be deemed always to have been void and of no effect.

(5) Any appeal or cross appeal against any such order of any court as is referred to in clause (4) pending immediately before the commencement of the Constitution (Thirty-ninth Amendment) Act, 1975, before the Supreme Court shall be disposed of in conformity with the provisions of clause. (4).

(6) The provisions of this article shall have effect notwithstanding anything contained in this Constitution"

513. Counsel for both sides are agreed that, for the purposes of the case before us, we need not consider the constitutional validity of clauses (1) to (3) of the newly introduced Article 329A of the Constitution. I will therefore, concern myself only with the constitutional validity of clause (4) of Article 329A of the Constitution

'CONSTITUENT POWER' MISUSED POWER UNDER ARTICLE 368 – CLAUSE (4) OF ARTICLE 329A DECIDED AN ELECTION DISPUTE ARBITRARILY – REVERSED A JUDGEMENT – IT DAMAGES FREE AND FAIR ELECTIONS – DESTROYS BASIC STRUCTURE OF THE CONSTITUTION – SUBMITS RESPONDENT

514. Learned Counsel for the election-petitioner contended that the constituent or amending power contained in Article 368 of our Constitution had been misused to achieve some purpose which was either outside the Article or which struck at the roots of the "basic structure" or "the essential features" of our Constitution. It was submitted that the amendment is invalid on an application of the tests laid down by a majority of the 13 Judges who indicated certain basic and inviolable principles of our Constitution in **Kesavananda Bharti's** case (supra). It was contended that the newly added Article 329A(4) of the Constitution, far from constituting a Constitutional law, which alone could be made under Article. 368, did not even satisfy the tests of a law, in as much as it did not lay down any general rule applicable to all cases of a particular class but was really designed to decide one particular election case, which is now before us for hearing, in a particular way.

According to learned Counsel, the amending bodies had, under the guise of an exercise of constituent power, really decided a particular election dispute arbitrarily without following the elementary principles of judicial procedure or applying any intelligible norms or principles of justice either as a Court of law would have done or as any body of persons entrusted with the duty to decide a matter justly or *quasi*-judicially could possibly have done. The assumption underlying this argument was that setting aside the results of a judicially recorded judgment and order by declaring it void and the validation of an election held by a Court of law to be invalid necessarily involves the adoption of a judicial or a *quasi*-judicial procedure if the results are to appear just and not violative of the basic principles of natural justice which must be held to be parts of the Rule of law envisaged by our Constitution. What had been done by clause (4) according to the learned Counsel for the election petitioner, was nothing short of lifting and placing the elections of the first four dignitaries of State outside, the range of questionability before any authority whatsoever either in the past, present or future.

As the only election out of these dignitaries still in dispute at the time of the passing of the 39th Amendment was the election of the Prime Minister to the House of the People, now under consideration in the appeals before us, it was suggested that all this was done, wholly and solely though indirectly, with the object of validating the Prime Minister's election as a Member of the House of Representatives in 1971. It sought to place the Prime Minister and the Speaker in a separate class by themselves as candidates at a general election for the membership of the House of Representatives. It was urged that there could be no reasonable or logical nexus between the alleged objects of such a classification and the results of the amendment made. It was urged that, in as much as a Prime Minister holds the pivotal position in the governance of the country there could not be a less and not more need to ensure that the election of the holder of such a high office to a Parliamentary seat had been free from any corrupt practice. It was urged that the test and the procedure for determining whether the holder of such an exalted, responsible, and important office was duly elected as a Member of Parliament could not, logically or reasonably be different from that which ordinary Members of the Parliament had to go through. It was pointed out that, in a case covered by this clause, there could be no consideration at all, if the amendment is upheld, of the validity of a past election by any authority in the future as all elections in this very special end exceptional class had been validated without any qualification and quite unconditionally.

The effect was, it was urged, that the present Prime Minister was placed in a very privileged and exalted position which was not enjoyed by a past Prime Minister and which was not meant to be occupied by any future Prime Minister. Such a procedure and such a result, it was contended, made a mockery of the concept of free and fair elections under a democratic system. Furthermore, it was urged that it was destructive of the concepts of rule of law, of equality before law, and of just determination of Judicially Tribunal disputes. Taking away of even the supervisory jurisdiction of superior Courts in elections of a certain class of dignitaries was characterised as a gross violation of a basic principle of our Constitution.

It was also submitted that if what was intended to be conveyed by the amendment was that Parliament had withdrawn the case before us from the sphere of judicial scrutiny and determination and had decided in itself, as was stated in his opening address by the learned counsel for the original respondent, not merely was the basic constitutional principle of separation of powers set at naught but the primordial rule of natural justice, that no one should be a judge in his own cause, had been infringed in as much as the dispute was really between a majority party and the numerically minority groups or parties in the Houses of Parliament. No hearing could be given to leaders of the numerically minority groups of parties in Parliament because they were, it was submitted illegally detained under Preventive Detention laws after a declaration of emergency by the President of India, with the result that members of Parliament who did not support the ruling party were denied access to Courts so as to secure their release from detention and could not take part in proceedings which produced the Acts amending the Act of 1951, and, the 39th Amendment. I have already dealt with and rejected the objection to the proceedings of the Houses of Parliament, on the collateral ground of allegedly illegal detentions of opposition leaders.

515. All the contentions of learned Counsel for the election Petitioners, apart from the alleged procedural defect in amending the Act of 1951 and the Constitution when a number of opposition Members of Parliament are detained under the Preventive Detention laws, already dealt with by me, seemed directed towards producing two results either simultaneously or alternatively: *firstly*, to persuade us to hold that the constituent power had been exceeded or sought to be utilised for extraneous purposes falling outside the purview of Article 368 of the Constitution altogether; and *secondly*, to convince us that the effects of the 4th clause of Article 329A must be such that, if this purported addition to our Constitution was upheld, the "basic structure" or the "basic features" or "the underlying principles" of our Constitution will be irreparably damaged so that it could not any longer be looked upon as the same Constitution. It was submitted that the majority view in **Kesavananda Bharati's** case (supra) which was binding upon us, will compel us to invalidate clause (4) of Article 329A. There was, in the course of argument, considerable overlapping between tests and considerations appertaining to the purposes and those involving the effects, consequences, or implications of clause (4) if it was upheld. It was proposed that purposes should be ascertained and their validity determined, inter alia, in the light of the consequences and implications of upholding the validity of the impugned clause. Both sets of contentions involved a definition of the scope of Article 368 and a determination of the exact nature of the function actually performed by the constituent authorities in passing the impugned clause (4) of Article 329A.

CLAUSE (4) OF ARTICLE 329A – 39TH CONSTITUTIONAL AMENDMENT IS VALID – PARLIAMENT ITSELF EXAMINED VALIDITY OF THE ORDER AND FINDINGS AND FOUND IT VOID – SUBMITS ATTORNEY-GENERAL

516. We have heard the learned Attorney-General and the learned Solicitor-General of India, in defence of the 4th clause of Article 329A sought to be added by the 39th Amendment, as well as Mr. A.K. Sen and Mr. Jagannath Kaushal, learned Counsel for the original respondent, who also supported the validity of the impugned clause. The 1st contention of the learned Counsel seemed directed toward inducing us not to look beyond the language to discover the purposes or the nature of the function performed in passing clause (4) of Article 329A or its effects. This contention had necessarily to rest upon the assumption that provisions of clauses (4) and (5) and (6) of Article 329A, sought to be introduced by the 39th Amendment, were valid and had the effect of depriving this Court of jurisdiction to determine the validity of clause (4) by exploring the purposes and objects which may lie behind the plain meaning of clause (4).

PARLIAMENT IN ITS CONSTITUENT POWER ACTED AS COURT OF APPEAL OVER HIGH COURT JUDGMENT – CLAUSE (4) ALSO DOES AWAY WITH THE APPLICATION OF SECTION 100 OF RP ACT – SUBMITS ATTORNEY-GENERAL

Our difficulty, however, is that even an attempt to give its natural and literal meaning to every word used in clause (4), after hearing the statements made by learned counsel supporting the 39th Amendment, to the effect that Parliament had itself examined the validity of whatever order and findings on question of fact or law are referred to there, and, had reached the conclusion that the order and each of the findings of fact on which it was based must be adjudged to be void and of no effect, baffles us very much. This could only mean that Parliament, in its constituent capacity, had functioned as though it was a direct Court of Appeal from a judgment of the High Court while an appeal in the last Court is pending – a procedure which has not been shown to have been followed so far in any case brought to our notice either decided in this country or anywhere else in the world, all the cases cited to support such a view being distinguishable on facts and law applicable.

517. In the circumstances of this case, set out above, the finding on contested questions of fact and law and the order indicated by clause (4) could only be those contained in the judgment under appeal by both sides before us. The language of clause (4) was, according to the submissions of learned Counsel supporting the amendment itself meant to convey that after going into the disputed questions of fact, the constituent bodies had reached the conclusion that the order and the findings must have no legal effect. Indeed, the Solicitor-General went so far as to submit that Parliament must be deemed to be aware of the contents of the whole record of the proceedings in the High Court, including the pleadings, the evidence, and the findings in the Judgment of the High Court, as these were all available to it. In other words, we must imagine and suppose that, whatever may be the actual position. Parliament had sat in judgment over the whole case as a Court of appeal would have done. But, the impugned clause (4), if valid, would compel us to make a contrary assumption in as much as it declares that all laws prior to the 39th Amendment, relating to election petitions and "matters connected therewith", which must include the grounds given in section 100 of the Representation of the People Act, 1951, were neither to be applied nor ever deemed to have applied to such a case as the one before us. This surely meant that they must be "deemed" not to have been applied by Parliament itself, according to the well-known rule of construction that a legal fiction, introduced by a deeming provision, must be carried to its logical conclusion and we must not allow our imagination to boggle at the consequences of carrying the fiction to its logical conclusions; *See:* **East End Dwellings. Co. Ltd. v. Finsbury Borough Council, (1952) AC 109.**

CONSTITUENT POWER ABROGATED PRE-EXISTING ELECTION LAW – SUBMITS APPELLANT

518. At the same time, it was contended, and this was especially emphasised by Mr. Jagannath Kaushal, that Parliament and the ratifying legislatures of the State

– participating in the constitution making process – had not applied any pre-existing norms but had merely declared and registered, almost automatically without any need to consider anything further or to apply any law whatsoever to any facts, what followed from the abrogation of all pre-existing law, with its procedure and norms, so far as the election-petition against the original respondent was concerned. This meant that the constituent bodies, proceeding on the assumption that the High Court had rightly held the original respondent's election to be invalid by applying the provisions of the 1951 Act, had considered it necessary to validate what really was invalid according to the 1951 Act. In view of what I have already held on merits, such an assumption, if it was there at all, could only be based on a misconception.

CLAUSE (4) DIVESTED COURTS OF THEIR JURISDICTION – JUDGMENT WASHED AWAY WITHOUT APPLYING ANY LAW OR PROCEDURE – SUBMITS RESPONDENT

519. The conflicting points of view, advanced in support of the amendment, enabled the election-petitioner's counsel to find support for his contention that the impugned clause (4) obviously meant that a considered judgment on, *inter alia*, disputed questions of fact, however, erroneous, had been swept aside, quite unceremoniously, mechanically, and, without a semblance of a *quasi*-judicial procedure, by a purported exercise of constituent power by the constituent bodies, consisting of the two Houses of Parliament and the ratifying legislatures of the various States. He urged that the alternative contentions of Mr. Kaushal constituted an admission that no procedure whatsoever, which could be considered either reasonable or appropriate for a judicial or *quasi*-judicial determination of any question of fact or law was followed. He contended that whichever of the two alternative contentions of counsel supporting the 39th Amendment was accepted by us, his submission, that the amendment was *ultra vires*, arbitrary and improperly motivated was made out.

520. The essence of judicial or *quasi*-judicial function is the application of a law which is already given by the law making authority to the judicial or *quasi*-judicial authority to apply. This law has to be applied to certain findings after determining the disputed questions of fact in a manner which must conform to the canons of natural justice. Learned Counsel for the election petitioner contended that it was not necessary to go beyond clause (4) to reach the conclusion that what was being done was to decide a dispute which could, under the law as it existed till then, only be judicially determined in the mode prescribed by Article 329(b) read with the Act of 1951 which could not be circumvented even before Article 329A engrafted exceptions on it and the Act of 1951 had been repealed retrospectively in its application to the Prime Minister. The result of a sort of consolidated legislative-cum-adjulicatory function was sought to be embodied in Article 329A(4) by purported Constitutional amendment. He contended that we were bound to consider and decide whether the "constituent power" contained in Article 368 of the Constitution was meant to be used in this manner. Such use would, he submitted, fall outside Article 368. Hence, he submitted, there was no need to resort to principles emerging from a consideration of what may be spoken of as the basic structure or essential features of the Constitution. It was enough if we held that "constituent power" did not cover such a use made of it.

CONSTITUENT POWER CONTAINED IN ARTICLE 368 HAS TO BE INTERPRETED PROPERLY – ITS EXTENT HAS TO BE FOUND OUT – OBSERVES BEG, J.

Learned Counsel for the election petitioner had thus advanced an alternative contention based upon the meaning of the term "constituent power" introduced by the 24th Amendment; and, in my opinion, we are duty bound to interpret Article

368 and determine the precise meaning of "constituent power" when properly called upon by a party before us to do so. Indeed, the very contention that we should so construe "constituent power" as to deny ourselves the jurisdiction to decide the validity of what was done under a purported exercise of such a power involves a determination of its meaning. I fail to see how our jurisdiction to do this could be barred by the provisions of the very amendment whose constitutional validity is challenged before us was repealed.

POWER TO AMEND CONSTITUTION UNDER ARTICLE 368 "IS THE VERY ORIGINAL POWER OF THE PEOPLE WHICH IS UNBROKEN INTO THE LEGISLATIVE – THE EXECUTIVE – THE JUDICIAL – SUBMITS SOLICITOR-GENERAL

521. Learned Counsel supporting the 39th Amendment, had, in defence of the Amendment, advanced arguments which go beyond the position which was adopted to support the amendments considered by us in **Kesavananda Bharati's** case (supra). The new argument now advanced, to use the language of the Solicitor-General in his last written submissions, is that "the power of amendment under Article 368 is "the very original power of the people which is unbroken into the legislative and the executive and the judicial." He submitted that the implied limitations, to which the majority decision in **Kesavananda Bharati's** case (supra) has committed this court for the time being, are no longer available when considering this "unbroken" power. Mr. A.K. Sen, learned Counsel for the original respondent, puts this very argument in the following words in his written submissions:

> "In the hands of the constituent authority there is no demarcation of powers. But the demarcation emerges only when it leaves the hands of the constituent authority through well-defined channels into demarcated pools. The constituent power is independent of the fetters or limitations imposed by separation of powers in the hands of the organs of the Government, amongst whom the supreme authority of the State is allocated.
>
> The constituent power is independent of the doctrine of separation of powers. Separation of powers is when the constitution is framed laying down the distribution of the powers in the different organs such as the legislative, executive and the judicial power. The constituent power springs as the fountain head and partakes of sovereignty and is the power which creates the organ and distributes the powers. Therefore, in a sense the constituent power is all embracing and is at once judicial, executive and legislative, or in a sense super power. The constituent power can also change the system of checks and balances upon which the separation, of powers is based."

522. The theory advanced before us may have been designed to escape the logical consequences of the majority view in **Kesavananda Bharati's** case (supra) which we cannot sitting as a Bench of five Judges in this Court, overrule. The theory is however quite novel and has to be, I think, dealt with by us. It postulates an undifferentiated or amorphous amalgam of bare power constituting the "constituent power" According to this theory, the power which constitutes does not need to be either constituted or prevented from exercising a power assigned by it already to a constituted authority. Hence, it is a power of a kind which is above the Constitution itself. If I am not mistaken, the learned Solicitor-General did say that the constituent power lies "outside" the Constitution. In other words, it is independent and above the Constitution itself because it operates on the Constitution and can displace it with, so to say one stroke of its exercise.

I do not think that such an extreme theory could be supported by the citation of either the majority or minority views of Judges, barring stray remarks made in other contexts, either in the **I.C. Golaknath v. State of Punjab's case, (1967) 2 SCR 672** or in the **Kesavananda Bharati's** case (supra). In fact; in neither of these two cases was the question raised or considered at all by this Court whether the amending power or the "Constituent power" itself constituted such an amalgamated concentration of power, said to be distributed by the Constitution between the three different organs of State at a "subsequent stage" whatever this may mean. The distribution of power of different kind between the three organs was compared to delegation of authority to agents which could be withdrawn at any time by the constituent bodies.

523. If we were to accept the theory indicated above, it would make it unnecessary to have a constitution beyond one consisting of a single sentence laying down that every kind of power is vested in the constituent bodies which may by means of a single consolidated order or declaration of law, exercise any or all of them themselves whenever they please whether such powers be executive, legislative, or judicial, Could this be the ambit of "constituent power" in our Constitution? Would such a view not defeat the whole purpose of a Constitution? Does the whole constitution so crumble and melt in the crucible of constituent power that its parts cannot be made out ? Before we could accept a view which carries such drastic implications with it we will have to overrule the majority view in **Kesavananda Bharati's** case (supra). The majority view in that case, which is binding upon us, seemed to be that both the supremacy of the Constitution and separation of powers are parts of the basic structure of the Constitution.

'CONSTITUENT POWER' CANNOT BE QUESTIONED AS IT EXERCISES 'SOVEREIGN POWER' – SUBMITS APPELLANT

524. If "constituent power", by itself, is so transcendental and exceptional as to be above the provisions of the Constitution itself it should not, logically speaking be bound even by the procedure of amendment prescribed by Article 368(2). I have not found any opinion expressed so far by any learned Judge of this Court to show that the constituent power is not bound by the need to follow the procedure laid down in Article 368(2) of the Constitution. Indeed, rather inconsistently with the theory of an absolute and unquestionable power in some undifferentiated or raw and unfettered form, operating from above and outside the Constitution, learned Counsel, supporting the impugned 4th Clause in the 39th Amendment, concede that the constituent power is bound by the expropriate procedure laid down in Article 368 for the amendment of the Constitution. What they urge is that, subject to this procedure, which has been followed here the constituent power cannot be questioned because it is a "sovereign power". The logical consequence of such an argument also is that the majority view in **Kesavananda Bharati's** case (supra) was erroneous. It also overlooks that judicial review of laws made by Parliament is always a review of an exercise of "sovereign power." It may be that the object of the learned Counsel in advancing this extraordinary theory was to induce us to refer this case to a much larger bench so that the majority view in **Kesavananda Bharati's** case (supra) may if necessary, be overruled. I, however, doubt whether putting forward such extreme and untenable propositions is the best method of securing such a result.

SUBMISSION OF SOLICITOR-GENERAL NEEDS SERIOUS CONSIDERATION – OBSERVES BEG, J.

525. I think that the possibly theoretical question indicated above, whatever may be the object of raising it does deserve to be seriously considered and answered by us because it discloses a basic misconception. Therefore I propose to consider it at a length which seems to me to be justified by our need to clarify our thinking on a basic or "key" concept without a final commitment to a particular view on it. Clearer thinking, by examining a basic theoretical question from every conceivable angle, leads. I believe, to that open-mindedness which is needed by lawyers no less than by any other class today so that we may, contrary to our reputation, be responsive to the inevitable challenges of change. Justice Holmes once said : "Theory is the most important part of the dogma of law, as the architect is the most important man who takes post in the building of a house"; Holmes, *Collected Papers* (1921) 200.

'SOVEREIGNTY AND 'SOVEREIGN POWER' ARE TWO DIFFERENT CONCEPTS DENOTING DIFFERENT MEANING – OBSERVES BEG, J.

526. It seems to me that the words "sovereignty" and "sovereign power" used repeatedly by learned Counsel defending the 39th Amendment to describe the constituent power, should, for several good reasons, be avoided, so far as possible, by lawyers who seek that clarity of thought for which precision in language is the first requirement. One of these reasons was given by Lord Bryce (Studies in *"History and Jurisprudence"* (1901) (503-504)). "The frontier districts, if one may call them so, of Ethics of Law, and of political science have been thus infested by a number of vague or ambiguous terms which have produced many barren discussions and caused much needless trouble to students .... No offender of this kind has given more trouble than the so-called Doctrine of 'Sovereignty', Prof.' Mellwain, however, opined: "But this very fact is proof of its vital importance in our modern world, and the wide variety of the views held concerning its essence, as well as the conflicting conclusions to which these views still lead, may furnish sufficient excuse for another attempt to clarify some of our ideas touching this central formula under which we try to rationalize the complicated facts of our modern political life." Another reason for eschewing such expressions, so far as possible, is that they are "emotive" or of a kind about which Mr. Leonard Schapiro, (writing on "Key concepts in Political Science" Series, at p. 7) rightly observed, "Emotive words such as 'equality', 'dictatorship', 'elite' or even 'power' can often, by the very passions which they raise, obscure a proper understanding of the sense in which they are, or should be, or should not be, or have been used. Confucius regarded the 'rectification of names' as the first task of government. 'If names are not correct, language will not be in accordance with the truth of things', and this in time would lead to the end of justice, to anarchy and to war." At any rate, in America, the concept of State Sovereignty, ranged against that of national sovereignty, did produce a civil war which is said to have been precipitated by the decision of the American Supreme Court in **Red Scott v. Sanford, (1856) 19 How 393.**

527. I must preface my observations here about the concepts of "sovereignty" and exercise of "sovereign power" between which I make a distinction, with two kinds of explanation. The first kind involves an exposition of a functional or sociological point of view. I believe that every social political, economic, or legal concept or doctrine must answer the needs of the people of a country at a particular time. I see the development of concepts, doctrines, and institutions as responses to the changing needs of society in every country. They have a function to fulfil in relation to national needs. The second type of explanation may be called historical or meant merely to indicate and illustrate notions or concepts put forward by thinkers at various times in various countries so as to appropriately relate them to what we may find today under our Constitution. We have to appreciate the chronology or stages of their development if we are to avoid trying to fit into our Constitution something which has no real relevance to it or bearing upon its contents or which conflicts with these. It must not, if I may so put it, be constitutionally "indigestible" by a constitution such as ours.

Of course, it is not a secret that we have taken some of the basic concepts of our Constitution from British and American Constitutions in their most developed stages.

That too must put us on our guard against attempts to foist upon our Constitution something simply because it happens to be either a British or American concept of some particular period which could not possibly be found in it today. Therefore, both types of explanation appear to be necessary to an exposition of what may or may not be found in our Constitution.

CONSTITUTION SHOULD BE INTERPRETTED WHAT IT SAYS, DECLARES OR IMPLIES – BEG, J.

528. I certainly do not think that Judges of this Court have or should think that they have the power to consciously alter, under the guise of judicial interpretation, what the Constitution declares or necessarily implies even though our pronouncements, interpreting the Constitution, may have the effect of contributing something to the growth or even change of Constitutional law by clearing doubts, removing uncertainties, or filling-up of gaps to a limited extent. If the law embodied in our Constitution, as declared by this Court, is not satisfactory, I do not think that we can or should even attempt to stand in the way of a change of any kind sought through appropriate constitutional means by the constitutionally appointed organs and agencies of the State. If, however, this Court is asked to declare as valid what seems to it to fall clearly outside the ambit of the Constitution, and, indeed, what is even claimed to be operating from outside the Constitution and described as a supra-Constitutional power, there may be no alternative left to it except to declare such a claim to be really outside the Constitution. If we were to do that we would only be accepting the professed basis of the claim without conceding its constitutional validity. After all, we are really concerned with the questions of constitutional validity which can only be resolved by references to what the Constitution contains, either expressly or by a necessary implication, and not with what is beyond its range except insofar as this also may be necessary to explain what is or what is deemed to be a part of our Constitution.

THE WORD 'SOVEREIGN' IS DERIVED FROM A LATIN WORD – INDICATING HIGHEST SUPERIOR IN POLITICAL HIERARCHY – WHO RENDERS HELP TO THE NEEDY – BEG, J.

529. The term "sovereign" is derived from the Latin word "Superanus" which was akin to "Suzerian" suggesting a hierarchy of classes which characterised ancient and medieval societies. In its origin, it is an attribute assigned to the highest living human superiors in the political hierarchy and not some abstract quality of a principle or of a law contained in a document, a meaning, as will be shown here, which emerges clearly later. In times of anarchic disorder or oppression, by local satraps or chieftains or barons or even bullies and criminals, ordinary mortals have sought the protection of those who could give it because of their superior physical might. No book or document could provide them with the kind of help they needed. They looked upto their 'sovereign liege and Lord", as the medieval monarch was addressed by his subjects, for protection against every kind of tyranny and oppression.

GREEKS HAD DEVELOPED 'LAW OF NATURE' – IT WAS ABOVE THE LAW ACTUALLY ENFORCED – ROMAN JURISTS LIKED IT – ARISTOTLE FURTHER REFINED IT – BEG, J.

530. The Greeks and Romans were not doubled by theories of "Sovereignty" in a State. The principle that Might was Right was recognised as the unquestioned legally operative principle at least in the field of their Constitutional laws. Greek philosophers had, however, formulated a theory of a Law of Nature which was, morally, above the laws actually enforced. In later stages of Roman Law, Roman jurists also, saturated with Greek notions of an ethically superior law of Nature, said that the institution of slavery, which gave the owner of a slave theoretically absolute powers of life and death over the slave, just like the powers of a paterfamilies over his children, was contrary to jus natural although it was recognised by jus gentian, the laws of then civilised world. Aristotle, in his analysis of forms of Government, had emphasized the importance of the condition of a State as a test or determinant of sovereign power in the State. And, Roman jurists, had, indirectly, cleared the path for the rise of modern legalism and constitutionalism by rescuing law itself from the clutches of a superstitious reverence for customs, surrounded with ceremonial and ritualistic observances and cumbersome justice defeating formalism, through fiction and equity, and forged a secular and scientific weapon of socio-economic transformation. All this was very useful in preparing for an age in which secular law could displace religion as the "control of controls" (*see* Julius Stone's *"Province and Function of Law,"* 1961 Edn., pp. 734, 767).

* * * * *

IN MEDIEVAL EUROPE CHURCH AND THE KING TRIED TO DEVELOP SPIRITUAL AND TEMPORAL MEANS FOR CHECKING WRONG AND OPPRESSION – ULTIMATELY KING SUCCEEDED TO WEAR SPIRITUAL CROWN – BEG, J.

532. After the break-up of the Roman Empire, there were attempts in medieval Europe, both by the Church and the Kings, to develop spiritual and temporal means for checking wrong and oppression. Quests for the superior or a sovereign power and its theoretical justifications by both ecclesiastical and lay thinkers were parts of an attempt to meet this need. The claims of those who, as vicars of God on earth, sought to meddle with mundane and temporal affairs and acquire even political power and influence were, after a struggle for power, which took different forms in different countries, finally defeated by European Kings with the aid of their subjects. Indeed these Kings tried to snatch, and, not without success, to wear spiritual crowns which the roles of "defenders of the faith" carried with them so as to surround themselves with auras of divinity.

THEORY OF 'SOVEREIGN AUTHORITY' OF THE KING WAS PREVALENT IN ALMOST ALL ANCIENT RELIGIONS ALSO – IN INDIA KING DELEGATED POWER TO DELIVER JUSTICE TO JUDGES – OBSERVES BEG, J.

533. The theory of a legally sovereign unquestionable authority of the King, based on physical might and victory in battle, appears to have been developed in ancient India as well, by Kautaliya, although the concept of a Dharma, based on the authority of the assemblies of those who were learned in the Dharma Shastras also competed for control over exercise of royal secular power. High philosophy and religion, however, often seem to have influenced and affected the actual exercise of sovereign power and such slight law-making as the King may have attempted. The ideal King in ancient India, was conceived of primarily as a Judge deciding cases or giving orders to meet specific situations in accordance with the Dharma Shastras. It also appears that the actual exercise of the power to administer justice was often delegated by the King to his judges in ancient India. Indeed, according to some, the theory of separation of powers appears to have been carried so far (*See*: K.P. Jayaswal in *"Manu and Yajnavalkya" – A basic History of Hindu Law* – 1930 Edn., p. 82) that the King could only execute the legal sentence passed by the Judge.

534. We know that Semitic prophets, as messengers of God, also became rulers wielding both spiritual and political temporal power and authority although to Jesus Christ, who never sought temporal power, is ascribed the saying: "render unto Caesar the things that are Caesar's and to God things that are God's". According to the theory embodied in this saying, spiritual and temporal powers and authorities had to operate in different orbits of power altogether. Another theory, however, was that the messenger of God had been given the sovereign will of God Almighty which governed all matters and this could not be departed from by any human authority or ruler. In the practical administration of justice, we are informed, Muslim caliphs acknowledged and upheld the jurisdiction of their Kazis to give judgment against them personally. There is an account of how the Caliph Omar, being a defendant in a claim brought by a Jew for some money borrowed by him for purposes of State, appeared in person in the Court of his own Kazi to answer the claim. The Kazi rose from his seat out of respect for the Caliph who was so displeased with this unbecoming conduct that he dismissed him from office. (*See*: *Sir A. Rahim's "Muhammadan Jurisprudence"*, (1958) p. 21).

THEORY OF 'SEPARATION OF POWER' WAS EMBEDDED IN OUR BEST TRADITIONS – OBSERVES BEG, J.

535. "The theory, therefore, that there should be a separation of functions between the making of laws, the execution of laws, and the application of laws, after ascertaining facts satisfactorily, is not new. It is embedded in our own best traditions. It is dictated, if by nothing else, by common sense and the principle of division of labour, without an application of which efficient performance of any duties cannot be expected.

IN EUROPE – THERE WAS SEPARATION OF POWER – EXECUTIVE, LEGISLATIVE AND JUDICIAL – BEG, J.

536. We may now look back at the theory and practice of sovereignty in Europe. There, wise Kings, in the Middle ages, sought the support of their subjects in gatherings or "colloquia", which in the words of Mr. De Jouvenel (*See*: "Sovereignty an Inquiry into the Political Good" p. 177), "had the triple character of a session of justice, a council of State and the timid beginnings of a legislative assembly were the means by which the affairs of the realm came more and more into the hands of the King". He goes on to observe: "The council of the King and the Courts of justice progressively developed an independent life, the assembly remaining under the name of Parliament in England and States-General in France."

IN FRANCE SOVEREIGNTY VESTED IN THE KING – BUT HE WAS BOUND BY DIVINE LAW AND THE LAW OF NATURE – BEG, J.

537. Bodin, writing in the reign of Henry the III of France (1551 to 1589), viewed sovereignty as an absolute unlimited power which, though established by law, was not controlled by it. According to him, under an ideal system, sovereignty was vested in the King by divine right. The King's word was law. But, even according to Bodin, although the Sovereign was free from the trammels of positive law, as he was above it, yet, he was "bound by divine law and the law of nature as well as by the common law of nations which embodies principles distinct from these" (*See*: Dunning's "History of Political Theories": Ancient and Medieval" p. 28). Hobbes, a century later continued this line of thinking on an entirely secular and non-moral plane. He opined: "Unlimited power and unfettered discretion as to ways and means are by the sovereign for the end with a view to which civil society is constituted namely, and escape from the evils of the state of nature," in which the life of individuals was "nasty, brutish, and short". Although Hobbes visualised the existence of a social compact as the source of the authority of the sovereign, yet, he looked upon the compact only as a mode of surrender by the subject of all their individual fights and power to the sovereign who could be either an individual or a body of person. Subjects, according to him, had no right to rely upon the compact as means of protection against the soverign. He provided the fullest theoretical foundations of a machiavellian view of sovereignty.

IN 17TH AND 18TH CENTURIES – THERE WERE REVOLUTIONARY CHANGES IN EUROPE – BEG, J.

538. As we know, in the 17th and 18th centuries, European monarchs came in sharp conflict with the representatives of their subjects assembled in "Parliament" in England and in "States-General" in France. And, theories were put forward setting up, as against the claims of Kings to rule as absolute sovereigns by indefeasible divine right, no lesser claims to inviolability and even divinity of the rights of the people. But, theories apart, practice of the art of Government proves, that the effective power to govern, by the very nature of conditions needed for its efficient exercise, has had to be generally lodged in one or few especially in times of crisis, but not in all those who represent the people even under democratic forms of Government. Direct democracy, except in small city States such as those of ancient Greece, is not practically feasible.

539. Theories of popular sovereignty put forward by Locke and Rousseau came to the fore-front in the 17th and 18th centuries – an era of revolutionary changes and upheavels. The thory of certain immutable individual natural rights, as the basis of a set of positive legal rights, essential and necessary to the fulfilment of the needs of human beings as individuals, was advanced by Locke. He visualised a social contract as a means of achieving the welfare of individuals composing Society. He also advocated separation of powers of Government in a Constitution as a method of securing rights of individual citizens against even their own Governments. Montesquieu elaborated this theory. The ideas of Rousseau were amongst those which contributed to produce that great conflagration, the French Revolution, which was described by Carlyle as the "bonfire of feudalism." Government, according to Rousseau, in all its departments, was the agent of the general will of the sovereign people whose welfare must always be its aim and object. But, the general will for the time being was also liable to err about the particular means chosen to achieve the ends of good government. There was, according to Rousseau, also another part of the "General Will" which was more permanent and stable and unerring and decisive. He hinted that there was what Bosanquet (*See*: The Philosophical Theory of the State – Chap. V) called the "Real Will", the basis of which was found in Rousseau's philosophy. As pointed out by T.H. Green, in his Lectures on "Principles of Political Obligation" (1931 Edn., p. 82) Rousseau's theorry of sovereignty was designed to bring out that:

> there's on earth a yet auguster thing. Veiled though it be, than Parliament and King".

T.H. Green said: "It is to this 'augustes thing', not to such supreme power as English lawyers held to be vested in 'Parliament and King', that Rousseau's account of the soverign is really applicable."

AMERICAN CONSTITUTION-MAKERS – INTRODUCED SEPARATION OF POWER – BEG, J.

540. The ideas of Rousseau were subsequently used by Hegelian and Idealist political philosophers to deify the state as the repository of the "Real Will" of the people and by Marxists to build their theory of a dictatorship of the proletariat. But, the views of Locke and Montesquieu were sought to be given a practical form by American Constitution-makers, who imbued with them, devised a machinery for the control of sovereign powers of the people placed in the hands of the three organs of State so that it may not be misused. Suspicion of Governmental power and fear of its misuse, which characterised liberal democratic thinking, underlay the doctrine of separation of powers embodied in the American Constitution.

MERITS OF DEMOCRACY WERE LOOKED AT DIFFERENTLY – SOME DESCRIBED AS PROTECTION FROM EVIL – OTHER THOUGHT MAY NOT ENSURE GOOD GOVERNANCE – BEG, J.

541. "The merits of democracy", according to Bertrand Russsal (*See*: "Power: A new Social Analysis" p. 187) "are negative: it does not insure good Government, but it prevents certain evils." He pointed out (at p. 188):

> "It is possible, in a democracy, for the majority to exercise a brutal and wholly unnecessary tyranny over a minority ....The safeguarding of minorities so far as is compatible with orderly Government, is an essential part of the taming of power."

He also said (at p. 192):

> "Where democracy exists, there is still need to safeguard individuals and minorities against tyranny, both because tyranny is undescribable in itself, and because it is likely to lead to breaches of order, Montesquieu's advocacy of the separation of legislative executive, and judiciary, the traditional English belief in checks and balances, Bentham's political doctrines and the whole of nineteenth century liberalism, were designed to prevent the arbitary execise of powers. But such methods have come to be considered incompatible with efficiency."

542. Some quite honest, upright, and intelligent people think that the inefficiency, the corruption, the expense, the waste of time and efforts, and the delay in accomplishing what they regard as much too urgently needed socio economic and cultural transformations of backward people today, involved in treading the democratic path, are so great that they would readily sacrifice at least some of the democratic processes and such safeguards against their misuses as separation of powers and judicial review are meant to provide. They would not mind taking the risk of falling into the fire to escape from what they believe to be a frying pan. Some may even agree with Bernard Shaw, who liked to look at everything turned upside down in attempts to understand them, that Democracy, with all its expensive and time-consuming accompaniments, is even in the most advanced countries, only a method of deluding the mass of the people into believing that they are the rulers whilst the real power is always enjoyed by the few who must be judged by the results they produce and not by their professions. Others regard democracy as the only means of achieving the highest good and the greatest happiness of the greatest number. They consider its maintenance to be inextricably bound up with the preservation of the basic individual freedoms and a supporting mechanism or structure of checks and balances, separation of powers, and judicial review. What some believe to be obstacles to any real progress are looked upon by others as almost sacred institutions essential for the protection of their lives and liberties, hearths and homes, occupations and means of livelihood, religions, languages, and cultures. Inevitability of change is according to some, the basic and inescapable law of all life, the only questions to be considered being its pace and direction: how soon or how late and whether the change is to be for the better or for the worse? "El Dorado", some believe, lies ahead. Our march towards it, they say, should be orderly and disciplined. To others all change is anathema as it is generally for the worse. The Golden Age, some believe, lay in the past. Salvation of mankind, they think, lies in a return to the imagined pristine virtues of that past. Some assert that certain amendments of our Constitution have "defaced and defiled" it (*See*: Mr. Palkhivala's "Our Constitution"). Others maintain that these very amendments have made our Constitution a more potent instrument of those socio-economic and cultural transformation for which the Constitution was designed (*See*: Dr. V.A. Seyid Muhammad's "Our Constitution for Haves or Have nots ?"

JUDGES MUST BE IMPARTIAL AND INDEPENDENT – MAY HAVE THEIR OWN VIEWS – OBSERVES BEG, J.

543. Judges must, no doubt, be impartial and independent. They cannot, in a period of intensified socio-economic conflicts, either become tools of any vested interests, or function, from the bench, as zealous reformers propagating particular course. Nevertheless, they cannot be expected to have no notions whatsoever of their own, or to have completely blank minds on important questions indicated above which, though related to law, really fall outside the realm of law. They cannot dwell in ivory towers or confine their processes of thinking in some hermetically sealed chambers of purely legal logic artificially cut off from the needs of life around to which law must respond. Their differing individual philosophies, outlooks, and attitudes on vital questions, resulting from differences in temperament, education, tradition, training, interests and experiences in life, will often determine their honest choices between two or more reasonably possible interpretations of such words as "amendment" or "constituent power" in the Constitution.

But, on certain clear matters of principle, underlying the Constitution, no reasonable person could entertain two views as to what was or could be really intended by the Constitution makers. One of these matters, clear beyond the region of all doubt, seems to me to be that the judicial and law making functions, however broadly conceived, could not possibly have been meant to be interchangeable. They are not incapable of distinction and differentiation, in any constitutionally prescribed sphere of operation of power including that of "constituent power". Each has its own advantages and disadvantages and its own natural *modus operandi*.

* * * * *

AS PER COKE COURTS COULD INVALIDATE ACTS OF PARLIAMENT IF THEY CONTRAVENED RULES OF NATURAL JUSTICE – BEG, J.

547. We know that Coke even advanced the claim, in **Bonham's** case, (1610) 8 Co Rep 118A that Courts could invalidate acts of Parliament if they contravened rules of natural justice such as that a man shall not be heard before he is condemned or that he should be a Judge in his own cause. As Ivor Jennings points out, in an appendix to *"The Law and the Constitution"* (5th Edn. 1959 p. 318) the theory of Parliamentary sovereignty or supremacy could, by no means, be said to be firmly established in England in Coke's time.

BLACKSTONE SPOKE ABOUT PARLIAMENTARY SOVEREIGNTY – DICEY SAID LAW OF NATURE WAS COMMON TO ALL MANKIND – BEG, J.

548. Blackstone, while enunciating the theory of Parliamentary sovereignty in the 19th century, as it was to be later expounded in the 20th century by Prof. A. V. Dicey, also claimed superiority for "the law of nature which was common to all mankind". He said about this law:

> "It is binding over all the globe, in all countries, and at all time; no human laws are of any validity if contrary to this, and such of them as are valid derive all their force and all their authority, medially or immediately, from this original".

(*See*: Dicey – *Law of the Constitution*, p. 62).

549. It is a matter of legal and constitutional history that English Judges finally rejected claims based upon vague philosophical concepts or upon a law of nature or appeals to the "yet auguster thing" pitted against statutory law except insofar as certain rules of natural justice and reason could impliedly be read into acts of Parliament due to absence of statutory prohibition and the need to observe them having regard to the character of the function required by a statute to be performed.

Constitutional historians, such as Holdsworth, have pointed out how English Common Lawyers, some presiding as Judges over King's Courts of Justice, others sitting in Parliament as Legislators, joined hands to evolve, sustain, and, give life to principles of "Sovereignty of Parliament" and the "Rule of Law" as understood by them. Dicey asserted, in his "Law of the Constitution", that both these principles so operated as to reinforce each other instead of coming into conflict with each other. One wonders whether this could be said of later times when the need for more rapid transformations of social and economic orders, in an effort to build up a welfare State in Britain, led to serious curtailments of what were at one time considered natural and inviolable rights and to adoption of legislative devices such as Henry VIIIth clause. We know that these developments evoked a powerful protest from a Chief Justice of England, Lord Hewart, who wrote a book on the subject: "New Despotism". Today, however, it cannot be said that the Courts of justice in England do not see the implications of a welfare Socialistic State which may demand the curtailment of liberties of subjects in many directions in order that the substance of democratic freedom only attainable through removal of economic, social, and educational disparities and barriers, may be attained.

COKE'S DICTUM REJECTED IN ENGLAND – BUT IN AMERICA SUPREMACY OF SUPREME COURT PREVAILED OVER LEGISLATION – BEG, J.

550. Willis, dealing with the development of American Constitutional Law, wrote about the claim of Coke, mentioned above, to invalidate Acts of Parliament by reference to certain fundamental principles of natural justice and of common law (See *Willis on Constitutional Law* – Edn. 1936 p. 76):

> "This dictum of Coke, announced in **Dr. Monham's** case, (1610) 8 Co. Rep, 118A was soon repudiated in England, but the doctrine announced in Coke's dictum found fertile soil in the United States and sprouted into such a vigorous growth that it was applied by the United States Supreme Court in the decision of cases coming before it, and it has been said that the doctrine of the supremacy of the Supreme Court is the logical conclusion of Coke's doctrine of control of the Courts over legislation".

JUDICIAL REVIEW WITH REFERENCE TO BASIC PRINCIPLES CONTAINED IN A CONSTITUTION WERE CONSIDERED INVIOLABLE – IT IS EMBEDDED IN OUR CONSTITUTION ALSO – BEG, J.

551. It seems to me that judicial review of all law-making, whether it appertains to the sphere of fundamental law or of ordinary law, is traceable to this doctrine of judicial control by reference to certain basic principles, contained in a Constitution and considered too inviolable to be easily alterable. It may be that this doctrine is unsuitable for our country at a time when it is going through rapid socio-economic transformation. Nevertheless, so long as the doctrine is found embodied in our Constitution, we cannot refuse to recognise it.

IN AMERICA JUDICIAL REVIEW – CONSTITUTION AS THE BASIC DOCUMENT – FUNDAMENTAL LAW OF THE LAND – SUPREME COURT AS MOUTHPIECE OF THE CONSTITUTION – 'REAL WILL' OF THE PEOPLE – BEG, J.

552. In America, there was some doubt whether the doctrine of judicial review of all legislation naturally flowed out of the vesting of judicial power by section 1 of Article 3 of their Constitution which says:

> "The judicial power of the United States shall be vested in one Supreme Court, and in such inferior Courts as the Congress may, from time-to-time, ordain and establish."

(Willis on *Constitutional Law* – p. 1020). There is no article there, like Article 13 of our Constitution, which declared any kind of legislation abridging or taking away fundamental rights to be "void". The doubt was not without substance. It was removed by Chief Justice Marshall whose judgment in **Marbury v. Madison, 1803 Cranch 137** firmly established the doctrine of judicial review and the supremacy of the Supreme Court of America, in the judicial field of interpretation, as the mouthpiece of the Constitution, and, therefore, of the "Real Will" of the people themselves. The Constitution, as the basic or fundamental law of the land, was to operate there as the touchstone of the validity of ordinary laws just as the validity of laws made by British colonial legislatures was tested by reference to the parental Act of the British Parliament.

ARTICLE 141 OF CONSTITUTION VESTED AUTHORITY IN SUPREME COURT TO DECLARE THE LAW – BEG, J.

553. Under our Constitution, by Article 141 of the Constitution, power is vested only in the Supreme Court and in no other organ or authority of the Republic to declare the law "which shall be binding on all Courts within the territory of India." Article 143 of the Constitution of India also shows that whenever questions of fact or law have either arisen or are likely to 'arise' the President of India may, in view of their public importance, seek the opinion of the Supreme Court, by a reference made to the Court. The procedure on such a reference is that of a judicial authority which hears those interested and then gives its opinion. Article 32 of the Constitution gives a wide power to the Supreme Court "to issue directions or orders or writs", which is larger than that of the British Courts issuing prerogative writs. Although it is confined to the enforcement of the rights conferred by part 3 dealing with fundamental rights.

The power of the High Courts of the various States under Article 226 of the Constitution to issue appropriate directions, orders or writs "to any person or authority including in appropriate cases any Government", within the territories under its jurisdiction, extends to "any other purpose", that is to say, to purposes other than enforcement of fundamental rights. Article 227 also contains the power of a High Court to superintend the functioning of "all Courts and Tribunals" within its jurisdiction. These powers of the High Courts are subject to appeals to the Supreme Court, which is also a repository of a special jurisdiction under Article 136 to grant special leave to appeal "from any judgment, decree, determination sentence or order in any cause or matter passed or made by any Court or Tribunal in the territory of India." It is true that these is no mention or vesting of judicial power, as such, in the Supreme Court by any Article of our Constitution, but, can it be denied that what vests in the Supreme Court and High Courts is really judicial power?

The Constitution undoubtedly specifically vests such power, that is to say, power which can properly be described as "judicial power", only in the Supreme Court and in the High Courts and not in any other bodies or authorities, whether executive or legislative, functioning under the Constitution. Could such a vesting of power in Parliament have been omitted if it was the intention of Constitution makers to clothe it also with any similar judicial authority or functions in any capacity whatsoever?

NO 'SOVEREIGN POWER' IS VESTED IN THE 'CONSTITUENT POWER' – SOVEREIGN POWER IS VESTED – IN LEGAL FICTION IT VESTS IN 'THE PEOPLE OF INDIA' – SUPREME COURT EXERCISING POWER UNDER THE CONSTITUTION DECLARES THE LAW OF THE LAND – CONSTITUENT POWER CANNOT EXERCISE JUDICIAL POWER – BEG, J.

554. The claim, therefore, that an amalgam or some undifferentiated residue of inherent power, incapable of precise definition and including judicial power, vests in

Parliament in its role as a constituent authority, cannot be substantiated by a reference to any Article of the Constitution whatsoever, whether substantive or procedural. Attempts are made to infer such a power from mere theory and speculation as to the nature of the "Constituent power" itself. I do not think that, because the constituent power necessarily carries with it the power to constitute judicial authorities, it must also, by implication, mean that the Parliament, acting in its constituent capacity, can exercise the judicial power itself directly without vesting it in itself first by an amendment of the Constitution. The last mentioned objection may appear to be procedural only, but, as a matter of correct interpretation of the Constitution, and, even more so, from the point of view of correct theory and principle, from which no practice should depart without good reason, it is highly important.

555. This impels me to consider such theories of sovereignty as we may find embedded in our Constitution. The term "sovereign" is only used in the preamble of our Constitution, which says:

> "We, the people of India, having solemnly resolved to constitute India into a Sovereign, Democratic Republic and to secure to all its citizens:
>
> ... . : ... ... : ...
>
> In our Constituent Assembly this twenty-sixth day of November, 1949, do hereby adopt, enact and give to ourselves this Constitution".

556. This Court, exercising the powers vested in it under the Constitution to declare the law of the land, cannot go behind the clear words of the Constitution on such a matter. We have to presume that the Constitution was actually made by the people of India by virtue of their political sovereignty which enabled them to create a legally Sovereign Democratic Republic to which they consigned or entrusted, through the Constitution, the use of sovereign power to be exercised, in its different forms, by the three different organs of Government, each acting on behalf of the whole people, so as to serve the objects stated in the Preamble. This reference to "the people of India" is much more than a legal fiction. It is an assertion in the basic legal instrument for the governance of this country of the fact of a new political power. The legal effect of the terms of the instrument is another matter.

KESAVANANDA BHARATI'S JUDGMENT LAYS DOWN THEORIES OF 'BASIC STRUCTURE' 'SEPARATION OF POWER' – NONE CAN ENCROACH ON EACH OTHER'S AREA – IT CANNOT BE CHANGED EVEN BY RESORTING TO ARTICLE 368, BEG, J.

557. It has been pointed out in the **Keshvananda Bharati's** case (supra), that the preamble of our Constitution did not, like that of the American Constitution, "walk before the Constitution", but was adopted after the rest of the Constitution was passed so that it is really a part of the Constitution itself. It means that the Constitution is a document recording an act of entrustment and conveyance by the people of India, the political sovereign, of legal authority to act on its behalf to a "Sovereign Democratic Republic." "This Constitution" has a basic structure comprising the three organs of the Republic the Executive, the Legislature, and the Judiciary. It is through each of these organs that the Sovereign Will of the People has to operate and manifest itself and not through only one of them. Neither of these three separate organs of the Republic can take over the function assigned to the other. This is the basic structure or scheme of the system of Government of the Republic laid down in this Constitution whose identity cannot, according to the majority view in **Kesavananda's** case (supra) be changed even by resorting to Article 368.

It necessarily follows, from such a view, that Sovereignty, as the power of taking ultimate or final decisions on broad politico-legal issues involved in any proposed changes in the law, becomes divisible. The people are not excluded from the exercise of it. They participate in all the operations of the Republic through the organs of the State. They bind themselves to exercise their individual and collective rights and powers only in the ways sanctioned and through agencies indicated by the Constitution. The Republic is controlled and directed by the Constitution to proceed towards certain destinations and for certain purposes only. The power to change even the direction and purposes is itself divided in the sense that a proposed change, if challenged, must be shown to have the sanction of all the three organs of the Republic, each applying its own methods and principles and procedure for testing the correctness or validity of the measure.

This result, whether we like it or not, necessarily follows from our present constitutional structure and scheme. If the judicial power operates here like a brake or a veto, it is not one which can be controlled by any advice or direction to the judiciary as is the case in totalitarian regimes. In our system, which is democratic, its exercise is left to the judicial conscience of each individual judge. This is also a basic and distinguishing feature of democracy as Prof. Friedman indicated in his *"Law in a Changing Society"* (p. 61) quoted by me in **Kesavananda Bharati's** case (supra) at p. 859.

558. In **Kesavananda Bharati's** case (supra), I had approvingly quoted the views of Prof. Ernest Barker, who, in his "Social and Political Theory", claiming to be elaborating the theory underlying the preamble to our own Constitution, pointed out that, in as much as the Constitution is the instrument which regulates the distribution between and exercise of sovereign power, by the three organs of the State, and it is there constantly to govern and to be referred to and to be appealed to in any and every case of doubt and difficulty, it could itself, conceptually, be regarded as the true or "ultimate" sovereign, that is to say, Sovereign as compared with "immediate" sovereignty of an organ of the Republic acting within its own sphere and at its own level.

CONSTITUTION IS KING OF KINGS – ALL FUNCTIONARIES SWEAR ALLEGIANCE TO THE CONSTITUTION – BEG, J.

559. Of course, in as much as the power of altering every feature of the Constitution remains elsewhere politically, the Constitution is neither the ultimate "political" sovereign nor a legally unalterable and absolute sovereign. All constitutional and "legal" sovereigns are necessarily restrained and limited sovereigns. I thought and still think that such a working theory should be acceptable to lawyers, particularly as the dignitaries of State, including Judges of superior Courts, and all the legislators, who have to take oaths prescribed by the Third Schedule of our Constitution, swear "allegiance" to the Constitution as though the documents itself is a personal Ruler. This accords with our own ancient notions of the law as "The King of Kings" and the majesty of all that it stands for: The Rightfulness of the Ends as well as of the Means.

DIFFERENT SCHOOLS OF THOUGHT INTERPRET 'SOVEREIGNTY' DIFFERENTLY – JURISTS LOOK AT IT FROM DIFFERENT ANGLES – DESCRIBE STATUS DIFFERENTLY – BEG, J.

560. The theory outlined above would, of course, be unacceptable if sovereignty must necessarily be indivisible and located in a determinate living person or persons ......, a really medieval concept which is not generally employed today even to describe the titular hereditary monarchs as "sovereigns", although the dictionaries may still give the derivative meaning of "sovereign" as the human ruler. Modern theories of even political sovereignty advanced by the Pluralist School ......e.g. Gierke, Duguit, McIyer, Laski ....., look upon it as divisible and not as absolute and unlimited. Indeed, they go to the extent of practically denuding sovereignty of all its customary connotations. Duguit abandons "sovereignty" as an obsolescent doctrine and displaces it by the ruling principle of "social solidarity." McIyer thinks that the traditional concept of sovereignty, dominated too long by legalistic Austinian views, needs to be discarded. His conclusion is that the State, with which doctrine of sovereignty has been bound up, is "the association of associations", merely regulates "principles of association" or relations between individuals and associations in the interests of Society as a whole. He wrote:

> "At any moment the State is more the official guardian than the maker of the law. Its chief task is no uphold the rule of law, and this implies that it is itself also the subject of law, that it is bound in the system of legal values which it maintains. "

(*See*: R.M. MacIyer: "The Modern State" p. 478).

Laski, while mainly accepting this rather negative approach, reminiscent of 19th century Liberalism, would accord the State a much more positive role in the interests not only of social order but also of socio-economic engineering and progress.

561. Marxists, who saw in the State and its laws and all institutions supporting an existing social order, the means of oppression and exploitation of the mass of the people, dreamt of the "withering away" of the State with its claims to 'Sovereignty'. But, the Russian Revolution was followed by the vastly increased powers of the State run for the benefit of the proletariat. Nevertheless, the Constitution of the U.S.S.R. guarantees to citizens not merely fundamental rights, including the right to work, but has a special department of the Procurator General to enforce due observance of legality, according to the law of the Constitution, by all the functionaries of State. Article 104 of their Constitution reads:

> "104. The Supreme Court of the U.S.S.R, is the highest judicial organ. The Supreme Court of the U.S.S.R, is charged with the supervision of the judicial activities of all the judicial organs of the U.S.S.R, and of the Union Republic within the limits established by law."

(*See*: A Denisov, M. Kirichenko, Soveit State-Law, p. 400).

562. It is true that legality is enforced in the U.S.S.R, not merely through the organs of the State but the vigilance of the Communist Party which consists of selected persons keeping a watch on the policy of the State. A.Y. Vyshinski, however, explained (*See*: Fundamental Tasks of Soviet Law 1938) that Soviet "law can no more be reduced simply to policy than cause can be identified with effect. " Strict observance of "Socialist Legality", under the supremacy of the Constitution, is entrusted to the care of the State, with its three organs, the Communist Party, and the people of the U.S.S.R. (*See*: "The Soviet Legal System" by M/s. John N. Howard and Issac Shapiro). Although, Article 15 of the Constitution of the U.S.S.R., speaks of the "Sovereignty'" and "Sovereign Rights" of the Union Republics, yet, it is made clear that these Republics function subject to the supremacy of the Constitution. Hence, the supremacy of the Constitution is a principle recognised by the Constitution of the U.S.S.R. also as operating above and limited the Sovereignties of the Socialist Republics.

563. Gierke made a wide survey and a penetrating analysis of juristic thinking, up to the end of the 19th century, on sovereignty, derived, on the one hand, from theories of the sovereignty of the Ruler, and, on the other, from theories of popular sovereignty. He observed: (*See*: "Natural Law and Theory of Society" by Otto Gierke translated by Ernest Barker, Vol. I, p, 153) about the approach of Kant:

> "Kant sketches, indeed, an ideal Constitutional State in which popular sovereignty is nominally present, but no living 'subject' of supreme authority

is anywhere really to be found in this State. The 'bearers' of the different powers (legislative, executive and judicial) are supposed to govern, but each is subject to strict legal obligation appropriate to its own sphere, and over them all, as the Sovereign proper, the abstract Law of Reason is finally enthroned."

He concluded (at p. 153):

"The history of the theory of constitutionals shows how a doctrine derived from the principle of popular sovereignty could produce almost the same results as the other (and apparently opposite) system of thought which started from the principle of the sovereignty of the Ruler. In the one case, just as in the other, the inviolability of sovereignty and the unity of the personality of the State are sacrificed, in order to attain the possibility of a constitutional law which is binding even on the Sovereign."

SOVEREIGNTY DEMARCATES THE SPHERE FOR PROPER OPERATION – HATES MERE USE OF POWER DIVORCED FROM HUMAN REASON AND NATURAL JUSTICE – OUR CONSTITUTION REGULATES THE OPERATION OF THE ORGANS OF THE STATE – IT OPERATES THROUGH LAW – BEG, J.

564. A theory of a "Legal Sovereignty" must necessarily demarcate the sphere of its "legal" or proper operation as opposed to mere use of power either capriciously or divorced from human reason and natural justice. Ernest Barker's statement of it, quoted by me in **Kesavananda's** case (supra), seemed to me to satisfy this requirement. After pointing out that Sovereignty, by which I understand one recognised by law, is limited both by its own "nature" as well as its "mode of action", it concludes: (at pp. 867 868 (of SCR) = (at p. 1973 of AIR)):

"Sovereignty moves within the circle of the legal association, and only within that circle it decides upon questions of a legal order, and only upon those questions. Moving within that circle, and deciding upon those questions, sovereignty will only make legal pronouncements, and it will make them according to regular rules of legal procedure. It is not a capricious power of doing anything in any way: it is a legal power of settling finally legal questions in a legal way."

There should be no difficulty in accepting such a theory if one can conceive of an ordered system or "Government of laws' as opposed to a "Government of men" placed beyond limitations of this kind. At any rate, it is implicit in the very idea of a Constitution. Our Constitution not only regulates the operations of the organs of State but symbolises the unity of the Republic and contains the inspiring hopes and aspirations and cherished goals of all the efforts of the nation. It operates not merely through the law but also on the minds and feelings of the people.

AMERICAN JURIST ADVOCATES DOCTRINE OF 'SOVEREIGNTY OF THE PEOPLE' – BEG, J.

565. Prof. Willis, in his "Constitutional Law of the United States" advocates the doctrine of "sovereignty of the People" for which he finds support in Abraham Lincoln's well-known description of the American system as "a Government of the people, for the people, by the people" as well as in a number of pronouncements of the American Supreme Court. After considering and rejecting a whole host of theories of political philosophers and jurists, including those of Bodin, Hegel, Hooker, Hobbes, Locke, Rousseau, Fichte, Kant, Austin, Brown, Dicey, Willoughby, Duguit, and Laski, he opines: (at p. 51):

> "As Dewey says, the forces which determine the Government are sovereign. The effective social forces are not the Union, nor the States, nor the oligarchy of States, nor the organs of Government, nor the Constitution, nor natural law, but those forces which created these organisations and agents and institutions, and to whom they are all ultimately responsible."

According to him, the "Sovereignty of the People" which he advocates does not mean an anarchic license given to each individual or group to do as he or it pleases, but stands for the power of the people, "organised in Government to express and adjust their will either directly or through representatives". He explains, in the rest of his work, how the Government of the U.S.A., in the broader sense of all that social control which, operating through the three departments of State, has to take place in accordance with the Constitution. This concept of a nation "organised in Government" appears to me to clearly introduce the idea of a Constitution which lays down what that organisation is and how it must operate. Although Prof. Willis rejects the view that the Constitution is "Sovereign", because it can be altered by the people, he is obliged to accept something resembling it because he sees that the "people", thought of as a mere aggregation or an amorphous mass, is too nebulous. Any satisfactory theory of sovereignty must account for the power of the people to act in certain ways or to move in certain directions. A 'hydra-headed' multitude or mass of people will not know how to act or in which direction to move. It is its "Organisation" which provides that. And, its effort to organise itself and to rationalise will produce a Constitution for it which embodies its will as organised in the form of a Government. The will of the people is thus inseparable from a Constitution which enables it to be expressed and then to govern. The Constitution neither is nor can be sovereign in the sense that the people who made it cannot unmake it or change it. It only prescribes the correct mode of doing everything, including that of changing the very system of Government. It is only in this sense that it can be "Sovereign" or "Supreme" and rule the life of a nation."

566. Another American writer, Willoughby, has put forward the view that sovereignty, as an attribute of the State, conceived of as a juristic entity apart from its governmental organs, cannot be legally limited. According to him, to limit it is to destroy it. He says (*See*: Willoughby on *"Fundamental Concepts of Public Law, Tagore Law Lectures*, 1924, at p. 77): "There would seem to be no more value in attaching legal rights and duties to the sovereign State than there is in predicating the attributes of goodness and justice of a Divine Being who is regarded as Himself the creator, by His own unrestrained Will, of all distinctions between goodness and badness". But, this seems more a metaphysical than a realistic, more amoral Hobbes-Machiavellian than a Dante Gandhian stance. If one's concepts of the Divine Being are to be introduced into law, one could refer to those also which see Divinity only in that order and that law which seems to pervade and govern the whole physical world and the universe. Indeed, there are judicial dicta to the effect that God Himself considered Himself bound by those elementary principles of justice whose love was planted in man by him. In **Cooper v. Wandsworth Board of Works, (1863) 14 CB (NS) 180** Byles, J., observed:

> "The laws of God and man both give the party an opportunity to make his defence, if he has any. I remember to have heard it observed by a very learned man, upon such an occasion, that even God himself did not pass sentence upon Adam before he was called upon to make his defence. 'Adam'(says God), 'where art thou? Hast thou not eaten of the tree whereof I commanded thee that thou shouldest not eat? And the same question was put to Eve also".

CONSTITUTIONAL GOVERNMENT PRESCRIBES DEFINITE WAYS IN WHICH THE SOVEREIGN POWER SHALL BE EXERCISED BY THE STATE – THEORY OF SOVEREIGN PRE-SUPPOSES ORDERLY EXISTENCE OF GOVERNMENT – BEG, J.

567. It is clear that no simple theory of sovereignty fits the complex facts of modern life. Every theory of today, ultimately, rests on concepts more refined than the physical or spiritual might of some ruler, in whom executive, legislative, and judicial powers coalesce to take away all legal distinctions between them. Even if that was ever the concept of sovereignty anywhere, it was certainly not that of our Constitution makers and it is not ours today. Even Willoughby, dealing with Constitutionals (Willoughby on "Nature of the State" 1928, at p. 302) says: "the value of constitutional Government is not that places sovereignty in the hands of the people, but that it prescribes definite ways in which this sovereign power shall be exercised by the State". Hence, he too admits that the Constitution does place some limitation on exercise of sovereign power. That seems to me to be the essence of a Constitution and the rationale of its existence.

568. Still another American writer, Orfield, in the course of his discussion (*see*: "The Amending of the Federal Constitution" by Lester B. Orfield 1971), of a number of concepts of sovereignty seems sometimes to almost consider Article 5 of the American Constitution, containing the constituent power and its procedure, to be sovereign. He concludes his discussion on the subject as follows (at p, 166):

> "Each part of the amending body is subject to law, and may be altered or abolished. The amending body itself may be altered through the amending process, and limitations on the future amending capacity may be imposed. The amending body is an artificial sovereign deriving its being from a law in the form of Article Five. The amending groups hold office for but a short time, and may be supplanted by others in the elections in which an increasingly larger electorate participates. The theory of sovereignty, moreover, presupposes the continued orderly existence of the Government. In case of a revolution the commands of the sovereign would be disregarded, and authority could no longer be ascribed to the amending body either in fact or in law. The moral, religious, physical, and other factual limitations on the supposed sovereign are so important that it may perhaps be correct to say that they are also legal limitations, as there comes a time when law and fact shade into one another. Finally, when it is remembered that throughout all history, American as well as European, there never has been a consensus as to the meaning of sovereignty, it seems that the term should be used only with the greatest circumspection."

He rejects the concept of sovereignty of the people as too vague and meaningless. And, for the reasons given above, he rejects the theory of a sovereignty of the amending body. His final conclusion seems to be that it is better to avoid altogether entanglement in the concept of sovereignty. This view, however, overlooks the fact that lawyers need a working theory of sovereignty to be able to decide legal questions before them. As between the sovereignty of the amending Article and the sovereignty of the Constitution there should be little doubt that lawyers should and would prefer the sovereignty or supremacy of the whole Constitution rather than of any part of it. On the face of it, it appears more reasonable and respectable to swear allegiance to the whole Constitution, as we actually do, rather than to Article 368 or to the amending powers contained in it. If there is a part of our Constitution which deserves greater devotion than any other part of it, it is certainly the preamble to our Constitution.

568A. The American Supreme Court, in the context of the especially American conditions and needs, after leaning sometimes towards a recognition of "State

Sovereignty" (*See*: Ware v. Hylton, (1876) 3 Dall 199; Dred Scott v. Sandford, (1856) 19 How 393) and at others towards a recognition of the dual system of Government which has prevailed in America (*See*: e.g. **Gibbus v. Ogden, (1824) 9 Wheat 1)** has on the whole opted for the "Sovereignty of the People" which unifies the nation (*See*: e.g. **White v. Heart, (1871) 13 Wall 646; Keith v. Clark, (1878) 97 US 454; National Prohibition** cases, (1920) 253 US 350).

569. I cannot, while I am on the subject of American conditions, resist the temptation to quote the trenchant, comments of Prof. Willis on what he considers to be the dangers of the American system of Government. He wrote (at pp. 68-69).

> "But the greatest danger in popular sovereignty does not lie in the intellectual field, but in the moral. While our intellectual level is not as high as it ought to be, our moral level is much lower than it can safely be if our form of Government is to endure permanently. Millions of our citizens are already members of the criminal class. Millions of other citizens who are not yet members of the criminal class are in the economic world doing things just as bad as the things which members of the criminal class are doing. Millions of our people are concerned with their own selfish interests instead of the cornpone good. Millions of our citizens are only too ready to ruin themselves and the rest of our people physically, intellectually, and morally by drugs and intoxicating liquors and vices. Our people do not seem to be much concerned with high ideals in any of the fields of human endeavor. Our people as a whole do not seem to be seriously concerned with social planning for the purpose of obtaining an ideal social order. They are more interested in rotation in office than they are in good Government. They are more interested in winning law suits than in ideal system for the administration of justice. They are more interested in making fortunes in the practice of medicine than in the prevention of disease. They are more interested in profits in the business world than they are in a well-planned system of business organisation adapted to the needs of our social order. They are more interested in individualism than they are in collective planning for the good of all.
>
> The effects of the moral standards of our people are already manifest. As a result of our political and economic theories, there has developed a concentration of wealth unparalleled in human history. While on the whole the economic level is comparatively high in the United States, the difference between the wealth of the many and that of the few is startling. One-fourth of the families in the United States before the depression had incomes of less than $ 500 and two thirds of the families in the United States incomes of less than $ 1,000 while 2 per cent of our population owned 65 per cent of the wealth. There were four men any one of whom had an income as large as five million of the poorest people in the United States. This concentration of wealth was probably one of the primary causes of the depression, and the depression has threatened our capitalistic system. This only shows the danger inherent in our political organisation."

AFTER NOTICING PROF. WILLIS'S VIEWS – IT CAN BE SAID THAT CONCEPT OF SUPREMACY OF OUR CONSTITUTION IS UNDOUBTEDLY MORE SUITED TO NEEDS OF OUR COUNTRY – IT PLACES GOALS BEFORE THE NATION – COMPELS THREE ORGANS OF SOVEREIGN REPUBLIC TO ACHIEVE IT – BEG, J.

570. If the people of an advanced country like the U.S.A., left entirely to the concept of popular sovereignty, have revealed the need for a more positive guiding or moulding role of their State so as to overcome the dangers adverted to by Prof.

Willis, how much greater are the needs of a people potentially so great but actually so backward economically and educationally as ours, taken *en masse,* still are? Our concepts of sovereignty must accord with the needs of the people of our country. Our Constitution, which has been described by G. Austin as "the cornerstone of the Nation", was devised as a means to serve those needs. It has not only the elevating Preamble, deserving the allegiance of every rational human being, but, unlike the American Constitution, the whole of Part IV of our Constitution which contains "Directive Principles of State Policy" to guide the future course of State action particularly in the legislative field. It is true that provisions of Part IV are not enforceable through the Courts against the State, but they are declared as fundamental in the governance of the country and are used to interpret the Constitution and to fix its meaning. I think, from this point of view also, we can say that the concept of the Supremacy of the Constitution is, undoubtedly, more suited to the needs of our country than any other so far put forward. It not only places before us the goals towards which the nation must march but it is meant to compel our Sovereign Republic, with its three organs of Government to proceed in certain directions. It assumes that each organ of State will discharge its trust faithfully. Can we deny it that supremacy which is the symbol and proof of the level of our civilisation?

'SUPREMACY' OR 'SOVEREIGNTY' HAS BEEN VESTED IN OUR 'CONSTITUTION' BY A SEVEN–JUDGE BENCH OF SUPREME COURT – ALSO HELD BY MAJORITY IN KESHVANANDA'S JUDGMENT DECLARING ITS 'BASIC STRUCTURE' – BEG, J.

571. I find that the doctrine of the supremacy or sovereignty of the Constitution was adopted by a Bench of seven learned Judges of this Court in **Special Reference No. 1 of 1964, (1965) 1 SCR 413** where Gajendragadkar, C.J., speaking for six learned Judges of this Court said (at p. 446) (of SCR): (at pp. 762-763 of AIR):

> "In a democratic country governed by a written Constitution, it is the Constitution which is supreme and sovereign. It is no doubt true that the Constitution itself can be amended by the Parliament, but that is possible because Article 368 of the Constitution itself makes a provision in that behalf, and the amendment of the Constitution can be validly made only by following the procedure prescribed by the said article. That shows that even when the Parliament purports to amend the Constitution, it has to comply with the relevant mandate of the Constitution' itself. Legislators, Ministers, and Judges all take oath of allegiance to the Constitution, for it is by the relevant provisions of the Constitution that they derive their authority and jurisdiction and it is to the provisions of the Constitution that they owe allegiance. Therefore, there can be no doubt that the sovereignty which can be claimed by the Parliament in England, cannot be claimed by any Legislature in India in the literal absolute sense."

572. The principle of the supremacy of the Constitution was then declared by the majority of the learned Judges of this Court in **Kesavananda's** case (supra) to be a part of the basic structure of the Constitution. The minority opinion, while not specifically dissenting from this view, was that even what was considered by the majority to be a part of "basic structure" was alterable under Article 368. But, no Judge of this Court has so far held that, without even attempting to change what may be the basic structure of Constitution itself, by appropriate amendments, judicial power could be exercised by Parliament under Article 368 on the assumption that it was already there.

573. M.C. Setalvad, a distinguished jurist of India, said (*See*: *"The Common Law of India"* Hamlyn Lectures 12th series – 1960) (at pp, 174-175):

"The Constitution divides the functions of the Union into the three categories of executive, legislative and judicial functions following the pattern of the British North America Act and the Commonwealth of Australia Act. Though this division of functions is not based on the doctrine of separation of powers as in the United States yet there is a broad division of functions between the appropriate authorities so that, for example, the legislature will not be entitled to arrogate to itself the judicial function of adjudication. The Indian Constitution has not indeed recognised the doctrine of separation of powers in its absolute rigidity but the functions of the different parts or branches of the Government have been sufficiently differentiated and consequently it can very well be said that our Constitution does not contemplate assumption, by one organ or part of the State, of functions that essentially belong to another', (*See*: **Rai Saheb R.J. Kapur v. State of Punjab, (1955) 2 SCR 225 (235, 555-56)**. This will no doubt strike one accustomed to the established supremacy of Parliament in England as unusual. In the course of its historical development Parliament has performed and in a way still performs judicial functions. Indeed the expression 'Court of Parliament' is not unfamiliar to English lawyers. However, a differentiation of the functions of different departments is an invariable feature of all written constitutions. The very purpose of a written constitution is the demarcation of the powers of different departments of Government so that the exercise of their powers may be limited to their particular fields. In countries governed by a written constitution, as India is, the supreme authority is not Parliament but the Constitution. Contrasting it with the supremacy of Parliament, Dicey has characterised it as the supremacy of the Constitution."

IN AMERICA ALSO THE THEORY IS THAT 'CONSTITUTION IS SUPREME' – BEG, J.

574. A.V. Dicey, the celebrated profounder of the doctrine of the sovereignty of Parliament, had critised Austin for frequently mixing up "legal sovereignty" and "political sovereignty" (*See* Law of the Constitution by A.V. Dicey – 10th Edn. p. 72). He contrasted the British principle of "parliamentary sovereignty" with what was described by him the "Supremacy of the Constitution" in America. He observed (at p. 165).

"But, if their notions were conceptions derived from English law, the great statesman of America gave to old ideas a perfectly new expansion and for the first time in the history of the world formed a constitution which should in strictness be 'the law of the land', and in so doing created modern federalism. For the essential characteristics of federalism – the supremacy of the constitution – the distribution of powers – the authority of the judiciary- reappear, though no doubt with modifications, in every true federal state."

He said (at p, 144):

"A federal state derives its existence from the constitution, just as a corporation derives its existence from the grant by which it is created. Hence, every power, executive, legislative, or judicial, whether it belongs to the nation or to the individual States, is subordinate to and controlled by the constitution."

He wrote about the American Supreme Court (at p, 159):

"Of the nature and position of the Supreme Court itself this much alone need for our present purpose be noted. The court drives its existence from the Constitution, and stands, therefore, on an equality with the President and with Congress, the members thereof (in common with every Judge of the Federal Judiciary) hold their places during good behaviour, at salaries which cannot be diminished during a judge's tenure of office."

SUPREME COURT IS MOUTHPIECE OF THE "REAL WILL" OF THE PEOPLE – SCOPE OF ARTICLE 368 IS LIMITED – BASIC STRUCTURE OF THE CONSTITUTION CANNOT BE TOUCHED EVEN BY CONSTITUENT POWER – HELD BEG, J.

575. The theory of the Supremacy of the Constitution is thus not a new one at all. It is inherent in the very concept of "the auguster thing" which lies behind Parliament or king and is sought to be embodied in the Constitution of a country. The Judges, who are vested with the authority and charged with the duty to uphold the Constitution, do so as the mouthpieces of what has been called the "Real will" of the people themselves by political philosophers such as Bosanquet. That, as I have indicated earlier, is the theory underlying the system of judicial review. Such a system may delay changes but should not, I think, speaking entirely for myself deny or defeat the right of the people to bring about any change, whether basic or not, in the Constitution. Indeed, in **Kesavananda's** case (supra), I indicated that I thought that the most proper and appropriate function of the amending power in a Constitution, which is also a part of the Constitution, and, indeed, its most potent part - was that of making basic changes so as to avert constitutional break downs and revolutions if possible. However, we are precluded from acting upon such a broad view of amending power in this case as we are bound by the majority opinion in **Kesavananda's** case (supra) that implied limitations of "a basic structure", operating from even outside the language of Article 368, as it stood before the 24th amendment, restrict its scope. These limitations must however, be related to provisions of the Constitution.

576. It has not been argued before us that the introduction by the 24th amendment of the new clause (1) in Article 368, containing the "constituent power", itself amplifies or increases the contents or changes the character of the power in Article 368 by making, a composite power so as to include a new type of judicial or quasi-judicial power also within its fold now. It is evident from the judgments of learned Judges of this Court in **Golaknath's** case (supra) that possible distinctions between amending power and "constituent power" and "Sovereign power" figured prominently in arguments in that case. Wanchoo, J., in his minority opinion (*see* **1967 (2) SCR 762 (833)** said that, it was not necessary, for the purpose of that case, to decide whether the amending power was as wide as the "sovereign power" of the Constituent Assembly which had framed our Constitution. After all the discussion that had taken place then, came the 24th amendment. It does not use the words "sovereignty" or "sovereign power" presume that the words "constituent power" were advisedly used in it so as to clarify the position and not to put in or to include anything beyond constitution making power in Article 368.

577. The "constituent power" is still bound by the exclusively prescribed procedure to "amend by way of addition, variation, or repeal" any provision of the Constitution. It is entirely a law making procedure elaborately set out in clause (2). In fact, Article 368 contains so much of the fundamental law making or legislative procedure that five judges of this Court, led by Subba Rao, C.J., opined in **Golaknath's** case (supra), that it was confined to procedure and did not contain at all the substantive power to amend. Clause (1) of Article 368, introduced by the 24th amendment, was, apparently, meant to remove this objection and to do no more. It could not be intended to pour some new amalgam of executive and judicial or quasi-judicial substantive powers into it also by some implication so as to do away with the very need for such an elaborate and carefully drawn up Constitution such as ours. The absence of any *quasi*-judicial procedure, from the comprehensively framed procedural provisions of Article 368, seems extremely significant. It indicates that it was the clear intention of Constitution-makers that no judicial or *quasi*-

judicial function could be performed by Parliament whilst operating in the special Constituent field of law making. An omission to provident *quasi*-judicial procedure in Article 368; which, apparently, furnishes a self-contained code, means that no such power was meant to be included here at all. Proper exercise of judicial power is inseparable from appropriate procedure.

578. Learned counsel supporting the 39th Amendment tried to find the meaning of "constituent power" in theoretical' speculations about the meaning of "the sovereignty of the people", on the one hand, and the sovereignty of the medieval monarch on the other, instead of looking to the legislative history of the "constituent power". I have, therefore, also referred to some of these theories and practices from ancient times so as to be able to indicate the precise significance or relevance of various concepts and decisions placed before us. These theories and practices could have only an indirect bearing on the meaning of the term "constituent power" in Article 368. They are more germane to a statement of a correct theory of sovereignty which underlies what has been called the "basic structure" of our Constitution.

'SOVEREIGNTY OF THE PEOPLE' FINDS EXPRESSION THROUGH THREE ORGANS OF 'STATE' – LEGISLATURE, EXECUTIVE, JUDICIARY – HELD BEG, J.

579. There are scattered dicta in the judgments of the Court speaking of the "sovereignty of the people" which, in my opinion, can only be related to the political sovereignty of the people recognised by the preamble to our Constitution where the people are described as the Constitution makers who gave the Constitution unto themselves. This, however, does not, in my opinion, mean that the people retained upto themselves any residue of legal sovereignty. They did not prescribe, apart from dividing the exercise of sovereign power roughly between the three organs of the Republic, each with its own *modus operandi*, any other or direct method, such as Initiative or Referendum, for exercising their politically sovereign power. The view I have tried to put forward in the foregoing pages is that the people entrusted to the three organs of the Sovereign Democratic Republic they constituted the exercise of three aspects of sovereign power on behalf of the people. This seems to me to be the only way of reconciling the idea of a sovereign people, in the political sense, and the sovereignty of the Republic, represented by a legally supreme constitution, so that the "sovereign" powers of each of the three organs of the Republic had to be exercised in conformity with the mandates, both positive and negative, express and implied, of the Constitution. I would prefer to describe this concept as one of the "supremacy of the Constitution" instead of "sovereignty" of the Constitution because of the theoretical, speculative, and "emotive" clouds which have gathered around the term "sovereignty".

JURISTS ARE DIFFERING TO INTERPRET 'SOVEREIGNTY' – POLITICAL THEORISTS ARE MAINLY CONCERNED WITH THE 'CONSTITUENT POWER' – BEG, J.

580. I have tried to point out that the term sovereignty in its origin is associated with the actual human ruler or authority wielding theoretically absolute or final powers. Political philosophers are particularly concerned with the problem of determining the location and manner of exercise of such powers if any. Jurists, however, have also occupied themselves with these problems partly because constitutional law, as Dicey once pointed out, has some overlapping territory with the political theory which underlies it. Some Constitutional lawyers, such as Ivor Jennings, have said that it is flirtation with political theory which has brought into the juristic fold a term such as 'sovereignty'. On the other hand, political theorists, such as McIver, have blamed, far less justly, jurists like Austin for infecting political theory with legalistic authoritarian notions of sovereignty. Political theorists, in their attempts to understand and rationalize, and sometimes to justify to condemn a system are more concerned with the operations of all those socio-economic-cum-political forces which govern society. Law is, for them, one of these forces and reflects them. Lawyers have been compelled to "Flirt' (if I may employ the term used by Sir Ivor Jennings with sovereignty) only because they have to look for some final authority which determines the validity of the claims they have to deal with, Political theory, faced with the complexities of modern life, finds location of sovereignty as a power concept too elusive and difficult a task to be satisfactorily carried out. Some of them would like to banish the term to the region of purely moral philosophy where it could be reserved for such freedom of thought and Will and action as even the most powerful totalitarian State, employing all the techniques based on Prof. Pavlov's theories for purposes of propaganda, cannot take away from the individual. Others find it of use only in International Law to denote that independence of the national State and the freedom which it claims and is entitled to from outside interference. Jurists as well as practical lawyers have to be content with finding an ultimate measuring rod in a fundamental law which could test the validity of exercise of every kind of Governmental power. Their quest for certainty is even more pressing and urgent than that of the political theorist. For their purposes, the supremacy of the Constitution, of which a very vital and necessary part is the constituent power, is sufficient. Of course, they have to determine the content of "constituent power" itself in the light of all relevant considerations which, as I have indicated above, may take us outside the ordinary range of Law. Nevertheless, our deviation from the orthodox canons of construction and interpretation, when faced with such a problem must not be so wide as to rob our method of construction itself of legal propriety or give rile to the suspicion that we have ourselves clearly trespassed into the territory of law-making. The lines of demarcation, though difficult to draw sometimes, are, nevertheless, there.

581. I do not think that it is at all helpful to refer to certain authorities of this Court which were, rather surprisingly, relied upon by learned counsel supporting the 39th amendment to discover the nature of the "constituent power" contained in Article 368. I will content myself by citing a passage from the last of these cases relied upon which mentions the earlier cases of this Court also on the effect of a "Firman", in **Tilkayat Shri Govindlalji Maharaj v. The State of Rajasthan, (1964) 1 SCR 561** Gajendragadkar J., speaking for this Court said (at p. 591 of SCR); (at p, 1650 of AIR):

> "In appreciating the effect of this Firman, it is first necessary to decide whether the *Firman* is a law or not. It is matter of common knowledge that at the relevant time the Maharana of Udaipur was an absolute monarch in whom vested all the legislative, judicial and executive powers of the State. In the case of an absolute Ruler like the Maharana of Udaipur, it is difficult to make any distinction between an executive order issued by him or a legislative command issued by him. Any order, issued by such Ruler has the force of law and did govern the rights of the parties affected thereby. This position is covered by decisions of this Court and it has not been disputed before us, *Vide* **Madhaorao Phalke v. The State of Madhya Bharat, (1960) 1 SCR 957; Ammer-un-Nisa Begum v. Mahboob Begum, AIR 1955 SC 352**, and **Director of Endowments, Government of Hyderabad v. Akram Ali, AIR 1956 SC 60.**"

582. It is evident, from the quotation, relied upon by the Solicitor-General, that this Court was not deciding whether the Firman was even a "law" in the sense of a general nor which had to be applied to the decision of cases. It was held that whatever be its juristic character it had the "force of law" in as much as the Ruler of Udaipur was an absolute ruler, who combined in his person the legislative, the judicial, and executive authority of the State. That was the Constitution of Udaipur. The doctrine of separation of powers, in such a context, was really irrelevant. Article 368 of our Constitution, however, is not a power acquired by our Republic by State Succession from the powers of Indian ruling princes. The legislative history behind it is entirely different.

INDIAN INDEPENDENCE ACT GAVE ONLY LAW-MAKING CONSTITUENT POWERS – NO LAW FRAMED AFTER REPEALING ACT OF 1951 PRIOR TO 39TH CONSTITUTION AMENDMENT – NO JUDICIAL POWER VESTED IN PARLIAMENT – CLAUSE 4 OF ARTICLE 329A WAS NOT AN 'UNBROKEN' COMBINATION OF LEGISLATIVE AND JUDICIAL POWER – BEG, J.

583. As a matter of legislative history, we will find the source of the "constituent power" in sections 6 and 8 of the Indian Independence Act passed by the British Parliament. Section 6 of that Act constituted a "Legislature" for each of two Dominions set up with plenary powers of legislation. The legislative powers of the Legislature of each Dominion were so enlarged by section 8 that it could frame the Constitution of the Dominion concerned. This was a transfer of only a legislative power. Section 8 said: "for the purpose of making provision as to the Constitution of the Dominion, the legislature of the dominion was recognised as the constituent assembly of the Dominion". These powers were "plenary" in the sense in which this term is used in **Queen v. Burah, (1878) 5 Ind App 178 (PC)** but they were confined to law making and did not extend to adjudication or decision of individual cases which is certainly distinguishable from a law-making power. For purposes other than framing of the Constitution, provisions of the Government of India Act operated until they were repealed and replaced by other relevant provisions. Such was the process of a legislative succession through which institutional transformation or transition to a new but corresponding set of institutions was brought about. In the eyes of law, this was an evolutionary process through constitutional channels and not a revolutionary break with the past.

584. It is true that, in the exercise of the law making constituent power, brought in by section 8 of the Indian Independence Act, the legislatures could be armed with judicial powers as well if appropriate laws were made to that effect. But, as no law, either Constitutional or ordinary was passed, preceding 39th amendment, to repeal the Act of 1951 and then to vest a judicial power in Parliament, so as to enable it to take over and decide election disputes itself directly, I do not see how clause (4) of Article 329A, if it contained certain provisions on the assumption that such a judicial power was already there in Parliament, could be valid as a piece of mere law making. However, counsel supporting the 39th Amendment had submitted that Article 329A(4) evidenced and constituted an exercise of some "unbroken" or a combined legislative and judicial power – proposition for which no precedent of any such consolidated action of a constituent body was cited from any part of the world. The Firmans of former Indian ruling princes were hardly suitable or applicable precedents.

WHAT WAS NOT CONFERRED ON PARLIAMENT BY 'CONSTITUENT POWER' CANNOT BE PROVIDED BY ARTICLE 105(3) – HELD BEG, J.

585. An attempt was made to convince us that what may not have been otherwise possible for Parliament to do became possible by invoking the presumed exercise of some judicial power imported by Article, 105(3) of the Constitution which says:

> "105(3)...... the powers, privileges and immunities of each House of Parliament, and of the members and the committees of each House, shall be such as may from time to time be defined by Parliament by law, and, until

so defined, shall be those of the House of Commons of the Parliament of the United Kingdom, and of its members and committees, at the commencement of this Constitution."

586. I am unable to see how what was not conferred upon Parliament itself, in its constituent capacity, could be impliedly assumed to be there by virtue of certain "powers, privileges and immunities" which belong separately to each House of Parliament. Such a claim could not be based upon what is to be found directly in Article 368. It is sought to be derived from Article 105. This reasoning would, obviously, conflict with the provisions of Article 329(b) of the Constitution which indicates that an election dispute can only be resolved by an election petition before a forum provided by an ordinary enactment. Article 329(b) says:

> "329(b) No election to either House of Parliament or to the House or either House of the Legislature of a State shall be called in question except by an election petition presented to such authority and in such manner as may be provided for by or under any law made by the appropriate Legislature."

587. In exercise of its powers under Article 329(b) our Parliament had enacted the Act of 1951. The procedure provided by the Act had the binding force of a constitutionally prescribed procedure. It could not be circumvented unless, with reference to cases covered by Article 329A(4), it had been first repealed. Only after such a repeal could any other forum or procedure be legally adopted. It could not be assumed, by reason of Article 105(3), that the prescribed forum had shifted to Parliament itself, and that Parliament, in exercise of its constituent function, had both legislated and adjudicated. This is what we were asked to accept.

588. The well recognised rule of construction of statutes, which must apply to the interpretation of the Constitution as well, is: *"Expressio Unius Est Exclusio Alterius"*. From this is derived the subsidiary rule that an expressly laid down mode of doing something necessarily prohibits the doing of that thing in any other manner. The broad general principle is thus summarised in CRAWFORD's "Statutory Constructions" (1940) at p. 334:

> "Express Mention and Implied Exclusion (Expressio Unius Est Exclusio Alterius) – As a general rule in the interpretation of statutes, the mention of one thing implies the exclusion of another thing. It, therefore, logically follows that if a statute enumerates the things upon which it is to operate, everything else must necessarily, and by implication, be excluded from its operation and effect. For instance, if the statute in question enumerates the matters over which a court has jurisdiction, no other matters may be included. Similarly, where a statute forbids the performance of certain things, only those things expressly mentioned are forbidden. So also, if the statute directs that certain acts shall be done in a specified manner, or by certain person, their performance in any other manner than that specified, or by any other person than one of those named, is impliedly prohibited."

589. It is interesting to note that in the Australian Constitution, where there is Article 49, using language very similar to that of Article 105(3) of our Constitution, there is also a separate but differently cast Article 47 of the Australian Constitution corresponding to Article 329(b) of our Constitution. This article runs as follows:

> "Article: 47. Until the Parliament otherwise provides, any question respecting the qualification of a senator or of a member of the House of Representatives, or respecting a vacancy in either House of the Parliament, and any question of a disputed election to either House, shall be determined by the House in which the question arises."

WHAT IS PROVIDED BY ARTICLE 329(B) FALLS OUTSIDE THE SCOPE OF ARTICLE 105(3) – THESE PROVISIONS OPERATE SEPARATELY – HELD BEG, J.

590. What is separately, expressly, and especially provided for by Article 329(b) must necessarily fall outside the purview of Article 105(3) on the principle stated above. Moreover, Article 105(3) contained a temporary provision until other provision was made by Parliament in that behalf. Appropriate provisions were enacted by the Act of 1951 in compliance with Article 329(b) because that was the proper Article for it. It would be idle to contend that these provisions suddenly lapsed or ceased to exist as soon as Parliament took up consideration of the issue and the grounds of the decision on them by the High Court to which reference is made in Article 329A(4). Again, a purported exercise of power, in enacting Article 329A(4), could only be a law making power and not any other power which could conceivably fall under Article 105, sub-art. (3). Nevertheless, it was suggested, by copious references to the origin of the power of the House of Commons to decide disputes relating to elections, that such a power exists in each House of our Parliament as its inherent power. Such an argument completely overlooks that, quite apart from the great difference made by providing both the forum and the procedure for deciding election disputes indicated by Article 329(b) of our Constitution, Article 105(3) itself could only refer to such powers as were still exercisable by the House of Commons at the time when our Constitution was passed. Long before that, the House of Commons in England had ceased to decide election disputes itself. It had transferred this power to Courts by statute and has not resumed it. In fact, the law enacted in the Representation of the People Act, 1949, by the British Parliament confirmed this transfer or delegation of power. Section 107 of that Act makes it clear, like Article 329(b) of our Constitution, that the statutory remedies are the only ones open for election disputes.

* * * * *

ARTICLE 194(3) VEST POWER TO PUNISH FOR ITS CONTEMPT – ARTICLE 105(3) GIVES SAME POWER TO PARLIAMENT – IT DOES NOT EMPOWER IT TO DECIDE ELECTION DISPUTE – HELD BEG, J.

594. The confusions mentioned above misled some people in this country, due to the provisions of Article 194(3) of our Constitution, on the question whether a House of a Legislature had not only the power to punish a citizen for contempt but also to exercise what is really a judicial power to interpret and determine the ambit of its own jurisdiction. Gajendragadkar, C.J. speaking for this court in Special **Reference No. 1 of 1964** (supra), rejected this claim and explained the English law on the subject. The learned Chief Justice pointed out the incidental character of any claim to a power, privilege, or immunity which could be covered by Article 194(3), a provision identically similar to Article 105(3), He pointed out that the only exception to this rule was the power to punish for its own contempt which, since the decision of Privy Council in **Kielley v. Carson, (1842) 4 Moo PC 63** could be thought of as a power of the House of Commons even acquired as a kind of "inheritance" from the powers once possessed by the High Court of Parliament in England. But, as all judicial or *quasi*-judicial power is, under our Constitution, expressly made exercisable under the supervision of the judicial organs of the State, it was held that a decision about the existence of the power to punish for contempt, on the facts of a particular case, is vested in the High Court. Even Sarkar, J., in his dissenting minority opinion, said (at p. 513) (of SCR): (at p. 796 of AIR): "I do not think that the House of Commons was itself ever a Court. The history of that House does not support such a contention." The result is similar to that in England where Courts do determine the orbit of a claim to a power as a Parliamentary preserve, on the facts of a case, although, once it is established that the claim is to a power confined to its proper sphere, they will not decide a mere question of its proper exercise.

595. Whatever view one may take of any other powers of Parliament, by reason of Article 105(3) of the Constitution, I am unable to see how exercise of the jurisdiction to determine an election dispute, which was in accordance with Article 329(b), already vested in the High Court by the Act of 1951 for all elections to House of the People, could not only be taken away by a Constitutional amendment, purporting to repeal retrospectively the provisions of the Act of 1951, a piece of ordinary legislation, in their application to particular class of cases, but at the same time, making a declaration of the rights of the parties to a judgment, without first performing a judicial function also which was not included in the "constituent' or any other law making power.

'CONSTITUENT POWER' CAN AMEND CONSTITUTION – IT DID NOT CONTAIN JUDICIAL POWER IN ITSELF – IT IS DISTINCT FROM ORDINARY LEGISLATIVE POWER – HELD BEG, J.

596. The question was not clearly raised before us whether a Constitutional amendment could partially repeal the provisions of an ordinary piece of legislation, that is to say, the Act of 1951, in so far as its application to a certain class of cases is concerned. One of the submissions of the learned Counsel for the election petitioner, however, was that, in as much as the Constitution lays down the norms to which ordinary legislation must conform, its proper sphere of operation is different from that of ordinary legislation which takes place under the provisions of Articles 245 to 255 of the Constitution. The argument seemed to be, that, if ordinary law making and constitution making took place in different orbits or on different planes of law making power what could be done by one method was necessarily prohibited by the other. Learned Counsel relied upon a number of passages from the judgment in **Keshvananda Bharati's** case (supra), and, in particular, on what Ray, J., (as he then was) said (at p. 386) (of SCR: (at p. 1688 of AIR):

> "The constituent power is *sui generis*. The majority view in **Golak Nath** case that Article 13(2) prevails over Article 368 was on the basis that there was no distinction between constituent and legislative power and an amendment of the Constitution was law and that such law attracted the opening words of Article 245 which in its turn attracted the provisions of Article 13(2), Parliament took notice of the two conflicting views which had been taken of the unamended Article 368, took notice of the fact that the preponderating judicial opinion, namely, the decision in **Shankari Prasad** case, **Sajjan Singh** case and the minority views of five larned Judges in **Golak Nath** case were in favour of the view that Article 368 contained the power of amendment and that power was the constituent power belonging to Parliament. Wanchoo, J. rightly said in **Golak Nath** case that the power under Article 368 is a constituent power to change the fundamental law, that is to say, the Constitution and is distinct from ordinary legislative power. So long as this distinction is kept in mind Parliament will have power under Article 368 to amend the Constitution and what Parliament does under Article 368 is not ordinary law making which is subject to Article 13(2) or any other Article of the Constitution. This view of Wanchoo, J. was adopted by Parliament in the Constitution 24th Amendment Act which made explicit that under Article 368 Parliament has the constituent power to amend this Constitution".

597. On the other hand, learned Counsel defending the 39th Amendment relied on a number of passages from various judgments, including mine, in **Kesavananda**

Bharati's case (supra), indicating that at least the minority view there was that the power of amendment contained in Article 368 was only limited by the procedure laid down in Article 368(2) of the Constitution and nothing else. It is true that this is what was emphasized by several learned judges, including myself, in dealing with a case where the real question was whether the constituent power embraced an amendment of the Constitution in such a way as to take away fundamental rights. But, neither the question whether "constituent power" itself contained judicial power within its fold nor the question whether "constituent power" operated on a plane or in a sphere which excluded altogether what could be done through ordinary legislation were under the consideration in **Kesavananda's** case (supra). Some passages were cited from my judgment in that case indicating that the constituent plane of basic changes excluded the ordinary law making plane of legislation, the two belonging, so to speak, to different spheres or orbits of operation. I think I had only cited Prof. Ernest Barker's statements of his theory some of which could convey that sense. But, I had not committed myself to a view on the question whether there was a limit on the subject matter of constituent law making.

598. It could be and has been argued, not without force, that there are no legal limitations upon the subject matter which may be considered fit for inclusion or incorporation in a constitution. This is left to the good sense of the Constitution makers. Constitutions differ greatly in this respect (*See*: Wheare's "Modern Constitution pp. 49 to 51). What may be the ideal, from this point of view, is not always the actual. Reference was also made in support of this submission to Rottschaefer on "*Constitutional Law*" (1939 Edn, p. 10). It is not necessary to pursue this question any further here.

599. I had said, in **Kesavananda's** case (supra) after dealing with amending power in Article 368, on the assumption at it was an exercise of a "sovereign power" (at p. 870) (of SCR) = (at p. 1975 of AIR):

"No doubt the judicial organ has to decide the question of the limits of a sovereign authority as well as that of other authorities in cases of dispute. But when these authorities act within these limits, it cannot interfere." In other words, I look upon a "sovereign power" itself, under the Constitution, as limited by the supremacy of the Constitution.

NO JUDICIAL POWER IS INCLUDED IN 'CONSTITUENT POWER' – CLAUSE (4) ARTICLE 329A CANNOT PERFORM JUDICIAL FUNCTIONS – PROCEDURE LAID DOWN IN 1951 ACT CANNOT BE CIRCUMVENTED – PARLIAMENT COULD NOT TAKE IN ITS OWN HANDS THE ELECTION APPEAL PENDING IN SUPREME COURT NOR DECIDE IT – HELD BEG, J.

600. If the constitutional provisions compel us to hold, as I think they do, that no form of judicial or *quasi*-judicial power is included in the "constituent power", contained in Article 368 of the Constitution, no further question need really be considered by us if we were to hold that the insertion of clause (4) in Article 329A necessarily involved, as a condition precedent to the making of the declaration found at the end of it, the performance of a *quasi*-judicial or judicial function. But, I do not think that we could go so far as that. The Act of 1951, enacted under the provisions of Article 329(b) of the Constitution, provided a procedure which could not be circumvented. This procedure was certainly applicable until 10-8-1975 when the 39th Amendment received Presidential assent. Rights of appeal under section 116A of the Act having been invoked by the Original Respondent as well as by the election petitioner, and the operation of the High Court's order having been suspended, the position was, in the eyes of law, that the election dispute was continued by a proceeding, exclusively prescribed by article 329(b) for the resolution of the dispute, pending in this Court. I do not think, that despite the impression created by the terms of the declaration at the end of clause (4) of Article 329A and the opening statement of the counsel for the original respondent, we can assume that Parliament took over the case into its own hands to decide it and to incorporate the result in the form of Article 329A(4) so that this may take the place of a possible judgment of this Court. Parliament could not be deemed to be unaware of the bar created by Article 329(b) and the 1951 Act.

601. At one stage, counsel supporting the 39th amendment said that the norms of the Act of 1951, together with the amendment of the Act in 1974 and the very recent ones of 1975, must have been present in the minds of members of Parliament and applied to the facts of the case. Such a contention, apart from overlooking the effect of the bar of Article 329(b), which operated against the case being taken up in Parliament directly until at least 10-8-1975, just as section 107 of the British Representation of People Act, 1949, operates against the adoption of such a course in England, overlooked the legal effect of the deeming provision which, if valid, would repeal such a submission of counsel supporting the 39th amendment. The deeming provision appeared to be quite sweeping. It said:

> "No law made by Parliament before the commencement of the Constitution (Thirty-ninth Amendment) Act, 1975, in so far as it relates to election petitions and matters connected therewith, shall apply or shall be deemed ever to have applied to or in relation to the election of any such person as is referred to in clause (1) to either House of Parliament."

602. The effect of such a provision is thus stated, in the oft quoted passage from **East End Dwellings Co. Ltd. v. Finsbury Borough Council, (1952) AC 109**:

> "If you are bidden to treat an imaginary state of affairs as real, you must surely, unless prohibited from doing so, also imagine as real the consequences and incidents which, if the putative state of affairs had in fact existed, must inevitably have flowed from or accompanied it........... The statute says that you must imagine a certain state of affairs, it does not say that having done so, you must cause or permit your imagination to boggle when it comes to the inevitable corollaries of that state of affairs."

THERE IS NO EVIDENCE AS TO WHAT NORMS WERE APPLIED BY THE PARLIAMENT AND WHAT PROCEDURE FOLLOWED IN NULLIFYING THE HIGH COURT JUDGMENT AS PER CLAUSE (4) OF ARTICLE 329A – HELD BEG, J.

603. When the effect of Article 329(b) and of the deeming provision was pointed out to learned counsel supporting the 4th clause of Article 329A, they took up the position that Parliament must have applied its own norms. We, however, do not know at all and cannot guess what matters were considered or the norms applied by Parliament. No speeches made in Parliament on the proposed 39th amendment were cited before us by either side. We only know that the Objects and Reasons of the 39th Amendment contain the following statements to show us why Article 329A (4) was believed to be necessary:

> "Article 71 of the Constitution provides that disputes arising out of the election of the President or Vice-President shall be decided by the Supreme Court. The same article provides that matters relating to their election shall be regulated by a parliamentary law. So far as the Prime Minister and the Speaker are concerned, matters relating to their election are regulated by the provisions of the Representation of the People Act, 1951. Under this Act the High Court has jurisdiction to try an election petition presented against either of them.

2. The President, the Vice President, the Prime Minister and the Speaker are holders of high offices. The President is not answerable to a Court of law for anything done, while in office, in the exercise of his powers. A fortiori matters relating to his election should not be brought before a court of law but should be entrusted to a forum other than a court. The same reasoning applies equally to the incumbents of the office of Vice-President, Prime Minister and Speaker. It is accordingly proposed to provide that dispute relating to the election of the President and Vice-President shall be determined by a forum as may be determined by a Parliamentary law. Similar provision is proposed to be made in the case of the election to either House of Parliament or, as the case may be, to the House of the People of a person holding the office of Prime Minister or the Speaker. It is further proposed to render pending proceedings in respect of such election under the existing law null and void. The Bill also provides that the Parliamentary law creating a new forum for trial of election matters relating to the incumbents of the high offices above-mentioned shall not be called in question in any court".

604. I think that this statement of Objects and Reasons and other reasons mentioned above by me lend support to the submission, to which Mr. Kaushal confined himself whilst other counsel supporting the validity of Article 329A(4) offered it only as an alternative submission. This was that the whole procedure adopted and needed being a law making procedure and nothing more there was no need to look for norms of for law applied as no judicial or *quasi*-judicial proceeding was involved. This approach certainly avoids the extraordinary anomalies and results involved in the proposition that "constituent power" embraces some indefinable or "unbroken" power to override laws and to withdraw and decide all disputes, particularly in election matters, in Parliament itself. As already indicated, there is no provision anywhere for the exercise of overriding judicial or *quasi*-judicial powers by Parliament. It is difficult to conceive a case being considered by Parliament and the ratifying legislatures a case on trial. Parliament could not, therefore, be assumed to have withdrawn and then to have decided a particular case in a particular way by applying its own norms. It is presumed to know the law. Ostensibly, Article 329A(4) is part of an amendment of the Constitution for the purposes found in the Statement of Objects and Reasons. Only the declaration given at the end of it suggests that, in the course of it, the effect upon the case before us was considered and dealt with.

605. If Article 329A(4) constituted only a piece of purported law making, the next question, which deserves very serious consideration by us, is whether such purported law making is not fully covered by the undoubted law making power of Parliament to make law prospectively as well as retrospectively, *inter alia,* to get rid of the legal effect or result of a judgment considered erroneous by it or to retrospectively validate an election it considers valid whatever may be its reasons for reaching this conclusion. I will answer this question after considering the relevant case law cited on the subject.

CASE-LAW RELIED UPON BY THE SOLICITOR-GENERAL IN SUPPORT OF HIS SUBMISSION DO NOT APPLY TO THE FACTS OF THIS CASE – HELD BEG, J.

606. A number of cases have been cited before us: some on retrospective validation of taxing provisions, by removing defects.

Others on removal of the basis of or grounds of decisions given by Courts making their judgments ineffective, others affecting the jurisdiction of Courts in cases pending, either in the original Courts or in Courts of Appeal so as to render proceedings infructuous, and still others curing legally defective appointments or elections. It is not necessary to discuss these cases separately and individually as the principles laid down there are well recognised. I will be content with mentioning the cases cited. They were **M.P.V. Sundararamier and Co. v. The State of Andhra Pradesh, 1958 SCR 1422; Shree Vinod Kumar v. State of Himachal Pradesh, 1959 Supp 1 SCR 160; Jadab Singh v. The Himachal Pradesh Administration, (1960) 3 SCR 755; Udai Ram Sharma v. Union of India, (1968) 3 SCR 41; Rustom Cavasjee Cooper v. Union of India, (1970) 3 SCR 530; Jagannath v. Authorised Officer, Land Reforms, (1972) 1 SCR 1055; Khyerban Tea Co. Ltd. v. The State of Assam, (1964) 5 SCR 975; Tirath Ram Rajindra Nath, Lucknow v. State of Uttar Pradesh, AIR 1973 SC 405; Krishna Chandra Gangopadhyaya v. The Union of India, AIR 1975 SC 1389; Pandia Nadar v. The State of Tamil Nadu, (1974) 2 SCC 539; State of Orissa v. B.K. Bose, 1962 Supp 2 SCR 380.**

607. Cases were also cited where rights having been altered during the pendency of proceedings. Courts had to give effect to the rights as altered, and judgments already given on the strength of the previous law had ceased to have a binding force as *res judicata* between parties or had to be set aside where appeals against them were pending. These were; **State of Uttar Pradesh v. Raja Anand Brahma Shah, (1967) 1 SCR 362; Shri Prithvi Cotton Mills Ltd. v. Broach Borough Municipality, (1970) 1 SCR 388 (392); Janapada Sabha Chhindwara v. The Central Provinces Syndicate Ltd., (1970) 3 SCR 745; Municipal Corporation of the City of Ahmedabad v. New Shorock Spg. and Wvg. Co. Ltd., (1970) 1 SCR 288; State of Tamil Nadu v. M.R. Gounder, AIR 1971 SC 231; Amarjit Kaur v. Pritam Singh, AIR 1974 SC 2068; Qudrat Ullah v. Municipal Board, Bareilly, AIR 1974 SC 396.**

608. Cases were also cited of the exercise of Constitutional power of amendment, by placing Acts in the 9th Schedule, under the provisions of Article 31B of the Constitution, such as **Jagannath v. Authorised Officer, Lond Reforms,** (supra) so that Acts so included in the 9th Schedule were immune from attack on the ground of alleged violation of any fundamental rights. It is not necessary to cite them as this is now a well recognised constitutional device whose validity has been upheld by this Court in **Keshvananda Bharati's** case, (supra).

609. Our attention was especially invited to passages from **Udai Ram Sharma v. Union of India,** (supra), where it was said (at page 54):

> "In our opinion no useful purpose will be served by referring to the clear demarcation between the judicial powers and legislative powers in America and attempt to engraft the said principle in the working of our Constitution. This development of the law, as pointed out in **A.K. Gopalan v. State, 1950 SCR 88 (198)** was due to historical reasons."

610. After that, the following passage from the judgment of Das, J. in **A.K. Gopalan's case, AIR 1950 SC 27** was quoted (at page 55):

> "The Supreme Court of the United States, under the leadership of Chief Justice Marshall, assumed the power to declare any law unconstitutional on the ground of its not being in "due process of law," .... It is thus that the Supreme Court established its own supremacy over the executive and the Congress. In India the position of the Judiciary is somewhere in between the Courts in England and the United States. While in the main leaving our Parliament and the State Legislatures supreme in their respective legislative fields, our Constitution has, by some of the articles, put upon the Legislature certain specified limitations :....... Our Constitution, unlike the English Constitution, recognises the Court's supremacy over the legislative authority, but such supremacy is a very limited one, for it is confined to the field where the legislative power is circumscribed by limitations put upon it by the Constitution itself. Within this restricted field the Court may, on a scrutiny of the law made by the Legislature, declare it void if it is found to have transgressed the conditional limitation."

611. In **Udai Ram Sharma's** case (supra) the following passage from *Willoughby's Constitution of the United States*, 2nd Edn., Vol. 3, was also cited:

> "If the legislature would prescribe a different rule for the future from that which the Courts enforce, it must be done by statute, and cannot be done by a mandate to the Courts which leaves the law unchanged, but seeks to compel the Courts to construe and apply it not according to the judicial, but according to the legislative judgment......... If the legislature cannot thus indirectly control the action of the Courts, by requiring of them a construction of the law according to its own views, it is very plain it cannot do so directly, by setting aside their judgments, compelling them to grant new trials, ordering the discharge of offenders, or directing what particular steps shall be taken in the progress of a judicial inquiry."

612. Willoughby's statement of law in the United States of America showing that retroactive legislation which does not impair vested or substantial rights or constitutional prohibitions, is permissible and his conclusion, relying on *Cooley's "Constitutional Limitations"*, was also quoted:

> "The legislature does, or may, prescribe the rules under which the judicial power is exercised by the Courts: and in doing so it may dispense with any of those formalities which are not essential to the jurisdiction of the Court; and whatever it may dispense with by statute anterior to the proceedings, we believe it may also dispense with by statute after the proceedings have been taken, if the Court has failed to observe any of those formalities. But it would not be competent for the legislature to authorise a Court to proceed and adjudicate upon the rights of parties, without giving them an opportunity to be heard before it and, for the same reason it would be incompetent for it, by retrospective legislation, to make valid any proceedings which had been had in the Courts, but which were void for want of jurisdiction over the parties."

613. In **Udai Ram Sharma's** case (supra) an argument based on some observations in **B.C. Ghose v. King Emperor, 1944 FCR 295** was that the provisions of an amending Act amounted to passing a decree. But, this Court repelled this argument reliving on principles laid down in **Q. v. Burah**, (supra):

> "If what has been done is legislation, within the general scope of the affirmative words which give the power, and if it violates no express condition or restriction by which that power is limited (in which category would, of course, be included any Act of the Imperial Parliament at variance with it), it is not for any Court of Justice to inquire further, or to enlarge constructively those conditions and restrictions."

614. A case strongly relied upon by learned Counsel supporting the validity of Article 329A(4) was: **Kanta Kathuria v. Manak Chand Surana, (1970) 2 SCR 835.** In this case, decided by five Judges of this Court, there was unanimity on the conclusion that the State Legislature had power to retrospectively remove the disqualification of a candidate. The following quotation from the judgment (at page 851 of SCR) shows the reasoning adopted:

> "Mr. Chagla, learned Counsel for the respondent, contends that the Rajasthan State Legislature was not competent to 'declare retrospectively' under Art, 191(1)(a) of the Constitution. It seems to us that there is no force in this contention. It has been held in numerous cases by this Court that the State Legislatures and Parliament can legislate retrospectively subject to the provisions of the Constitution. Apart from the question of fundamental rights, no express restriction has been placed on the power of the Legislature of the State, and we are unable to imply in the context, any restriction.

Practice of the British Parliament does not oblige us to place any implied restriction. We notice that the British Parliament in one case validated the election: (*Erskine May's Treatise on the Law, Privileges Proceedings and Usage of Parliament*, Seventeenth (1964) Edition)—

"After the general election of 1945 it was found that the persons elected for the Coatbridge Division of Lanark and the Springbourn Division of Glassgow were disqualified at the time of their election because they were members of tribunals appointed by the Minister under the Rent of Furnished Houses Control (Scotland) Act, 1943, which entitled them to a small fee in respect of attendance at a Tribunal. A Select Committee reported that the disqualification was incurred inadvertently, and in accordance with their recommendation the Coatbridge and Springbourn Elections (Validation) Bill was introduced to validate the irregular elections (H,C. Deb (1945-46) 414, c. 564-6). *See* also HC 3 (1945-46); *ibid.*, 71 (1945-46) and *ibid.*, 92 (1945-46)."

We have also noticed two earlier instances of retrospective legislation, *e.g.* The House of Commons (Disqualification) Act, 1813 (Halsbury Statutes of England P. 467) and section 2 of the Re-election of Ministers Act, 1919 (ibid, p. 515).

Great stress was laid on the word 'declared' in Article 19(1)(a), but we are unable to imply any limitation on the powers of the Legislature from this word. Declaration can be made effective as from an earlier date.

The apprehension that it may not be a healthy practice and this power might be abused in a particular case are again no grounds for limiting the powers of the State Legislature."

615. Another case on which a great deal of reliance was placed by Mr. A.K. Sen, was the case of the validation of the elections of John Clarke George, Esquire and Sir Roland Jennings, Knight 1955 Law Reports Statutes 4 Eliz 2 by the British Parliament. Here, the two gentlemen named above were "discharged, freed and indemnified from all penal consequences whatsoever incurred by them respectively by sitting or voting as Members of the Commons House of Parliament while holding their said offices." It was also declared that they "shall be deemed not to have been incapable of being elected members of the Commons House of Parliament, or to have been or to be incapable of sitting or voting as members thereof, by reason only of having at any time before the passing of this Act held office:

"(a) in the case of the said John Clarke George, as Director appointed by the Minister of Works of Scottish Slate Industries Limited.

(b) in the case of the said Sir Roland Jennings, as Approved Auditor appointed under the Industrial and Provident Societies Act, 1893, and the Friendly Societies Act, 1896."

616. Learned Counsel for the election petitioner replied that it is noticeable that no English case could be cited where any attempt was made by the British Parliament to circumvent section 107 of the Representation of the People Act, 1949, which laya down:

"Section 107, Method of questioning Parliamentary election.

(1) No Parliamentary election and no return of Parliament shall be questioned except by a petition complaining of an undue election or undue return (hereinafter referred to as Parliamentary election petition) presented in accordance with this Part of this Act.

(2) A petition complaining of no return shall be deemed to be a Parliamentary election petition and the High Court may make such order thereon as they think expedient for compelling a return to be made or may allow the petition to be heard by an election court as provided with respect to ordinary election petitions."

617. He also submitted that, in none of the cases of validation, was any election dispute shown to be pending. No judgment was actually set aside in contravention of the binding conditionally prescribed procedure to decide such disputes. He submitted that, in the case of an election to a Parliamentary seat in this country, this could be done by; parliament itself only after first repealing the application of the 1951 Act and amending Article 329(b) in such a way as to vest the power in itself to decide the dispute.

618. Learned Counsel, for the election petitioner relied upon the following statement in the *American Jurisprudence*, 2nd Edn. Vol. 46, at page 318:

> 'The general rule is that the legislature may not destroy, annul, set aside, vacate, reserve, modify, or impair the final judgment of a Court of competent jurisdiction, so as to take away private rights which have become vested by the judgment. A statute attempting to do so has been held unconstitutional as an attempt on the part of the legislature to exercise judicial power, and as a violation of the constitutional guarantee of due process of law. The legislature is not only prohibited from reopening cases previously decided by the Courts, but is also forbidden to affect the inherent attributes of a judgment. That the statute is under the guise of an Act affecting remedies does not alter the rule".

619. On the other hand, learned Counsel supporting the validity of Article 329A (4) relied on the following passage:

> "It is worthy of notice, however, that there are cases in which judgments requiring acts to be done in the future may validly be affected by subsequent legislation making illegal that which the judgment found to be legal, or making legal that which the judgment found to be illegal" They also pointed out:
>
> "With respect to legislative interference with a judgment, a distinction has been made between public and private rights under which distinction a statute may be valid even though it renders ineffective a judgment concerning a public right. Even after a public right has been established by the judgment of the Court, it may be annulled by subsequent legislation".

CONSTITUTION IS SUPREME WHICH CANNOT BE CHALLENGED – VALIDITY OF CONSTITUTIONAL AMENDMENT BY 'CONSTITUENT POWER' HAS TO BE TESTED BY CONSTITUTIONAL PROVISIONS – HELD BEG, J.

620. It is contended that the election of a candidate is the result of the exercise of their rights of voting by the electorate. An election results from public action and produces a "public right" in as much as the electorate and the public become interested parties acquiring the right to be represented by the elected candidate. The right to challenge that election is a statutory right. What the statute gives can be taken away by statute. The grounds for challenging the election could also be altered. No one, it was urged, could be heard to say that he had any vested or inherent right to challenge an election. It was contended that once the applicability of all law previous to the 39th amendment to the class dealt with by Article 329A(4) was removed retrospectively, the resulting legislative declaration followed automatically even if it had not been inserted. Its inclusion was a superfluity. Article 329A(4) was said to be merely incidental and consequential to what was done by earlier clauses (1) to (3). It is difficult to see how Article 329A(4) which relates to what was past could be incidental or consequential to what was intended to be done in future. Moreover, more serious difficulties, dealt with below, are found here than those which could arise in ordinary cases of retroactive validation.

* * * * *

622. If the constituent bodies, taken separately or together, could be legally sovereign, in the same way as the British Parliament is, the Constitutional validity of no amendment could be called in question before us. But, as it is well established that it is the Constitution and not the constituent power which is supreme here, in the sense that the Constitutionality of the Constitution cannot be called in question before us, but the exercise of the constituent power can be. We have to judge the validity of exercise of constituent power by testing it on the anvil of constitutional provisions. According to the majority view in **Keshvananda's case** (supra), we can find the test primarily in the Preamble to our Constitution.

VALIDITY OF CONSTITUTIONAL AMENDMENT – ORDINARY LAW – BOTH TO BE TESTED ON THE TOUCHSTONE OF 'BASIC STRUCTURE' – HELD BEG, J.

623. A point emphasized by J.C. Gray (*See*: *"Nature and Sources of Law"* p. 96) is that unless and until Courts have declared and recognised a law as enforcible it is not law at all. Kelsen (*See*: *"General Theory of Law and State"* p. 150) finds Gray's views to be extreme. Courts, however, have to test the legality of laws, whether purporting to be ordinary or constitutional, by the norms laid down in the Constitution. This follows from the Supremacy of the Constitution. I mention this here in answer to one of the questions set out much earlier: Does the "basic structure" of the Constitution test only the validity of a constitutional amendment or also ordinary laws? I think it does both because ordinary law making itself cannot go beyond the range of constituent power. At this stage, we are only concerned with a purported constitutional amendment. According to the majority view in **Kesavananda Bharati's** case the Preamble furnishes the yard-stick to be applied even to constitutional amendments.

IF A MAJORITY PARTY HAS TO DECIDE ELECTION DISPUTE – MINORITY PARTY CAN NEVER BE HEARD – CLAUSE (4) CREATED SUCH A LEGAL ISSUE – HELD BEG, J.

624. Learned Counsel for the election petitioner has strongly relied upon the very first purpose of the Constitution stated in the preamble to be Justice (with a capital "J") which includes "political justice". His contention is that, if a majority party is to virtually act as the judge in an election dispute between itself and minority parties whose cause, according to the learned Counsel, the election petitioner represents, it would be a plain denial of "political" justice. I do not know why this question should be termed as one of "political justice" and not of plain and simple elementary justice except that the contending parties represent political causes which are, for purposes of plain and simple justice with which we are really concerned, irrelevant. We are not asked to judge a political issue directly as to who should be the Prime Minister of this country. We are only asked to hold that even a constitutional amendment, when made by Members of a majority party to enforce their own views of what is politically and legally right, as against the views, on these matters, of minority parties, when the representatives of the minority parties allege a misuse of constitutional powers by deviation from a constitutionally laid down purpose such a legal question of fact and law should be capable of trial and decision by an independent authority on such exclusively legal grounds as may be open. That is the simple principle on which learned Counsel for the election petitioner rests his case, irrespective of the right and wrongs or the merits of his client's case ...., and, I have found it impossible to decide it, as I have decided it against the election petitioner, without going into facts and merits of the appeals – for the submission that our jurisdiction to try this case on merits cannot be taken away without injury to the basic postulates of the rule of law and of justice within a politically democratic constitutional structure. I do not think that we can, consistently with the objects of justice, including what is claimed as "political justice", which are parts of what is called the "basic structure", deny the right to claim and adjudication from this Court on exclusively legal issues (not political ones) between the majority party and the minority groups of parties, however, large and legally right the majority party may be and however small and legally wrong the minorities groups or parties may be. Can the legal rights and wrongs, on such an issue, be resolved, in accordance with the objects of the Preamble, anywhere other than this Court now? I think that it would be a very dangerous precedent to lay down that they can be and need be determined nowhere at all. That is what acceptance of total validity of Article 329A(4) may mean if it bars our jurisdiction to hear and decide such a case on merits.

625. What was sought to be done by the Constitutional amendment may be politically very justifiable. The question before us, however, is whether it is also legally justifiable. Here, we are back again in the realm of basic principles of justice. We are not to decide a political question here at all. But, we have to decide legal questions even if they have, as many legal issues have, political consequences and repercussions which we cannot entirely ignore. Perhaps we have to go back to **Marbury v. Madison**, (supra) where Chief Justice Marshal said (at. p. 162):

> "The very essence of civil liberty certainly consists in the right of every individual to claim the protection of the laws, whenever he receives an injury. One of the first duties of Government is to afford that protection. In Great Britain the King himself is sued in the respectful form of a petition, and he never fails to comply with the judgment of his court.
>
> In the 3rd, Vol. of his Commentaries, p. 23 Blackstone states two cases in which a remedy is afforded by mere operation of law.
>
> 'In all other cases', he says it is a general and indisputable rule, that where there is a legal right, there is also a legal remedy by suit, or action at law, whenever that right is invaded."

RESPONDENT CLAIMS PURELY A STATUTORY RIGHT – HE CANNOT BE DENIED EVEN A RIGHT TO BE HEARD – MAY NOT HAVE ANY MERIT – HELD BEG, J.

626. It is true that the right which the election petitioner claims is a purely statutory right. The right to come to this Court under section 116A of the Act of 1951 is also a creature of statute and can be taken away retrospectively. But, where this taking away also involves the taking away of the right to be heard by this Court on a grievance, whether justifiable or not, that a minority party is being oppressed by the majority, can we deny the spokesman of the minority even a right to be heard on merits ? Such an issue is constitutional. Confession of our inability to resolve it judicially would be, according to learned Counsel for the election petitioner, a denial of "political justice". This issue is extrinsic so far as the Act of 1951 is concerned. The election petitioner has complained of the taking away of his right to be heard with a view to depriving him of "political" justice with an ulterior object and political motivation. I have dealt with the merits of the case to show that, from the legal aspect, his grievance, on the merits of his case, is misconceived. He has no vested right under a palpably erroneous judgment which was the subject-matter of the two appeals to this Court. Nevertheless, this could only be demonstrated after we had gone into the merits of the case and rendered our decision on the issues in accordance with the law in the 1951 Act. Thus, what is involved is the right of the election, petitioner to be heard on merits and the power of this Court to look into merits of the case in order to determine whether the election-petitioner's grievances could have any real legal foundations. I think that this is a basic consideration which must compel us, in the light of the principles laid down by us in **Kesavananda Bharati's** case (supra), to hold that we must look into his grievances and determine, for ourselves, : where his case stood, on the law before it was amended. Our jurisdiction, at any rate, cannot be barred without creating the impression that what the election petitioner calls "political justice" is being denied to him.

DO CLAUSES (4)(5)(6) OF ARTICLE 329A BAR JURISDICTION OF SUPREME COURT – IF IT IS SO, IT WOULD EVEN BAR APPELLANT FROM BEING HEARD – BUT PARLIAMENT NEVER INTENDED TO DEFEAT JUSTICE – HELD BEG, J.

627. The question which arises now is: Was clause (4) of Article 329A, read with clauses (5) and (6), really meant to bar our jurisdiction to consider the grievances of the petitioner and to decide them, or, can they be so interpreted as to preserve this court's jurisdiction?

628. Broadly speaking, the election petitioner has two heads of grievance: *firstly*, that the election of the original respondent is vitiated by corrupt practices which, as I have indicated, after considering the case set-up by him and the evidence tendered and the law applicable, could not possibly succeed even under the law as it stood before the amendment, and, *secondly*, that our very jurisdiction to go into these grievances is sought to be debarred by clauses (4), (5) and (6) of Article 329A with the political object of stifling opposition, and, therefore, according to the election petitioner, we must declare clause (4) and the connected clauses (5) and (6) of Article 329A to be invalid. Although, the 1st set of complaints is based upon the provisions of the Act of 1951, the second set arises because of impugned clauses of the 39th Amendment. For the second set of grievances, the action complained of is that of the State itself acting through its law making organs. It is because of this interest of the Union of India, acting in its law making capacity, that we have heard the Attorney General and the Solicitor-General. Although, the second set of grounds may arise as a result of the 1st set, yet, they are different. Our jurisdiction to consider these different grounds of complaint does not ordinarily arise at all in the exercise of our jurisdiction under section 116A of the Act of 1951. It is for this reason, that the election petitioner had filed a separate Writ Petition in the High Court to challenge an amendment of the Act. But, we decided to hear arguments on constitutional issues also without a separate proceeding. The causes of action arising out of the amendments have become attached if I may so put it, to the appeals under section 116A of the Act because we could not, under the law, hear the appeals unless these obstacles, if any, were overcome.

629. Indeed, so far as the original respondent is concerned, the effect of clauses (4), (5) and (6) of Article 329A would be, if we were to hold that they bar our jurisdiction to go into the merits of the appeals under section 116-A of the Act, that her grievance against the judgment under appeal also could not be gone into or dealt with. In other words, the original respondent would also be denied an opportunity of asserting her rights under the 1951 Act and of vindicating her stand in the case by showing that there was really no sustainable ground for the findings given by the learned Judge of the High Court against her. We would, therefore, be prevented from doing justice to her case as well if we were to accept the contention that the 39th Amendment bars our jurisdiction to hear the appeals under section 116-A of the Act on merits. The total effect would be that justice would appear to be defeated even if, in fact, it is not so as a result of the alleged bar to our jurisdiction if it, were held to be there. Could it be the intention of Parliament that justice should appear to be defeated? I think not.

EVEN AMERICAN LAW DOES NOT BAR THIS COURT FROM HEARING 'POLITICAL JUSTICE CASE' AS MADE OUT IN THIS CASE – HELD BEG, J.

630. It was also contended before us that we should not go at all into the merits of the case before us as it was a political matter. In other words, the "political question" doctrine was invoked in aid of the submission that we should voluntarily abstain from deciding a question of a "political nature". It is true that the "political question doctrine" has been sometimes invoked, in the past, by the American Supreme Court to abstain from taking a decision. In answer to this argument, learned Counsel for the election petitioner cited before us from comments on the Constitution of the United States of America (Analysis and Interpretation by the Congressional Research Service – 1973 Edn. p. 665) that the "political question" doctrine is the result of a "prudential" attitude Courts adopt when they find that their judgments may not be enforced. It was described there as "a way of avoiding a principled decision damaging to the Court or an expedient decision damaging to the principle." It was also pointed out there that this doctrine has been rationalized and considerably narrowed down by the American Supreme Court in **Baker v. Carr, (1962) 369 US 186** where it was explained that "non-justifiability" of a political question is primarily function of separation of power." It really means that there are matters about which declarations made or certificates granted by the executive wing of Government would be treated as conclusive so that Courts will not go behind them. It was also said there:

> "Deciding whether a matter has in any measure been committed by the Constitution to another branch of government, or whether the action of that branch exceeds whatever authority has been committed, is itself a delicate exercise in constitutional interpretation and is a responsibility of this Court as ultimate interpreter of the Constitution".

ORDERS PASSED IN A DEMOCRATIC COUNTRY CAN BE CHALLENGED BEFORE A LAWFULLY CONSTITUTED COURT – SUBMITS RESPONDENT

631. Learned Counsel for the election petitioner also relied upon **H.H. Maharajadhiraja Madhav Rao Jiwaji Rao Scindia Bahadur v. Union of India, (1971) 3 SCR 9** where this Court said: (at p. 75) (of SCR): (at p. 563 of AIR):

> "The functions of the State are classified as legislative, judicial and executive; the executive function is the residue which does not fall within the other two functions. Constitutional mechanism in a democratic policy does not contemplate existence of any function which may *qua* the citizens be designated as political and orders made in exercise whereof are not liable to be tested for their validity before the lawfully constituted courts: **Raj Sahib Ram Jawaya Kapur v. State of Punjab (1955) 2 SCR 225; Jayantilal Amritlal Shodhan v. F.N. Rana, (1964) 5 SCR 294)**; and *Halsbury's Laws of England,* 3rd Edn. Vol. 7, Article 409, at p. 192".

CLAUSE (4) ARTICLE 329B HAS BEEN PASSED IN VIEW OF INTERNAL AND EXTERNAL DANGERS – PRIME MINISTER'S POSITION HAS TO BE KEPT UNASSAILABLE – SHOULD BE INTERPRETED IN THAT CONTEXT – SUBMITS SOLICITOR-GENERAL

632. Learned Solicitor General also contended that we were passing through critical times when a state of Emergency had been declared. He submitted that the decision of the constituent authorities, in excluding a particular case from the jurisdiction of this Court, should be treated as an exercise of very special power under very unusual conditions in which internal and external dangers, with which the country was surrounded, required that the position of the Prime Minister should be declared unequivocally unassailable so that the need for further examination of the question of her election to Parliament may not be raised anywhere else. This seems to be another form in which "political question' argument could be and was addressed to us. Undoubtedly, clause (4) of Article 329A the context in which it was introduced, and we could perhaps take judicial notice of this context.

THERE WAS NO NEED TO EXCLUDE JURISDICTION OF SUPREME COURT – HOLDS BEG, J.

Even if it was possible to go beyond the statement of objects and reasons and to hold that clause (4) of Article 329A is there essentially for demonstrating the strong position of the Government and of the Prime Minister of this country to all inside and outside the country so as to inspire the necessary confidence in and give the necessary political and legal strength to the Government to enable it to go forward boldly to deal with internal, economic, law and order problems and international questions. Yet, I fail to see why this could make it necessary to exclude the jurisdiction of this Court so as to prevent it from considering a case which would have been over much sooner if we had not been confronted with difficulties, at the very outset, in examining the merits of the case. Speaking for myself, I fail to see what danger to the country could arise or how national interests could be jeopardised by a consideration and a decision by this Court of such a good case as I find that and the law.

IF THERE WAS POLITICAL OBJECTIVE AND UTILITY FOR CLAUSE (4) – NOT INTENDED TO INJURE INTEREST OF MINORITY PARTY – IT MAY BE RELEVANT – HELD BEG, J.

Nevertheless I am prepared to concede that there may be and was some very useful political objective to be served by demonstrating the strength and ability of the Government to face the difficulties with which it had been confronted. If that be so, we can certainly say that clause (4) of Article 329A had a political objective and utility which has been served. And, if that was the real object behind its enactment, it could not be really to injure the interests of minority political parties or groups which is what is contended for on behalf of the election petitioner. I think that the context and the political considerations placed before us could be relevant in understanding the real meaning of clause (4) of Article 329A of the Constitution.

TWO WAYS OF INTERPRETATION – ONE TO PREVENT UNCONSTITUTIONALITY – 2ND TO CREATE A LEGAL FICTION OF DEEMING PROVISION FOR DEFINITE PURPOSE – NOT FOR OUSTING JURISDICTION OF SUPREME COURT – OBSERVES HON'BLE JUDGE

633. It is a well-established canon of interpretation that, out of two possible interpretations of a provision, one which prevents it from becoming unconstitutional should be preferred if this is *possible-ut res magis valeat quam pereat*. It is true that the deeming provision seems to stand in the way of our examination of the merits of the case even though there is no direct provision taking away our jurisdiction to consider the merits of the appeals before us. It has, however, been repeatedly laid down that a deeming provision introducing a legal fiction must be confined to the context of it and cannot be given a larger effect: (*See* **Radha Kishan v. Durga Prasad, AIR 1940 PC 167**). In **Bengal Immunity Co. Ltd. v. The State of Bihar, (1955) 2 SCR 603** it was held by this Court that a legal fiction is created for some definite purposes and should not be extended beyond its legitimate field determined by its context. The same view has been expressed by this Court in other cases; **C.I.T., Bombay v. James Anderson, (1964) 5 SCR 590; C.I.T., Madras v. Express Newspapers Ltd., Madras, (1964) 8 SCR 189; Sri Jagadguru Kari Basava Rajendraswami of Gavimutt v. Commissioner of Hindu Religious Charitable Endowments, Hyderabad, (1964) 8 SCR 252.**

* * * * *

SUPREME COURT JURISDICTION SAVED BY CLAUSE 5 – NATIONAL INTEREST PREVAILS OVER OTHER CONSIDERATIONS – VALIDITY OF CLAUSE (4) UPHELD – HELD BEG, J.

635. If the purpose of the clause (4) of Article 329A was purely to meet the political needs of the country and was only partly revealed by the policy underlying the statement of objects and reasons it seems possible to contend that it was not intended at all to oust the jurisdiction of the Court, Hence, Article 329A clause (5) will not, so understood, bar the jurisdiction of the Court to hear and decide the appeals when it says that the appeal shall be disposed of in conformity with the provisions of clause (4).

636. In the circumstances of this case, it would seem that conformity with the declaration embodied in Article 329A clause (4) is possible, if we confine the meaning and effect of the deeming provision to what was needed only for the declaration to be given at the end of clause (4) by the constituent bodies, with a political object, and not for the purposes of affecting our jurisdiction which determines legal effects of what is sought to be done. Of course, the more natural interpretation would appear to be that the deeming provision should apply for "all purposes" including those for consideration of the appeals before us. But if it is not possible to decide those appeals without giving a different meaning to the deeming provision, on which the final declaration in clause (4) rests, and clause (5) leaves us free to decide how we could conform with clause (4) need our jurisdiction to decide factual and legal issues judicially be said to be affected? If the fiction was only a logical step in the process of the declaration to be made by constituent authorities but not of ours, it would only attach to the declaration contained at the end of clause (4). Perhaps it could be argued, by applying the doctrine of "reading down', that clause (4) was not intended to oust the jurisdiction of this Court altogether to try the case. No such attempts at reading it down have, however, been made by learned Counsel supporting the validity of Article 329A(4). It is not unlikely that Article 329A(4) was based on the misapprehension that the High Court's judgment may be legally cannot or that there was a possibility, even for a case so ill founded in fact and in law as the one put forward on behalf of the election-petitioner, to succeed in this Court if it had succeeded in the High Court. We cannot indulge in guess work on these matters. In any case, no useful purpose will be served now by our declaring anything beyond that clause 329A(4) does not so operate as to bar the jurisdiction of this court to go into and determine the merits of the appeals before us by applying the Act of 1951. Even if we were to consider matters of expediency and national interest, as we should in appropriate cases, it does not appear to me to be either expedient or in conformity with national interests to leave the matter in doubt whether the judgment under appeal before us could or could not legally stand on its own legs under the unmanned law.

ARTICLE 329A(4) DOES NOT BAR JURISDICTION OF SUPREME COURT TO CONSIDER APPEAL ON MERITS – APPEAL NO. 887 OF APPELLANT ACCEPTED – CROSS APPEAL NO. 909 OF 1975 DISMISSED

637. For the reasons given above, I declare that Article 329A(4) does not stand in the way of the consideration of the appeals before us on merits under the Act of 1951 or the validity of the amendments of the Act. On a consideration of the merits of Appeal. Nos. 887 and 909 of 1975, I have come to the conclusion, as indicated above, that Appeal No. 887 must be allowed and the Cross Appeal No. 909 of 1975 must fail. The result is that the judgment and orders passed by the learned Judge of the Allahabad High Court on the election case are set aside, and, in such conformity with Article 329A clause (4) as is possible for us, I also declare the judgment and the findings contained in it to be void and of no effect whatsoever. It is not necessary for me to add that the order of the learned Judge, holding the original respondent disqualified from occupying her office, disappears ipso facto and it neither has nor will be deemed over to have had any legal effect whatsoever. In the circumstances of the case, I think the parties should bear their own costs throughout.

Chandrachud, J.—638. The Election Petition out of which these appeals arise involved the question of the validity of the election of Smt. Indira Nehru Gandhi to the Lok Sabha. In the General Parliamentary Elections of 1971, she was declared as the successful candidate from the Raebareli constituency in Uttar Pradesh. She won the election by a margin of 1,11,810 votes over her nearest rival, Shri Raj Narain.

RESPONDENT FILED ELECTION PETITION UNDER SECTION 80 READ WITH SECTION 100 OF RP ACT, 1951 TO CHALLENGE ELECTION RESULT – CHANDRACHUD, J.

639. Shri Raj Narain, who was sponsored by the Samyukta Socialist Party, filed an election petition under section 80 read with section 100 of the Representation of the People Act, 1951, to challenge the election of the successful candidate. Originally, the challenge was founded on numerous grounds but during the trial of the petition in the High Court of Allahabad, the challenge was limited to seven grounds.

ALLAHABAD HIGH COURT ACCEPTED ELECTION PETITION ON TWO GROUNDS *VIDE* JUDGMENT DATED 12.6.1975 – SET ASIDE ELECTION OF THE APPELLANT – CHANDRACHUD, J.

640. A learned Single Judge of the High Court, M.L. Sinha, J., upheld the challenge on two grounds, rejecting the other grounds of challenge. That explains the cross appeals.

641. The High Court held that the successful candidate was guilty of having committed two corrupt practices within the meaning of section 123(7) of the Representation of the People Act: *Firstly*, she obtained the assistance of the Gazetted Officers of the Government of Uttar Pradesh for furthering her election prospects; and *secondly*, she obtained the assistance of Shri Yashpal Kapur, a Gazetted Officer in the Government of India holding the post of Officer on Special Duty in the Prime Minister's Secretariat, for furthering the same purpose. Acting under section 8A of the Act the learned Judge declared that the successful candidate would stand disqualified for a period of six years from June 12, 1975 being the date of the judgment. Aggrieved by this part of the judgment, Smt. Indira Gandhi has filed Appeal No. 887 of 1975.

DECIDED FIVE OTHER GROUNDS AGAINST THE RESPONDENT – HE FILED APPEAL NO. 909 OF 1975 – CHANDRACHUD, J.

642. The other five grounds of challenge were: (1) The successful candidate procured the assistance of the Armed Forces for arranging her flights by Air Force aeroplanes and helicopters; (2) Her election agent, Shri Yashpal Kapur, and others distributed clothes and liquor to induce the voters to vote for her; (3) She and her election agent made appeals to the religious symbol of cow and calf; (4) Her election agent and others procured vehicles for the free conveyance of voters to the polling stations; and (5) She and her election agent incurred or authorised expenditure in violation of section 77(3) of the Act read with Rule 90 of the Conduct of Election Rules, 1961. These grounds having been rejected by the High Court, the defeated candidate has filed appeal No. 909 of 1975. The first two grounds were given up in appeal for the reason that the evidence on record was not likely to be accepted by this Court in proof thereof.

643. The defeated candidate did not lead evidence in the High Court to show that any part of the expenditure in excess of the permissible limit of Rs. 35,000 was incurred by the successful candidate or her election agent. His contention was that the expenditure incurred for her election by the political party which had sponsored her candidature, the Congress (R), was liable to be included in the expenses incurred or authorised by her. This contention was founded on a decision rendered by a Division Bench of this Court on October 3, 1974 in **Kanwar Lal Gupta v. Amarnath Chawla, AIR 1975 SC 308.**

DURING PENDENCY OF ELECTION PETITION – AN ORDINANCE ON 19.10.1974 AMENDED SECTION 77(1) RP ACT – REPLACED BY ACT 58 OF 1975 – CHANDRACHUD, J.

644. On October 19, 1974 the President of India promulgated The Representation of the People (Amendment) Ordinance, 1974 providing that "Notwithstanding any judgment, order or decision of any court to the contrary, any expenditure incurred or authorized in connection with the election of a candidate by a political party or by any other association or body of persons or by any individual (other than the candidate or his election agent) shall not be deemed to be, and shall not ever be deemed to have been, expenditure in connection with the election incurred or authorized by the candidate or by his election agent ...." This provision was added by the Ordinance by way of an *Explanation* to section 77(1) of the Representation of the People Act, 1951. It expressly excepted from its operation decisions of the Supreme Court voiding an election before the commencement of the Ordinance. Shri Amarnath Chawla fell outside the Ordinance. It also excepted similar decisions of High Courts provided that they had become final or unappealable. The Ordinance was replaced by the Representation of the People (Amendment) Act, 58 of 1974, which was brought into force retrospectively from October 19, 1974.

RESPONDENT CHALLENGED LEGALITY OF ACT BY FILING WRIT PETITION – DISMISSED HOLDING EXPENSES WERE WITHIN PRESCRIBED LIMIT – TAKEN UP BY SUPREME COURT WITH OTHER APPEAL – CHANDRACHUD, J.

645. The defeated candidate filed Writ Petition 3761 of 1975 in the High Court to challenge the constitutional validity of the Ordinance and the Act of 1974. In view of his finding that the total amount of expenditure incurred or authorised by the successful candidate or her election agent, together with the amount proved to have been incurred by the political Party or the State Government in connection with her election, did not exceed the prescribed limit, the learned Judge thought it unnecessary to inquire into the constitutionality of the Ordinance and the Act of Bench of the High Court from the aforesaid order but, by consent of parties, this Court decided to hear the points involved in the Writ Petition and in the appeal therefrom.

DURING PENDENCY OF APPEAL – CROSS APPEAL IN SUPREME COURT – PARLIAMENT PASSED ELECTION LAWS (AMENDMENT) ACT, 40 OF 1975 ON 6-8-1975 – SEALS THE FATE OF THE APPEAL – CHANDRACHUD, J.

646. During the pendency of these cross-appeals, the Parliament passed the Election Laws (Amendment) Act, 40 of 1975, which came into force on August 6, 1975. This Act, if valid, virtually seals the controversy in the appeal filed in this Court by the successful candidate from the decision of the Allahabad High Court. It also takes care of a considerable gamut of the appeal filed in this court by the defeated candidate. It substitutes a new section 8A in the Representation of the People Act, 1951 empowering the President to decide whether a person found guilty of corrupt practice shall be disqualified and if so, for what period. By section 6, it amends section 77 of the Act of 1951 making pre-nomination expenses a matter of irrelevant consideration. It declares that the expenditure incurred by a Government servant in the discharge of his official duty in connection with any arrangements or facilities and such arrangements or facilities shall not be deemed to be expenditure or assistance incurred or rendered for the election prospects of the candidate concerned. By section 7, it re-defines a "candidate" to mean a person who has been or claims to have been duly nominated as a candidate at any election. By section 8, it provides that no symbol allotted to a candidate shall be deemed to be a religious or a national symbol. And it says, to the extent relevant, that the publication in the Official Gazette of the resignation of a Government servant shall be conclusive proof of the fact of resignation. If the effective date of the resignation is stated in the publication, it shall also be conclusive proof of the fact that the Government servant ceased to be in service with effect from the particular date. The amendments made by sections 6, 7 and 8 of the amending Act have retrospective effect and expressly govern election appeals pending in this Court, among other proceedings.

BESIDES AMENDMENT ACTS 58 OF 1974 – ACT 40 OF 1975, PARLIAMENT PASSED CONSTITUTION (THIRTY-NINTH AMENDMENT) ACT ON 10-8-1975 – CHANDRACHUD, J.

647. The amendments brought about by Act 58 of 1974 and Act 40 of 1975 have an incisive impact on the cross-appeals but their edge was blunted by the Constitution (Thirty-ninth Amendment) Act which came into force on August 10, 1975.

BY CONSTITUTIONAL AMENDMENT ARTICLE 71 WAS SUBSTITUTED AND 329A WAS ADDED AND THREE ACTS WERE KEPT IN 9TH SCHEDULE OF THE CONSTITUTION – DECLARED ELECTION OF THE APPELLANT VALID – BARS JURISDICTION OF SUPREME COURT – CHANDRACHUD, J.

The 39th Amendment introduces two new articles in the Constitution: Articles 71 and 329A; and it puts in the Ninth Schedule three Acts: (i) The Representation of the People Act, 43 of 1951; (ii) The Representation of the People (Amendment) Act, 58 of 1974; and (iii) The Election Laws (Amendment) Act, 40 of 1975. The new Article 71 which replaces its precursor empowers the Parliament to pass laws regulating the elections of the President and the Vice-President, including the making of a provision for the decision of disputes relating to their election. Article 329A has six clauses out of which the first three deal with the future election to the Parliament of persons holding the office of Prime Minister or Speaker at the time of the election or who are appointed to these offices after their election to the Parliament. These clauses aim at depriving the courts of their jurisdiction to try election petitions in which the election of the Prime Minister or the Speaker to the Parliament is challenged. Clause 4 frees the disputed election of the Prime Minister and the Speaker to the Parliament from the restraints of all election laws. It declares such election as valid notwithstanding any judgment and clause 5 ordains that any appeal or cross appeal pending before the Supreme Court shall be disposed of on the assumption that the judgment under appeal is void, that the findings contained in the judgment never had any existence in the eye of law and that the election declared void by the judgment shall continue to be valid in all respects. Clause 6 provides that Article 329A shall have precedence over the rest of the Constitution.

648. At first blush, what remains to be decided judicially in face of the 39th Amendment? As an exercise of Constituent power, the 39th Amendment must reign supreme. The political sovereign having re-posed its trust in the legal sovereign, the doings of the Constituent Assembly have an aura of sanctity that legal ingenuity may be powerless to penetrate. But that is an uninformed approach to a field strewn with various shades of legal landmarks.

PRIOR LAW ON CONSTITUTIONAL AMENDMENTS DISCUSSED – CHANDRACHUD, J.

649. While repelling the challenge to the First Constitutional Amendment which was passed in June 1951, this Court held in **Sri Sankari Prasad Singh Deo v. Union of India and State of Bihar, (1952) 3 SCR 89** that the power of amendment conferred by Article 368 was not subject to any limitations, express or implied, and that fundamental rights were within the sweep of the amending power. The Seventeenth Constitutional Amendment passed in June 1964 was similarly upheld by a majority decision of this Court in **Sajjan Singh v. State of Rajasthan, (1965) 1 SCR 933** which took the view that the fundamental rights were not intended by the framers of the Constitution to be finally and immutably settled when the Constitution was passed. But the Seventeenth Amendment came to be challenged once again in **I.C. Golak Nath v. State of Punjab, (1967) 2 SCR 672.** By a majority of 6 : 5, this Court held that the Seventeenth Amendment was ultra vires the Parliament's power to amend the Constitution. Five out of the six learned Judges held that Article 368 did not confer any power to amend but merely prescribed the procedure for amendment. The sixth learned Judge held that Article 368 did contain the power of amendment but that the Parliament must amend Article 368 to convoke another Constituent Assembly, pass a law under item 97 of List I of Schedule 7 to call a Constituent Assembly and then that Assembly may be able to abridge or take away the Fundamental Rights if desired.

GOLAK NATH'S CASE RESTRICTED PARLIAMENT TO AMEND FUNDAMENTAL RIGHTS – PARLIAMENT AMENDED CONSTITUTION TO RESTORE ITS POWER – CHANDRACHUD, J.

650. The decision in **Golak Nath's** case raised a debate of national dimensions as the Parliament's power to amend the Constitution so as to abridge or take away the fundamental rights virtually became a dead letter. Under the majority judgment, the Constituent Assembly alone, called by virtue of a law to be passed under Entry 97 of List I, could abridge or take away the fundamental rights. The Parliament, in a resolve to reaffirm its powers, passed the Constitution (Twenty-fourth Amendment) Act on November 5, 1971 and the Constitution (Twenty fifth Amendment) Act on April 20, 1972. By the 24th Amendment, the Parliament amended Articles 13 and 368 of the Constitution so as to provide that nothing contained in Article 13 shall apply to any amendment of the Constitution made under Article 368 and that notwithstanding anything in the Constitution, Parliament may, in the exercise of its constituent power, amend by way of addition, variation or repeal any provision of the Constitution in accordance with the procedure laid down in Article 368. As an instance of the amendatory power re-acquired under the 24th Amendment, Parliament, by the 25th Amendment, substituted a new clause (2) in Article 31 and introduced a new Article 31-C in the Constitution. By the 29th Amendment, Parliament placed the Kerala Law Reforms (Amendment) Acts of 1969 and 1971 in the Ninth Schedule.

IN *KESVANANDA BHARATI'S* CASE A BENCH OF 13 JUDGES OF SUPREME COURT BY MAJORITY HELD – CONSTITUENT POWER UNDER ARTICLE 368 CANNOT ALTER OR DESTROY 'BASIC STRUCTURE' OF THE CONSTITUTION – IT STILL PREVAILS – LAW DECLARED BY SUPREME COURT BINDING ON ALL – CHANDRACHUD, J.

651. A Bench of thirteen Judges of this Court sat to consider the constitutionality of the 24th, 25th and 29th Amendments. The eleven judgments delivered in that case are reported in **Kesavananda Bharati v. State of Kerala, 1973 (Supp) SCR 1** commonly known as the **Fundamental Rights** case. **Golak Nath's** case stood over ruled as a result of the decision in this case. But six learned Judges out of the thirteen (Sikri, C.J. and Shelat, Grover, Hegde, Reddy and Mukherjea, JJ.) accepted the contention of the petitioners that though Article 368 conferred the power to amend the constitution, there were inherent or implied limitations on the power of amendment and therefore, Article 368 did not confer power to amend the Constitution so as to damage or destroy the essential elements or basic features of the Constitution. Fundamental Rights, being a part of the essential features of the Constitution, could not, therefore, be abrogated or emasculated in the exercise of the power conferred by Article 368, though a reasonable abridgement of those rights could be effected in the public interest.

Brother Khanna, J. found it difficult, in face of the clear words of Article 368, to exclude from their operation the articles relating to fundamental right, in Part III of the Constitution. But proceeding to consider "the scope of the power of amendment under Article 368", the learned Judge held that the power to amend did not include the power to abrogate the Constitution, that the word "amendment" postulates that the old Constitution must survive without loss of identity, that the old Constitution must accordingly be retained though in the amended form, and, therefore, the power of amendment does not include the power to destroy or abrogate the basic structure or framework of the Constitution. The remaining six Judges took the view that there were no limitations of any kind on the power of amendment, though three of them seemed willing to foresee the limitation that the entire Constitution could not be abrogated, leaving behind a State without a Constitution. Some scholars have clapped and some scholars have scoffed at the decision in the Fundamental Rights case. These criticisms, I cannot deny, cause a flutter in the ivory tower. But by Article 141 of the Constitution, the law declared by the Supreme Court is binding on all courts within the territory of India. The law declared by the majority of 7 : 6 in the Fundamental Rights case must, therefore, be accepted by us, dutifully and without reserve as good law. The history of law courts abounds with memorable decisions based on a thin majority.

THESE APPEALS ARE TO BE DECIDED KEEPING IN VIEW THESE BINDING PRINCIPLES – CHANDRACHUD, J.

652. These appeals have, therefore, to be decided in the light of the principle emerging from the majority decision in the Fundamental Rights case that Article 368 does not confer power on the Parliament to alter the basic structure or framework of the Constitution. Arguments of the learned counsel appearing on both sides have taken many forms and shapes but they ultimately converge on the central theme of basic structure.

SUBMISSIONS OF RESPONDENT RELATING TO 39TH CONSTITUTIONAL AMENDMENT – CHANDRACHUD, J.

653. I would like first to deal with the constitutional validity of the 39th Amendment. On that question, the arguments of Mr. Shanti Bhushan, who appears for Shri Raj Narain, may be summed up thus:

(i) The 39th Amendment affects the basic structure or framework or the institutional pattern adopted by the Constitution and is, therefore, beyond the amending power conferred by Article 368. It destroys the identity of the Constitution.

(ii) Separation of powers is a basic feature of the Constitution and, therefore, every dispute involving the adjudication of legal rights must be left to the decision of the judiciary. Clause (4) of Article 329A introduced by the 39th Amendment takes away that jurisdiction and is, therefore, void.

(iii) The function of the legislature is to legislate and not decide private disputes. In the instant case the Constituent Assembly has transgressed its constituent function by adjudicating upon a private dispute.

(iv) Democracy is an essential feature of the Constitution. Free and fair elections are indispensable for the successful working of any democratic government. By providing that the election of the Prime Minister shall not be open to challenge and shall continue to be valid despite the judgment of the Allahabad High Court holding that the election is vitiated by corrupt practices, the Constituent Assembly has destroyed the very core of democracy.

(v) Equality is an essential feature of a Republican Constitution. The 39th Amendment puts the Prime Minister and the Speaker above the law and beyond the reach of the equality principle. The classification made by the 39th Amendment bears no nexus with the sort of immunity granted to two high personages, from the operation of election laws.

(vi) Rule of law and judicial review are also basic features of the Constitution. To free certain persons from the constraints of law and to place their conduct beyond judicial review is to destroy the identity of the Constitution. No freedom is secure without the court to protect it. The organic balance between the three branches, the legislature, executive and the judiciary, is upset by eroding the authority of the Supreme Court in a vital matter like elections. And the Rule of Law is abrogated by providing that the election of the Prime Minister shall continue to be valid and will be open to no challenge before any court or any authority whatsoever.

(vii) The concept of political justice recognised by the Preamble is violated by the 39th Amendment. The Constitution can always be subverted by revolutionary methods. The question is whether it is permissible to the Parliament to use the legitimacy of constitutional provisions for effecting revolutionary changes.

(viii) The constituent power partakes of legislative power and can only be exercised within the highest ambit of the latter power. Therefore, even with a two-third majority, the constituent body cannot exercise executive or judicial power. For example, the power to appoint or dismiss a Government servant or the power to declare war which are executive powers cannot be exercised by the Constituent Assembly. Similarly, it cannot, in the guise of amending the Constitution, provide that an accused arraigned before a criminal court shall be acquitted and shall be deemed to be innocent. The constituent body can make changes in the conditions of the exercise of judicial power but it cannot usurp that power; and lastly.

(ix) The question in the Fundamental Rights case was whether Parliament can, in the exercise of its power of amendment abridge or take away Fundamental Rights and, whether there are any inherent or implied limitations on the Parliament's power of amendment.

CORE QUESTION IS: CAN 'AMENDING POWER' DESTROY THE 'BASIC STRUCTURE' – CHANDRACHUD, J.

In other words, the question was whether the power of amendment can be exercised so as to destroy or mutilate the basic structure of the Constitution. The Fundamental Rights case did not involve the consideration of the question as to what the power of amendment comprehends. Promoting and demoting Government servants, passing and failing students who have appeared in an examination, granting or withdrawing building contracts and last but not the least, declaring who has won and who has lost an election are matters clearly outside the scope of the amending power under Article 368, which means and implies the power to alter the fundamental instrument of country's governance.

COUNSEL FOR APPELLANT AGREE – APPEALS BE DECIDED AS PER PREVAILING LAW – CHANDRACHUD, J.

654. Learned counsel appearing for the Union of India and for Smt. Indira Gandhi did not dispute the contention that the appeals before us must be disposed of on the basis of the law laid down by the majority in the Fundamental Rights case.

SUBMISSIONS OF ATTORNEY-GENERAL FOR THE UNION OF INDIA – CHANDRACHUD, J.

655. The learned Attorney General contended that:

(i) The majority decision in the Fundamental Rights case is not an authority for the proposition that there could be no free or fair elections without judicial review. The Constitutions and laws of several countries leave the decision of election disputes to the judgment of the legislatures themselves. The history of the Representation of the People Act, 1951 as also various articles in our Constitution show that judicial review can be excluded in appropriate cases as a matter of policy.

(ii) That validation of elections is a process well-known to democratic forms of Government.

(iii) That a law may be constitutional even if it relates to a single individual if on account of special reasons, the single individual could be treated as a class by himself.

(iv) That it is clear from Articles 326 and 327 of the Constitution that the Constitution makers thought that as a matter of high policy elections ought to be dealt with by the Constitution itself and not by ordinary legislation passed within the framework of the Constitution. How much of elections should be dealt with by the Constitution and how much should be relegated to ordinary legislation is not a matter for the courts to decide. If the constituent body thought that the offices of the Prime Minister and the Speaker are important enough to be dealt with by the Constitution itself in the matter of their elections to the Parliament, it cannot be said that the decision is frivolous or without jurisdiction; and that

(v) The contention that the 39th Amendment is not an exercise of constituent power should not be allowed to be taken up because every possible aspect of the matter was argued in **Sankari Prasad's** case, **Sajjan Singh's** case and the Fundamental Rights case. The basic question involved in these cases was as to what is the meaning of the word 'amendment'. The argument now is that there is a further limitation on the amending power. If it is the same question and has been decided, it cannot be reopened by saying that the question has a new aspect which was not considered then. If the question is new, the principle of the Fundamental Rights case cannot be extended any further. Therefore, the constituent power must be held to be a plenary power on which the only limitation is as regards the inviolability of the basic structure.

SUBMISSIONS OF SOLICITOR-GENERAL FOR THE APPELLANT – CHANDRACHUD, J.

656. The learned Solicitor-General who continued the unfinished arguments of the learned Attorney-General urged that

(i) Article 14 is founded on a sound public policy recognised and followed in all civilised States. The exclusion of judicial review does not by itself mean the negation of equality. Article 31-B which on the face of it denied equality to different sections of the community attained the ideal of economic justice by bringing about economic equality. Article 33 also shows that the demands of public problems may require the adjustment of Fundamental Rights for ensuring greater equality.

(ii) What a Constitution should contain depends on what permanency is intended to be accorded to a particular provision included in the Constitution.

(iii) Exclusion of judicial review is at least permissible in those fields where originally the Constitution did not provide for or contemplate judicial review.

(iv) If the election law does not apply, as it means to apply by virtue of Article 329A(4) it is the function of the legislature to declare whether or not a particular election is good or bad; and that Rule of Law is not a part of the basic structure of the Constitution and apart from Article 14, our Constitution recognises neither the doctrine of equality nor the Rule of Law.

SUBMISSIONS OF THE COUNSEL FOR THE APPELLANT – CHANDRACHUD, J.

657. Shri A.K. Sen who appears for Smt. Indira Gandhi defended the 39th Amendment by contending that:

(i) The Amendment follows the well-known pattern of all validation Acts by which the basis of judgments or orders of competent courts and Tribunals is changed and the judgments and orders are made ineffective.

(ii) The effect of validation is to change the law so as to alter the basis of any judgment, which might have been given on the basis of old law and thus to make the Judgment ineffective.

(iii) A formal declaration that the judgment rendered under the old Act is void, is not necessary. If the matter is pending in appeal, the appellate court has to give effect to the altered law and reverse the judgment. If the matter is not pending in appeal, then the judgment ceases to be operative and binding as *res judicata*.

(iv) The rendering of a judgment ineffective by changing its basis by legislative enactment is not an encroachment on judicial power but a legislation within the competence of the legislature rendering the basis of the judgment *non-est*.

(v) The constituent power has retrospectively changed the law in so far as it relates to election. The constituent authority could have left the application of the changed law either to Parliament or to any other body. But it has chosen to assume the duty of determination in this particular case for itself.

(vi) The determination of election disputes and the validity of elections is not an exercise of judicial power. This function may be left either to courts, properly so-called or to Tribunals or to other bodies including the legislature itself.

(vii) The rigid separation of powers as it obtain in the United States or in a lesser degree under the Australian Constitution does not apply to India. Many powers, which are strictly judicial, have been excluded from the purview of the courts. There is therefore, no question of any separation of powers being involved in matters concerning elections and election petitions.

(viii) There is no question of separation of powers when the constituent authority exercises either a power which is allocated to the Legislature, or to the Executive or to the Judiciary under the Constitution. In the hands of the constituent authority there is no demarcation of powers. But the demarcation emerges only when it leaves the hands of the constituent authority through well-defined channels into demarcated pools. The constituent power is independent of the fetters of limitations imposed by separation of powers in the hands of the organs of the Government, amongst whom the supreme authority of the State is allocated.

(ix) The Constituent power springs as the fountainhead and partakes of sovereignty and is the power which creates the organs and distributes the powers. Therefore, in a sense, the constituent power is all-embracing and is at once judicial, executive and legislative. It is, in a sense, a "super power".

(x) Even if the preamble lays down as its objective the attainment of equality, the 39th Constitution Amendment does not violate the said concept of equality as the same is based on a national classification and has a reasonable nexus with the object of the Amendment.

(xi) The Preamble to the Constitution only refers to securing "equality of status and opportunity." Equality of status and opportunity has got many facets: some of these facets are guaranteed as fundamental rights under Articles 14 to 18 of the Constitution. These facets alone can be considered to be basic features of the Constitution, assuming that equality was a basic feature of the Constitution.

(xii) 'Free and fair election" does not postulate that there must be a constitutional provision for determining election disputes by a separate Tribunal or Court.

(xiii) The 39th Amendment Act does not affect the structure of a Republican Democracy, assuming that the same is a basic feature of the Constitution. The validation of one election does not alter the character of the democracy; and

(xiv) A Constitutional amendment need not necessarily relate to the structural organisation of the State.

SUBMISSIONS OF ANOTHER COUNSEL FOR THE APPELLANT – CHANDRACHUD, J.

658. Shri Jagannath Kaushal supported the arguments of Shri Sen by citing pragmatic illustrations. He gave interesting statistics showing that a very small percentage of election petitions succeed eventually which, according to him, is evidence that such petitions are used by defeated candidates as an instrument of oppression against successful candidates. Parliament, therefore, wanted to save high personages from such harassment. A law may benefit a single individual and may still be valid. According to Shri Kaushal, the judgment of the Allahabad High Court became a nullity by reason of that Court ceasing retrospectively to have jurisdiction over the dispute and a judgment which is a nullity need not be set aside. It can even be challenged in a collateral proceeding.

DISCUSSION ON 39TH CONSTITUTIONAL AMENDMENT – ON VALIDITY OF CLAUSES (4) TO (6) OF ARTICLE 329A – CHANDRACHUD, J.

659. I thought it only fair to indicate broadly the line of approach adopted by the various learned counsel to the question as regards the validity of the

39th Amendment. It will serve no useful purpose to take up each one of the points for separate consideration and indeed many an argument is interrelated. It would be enough for my purpose to deal with what I consider to be points of fundamental importance, especially as my learned Brethren have dealt with the other points.

660. This Court has strictly adhered to the view that in Constitutional matters one must decide no more than is strictly necessary for an effective adjudication of the points arising in any case. By that test, a numerically substantial part of the 39th Amendment has to be deferred for consideration to a future occasion. We are clearly not concerned in these appeals with the new Article 71 introduced by the 39th Amendment, which deals with the election of the President and the Vice-President. We are concerned with the new Article 329A but not with the whole of it. Clauses (1) to (3) of that article deal with future events and the validity of those clauses may, perhaps, be examined when those events come to happen. Clauses (4) to (6) of Article 329A are the ones that are relevant for our purpose and I propose to address myself to the validity of those provisions.

661. Clause (4) of Article 329A, which is the real focus of controversy, may conveniently be split up as follows for understanding its true nature and effect:

(i) The Laws made by Parliament prior to August 10, 1975 in so far as they relate to election petitions and matters connected therewith cease to apply to the Parliamentary election of Smt. Indira Gandhi which took place in 1971.

(ii) Such Laws are repealed retrospectively in so far as they governed the aforesaid election, with the result that they must never be deemed to have applied to that election.

(iii) Such an election cannot be declared to be void on any of the grounds on which it could have been declared to be void under the Laws which were in force prior to August 10, 1975.

(iv) The election shall not be deemed ever to have become void on any ground on which, prior to August 10, 1975 it was declared to be void

(v) The election shall continue to be valid in all respects notwithstanding the judgment of any court, which includes the judgment dated June 12, 1975 of the High Court of Allahabad.

(vi) The judgment of the Allahabad High Court and any finding on which the judgment and order of that court is based are void and shall be deemed always to have been void.

DISCUSSION ON THE VALIDITY OF 39TH AMENDMENT OF THE CONSTITUTION – CHANDRACHUD, J.

662. Shri Shanti Bhushan has as it were, a preliminary objection to the 39th Amendment that the election of a private individual and the dispute concerning it cannot ever be a matter of Constitutional amendment. Whether this contention is sound is another matter but I do not see the force of the argument of the Attorney-General that in view of the decisions in **Sankari Prasad's** case, **Sajjan Singh's** case and the **Fundamental Rights** case, the contention is not open to be taken. The question raised by Shri Shanti Bhushan was not raised or considered in either of the three aforesaid cases and I do not see how the question can be shelved. The argument is not a new facet of the theory of inherent or implied limitations on the amending power, in which case it might have been plausible to contend that the last word was said on the subject by the Full Court in the Fundamental Rights case. The question now raised touches a totally new dimension of the amending power:

Can the Constituent Assembly, while amending the Constitution, pronounce upon private disputes or must it only concern itself with what may be termed organisational matters concerning the country's governance? The question has the merit of novelty, but I see no substance in it. But I must clarify that I prefer to examine the point in isolation, that is, divorced from considerations arising from the theory of separation of powers. Whether the amendment constitutes an encroachment on judicial functions and thereby damages one of the basic structures of the Constitution may best be examined separately. The reason why I see no substance in Shri Shanti Bhushan's contention is that what the Constitution ought to contain is not for the Courts to decide. The touchstone of the validity of a Constitutional amendment is firstly whether the procedure prescribed by Article 368 is strictly complied with and secondly whether the amendment destroys or damages the basic structure of the Constitution. The subject-matter of constitutional amendments is a question of high policy and Courts are concerned with the interpretation of laws, not with the wisdom of the Policy underlying them. I do not see why the Constitution cannot be amended so as to provide that wagering contracts shall be void or that bigamous marriages shall be unlawful or that economic offenders shall be visited with a higher penalty. The Indian Constitution is not like the American Constitution an instrument of few words.

The range of topics it covers would bemuse any student of foreign Constitutions which do not even skirt the problems with which our constitution deals in copious details. In fact, there is hardly any important facet of national life which our Constitution does not touch. Alongwith matters of high priority like citizenship. Fundamental Rights, Directive Principles of state policy and the relations between the Union and the States, it deals with matters not normally considered constitutionally important like the salaries of high dignitaries, the power of the Supreme Court to frame rules for regulating its practice and procedure, official language for communication between one State and another and last but not the least, elections to the Parliament and the State Legislatures. Those to whose wisdom and judgment the constituent power is confided, will evoke scorn and derision if that power is used for granting or withdrawing building contracts, passing or failing students or granting and denying divorces. But the electorate lives in the hope that a sacred power will not so flagrantly be abused and the moving finger of history warns of the consequences that inevitably flow when absolute power has corrupted absolutely. The fear of perversion is no test of power.

663. But the comparison is odious between the instances given by Shri Shanti Bhushan and the subject-matter of Article 329A(4) of the Constitution. In the *first* place, elections to legislatures were considered by Constitution-makers to be a matter of constitutional importance. *Secondly*, though the powers of the Prime Minister in a cabinet form of democracy are not as unrivalled as those of the President in the American system, it is undeniable that the Prime Minister occupies a unique position. The choice of the subject for constitutional amendment cannot, therefore, be characterised as trifling, frivolous or outside the framework of a copious Constitution. In America, the challenge to the 18th Amendment on the ground that ordinary legislation cannot be embodied in a constitutional amendment was brushed aside as unworthy of serious attention, Rottschaefer endorsed it as consistent with the ultimate political theory on which the American constitutional system is based. "The people, acting through the machinery provided by the existing Constitution, must be accorded the legal power to change their basic law by peaceable means."* In fact, it is wrong to think that elections to the country's legislatures are a private affair of the contestants. They are matters of public interest and of national importance. Every citizen has a stake in legislative elections for, his social and economic well-being depends upon the promises and performance of the legislators. Such elections,

* Rottschaefer on Constitutional Law Edn. 1939, page 397.

and moreso the election of the Prime Minister who is atleast *primus inter pares*, can legitimately form the subject-matter of a constitutional provision. The form of what is brought into the Constitution has to be judged by different standards.

BROAD OUTLINES OF CONSTITUTION ARE 'BASIC STRUCTURE' – LIKE 'DEMOCRATIC FORM OF GOVERNMENT', 'SECULAR CHARACTER OF THE STATE' OR 'SUPREMACY OF THE CONSTITUTION' ETC. – ARE ONLY ILLUSTRATIVE BUT NOT EXHAUSTIVE – CHANDRACHUD, J.

664. There was some discussion at the Bar as to which features of the Constitution form the basic structure of the Constitution according to the majority decision in the Fundamental Rights case. That, to me, is an inquiry both fruitless and irrelevant. The ratio of the majority decision is not that some named features of the Constitution are a part of its basic and structure but that the power of amendment cannot be exercised so as to damage or destroy the essential elements or the basic structure of the Constitution, whatever these expressions may comprehend. Sikri, C.J., mentions supremacy of the Constitution, Republican and Democratic form of the Government, secular character of the Constitution, separation of powers, federalism and dignity and freedom of the individual as essential features of the Constitution. Shelat and Grover, JJ., have added to the list two other features: the mandate to build a welfare State and unity and integrity of the Nation, Hegde and Mukherjea, JJ., added sovereignty of India as a fundamental feature of the Constitution. Reddy. J., thought that a sovereign democratic republic, Parliamentary democracy and the three organs of the State form the basic structure of the Constitution.

Khanna. J., held that fundamental rights are not a part of the basic structure and, therefore, they can be abrogated like many other provisions. He observed that basic structure indicates the broad outlines of the Constitution and since the right to property is a matter of details, it is not a part of that structure. The democratic form of Government, the secular character of the State and possibly judicial review are according to Brother Khanna a part of the basic structure of the Constitution. It is obvious that these are merely illustrations of what constitutes the basic structure and are not intended to be exhaustive. Shelat and Grover. JJ., Hegde and Mukherjea, JJ., and Reddy, J., say in their judgments that their list of essential features which form the basic structure of the Constitution is illustrative or incomplete. For determining, whether a particular feature of the Constitution is a part of its basic structure, one has perforce to examine in each individual case the place of the particular feature in the scheme of our Constitution, its object and purpose, and the consequences of its denial on the integrity of the Constitution as a fundamental instrument of country's governance. But it is needless for the purpose of these appeals to ransack every nook and cranny of the Constitution to discover the bricks of the basic structure. Those that are enumerated in the majority judgments are massive enough to cover the requirements of Shri Shanti Bhushan's challenge.

665. I consider it beyond the pale of reasonable controversy that if there be any unamendable features of the Constitution on the score that they form a part of the basic structure of the Constitution, they are that:

(i) India is a Sovereign Democratic Republic;

(ii) Equality of status and opportunity shall be secured to all its citizens;

(iii) The State shall have no religion of its, own and all persons shall be equally entitled to freedom of conscience and the right freely to profess, practice and propagate religion and that;

(iv) the Nation shall be governed by a Government of laws, not of men. These, in my opinion, are the pillars of our constitutional philosophy, the pillars, therefore, of the basic structure of the Constitution.

PREAMBLE OF THE CONSTITUTION IS NOT A KEY TO THE 'BASIC STRUCTURE' – CHANDRACHUD, J.

666. I find it impossible to subscribe to the view that the Preamble of the Constitution holds the key to its basic structure or that the preamble is too holy to suffer a human touch. Constitutions are written if they are written, in the rarefied atmosphere of high ideology, what, ever be the ideology. Preambles of written Constitutions are intended primarily to reflect the hopes and aspirations of people. They resonate the ideal which the Nation seeks to achieve, the target, not the achievement. In parts, therefore, they are metaphysical like slogans. For example, the concept of Fraternity which is referred to in our Preamble is not carried into any provision of the Constitution and the concept is hardly suitable for encasement in a coercive legal formula. The Preamble, generally, uses words of "Passion and power" in order to move the hearts of men and to stir them into action.* Its own meaning and implication being in doubt, the Preamble cannot affect or throw light on the meaning of the enacting words of the Constitution.** Therefore, though our Preamble was voted upon and is a part of the Constitution, it is really "a preliminary statement of the reasons" which made the passing of the Constitution necessary and desirable.*** As observed by Gajendragadkar, J., **In re: Beriberi Union and Exchange of Enclaves, (1960) 3 SCR 250, 282** what Willoughby has said about the Preamble to the American Constitution, namely that it has never been regarded as the source of any substantive power, is equally true about the prohibitions and limitations. The Preamble of our Constitution cannot, therefore, be regarded as a source of any prohibitions or limitations.

JUDICIAL REVIEW IS NOT A PART OF BASIC STRUCTURE – AS A MATTER OF RULE – NOT EVEN ELECTION MATTERS – TO BE CONSIDERED IN INDIVIDUAL CASE – CHANDRACHUD, J.

667. Judicial review, according to Shri. Shanti Bhushan is a part of the basic structure of the Constitution and since the 39th Amendment by Article 329A(4) and (5) deprives the courts, including the Supreme Court, of their power to adjudicate upon the disputed election, the Amendment is unconstitutional. The fundamental premise of this argument is too broadly stated because the Constitution, as originally enacted, expressly excluded judicial review in a large variety of important matters. Articles 31(4), 31(6), 136(2), 227(4), 262(2) and 329(a) are some of the instances in point. True, that each of these provisions has a purpose behind it but these provisions show that the Constitution did not regard judicial review as an indispensable measure of the legality or propriety of every determination. Article 136(2) expressly took away the power of the Supreme Court to grant special leave to appeal from the decisions of any court or Tribunal constituted by a law relating to the Armed Forces. Article 262(2) authorized the Parliament to make a law providing that the Supreme Court or any other court shall have no jurisdiction over certain river disputes. But what is even more to the point are the provisions contained in Articles 103(1) and 329(b).

Article 102 prescribes disqualification's for membership of the Parliament. By Article 103(1), any question arising under Article 102 as to whether a member of the Parliament has become subject to any disqualification has to be referred to the President whose decision is final. The President is required by Article 103(2) to obtain the opinion of the Election Commission and act according to its opinion. Thus, in a vital matter pertaining to the election for membership of the Parliament, the framers

* Constitutional Law of India, 2nd Edn, (1975) Vol. *76-H.M. Seervai.*

** (1957) AC 436 (463).

*** Halsbury's Laws of England, 3rd Edn. p. 6570, para 343.

of the Constitution had left the decision to the judgment of the executive. Articles 327 and 328 give power, to the Parliament and the State legislatures to provide by law for all matters relating to elections to the respective legislatures, including the preparation of electoral rolls and the delimitation of constituencies. By Article 329(a) the validity of any law relating to the delimitation of constituencies or the allotment of seats to such constituencies cannot be called in question in any court.

668. The provision contained in Article 329(b) is decisive on the question under consideration. That article provides that no election to the Parliament or the State legislature shall be called in question except by an election petition presented to such authority and in such manner as may be provided for by or under any law made by the appropriate Legislature. It was, therefore, open to the legislature to leave the adjudication of election disputes to authorities other than those in the hierarchy of our judicial system. In fact, until the passing of the Representation of the People (Amendment) Act, 47 of 1966, by which High Courts were given jurisdiction to try election petitions, that jurisdiction was vested first in a Tribunal consisting of three members and later in a tribunal consisting of a single member who was to be a sitting District Judge. The decisions of those tribunals could eventually be brought before the Supreme Court under Article 136(1) of the Constitution but it is at least plausible that were the Legislatures to pass laws leaving the decision of election disputes to themselves, judicial review might have stood excluded. Since the Constitution, as originally enacted, did not consider that judicial power must intervene in the interests of purity of elections, judicial review cannot be considered to be a part of the basic structure insofar as legislative elections are concerned. The theory of Basic Structure has to be considered in each individual case, not in the abstract, but in the context of the concrete problem. The problem here is whether under our Constitution, judicial review was considered as an indispensable concomitant of elections to country's legislatures. The answer, plainly is no.

* * * * *

KEEPING ELECTION OF PRIME MINISTER APART FROM JUDICIAL REVIEW BY ARTICLE 329A(4) AND (5) DOES NOT MAKE IT UNCONSTITUTIONAL – HELD CHANDRACHUD, J.

671. I am therefore, unable to accept the contention that Articles 329A(4) and (5) are unconstitutional on the ground that by those provisions, the election of the Prime Minister is placed beyond the purview of courts.

672. Equally, there is no substance in the contention that the relevant clauses of the 39th Amendment are in total derogation of 'political justice' and are accordingly unconstitutional. The concept of political justice of which the Preamble speaks is too vague and nebulous to permit by its yardstick the invalidation of a Constitutional amendment. The Preamble, as indicated earlier, is neither a source of power nor of limitation.

DEMOCRACY IS ESSENTIALLY 'BASIC STRUCTURE' OF THE CONSTITUTION – ARTICLE 329A(4) AND (5) DO NOT DESTROY DEMOCRACY – HELD CHANDRACHUD, J.

673. The contention that 'Democracy' is an essential feature of the Constitution is unassailable. It is therefore, necessary to see whether the impugned provisions of the 39th Amendment damage or destroy that feature. The learned Attorney-General saw an insurmountable impediment in the existence of various forms of democracies all over the world and he asked: What kind and form of democracy constitutes a part of our basic structure? The cabinet system, the Presidential system, the French, the Russian or any other? This approach seeks to make the issue unrealistically complex.

If the democratic form of government is the corner-stone of our Constitution, the basic feature is the broad form of democracy that was known to Our Nation when the Constitution was enacted, with such adjustment and modifications as exigencies may demand but not so as to leave the mere husk of a popular rule. Democracy is not a dogmatic doctrine and no one can suggest that a rule is authoritarian because some rights and safeguards available to the people at the inception of its Constitution have been abridged or abrogated or because, as the result of a constitutional amendment, the form of government not strictly comport with some classical definition of the concept. The needs of Nation may call for severe abnegations though never the needs of the Rulers and evolutionary changes in the fundamental law of the country do not necessarily destroy the basic structure of its government. What does the law live for, if it is dead to living needs? We cannot therefore, as lawyers and Judges, generalize on what constitutes 'Democracy' though we all know the highest form of that idealistic concept – the state of bliss – in political science.

674. The question for consideration is whether the provisions contained in Articles 329A(4) and (5) are destructive of the democratic form of Government. The answer does not lie in comparisons with what is happening in other parts of the world, those that stake their claim to 'democracy', because we are not concerned to find whether despite the 39th Amendment we are still not better off, democratically than many others. The comparison has to be between the pre-39th amendment period and the post-39th Amendment period in the context of our Constitution.

675. "Those of us who have learned humility have given over the attempts to define law". This statement of Max Radian* may be used to express a similar difficulty in defining 'Democracy' but just as legal scholars, not lacking in humility, have attempted to define 'Law', so have political scientists attempted a satisfactory definition of 'Democracy'. The expression is derived from the Greek word 'Demos', which was often used by the Greeks to describe the many, as distinct from the few, rather than the people as a whole. And Aristotle defined democracy as the rule of the poor, simply because they formed, always and necessarily, the more numerous class. But the word is commonly used "In the sense of the rule of the majority of the community as a whole, including 'classes' and 'masses' .... since that is the only method yet discovered for deterring what is deemed to be the will of a body politic which is not unanimous. This will is expressed through the election of representatives".** C.F. Strong defines democracy to mean "that form of government in which the ruling power of a State is legally vested, not in any particular class or classes, but in the members of a community as a whole". This may more aptly be called a description rather than a definition of democracy became it is beyond human ingenuity to foresee the possible permutations and combination of circumstances to which a generalisation may have to be applied.

676. Forgetting mere words which Tennyson said: 'Like Nature, half reveal and half conceal the Soul within'. The substance of the matter is the rule of the majority and the manner of ascertaining the will of the majority is through the process of elections. I find myself unable to accept that the impugned provisions destroy the democratic structure of our government. The rule is still the rule of the majority despite the 39th Amendment and no law or amendment of the fundamental instrument has provided for the abrogation of the electoral process. In fact it is through that process that the electorate expressed its preference for Smt. Indira Gandhi over Shri Raj Narain and others. Article 326 of the Constitution by which the elections to the house of the People and to the State Legislative Assemblies shall

* "A Restatement of Honfeld". Harvard Law Review (1938) Vol. 51 pp. 1141, 1145.

** Modern Political Constitutions by C.F. Strong: (E.L.B.S. Ed., 2nd Impression, 1970), p. 172.

be on the basis of Adult Suffrage still stands. Article 79 which provides that "There shall be a Parliament .... which shall consist of .... two Houses". Articles 80 and 81 which prescribe the composition of the two Houses. Article 83 which provides for the duration of the Houses. Article 85 which directs that six months shall not intervene between the two sessions of Parliament. Article 100(1) which provides that all questions shall be determined by a majority of votes of the members present and voting, article 105 which preserves the powers and privileges of the members of Parliament and the counterparts of these articles in regard to State Legislatures retain their pristine primacy. These articles, unimpaired as they remain even after the 39th Amendment, are enough assurance that the Parliament is not leading the country to a totalitarian path.

677. This is not to put a seal of approval on the immunity conferred on any election but it is hard to generalize from a single instance that such an isolated act of immunity has destroyed or threatens to destroy the democratic frame-work of our government. One swallow does not make a summer. The swallow with its pointed wings, forked tail, a curving flight and twittering cry is undoubtedly harbinger of summer but to see all these in the 39th Amendment and to argue that the summer of a totalitarian rule is knocking at the threshold is to take an unduly alarmist view of the political scene as painted by the amendment. Very often, as said by Sir Frederick Pallock, "If there is any real danger it is of the alarmist's own making".*

CLAUSES (4) AND (5) OF ARTICLE 329A DESTROY 'EQUALITY BEFORE LAW' AND 'EQUAL PROTECTION OF LAW' AS CONTAINED IN ARTICLE 14 – IT IS A 'BASIC FEATURE' OF OUR CONSTITUTION – CHANDRACHUD, J.

678. The 39th Amendment is however, open to grave objection on other grounds, in so far as clauses (4) and (5) of Article 329A are concerned. Generality and equality are two indelible characteristics of justice administered according to law. The Preamble to our Constitution by which the people of India resolved solemnly to secure to all its citizens equality of status and opportunity finds its realisation in an ampler measure in Article 14 which guarantees equality before the law and the equal protection of laws to all persons, citizens and non-citizens alike. Equality is the faith and creed of our Democratic Republic and without it, neither the Constitution nor the laws made under it could reflect the common conscience of those who owe allegiance to them. And if they did not, they would fail to command respect and obedience without which any Constitution would be doomed to founder on the rocks of revolution. A Constitution which, without a true nexus, denies equality before the law to its citizens may in a form thinly disguised, contain reprisals directed against private individuals in matters of private rights and wrongs. The English Acts of Attainder beginning with the one passed by the English Parliament in 1459 after the commencement of the wars of Roses or the 'Pervigilium' in Rome are only some of the historical instances in point. Speaking of Bracton's famous passage which contains the admonition that the King ought to be under the law because the law makes him King, Sir Frederick Pollock says that there you have in a nutshell the great point of Constitutional freedom that law is not merely the instrument of Government, but the safeguard of each individual citizen's public rights and liberties.**

679. Article 329A(4) makes, the existing election laws retrospectively inapplicable in a very substantial measure, to the Parliamentary elections of the Prime Minister and the Speaker. The inapplicability of such laws creates a legal vacuum the repeal, so to say, of existing laws is only a step-in-aid to free from the restraints and obligations of all election laws, indeed of all laws. The plain intendment and meaning of clause

* Ethics and Morals (Essays in jurisprudence), p. 303.

** Jurisprudence and Legal Essays (1964), p. 195.

(4) is that the election of the two personages will be beyond the reach of any law, past or present. What follows is a neat logical corollary. The elections of the Prime Minister could not be declared void as there was no law to apply to that election: the judgment of the Allahabad High Court declaring the election void is itself void; and, the election continues to be valid as it was before the High Court pronounced its judgment.

680. These provisions are an outright negation of the right of equality conferred by Article 14 a right, which more than any other is a basic postulate of our Constitution. It is true that the right, though expressed it an absolute form, is hedged in by a judge-made resurrection that it is open to the Legislature to make a reasonable classification so that the same law will not apply to all persons alike or different laws may govern the rights and obligations of different persons falling within distinct classes. The boast of Law that it is no respecter of persons is the despair of drawers of waters and hewers of wood who clamour for a differential treatment. The Judge takes that boast to mean that in an egalitarian society no person can be above the law and that justice, must be administered with an even hand to those who are situated equally. In other words, all who are equal are equal in the eye of Law and it will not accord a favoured treatment to, person within the same class. Laws as Plato said, would operate "like an obstinate and ignorant tyrant if they imposed inflexible rules without allowing for changed circumstances or exception cases."*

(*See* "The Sense of Injustice" by Edmond Cahn (1964), p. 461 in which the reference is made to Plato's 'Politicus', p. 294.)

CLASSIFICATION MUST BE FOUNDED ON AN INTELLIGIBLE DIFFERENTIA HAVING RELATION TO THE OBJECT SOUGHT TO BE ACHIEVED – NO BASIS FOR TREATING PM AND SPEAKER ABOVE THE LAW – ELECTION DECLARED VOID BY HIGH COURT JUDGMENT MADE VALID – CLAUSES (4)(5) DESTROY BASIC FEATURE OF THE CONSTITUTION "RULE OF LAW" – HENCE UNCONSTITUTIONAL – CHANDRACHUD, J.

681. This Court, at least since the days of **Anwar Ali Sarkar's case, 1952 SCR 284**, has consistently taken the view that the classification must be founded on an intelligible difference which distinguishes those who are grouped together from those who are left out and that the differentia must have a rational relation to the object sought to be achieved by the particular law. The first test may be assumed to be satisfied since there is no gainsaying that in our system of Government, the Prime Minister occupies a unique position. But what is the nexus of that uniqueness with the law which provides that the election of the Prime Minister and the Speaker to the Parliament will be above all laws, that the election will be governed by no norms or standards applicable to all others who contest that election and that a election declared to be void by a High Court judgment shall be deemed to be valid, the judgment and its finding being themselves required to be deemed to be void? Such is not the doctrine of classification and no facet of that doctrine can support the favoured treatment accorded by the 39th Amendment to two high personages. It is the common man's sense of justice which sustains democracies and there is a fear that the 39th Amendment, by its impugned part, may outrage that sense of justice. Different rules may apply to different conditions and classes of men and even a single individual may, by his uniqueness, form a class by himself. But in the absence of a differentia reasonably related to the object of the law, justice must be administered with an even hand to all.

682. It follows that clauses (4) and (5) of Article 329A are arbitrary and are calculated to damage or destroy the Rule of Law. Imperfections of language. Law as

* Jurisprudence and Legal Essays (1964), p. 195.

of the definition of 'Law' itself. And the Constitutional Law of 1975 has undergone many changes since A.V. Dicey, the great expounder of the rule of law, delivered his lectures as Vinerian Professor of English Law at Oxford, which were Published in 1855 under the title, 'Introduction to the Study of the Law of the Constitution'. But so much, I suppose, can be said with reasonable certainty that the rule of law means that the exercise of powers of government shall be conditioned by law and that subject to the exceptions to the doctrine of Equality, no one shall be exposed to the arbitrary will of the Government. Dicey gave three meanings to rule of law: Absence of arbitrary power, equality before the law or the equal subjection of all classes to the ordinary law of the land administered by ordinary law courts and that the Constitution is not the source but the consequence of the rights of individuals, as defined and enforced by the Courts. The second meaning grew out of Dicey's unsound dislike of the French Droit Administrative which he regarded "as a misfortune inflicted upon the benighted folk across the Channel".* Indeed, so great was his influence on the thought of the day that as recently as in 1935 Lord Hewart, the Lord Chief Justice of England, dismissed the term "administrative law" as "continental jargon".

The third meaning is hardly apposite in the context of our written Constitution for, in India, the Constitution is the source of all rights and obligations. We may not, therefore, rely wholly on Dicey's exposition of the rule of law but ever since the second World War the rule has come to acquire a positive content in all democratic countries.** The International Commission of Jurists, which has a consultative status under the United Nations, held its Congress in Delhi in 1959 where lawyers, judges and law teachers representing fifty-three countries affirmed that the rule of law is a dynamic concept which should be employed to safeguard and advance the political and civil rights of the individual in a free society. One of the committees of that Congress emphasised that no law should subject any individual to discriminatory treatment. These principles must vary from country to country depending upon the provisions of its Constitution and indeed upon whether there exists a written Constitution. As it has been said in a lighter vein, to show the supremacy of the Parliament, the charm of the English Constitution is that "it does not exist". Our Constitution exists and must continue to exist. It guarantees equality before law and the equal protection of laws to every one. The denial of such equality, as modified by the judicially evolved theory of classification, is the very negation of rule of law.

'SEPARATION OF POWER' IS NOT STRICTLY REGARDED AS 'BASIC STRUCTURE' OF THE CONSTITUTION – BUT INSTITUTIONS HAVE TO RESPECT THEIR LIMITS – HELD CHANDRACHUD, J.

683. The argument directed at showing the invalidation of the 39th Amendment on the ground that it abrogates the principle of "Separation of Powers' is replete with many possibilities since it has several sidelights. But I will be brief since I have already held that clauses (4) and (5) of Article 329A are unconstitutional. I cannot regard the point as unnecessary for my determination since the point seems to me of great constitutional importance.

684. The Indian Constitution was enacted by the Constituent Assembly in the backdrop of the National struggle for Independence. The Indian people had gone through a travail and on the attainment of Independence, the country had to face unique problems which had not confronted other federations like America, Australia. Canada or Switzerland. These problems had to be solved pragmatically and not by confining the country's political structure within the straitjacket of a known or

* *See* Judicial Review of Administrative Action – S.A, de Smith, (1968), p. 5.

** *See* Wade and Phillips' Constitutional Law' (Sixth Edn.), pp. 70-73).

established formula. The Constituent Assembly, therefore, pursued the policy of pick and choose to see what suited the genius of the Nation best. "This process produced new modifications of established ideas -about the construction of federal governments and their relations with the governments of their constituent units. The Assembly in fact, produced a new kind of federalism to meet India's peculiar needs."* While introducing the Draft Constitution in the Constituent Assembly. Dr. Ambedkar who was one of the chief architects of the Constitution said that our Constitution avoided the tight mould of federalism in which the American Constitution was caught and could be "both unitary as well as federal according to the requirements of time and circumstances". We have what may perhaps be described by the phrase, 'co-operative federalism', a concept different from the one in vogue when the federations of United States or of Australia were set-up.

685. The American Constitution provides for a rigid separation of governmental powers into three basic divisions – the executive, legislative and judicial. It is an essential principle of that Constitution that powers entrusted to one department should not be exercised by any other department. The Australian Constitution follows the same pattern of distribution of powers. Unlike these Constitutions, the Indian Constitution does not expressly vest the three kinds of power in three different organs of the State. But the principle of separation of powers is not a magic formula for keeping the three organs of the State within the strict confines of their functions. As observed by Cardozo, J., in his dissenting opinion in **Panama Refining Company v. Ryan, (1934) 293 US 388 (440)** the principle of separation of powers "is not a doctrinaire concept to be made use of with pedantic rigour. There must be sensible approximation, there must be elasticity of adjustment in response to the practical necessities of Government which cannot foresee today the developments of tomorrow in their nearly infinite variety." Thus, even in America, despite the theory that the legislature cannot delegate its power to the executive, a host of rules and regulations are passed by non-legislative bodies, which have been judicially recognised as valid. See the judgment of Mukherjea. J., in the **Delhi Laws Act case, 1951 SCR 747 (964).**

686. The truth of the matter is that the existence, and the limitations on the powers of the three departments of Government are due to the normal process of specialisation in governmental business which becomes more and more complex as civilisation advances. The legislature must make laws, the executive enforce them and the judiciary interpret them because they have in their respective fields acquired an expertise which makes them competent to discharge their duly appointed functions. The Moghal Emperor, Jehangir, was applauded as a reformist because soon after his accession to the throne in 1605, he got a golden chain with sixty bells hung in his palace so that the common man could pull it and draw the attention of the Ruler to his grievances and sufferings. The most despotic Monarch in the modern world prefers to be armed, even if formally with the opinion of his Judges on the grievances of his subjects.

687. The political usefulness of the doctrine of separation of powers is now widely recognized though a satisfactory definition of the three functions is difficult to evolve. But the function of the Parliament is to make laws, not to decide cases. The British Parliament in its unquestioned supremacy could enact a legislation for the settlement of a dispute or it could, with impunity, legislate for the boiling of the Bishop of Rochestor's cook. The Indian Parliament will not direct that an accused in a pending case shall stand acquitted or that a suit shall stand decreed. Princely India, in some parts, often did it.

---

* The Indian Constitution: Cornerstone of a Nation by Granville Austin. (1972). page 186.

688. The reason of this restraint is not that the Indian Constitution recognizes any rigid separation of powers. Plainly, it does not. The reason is that the concentration of powers in any one organ may by upsetting that fine balance between the three organs, destroy the fundamental premises of a democratic government to which we are pledged. Sir Carleton K. Allen says in his 'Law and Orders' (1965 Edn.. D. 8) that neither in Montesquieu's analysis nor in Locke's are the governmental powers conceived as the familiar trinity of legislative, executive and judicial powers. Montesquieu's "separation" took the form not of impossible barriers and unalterable frontiers, but of mutual restraints, or of what afterwards came to be known as "checks and balances", (p. 10).

The three organs must act in concert, not that their respective functions should not ever touch one another. If this limitation is respected and preserved, "it is impossible for that situation to arise which 'Locke and Montesquieu regarded as the eclipse of liberty the monopoly or the disproportionate accumulation, of power in one sphere". (p. 19; Allen), In a federal, system which distributes powers between three co-ordinate branches of government, though not rigidly, disputes regarding the limits of constitutional power have to be resolved by courts and therefore, as observed by Paton, "the distinction between judicial and other powers may be vital to the maintenance of the Constitution itself".* Power is of an encroaching nature, wrote Madison in 'The Federalist'. The encroaching power which the Federalists feared most was the legislative power and that, according to Madison, is the danger of all republics. Allen says that the history of both the United States and France has shown on many occasions that the fear was not unjustified.**

PARLIAMENT BY CLAUSE (4) HAS DECIDED A MATTER WITHOUT HEARING PARTIES – IN DEFIANCE OF PRINCIPLES OF NATURAL JUSTICE – OF WHICH SUPREME COURT WAS LAWFULLY SEIZED – CLAUSE (5) COMMANDS SUPREME COURT TO DISPOSE OF APPEALS AS PER 'JUDGMENT' DELIVERED BY PARLIAMENT IN CLAUSE (4) – IMPOSSIBLE TO SUSTAIN – HELD CHANDRACHUD, J.

689. I do not suggest that such an encroaching power will be pursued relentlessly or ruthlessly by our Parliament. But no Constitution can survive without a conscious adherence to its fine checks and balances. Just as Court ought not to enter into problems entwined in the "political thicket", Parliament must also respect the preserve of the Courts. The principle of separation of powers is a principle of restraint which "has in it the precept, innate in the prudence of self-preservation (even if history has not repeatedly brought it home), that discretion is the better part of valour"*** Courts have, by and large, come to check their valorous propensities. In the name of the Constitution, the Parliament may not also turn its attention from the important task of legislation to deciding court cases for which it lacks the expertise and the apparatus. If it gathers facts, it gathers facts of policy. If it records findings it does so without a pleading and without framing any issues. And worst of all, if it decides a Court case, it decides without hearing the parties and in defiance of the fundamental principles of natural justice.

690. The Parliament, by clause (4) of Article 329A, has decided a matter of which the country's Courts were lawfully seized. Neither more nor less. It is true, as contended by the learned Attorney General and Shri Sen, that retrospective validation is a well known legislative process which has received the recognition of this Court in tax cases, pre-emption cases, tenancy cases and a variety of other

* A textbook of Jurisprudence (1964), page 295.

** Allen, Law and Orders, p. 12.

** Social Dimentions of Law and Justice-Julius Stone, (1996) p. 668.

matters. In fact, such validation was resorted to by the legislature and upheld by this Court in at least four election cases, the last of them being **Kanta Kathuria v. Manak Chand Surana, (1970) 2 SCR 835**. But in all of these cases, what the legislature did was to change the law retrospectively so as to remove the reason of disqualification leaving it to the Courts to apply the amended law to the decision of the particular case. In the instant case the Parliament has withdrawn the application of all laws whatsoever to the disputed election and has taken upon itself to decide that the election is valid. Clause (5) commands the Supreme Court to dispose of the appeal and the cross-appeal in conformity with the provisions of clause (4) of Article 329-A, that is, in conformity with the "judgment" delivered by the Parliament. The "separation of powers does not mean the equal balance of powers", says Harold Laski, but the exercise by the legislature of what is purely and indubitably a judicial function is impossible to sustain in the context even of our co-operative federalism which contains no rigid distribution of powers but which provides a system of salutary checks and balances.

CONSTITUENT AUTHORITY HAS ITS LIMITATIONS WITHIN WHICH IT HAS TO OPERATE – HELD CHANDRACHUD, J.

691. I find it contrary to the basic tenets of our Constitution to hold that the Amending Body is an amalgam of all powers – legislative, executive and judicial. "Whatever pleases the emperor has the force of law" is not an article of democratic faith. The basis of our Constitution is a well-planned legal order, the presuppositions of which are accepted by the people as determining the methods by which the functions of the Government will be discharged and the power of the State shall be used.

ACT 58 OF 1974 AND ACT 40 OF 1975 ARE VALID – NOT PARADOXICAL THAT CONSTITUTIONAL AMENDMENT HAS LIMITATIONS BUT ORDINARY LAW HAS OTHER GROUNDS – HELD CHANDRACHUD, J.

692. So much for the 39th Amendment. The argument regarding the invalidity of the Representation of the People (Amendment) Act, 58 of 1974, and of the Election Laws (Amendment) Act, 1975 has, however, no substance. The Constitutional amendments may, on the ratio of the **Fundamental Rights** case, be rested on the anvil of basic structure. But apart from the principle that a case is only an authority for what it decides, it does not logically follow from the majority judgment in the Fundamental Rights case that ordinary legislation must also answer the same test as a constitutional amendment. Ordinary laws have to answer two tests for their validity:

(1) The law must be within the legislative competence of the legislature as defined and specified in Chapter I, Part XI of the Constitution and

(2) it must not offend against the provisions of Article 13(1) and (2) of the Constitution. 'Basic structure', by the majority judgment, is not a part of the fundamental rights nor indeed a provision of the Constitution. The theory of basic structure is woven out of the conspectus of the Constitution and the amending power is subjected to it because it is a constituent power. 'The power to amend the fundamental instrument cannot carry with it the power to destroy its essential features' – this, in brief, is the arch of the theory of basic structure. It is wholly out of place in matters relating to the validity of ordinary laws made under the Constitution.

693. Shri Shanti Bhushan thought it paradoxical that the higher power should be subject to a limitation which will not operate upon a lower power. There is no paradox, because certain limitations operate upon the higher power for the reason that it is a higher power. A constitutional amendment has to be passed by a special majority and certain such amendments have to be ratified by the Legislatures of not less than one-half of the States as provided by Article 368(2) An ordinary legislation can be passed by a simple majority. The two powers, though species of the same genus, operate in different fields and are, therefore, subject to different limitations.

694. No objection can accordingly be taken to the constitutional validity of the two impugned Acts on the ground that they damage or destroy the basic structure. The power to pass these Acts could be exercised retrospectively as much as prospectively.

ACT 40 OF 1975 REMOVES TWO GROUNDS OF 'CORRUPT PRACTICE' – PUT AN END TO THE TOTALITY OF OBJECTIONS OF RESPONDENT – ACT 58 OF 1974 BECOMES ACADEMIC – DETENTION OF 21 MPs OF LOK SABHA AND 10 MEMBERS OF RAJYA SABHA – DOES NOT INVALIDATE THESE ACTS – HELD CHANDRACHUD, J.

695. These Acts effectively put an end to the two appeals before us for they answer the totality of the objections which were raised by Shri Raj Narain against the election of Smt. Indira Gandhi. The basis of the findings on which the High Court held against the successful candidate is removed by Act 40 of 1975 retrospectively. Were the law as it is under the amendments introduced by that Act, the High Court could not have held that the election is vitiated by the two particular corrupt practices. In regard to the cross-appeal filed by Sri Raj Narain, Shri Shanti Bhushan thought that a part of it escapes through the crevices in the Act but I see no substance in that contention either. I would like to add that the findings recorded by the High Court in favour of Smt. Indira Gandhi are amply borne out by the evidence to which our attention was drawn briefly by the learned counsel for the parties. The expenses incurred by the political party together with the expenses incurred by her are not shown to exceed the prescribed ceiling. Apart from that, Act, 58 of 1974 makes that issue academic.

696. Finally, there is no merit in the contention that the constitutional amendment is bad because it was passed when some members of the Parliament were in detention. The legality of the detention orders cannot be canvassed in these appeals collaterally. And from a practical point of view, the presence of 21 members of the Lok Sabha and 10 members of the Rajya Sabha who were in detention could not have made a difference to the passing of the Amendment.

CLAUSES (4)(5) OF ARTICLE 329A ARE UNCONSTITUTIONAL – APPEAL NO. 887 OF 1975 IS ACCEPTED – CROSS APPEAL 909 OF 1975 IS DISMISSED – CHANDRACHUD, J.

697. In the result. I hold that clauses (4) and (5) of Article 329A are unconstitutional and, therefore, void. But for reasons aforesaid I allow Civil Appeal No. 887 of 1975 and dismiss Civil Appeal No. 909 of 1975. There will be no order as to costs throughout.

Civil Appeal No. 887 of 1975. Allowed.
Civil Appeal No. 909 of 1975. Dismissed.

The Tribune

ESTABLISHED 1881

Chandigarh, Wednesday, January 19, 1977

LOK SABHA ELECTION IN MARCH

Opportunity to cleanse public life of confusion

— Mrs. Gandhi

NEW DELHI, Jan. 18 (Samachar)—Prime Minister Indira Gandhi tonight announced election to the Lok Sabha in March next.

In a broadcast to the nation tonight Mrs Gandhi said she had recommended to the President dissolution of the present Lok Sabha.

Mrs. Gandhi referred to the gains of the emergency and the economic progress achieved by the country.

She said the question before them now was to restore those political processes "on which we were compelled to put some curbs".

Although the present Lok Sabha could continue for another 12 months, "we also strongly believe that the parliamentary Government must report back to the people and seek sanction from them to carry out programmes and policies for the nation's strength and welfare".

"Because of this unshakeable faith in the power of the people, I have advised the President to dissolve the present Lok Sabha and order fresh election," she said.

"We expect the poll to take place in March".

The Prime Minister said that the emergency had been further relaxed to permit legitimate political activity for recognised political parties.

"I earnestly appeal to political parties to eschew violence and refrain from vilification and calumny," she said.

The people should neither believe in nor give currency to rumours and gossip.

Every election, Mrs. Gandhi continued, "is an act of faith. It is an opportunity to cleanse public life of the confusion".

She asked the nation to go to the polls with the "resolve to reaffirm the power of the people and to uphold the fair name of India as a land committed to the path of reconciliation, peace and progress".

She ended her broadcast by giving her good wishes to the people.

The original term of the current Lok Sabha was to expire in March 1976. Its tenure was, however, extended till March 1978 through two extensions of one year each.

The Prime Minister called on the President twice during the day—at 1 p.m. and again at 7 p.m., immediately after the meeting of the Union Cabinet.

THE TRIBUNE

Chandigarh, Wednesday, January 19, 1977

LOK SABHA ELECTION IN MARCH

NEW DELHI, January, 18 (Samachar)—Prime Minister Indira Gandhi tonight announced election to the Lok Sabha in March next.

In a broadcast to the nation tonight Mrs Gandhi said she had recommended to the President dissolution of the present Lok Sabha.

Mrs. Gandhi referred to the gains of the emergency and the economic progress achieved by the country.

She said the question before them now was to restore those political processes "on which we were compelled to put some curbs".

Although the present Lok Sabha could continue for another 12 months. "We also strongly believe that the parliamentary Government must report back to the people and seek sanction from them to carry out programmes and policies for the nation's strength and welfare".

"Because of this unshakable faith in the power of the people, I have advised the President to dissolve the present Lok Sabha and order fresh election." She said. "We expect the poll to take place in March".

The Prime Minister said that the emergency had been further relaxed to permit legitimate political activity for recognised political parties.

"I earnestly appeal to political parties to eschew violence and refrain from vilification and calumny," she said.

The people should neither believe in nor give currency to rumours and gossip.

Every election, Mrs. Gandhi continued, "is an act of faith. It is an opportunity to cleanse public life of the confusion".

She asked the nation to go to the polls with the "resolve to reaffirm the power of the people and to uphold the fair name of India as a land committed to the path of reconciliation, peace and progress".

She ended her broadcast by giving her good wishes to the people.

The original term of the current Lok Sabha was to expire in March, 1976. Its tenure was, however, extended till March, 1978 through two extensions of one year each.

The Prime Minister called on the President twice during the day at 1 p.m. and again at 7 p.m., immediately after the meeting of the Union Cabinet.

The following is the text of the Prime Minister's broadcast:

> It is some time since I last spoke to you on the radio. However, through my continuous travels in various parts of the country, and through the groups of large number of individuals whom I meet in Delhi and elsewhere, I have continued to be in close touch with you all. Your support, your affection and your trust enabled me to serve India to the best of my ability.

On my journeys up and down the country, I have been glad to find that our people have shaken off their sense of defeatism and gloom. There is a new pride in being Indians. Indeed it can be said that in the year just completed the nation has rediscovered its sense of purpose and potential strength.

Some 18 months ago our beloved country was on the brink of disaster. Violence was openly preached, workers were exhorted not to work, students not to study and Government servants to break their oath. Massive paralysis was propagated in the name of revolution.

The democratic way would have been to work towards the next elections, which were not far off.

The Government had to act and did act. Without purposive Government, a nation, specially a developing one, cannot survive. At that time I made it clear that the restrictions imposed would be temporary. They have been gradually eased. The leaders and many of the rank and file, who had been detained, have been released. For some time past press censorship has been relaxed and newspapers have been reporting the activities of people and parties. Restrictions would have been lifted earlier, had violence and sabotage been given up, had there been no attempt to stir up communal and other unrest.

This discipline and feeling of hope enabled us to initiate and pursue many policies to help those sections of the population who had not greatly benefited from development plans. The constitution has been amended to remove impediments to policies which are designed to serve the people. We have also undertaken programmes to combat social evils such as dowry, which is a burden on our middle classes, and family planning, which aims at healthier and better-cared for children. Any act of compulsion or harassment will be dealt with severely.

May I remind you that the emergency was proclaimed because the nation was far from normal. Now that it is being nursed to health, we must ensure that there is no relapse.

Normality means the orderly conduct of business. This is possible only if people live by certain codes and norms of behavior. Democracy also has certain rules. The Government functioning cannot be obstructed. None should imperil the welfare of any section of the people or the safety of the nation. If India is to live and prosper, there can be no preaching of hatred, no practising of violence, no encouragement of subversive activities, or lowering of standards of public life.

INDIAN EXPRESS

Largest combined net sales among all daily newspapers in India

Vol. XLV No. 120 New Delhi: Monday March 21, 1977 35 p

JANATA PARTY LEADING IN NORTH

Congress showing better in south

Express Correspondent

NEW DELHI, March 20. The Janata Party and CFD combination was set on a resounding spree of election victories in most northern states and the Congress was poised for a highly satisfactory showing in the south as results came in this evening.

The key states of UP and Bihar appeared to be going full steam to

Pradesh where all eleven seats which were declared by the evening went to the Congress. According to unofficial sources, 33 of the 39 seats in Tamil Nadu have been won by the Congress-AIDMK-CPI front. Early in the evening the Congress was leading in 16 out of 19 constituencies where counting was on.

Leading Congressmen in trouble today were the Defence Minister, Mr Bansi Lal, who was trailing by 1,03,000, and his deputy, Mr J. B. Patnaik, Minister of State for Defence, who was trailing by 25,000 in Orissa.

also trounced from Bayana in Rajasthan.

One of the expected Janata victories came in Chandigarh when Mr Krishna Kant won against his Congress rival, Mr Satpal Kapur by over 40,000 votes. Mr Kapur had never been comfortable against Mr Krishna Kant.

INDIAN EXPRESS

New Delhi, Monday March 21, 1977

JANATA PARTY LEADING IN NORTH

NEW DELHI, March 20: The Janata Party and CFD combination was set on a resounding spree of election victories in most northern states and the Congress was poised for a highly satisfactory showing in the south as results came in this evening.

The key states of UP and Bihar appeared to be going full steam to give a landslide victory to the Janata Party. As first reports of counting were coming in with many more votes yet to be counted – Mrs. Gandhi was reported to be trailing behind by 12,000 votes in Raebareli and Mr. Sanjay Gandhi by 34,650 votes in Amethi. It remained to be seen how they would be able to make up the deficit.

In Bihar the Congress was not in any better shape. It was trailing in all 11 constituencies where the counting was in progress this evening. The same was the party's fate in Madhya Pradesh, where in the very early hours the first "Kill" for the opposition was the Union Minister for communications, Dr. S.D. Sharma. In Rajasthan it was in for a major upset, while it was facing troublesome early hours in Punjab and Haryana. Judging by the leads obtained by some of the Janata candidates, there was little comfort on the way for the ruling party.

This dismal showing for the Congress was greatly relieved in Andhra Pradesh where all eleven seats which were declared by the evening went to the Congress. According to unofficial sources, 33 of the 39 seats in Tamil Nadu have been won by the Congress-AIDMK-CPI front. Early in the evening the Congress was leading in 16 out of 19 constituencies where counting was on.

Leading Congressmen in trouble today were the Defence Minister, Mr. Bansi Lal, who was trailing by 1,03,000, and his deputy, Mr J.B. Patnaik, Minister of State for Defence, who was trailing by 25,000 in Orissa.

The Union Minister for Housing Mr Hitendra Desal, had a slender lead of 1,300 from Godhra against his Janata rival, Mr. Piloo Mody. The Congress President Mr. D.K. Barooah, was leading by more than 23,000 votes over his Janata competitor. Mr. Morarji Desai, Janata Party Chairman, who had early established a lead of 6,000 improved his position to 16,000 in his Surat constituency. The External Affairs Minister, Mr. Chavan, had early established a comfortable lead.

Mr. Raj Bahadur former Union Minister for Communications, lost from Baratpur. Mr. Jagannath Pahadia, Union Minister of State, was also trounced from Bayana in Rajasthan.

One of the expected Janata victories came in Chandigarh when Mr. Krishna Kant won against his Congress rival, Mr. Satpal Kapur by over 40,000 votes. Mr. Kapur had never been comfortable against Mr. Krishna Kant.

INDIAN EXPRESS

Largest combined net sales among all daily newspapers in India

Vol. XLV No. 120 New Delhi: Monday March 21, 1977 35 p

Respect the verdict

INDIA'S most momentous and keenly-fought election since Independence is over. There will be profound relief and satisfaction all over the country that the polls have been conducted peacefully except for stray incidents. All praise is due to the millions of electors who have conducted themselves with exemplary discipline and vindicated their abiding faith in the democratic process. The election authorities and the forces of law and order who had to bear the brunt of the burdens connected with the holding of fair and free polls, have acquitted themselves creditably.

By the time this appears in print the broad trend of voting will have become clear from the available results. Whatever the final pattern of party alignments in the new Lok Sabha the supreme obligations of all the parties elected to Parliament are clear. After the gruelling ordeal of the past two years and the bitter contest at the polls, the country must enter on a new era of peace and orderly progress. This means that the harsh legacy of the emergency period must be forgotten by both sides. Admittedly there have been faults on each side and there is no point in harbouring ill-will or rancour. There is no need for witchhunting or for acting in a vindictive spirit. The wounds caused in the past must be healed quickly so that no scars are left behind.

It is in a true Gandhian spirit of forgive and forget that all parties should act so that a new co-operative approach to the nation's formidable problems may be possible. In a democratic election, there are no victors or vanquished. The majority party as well as the opposition minority has an overwhelming obligation to the electorate to observe the norms of democracy and ensure the smooth and efficient working of the parliamentary system. This means, above all, that the true will of the electorate as expressed at the polls should be allowed to prevail in the formation of the government as well as in the conduct of the opposition. If the vote goes against the ruling party it must accept the verdict of the electorate with good grace and be ready to play the role of a responsible and co-operative opposition. If the opposition parties do not secure a majority, their role in the opposition in the new context created by the elections will be no less important than if they had been voted to power. The emergence of a large and viable opposition, irrespective of its party complexion, will invest the new Parliament with a character and significance which none of the earlier parliaments enjoyed. The disparate multiplicity of parties which had constituted the opposition in the past had led to virtual one-party rule, with the Government often being indifferent to the raucous voices of the opposition, while the latter tended to be irresponsible and obstructive because of the unlikelihood of their ever coming to power.

It will be no small gain if after the current elections we have more or less a two-party system, with a government sustained by a not very large majority and an opposition sufficiently unified and strong to keep the government on its toes and to offer itself as an effective alternative at the polls. This will be an ideal situation in which responsible and constructive co-operation is possible between the government and the opposition. In a way such co-operation will be a more genuine desirable response to the will of the electorate than a continuous and sterile confrontation between the ruling party and the opposition.

The orderly establishment of a new government reflecting the verdict of the electorate and its dedication to the challenging tasks that will face it in a spirit of true devotion to the interests of the people will mark the greatest and most enduring triumph of the hopes and aspirations with which India began its career as an independent democratic nation. India today is the cynosure of the world's eyes. The hopes of all free countries are centred on the successful survival of Indian democracy. The resurgence among the people that was witnessed in recent weeks is an assurance that these hopes will be fulfilled.

Page No. 4 **Editorial**

THE INDIAN EXPRESS

New Delhi, March 21, 1977

RESPECT THE VERDICT

INDIA'S most momentous and keenly-fought election since independence is over. There will be profound relief and satisfaction all over the country that the polls have been conducted peacefully except for stray incidents. All praise is due to the millions of electors who have conducted themselves with exemplary discipline and vindicated their abiding faith in the democratic process. The election authorities and the forces of law and order who had to bear the brunt of the burdens connected with the holding of fair and free polls, have acquitted themselves creditably.

By the time this appears in print the broad trend of voting will have become clear from the available results. Whatever the final pattern of party alignments in the new Lok Sabha, the supreme obligations of all the parties elected to Parliament are clear. After the gruelling ordeal of the past two years and the bitter contest at the polls, the country must enter on a new era of peace and orderly progress. This means that the harsh legacy of the emergency period must be forgotten by both sides. Admittedly there have been faults on each side and there is no point in harboring ill-will or rancour. There is no need for witchhunting or for acting in a vindictive spirit. The wounds caused in the past must be healed quickly so that no scars are left behind.

It is in a true Gandhian spirit of forgive and forget that all parties should act so that a new co-operative approach to the nation's formidable problems may be possible. In a democratic election, there are no victors or vanquished. The majority party as well as the opposition minority has an overwhelming obligation to the electorate to observe the norms of democracy and ensure the smooth and efficient working of the Parliamentary system. This means, above all, that the true will of the electorate as expressed at the polls should be allowed to prevail in the formation of the government as well as in the conduct of the opposition. If the vote goes against the ruling party it must accept the verdict of the electorate with good grace and be ready to play the role of a responsible and co-operative opposition. If the opposition parties do not secure a majority, their role in the opposition in the new context created by the elections will be no less important than if they had been voted to power. The emergence of a large and viable opposition, irrespective of its party complexion, will invest the new Parliament with a character and significance which none of the earlier parliaments enjoyed. The disparate multiplicity of parties which had constituted the opposition in the past had led to virtual one-party rule, with the Government often being indifferent to the raucous voices of the opposition, while the latter tended to be irresponsible and obstructive because of the unlikelihood of their ever coming to power.

It will be no small gain if after the current elections we have more or less a two-party system, with a government sustained by a not very large majority and an opposition sufficiently unified and strong to keep the government on its toes and to offer itself as an effective alternative at the polls. This will be an ideal situation in which responsible and constructive co-operation is possible between the government and the opposition. In a way such co-operation will be a more genuine desirable response to the will of the electorate than a continuous and sterile confrontation between the ruling party and the opposition.

The orderly establishment of a new government reflecting the verdict of the electorate and its dedication to the challenging tasks that will face it in a spirit of true devotion to the interests of the people will mark the greatest and most enduring triumph of the hopes and aspirations with which India began its career as an independent democratic nation. India today is the cynosure of the world's eyes. The hopes of all free countries are centred on the successful survival of Indian democracy. The resurgence among the people that was witnessed in recent weeks is an assurance that these hopes will be fulfilled.

CITY EDITION *

The Tribune

ESTABLISHED 1881

VOL. XCVII NO. 80 Chandigarh, Tuesday, March 22, 1977

JANATA PARTY FORGES AHEAD IN NORTH

Record Victory For Fernandes

Ram, Sanjiva Reddy, Barooah Elected

V.C. Shukla Among 5 Ministers Defeated

NEW DELHI, March 21 (Samachar) — The Janata Party's elector al floodtide in northern States swept more of its candidates to victory to widen its lead over the Congress tonight.

The Janata Party, with a tally of 177 seats, had forged a 43-seat lead over the Congress as more results were announced, taking the total of seats filled to 384.

The message of first returns

Jagjivan Ram

from West Bengal and Orissa was that the Janata Party would overwhelm the Congress in these States.

In Orissa, it had secured 11 seats and was comfortably placed in five more constituencies while its electoral allies the CFD and the CPI(M) had captured one each. Congress had secured four seats all in South Orissa. [illegible] Congress had win in the [illegible] of Mr. P. K. Deo (Ind), whom it had supported in Kalahandi.

The party's prospects were no better in West Bengal, where all the 10 results declared fell to the Opposition combination.

The Congress was routed in Haryana, where all 10 seats went in favour of the Janata Party.

In Punjab the Opposition combine nominees had been returned in 11 constituencies. In Ferozepore the Pradesh Congress chief, Mr. Mohinder Singh Gill, was battling grimly to retain the seat.

Mr George Fernandes (Janata) won the Muzaffarpur seat by a record margin of over three lakh votes.

CFD General Secretary H. N. Bahuguna defeated the sitting Congress member Mrs. Sheela Kaul in Lucknow by a convincing margin.

In Madhya Pradesh the Janata Party picked all but one of the 27 seats declared. The party dealt a severe blow to the Congress when it unseated the Minister for Information and Broadcasting, Mr. Vidya Charan Shukla, in Raipur.

Mr. Shukla, who had fought hard for a victory, lost by a huge margin of about 86,000 votes to Mr. Purshottam Lal Kaushik

Mr. Shukla's deputy, Mr. Dharam Bir Sinha, was overthrown in Barh, Bihar, by Mr. Shyam Sunder Gupta (Janata), a former Mayor of Calcutta, by more than 200,000 votes. Besides them, two more ministers Mr. A. P. Sharma and J. B. Fatnaik also lost.

The Congress, however, continued to hold its own in the south. In Karnataka, with 17 of the 19 seats declared already in its bag, the party was leading in all the remaining nine constituencies.

The Congress and its allies

H. N. Bahuguna

made a clean sweep of all the 20 seats in Kerala and conceded only four out of 39 in Tamil Nadu. The only other State where the party seemed to be doing well was Assam. It claimed six of the eight seats filled. the party President, Mr. D. K. Barooah [illegible] an unequivocal victory in [illegible]gong.

Mr. Arvind Netam, Union Deputy Minister for Education and Social Welfare, was defeated [illegible] Mr. [illegible]ghan Singh Thakur [illegible]ta) by a margin of 53,777 votes.

Mr. Biju Patnaik (Janata) was declared elected from the Kendrapara Constituency defeating his sole Congress rival, Mr. Bhagabat

THE TRIBUNE

Chandigarh, Tuesday, March 22, 1977

JANATA PARTY FORGES AHEAD IN NORTH

Record Victory For Fernandes *Ram, Sanjiva Reddy, Barooah Elected*

NEW DELHI, March 21 (Samachar)-The Janata Party's electoral floodtide in northern States swept more of its candidates to victory to widen its lead over the Congress tonight.

The Janata Party, with a tally of 177 seats, had forged a 43-seat lead over the Congress as more results were announced, taking the total of seats filled to 384.

The message of first returns from West Bengal and Orissa was that the Janata Party would overwhelm the Congress in these States.

In Orissa, it had secured 11 seats and was comfortably placed in five more constituencies while its electoral allies the CFD and the CPI(M) had captured one each. Congress had secured four seats all in South Orissa.

The Congress had win in the election of Mr. P.K. Deo (Ind) whom it had supported in Kalahandi

The party's prospects were no better in West Bengal, where all the 10 results declared fell to the Opposition combination.

The Congress was routed in Haryana where all 10 seats went in favour of the Janata Party.

In Punjab Opposition combine nominees had been returned in 11 constituencies. In Ferozepore the Pradesh Congress chief, Mr. Mohinder Singh Gill was battling grimly to retain the seat.

Mr. George Fernandes (Janata) won the Muzaffarpur seat by a record of over three lakh votes.

CFD General Secretary H.N. Bahuguna defeated the sitting Congress member Mrs. Sheela Kaul in Lucknow by a convincing margin.

In Madhya Pradesh the Janata Party picked all but one of the 27 seats declared. The party dealt a severe blow to the Congress when it unseated the Minister for Information and Broadcasting, Mr. Vidya Charan Shukla, in Raipur.

Mr. Shukla who had fought hard for a victory lost by a huge margin of about 86,000 votes to Mr. Purshottam Lal Kaushik.

Mr. Shukla's deputy, Mr. Dharam Bir Sinha, was overthrown in Barh, Bihar by Mr. Shyam Sunder Gupta (Janata), a former Mayor of Calcutta, by more than 2,00,000 votes. Besides them, two more ministers Mr. A.P. Sharma and J.B. Patnaik also lost.

The Congress, however, continued to hold its own in the south. In Karnataka, with 17 of the 19 seats declared already in its bag, the party was leading in all the remaining nine constituencies.

The Congress and its allies made a clean sweep of all the 20 seats in Kerala and conceded only four out of 39 in Tamil Nadu. The only other state where the party seems to be doing well was Assam. It claimed six of the eight seats filled, the party President, Mr. D.K. Barooah is nearing an unequivocal victory in Nowgong.

Mr. Arvind Neon, Union Deputy Minister for Education and Social Welfare was defeated by Mr. Faghan Singh Thakur (Janata) by a margin of 53,777 votes.

Continued from page 1 col. 4

Prasad Mohanty by a margin of 1,15,000 votes.

Big guns of the Congress among them the Prime Minister, Mrs. Indira Gandhi, the Union Defence Minister, Mr. Bansi Lal and Mr. Sanjay Gandhi, suffered defeat at the hands of their Janata Party rivals as results of the Lok Sabha elections last night.

The Prime Minister was defeated by over 55,000 votes in Rae Bareli by Mr. Raj Narain (Janata). And the Congress appeared to be heading for a severe mauling in the northern States.

Mr. Sanjay Gandhi lost to his Janata Party rival Mr. Ravindra Pratap Singh by over 75,000 votes. Mr. Bansi Lal lost by over 1.60 lakh votes to Mrs. Chandravati (Janata) in Bhiwani.

Other top Congress leaders also fell by the way side in the Janata onslaught.

Among the Union Ministers defeated were Law Minister H. R. Gokhale, Minister of State for Defence Production V. N. Gadgil, and Mr. K. C. Pant, Union Energy Minister, Mr. H.K.L. Bhagat, Minister of State for Works and Housing, and Mr. Jagannath Pahadia, Deputy Minister for Labour.

Dr. Shankar Dayal Sharma, Minister for Communications, conceded defeat before the declaration of the result.

The Returning Officer of Rae Bareli Parliamentary constituency, Mr. Vinod Malhotra, announced the result of Mrs. Gandhi after rejecting a plea by Mr. M. L. Fotedar, election agent of Mrs. Gandhi, seeking time to file petition for recounting.

Mr. Malhotra, before announcing the result, also turned down a plea of Mr. Fotedar asking for re-poll on several grounds, including alleged tampering of official seals on one of the ballot boxes.

Mrs. Gandhi polled 1.22.517 votes against 1.77.729 votes secured by Mr. Raj Narain.

The solitary Congress victory in Rajasthan was that of Mr. N. R. Mirdha, a member of the dissolved Lok Sabha.

Mr. Nathu Ram Mirdha retained the Nagaur seat by defeating his nearest Janata rival Mr. Kishan Lal Shah by a margin of over 20.000 votes in a triangular contest.

Those who fell before the Janata onslaught included Mr. Jagannath Pahadia, Union Deputy Minister for Labour, Mr. Raj Bahadur, former Tourism and Civil Aviation Minister, Dr. K. L. Shrimali, a former Union Education Minister and former Vice-Chancellor of Banaras Hindu University, and Mr. Khet Singh State Minister for Law. All these leaders lost by decisive margins.

Mr. Khet Singh was defeated in the Barmer constituency by Mr. Tan Singh (Janata) former MP, in a triangular contest by a margin of over 88,000 votes.

GREAT PERFORMANCE

The Congress, however, put up a great performance in Andhra Pradesh and did well in Tamil Nadu.

Mr. C. Subramaniam, Finance Minister, scored a spectacular victory trouncing his nearest DMK rival, Mr. K. N. Swaminathan in Palani by a margin of more than 2.2 lakh votes.

In Maharashtra, the External Affairs Minister Mr Y. B. Chavan, also scored a big victory, defeating his nearest rival, Mr. N. J. Bavangare (Janata) by a margin of over 1.9 lakh votes.

A blow the Congress had already suffered in U.P. was the defeat of Mr. Dinesh Singh, a former External Affairs Minister, at the hands of Mr. Roopnath Singh Yadav (Janata) in Pratapgarh, long considered his stronghold.

The Janata Party Chairman, Mr. Morarji Desai, led 13 of his party candidates to victory in Gujarat, where the Congress captured only five seats.

Notable Congress victories were those of Mr. T. A. Pai, Industry Minister, in Udipi (Karnataka) and Mr K. Brahmananda Reddy, Home Minister in Narasaraopet (Andhra Pradesh).

Mr. Mani Ram Bagri (Janata) was elected from the Mathura constituency in UP.

The Union Energy Minister Mr K.C. Pant was defeated by Mr. Bharat Bhooshan (Janata).

Mr. P. V. G Raju (Cong) elected from Bobbli defeating Mr P. P. Undarikakshachar (Janata) and five others.

The Congress tally included two seats won from the Union Territories of Dadra and Nagar Haveli and Lakshadweep

Mr. Ramji Lal Yadav Janata defeated Mr Hari Prasad Sharma (Congress) by a margin of over 1.72.000 votes in multi-cornered contest in Alwar

Mr Mohammed Ismail Arif Congress member of the Rajya Sabha was defeated from the Churu constituency by Mr Daulat Ram Saran (Janata by a margin of about 1.00.000 votes in a multi-cornered contest

In Ajmer Mr. Shri Karan Sharda (Janata) defeated Mr. V. N. Bhargwa (Congress) by a margin of over 100.000 votes.

Ravindra Pratap Singh

Mr. Ram Kanwar Berwa (Janata) retained the Tonk (SC) seat defeating his nearest Congress rival, Mr. Banwarilal, Rajasthan Minister of State for Jails, by a margin of more than 1,60.000 votes.

Mr. Krishna Kumar Goel (Janata) was declared elected from the Kota constituency defeating his nearest Congress rival, Mr. Kirit Bhai, by a margin of over 1,40,000 votes in a multi-cornered contest.

In the Salumber (ST) constituency Mr. Lalia (Janata) defeated Mr. Devi Lal (Cong.) MLA in a straight contest by a margin of over 98,000 votes.

Mr. Bega Ram (Janata) declared elected, defeating the Congress rival, Mr. Birbal in a triangular contest in Ganganagar.

In the Bayana (SC) constituency, Mr. Jagannath Pahadia, Union Deputy Labour Minister, was defeated by Mr. Sham Sunder Lal (Janata) by a margin of over 110,000 votes in a multi-cornered contest.

Mr. Raj Bahadur, former Union Minister for Tourism and Civil Aviation, was defeated by Mr. Ram Kishan (Janata) MLA, in the Bharatur constituency by a margin of over 150,000 votes in a triangular contest.

Mr. Shyam Sunder Somani (Janata) was declared elected from Chittorgarh defeating his Congress rival Mr. Bhawar Lal Jhanwar in a straight contest by a margin of over 1,37,000 votes.

In Andhra Pradesh Mr. S.B.P. Pattabhi Ramarao (Cong) defeated his nearest Janata rival Mr. M.V.S. Rubba Raju in the Rajahmundry constituency.

In Amreli, Gujarat, Mr. Dwarkadas Mohanlal Patel (Cong.-sitting) retained his seat defeating his nearest rival Mr. Gondhiva Narsinhdas Gordhandas (BLD).

Mr. R. K. Amin (BLD) defeated Mr Manubhai M Shah (Cong.) and two others in Surendranagar.

In Bulsar Mr. Nanubhai N Patel (Janata) was declared elected. He retains the Bulsar seat Mr.

Raj Narain

Ahmedbhai M. Patel (Cong.) was declared elected from Broach.

The Congress retained the Mandvi seat when its candidate Mr. Chhitubhai Gamit was declared elected in a straight contest with Mr. Mukundbhai Chaudhury (BLD).

Mr. P G. Mavlankar (Janata) was declared elected, defeating his immediate rival Mr. Govindbhai Patel, from Gandhinagar.

In Mah[illegible] Mr. Nana Mahadeo Bonde (Congress) [illegible] Amravati seat, defeating Mr. Haribhau Kaloti (Janata Party), his nearest rival, by over [illegible]0,000 votes.

The Defence Production Minister, Mr. V. N. Gadgil (Congress), Rajya Sabha member was defeated by Mr. S. S. Kakade (Janata) by a margin of 30,700 votes in a straight contest in the Baramati constituency, in Pune district.

Mr. Dinkar Balu Patil of the Peasants and Workers' Party defeated Mr. Shankar Babaji Sawant (Cong) in a straight contest to win the Kolaba seat.

Mr. Keshavrao S. Dhondge (PWP-Janata supported) wrested the Nanded seat from the Congress, defeating Prof. G. R. Mhaisekar, Congress member of the Rajya Sabha, in a straight fight.

Dr. Bapusaheb Kaladate (Janata) wrested the Aurangabad seat from the Congress, defeating his nearest rival Mr. Chandrashekhar Rajurkar (Congress) by 57,114 votes.

Mr. Santoshrao Vyamkatrao Gode (Cong) retained the Wardha seat.

Mr. E. V. Vikhe (Congress-sitting) retained the Kopargaon seat, defeating his nearest rival Mr. Kishor Pawar (Janata) by a margin of 98,544 votes.

Mr. Lahanu Shidva Kom of the CPI-M won the Dahanu (Scheduled Tribes) seat, defeating his Congress rival Mr. L. K. Dumada who held the seat in the dissolved Lok Sabha.

Mr. Tukaram Sadashiv Shingare (Cong) was declared elected from the Osmanabad constituency.

Mrs. Premalabai Dajisaheb Chavan retained the Karad seat for the Congress in a four-cornered contest.

Mr. Pundlik Danave (Janata) wrested the Jalna seat, defeating Mr. Manikrao Palodkar (Cong) by 24,645 votes in a straight fight.

The former Chief Minister of Maharashtra, Mr. V. P. Naik (Cong) was declared elected from the Washim (SC) constituency defeating two others.

Mr. Biju Patnaik (Janata) was declared elected from the Kendrapara Constituency defeating his sole Congress rival Mr. Bhagabat Prasad Mohanty by a margin of 1,15,000 votes.

Big guns of the Congress, among them the Prime Minister, Mrs. Indira Gandhi, the Union Defence Minister, Mr. Bansi Lal and Mr. Sanjay Gandhi, suffered defeat at the hands of their Janata Party rivals as results of the Lok Sabha elections declared last night.

The Prime Minister was defeated by over 55,000 votes in Raebareli by Mr. Raj Narain (Janata). And the Congress appeared to be heading for a severe mauling in the northern States.

Mr. Sanjay Gandhi lost to his Janata Party rival Mr. Ravindra Pratap Singh by over 75,000 votes. Mr. Bansi Lal lost by over 1.60 lakh votes to Mrs. Chandravati (Janata) in Bhiwani.

Other top Congress leaders also fell by the way side in the Janata onslaught.

Among the Union Ministers defeated were Law Minister H.R. Gokhale, Minister of State for Defence Production V.N. Gadgil, and Mr. K.C. Pant, Union Energy Minister, Mr. H.K.L. Bhagat, Minister of State for Works and Housing and Mr. Jagannath Pahadia, Deputy Minister for Labour.

Dr. Shankar Dayal Sharma Minister for communications conceded defeat before the declaration of the result.

The Returning Officer of Raebareli Parliamentary constituency, Mr. Vinod Malhotra, announced the result of Mrs. Gandhi after rejecting a plea by Mr. M.L. Fotedar, election agent of Mrs. Gandhi, seeking time to file petition for recounting.

Mr. Malhotra, before announcing the result, also turned down a plea of Mr. Fotedar asking for re-poll on several grounds, including alleged tampering of official seals on one of the ballot boxes.

Mrs. Gandhi polled 1,22,517 votes against 1,77,729 votes secured by Mr. Raj Narain.

The solitary Congress victory in Rajasthan was that of Mr. N.R. Mirdha, a member of the dissolved Lok Sabha.

Mr. Nathu Ram Mirdha retained the Nagaur seat by defeating his nearest Janata rival Mr. Kishan Lal Shah by a margin of over 20,000 votes in a triangular contest.

Those who fell before the Janata onslaught included Mr. Jagannath Pahadia, Union Deputy Minister for Labour, Mr. Raj Bahadur, former Tourism and Civil Aviation Ministers, Dr. K.L. Shrimali, a former Union Education Minister and former Vice-Chancellor of Banaras Hindu University, and Mr. Khet Singh, State Minster for Law. All these leaders lost by decisive margins.

Mr. Khet Singh was defeated in the Barmer constituency by Mr. Tan Singh (Janata) former MP, in a triangular contest by a margin of over 88,000 votes.

The Congress, however, put up a great performance in Andhra Pradesh and did well in Tamil Nadu.

Mr. C. Subramaniam, Finance Minister, scored a spectacular victory trouncing his nearest DMK rival, Mr. K.N. Swaminathan in Palani by a margin of more than 2.2 lakh votes.

In Maharashtra, the External Affairs Minister Mr. Y.B. Chavan, also scored a big victory, defeating his nearest rival, Mr. N.J. Bavangare (Janata) by a margin of over 1.9 lakh votes.

A blow the Congress had already suffered in U.P. was the defeat of Mr. Dinesh Singh, a former External Affairs Minister, at the hands of Mr. Roopnath Singh Yadav (Janata) in Pratapgarh, long considered his stronghold.

The Janata Party Chairman, Mr. Morarji Desai, led 13 of his party candidates to victory in Gujarat, where the Congress captured only five seats.

Notable Congress victories were those of Mr. T.A. Pai, Industry Minister, in Udipi (Karnataka) and Mr. K. Brahmananda Reddy, Home Minister in Narasaraopet (Andhra Pradesh).

Mr. Mani Ram Bagri (Janata) was elected from the Mathura constitutency in UP.

The Union Energy Minister Mr. K.C. Pant was defeated by Mr. Bharat Bhooshan (Janata).

Mr. P.V.G. Raju (Cong) elected from Bobbli defeating Mr. P.P. Undarikakshachar (Janata) and five others.

The Congress tally included two seats won from the Union Territories of Dadra and Nagar Haveli and Lakshadweep.

Mr. Ramji Lal Yadav (Janata) defeated Mr. Hari Prasad Sharma (Congress) by a margin of over 1,72,000 votes in multi-cornered contest in Alwar.

Mr. Mohammed Ismail Arif Congress member of the Rajya Sabha was defeated from the Churu constituency by Mr. Daulat Ram Saran (Janata) by a margin of about 1,00,000 votes in a multi-cornered contest.

In Ajmer Mr. Shri Karan Sharda (Janata) defeated Mr. V.N. Bhargwa (Congress) by a margin of over 1,00,000 votes.

Mr. Ram Kanwar Berwa (Janata) retained the Tonk (SC) seat defeating his nearest Congress rival, Mr. Banwarilal, Rajasthan Minister of State for Jails, by a margin of more than 1,60,000 votes.

Mr. Krishna Kumar Goel (Janata) was declared elected from the Kota constituency defeating his nearest Congress rival, Mr. Kirit Bhai, by a matgin of over 1,40,000 votes in a multi-cornered contest.

In the Salmber (ST) constituency Mr. Lalia (Janata) defeated Mr. Devi Lal (Cong.) MLA in a straight contest by a margin of 98.000 votes.

Mr. Bega Ram (Janata) declared elected, defeating the Congress rival, Mr. Birbal in a triangular contest in Ganganagar.

In the Bayana (SC) constitutency, Mr. Jagannath Pahadia, Union Deputy Labour Minister was defeated by Mr. Sham Sunder Lal (Janata) by a margin of over 1,10,000 votes in a multi-cornered contest.

Mr. Raj Bahadur, former Union Minister for Tourism and Civil Aviation, was defeated by Mr. Ram Kishan (Janata) MLA in the Bharatpar constituency by a margin of over 1,50,000 votes in a triangular contest.

Mr. Shyam Sunder Somani (Janata) was declared elected from Chittorgarh defeating his Congress rival Mr. Bhawar Lal Jhanwar in a straight contest by a margin of over 1,37,000 votes.

In Andhra Pradesh Mr. S.B.P. Pattabhi Ramarao (Cong) defeated his nearest Janata rival Mr. V.S. Rubba Raju in the Rajahmundry constituency.

In Amareli, Gujarat Mr. Dwarkadas Mohanlal Patel (Cong-sitting) retained his seat defeating his nearest rival Mr. Gondhiva Narsinhdas Gordhandas (BLD).

Mr. R.K. Amin (BLD) defeated Mr. Manubhai M. Shah (Cong.) and two others in Surendranagar.

In Bulsar Mr. Nanubhai N. Patel (Janata) was declared elected. He retains the Bulsar seat. Mr. Ahmedbhai M. Patel (Cong.) was declared elected from Broach.

The Congress retained the Mandvi seat when its candidate Mr. Chhitubhai Gavit was declared elected in a straight contest with Mr. Mukundbhai Chaudhury (BLD).

Mr. P.V. Mavlankar (Janata) was declared elected, defeating his immediate rival Mr. Govindbhai Patel from Gandhinagar.

In Maharashtra Mr. Nana Mahadeo Bonde (Congress) won Amrawati seat, defeating Mr. Haribhau Kaloti (Janata Party), his nearest rival by over 1,60,000 votes.

The Defence Production Minister Mr. V.N. Gadgil (Congress), Rajya Sabha member was defeated, by Mr. S.S. Kakade (Janata) by a margin of 30,700 votes in a straight contest in the Baramati constituency, in Pune district.

Mr. Dinkar Balu Patil of the Peasants and Workers' Party defeated Mr. Shankar Babaji Sawant (Cong) in a straight contest to win the Kolaba seat.

Mr. Keshavrao S. Dhondge (PWP-Janata supported) wrested the Nanded seat from the Congress defeating Prof. G.R. Mhaisekar, Congress member of the Rajya Sabha, in a straight fight.

Dr. Bapusaheb Kaladate (Janata) wrested the Aurangabad seat from the Congress, defeating his nearest rival Mr. Chandrashekhar Rajurkar (Congress) by 57,114 votes.

Mr. Santoshrao Vyamkatrao Gode (Cong) retained the Wardha seat.

Mr. E.V. Vikhe (Congress-sitting) retained the Kopargaon seat, defeating his nearest rival Mr. Kishor Pawar (Janata) by a margin of 98,544 votes.

Mr. Luhanu Shidva Kom of the CPI-M won the Dahanu (Scheduled Tribes) seat, defeating his Congress rival Mr. L.K. Dumada who held the seat in the dissolved Lok Sabha.

Mr. Tukaram Sadashiv Shingare (Cong.) was declared elected from the Osmanabad constituency.

Mrs. Premalabai Dajisahey Chavan retained the Karad seat, defeating Mr. Manikrao Palodkar (Cong) by 24645 votes in a straight fight.

The former Chief Minister of Maharashtra Mr. V.P. Naik (Cong.) was declared elected from the Washim (SC) constituency defeating two others.

CITY EDITION ✱

The Tribune

ESTABLISHED 1881

VOL. XCVII NO. 80 Chandigarh, Tuesday, March 22, 1977

JANATA-CFD COMBINE TO HAVE ONE LEADER

From Our Special Correspondent

NEW DELHI, March 21. — The Janata Party and the Congress for Democracy (CFD) will form one single block in Parliament and function as one party under one leader.

Announcing this, Mr. Surendra Mohan, Janata Party General Secretary, said that the leader of the Janata Party-CFD combine would be elected here on March 24 at a meeting of members of Parliament belonging to the combine to be held at 11 a.m.

The meeting will also elect other office-bearers of the common Parliamentary group. Mr. Jayaprakash Narayan will be present here on that day, he added.

He said: "My clear understanding is that there will be one Parliamentary group, one leader and one Government in which there will be full participation."

This was the outcome of the meeting of the Standing Committee of the National Committee of the Janata Party this morning. Mr H N Bahuguna, General Secretary, CFD attended the meeting as special invitee.

In the afternoon, the National Committee of the Janata Party met again and fixed priorities for the proposed Janata-CFD Government.

Mr Jagjivan Ram, Chairman, CFD, did not participate in the morning meeting. But he explained to newsmen later that he had kept awake till very late last night and, therefore, could not get ready for the morning meeting. Mr. Bahuguna attended. There was no other special reason.

He said that the meeting discussed steps for the change-over of the Government and it involved the question of leadership. He, however, declined to say anything about leadership but added that efforts would be made to evolve a consensus to avoid a contest. But he said that in a democracy a contest should not be considered bad.

The question of the merger of the Janata Party and the CFD would be considered when the Executive Committee of the CFD meets and discusses the issue. No date has yet been fixed for the meeting.

He said that the first priority of the Janata-CFD Government would be "economic development".

Meanwhile the National Committee of the Janata Party, this afternoon decided upon a programme of action which the Janata-CFD Government would implement on priority basis.

Mr. Surendra Mohan said the Janata-CFD priorities included restoration of civil liberties and democratic rights, repeal of the Prevention of Publication of Objectionable Matters Act and restoration of the Feroze Gandhi Act providing immunity to the press for covering Parliamentary proceedings. The Janata-CFD Government would withdraw the external emergency which had been there for a long time, release all detenus, review special cases and cancel the pending warrants.

Mr Surendra Mohan said that the Janata-CFD Government would also revoke the Maintenance of Internal Security Act (MISA) as far as its application to detenus is concerned. Certain amendments to MISA would be nullified and the question of repealing MISA altogether would be seriously examined. The Janata Party was of the view that none should be detained without trial, he added.

The action programme would also include removal of ban on certain organisations commensurate with the Party's election promise that no organisation should be banned without prior judicial enquiry into its activities.

The Janata-CFD Government would insist on austerity and discourage ostentatious living. At the party level a small committee would be set up to formulate a code of conduct for Ministers and party members on public behaviour and also for government behaviour.

All Ministers might be asked to declare their assets.

Asked about the Baroda dynamite case in which one of the Janata Party leaders, Mr. George Fernandes, successfully contested the Muzaffarpur Parliamentary constituency, is involved had two aspects, he explained. In that case some of the accused persons were arrested under MISA; this would be revoked. A court case was also on. The Law Ministry would examine this case.

Before the Janata-CFD members of Parliament embark on their Parliamentary work of electing the leader and other office-bearers, they will go to Rajghat, Mahatma Gandhi's Samadhi, on March 24 in the morning and take a pledge.

Answering a question about the pattern of relationship between the combine and its allies like the Akali Dal of Punjab, the DMK of Tamil Nadu and the CPI (M), Mr. Surendra Mohan said they would like to have discussions with them on this issue.

Although he said that the leadership issue would pose no problem, it is learnt that the question would be discussed both formally and informally among the Janata Party and CFD leaders, both separately and jointly, before election of the leader.

These discussions could not be held because many of the important members are still out of Delhi.

Front Page

THE TRIBUNE

Chandigarh, Tuesday, March 22, 1977

JANATA–CFD COMBINE TO HAVE ONE LEADER

New Delhi March 21.—The Janata Party and the Congress for Democracy (CFD) will form one single block in Parliament and function as one party under one leader.

Announcing this Mr. Surendera Mohan. Janata Party General Secreatary said the leader of the Janata Party-CFD combine would be elected here on March 24 at a meeting of members of Parliament belonging to the combine to be held at 11 a.m.

The meeting will also elect other office-bearers of the common Parliamentary group, Mr. Jayaprakash Narayan will be present here on that day, he added.

He said: "**My clear understanding is that there will be one Parliamentary group, one leader and one Government in which there will be full participation.**"

This was the outcome of the meeting of the Standing Committee of the National Committee of the Janata Party this morning. Mr. H.N. Bahuguna. General Secretary CFD attended the meeting as special invitee.

In the afternoon, the National Committee of the Janata Party met again and fixed priorities for the proposed Janata-CFD Government.

Mr. Jagjivan Ram, Chairman, CFD did not participate in the morning meeting. But he explained to newsmen later that he had kept awake till very late last night and, therefore, could not get ready for the morning meeting. Mr. Bahuguna attended. There was no other special reason.

He said that the meeting discussed steps for the change-over of the Government and it involved the question of leadership. He, however, declined to say anything about leadership but added that efforts would be made to evolve a consensus to avoid a contest. But he said that in a democracy a contest should not be considered bad.

The question of the merger of the Janata Party and the CFD would be considered when the Executive Committee of the CFD meets and discusses the issue. No date has yet been fixed for the meeting.

He said that the first priority of the Janata-CFD Government would be "economic development".

Meanwhile the National Committee of the Janata Party, this afternoon decided upon a programme of action which the Janata-CFD Government would implement on priority basis.

Mr. Surendra Mohan said the Janata-CFD priorities included restoration of Civil liberties and democratic rights, repeal of the Prevention of Publication of Objectionable Matters Act and restoration of the Feroze Gandhi Act providing immunity to the press for covering Parliamentary proceedings. The Janata-CFD Government would withdraw the external emergency which had been there for a long time, release all detenus, review special cases and cancel the pending warrants.

Mr. Surendra Mohan said that the Janata-CFD Government would also revoke the Maintenance of Internal Security Act (MISA) as far as its application to detenus is concerned. Certain amendments to MISA would be nullified and the question of repealing MISA altogether would be seriously examined. The Janata Party was of the view that none should be detained without trial, he added.

The action programme would also include removal of ban on certain organisations commensurate with the Party's election promise that no organisation should be banned without prior judicial enquiry into its activities.

The Janata-CFD Government would insist on austerity and discourage ostentatious living. At the party level a small committee would be set up to formulate a code of conduct for Ministers and party members on public behavior and also for government behaviour.

All Ministers might be asked to declare their assets.

Asked about the Baroda dynamite case in which one of the Janata Party leaders, Mr. George Fernandes, successfully contested the Muzaffarpur Parliamentary constituency, is involved had two aspects, he explained. In that case some of the accused persons were arrested under MISA: this would be revoked. A court case was also on. The Law Ministry would examine this case.

Before the Janata CFD members of Parliament embark on their Parliamentary work of electing the leader and other office bearers, they will go to Rajghat, Mahatma Gandhi's Samadhi on March 24 in the morning and take a pledge.

Answering a question about the pattern of relationship between the combine and its allies like the Akali Dal of Punjab, the DMK of Tamil Nadu and the CPI(M), Mr. Surendra Mohan said they would like to have discussions with them on this issue.

Although he said that the leadership issue will pose no problem, it is learnt that the question would be discussed both formally and informally among the Janata Party and the CFD leaders, both separately and jointly before election of the leader.

These discussions could not be held because many of the important members are still out of Delhi.

Among those who attended the National Committee meeting in the afternoon included Mr. L.K. Advani, Mr. Ashok Mehta, Mr. Atal Bihari Vajpayee, Mr. Surendra Mohan, Mr. Harbhajan Singh, Mr. Sikandar Bakht, Mrs. Mohinder Kaur and Mr. Shanti Bhushan, Mr. Morarji Desai, Chairman, Janata Party, presided.

Mr. Charan Singh, Deputy Chairman and Mr. P. Ramchandran as also leaders from West Bengal did not attend the meeting as they could not reach Delhi.

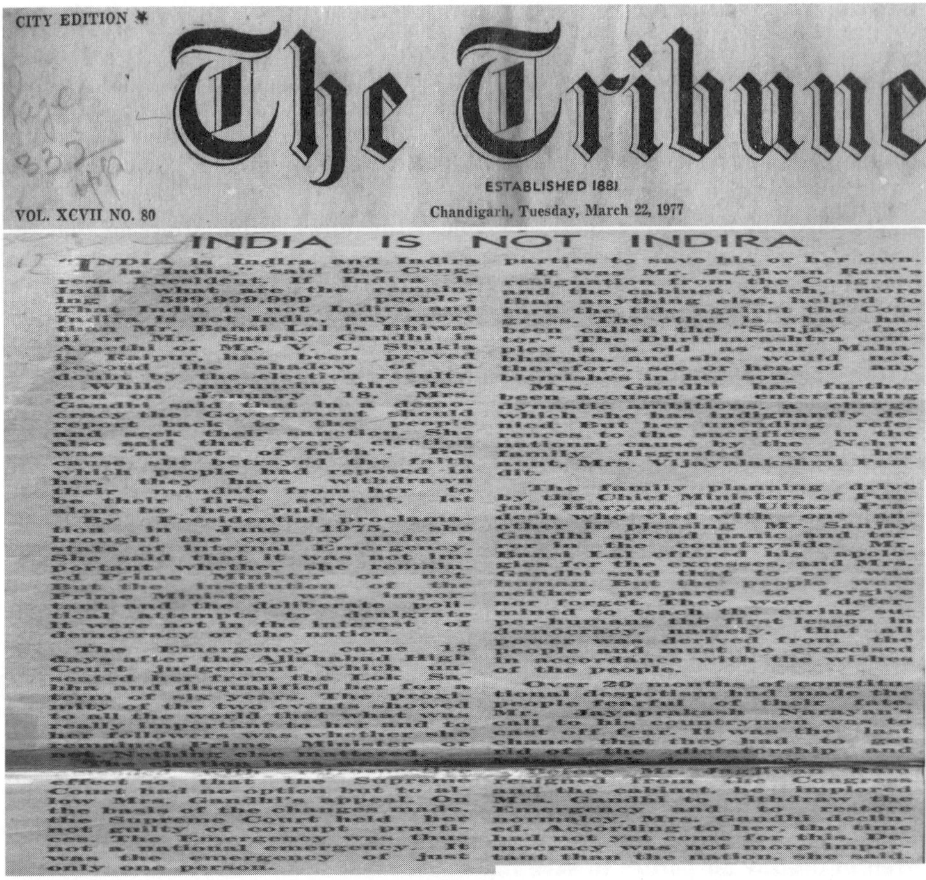
CITY EDITION ✱

The Tribune

ESTABLISHED 1881

VOL. XCVII NO. 80

Chandigarh, Tuesday, March 22, 1977

INDIA IS NOT INDIRA

Page No. 4 **Editorial**

THE TRIBUNE

Chandigarh, Tuesday, March 22, 1977

INDIA IS NOT INDIRA

"INDIA is Indira and Indira is India," said the Congress President. If Indira is India, what are the remaining 59,99,99,999 people? That India is not Indira and Indira is not India, any more than Mr. Bansi Lal is Bhiwani or Mr. Sanjay Gandhi is Amethi or Mr. V.C. Shukla is Raipur, has been proved beyond the shadow of a doubt by the election results.

While announcing the election on January 18, Mrs. Gandhi said that in a democracy the Government should report back to the people and seek their sanction. She also said that every election was "an act of faith". Because she betrayed the faith which people had reposed in her, they have withdrawn their mandate from her to be their first servant, let alone be their ruler.

By Presidential proclamation in June 1975, she brought the country under a state of internal Emergency. She said that it was not important whether she remained Prime Minister or not. But the institution of the Prime Minister was important and the deliberate political attempts to denigrate it were not in the interest of democracy or the nation.

The Emergency came 13 days after the Allahabad High Court judgment which unseated her from the Lok Sabha and disqualified her for a term of six years. The proximity of the two events showed to all the world that what was really important to her and to her followers was whether she remained Prime Minister or not. Nothing else mattered.

The election laws were then amended with retrospective effect so that the Supreme Court had no option but to allow Mrs. Gandhi's appeal. On the basis of the changes made, the Supreme Court held her not guilty of corrupt practices. The Emergency was thus not a national emergency. It was the emergency of just only one person.

The drastic amendment of MISA so as to leave the citizen completely at the mercy of the executive, the introduction of Press censorship, the enactment of the Publication of Objectionable Matters Act, the repeal of the Feroze Gandhi Act ensuring immunity for the publication of parliamentary proceedings and various other measures followed in logical sequence. Not only the opposition leaders but also the rank and file of opposition parties and individual dissenters were arrested in thousands and kept in detention without trial.

The opportunity provided by this enforced absence of the opposition from Parliament and the censorship of the press was utilized to bring about wholesale changes in the basic structure of the Constitution. The judiciary was reduced to impotence in the process. Mrs. Gandhi, however, has been very much sensitive to the criticism that she had made herself a dictator.

She has argued that if she wanted to be a dictator, she need not have called any elections at all, forgetting that even dictators like Hitter at one end and Ayub Khan and Yahya Khan at the other had also held elections. The timing and manner in which she announced the elections left no doubt that she wanted the Congress and the Congress alone, to come out victorious and glorious. A dictator is always driven to destroy all parties to save his or her own.

It was Mr. Jagjivan Ram's resignation from the Congress and the cabinet which, more than anything else helped to turn the tide against the Congress. The other is what has been called the "Sanjay factor." The Dhritharashtra complex is as old as our Mahabharata, and she would not, therefore, see or hear of any blemishes in her son.

Mrs. Gandhi has further been accused of entertaining dynastic ambitions, a charge which she has indignantly denied. But her unending references to the sacrifices in the national cause by the Nehru family disgusted even her aunt, Mrs. Vijayalakshmi Pandit.

The family planning drive by Chief Ministers of Punjab, Haryana and Uttar Pradesh who vied with one another in pleasing Mr. Sanjay Gandhi spread panic and terror in the countryside. Mr. Bansi Lal offered his apologies for the exercises, and Mrs. Gandhi said that to err was human. But the people were neither prepared to forgive nor forget. They were determined to teach the erring super-humans the first lesson in democracy, namely, that all power was derived from the people and must be exercised in accordance with the wishes of the people.

Over 20 months of constitutional despotism had made the people fearful of their fate. Mr. Jayaprakash Narayan's call to his countrymen was to cast off fear. It was the last chance that they had to get rid of the dictatorship and bring back democracy.

Before Mr. Jagjivan Ram resigned from the congress and cabinet, he implored Mrs. Gandhi to withdraw the Emergency and to restore normalcy. Mrs. Gandhi declined. According to her, the time had not yet come for this. Democracy was not more important than the nation, she said.

Mr. Jayaprakash Narayan asked whether she was the only one who cared for the nation. He wrote to her on July 27, 1975: "Among those whom you have detained or imprisoned there are many who have done much more for the nation than you. And every one of them is as good a patriot as yourself. So, please do not apply salt to our wounds by lecturing to us about the nation."

When Lorenzo the Magnificant was on his death-bed, he summoned the Prior of St. Mark. Savonarola reluctantly came and offered absolution on three conditions. Lorenzo asked what they were. Savonarola said: "You must repent and feel true faith in God's mercy". Lorenzo agreed. "Secondly", said Savonarola, "You must give up all your worldly possession." This too Lorenzo agreed. But upon hearing the third and last condition: "You must restore the liberties of Florence" Lorenzo turned his face to the wall and made no reply, and Savonarola walked away.

Mrs. Gandhi did not agree to lift the Emergency when so many people appealed to her to do so. What she resolutely refused to do when she thought she had the world at her feet, she has now done in the hour of her defeat. This is more than what Lorenzo was prepared to do for his Floreatines even in his last moments. It is thus something to be thankful for by all her countrymen.

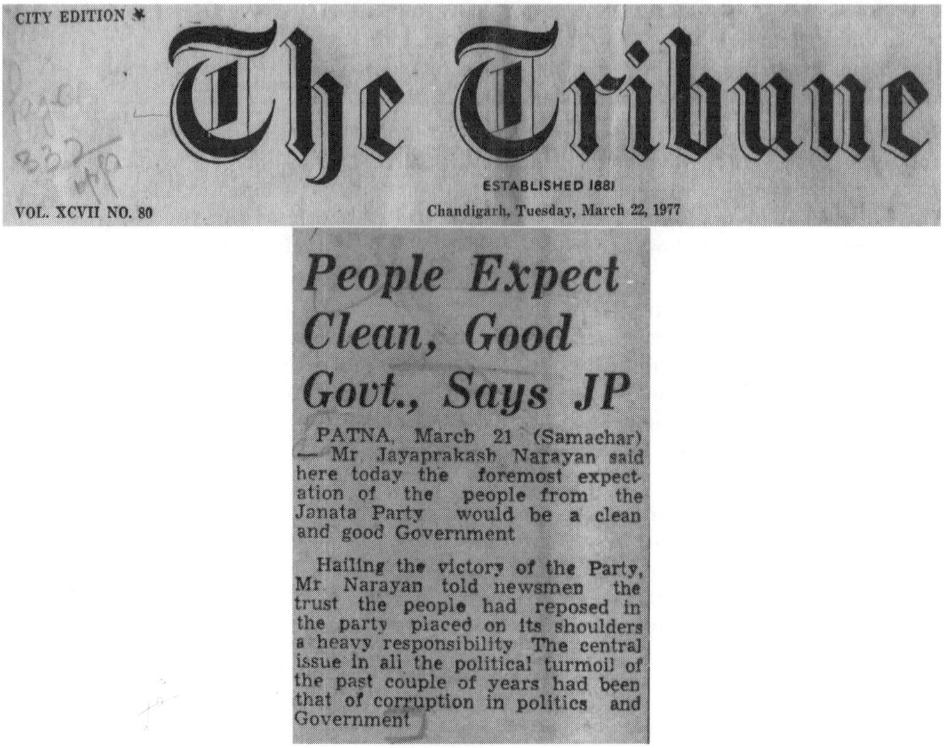

CITY EDITION ✱

The Tribune

ESTABLISHED 1881

VOL. XCVII NO. 80 Chandigarh, Tuesday, March 22, 1977

People Expect Clean, Good Govt., Says JP

PATNA, March 21 (Samachar) — Mr. Jayaprakash Narayan said here today the foremost expectation of the people from the Janata Party would be a clean and good Government

Hailing the victory of the Party, Mr. Narayan told newsmen the trust the people had reposed in the party placed on its shoulders a heavy responsibility. The central issue in all the political turmoil of the past couple of years had been that of corruption in politics and Government

Page 10

THE TRIBUNE

Chandigarh, Tuesday, March 22, 1977

PEOPLE EXPECT CLEAN GOVERNMENT, SAYS JP.

PATNA, March 21 (Samachar) – Mr. Jayaprakash Narayan said here today the foremost expectation of the people from the Janata Party would be a clean and good Government.

Hailing the victory of the Party Mr. Narayan told newsmen the trust the people had reposed in the party placed on its shoulders a heavy responsibility. The central issue in all the political turmoil of the past couple of years had been that of corruption in politics and Government.

Published from New Delhi, Bombay and Ahmedabad.

THE TIMES OF INDIA

NO. 79, VOL. CXXXIX ★★★ NEW DELHI: TUESDAY, MARCH 22, 1977 35 PAISE

MRS. INDIRA GANDHI DEFEATED

Recount plea rejected: Sanjay too loses

By Our Special Correspondent

NEW DELHI, March 21

THE Prime Minister, Mrs. Indira Gandhi, was defeated by over 55,000 votes in Rae Bareli at the hands of Mr. Raj Narain as the Janata Party mauled the Congress in northern states to register a tally of 101 out of 207 Lok Sabha seats the results of which have been declared so far.

THE TIMES OF INDIA

New Delhi, Tuesday, March 22, 1977

MRS. INDIRA GANDHI DEFEATED

RECOUNT PLEA REJECTED-SANJAY TOO LOSES

By Our Special Correspondent

The Prime Minister, Mrs. Indira Gandhi, was defeated by over 55,000 votes in Raebareli at hands of Mr. Raj Narain as the Janata Party mauled the Congress in northern states to register a tally of 101 out of 207 Lok Sabha seats the results of which have been declared so far.

Mrs. Gandhi polled 1,22,517 votes as against 1,77,729 votes secured by Mr. Raj Narain (Janata).

The returning officer of the Raebareli Parliamentary constituency, Mr. Vinod Malhotra, announced the result of Mrs. Gandhi after rejecting a plea by Mr. M.L. Fotedar, election agent of Mrs. Gandhi, seeking time to file petition for recounting.

Before announcing the result, Mr. Malhotra also turned down a plea by Mr. Fotedar asking for re-poll on several grounds, including alleged tampering of official seals on one of the ballot boxes.

In the neighbouring constituency of Amethi, Mr. Sanjay Gandhi has lost to Mr. Ravindra Pratap Singh (Janata) by 75,884 votes.

Published from New Delhi, Bombay and Ahmedabad. ESTABLISHED 1839

THE TIMES OF INDIA

NO. 79, VOL. CXXXIX ★★★ NEW DELHI: TUESDAY, MARCH 22, 1977 35 PAISE

2-hour arguments before rejecting PM's recount plea

RAE BARELI, March 21 (Samachar): Before rejecting the application filed by Mr. Fotedar, Mrs. Gandhi's poll agent, for a repoll, the returning officer said yesterday he could give half an hour to file a formal petition since the result could not be withheld for a long time.

Mr. Fotedar pleaded for a minimum of two hours as he had to consult his counsel and collect evidence.

Mr. Malhotra said since the petitioner has expressed his inability to file a formal application within the time he could permit, he had no option but to reject the plea and announce the result.

Earlier, Mr. Malhotra heard for about two hours arguments from both sides on an application of Mr. Fotedar seeking immediate adjournment of counting and recommending to the Chief Election Commission repoll in Rae Bareli constituency.

Mr. Fotedar, in his petition, argued that there were several instances of "malpractices" with regard to tampering of ballot papers. He alleged that seals of some ballot boxes were found broken.

Mr. Fotedar produced before the returning officer one such instance wherein one of the Congress agents during the counting of total member of votes polled yesterday morning had raised an objection to a broken official seal on one ballot box.

Mr. Fotedar, who was assisted by an advocate, Mr. Dinesh Chandra, also alleged in his plea that many such people were allowed to cast vote who were not found to be on electoral rolls.

Such complaints, they said, had been lodged with the concerned polling officers on the day of polling. They also alleged that many "spurious" ballot papers were found during the counting at some places.

Asked by Mr. Malhotra to produce evidence in support of any of such allegations, Mr. Fotedar said he wanted sufficient time to collect it.

Appearing on behalf of Mr. Raj Narain, Mr. R. S. N. Kakkar, a former advocate general of U.P., argued that no objection with regard to the allegations made in the petition, had been raised during the counting.

For demanding recount, Mr. Kakkar said, the petitioner should at least put forward sufficient allegations.

NO EVIDENCE

There is no allegation in compliance with such sections of People's Representation Act under which a returning officer could recommend to the Chief Election Commission repoll in a particular constituency.

In this ruling, Mr. Malhotra said there is no evidence in support of the allegation of tampering with the ballot boxes.

He said he found it difficult to accept any of the allegations for lack of proper evidence.

Mr. P. B. Dutta, an observer of the Chief Election Commission, was present during the counting yesterday and also during the hearing of Mr. Fotedar's petition.

The moment Mr. Malhotra read out the certificate he allotted to Mr. Raj Narain declaring him elected from Rae Bareli constituency, a packed courtroom of the district magistrate, burst into cheers.

The slogans of 'Raj Narain zindabad', 'Lok Nayak Jayaprakash zindabad' rented the air outside the collectorate where a 10,000-strong crowd listened to the result on the public address system.

After the declaration of the result, the supporters of Mr. Raj Narain took out a victory procession through the main thoroughfares of Rae Bareli.

Page 2

THE TIMES OF INDIA

New Delhi, Tuesday, March 22, 1977

2-HOUR ARGUMENTS BEFORE REJECTING PM'S RECOUNT PLEA

Raebareli, March 21 (Samachar): Before rejecting the application filed by Mr. Fotedar, Mrs. Gandhi's poll agent, for a repoll, the returning officer said yesterday he could give half an hour to file a formal petition since the result could not be withheld for a long time.

Mr. Fotedar pleaded for a minimum of two hours as he had to consult his counsel and collect evidence.

Mr. Malhotra said since the petitioner has expressed his inability to file a formal application within the time he could permit, he had no option but to reject the plea and announce the result.

Earlier, Mr. Malhotra heard for about two hours arguments from both sides on an application of Mr. Fotedar seeking immediate adjournment of counting and recommending to the Chief Election Commission repoll in Raebareli constituency.

Mr. Fotedar, in his petition, argued that there were several instances of "malpractices" with regard to tampering of ballot papers. He alleged that seals of some ballot boxes were found broken.

Mr. Fotedar produced before the returning officer one such instance wherein one of the Congress agents during the counting of total number of votes polled yesterday morning had raised an objection to a broken official seal on one ballot box.

Mr. Fotedar who was assisted by an advocate, Mr. Dinesh Chandra, also alleged in his plea that many such people were allowed to cast vote who were not found to be on electoral rolls.

Such complaints, they said, had been lodged with the concerned polling officers on the day of polling. They also alleged that many "spurious" ballot papers were found during the counting at some places.

Asked by Mr. Malhotra to produce evidence in support of any of such allegations. Mr. Fotedar said he wanted sufficient time to collect it.

Appearing on behalf of Mr. Raj Narain. Mr. R.S.N. Kakkar, a former advocate general of U.P. argued that no objection with regard to the allegations made in the petition, had been raised during the counting.

For demanding recount, Mr. Kakkar said, the petitioner should at least put forward sufficient allegations.

There is no allegation in compliance with such sections of People's Representation Act under which a returning officer could recommend to the Chief Election Commission repoll in a particular constituency.

In this ruling, Mr. Malhotra said there is no evidence in support of the allegation of tampering with the ballot boxes.

He said he found it difficult to accept any of the allegations for lack of proper evidence.

Mr. P.B. Dutta, an observer of the Chief Election Commission, was present during the counting yesterday and also during the hearing of Mr. Fotedar's petition.

The moment Mr. Malhotra read out the certificate he allotted to Mr. Raj Narain declaring him elected from Raebareli constituency, a packed courtroom of the district magistrate, burst into cheers.

The slogans of 'Raj Narain Zindabad', 'Lok Nayak Jayaprakash Zindabad' rented the air outside the collectorate where a 10,000-strong crowd listened to the result on the public address system.

After the declaration of the result, the supporters of Mr. Raj Narain took out a victory procession through the main thoroughfares of Raebareli.

Published from New Delhi, Bombay and Ahmedabad. ESTABLISHED 1838

THE TIMES OF INDIA

NO. 79, VOL. CXXXIX ★★★ NEW DELHI: TUESDAY, MARCH 22, 1977 35 PAISE

GONE WITH THE WIND

By K. K. SASTRY

LUCKNOW, March 21.
HOW the mighty have fallen, seeded Congress candidates blown off like chaff and the newcomers knocked down like nine pins!

Mr. Indira Gandhi and Mr. Sanjay Gandhi went the way of 29 other Congress nominees who were swept off by the Janata wave.

Election Result No. 14, coming after 2 a.m., gave the Rae Bareli seat to Mr. Raj Narain, Mrs. Gandhi's old electoral foe, by 55,000 votes, the margin by which she triumphed in 1971.

For Mr. Narain, it was a popular endorsement of the election petition he had won, futilely at that time, in the Allahabad High Court in June 1975.

Shortly afterwards came the announcement that Mr. Sanjay Gandhi had lost by 75,000 votes to Mr. Ravindra Pratap Singh, the 37-year-old moustachioed lawyer who swayed the electorate with his personality and folksy oratory.

Twenty-three candidates who were members of the dissolved Lok Sabha, including six members of the Union ministry, lost their electoral battle in this state. Twentyone of the Janata Party nominees were elected by margins exceeding one lakh votes.

Front Page

THE TIMES OF INDIA

New Delhi, Tuesday, March 22, 1977

GONE WITH THE WIND

BY K.K. SASTRY

LUCKNOW, MARCH 21. How the mighty have fallen, seeded Congress candidates blown off like chaff and the newcomers knocked down like nine pins!

Mrs. Indira Gandhi and Mr. Sanjay Gandhi went the way of 29 other Congress nominees who were swept off by the Janata wave.

Election Result No. 14 coming after 2 a.m. gave the Raebareli seat to Mr. Raj Narain, Mrs. Gandhi's old electoral foe, by 55,000 votes, the margin by which she triumphed in 1971.

For Mr. Narain it was a popular endorsement of the election petition he had won, futilely at that time, in the Allahabad High Court in June 1975.

Shortly afterwards came the announcement that Mr. Sanjay Gandhi had lost by 75,000 votes to Mr. Ravindra Pratap Singh, the 37-year-old moustached lawyer who swayed the electorate with his personality and folky oratory.

Twenty-three candidates who were members of the dissolved Lok Sabha, including six members of the Union Ministry, lost their electoral battle in this state. Twenty-one of the Janata Party nominees were elected by margins exceeding one lakh votes.

Published from New Delhi, Bombay and Ahmedabad. ESTABLISHED 1838

THE TIMES OF INDIA

NO. 79, VOL. CXXXIX *** NEW DELHI: TUESDAY, MARCH 22, 1977 35 PAISE

Emergency revoked

NEW DELHI, March 21 (Samachar): The proclamation of emergency issued on June 25, 1975, has been revoked by the Vice-President, Mr. B. D. Jatti, acting in his capacity as President.

The text of the proclamation said: "In exercise of the powers conferred by sub-clause (A) of clause (2) of Article 352 of the Constitution, I, Basappa Danappa Jatti, Vice-President acting as President of India, hereby revoke the proclamation of emergency issued under clause (1) of that Article on the 25th June 1975, and published with the notification of the Government of India in the Ministry of Home Affairs No. GSR 353 (E) dated the 26th June, 1975."

Front Page

THE TIMES OF INDIA

New Delhi, Tuesday, March 22, 1977

EMERGENCY REVOKED

NEW DELHI, March 21 (Samachar); The proclamation of emergency issued on June 25, 1975, has been revoked by the Vice-President, Mr. B.D. Jatti, acting in his capacity as President.

The text of the proclamation said: "In exercise of the powers conferred by sub-clause (A) of clause (2) of Article 352 of the Constitution, I, Bassappa Danappa Jatti, Vice-President acting as President of India, hereby revoke the proclamation of emergency issued under clause (1) of that Article on the 25th June, 1975, and published with the notification of the Government of India in the Ministry of Home Affairs No. GSR 353 (E) dated the 26th June, 1975."

THE TIMES OF INDIA

NO. 80, VOL. CXXXIX ★★★ NEW DELHI: WEDNESDAY, MARCH 23, 1977 35 PAISE

P.M. resigns, will continue till new govt.

By Our Special Correspondent

NEW DELHI, March 22.

THE Prime Minister, Mrs. Indira Gandhi, has submitted her resignation and that of her colleagues in the Council of Ministers.

A Rashtrapati Bhavan communique announced this morning that the President had accepted the resignation and asked Mrs. Gandhi and her colleagues to continue till a new council of ministers is appointed.

Mrs. Gandhi called on Mr. B. D. Jatti, the acting President, at his residence, this morning to submit the resignation.

Prior to her submitting the resignation, a Cabinet meeting was held. Mrs. Gandhi accompanied by her principal secretary, Mr. P. N. Dhar, drove from her South Block office to the acting President's residence on Maulana Azad Road. She was with Mr. Jatti for about 20 minutes.

As she came out of Mr. Jatti's residence she smilingly greeted a handful of correspondents and cameramen who were waiting outside.

Her resignation brings to an end her 11-year stewardship of the country. She had assumed office on January 24, 1966 after the demise of Mr. Lal Bahadur Shastri at Tashkent.

The resignation followed the sensational debacle of the Congress Party in the general elections held last week. Mrs. Gandhi herself lost the election at Rae Bareli.

LAST ACT

Her last major official act was to recommend revocation of the Emergency, her own brain child, the rigours of which wrecked the party's chances of returning to power and humbled her at the hustings.

Mrs. Gandhi's resignation signifies the fall of one of the most powerful personages in south Asia, particularly in the last six years after she had returned with a massive mandate on a platform of 'garibi hatao'.

More than the resounding electoral triumph of 1971, the crowning achievement of her public life was the political direction she gave to the Bangladesh liberation.

Even otherwise, it was an event-studded term as Prime Minister. The great split in the Congress, the mid-term poll, the period of economic strains, the euphoric nuclear implosion, launching "Aryabhata", the Opposition challenges and the sweeping changes in the Constitution which invested her with extraordinary powers were significant landmarks in the country's history.

The turning point in her public life came on June 12, 1975 when the Allahabad High Court upheld Mr. Raj Narain's petition challenging her election. Developments since then provide the scenario that [illegible] in the rejection of her rule.

Incidentally, the [illegible] of Mr. Raj Narain this time was: "My election petition was upheld by the high court. I was jailed. The law of the land was changed. Even the Supreme Court could not do anything. Now I come to the highest court, you, electors, for the final verdict."

The final verdict came on Sunday night when the voters gave her Lok Sabha seat to her rival.

It was only a year ago that the official media made a big effort to celebrate the "decade of progress" under her rule. One could not fail to notice a coincidence in this regard in the rise and fall of a regime in Pakistan. The tenth year of Field Marshal Ayub's rule was celebrated with a fanfare of publicity. It was stated that a new ethos had developed in the country—a familiar phrase for the media in India for the last 19 months. A year later he was toppled from power.

Following are the texts of the letters of resignation of the Prime Minister and the reply of the acting President, Mr. B. D. Jatti:

Dear Rashtrapatiji,

Consequent on the announcement of the results of the general elections, I tender my own and the resignation of the Council of Ministers.

I am grateful to you for the consideration you have consistently shown to me and my colleagues.

Yours Sincerely,
Indira Gandhi.

In his letter accepting the resignation, Mr. Jatti said:

My dear Prime Minister,

I have received your letter dated March 22, 1977, tendering your resignation and that of your colleagues in the Council of Ministers. I accept the resignation and request you and your colleagues to continue in office till a new government is formed.

I would like to take this opportunity to thank you for the services rendered to the nation by you and your colleagues in the outgoing Council of Ministers.

With regards,

Yours sincerely,
B. D. Jatti.

THE TIMES OF INDIA

New Delhi, Wednesday, March 23, 1977

P.M. RESIGNS, WILL CONTINUE TILL NEW GOVERNMENT

The Prime Minister, Mrs. Indira Gandhi, has submitted her resignation and that of her colleagues in the Council of Ministers.

A Rashtrapati Bhavan Communique announced this morning that the President had accepted the resignation and asked Mrs. Gandhi and her colleagues to continue till a new council of ministers is appointed.

Mrs. Gandhi called on Mr. B.D. Jatti, the acting President, at his residence, this morning to submit the resignation.

Prior to her submitting the resignation, a Cabinet meeting was held. Mrs. Gandhi accompanied by her principal secretary, Mr. P.N. Dhar, drove from her South Block office to the acting President's residence on Maulana Azad Road. She was with Mr. Jatti for about 20 minutes.

As she came out of Mr. Jatti's residence she smilingly greeted a handful of correspondents and cameramen who were waiting outside.

Her resignation brings to an end her 11- year stewardship of the country. She had assumed office on January 24, 1966 after the demise of Mr. Lal Bahadur Shastri at Tashkent.

The resignation followed the sensational debacle of the Congress Party in the general elections held last week. Mrs. Gandhi herself lost the election at Raebareli.

Last Act

Her last major official act was to recommend revocation of the Emergency, her own brain child, the rigours of which wrecked the party's chances of returning to power and humbled her at the hustings.

Mrs. Gandhi's resignation signifies the fall of one of the most powerful personages in South Asia, particularly in the last six years after she had returned with a massive mandate on a platform of 'garibi hatao."

More than the resounding electoral triumph of 1971, the crowning achievement of her public life was the political direction she gave to the Bangladesh liberation.

Even otherwise, if was an event-studded term as Prime Minister. The great split in the Congress, the mid-term poll, the period of economic strains, the euphoric nuclear implosion, launching "Aryabhata", the Opposition challenges and the sweeping changes in the Constitution which invested her with extraordinary powers, were significant landmarks in the country's history.

The turning point in her public life came on June 12, 1975 when the Allahabad High Court upheld Mr. Raj Narain's petition challenging her election. Developments since then provide the scenario that culminated in the rejection of her rule.

Incidentally, the election refrain of Mr. Raj Narain this time was: "My election petition was upheld by the High Court. I was jailed. The law of the land was changed. Even the Supreme Court could not do anything. Now I come to the highest court, you, electors, for the final verdict."

The final verdict came on Sunday night when the voters gave her Lok Sabha seat to her rival.

It was only a year ago that the official media made a big effort to celebrate the "decade of progress" under her rule. One could not fail to notice a coincidence in this regard in the rise and fall of a regime in Pakistan. The tenth year of Field Marshal Ayub's rule was celebrated with a fanfare of publicity. It was stated that a new ethos had developed in the country – a familiar phrase for the media in India for the last 19 months. A year later he was toppled from power.

Following are texts of the letters of resignation of the Prime Minister and reply of the acting President, Mr. B.D. Jatti.

Dear Rashtrapatiji,

Consequent on the announcement of the results of the general elections, I tender my own and the resignation of the Council of Ministers.

I am grateful to you for the consideration you have consistently shown to me and my colleagues.

Yours Sincerely,
Indira Gandhi.

In his letter accepting the resignation, Mr. Jatti said:

My dear Prime Minister,

I have received your letter dated March 22, 1977, tendering your resignation and that of your colleagues in the Council of Ministers. I accept the resignation and request you and your colleagues to continue in office till a new government is formed.

I would like to take this opportunity to thank you for the services rendered to the nation by you and your colleagues in the outgoing Council of Ministers.

With regards,

Yours Sincerely
B.D. Jatti.

THE TIMES OF INDIA

NO. 80, VOL. CXXXIX *** NEW DELHI: WEDNESDAY, MARCH 23, 1977 35 PAISE

PM deserved defeat, says JP

By Our Staff Correspondent

Page No. 3

THE TIMES OF INDIA

New Delhi, Wednesday, March 23, 1977

PM DESERVED DEFEAT, SAYS JP

By Our Staff Correspondent

PATNA, March 21: "I think Mrs. Gandhi deserved the defeat. She has got her deserts," Mr. Jayaprakash Narayan said here today when asked whether, he felt sorry for Mrs. Gandhi's defeat.

Asked whether he anticipated the Raebareli and Amethi results, he said: "I am not surprised." But he did not expect them to be defeated by such a wide margin.

"You can say it is one of the happiest days in my life", he smilingly told a correspondent who asked him how he felt now that the tide had changed and a new government would be installed for the first time in 30 years. He added: "But I am not such a political being as I used to be once."

Was the victory symbolic of a negative vote for the Congress or a positive vote for the Janata Party? "It's more of an anti-Mrs. Gandhi vote than a pro-Janata Party vote", he replied.

But he agreed that the anti-Mrs. Gandhi vote would not have crystallized but for the coming together of parties and fulfilling the need for a viable alternative to the Congress in the shape of the Janata Party whose leadership had won the confidence and trust of the people.

He likened the Congress to a sinking ship and said the "rats" which might like to desert it at this juncture would not be welcome in the new ruling party.

In reply to a question on the desirability of the assembly elections, Mr. Narayan said that in the context of the massive anti-Congress vote all assemblies had become unrepresentative.

Elections to the assemblies should be held and he would like the Janata Party to expedite the poll so that there were new and representative government in the states, he said.

He also spoke of the plan to form popular people's committees or vigilance committees in every constituency. The plan was not for Bihar alone but for the entire country.

THE TIMES OF INDIA

NO. 80, VOL. CXXXIX *** NEW DELHI: WEDNESDAY, MARCH 23, 1977 35 PAISE

J.P. expects Janata not to belie people's hopes

By Our Staff Correspondent

PATNA, March 21.

MR. JAYAPRAKASH NARAYAN said here today that the entire edifice built by Mrs. Indira Gandhi to convert Indian democracy into dictatorship would have to be dismantled and constitutional and legal measures taken to make it impossible for any future prime minister or head of government to weaken or disfigure the country's democratic structure.

Addressing a Press conference at his Kadamkuan residence, Mr. Narayan expressed the hope that the Janata Party would belie Mrs Gandhi's contention that the opposition could never provide a stable government at the Centre by presenting and preserving a solid front. "In this connection, it seems desirable that in the interest of the country and to provide it with a stable and efficient government, the Congress for Democracy should unite with with the Janata Party to form a single and solid political entity," he observed.

Congratulating the people, particularly the youth, on the magnificent success achieved at the polls, Mr. Narayan said the trust reposed in the Janata Party placed on its shoulders a heavy responsibility.

ERADICATION OF CORRUPTION

The central issue in the political turmoil of the past few years had been that of corruption in politics and government. Therefore, the foremost expectation of the people from the Janata Party would be that it offered them a clean and good government.

To that end, the people would expect the Janata Party government to set up an effective and independent machinery to check and eradicate corruption from the government in particular and politics in general.

He cautioned against the appointment of a fresh commission to study the problems and to make recommendations as the subject of corruption had been under official and non-official study for a number of years. There already existed enough recommendations that could be acted upon immediately. For instance, there were the reports of the Tarkunde commission and the Santhanam committee.

Similarly the issue of administrative reforms had also been receiving close official and non-official attention in the past few years and there were proposals that could be put into force without delay.

Much groundwork had already been done in the important fields of socio-economic, constitutional, electoral and other reforms. Quite a number of measures could be given effect to without delay.

Page No. 3

THE TIMES OF INDIA

New Delhi, Wednesday, March 23, 1977

J.P. EXPECTS JANATA NOT TO BELIE PEOPLE'S HOPES

PATNA, March 21. Mr. JAYAPRAKASH NARAYAN said here today that the entire edifice built by Mrs. Indira Gandhi to convert Indian democracy into dictatorship would have to be dismantled and constitutional and legal measures taken to make it impossible for any future prime minister or head of Government to weaken or disfigure the country's democratic structure.

Addressing a Press conference at his Kadamkuan residence, Mr. Narayan expressed the hope that the Janata Party would belie Mrs. Gandhi's contention that the opposition could never provide a stable government at the Centre by presenting and preserving a solid front. "In this connection, it seems desirable that in the interest of the country and to provide it with a stable and efficient Government, the Congress for Democracy should unite with the Janata Party to form a single and solid political entity," he observed.

Congratulating the people, particularly the youth, on the magnificent success achieved at the polls, Mr. Narayan said the trust reposed in the Janata Party placed on its shoulders a heavy responsibility.

The central issue in the political turmoil of the past few years had been that of corruption in politics and government. Therefore, the foremost expectation of the people from the Janata Party would be that it offered them a clean and good government.

To that end, the people would expect the Janata Party Government to set-up an effective and independent machinery to check and eradicate corruption from the Government in particular and politics in general.

He cautioned against the appointment of a fresh commission to study the problems and to make recommendations as the subject of corruption had been under official and non-official study for a number of years. There already existed enough recommendations that could be acted upon immediately. For instance, there were the reports of the Tarkunde commission and the Santhanam committee.

Similarly the issue of administrative reforms had also been receiving close official and non-official attention in the past few years and there were proposals that could be put into force without delay.

Much groundwork had already been done in the important fields of socio-economic, constitutional, electoral and other reforms. Quite a number of measures could be given effect to without delay.

THE TIMES OF INDIA

NO. 80, VOL. CXXXIX *** NEW DELHI: WEDNESDAY, MARCH 23, 1977 35 PAISE

THE GREAT DEFEAT

It was neither a general election nor a referendum in the normal sense of the terms. For a vast majority of the people from metropolitan towns like Bombay, Calcutta and Delhi to tiny hamlets in the most backward districts of U.P., and Bihar, it has been a second liberation struggle. And so, indeed, it has been on any reckoning. For most people, specially in the countryside, the issue was doubtless not joined till last summer when the police force was extensively used to drag hundreds of thousands to hastily set up and ill-equipped vasectomy camps for "voluntary" sterilisation. But these often [illegible] and desperately poor people were quick to realise that their dignity as human beings could not have been trampled upon in so brazen and unashamed a fashion unless the press had been completely muffled, the courts deprived of their authority and Parliament reduced to a rubber stamp and cabinet ministers to the status of helpless spectators or court jesters. From that time onwards, they were waiting for an opportunity when they could sweep away the oppressors, and when it came with the announcement of the election last January, they seized it with an enthusiasm that has never been witnessed in this country before. The result is there for all to see.

On a surface view, the Indian nation lay prostrate for 19 long months at the feet of the all-powerful prime minister, her would-have-been successor, Mr. Sanjay Gandhi, and the small coterie of evil and not wholly evil men and women around them, that is between June 26, 1975, when Mrs. Gandhi pushed thousands of public spirited Indians, including men like Mr. Jayaprakash Narayan and Mr. Morarji Desai, into prison under the cover of darkness and imposed the emergency on an unsuspecting nation and January 18 when she announced the sixth general election to the Lok Sabha. But the reality was different. The Indian people practised non-violent non-co-operation with the government on a far bigger scale than during the freedom struggle itself when Gandhiji himself was in command. The resistance was not active in most cases and therefore not visible. But it was there and it took many forms. The government could not, for instance, win over even a couple of dozen leading journalists, lawyers and academics to its side, though it had so much patronage to shower on them. The alienation of the intelligentsia is best illustrated by the fact that it tried and failed to persuade any major figure in any walk of life to sign an advertisement it wanted to place in a British daily in reply to one by leading European public figures and intellectuals demanding Mr. Narayan's release. Scores of high court judges refused to be intimidated and gave inconvenient judgements at considerable risk to themselves. A large number of senior civil servants made no secret of their abhorrence of what was going on in the name of discipline and what not. Above all, crowds had to be hired and transported for so-called public meetings to be addressed by the once genuinely popular prime minister and her son who was to be projected not only as the ideal of the youth but the saviour of the nation.

All in all, the government or what passed for government functioned in steadily increasing isolation. Its loud claims—the "dynamic" decade under Mrs. Gandhi's leadership, "gains" of the emergency in terms of stable prices, the record rise in exports and the highest ever foreign exchange holdings—did impress a section of the community for a few brief months. But as the recession continued, unemployment rose and the prices inevitably began to move up once again, the official propaganda invited only ridicule. Mr. V. C. Shukla managed the press for Mrs. Gandhi and Mr. Gandhi but the people trusted rumours more than newspapers.

No one can say what form the struggle for liberty could have taken if the prime minister had heeded the interested counsel of toughs like Mr. Bansilal who constituted the Sanjay court and cared nothing for such "foreign" concepts as legitimacy and credibility. Fortunately, she did not, not because she suddenly developed a democratic conscience but because she was convinced that she had everything sewed up neatly for her. The opposition, she calculated, would remain splintered, would be in no position to raise the necessary resources in men or money, indeed, might not be able to even field a sufficient number of candidates; the press was too terrorised to raise its voice; the mass media were firmly under control; Samachar could be depended upon to manufacture reports as in connection with the officially sponsored anti-CPI campaign and the people could be managed with the help of an "obliging" bureaucracy. In the process, she thought, she would not only regain her legitimacy but also pave the way for the son by choosing 150 to 200 candidates from among the youth Congress. The last part of the plan misfired with the resignation of Mr. Jagjivan Ram and the other parts collapsed one by one as the people took up the struggle in right earnest. But that is a different matter. The pertinent point is that if in the absence of a decision to go to the polls, the struggle for restoration of liberty had taken a violent form, the result could have been catastrophic for the country. Violence in our era has almost in every case produced as great a tyranny as the one it has sought to overthrow, if not a worse one.

As is unavoidable [illegible] convulsions, the success of the struggle has created problems. The 90-year-old Congress, which has provided coherence to Indian polity in the 30 years of independence, has, in terms of seats, been reduced to a party confined to the southern and western states, and it is open to question whether it can survive out of office. For, so used have its leaders become to the comforts of office and the enormous patronage that goes with it that it is difficult to believe that the survivors among them will be able to resist the temptation to cross to the other side. The Janata Party, on the other hand, has in spite of its elan, just been born and its constituents need a long time before they can acquire the necessary hierarchy and discipline. The political spectrum it covers may not be wider than that of the Congress. But the Congress was already over 60 years old when it was called upon to shoulder the responsibility of governing the country and men like Mr. Nehru and Sardar Patel had been its leaders for almost three decades. Equally important, most of the states are still under Congress governments and no one can say whether all of them or many of them will stay that way and how long. The exodus from the Congress in the states may solve certain problems for the Janata Party leadership in New Delhi but it will also create some others. The large number of aspirants to elective and high offices cannot be easily accommodated in a new party. Above all, it has been demonstrated as never before that the people have become highly politicised even in the countryside and are, therefore, going to be far more assertive of their rights than ever before.

These are not long-term but immediate problems and will need to be faced as the Janata Party elects its leader and the new government is sworn in. But the pall of fear has lifted and the people can breathe in freedom once again. And that is as big a gain as anyone can ask for after 21 months of emergency. Also the people have learnt the bitter lesson that it is dangerous to entrust the country's destiny to one person, however well motivated to begin with, and they have learnt it at a relatively small price. Comparisons are invidious. But the people here have been luckier than many others. They have escaped what could have developed into a great disaster for them. For it will not be a gross exaggeration to say a victory for the Congress on the 1971 scale or even a somewhat smaller scale would have meant eclipse of liberty for decades.

Page No. 6 **Editorial**

THE TIMES OF INDIA

New Delhi, Wednesday, March 23, 1977

THE GREAT DEFEAT

It was neither a general election nor a referendum in the normal sense of the terms. For a vast majority of the people from metropolitan towns like Bombay, Calcutta and Delhi to tiny hamlets in the most backward districts of U.P., and Bihar, it has been a second liberation struggle. And so, indeed, it has been on any reckoning. For most people, specially in the countryside, the issue was doubtless not joined till last summer when the police force was extensively used to drag hundreds of thousands to hastily set-up and ill-equipped vasectomy camps for "voluntary" sterilization. But these often illiterate and desperately poor people were quick to realize that their dignity as human beings could not have been trampled upon in so brazen and unashamed a fashion unless the press had been completely muffled, the courts deprived of their authority and Parliament reduced to a rubber stamp and cabinet ministers to the status of helpless spectators or court jesters. From that time onwards, they were waiting for an opportunity when they could sweep away the oppressors, and when it came with the announcement of the election last January, they seized it with an enthusiasm that has never been witnessed in this country before. The result is there for all to see.

On a surface view, the Indian nation lay prostrate for 19 long months at the feet of the all - powerful Prime Minister, her would-have-been successor, Mr. Sanjay Gandhi, and the small coterie of evil and not wholly evil men and women around them, that is between June 26, 1975, when Mrs. Gandhi pushed thousands of public spirited Indians, including men like Mr. Jayaprakash Narayan and Mr. Morarji Desai, into prison under the cover of darkness and imposed the emergency on an unsuspecting nation and January 18 when she announced the sixth general election to the Lok Sabha. But the reality was different. The Indian people practised non-violent non-cooperation with the Government on a far bigger scale than during the freedom struggle itself when Gandhiji himself was in command. The resistance was not active in most cases and therefore not visible. But it was there and it took many forms. The Government could not, for instance, win over even a couple of dozen leading journalists, lawyers and academics to its side, though it had so much patronage to shower on them. The alienation of the intelligentsia is best illustrated by the fact that it tried and failed to persuade any major figure in any walk of life to sign an advertisement it wanted to place in a British daily in reply to one by leading European public figures and intellectuals demanding Mr. Narayan's release. Scores of High Court Judges refused to be intimidated and gave inconvenient judgements at considerable risk to themselves. A large number of senior civil servants made no secret of their abhorrence of what was going on in the name of discipline and what not. Above all, crowds had to be hired and transported for so-called public meetings to be addressed by the once genuinely popular prime minister and her son who was to be projected not only as the ideal of the youth but the saviour of the nation.

All in all, the government or what passed for government functioned in steadily increasing isolation. Its loud claims-the "dynamic" decade under Mrs. Gandhi's leadership, "Gains" of the emergency in terms of stable prices, the record rise in exports and the highest ever foreign exchange holdings- did impress a section of the community for a few brief months. But as the recession continued, unemployment rose and the prices inevitably began to move up once again, the official propaganda invited only ridicule. Mr. V.C. Shukla managed the press for Mrs. Gandhi and Mr. Gandhi but the people trusted rumours more than newspapers.

No one can say what form the struggle for liberty could have taken if the prime minister had heeded the interested counsel of toughs like Mr. Bansilal who constituted the Sanjay court and cared nothing for such "foreign" concepts as legitimacy and credibility. Fortunately, she did not, not because she suddenly developed a democratic conscience but because she was convinced that she had everything sewed up neatly for her. The opposition, she calculated, would remain splintered, would be in no position to raise the necessary resources in men or money, indeed, might not be able to even field a sufficient number of candidates; the press was too terrorized to raise its voice; the mass media were firmly under control; Samachar could be depended upon to manufacture reports as in connection with the officially sponsored anti-CPI campaign and the people could be managed with the help of an "obliging" bureaucracy. In the process, she thought, she would not only regain her legitimacy but also pave the way for the son by choosing 150 to 200 candidates from among the youth Congress. The last part of the plan misfired with the resignation of Mr. Jagjivan Ram and the other parts collapsed one by one as the people took up the struggle in right earnest. But that is a different matter. The pertinent point is that if in the absence of a decision to go to the polls, the struggle for restoration of liberty had taken a violent form, the result could have been catastrophic for the country. Violence in our era has almost in every case produced as great a tyranny as the one it has sought to overthrow, if not a worse one.

As is unavoidable in such convulsions, the success of the struggle has created problems. The 90-year-old congress, which has provided coherence to Indian Polity in the 30 years of independence, has, in terms of seats, been reduced to a party confined to the southern and western states, and it is open to question whether it can survive out of office. For, so used have its leaders become to the comforts of office and the enormous patronage that goes with it that it is difficult to believe that the survivors among them will be able to resist the temptation to cross to the other side. The Janata Party, on the other hand, has in spite of its elan, just been born and its constituents need a long time before they can acquire the necessary hierarchy and discipline. The political spectrum it covers may not be wider than that of the Congress. But the Congress was already over 60 years old when it was called upon to shoulder the responsibility of governing the country and men like Mr. Nehru and Sardar Patel had been its leaders for almost three decades. Equally important most of the states are still under Congress governments and no one can say whether all of them or many of them will stay that way and how long. The exodus from the Congress in the states may solve certain problems for the Janata Party leadership in New Delhi but it will also create some others. The large number of aspirants to elective and high offices cannot be easily accommodated in a new party. Above all, It has been demonstrated as never before that the people have become highly politicized even in the countryside and are therefore, going to be far more assertive of their rights than ever before.

These are not long-term but immediate problems and will need to be faced as the Janata Party elects its leader and the new government is sworn in. But the pall of fear has lifted and the people can breathe in freedom once again. And that is as big a gain as anyone can ask for after 21 months of emergency. Also the people have learnt the bitter lesson that it is dangerous to entrust the country's destiny to one person, however well motivated to begin with, and they have learnt it at a relatively small price. Comparisons are invidious. But the people here have been luckier than many others. They have escaped what could have developed into a great disaster for them. For it will not be a gross exaggeration to say a victory for the Congress on the 1971 scale or even a somewhat smaller scale would have meant eclipse of liberty for decades.

THE TIMES OF INDIA

NO. 80, VOL. CXXXIX *** NEW DELHI: WEDNESDAY, MARCH 23, 1977 35 PAISE

Australian Press calls it 'triumph of common man'

SYDNEY, March 22 (Reuter).

AUSTRALIA's metropolitan newspapers frontpaged the election debeat of Mrs. Indira Gandhi today, hailing the result in a rare show of unanimity as, in the words of the nationally-circulated Australian, "a triumph for the common man in India."

Describing the result as an earthquake after which the dust had yet to settle, the Australian posed a handful of immediate conclusions, among them the assertion that it represented a reassurance to the supporters of the democratic system everywhere.

"Primarily there must be admiration on an international level for the outstanding independence just demonstrated by that ordinary, and for the most part illiterate, Indian voter —who after 30 years of Congress Party rule and 11 by Mrs. Gandhi has had the wit and the spirit to give an uncompromising thumbs down to the dictatorial clique," the newspaper declared.

The Sydney Morning Herald described the outcome as "a truly remarkable vindication of the democratic process."

" .. Whatever difficulties there may be in forming a stable and cohesive government amid the ruins of the Congress monopoly, it is reasonably sure that the (Mrs.) Gandhi experiment in dictatorship will not lightly be resorted to again," it said.

CRUCIAL DIFFERENCE

The influential Melbourne Age said the election showed India was shuddering at the brink of fundamental change and described the result as a censure of Mrs. Gandhi.

Mrs. Gandhi, said the Age, failed to discern the crucial difference between being the world's most powerful woman and being a dictator.

"The lesson is that democracy lies deep in the heart of India's 320 million electors".

In the nation's capital, the Canberra Times noted that had Mrs. Gandhi relaxed India's emergency strictures and withdrawn what it called the "brutal" sterilisation programme before calling the poll, then she might have survived.

And in the cautionary note, the newspaper added, the defeat could also herald the end of political stability in India.

Page No. 13

THE TIMES OF INDIA

New Delhi, Wednesday, March 23, 1977

AUSTRALIAN PRESS CALLS IT "TRIUMPH OF COMMON MAN"

SYDNEY, March 22 (Reuter): Australia's metropolitan newspapers front paged the election defeat of Mrs. Indira Gandhi today, hailing the result in a rare show of unanimity as, in the words of the nationally-circulated Australian, "a triumph for the common man in India."

Describing the result as an earthquake after which the dust had yet to settle, the Australian posed a handful of immediate conclusions, among them the assertion that it represented a reassurance to the supporters of the democratic system everywhere.

"Primarily there must be admiration on an international level for the outstanding independence just demonstrated by that ordinary, and for the most part illiterate, Indian voter – who after 30 years of Congress Party rule and 11 by Mrs. Gandhi has had the wit and the spirit to give an uncompromising thumbs down to the dictatorial clique," the newspaper declared.

The Sydney Morning Herald described the outcome as "a truly remarkable vindication of the democratic process."

"...... Whatever difficulties there may be in forming a stable and cohesive government amid the ruins of the Congress monopoly, it is reasonably sure that the (Mrs.) Gandhi experiment in dictatorship will not lightly be resorted to again," it said.

CRUCIAL DIFFERENCE

The influential Melbourne Age said the election showed India was shuddering at the brink of fundamental change and described the result as a censure of Mrs. Gandhi.

Mrs. Gandhi, said the Age, failed to discern the crucial difference between being the world's most powerful woman and being a dictator.

"The lesson is that democracy lies deep in the heart of India's 320 million electors."

In the nation's capital the Canberra Times noted that had Mrs. Gandhi relaxed India's emergency strictures and withdrawn what it called the "brutal" sterilization programme before calling the poll, then she might have survived.

And in the cautionary note, the newspaper added the defeat could also herald the end of political stability in India.

THE TIMES OF INDIA

NO. 80, VOL. CXXXIX *** NEW DELHI: WEDNESDAY, MARCH 23, 1977 35 PAISE

'Democracy reasserts'

LONDON, March 22 (Samachar): First reaction of western observers here to the stunning and sensational reverses for Mrs. Indira Gandhi and the Congress party has been that India's vibrant democracy has reasserted itself.

Observers here were baffled and bewildered as reports of the Congress rout engulfing the Prime Minister and her senior Cabinet colleagues started coming.

The Samachar office received unending telephone calls from members of the Indian community anxious to know the outcome of the most keenly fought elections since independence. At India House, scores of people gathered to see the election results displayed on specially erected boards.

While news of Mrs. Gandhi's defeat caused gloom among Indians here, the general view was that it was brought about by what has come to be regarded as the "extra-constitutional authority" functioning during the last few months.

British newspapers and other media gave lead or front page treatment to the Indian landslide pushing aside to second place reports on the fate of the Callaghan government in the face of a no confidence motion tabled for debate on Wednesday. Many of newspapers carried the photograph of Mr. Jagjivan Ram captioned variously as the face of victory and the smile of victory. Some papers also published the photograph of Mrs. Gandhi.

Although fears are vaguely expressed about the future stability of India, there is a strong undercurrent of hope that in the event of the final defeat of the Congress the opportunity that has come to the opposition will not be lost in infighting and its leaders will be able to form a viable government.

It is noted that there is enough administrative talent in men like Mr. Morarji Desai, Mr. Jagjivan Ram, Mr. Charan Singh and Mr. Bahuguna.

The general impression among observers here is that resentment against the emergency and the sterilisation programme has been reflected in the massive vote against the Congress. Observers acknowledge Mrs. Gandhi's [illegible] stewardship of the country's [illegible] a decade and give her the credit for restoring liberty and fundamental rights to the citizens. In their view the Indian elections have served to destroy the myth that the rural folk are more interested in bread than in freedom of expression.

Page No. 13

THE TIMES OF INDIA

New Delhi, Wednesday, March 23, 1977

DEMOCRACY REASSERTS

LONDON, March 22 (Samachar): First reaction of western observers here to the stunning and sensational reverses for Mrs. Indira Gandhi and the Congress party has been that India's vibrant democracy has reasserted itself.

Observers here were baffled and bewildered as reports of the Congress rout engulfing the Prime Minister and her senior Cabinet colleagues started coming.

The Samachar office received unending telephone calls from members of the Indian community anxious to know the outcome of the most keenly fought elections since independence. At India House, scores of people gathered to see the election results displayed on specially erected boards.

While news of Mrs. Gandhi's defeat caused gloom among Indians here, the general view was that it was brought about by what has come to be regarded as the "extra-constitutional authority" functioning during the last few months.

British newspapers and other media gave lead or front page treatment to the Indian landslide pushing aside to second place reports on the fate of the Caliaghan Government in the face of a no confidence motion tabled for debate on Wednesday. Many of newspapers carried the photograph of Mr. Jagjivan Ram captioned variously as the face of victory and the smile of victory. Some papers also published the photograph of Mrs. Gandhi.

Although fears are vaguely expressed about the future stability of India, there is a strong undercurrent of hope that in the event of the final defeat of the Congress the opportunity that has come to the opposition will not be lost in infighting and its leaders will be able to form a viable Government.

It is noted that there is enough administrative talent in men like Mr. Morarji Desai, Mr. Jagjivan Ram, Mr. Charan Singh and Mr. Bahuguna.

The general impression among observers here is that resentment against the emergency and the sterilisation programme has been reflected in the massive vote against the Congress. Observers acknowledge Mrs. Gandhi's able stewardship of the country's affairs for more than a decade and give her the credit for restoring liberty and fundamental rights to the citizens. In their view the Indian elections have served to destroy the myth that the rural folk are more interested in bread than in freedom of expression.

The Tribune

ESTABLISHED 1881

Chandigarh, Wednesday, March 23, 1977

Mrs Gandhi bows out of office

From Our Special Correspondent

NEW DELHI, March 22 – Mrs. Indira Gandhi today submitted her resignation as Prime Minister and that of the Council of Ministers to the Acting President, Mr. B. D. Jatti, at 11 this morning.

Mr. Jatti accepted the resignation but asked Mrs. Gandhi and her colleagues to continue in office till a new Council of Ministers is appointed.

Before the submission of the resignation, Mrs. Gandhi presided over a Cabinet meeting which took the resignation decision. The meeting was held at 10 a.m. Thereafter, she drove to the residence of Mr. Jatti at Maulana Azad Road. Mrs. Gandhi spent 20 minutes with Mr. Jatti.

The new Council of Ministers to be formed by the Janata Party-Congress for Democracy combine is expected to take office on March 24 soon after it elects its leader who will head the new Ministry.

Mrs. Gandhi, who was the third Prime Minister of independent India, joined the Central Government as Minister of Information in the Cabinet, headed by Mr. Lal Bahadur Shastri, after the death of her father Jawahar lal Nehru.

Her 11-year stewardship of the country began on January 24, 1966, when she was elected leader of the Congress Party and became Prime Minister on the death of Mr. Lal Bahadur Shastri. Mrs. Gandhi led the party to success in two general elections in 1967 and 1971. The 1971 elections which followed the split in the Congress Party gave it a massive mandate in the dissolved Lok Sabha.

THE TRIBUNE

Chandigarh, Wednesday, March 23, 1977

MRS. GANDHI BOWS OUT OF OFFICE

From Our Special Correspondent

NEW DELHI, March 22 – Mrs. Indira Gandhi today submitted her resignation as Prime Minister and that of the Council of Ministers to the Acting President, Mr. B.D. Jatti, at 11 this morning.

Mr. Jatti accepted the resignation but asked Mrs. Gandhi and her colleagues to continue in office till a new Council of Ministers is appointed.

Before the submission of the resignation, Mrs. Gandhi presided over a Cabinet meeting which took the resignation decision. The meeting was held at 10 a.m. Thereafter, she drove to the residence of Mr. Jatti at Maulana Azad Road. Mrs. Gandhi spent 20 minutes with Mr. Jatti.

The new Council of Ministers to be formed by the Janata Party-Congress for Democracy combine is expected to take office on March 24 soon after it elects its leader who will head the new Ministry.

Mrs. Gandhi, who was the third Prime Minister of independent India, joined the Central Government as Minister of Information in the Cabinet, headed by Mr. Lal Bahadur Shastri, after the death of her father Jawaharlal Nehru.

Her 11-years stewardship of the country began on January 24, 1966, when she was elected leader of the Congress party and became Prime Minister on the death of Mr. Lal Bahadur Shastri. Mrs. Gandhi led the party to success in two general elections in 1967 and 1971. The 1971 elections which followed the split in the Congress Party gave it a massive mandate in the dissolved Lok Sabha.

The Tribune

ESTABLISHED 1881

Chandigarh, Wednesday, March 23, 1977

The Parting Message

NEW DELHI, March 22 (Samachar) — Mrs. Indira Gandhi conveyed her good wishes to the new Government to be formed at the Centre and said she and her Congress party were ready to give "constructive cooperation" in the common tasks that face our nation."

In a statement a few hours after resigning as Prime Minister today, Mrs. Gandhi referred to the poll verdict and said "the collective judgement of the people must be respected.

"My colleagues and I accept their verdict unreservedly and in a spirit of humility."

Mrs. Gandhi said she hoped that the secular, Socialist and democratic foundations of India would be reinforced.

The following is the text of Mrs. Gandhi's statement:

"The collective judgement of the people must be respected. My colleagues and I accept their verdict unreservedly and in spirit of humility.

"Elections are part of the democratic process to which we are deeply committed. I have always said, and I do believe, that the winning or losing of an election is less important than the strengthening of our country and ensuring a better life for our people.

"I give my good wishes to the new Government that will be formed. I hope that the secular, Socialist and democratic foundations of India will be reinforced. The Congress and I are ready to give constructive cooperation in the common tasks that face our nation.

"We are proud of our great country. As I take leave of you as Prime Minister, I should like to express my gratitude to my colleagues, to my party and to the millions of men, women and children who have given me their trust, cooperation and even deep affection over the years. My love and concern for the welfare of every section of the people remain unchanged. Since childhood, my aim has been to serve the people to the limit of [illegible] This I shall [illegible] wishes to you [illegible]"

Front page

THE TRIBUNE

Chandigarh, Wednesday, March 23, 1977

THE PARTING MESSAGE BY MRS. INDIRA GANDHI

New Delhi, March 22 (Samachar)—Mrs. Indira Gandhi conveyed her good wishes to the new Government to be formed at the Centre and said she and her Congress party were ready to give "constructive cooperation in the common tasks that face our nation."

In a statement a few hours after resigning as Prime Minister today, Mrs. Gandhi referred to the poll verdict and said "the collective judgment of the people must be respected."

"My colleagues and I accept their verdict unreservedly and in a spirit of humility."

Mrs. Gandhi said she hoped that the secular, socialist and democratic foundations of India would be reinforced.

The following is the text of Mrs. Gandhi's statement:

> "The collective Judgement of the people must be respected. My colleagues and I accept their verdict unreservedly and in spirit of humility.
>
> "Elections are part of the democratic process to which we are deeply committed. I have always said, and I do believe, that the winning or losing an election is less important than the strengthening of our country and ensuring a better life for our people.
>
> "I give my good wishes to the new Government that will be formed. I hope that the Secular, Socialist and Democratic foundations of India will be reinforced. The Congress and I are ready to give constructive cooperation in the common tasks that face our nation.
>
> "We are proud of our great country. As I take leave of you as Prime Minister, I should like to express my gratitude to my colleagues, to my party and to the millions of men, women and children who have given me their trust, cooperation and even deep affection over the years. My love and concern for the welfare of every section of the people remain unchanged. Since childhood, my aim has been to serve the people to the limit of my endurance. This I shall continue to do.
>
> My good wishes to you now and always."

The Tribune

ESTABLISHED 1881

Chandigarh, Wednesday, March 23, 1977

Janata Govt. On March 24

— ADVANI

From Our Special Correspondent

NEW DELHI, March 22.— Mr. L. K. Advani, Janata Party General Secretary, said here today that the Janata Party-Congress for Democracy Government would assume office on March 24 soon after the election of the Party leader.

Talking to newsmen, he said that Parliament would meet, as tentatively decided, from March 25 onwards. Due to constraints of time, there would have to be a vote of account not only for the Centre but also for the States which are under Presidential rule — Tamil Nadu, Nagaland and Pondicherry — before March 31.

Mr. Advani said that the National Committee of the Janata Party today decided that its Ministers should have a code of conduct as the Party wanted its Ministers to set an example in matters of austere living and governmental behaviour.

A small committee with Mr. C. B. Gupta, Mr. Biju Patnaik and Mr. V. K. Shaklecha has been formed to draw up the code which would be placed before the National Committee for finalisation tomorrow.

There would also be a code of conduct for Members of Parliament belonging to the Party, Mr. Advani said. Details of this would be worked out later.

Asked to give his Party's view about the admissibility of members who might defect from other parties, Mr. Advani said that the Party would take a stand on the issue. But generally the Party did not favour floor-crossing after a member had been elected on a mandate.

He said that the formation of the Cabinet was the prerogative of the leader of the Party. Nevertheless, the general view of the party was that the size of the Cabinet should not be large, although regional representation on the Cabinet had to be considered.

Mr. Advani said that the Party proposed to make an in-depth analysis of the factors that led to the failure of the Janata Party in Tamil Nadu, Andhra Pradesh, Karnataka and Kerala.

Front page

THE TRIBUNE

Chandigarh, Wednesday, March 23, 1977

JANATA GOVERNMENT ON MARCH 24 – ADVANI

From Our Special Correspondent

NEW DELHI, March 22.—Mr. L.K. Advani, Janata Party General Secretary, said here today that the Janata Party-Congress for Democracy Government would assume office on March 24 soon after the election of the Party leader.

Talking to newsmen, he said that Parliament would meet, as tentatively decided, from March 25 onwards. Due to constraints of time, there would have to be a vote of account not only for the Centre but also for the States which are under Presidential rule – Tamil Nadu, Nagaland and Pondicherry – before March 31.

Mr. Advani said that the National Committee of the Janata Party today decided that its Ministers should have a code of conduct as the Party wanted its Ministers to set an example in matters of austere living and governmental behaviour.

A small committee with Mr. C.B. Gupta, Mr. Biju Patnaik and Mr. V.K. Shaklecha has been formed to draw up the code which would be placed before the National Committee for finalization tomorrow.

There would also be a code of conduct for Members of Parliament belonging to the Party, Mr Advani said. Details of this would be worked out later.

Asked to give the Party's view about the admissibility of members who might defect from other parties, Mr. Advani said that the Party would take a stand on the issue. But generally the Party did not favour floor-crossing after a member had been elected on a mandate.

He said that the formation of the Cabinet was the prerogative of the leader of the Party. Nevertheless, the general view of the party was that the size of the Cabinet should not be large, although regional representation on the Cabinet had to be considered.

Mr. Advani said that the Party proposed to make an in-depth analysis of the factors that led to the failure of the Janata Party in Tamil Nadu, Andhra Pradesh, Karnataka and Kerala.

The Tribune

ESTABLISHED 1881

Chandigarh, Wednesday, March 23, 1977

EXIT CONGRESS, ENTER JANATA

THE wheel of change, said Mr. Nehru many years ago, moves on and those who were up come down and those who were down go up. In fact, everything changes and nothing remains static. If Mrs. Gandhi thought that she would remain Prime Minister in perpetuity and could therefore make mincemeat of the Constitution and trample upon the people's basic liberties without ever getting a telltale rebuff, she was sadly mistaken. The harsh realities of public fury must have dawned upon her when she went to Rashtrapati Bhavan to tender her and her cabinet's resignation. The Congress defeat and her personal humiliation have to be accepted sportingly, in the manner of matured politicians. It is good that no attempt has been made to bypass the nation's verdict and that this time the democratic norm has been maintained.

Mrs. Gandhi's exit from the citadel of power comes as a nemesis. This and the imminent induction of a truly popular Janata ministry are bound to go down in the nation's history as distinct landmarks. In fact the current year may prove a year of the people in which they fully and fearlessly asserted themselves. For the first time the Congress will be out of power and occupy the Opposition benches. Few could have imagined such a reversal of roles, but there need be no doubt that the chastening of the top Congress leadership and the transformation of the scene will be good for the country. It will be good also for the Congress which has had an unduly long innings which is full of blemishes. The lifting of the Emergency and the restoration of basic freedoms are especially welcome. They will help people breathe fresh air after a long period of stagnation.

The thumping majority which the Janata has secured in the Lok Sabha has come as a very pleasant surprise even to the party leaders themselves. Answering a question, Mr. Jayaprakash Narayan conceded that Monday was the happiest day in his life. He was not surprised at the election results of Mrs. Gandhi and her son, but he did not expect such margins. "She has got her deserts; she deserved it," he said. That would be the reaction of countless others who feel greatly relieved at the end of a virtual nightmare.

The task now facing the Janata Party and its allies is a challenging one — to ensure a good, clean Government that would accord the utmost respect to the human personality and work ceaselessly for the nation's welfare. The Rule of Law has to be maintained. The task of governance is far more complex than winning an election. In this task the new Janata leadership will have the fullest cooperation of the crores of people who have voted the party into power with impressive margins. The party has to justify the confidence placed in it. Of course there are numerous pitfalls which the new Government should avoid. One danger against which the leadership should safeguard itself is getting surrounded by a coterie of sycophants like the one which created for Mrs. Gandhi a world of make-believe and isolated her from the man in the street. Yet she thought she had a finger on the pulse of the people! The second is that of a split in the ranks and among the leaders of the Janata party's diverse constituents whose ideologies differ in some respects. The crucial test of their declarations of unity in thought and action will come in the coming months. A stunning victory should be followed up by a stunning performance.

A good start has been made with the announcement that the Janata and the Congress for Democracy will form a single bloc in Parliament and function as one party under one leader. The all-out quest for a consensus on the leadership issue, which the Congress party made a feature of its political functioning, often created undemocratic situations. A contest for the top post is in fact a healthy sign in a democracy. The unhealthy reaction comes in when the losers do not accept the majority verdict and sulk in their tents. Such mental reservations have to be avoided at all costs and the fullest cooperation of all wings of the ruling alliance ensured. The Congress in its new role would do well to conduct itself as a responsible opposition and not as a party that merely scoffs at every other.

Page No. 4 **Editorial**

THE TRIBUNE

Chandigarh, Wednesday, March 23, 1977

EXIT CONGRESS, ENTER JANATA

THE wheel of change, said Mr. Nehru many years ago, moves on and those who were up come down and those who were down, go up. In fact, everything changes and nothing remains static. If Mrs. Gandhi thought that she would remain Prime Minister in perpetuity and could therefore make mincemeat of the Constitution and trample upon the people's basic liberties without ever getting a telltale rebuff, she was sadly mistaken. The harsh realities of public fury must have dawned upon her when she went to Rashtrapati Bhavan to tender her and her cabinet's resignation. The Congress defeat and her personal humiliation have to be accepted sportingly, in the manner of matured politicians. It is good that no attempt has been made to bypass the nation's verdict and that this time the democratic norm has been maintained.

Mrs. Gandhi's exit from the citadel of power comes as a nemesis. This and the imminent induction of a truly popular Janata ministry are bound to go down in the nation's history as distinct landmarks. In fact the current year may prove a year of the people in which they fully and fearlessly asserted themselves. For the first time the Congress will be out of power and occupy the Opposition benches. Few could have imagined such a reversal of roles, but there need be no doubt that the chastening of the top Congress leadership and the transformation of the scene will be good for the country. It will be good also for the Congress which has had an unduly long innings which is full of blemishes. The lifting of the Emergency and the restoration of basic freedoms are especially welcome. They will help people breathe fresh air after a long period of stagnation.

The thumping majority which the Janata has secured in the Lok Sabha has come as a very pleasant surprise even to the party leaders themselves. Answering a question, Mr. Jayapraksh Narayan conceded that Monday was the happiest day in his life. He was not surprised at the election results of Mrs. Gandhi and her son, but he did not expect such margins. "She has got her deserts: she deserved it," he said. That would be the reaction of countless others who feel greatly relieved at the end of a virtual nightmare.

The task now facing the Janata Party and its allies is a challenging one – to ensure a good, clean Government that would accord the utmost respect to the human personality and work ceaselessly for the nation's welfare. The Rule of Law has to be maintained. The task of governance is far more complex than winning an election. In this task the new Janata leadership will have the fullest cooperation of the crores of people who have voted the party into power with impressive margins. The party has to justify the confidence placed in it. Of course there are numerous pitfalls which the new Government should avoid. One danger against which the leadership should safeguard itself is getting surrounded by a coterie of sycophants like the one which created for Mrs. Gandhi a world of make-believe and isolated her from the man in the street. Yet she thought she had a finger on the pulse of the people! The second is that of a split in the ranks and among the leaders of the Janata Party's diverse constituents whose ideologies differ in some respects. The crucial test of their declarations of unity in thought and action will come in the coming months. A stunning victory should be followed up by a stunning performance.

A good start has been made with the announcement that the Janata and the Congress for Democracy will form a single bloc in Parliament and function as one party under one leader. The all-out quest for a consensus on the leadership issue, which the Congress party made a feature of its political functioning, often created undemocratic situations. A contest for the top post in fact is a healthy sign in a democracy. The unhealthy reaction comes in when the losers do not accept the majority verdict and sulk in their tents. Such mental reservations have to be avoided at all costs and the fullest cooperation of all wings of the ruling alliance ensured. The Congress in its new role would do well to conduct itself as a responsible opposition and not as a party that merely scoffs at every other.

The Tribune

ESTABLISHED 1881

Chandigarh, Wednesday, March 23, 1977

Fall Of Nehru Dynasty, Says London "Times"

LONDON, March 22 (Reuter) — The London Times has said that it seemed certain that Mrs. Indira Gandhi's political career was at an end.

In an editorial, 'Fall of the Nehru Dynasty' the newspaper yesterday said: "Her rule, her leadership and her emergency have been rejected.... it will be seen as the end of a Nehru family dynasty that has ruled India for 30 years since independence".

"The dynasty threatened to continue, as an outcome of the emergency, with rise to power—while not holding any party or national office—of Mr. Sanjay Gandhi", the Times said.

However, the overwhelming defeat of Mrs. Gandhi's son too, marked the end of the dynasty which served India well in its day but which India might have felt was due to end, the paper added.

"That conclusion should be coupled with the other obvious answer in this election: The positive preference for democracy," the Times said.

The newspaper added that the Congress party would remain the dominant party in India since no other party with national appeal was even in the making. But, unfortunately the election had thrown up no new leaders, it said.

The task of building a new Government from the wreck of the old may not be easy, it said.

The Guardian, commenting on the election results, said: "It is a political earthquake, an upheaval so stunning that nobody can fully assess it or tell where it will lead."

The newspaper said the Indian people "have taken a massive gamble: But they have also decisively shown that a dictatorship could not have lasted resentment, righteous wrath, would have blown it to bloody smithereens."

"But there is a chance, a heady and exhilarating chance, that the imperatives of Government will now give Indian democracy one priceless boon—two coherent national parties and the opportunity, buoyed on the Janata wave of hatred towards despotism, to make freedom stick and stick," the newspaper said.

AP adds: The Daily Telegraph said at one stroke, India seems to have brought to a close 21 months of emergency tyranny, 11 years of Mrs. Gandhi and 30 years of Congress supremacy—in other words an era.

The hasty revocation of the emergency decrees was widely attributed to fears of their being used against Mrs. Gandhi and her defeated accomplices.

SINGAPORE, (Samachar): Influential Singapore daily, the Straits Times, said today: "India has once again demonstrated that in a choice between democratic freedom and trains running on time, it will instinctively go for democracy."

The daily said that "incredibly for such an astute politician, Mrs Indira Gandhi was unaware of the depth of anger over the excesses perpetrated in the name of emergency and the amount of ill-feeling against her son. She had become isolated from reality and did not realise this until she went campaigning. By then it was too late."

Page 4

THE TRIBUNE

Chandigarh, Wednesday, March 23, 1977

FALL OF NEHRU DYNASTY, SAYS LONDON "TIMES"

LONDON, March 22 (Reuter)—The London Times has said that it seemed certain that Mrs. Indira Gandhi's political career was at an end.

In an editorial, 'Fall of the Nehru Dynasty' the newspaper yesterday said: "Her rule, her leadership and her emergency have been rejected....it will be seen as the end of a Nehru family dynasty that has ruled India for 30 years since independence".

"The dynasty threatened to continue as an outcome of the emergency with rise to power-while not holding any party or national office-of Mr. Sanjay Gandhi" the Times said.

However, the overwhelming defeat of Mrs. Gandhi's son too, marked the end of the dynasty which served India well in its day but which India might have felt was due to end, the paper added.

"That conclusion should be coupled with the other obvious answer in this election. The positive preference for democracy," the Times said.

The newspaper added that the Congress party could remain the dominant party in India since no other party with national appeal was even in the making. But unfortunately the election had thrown up no new leaders, it said.

The Guardian, commenting on the election results, said: "It is a political earthquake, an upheaval so stunning that nobody can fully assess it or tell where it will lead."

The newspaper said the Indian people "have taken a massive gamble: But they have also decisively shown that a dictatorship could not have lasted resentment, righteous wrath, would have blown it to bloody smithereens."

"But there is a chance, a heady and exhilarating chance. That the imperatives of Government will now give Indian democracy one priceless boon-two coherent national parties and the opportunity, buoyed on the Janata wave of hatred towards despotism to make freedom stick and stick," the newspaper said.

AP add: The Daily Telegraph said at one stroke, India seems to have brought to a close 21 months of emergency tyranny, 11 years of Mrs. Gandhi and 30 years of Congress supremacy- in other words an era.

The hasty revocation of the emergency decrees was widely attributed to fears of their being used against Mrs. Gandhi and her defeated accomplices.

SINGAPORE: (Samachar): Influential Singapore daily, the Straits Times, said today, "India has once again demonstrated that in a choice between democratic freedom and trains running on time, it will instinctively go for democracy."

The daily said that "incredibly for such an astute politician, Mrs. Indira Gandhi was unaware of the depth of anger over the excesses perpetrated in the name of emergency and the amount of ill-feeling against her son. She had become isolated from reality and did not realize this until she went campaigning. By then it was too late."

The Tribune

ESTABLISHED 1881

Chandigarh, Wednesday, March 23, 1977

CARTER PRAISES INDIAN DEMOCRACY

WASHINGTON, March 22 (AFP). — President Jimmy Carter has praised India for practising democracy in the choice of its leadership.

Mr. Carter's spokesman, Mr. Jody Powell, yesterday said Mr. Carter held that the Indian elections "should be an inspiration" to the rest of the world.

"Large numbers of people" elsewhere did not enjoy the right to freely choose their leadership, he added.

COLUMBUS, (Ohio): Mr. William Saxbe, former US Ambassador to India has said Mrs. Indira Gandhi's defeat in the Parliamentary elections this week, coupled with the fall of the Congress Party, could lead to an improvement in US relations with that country.

But Mr. Saxbe, who retired in January as Ambassador after two years, said here yesterday he believed the United States should not interfere in Indian affairs during its transition period. He recommended that American support to India be given in the form of technical aid and increased trade.

NEW YORK (Samachar, Reuter): Newspaper and mass media commentators view the Indian elections as having proved indisputably that India is "the world's largest democracy".

Analysts here predict that the relations between the Carter Administration and the new Government to be formed in India are likely to improve. President Jimmy Carter in his policy statement has said that the USA would follow a closer policy towards sister democracies.

When Mrs. Gandhi announced the Parliamentary elections, Mr. Carter lost no time in welcoming the decision. He also made a gesture to India by sending his mother, Miss Lillian Carter, and his son to New Delhi to represent him at the funeral of President Fakhruddin Ali Ahmed.

The two-month electoral campaign in India occupied a prominent place in the country's newspapers. The results being announced from New Delhi make the major story in the newspapers across the nation while television and broadcast stations are headlining the news hourly.

The personal reversal of Mrs. Indira Gandhi at the Rae Bareli constituency has surprised Americans. While a close contest between the Congress and the Janata Party was forecast by American newsmen, Mrs. Gandhi's defeat was not foreseen.

In yesterday's papers, the municipal elections in France in which the Socialists and Communists won a decisive victory for the Gaullist and Centrist coalition that had ruled for 19 years also made the headlines but the US papers carried a more detailed account of the outcome of the Indian elections and speculated on the future political set-up at New Delhi.

The names of Mr. Morarji Desai and Mr. Jagjivan Ram were mentioned for Prime Ministership.

The CBS commentator said India, with the second largest population in the world, is undoubtedly "the largest democracy in the world"

A radio commentator took the line that the elections have "re-established the credibility of Indian democracy".

Others have said the outcome had shown that the general elections in India have been "free and fair".

The Washington Post, the first newspaper to comment on the Indian elections, yesterday urged the United States to "encourage" Indian democracy by "nourishing" economic conditions in India.

The paper said the electoral developments in India, including the personal reverse suffered by Mrs. Indira Gandhi were "mind boggling" and reflected a reversal, undreamed of just a few months ago".

The paper referred to the two election slogans in India — 'Democracy or Dictatorship' raised by the Opposition and 'Stability or Chaos' by the ruling party and said: "The irony and tragedy of India, of course, is that both slogans have a measure of validity.

If Indians have shown that dictatorship is not their preferred political style, then there are grounds to fear that the Janata Opposition, if it comes to power, will have immense difficulty governing India the paper said.

The Daily News, New York, said today that the general elections in India proved that democracy was very much alive there.

"Mrs. Indira Gandhi and her experiment in totalitarian rule took a deserved drubbing from the voters . . . . The Congress Party, which has reigned supreme since India gained its independence 30 years ago, apparently was dragged down with her", the largest paper in the U.S. said in an editorial headlined "Exit Indira."

"Mrs. Gandhi signed her own political death warrant when she manufactured the "national emergency" to institute dictatorial measures.

"Excercising powers acquired by illegal extra-legal means, she altered the Constitution by fiat, jailed opponents without charges, imposed press censorship and generally trampled on individual liberties," the News said.

"Only a person with Mrs. Gandhi's armour-plated arrogance could have believed that the people of India would forget such outrages and indignities, and ratify her home-grown brand of tyranny.

"The victors are an assorted lot, whose only common goal was a desire to rid India of Mrs. Gandhi's authoritarian ways. What they will do with their mandate is a mystery only time can solve.

"But the election did prove that the democratic spirit is very much alive in India — and that alone is cause for rejoicing," the News said.

Page 4

THE TRIBUNE

Chandigarh, Wednesday, March 23, 1977

CARTER PRAISES INDIAN DEMOCRACY

WASHINGTON, March 22 (AFP).—President Jimmy Carter has praised India for practising democracy in the choice of its leadership.

Mr. Carter's spokeman, Mr. Jody Powell, yesterday said Mr. Carter held that the Indian elections "should be an inspiration" to the rest of the world.

"Large numbers of people" elsewhere did not enjoy the right to freely choose their leadership he added.

COLUMBUS (Ohio): Mr. William Saxbe, former US Ambassador to India has said Mrs. Indira Gandhi's defeat in the Parliamentary elections this week, coupled with the fall of the Congress Party could lead to an improvement in US relations with that country.

But Mr. Saxbe, who retired in January as Ambassador after two years, said here yesterday he believed the United States should not interfere in Indian affairs during its transition period. He recommended that American support to India be given in the form of technical aid and increased trade.

New York (Samachar, Reuter): Newspaper and mass media commentators view the Indian elections as having proved indisputably that India is "the world's largest democracy."

Analysts here predict that the relations between the Carter Administration and the new Government to be formed in India are likely to improve. President Jimmy Carter in his policy statement has said that the USA would follow a closer policy towards sister democracies.

When Mrs. Gandhi announced the Parliamentary elections, Mr. Carter lost no time in welcoming the decision. He also made a gesture to India by sending his mother, Miss Lillian Carter, and his son to New Delhi to represent him at the funeral of President Fakhruddin Ali Ahmad.

The two-month electoral campaign in India occupied a prominent place in the country's newspapers. The results being announced from New Delhi make the major story in the newspapers across the nation while television and broadcast stations are headlining the news hourly.

The personal reversal of Mrs. Indira Gandhi at the Raebareli constituency has surprised Americans. While a close contest between the Congress and the Janata party was forecast by American newsmen, Mrs. Gandhi's defeat was not foreseen.

In Yesterday's papers the municipal elections in France in which the Socialists and Communists won a decisive victory for the Gaullist and Centrist coalition that had ruled for 19 years also made the headlines but the US papers carried a more detailed account of the outcome of the Indian elections and speculated on the future political set-up at New Delhi.

The names of Mr. Morarji Desai and Mr. Jagjivan Ram were mentioned for Prime Ministership.

The CBS commentator said India, with the second largest population in the world, is undoubtedly "the largest democracy in the world."

A radio commentator took the line that the elections have "re-established the credibility of Indian democracy".

Others have said the outcome had shown that the general elections in India have been "free and fair."

The Washington Post the first newspaper to comment on the Indian elections, yesterday urged the United States to "encourage" Indian democracy by "nourishing" economic conditions in India.

The paper said the electoral developments in India, including the personal reverse suffered by Mrs. Indira Gandhi were "mind boggling" and reflected a reversal, undreamed of just a few months ago.

The paper referred to the two election slogans in India – 'Democracy or Dictatorship' raised by the Opposition and 'Stability or Chaos' by the ruling party and said: "The irony and tragedy of India, of course, is that both slogans have a measure of validity."

If Indians have shown that dictatorship is not their preferred political style, then there are grounds to fear that the Janata Opposition , if it comes to power, will have immense difficulty governing India, the paper said.

The Daily News, New York said today that the general elections in India proved that democracy was very much alive there.

"Mrs. Indira Gandhi and her experiment in totalitarian rule took a deserved drubbing from the voters.... The Congress Party, which has reigned supreme since India gained its independence 30 years ago, apparently was dragged down with her", the largest paper in the U.S. said in an editorial headlined "Exit Indira."

"Mrs. Gandhi signed her own political death warrant when she manufactured the "national emergency" to institute dictatorial measures.

"Exercising powers acquired by illegal extra-legal means, she altered the Constitution by fiat, jailed opponents without charges, imposed press censorship and generally trampled on individual liberties," the News said.

"Only a person with Mrs. Gandhi's armour-plated arrogance could have believed that the people of India would forget such outrages and indignities, and ratify her home-grown brand of tyranny.

"The victors are an assorted lot, whose only common goal was a desire to rid India of Mrs. Gandhi's authoritarian ways. What they will do with their mandate is a mystery only time can solve.

"But the election did prove that the democratic spirit is very much alive in India – and that alone is cause for rejoicing," the News said.

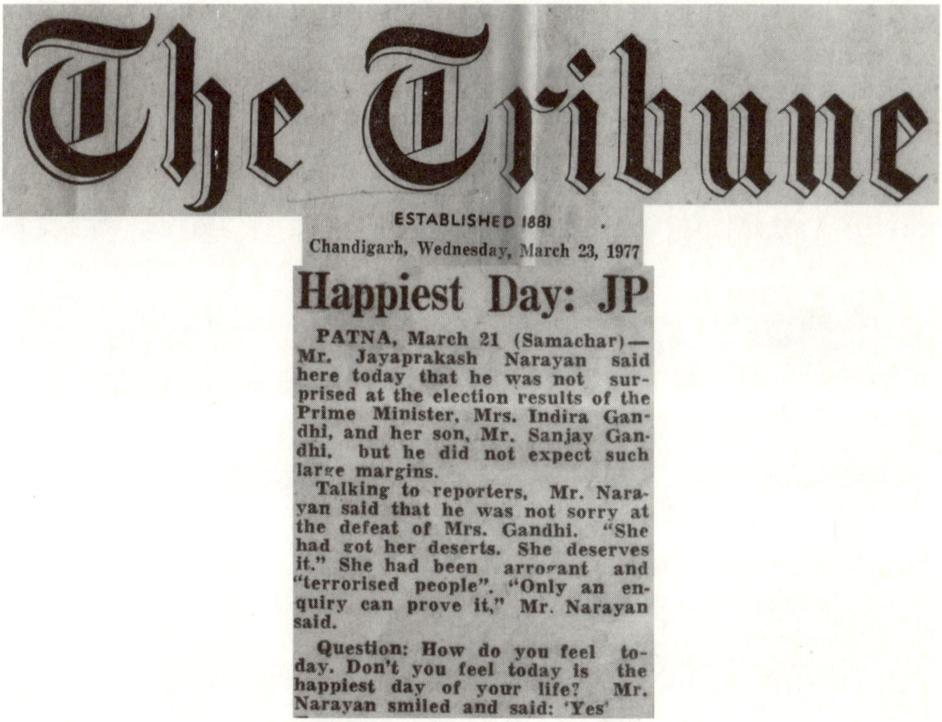

The Tribune

ESTABLISHED 1881

Chandigarh, Wednesday, March 23, 1977

Happiest Day: JP

PATNA, March 21 (Samachar)—Mr. Jayaprakash Narayan said here today that he was not surprised at the election results of the Prime Minister, Mrs. Indira Gandhi, and her son, Mr. Sanjay Gandhi, but he did not expect such large margins.

Talking to reporters, Mr. Narayan said that he was not sorry at the defeat of Mrs. Gandhi. "She had got her deserts. She deserves it." She had been arrogant and "terrorised people". "Only an enquiry can prove it," Mr. Narayan said.

Question: How do you feel today. Don't you feel today is the happiest day of your life? Mr. Narayan smiled and said: 'Yes'

Page 8

THE TRIBUNE

Chandigarh, Wednesday, March 23, 1977

HAPPIEST DAY: JP

PATNA, March 21 (Samachar).—Mr. Jayaprakash Narayan said here today that he was not surprised at the election results of the Prime Minister, Mrs. Indira Gandhi, and her son, Mr. Sanjay Gandhi, but he did not expect such large margins.

Talking to reporters, Mr. Narayan said that he was not sorry at the defeat of Mrs. Gandhi. "She had got her deserts. She deserves it." She had been arrogant and "terrorized people". "Only an enquiry can prove it," Mr. Narayan said.

Question: How do you feel today. Don't you feel today is the happiest day of your life? Mr. Narayan smiled and said: 'Yes'.

INDIAN EXPRESS

Largest combined net sales among all daily newspapers in India

New Delhi: Wednesday March 23, 1977

Mrs Gandhi resigns; wishes new Govt well

Constructive cooperation in common tasks assured

Express Correspondent
NEW DELHI, March 22.

Soon after submitting her resignation as Prime Minister, Mrs Indira Gandhi offered to the new government "constructive cooperation" in the common tasks that face our nation".

She said this on behalf of the Congress party as well as herself. She also said: "The collective judgment of the people must be respected. My colleagues and I accept their verdict unreservedly and in a spirit of humility." Elections are part of the democratic process to which we are deeply committed, she said.

The stout-hearted heroine of many a political upheavel in India's modern history who succumbed in the last battle of the ballot she fought was serene and dignified as she went through the motions of winding up the last vestiges of her 11-year historic and deeply controversial rule. She had a busy day.

She rose early and met a large number of callers. At 10 a.m. the members of her Council of Ministers, many of whom like herself have fallen under the bulldozer effect of the country's sixth general election, were called for a cabinet meeting, the last of her tumultous reign. She told them of the letter of resignation she was submitting to the acting President, Mr B. D. Jatti, and her colleagues passed a resolution placing on record their "deep appreciation" of her outstanding services.

These formalities over, she talked to them informally before driving with her Secretary, Mr P. N. Dhar, to the Maulana Azad residence of Mr Jatti. She gave him her letter of resignation. In his reply, accepting her resignation and requesting her to continue until the new government is formed, Mr Jatti thanked her "for the services rendered to the nation by you and your colleagues in the outgoing Council of Ministers." She spent half an hour with him and the members of his family before returning home which she will be vacating shortly to live as private citizen and Congress leader.

She did not visit her office. Although she is still the caretaker Prime Minister, she has stopped dealing with policy issues all of which are being kept apart for the new government to handle. Only the very routine questions are being dealt with. The kind of changeover that is being gone through now is without precedent for the country and Mrs Gandhi and her aides are said to be keen to establish proper norms which will be followed in the future.

Mrs Gandhi has another appointment in the afternoon when all senior officials, including Secretaries of all Ministries and personal staff, called on her at her house to bid her farewell. There were no speeches, but Mrs Gandhi, in good humour and well composed after the shattering defeat she and her party have suffered, moved among them, chatting with them and wishing them well.

INDIAN EXPRESS

New Delhi, Wednesday March 23, 1977

MRS. GANDHI RESIGNS; WISHES NEW GOVT. WELL

Constructive cooperation in common tasks assured

EXPRESS CORRESPONDENT

NEW DELHI, March 22.—Soon after submitting her resignation as Prime Minister, Mrs. Indira Gandhi offered to the new government "Constructive cooperation in the common tasks that face our nation".

She said this on behalf of the Congress party as well as herself. She also said: "The collective Judgement of the people must be respected. My colleagues and I accept their verdict unreservedly and in a spirit of humility." Elections are part of the democratic process to which we are deeply committed, she said.

The stout-hearted heroine of many a political upheaval in India's modern history who succumbed in the last battle of the ballot she fought, was serene and dignified as she went through the motions of winding up the last vestiges of her 11-year historic and deeply controversial rule. She had a busy day.

She rose early, met a large number of callers. At 10 a.m. the members of her Council of Ministers, many of whom like her have fallen under the bulldozer effect of the country's sixth general election, were called for a cabinet meeting, the last of her tumultuous reign. She told them of the letter of resignation she was submitting to the Acting President, Mr. B.D. Jatti, and her colleagues passed a resolution placing on record their "deep appreciation" of her outstanding services.

These formalities over, she talked to them informally before driving with her Secretary, Mr. P.N. Dhar, to the Maulana Azad residence of Mr. Jatti. She gave him her letter of resignation. In his reply, accepting her resignation and requesting her to continue until the new government is formed, Mr. Jatti thanked her "for the services rendered to the nation by you and your colleagues in the outgoing council of Ministers." She spent half an hour with him and the members of his family before returning home which she will be vacating shortly to live as private citizen and Congress leader.

She did not visit her office. Although she is still the caretaker Prime Minister, she has stopped dealing with policy issues all of which are being kept apart for the new government to handle. Only the very routine questions are being dealt with. The kind of change-over that is being gone through now is without precedent for the country and Mrs. Gandhi and her aides are said to be keen to establish proper norms which will be followed in the future.

Mrs. Gandhi has another appointment in the afternoon when all senior officials, including Secretaries of all Ministries and personal staff, called on her at her house to bid her farewell. There were no speeches, but Mrs. Gandhi, in good humour and well composed after the shattering defeat, she and her party has suffered, moved among them chatting with them and wishing them well.

INDIAN EXPRESS

Largest combined net sales among all daily newspapers in India

New Delhi: Wednesday March 23, 1977

The end of an era

By KULDIP NAYAR

NEW DELHI, March 22.

The departure of Mrs Gandhi ends an era which is neither altogether white nor black.

Her efforts to keep the country secular and together is by no standard a [illegible] contribution. She showed courage in fighting cant and convention, and even in political matters she took the path which most would fear to tread.

But courage is no substitute for good deeds or for the methods you employ to achieve them. This has been the strongest and the weakest point of Mrs Gandhi's tenure of eleven years as the Prime Minister. Methods to her were not important, results were.

Whether it was the split of the Congress party in 1969 or the imposition of internal emergency in June 1975, it showed that she would spare no weapon to win. It was success that mattered to her, not how she achieved it.

It is true that she believed in a left-of-centre programme but ideology was primarily the means to an end. The nationalisation of banks she effected in 1969 was a commendable step but it was essentially meant to crowd out her rival, Mr Morarji Desai. Ideology also gave her a progressive image which went down well with the masses. But in her time another 160 million people went below the poverty line, thus making the impressive total of 68 per cent of our population.

And, as days went by, she convinced herself that she, and she alone, knew what was right or wrong for the country. This gave her a feeling of being indespensable and she built a strong secretariat which controlled every segment of the government and a spy network which kept an eye on real and imaginary opponents.

This also cut her away from all advice because everything fed to her had to fit into her assumption that she was indespensable. Those who tried to place another point of view were motivated by the desire to oust her, she rationalised.

At Cabinet meetings she would tend to behave like a school-teacher and most ministers, fearing her displeasure, would not even open their mouths. She was the government and she left no one in doubt about it.

She did not care whether the concentration of power would expose her to the charge of dictatorship. She knew she had the power and was ready to use it. The only role she set for the opposition was that of a scapegoat—for anything that went wrong with her government's policies or programmes. She wanted control, overt or covert, over every field.

For a particular matter, she would pick up somebody who knew the ropes. But later he was drop- ed to be her Waterloo, she thought ed. There was no permanent adviser. She would not trust one.

In this atmosphere, only the man who had no scruples, Mr Bansi Lal, or the one she trusted most, Mr Sanjay Gandhi, her son, could survive. They could do no wrong because they were the ones she depended on. It was tragic for such a courageous person to look for crutches. But she was confident that she could do away with them when she so desired.

And when she ordered the elections which proved to be her Waterloo, she thought that she knew the best, not her son or Bansi Lal, who wanted her to postpone the poll for many years to come. She felt she could win now and tell them all that the people were behind her no matter what she did. This would once again prove that she had not lost touch with the masses and that she was still courageous.

What she did not realise was that cut off as she were, she had lost contact with the mases. But she should have one satisfaction that she did disprove those who compared her with Hitler or Mussolini. They never had free and fair elections; she at least had that.

Front page

INDIAN EXPRESS

New Delhi, Wednesday March 23, 1977

THE END OF AN ERA

NEW DELHI, March 22. The departure of Mrs. Gandhi ends an era which is neither altogether white nor black.

Her effort to keep the country secular and together is by no standard a mean contribution. She showed courage in fighting cant and convention, and even in political matters she took the path which most would fear to tread.

But courage is no substitute for good deeds or for the methods you employ to achieve them. This has been the strongest and the weakest poll in Mrs. Gandhi's tenure of eleven years as the Prime Minister. Methods to her were not important, results were.

Whether it was the split of the Congress party in 1969 or the imposition of internal emergency in June 1975, it showed that she would spare no weapon to win. It was success that mattered to her, not how she achieved it.

It is true that she believed in a left-of-centre programme but ideology was primarily the means to an end. The nationalisation of banks she effected in 1969 was commendable step but it was essentially meant to crowd out her rival, Mr. Morarji Desai. Ideology also gave her a progressive image which went down well with the masses. But in her time another 160 million people went below the poverty line thus making the impressive total of 68 percent of our population

And as days went by, she convinced herself that she and she alone, knew what was right or wrong for the country. This gave her a feeling of being indispensable and she built a strong secretariat which controlled every segment of the government and a spy network which kept an eye on real and imaginary opponents.

This also cut her away from all advice because everything fed to her had to fit into her assumption that she was indispensable. Those who tried to place another point of view were motivated by the desire to oust her, she rationalised.

At Cabinet meetings she would tend to behave like a school- teacher and most ministers, fearing her displeasure, would not even open their mouths. She was the government and she left no one in doubt about it.

She did not care whether the concentration of power would expose her to the charge of dictatorship. She knew she had the power and was ready to use it. The only role she set for the opposition was that of a scapegoat- for anything that went wrong with her government's policies or programmes. She wanted control, overt or covert, over every field.

For a particular matter, she would pick up somebody who knew the ropes. But later he was dropped to be her Waterloo, she thought. There was no permanent adviser. She would not trust one.

In this atmosphere, only the man who had no scruples, Mr. Bansi Lal, or the one she trusted most, Mr. Sanjay Gandhi, her son, could survive. They could do no wrong because they were the ones she depended on. It was tragic for such a courageous person to look for crutches. But she was confident that she could do away with them when she so desired.

And when she ordered the elections which proved to be her Waterloo, she thought that she knew the best, not her son or Bansi Lal, who wanted her to postpone the poll for many years to come. She felt she could win now and tell them all that the people were behind her no matter what she did. This would once again prove that she had not lost touch with the masses and that she was still courageous.

What she did not realise was that cut off as she were, she had lost contact with the masses. But she should have one satisfaction that she did disprove those who compared her with Hitler or Mussolini. They never had free and fair elections; she at least had that.

MORARJI DESAI WAS ELECTED AS LEADER BY THE COMBINE OF 'JANATA PARTY' AND THE 'CONGRESS FOR DEMOCRACY'. THE COMBINE TOGETHER CONSTITUTED ABSOLUTE MAJORITY. MORARJI DESAI TOOK OVER AS PRIME MINISTER ON 24 MARCH, 1977.

The Janata Party was a combination of numerous groups and Congress for Democracy was a party led by Jagjivan Ram once a confident of Indira Gandhi. Moreover the uniting force of the Janata Party, Jayaprakash Narayan had become very weak due to long illness and he was virtually bed-confined. Dissent appeared between different groups. As a result Morarji Desai Government could not last long. Morarji Desai resigned on 15 July, 1979. He remained the Care-Taker Prime Minister till 28 July as advised by the President of India.

CHARAN SINGH was invited by the President of India on 26 July, 1979 to be the new Prime Minister. The news in bold letters appeared in the Indian Express dated 27 July, 1979,"CHARAN SINGH TO BE NEW PM", 'Vote of Trust by August 3rd week'. It is also reported that Charan Singh had the support of 262 members against the needed number of 236 members. It appeared that he was supported by the Congress Party also.

CHARAN SINGH TOOK OVER AS PRIME MINISTER ON 28 JULY, 1979. However, it was reported in the Tribune dated 23 August, 1979 that, 'MID-TERM POLL IN NOV-DEC; Lok Sabha Dissolved by President; Charan Singh to be the Caretaker Prime Minister, this decision was taken by the President of India on 22 August, 1979. CHARAN SINGH CONTINUED AS CARE TAKER PRIME MINISTER UPTO 14 JANUARY, 1980.

Mid-term elections to Lok Sabha were held and the Congress Party got absolute majority. Smt. Indira Gandhi was elected as the leader. Indira Gandhi took over as Prime Minister on 14 January, 1980. However unfortunately she could not complete her full term as she was assassinated on 31 October, 1984 by her own Security Guards.

P.V. NARASIMHA RAO

At this stage it deserves to be noticed that for existence of democracy and rule of law, which is life and blood of Constitution of India, probity in public life has to be maintained at every cost, whosoever may be the casualty and irrespective of height and might of person or his office.

Delhi High Court

Para 16 of the Judgment dated 24 May, 1996

P.V. NARASIMHA RAO

DELHI HIGH COURT

Rashtriya Mukti Morcha

v.

Suraj Mandal

1996 (38) DRJ 250

Hon'ble Y.K. Sabharwal, J.
Hon'ble D.K. Jain, J.

C.W. No. 789 of 1996. Dated 24.5.1996.

For the Petitioner:—Mr. P.N. Lekhi , Sr. Adv. with Mr. Vijay Chaudhary and Mr. Ravinder Kumar, Advocates.

For the Respondent No. 1:—Mr. A.M. Singhvi, Sr. Adv. with Mr. Prem Pankaj, Advocate.

For the Respondent No. 2:—Mr. S. Lal, Advocate.

For the Respondent Nos. 2 and 3:—Mr. Madan Lokur, Advocate.

JUDGMENT

Y.K. Sabharwal, J.—On 26th July, 1993 motion of No confidence was moved against the Government headed by the Congress Party. Since the effective strength of the 10th Lok Sabha at that time was 528. Congress Party needed 265 votes to defeat the Motion of No Confidence but had 250 members in the House. When the votes on No Confidence Motion were cast on 28th July, 1993, the motion was defeated by 265 votes against and 251 in favour. Briefly stated the case of the petitioner, as set out in the writ petition is:

MAJORITY WAS SECURED BY PRIME MINISTER BY BRIBING RESPONDENT NO. 1 AND OTHER MPs OF JMM AND JANATA DAL (A) - PLEADS PETITIONER

2. The result of defeating Motion of No Confidence was achieved by Congress Party by indulging in political horse trading and violation of Constitutional morality. The whisker majority of one (264 4-1) in the 10th Lok Sabha was manipulated by Sh. P.V. Narsimha Rao, President of Congress(l) who was also the Prime Minister and for this purpose he was responsible to offer bribes and utilised the monies he had collected by offering inducements. These bribes helped Sh. Rao to muster whisker majority of one vote to defeat the No-Confidence motion. Shri Suraj Mandal, a member of Lok Sabha who is Respondent No. 1 before us, was one such members who was paid handsomely to switch over his support in favour of Congress. The other members of the opposition who voted to defeat the No Confidence motion included Sh. Simon Marandi, Shailendra Mehto and Shibu Soren, all members of Lok Sabha belonging to Jharkhand Mukti Morcha and Sh. Govinda Chandra Munda and Gulam Mohd. Khan, members of Parliament (Janata Dal-A) who had earlier defected and were declared disqualified but their disqualification was stayed by this court.

STATEMENT OF SB ACCOUNT NO. 17108 FROM PNB SHOWS THAT RESPONDENT NO. 1 HAD DEPOSITED RS. 30 LAKHS ON 1 AUGUST, 1993 – SUBMITS PETITIONER

The petitioner to illustrate that bribe was offered has been able to collect credible information regarding one of the bank accounts of Respondent No. l, who is one of the four members of Jharkhand Mukti Morcha, a regional political party of Bihar, who voted against the No Confidence motion. That credible information is a Saving Bank account No. 17108 maintained by Respondent No. l with Punjab National Bank, Naroji Nagar Branch, New Delhi. The address *i.e.* M-12, Green Park, New Delhi, given to the bank by respondent No. 1 is false. The entries in the said account showing deposit of huge amounts in cash have been set out in petition. The crucial entry in that account is of Rs. 30,00,000.00 which was deposited in cash on 1st August, 1993, a date proximate in time to the date when Respondent No. l split from Jharkhand Mukti Morcha (alongwith 3 others) to enable him and his other detectors to swell support in the 10th Lok Sabha in opposition to the No Confidence motion.

RESPONDENT NO. 1 GOT IT ILLEGALLY – PLEADS PETITIONER

Respondent No. 1 is neither gainfully employed nor connected with any business to enable him to earn a wind fall of three million rupees and that he has not received this amount by inheritance or under any bequest and it is a bumper for the fall from constitutional morality, wages of political sin, which is an offence under Penal Code and Prevention of Corruption Act and if the primary source of this money is traced, offence under Foreign Contribution Regulation Act, 1978 is also made out.

S.K. JAIN GAVE RS. 3 CRORE TO GET A CONTRACT – SATISH SHARMA USED THIS MONEY TO WIN OVER MPs – PLEADS PETITIONER

The statement of one Sh. S.K. Jain recorded under Section 161 Criminal Procedure Code has been reproduced in the petition, *inter alia,* stating that he expected some works in the plant (at Rourkela) to be given to him and in that expectation he agreed to pay Rs. 3 crores; these payments were required for the purposes of effecting defections of some Members of Parliament in support of the Congress Party which was being planned during those days by Satish Sharma and Chandraswamy.

CBI ACTED TO COVER UP THE MATTER – BAIL OUT THE GUILTY – PLEADS PETITIONER

3. The petitioner has also alleged that this petition has nothing to do with Hawala. The petitioner further says that the history of Hawala case (the present one is not based on Jain diaries) shows that CBI has done its worst in ensuring a cover up on the involvement of persons described in the diaries and unless supervision of the court is imposed, the CBI is sure to play all the tricks to bail out Sh. Rao.

COMPLAINT LODGED WITH CBI ON 1 FEBRUARY, 1996 – CRIMINAL CONSPIRACY OF BRIBING JMM AND JD(A) MPs – PLEADS PETITIONER

4. The further case of the petitioner is that on 1st February, 1996 it lodged a complaint with Central Bureau of Investigation. A photostat copy of the said complaint has been annexed with the petition. The said complaint, *inter alia*, sets out the details of the bank account referred to above, opened by Sh. Suraj Mandal in Punjab National Bank. The complaint further states that immediately when Sh. P.V. Narasimha Rao's government was facing 'No Confidence Motion' in the House of People, a criminal conspiracy with the common intention and object was hatched by Sh. Rao, Sh. V.C. Shukla, Sh. R.K. Dhawan, Capt. Satish Sharma, Sh. Ajit Singh, Sh. Bhajan Lal and Sh. Lalit Suri to prove majority on the floor of the House on 28th July 1993. The complaint further states that the said named persons started horse trading of Members of Parliament by giving them and bribing huge amount of over Rs. 3 crores to the Members of Parliament of different political parties - individuals and groups and succeeded in their nefarious designs to win over 4 Members of Parliament belonging to Jharkhand Mukti Morcha and Sh. Suraj Mandal was one of them who defected and joined illegal hands with the Government headed by Sh. Rao. It has been further alleged that on 28th July, 1993 about Rs. 1,10,00,000.00 was handed over to Sh. Suraj Mandal and part of the said amount amounting to Rs. 30 lakhs was deposited by Sh. Suraj Mandal in Saving Bank Account on 1st August, 1993 with the Punjab National Bank. Alongwith the complaint photocopies and statement of account were annexed.

CBI INVESTIGATION NOT STARTED – ONLY COVER UP TO SHIELD GUILTY – PLEADS PETITIONER

The complainant also refers to an earlier similar complaint dated 1st January, 1996. A request was thus made to CBI for independent investigation being held and the accused persons be prosecuted under the provisions of law. The petitioner has alleged that CBI has not started investigations and has not even asked the petitioner to get the statement recorded.

5. The petitioner, under the circumstances, prays that it be declared that CBI has so far failed to perform its statutory duty of investigation and has launched cover up operation for the protection of Sh. Rao and has dismally failed to conduct investigations in the manner laid down in the Vigilance Manual and further it be declared that Sh. Suraj Mandal received bribes from or at the instance of Sh. Rao for switching over support to Congress (1) during the vote on No Confidence Motion. The petitioner has further prayed for issue of order, directions or writ in the nature of writ of mandamus directing investigation into the statement of Sh. S.K. Jain, referred to in Para 25 of the petition and to register regular case on the complaint dated 1st February 1996 lodged by the petitioner and investigation to be conducted under the supervision of this court.

IF FIR REGISTERED ON BASIS OF COMPLAINT DATED 1 FEBRUARY, 1996 – QUESTION BEFORE COURT – HIGH COURT

6. At this stage, however, the main question which falls for our determination is whether regular case has been registered on the complaint of the petitioner dated 1st February, 1996. What is the purport of the regular case which has been registered by CBI during the pendency of this petition? If regular case on the basis of complaint dated 1st February 1996 has not been registered, has the petitioner made out a case for issue of directions to CBI to register a regular case on the basis of the complaint of the petitioner dated 1st February 1996. Firstly, it would be useful to notice briefly how the petition proceeded from stage to stage in this court.

NOTICE ISSUED TO CBI – UOI – BY THE COURT – TO EXPLAIN

7. On 22nd February, 1996 this court directed that notice be issued to CBI and Union of India to show cause why investigation has not been conducted in regard to the source of huge amount deposited by Sh. Suraj Mandal in cash in Saving Bank

Account No. 17108 in Punjab National Bank, Naroji Nagar Branch, New Delhi, and on this limited question notice be also issued to Sh. Suraj Mandal.

COMPLAINT REGISTERED FOR VERIFICATION – ASG SUBMITTED

8. On 18th March 1996 learned Additional Solicitor General submitted before us that Preliminary Enquiry (PE) has not been registered and only a complaint has been registered in the Complaint Register and it is being verified. The reference to the complaint is necessarily to complaint of petitioner dated 1st February, 1996. Learned Additional Solicitor General further submitted that, as at present, it cannot be said that this case relates to hawala matter and that CBI would be in a position to make up its mind after completion of verification.

COMPLETE INVESTIGATION SOON – HIGH COURT

9. On 20th March, 1996 learned Additional Solicitor-General submitted that CBI is on the eve of registering a regular case and is going to commence the investigation. Here again reference is obviously to registration of regular case and commencement of investigation on the basis of complaint dated 1st February 1996. In this view we directed on 20th March, 1996 that at this stage we would not like to make any comment but would only note that considering the nature of the case, investigation cannot brook any delay whatsoever and expressed the hope that CBI would try to complete the investigation in approximately one week.

CASE REGISTERED AGAINST RESPONDENT NOs. 1 AND 3 MPs OF JMM – ASG SUBMITTED

10. On 27th March, 1996 on submissions made by learned Additional Solicitor General it was noticed that regular case for offences punishable under section 13(2) read with section 13(1)(d)(iii) of Prevention of Corruption Act, 1988 have been registered against Sh. Suraj Mandal and 3 others, namely, Sh. Shibu Soren, Sh. Simon Marandi and Sh. Shailendra Mehto, Members of Lok Sabha. Once again we were not informed that the regular case that had been registered was not on the complaint of petitioner dated 1st February, 1996 and, therefore, after noticing the submission of learned Additional Solicitor General that investigation is going on and it is likely to take considerable time - may be six months, we again reiterated that considering the nature of the case all efforts should be made to expedite the investigation.

CBI DIRECTED TO SUPPLY COPY OF THE FIR – HIGH COURT

11. On 12th April, 1996 after noticing the submission of learned counsel for the petitioner and Sh. Suraj Mandal, we directed CBI to supply copy of FIR registered and referred to in our order dated 27th March, 1996.

ACCOUNT IN PNB VERIFIED – CBI

12. We may also notice that in reply dated 29th February, 1996 filed on behalf of CBI, it was, interalia, stated that soon after the receipt of the complaint dated 1st February, 1996 CBI has started preliminary verification of the allegations and has secured information through sources to the effect that Saving Bank Account as mentioned in the complaint exists in Punjab National Bank, Nauroji Nagar branch in the name of Sh. Suraj Mandal and further verification as to the source of these funds is continuing and after completing the said verification action would be taken as per law. Now we would notice the stage at which it came to the notice of this court as to what regular case was registered by CBI.

REGULAR CASE REGISTERED BY CBI – WAS NOT BASED ON COMPLAINT DATED 1.2.1996 – PRAYS FIR ON THE COMPLAINT BASIS – SUBMITS PETITIONER

13. Sh. Ravinder Kumar, President of the petitioner in his affidavit dated 22nd April, 1996, *inter alia*, submitted that perusal of the four copies of RCs supplied by

CBI shows that CBI is acting malafide by making a mockery of investigation and its effort is to misdirect and mislead this court. The copies of these RC's were supplied by CBI to the petitioner pursuant to our directions dated 12th April, 1996. The affidavit says that a bare perusal of the said RCs would show that there is total omission of facts alleged in the complaint made to CBI. It has been submitted that investigation must search for material and facts in order to Find out whether or not an offence has been committed but RCs show total absence of such intention particularly in view of the total omission in RCs of the facts as alleged in the complaint made to CBI. It has further been alleged that CBI has purposely avoided performance of its statutory duties with a view to shield the persons in authority and power.

14. The affidavit further says that according to Vigilance Manual or according to the prayer made in the writ petition and also according to the accepted practice of Police force, the complaint should have been reduced as a text of the regular case. It further says that in the matters where issue is deep rooted conspiracy to commit offence of bribery the standard of proof, unlike other criminal offences is not proof beyond reasonable doubt but preponderance of probabilities. We, however, feel that this is not the stage to go into such a question. The petitioner further says that despite sufficient material being placed before CBI to record an honest regular case, CBI would have succeeded in misleading this court with a perfunctory exercise, aimed not for conducting proper investigation but with an eye to close it, had this court not ordered supply of copies of RCs.

15. Under the aforesaid circumstances, the petitioner has prayed for registration of regular case on the basis of his complaint dated 1st February, 1996.

PROBITY IN PUBLIC LIFE IS ESSENTIAL – HIGH COURT

16. At this stage it deserves to be noticed that for existence of democracy and rule of law, which is life and blood of Constitution of India, probity in public life has to be maintained at every cost, whosoever may be the casualty and irrespective of height and might of person or his office. We may also notice that exercise of registration of a regular case/First Information Report under section 154 Criminal Procedure Code is not an idle formality.

FIR REGISTERED BY CBI – UNRELATED TO THE COMPLAINT – SUBMITS PETITIONER

17. According to the petitioner the exercise undertaken by CBI in the present case in registering the RC is not only an idle formality to mislead the petitioner and this court but that has been done with specific and deliberate intention to protect the persons in authority and power. The petitioner submits that the regular case/ FIR which has been registered by CBI is unrelated to complaint dated 1st February, 1996. It is not in consonance with section 154 Criminal Procedure Code. According to the petitioner it is the statutory duty of the CBI to register a case in accordance with law on the basis of its complaint dated 1st February, 1996.

CONTENTS OF FIR REPRODUCED

18. Against the column wherein name of complainant or informant with address is required to be given in First Information Report, the CBI has stated 'source' information. Why not Complainant ? We do not know. This FIR registered under section 13(2) read with section 13(l)(d)(iii) of the Act is a short document which reads:

> **INFORMATION**
>
> "Information has been received that Shri Suraj Mandal was elected as Member of Parliament to the Lok Sabha in 1991. He while holding office as

Public Servant in his capacity as Member of Parliament (Lok Sabha) during 1993 obtained pecuniary advantage to the extent of Rs. 30 lakhs from some unknown source without any public interest and deposited the said amount in his Saving Fund Account No. 17108 in Punjab National Bank, Nauroji Nagar, New Delhi on 1.8.1993.

The above facts constitute offence punishable under section 13(2) read with 13(1)(d)(iii) of Prevention of Corruption Act, 1988 (Act 49 of 1988). Therefore, a Regular Case is registered and entrusted to Shri G.N. Gupta, DSP, CBI, ACU. VIII, New Delhi for investigation."

CBI FAILED TO EXPLAIN WHY CONTENTS OF COMPLAINT NOT GIVEN IN FIR – NOT EVEN EXPLAINED IN REPLY – HOLDS HIGH COURT

19. None of the facts of which information was given to CBI in the complaint dated 1st February 1996 find any mention in the FIR. Why it is so-no answer was given by the CBI. The CBI did not even attempt to give an answer much less plausible answer even in written submissions filed before us.

CONTENTS OF SECTION 13 OF THE PREVENTION OF CORRUPTION ACT, 1988 REPRODUCED

20. Since FIR has been registered under section 13, it may be useful, for facility of reference, to reproduce section 13 of the Act as under:

"13.*Criminal misconduct by a public servant.*—(1) A public servant is said to commit the offence of criminal misconduct—

(a) if he habitually accepts or obtains or agrees to accept or attempts to obtain from any person for himself or for any other person any gratification other than legal remuneration as a motive or reward such as is mentioned in section 7; or

(b) if he habitually accepts or obtains or agrees to accept or attempts to obtain for himself or for any other person, any valuable thing without consideration or for a consideration which he knows to be inadequate from any person whom he knows to have been, or to be, or to be likely to be concerned in any proceeding or business transacted or about to be transacted by him, or having any connection with the official functions of himself or of any public servant to whom he is subordinate, or from any person whom he knows to be interested in or related to the person so concerned; or

(c) if he dishonestly or fraudulently misappropriates or otherwise converts for his own use any property entrusted to him or under his control as a public servant or allows any other person so to do; or

(d) if he,—

(i) by corrupt or illegal means, obtains for himself or for any other person any valuable thing or pecuniary advantage; or

(ii) by abusing his position as a public servant, obtains for himself or for any other person any valuable thing or pecuniary advantage; or

(iii) while holding office as a public servant, obtains for any person any valuable thing or pecuniary advantage without any public interest; or

(e) if he or any person on his behalf, is in possession or has, at any time during the period of his office, been in possession for which the public servant cannot satisfactorily account, of pecuniary resources or property disproportionate to his known sources of income.

Explanation.—For the purposes of this section, "known sources of income" means income received from any lawful source and such receipt has been intimated in accordance with the provisions of any law, rules or orders for the time being applicable to a public servant.

(2) Any public servant who commits criminal misconduct shall be punishable with imprisonment for a term which shall be not less than one year but which may extend to seven years and shall also be liable to fine."

SUBMISSION OF PARTIES

21. Learned counsel for the parties also made submissions on the question whether sub-clause (iii) of section 13(1)(d) would cover a case where it is alleged that pecuniary consideration is received by accused for himself. According to CBI clause (d)(iii) would cover such a case. According to petitioner it would not be covered in view of the absence of the word 'for himself in sub-cause (iii) of clause (d), unlike the use of the word 'for himself in sub-clauses (i) and (ii) and other parts of section 13. At this stage we express no opinion on this aspect since in our view it is not necessary for determination of the question which we are presently considering.

ORIGINALLY CASE REGISTERED UNDER SECTION 13(1)(d) OF PC ACT – LATER ON (iii) ADDED – HIGH COURT LEAVES QUESTIONS OPEN

We may, however, notice that a perusal of the file of CBI shows that decision had first been taken to register a case under section 13(1)(d) but later at some stage after the draft FIR had been prepared it was decided to incorporate clause (iii) after section 13(l)(d). Who did it? With what intention it was done? These questions, for the present, we leave open without expressing our opinion at this stage so that it may not cause any prejudice to the accused or hamper the investigation.

MAINTAINABILITY OF THIS PETITION – CBI AND RESPONDENT NO. 1 QUESTION

22. Before dealing with the question which falls for our determination, we may first consider the objection raised by CBI and Respondent No.1 to the maintainability of this petition in this court in view of the order of the Supreme Court dated 22nd February, 1996 in the case of Vineet Narain and others.

OBJECTION ABOUT ITS MAINTAINABILITY – REJECTED HIGH COURT

We have perused the said order. In our considered view there is no substance in the objection raised about the maintainability of the writ petition. In the writ petition it has been alleged that this petition has nothing to do with hawala. Insofar as CBI is concerned, it was submitted before us on 18th March, 1996 that as at present it cannot be said that this case relates to hawala matter and that CBI may be in a position to make up its mind after completion of verification. Thereafter, till date it has not been submitted before us by CBI that now after verification it is in a position to say that the case relates to hawala. Although the petitioner has also made allegations as to the source of amount which was alleged to have been given as bribe to Respondent No. 1, but the gravaman of accusation of the petitioner is that huge amounts were paid as bribery with a view to buy votes to ensure that No Confidence Motion moved against the Government is defeated and the petitioner has given details of huge amounts deposited in cash in Bank account by Respondent No. 1 proximate in point of time with the date of vote on No Confidence Motion.

23. In view of the aforesaid, it is not possible to accept the submission that the writ petition in this court is not maintainable in view of the order of Supreme Court dated 22nd February, 1996 in the case of Vineet Narain and others. Thus, the objection about the maintainability of the writ petition is rejected.

REGISTER FIR ON COMPLAINT DATED 1.2.1996 – HOLDS HIGH COURT

24. Reverting now to the main question which falls for our determination, we have to see as to what are the allegations in the complaint dated 1st February 1996 and what is stated in the FIR. The FIR has already been reproduced earlier. We have also noticed hereinbefore in brief as to what is the complaint of the petitioner dated 1st February, 1996.

25. The Supreme Court in the case of *State of Haryana* v. *Bhajan Lal,* 1992 Supp (1) SCC 335, has laid down the law regarding the statutory duly of police to register the FIR and also law relating to power of police to investigate. The recording of the First Information Report in criminal cases is extremely vital and important. At times the non-recording of proper First Information Report can be fatal to the case. If any information disclosing a cognizable offence is laid before an officer incharge of a Police Station satisfying the requirement of section 154(1) of the Code of Criminal Procedure, the said Police Officer has no other option except to enter the substance thereof in the prescribed form, that is to say, to register a case on the basis of such information. In the present case that information has been furnished in writing in the form of complaint dated 1st February, 1996. When a police officer enters on investigation he has to satisfy himself on the basis of allegations mentioned in FIR as to whether these allegations constitute a cognizable offence warranting an investigation. In other words the existence of the reason to suspect the commission of a cognizable offence is a condition precedent to the commencement of the investigation.

WILL NOT EXAMINE FACTS OF COMPLAINT AT THIS STAGE – HIGH COURT

At this stage we are not called upon to embark upon an enquiry whether the allegations in the complaint are truthful or not. These matters can be examined only by the concerned court after the entire materials are placed before it on a thorough investigation. Therefore, at this stage the question of our examining the truth or otherwise of the allegations made in the complaint does not arise.

CBI FAILED TO REGISTER FIR ON BASIS OF COMPLAINT DATED 1.2.1996 – CLAUSES 3.2 AND 3.3 VIGILANCE MANUAL REPRODUCED – HIGH COURT

26. It is the paramount duty of a police officer to whom the commission of a cognizable offence is reported, to register a case and promptly commence investigation without perverting or subverting the law. That does not appear to have been done in the present case since what has been registered does not contain anything of significance from the information contained in the complaint dated 1st February, 1996. The CBI has also not said before us that on verification it has been decided not to register the case on information as contained in complaint of the petitioner. The method of registration of a regular case by CBI has been provided for in Vigilance Manual, relevant clauses 3.2 and 3.3 whereof read as under:—

> "3.2. In cases in which the information available appears to be authentic and definite so as to make out a clear cognisable offence or to have enough substance in it, the CBI may register a regular case (R.C.) straightaway under section 154 of the Criminal Procedure Code. (Emphasis has been supplied by us).

3.3. If the available information appears to require verification before formal investigation is taken up, a preliminary enquiry (P.E.) is first made. As soon as the preliminary enquiry reveals that there is substance in the allegations, a regular case may be registered for formal investigation."

CBI REFERS TO PRIOR LAW – NOT APPLICABLE TO FACTS OF THIS CASE – HIGH COURT

27. In its written submission, CBI has referred to the decision of Supreme Court in the case of *P. Sirajuddin* v. *State of Madras*, 1970 SCC (Cri) 240. In the said decision it was held that before a public servant, whatever be his status is publicly charged with acts of dishonesty which amount to serious misdemeanour or misconduct and First Information is lodged against him, there must be some suitable preliminary enquiry into the allegations by a responsible officer. The lodging of such a report against a person who occupies top position in the department, even if baseless, would do incalculable harm not only to him in particular, but also to the department to which he belongs, in general. The CBI except referring to this decision in the written submissions filed on last date of hearing, has not explained as to how the said decision is applicable to the facts and circumstances of the present case. It is not a case of departmental preliminary enquiry before lodging a FIR.

DEPENDS ON MATERIAL – TO REGISTER RC OR PE – IN PRESENT CASE CBI REGISTERED RC – HIGH COURT

28. In the present case, it was for investigating agency to conduct or not a preliminary enquiry as registration of PE depends upon the facts and circumstances of each case. In one given case the investigating agency may first register PE before registration of a Regular Case (RC) and in yet another case it may straightaway register RC. It will all depend upon the material placed before the investigating agency. In the present case the CBI registered a 'RC' without registering 'PE'. We would at this stage notice the course which was adopted by CBI on receipt of the complaint dated 1st February, 1996.

NO ACTION WAS TAKEN BY CBI ON THE RECEIPT OF COMPLAINT DATED 1.2.1996 – AFTER SHOW CAUSE NOTICE ISSUED – RC WAS REGISTERED ON 25.3.1996 – HIGH COURT

29. It seems clear from the material placed before us that on receipt of complaint from the petitioner the CBI initially did not take any action. When this petition was filed and notice to show cause, as noticed hereinbefore, was issued to respondents including CBI we were told that preliminary enquiry has not been registered and only a complaint has been registered in the Complaint Register and it is being verified. Two days later we were informed by CBI that it is on the eve of registering a regular case and going to commence the investigation. That was stated on 20th March, 1996. The regular case was registered on 25th March, 1996, which is the FIR reproduced above, and we were informed about it on 27th March, 1996. It is, therefore, obvious that after registration of the complaint for verification, the CBI instead of registering a preliminary enquiry decided to register the regular case. In the regular case which was registered there is neither whisper nor mention of the complaint dated 1st February, 1996 nor it mentions any facts stated in the complaint. When this court was informed on 20th March, 1996 that CBI is on the eve of registration of a regular case and again on 27th March, 1996 that regular case has been registered, we were not informed further that what has been registered is not on the basis of the complaint dated 1st February, 1996. At this stage we may only say that CBI did not bring to the notice of this court the correct facts in correct prospective.

COMPLAINT DATE 1.2.1996 WAS NOT MADE BASIS OF FIR REGISTERED – HIGH COURT

30. It would not be appropriate for us to say at this stage that regular case which has been registered discloses or not the commission of offence under the Act. We have, however, no hesitation in holding that FIR registered is not on the basis of the complaint dated 1st February, 1996. It was not the case before us that the complaint dated 1st February, 1996 does not disclose commission of offence under the Act or the information does not 'appear to be' authentic and definite. When CBI decided to register the RC without registering a 'PE', it had to register it on the basis of the complaint dated 1st February, 1996 or they could have taken the stand that verification made by them shows that it is not necessary to register the regular case. Nothing of the kind was, however, done by CBI. The purported registration of 'RC' being not on the basis of complaint dated 1st February, 1996, on the facts and circumstances of the present case, is neither in consonance with the provisions of Vigilance Manual nor section 154 Criminal Procedure Code. We are constrained to observe that the manner in which the court was told about the registration of the case was clearly an attempt to mislead and over-reach this court. The court learnt about the registration of the case, as reproduced above, only after 12th April, 1996 when CBI was directed to supply copies of FIR to the petitioner and respondent No. 1 and after that when the petitioner filed affidavit dated 22nd April, 1996.

QUALITY OF A NATION'S CIVILISATION – DEPENDS ON ENFORCEMENT OF CRIMINAL LAW – SC QUOTED – HIGH COURT

31. Before issuing directions to CBI we may reproduce what has been said in the case of *Rampal Pithwa Rahidas* v. *State of Maharashtra,* 1994 Supp (2) SCC 73. "The quality of a nation's civilisation can be largely measured by the methods it uses in the enforcement of criminal law." In the present case we feel concerned about the manner in which the CBI has gone about in the matter of registration of the case while this petition was pending.

CBI DIRECTED TO REGISTER FIR ON THE BASIS OF COMPLAINT DATED 1.2.1996 – HIGH COURT

32. Under circumstances as aforesaid, in our view, it is just, fit and proper to direct CBI to register a regular case on the basis of the complaint of the petitioner. Learned counsel for respondents submitted before us that right of investigation is the function of the investigating agency. We have no doubt or quarrel with this proposition. The process of investigation is initiated with the registration of a FIR under section 154 of the Code and it culminates in a report under section 173(2) of the Code which has to be presented before a court competent to take cognizance of an offence. The process of investigation is set into motion upon registration of FIR. The right of the Police to investigate the circumstances of an alleged cognizable offence and its duty to carry out that investigation are codified in various provisions under the Code. These rights and duties of the Police have been recognised in a catena of judgments [See: *Emperor* v. *Khwaja Nazir Ahmad, Bhajan Lal's* case (supra) and *State of Bihar* v. *P.P. Sharma, IAS,* 1992 Supp (1) SCC 222]. We are in no manner questioning the right of CBI to investigate. After registration of the case as directed by us, it would be for CBI to investigate the matter in accordance with law. After investigation is complete the CBI would proceed in the manner provided in section 173 of the Code of Criminal Procedure by either filing charge sheet or a report disclosing that no case has been established.

NO DECLARATION CAN BE GIVEN – HIGH COURT

33. We have noticed in the earlier part of this judgment that the petitioner has sought a declaration to the effect that Sh. Suraj Mandal received bribe from or at the instance of Sh. P.V. Narasimha Rao for switching over support to Congress (1) during the vote on No Confidence Motion. Such declarations cannot be given in these proceedings, particularly, at this stage. If at all, this would be the last stage after completion of investigation, filing of charge-heet, if any, conclusion of the trial in a criminal court and on pronouncement of the judgment.

OBSERVATIONS MADE – WILL HAVE NO EFFECT – HIGH COURT

34. Some apprehensions were expressed by learned counsel for Respondent No. 1 that any observations made by us may cause prejudice to the rights of his clients. We attach paramount importance to the rights of the accused and therefore, make it clear that any observations made in this judgment would not have any effect whatsoever on the rights of Respondent No. 1 or any other person named or unnamed in the complaint of the petitioner.

CBI DIRECTED TO REGISTER FIR – NO DELAY IN INVESTIGATION – PROCEED ACCORDING TO LAW – HIGH COURT

35. Accordingly, we direct CBI to forthwith register a regular case on the basis of the complaint of the petitioner dated 1st February, 1996. Since 20th March, 1996 we have been noticing in our order that considering the nature of the case investigation cannot brook any delay. We reiterate it again with the hope that CBI would expedite and promptly complete the investigation. After completion of the investigation, it will proceed in the matter in accordance with law.

36. List the matter for further proceedings on 2nd August, 1996.

Author's note: After the registration of the case, presentation of challan in the CBI Court after the accused including P.V. Narasimha Rao were summoned by the trial court to appear before the trial court on 30th October, 1996, P.V. Narasimha Rao and other accused filed applications for Anticipatory bail in the Delhi High Court bearing Crl. M (m) Nos. 2733 of 1996. It was accepted by the Delhi High Court *vide* orders dated 3 January, 1997.

IN THE COURT OF
SHRI AJIT BHARIHOKE, SPECIAL JUDGE,
VIGYAN BHAWAN, NEW DELHI
SC. S(A)/96-ACU-VIII/CBI, New Delhi

CBI
v.
P.V. NARASIMHA RAO

ORDER

NAMES OF THE ACCUSED AND NUMBER OF CHARGESHEETS FILED BY CBI

Prosecution is seeking to try accused Sh. P.V. Narasimha Rao (herein referred to as A-1), accused Capt. Satish Sharma (here referred to as A-2), accused Suraj Mandal (herein referred to as A-3), accused Shibu Soren (herein referred to as A-4), accused Simon Marandi (herein referred to as A-5), accused Shailendra Mahto, subsequently turned approver (herein referred to as approver) (A-6), accused Buta Singh (herein referred to as A-7), accused V. Rajeshwar Rao (herein referred to as A-8), accused H.M. Revanna (herein referred to as A-9), accused Ramalinga Reddy (herein referred to as A- 10), accused M. Veerappa Moily (herein referred to as A-11), accused D.K. Audikesavulu (herein referred to as A-12), accused H. Thimmegowda (herein referred to as A-13), accused Bhajan Lal (herein referred to as A-14), accused Ajit Singh (herein referred to as A-15), accused Ram Lakhan Singh Yadav (herein referred to as A-16), accused Ram Sharan Yadav (herein referred to as A-17), accused Roshan Lal (herein referred to as A-18), accused Anadi Charan Das (herein referred to as A-19), accused Abhay Pratap Singh (herein referred to as A-20 and accused Haji Gulam Mohd. Khan (herein referred to as A-21) charge-sheeted in case PC. 5 (A)/96- ACU-VIII/CBI New Delhi *vide* three different reports under section 173 Cr. P.C. First charge-sheet was filed in the court on 30-10-1996. In furtherance of that charge-sheet, second and third charge sheets were filed on 9-12-1996 and 22-1-1997 respectively.

VERSION OF CBI

2. The relevant facts for deciding the question of framing of charge are as follows:—

(A) That in the General Election of 10th Lok Sabha in 1991 Congress (I) emerged as a single largest party and it formed the Government at the Centre under the leadership of Shri P.V. Narasimha Rao (A-1). Monsoon Session of Lok Sabha was to commence on 26th of July, 1993 with a 'No Confidence Motion' being moved against the Government by Sh. Ajay Mukh Upadhiya, a CPI (M). The effective strength of Lok Sabha at that time was 528 and the Congress (I) had 251 Members in the Lok Sabha. Thus, the Government headed by (A-1) was short of 14 members of Parliament for a simple majority since it required 265 votes to defeat the Motion of 'No confidence'. It is alleged that the opposition parties had made their intention clear to move a 'no confidence motion' on or well before 26-7-1993. On 28-7-1993 'No Confidence Motion' was put to vote and it was defeated with the support of (A-3 to A-6), the JMM., IPs. and (A-16 to A-21) as well as late Shri G.C. Munda, the Break away TDA M.Ps. group.

ON HIGH COURT DIRECTION FIR OF CRIMINAL CONSPIRACY AND BRIBING OF MPs REGISTERED BY CBI

(B) one Ravinder Kumar President of Rashtriya Mukti Morcha filed a complaint with CBI alleging that (accused no.1) had hatched a criminal conspiracy with Sh. V.C. Shukla, R.K. Dhawan, Capt. Satish Sharma (A-2), Ajit Singh (A-15). Bhajan Lal (A-14) and Lalit Suri with the object to prove the majority of the Government on the floor of the House by bribing some of the Members of the Parliament to the extent of over Rs. 3 crores. Even though the complaint disclosed the commission of cognizable offence, no FIR was registered and the said Ravinder Kumar, therefore, filed a petition in the High Court of Delhi for a direction to CBI to register the FIR. After direction had been given by a Division Bench of Hon'ble High Court, the CBI ultimately registered case RC No. 5A/96-ACU-VIII against the accused named in the complaint.

(C) Sum and substance of the allegations in the respective charge sheets is that the above-referred accused persons namely A-1 to A-21 entered into a criminal conspiracy to defeat the 'No Confidence Motion' by resorting to giving and accepting of illegal gratification as a motive or reward and in pursuance thereof four JMM MPs namely A-4 to A-5 and the approver Shailendra Mahto and also A-15 Ajit Singh and A-16 to A-21 the break-away JD(A) group of MPs, accepted illegal gratification to vote against the 'no confidence motion' to ensure the survival of the Government led by Shri P.V. Narasimha Rao (A-1).

ACCUSED ENTERED INTO CRIMINAL CONSPIRACY IN PAYING BRIBE TO THE MPs – SAYS CBI

(D) It is alleged that on 24-7-1993 there was a party hosted by Capt. Satish Sharma (A2) at his residence and during said party some suit cases were brought in a gypsy from the Farm House of A-2. On the morning of 25-7-1993 Capt. Satish Sharma (A-2) visited the residence of Shri P.V. Narasimha Rao (A-1). It is alleged that on 26-7-1993 Shri Buta Singh (A-7) and one other senior leader of Congress approached four JMM MPs namely A-3 to A-5 and the approver for securing their votes against 'No Confidence Motion'. Initially said JMM MPs had a meeting with A-7 at his residence and thereafter Shri Buta Singh (A-7) arranged a secret meeting between JMM MPs. and Shri P.V. Narasimha Rao at the latter's residence. On 27-7-1993 JMM MPs, had another meeting with A-7 during night time at his residence. Investigation has further revealed that accused Buta Singh (A-7) met with Shri P.V. Narasimha Rao at latter's residence on 15-7-1993, 25-7-1993 and 26-7-1993. On 28-7-1993, 'No Confidence Motion' was defeated with the help of the votes of JMM MPs. and the MPs. belonging to break-away group of JD (A).

BRIBE MONEY PAID TO JMM MPS ON 29-31 JULY IN BAGS AND SUIT CASES – SAYS CBI

(E). It is alleged that on 29-7-1993 at about 8 AM, 4/5 unknown persons visited the residence of Suraj Mandal (A-3) in two vehicles and delivered five suit cases and one bag which were locked in a room and keys were kept by A-3. In the next morning *i.e.,* on 30-7-1993 Suraj Mandal (A-3) received three boris and one suit-case which were seen lying in the verandah by Shri Dara Ravani. In the forenoon of the same day Simon Marandi (A-5) visited the house of Suraj Mandal (A-3) and took three boris and one suit-case away in his car.

(F). Thereafter, accused Simon Marandi (A-5) went to the house of Shailendra Mahto approver and both of them went together to the residence of Shri R.K. Jaitley. They unloaded three boris and one suit-case in the house of R.K. Jaitley. After sometime Shri Bal Kishan an employee of R.K. Jaitley went to the nearby market alongwith the driver of Simon Marandi and brought three new suit cases. Accused Simon Marandi (A-5) and the approver Shailendra Mahto then transferred the currency notes contained in three boris and one suit-case into four suit-cases then available with them after counting the cash. Thereafter, both of them left the flat of Jaitley with two suit cases, leaving the two suit cases behind. On the same day at about 9 PM, accused Shibhu Soren visited the residence of accused Suraj Mandal and collected from there one bag and a suit case.

(G). It is further alleged that on 31-7-1993 at about 7 AM accused Simon Marandi went to the house of Jaitley and from there he picked up accused Shailendra Mahto (approver) alongwith two suit cases and then they went to the residence of Shibhu Soren (A-4). Approver Sheilendra Mahto stayed back at the house of Shibhu Soren alongwith the suit cases and Simon Marandi left.

JMM MPs DEPOSITED SOME MONEY IN PNB IN DIFFERENT ACCOUNTS – SAYS CBI

(H). It is further alleged that thereafter huge amount of cash as per details given hereinafter were deposited by the aforesaid four JMM MPs. in Punjab National Bank, Naroji Nagar Branch, New Delhi. Although, the amounts pertaining to those accounts was collected by the bank officials in the late hour of 31-7-1993, but those accounts were formally opened on next day *i.e.* 1-8-1993, it is alleged that Rs. 30 lakhs was deposited in the SF Account No. 17108 of Suraj Mandal (A-3). One FD Account No. 195 worth Rs. 30 lakhs was opened in the joint name of said four JMM MPs. and one joint SF Account was opened in the joint names of said MPs. with a deposit of Rs. 10,000. As per instructions of Shailendra Mahto (approver) one Sugam FD account No. 196 was opened with Rs. 39.80 lakhs in the joint names of approver and his wife Smt, Abha. Another PD Account No. 194 was opened in the joint names of Shibhu Soren (A-4), his wife and two sons with Rs. 30 lakhs and one FD Account No. 197 with deposit of Rs. 12 lakhs was opened in the joint name of Simon Marandi (A-5) and his wife. All these accounts were introduced by Sushil Kumar, Chartered Accountant. It is alleged that on 2-8-1993 Simon Marandi (A-5) again visited Punjab National Bank, Naroji Nagar and deposited a sum of Rs. 21 lakhs in FD Account No. 197.

(I) After opening above-referred accounts, Saving Fund Account was also opened by all the four JMM MPs, in the same bank with a view to facilitate the transfer of money from FD Accounts to SF Account.

CAPT. SATISH SHARMA, MINISTER PETROLEUM HAD COLLECTED Rs. 4 CRORES FROM 4 INDUSTRIAL HOUSES – SAYS CBI

(J) It is further alleged that investigation has revealed that Capt. Satish Sharma (A-2) was the then Minister of Petroleum and he had received huge payments worth four crores from various industrial houses like Jindal Pipes, Videocon International Limited, Reliance Industries and Bindal Agro Industries during the period with effect from April, 1993 till July, 1993. It is also alleged that Shri B.N. Safaye the Additional Private Secretary of A-2 used to collect aforesaid money on behalf of Capt. Satish Sharma. It is also alleged that around 30th or 31st July, 1993 Simon Marandi visited the residence of Shri Safaiya to collect Rs. 10 lakhs promised by Capt. Satish Sharma (A-2). After confirming from Capt. Satish Sharma, Shri Safaiya asked Simon Marandi (A-5) to come later and paid him Rs. 10 lakhs which Shri Safaiya had meanwhile brought from Capt. Satish Sharma's residence. It is also alleged that the above referred JMM MPs. in order to conceal their involvement in the present crime fabricate false documents such an donation coupons, minute books of JMM party and the books of accounts in order to justify the amounts found deposited in their personal accounts.

(K) As per charge-sheet No. 2 filed against A-8 to A-13 it is alleged that investigation has revealed that approver Shailendra Mahto met Shri Ashok Rao Deshmukh few days before the voting on 'no confidence motion' and requested him to arrange a meeting between him and Shri P.V. Narasimha Rao (A-1). On 25-7-1993 Sh. Ashok Rao Deshmukh met A-1 and apprised him about his meeting with Shailendra Mahto (approver). On this A-1 told him to ascertain the demand of JMM MPs. but approver Shailendra Mahto insisted on direct meeting with the P.M. Shri Deshmukh informed Shri P.V. Narasimha Rao (A-1) accordingly and in the same evening A-1 advised Shri Ashok Deshmukh to take JMM MPs. to Sh. V. Rajeshwar Rao (A-8) for further discussion.

(L) On 26-7-1993 at about 11 A.M. Sh. Ashok Rao Deshmukh took four JMM MPs to Shri V. Rajeshwar Rao (A-8) at 7, Swaranmukhi Apartment, Andhra Bhawan. Since JMM MPs wanted to discuss their demands for supporting Congress (I) Government in privacy Shri Deshmukh left the flat. It is also alleged that Shri Shailendra Mehto (approver) had also taken the help of his old acquaintance Shri Harsharan Lal in having a meeting with Shri V. Rajeshwar Rao (A-8). After the voting on 'no-confidence motion' on 29-7-1993 the JMM MPs. namely A-3 to A-6 complained to Harsharan Lal that Rao Sahib has not fully met their demands. This protest was conveyed by Harsharan Lal to Shri V. Rajeshwar Rao (A-8) who assured that he would take care of the demand of JMM MPs.

M. VEERAPPA MOILY CM KARNATAKA REMAINED IN DELHI FROM 25-29 JULY, 1993 AND MET PM FREQUENTLY – SAYS CBI

(M) it is also alleged that during the relevant period M. Veerappa Moily (A-11) was camping in Delhi from 25-7-1993 to 29-7-1993 and during his stay he called on Shri P.V. Narasimha Rao (A-1) repeatedly and he also met V. Rajeshwar Rao (A-8). He also called Capt. Satish Sharma (A-2), Shri K. Karna Karan and Shri Ajit Singh (A-15). It is alleged that during the relevant period hectic political activities were going on at the residence of M. Veerappa Moily (A-11) at Bangalore and H.M, Revanna (A-9), Ramalinga Reddy (A-10) , D.K. Audikesavulu (A.12), M. Thimmegowda (A-13) and others had been frequently visiting his residence and some suit cases were also delivered by them.

A-12 WENT TO BANGALORE ON 29 JULY – CONDUCTED BANK TRANSACTIONS – SAYS CBI

(N) It is alleged that Shri D.K. Audikesavulu (A-12) was also camping at Delhi from 24-7-1993 to 29-7-1993 and he was also seen at the residence of V. Rajeshwar Rao (A-8) on 26-7-1993, the date on which A-8 had a meeting with JMM MPs. Shri D.K. Audikesavulu (A-12) left for Bangalore on 29-7-1993 by evening flight.

(O) It is alleged that at Bangalore accused D.K. Audikesavulu (A-12) drew cheque No. 348507 dated 29.7.93 worth Rs. 30 lakhs on the account of his firm M/s. Sapthagiri Enterprises drawn on Canara Bank, RMV Extension in favour of M/s. Siri Padmavati Enterprises. He also issued two cheques bearing Nos. 372415 and 372414 both dated 30.7.1997(?1993) for Rs. 61,7349 and Rs. 14,78125 respectively favouring Shri B.P. Ramakrishan, an employee of the Company M/s. K.B.D.L. The cheque worth Rs. 30 lakhs was credited to the current account No. 754 of M/s. Siri Padmawati Enterprises on 30-7-1993 and the said amount was withdrawn from the account on the same day through a cheque purported to have been signed by K. Muniraja proprietor of the said firm. However, the cash payment against the said cheque was received by Dwarka Nath an employee of M/s. K.B.D.L. The funds of other two cheques were also withdrawn in cash on 30-7-1993. Thereafter the aforesaid cash amount was delivered by Dwarka Nath to accused D.K. Audikesavulu.

(P) It is alleged that investigation has revealed that M/s. Siri Padmawati Enterprises is a non-existent firm and the account opening form pertaining to its bank account was filled by Shri Dwarka Nath a close relative of A-12 and also an employee of KBDL. It is alleged that said Account Opening Form was filled up by Dwarka Nath at the instance of A-12 and aforesaid amount was also introduced by one Sreovari Enterprises which was also found to be non-existent.

(Q). It is further alleged that M. Thimmegowda is the Managing Director of S.P.R. Group Holdings (P) Ltd. having current account No. 1968 with Canara Bank, Sheshadari-puram Branch, Bangalore.

A-13 WITHDREW RS. 1 CRORE OVERDRAFT FROM CANARA BANK- SAYS CBI

(R) It is alleged that on 30-7-1993, M. Thimmegowda (A-13) approached the Branch Manager of the said bank and applied for temporary over-draft of Rs. one crore for ten days on the pretext of meeting some urgent business commitments. The Branch Manager sought oral approval of Shri V.A. Prabhu the then General Manager, Circle Office, Canara Bank, Bangalore on telephone and V.A. Prabhu in turn obtained approval from the Chairman, Canara Bank on telephone and conveyed the sanction to the Sheshadari Puram Branch after banking hours. However, Shri M. Thimmegowda (A-13) insisted on withdrawing the whole amount on 30-7-1993 itself and, therefore the Branch Manager directed the Manager (Cash) for placing indent on cash chest Canara Bank, RMV Extension for issue of currency notes amounting to Rs. one crore. Thereafter the Manager (Cash) alongwith two other officers visited the Cash Chest and withdrew the sum of Rs. 95 lakhs after normal banking hours.

(S) It is further alleged that on 30-7-1993 M. Thimmegowda (A-13) issued two cheques for Rs. 60 lakhs and Rs. 25 lakhs in favour of M/s. Ranganathan Group and M/s Yellamma Group. He also issued one self cheque dated 30-7-1993 for Rs. 15 lakhs on the account of M/s. SPR Group holdings (P) Ltd.

The funds against the cheques issued in favour of said two companies were credited to their accounts and thereafter Sh. M.S. Chelavuraju partner of M/s. Ranganathan Group and Sh. T. Surarmia Proprietor of M/s. Yellamma Group Enterprises withdrew the respective amounts of Rs. 60 lakhs and Rs. 25 lakhs in cash. Similarly, A-13 also withdrew Rs. 15 lakhs in cash and took the entire amount of Rs. one crore in two big VIP suit-cases. It is alleged that M/s. Ranganathan actually belongs to A-3 and Shri M.S. Chelavuraju is shown as Managing partners of firm only for name-sake. It is also alleged that M/s. Yellemma Enterprises is also controlled by A-13.

A-13 WITHDREW RS. 1 CRORE OVERDRAFT FROM CANARA BANK – SAYS CBI

A-13 DELIVERED SUIT CASES IN CM'S BANGALORE HOUSE ON 30 JULY 1993 – LEFT FOR DELHI WITH A7-A12 – SAYS CBI

(T). It is further alleged that after withdrawing the cash M. Thimmegowda (A-13) visited the residence of Shri M. Veerappa Moily (A-11) at Bangalore in the evening of 30-7-1993 and delivered said two suit-cases. Sh. H.M. Revanna (A-9) and Sh. Ramalinga Reddy (A-10) were also present there at that time. Subsequently, in the same evening Shri H.M. Revanna (A-9) and Ramalinga Reddy (A-10) left the residence of M. Veerappa Moily in a car with three suit-cases and one hand bag and proceeded to Bangalore Airport. Shri D.K. Audikesavulu (A-12) also reached at Bangalore Airport with one VIP suit-case and thereafter A-9, A-10 and A-12 left for Delhi by Indian Airlines flight No. IC-404 and reached Delhi at 10-30 hrs. Shri Buta Singh (A-7) also travelled from Bangalore to Delhi in the same flight.

(U). It is further alleged that at Delhi above-referred accused persons were received by Bachan Singh, Rup Ram and Darmian Singh. They loaded three VIP suit-cases and one bag in the taxi driven by Rup Ram whereas D.K. Audikesavulu (A-11) Kept his VIP suit-cases in the Maruti car of M/s. MBDL. Thereafter they all went to Andhra Bhawan and called on Shri V. Rajeshwar Rao at his apartment. After some discussion they left for hotel Claridges. Sh. H.M. Revanna and Ramalinga Raddy stayed at the hotel and D.K. Audikesavulu went to MBDL Guest House at New Friends Colony.

(V). It is alleged that in the morning of 31-7-1993 Shri D.K. Audikesavulu (A-12) brought his VIP suit-case to hotel Claridges. Shri Rup Ram also brought his taxi to the hotel. VIP suit-cases and hand bag were loaded in the taxi and thereafter Shri D.K. Audikesavulu (A-12), H.M. Revanna (A-9) and Ramalinga Reddy (A-10) left for Andhra Bhawan. Shri H.M. Revanna and Ramalinga Reddy had followed the taxi to Andhra Bhawan in a Maruti Car of Vijay Handa alongwith him to Shri Harsharan Lal. At Andhra Bhawan A-9, A-10 and A-12 and other persons went up-stairs and they came back after about one hour with Shri V. Rajeshwar Rao. Thereafter at the instance of Shri D.K. Audikesavulu hand bag and one VIP suit-case which was kept at the back seat of the taxi and one VIP suit-case brought by him were shifted to the white Maruti car of Shri Vijay Handa. H.M. Revanna thereafter sat in the taxi driven by Rup Ram. The Maruti car driven by Vijay Handa with Shri Harsharan Lal and Ganga Singh left for the residence of Suraj Mandal (A-3) at Ferozeshah Road, New Delhi and Rup Ram taxi driver was asked to follow them. The said vehicles visited the residence of Suraj Mandal (A-3) and delivered aforesaid VIP suit-case and the hand bag to him.

ON 24 JULY 1993 BHAJAN LAL CM HARYANA VISITED AJIT SINGH RESIDENCE A-15 AND DELIVERED HIM 3 PACKETS OF MONEY – SAYS CBI

(w) In the third charge-sheet it is alleged that with a view to win over the votes of JD(A) MPs. Shri Bhajan Lal (A-14) visited the residence of Sh. Ajit Singh (A-15) on 24-7-1993 and requested him to support Congress (I) Government. He also delivered three packets to Shri Ajit Singh. After Shri Bhajan Lal left Sh. Ajit Singh asked Capt. Dilawar Singh to open one of the packets which was found to contain 200 wads of currency notes of Rs. 50 denomination which indicated that the packets delivered by Bhajan Lal contained Rs. One crore each. It is also alleged that on 26-7-1993 Sh. Ram Lakhan Singh Yadav (A-16) visited Shri Ajit Singh (A-15) and during their discussion heated arguments took place. Sh. Ram Lakhan Singh demanded his share of Rs. 15 lakhs out of the amount received by Ajit Singh from Bhajan Lal. However, Ajit Singh denied having received any money from Bhajan Lal. Thereafter Ajit Singh called the party meeting wherein it was decided to support 'no confidence motion'.

A-16 MADE A BREAK-AWAY GROUP OF JD(A) OF A16-A21 – ASSURED OF MONEY – PETROL PUMPS – SAYS CBI

(X) It is further alleged that investigation has revealed that 7 MPs. namely A-16 to A-21 and late Shri G.C. Munda assembled at the residence of Ram Lakhan Singh Yadav on 27-7-1993 at 4 PM and they decided to form a separate group under the leadership of Ram Lakhan Singh Yadav (A-16) and to vote against the 'no confidence motion'. During this meeting Sh. Bhajan Lal visited Shri Ram Lakhan Singh Yadav (A-16) and had some secret discussions and Shri Ram Lakhan Singh Yadav (A-16) spoke telephonically to Shri Narasimha Rao (A-1) and assured that his group would split from JD (A) by the evening and PM should take care of rest of the things. It is further alleged that accused Capt. Satish Sharma (A-2) also attended the meeting and during said discussion Shri Bhajan Lal assured that said MPs. would be paid huge some in cash while Capt. Satish Sharma assured them allotments of Petrol Pumps either in their names or in their family members.

ON 28 JULY 1993 A2, A14 MET A16-A21 AT HOUSE OF A16-A14 GAVE RS. 20 LAKHS EACH – ASSURED EQUAL AMOUNT AFTER VOTING – SAYS CBI

(Y) It is further alleged that on 28-7-1993 above-referred MPs. of break-away JD(A) group met at the residence of Ram Lakhan Singh Yadav (A-16). Shri V.C. Shukla, Capt. Satish Sharma (A-2), Bhajan Lal (A-14) and others also visited these MPs. On the said day Sh. Bhajan Lal delivered suit-cases at the residence of Shri Ram Lakhan Singh Yadav, his son Parkash Yadav informed the members belonging to its break-away groups of the JD (A) that Sh. Bhajan Lal had fulfilled his promise. It is alleged that Bhajan Lal and Capt. Satish Sharma had assured them that Petrol Pumps and sum of Rs. 20 lakhs would be paid to every member of break-away JD(A) group led by Ram Lakhan Singh Yadav before the voting and another sum of Rs. 20 lakhs each would be paid after the voting. Thereafter from the residence of Ram Lakhan Singh Yadav all seven MPs of break-away group proceeded to Parliament House along with Shri Bhajan Lal (A-14) and each of those MPs. had received Rs. 20 lakhs before leaving for Parliament on 28-7-1993. It is also alleged that from 23-7-1993 to 2-8-1993 Bhajan Lal (A-14) was camping at Delhi except on 26-7-1993 and during this period, he was constantly in touch with Sh. P.V. Narasimha Rao (A-1), A-2 and the other accused persons. It is further alleged that accused Bhajan Lal was also mobilizing the funds during the period immediately before the 'no-confidence motion' and he had obtained Rs. 30 to Rs. 40 lakhs from the office bearers of Saraswati Kunj House Building Society for granting them license for colonization. It is also alleged that during the relevant period Bhajan Lal had arranged for the stay of accused Haji Gulam Mohd. Khan and late Shri G.C. Munda at Hotal Raj Hans, Suraj Kund from 1-8-1993 to 3-8-1993 and he had borne the bill of Rs. 40,000. It is further alleged that in a public meeting at hotel on 11-8-1993 Shri Bhajan Lal had voluntarily admitted having engineered the defection of 7 MPs. of JD (A) within 48 hrs., which led to survival of the Government.

BREAK-AWAY GROUP DEPOSITED MONEY IN BANK OR INVESTED IN PROPERTY – SAYS CBI

(2) It is further alleged that from the investigation it is revealed that immediately after the defeat of 'no-confidence motion' MPs. of break-away JD (A) group have either made substantial deposits or made substantial investments in properties.

(3) On the aforesaid allegations made in the three charge-sheets, prosecution is seeking to try the above referred 21 accused persons under sections 120B, IPC read with sections 7.12.13(2) read with sections 13(1)(a) of the P.C. Act, 1988 as well as the substantive offences.

DISCUSSION IF CHARGE MADE OUT – CBI COURT

(4) I have heard respective counsels for the accused persons as well as Ld. Prosecutor and perused the material on record.

(5) Besides arguing that no case for framing of charges is disclosed against the accused persons, their respective counsels have also raised various legal pleas.

JURISDICTION OF THE CBI COURT DISPUTED BY ACCUSED – REJECTED BY CBI COURT

(6) First contention on behalf of the accused persons is that jurisdiction of this court to try this case is barred under section 105(2) of the Constitution of India because such a trial would amount to breach of privilege and immunity of Parliament as well as its members. It is submitted on behalf of the accused persons that foundation of the present charge-sheet is the allegation of acceptance of bribe by some members of parliament for voting against the 'no confidence motion'. It is contended that the controversy to be decided in this case would be in respect of motive and action of members of Parliament pertaining to the vote given by them in relation to the motion of 'no confidence'.

(7) In order to properly appreciate this contention it is necessary to go through article 105(2) of the constitution of India which is reproduced as follow:

Article 105(2)

> "No member of Parliament shall be liable to any proceedings in any Court in respect of anything said or any vote given by him in Parliament or any committee thereof, and no person shall be so liable in respect of the publication by or under the authority of either house of Parliament of any report, paper, votes or proceedings.
>
> (3)..............................".

Perusal of this Article would reveal that no Member of Parliament can be made liable in any proceedings in any court in respect of any vote given by him in the

Parliament or any committee thereof. In my opinion, the object of this Article is that Members of Parliament in exercise of their functions must act fearlessly and they should speak their mind and exercise their franchise without any fear of legal proceedings for anything said or done in the Parliament. However, this does not imply that Article 105(2) has granted a license to Member of Parliament to sell his vote. If such an interpretation is given to Article 105(2), it would amount to defeating the main object of Parliamentary democracy provided in Constitution of India. Thus, I do not agree with the contention raised on behalf of the accused persons. In the present case voting pattern of the accused persons (Members of Parliament) is not under adjudication. They are ought to be tried for their illegal acts committed outside the Parliament *i.e.* demanding and accepting the bribe for exercising their franchise in a particular manner. It is not that the accused persons Members of Parliament are being prosecuted for exercising their right of vote but they are being prosecuted on the allegations that they while holding a public office demanded and accepted illegal gratification for exercising their franchise in a particular manner which is an offence punishable under P.C. Act, 1988. Thus, under the circumstances I am of the view that Article 105 of the Constitution of India do not provide any protection to the accused persons.

MP IS NOT A 'PUBLIC SERVANT' – SUBMIT ACCUSED – REJECTED BY CBI COURT

(8) Second submission on behalf of almost all the accused persons is that a Member of Parliament is not a public servant for the purpose of P.C. Act, 1988 and as such giving and taking of alleged gratification does not amount to any offence punishable under the provisions of P.C. Act. Thus, there cannot be any offence of conspiracy of giving and taking of bribe by the MPs.

(9) Ld. Prosecutor, on the other hand, has contended that the term 'public servant' has been defined in section 2(C) of the P.C. Act, 1988 and a Member of Parliament falls within the ambit of section 2(C)(VIII) of the P.C. Act because he holds an office as a member of Parliament by virtue of which he is required to perform public duty.

(10) From the contentions put forward by the respective parties, the point which arises for adjudication is, whether or not M.P. is a public servant? This controversy has already been set at rest by the orders of Hon'ble Justice Mohd. Shamin of Delhi High Court pronounced in Criminal Revision petition Nos. 265, 124, 166, 167, 256, 257, 328, 329, 330 and 311 of 1996 in the matters of Shri L.K. Advani and Sh. P.C. Shukla. In the aforesaid judgment, Hon'ble Justice Mohd. Shamim after thoroughly discussing the provisions of P.C. Act and its object have held that MP is a public servant. In view of the aforesaid judgment, I do not find any merit in the submission made on behalf of the accused persons.

PRIOR SANCTION UNDER SECTION 19 OF P.C. ACT NOT OBTAINED – COGNIZANCE CANNOT BE TAKEN BY THE COURT – SUBMIT SOME OF THE ACCUSED – REJECTED CBI COURT

(11) It is also submitted on behalf of most of the accused persons that present case cannot proceed for want of previous sanction for prosecution under section 19 of the P.C. Act, 1988.

(12) This section provides that no court shall take cognizance for offences punishable under sections 7, 10, 11, 13 and 15 alleged to have been committed by a public servant except with the prior sanction of Central Government or the State Government or the Authority competent to remove him from the office, as the case may be.

(13) Scope of the provision in respect of previous sanction was considered by Hon'ble Supreme court is **S.A. Venkataraman v. State, AIR 1958 SC 107,** while discussing a parallel provision *i.e.* section 6 of the previous Anti-Corruption Act of 1947. In the aforesaid judgment it was held that no previous sanction for prosecution was necessary before a court could take cognizance of the offences under P.C. Act if the accused person had ceased to be a public servant at the time of taking of cognizance. This view has been followed in **C.R. Bansi v. State of Maharashtra** and in the case of **K. Veeraswami v. Union of India, (1991) 3 SCC 655**. Thus, it is obvious that no sanction for prosecution of an accused under section 19 is necessary if he is ceased to hold the public office which was allegedly misused by him.

(14) In the present case, at the time of filling of the charge-sheet and on the date of taking cognizance of offence by the court A-1, A-2, A-4 and A-14 were Members of existing Lok Sabha while A-8 was a Member of Rajya Sabha. Similarly, A-10 and A-11 were Members of Karnataka Assembly while A-14 was the Member of Haryana State Assembly. A-4 was Chairman and A-3 was Vice Chairman and A-5 and A-6 were Member of Jharkhand Area Autonomous Council constituted vide Act of 1944. All the other accused persons were private persons. Perusal of the record would reveal that offence is alleged to have been committed, while A-1 was Prime Minister, A-2 was Union Minister, A-11 and A-14 were Chief Ministers of States of Karnataka and Haryana. A-10 was a Minister and A-9 was MLA in the State of Karnatka. A-3 to A-5, A-7, A-8 and A-15 to A-21 were the Members of 10th Lok Sabha.

(15) It may be noted that 10th Lok Sabha have come to an end and after the Elections in 1996, 11th Lok Sabha has come into operation. This imply that all the accused persons who were the Members of 10th Lok Sabha have ceased to hold the office as Members of said Lok Sabha which has come to an end. Therefore, under law no sanction for their prosecution is required. Further more accused persons are sought to be tried for criminal conspiracy under section 120B, IPC read with sections 7, 12, and 13(2) P.C. Act, 1988 as well as the substantive offences. According to section 19 of the P.C. Act, sanction is required only in respect of the offences punishable under section 7 and 13. These substantive offences have allegedly been committed by the Members of Parliament who have accepted the illegal gratification for voting against the 'no confidence motion'. In **Habib Ullah Khan v. State of Orissa, 1993 Cr LJ 3604,** Hon'ble High Court has discussed this proposition and held that in case of MLA no sanction is required, though he is a public servant because there is no sanctioning authority qua him. Case of the MP is also on a similar footing so far as question of sanctioning authority is concerned. Therefore, applying the ratio of said judgment, I am of the view that no sanction for prosecution under section 19 of the P.C. Act is required against the above referred MPs. who have allegedly accepted the bribe.

NO CASE FOR CHARGE IS MADE OUT – SUBMIT ACCUSED – *PRIMA FACIE* CASE MADE OUT – HELD CBI COURT

(16) On Merits, it has been argued on behalf of all the accused persons that on the basis of evidence submitted alongwith the report under section 173, Cr. P.C., no case for framing of charges against the accused persons is made out. It is also submitted that in this matter prosecution has filed three charge-sheets and the allegations in the charge-sheets are contradictory which makes prosecution case highly improbable and as such the accused persons should be discharged.

(17) On the other hand, Ld. Prosecutor has vehemently argued that there is sufficient evidence on the record to raise strong suspicion of participation of all the accused in the conspiracy. He has submitted that conspiracy is normally hatched behind the closed doors and, therefore, it is very difficult to collect direct evidence of conspiracy. Thus under law, Court is supposed to draw its conclusion and presumption regarding conspiracy from the various circumstances established by the evidence. He has submitted that the investigating agency has been able to collect sufficient *prima-facie* evidence of relevant circumstances which raise a grave suspicion of participation of all the accused persons in the conspiracy of offer and payment of bribe to the Members of Parliament and acceptance of the same by them. Thus, he has submitted that this is a fit case in which charges against the accused persons should be framed.

(18) I have carefully considered the report under section 173, Cr.P.C., statements of witnesses recorded under section 161, Cr.P.C. documents relied upon by the prosecution, written submissions made by some of the accused persons and the oral submissions made one behalf of the respective parties.

(19) Before referring to the evidence on the record I may point out that number of judgments of Hon'ble Supreme Court and various High Courts have been cited by the respective parties to throw light upon the standard of evaluation of evidence at the time of charge. After going through the said judgments. I am of the view that settled position of law is that at the time of framing of charge, court is supposed to take a *prima-facie* view of the evidence submitted alongwith the report under section 173, Cr.P.C. and to test the same on the anvil of probability. If the court is of the view that the evidence submitted by the prosecution is sufficient to raise grave suspicion of complicity of the accused or accused persons in the crime, then the charge should be framed. On the other hand, if the evidence submitted along with the report under section 173, Cr.P.C. seem to be improbable or it raises a more suspicion, then the accused must be discharged.

(20) In the light of above legal position. I have considered the material on record and after going through the same, I am of the view that there is sufficient evidence on the record to raise a strong suspicion of existence of conspiracy and complicity of all the accused persons in the same. There is *prima-facie* evidence on the record to suggest participation of all the accused persons to achieve the object of the conspiracy *i.e.* to defeat the 'no confidence motion' by illegal means, at one stage or the other.

DISCUSSION OF THE CASE OF INDIVIDUAL ACCUSED AND HIS INVOLVEMENT – CBI COURT

(21) Now, I propose to high light silent circumstances which raise strong suspicions of existence of conspiracy and involvement of respective accused persons in the same.

(a) INVOLVEMENT OF SHRI P.V. NARASIMHA RAO (A-1) – CBI COURT

(A) It is admitted fact on the record that at the relevant time accused A-1 was heading a minority Government of Congress I which was required to face the 'no confidence motion' on 28-7-1993. This circumstance provides a motive for the hatching of conspiracy to win over the votes of opposition MPs. by extra legal means.

(B) PW 144 Shri Ashok Rao Deshmukh has stated during investigation that few days prior to the voting Shailendra Mahto approver requested him to arrange a direct meeting between JMM MPs. and A-1 when he apprised A-1 of the request he told him to find out the demands and conditions of JMM MPs. (A-3 to A-6). Thereafter, he again contacted A-6 in presence of either accused Suraj Mandal or Shibu Soren to find out their demands and conditions for supporting the Government but they insisted on direct meeting with the P.M. Thereafter, he again contacted A-1 in the same evening and apprised him about the outcome of his meeting with JMM MPs. and on this A-1 advised him to take the concerned MPs. to Shri V. Rajeshwar Rao (A-8). On this, the witness took the JMM MPs to the residence of V. Rajeshwar Rao at Andhra Bhawan, where they had a private discussion with A-8. There is also evidence on record (to be discussed later) to show that thereafter A-8 with the help of A-9 to A-13 got involved in the mobilization of huge funds which were brought from Bangalore and delivered at the residence of one of the JMM MPs. Suraj Mandal (A-3). There is also evidence on the record that on 25-7-1993 accused Capt. Satish Sharma (A-2) and accused Buta Singh (A-7) had visited the house of A-1. (Reference may be made to be statement of PW71 to PW73 and PW-93.

(C) From the statements of witnesses PW. 39, PW 42 to PW 44, PW 54, PW 85 and PW 95, it appears that in the night of 26.7.1993 JMM MPs. (A-3 to A-6) visited the house of A-7 and thereafter A-7 took them to the house of A-1 for a secret meeting. As per the statements of driver and PSOs. of A-3 and A-4, they were sent back from the house of A-7 and visit of Buta Singh to the house of A-1 on the said night is also established by NSG record and statement of PW-93. This fact is also corroborated by the statement of approver Shailendra Mahto recorded under section 164, Cr.P.C. on 22-3-1997 in which he has stated that during said meeting Suraj Mandal had a private talk with A-1 and A-7 and after the conclusion of meeting on the asking of Simon Marandi, he had told that matter of payment of money has also been discussed with the PM.

(D) There is also prima facie evidence on the record (to be discussed later) to show that ultimately huge amounts of bribe were paid to JMM MPs. which they deposited in PNB, Naroji Nagar, New Delhi.

(E) All the circumstances give rise to a strong suspicion of hatching up of conspiracy by A-1 and his participation in the same by having negotiations with JMM MPs. directly as well as through V. Rajeshwar Rao (A-B).

(b) INVOLVEMENT OF CAPT. SATISH SHARMA (A-2) – CBI COURT

(A) From the statements of PW 74, PW 76 to PW 78, PW 94 and PW 96, it *prima facie* appears that just prior to the 'no confidence motion' Capt. Satish Sharma had received cash amount about Rs. Four crores from various industrial houses during April to July, 1993. This circumstance shows that Capt. Satish Sharma was in a position to provide funds for bribing the MPs.

(B) From the statement of PW. 75 D.K. Mukhiya, it *prima facie* appears that Simon Marandi (A-5) met Capt. Satish Sharma at his office in presence of B.D. Paswan and D.K. Mukhiya and Capt. Satish Sharma (A-2) promised money. Petrol pump and gas agency in lieu of the support of JMM MPs. against 'no confidence motion'. Simon Marandi (A-5) promised to reply after consulting the other JMM MPs.

(C) PW 75 has also stated about a meeting dated 22-7-1993, between Capt. Satish Sharma (A-2), Simon Marandi (A-5), Ram Lakhan Singh Yadav (A-16), Roshan Lal (A-18), Haji Gulam Mohd. Khan (A-21) and late Shri G.C. Munda at about 6-30 PM in the old Ashram of Chandraswami. He has stated that in the aforesaid meeting, promise of payment of money, plot, and petrol pump was made by Capt. Satish Sharma.

(D) PW. 73 Rakesh Kumar has also stated about a party hosted by Capt. Satish Sharma at his residence which was also attended by Ajit Singh (A-15). He has also stated that driver of A-2 Shri Shiv Mangal brought one Gypsy full of suit-cases from Mehrauli Farm House on the said night.

(E) PW. 74 B.N Safaiya PA to Capt. Satish Sharma has stated that either on 30th or 31st July 1993 Suraj Mandal visited his residence at about 8.30 or 9 PM and demanded some payment promised by Capt. Satish Sharma. On this, he contacted Capt. Satish Sharma (A-2) on telephone and he confirmed that payment was to be made. He has stated that since he did not have the money. He went to the house of Capt. Satish Sharma at Mehruli and collected Rs. 10 lakhs contained in a card-board box. Thereafter, he returned back to his residence and delivered the money to Simon Marandi (A-5).

(F) There is also evidence on the record that on 27-7-1993 meeting of 7 MPs. Belonging to break- away groups of JD (A) took place at the residence of Ram Lakhan Singh Yadav (A-16). Said meeting was also attended by Shri Bhajan Lal (A-14) and Capt. Satish Sharma (A-2). During said meeting Capt. Satish Sharma assured the allotment of Petrol Pump to the aforesaid MPs. or their family members (reference may be made to the statement of PW81 Capt. Dilawar, PW 237 Gopi, PW 210 Praduyman). Similarly, there is also evidence in the form of statements of aforesaid witnesses to prime facie show that on 28-7-93 also meeting of six MPs. of JD(A) break-away group namely A-16 to A-20 and late Shri G.C. Munda took place at the residence of A-16. Sh. Bhajan Lal and Capt. Satish Sharma also visited them and assured them that the petrol pumps and a sum of Rs. 20 lakhs would be paid to every member of the group before the voting and another Rs. 20 lakhs each would be paid after the voting. On the said date Sh. Bhajan Lal had also delivered suit cases at the residence of A-16 after which Shri Parkash Yadav son of A-16 informed the MPs, present there that Bhajan Lal has fulfilled his promise.

(G) These circumstance raise a strong suspicion of involvement of Capt. Satish Sharma (A-2) in the conspiracy and his active participation in inducing and winning over vote of the JMM MPs. and MPs., belonging to break-away group of JD (A) by offering them cash bribe and promise of allotment of petrol pumps. etc.

(c) CIRCUMSTANCES AGAINST ACCUSED SURAJ MANDAL, SHIBU SOREN AND SIMON MARANDI – CBI COURT

(A) I have already discussed the evidence pointing out to the role of JMM MPs. seeking meeting with A-1 through Buta Singh (A-7) and their having discussed their demands and conditions for supporting the Government with A-1. I have also pointed out the evidence relating to JMM MPs. Having a meeting with Shri V. Rajeshwar Rao (A-8) while discussing circumstances against accused A-1. I have also pointed out the evidence relating to the talks between accused Simon Marandi (A-5) and accused Capt. Satish Sharma (A-2) in which bribe was offered by A-2 and A-5 promised to reply after consulting the other JMM MPs.

(B) From the statements of PW 46 Dara Rawani servant-cum-cook of A-3 and PW 45 Mitlesh Mandal PW 4 to A-3, it *prima facie* appears that on 29-7-1993, at about 8 A.M., 4/5 unknown persons visited the residence of accused Suraj Mandal (A-3) and delivered five suit-cases and one bag supposed to contain money. According to PW-46 Dara Rawani on 30-7-1993 he saw accused Suraj Mandal with three boris and one suit-case which he kept inside the room. In the same afternoon Simon Marandi (A-5) visited the residence of Suraj

Mandal (A-3) and collected three boris and one suit-case which were loaded in presence of accused Suraj Mandal.

(C) From the statements of PW 85, Sanjay, PW 92 Smt. Nita Jaitley, PW 83 Miss Pooja Jaitley and PW 94 Master Amber Jaitley, it *prima facie* appears that Simon Marandi (A-5) thereafter visited the residence of, Shailendra Mahto (A-6). Then both of them visited the residence of PW 1 R.K. Jaitley, who was out of station. The suit cases and boris were taken to the flat of R.K. Jaitley. The cash contained therein was counted and was re-packed in four suit-cases including three new suit-cases which were brought from the market by PW 89 Bal Kishan.

(D) PW 44 Sh. Kamal Yadav has stated that on 30-7-1993 at about 9/9.30 PM accused Shibu Soren visited the residence of accused Suraj Mandal in his Gypsy in which one suit-case and a bag were kept on the instruction of accused Suraj Mandal and thereafter he drove the gypsy of accused Shibu Soren to his residence.

(E) PW 74 B.N. Safaya has stated that either on 30th or 31st of July, 1993 accused Simon Marandi visited him at around 8-30 to 9 PM alongwith Sh. B.D. Paswan MP and demanded some payment to be made immediately. On this, he contacted accused Capt. Satish Sharma on telephone and he confirmed that payment was to be made to the accused Simon Marandi. He has stated that since he did not have the money he went to the house of Capt. Satish Sharma at Mehrauli and collected Rs. Ten lakhs contained in a card-board box there. Thereafter, he returned back to his residence and delivered said money to Simon Marandi.

(F) PW 141 Harsharan Lal has stated that on 29-7-1993 he visited the house of A-4 where the approver Shailendra Mahto was also present and both of them complained to him of non-fulfillment of promise made by V. Rasjeshwar Rao (A-8). The witness has stated that he conveyed this complaint to Vijay Handa (PW 140) who in turn conveyed the complaint to A-8.

(G) Further, there is evidence on the record in the form of statements of PW 146 Rup Ram, PW 142 Bachan Singh, PW 140 Vijay Handa and PW 141 Harsharan Lal and PW 139 Ganga Singh that the money which was brought from Bangalore (evidence to be discussed later on) was kept at Hotel Claridges during the night of 30-7-1993 and on the next day said money was carried to Andhra Bhawan, where A-9, A-10, A-12, Vijay Handa and Harsharan Lal went up-stairs and came back alongwith the accused V. Rajeshwar Rao (A-8) and thereafter aforesaid money was carried to the residence of Suraj Mandal (A-3) and delivered to him.

(H) There is also evidence of PW 4 Sushil Kumar Chartered Accountant a close associate of A-3 and the officials of PNB, PW5 to PW-14 and the documents D-6 to D-23, D-73 to D-77 to show that on 1st August and 2nd August, 1993 huge deposits were made by these JMM MPs, in the bank either jointly or individually for which there is no cogent explanation as to from where the money came. There is also evidence on record to show that after the registration of the case JMM MPs, have fabricated certain donation coupons and the minutes pertaining to the proceedings of the party so to create evidence that the aforesaid deposits related to the political donation received by the party.

(I) Aforesaid circumstances raise strong suspicion of complicity of these JMM MPS. in the conspiracy and their having accepted illegal gratification and fabricated the evidence to create a defence.

(d) CIRCUMSTANCES AGAINST BUTA SINGH (A-7) – CBI COURT

(A) I have already discussed the role of accused Buta Singh in arranging the secret meeting between JMM MPs, and A-1 and his participation in the discussion which took place between A-1, A-7 and accused Suraj Mandal. Approver Shailendra Mahto has also corroborated this fact in his statement under section 164, Cr.P.C. wherein he has deposed that during the meeting dated 26-7-1993, Buta Singh (A-7), Shri P.V Narasimha Rao (A-1) and Suraj Mandal (A-3) had a conversation in a separate room and after the conclusion of meeting Suraj Mandal had confirmed that talks regarding payment of money had also taken place.

(B) There is evidence on the record in the form of flight documents to show that Buta Singh had gone to Bangalore and came back to Delhi in the same flight in which A-9, A-10 and A-12 had brought the bribe money.

(C) These circumstances raise a strong suspicion of involvement of Buta Singh (A-7) in the conspiracy.

(e) CIRCUMSTANCES AGAINST SH. V. RAJESHWAR RAO (A8) – CBI COURT

(A) I have already pointed out in the circumstance discussed against Shri P.V. Narasimha Rao as to how JMM MPs. have tried to have a meeting with A-1 and how they where directed by A-1 to have talks with A-8. PW. 144 Ashok Rao Deshmukh has stated that at the instance of A-1 he took JMM MPs. to the residence of A-8 where they had a private meeting.

(B) It is also in evidence that D.K. Audikesavulu (A-12) was camping in Delhi from 24th to 29th July, 1993 (reference may be made to statement of PW 138 and documents D-648 and D-676).It is also in evidence that M. Veerappa Moily (A-11) was camping in Delhi from 25-7-1993 to 29-7-1993 and during this stay, he met A-1 repeatedly and also met A-2 and A-9 as well as others. (Reference may be made to statements of PW 183, PW 176 and documents D-575 to D-580 and D-644).

(C) There is statement of PW 141 Harsharan Lal that on 29-7-1993 Shibu Soren (A-4) and the approver Sailendra Mahto protested to him that Sh. V. Rajeshwar Rao (A-8) has not fulfilled promise. He conveyed this protest to P.W. 140 Vijay Handa who in turn conveyed it to A-8 on the same day.

(D) It is in evidence that on 30-7-1993 Shri D.K. Audikesavulu (A-12) withdrew cash to the tune of Rs. 50,95,474 and M. Thimmegowda (A-13) got a temporary over draft of Rs. one crore sanctioned and withdrew the said amount. It is also in the evidence that both these accused took care to withdraw these amounts with multiple bank transactions so that the withdrawals may not be directly linked to them. (Reference may be made to the statements of PW 158, PW 159, PW 162 to PW 165 and documents 602 to 608, 655, 656, 644, 665 of A-12 and PW 155 to PW 157, PW 160, 167 and documents Nos. D-594 to 601, 609, to 643, 652 for A-13.

(E) It has also come in evidence that on 30-7-1993, A-13 delivered two suit cases at the residence of M. Veerappa Moily (A-11) and thereafter on the same day by evening flight A-9 and A-10 left Bangalore for Delhi alongwith three suit-cases and one bag which they took from the residence of A-11 (Reference may be made to the statements of PW-173 Parameshwar cook of A 11, PW 174 Shri P.V. Nagraj and PW-175 Shri T.R. Suresh, staff member at official residence of A-11.

(F) It is in evidence that Sh. Buta Singh also travelled to Delhi in the same flight and Shri D.K. Audikesavulu (A-12) also travelled to Delhi by the same flight with one suit case.

(G) It has also come in the evidence discussed above that aforesaid suit-cases of money which were brought from Bangalore were carried on 31.7.1993 to Andhra Bhawan, where A-9 to A-12 and others met V. Rajeshwar Rao at his flat and thereafter they all came down and ultimately aforesaid suit cases and the bag were delivered at the residence of Suraj Mandal. (A3).

(H) All these circumstances show active involvement of V. Rajeshwar Rao (A-8) in the conspiracy in the form of participation in negotiations with JMM MPs. and arrangement of money and delivery thereof at the residence of Suraj Mandal (A-3).

(f) CIRCUMSTANCES AGAINST ACCUSED H.M. REVANNA, RAMALINGA REDDY, M VEERAPPA MOILY, D.K. AUDIKESAVULU. AND M. THIMOOGOWDA – CBI COURT

(A) while discussing the prima facie evidence against A-8, I have enumerated the evidence to the effect that A-8 and A-12 were camping at Delhi during the crucial period and thereafter an exercise of mobilisation of huge funds was carried on at Bangalore by A-12 and A-13 with a sense of urgency and with an apparent effort to cover their effect by indulging in multiple bank transactions for withdrawal of the cash.

(B) It is also in the evidence collected by the prosecution that A-11 and A-12 had left Delhi for Bangalore on 29-7-1993 (reference be made to D-591). From the statements of staff at the official residence of A-11, referred to above, it is *prima facie* clear that A-9 and A-10, had arrived at the residence of A-11 on 30-7-1993. On the same day A-13 delivered two suit-cases at the residence of A-11. Thereafter, in the evening A-9 and A-10 left the residence of A-11 alongwith the said two suit-cases as well as one other suit-case and a bag and took flight for Delhi. A-12 also reached the Airport with one suit-case and boarded the same flight. Similarly, A-7 also left for Delhi in the same flight.

(C) It has also come in evidence that after reaching at Delhi A-9, A-10 and A-12 went to Andhra Bhawan and met A-8. Thereafter, they went to Hotel Claridges where A-9 and A-10 stayed while A-12 went to MBDL Guest House, New Friends Colony. On the next morning A-12 reached at Claridges Hotel and from there he alongwith A-9 and A-10 went to Andhra Bhawan and met A-8 and thereafter the aforesaid suit-cases and bag brought by them were delivered at the residence of Suraj Mandal in the forenoon of 31-7-1993. (Reference may be made to the statements of PW 143, PW 181, PW 121, PW 146, PW 142, PW 147, PW 172 to PW 175 and documents D-581 to D-585, D-589 to D-590 and D-759).

(D) These circumstances raise a strong suspicion to the effect that accused Nos. A-9 to A-13 have taken active part in mobilisation of funds from Bangalore and delivery thereof to accused Suraj Mandal (A-3).

(E) It has been argued on behalf of A-9 to A-13 that their alleged role as per prosecution is after the defeat of 'no confidence motion' *i.e.* the accomplishment of object of conspiracy. As such they cannot be termed as conspirators.

(F) It is also submitted that there is nothing on the record to suggest that A-9 to A-13 were aware of the purpose for which the money was allegedly brought to Delhi and as such they should be discharged.

(G) I do not agree with this contention firstly because the conspiracy continued till the illegal act of payment of bribe to the respective MPs was accomplished.

(H) From the circumstances enumerated here, the money brought from Bangalore was delivered to A-3, therefore, its moblisation and delivery to A-3 was an act in furtherance of the conspiracy.

(I) Further more circumstances discussed above show that money has been withdrawn from the bank with the sense of urgency and in clandestine manner which raise a presumption of effort to cover up their tracks on the part of A-12 and A-13. This circumstance raise a presumption about their knowledge of purpose for which the money was being arranged and sent to Delhi. Moreover, it is also in evidence that after bringing the money A-9, A-10 and A-12 had met A-8 and even before sending the money for delivery, they had met A-8. This circumstance also raise a strong suspicion of their complicity in the conspiracy with the knowledge.

(g) CIRCUMSTANCES OF SH. BHAJAN LAL (A-14) – CBI COURT

(A) From the statements of PW-191 to PW 193 it prime facie appears that Bhajan Lal (A-14) visited the residence of A-15 on 24-7-1993 in the morning. He requested Ajit Singh (A-15) to support Congress (I) and stated that fate of the Government headed by A-1 was in his hand. PW 191 has also stated that on the said morning A-14 also delivered three packets to Ajit Singh. One of which packets was later on opened by Ajit Singh and it was found to contain 200 wads of currency notes of Rs. 500 denomination so as to suggest the delivery of Rs. 300 crores to A-15.

(B) Besides, that I have already discussed the role of Bhajan Lal (A-14) to win over the members of JD-A break-away group while discussing the role of Capt. Satish Sharma (A-2).

(C) PW 75 Shri Mukhiya has stated that on 23-7-1993 A-4 had meeting with JMM. MPs. in hotel Holiday-Inn and he later on admitted about the payments to be made to JMM MPs.

(D) PW 191 Dilawar Singh has stated that on 26-7-1993 R.L.S. Yadav (A-16) visited Ajit Singh (A-15) and demanded his share of Rs. 15 lakhs from the amount which he had received from Shri Bhajan Lal.

(E) On 27-7-1993 Sh. Bhajan Lal (A-15) visited the residence of A-1 during night time at 2-30 AM and remained there for one hour (reference be made to PW 190).

(F) on. 27-7-1993 meeting of 7 MPs, belonging to break-away group of JD(A) took place at the residence of Ram Lakhan Singh Yadav (A-16) which was also attended by Bhajan Lal (A-14) and Capt. Satish Sharma (A-2). During said discussion A-14 assured those MPs, the payment of large sum in cash while Capt. Satish Sharma (A-2) assured them petrol pumps (reference be made to statements of PW. 191, PW 237, PW 210 and PW 240).

(G) On 28-7-1993 six MPs, of JD (A) break-away group met at the residence of A-16. A-14 and A-2 also visited them. During said meeting A-14 and A-2 assured petrol pumps and Rs. 20 lakhs each to every member of said group before the voting and another Rs. 20 lakhs each after the voting. Sh. Bhajan Lal also delivered suit- cases at the residence of Ram Lakhan Singh Yadav (A-16) on the same day after which son of A-16 informed the MPs. present there that Bhajan Lal (A-14) has fulfilled his promise. During the said meeting, Bhajan Lal on the receipt of telephone call from Shri V.C. Shukla had gone away for half an hour and returned back alongwith Haji Gulam Mohd. Khan (A-21) (reference may be made to statements of witnesses PW- 191, PW 210, PW 240, PW 237 and PW 244).

(H) Besides this, there is also evidence of meeting of Bhajan Lal with various participants of this conspiracy on several occasions. There is also evidence on record in the form of statements of PW 227 to PW 229 that during the relevant period, Bhajan Lal was actively mobilising the funds and witness PW 199 Varinder Singh has stated that during the public meeting at Hissar on 11-8-1993, Bhajan Lal had voluntarily admitted of having engineered defection of 7 MPs. of JD(A) within 48 hrs.

(I) All these circumstances raise a strong suspicion of complicity of accused Bhajan Lal (A-14) in the conspiracy of and his active participation in mobilizing the funds and inducement and bribing of the MPs.

(h) CIRCUMSTANCES AGAINST SH. AJIT SINGH (A-15) – CBI COURT

(A) Main circumstances against him is that on 24-7-1993 Bhajan Lal (A-14) visited his residence for a break-fast meeting where he requested him to save Government of Shri P.V. Narasimha Rao (A-1). PW 191 Capt. Dilawar Singh has stated that while leaving A-14 delivered three packets to A-15. One of those packets was later on opened and it was found to contain 20 packets of Rs. 500 currency notes. He has also stated that Ajit Singh (A-15) made him to promise to keep the transaction secret. This circumstance prima facie show the involvement of Ajit Singh (A-15) in the conspiracy and also the factum of his having accepted illegal gratification.

(B) It is argued on behalf of A-15 that version of PW 191 is not reliable because it is not corroborated by the statement of any other witness and also because no money had been recovered from the possession of Ajit Singh. He has submitted that if such a huge amount had been paid to the accused, some of which should have been recovered during investigation.

(C) This is the stage of framing of charge and at this stage, court is to take a *prima facie* view of the matter and it is not supposed to analyse the evidence with a view to determine the correctness or falsehood of the statements of witnesses made during investigation. PW 191 is categorical in his statement, therefore this testimony cannot be rejected. There can be so many reasons for non-recovery of the amount on which I do not wish to comment at this stage. Thus, I do not find any force in contention of Ld. Counsel for A-15.

(i) CIRCUMSTANCES AGAINST ACCUSED RAM LAKHAN SINGH YADAV, RAM SHARAN YADAV, ROSHAN LAL, ANANDI CHARAN DAS, ABHAY PRATAP SINGH AND HAJI GULAM MOHD. KHAN – CBI COURT

(A) PW 191 Capt. Dilawar Singh has stated that on 26-7-1993, Ram Lakhan Singh Yadav visited the house of A-15 and demanded his share of Rs. 15 lakhs from the amount which A-15 had received from Sh. Bhajan Lal.

(B) On 27-7-1993 Ajit Singh called a meeting of JD (A) MPs. in which Ram Lakhan Singh Yadav (A-16), charged Ajit Singh (A-15) for hob-nobbing and bargaining with Congress Leaders and thereafter he left the meeting alongwith A-17 to A-20 and late Shri G.C. Munda. (Reference be made to statement of PWs. 191, 210, 225 and 240).

(C) On the same day meeting of 7 MPs belonging to JD (A) break- away group took place at the residence of A-16 which was also attended by Bhajan Lal and Capt. Satish Sharma in which they were assured payment of large sum in cash as well as allotment of petrol pumps to them and their family members. In the said meeting A-16 also spoke to A-1 and assured that his Group would split by the evening (reference be made to statements of PWs. 191, 237. 210 and 240).

(D) On 28-7-1993 six MPs. namely A-16 to A-20 and late Shri G.C. Munda again assembled at the residence of A-16. Capt. Satish Sharma and Bhajan Lal also visited them. During that meeting they offered them petrol pumps and a sum of Rs. 20 lakhs each before the voting and another sum of Rs. 20 lakhs each after the voting. Bhajan Lal also delivered suit-cases at the residence of A-16 on the same day and son of A-16 thereafter informed the MPs. present there that Bhajan Lal had fulfilled his promise. During this meeting on the receipt of telephone call from V.C. Shukla, Bhajan Lal (A-14) left for sometime and came back alongwith Haji Gulam Mohd. Khan (A-21) (reference may be made to statements of PWs. 191, 210, 240, 237 and 244)

(E) From the statements of PWs. 213, 232, and 238 and documents D-686 to 717, 753 and 754, it is *prima facie* clear that sometime after defeat of 'no confidence motion' huge amounts were laundered by Prakash Singh son of Ajit Singh (A-16) with the advice of Anil Sanghi Chartered Accountant. There are also circumstances regarding investments made by A-17 and A-18 in property as well as banks.

(F) From the statements of PW. 110 R.K. Jain and PW. 237 Gopi, it *prima facie* appears that later on altercation took place between late G.C. Munda, and Ram Lakhan Singh Yadav regarding the distribution of money and Sh. Munda also made complaint to A-4 and A-14 about non-fulfillment of promises made by them.

(G) All these circumstances raise a strong suspicion of complicity of JD (A) break-away Group MPs. A-16 to A-20 in the conspiracy and also regarding their having received illegal gratification for using their franchise against 'no-confidence motion'.

CASE IS MADE OUT FOR FRAMING OF CHARGES AGAINST ALL ACCUSED – CBI COURT

22. In view of the circumstances discussed above, I am of the opinion that there is sufficient evidence on the record to justify framing of charges against all the accused persons.

23. So far as accused Nos. A-1, A-2, A-7, A-8 to A-14 are concerned there is sufficient evidence on record to justify framing of charge under section 120B, IPC read with sections 7, 12 and 13(2) read with section 13(1)(d) of the P.C. Act and also for substantive offence punishable under section 12 of the P.C. Act, 1988 against all of them.

24. So far as accused nos. 3 to 5 and 15 to 21 are concerned, there is sufficient evidence on record to justify framing of charges under section 120B, IPC read with sections 7, 12 and 13(2) read with section 13(1)(d) as well as charges for substantive offence punishable under section 7 of the P.C. Act and section 13(2) read with section 13(1)(d) of the P.C. Act. There is also prima facie evidence of commission of offence under section 193, IPC by accused Nos. 3 to 5. Therefore, they are to be charged for that offence also.

ANNOUNCED IN open court.
Dated: 6-5-1997

Sd/-
(AJIT BHARIHOKE)
SPECIAL JUDGE: NEW DELHI.

HIGH COURT OF DELHI

P.V. Narasimha Rao
v.
C.B.I.

Cr. R. Nos. 194, 195, 197, 213, 214, 215, 218, 220, 231, 233, 234, 246, 249, 270, 284, 285, 305, 308 of 1997

Decided on 12 September 1997

The Judgment was delivered by: JUSTICE JASPAL SINGH

Jaspal Singh, J.—1. What is the best way to win political foes? Persuasion? Understanding? Love? Compassion? Dale Conegie's Sermons? The sordid facts giving rise to these revision petitions against framing of charges show that the secret of success lies, at least with regard to some, in mastering the art of transferring one's own bulging wallets into the eager pockets of others.

2. More a little later.

IN 1991 ELECTIONS – P.V. NARASIMHA RAO OF CONGRESS PARTY WAS PRIME MINISTER – HIGH COURT

3. Narasimha Rao, one may recollect, was, not long time ago, the Prime Minister of India. In the General Elections in 1991 though his party, the Congress (I), had emerged as a single largest party, yet it needed the support of at least 14 more members of Lok Sabha for a simple majority.

NO CONFIDENCE MOVED ON 26 JULY, 1993 – VOTING FIXED FOR 28 JULY, 1993 – MOTION WAS DEFEATED – HIGH COURT

Lack of clear majority and need to win over at least 14 other members of Lok Sabha was felt more acutely when the Government came to know of an impending "Motion of No-confidence", which, in fact, came to be moved on the 26th day of July in the fateful year of 1993. On July 28, 1993, the Motion was lost. How did it happen?

INFLUENTIAL PARTY MEN HELPED TO WIN 14 MPs WITH MONEY – SAYS CBI

Simple. The Prime Minister succeeded in mustering the support of fourteen more Members of Lok Sabha. And, how did he manage to win their support? Well, as we all know no bird soars too high if he soars with his own wings and Narasimha Rao had the wings of many others, available at his elbow. The C.B.I. tells us that Captain Satish Sharma, Buta Singh, V. Rajeshwara Rao, H.M. Revanna, Ramalinga Reddy, M. Veerappa Moily, D.K. Audikeshavalu, M. Thimmegowda and Bhajan Lal were some of the persons to lend their wings. And, how was the task accomplished? "Elementary!", tells the C.B.I. in the manner reminiscent of Sherlock Holmes. "With the applause of money indeed"!

JMM MPs – MPs OF BREAK-AWAY JD(A) GROUP WERE WON OVER – SAYS CBI

4. It is said that there is no more miserable being than one in whom nothing is habitual but indecision. But here with the news of impending No-confidence Motion, the time was running out and indecision could indeed spell doom. The stage was thus set and the assigned roles played and if CBI is to be believed though the centre-stage remained to be Delhi, no mean role was to be played on the stage set in Bangalore. In Delhi the targets were the JMM MPs and the MPs belonging to JD (A) led initially by Ajit Singh but later some of them hijacked by Ram Lakhan Singh Yadav. The first group was to be tackled by a Captain known by the name of Satish Sharma with Buta Singh, V. Rajeshwara Rao and others in the toe and the second by yet another hero of many a political battles Bhajan Lal though the Captain's shadow was to cast its own spell there too. As for Bangalore, it was principally there where money was to be largely collected to make the proverbial mare go.

JMM MPs MET NARASIMHA RAO THROUGH BUTA SINGH ON 26 JULY 1993 – DEAL SETTLED – SAYS CBI

5. With the "No-confidence Motion" hanging over the head of the Government like the Sword of Democles, the JMM MPs scented blood. While Simon Marandi got in touch with Captain Satish Sharma and found him too willing to extend promises of reward in cash and kind, Bhajan Lal too was found as willing as David Coperfield's Barkes. But then JMM MPs were in no mood to take chances, Shailendra Mahto met Ashok Rao Deshmukh and expressed his desire to meet the Supremo Narasimha Rao. On July 25 Deshmukh contacted Narasimha Rao and told him about his meeting with Mahto. Rao asked him to ascertain the demand of the JMM MPs. Shailendra Mehto, however, insisted upon meeting Rao directly. When informed about it, Narasimha Rao advised Ashok Rao Deshmukh to take them to V. Rajeshwara Rao. So directed, Deshmukh took them on the 26th to V. Rajeshwara Rao. It appears that the meeting was not a success since the amount offered was felt to be not enough. The same night Buta Singh took the JMM MPs to the residence of Prime Minister Narasimha Rao, who, too, realising that it was time to do or die, promised with great alacrity reward in cash in exchange of help. The die was thus, cast.

BREAK-AWAY GROUP OF JD(A) MPs LED BY RAM LAKHAN PROMISED SUPPORT – IN LIEU OF MONEY – PETROL PUMPS – SAYS CBI

6. In the meanwhile, Bhajan Lal, who was in constant touch with Narasimha Rao, had opened yet another front. His target was the JD (Ajit Singh) and its MPs. On July 24 he visited the house of Ajit Singh, the leader of the group, told him that he had been sent by Prime Minister Narasimha Rao for seeking his help, gave him rupees two crores and in return demanded not only his own but his group's support as well. It appears that though the booty was meant to be shared, Ajit Singh wanted to have the whole of it. It so happened that on July 26 when Ram Lakhan Singh Yadav, demanded his own share, Ajit Singh refused. He rather denied having received any amount from Bhajan Lal. However, Ram Lakhan Singh remained unconvinced and determined not to let the great opportunity pass by, formed a breakaway group of his own. In the meeting of that group on the 27th, Bhajan Lal assured them huge sums of money in cash, and Captain Satish Sharma assured allotment of Petrol Pumps either in their names or in the names of their relatives. The payment in cash was to be made in two instalments of Rs. 20 lakhs each. The first before the voting and the second thereafter. And, honouring that commitment, all the seven MPs of the break-away group led by Ram Lakhan Singh Yadav received Rs. 20 lakhs each on the 28th and that too before leaving for the Parliament.

NO-CONFIDENCE MOTION DEFEATED ON 28 JULY, 1993 AS PLANNED – SAYS CBI

7. The No-confidence Motion was lost on the 28th. The four JMM MPs and seven MPs of the Ram Lakhan Singh Yadav group voted against the Motion. And, on the 29th and the 30th, the JMM MPs received a part of the promised booty. For the rest, arrangements were being made in Bangalore.

MONEY PAID TO JMM MPs IN GUNNY BAGS AND SUIT-CASES – SAYS CBI

8. What was cooking at Bangalore? This is what the C.B.I. tells us.

9. M. Veerappa Moily, the Chief Minister of Karnataka who had camped at Delhi and had been in touch with the Prime Minister and men like V. Rajeshwara Rao and Captain Satish Sharma, rushed back to Bangalore. He was followed by D.K. Audikeshavalu a close friend of Moily. On the 29th and the 30th D.K. Audikeshavalu collected a total sum of Rs. 50,95,474 from the Banks by means of three cheques. M. Thimmegowda, yet another close friend of Moily, was also not sitting idle. On the 30th of July he approached the Branch Manager of the Canara Bank, Sheshadaripuram Branch, Bangalore for an over-draft of rupees one crore for ten days and the same evening but after banking hours got the amount in cash. He also issued three cheques, one for Rs. 60 lakhs, the second for Rs. 25 lakhs and the third for Rs. 15 lakhs. The first was in favour of M/s. Ranganathan Group and the second in favour of M/s. Yellamma Group. The third was drawn in favour of self. The amounts were withdrawn in cash the same day. After having made the withdrawals, M. Thimmegowda put the money in two big V.I.P. suit-cases and delivered the same to M. Veerappa Moily in the presence of H.M. Revanna and Ramalinga Reddy. The same evening H.M. Revanna and Ramalinga Reddy left the residence of M. Veerappa Moily with three suit-cases and a hand bag for Bangalore Airport. Those suit-cases included the two brought by M. Thimmegowda. D.K. Audikeshavalu also reached there with one V.I.P. suit-case and then all the three reached Delhi at 10.30 hours and went straight to Andhra Bhawan spending some time with V. Rajeshwara Rao. On the morning of 31st July D.K. Audikeshavalu, H.M. Revanna and Ramalinga Reddy alongwith their suit-cases and the hand-bag went again to Andhra Bhawan in a taxi and a Maruti car accompanied by Vijay Handa and one Harsharan Lal and after having remained closeted with V. Rajeshwara Rao for about half-an-hour delivered the precious cargo to Suraj Mandal, the JMM MP.

10. We are told that two days before the deliveries made by D.K. Audikeshavalu and H.M. Revanna, that is on the 29th, five suit-cases and one bag had been delivered at the residence of Suraj Mandal and that on the 30th too he had received an assignment comprising three gunny bags and one suit-case The same day Simon Marandi after having collected three of the said gunny bags and a suit-case, rushed to the house of Shailendra Mahto. Out of the said gunny bags and suit-cases, Simon Marandi collected three gunny bags and one suit-case. This was on the 30th. The same day he also collected a sum of Rs. 10 lakhs from B.N. Safaya, Addl. Private Secretary of Capt. Satish Sharma. We are further told that the same evening Shibu Soren too collected one bag and a suit-case from the residence of Suraj Mandal.

FOUR JMM MPs DEPOSITED SOME MONEY IN INDIVIDUAL AND JOINT ACCOUNT IN PNB DELHI – SAYS CBI

11. Confucius says that when prosperity comes, do not use all of it. Inspired, perhaps, by the advice of the Sage-philosopher, the four JMM MPs namely Suraj Mandal, Shibu Soren, Simon Marandi and Shailendra Mahto decided to keep a part of the booty in the safe lockers of a Bank. They thus went to the Punjab National Bank, Noroji Nagar Branch, New Delhi on the 31st, where Suraj Mandal made a deposit of Rs. 30 lakhs in his own name in the S.F. Account No. 17108. Shailendra Mahto got opened one Sugam F.D. Account No. 196 by making a deposit of Rs. 39.80 lakhs. It was joint in his own name and in the name of his wife Abha. Shibu Soren too got opened a joint F.D. account in his own name and in the names of his wife and two sons with a deposit of Rs. 30 lakhs. Simon Marandi too did not lag behind. While on the 1st of August he deposited Rs. 12 lakhs and had got opened a joint F.D. account in his own name and in the name of his wife, on the 2nd he deposited another sum of Rs. 21 lakhs in the F.D. account got opened by him a day earlier. All the four of them also got opened one joint Fixed Deposit Account No. 195 for Rs. 30 lakhs besides one joint S.F. account with a deposit of Rs. 10,000.

3 SEPARATE CHALLANS FILED BY CBI – CBI COURT ORDERS FRAMING OF CHARGES – HIGH COURT

12. The sordid story of political corruption as unfolded above, led to the filing of three separate charge-sheets by the C.B.I. and on May 6, 1997 the learned Special Judge ordered framing of charges against P.V. Narasimha Rao, Captain Satish Sharma, Buta Singh, V. Rajeshwara Rao, H.M. Revanna, Ramalinga Reddy, M. Veerappa Moily, D.K. Audikeshavalu, M. Thimmegowda and Bhajan Lal under section 120B of the Indian Penal Code read with sections 7, 12 and 13(2) read with section 13(1)(d) of the Prevention of Corruption Act, 1988 and so also under section 12 of the Prevention of Corruption Act, 1988.

13. The learned Special Judge also ordered framing of charges against Suraj Mandal, Shibu Soren, Simon Marandi, Ajit Singh, Ram Lakhan Singh Yadav, Ram Saran Yadav, Roshan Lal, Anandi Charan Das, Abhey Pratap Singh and Haji Mohd. Khan under section 120B of the Indian Penal Code read with sections 7, 12, 13(2) read with section 13(1)(d) as well as under sections 7 and 13(2) read with section 13(1)(d) of the Prevention of Corruption Act, 1988.

14. As against Shibu Soren and Suraj Mandal charge was also ordered to be framed under section 193 of the Indian Penal Code.

15. The narrative that we find above, is shorn of details, some perhaps material. However, I thought it necessary to give a thumb-nail view of the case only with an idea to give a feel of the case and to prepare for what is to follow.

ORDER OF CBI COURT CHALLENGED ON 6 GROUNDS – NARRATED IN BRIEF – HIGH COURT

16. Broadly speaking, the challenge to the impugned order was six-fold. The first ground of attack rested on Article 105 of the Constitution of India. My attention was particularly drawn to clauses (2) and (3) of Article 105 of the Constitution and it was contended that even if the allegations of the prosecution were accepted, the Court would have no jurisdiction to fasten any criminal liability on the petitioners as whatever allegedly happened was in respect of the votes given by some of them in the Lok Sabha and that, in any case, whatever transpired, touched the privileges of the House within the meaning of clause (3) of Article 105 of the Constitution. The second contention was that the members of Lok Sabha hold no office and as such are not public servants within the meaning of section 2(c) of the Prevention of Corruption Act, 1988 (hereinafter referred to as the Act of 1988) and that for that reason the Act of 1988 would not apply to the alleged acts of omission and commission of the petitioners. *Thirdly*, it was argued that even if it be taken that members of Lok Sabha do fall within the definition of section 2(c) of the Act and are thus taken to be public servants, yet the Act would not apply for the simple reason that in the case of Lok Sabha members there is no authority competent to remove them from their office within the meaning of section 19(1)(c) of the Act. The next argument was that sanction was required under section 197 of the Code of Criminal Procedure to prosecute P.V. Narasimha Rao. Fifthly it was contended that in case of P.V. Narasimha Rao, M. Thimmegowda, H.M. Revanna, Ramalinga Reddy and Moily there was nothing to show that they had conspired or were part of any conspiracy. Lastly, it was argued that even on facts no case was made out for framing of the charges.

PETITIONERS PROTECTED BY ARTICLES 105 AND 19 OF THE CONSTITUTION – LAW COURTS HAVE NO JURISDICTION – SUBMIT PETITIONERS – ARTICLE 105 REPRODUCED – HIGH COURT

17. Since the first contention revolved around Article 105 of the Constitution of India, I think I would rather do well to reproduce it at this very stage. It reads as under:

> "105. Powers, privileges, etc., of the Houses of Parliament and of the members and committees thereof.—
>
> (1) Subject to the provisions of this Constitution and to the rules and standing orders regulating the procedure of Parliament, there shall be freedom of speech in Parliament.
>
> (2) No member of Parliament shall be liable to any proceedings in any Court in respect of anything said or any vote given by him in Parliament or any committee thereof, and no person shall be so liable in respect of the publication by or under the authority of either House of Parliament of any report, paper, votes or proceedings.
>
> (3) In other respects, the powers, privileges and immunities of each House of Parliament, and of the members and the committees of each House, shall be such as may from time to-time be defined by Parliament by law, and, until so defined, shall be those of that House and of its members and committees immediately before the coming into force of section 15 of the Constitution (Forty-fourth Amendment) Act, 1978.
>
> (4) The provisions of clauses (1), (2) and (3) shall apply in relation to persons who by virtue of this Constitution have the right to speak in, and otherwise to take part in the proceedings of, a House of Parliament or any committee thereof as they apply in relation to members of Parliament."

18. Before the Constitution (44th Amendment) Act, 1978 in clause (3) instead of the words "shall be those of that House and of its members and committees immediately before the coming into force of section 15 of the Constitution (Forty-fourth Amendment) Act, 1978 ", the words were:

> "Shall be those of the House of Commons of the Parliament of the United Kingdom, and of its members and committees at the commencement of this Constitution."

19. It was contended that while clause (1) of the Article confers freedom of speech on members of Parliament independently of, and uncontrolled by, anything in Article 19(1)(a), Clause (2) goes one step further than clause (1), in one respect, namely, legal immunity of Members of Parliament for anything said in the Parliament or in respect of any vote given by them in Parliament or in any Committee thereof. It was argued that in view of clause (2) no action in a Court of law lies "in respect of" anything said or any vote given and that the immunity is complete and is based on the principle that it is of the essence of the Parliamentary system of Government that people's representatives should be free to express themselves and/or to vote without fear of legal consequences. Laying particular emphasis on the words "in respect of" it was contended that whatever happens even outside the precincts of the Parliament but in respect of any voting in Parliament would also be immune from legal consequences in a Court of Law. In other words, the contention was that even if the allegations of the prosecution were to be accepted, as the process of winning over the voters even by means of illegal gratification, was "in respect of" the voting in Parliament, the immunity extended to those acts as well and that any action taken under the Act of 1988 with regard to the same would be in violation of Article 105. In support my attention was drawn to certain authorities to which reference may be made.

PRIOR LAW RELIED UPON BY THE PETITIONERS – HIGH COURT

20. The first judgment on which reliance was placed is by a Full Bench of this Court in **Tej Kiran Jain v. N. Sanjiva Reddy, 1971 (7) DLT 1 (FB)** wherein it was held that the words "anything said" in clause (2) of Article 105 were of the widest amplitude and it was not permissible to read any limitation therein and further that the object of the provision obviously was to secure absolute freedom of discussion in Parliament and to allay any apprehension of a legal proceeding in respect of anything said in Parliament by a member thereof.

* * * * *

25. To continue with the narrative of the points urged on behalf of the petitioners, I may mention that it was also argued that the Courts cannot look into the pattern of voting in the Lok Sabha nor can the Courts use the same as evidence to support of the charge of corruption and in support reliance was placed on **Church of Scientology v. Johnson Smith, (1972) 1 QB 522 and R. v. Secretary of State, (1983) 2 All ER 233.**

In England, the concept of "Parliamentary privilege" had begun to assume a coherent form by 1450 with an address by the Speaker to the Monarch claiming "the ancient rights and privileges of the Commons." Earlier analysis of privilege assumed the Commons and Lords were "Superior Courts" having exclusive power over all matters within their claimed jurisdiction. As expressed by Coke CJ (1 Inst. 15):

> "Every Court of Justice hath rules and customs for its directions... It is lex *et consuetude parliamenti* that all weighty matters in any Parliament moved concerning the peers of the realm, or common in Parliament assembled, ought to be determined, adjudged, and discussed by the course of the Parliament, not by the civil law nor yet by the common laws of this realm used in more inferior Courts".

Coke's treatise, however, offers no clear guidance as to the legal status of the *lex et consuetude parliamenti vis-a-vis* statute and common law. However, much before the Revolution was fought, three cases of great significance stood decided. They were **Haxey's** case **(1397), Strode's** case **(1512) and Sir John Elliot's** case **(1629).** In each of these cases the freedom of speech, debate and proceeding as the privilege of the House was established. Finally, and after having witnessed the saga of Peter Wentworth's defence of freedom of discussion in the Commons and the case of the Five Members (1641) which heard the courageous speaker say, while defying the King's direct command to reveal the whereabouts of the five Members:

> "May it please Your Majesty, I have neither eyes to see, nor tongue to speak in this place but as this House is pleased to direct, whose servant I am."

Came the Revolution and with it came the Declaration of Right which stressed the Commons' "independence" from interference of the Crown and the Courts. This later came to be expressed in Article 9 of the Bill of Rights, 1689 which expressed:

> "That the freedom of speech, and debates or proceedings in Parliament ought not to be impeached or questioned in any Court or place out of Parliament."

Though it was felt by some that by enacting Article 9, the pre-existing privileges enjoyed by the two Houses stood abolished, many feel that Article 9 was merely declaratory and not enacting (See: *Erskine May, Parliamentary Practice*). Just twelve years after the 1688 settlement, a legislation was enacted entitled:

> "An Act for preventing any inconveniences that may happen by privilege of Parliament". Its main provision, as restated in section 1 of the Parliamentary Privilege Act, 1770, was that:
>
> "Any person may at any time commence and prosecute any action of suit against any Lord of Parliament or any (member) of the House of Commons... or any other person entitled to the privilege of Parliament... and no such action shall at any time be impeached, stayed or delayed by or under colour or pretence of any privilege of Parliament."

This too raised doubts. Did it abolish all aspects of privilege insofar as they restricted access to the Courts, including Article 9? The Privy Council **in Re Parliamentary Privilege Act, 1770, [1958] AC 331** held that the Act did not do away with the MPs' freedom of speech and that the 1700 Act and its successors reached only those legal actions whose origin did not lie in a "proceeding in Parliament" (see *Ian Loveland: Constitutional Law: A Critical Introduction, Butterworths*, 1996). However, the fact remains that a number of privileges have been surrendered or modified over the years. For example, following the Parliamentary Privilege Act, 1770 the privilege of freedom from arrest previously enjoyed by the servants of the Members was extinguished. Similarly, at the beginning of the Second World War, the Privileges Committee concluded that detention of a Member under Emergency Powers legislation should be regarded as akin to arrest under the criminal law, so that no breach of privilege was involved. (See *Erskine May: Parliamentary Practice*).

Despite all the ups and downs some of the privileges remain well-entrenched. The main privileges may be enumerated. They are as under:

> "(i) Freedom of the Members from civil arrest for a period of forty days before to forty days after the meeting of the Parliament. However, this protection was not available with regard to arrests made on criminal charges for an offence or where there was preventive detention by an order of the executive authorities under statutory powers.
>
> (ii) Freedom of speech, debate and proceeding. These freedoms could neither be impeached nor questioned in any Court.
>
> (iii) Power and privilege to commit for contempt. As per Erskine May the main value of this power lay "in upholding the dignity of Parliament and defending it against disrespect and affronts which could not be brought or could only be brought by implication under the head of any of the specific privileges."

LAWS ON PRIVILEGES OF MPs DIFFERENT IN DIFFERENT COUNTRIES – HELD HIGH COURT

26. As would be borne out from above immunities relate primarily to the exercise of parliamentary duties and endorse the principle of non-accountability. Some Constitutions do set limits to the principle of non-accountability with a view to prevent its abuse. For example, under the Constitution of the Federal Republic of Germany immunity does not cover defamation of character and insult even when committed in the course of Parliamentary duties. In Denmark and Iceland too member may be held accountable for their actions if the assembly to which they belong authorises. To some extent similar is the position in Finland and Sweden.

PRIVILEGES AND IMMUNITIES AVAILABLE TO MPs – HELD HIGH COURT

27. In India, clause (3) of Article 105 protects and makes available to the members the same powers privileges and immunities as were enjoyed on the 26th day of January, 1950 by the British House of Commons. I have enumerated above those three main privileges. What is further to be noticed is that in view of clause (2) of Article 105 besides the powers, privileges and immunities enjoyed under clause (3), no member of Parliament shall be liable to any proceedings in any Court in respect of anything said or any vote given by him in Parliament or any Committee thereof.

MPs ENTITLED TO ACTS DONE OUT SIDE THEIR OFFICE – SUBMIT PETITIONERS

28. The argument advanced by Mr. R.K. Anand and others seems to suggest that besides non-accountability, clause (2) of Article 105 benefits the Members from "inviolability" (though this term was not put to use by any Counsel) or protection from legal process which ensures that members of Parliament are protected against legal actions brought against them for acts committed outside the orbit of their office.

29. The powers, privileges and immunities enjoyed both under clauses (2) and (3) proceed on the same ground, *viz.* the necessity that the Parliament and its members should in no way be obstructed in the performance of their high office and important duties and that if there is any such obstruction caused either to the Parliament or to any Member, the remedy should be in the hands of the House. Undoubtedly, the powers, privileges and immunities as provided by clauses (2) and (3) of Article 105 are necessary for the protection of the Parliament and its members. But then "inviolability" has not met with unanimous approval in all Constitutions. Canada and Netherlands, for example, consider that members are well enough protected in criminal and civil matters by the ordinary law.

30. The Members may enjoy all privileges and immunities which may be necessary to ensure freedom of speech and right of vote inside the Parliament, but then in England there has never been any suggestion that "inviolability" could interfere with the working of the Penal law. It applies only in case of civil matters and that too to prevent the arrest of Members for a few days during and after the Session. I have no manner of doubt that with regard to the Penal law the position is no different in India.

NO AUTHORITY IN ENGLISH LAW IF CRIMES COMMITTED IN PARLIAMENT CANNOT BE PUNISHED BY ORDINARY COURTS – HELD HIGH COURT

31. It is true that in **Eliot's** case, **(1629) 3 St Tr 294**; the question whether or not the Court could deal with the assault on the Speaker committed in the House of Commons was expressly left open when the judgment was declared illegal by both Houses but then, as observed by Wade and Phillips, while commenting on that case, there is no authority showing the crimes committed in the precincts of the Parliament cannot be punished by the ordinary courts [See: *Wade and Phillips: Constitutional Law* (8th Edn.) p. 167].

TAKING OF BRIBE BY MPs TO VOTE IN PARTICULAR WAY – MAY BE BREACH OF PRIVILEGE OF BRITISH PARLIAMENT – CANNOT BE USED AS LICENCE TO COMMIT CRIME – DOES NOT OUST JURISDICTION OF CRIMINAL COURTS – SO IS IN INDIA – HELD HIGH COURT

32. Undoubtedly, acceptance of a bribe by any Member of either House to influence him in his conduct as such Member is a breach of privilege and there have been cases where Members of the Commons found guilty of such offence have either been committed [CJ (169-97) 236] or expelled (CJ [(1667-87) 24], (CJ (1693-97) 274]. There is also no doubt that influencing or attempting to influence Members of Parliament may be considered contempt. In 1695 the House of Commons had resolved that "the offer of money, or other advantage, to any Member of Parliament for the promoting of any matter whatsoever, depending or to be transacted in Parliament is a high crime and misdemeanor and tends to the subversion of the English Constitution [CJ (1693-97) 331]. Thus, to offer bribe to a Member of Parliament to influence him in his conduct as a Member has been treated as a breach of privilege [CJ (1697-99) 528]. But then, merely treating the commission of a criminal offence as breach of privilege does not amount to ouster of jurisdiction of the ordinary Courts to try penal offences. To claim that in such matters the Courts would have no jurisdiction would amount to claiming a privilege to commit a crime. And, in this respect reference may be made to **Rex v. Sir R.F. Graham-Campbell, [1935] 1 KB 594**. It was a case relating to sale of intoxicating liquor without licence within the precincts of House of Commons. The applicant applied in the Police Court for summonses against certain members of the Kitchen Committee of the House of Commons and the Managers of the Refreshment department of the House. Of course, the attempt to convict them failed but it was not because Courts have no jurisdiction over criminal offences committed within the precincts of the Parliament but primarily on the ground of the right of the House to regulate its internal affairs.

33. In **Edinburgh & Dalkeith Railway Co. v. Wallchope, (1842) 8 C&F 710**, the House of Lords was asked, but refused to declare a private Act invalid on the ground that it had been passes without notice of intention to introduce having been given to interested parties as required by the Standing Orders of the House of Commons. In **Lee v. Bude & Torrington Junction Railway Co., [1884] 12 QB 271**, the Court of Common Pleas refused to declare a private Act invalid on the ground that it had been obtained by fraudulent recitals. In **Bradlaugh v. Gossett, 1871 (6) LR (CP) 577,** Mr. Charles Bradlaugh, who had been excluded from the House of Commons and from taking the oath upon his election, challenged the order of the House on the ground, *inter alia,* that his position was regulated by the Parliamentary Oaths Act, 1899. The action did not meet with success. These cases and so also the cases referred to by Mr. Anand establish only the elementary proposition that the Houses of the British Parliament are privileged to be the exclusive arbiters of the regularity of their own proceedings. None of the authorities referred to lay down a proposition that ordinary Courts can have no jurisdiction to try criminal offences committed by the Members of Parliament whether within or outside the precincts of the Parliament. And while I am on it, I may mention in some detail the history of the reference by the Commons to the Privy Council **Re. Parliamentary Privilege Act, 1770, [1958] AC 331**. I am doing so only with a view to meet the argument of Mr. Anand that the British Parliament had accepted communications between members and ministers initiated with a view to placing a question as part of "proceeding in Parliament". The cause of Common's reference to the Privy Council was an episode involving Labour MP George Strauss. Strauss had sent a letter to a minister criticizing the London Electricity Board (LEB). The minister forwarded the letter to the Chairman of the LEB who considered the comments in the letter defamatory and threatened libel action. Strauss; claiming that the threat was breach of privilege, referred the matter to the House. The Committee of Privileges felt that the letter was a "proceeding" but the House rejected the Committee's conclusion. Truly, there are still many "grey areas" as suggested by Griffith and Ryle but not, in my view, with regard to the jurisdiction of the Courts to try criminal offences committed by Members as referred to above.

34. It is true that in **Tej Kiran Jain's** case a Full Bench of this Court had held that the words "anything said" are of wide amplitude. It is also true that the words "any proceeding" would cover within their sway civil and criminal action but then these words, as already noticed, only make the Parliament exclusive arbiter of the regularity of its proceedings. These words do not make the Members acquire a prescriptive right to commit a crime. Any such approach would start a thoroughly vicious and destructive process. The privileges of British Parliament do not apply to criminal matters and members of either House are subject to ordinary course of criminal justice (See *Halsbury's Laws of England,* 2nd Edn. Vol. XX, p. 25) and the English Courts have more than once intimated that a crime committed in the House of Commons or by its order would not thereby be considered outside their jurisdiction (See: *Sir William Anson, The Law and Custom of the Constitution,* 5th Edn., Vol. I, p. 186). The position in India is no different.

LOK SABHA LEFT THE DISPUTE TO BE DECIDED BY COURTS – PARLIAMENTARY PROCEEDINGS REPRODUCED – HELD HIGH COURT

35. That jurisdiction of Courts is not ousted is accepted by Lok Sabha also. It appears that on the 11th and 12th of March, 1996 notices of question of privilege were taken up by the Lok Sabha with regard to JMM MPs and were disallowed. I am tempted to reproduce below what appears in '*The Journal of Parliamentary Information*', Volume XLII No. 2, June, 1996, pp. 186-187:

"PRIVILEGE

LOK SABHA

"Alleged payment of large sums of money to some members of the Jharkhand Mukti Morcha in the Lok Sabha for voting against the Motion of No-confidence in the Council of Ministers in July, 1993. Four notices of a question of privilege regarding the alleged payment of large sums of money to some members of the Jharkhand Mukti Morcha (JMM) in the Lok Sabha for voting against the Motion of No-confidence in the Council of Ministers in July, 1993 were received from Sarvashri Jaswant Singh, Indrajit Gupta, Arjun Singh and Jagmeet Singh Brar, all members. The notices dated 26 and 27 February, 1996, received from Shri Jaswant Singh and Shri Indrajit Gupta, respectively, were against their Prime Minister. The notice dated 27 February, 1996, given by Shri Arjun Singh and Shri Jagmeet Singh Brar was against the Prime Minister and Sarvashri Shibu Soren, Suraj Mandal, Simon Marandi and Shailendra Mahto, all members belonging to the JMM in the Lok Sabha (who were said to be the beneficiaries of the alleged pay-offs).

All the said four notices, in support of the contention made therein, relied upon a Press statement issued by Shri Shailendra Mahto, a member. The statement, a copy of which was enclosed by Shri Jaswant Singh with his notice, stated that a meeting of the said four members of the JMM in the Lok Sabha was held with the Prime Minister in the presence of Shri Buta Singh, a member, two days before the voting on the No-confidence on 28 July, 1993. On the basis of an agreement allegedly reached at the said meeting, the members had voted against the Motion of No-confidence and large sums of money were subsequently paid into various Bank Accounts of the said members.

The main contention of the members in their notices was that the Prime Minister was in contempt of the House by allegedly offering inducements to the said four members of the JMM and by trying to influence them in their parliamentary conduct. Shri Arjun Singh further contended that the Prime Minister had aided and abetted the conduct of the said members. Shri Arjun Singh and Shri Jagmeet Singh Brar also contended that those members had committed a breach of privilege and contempt of the House by accepting the 'improper gratification in matter of voting'.

Copies of all the four notices were forwarded to the Prime Minister for his comments. Copies of the notices of Shri Arjun Singh and Shri Jagmeet Singh Brar were also forwarded to the said four members of the JMM for their comments in the matter.

The Prime Minister's comments on the notices of Shri Jaswant Singh were received on 28 February, 1996. In his comments, the Prime Minister, inter alia stated as follows:

The news item appearing in a section of Press and the press release by Shri Shailendra Mahto, MP, are baseless and false. Neither any payments of money were made or arranged to be paid by me to any member of Parliament, nor was any member of Parliament influenced through improper means in his parliamentary conduct, nor was any member of Parliament offered any inducements, fee or reward on the occasion of the Motion of No-confidence moved against the Council of Ministers in July, 1993.

It is also to submit further that no attempt whatsoever has been made to prevent the will of the House and never was there any question of violation of the oath of office under the Constitution.

I would therefore submit to the Hon'ble, Speaker that no breach of privilege has been committed.

The same day, comments of the Prime Minister on the notice of Shri Indrajit Gupta were also received. In his comments, the Prime Minister stated *inter alia* as follows:

The allegations in the published statement of Shri Shailendra Mahto are false and baseless and hence denied. In view of this, the question of, denigration of Parliament does not arise.

I would, therefore, submit to the Hon'ble Speaker that no breach of privilege has been committed.

The comments of the Prime Minister on the notices of Shri Arjun Singh and Shri Jagmeet Singh Brar were received on 6 March, 1996. The Prime Minister, in his comments, stated *inter alia* as under:

The allegation that I have aided and abetted the alleged conduct of the MPs mentioned in the aforesaid notice is false and baseless and hence denied.

I would therefore submit to the Hon'ble Speaker that no breach of privilege or contempt of the House has been committed.

Shri Buta Singh, Member, also addressed a letter to the Speaker, Lok Sabha in which he denied the allegations, stating inter alia that "I totally deny the consideration of any financial dealing. At no stage any money was offered or given to anybody either by me or through me. He also made a personal explanation in this regard during the debate in the House on 28 February, 1996.

Shri Suraj Mandal, Member, while speaking in the House on 28 February, 1996 during the discussion on Motion under Rule 184 regarding the Government's failure to answer charges relating to the '**Hawala**' case and illegal pay-offs to some members of Parliament, also categorically denied the allegations.

On 29 February, 1996, Shri Shailendra Mahto, Member, during his personal explanation in the House, denied the allegation in respect of acceptance of improper gratification by him for not voting in favour of the No-confidence Motion against the Council of Ministers on 28 July, 1993.

On 11 March, 1996, Shri Arjun Singh raised the matter in the House with the permission of the Speaker, Lok Sabha, Shri Shivraj V. Patil. After a prolonged discussion, during which members of all parties expressed their views, the Speaker, disallowing Shri Arjun Singh's notice of question of privilege, observed as follows:

> **... The matter is before the Court which may take a proper decision on the basis of evidence that may be produced before it. Three years back some allegation were voiced about the illegal payments. At that time itself, the House could have been asked to look into it. On the basis of other kinds of inducements, the matter could have been asked to be looked into the House. In view of these facts and the available evidence, I find it very difficult to give the consent.**

The notices of question of privilege given by Sarvashri Jaswant Singh, Indrajit Gupta and Shri Jagmeet Singh Brar were disallowed by the Speaker on 12 March, 1996 in view of his ruling in the House on 11 March, 1996.

36. It was also contended that it is for the Parliament to decide as to whether the act complained of falls within the ambit and scope of the words "in respect of" and that the Courts by embarking upon any enquiry on that aspect of the matter would be in contempt of the House.

CLAUSES (2) AND (3) ARE INTER-CONNECTED – COURTS ALONE CAN INTERPRET IT – HELD HIGH COURT

37. It is, indeed, true that the members of each House of Parliament are the sole Judges whether their privileges have been violated, and whether thereby any person has been guilty of a contempt of their authority [See **Stockdale v. Hansard**] But, then, the rights and privileges spoken of in clause (2) of Article 105 are the creation of the Constitution. Without clause (2), the Houses of Parliament would enjoy no greater privileges than those which fall under clause (3). Thus, clause (2), has to be interpreted by the Courts independently of the Houses of Parliament. In other words, the question as to whether the act complained of falls within the ambit and scope of the words "in respect of anything said or any vote given by him in Parliament" would not be beyond the jurisdiction of the Court. I am conscious of the French view that the ordinary Courts cannot even question the validity of an Act of the legislature but then it is based on French history [See: Prof. A.T. Von Mehren: *"The Judicial Process in the United States and France"* 22 Revista Juridica de La Universidad de Puerto Rica, 1952] and legislation [See: *Constitution of 1971,* Ch. V, Tit. III, Article 3: Article 127 of the Penal Code of 1810] and an extreme form of the doctrine of separation of powers [*See*: Prof. Max Radin, "Judicial Review of Statutes in Continental Europe" 41. West Virginia Law Quarterly, 112 at p. 116] but then the position in India is different. It is the Constitution of India which carves the boundaries and the boundaries so carved are neither fluid, nor elusive, nor obscure.

38. It is pre-eminently desirable that there should arise no dispute between the judiciary and the legislature and that if, unfortunately, it does arise, it should be resolved amicably. As observed by Gajendragadkar, C.J. in **The President's Reference No. 1 of 1964,** (1965) 1 SCR 413:

> **"These two august bodies as well as the Executive which is another constituent of a democratic state must function not in antimony (sic) nor in a spirit of hostility, but rationally, harmoniously and in a spirit of understanding within their respective spheres." I must say, the Lok Sabha, with all respect, did display that spirit of understanding in dealing with the privilege issue referred to above. Surely, one is not to define Parliamentary sovereignty in the formalistic Diceyan sense of blind obedience to statutory words, but in a much more functionalistic vein of giving effect to legislative intent. But to say that Court has no jurisdiction at all to interpret and look at the ambit and scope of clause (2) of Article 105 is a very different thing.**

I regard it, not with tenderness, but with jealousy. True, clause (2) protects individual MPs from criminal or civil liability for statements made inside the Parliament, True also that an MP cannot be prosecuted or made civilly liable for having voted for or against a motion but then I say so because I regard it to be the plain meaning of clause (2) of Article 105. And, it is again for the Court and not for the Parliament to determine in the particular case whether it falls within the fold of clause (2) of Article 105. And, it is in the context that I adopt what was said long-time back in **Stockdale v. Hansard** (supra): If I am to pronounce a judgment at all in this or any other case, it must and shall be the judgment of my own mind, applying the law of the land as I understand it according to the best of my abilities, and with regard to the oath which I have taken to administer justice truly and impartially.

39. I need say no more.

EXPRESSION 'PUBLIC SERVANTS' HAS BEEN DEFINED IN SECTION 2(C) OF THE P.C. ACT, 1988 – HIGH COURT

Are members of Lok Sabha public servants within the meaning of section 2(c) of the Act" This, then, is the next question.

Section 2(c) of the Act defines 'public servant' as follows:

"2 (c) "public servant" means—

(i) any person in the service or pay of the Government or remunerated by the Government by fees or commission for the performance of any public duty;

(ii) any person in the service or pay of a local authority;

(iii) any person in the service or pay of a Corporation established by or under a Central, Provincial or State Act, or an authority or a body owned or controlled or aided by the Government or a Government Company as defined in section 617 of the Companies Act, 1956 (1 of 1956);

(iv) any Judge, including any person empowered by law to discharge, whether by himself or as a member of any body of persons, any adjudicatory functions;

(v) any person authorised by a Court of justice to perform any duty, in connection with the administration of justice, including a liquidator, receiver or commissioner appointed by such Court;

(vi) any arbitrator or other person to whom any cause or matter has been referred for decision or report by a Court of justice or by a competent public authority;

(vii) any person who holds an office by virtue of which he is empowered to prepare, publish, maintain or revise an electoral roll or to conduct an election or part of an election;

(viii) any person who holds an office by virtue of which he is authorised or required to perform any public duty;

(ix) any person who is the president, secretary or other office-bearer of a registered co-operative society engaged in agriculture, industry, trade or banking, receiving or having received any financial aid from the Central Government or a State Government or from any Corporation established by or under a Central, Provincial or State Act, or any authority or body owned or controlled or aided by the Government or a Government Company as defined in section 617 of the Companies Act, 1956 (1 of 1956);

(x) any person who is a chairman, member or employee of any Service Commission or Board, by whatever name called, or a member of any selection committee appointed by such commission or Board for the conduct of any examination or making any selection on behalf of such Commission or Board;

(xi) any person who is a Vice-Chancellor or member of any governing body, professor, reader, lecturer or any other teacher or employee, by whatever designation called, of any University and any person whose services have been availed of by a University or any other public authority in connection with holding or conducting examinations;

(xii) any person who is an office-bearer or an employee of an educational, scientific, social, cultural or other institution, in whatever manner established, receiving or having received any financial assistance from the Central Government or any State Government, or local or other public authority.

PUBLIC SERVANT IS ALSO DEFINED IN SECTION 21 OF INDIAN PENAL CODE – HIGH COURT

40. Before the coming into force of the Act of 1988, for determining the question as to whether a person was a public servant or not, one had to look towards section 21 of the Indian Penal Code for an answer. Section 21 of the Indian Penal Code does not define what a "public servant" means but enumerates the various functionaries who will be designated as public servants. The section runs as under:

"21. "Public Servant".—The words "public servant" denote a person falling under any of the descriptions hereinafter following, namely:

First: [Repealed by A.D. 1950];

Second: Every Commissioned Officer in the Military Naval or Air Forces of India;

Third: Every Judge including any person empowered by law to discharge, whether by himself or as a member of any body of persons, any adjudicatory functions;

Fourth: Every officer of a Court of Justice (including a liquidator, receiver or commissioner) whose duty it is, as such officer, to investigate or report on any matter of law or fact, or to make, authenticate, or keep any document, or to take charge or dispose of any property, or to execute any judicial process, or to administer any oath, or to interpret, or to preserve order in the Court, and every person specially authorised by a Court of Justice to perform any of such duties;

Fifth: Every juryman, assessor, or member of a Panchayat assisting a Court of justice or public servant;

Sixth: Every Arbitrator or other person to whom any cause or matter has been referred for decision or report by any Court of Justice, or by any other competent public authority;

Seventh: Every person who holds any office by virtue of which he is empowered to place or keep any person in confinement;

Eighth: Every officer of the Government whose duty it is, as such officer, to prevent offences, to give information of offences, to bring offenders to justice or to protect the public health, safety or convenience;

Ninth: Every officer whose duty it is, as such officer, to take, receive or expend any property on behalf of the Government, or to make any survey, assessment or contract on behalf of the Government, or to execute any revenue-process, or to investigate, or to report, on any matter affecting the pecuniary interests of the Government, or to make, authenticate or keep any document relating to the pecuniary interests of the Government, or to prevent the infraction of any law for the protection of the pecuniary interests of the Government;

Tenth: Every officer whose duty it is, as such officer, to take, receive, keep or expend any property, to make any survey or assessment or to levy any rate of tax for any secular common purpose of any village, town or district or to make, authenticate or keep any document for ascertaining the rights of the people of any village, town or district;

Eleventh: Every person who holds any office by virtue of which he is empowered to prepare, publish, maintain or revise an electoral roll or to conduct an election or part of an election; an electoral roll or to conduct an election or part of an election.

Twelfth: Every person—

(a) in the service or pay of the Government or remunerated by fees or commission for the performance of any public duty by the Government;

(b) in the service or pay of a local authority, a corporation established by or under a Central, provincial or State Act or a Government company as defined in section 617 of the Companies Act, 1956 (1 of 1956).

MLA IS NOT A PUBLIC SERVANT UNDER THE OLD PC ACT, 1947 – HELD SUPREME COURT – HIGH COURT

41. In **R.S. Nayak v. A.R. Antulay, (1984) 2 SCC 183** a question arose as to whether an M.L.A. is a public servant or not within the meaning of section 21 of the Indian Penal Code. It was a case under the Prevention of Corruption Act, 1947. It was held by the Supreme Court that, as an M.L.A. does not discharge any judicial function he is not covered by the Third Clause of section 21 and as an M.L.A. is also not empowered to place or keep any person in confinement, he does not fall within the Seventh Clause as well. As regards the Twelfth Clause, it was held that the expression "Government" in section 21(12)(a) denotes the Executive and not the legislative and that even though an M.L.A. receives pay and allowances, he cannot be said to be in the pay of the Government *i.e.* the Executive and as such an M.L.A. would not be a public servant within the meaning of Clause Twelfth also. In paragraph 23 of the judgment it was observed:

"A public servant occupies office which renders him a public servant and occupying the office carries with it the powers conferred on the office. Power generally is not conferred on an individual person. In a society governed by Rule of Law power is conferred on office or acquired by statutory status and the individual occupying the office or on whose status is conferred enjoys the power of office or power flowing from the status. The holder of office alone would have opportunity to abuse or misuse the office. The sections codify a well-recognised Truism that power has the tendency to corrupt. It is the holding of the office which gives an opportunity to use it for corrupt motives. Therefore, the corrupt conduct is directly attributable and flows from the power conferred on the office. Each of the three clauses of sub-section (1) of section 6 uses the expression "office" and the power to grant sanction is conferred on the authority competent to remove the public servant from his office and section 6 requires a sanction before taking cognizance of offences committed by public servants. The removal would bring about cessation of inter-relation between the office and abuse by the holder of the office...... The expression "office" in the three sub-Clauses of section 6(1) would clearly denote that office which the public servant misused or abused for corrupt motives for which he is to be prosecuted and in respect of which a sanction to prosecute him is necessary the competent authority entitled to remove him from that office which he has abused. The inter-relation between the office and its abuse if severed would render section 6 devoid of any office."

MPs ARE NOT PUBLIC SERVANTS – SUBMIT PETITIONERS

42. On the basis of the observations of the Supreme Court reproduced above and the findings arrived at in the judgment, it was contended by Mr. R.K. Anand, Senior Advocate appearing for P.V. Narasimha Rao that an MP not being in the service or pay of the Government or in the service or pay of a local authority or of a corporation established by or under a Central, Provincial or State Act or an authority or a body owned or controlled or ordered by the Government or a Government Company as defined in section 617 of the Companies Act, 1956, he is not covered by clauses (i), (ii) and (iii) of section 2(c) of the Act of 1988 and as he is neither a Judge nor a person empowered by law to discharge, whether by himself or as a member of any body of persons any adjudicatory functions and further as he is neither an Arbitrator nor empowered to prepare, publish, maintain or reverse an electoral roll or to conduct an election or part of an election, he is not covered even under clauses (iv), (v), (vi) and (vii), and further that clause (ix) which relates to an office-bearer of a registered co-operative society, clause (x) which relates to an employee of any Service Commission or Board, clause (xi) which confines itself to a Vice-Chancellor etc. and Clause (xii) which relates to an office-bearer or an employee of an educational and certain other institutions established, receiving or having received financial assistance from the Central or any State Government etc., would also not be attracted.

ADMITTEDLY MPs PERFORM 'PUBLIC DUTIES' – BUT DO NOT HOLD ANY 'OFFICE' – HENCE NOT COVERED BY P.C. ACT, 1988 – SUBMIT PETITIONERS

43. As would be noticed, I left out above any comment on clause (viii). I did it purposely for, while the State banked upon it, Mr. R.K. Anand directed much of the ammunition at it. Let us have another look at clause (viii). As per it:

"2(c) 'public servant' means—

(viii) any person who holds an office by virtue of which he is authorised or required to perform any public duty."

44. It must be said, in all fairness to Mr. R.K. Anand, that it was not disputed that an MP is not only authorised but is required also to perform public duties. However, it was contended that despite the fact that an M.P. is authorised or required to perform certain public duties, he performs them not by virtue of any office. In other words, the contention was that an M.P. occupies no "office" and that as he holds no "office" and as, according to the Supreme Court in **R.S. Nayak v. A.R. Antulay** (supra) the corrupt conduct as delineated in the Prevention of Corruption Act, is directly attributable to and flows from, the power conferred on the office and as there has to be an inter-relation between the office and abuse by the holder of the office, in the case of an M.P., these requirements are wanting thus taking the case out of the reach of the Act.

45. Does an MP hold an "office" within the meaning of clause (viii) of section 2(c) of the Act?

46. To show that an MP was never meant or intended to be included within the definition of 'public servant', I was taken through the history of legislation on the point and upon the Parliamentary debates relating to the Act of 1988.

47. I need not dabble into the historical background as far as it relates to section 21 of the Indian Penal Code. The same stands noticed by the Supreme Court in **R.S. Nayak v. A.R. Antulay** (supra). The Court, after noticing the historical evolution of section 21 and adopting it as an external aid to construction, held that an MLA is not a "public servant' within the meaning of the expression in any of the Clauses of section 21 of the Indian Penal Code.

PETITIONERS REFERRED TO THE PARLIAMENTARY PROCEEDINGS TO SHOW THAT MPs ARE NOT COVERED BY THE PROVISIONS OF P.C. ACT, 1988 – HIGH COURT

48. It was contended that the Prevention of Corruption Act, 1988 brought about no change in the position and that the definition of 'public servant' as contained in Clause (viii) of section 2(c) of the Act does not include MLAs or MPs and in support, my attention was drawn to the following appearing in the Lok Sabha and the Rajya Sabha debates on the Bill which led to the passing of the Act of 1988:

Lok Sabha

"Prevention of Corruption Bill, 1987 page 362

Now, what are the changes this Bill is trying to bring about? Sir, I may submit that this Bill has merely compiled the various provisions of the Indian Penal Code which were prevalent and the Prevention of Corruption Act and the Ordinance put together which as I could see, there is no doubt an enlargement of the definition of a "Public Servant". I do not see what is the rationale behind this enlargement of the public servant. You were anxious to enlarge your jurisdiction. While the investigating agencies and the prosecuting agencies were not even able to meet the fringe of the problem with regard to the corruption that was prevalent among the public servants as defined previously under section 21 of the Indian Penal Code, where was the necessity for you to expand it? Are you able to say that on account of this non-expansion, on account of the original definition which was prevailing previously, the agencies were prevented or were not able to get at the roots of corruption. It is not your case at all. Now in the expanded definition you have included elected presidents of cooperative societies. If I am not wrong, in this definition you have included also elected MLAs and MPs within the definition of public servant. You have not stated that elected MPs as well as MLAs also come within the meaning of this Bill. Is it your intention to include MLAs and MPs within the sphere of this Bill. Please make it clear because by reading the definition one gets the impression that if he is merely discharging his public duties whether he is appointed by a Government or not, he will be deemed to be a public servant. The definition is very sweeping:

"Any person who holds an office by virtue of which he is authorised or required to perform any public duty"

Explanation I says:

> "Persons falling under any of the above sub-clauses are public servants, whether appointed by the Government or not."

Prevention of Corruption Bill, 1987 pages 422-424

SHRI P. CHIDAMBARAM

You cannot do it in that manner. That kind of Code will take decades to pass. What we are trying to do is to make a penal law, a bill for a penal law which can only create offences and specify penalties and this Bill, I believe, does it. We have to supplement this with other laws. Sir, a number of questions have been raised about certain provisions of the Bill. Since Members by and large have accepted the provisions of the Bill, I do not want to dilate upon them. Let me point out one or two things. For example, a Minister is a public servant. Therefore, there is no doubt about the fact that a Minister would certainly be covered by this Bill. A question has been raised what is the position of a Member of Parliament or a member of a Legislative Assembly? We have not done anything different or contrary to the law as it stands today. Under the law, as it stands today, the Supreme Court has held in **Antulay's** case that a Member of the Legislative Assembly is not a public servant within the meaning of section 21 of the Indian Penal Code.

I personally think that it is very difficult to say when an MLA or an MP becomes a public servant. I believe that when an MP functions *qua* MP, perhaps he is not a public servant and therefore, we are not attempting a definition which will lead to difficulties. We think that there could be situations when an MP or an MLA does certain things which are really not part of his duties as an MP or an MLA. We think that an MP or an MLA could in certain circumstances hold an office where he will be discharging certain public duties. These two situations are covered by this Act. If an MP or an MLA does certain acts not *qua* MP or *qua* MLA, but as an individual, abusing his position, I am not using the word 'Office', I think he will be covered like any other individual under sections 8, 9 and 12. When an MP or an MLA holds an office, and by virtue of that office he has to discharge certain public duties, I think he will be covered under section 2 clause (b) read with section 2 clause (c), sub-clause (viii). I think these two situations are quite adequate to take care of defaulting Members of Parliament and defaulting members of the Legislative Assemblies. If any other situation arises in future, we shall certainly consider amending the Act at a suitable time. We are trying to fit this in with the pronouncement of the Supreme Court and at the same time taking note of the felt needs of the situation.

Sir, a question has been asked who will be the competent authority to sanction such a prosecution. The question itself is wrongly addressed. Sanction for prosecution is required only in the case of public servant. In the case of a person other than a public servant and in the case of a person committing offences under section 8 or section 9 or section 12, no sanction is necessary. If you will kindly see the section which requires sanction, namely section 19, it requires sanction only in respect of offences punishable under sections 7, 10, 11, 13 and 15 committed by a public servant. The question may not arise in the case of an MP or an MLA. Therefore, I do not think there is any problem.

Rajya Sabha

Prevention of Corruption Bill, 1987 pages 252-254

SHRI P. CHIDAMBARAM

One of the Hon. Members raised question about the position of the Ministers. I think the position is beyond doubt. Ministers are public servants. They have always been public servants and they are public servants under this law and Ministers will come under the purview of this Bill.

An HON. MEMBER: What about MPs?

SHRI P. CHIDAMBARAM: I am coming to that. A question was asked about the Members of Parliament and members of Legislative Assembly. Madam, under the law declared by the Supreme Court a Member of Parliament or a member of the Legislative Assembly per sec.... is not a public servant but there can be a number of situations where an MP or an MLA holds an office and discharges other duties which brings him under this Bill. If he holds another office in a Coop. Society, if he holds another office in an public institution, if he discharges certain duties which will come under the defection of public duty clearly, then he would be within the definition of 'public servant' under this Bill. But these are matters in which you cannot make a prior assumption. One has to look into the facts of each case and then the Courts will decide on the facts of that case.

MPs HOLD 'SEAT' NOT 'OFFICE' – A DISTINCTION NOTICED BY THE CONSTITUTION – HENCE MPs NOT COVERED BY THE P.C. ACT, 1988 – SUBMIT PETITIONERS

49. It was also argued that the Constitution of India has made a marked distinction between the expressions "office" and "seat" and that as and when reference is made to an MP the expression used is "seat" and not "office" and that wherever the expression "office" is used its duties are also invariably mentioned. In this respect my attention was particularly drawn to Articles 59(1), 67, 75, 84, 93, 94 and 99 which run as under:

"59. Conditions of President's office.—(1) The President shall not be a member of either House of Parliament or of a House of the Legislature of any State, and if a member of either House of Parliament or of a House of the Legislature of any State be elected President, he shall be deemed to have vacated his seat in that House on the date on which he enters upon his office as President."

"67. Term of office of Vice-President:— The Vice-President shall hold office for a term of five years from the date on which he enters upon his office. Provided that —

(a) ....

(b) A Vice-President may be removed from his office by a resolution of the Council of States passed by a majority of all the then members of the Council and agreed to by the House of the People; but no resolution for the purpose of this Clause shall be moved unless at least fourteen days' notice has been given of the intention to move the resolution;

(c) a Vice-President shall, notwithstanding the expiration of his term, continue to hold office until his successor enters upon his office."

....

"75. Other provisions as to Ministers.—(1) The Prime Minister shall be appointed by the President and the other Ministers shall be appointed by the President on the advice of the Prime Minister.

(2) The Ministers shall hold office during the pleasure of the President.

(3) ......

(4) Before a Minister enters upon his office, the President shall administer to him the oaths of office and of secrecy according to the forms set out for the purpose in the Third Schedule.

(5) ....

(6) ....;

"84. Qualification for membership of Parliament.—A person shall not be qualified to be chosen to fill a seat in Parliament unless he—

(a) is a citizen of India, and makes and subscribes before some person authorized in that behalf by the Election Commission on oath or affirmation according to the form set out for the purpose in the Third Schedule;

(b) is, in the case of a seat in the Council of States, not less than thirty years of age and, in the case of a seat in the House of the People, not less than twenty-five years of age; and

"93. The Speaker and Deputy Speaker of the House of the People—The House of the People shall, as soon as may be, choose two members of the

House to be respectively Speaker and Deputy Speaker thereof and, so often as the office of Speaker or Deputy Speaker becomes vacant, the House shall choose another member to be Speaker or Deputy Speaker, as the case may be."

"94. Vacation and resignation of, and removal from, the offices of Speaker and Deputy Speaker—A member holding office as Speaker or Deputy Speaker of the House of the People—

(a) Shall vacate his office if he ceases to be a member of the House of the People;

(b) May at any time, by writing under his hand addressed, if such member is the Speaker, to the Deputy Speaker, and if such member is the Deputy Speaker, to the Speaker, resign his office, and

(c) May be removed from his office by a resolution of the House of the People passed by a majority of all the then members of the House:

Provided that no resolution for the purpose of clause (c) shall be moved unless at least fourteen days' notice has been given of the intention to move the resolution:

Provided further that, whenever the House of the People is dissolved, the Speaker shall not vacate his office until immediately before the first meeting of the House of the People after the dissolution."

"99. Oath or affirmation by members—Every member of either House of Parliament shall, before taking his seat, make and subscribe before the President, or some person appointed in that behalf by him, an oath or affirmation according to the form set out for the purpose in the Third Schedule." (Emphasis supplied)

SUPREME COURT HELD WORD 'OFFICE' HAS MANY MEANINGS – HIGH COURT

50. Besides the provisions of the Constitution of India to which reference has been made above my attention was drawn to certain judgments also which, it was felt, throw some light on the ambit and scope of the expression "office". The first such judgment is **State of Gujarat v. M.P. Dwivedi, 1972 Cr LJ 1247.** It related to the Ninth Clause of section 21 of the Indian Penal Code before its amendment by Act 40 of 1964. The Ninth Clause was in the following terms:

"Ninth: Every officer whose duty it is, as such officer, to take, receive, keep or expend any property on behalf of the Government, or to make any survey, assessment or contract on behalf of the Government, or to execute any revenue-process, or to investigate, or to report, on any matter affecting the pecuniary interests of the Government, or to make, authenticate or keep any document relating to the pecuniary interests of the Government, or to prevent the infraction of any law for the protection of the pecuniary interests of the Government and every officer in the service or pay of the Government or remunerated by fees or commission for the performance of any public duty."

The High Court while dealing with this Clause observed:

"The person to be an officer must hold some office. The holding of office implied charge of a duty attached to that office."

51. The other judgment to which my attention was drawn is reported as **Kanta Kathuria v. Nanak Chand, AIR 1970 SC 694.** In the said case an Advocate was appointed as a Special Government Pleader to assist the Government Pleader in a particular case. Question arose as to whether he could be taken to be holding "any office of profit" incurring disqualification under Article 191 of the Constitution of India. The relevant portion of Article 191 of the Constitution of India reads as under:

"191. Disqualifications for membership—

(1) A person shall be disqualified for being chosen as, and for being, a member of the Legislative Assembly or Legislative Council of a State—

(a) if he holds any office of profit under the Government of India or the Government of any State specified in the First Schedule, other than an office declared by the Legislature of the State by law not to disqualify its holder;

(b) if he is of unsound mind and stands so declared by a Competent Court;

(c) if he is an undischarged insolvent;

(d) if he is not a citizen of India, or has voluntarily acquired the citizenship of a foreign State, or is under any acknowledgements of allegiance or adherence to a foreign State;

(e) if he is so disqualified by or under any law made by Parliament.

Explanation: For the purpose of this Clause, a person shall not be deemed to hold an office of profit under the Government of India or the Government of any State specified in the First Schedule by reason only that he is a Minister either for the Union or for such State.

(2) A person shall be disqualified for being a member of the Legislative Assembly or Legislative Council of a State if he is so disqualified under the Tenth Schedule."

The Supreme Court while observing that the word "office" had various meanings, held that the words "its holder" occurring in Article 191(1)(a) indicated that there must be an office existing independently of the holder of the office and that in the case of the petitioner neither any "office" had been created nor the legislature had declared a legal practitioner like the petitioner to be attracted by Article 191(1)(a).

R.S. NAYAK SC JUDGMENT NOT APPLICABLE TO FACTS OF THIS CASE – HELD HIGH COURT

52. As already noticed, while dealing with section 21 of the Indian Penal Code, the Supreme Court in **R.S. Nayak v. A.R. Antulay, AIR 1984 SC 546,** did hold an MLA to be not a public servant. But then, as we know, the Supreme Court was dealing with sub-clause (a) of the Twelfth clause of section 21 which, if I may say so, was materially different from clause (viii) of section 2(c) of the Act of 1988. It is for this reason that I feel that Antulay's judgment can neither provide a cushion nor a bastion to the plea raised by Mr. Anand.

'OFFICE' AND 'PUBLIC DUTY' ESSENTIAL FOR CLAUSE (viii) OF SECTION 2(c) – HELD HIGH COURT

53. Confining myself to clause (viii) of section 2(c) of the Act of 1988, apparently two conditions must necessarily be satisfied to attract it. First that an MP or for that matter an MLA must hold an office and second that by virtue of the office he must be authorised or required to perform any public duty. However, and as already noticed, as far as the second requirement is concerned I need not lose my breath for the simple reason that it was admitted that MPs do perform public duties on account of the 'seat' they occupy. I am thus, for this reason, confining myself only to the first requirement.

FOR PURPOSES OF CLAUSE (viii) OF SECTION 2(c) OF PC ACT, 1988 READ WITH *EXPLANATION* 2, WORD 'OFFICE' COVERS MPs/MLAs – HELD HIGH COURT

54. Does an MP hold an "office"? But, then, before this question is answered, we shall have to know as to what precisely is meant by the word "office". What does it imply? What does it signify? Let us first have a look at the dictionaries. In *Black's Law Dictionary,* it is defined as an "assigned duty" or "function". Its synonyms are "post" "appointment", "situation", "place", "position". *The Oxford English Dictionary,* IInd Edn., Vol. X defines "office" as "duty attaching to one's station, position, or employment; a duty, service, charge falling or assigned to one; a service or task to be performed; A position or place to which certain duties are attached, especially one of a more or less public character; a position of trust, authority or service under constituted authority; a place in the administration of Government, the public service, the direction of a Corporation, company, society, etc.". And, as per Stroud's *Dictionary of Words and Phrases,* Vth Edn. an office "necessarily implies that there is some duty to be performed". This definition seems to have been lifted from what Cockburn C.J. said in **Heartley v. Banks, 5 CBNS 55.**

55. If we accept what the Dictionaries want us to accept then clearly an MP holds an "office". But then, though the dictionaries do refer to various shades of meaning and provide many meanings in which a word has been used or may be used in different contexts and connections, we can ill-afford to ignore the well-known canon of construction that the meaning of the words and expressions used in a statute ordinarily take their colour from the context in which they are used. As said by Krishna Iyer, J. in **State Bank of India v. Sundara Money, AIR 1976 SC 1111,** "dictionaries are not dictators of statutory construction where the benignant mood of a law may furnish a different denotation." But then the question is: Does the word "office" in clause (viii) of section 2(c) of the Act of 1988 furnish a different denotation?

56. It is not that the word "office" is coming up for consideration for the first time. Rather, it has been under close judicial scrutiny in number of cases including those referred to above. For example, in **Champalal v. State of Madhya Pradesh** "office" was taken to mean "A position or station in which a person is employed to perform certain duty. The Constitution Bench in **Statesman v. H.R. Deb, AIR 1968 SC 1495** opined that "an 'office' means no more than a position to which certain duties are attached".

57. The word "office" is of indefinite content and its various meanings cover four columns of the *New English Dictionary*. But, then, which is the appropriate meaning to be ascribed to this word in the context? I think, when we examine the language employed in clause (viii) of section 2(c) for purposes of discerning the real meaning of the word "office", we need to look at *Explanation* 2 also which, to my mind, does throw some light on the point. It says:

> "*Explanation* 2.—Wherever the words 'public servant' occur, they shall be understood of every person who is in actual possession of the situation of a public servant, whatever legal defect there may be in his right to hold that situation." (emphasis supplied)

58. Thus, in the *Explanation* the Legislature has, by using the word "situation", made it clear that the word "office" as used in clauses (vii) and (viii) means merely a position, or station or situation or place to which certain duties are attached of public character. This, then, is the meaning which, in the context, I attach to the word "office" as used in clause (viii) of section 2(c) of the Act of 1988, and if I am correct, then, surely, Members of Parliament would be taken as public servants within the meaning of section 2(c) of the Act of 1988.

WORDS "OFFICE" AND "SEAT" INTERCHANGEABLE – HELD BY DELHI HIGH COURT IN L.K. ADVANI'S CASE – HENCE MPs HOLD AN "OFFICE" – HELD HIGH COURT

59. I shall be failing in my duty in not touching upon the argument advanced by Mr. R.K. Anand and enthusiastically adopted by others that the Constitution itself distinguishes between an "office" and a 'seat'. I find that this very argument was advanced before my brother Mohd. Shamim, J. in **L.K. Advani v. Central Bureau of Investigation, 1997 (3) AD (Del) 53.** The argument was rejected with the observation:

> "The mere fact that the position which an MP occupies in the Parliament has been referred to as seat instead of office is not a sure indicium of the fact that an MP is not a public servant."

The Court noticed that in the Salary, Allowances and Pension of Members of Parliament Act, 1954 a Member of Parliament has been adverted to as a person having an "office" and, on its basis, observed that the words "seat" and "office" are interchangeable. With respect, I feel the terms "seat" and "office" have been used to distinguish legislators from the Executive and to approve the principle of holding two offices one of the legislator and the other of a ministerial post. Casell London in his Parliaments explains it as under:

> "In Great Britain, for many years members who were appointed ministers" had to submit themselves for re-election in order that their position as a member should be confirmed. The point of this provision which was repealed in 1926 was that the electors were considered to be entitled to approve (or disapprove) the election of any member of Parliament who was appointed to a ministerial post and so to bless officially the principle of holding both offices."

THERE IS NO AUTHORITY TO REMOVE MPs UNDER SECTION 19(1)(c) OF PC ACT – RELY UPON PRIOR LAW – HENCE PC ACT, 1988 NOT APPLICABLE TO MPs – SUBMIT PETITIONERS

60. Coming to the third contention, it was inspired by section 19(1)(c) of the Act of 1988 which reads as under:

> "19. Previous sanction necessary for prosecution:
>
> (1) No Court shall take cognizance of an offence punishable under sections 7, 10, 11, 13 and 15 alleged to have been committed by a public servant, except with the previous sanction:
>
> (a) ....
>
> (b) ....
>
> (c) In the case of any other person, of the authority competent to remove him from his office."

61. It was argued by Mr. R.K. Anand that section 2(c) has necessarily to be read in conjunction with section 19 and that even if a person is a 'public servant' within the meaning of section 2(c) but there is no authority competent to remove him from his office within the meaning of section 19(1)(c) of the Act then, in such a case, such a person, despite being a public servant, cannot be prosecuted under the Act of 1988. The contention was that even if some of the petitioners be taken as public servants within the meaning of section 2(c) of the Act, as there is no authority competent to remove an MP from his office, therefore, for that reason the requirement of section 19(1)(c) of the Act of 1988 remains unfulfilled, and, if that be so, the Act of 1988 would have no application. In support, my attention was drawn to a judgment of the Supreme Court in **K. Veeraswami v. Union of India, (1991) 3 SCC 655.**

62. K. Veeraswami v. Union of India, (supra) was a case under the Prevention of Corruption Act, 1947 and revolved mainly around section 6(1)(c) of the said Act which was as follows:

> "6(1) No Court shall take cognizance of an offence punishable under section. 161 or section 164 or section 165 of the Indian Penal Code (45 of 1860) under sub-section (3A) of section 5 of this Act, alleged to have been committed by a public servant, except with the previous sanction,
>
> ....
>
> (c) in the case of any other person, of the, authority competent to remove him from office."

THERE IS NO AUTHORITY TO GRANT SANCTION FOR PROSECUTION OF MPs – PC ACT NOT APPLICABLE – SUBMIT PETITIONERS – PRIOR LAW RELIED

63. It is not disputed that in case of Members of Parliament there is no authority competent to remove them from their office. In **K. Veeraswami v. Union of India, (1991) 3 SCC 655** it was observed by Verma J. (as his Lordship then was):

> "Clauses (a), (b) and (c) in sub-section (1) of section 6 exhaustively provide for the competent authority to grant sanction for prosecution. Admittedly, such previous sanction is a condition precedent for taking cognizance of an offence punishable under the Act, of a public servant who is prosecuted during his continuance in the office. It follows that the public servant falling within the purview of the Act must invariably fall within one of the three clauses in sub-section (1) of section 6. It follows that the holder of an office, even though a public servant, according to the definition of the Act, who does not fall within any of the clauses (a), (b) or (c) of sub-section (1) of section 6 must be held to be outside the purview of the Act since the special enactment was not enacted to cover that category of public servants in spite of the wide definition of public servant in the Act."

And:

> "The grant of previous sanction under section 6 being a condition precedent for the prosecution of a public servant covered by the Act, it must follow that the holder of an office who may be a public servant according to the wide definition of the expression in the Act but whose category for the grant of sanction for prosecution is not envisaged by section 6 of the Act, is outside the purview of the Act, not intended to be covered by the Act. This is the only manner in which a harmonious construction of the provisions of the Act can be made for the purpose of achieving the object of that enactment."

And, further that:

> "The concept of sanction for prosecution by a superior is so inextricably woven into the fabric of the enactment that the pattern is incomplete without it. The clear legislative intent is that the enactment applies only to those in whose case sanction of this kind is contemplated and those to whom the provision of sanction cannot squarely apply are outside its ambit. The provision for sanction is like the keystone in the arch of the enactment. Remove the keystone of sanction and the arch crumbles."

It was contended by Mr. R.K. Anand that since the other members of the Bench had neither touched the above-noted point nor had they disagreed with the view expressed by Verma J., therefore, the said observations would be binding on me.

PRIOR LAW WAS ON 1947 ACT – NOT 1988 ACT – MATERIAL CHANGES IN NEW LAW – IT WAS A MINORITY VIEW – HENCE NOT APPLICABLE – BRIBERY, CORRUPTION CAN'T BE CONDONED – HIGH COURT HELD

65. I do not think Mr. Anand is very correct in his submission. The perusal of the judgments delivered by the other Hon'ble Judges of the Bench would go to show that they had before them the draft judgment prepared by Verma J. and yet they did not agree with that judgment and that is why Verma J. after going through the opinions of the other Judges constituting the majority, had to observe that his dissenting opinion was at best only academic.

66. I think, and I say so with utmost respect, that the opinion of Verma J. in **Veeraswami's** case is no precedent for the following reasons: (i) It is a minority judgment. The majority has taken a contrary view; (ii) It is a judgment under the Act of 1947 and not under the Act of 1988; (iii) There have been significant changes in, the Act of 1988. For example, there was no provision like sub-section (3) of section 19 in the Act of 1947; (iv) By taking the view that in the absence of any authority to remove, the Act would not apply we shall be condoning the offence of bribery and corruption by public servants. Such immunity from prosecution would lead to disturbing results.

NARASIMHA RAO "WHILE ACTING OR PURPORTING TO ACT IN DISCHARGE OF HIS OFFICIAL DUTY" HAS DONE TO DEFEAT 'NO-CONFIDENCE MOTION' – SANCTION UNDER SECTION 197, CR.P.C. – SUBMIT PETITIONERS

67. Coming to the charge framed under section 120B of the Indian Penal Code it was argued on behalf of P.V. Narasimha Rao that the same cannot be sustained for want of sanction under section 197 of the Code of Criminal Procedure. It was contended that as, in view of Article 75(2) of the Constitution it was the constitutional duty of P.V. Narasimha Rao as Prime Minister to defeat the No-confidence Motion, therefore, whatever he did was covered by the words "while acting or purporting to act in discharge of his official duty" and that consequently sanction was required under section 197 of the Code of Criminal Procedure.

MEANING OF WORDS "ANY OFFENCE ALLEGED TO HAVE BEEN COMMITTED WHILE ACTING OR PURPORTING TO ACT IN THE DISCHARGE OF HIS OFFICIAL DUTY" – PRIOR LAW REFERRED – HIGH COURT

68. The entire dispute hinges upon the meaning and scope of the expression "any offence alleged to have been committed by him while acting or purporting to act in the discharge of his official duty." What do these words mean" It was observed in **S.B. Saha v. M.S. Kochar, AIR 1979 SC 1841:**

> "The words any offence alleged to have been committed by him while acting or purporting to act in the discharge of his official duty employed in section 197(1) of the Code, are capable of a narrow as well as a wide interpretation. If these words ale construed too narrowly, the section will be rendered altogether sterile, for, it is no part of an official duty to commit an offence, and never can be. In the wider sense, these words will take under their umbrella every act constituting an offence, committed in the course of the same transaction in which the official duty is performed or purports to be performed. The right approach to the import of these words lies between these two extremes. While on the one hand, it is not every offence committed

> by a public servant while engaged in the performance of his official duty, which is entitled to the protection of section 197(1), an act constituting an offence , directly and reasonably connected with his official duty will require sanction for prosecution under the said provision."

In **P. Arulswami v. State of Madras, AIR 1967 SC 776,** the Supreme Court after reviewing the earlier case law held:

> "....It is not, therefore, every offence committed by a public servant that requires sanction for prosecution under section 197(1) of the Criminal Procedure Code; nor even every act done by him while he is actually engaged in the performance of his official duties; but if the act complained of is directly concerned with his official duties so that, if questioned, it could be claimed to have been done by virtue of the office, then sanction would be necessary. It is the quality of the act that is important and if it falls within the scope and range of his official duties the protection contemplated by section 197 of the Criminal Procedure Code will be attracted. An offence may be entirely unconnected with the official duty as such or it may be committed within the scope of the official duty. Where it is unconnected with the official duty there can be no protection. It is only when it is either within the scope of the official duty or in excess of it that the protection is claimable."

70. In **Matajog Dubey v. H.C. Bhari, AIR 1956 SC 44,** while explaining to what extent an act or omission performed by a public servant in discharge of his duty can be deemed to be official, the Supreme Court said:

> "The offence alleged to have been committed (by the accused) must have something to do, or must be related in some manner with the discharge of official duty... there must be a reasonable connection between the act and the discharge of official duty; the act must bear such relation to the duty that the accused could lay a reasonable (claim) but not a pretended or fanciful claim, that he did it in the course of the performance of his duty."

71. The legal position which emerges from above, has been summed up by the supreme Court in **State of Maharashtra v. Dr. Budhikote Subbarao, (1993) 3 SCC 339** is under:

> "Use of the expression, official duty implies that the act or omission must have been done by the public servant in the course of his service and that it should have been in discharge of his duty. The section does not extend its protective cover to every act or omission done by a public servant in service but restricts its scope of operation to only those acts or omissions which are done by a public servant in discharge of official duty."

> "It has been widened further by extending protection to even those acts or omissions which are done in purported exercise of official duty. That is under the colour of office. Official duty therefore implied that the act or omission must have been done by the public servant in course of his service and such act or omission must have been performed as part of duty which further must have been official in nature. The section has, thus, to be construed strictly, while determining its applicability to any act or omission in course of service. Its operation has to be limited to those duties which are discharged in course of duty. But once any act or omission has been found to have been committed by a public servant in discharge of his duty then it must be given liberal and wide construction so far its official nature is concerned. For instance a public servant is not entitled to indulge in criminal activities. To that extent the section has to be construed narrowly and in a restricted manner. But once it is established that act or omission was done by the

public servant while discharging his duty then the scope of its being official should be construed so as to advance the objective of the section in favour of the public servant. Otherwise the entire purpose of affording protection to a public servant without sanction shall stand frustrated. For instance, a police officer in discharge of duty may have to use force which may be an offence for the prosecution of which the sanction may be necessary. But if the same officer commits an act in course of service but not in discharge of his duty then the bar under section 197 of the Code is not attracted."

"If on facts, therefore, it is *prima facie* found that the act or omission for which the accused was charged had reasonable connection with discharge of his duty then it must be held to be official to which applicability of section 197 of the Code cannot be disputed."

TAKING PART IN CONSPIRACY AND BRIBING THE MPs WAS 'NOT IN THE PERFORMANCE OF HIS OFFICIAL DUTIES' AS PM – HELD HIGH COURT

72. The law being as noticed above, let us have yet another look at the case set up by the C.B.I. against P.V. Narasimha Rao. He, with a view to save the Government headed by him, was prima facie a party to a conspiracy to bribe MPs and thereby to win over their support. He was also a party to actual bribing of the MPs. It is no job of a Prime Minister to hatch or be a party to such a criminal conspiracy. Power intoxicates the best hearts as wine the strongest heads but then no body can thrive on corruption. It is the froth on water - an inch deep and then the mud. A Prime Minister must not sustain his power and position on the crutches of corruption. It is unfortunate that P.V. Narasimha Rao thinks he was justified under Article 75(2) of the Constitution. The plea demeans the provision. He is looking out for something which is not there. All ambitions, including the ambition to remain perennially in power, are lawful except those which climb upward by means unlawful. If the prosecution is to be believed, what P.V. Narasimha Rao did, cannot, to my mind, fall within the words "while acting or purporting to act in the discharge of his official duty".

EVIDENCE OF CONSPIRACY WAS NOT ADMISSIBLE QUA NARASIMHA RAO – SUBMIT PETITIONERS – REJECTED – HIGH COURT

73. It was argued, not only by Mr. R.K. Anand but also by Mr. Murli Bhandare representing M. Thimmegowda, Mr. Santosh Hegde and Mr. B.V. Acharya representing M. Moily, and Mr. Arunachalam representing D.K. Audikeshavalu that there was no evidence to prove that any of their clients had entered into any conspiracy. Mr. R.K. Anand was of the view that the so-called incriminating evidence against P.V. Narasimha Rao was not admissible even under section 10 of the Evidence Act.

74. As we all know conspiracy consists simply in the agreement or confederacy to commit an offence. It is not an ingredient of the offence under section 120B that all the parties should agree to do a single act. It may, in fact, comprise the commission of a number of acts. It is also not necessary that each member of the conspiracy must know all the details of conspiracy. As rightly pointed out by Mr. Murli Bhandare, and so also by Mr. Santosh Hegde, Mr. B.V. Acharya and Mr. Arunachalam the gist of the offence of conspiracy is an agreement to do an unlawful act, or to do a lawful act by unlawful means.

DIRECT EVIDENCE OF CONSPIRACY NEVER AVAILABLE – GENERALLY PROVED BY CIRCUMSTANTIAL EVIDENCE – HOLDS HIGH COURT

75. "How is a conspiracy to be proved". The moment we are faced with this question, what immediately comes to mind are the observations of Ele J. in **Reg. v. Duffield, (1851) 5 Cox 404**. He said:

> "It does not happen once in a thousand times, when the offence of conspiracy is tried, that anybody comes before the jury to say – 'I was present at the time when these parties did conspire together, and when they agreed to carry out their unlawful purpose'; that species of evidence is hardly ever to be adduced before a jury, but the unlawful combination and conspiracy is to be inferred from the conduct of the parties, and if you see several men taking several steps, all tending towards one obvious purpose, and you see them through a continued portion of time, taking steps that lead to an end, why it is for you to say whether persons had not combined together to bring about that end, which their conduct so obviously appears adapted to effectuate."

Coleridge J. dealt with the question in **Regina v. Murphy, 1837 (8) CVP 297, 310]** as follows:

> "Although the common design is the root of the charge, it is not necessary to prove that these two parties came together and actually agreed in terms to have this common design and to pursue it by common means, and so to carry it into execution. This is not necessary, because in many cases of the most clearly established conspiracies there are no means of proving any such thing, and neither law nor common sense requires that it should be proved. If you find that these two persons pursued by their acts the same object, often by the same means, one performing one part of an act, and the other another part of the same act, so as to complete it, with a view to the attainment of the object which they were pursuing, you will be at liberty to draw the conclusion that they have been engaged in a conspiracy to effect that object."

In short thus, conspiracy is a matter of inference. It is not necessary to prove that the conspirators actually met; nor is it necessary to show that they communicated in any way. In fact the Court may infer a conspiracy even though the conspirator may not have even known each other.

76. I have made a little *sojourn* into the realm of the law of conspiracy only with a few to show that while dealing with each of the petitioners I would be guided by the principles referred to above though I may not henceforth be making a specific reference to them.

77. Since Mr. Anand was apprehensive that I may in my assessment of the material on record take note of section 10 of the evidence Act, I may mention that I have been constantly reminding myself that as a general rule some *prima facie* satisfactory evidence should in the first instance be on the record of there being reasonable grounds to believe in the existence of the conspiracy before evidence may be given of acts or declarations of the alleged conspirators in order to make them admissible against their fellows. And, while I am on it, I may mention that I do feel, and this feeling has stemmed out of repeated examination of the material on the record, that there is *prima facie* and satisfactory evidence to that effect. It is because of this that, to my mind, benefit can be availed of section 10 of the Evidence Act.

BENEFIT OF SECTION 10 EVIDENCE ACT READ WITH ILLUSTRATION IS AVAILABLE IN INDIA – SCOPE BECOMES WIDER THAN IN ENGLAND – HOLDS HIGH COURT

78. Mr. Anand had, in support of his submissions, chiefly relied upon the well-known English judgment in **R. v. Blake, [1844] 6 QB 126**. What in that case was held to be admissible against the conspirator was the evidence of entries made by the fellow conspirator contained in various documents actually used for carrying out the fraud. But a document not created in the course of carrying out the transaction, but made by one of the conspirators after the fraud was completed (although what it contained amounted to a statement evidencing what had been done) was held to be inadmissible against the other "on the principle that a mere statement, made by one conspirator to a third party, or any act of such conspirator not done in pursuance of the conspiracy, is not evidence for or against another conspirator" (per Lord Denman C.J.). Patherson, J. described it as "a statement made after the conspiracy was effected". Williams, J. said that if merely related "to a conspiracy at that time completed". Coleridge, J. said that it "did not relate to the furtherance of the common object".

However, what needs to be kept in mind is that section 10 has a wider scope than the English law as under section 10 anything said or done in reference to the common intention, although it may not be in support or in furtherance of the conspiracy, is relevant against the others, and that is why in **R. v. Amiruddin (15 WR Cr 25)**, a letter containing an account of the conspiracy was admitted even though not written in support of or in furtherance of it. Yet, what more needs to be mentioned is, and it is borne out from the illustration to section 10, that whereas under the English law what is said or done by other conspirators after one terminates his connection with the conspiracy is not admissible against the latter, under section 10 it is admissible against him. I am laying emphasis on it because, at one stage, it was emphasised by Mr. Bhandare that even if it be taken, for argument's sake, that M. Thimmegowda was a co-conspirator, it terminated soon after his having handed over the bags at the residence of M. Moily and that what the other conspirators said or did thereafter could not be used against his client. I am laying emphasis on it because, at one stage, it was emphasised by Mr. Bhandare that even if it be taken, for argument's sake, that M. Thimmegowda was a co-conspirator, it terminated soon after his having handed over the bags at the residence of M. Moily and that what the other conspirators said or did thereafter could not be used against his client.

THREE CHARGE-SHEETS ARE TO BE READ TOGETHER – SUFFICIENT EVIDENCE OF CONSPIRACY – OFFENCE UNDER SECTION 120B MADE OUT AGAINST THEM – HOLDS HIGH COURT

79. The law being as noticed above, is there material on the record to show that P.V. Narasimha Rao, M. Thimmegowda, H.M. Revanna, Ramalinga Reddy and M. Veerappa Moily were party to the conspiracy? I am confining myself to the above-noted persons because it was on their behalf that this question was specifically raised during arguments.

80. Before I proceed to examine as to whether charge as against them under section 120B is made out or not, I may mention that it was strenuously emphasised by the Counsel representing the above petitioners excepting Mr. Anand representing P.V. Narasimha Rao, that since the names of the above petitioners did not figure in the first charge sheet and as, according to them, the first charge-sheet was complete in itself, the question of conspiracy or the above-named petitioners being a party to it, did not arise. I may say, at the outset, that I remain unconvinced. All the three charge-sheets have to be read and considered together. It was a conspiracy with different facets. The goal was the same though some of the players faded out after performing their roles. Thus, when we proceed to examine the conspiracy angle, the whole of the script has to be borne in mind. The three charge-sheets are intertwined and cannot be fragmented or separated. Each constitutes a part of the whole.

MPs ACCEPTING BRIBE – HAD DIRECT TALK WITH NARASIMHA RAO – BHAJAN LAL AND CAPTAIN SATISH SHARMA WERE ALSO IN DIRECT TOUCH – HELD HIGH COURT

81. Let us then, revert back to the question posed. P.V. Narasimha Rao was the Prime Minister but his party was not in majority. The threat of No Confidence Motion stood extended much before July 26, 1993 when it was actually moved. P.V. Narasimha Rao needed the support of at least 14 members for simple majority

(*See* PW-1 Ravinder Kumar, PW 2 Ajoy Mukhopadhyay, PW 3 Manoranjan Bhakta and PW-144 Ashok Rao Deshmukh.) This created a situation of crisis and Narasimha Rao decided to win over Ajit Singh who was leading a faction of Janta Dal which had six members in the Lok Sabha (See PW-1 Ravinder Kumar). With that in view on 23rd July he offered ministership to Ajit Singh or in the alternative Chairmanship of a public Undertaking (See PW 192 Captain Dilawar Singh). However, Ajit Singh refused. On the very next day, Bhajan Lal went to the house of Ajit Singh and told him "**Chaudhary Sahib Narasimha Rao Ji ki kursi ab aapke haath mein hai. Chahe chhuda do ya bachha do aur ise bachhane ke liye hi Narasimha Rao Ji ne mujhe aap ki sewa mein bheja hai.**" (Chaudhary Sahib, Narasimha Rao Ji's remaining in power now depends upon you. It is upto you now whether you want him to remain in power or not. Narasimha Rao Ji has sent me to you to request you for your help). Thereafter Bhajan Lal delivered packets containing currency notes each of Rs. 500 denomination as price for his support. Same Bhajan Lal with active support of Captain Satish Sharma, allegedly bribed Ram Lakhan Singh Yadav and his group and won support for P.V. Narasimha Rao's Government. [See PW 240 Pradyuman Singh). However before that, on July 27, 1993 at about 4 p.m. while Bhajan Lal was with Ram Lakhan Singh Yadav, Prime Minister P.V. Narasimha Rao had a telephonic conversation with Ram Lakhan Singh Yadav. This is what Ram Lakhan Singh Yadav told P.V. Narasimha Rao. **Sir Nischint Rahiyega! Shamm Tak Split Ho Jayegi! Chaar Aa Gaye Hein! Munda Abhi Aane Wala Hai! Yeh Mera Vaida Hai Sir. Aapki Sarkar Nahin Jane Doonga! Baki Aaap Dekh Lena! Achcha Sir, Namaskar! Sir, Veh Dono Bhi Aa Gaye Hein! Namaskar Sir .... Achcha Hai PM Sahib Se Bhi Baat Ho Gayee**". Soon, thereafter, there was yet another telephonic call apparently from P.V. Narasimha Rao. It was meant for Bhajan Lal. It was at that moment that Ram Lakhan Singh Yadav told Captain Dilawar Singh while referring to Ajit Singh: **"Yeh to theek hae bina paise politics nahin hoti, parantu Saathiyon kaa vishwas bhi to chahiye!"**

82. It appears that P.V. Narasimha Rao had been telephonically in touch with Ram Saran Yadav and on July 26, 1993 he had, for return of support, assured him Deputy Ministership. He was also offered bribe in cash through Bhajan Lal and Captain Satish Sharma.

83. It is in evidence that both Bhajan Lal and Captain Satish Sharma were, during the relevant period, in constant touch with P.V. Narasimha Rao.

JMM MPs WERE TAKEN BY BUTA SINGH TO NARASIMHA RAO AND DEAL WAS STRUCK – NARASIMHA RAO WAS IN TOUCH WITH DESHMUKH AND RAJESHWAR RAO – HIGH COURT HELD

84. Besides, what has been noticed above, P.V. Narasimha Rao was making efforts to win over the support of JMM MPs also. Captain Satish Sharma, who, as already noticed above, was already in touch with Prime Minister P.V. Narasimha Rao and Bhajan Lal had lost no time in offering them bribes in return for voting for the Government (*See* PW 75 Devinder Kumar Mukhiya and Approver Shailendra Mahto). While all this was going on P.V. Narasimha Rao had been in touch with PW 144 Ashok Anand Rao Deshmukh. When told by Deshmukh that JMM MPs were keen in personally meeting him as they wanted some "conditions" to be met, P.V. Narasimha Rao asked him to ascertain the conditions and advised him to take them to Rajeshwara Rao. They were thus taken to Rajeshwara Rao but since the amount of money offered by V. Rajeshwara Rao was not considered to be sufficient, Buta Singh arranged their meeting with P.V. Narasimha Rao where terms including payment of money were settled. (See Statements of PW 144 Deshmukh, PW 93 Sunder Singh and the statement of Approver) and ultimately payments were made.

M. VEERAPPA MOILY, CM, KARNATAKA REMAINED IN TOUCH WITH NARASIMHA RAO – ARRANGED MONEY AT BANGALORE IN CRORE – DELIVERED THROUGH HIS MEN TO JMM MPs – CONSPIRACY OF MOILY AND NARASIMHA RAO MADE OUT – HIGH COURT HELD

85. Let us now have a look at what M. Veerappa Moily the then Chief Minister of Karnataka was doing. He was in Delhi from 25th July, 1993 to 29th July, 1993 (*See* S.K. Anand Rao PW 183, PW 177 Bhupinder Singh and PW 176 P. Armugham). This was a period when he moved "at a very hectic speed". (*See* PW 176). He not only met P.V. Narasimharao but V. Rajeshwara Rao also. He was in Parliament on the day when voting had taken place on the No Confidence Motion (*See* PW 176). Not only this he had made a significant remark in Kannada on that very day which when translated runs as under: "Had they given me sufficient time I would have done the work easily. Now what to do" He left for Bangalore on the 29th and was constantly in touch with the Prime Minister on telephone (*See* T.R. Suresh PW 175). On the 30th and 31st he had talked to V. Rajeshwara Rao also. While in Bangalore he was in touch with his close confidants H.M. Revanna, Ramalinga Reddy and M. Thimmegowda. On July 30, 1993 M. Thimmegowda went to the Branch Manager of Seshadipuram Branch of the Canara Bank where M/s. SPR Group Holdings (P) Ltd. of which he is the Managing Director, maintains current Account and applied for a Temporary Over Draft of Rs. 1 crore for ten days. The Branch Manager contacted the General Manager on telephone and the General Manager got in touch with the Chairman who, incidentally, was camping at Bombay. With the approval obtained, though after banking hours, M. Thimmegowda insisted upon having the cash and that too on the same day. It so happened that the Seshadipuram Branch did not have sufficient funds. But then urgency being writ large, the Manager (cash) alongwith two other officers visited the cash chest, withdrew an amount of Rs. 95 lakhs and so met the demand of M. Thimmegowda. But then, M. Thimmegowda needed more money. He issued two cheques both dated July 30, 1993 one for Rs. 60 lakhs and the second for Rs. 25 lakhs in favour of M/s. Ranganatha Group and M/s. Yellama Enterprises respectively which were credited the same day by way of transfer and the amounts were withdrawn also the same day by M.S. Cheluvarajee Partner of M/s. Ranganatha Group and T. Shivarama, Proprietor of M/s. Yellamma Enterprises. In the meanwhile N. Thimmegowda also withdrew a sum of Rs. 15 lakhs against a self-cheque drawn on account of M/s. SPR Group Holdings (P) Ltd. All the money so withdrawn then reached through a circutous route, the hands of M. Thimmegowda which was later transferred into two big V.I.P. suit-cases. With money safe into two big VIP suitcases Thimmegowda rushed to the house of Moily and delivered the same to him. H.M. Revanna and Ramalinga Reddy were also there at the house of Moily. All of them had a half hour meeting and soon thereafter Ravanna and Ramalinga Reddy left for the airport with the four bags two of which had been earlier brought by Mr. Thimmegowda (*See* PW 174 Nagaraju and PW 173 Parmesh). Immediately on reaching Delhi H.M. Revanna and Ramalinga Reddy went straight to V. Rajeshwara Rao. On the 31st those very suitcases were delivered at the residence of Suraj Mandal. On 1st of August Ravanna was in touch with Moily on telephone. (*See* PW 175 T.R. Suresh).

MAN'S MIND CAN ONLY BE READ FROM HIS ACTIONS – HELD HIGH COURT

86. Invariably, as Devlin J. pointed out in **Roper v. Taylor's Central Garages, 1951 (2) TLR 284**, it is impossible to prove the state of another man's mind, with the result that defendant's knowledge is generally inferred from the nature of the act done. There is of course, nothing new in this doctrine which is sometimes expressed in the time-honoured maxim that a man is taken to intend the natural consequences of his own conduct. Its application in the realm of *mens rea* was well explained in **Lee v. Taylor & Gill, (1912) 77 JP 66** by Chaunel, J. who said:

> "In all cases where it is necessary to prove anything which depends upon the state of a man's mind, whether it is malice, whether it is intent, whether it is knowledge, whether it is suffering or conniving, which all depend upon what is in the man's mind, in any of those cases the way in which it certainly may be and generally must be proved is by inferring it from the facts."

CONSPIRACY AGAINST ALL PETITIONERS IS PROVED BY CIRCUMSTANCES – HELD HIGH COURT

87. As already noticed above, though to establish charge of conspiracy, there must be agreement, there need not be proof of direct meeting or combination, nor need the parties be brought into each other's presence; the agreement may be inferred from circumstances raising a presumption of a common concerted design. It is in this context that the evidence is to be looked into and if we examine the material on record in the light of what is noticed above, none of the petitioners, escape.

88. However, since Mr. Murli Bhandare thought that there was absolutely nothing to rope in M. Thimmegowda, I have with special reference to him, detailed above some of the facts concerning him. Acting in unlikely haste, withdrawing money in an unlikely hour handing over the same to a man who was more than knee deep into the conspiracy, remaining closeted for half-an-hour with other conspirators, seeing them off to the airport and their delivering the precious cargo, at the instance of Rajeshwara Rao, to Suraj Mandal, show that there was meeting of mind. In any case, this gentleman who ought to have known was shutting his eyes to what ought to have been known and was thereby conniving at what was going on.

89. Somebody said: "When I see a bird that walks like a duck and swims like a duck and quacks like a duck, I call that bird a duck". The Judges have always been calling a duck a duck. Ingredients of conspiracy being clear from the evidence I have no hesitation in *prima facie* proclaiming them the conspirators.

STATEMENT OF APPROVER RECORDED UNDER SECTION 164, CR.P.C. IS VALID – HELD HIGH COURT

90. It was also argued by Mr. R.K. Anand that the statement of the Approver recorded under section 164 of the Code of Criminal Procedure cannot be looked into as it was recorded during the pendency of the trial and as such in violation of the provisions of sub-section (1) of section 164 of the Code. I may mention that this question has been raised in separate revision petitions as well in support of which the same argument was advanced. The discussion which follows shall dispose off those petitions too.

91. Sub-section (1) of section 164 of the Code of Criminal Procedure is as follows:

> "164. *Recording of confessions and statements.*—(1) Any Metropolitan, Magistrate or Judicial Magistrate may whether or not he has jurisdiction in the case record any confession or statement made to him in the course of an investigation under this Chapter or under any other law for the time being in force, or at any time afterwards before the commencement of the inquiry or trial:
>
> Provided that no confession shall be recorded by a Police officer on whom any power of a Magistrate has been conferred under any law for the time being force"

92. Undoubtedly, the statement of the Approver was recorded during trial. What is more, it appears to have been recorded under section 164 of the Code. Does it mean that the statement so recorded becomes inadmissible? It may be noticed that before recording the statement all the precautions as required under section 164 of the Code, were taken. This being the position, I do not think that the statement purported to have been recorded under section 164 would become inadmissible merely because it came to be recorded during trial. I do not think that a statement or a confession of an accused can be recorded only at the stage envisaged by section 164 of the Code. There is nothing in section 164 of the Code to warrant the proposition that if a statement or a confession is recorded during trial, the same becomes inadmissible. In any case it is not a defect of substance.

93. There is yet another way of looking at the statement of the Approver. When I say so, I have in my mind sub-section (2) of section 5 of the Prevention of Corruption Act, 1988. It runs as under:

> "5(1).........
>
> (2) A Special judge may, with a view to obtaining the evidence of any person supposed to have been directly or indirectly concerned in, or privy to, an offence, tender a pardon to such person on condition of his making a full and true disclosure of the whole circumstances within his knowledge relating to the offence and to every other person concerned, whether as principal or abettor, in the commission thereof and any pardon so tendered shall, for the purposes of sub-sections (1) and (5) of section 308 of the Code of Criminal Procedure, 1973 (2 of 1974), be deemed to have been tendered under section 307 of that Code."

94. As would be borne out from the sub-section, it is enabling and wide enough. The powers of the Special Judge are not circumscribed by any condition excepting that the person must be one who is supposed to have been directly or indirectly concerned in, or privy to, an offence. The power so conferred can be exercised at any time after the case is received and before its conclusion. But then, before the Special Judge acts or tenders pardon, he must know the nature of the evidence the person seeking conditional pardon is likely to give, the nature of his complicity and the degree of his culpability in relation to the offence and in relation to the co-accused **(See: Andhra Sugars Ltd. v. State of Andhra Pradesh, AIR 1967 SC 594)**. After all, it is the duty of the Special Judge to be very cautious as to whom he admits to give evidence as an approver and should carefully inquire to what extent the approver is mixed up with the transaction, and if he be an accomplice, into the extent of his guilt. **[See Reg. v. Robert Dunne, (1851) 5 Cox Cr Cas 507]**. If that be so, I feel that while proceeding under sub-section (2) of section 5 of the Act of 1988, the Special Judge may, by way of caution and to satisfy himself record the statement of the person concerned and if he does so, the statement so recorded shall be taken to be one recorded under sub-section (2) of section 5 of the Act though it may, by mistake, be mentioned that it was being recorded under section 164 of the Code of Criminal Procedure. The statement so recorded shall be admissible in evidence.

95. It was next contended that the Approver had been changing his colours and was therefore totally unreliable. I think, this is no stage to firmly comment on it. I would rather leave it to the Special Judge, for after all, this is a stage to examine merely the question as to whether a case is made out for Charge or not. Of course, while assessing the statement of the approver, I have kept and will keep in view the observations made by the Supreme Court in **Sarwan Singh v. State of Punjab, AIR 1957 Punj 587** and what has been said by the Apex Court in **Saravana Bhawan v. State of Madras, AIR 1966 SC 1273.** I am mentioning this only to show that while assessing the worth of the statement of the Approver, I have been guided by what has been observed by the Supreme Court.

96. Before I proceed to bring forth the facts concerning each of the other petitioners I do feel that I must spell out how I propose to look into the material on the record and what is going to be my approach. I am touching this aspect at the threshold because I shall not be referring to the principles over and over again while dealing with each of the remaining petitioners. The discussion is meant only to give an inkling of the mental process.

WARNING OF SUPREME COURT THAT CASE SHOULD NOT BE TO PERSECUTE PETITIONERS – KEPT IN MIND – ORDER OF SPECIAL JUDGE JUSTIFIED – HELD HIGH COURT

97. The primary consideration before me, of course, is whether the learned Special Judge was justified in ordering the framing of the charges and while considering the same I would keep in mind the warning given by the Supreme Court in the **State of Karnataka v. L. Muniswamy, AIR 1977 SC 1489** that a Court proceeding ought not to be permitted to degenerate into a weapon of harassment or persecution. I am making myself conscious of this warning for it was time and again argued by Mr. D.C. Mathur, Senior Advocate, Mr. P.P. Malhotra, Senior Advocate and Mr. N.N. Aggarwal, Advocate, that the proceedings initiated at the instance of the C.B.I. were inspired by the political foes of the petitioners not only to harass and persecute them but also to tarnish their image and thereby herald their political death.

98. Section 227 of the Code of Criminal Procedure which undoubtedly has bearing on the matters in hand provides:

> "227. *Discharge.*—If, upon consideration of the record of the case and the documents submitted therewith, and after hearing the submissions of the accused and the prosecution in this behalf, the Judge considers that there is not sufficient ground for proceeding against the accused, he shall discharge the accused and record his reasons for so doing."

Yet another provision which needs to be noticed is section 228 of the Code of Criminal Procedure. It reads as under:

> "228. *Framing of charge.*—(1) If, after such consideration and hearing as aforesaid, the Judge is of opinion that there is ground for presuming that the accused has committed an offence which—
>
> (a) is not exclusively triable by the Court of Session, he may frame a charge against the accused and, by order, transfer the case for trial to the Chief Judicial Magistrate, and thereupon the Chief Judicial Magistrate shall try the offence in accordance with the procedure for the trial of warrant cases instituted on a police report;
>
> (b) is exclusively triable by the Court, he shall frame in writing a charge against the accused.
>
> (2) Where the Judge frames any charge under clause (b) of sub-section (1), the charge shall be read and explained to the accused and the accused shall be asked whether he pleads guilty of the offence charged or claims to be tried."

99. Sections 227 and 228 of the Code interplay and interact. What is the scope of the said provisions" The Supreme Court has answered the question for us in **State of Bihar v. Ramesh Singh, AIR 1977 SC 2018.** While explaining the scope of the said section it was observed:

> "Reading the two provisions together in juxtaposition, as they have got to be; it would be clear that at the beginning and the initial stage of the trial, the truth, veracity and effect of the evidence which the prosecutor proposes to adduce are not to be meticulously judged. Nor is any weight to be attached to

the probable defence of the accused. It is not obligatory for the Judge at that stage, of the trial to consider in any detail and weigh in a sensitive balance whether the facts, if proved, would be incompatible with the innocence of the accused or not. The standard of test and judgment which is to be finally applied before recording a finding regarding the guilt or otherwise of the accused is not exactly to be applied at the stage of deciding the matter under sections 227 or section 228 of the Code. At that stage the Court is not to see whether there is sufficient ground for conviction of the accused or whether the trial is sure to end in his conviction. Strong suspicion against the accused, if the matter remains in the region of suspicion cannot take the place of proof of his guilt at the conclusion of the trial. But at the initial stage if there is a strong suspicion which leads the Court to think that there is ground for presuming that the accused has committed an offence then it is not open to the Court to say that there is no sufficient ground for proceeding against the accused. The presumption of the guilt of the accused which is to be drawn at the initial stage is not in the sense of the law governing the trial of criminal cases in France where the accused is presumed to be guilty unless the contrary is proved. But it is only for the purpose of deciding *prima facie* whether the Court should proceed with the trial or not. If the evidence which the Prosecutor proposes to adduce to prove the guilt of the accused even if fully accepted before it is challenged in cross-examination or rebutted by the defence evidence, if any, cannot show that the accused committed the offence, then there will be no sufficient ground for proceeding with the trial. An exhaustive list of the circumstances to indicate as to what will lead to one conclusion or the other is neither possible nor advisable. We may just illustrate the difference of the law by one more example. If the scales of pan as to the guilt or innocence of the accused are something like even at the conclusion of the trial, then, on the theory of benefit of doubt, the case is to end in his acquittal. But if, on the other hand, it is so at the initial stage of making an order under section 227 or section 228, then in such a situation ordinarily and generally the order which will have to be made will be one under section 228 and not under section 227, **State of Bihar v. Ramesh Singh, AIR 1977 SC 2018.**

In **Union of India v. Prafulla Kumar Samal, (1979) 3 SCC 4,** the principles were summarised as under:

"(1) That the Judge while considering the question of framing the charges under section 227 of the Code has the undoubted power to sift and weight the evidence for the limited purpose of finding out whether or not a *prima facie* case against the accused has been made out.

(2) Where the materials placed before the Court disclose grave suspicion against the accused which has not been properly explained the Court will be fully justified in framing a charge and proceeding with the trial.

(3) The test to determine a *prima facie* case would naturally depend upon the facts of each case and it is difficult to lay down a rule of universal application. By and large however if two views are equally possible and the Judge is satisfied that the evidence produced before him while giving rise to some suspicion but not grave suspicion against the accused, he will be fully within his right to discharge the accused.

(4) That in exercising his jurisdiction under section 227 of the Code the Judge which under the present Code is a senior and experienced Court cannot act merely as a post office or a mouthpiece of the prosecution, but has to consider the broad probabilities of the case, the total effect of the evidence and the

document produced before the Court, any basic infirmities appearing in the case and so on. This however does not mean that the judge should make a roving enquiry into the pros and cons of the matter and weight the evidence as if he was conducting a trial."

Dealing with the two decisions referred to above, the Supreme Court observed in **Stree Atyachar Virodhi Parishad v. Dilip Nathumal Chordia, (1989) 1 SCC 715:**

"These two decisions do not lay down different principles. Prafulla Kumar Case has only reiterated what has been stated in Ramesh Singh case. In fact section 227 itself contains enough, guidance as to the scope of enquiry for the purpose of discharging an accused. It provides that the judge shall discharge when he considers that there is no sufficient ground for proceeding against the accused. The ground in the context is not a ground for conviction, but a ground for putting the accused on trial. It is in the trial, the guilt or the innocence of the accused will be determined and not at the time of framing of charge. The Court, therefore, need not undertake an elaborate inquiry into sifting and weighing the material. Nor is it necessary to delve deep into various aspects. All that the Court has to consider is whether the evidentiary material on record if generally accepted, would reasonably connect the accused with the crime. No more need be enquired into."

100. I do not think anything more need be said. However, since, during arguments, it was time and again contended that the material on the record was neither truthful nor its veracity could be vouchsafed and as I was urged repeatedly to meticulously judge the material I may, only by way of emphasis, and not because these points have not been met squarely in the judgments referred to above, make a mention to yet another judgment of the **Supreme Court in Superintendent and Remembrancer of Legal Affairs, West Bengal v. Anil Kumar Bhinja, AIR 1979 SC 1841** wherein, while relying upon the judgment in **State of Bihar v. Ramesh Singh, AIR 1977 SC 2018** it was observed that at the time of the framing of the charge "the truth, veracity and effect of the evidence which the prosecutor proposes to adduce are not to be meticulously judged. The standard of test, proof and judgment which is to be applied finally before finding the accused guilty or otherwise, is not exactly to be applied at the stage of section 227 or 228 of the Code of Criminal procedure, 1973". To the same effect are the observations of the Supreme Court in **Mohd. Akbar Dar v. State of Jammu and Kashmir, AIR 1980 SC 52; Radhey Shyam v. Kunj Behari, (1989) 1 SCC 715.**

PRINCIPLES OF LAW APPLIED WHILE DEALING WITH P.V. NARASIMHA RAO – OTHER PETITIONERS – HELD HIGH COURT

101. My entire approach has been, while dealing with P.V. Narasimha Rao, M. Thimmegowda, H.M. Revanna, Ramalinga Reddy and M.V. Moily, on the lines suggested above and the principles delineated above would guide me in the case of others too. With these observations, let me proceed to deal with the remaining petitioners. However, before I do so, I may mention by way of clarification that the observations made in the preceding paragraphs and those which I propose to make presently while dealing with the petitioners must, in no case, be taken to be any expression of opinion on the merits of the case. Rather they must be taken as merely a presumptive opinion as to the existence of the factual ingredients constituting the, offences alleged.

102. Like M. Thimme Gowda, D.K. Audikeshavalu too is stated to be a liquor baron of Karnataka, and like him, he too figures neither in the first or the third charge sheet. However, as far as the second charge-sheet is concerned he is at the centre-stage, I mean, almost. He is not a politician but appears to have lot to do with them. It is said that business is like oil. It won't mix with anything but business. I do not know whether this particular businessman when mixing with politicians was actually mixing with business or not. What really does emerge out is that here was a business magnate who, believing perhaps in what Jesus said: he that cometh to me shall never hunger (John VI, 35), rather himself went to those who believe that power lies in other people's money, and proved to be a friend in need. There is material on the record to show that he is very close to V. Rajeshwara Rao and so also to M.V. Moily. After staying in Delhi from July 24 to July 29, 1993 he went back to Bangalore. On the 29th itself he issued a cheque for Rs. 30 lakhs and on the next day he issued three cheques one for Rs. 6,17,349, the second for Rs. 14,78,125 and the third for Rs. 30 lakhs Though all those cheques were in favour of different persons, the cash flowing from the withdrawal of those cheques came finally into the hands of none other but D.K. Audikeshavalu himself. With the cash in his pocket on the 30th itself, he too put the same in a V.I.P. suit-case and found himself at the Bangalore Airport. However, before leaving for Delhi, he had contacted K. Narayanan, Resident Manager of the Guest House of M/s. Mohan Breweries and Distilleries Ltd. at New Friends Colony, New Delhi and had asked him to arrange Company's vehicle as well as one taxi as some V.I.P.s were to accompany him to Delhi. And, who were these VIPs? Well, none other but H.M. Revanna and Ramalinga Reddy who had collected three suitcases and one bag from the residence of M. Veerappa Moily, the then Chief Minister of Karnataka. Two of those suit-cases had been delivered to Moily by his businessman friend M. Thimmegowda after having stuffed them with the withdrawals in cash from the Canara Bank.

Coming back to the Bangalore Airport. D.K. Audikeshavalu along with H.M. Revanna and Ramalinga Reddy boarded Indian Airlines flight No. K.404. They were in Delhi at about 22.30 hrs. Bachan Singh, driver of the Company's Maruti car and one Darmayan Singh an attendant detailed by K. Narayanan of M/s. Mohan Breweries and Roop Ram, a taxi driver with his taxi received them at the Airport. It may be mentioned that Roop Ram too had been detailed by Naraynan. The three V.I.P. suit-cases and a handbag brought by H.M. Revanna and Ramalinga Reddy were loaded in the taxi of Roop Ram while the suitcase brought D.K. Audikeshavalu was kept in the Maruti car of the Mohan Meaken Breweries with Bachan Singh on the wheel. On the instructions of D.K. Audikeshavalu the taxi and the Maruti car left for Andhra Bhawan. At the Andhra Bhawan D.K. Audikesavalu, H.M. Revanna and Ramalinga Reddy had a closed door meeting with V. Rajeshwara Rao. With the meeting over, all the three with the suit cases and the bag, left for Hotel Claridges. Leaving H.M. Revanna and Remalinga Reddy there along with their three VIP suit-cases and one hand-bag, D.K. Audikeshavalu left for the Company's Guest House at New Friends Colony. Lest I forget, may mention that the VIP suit-case brought by D.K. Audikeshavalu from Bangalore remained with him. The next day, that is, July 31 he took that suit case in the same Maruti car with Bachan Singh again on the wheel, to Claridges Hotel. The time was about 0700 hours. In the meanwhile Roop Ram too reached there with his taxi. After about half-an-hour all the VIP suit cases and the hand-bag were loaded in the taxi. The visitors from Karnataka and their cargo then again left for Andhra Bhawan with two more persons. They were Vijay Handa and Harsharan Lal. Vijay Handa was in his white Maruti car. They remained at the Andhra Bhawan for an hour and when finally they did come out, V. Rajeshwara Rao was with them. At the instance of D.K. Audikeshavalu the handbag and one VIP suit-case lying at the back seat of the taxi and the VIP suit-case brought by him were loaded in the white Maruti car of Vijay Handa. With this done, H.M. Revanna made himself comfortable in the taxi of Roop Ram while Harsharan Lal and Ganga Singh sat down in the white Maruti car with Vijay Handa on the wheel.

They left for the residence of Suraj Mandal, the JMM MP, and delivered to him the aforesaid VIP suitcases and the Hand-bag brimming with currency notes. I am sorry, I forgot to mention that as per the prosecution after seeing off H.M. Revanna, Vijay Handa, Harsharan Lal and Ganga Singh, the three remaining persons namely D.K. Audikeshavalu, Ramalinga Reddy along with V. Rajeshwara Rao were closeted again inside the Andhra Bhawan.

103. It was argued by Mr. T.S. Arunachalam that though D.K. Audikeshavalu was in Delhi from July 24 to July 29, 1993, the visit was in connection with a writ petition moved by him in the Supreme Court and that the learned Special Judge was not justified in saying that on July 26 he was seen by Ashok Rao Deshmukh at the residence of V. Rajeshwara Rao. It was further contended by him that even if the entire version put up by the prosecution was accepted, it would not be sufficient to sustain the charge of criminal conspiracy or abetment and that consequently, the learned Special Judge was not justified in ordering the framing of charges under section 120B of the Indian Penal Code read with sections 7, 12 and 13(2) read with section 13(1)(d) of the Act of 1988. Of course, I will be failing in my duty by not mentioning that Mr. Arunachalam had also contended that as the conspiracy was complete with the first charge-sheet and as the Approver too had not named D.K. Audikeshavalu, there was absolutely no justification for invoking section 120B as against him. The same argument was adopted by Mr. Bhandare and Mr. Hegde also. I may mention that the order for framing of the charges was also challenged on the ground that as the JMM MPs had allegedly already received full payment by the evening of the 30th in terms of the understanding, any payment allegedly received on the morning of the 31st could not, therefore, be either in terms of or in connection with the conspiracy.

THERE IS STRONG EVIDENCE TO HOLD THAT D.K. AUDIKESHAVALU WAS A PARTY TO THE CONSPIRACY – HELD HIGH COURT

104. I have already discussed above the law of conspiracy and the requirements to prove its existence. I need not repeat the, same again. However, what I do need to say is that the material on the record is sufficient enough to raise a strong suspicion that D.K. Audikeshavalu was a party to the conspiracy and rather had a significant role to play. I have also dealt with above the plea regarding persons like D.K. Audikeshavalu, Ramalinga Reddy and H.M. Revanna etc. not finding any mention in the first charge sheet. As already noticed, I find it to be of no consequence since all the three charge sheets constitute parts of one conspiracy with different facets.

105. As regards the argument that payments made to Suraj Mandal on the 31st were of no consequence as, in terms of the conspiracy, entire payment stood already made on the 30th, I may merely refer to the statement of PW 29 Vijay Kumar Handa which shows *prima facie* that payments made on the 31st were part of the same transaction.

106. The role played by V. Rajeshwara Rao has already been dealt with in some detail in the introductory part of this judgment. However, even though it may appear to be repetitive, since I am at the moment, dealing specifically with his role I may recall what the prosecution alleges against him.

107. The JMM MPs were, it appears, seeing great opportunity in the No Confidence Motion and had come to realize that wealth is not the fruit of labour but the result of organized bribery and in pursuit of wealth Simon Marandi approached Captain Satish Sharma. Shailendra Mahto, on the other hand, requested Ashok Rao Deshmukh to arrange a direct meeting with Prime Minister P.V. Narasimha Rao making it clear at the same time that for support to the Government some conditions shall have to be met – a hint intelligent enough for an intelligent man and luckily for the Government of the day there was no dirth on its side of intelligent people. Getting the message, which, in fact, was clear and loud, P.V. Narasimha Rao advised Deshmukh to take the JMM group to the residence of V. Rajeshwara Rao at Andhra Pradesh Bhawan. The very next day, that is 25th July, 1993 four of the JMM MPs namely Shailendra Mahto, Suraj Mandal, Shibu Soren and Simon Marandi met Rajeshwara Rao who confirmed having received a personal message from the Prime Minister. (*See* Ashok Rao Deshmukh and the Approver) The meeting, it appears, was not very fruitful because after having held a closed down dialogue with Rajeshwara Rao, Suraj Mandal informed his companions that since "they do not intend to give us sufficient amount of money, therefore, we should meet the Prime Minister only" (See the statement of the Approver Shailendra Mahto).

108. On the 26th, thanks to Buta Singh, the JMM MPs met Prime Minister P.V. Narasimha Rao where the mystic bond of money made all of them one. Mandal told his colleagues: "Have a heart, money has also been settled" and on the morning of 29th of July Suraj Mandal told the approver in the presence of Rajeshwara Rao that Rs. 50 lakhs stood paid and that rest would come in a day or two. It was then left to V. Rajeshwara Rao to disclose that Rs. 50 lakhs, a petrol pump and a HUDA plot were being given to Ram Lakhan Singh Yadav and his group and that "you (JMM group) are also being given Rs. 50 lakhs each and it has been decided that Rs. 30 lakhs each shall be given to those who supported on the day of voting by abstaining or remaining silent" (*See* statement of the approver).

109. On the evening of 29th Vijay Kumar Handa (PW 140) was told by V. Rajeshwara Rao that efforts to fulfil the commitment made to JMM MPs was being made.

110. On the 30th H.M. Revanna, Ramaling Reddy and D.K. Audikesavulu who had brought money bags from Bangalore rushed to the residence of V. Rajeshwara Rao and had a meeting with him. The same night V. Rajeshwara Rao informed Vijay Kumar Handa that some arrangement had been made to please the persons who had helped the Government to survive. The next day, Vijay Kumar Handa and Harsharan Lal, at the instance of V. Rajeshwara Rao, went to Claridges Hotel, brought the visitors from Bangalore to the residence of V. Rajeshwara Rao with the suit-cases and the hand-bag and from their, under the watchful eyes of V. Rajeshwara Rao, they left for the residence of Suraj Panday (Mandal) where the suit-cases and the handbag bulging with currency notes were delivered. After having made the delivery, Vijay Handa (PW 140) reported back to V. Rajeshwara Rao to inform about the deliveries made at the residence of Suraj Mandal.

111. Besides all that has been noticed above, there is also material on the record that D.K. Audikesavulu, M. Veerappa Moily while in Delhi had been in touch with V. Rajeshwara Rao and that D.K. Audikesavulu and M. Thimmegowda had withdrawn moneys while in Bangalore which they had taken to the residence of M. Veerappa Moily and it was from there that the suitcases and the handbag containing currency notes were brought to Delhi on the 30th and delivered to Suraj Mandal on the 31st.

THERE IS OVERWHELMING EVIDENCE IMPLICATING V. RAJESHWAR RAO – HELD HIGH COURT

112. Despite the overwhelming material on the record implicating V. Rajeshwara Rao, Mr. R.D. Rana appearing for him made a valiant effort to defend him. My compliments. It was perhaps Emerson who said: "What you do speak so loud that I cannot hear what you say." What V. Rajeshwara Rao did do was surely so loud that it reduced the arguments of Mr. R.D. Rana to nothingness. However, I do need to mention one argument advanced by Mr. Rana. It was contended that Prime Minister

P.V. Narasimha Rao was not so naive as to involve so many persons in the operation, more so when he could meet the situation alone. In politics, it was said by Napoleon Bonaparte, an absurdity is not a handicap. In any case, in the Executive ability lies in deciding quickly and getting somebody else to do the work. Narasimha Rao, having decided, was getting the work done through men like V. Rajeshwara Rao.

113. The material against V. Rajeshwara Rao is so overwhelming and his role in the entire episode is so pronounced that I find no fault with the impugned order.

114. The role assigned to Buta Singh reminds of a sprint. Quick in finish but full of bursting energy. Admittedly, and I am saying so because it was not disputed, he had met the then Prime Minister P.V. Narasimha Rao on 25th of July, 1993. What transpired at that meeting, we know not. Admittedly again, the JMM MPs had gone to the residence of Buta Singh on the evening of the 26th from where all the four JMM MPs accompanied Buta Singh to the residence of P.V. Narasimha Rao. Why? Well, as per the statement of the Approver when they went to the residence of Buta Singh they found him waiting for them. After they had settled down in the Drawing Room, Buta Singh told them that the Prime Minister was "remembering" them. On this Suraj Mandal retorted: "How does it matter if the Prime Minister is remembering us; Our Jharkhand issue is still pending and he has not solved it so far." Buta Singh's reply was "O.K. we'll talk to the Prime Minister on it straight away". Thereafter, the JMM MPs accompanied by Buta Singh went to the residence of the Prime Minister Narasimha Rao. What happened thereafter needs to be described in the words of the Approver himself. This is how he describes the meeting:

> "After a while we were called inside the Prime Minister's room, where he (the Prime Minister) was sitting alone in a contemplative mood. Buta Singh broke the ice and appraised the Prime Minister that talks on Jharkhand matter had begun and a Committee was formed when he was the Home Minister and that Committee had submitted its report also but its decision was reversed. At this, Suraj Mandal said, "So far you have not done anything on Jharkhand issue, how can we help you." The Prime Minister said "O.K. I'll send for all the files regarding Jharkhand issue and shall myself finalise the matter." After this Mr. Mandal and Mr. Singh went to a separate room alongwith the Prime Minister. They came back after a while and then the Prime Minister told us: "At present you help me and I shall help you." The Prime Minister also said that he had held separate talks with Suraj Mandal also and those will also be honoured. After this we walked down up to the gate from where Buta Singh went of his own while we four MPs also went back. On our way back I asked Suraj Mandal "What transpired amongst three of you?" Mandal replied: "The talks were for your benefit and I shall let you know later on." At this Simon Marandi interjected: "Suraj, say clearly, what happened" Or else we shall not vote." At this Mandal said: "Have a heart, money has also been settled though the exact amount has not been decided."

This then is the direct evidence against Buta Singh.

115. It was contended by Mr. N.N. Aggarwal and Mr. Rajiv Awasthi, the learned Counsel for Buta Singh, that barring the solitary bald statement of the Approver, there was nothing to corroborate the same and that even if the statement was accepted it merely showed that Buta Singh had arranged the meeting with Prime Minister P.V. Narasimha Rao only to plead for their demand for Jharkhand and that as after the said meeting Buta Singh was not shown to have played any role, he could not be said to be a party to any conspiracy.

116. The argument advanced by Mr. Aggarwal tends to see the role played by Buta Singh in total isolation. This, I feel, would not be the correct approach. We have to look at the case in its totality and then see as to where and to what extent the role played by Buta Singh fits into the scenario.

ROLE PLAYED BY BUTA SINGH – ARRANGING OF MEETING OF JMM MPs WITH P.V. NARASIMHA RAO – SETTLEMENT OF MONETARY DEAL FOR VOTES – SUFFICIENT FOR CHARGE-SHEET – HELD HIGH COURT

117. The Approver is silent on the point as to how the meeting was fixed with Buta Singh and when. However, his statement does show that Suraj Mandal had played some role in it as it was he who had told others that they were to go to the House of Buta Singh. The very, fact that Buta Singh was found "waiting" for them shows that it was a pre-arranged meeting. Similarly, the fact that during tea, Buta Singh had said: "The Prime Minister is remembering you" shows that meeting with the Prime Minister had been fixed earlier in time. It is important to note that much before the 26th of July Simon Marandi had held a meeting with Captain Satish Sharma who had assured: "If we support the Government, then we will be given money and petrol pump." And that on the 25th Shailendra Mahto too had met Ashok Rao Anand Rao Deshmukh and had asked him to arrange a meeting with Prime Minister P.V. Narasimha Rao and that the meeting was to be with respect to JMM MPs support to the Government in the No Confidence Motion. It appears that when Deshmukh talked to Narasimha Rao about it, he (Narasimha Rao) told him to discuss the matter in detail with him after knowing their (JMM MPs) stand and ascertaining the conditions which they wanted to be fulfilled and that the same day at about 5 p.m. when Deshmukh met Shailendra Mahto and another JMM MP, and told them about his talk with the Prime Minister, "they maintained their stand that they would like to meet the Prime Minister directly." Deshmukh tells us that thereupon when he again contacted the Prime Minister and told him that the JMM MPs "were insisting upon meeting him to discuss their conditions," the Prime Minister said that he was busy with some other matter and that the MPs should be taken to the residence of Rajeshwara Rao. It appears that on the morning of the 26th the JMM MPs had met Rajeshwara Rao through the good offices of Deshmukh and after the meeting Suraj Mandal who had held closed-door talks with Rajeshwara Rao, had declared that he (Rajeshwara Rao) was not intending "to give us sufficient amount of money and therefore we should meet the Prime Minister only". It is in this sequence of events that we have to look at the meeting with Buta Singh on the evening of the 26th. And, the events narrated above show that it was the anxiety to strike a deal with the Prime Minister over the No Confidence Motion which was the driving force and that Jharkhand was no where in their mind.

118. That the JMM MPs met Buta Singh not to canvass for Jharkhand but to satiate their thirst for money is further borne out from the tenor of the talk which took place at Buta Singh's residence. Let us recapture the scene. JMM MPs and Buta Singh are having tea. Buta Singh says: "The Prime Minister is remembering you". This invites a retort from Suraj Mandal. "How does it matter if the Prime Minister is remembering us; our Jharkhand issue is still pending and he has not solved it so far." Had the meeting been arranged to discuss the Jharkhand issue would Suraj Mandal have reacted in that manner? Surely not. The reaction was sudden, unpremeditated and that is why Buta Singh replied: "O.K. we'll talk to the Prime Minister on it straight away." Had the meeting been arranged for discussing the Jharkhand issue, the response of Buta Singh would have been to the effect; "Well, we are meeting him for that very purpose." No, the response was not to that effect. Rather, as noticed, it was "O.K. we'll talk to the Prime Minister on it straightaway." Does it not show that the purpose of meeting was different or very different"

119. True, Buta Singh did initiate the meeting with a reference to Jharkhand issue but then let us look at what Suraj Mandal abruptly told the Prime Minister,

"So far", he said "you have not done anything on Jharkhand issue. How can we help you?" Let us pause on the words: "How can we help you?" If the meeting was for discussing the Jharkhand issue and that issue alone, where was the occasion for Suraj Mandal to say: "How can we help you?" And then, help him over what?

120. No, this is not all. The Prime Minister gives an assurance to finalise the Jharkhand issue. So far, so good. But then why a separate meeting in a separate room with Suraj Mandal and Buta Singh only" What else was left after the assurance already given? Well, the proverbial cat jumps out of the bag just soon after the meeting. The Prime Minister, who only a few minutes earlier was found in a pensive mood and all to himself, was altogether a changed man. He announced to his captive audience that the promises made to Suraj Mandal in the separate meeting would be honoured, With a promise already made earlier in the open, what was this promise in the secret? Surely it could not be the same promise again. And, indeed it was not. When Suraj Mandal was asked by his companions to spell out the promise, he said: "These talks were for our benefit and I shall let you know later." But then, it seems, his companions were too anxious to know and that too only there and then. Suraj Mandal then had to say: "Have a heart, money has also been settled. How much has not been decided."

121. Was it all? No. The Approver tells us that on the day of voting, that is the 28th of July Sita Ram Kesari (only C.B.I. knows why he has been left out) called the four of the JMM MPs and said: "Look here Shibu. I have known you and Suraj for the past 15 to 20 years. At present the Government is in trouble. Each and every vote matters. We have settled a lot. You give your votes so that the Government is saved and all the talks with the Prime Minister shall be honoured". And, we are told, the day after the voting the first instalment of bags brimming with money had been delivered.

The role of Buta Singh is to be looked into in that perspective and once we look at it that way, order for framing charges appears to be pre-eminently justified.

122. In the opening lines of Henry V, using the humble voice of the narrator, Shakespeare cajoles the audience to suspend disbelief. It's a bit much to ask, he admits, but might we transform "This unworthy scaffold" of the stage into the vasty fields of France? Or may be cram/Within this Wooden O the very casquesd. That did affright the air at Agni-Court?" The house of Ajit Singh may be no replica of Shakespeare's "Wooden O" but we are told, it did provide a stage with Ajit Singh in at the centre playing such a role "That did affright the air" though obviously not at Agni-Court but certainly at the headquarters of P.V. Narasimha Rao and Bhajan Lal, if not others.

123. Ajit Singh was a leader of a group of 60 MPs and was thus targeted by Bhajan Lal who, at that time, was the Chief Minister of Haryana. We are told by Captain Dilawar Singh (PW 191) allegedly a long-time associate and confidante of Ajit Singh that on July 24, 1993 Bhajan Lal called on Ajit Singh at the latter's residence at about 8.00 a.m. and that after about five minutes of formal talk about health and family welfare, Bhajan Lal switched on to the No Confidence Motion and said: **"Chaudhary Sahib, Narasimha Rao Ji Ki Kursi ab aapke haath mein hai! Chaho Chudda do ya bacha do aur isse bachaane ke liye hi Narasimha Rao Ji ne mujhe aapki sewa mein bheja hai" (Chaudhary Sahib, Narasimha Rao Ji's remaining in power now depends upon you. It is upto you now whether you want him to remain in power or not. Narasimha Rao Ji has sent me to you to request you for your help).**

124. Dilawar Singh tells us that after the above-quoted conversation, Ajit Singh and Bhajan Lal went into the dinning room for their breakfast. After about

40 minutes Ajit Singh accompanied by Bhajan Lal, went to the car of Bhajan Lal and asked Dilawar Singh to take out from it the three packets. The packets, being too heavy could be taken inside the bed room only with the help of the person who had come with Bhajan Lal but had remained seated in the car. **However, what is significant to note is that while the first packet which weighed about 20-25 Kgs. was being lifted, Ajit Singh jokingly remarked: "Bhajan Lal Ji Harshad Mehta ke suitcase ke muqable main yeh packets chote hein inke andar ka maal to sahi hai?" (Bhajan Lal Ji these packets are smaller in size than Harshad Mehta's suit case. Are their contents all right?). On this Bhajan Lal replied: "Chaudhary Sahib mein pucca businessman hoon – jiski sabhi deals pucci hoti hain! Yeh Harshad Mehta ke nahin Bhajan Lal ke packets hein jo 500 rupees ke noton ki wajah se chhote hein." (Chaudhary Sahib I am a solid businessman. My all deals are solid. These are my packets and not of Harshad Mehta. They are small in size because they contain currency notes of the denomination of Rs. 500 each.)**

125. After the departure of Bhajan Lal Ajit Singh came inside his bed room, gave Dilawar Singh a cutter and directed him to cut open one of the packets. Dilawar Singh did so and to Ajit Singh's relief, it was found to contain 200 wads of currency notes with each currency note of the denomination of Rs. 500.

126. It appears from the statement of Dilawar Singh that Ajit Singh had left for Mirzapur on the night of the 24th and had returned to Delhi on the morning of 26th.

THE WHOLE CONVERSATION SURROUNDING AJIT SINGH MAKES OUT A CASE FOR CHARGE AGAINST HIM AS WELL – HELD HIGH COURT

127. According to Dilawar Singh on the 26th at about 9 a.m. Ram Lakhan Singh Yadav who too is an accused and was an MP belonging to Ajit Singh group came to meet Ajit Singh. What transpired at the meeting? Well, let us know it in Dilawar Singh's own-words:

> **"They both met in the personal office Chamber of Sh. Ajit Singh. After about 5 minutes there was some heated and loud exchanges between the two. I went near the chamber door which was closed and I heard the name of Sh. Bhajan Lal being abused by Sh. Ajit Singh repeatedly saying among others "Bhajan Lal Saala khud Beiman hai aur doosron ko beiman banaata hai, mujhe koi kissi ka paisa nahin de gaya" and Sh. Yadav was demanding Rs. 15 lakhs from Sh. Ajit Singh as his share. I immediately asked two other visitors to vacate the sitting room for some time. After about 2 minutes Sh. Ram Lakhan Yadav came out fuming with anger and left in a huff saying "Pichhali bar kee tarhan paisa hazam nahin karne doonga". Sh. Ajit Singh also came out and went to his residence. Sh. Ajit Singh was so furious and tensed up at that time that he even tore up an application and pushed aside one old man from Madhya Pradesh who had come to seek his help for transfer of his son serving in BSF. While going he asked me to get Sh. Bhajan Lal on phone which I did and connected the call to Sh. Ajit Singh in his residence. The phone talk lasted for about 2 minutes. Sh. Ajit Singh then asked me to call Sh. Surya Narain Yadav, Sh. Sonkar Shastri, Rasheed Masood, all MPs and Sh. Sunil Shastri, General Secretary of JD(A) immediately for a meeting. They all came by 10.00 a.m. and Sh. Ajit Singh told them that JD(A) will go in the favour of the No Confidence Motion and asked Shri Surya Narain Yadav to call a meeting of all other Party MPs next day *i.e.* 27th July at 10.00 a.m. in Party office at 15 Windsor Place and till then hold announcement of the decision officially."**

Dilawar Singh also tells us something about his meeting with Ajit Singh the same day at about 7 p.m. This is what he says:

> "In the evening, I met Sh. Ajit Singh at about 7.00 p.m. and requested him about the morning episode between him and Sh. Ram Lakhan Yadav. He told me, **'that idiot pimp Bhajan Lal disclosed to all the sundry including Ram Lakhan Yadav about the monetary transaction between us on 24th July, 1993 morning and Ram Lakhan tried to show me down on the issue by asking for his share.'** I advised Sh. Ajit Singh that he should not fight with his colleagues on this matter to which he replied that he could not care less as there is no proof."

He further says:

> "The Congress circles were highly demoralised by this shocking development and Sh. Karunakaran and Sh. Vidya Charan Shukla made two attempts to persuade Sh. Ajit Singh to reconsider his decision but he remained unmoved. He was bitter and extremely annoyed with Sh. Bhajan Lal who had disclosed to various people including Sh. Ram Lakhan Yadav the fact of money having been paid to Sh. Ajit Singh by Sh. Bhajan Lal and thus lowered him in the eyes of his colleagues. The volte-face was a natural reaction and logically the one and only one solution for him to save his honour, respect and political standing and this was what he had to perforce do and thus he decided for voting in favour of the no-confidence motion along with other opposition parties."

This, however, is still not the end of the matter.

128. Finding Ajit Singh bent upon voting for the No Confidence Motion, Ram Lakhan Singh Yadav decided to have his own splinter group. Realising the gravity of situation, Dilawar Singh requested Ajit Singh to save the situation. Ajit Singh then sent Dilawar Singh to the residence of Ram Lakhan Singh Yadav. To his surprise he found Bhajan Lal also there and when he asked Bhajan Lal to talk to Ajit Singh on telephone, Bhajan Lal said "Isko ek C.M. se baat karne ki tameez to honi chahiye! Aakhir main us se umar main bhi bara hoon! Paise ki kami thi aur maang leta, Gaali galoch aur dhamki se bolna kaun bardasht karega! Paise usne liye the, maine nahin." (Atleast he should know how to talk to a C.M. After all I am elder to him in age also. If he was short of money he could ask for more. Who will tolerate abuses and threats. Money had been taken by him, not by me).

That Bhajan Lal was present at the meeting finds support and corroboration from the statements of PW 210 R.K. Jain, PW 237 Gopi Krishan Yadav and PW 240 Pradyuman Kumar.

129. It was contended by Mr. R.K. Jain, Senior Advocate for Ajit Singh that barring the bald statement of Captain Dilawar Singh there was nothing on the record to substantiate the allegation that Bhajan Lal had brought money to the residence of Ajit Singh and that Ajit Singh in turn, had accepted the same. He drew my attention to the fact that as per Captain Dilawar Singh, Bhajan Lal had come to the residence of Ajit Singh in a vehicle driven by another person and that it was allegedly with the help of that person that the packets allegedly containing currency notes had been taken out of the vehicle and kept inside the house of Ajit Singh. It was contended that the said driver would have been the best witness to lend support to the version of Captain Dilawar Singh but strangely he had not only been left out but his identity too had not been disclosed and this in itself was sufficient to cast grave doubts on the integrity of the investigation.

130. Mr. Jain emphasised that since Bhajan Lal had been provided with Z Category of security and as the security officials were supposed to keep a close vigil, it could not escape their sharp eyes that heavy packets were being loaded and unloaded and that the fact that none of those security personnel had come forward to support the prosecution version regarding the packets was sufficient to cast grave doubts on the veracity of the statement of Capt. Dilawar Singh.

131. It was further argued that the facts and circumstances around the alleged involvement of Ajit Singh rather showed that despite pulls and pressures Ajit Singh stood by his conviction and voted for the No Confidence Motion and that had Ajit Singh taken the bribe money as alleged, he would not have abused and insulted Bhajan Lal on telephone nor would he have said: "Bhajan Lal Saala khud beiman hai aur doosron ko beiman banaata hai. Mujhe koi kisi ka paisa nahin de gaya".

132. Undoubtedly, excepting the solitary statement of Captain Dilawar Singh, there is nothing on the record to show that Ajit Singh took money from Bhajan Lal. It is also true that the C.B.I. has failed to trace the person who had allegedly helped Captain Dilawar Singh in taking out the packets containing currency notes from Bhajan Lal's vehicle. Unfortunately, the C.B.I. has also failed to gather any incriminating evidence from the security personnel of both Bhajan Lal and Ajit Singh. We are not even told as to from where those packets came and from where they were loaded. One really feels sad about these obvious lapses. It, surely, is not a job well done. But then, the fact remains that Captain Dilawar Singh is there and he says all which is enough to invite an order of framing of charge, for, after all, his statement does raise a strong suspicion with regard to Ajit Singh's complicity.

133. Carl Sandburg who was Whitman's disciple said:

> "Money buys everything except love, personality, freedom, immortality, silence, peace. Therefore, men fight for money. Therefore, men steal, kill, swindle walk as hypocrites and whited sepulchres, therefore men speak softly carrying plans, prisons, weapons, each in the design; The words of his mouth were Butter but war was in his heart."

If the prosecution is to be believed, Bhajan Lal is one man who knows what money can do.

134. At the relevant time, he was the Chief Minister of Haryana and was heading there a Congress (I) Government. His anxiety to save his party's Government at the Centre was thus natural. He camped at Delhi from July 23, 1993 to July 25 and then from July 27 to August 2, 1993. During this period he was often having long meetings with Captain Satish Sharma (*See* PWs 73, 74, 190, 193 and 194 Rakesh Kumar, B.N. Safaya, Shiv Narayan, Ram Kumar and Ashok Jolly respectively). During this very period he met Prime Minister P.V. Narasimha Rao (*See* PW 190 Shiv Narain) and several other Congress leaders including Buta Singh. On the 23rd he had met JMM MPs at Hotel Holiday Inn, New Delhi with a view to win their support and on July 24 he was at the house of Ajit Singh at about 8 am. (*See* PW 191 Dilawar Singh, PW 192 Constable Onkar Prasad and PW 193 Ram Kumar). What transpired at the house of Ajit Singh has already been mentioned by me in sufficient detail while dealing with the case of Ajit Singh. I need not repeat it again. Suffice to say that at that meeting Bhajan Lal made it known to Ajit Singh that he had been sent by Narasimha Rao, that it was upto Ajit Singh to either save the Government of Narasimha Rao or to topple it and that ultimately packets containing wads of currency notes of the denomination of Rs. 500 each were delivered to Ajit Singh. The conversation between the two has already been reproduced by me in my description of role played by Ajit Singh. However, I do feel tempted to reproduce the same for it throws light on how their minds were working.

Bhajan Lal to Ajit Singh

> **"Chaudhary Sahib, Narasimha Rao Ji ki kursi ab aapke haath mein hai Chaho Chhuda do ya bacha do aur isse bachaane ke liye hi Narasimha Rao**

Ji ne mujhe aapki sewa mein bheja hai" (Choudhary Sahib, Narasimha Rao Ji's remaining in power now depends upon you. It is upto you now whether you want to remain him in power or not. Narasimha Rao Ji has sent me to you to request you for your help)."

Ajit Singh to Bhajan Lal while the packets were being taken out of Bhajan Lal's car:

"Bhajan Lal Ji Harshad Mehta ke suitcase ke muqable main ye packets chhote hain inke undar kaa maal to sahi hai"? (Bhajan Lal Ji these packets are smaller in size as compared to Harshad Mehta's suit-case. Are their contents all right"?)

Reply by Bhajan Lal

"Chaudhary Sahib main pucca businessman hoon jiski sabhi deals pucci hoti hein! Yeh Harshad Mehta ke nahin Bhajan Lal ke packets hein jo 500 rupees ke noton ki wajah se chhote hein" (Chaudhary Sahib I am a pucca businessman. All my deals are solid. These are my packets and not of Harshad Mehta. They are small in size because they contain currency notes of the denomination of Rs. 500 each)

BHAJAN LAL HAD TALKED TO AJIT SINGH AND SEPARATELY TO THE BREAK AWAY GROUP OF JD(A) – GOT CONNECTED RAM LAKHAN WITH NARASIMHA RAO ON PHONE – PAID MONEY TO BOTH – SUFFICIENT CAUSE TO CHARGE-SHEET HIM – HELD HIGH COURT

135. As detailed by me while dealing with Ajit Singh, the media came to know of the meeting. Rumours spread about the deal and Ajit Singh became panicky. Things came to a head when Ram Lakhan Singh asked for a share in the booty. Ajit Singh took it that it was Bhajan Lal who had leaked out the proceedings, and in order to save his face, had a somersault and decided to vote for the No Confidence Motion. He even abused Bhajan Lal on telephone (*See* PW 191 Dilawar Singh). This was a shocking development for the Congress. But then, as per the prosecution Bhajan Lal was in no mood to drop the hat. He met Prime Minister P.V. Narasimha Rao at the unearthly hour of 2.30 a.m. on the 27th and (*see* PW 190 Shiv Narain) later targeted Ram Lakhan Singh and his supporters.

136. Before I come to deal with what transpired with Ram Lakhan Singh and his supporters, I may reproduce yet another dialogue of Bhajan Lal which he delivered with obvious anguish at the residence of Ram Lakhan Singh on being requested by Captain Dilawar Singh to get in touch with Ajit Singh on telephone.

"Isko ek C.M. se baat karne ki tameez to honi chahiye! Aakhir main us se umar main bhi bara hoon! Paise ki kami thi aur maang leta, Gaali galoch aur dhamki se bolna kaun bardasht karega! Paise usne liye the, maine nahin." (At least he should know how to talk to a C.M. After all I am elder to him in age also. If he was short of money he could ask for more. Who will tolerate abuses and threats. Money had been taken by him, not by me)."

Coming back to Ram Lakhan Singh Yadav, a meeting of the breakaway group took' place on the 27th at the residence of Ram Lakhan Singh Yadav. During this very meeting Bhajan Lal had a talk with Ram Lakhan Singh Yadav. This was followed by a telephonic conversation with Prime Minister P.V. Narasimha Rao. During this very meeting Bhajan Lal assured the seven MPs of the breakaway group of large sums of money in cash. Captain Satish Sharma, who too was present at the meeting, assured them allotment of petrol pumps (*See* PW 191, PW 237, PW 210 and PW 240 Captain Dilawar Singh, Gopi Krishan Yadav, R.K. Jain and Pradyuman Kumar).

137. The voting on the No Confidence Motion was to take place on the 28th of July, 1993. On the morning Bhajan Lal asked R.S. Yadav on phone to reach the house of Ram Lakhan Singh Yadav (*See* PW 240 Pradyuman Kumar) Besides R.S. Yadav, the other MPs of the breakaway group also collected at the residence of Ram Lakhan Singh. They were not only met there by Bhajan Lal and Captain Satish Sharma but were also delivered suitcases brought by Bhajan Lal on which Prakash Chandra Yadav son of Ram Lakhan Singh Yadav informed the gathering that Bhajan Lal had fulfilled his promise. Not only this, Bhajan Lal and Captain Satish Sharma assured the MPs collected there that they would be allotted petrol pumps and would also be paid Rs. 20 lakhs each before voting and Rs. 20 lakhs each after the voting. Thereupon, each one of the said MPs were delivered one suitcase each (*See* PWs 191, 210, 212, 226, 237, 240, 244 Captain Dilawar Singh, R.K. Jain, Manoj Rana, Om Prakash, Gopi Krishan Yadav, Pradyuman Kumar and R.K. Dayal respectively besides documents D 750 and 751).

138. Long after the voting Haji Gulam Mohd. Khan and R.S. Yadav of the breakaway group admitted before Captain Dilawar Singh that each of them had received Rs. 20 lakhs in cash from Bhajan Lal and that there was a promise to allot Petrol Pumps too.

139. What is more to be noticed is that on August 11, 1993 Bhajan Lal claimed in a public meeting in Hissar that it was he who had engineered the defection of seven MPs within 48 hours and had thereby saved the Government at the centre. (*See* PW 199, Varinder Singh and Video cassette D-684)

140. This, then is the material against Bhajan Lal.

141. It was argued by Mr. D.C. Mathur, Senior Advocate that Bhajan Lal being the Chief Minister and being of the same political party which was ruling at the Centre, it was expected of him to save his party's Government at the Centre and that consequently even if it be assumed that he had met the Prime Minister at an odd hour of the day or had met certain MPs to win their support, no fault could be found with the same. However, he dismissed the evidence regarding payments made in cash and promises made orally as totally unworthy of reliance. He argued that on the basis of the material on record no order for framing of charges could legally be passed. Of course, he too adopted the arguments advanced by Mr. R.K. Anand on Article 105 of the Constitution and on other points including want of sanction which already stand discussed.

142. The role allegedly played by Bhajan Lal has been referred already by me above in some detail. On the basis of the material collected it cannot be said that the C.B.I. has tried to churn out an epic out of a shoe- string. The material on the record speaks of the conspiracy hatched, of the abetment and so also of the payments in cash and of the promises made. The role allegedly played is clear and unambiguous and speaks for itself. Keeping the same in view and so also the law with regard to the framing of charges as noticed above, I find no infirmity factual or legal in the impugned order.

143. The prosecution alleges that Captain Satish Sharma who, at the relevant time, was a Union Minister of State for Petroleum and Natural Gas, had the dubious distinction of being one of those who were in the forefront to bribe some of the MPs of different political parties so as to defeat the No Confidence Motion. As already noticed, while some of the leading lights of the Congress party were chalking out their game plan, the JMM MPs were also seeing in the No Confidence Motion an opportunity to enrich their coffers. Simon Marandi got in touch with Captain Satish Chandra who lost no time in assuring cash payments and allotment of petrol pumps (*See* the statement of the Approver Shailendra Mahto and of PW 75 Devendu

Mukhiya). In the meantime Bhajan Lal who was to play no less a role in this sinister game of power politics was constantly in touch with Captain Satish Sharma (*See* PWs Rakesh Kumar, B.N. Safaya, Shiv Narayan, Ram Sumer and Ashok Jolly PWs 73, 75, 190, 193 and 194 respectively). Significantly M. Veerappa Moily the then Chief Minister of Karnataka was also in touch with Captain Satish Chandra and others. At a later stage Moily was destined to play no mean a role. Going back to the offer made by Captain Satish Sharma to Simon Marandi, the Captain, on the same day *i.e.* July 22, 1993 had a meeting with Ram Lakhan Singh Yadav, Roshan Lal, Haji Gulam Mohd. And late G.C. Munda and they too were promised money, petrol pumps and housing plots for voting against the Motion.

CAPTAIN SATISH CHANDRA MINISTER FOR PETROLEUM PROMISED PETROL PUMPS TO MPs OF JD(A) BREAK-AWAY GROUP – PAID MONEY TO JMM MPs – CHARGE-SHEETED – HELD HIGH COURT

144. On the morning of 24th Bhajan Lal had delivered hefty packets of currency notes of the denomination of Rs.500 each to win Ajit Singh's support and the same evening Captain Satish Sharma had hosted a party with Ajit Singh as one of the guests. The same evening the personal driver of Captain Satish Sharma brought suit cases and delivered the same at the venue of the party (*See* PW 73 Const. Rakesh Kumar). On the morning of the 25th Captain Satish was given an audience by Prime Minister Narsimha Rao. (*See* PWs Haridas, Rajmal, Constable Rakesh Kumar and Rojnamcha D-502).

145. As already noticed Ajit Singh, even after having allegedly accepted the bribe money paid by Bhajan Lal, declared his intention to support the Motion sending shock waves in the Congress camp. Consequently Bhajan Lal and Captain Satish Sharma directed their energies towards the breakaway group of Ram Lakhan Singh Yadav. On the 27th they were present at the 'meeting called by Ram Lakhan Singh at his residence. During that meeting while Bhajan Lal assured large sums of money in cash in return for their support, Captain Satish Sharma assured allotment of petrol pumps to them or their family members (*See* Captain Dilawar Singh, Gopi Krishan Yadav, R.K. Jain and Pradyuman Kumar PWs 191, 237, 210 and 240 respectively).

146. The voting on the No Confidence Motion was to take place on the 28th day of July, 1993. On the morning of that day the six MPs of the breakaway group of JD(A) namely Ram Lakhan Singh Yadav, R.S. Yadav, Roshan Lal, Anandi Charan Das, Abhay Pratap Singh and late G.C. Munda assembled at the residence of Captain Satish Sharma. While they were still there Bhajan Lal brought suitcases and soon thereafter Prakash Chandra Yadav son of Ram Lakhan Singh Yadav happily proclaimed to the breakaway group that Bhajan Lal had fulfilled his promise. Obviously, the suitcases did not contain pornographic material though the contents were sufficient to prostitute politics. Anyhow, in the same meeting six of our worthy representatives in the Lok Sabha were once again assured by Captain Satish Sharma and Bhajan Lal that (being men of honour?) they would honour their commitment of allotment of petrol pumps, payment of Rs. 20 lakhs to each one of them before voting and Rs. 20 lakhs to each one of them after the voting. Each one of the six of them got their prized suitcases. All the six of them being themselves no less honourable, honoured their commitment. The No Confidence Motion was defeated with their support.

147. This, in short, is the story of how a Captain with the help of his crew, saved the sinking ship of P.V. Narsimha Rao.

148. However, one thing more before I close the narrative. On the 30th (or was it 31st?) of July, 1993 Simon Marandi had contacted B.N. Safaya, the confidant of Captain Satish Sharma, and Safaya after receiving Rs. 10 lakhs from the Captain, had handed over the same to Marandi. Thus yet another promise stood honoured.

149. Mr. P.P. Malhotra, Senior Advocate for Captain Satish Sharma while adopting the arguments advanced by Mr. R.K. Anand on the law points involved regarding the scope of Article 105 of the Constitution and whether MPs are to be taken as public servants or not and if so whether any sanction is required under section 197 of the Code of Criminal procedure, assailed the prosecution version as a "cock and bull" story invented to tarnish what he called "the great image" of his client. However, I see no "Cock" in the prosecution story, though, if the prosecution is to be believed, then, proverbially speaking, a "Bull" of course, was there but in the China shop of the Opposition hitting at the No Confidence Motion with the aid of money bags and promises ***a la galore***.

150. The law points referred to above have already been dealt with by me above. I need say no more on them.

151. What these gentlemen allegedly did need not be repeated ad nauseam. What has already been highlighted with regard to others highlights the roles played by these gentlemen as well. The JMM MPs, as already noticed above, found in the No Confidence Motion, a great opportunity to make what the Americans call, a quick buck. They contacted Captain Satish Sharma and secured promises from him. They approached Deshmukh. They approached V. Rajeshwara Rao also. Not, content, they came in contact with Buta Singh and ultimately reached the Supremo, P.V. Narsimha Rao. Politics is not for the novices and as for them they used the chessboard of peff, power and money like Grandmasters and ultimately succeeded (or is it nearly?) in filling their coffers.

152. As for Ram Lakhan Singh Yadav and his break-away group, the very foundation of that group was allegedly laid with greed. Finding that Ajit Singh was not willing to share what he had allegedly got from Bhajan Lal, he lost no time in breaking away from his political mentor. Bhajan Lal and Captain Satish Sharma were already prowling for a kill. So was P.V. Narsimha Rao. Assurances were made and later honoured though only with regard to payments in cash.

153. It was allegedly a game where each player exploited the weakness of the other and where ultimately all the players collected their respective "winnings" but at the cost of the game which, unfortunately, was never played in the spirit of the game.

154. A word or two before dropping the curtain. While a long line of senior and seasoned Advocates representing the petitioners argued for days together, the C.B.I. Prosecutor took a little over ninety minutes to conclude his reply. I must say he did his best but then in a case of corruption and bribery raising number of legal and Constitutional issues and involving a former Prime Minister, Cabinet Ministers, a Minister of State, two Chief Ministers, two State Ministers and number of Members of Parliament, could not the C.B.I. engage a lawyer to meet the legal challenges thrown by some of the best legal brains and to be of some assistance to the Court? But then, who dare investigate the Investigator"

PETITIONS ARE DISMISSED – HIGH COURT

155. The petitions are dismissed. Trial court record be sent back forthwith.

156. The parties are directed to appear before the learned Special Judge on 19th September, 1997.

SUPREME COURT OF INDIA

P.V. Narasimha Rao
v.
State (CBI/SPE)

1998 (4) RCR (Cri) 260: AIR 1998 SC 2120

Before: S.C. Agrawal, G.N. Ray, Dr. A.S. Anand, S.P. Bharucha and S. Rajendra Babu, JJ.

Crl. Appeals Nos. 1207-1208 of 1997 with Crl. A. Nos. 1209-1222 of 1997 and 186 of 1998 (Arising out of SLP (Cri.) Nos. 2, 1987 and 366 of 1998)
Dated 17 April, 1998

JUDGMENT

S.C. Agrawal, J. (for himself and on behalf of Dr. A.S. Anand, J.)—1. Whether by virtue of Article 105 of the Constitution a Member of Parliament can claim immunity from prosecution on a charge of bribery in a criminal Court, and whether a Member of Parliament is a "public servant" falling within the purview of the Prevention of Corruption Act, 1988 (hereinafter referred to as 'the 1988 Act'). These are the two questions which have come up for consideration before this Bench in these matters.

P.V. NARASIMHA RAO PRIME MINISTER – SHORT BY 14 MPs OF ABSOLUTE MAJORITY – FACES 'NO CONFIDENCE MOTION' MOVED ON 26 JULY, 1993 – VOTING ON 28 JULY, 1993 – MOTION DEFEATED – FACTS

2. In the General Election for the Tenth Lok Sabha held in 1991 the Congress (I) party emerged as the single largest party and it formed the Government with P.V. Narasimha Rao (hereinafter referred to as 'A-1') as the Prime Minister. In the Monsoon Session of Lok Sabha in July, 1993 a 'No-Confidence Motion' was moved against the Government by Shri Ajay Mukhopadhyaya, a CPI (M) M.P. At that time the effective strength of the House (Lok Sabha) was 528 and Congress (I) party had 251 members. It was short by 14 members for simple majority. The Motion of No-Confidence was taken up for discussion in the Lok Sabha on July 26, 1993 and the debate continued till July 28, 1993. The motion was defeated with 251 members voting in favour of the motion, while 265 voting against it.

COMPLAINT DATED 1 FEBRUARY, 1996 FILED ALLEGING CRIMINAL CONSPIRACY – BRIBERY TO JMM – JD(A) BREAK-AWAY GROUP MPs – FACTS

On February 28, 1996, one Shri Ravindra Kumar of Rashtriya Mukti Morcha filed a complaint dated February 1, 1996 with the Central Bureau of Investigation (for short 'CBI') wherein it was alleged that in July, 1993 a criminal conspiracy was hatched by A-1, Satish Sharma (hereinafter referred to as 'A-2'), Ajit Singh (hereinafter referred to as 'A-13'), Bhajan Lal (hereinafter referred to as 'A-14'), V.C.

Shukla, R.K. Dhawan and Lalit Suri to prove a majority of the Government on the floor of the House on July 28, 1993 by bribing Members of Parliament of different political parties, individuals and groups of an amount of over Rs. 3 crores and that in furtherance of the said criminal conspiracy a sum of Rs. 1.10 crores was handed over by the aforementioned persons, except A-15, to Suraj Mandal (hereinafter referred to as 'A-3').

FIR REGISTERED BY CBI ON DELHI HIGH COURT ORDER DATED 24 MAY, 1996 – ANOTHER ON 11 JUNE, 1996 – CBI SUBMITTED 3 CHARGE-SHEETS ON DIFFERENT DATES – IN ALL AGAINST A1 TO A22 – FACTS

On the basis of the said complaint the CBI registered four cases under section 13(2) read with section 13(1)(d)(iii) of the 1988 Act against A-3, Shibu Soren (hereinafter referred to as 'A-4'), Simon Marandi (hereinafter referred to as 'A-5') and Shailendra Mahto (hereinafter referred to as 'A-6'), Members of Parliament belonging to the Jharkhand Mukti Morcha party (for short 'JMM'). Subsequently in pursuance of the order dated May 24, 1996 passed by the Delhi High Court in Civil Writ Petition No. 23/96 another case was registered on June 11, 1996 against A-1, A-2, A-3, A-4, A-5, A-6, A-14, A-15, V.C. Shukla, R.K. Dhawan, Lalit Suri and others under section 120-B, Indian Penal Code and sections 7, 12, 13(2) read with section 13(1)(d)(iii) of the 1988 Act. After completing the investigation, the CBI submitted three charge-sheets dated October 30, 1996, December 9, 1996 and January 22, 1997 in the Court of Special Judge, New Delhi. In the first charge-sheet dated October 30, 1996 it was stated that investigation had revealed that A-1, A-2, A-3, A-4, A-5, A-6, Buta Singh (hereinafter referred to as 'A-7'), and other unknown persons entered into a criminal conspiracy to defeat the 'No-Confidence Motion' by resorting to giving and accepting of gratification as a motive or reward and in pursuance thereof four Members of Parliament belonging to JMM (A-3, A-4, A-5 and A-6) accepted illegal gratification to vote against the Motion and because of their votes and some other votes the Government led by A-1 survived. It was also stated in the charge-sheet that investigation has also revealed that the four Members of Parliament belonging to JMM had been bribed in crores of rupees for voting against the 'No-Confidence Motion'. The said charge-sheet was filed against A-1, A-2, A-3, A-4, A-5, A-6 and A-7 and other unknown persons in respect of offences under section 120-B, Indian Penal Code and sections 7, 12, 13(2) read with section 13(1)(d)(iii) of the 1988 Act and substantive offences thereunder. The second charge-sheet dated December 9, 1996 was in the nature of a supplementary charge-sheet wherein it was stated that investigation has further revealed that V. Rajeshwar Rao (hereinafter referred to as 'A-8'), N.M. Revanna (hereinafter referred to as 'A-9'), Ramalinga Reddy (hereinafter referred to as 'A-10'), M. Veerappa Moily (hereinafter referred to as 'A-11'), D.K. Audi Kesavulu (hereinafter referred to as 'A-12') and M. Thimmegowda (hereinafter referred to as 'A-13') were also parties to the criminal conspiracy which is the subject-matter of the first charge-sheet filed on October 30, 1996 and in pursuance to the said criminal conspiracy they had arranged funds and bribed the four JMM MPs as the motive or award to secure their support to defeat the 'No-Confidence Motion' and thereby committed the offences punishable under section 120-B, Indian Penal Code and sections 7, 12, 13(2) read with section 13(1)(d)(iii) of the 1988 Act and substantive offences thereunder along with the original seven accused. In the third charge-sheet dated January 22, 1997, which was described as 'Supplementary Charge-sheet No. 2', it was stated that further investigation has been carried on under section 173(8) of Criminal Procedure Code and as a result identity of remaining accused persons has been established and that they are A-14, A-15, Ram Lakhan Singh Yadav (hereinafter referred to as 'A-16'), Ram Sharan Yadav (hereinafter referred to as 'A-17'), Roshan Lal (hereinafter referred to as 'A-18'), Abhay Pratap Singh (hereinafter referred to as 'A-19'), Anadi Charan Das (hereinafter referred to as 'A-20'), Haji Gulam Mohd. Khan (hereinafter referred to as 'A-21') and late G.C. Munda (hereinafter referred to as 'A-22'). It was stated that even after securing the support of four JMM MPs in the manner stated in the first charge-sheet dated October 30, 1996 and second charge-sheet dated December 9, 1996 the Congress (I) Government still required the support of some more MPs and that with this objective the Congress (I) led by A-1 was making efforts to win the support of some other MPs including MPs belonging to Janta Dal (Ajit Group) (for short 'JD(A)'). In the charge-sheet it was also stated that A-14, A-15, A-16, A-17, A-18, A-19, A-20, A-21 and A-22 were parties to the criminal conspiracy along with A-1 to A-13 already named in the earlier two charge- sheets and in pursuance to the said criminal conspiracy A-14 had arranged funds and had paid bribes to A-15 and the seven MPs of the breakaway JD(A) as a motive or award to secure their support to defeat the 'No-Confidence Motion' and thereby committed the offences punishable under section 120-B, Indian Penal Code and sections 7, 12, 13(2) read with section 13(1)(d)(iii) of the 1988 Act and substantive offences thereunder.

A6 (SHAILENDRA MAHTO) BECAME APPROVER – SPECIAL JUDGE ORDER ON 5 APRIL, 1997 – ORDER DATED 6 MAY, 1997 FOR FRAMING OF CHARGES AGAINST ALL ACCUSED UNDER VARIOUS OFFENCES OF CONSPIRACY AND BRIBERY AGAINST BOTH – GIVERS AND TAKERS – FACTS

3. An application was submitted by A-6 (Shailendra Mahto) under section 306, Criminal Procedure Code for grant of pardon for being treated as an approver. The said application was referred to the Magistrate for recording his statement under section 164, Criminal Procedure Code and after considering the said statement the Special Judge, by order dated April 5, 1997, allowed the application of A-6 and tendered pardon to him on the condition of his making a full and true disclosure of all the circumstances within his knowledge relating to the offences of every other person concerned, whether as a principal or abettor in the commission of the offences under the charge-sheets. After hearing the arguments on charges, the Special Judge passed the order dated May 6, 1997 wherein he held that there is sufficient evidence on record to justify framing of charges against all the appellants. Insofar as A-1, A-2, A-7 and A-8 to A-14 are concerned, the Special Judge held that there is sufficient evidence on record to justify framing of charges under section 120-B, Indian Penal Code read with sections 7, 12, 13(2) read with section 13(1)(d) of the 1988 Act and also for substantive offence punishable under section 12 of the 1988 Act against all of them. So far as A-3, A-5 and A-15 to A-21 are concerned, the Special Judge held that there is sufficient evidence on record to justify framing of charges under section 120B, Indian Penal Code read with sections 7, 12, 13(2) read with section 13(1)(d) of the 1988 Act and as well as charges for substantive offence punishable under section 7 and section 13(2) read with section 13(1)(d) of the 1988 Act against all of them. The Special Judge also held that there is prima facie evidence of commission of offence under section 193, Indian Penal Code by accused Nos. A-3 to A-5.

MPs ARE PROTECTED BY ARTICLE 105 – MPs ARE NOT PUBLIC SERVANTS – SANCTION TO PROSECUTE NOT OBTAINED – SUBMISSIONS REJECTED BY SPECIAL JUDGE – FACTS

4. Before the Special Judge, an objection was raised on behalf of the accused persons that the jurisdiction of the Court to try the case was barred under Article 105(2) of the Constitution because the trial is in respect of matters which relate to the privileges and immunities of the House of Parliament (Lok Sabha) and its Members in as much as the foundation of the charge-sheets is the allegation of acceptance of bribe by some Members of Parliament for voting against the 'No-Confidence Motion' and that the controversy to be decided in this case would be in respect of the motive and action of Members of Parliament pertaining to the vote given by them in relation to the 'No- Confidence Motion'. The Special Judge rejected the said contention on the view that in the present case voting pattern of the accused persons was not under adjudication and they were sought to be tried for their illegal acts committed outside Parliament, *i.e.*, demanding and accepting the bribe for exercising their franchise in a particular manner, and the accused persons are not being prosecuted for exercising their right of vote but they are being prosecuted on the allegations that they while holding a public office demanded and accepted illegal gratification for exercising their franchise in a particular manner which is an offence punishable under the 1988 Act and that Article 105 of the Constitution does not provide any protection to the accused persons. Another contention that was urged before the Special Judge was that a Member of Parliament is not a public servant for the purpose of the 1988 Act and as such giving and taking of the alleged illegal gratification does not amount to any offence punishable under the provisions of the 1988 Act and there cannot be any offence of conspiracy of giving and taking of bribe by a Member of Parliament. The said contention was rejected by the Special Judge on the view that the question whether a Member of Parliament is a public servant is concluded by the decision of the Delhi High Court in the cases of **L.K. Advani v. Central Bureau of Investigation, 1997 Cr LJ 2559,** wherein it has been held that Member of Parliament is a public servant under the 1988 Act. It was also urged before the Special Judge that the case could not be proceeded against the accused persons since previous sanction for prosecution under section 19 of the 1988 Act had not been obtained. The said contention was also rejected by the Special Judge on the ground that no previous sanction of prosecution for an accused under section 19 is necessary if he has ceased to hold a public office which was allegedly misused by him and in the present case at the time of filing of the charge-sheets and on the date of taking of cognizance by the Court Tenth Lok Sabha had come to an end and after the Elections in 1996 and the accused persons who were the members of the Tenth Lok Sabha had ceased to hold the office as members of the said Lok Sabha and therefore under law no sanction for their prosecution is required and furthermore accused persons are sought to be tried for criminal conspiracy under section 120B, Indian Penal Code read with sections 7, 12, 13(2) of the 1988 Act as well as the substantive offences and that according to section 19 of the 1988 Act sanction is required only in respect of the offences punishable under sections 7 and 13 and these substantive offences were allegedly committed by Members of Parliament who had accepted the illegal gratification for voting against the 'No-Confidence Motion' and that no sanction is required in the case of a Member of Parliament or a Member of the State Legislature though he is a public servant because there is no sanctioning authority qua him.

REVISION PETITION DISMISSED BY DELHI HIGH COURT *VIDE* DETAILED ORDER – FACTS

Revision petitions filed by the appellants against the said order of the Special Judge have been dismissed by the impugned judgment of the Delhi High Court. In the High Court the following contentions were urged by the appellants:

(I) Even if the allegations of the prosecution were accepted, the Court would have no jurisdiction to fasten any criminal liability on the accused persons as whatever allegedly happened was in respect of votes given by some of them in the Lok Sabha and that, in any case, whatever transpired, touched the privileges of the House within the meaning of clauses (2) and (3) of Article 105 of the Constitution.

(II) Members of Lok Sabha hold no office and as such are not public servants within the meaning of section 2(c) of the 1988 Act and that for that reason the 1988 Act would not apply to the alleged acts of omission and commission of the accused persons.

(III) Even if it be taken that Members of Lok Sabha do fall within section 2(c) of the 1988 Act and are thus taken to be public servants, yet the Act would not apply for the simple reason that in the case of Lok Sabha Members there is no authority competent to remove them from their office within the meaning of section 19(1)(c) of the 1988 Act.

(IV) In the case of A-1, A-9, A-10, A-11 and A-13 there is nothing to show that they had conspired or were part of any conspiracy.

(V) Sanction was required under section 197, Criminal Procedure Code to prosecute A-1.

(VI) No case is made out for framing the charges against the appellants.

BRIBING AN MP MAY BE BREACH OF PRIVILEGE – IT DOES NOT OUST JURISDICTION OF COURTS TO TAKE COGNIZANCE – PRIVILEGE IS NOT TO TAKE BRIBE – MOREOVER PRIVILEGE DISALLOWED ON 11-12 MARCH 1996 – HELD HIGH COURT – AGRAWAL, J.

5. While dealing with the first contention based on clauses (2) and (3) of Article 105 of the Constitution the High Court has held that to offer bribe to a Member of Parliament to influence him in his conduct as a member has been treated as a breach of privilege in England but merely treating the commission of a criminal offence as a breach of privilege does not amount to ouster of jurisdiction of the ordinary Court to try penal offences and that to claim that in such matters the Courts would have no jurisdiction would amount to claiming a privilege to commit a crime. The High Court has also pointed out that four notices of a question of privilege dated February 26 and 27, 1996 were given by four members of Lok Sabha, namely, Sarva Shri Jaswant Singh, Inderjit Gupta, Arjun Singh and Jagmeet Singh Brar against A-1 and the four members belonging to JMM (A-3 to A-6). The notices were forwarded to the said accused for comments and after discussion on the said notices during which members of all parties expressed their views the Speaker disallowed the notice given by Shri Arjun Singh on March 11, 1996 and the notices of a question of privilege given by Sarva Shri Jaswant Singh, Inderjit Gupta and Jagmeet Singh Brar were disallowed by the Speaker on March 12, 1996.

AN MP HELD AN OFFICE – PERFORMS PUBLIC DUTIES – IS A PUBLIC SERVANT – HELD HIGH COURT – AGRAWAL, J.

The second submission that a Member of Parliament is not a public servant under section 2(c) of the 1988 Act was rejected by the High Court on the view that a Member of Parliament holds an office and is a public servant falling under clause (viii) of section 2(c) of the 1988 Act.

IF THERE WAS NO AUTHORITY TO REMOVE AN MP DOES NOT MEAN PC ACT WAS NOT APPLICABLE – HELD HIGH COURT – AGRAWAL, J.

The third contention that the 1988 Act is not applicable to a Member of Parliament since there is no authority competent to remove him from his office for the purpose of granting sanction under section 19(1)(c) of the 1988 Act was also not accepted by the High Court. It was held in the absence of an authority to remove a Member of Parliament does not mean that the 1988 Act would not be applicable to him.

ENTERING INTO A CONSPIRACY – BRIBING OF MPs BY PM WAS 'NOT ACT IN THE DISCHARGE OF HIS OFFICIAL DUTY' – HIGH COURT DISMISSED REVISION PETITION – AGRAWAL, J.

As regards the requirement of sanction under section 197, Criminal Procedure Code as against A-1, the High Court held that A-1 was a party to actual bribing of Members of Parliament and that it is no job of a Prime Minister to hatch or be a party to such a criminal conspiracy and that what A-1 did cannot fall within the ambit of the words "while acting or purporting to act in the discharge of his official duty" in section 197, Criminal Procedure Code. The High Court thereafter examined the material on record in relation to each accused person and found that there was no ground for interfering with the order passed by the Special Judge.

HENCE APPEALS – ORIGINALLY HEARD BY THREE JUDGE BENCH – SINCE SUBSTANTIAL QUESTION OF LAW INVOLVED – REFERRED TO CONSTITUTIONAL BENCH – AGRAWAL, J.

6. Feeling aggrieved by the said judgment of the High Court, the appellants have filed these appeals. The appeals were heard by a Bench of three Judges. After hearing the arguments of the learned counsel, the following order was passed by that Bench on November 18, 1997:

> "Among other questions, a substantial question of law as to the interpretation of Article 105 of the Constitution of India is raised in these petitions. These petitions are, therefore, required to be heard and disposed of by a Constitution Bench. Accordingly, the Registry is directed to place these petitions before Hon'ble the Chief Justice for necessary orders."

In pursuance of the said order, the matter has been placed before us. At the commencement of the hearing, we passed the following order on December 9, 1997:

> "By order dated November 18, 1997 these matters have been referred to this Court for the reason that among other questions, a substantial question of law as to the interpretation of Article 105 of the Constitution of India is raised in these petitions. These petitions are, therefore, required to be heard and disposed of by a Constitution Bench. The learned counsel for the parties agree that the Constitution Bench may only deal with the questions relating to interpretation of Article 105 of the Constitution and the applicability of the Prevention of Corruption Act to a Member of Parliament and Member of State Legislative Assembly and the other questions can be considered by the Division Bench."

DURING THE PENDENCY OF APPEALS – CHARGES FRAMED BY THE SPECIAL JUDGE – AGRAWAL, J.

During the pendency of the appeals in this Court the Special Judge has framed the charges against the accused persons (appellants herein) on September 25, 1997. All the appellants have been charged with the offence of criminal conspiracy punishable under section 120B, Indian Penal Code read with sections 7, 12 and 13(2) read with section 13(1)(d) of the 1988 Act. A-3 to A-5, belonging to JMM and A-15 to A-21, belonging to JD(A), have been further charged with offences under section 7 and section 13(2) read with section 13(1)(d) of the 1988 Act. A-3 to A-5 have also been charged with offence under section 193, Indian Penal Code. The other appellants, *viz.*, A-1, A-2 and A-7 to A-14 have been charged with the offence under section 193, Indian Penal Code. The other appellants, *viz.*, A-1, A-2 and A-7 to A-14 have been charged with offence under section 12 of the 1988 Act for having abetted the commission of the offence punishable under section 7 of the 1988 Act by the members of Parliament belonging to JMM and JD(A).

SECTIONS 7, 12, 13(1)(d) AND 13(2) OF PC ACT, 1988 REPRODUCED – AGRAWAL, J.

Sections 7, 12 and 13(1)(d) and 13(2) of the 1988 Act may be reproduced as under:

> "7. Public servant taking gratification other than legal remuneration in respect of an official act – Whoever, being, or expecting to be a public servant, accepts or obtains or agrees to accept or attempts to obtain from any person, for himself or for any other person, any gratification whatever, other than a legal remuneration, as a motive or reward for doing or forbearing to do any official act or for showing or forbearing to show, in the exercise of his official functions, favour or disfavour to any person or for rendering or attempting to render any service or disservice to any person, with the Central Government or any State Government or Parliament or the Legislature of any State or with any local authority, corporation or Government or Parliament or the Legislature of any State or with any local authority, corporation or Government company referred to in clause (c) of section 2, or with any public servant, whether named or otherwise, shall be punishable with imprisonment which shall be not less than six months but which may extend to five years and shall also be liable to fine.
>
> *Explanations.*—(a) "Expecting to be a public servant." If a person not expecting to be in office obtains a gratification by deceiving others into a belief that he is about to be in office, and that he will then service them, he may be guilty of cheating, but he is not guilty of the offence defined in this section.
>
> (b) "Gratification". The word "gratification" is not restricted to pecuniary gratifications or to gratifications estimable in money.
>
> (c) "Legal remunerations." The words "legal remuneration" are not restricted to remuneration which a public servant can lawfully demand, but include all remuneration which he is permitted by the Government or the organisation, which he serves, to accept.
>
> (d) "A motive or reward for doing". A person who receives a gratification as a motive or reward for doing what he does not intend or is not in a position to do, or has not done, comes within this expression.
>
> (e) Where a public servant induces a person erroneously to believe that his influence with the Government has obtained a title for that person and thus induces that person to give the public servant, money or any other gratification as a reward for this service, the public servant has committed an offence under this section."
>
> "*12. Punishment for abetment of offences defined in section 7 or 11.*—Whoever abets any offence punishable under section 7 to section 11 whether or not that offence is committed in consequence of that abetment, shall be punishable with imprisonment for a term which shall not be less than six months but which may extend to five years and shall also be liable to fine."
>
> "*13. Criminal misconduct by a public servant.*—(1) A public servant is said to commit the offence of criminal misconduct,—
>
> (a) to (c) x x x x x
>
> (d) If he,—
>
> (i) by corrupt or illegal means, obtains for himself or for any other person any valuable thing or pecuniary advantage; or

(ii) by abusing his position as a public servant, obtains for himself or for any other person any valuable thing or pecuniary advantage; or

(iii) while holding office as a public servant, obtains for any person any valuable or pecuniary advantage without any public interest; or

(e) x x x x

(2) Any public servant who commits criminal misconduct shall be punishable with imprisonment for a term which shall not be less than one year but which may extend to seven years and shall also be liable to fine."

CHARGES FRAMED AGAINST P.V. NARASIMHA RAO EX-PM AND OTHERS – AGRAWAL, J.

The charge of criminal conspiracy as against appellants who are alleged to have agreed to offer the gratification (A-1, A-2 and A-7 to A-14) is in these terms:—

"That you P.V. Narasimha Rao between July and August, 1993 at Delhi and Bangalore were party to a criminal conspiracy and agreed to or entered into an agreement with your co-accused Capt. Satish Sharma, Buta Singh, V. Rajeshwara Rao, H.M. Revanna, Ramlinga Reddy, M. Veerappa Moily, D.K. Audi Kesavalu, M. Thimmegowda, Bhajan Lal, JMM (Jharkhand Mukti Morcha) MPs Suraj Mandal, Shibu Soren, Simon Marandi, Shailendra Mahto (Approver, since granted pardon on 8.4.1997), Janata Dal (Ajit Group) MPs Ajit Singh, Ram Lakhan Singh Yadav, Ram Sharan Yadav, Roshan Lal, Anadi Charan Das, Abhay Pratap Singh, Haji Ghulam Mohd. Khan and late G.C. Munda to defeat the no-confidence motion moved on 26.7.1993 against the then Congress (I) Government headed by you by illegal mean *viz.*, to offer or cause to offer and pay gratification other than the legal remuneration to your co-accused persons namely JMM and Janata Dal (A) MPs named above as a motive or reward for their helping in defeating the said no-confidence motion moved by the opposition parties and in pursuance of the said agreement you paid or caused to pay several lakhs of rupees to the above referred JMM and Janata Dal (A) MPs who obtained or attempted to obtain the same in the manner stated above and thereby you have committed an offence punishable under section 120, Indian Penal Code read with sections 7, 12, 13(2) read with section 13(1)(d) of the P.C. Act, 1988 and within my cognizance."

The charge of criminal conspiracy as against appellants who are alleged to have agreed to receive the gratification (A-3 to A-5 and A-15 to A-21) is in these terms:

"Firstly, you between July and August, 1993 at Delhi and Bangalore were party to a criminal conspiracy and agreed to or enter into an agreement with your co-accused P.V. Narasimha Rao, Capt. Satish Sharma, Buta Singh, V. Rajeshwara Rao, H.M. Revanna, Ramlinga Reddy, M. Veerapa Moily, D.K. Audi Keshvalu, M. Thimmegowda, Bhajan Lal, JMM (Jharkhand Mukti Morcha) MPs Shibu Soren, Simon Marandi, Shailendra Mahto (Approver, since granted pardon on 8.4.1997), Janata Dal (Ajit Group) MPs Ajit Singh, Ram Lakhan Singh Yadav, Ram Sharan Yadav, Roshan Lal, Anandi Charan Dass, Abhey Partap Singh, Haji Ghulam Mohd. Khan and late G.C. Munda to defeat the no-confidence motion moved against the then Congress (I) Government headed by accused Shri P.V. Narasimha Rao on 26.7.1993 by illegal means *viz.* to obtain or agree to obtain gratification other than legal remunerations from your above named accused persons other than JMM and Janata Dal (A) MPs as a motive or reward for defeating the no-confidence motion and in pursuance thereof abovenamed accused persons other than JMM and Janata Dal (A) passed on several lakhs of rupees to you or your other co-accused namely JMM and Janata Dal (A) MPs which amounts were accepted by you or your said co-accused persons and thereby you have committed an offence punishable under section 120B read with sections 7, 12, 13(2) read with section 13(1)(d) of the P.C. Act and within my cognizance."

The charges under section 7 and section 13(2) read with section 13(1)(d) of the 1988 Act against A-3 to A-5 and A-15 to A-21 are in these terms:

> "*Secondly*, that you being a public servant while functioning in your capacity of Member of Parliament (10th Lok Sabha) during the aforesaid period and at the aforesaid places in pursuance of the aforesaid conspiracy demanded and accepted from your co-accused other than JMM and JD (A) MPs mentioned above a sum of Rs. 280 lakhs for yourself and other JMM MPs named above other than your legal remuneration as a motive or reward for defeating above referred no-confidence of Congress (I) headed by your co-accused P.V. Narasimha Rao and thereby you have committed an offence punishable under section 7 of P.C. Act and within my cognizance."
>
> "*Thirdly*, you during the aforesaid period and at the aforesaid places being a public servant while functioning in your aforesaid capacity of Member of Parliament by corrupt or illegal means and by abusing your position as a said public servant obtained for yourself or your other co-accused advantage to the extent of Rs. 280 lakhs and thereby committed an offence punishable under section 13(2) read with section 13(1)(d) of P.C. Act and within my cognizance."

The charge under section 12 of the Act against A-1, A-2, A-14 and A-15 is in these terms:—

> "*Secondly*, you P.V. Narasimha Rao in pursuance of the aforesaid criminal conspiracy during the aforesaid period and at the aforesaid place abetted the commission of offence punishable under section 7 of P.C. Act by above referred JMM and Janata Dal (A) MPs and thereby you have committed an offence punishable under section 12 of the P.C. Act and with my cognizance."

QUESTIONS WHICH WERE TO BE DECIDED BY THE CONSTITUTIONAL BENCH – AGRAWAL, J.

The two questions arising for consideration can be thus formulated :-

(1) Does Article 105 of the Constitution confer any immunity on a Member of Parliament from being prosecuted in a Criminal Court for an offence involving offer or acceptance of bribe?

(2) Is a Member of Parliament excluded from the ambit of the 1988 Act for the reason that:

   (a) he is not a person who can be regarded as a "public servant" as defined under section 2(c) of the 1988 Act, and

   (b) he is not a person comprehended in clauses (a), (b), and (c) of sub-section (1) of section 19 and there is no authority competent to grant sanction for his prosecution under the 1988 Act?

DISCUSSION BY THE SUPREME COURT – AGRAWAL, J.

Immunity from prosecution

7. In order to answer the first question it would be necessary to examine the scope and ambit of the protection available to a Member of Parliament under Article 105 which deals with the powers, privileges and immunities of the Houses of Parliament and it members. Before we undertake this task, we would briefly set out the prevailing state of law in the United Kingdom and other countries follows the common law.

LAW PREVAILING IN OTHER COUNTRIES REGARDING THE PRIVILEGES AVAILABLE TO THE MEMBERS OF PARLIAMENT – AGRAWAL, J.

8. UNITED KINGDOM: During the rule of the Tudor and Stuart Kings the Commons had to wage a bitter struggle to assert their supremacy which culminated in the Bill of Rights, 1689 whereby it was secured "that the freedom of speech and debates or proceedings in Parliament ought not to be impeached or questioned in any court or place out of Parliament" (Article 9). On May 2, 1965 the House of Commons passed a resolution whereby it resolved that "the offer of money, or other advantage, to any Member of Parliament for promoting of any matter whatsoever, depending or to be transacted in Parliament is a high crime and misdemeanour and tends to the subversion of the English constitution". In the spirit of this resolution, the offering to a Member of either House of a bribe to influence him in his conduct as a Member or of any fee or reward in connection with the promotion of or opposition to any bill, resolution, matter or thing submitted or intended to be submitted to the House or any committee thereof, has been treated as a breach of privilege. [See: *May's Parliamentary Practice,* 21st Edn., p. 128]. In its report submitted in July 1976 the Royal Commission on Standards of Conduct in Public Life (chaired by Lord Salmon) has pointed out that "neither the statutory nor the common law applies to the bribery or attempted bribery of a Member of Parliament in respect of his Parliamentary activities" but "corrupt transactions involving a Member of Parliament in respect of matters that had nothing to do with his parliamentary activities would be caught by the ordinary criminal law" (page 98, paras 307 and 308). The Salmon Commission has observed that sanctions against bribery introduced by the criminal law in other fields have now outstripped whatever sanctions may be exerted through Parliament's own powers of investigation and punishment and the Commission was of the view there is a strong case for bringing such malpractice within the criminal law. According to the Salmon Commission, the Committee of Privileges and the Select Committee on Members' Interests do not provide an investigative machinery comparable to that of a police investigation and that having regard to the complexity of most investigations into serious corruption special expertise is necessary for this type of inquiry (para 310, pp. 98, 99). The Salmon Commission has recommended :

> "Membership of Parliament is a great honour and carries with it a special duty to maintain the highest standards of probity, and this duty has almost invariably been strictly observed. Nevertheless in view of our report as a whole, and especially in the light of the points set out in the foregoing paragraph, we recommend that Parliament should consider bringing corruption, bribery and attempted bribery of a Member of Parliament acting in his parliamentary capacity within the ambit of the criminal law." [para 311 p. 99]

During the course of the debate in the House of Lords, Lord Salmon said:

> "To my mind equality before the law is one of the pillars of freedom. To say that immunity from criminal proceedings against anyone who tries to bribe a Member of Parliament and any Member of Parliament who accepts the bribe, stems from the Bills of Rights is possibly a serious mistake."

After quoting the Bill of Rights Lord Salmon continued:

> "Now this is a charter for freedom of speech in the House it is not a charter for corruption. To my mind, the Bill of Rights, for which no one has more respect than I have, has no more to do with the topic which we are discussing than the Merchandise Marks Act. The crime of corruption is complete when the bribe is offered or given or solicited or taken."

9. The correctness of the statement in the Report of the Salmon Commission that common law does not apply to bribery or attempted bribery of a Member of Parliament in respect of his parliamentary activities, has been doubted by Prof. Graham Zellick who has said that Sir James Fitzjames Stephen appears to be the only writer to have taken the same view in his Digest of Criminal Law (1878), Article 118, and that there is nothing in the English authorities which compels to the conclusion that a Member of Parliament is not a public officer and is not punishable at common law for bribery and breach of trust. [*See*: Grahma Zellick: Bribery of Members of Parliament and the Criminal Law, 1979 Public Law p. 31 at pp. 39, 40].

10. The question whether offering of a bribe to and acceptance of the same by a Member of Parliament constitutes an offence at common law came up for consideration before a criminal court (Buckley J.) in 1992 in **R.V. Currie**. In that case it was alleged that a Member of Parliament had accepted bribes as a reward for using his influence as a Member in respect of application for British nationality of one of the persons offering the bribe. The indictment was sought to be quashed on the ground that bribery of a Member of Parliament is not a crime and that in any event the Court has no jurisdiction and Parliament alone can try a member for bribery, the matter being covered by parliamentary privilege. The learned Judge rules against the contention and held:

> "That a member of Parliament against whom there is a *prime facie* case of corruption should be immune from prosecution in the Courts of law is to my mind an unacceptable proposition at the present time. I do not believe it to be the law." In 1994 the Attorney-General advised the Committee of Privileges of the House of Commons that, in his opinion, though bribery of a Member was not a statutory offence, it might be an offence at the common law. [See: *May's Parliamentary Practice*, 22nd End., p. 114]. The Committee on Standards in Public Life, chaired by Lord Nolan (Nolan Committee) in its first report submitted in May 1995, has said:
>
> "There is one area of conduct where a need already exists to clarify, and perhaps alter, the boundary between the Courts of Parliament. Bribery of a Member, or the acceptance of a bribe by a Member, is contempt of Parliament and can be punished by the House. The test which the House would apply for bribery would no doubt be similar to that which would apply under Common Law. However it is quite likely that Members of Parliament who accepted bribes in connection with their Parliamentary duties would be committing Common Law offences which could be tried by the courts. Doubt exists as to whether the courts or Parliament have jurisdiction in such cases." [para 103]
>
> "The Salmon Commission in 1976 recommended that such doubt should be resolved by legislation, but this has not been acted upon. We believe that it would be unsatisfactory to leave the issue outstanding when other aspects of the law of Parliament relating to conduct are being clarified. We recommend that the Government should now take steps to clarify the law relating to the bribery of or the receipt of a bribe by a Member of Parliament. This could usefully be combined with the consolidation of the statute law on bribery which Salmon also recommended, which the government accepted, but which has not been done. This might be a task which the Law Commission could take forward." [para 104]

It appears that the matter is being considered by the Law Commission. In the Law Commission, Consultation Paper No. 145, reference has been made to a document entitled 'Clarification of the law relating to the Bribery of Members of Parliament', published by the Home Office in December 1996, whereby the Select Committee on Standards and Privileges has been invited to consider the following four broad options:

(1) to rely solely on Parliamentary privileges to deal with accusations of the bribery by Members of Parliament;

(2) subject Members of Parliament to the present corruption statutes in full;

(3) distinguish between conduct which should be dealt with by the criminal law and that which should be left to Parliament itself, and

(4) make criminal proceedings subject to the approval of the relevant House of Parliament.

11. AUSTRALIA: Even though Article 9 of the Bill of Rights is applicable in Australia but as far back as in 1875 the Supreme Court of New South Wales held that an attempt to bribe a Member of the Legislative Assembly in order to influence his vote was a criminal offence, a misdemeanour at common law. [*See*: **R. v. White, 13 SCR (NSW) 332]**.

12. The said decision in White was approved by the High Court of Australia in **R.V. Boston, (1923) 33 CLR 386.** In that case three persons, namely, Walter James Boston, a member of the Legislative Assembly of New South Wales, John Andrew Harrison and Henry Ernest Mitchelmore, were alleged to have unlawfully conspired together and with other persons that certain large sums of money should be corruptly given to Walter James Boston to use his position to secure the inspection of, acquisition and the payment of cash for certain estates by the Government of New South Wales and which estates were to be paid for out of the public funds of the said State and to put pressure upon the Minister for Lands and other officers of the Crown to inspect, acquire and to pay cash for certain estates. The trial Judge upheld the demurrer to the charge by the defendants on the ground that the matters alleged did not include a provision respecting voting in Parliament. In the High Court it was not disputed by the defendants that an agreement to pay money to a member of Parliament in order to influence his vote in Parliament would amount to a criminal offence. It was urged that consistently with the allegations in the information, the agreement between the defendants might have been to pay money to Boston to induce him to use his position exclusively outside Parliament, not by vote or speech in the Assembly, and that the transaction in connection with which he was to use his position to put pressure on the Minister might, consistently with the information, be one which would never come before Parliament and which, in his opinion and in the opinion of those who paid him, was highly beneficial to the State; that such an agreement would not amount to a criminal offence, and that consequently the information is bad. Rejecting the said contention, Knox C.J. has observed:

> "In my opinion, the payment of money to, and the receipt of money by, a Member of Parliament to induce him to use his official position, whether inside or outside Parliament, for the purpose of influencing or putting pressure on a Minister or other officer of the Crown to enter into or carry out a transaction involving payment of money out of the public funds, are acts tending to the public mischief, and an agreement or combination to do such acts amounts to a criminal offence. From the point of view of tendency to public mischief I can see no substantial difference between paying money to a member to induce him to use his vote in Parliament in a particular direction and paying him money to induce him to use his position as a member outside Parliament for the purpose of influencing or putting pressure on Ministers. A member of

> Parliament cannot divest his position of the right which it confers to take part in the proceedings of Parliament—he cannot 'use his position as a member of Parliament' stripped of its principal attribute. The influence which his position as a member of Parliament enables him to exert on a Minister has its source in his right to sit and vote in Parliament, and it would be idle to pretend that in discussions and negotiations between a Minister and a member that right, or the power it confers on a member, can be disregarded or ignored. The tenure of office of the Minister and his colleagues may be dependent on the vote or on the abstention from voting of an individual member, or even on his words or his silence in Parliament." [pp. 392, 393]

Similarly, Isaacs and Rich JJ, have said:

> "It is impossible to sever the voluntarily assumed intervention departmentally from the legislative position to which by custom it is recognised as incidental. A member so intervening speaks as member and is dealt with as member, and not as a private individual. His ulterior power of action, though not intruded into observation, is always existent and is always known to exist. It is scarcely even camouflaged. The importance of even one parliamentary vote on a critical occasion is not entirely unknown." [p. 403]

Higgins J., after stating that it was not disputed by the counsel for the defendants that if the agreement were that the member should use his votes or his action in the House to secure the acquisition of the land, the agreement would be criminal conspiracy, expressed the view that he could not read the count as 'confining the agreement to action of the member outside the House' and that the words 'to use his position as such member' primarily refer to an action in the House. The learned Judge, however, held:

> "A member is the watch-dog of the public; and Cerberus must not be seduced from vigilance by a sop. I see no reason to doubt that even if the count were confined to an agreement as to the action of the member outside the House action in which the member used his position as member-the agreement would be an indictable conspiracy." [p. 410]

13. Gavan Duffy and Starke JJ., in their dissenting judgment, while holding that the acts charged as intended to be done by the defendant Boston, however, important they may be, would not be malversation in his office, or acts done in his office, unless they were done in the discharge of his legislative functions, have said:

> "It cannot be denied that a member of Parliament taking money or agreeing to take money to influence his vote in Parliament is guilty of a high crime and misdemeanour, and that an agreement to bring about such a state of things constitutes a criminal conspiracy; nor can it be denied that an agreement which has the effect of fettering Parliamentary or executive action may sometimes be as dangerous to the community as the direct purchase of a member's vote; and it may be that, under the words used in the count which we are considering, facts might be proved which would constitute a criminal conspiracy." [pp. 413, 414]

Section 73A of the Crime Act, 1914 in Australia makes it an offence for members of the Australian Parliament to accept or be offered a bribe. Under the said provision a member of either House of Parliament who asks for or receives or obtains, or offers or agrees to ask for or receive or obtain, any property or benefit of any kind for himself or any other person, on an understanding that the exercise by him of his duty or authority as such a member will, in any manner, be influenced of affected, is guilty of an offence. So also a person who, in order to influence or affect a member of either House of Parliament in the exercise of his duty or authority as such a member or to induce him to absent himself from the House of which he is a member, any committee of that house or from any committee of both House of the Parliament, gives or confers, or promises or offers to give or confer, any property or benefit of any kind to or on the member or any other person is guilty of an offence. [*See*: Gerard Carney – Conflict of Interest: A Commonwealth Study of Members of Parliament. p. 124].

14. CANADA: In the case of **R.V Bunting, (1984-5) 7 Ontario Reports 524**, the defendants had moved for quashing of an indictment for conspiracy to bring about a change in the Government of Province of Ontario by bribing members of the Legislature to vote against the Government. It was argued that bribery of a Member of Parliament is a matter concerning Parliament or Parliamentary business and is not an indictable offence at common law and that the exclusive jurisdiction to deal with such a case rests with the Legislative Assembly according to the law and custom of Parliament. Rejecting the said contention, Wilson CJ. held:

> "It is to my mind a proposition very clear that his Court has jurisdiction over the offence of bribery as at the common law in a case of this kind, where a member of the Legislative Assembly is concerned either in the giving or in the offering to give a bribe, or in the taking of it for or in respect of any of his duties as a member of that Assembly; and it is equally clear that the Legislative Assembly had not the jurisdiction which this Court has in a case of the kind; and it is also quite clear that the ancient definition of bribery is not the proper or legal definition of that offence." [p. 542]

Armour J. was of the same view and has said:

> "I think it beyond doubt that the bribery of a member of the Legislative Assembly of the Province of Ontario to do any act in his capacity as such is an offence at the common law, and is indictable and punishable as a misdemeanour." [p. 555]

O'Connor J, in his dissenting judgment, held that the bribe of a member of Parliament, in a matter concerning Parliament or Parliamentary business, is not an indictable offence at common law, and has not been made so by any statute.

15. Section 108 of the Criminal Code in Canada renders it an offence for a bribe to be offered to or accepted by a provincial or federal member, while in Federal Canada and several of the Provinces the acceptance of a reward etc., for promoting a matter within Parliament constitutes a breach of privilege. [*See*: Gerard Carney: Conflict of Interest: A Commonwealth Study of Members of Parliament, p. 123].

16. Other Commonwealth Countries: After examining the anti-corruption measures in the various Commonwealth countries, Gerard Carney has concluded:

> "Most countries treat corruption and bribery by Members of Parliament as a criminal offence rather than as a breach of privilege." [*See*: Gerard Carney: Conflict of Interest: A Commonwealth Study of Members of Parliament, p. 123].

17. UNITED STATES: Article 1(6) of the US Constitution contains the 'Speech or Debate Clause' which provides that "for any speech or debate in either House, they (Members of the Congress) shall not be questioned in any other place". In 1853 the Congress, by statute, declared a member liable to indictment as for a high crime and misdemeanour in any Court of the United States for accepting compensation intended to influence a vote or decision on any question brought before him in his official capacity. In 1862, the Congress enacted another statute to penalise legislators who received money for votes or influence in any matter pending before Congress and in 1864 Conflict of Interest statutes barred Congressmen from receiving compensation for their services before any agency. The Conflict of Interest Statutes were revised in 1962 and are contained in 18 U.S.C. (1964). [*See*: Note, The Bribed Congressmen's Immunity from Prosecution, (1965-66) 75 Yale L.J. 335, at p. 341].

18. A distinction is, however, made between the conduct of a member connected with the proceedings of the House and his conduct not in the House but in connection with other activities as a Member of the Congress. The speech and debate clause does not give any protection in respect of conduct "that is in no sense related to due functioning of the legislative powers". [*See*: **United States v. Johnson, 15 L Ed 2d 681 (684)**]. In **Burton v. United States, 202 US 344**, the US Supreme Court upheld the conviction of a Senator who had been bribed in order to get a mail fraud indictment quashed under the rationale that Burton's attempt to influence the Post Office Department was unprotected non-legislative conduct. The question regarding immunity in respect of actions connected with the proceedings of the House has been considered by the US Supreme Court in three decisions, namely, **Johnson, United State v. Brewster, 33 L Ed 2d 507**, and **United States v. Helstoski, 61 L Ed 2d 12**.

19. In Johnson a former US Congressman, named Johnson, and three co-defendants were found guilty of conspiracy consisting of an agreement among Johnson and another Congressman and two other co-defendants who were connected with a Maryland savings and loan institution whereby the two Congressmen would exert influence on the Department of Justice to obtain the dismissal of pending indictments of the loan company and its officers on mall fraud charges and as part of this general scheme Johnson read a speech favourable to independent savings and loan associations in the House and that the company distributed copies to allay apprehensions of potential depositors and that the two Congressmen approached the Attorney-General and Assistant Attorney-General in-charge of the Criminal Division and urged them to review the indictment and for these services Johnson received substantial sums in the form of campaign contribution and legal fees. Harlan J., delivering the opinion of the Court, held that the prosecution of the conspiracy count being dependent upon an intensive inquiry with respect to the speech or Debate Clause so as to warrant the granting of a new trial on the conspiracy count with all elements offensive to the Speech or Debate Clause to be eliminated. The Speech or Debate Clause was given a wider construction so as to exclude the motive for performing the legislative acts being enquired into in a criminal prosecution.

20. In **Brewster, 1972 (33) Law Ed 507** a former US Senator, named Brewster, had been charged with accepting bribes and the allegation was that while he was a Senator and a member of the Senate Committee on Post and Civil Service he received and agreed to receive sums in return for being influenced in his performance of official acts in respect of his action, vote and decision on postage rate legislation which had been pending before him in his official capacity. Brewster moved to dismiss the indictment on the ground that he was immune from prosecution for any alleged act of bribery because of the Speech or Debate Clause. The District Court accepted the said contention and dismissed the counts of the indictment which applied to Brewster. The said judgment of the District Court was reversed by the US Supreme Court and the matter was remanded. Burger CJ., who delivered the opinion of the Court on behalf of six Judges, held that the Speech or Debate Clause protects the members of Congress from inquiry into legislative acts or into the motivation for their actual performance of legislative acts and it does not protect from other activities they undertake that are political, rather than legislative, in nature and that taking a bribe for the purpose of having one's official conduct influenced is not part of any legislative process or function and the Speech or Debate Clause did not prevent indictment and prosecution of Brewster for accepting bribes. Brennan and White JJ. (joined by Douglas J.) disssented. The Court construed the Speech or Debate Clause as giving protection to an act which was clearly a part of the legislative process – the due functioning of the process. It was held that the purpose of the Speech or Debate Clause is to protect the individual legislator, not simply for his own sake, but to preserve the independence and thereby the integrity of the legislative process and that financial abuse, by way of bribes, would grossly undermine legislative integrity and defeat the right of the public to honest representation. The learned Chief Justice has observed:

> "Taking a bribe is, obviously, no part of the legislative process or function; it is not a legislative act. It is not, by any conceivable interpretation, an act performed as a part of or even incidental to the role of a legislator." [p. 526]

21. In **Helstoski, 1979 (61) Law Ed 2d 12** a former member of the House of Representatives, named Helstoski, was prosecuted for accepting money for promising to introduce and for introducing private bills which would suspend the application of the immigration laws so as to allow the aliens to remain in the country. Helstoski moved to dismiss the indictment in the District Court contending that the indictment violated the Speech or Debate Clause. The said motion was rejected by the District Court though it was held that the Government would not be allowed to offer evidence at trial of the performance of the past legislative acts by the Congressmen. The said judgment was affirmed by the Court of Appeals which judgment was also affirmed by the US Supreme Court by majority (Brennan J. dissenting). Burger CJ. has held that references to past legislative acts of a Member cannot be admitted without considering the values protected by the Speech or Debate Clause which was designed to preclude prosecution of Members for legislative act.

22. Having taken note of the legal position as it prevails in the various countries, we may now examine the legal position in this regard in India.

ACCEPTANCE OF BRIBE IN RELATION TO CONDUCT OF BUSINESS AS AN MP IN THE HOUSE AMOUNTS TO BREACH OF PRIVILEGE – IN OTHER CASES IT AMOUNTS TO LOWERING THE DIGNITY OF THE HOUSE – AGRAWAL, J.

23. Offering of a bribe or payment to a Member of Parliament influences him in his conduct as a member and acceptance of a bribe by such a Member is treated as a breach of privilege by Indian Parliament even though no money has actually changed hands. (*See*: M.N. Kaul and S.L. Shakdher: *Practice and Procedure of Parliament,* 4th Edn., p. 254). As early as in 1951 an *ad hoc* Committee of Parliament was appointed to investigate the conduct and activities of a member, H.G. Mudgal, in connection with some of his dealings with a business association which included canvassing support and making propaganda in Parliament on certain problems on behalf of that association in return for alleged financial and other business advantages. An *ad hoc* Committee of the House was appointed to consider whether the conduct of the member concerned was derogatory to the dignity of the House and inconsistent with the standards which Parliament is entitled to expect from members. The Committee found the member guilty of receiving monetary benefits for putting questions in Parliament, moving amendments to the Forward Contracts (Regulation) Bill and urging interviews with the Ministers, etc. and it held that the conduct of H.G. Mudgal was derogatory to the dignity of the House and inconsistent with the standards which Parliament was entitled to expect of its members. The Committee recommended the expulsion of the member from the House. While the said report was being considered by the House, the member, after participating in the debate, submitted his resignation from the membership of the House. In the resolution the House accepted the findings of the Committee and deprecated the attempt of the member to circumvent the effects of the motion expelling him from the House, by his resignation, which constituted a contempt of the House and aggravated the offence. (*See* Kaul and Shakdher at pp. 284, 285).

24. It does not, however, constitute breach or contempt of the House if the offering of payment of bribe is related to the business other than that of the House. In 1974 the Lok Sabha considered the matter relating to offer or payment of bribe in the Import Licences case wherein it was alleged that a Member of Lok Sabha had taken bribe and forged signatures of the Members for furthering the cause of certain applicants. The question of privilege was disallowed since it was considered that conduct of the Member, although improper, was not related to the business of the House. But at the same time it was held that as the allegation of bribery and forgery were very serious and unbecoming of a Member of Parliament, he could be held guilty of lowering the dignity of the House. (*See* Kaul and Shakdher, at pp. 254, 255).

NEVER CONSIDERED IF MP WAS ENTITLED TO IMMUNITY FROM PROSECUTION – ARTICLE 105 OF THE CONSTITUTION REPRODUCED – CONSIDERED – AGRAWAL, J.

25. The question whether a Member of Parliament can claim immunity from prosecution before a Criminal Court on charge of bribery in relation to proceedings in Parliament has not come up for consideration before the Court and it has to be examined in the light of the provisions contained in the Constitution. The relevant provision which provides for the powers, privileges and immunities of Parliament and its members and its Committees is contained in Article 105 of the Constitution. The said Article, in the original form, read as follows:

> "105. Powers, Privileges, etc. of the House of Parliament and of the Members and Committees thereof.—
>
> (1) Subject to the provisions of this Constitution and to the rules and standing orders regulating the procedure of Parliament, there shall be freedom of speech in Parliament.
>
> (2) No Member of Parliament shall be liable to any proceedings in any Court in respect of anything said or any vote given by him in Parliament or any committee thereof, and no person shall be so liable to in respect of the publication by or under the authority of either House of Parliament of any report paper, votes or proceedings.
>
> (3) In other respects, the powers, privileges and immunities of each House of Parliament, and of the members and the committees of each House, shall be such as may from time to time be defined by Parliament by law, and until so defined, shall be those of the House of Commons of Parliament of the United Kingdom, and of its members and committees, at the commencement of this Constitution.
>
> (4) The provisions of clauses (1), (2) and (3) shall apply in relation to persons who by virtue of this Constitution have the right to speak in, and otherwise to take part in the proceedings of, a House of Parliament or any Committee thereof as they apply in relation to Members of the Parliament."

By Constitution (Forty-fourth Amendment) Act, 1978, clause (3) was replaced by the following clause:—

> "(3) In other respects, the powers, privileges and immunities of each House of Parliament, and of the members and the Committees of each House, shall be such as may from time to time be defined by Parliament by law, and until so defined, shall be those of that House and of its members and committees

immediately before coming into force of section 15 of the Constitution (Forty-fourth Amendment) Act, 1978."

26. Clause (1) secures freedom of speech in Parliament to its members. The said freedom is "subject to the provisions of this Constitution and to the rules and standing orders regulating the procedure for Parliament." The words "subject to the provisions of this Constitution" have been construed to mean subject to the provisions of the Constitution which regulate the procedure of Parliament, viz., Articles 118 and 121. (*See*: **Pandit M.S.M. Sharma v. Shri Sri Krishna Sinha, 1959 Supp (1) SCR 806 (856): AIR 1959 SC 395 (408-9)** and Special Reference No. 1 of 1964, also known as the **Legislative Privileges case, 1965 (1) SCR 413 (441): AIR 1965 SC 745 (760)**. The freedom of speech that is available to Members of Parliament under Article 105(1) is not subject to the limitations contained in Article 19(2).

27. Clause (2) confers immunity in relation to proceedings in Courts. It can be divided into two parts. In the first part immunity from liability under any proceedings in any Court is conferred on a Member of Parliament in respect of anything said or any vote given by him in Parliament or any committee thereof. In the second part such immunity is conferred on a person in respect of publication by or under the authority of either House of Parliament of any report, paper, votes or proceedings. This immunity that has been conferred under clause (2) in respect of anything said or any vote given by a Member in Parliament or any Committee thereof and in respect of publication by or under the authority of either House of Parliament of any report, paper, votes or proceedings, ensures that the freedom of speech that is granted under Clause (1) of Article 105 is totally absolute and unfettered. (*See*: **Legislative Privileges case, pp. 441, 442: AIR 1965 SC 745 (760, 761).**

28. Having secured the freedom of speech in Parliament to the members under clauses (1) and (2), the Constitution, in clause (3) of Article 105, deals with powers, privileges and immunities of the House of Parliament and of the members and the committees thereof in other respects. The said clause is in two parts. The first part empowers Parliament to define, by law, the powers, privileges and immunities of each House of Parliament and of the Members and the Committees of each House. In the second part, which was intended to be transitional in nature, it was provided that until they are so defined by law the said powers, privileges and immunities shall be those of the House of Commons in the United Kingdom and of its members and committees at the commencement of the Constitution. This part of the provisions was on the same lines as the provisions contained in section 49 of the Australian Constitution and section 18 of the Canadian Constitution. Clause (3), as substituted by the Forty-fourth Amendment of the Constitution, does not make any change in the content and it only seeks to omit future reference to the House of Commons of Parliament in the United Kingdom while preserving the position as it stood on the date of coming into force of the said amendment.

29. Clause (4) of Article 105 makes the privileges and immunities secured under clauses (1), (2) and (3) applicable to persons who by virtue of the Constitution have the right to speak in and otherwise to take part in the proceedings of a House of Parliament or any Committee thereof as they apply in relation to Members of Parliament.

PROVISIONS OF ARTICLE 105(2) BE INTERPRETED WIDELY GRANTING IMMUNITY FROM LEGAL PROCEEDINGS – SUBMIT APPELLANTS

30. Shri P.P. Rao, Shri D.D. Thakur and Shri Kapil Sibal, the learned senior counsel appearing for the appellants, have submitted that having regard to the purpose underlying the grant of immunity under clause (2) of Article 105, namely, to secure full freedom for a Member of Parliament while participating in the proceedings in the House or its Committees by way of speech or by casting his vote, the said provision should be given a wide construction so as to enable the Member to exercise his said rights without being exposed to legal proceedings in a Court of law in respect of anything said or any vote given by him in Parliament or any Committee thereof. It has been submitted that the immunity from liability that has been conferred on a Member of Parliament under clause (2) of Article 105 would, therefore, extend to prosecution of member on a charge of bribery in making a speech or giving his vote in the House or any Committee as well as the charge of conspiracy to accept bribe for making a speech or giving the vote. It is claimed that by virtue of the immunity granted under clause (2) of Article 105 the offer to and acceptance by a Member of Parliament of bribe in connection with his making a speech or giving the vote would not constitute a criminal offence and, therefore, neither the member receiving the bribe nor the person offering this bribe can be prosecuted and so also there can be no offence of criminal conspiracy in respect of such offer and acceptance of bribe. It has been urged that on that view neither the charge of conspiracy under section 120B, Indian Penal Code nor the charges in respect of the substantive offences under the 1988 Act can be sustained against the appellants. Strong reliance has been placed on the decision of the Court of Queen's Bench in ***Ex Parte* Wason, 1869 LR 4 QBD 573,** as well as on the judgment of the U.S. Supreme Court (Harlan, J.) in Johnson, 1966 (15) Law Ed 2d 681 and on the dissenting judgments of Brennan, J. and White, J. in Brewster, 1972 (33) Law Ed 2d 507.

OFFER OF BRIBE MADE OR ACCEPTANCE OF BRIBE TO VOTE IN PARTICULAR WAY – IS A PENAL OFFENCE TO BE TRIED BY COURT – SUBMITTED ATTORNEY-GENERAL

31. The learned Attorney-General, on the other hand, has urged that the immunity granted under clause (2) of Article 105 gives protection to a Member of Parliament from any liability for a speech made by him or a vote given by him in the House or any Committee thereof, but the said immunity cannot be extended to confer immunity from prosecution of a Member for having received bribe or having entered into a conspiracy to receive bribe for the purpose of making a speech or giving a vote in the House or in any Committees thereof. The learned Attorney-General has placed reliance on the judgment of the U.S. Supreme Court (Burger, C.J.) in Brewster, 1972 (33) Law Ed 2d 507, the Canadian decision in Bunting (1884-5(7) Ontario Reports 524 and the Australian decisions in White (13 SCR (NSW) 332) and Boston (1923 (33) CLR 386) and the ruling of Buckley, J. in **R. v. Currie.**

BOTH PARTIES RELIED ON FOREIGN JUDGMENTS – THOSE JUDGMENTS DISCUSSED – AGRAWAL, J.

32. Before we proceed to consider these submissions in the light of the provisions contained in clause (2) of Article 105, we may refer to the decision in ***Ex Parte* Wason, 1869 LR 4 QBD 573** and the other decisions in which it has been considered.

33. In *Ex Parte* Wason information had been laid by Wason before the Magistrate wherein it was stated that he had given Earl Russell a petition to be presented in the House of Lords wherein the Lord Chief Baron was charged with wilful and deliberate falsehood and the object of the petition was that the Lord Chief Baron might be removed from his office by an address of both Houses of Parliament and that Earl Russell, Lord Chelmsford and the Lord Chief Baron conspired together to prevent the course of justice by agreeing to make statements which they knew to be untrue and that Earl Russell, Lord Chelmsford and the Lord Chief Baron agreed to deceive the House of Lords by stating that the charge of falsehood contained in the petition against the Lord Chief Baron was unfounded and false whereas they knew it to be true. The Magistrate refused to take applicant's recognisance on the ground that no indictable offence was disclosed by the information. The Court of Queen's Bench upheld the said order of the Magistrate and refused to grant the rule sought by the applicant. Cockburn, C.J., after referring to the information which was placed before the Magistrate, said:

> "Now in as much as these statements were alleged to have been for the purpose of preventing the prayer of the petition, and the statements could not have had that effect unless made in the House of Lords, it seems to me that the fair and legitimate inference is that the alleged conspiracy was to make, and that the statements were made, in the House of Lords. I think, therefore, that the Magistrate, looking at this and the rest of the information, was warranted in coming to the conclusion, that Mr. Wason charged and proposed to make the substance of the indictment, that these three persons did conspire to deceive the House of Lords by statements made in the House of Lords for the purpose of frustrating the petition. Such a charge could not be maintained in a Court of law. It is clear that statements made by members of either House of Parliament in their places in the House, though they might be untrue to their knowledge, could not be made the foundation of civil or criminal proceedings, however injurious they might be to the interest of a third person. And a conspiracy to make such statements would not make these persons guilty of it amenable to the criminal law." (p. 576)

Blackburn, J. said:

> "I perfectly agree with my Lord as to what the substance of the information is; and when the House is sitting and statements are made in either House of Parliament, the member making them is not amenable to the criminal law. It is quite clear that no indictment will lie for making them, nor for a conspiracy or agreement to make them, even though the statements be false to the knowledge of the persons making them. I entirely concur in thinking that the information did only charge an agreement to make statements in the House of Lords, and therefore did not charge any indictable offence." (p. 576)

Lush, J. also said:

> "I cannot doubt that it charges a conspiracy to deceive the House of Lords, and so frustrate the application, by means of making false statements in the House. I am clearly of opinion that we ought not to allow it to be doubted for a moment that the motives or intentions of members of either House cannot be inquired into by criminal proceedings with respect to anything they may do or say in the House." (p. 577)

The observations of Cockburn, C.J., with whom Blackburn, J. has concurred, show that the substance of the information laid by Wason was that the alleged conspiracy was to make false statements and that such statements were made in the House of Lords and that the said statements had been made the foundation of the criminal proceedings. Though in the judgment there is no reference to Article 9 of the Bill of Rights but the tenor of the abovequoted observations of the learned Judges leave no doubt that the judgment was based on that Article. It has been so understood in later judgments. (*See*: **R. v. Currie**)

34. Reliance has been placed by Shri Rao on the observations of Lush, J. that "the motives or intentions of members of either House cannot be inquired into by criminal proceedings with respect to anything they may do or say in the House."

35. In **Johnson, 1966 (15) Law Ed 2d 681** while dealing with the contention urged on behalf of the Government that the Speech or Debate Clause was meant to prevent only prosecutions based on the content of speech, such as libel actions, but not those founded on the antecedent unlawful conduct of accepting or agreeing to accept a bribe, Harian, J. has observed:

"Although historically seditious libel was the most frequent instrument for intimidating legislators, this has never been the sole form of legal proceedings so employed, and the language of the Constitution is framed in the broadest terms." (pp. 689, 690)

36. In order to show the broader thrust of the privilege reference was made by the learned Judge to the decision in ***Ex Parte* Wason, (1869) LR 4 QBD 573** and the observations of Cockburn, C.J. and Lush, J. have been quoted. The contention that the Speech or Debate Clause was not violated because the gravamen of the count was the alleged conspiracy, not the speech, was rejected by pointing out that "the indictment itself focused with particularity upon motives underlying the making of the speech and upon its contents." (p. 690). The learned Judge has further said:

"We emphasise that our holding is limited to prosecutions involving circumstances such as those presented in the case before us. Our decision does not touch a prosecution which, though as here founded on a criminal statute of general application, does not draw in question the legislative acts of the defendant member of Congress or his motives for performing them." (pp. 690, 691)

"The making of the speech, however, was only a part of the conspiracy charge. With all references to this aspect of the conspiracy eliminated, we think the Government should not be precluded from a new trial on this count, thus wholly purged of elements offensive to the Speech or Debate Clause". (p. 691)

37. In **Brewster, (1972 (33) Law Ed 2d 507)** Brennan, J. and White, J. in their dissenting judgments, have referred to the earlier judgment in **Johnson, (1966 (15) Law Ed 2d 681**) and the decision in *Ex Parte* Wason. Brennan, J. was of the view that Johnson "can only be read as holding that a corrupt agreement to perform legislative acts, even if provable without reference to the acts themselves may not be the subject of a general conspiracy prosecution." (p. 533). Burger, C.J. did not agree with this reading of Johnson and said:—

"Johnson thus stands on a unanimous holding that a Member of Congress may be prosecuted under a criminal statute provided that the Government's case does not rely on legislative acts or the motivation for legislative acts. A legislative act has consistently been defined as an act generally done in Congress in relation to the business before it. In sum, the Speech or Debate Clause prohibits inquiry only into those things generally said or done in the House or the Senate in the performance of official duties and into the motivation for those acts." (pp. 517, 518)

After pointing out that the history of the privileges in England is by no means free from grave abuses by Legislators, Burger, C.J. has observed:—

"The authors of our Constitution were well aware of the history of both the need for the privilege and the abuses that could flow from the sweeping safeguards. In order to preserve other values, they wrote the privilege so that it tolerates and protects behaviour on the part of Members not tolerated and protected when done by other citizens, but the shield does not extend beyond what is necessary to preserve the integrity of the legislative process." (p. 521)

The learned Chief Justice took note of the fact that "Congress is ill-equipped to investigate, try, and punish its Members for a wide range of behaviour that is loosely and incidentally related to the legislative process" and said:—

"In this sense, the English analogy on which the dissents place much emphasis, and the reliance on ***Ex Parte* Wason, (1869) LR 4 QB 573,** are inapt." (p. 521)

While referring to the observations made by Brennan, J., the learned Chief Justice has observed:

"Mr. Justice Brennan suggests that inquiry into the alleged bribe is inquiry into the motivation for a legislative act, and it is urged that this very inquiry was condemned as impermissible in Johnson. That argument misconstrues the concept of motivation for legislative acts. The Speech or Debate Clause does not prohibit inquiry into illegal conduct simply because it has some nexus to legislative functions. In Johnson, the Court held that on remand, Johnson could be retired on the conspiracy-to-defraud count, so long as evidence concerning his speech on the House floor was not admitted. The Court's opinion plainly implies that had the Government chosen to retry Johnson on that count, he could not have obtained immunity from prosecution by asserting that the matter being inquired into was related to the motivation for his House speech." (p. 527)

In his dissenting judgment White, J., after referring to *ex parte* Wason has observed:—

"The Wason Court clearly refused to distinguish between promise and performance; the legislative privilege applied to both." (p. 546)

The learned Judge then refers to Johnson and says:—

"I find it difficult to believe that under the statute there involved the Johnson Court would have permitted a prosecution based upon a promise to perform a legislative act." (p. 546).

But in Helstoski (1979 (61) Law Ed 2d 12) White, J. was a party to the majority judgment delivered by Burger, C.J. wherein it was held:

"Promises by a member to perform an act in future are not legislative acts." (p. 23)

"But it is clear from the language of the clause that protection extends only to an act that has already been performed. A promise to deliver a speech, to vote, or to solicit other votes at some future date is not 'speech or debate'. Likewise a promise to introduce a bill is not a legislative act." (p. 24).

In **Bunting, (1884-5 (7) Ontario Reports 524)** Wilson, C.J., has considered, *Ex Parte* Wason and has pointed out that in that case the alleged conspiracy could not fall under the head of an agreement to do an illegal act because the truth or falsity of statements made by members in Parliament could not be enquired into by the Court and that it did not also fall under the head of doing an act, not necessarily illegal, by illegal means because there were no illegal means used or to be used. The learned Chief Justice has, however, observed:

"But if these three persons had agreed that the two members of the House of Lords should make these false statements, or vote in any particular manner, in consideration of a bribe paid or to be paid to them, that would have been a conspiracy to do an act, not necessarily illegal perhaps, but to do the act by illegal means, bribery being an offence against the law; and the offence of conspiracy would have been complete by reason of the illegal means by which the act was to be effected.

That offence could have been inquired into by the Court, because the inquiry into all that was done would have been of matters outside of the House of Lords, and there could therefore be no violation of, or encroachment in any respect upon, the *lex parliamenti.*" (p. 554)

In **R. v. Currie,** Buckley, J. has referred to the observations of Wilson, C.J. in Bunting and has ruled that the reasoning in *Ex Parte* Wason would not apply to alleged bribery for the proof of which no reference to goings-on in Parliament would be necessary.

SCOPE OF ARTICLE 105 OF THE CONSTITUTION – CLAUSES (1) AND (2) ARE INTER-LINKED – EFFECT OF FOREIGN JUDGMENTS – DISCUSSED – AGRAWAL, J.

38. We may now examine whether the decision in *Ex Parte* Wason has any bearing on the interpretation of Article 105(2). Clauses (1) and (2) of Article 105 are interlinked, while clause (1) secures to the Members freedom of speech in Parliament, clause (2) safeguards and protects the said freedom by conferring immunity on the Members from liability in respect of anything said or any vote given by him in Parliament or in any Committee thereof. This is necessary because for a regulatory body like Parliament, the freedom of speech is of the utmost importance and a full and free debate is of the essence of Parliamentary democracy. In England that freedom of speech in Parliament is secured by Article 9 of the Bill of Rights. Though clause (2) of Article 105 appears to be similar to Article 9 of the Bill of Rights but a closer look would show that they differ in certain aspects. Article 9 of the Bill of Rights, by prescribing that "freedom of speech and debates or proceedings in Parliament ought not to be impeached or questioned in any Court or place out of Parliament," confers immunity in respect of speech, debates or proceedings in Parliament being questioned in any Court or place out of Parliament. The said immunity has been construed to preclude what was said or done in Parliament in the course of proceedings there being examined outside Parliament for the purpose of supporting a cause of action even though the cause of action itself arose out of something done outside Parliament. (See **Church of Scientology of California v. Johnson Smith, 1972 (1) All ER 378).**

In an Australian case **R. v. Murphy, 1986 (5) NSWLR 18,** a question arose whether in the course of criminal trial, the witness's earlier evidence to the Select Committee could be put to him in cross-examination with a view to showing a previous inconsistent statement. Hunt, J. in the Supreme Court of New South Wales, held that Article 9 of the Bill of Rights did not prohibit such cross-examination even if the suggestion was made that the evidence given to the Select Committee was a lie. He further held that the statements of the Select Committee could be used to draw inferences and could be analysed and be made the basis of submission.

39. In **Prebble v. Television New Zealand Ltd., 1994 (3) All ER 407,** Lord Browne Wilkinson, speaking for the Judicial Committee of the Privy Council, after taking note of decision of Hunt, J. in **R. v. Murphy,** (supra), has said:—

> "Finally, Hunt, J. based himself on a narrow construction of Article 9 derived from the historical context in which it was originally enacted. He correctly identified the mischief sought to be remedied in 1688 as being, inter alia, the assertion by the King's Courts of a right to hold a Member of Parliament criminally or legally liable for what he had done or said in Parliament. From this he deduced the principle that Article 9 only applies to cases in which a Court is being asked to expose the maker of the statement to legal liability for what he has said in Parliament. This view discounts the basic concept underlying Article 9, *viz.* the need to ensure so far as possible that a member of the legislature and witnesses before Committees of the House can speak freely without fear that what they say will later be held

against them in the Courts. The important public interest protected by such privilege is to ensure that the member or witness at the time he speaks is not inhibited from stating fully and freely what he has to say. If there were any exceptions which permitted his statements to be questioned subsequently, at the time when he speaks in Parliament he would not know whether or not there would subsequently be a challenge to what he is saying. Therefore he would not have the confidence the privilege is designed to protect." (p. 415)

The protection given under clause (2) of Article 105 is narrower than that conferred under Article 9 of the Bill of Rights in the sense that the immunity conferred by that clause is personal in nature and is available to the member in respect of anything said or in any vote given by him in the House or any Committee thereof. The said clause does not confer an immunity for challenge in the Court on the speech or vote given by a Member of Parliament. The protection given under clause (2) of Article 105 is thus similar to protection envisaged under the construction placed by Hunt, J. in **R. v. Murphy** (supra) on Article 9 of the Bill of Rights which has not been accepted by the Privy Council in **Prebble v. Television New Zealand Ltd**. The decision in ***Ex Parte* Wason** (supra), which was given in the context of Article 9 of the Bill of Rights can, therefore, have no application in the matter of construction of Clause (2) of Article 105. ***Ex Parte* Wason** (supra), which holds that the information laid by Wason did not disclose any indictable offence, proceeds on the basis that statements made by members of either House of Parliament in their places in the House, though they may be untrue to their knowledge, could not be made the foundation of civil or criminal proceedings.

The position under clause (2) of Article 105 is, however, different. The said clause does not prescribe that a speech made or vote given by a member in Parliament cannot be made the basis of civil or criminal proceedings at all. The said clause only gives protection to the member who has made the speech or is given the vote from liability in any proceeding in a Court of law. Therefore, on the basis of the decision in ***Ex Parte* Wason** (supra), it cannot be said that no offence was committed by those who are alleged to have offered the illegal gratification and by those who had received such gratification to vote against the No-Confidence Motion and for the reason the charge of conspiracy and abetment must also fail. On the basis of Article 105(2) the claim for immunity from prosecution can be made only on behalf of A-3 to A-5 and A-16 to A-21 who are alleged to have voted against the No-Confidence Motion. As to whether they are entitled to such immunity under Article 105(2) will, however, depend on the interpretation of the provisions of Article 105(2).

40. As indicated earlier, Article 105(2) is in two parts. In these appeals we are required to consider the first part which provides that no member of Parliament shall be liable to any proceedings in any Court in respect of anything said or any vote given by him in Parliament or any committee thereof. The immunity that has been conferred by this provision is: (i) only on the Member of Parliament, (ii) with regard to liability in any proceedings in any Court, which would include civil as well as criminal proceedings, (iii) in respect of anything said or any vote given by such Member, (iv) in Parliament or in any committee thereof.

APPELLANTS RELIED ON CLAUSE (2) READ WITH TEJ KIRAN JAIN'S CASE TO CLAIM IMMUNITY FROM PROSECUTION – AGRAWAL, J.

41. Shri Rao has submitted that having regard to the object underlying the provisions, *viz.*, to secure the freedom of speech in Parliament to the members, the immunity granted under clause (2) must be construed in a wide sense and just as the expression "anything" was construed in **Tej Kiran Jain v. N. Sanjiva Reddy,**

1971 (1) SCR 612: AIR 1970 SC 1573, as a word of widest import, the expression "in respect of" must also be given a wide meaning so as to comprehend an act having a nexus or connection with the speech made or a vote given by a member of Parliament or any committee thereof and would include, within its ambit, acceptance of bribe by a member in order to make a speech or to cast his vote in Parliament or any Committee thereof in a particular manner. In support of his submission for giving a wider meaning to the expression "in respect of" Shri Rao has relied upon the decisions of this Court in **State of Tripura v. Province of East Bengal, 1951 SCR 1: AIR 1951 SC 23; Tolaram Relumal v. State of Bombay, 1955 SCR 158: AIR 1954 SC 496** and **S.S. Railway Co. Ltd. v. Upper Doab Sugar Mills Ltd., 1960 (2) SCR 926: AIR 1960 SC 695** and the decision in **Paterson v. Chadwick, 1974 (2) All ER 772.**

CLAUSE (2) CANNOT SAVE FROM PROSECUTION THOSE MPs WHO COMMIT OFFENCE OF ENTERING INTO A CONSPIRACY – TAKING OF BRIBE – SUBMITS ATTORNEY-GENERAL

42. The learned Attorney-General has, on the other hand, urged that immunity granted under clause (2) of Article 105 is intended to protect a member from liability arising out of the speech made by him or vote given by him and it cannot be extended to cover the conduct of a member who has received bribe or has entered into a conspiracy to commit the offence of bribery in order to make a speech or cast his vote in Parliament. The submission is that the expression "in respect of" in clause (2) of Article 105 must be so construed as to ensure that the immunity conferred under clause (2) is only available in respect of legitimate acts of a member of Parliament and it cannot be invoked to secure immunity against any criminal acts committed by member in order to make a speech or to give his vote in Parliament or in any committee thereof. According to the learned Attorney-General, the expression "in respect of" in Article 105(2) must be construed to mean 'for'. Reliance has been placed by him on the decision of this Court in **State of Madras v. M/s. Swastik Tobacco Factory, Vedaranyam, 1966 (3) SCR 79: AIR 1966 SC 1000.**

RATIO OF LAW IN TEJ KIRAN JAIN'S CASE & ARTICLE 105 – DISCUSSED – AGRAWAL, J.

43. In **Tej Kiran Jain, AIR 1970 SC 1573,** the appellants had filed a suit for damages in respect of defamatory statements alleged to have been made by certain members of Parliament on the floor of the Lok Sabha during a calling attention motion. The said suit was dismissed by the High Court on the view that no proceedings could be initiated in respect of anything said on the floor of the House in view of Article 105(2) of the Constitution. Before this Court it was contended on behalf of the plaintiffs that the immunity under Article 105(2) was granted to what was relevant to the business of Parliament and not to something which was irrelevant. The said contention was rejected by the Court. It was observed:—

> "The article confers immunity inter alia in respect of 'anything said.... in Parliament.' The word 'anything' is of the widest import and is equivalent to 'everything'. The only limitation arises from the words 'in Parliament' which means during the sitting of Parliament and in the course of the business of Parliament. We are concerned only with speeches in Lok Sabha. Once it was proved that Parliament was sitting and its business was being transacted, anything said during the course of that business was immune from proceeding in any Court. This immunity is not only complete but is as it should be. It is of the essence of parliamentary system of Government that people's representatives should be free to express themselves without fear of legal consequences. What they say is only subject to the discipline of the rules

of Parliament, the good sense of the members and the control of proceedings by the Speaker. The Courts have no say in the matter and should really have none"; **AIR 1970 SC 1573 (1574).**

These observations in Tej Kiran Jain emphasise the object underlying the immunity that has been conferred under Article 105(2), namely, that the people's representatives should be free to exercise their functions without fear of legal consequences. Borrowing the words of Burger, CJ. it can be said that this immunity has been granted "to protect the integrity of the legislative process by ensuring the independence of the individual legislators". It cannot be given a construction which could lead to Article 105(2), a charter for freedom of speech in Parliament, being regarded, as per the phrase used by Lord Salmon, a "charter for corruption" so to elevate members of Parliament as "super citizens, immune from criminal responsibility". (Burger, CJ. in **Brewster, 1972 (33) Law Ed 2d 507)**. It would indeed be ironic if a claim for immunity from prosecution founded on the need to ensure the independence of Members of Parliament in exercising their right to speak or cast their vote in Parliament, could be put forward by a Member who has bartered away his independence by agreeing to speak or vote in a particular manner in lieu of illegal gratification that has been paid or promised. By claiming the immunity such a Member would only be seeking a licence to indulge in such corrupt conduct.

44. It is no doubt true that a member who is found to have accepted bribe in connection with the business of Parliament can be punished by the House for contempt. But that is not a satisfactory solution. In exercise of its power to punish for contempt the House of Commons can convict a person to custody and may also order expulsion or suspension from the service of the House. There is no power to impose a fine. The power of committal cannot exceed the duration of the session and the person, if not sooner discharged by the House, is immediately released from confinement on prorogation. (*See*: **May's Parliamentary Practice, 21st Edn. pp. 103, 109 and 111**). The House of Parliament in India cannot claim a higher power. The Salmon Commission has stated that "whilst the theoretical power of the House to commit a person into custody undoubtedly exists, nobody has been committed to prison for contempt of Parliament for a hundred years or so, and it is most unlikely that Parliament would use this power in modern conditions". (Para 306). The Salmon Commission has also expressed the view that in view of the special expertise that is necessary for this type of inquiry the Committee of Privileges do not provide an investigative machinery comparable to that of a police investigation. (Para 310)

45. The expression 'in respect of' has to be construed in this perspective. The cases cited by Shri Rao do show that this expression has been construed as having a wider meaning to convey 'some connection or relation in between the two subject-matters to which the words refer'. But as laid down by this Court in The **State Madras v. M/s. Swastik Tobacco Factory, Vendarayam, AIR 1966 SC 1000** (supra) the expression has 'received a wider interpretation, having regard to the object of the provisions and the setting in which the said words appeared'. The expression 'in respect of' in Article 105(5) has, therefore, to be construed keeping in view the object of Article 105(2) and the setting in which the expression appears in that provision.

46. As mentioned earlier, the object of the immunity conferred under Article 105(2) is to ensure the independence of the individual legislators. Such independence is necessary for healthy functioning of the system of parliamentary democracy adopted in the Constitution. Parliamentary democracy is a part of the basic structure of the Constitution. An interpretation of the provisions of Article 105(2) which would enable a Member of Parliament to claim immunity from prosecution in a criminal court for an offence of bribery in connection with anything said by him or a vote given by him in Parliament or any committee thereof and thereby place such Members above the law would not only be repugnant to healthy functioning of Parliamentary democracy but would also be subversive of the Rule of Law which is also an essential part of the basic structure of the Constitution. It is settled law that in interpreting the constitutional provisions the Court should adopt a construction which strengthens the foundational features and the basic structure of the Constitution. [See **Sub-Committee on Judicial Accountability v. Union of India, 1991 (4) SCC 699 (719)].**

The expression 'in respect of' precedes the words 'anything said or any vote given' in Article 105(2). The words 'anything said or any vote given' can only mean speech that has already been made or a vote that has already been given. The immunity from liability, therefore, comes into play only if a speech has been made or vote has been given. The immunity would not be available in a case where a speech has not been made or a vote has not been given. When there is a prior agreement whereunder a Member of Parliament has received an illegal consideration in order to exercise his right to speak or to give his vote in a particular manner on a matter coming up for consideration before the House, there can be two possible situations. There may be an agreement whereunder a Member accepts illegal gratification and agrees not to speak in Parliament or not to give his vote in Parliament. The immunity granted under Article 105(2) would not be available to such a Member and he would be liable to be prosecuted on the charge of bribery in a criminal Court. What would be the position if the agreement is that in lieu of the illegal gratification paid or promised the Member would speak or give his vote in Parliament in a particular manner and he speaks and gives his vote in that manner?

As per the wide meaning suggested by Shri Rao for the expression 'in respect of', the immunity for prosecution would be available to the Member who has received illegal gratification under such an agreement for speaking or giving his vote and who has spoken or given his vote in Parliament as per the said agreement because such acceptance of illegal gratification has a nexus or connection with such speaking or giving of vote by that Member. If the construction placed by Shri Rao on the expression 'in respect of' is adopted, a member would be liable to be prosecuted on a charge of bribery if he accepts bribe for not speaking or for not giving his vote on a matter under consideration before the House but he would enjoy immunity from prosecution for such a charge if he accepts bribe for speaking or giving his vote in Parliament in a particular manner and he speaks or gives his vote in Parliament in that manner.

It is difficult to conceive that the framers of the Constitution intended to make such a distinction in the matter of grant of immunity between a Member of Parliament who receives bribe for speaking or giving his vote in Parliament in a particular manner and speaks or gives his vote in that manner and a Member of Parliament who receives bribe for not speaking or not giving his vote on a particular matter coming up before the House and does not speak or give his vote as per the agreement so as to confer an immunity from prosecution on charge of bribery on the former but denying such immunity to the latter. Such an anomalous situation would be avoided if the words 'in respect of' in Article 105(2) are construed to mean 'arising out of'. If the expression 'in respect of' is thus construed, the immunity conferred under Article 105(2) would be confined to liability that arises out of or is attributable to something that has been said or to a vote that has been given by a Member in Parliament or any committee thereof.

The immunity would be available only if the speech that has been made or the vote that has been given is an essential and integral part of the cause of action for the proceedings giving rise to the liability. The immunity would not be available to give protection against liability for an act that precedes the making of the speech or giving of vote by a Member in Parliament even though it may have a connection with the speech made or the vote given by the Member if such an act gives rise to a liability which arises independently and does not depend on the making of the speech or the giving of vote in Parliament by the Member. Such an independent liability cannot be regarded as liability in respect of anything said or vote given by the Member in Parliament. The liability for which immunity can be claimed under Article 105(2) is the liability that has arisen as a consequence of the speech that has been made or the vote that has been given in Parliament.

47. An indication about the liability with regard to which immunity is granted by Article 105(2) is given in the **Legislative Privileges** case, **AIR 1965 SC 745** where in the context of clause (2) of Article 194, which confers immunity similar to that conferred by Article 105(2) on Members of the State Legislatures, it has been said:

> "Having conferred freedom of speech on the legislators, clause (2) emphasises the fact that the said freedom is intended to be absolute and unfettered. Similar freedom is guaranteed to the legislators in respect of the votes they may give in the Legislature or any committee thereof. In other words, even if a legislator exercises his right of freedom of speech in violation, say, of Article 21, he would not be liable for any action in any Court. Similarly, if the legislator by his speech or vote, is alleged to have violated any of the fundamental rights guaranteed by Part III of the Constitution in the Legislative Assembly, he would not be answerable for the said contravention in any Court. If the impugned speech amounts to libel or becomes actionable or indictable under any other provision of the law, immunity has been conferred on him from any action in any Court by this clause;" **AIR 1965 SC 745 (760).**

48. With regard to liability arising from giving of vote in the House an illustration is furnished by the decision of the US Supreme Court in **Kilbourn v. Thompson, 1879 (81) 26 Law Ed 377.** In that case one Hallet Kilbourn was found guilty of contempt of the House of Representatives and was ordered to be detained in custody under a resolution passed by that House. He brought an action in trespass for false imprisonment against the members of the House who had voted in favour of the resolution. The action was held to be not maintainable against the members in view of the immunity conferred by the Speech or Debate Clause in the US Constitution.

SPEAKING OR GIVING HIS VOTE IN A PARTICULAR MANNER ON A MATTER PENDING BEFORE THE HOUSE IS INDEPENDENT – IT DOES NOT ARISE OUT OF SOMETHING SAID OR VOTE GIVEN BY AN MP – OFFENCE OF BRIBERY IS COMPLETE WHEN MP AGREES TO TAKE BRIBE OR TAKES BRIBE FOR A PROMISE TO ACT IN A PARTICULAR WAY – AGRAWAL, J.

49. The construction placed by us on the expression 'in respect of' in Article 105(2) raises the question: Is the liability to be prosecuted arising from acceptance of bribe by a Member of Parliament for the purpose of speaking or giving his vote in Parliament in a particular manner on a matter pending consideration before the House an independent liability which cannot be said to arise out of anything said or any vote given by the Member in Parliament? In our opinion, this question must be answered in the affirmative. The offence of bribery is made out against the receiver if he takes or agrees to take money for promise to act in a certain way. The offence is complete with the acceptance of the money or on the agreement to accept the money being concluded and is not dependent on the performance of the illegal promise by the receiver. The receiver of the money will be treated to have committed the offence even when he defaults in the illegal bargain. For proving the offence of bribery all that is required to be established is that the offender has received or agreed to receive money for a promise to act in a certain way and it is not necessary to go further and prove that he actually acted in that way.

AN AGREEMENT TO DO AN UNLAWFUL ACT OR TO DO A LAWFUL ACT BY ILLEGAL MEANS MAKE OUT CRIMINAL CONSPIRACY – PROTECTION OF ARTICLE 105(2) NOT AVAILABLE TO SUCH MPs WHO DO IT – AGRAWAL, J.

The offence of criminal conspiracy is defined in section 120A, Indian Penal Code in these terms:

> "*120A. Definition of criminal conspiracy.*—When two or more persons agree to do, or cause to be done,—
>
> (1) an illegal act, or
>
> (2) an act which is not illegal by illegal mean, such an agreement is designated a criminal conspiracy:

Provided that no agreement except an agreement to commit an offence shall amount to a criminal conspiracy unless some act besides the agreement is done by one or more parties to such agreement in pursuance thereof.

Explanation.—It is immaterial whether the illegal act is the ultimate object of such agreement, or is merely incidental to that object."

The offence is made out when two or more persons agree to do or cause to be done an illegal act or when two or more persons agree to do or cause to be done by illegal means an act which is not illegal. In view of the proviso to section 120A, Indian Penal Code an agreement to commit an offence shall by itself amount to criminal conspiracy and it is not necessary that some act besides the agreement should be done by one or more parties to such agreement in pursuance thereof. This means that the offence of criminal conspiracy would be committed if two or more persons enter into an agreement to commit the offence of bribery and it is immaterial whether in pursuance of that agreement the act that was agreed to be done in lieu of payment of money was done or not.

50. The criminal liability incurred by a Member of Parliament who has accepted bribe for speaking or giving his vote in Parliament in a particular manner thus arises independently of the making of the speech or giving of vote by the member and the said liability cannot, therefore, be regarded as a liability 'in respect of anything or any vote given' in Parliament. We are, therefore, of the opinion that the protection granted under Article 105(2) cannot be invoked by any of the appellants to claim immunity from prosecution on the substantive charge in respect of the offences punishable under section 7, section 13(2) read with section 13(1)(d) and section 12 of the 1988 Act as well as the charge of criminal conspiracy under section 120B, Indian Penal Code read with section 7 and section 13(2) read with section 13(1)(d) of the 1988 Act.

APPELLANTS RELY ON CLAUSE (3) OF ARTICLE 105 – PRIOR JUDGMENTS – AGRAWAL, J.

51. Shri P.P. Rao has also invoked the privileges and immunities available to Members of Parliament under clause (3) of Article 105. It has been urged that since no law has been made by Parliament defining the powers, privileges and immunities of each of House of Parliament, the powers, privileges and immunities enjoyed by Members of Parliament of India are the same as those enjoyed by the Members of the House of Commons of the Parliament of the United Kingdom at the commencement of the Constitution on January 26, 1950. In order to show that on January 26, 1950 a Member of the House of Commons in the United Kingdom enjoyed an immunity from prosecution for bribery in connection with the exercise of his functions as such Member, Shri Rao has invited our attention to the following statement in *May's Parliamentary Practice*:

> "The acceptance by any Member of either House of bribe to influence him in his conduct as such Member or of any fee, compensation or reward in connection with the promotion of, or opposition to any bill, resolution, matter or thing submitted or intended to be submitted to the House or any committee thereof is a breach of privilege." (18th Edn. p. 138)

It has been submitted that since acceptance of a bribe by a Member of House of Commons was treated as breach of privilege and was not triable as an offence in any criminal court in the United Kingdom, the same privilege and immunity is available to a Member of Parliament in India by virtue of the second part of clause (3) of Article 105. It has been further contended that in a case where the conduct which constitutes the breach of privilege is also an offence at law, it is for the House to decide whether the punishment which the House is empowered to inflict is not adequate to the offence and it is necessary that the offender should be prosecuted in a criminal court and reliance is placed on the following passage in *May's Parliamentary Practice*:

> "In cases of breach of privilege which are also offences at law, where the punishment which the House has power to inflict would not be adequate to the offences, or where for any other cause the House has thought a proceeding at law necessary, either as a substitute for, or in addition to, its own proceeding, the Attorney-General has been directed to prosecute the offender." (18th Edn. p. 127).

In the **Legislative Privileges case, AIR 1965 SC 745** while construing clause (3) of Article 194, which was in the same terms as clause (3) of Article 105, this Court has said:—

> "This clause requires that the powers, privileges and immunities which are claimed by the House must be shown to have subsisted at the commencement of the Constitution, *i.e.*, on January 26, 1950. It is well known that out of a large number of privileges and powers which the House of Commons claimed during the days of its bitter struggle for recognition, some were given up in course of time, and some virtually faded out by desuetude; and so, in every case where a power is claimed it is necessary to enquire whether it was an existing power at the relevant time. It must also appear that the said power was not only claimed by the House of Commons, but was recognised by the English Courts. It would obviously be idle to contend that if a particular power which is claimed by the House was claimed by the House of Commons but was not recognised by the English courts, it would still be upheld that under the latter part of clause (3) only on the ground that it was in fact claimed by the House of Commons. In other words, the inquiry which is prescribed by this clause is: is the power in question shown or proved to have substituted in the House of Common at the relevant time"; **AIR 1965 SC 745 (761)**. (Emphasis supplied)

ATTORNEY-GENERAL ALSO DEPENDS ON FOREIGN JUDGMENTS – AGRAWAL, J.

The learned Attorney-General has submitted that till the decision in **R. v. Currie** the position in England was that acceptance of bribe by a Member of Parliament was not an offence at common law and since acceptance of bribe by a member of Parliament was not being treated as an offence at common law, the question whether a Member of Parliament enjoys an immunity from prosecution in a criminal court on a charge of bribery never came up before the English Courts and, therefore, it cannot be said that on January 26, 1950 the members of the House of Commons in the United Kingdom enjoyed a privilege, which was recognised by the English courts, that they could not be prosecuted on a charge of bribery in a criminal court and that such a privilege cannot, therefore, be claimed by Members of Parliament in India under clause (3) of Article 105. The learned Attorney-General has placed reliance on the following observations of Stephen, J. in **Bradlaugh v. Gossett, 1884 (12) QBD 271**:

> "I know of no authority for the proposition that an ordinary crime committed in the House of Commons would be withdrawn from the ordinary course of criminal justice."

52. The learned Attorney-General has also placed reliance on the following statement of law in *Halsbury's Laws of England,* Vol. 11 (1), Para 37 at page 40, wherein it is stated:

> "37. Members of Parliament, except in relation to anything said in debate, a member of the House of Lords or of the House of Commons is subject to the ordinary course of criminal justice, the privileges of Parliament do not apply to criminal matters."

In Footnote (1) to the said para it is stated that:

> "Although members are probably subject to the jurisdiction of the courts in respect of other conduct in Parliament they cannot be made criminally responsible in the courts for what is said by them in Parliament while it is sitting, see the Privileges of Parliament Act, 1512 (as amended)."

ARTICLE 105(3) DOES NOT PROVIDE PROTECTION TO APPELLANTS – AGRAWAL, J.

We find considerable force in the aforesaid submission of the learned Attorney General. Since offering of bribe to a Member of Parliament and acceptance of bribe by him had not been treated as an offence at common law by the courts in England when the Constitution was adopted in 1950, the fact that such conduct was being treated as a breach of privilege by the House of Commons in England at that time would not necessarily mean that the courts would have been precluded from trying the offence of bribery committed by a Member of Parliament if it were to be treated as an offence. In Australia and Cananda where bribery of a legislator was treated as an offence at common law the courts in White, Boston and Bunting had held that the legislator could be prosecuted in the criminal court for the said offence. It cannot, therefore, be said that since acceptance of bribe by a Member of House of Commons was treated as a breach of privilege by the House of Commons and action could be taken by the House for contempt against the Member, the Members of the House of Commons, on January 26, 1950, were enjoying a privilege that in respect of conduct involving acceptance of bribe in connection with the business of Parliament, they could only be punished for breach of privilege of the House and they could not be prosecuted in a court of law. Clause (3) of Article 105 of the Constitution cannot, therefore, be invoked by the appellants to claim immunity from prosecution in respect of the charge levelled against them.

POLITICIANS TAKE FINANCIAL CONTRIBUTIONS – MAKE PROMISES – WHEN CONTEST ELECTIONS – AS MPs THEY VOTE FOR BILL TO FULFILL PROMISE – WHY NOT IMMUNITY? – SUBMIT APPELLANTS – REJECTED – AGRAWAL, J.

53. Before we conclude on this aspect relating to the claim for immunity from prosecution, we would deal with the contention urged by Shri D.D. Thakur wherein he has laid emphasis on the practical political realities. The submission of Shri Thakur is that during the course of the election campaign a candidate receives financial contributions and also makes promises to the electorate and that if the immunity under Article 105(2) is not available he would be liable to be prosecuted if, after being elected as Member of Parliament, he speaks or gives his vote in Parliament in fulfilment of those promises. The learned counsel has placed reliance on the dissenting judgment of White, J. in Brewster, 1972(33) Law Ed 2d 507 wherein he has expressed the view that permitting the executive to initiate the prosecution of a member of Congress for the specific crime of bribery is subject to serious potential abuse that might endanger the independence of the legislature. Burger C.J. has, however, pointed out that there was no basis for such an apprehension in as much as no case was cited in which the bribery statutes which have been applicable to members of Congress for over 100 years have been abused by the Executive Branch. The learned Chief Justice has stated:

> "We do not discount entirely the possibility that an abuse might occur, but this possibility, which we consider remote, must be balanced against the potential danger flowing from either the absence of a bribery statute applicable to Members of Congress or a holding that the statute violates the Constitution. As we noted at the outset, the purpose of the Speech or Debate Clause is to protect the individual legislator, not simply for his own sake, but to preserve the independence and thereby the integrity of the legislative process. But financial abuses, by way of bribes, perhaps even more than Executive power, would gravely undermine legislative integrity and defeat the right of the public to honest representation. Depriving the Executive of the power to investigate and prosecute and the Judiciary of the power to punish bribery of Members of Congress is unlikely to enhance legislative independence". (p. 525).

In the earlier part of the judgment we have found that for the past more than 100 years legislators in Australia and Canada are liable to be prosecuted for bribery in connection with their legislative activities and, with the exception of the United Kingdom, most of the Commonwealth countries treat corruption and bribery by members of legislature as a criminal offence. In the United Kingdom also there is a move to change the law in this regard. There appears to be no reason why legislators in India should be beyond the pale of laws governing bribery and corruption when all other public functionaries are subject to such laws. We are, therefore, unable to uphold the above contention of Shri Thakur.

APPELLANT CANNOT CLAIM IMMUNITY UNDER ARTICLE 105(2)(3) FOR THE CHARGES LEVELLED AGAINST THEM – HELD AGRAWAL, J.

54. On a consideration of the submissions urged by the learned Counsel we arrive at the conclusion that on the basis of provisions contained in clauses (2) and (3) of Article 105, the appellants cannot claim immunity from prosecution on the charges that have been levelled against them.

55. We may now come to the question whether a Member of Parliament is a public servant for the purpose of the 1988 Act. Prior to the enactment of the 1988 Act the law relating to prevention of corruption was governed by the Prevention of Corruption Act, 1947 (hereinafter referred to as the 1947 Act). In section 2 of the 1947 Act it was provided that for the purpose of the said Act "public servant" means a public servant as defined in section 21, Indian Penal Code. Section 21, Indian Penal Code provide as follows:

> "21. *"Public servant"*.—The words "public servant" denote a person falling under any of the descriptions hereinafter following, namely:
>
> *First*.—(Repealed by the Adaptation of Laws Order, 1950).

Second.—Every Commissioned Officer in the Military, Naval or Air Forces of India;

Third.—Every Judge including any person empowered by law to discharge, whether by himself or as a member of any body of persons, any adjudicatory functions;

Fourth.—Every officer of a Court of Justice (including a liquidator, receiver or commissioner) whose duty it is, as such officer, to investigate or report on any matter of law or fact, or to make, authenticate, or keep any document, or to take charge or dispose of any property, or to execute any judicial process, or to administer any oath, or to interpret, or to preserve order in the court and every person specially authorised by a Court of Justice to perform any of such duties;

Fifth.—Every juryman, assessor, or member of a panchayat assisting a Court of Justice or public servant;

Sixth.—Every arbitrator or other person to whom any cause or matter has been referred for decision or report by any court of Justice, or by any other competent public authority;

Seventh.—Every person who holds any office by virtue of which he is empowered to place or keep any person in confinement;

Eighth.—Every officer of the Government whose duty it is, as such officer, to prevent offences, to give information of offences, to bring offenders to justice, or to protect the public health, safety or convenience;

Ninth.—Every officer whose duty it is, as such officer, to take, receive, keep or expend any property on behalf of the Government, or to make any survey, assessment or contract on behalf of the Government, or to execute any revenue-process, or to investigate, or to report, on any matter affecting the pecuniary interests of the Government, or to make, authenticate or keep any document relating to the pecuniary interests of the Government, or to prevent the infraction of any law for the protection of the pecuniary interests of the Government;

Tenth.—Every officer whose duty it is, as such officer, to take, receive, keep or expend any property, to make any survey or assessment or to levy any rate or tax for any secular common purpose of any village, town or district, or to make, authenticate or keep any document for the ascertaining of the rights of the people of any village, town or district;

Eleventh.—Every person who holds any office by virtue of which he is empowered to prepare, publish, maintain or revise an electoral roll or to conduct an election or part of an election;

Twelfth.—Every person—

(a) in the service or pay of the Government or renumerated by fees or commission for the performance of any public duty by the Government;

(b) in the service or pay of a local authority, a corporation established by or under a Central, Provincial or State Act or a Government company as defined in section 617 of the Companies Act, 1956 (1 of 1956)."

In **R.S. Nayak v. A.R. Antulay, 1984 (2) SCR 495: AIR 1984 SC 684** this Court construed the provisions of section 21, Indian Penal Code in order to determine whether a Member of the Legislative Assembly could be held to be a public servant for the purpose of the 1947 Act. The said question was considered in the light of clauses (3), (7) and (12)(a) of section 21, Indian Penal Code. It was pointed out that

Members of Parliament in the United Kingdom are not covered by the Prevention of Corruption Act, 1906, the Prevention of Corruption Act, 1916 and the Public Bodies Corrupt Practices Act, 1889. The Court has also referred to the Bill called the Legislative Bodies Corrupt Practices Act, 1925 introduced in 1925 to give effect to the recommendations of the Reforms Enquiry Committee (known as Mudiman Committee) which sought to fill in the lacuna in the existing law and to provide for punishment of corrupt practices by or relating to members of Legislative Bodies constituted under the Government of India Act, 1919, and has taken note that the said Bill was not enacted into law.

The Court has also referred to the Report of the Committee, known as the Santhanam Committee, appointed by the Government of India to suggest changes which would ensure speedy trial of cases of bribery, corruption and criminal misconduct and make the law otherwise more effective, which led to the amendments introduced in section 21, Indian Penal Code by the Anti-Corruption Laws (Amendment) Act, 1964 as well as the Statement made by Shri Hathi, Minister-in-charge, while piloting in the Lok Sabha the Bill which was enacted as the Anti-Corruption Laws (Amendment) Act, 1964. The Court held that a Member of the Legislative Assembly was not comprehended in the definition of 'public servant' in section 21, Indian Penal Code and that the amendments introduced in section 21, Indian Penal Code by the Amendment Act of 1964 did not bring about any change. While dealing with clause (12)(a) of section 21, Indian Penal Code, as amended by the Amendment Act of 1964, the Court observed that a person would be a public servant under clause 12(a) if (i) he is in the service of the Government, or (ii) he is in the pay of the Government, or (iii) he is remunerated by fees or commission for the performance of any public duty by the Government. It was held that even though a Member of Legislative Assembly receives his salary and allowances in his capacity as such Member, he is not a person in the pay of the Government in as much as the expression 'Government' connotes the executive and not the legislature and a Member of Legislative Assembly is certainly not in the pay of the executive. It was also held that a Member of Legislative Assembly is also not remunerated for performance of any public duty by the Government because he is not remunerated by fees paid by the Government, *i.e.* the Executive. At the same time, while dealing with the contention that a Member of Legislative Assembly is not performing any public duty it was observed:

> "It is not necessary to examine this aspect because it would be rather difficult to accept an unduly vide submission that MLA is not performing any public duty. However, it is unquestionable that he is not performing any public duty either directed by the Government or for the Government. He no doubt performs public duties cast on him by the Constitution and his electorate. He thus discharges constitutional functions for which he is remunerated by fees under the Constitution and not by Executive". (at p. 713 of AIR).

The Court also considered the question whether a Member of the Legislative Assembly is a public servant with reference to clauses (3) and (7) of section 21, Indian Penal Code and held that a member of the Legislative Assembly did not fall within the ambit of the said clauses.

56. In the 1988 Act the expression 'public servant' has been defined in section 2(c) which read as follows:

"2(c) 'Public servant' means—

(i) any person in the service or pay of the Government or remunerated by the Government by fees or commission for the performance of any public duty;

(ii) any person in the service or pay of a local authority;

(iii) any person in the service or pay of a corporation established by or under a Central, Provincial or State Act, or an authority or a body owned or controlled or aided by the Government or a Government company as defined in section 617 of the Companies Act, 1956 (1 of 1956);

(iv) any Judge, including any person empowered by law to discharge, whether by himself or as a member of any body of persons, any adjudicatory functions;

(v) any person authorised by a court of justice to perform any duty, in connection with the administration of justice, including a liquidator, receiver or commissioner appointed by such court;

(vi) any arbitrator or other person to whom any cause or matter has been referred for decision or report by a court of justice or by a competent public authority;

(vii) any person who holds an office by virtue of which he is empowered to prepare, publish, maintain or revise an electoral roll or to conduct an election or part of an election;

(viii) any person who holds an office by virtue of which he is authorised or required to perform any public duty;

(ix) any person who is the president, secretary or other office-bearer of a registered co-operative society engaged in agriculture, industry, trade or banking, receiving or having received any financial aid from the Central Government or a State Government or from any corporation established by or under a Central, Provincial or State Act, or any authority or body owned or controlled or aided by the Government or a Government company as defined in section 617 of the Companies Act, 1956 (1 of 1956);

(x) any person who is a chairman, member or employee of any Service Commission or Board, by whatever name called, or a member of any selection committee appointed by such Commission or Board for the conduct of any examination or making any selection on behalf of such Commission or Board;

(xi) any person who is a Vice-Chancellor or member of any governing body, professor, reader, lecturer or any other teacher or employee, by whatever designation called, of any University and any person whose services have been availed of by a University or any other public authority in connection with holding or conducting examinations;

(xii) any person who is an office-bearer or an employee of an educational, scientific, social, cultural or other institution, in whatever manner established, receiving or having received any financial assistance from the Central Government or any State Government, or local or other public authority.

Explanation 1.—Persons falling under any of the above sub-clauses are public servants, whether appointed by the Government or not.

Explanation 2.—Wherever the words "public servant" occur, they shall be understood of every person who is in actual possession of the situation of a public servant, whatever legal defect there may be in his right to hold that situation." Section 19 of the said Act deals with the previous sanction that is necessary for prosecution for the offences mentioned therein. It reads thus:

The expression 'public duty' is defined in section 2(b) in these terms:

"2. (b) 'Public duty' means a duty in the discharge of which the State, the public or the community at large has an interest;

Explanation.—In this clause 'State' includes a corporation established by or under a Central, Provincial or State Act, or an authority or a body owned or controlled or aided by the Government or a government company as defined in section 617 of the Companies Act, 1956 (1 of 1956);—

57. The clause relevant for our purpose is clause (viii) whereunder 'any person who holds an office by virtue of which he is authorised or required to perform any public duty' is to be treated as a public servant under the 1988 Act. The said clause postulates that the person must (i) hold an office and (ii) by virtue of that office (iii) he must be authorised or required to perform (iv) a public duty.

MP NEITHER HOLDS ANY OFFICE – NOR PERFORMS PUBLIC DUTY – HENCE NOT A PUBLIC SERVANT – SUBMIT APPELLANTS – DISCUSSION – AGRAWAL, J.

58. On behalf of the appellants it has been urged that a Member of Parliament does not fall within the ambit of this clause because (1) he does not hold an office; and (2) he is not authorised or required to perform any public duty by virtue of his office.

59. We will first examine the question whether a Member of Parliament holds an office. The word 'office' is normally understood to mean 'a position to which certain duties are attached, especially a place of trust, authority or service under constituted authority'. (See: *Oxford Shorter English Dictionary*, 3rd Edn., p. 1362.) In **McMillan v. Guest, 1942 AC 561: (1942) 1 All ER 606** Lord Wright has said:

"The word 'office' is of indefinite content. Its various meanings cover four columns of the *New English Dictionary*, but I take as the most relevant for purposes of this case the following: "A position or place to which certain duties are attached, especially one of a more or less public character."

In the same case Lord Atkin gave the following meaning:

"... an office or employment which was subsisting, permanent, substantive position, which had an existence independent of the person who filled it, which went on and was filled in succession by successive holders."

In **Statesman (P) Ltd. v. H.R. Deb, AIR 1968 SC 1495: (1968) 3 SCR 614: 1968 Lab IC 1525** and **Mahadeo v. Shantibhai, (1969) 2 SCR 422** this Court has adopted the meaning given by Lord Wright when it said:

"An office means no more than a position to which certain duties are attached."

60. In **Kanta Kathuria v. Manak Chand Surana, (1969) 3 SCC 268: (1970) 2 SCR 835: AIR 1970 SC 694** Sikri, J. (as the learned Chief Justice then was) speaking for the majority, while construing the words "holds any office of profit" in Article 19(1)(g), has said that "there must be an office which exists independently of the holder of the office". It was observed that there is no essential difference between the definitions given by Lord Wright and Lord Atkin.

61. In **White, 13 SCR (NSW) 332** the Supreme Court of New South Wales has held that a Member of the State Legislature holds an office. That view has been affirmed by the High Court of Australia in Boston. Isaacs and Rich, JJ. said:

"A Member of Parliament is, therefore, in the highest sense, a servant of the State; his duties are those appertaining to the position he fills, a position of no transient or temporary existence, a position forming a recognised place in the constitutional machinery of government. Why, then, does he not hold an 'office'? In **R. v. White**, it was held, as a matter of course, that he does. That decision is sound. 'Office' is defined in the *Oxford Dictionary* as including: '4. A position or place to which certain duties are attached, especially one of a more or less public character; a position of trust, authority, or service under constituted authority.' And 'officer' is defined (*inter alia*) as '2. One who holds an office, post, or place. (a) One who holds a public, civil, or ecclesiastical office; ... a person authoritatively appointed or elected to exercise some function pertaining to public life.' Clearly a Member of Parliament is a 'public officer' in a very real sense, for he has, in the words of Williams, J. in **Faulkner v. Upper Boddington Overseers** "duties to perform" which would constitute in law an office.... (p. 402)

62. In **Habibulla Khan v. State of Orissa, 1993 Cr LJ 3604: (1993) 3 Cri 198** the Orissa High Court has held that a Member of the Legislative Assembly holds an office and performs a public duty. The learned Judges have examined the matter keeping in view the meaning given to the expression 'office' by Lord Wright as well as by Lord Atkin in **McMillan v. Guest, 1942 AC 561: (1942) 1 All ER 606.** Taking into consideration the provisions of Articles 168, 170, 172 and 173 of the Constitution relating to the Legislative Assembly of the State, the learned Judges have held that the Member of the Legislative Assembly is created by the Constitution and that there is a distinction between the office and the holder of the office.

MP HOLDS A SEAT – NOT AN OFFICE – AS PER CONSTITUTION – SUBMIT APPELLANTS

63. Shri P.P. Rao has, however, pointed out that under the Constitution a distinction has been made between an 'office' and a 'seat' and that while the expression 'office' has been used in the Constitution in relation to various constitutional authorities such as President (Articles 56, 57, 59 and 62), Vice-President (Article 67), Speaker and Deputy Speaker of the Lok Sabha (Articles 93, 94, 95 and 96), Deputy Chairman of the Rajya Sabha (Article 90), Ministers (Article 90), Judges of the Supreme Court (Article 124), Judges of the High Court (Article 217) and the Attorney General of India (Article 76) but insofar as a Member of Parliament and a Member of the State Legislature is concerned the expression used is 'seat' and not 'office' which shows that the Constitution does not contemplate that a Member of Parliament or a Member of the State Legislature holds an office. In this context Shri Rao has invited our attention to Articles 84, 99 and 101 where the expression 'seat' has been used in respect of Members of Parliament and to Articles 173 and 190 where the word 'seat' has been used in respect of Members of the State Legislatures.

RP ACT MENTIONS 'TERM OF OFFICE' FOR MP OR MLA – SUBMITS ATTORNEY-GENERAL

64. The learned Attorney-General has, on the other hand, invited our attention to sections 12, 154 and 155 of the Representation of the People Act, 1951 wherein the expression 'term of office' has been used in relation to a Member of the Council of States (Rajya Sabha) and to sections 156 and 157 wherein the said expression has been used in relation to a Member of the Legislative Council of the State (Vidhan Parishad). The learned Attorney-General has also invited our attention to the provisions of the Salaries, Allowances and Pension of Members of Parliament Act, 1954 wherein the expression 'term of office', as defined in section 2(e) covering Members of the Council of States as well as the House of the People, has been used in section 3 (salaries and daily allowances), section 4 (travelling allowances), section 6(2) (free transit by railway), section 6-A(2) (free transit by steamer) and section 8-A(1) (pension).

LOOKING AT CONSTITUTIONAL AND STATUTORY PROVISIONS – MP OR MLA HOLDS 'OFFICE' – PERFORMS PUBLIC DUTIES – FALLS UNDER SECTION 2(c)(viii) OF PC ACT, 1988 – HELD AGRAWAL, J.

65. It would thus appear that although in the Constitution the word 'office' has not been used in the provisions relating to Members of Parliament and Members of the State Legislatures but in other parliamentary enactments relating to Members of Parliament the word 'office' has been used. Having regard to the provisions of the Constitution and the Representation of the People Act, 1951 as well as the Salaries, Allowances and Pension of Members of Parliament Act, 1954 and the meaning that has been given to the expression 'office' in the decisions of this Court, we are of the view that membership of Parliament is an 'office' in as much as it is a position carrying certain responsibilities which are of a public character and it has an existence independent of the holder of the office. It must, therefore, be held that the Member of Parliament holds an 'office'.

66. The next question is whether a Member of Parliament is authorised or required to perform any public duty by virtue of his office. As mentioned earlier, in **R.S. Nayak v. A.R. Antulay** this Court has said that though a Member of the State Legislature is not performing any public duty either directed by the Government or for the Government but he no doubt performs public duties cast on him by the Constitution and by his electorate and he discharges constitutional obligations for which he is remunerated fees under the Constitution.

67. In the 1988 Act the expression 'public duty' has been defined in section 2(b) to mean 'a duty in the discharge of which the State, the public or the community at large has an interest'.

The Form of Oath or Affirmation which is required to be made by a Member of Parliament (as prescribed in the Third Schedule to the Constitution) is in these terms:

> 'I, A.B., having been elected (or nominated) a Member of the Council of States (or the House of the People) do swear in the name of God/solemnly affirm that I will bear true faith and allegiance to the Constitution of India as by law established, that I will uphold the sovereignty and integrity of India and that I will faithfully discharge the duty upon which I am about to enter.'

The words 'faithfully discharge the duty upon which I am about to enter' show that a Member of Parliament is required to discharge certain duties after he is sworn in as a Member of Parliament. Under the Constitution the Union executive is responsible to Parliament and Members of Parliament act as watchdogs on the functioning of the Council of Ministers. In addition, a Member of Parliament plays an important role in parliamentary proceedings, including enactment of legislation, which is a sovereign function. The duties discharged by him are such in which the State, the public and the community at large have an interest and the said duties are, therefore, public duties. It can be said that a Member of Parliament is authorised and required by the Constitution to perform these duties and the said duties are performed by him by virtue of his office.

68. In **Horne v. Barber, (1920) 27 CLR 494 (500)**, Isaacs, J. has said:

> 'When a man becomes a Member of Parliament, he undertakes high public duties. Those duties are inseparable from the position: he cannot retain the honour and divest himself of the duties. One of the duties is that of watching on behalf of the general community the conduct of the executive, of criticising it, and if necessary, of calling it to account in the constitutional way by censure from his place in Parliament' censure which, if sufficiently supported, means

removal from office. That is the whole essence of responsible government, which is the keystone of our political system, and is the main constitutional safeguard the community possesses. (p. 402)

69. In **Boston, 1923 (33) CLR 386** while examining the nature of duties of a Member of Parliament, Isaacs and Rich, JJ. have reiterated the above-quoted observations in **Horne v. Barber** and have said:

> 'The fundamental obligation of a Member in relation to Parliament of which he is a constituent unit still subsists as essentially as at any period of our history. That fundamental obligation which is the key to this case is the duty to serve and, in serving, to act with fidelity and with a single-mindedness for the welfare of the community. (p. 400)
>
> Those duties are of a transcendent nature and involve the greatest responsibility, for they include the supreme power of moulding the laws to meet the necessities of the people, and the function of vigilantly controlling and faithfully guarding the public finances.' (p. 401)

70. We are, therefore, of the view that a Member of Parliament holds an office and by virtue of such office he is required or authorised to perform duties and such duties are in the nature of public duties. A Member of Parliament would, therefore, fall within the ambit of sub-clause (viii) of clause (c) of section 2 of the 1988 Act.

LOK SABHA – RAJYA SABHA PROCEEDINGS WHILE ENACTING PC ACT – MPs OR MLAs ARE NOT INTENDED TO BASE 'PUBLIC SERVANTS' UNDER SECTION 2 OF PC ACT, 1988 – SUBMIT APPELLANTS

71. The learned counsel for the appellants have, however, urged that while enacting the 1988 Act Parliament did not intend to include Members of Parliament and Members of the State Legislatures within the ambit of the Act and that the expression 'public servant' as defined in section 2(c) of the 1988 Act should be so construed as to exclude Members of Parliament and Members of the State Legislatures. The learned counsel have placed strong reliance on the speeches of Shri P. Chidambaram, the then Minister of State in the Ministry of Personnel, Public Grievances and Pensions and in the Ministry of Home Affairs during the course of debate on the Prevention of Corruption Bill, 1987 in the Lok Sabha as well as in the Rajya Sabha. Reliance has been placed on the following excerpts from the speech of the Minister in the Lok Sabha on 7-5-1987 and in the Rajya Sabha on May 11-5-1987 and 11-8-1987:

Lok Sabha

'A question has been raised what is the position of a Member of Parliament or a Member of a Legislative Assembly? We have not done anything different or contrary to the law as it stands today. Under the law, as it stands today, the Supreme Court has held in **Antulay** case that a Member of the Legislative Assembly is not a public servant within the meaning of section 21 of the Indian Penal Code.

I personally think that it is very difficult to say when an MLA or an MP becomes a public servant. I believe that when an MP functions *qua* MP perhaps he is not a public servant and, therefore, we are not attempting a definition which will lead to difficulties. We think that there could be situations when an MP or an MLA does certain things which are really not part of his duties as an MP or an MLA. We think that an MP or an MLA could in certain circumstances hold an office where he will be discharging certain public duties. These two situations are covered by this Act. If an MP or an MLA does certain acts not *qua* MP or *qua* MLA, but as an individual, abusing his position, I am not using the word 'office', I think he will be covered like any other individual under sections 8, 9 and 12. When an MP or an MLA holds an office, and by virtue of that office he has to discharge certain public duties, I think he will be covered under section 2 clause (b) read with section 2 clause (c) sub-clause (viii). I think these two situations are quite adequate to take care of defaulting Members of Parliament and defaulting Members of the Legislative Assemblies.'

Rajya Sabha

'Now I will reply to the best of my ability how an MP or an MLA comes within the ambit of this Bill. I have tried to explain it in the Lok Sabha and I will try to do so here within my limits and to the best of my capacity. But if you are quoting my speech, please quote the entire paragraphs. Don't take one sentence and then paraphrase it and give your commentary on it. Read the whole paragraph, it is very clear. I have said that an MP or an MLA will in my opinion, come within the scope of this Bill in two situations....

A law has to be made by Parliament. We make a law with certain intentions. We use a certain language. In my view and in my best judgment and on the best advice that I have, this is how we think an MP or an MLA will be covered. This is all that we can say while we are making a law. We believe that our interpretation will be accepted by the courts. If you find fault with our interpretation tell us where we should improve the Bill, tell us how we should improve the language. A law is a matter of interpretation. We are acting according to the legal advice available to us.

A question was asked about the Members of Parliament and Members of the Legislative Assembly. Madam, under the law declared by the Supreme Court, a Member of Parliament or a Member of the Legislative Assembly *per se* is not a public servant. But there can be a number of situations where an MP or an MLA holds another office and discharges other duties which will bring him under this Bill. If he holds another office in a cooperative society, if he holds another office in a public institution or if he discharges certain duties which will come under the definition of public duty clearly, then he would be within the definition of 'public servant' under this Bill. But these are matters in which you cannot make on a prior assumption. One has to look into the facts of each case and then the courts will decide on the facts of that case.'

72. It has been urged that these excerpts from the speeches of the Minister who had moved the Bill for consideration in both the Houses of Parliament throws considerable light on the meaning of the expression 'public servant' as defined in section 2(c) of the 1988 Act and that provisions of section 2(c)(viii) of the 1988 Act should be given a construction which is in accord with these statements of the Minister. Relying upon the decisions of this Court in **K.P. Varghese v. ITO, (1981) 4 SCC 173: 1981 SCC (Tax) 293: (1982) 1 SCR 629**; **R.S. Nayak v. A.R. Antulay** (supra); **State of Orissa v. Mahanadi Coalfields Ltd., 1995 Supp (2) SCC 686** and **Narendra Kumar Maheshwari v. Union of India, 1990 Supp SCC 440: (1989) 3 SCR 43**, Shri Rao has urged that the speech of the mover of the Bill can be looked into for construing the provisions of the enactment. It has been pointed out that in the recent decision in **Pepper v. Hart, (1993) 1 All ER 42: 1993 AC 593: (1992) 3 WLR 1032 (HL)**, the House of Lords has also departed from the earlier position taken by the courts in England in this regard and that it has been held that the statement of the Minister who had moved the Bill in Parliament can be taken into consideration for the purposes of interpreting the provisions of the enactment.

73. The view which prevailed earlier with the courts in England was that references to parliamentary material as an aid to statutory construction is not permissible. The said exclusionary rule precluded the court from looking even at reports made by Commissioners on which legislation was based. The rigidity of the said rule was relaxed in later decisions so as to permit reports of Commissioners, including Law Commissioners, and white papers to be looked at for the purpose solely of ascertaining the mischief the statute is intended to cure but not for the purpose of discovering the meaning of the words used by Parliament to effect such cure. Parliamentary debates were, however, not looked at as an aid to construction. The rationale for the exclusion of parliamentary debates is contained in the speech of Lord Reid in **Black-Clawson International Ltd. v. Papierwerke Waldhof-Aschaffenburg, 1975 AC 591: (1975) 1 All ER 810: (1975) 2 WLR 513 (HL).** The learned Lord Reid has said:

> "We often say that we are looking for the intention of Parliament, but that is not quite accurate. We are seeking the meaning of the words which Parliament used. We are seeking not what Parliament meant but the true meaning of what they said.
>
> ****
>
> The questions which give rise to debate are rarely those which later have to be decided by the courts. One might take the views of the promoters of a Bill as an indication of the intention of Parliament but any view the promoters may have had about questions which later come before the court will not often appear in Hansard and often those questions have never occurred to the promoters. At best we might get material from which a more or less dubious inference might be drawn as to what the promoters intended or would have intended if they had thought about the matter, and it would, I think, generally be dangerous to attach weight to what some other Members of either House may have said." (pp. 613-615)

74. The decision in **Pepper v. Hart, (1993) 1 All ER 42: 1993 AC 593: (1992) 3 WLR 1032 (HL)**, makes an advance. In that case Lord Browne-Wilkinson, who delivered the main judgment, has said:

> "... In my judgment, subject to the questions of the privileges of the House of Commons, reference to parliamentary material should be permitted as an aid to the construction of legislation which is ambiguous or obscure or the literal meaning of which leads to an absurdity. Even in such cases references in court to parliamentary material should only be permitted where such material clearly discloses the mischief aimed at or the legislative intention lying behind the ambiguous or obscure words. In the case of statements made in Parliament, as at present advised I cannot foresee that any statement other than the statement of the Minister or other promoter of the Bill is likely to meet these criteria. (p. 64)
>
> ... Given the purposive approach to construction now adopted by the courts in order to give effect to the true intentions of the legislature, the fine distinctions between looking for the mischief and looking for the intention in using words to provide the remedy are technical and inappropriate. Clear and unambiguous statements made by Ministers in Parliament are as much the background to the enactment of legislation as white papers and parliamentary reports." (p. 65)

75. In the earlier decisions this Court also adopted the rule of exclusion followed by the English courts. Parliamentary debates on a Bill were held to be inadmissible for construction of the Act. (See: **Aswini Kumar Ghose v. Arabinda Bose, AIR 1952 SC 369: 1953 SCR 1).** But in later judgments this Court has referred to the speech of the Minister while introducing the Bill in the legislature for the purpose of ascertaining the mischief sought to be remedied by the legislation and the object and purpose for which the legislation is enacted. In **K.P. Varghese v. ITO** (supra) Bhagwati, J. (as the learned Chief Justice then was) has said: (SCC p. 184, para 8)

> "Now it is true that the speeches made by the Members of the legislature on the floor of the House when a Bill for enacting a statutory provision is being debated are inadmissible for the purpose of interpreting the statutory provision but the speech made by the Mover of the Bill explaining the reason for the introduction of the Bill can certainly be referred to for the purpose of ascertaining the mischief sought to be remedied by the legislation and the object and purpose for which the legislation is enacted."

76. The other decisions of this Court cited by Shri Rao do not lay down any different principle. On the other hand in **Sanjeev Coke Manufacturing Co. v. Bharat Coking Coal Ltd., (1983) 1 SCC 147: (1983) 1 SCR 1000**, this Court has laid down: (SCC p. 172, para 25)

> "No one may speak for Parliament and Parliament is never before the court. After Parliament has said what it intends to say, only the court may say what the Parliament meant to say. None else. Once a statute leaves Parliament House, the court's is the only authentic voice which may echo (interpret) Parliament. This the court will do with reference to the language of the statute and other permissible aids."

SPEECH OF THE MOVER OF THE BILL MATERIAL IF THE ENACTMENT IS AMBIGUOUS – OBSCURE – LEADS TO ABSURDITY – SPEECH OF THE MINISTER DOES NOT RULE OUT IF MPs-MLAs – ARE NOT PUBLIC SERVANTS – HELD AGRAWAL, J.

77. It would thus be seen that as per the decisions of this Court the statement of the Minister who had moved the Bill in Parliament can be looked at to ascertain the mischief sought to be remedied by the legislation and the object and purpose for which the legislation is enacted. The statement of the Minister who had moved the Bill in Parliament is not taken into account for the purpose of interpreting the provisions of the enactment. The decision in **Pepper v. Hart** permits reference to the statement of the Minister or other promoter of the Bill as an aid to construction of legislation which is ambiguous or obscure or the literal meaning of which leads to an absurdity provided the statement relied upon clearly discloses the mischief aimed at or the legislative intention lying behind the ambiguous or obscure words and that such a statement of the Minister must be clear and unambiguous. This rule of construction laid in **Pepper v. Hart** has no application in the present case because sub-clause (viii) of section 2(c) of the 1988 Act cannot be said to be ambiguous or obscure nor can it be said that the literal meaning of the said clause leads to any absurdity.

78. Moreover, the excerpts from the statements of the Minister on which reliance has been placed by the learned counsel of the appellants cannot be regarded as clear and unambiguous on the question whether a Member of Parliament or the Member of the State Legislature would fall within the ambit of 'public servant' under the 1988 Act because according to the statements of the Minister a Member of Parliament and a Member of the State Legislature would be a 'public servant' under section 2(c)(viii) of the Act in certain situations. The statement of the Minister does not clearly indicate those situations. The provisions of the 1988 Act also do not give any indication about the situations in which a Member of Parliament or a Member of the State Legislature would be treated as a 'public servant' and the situations in which he will not be treated as a public servant. Shri Kapil Sibal has submitted that what the Minister meant was that if a Member of Parliament or a Member of the State Legislature is given some other assignment, *e.g.*, membership of a delegation, then in connection with that assignment his position would be that of a public servant under the 1988 Act. The language used in section 2(c)(viii) does not lend support to such a limited construction of the said provision.

79. Having regard to the object of the 1988 Act as indicated in the Statement of Objects and Reasons, namely, to widen the scope of the definition of the expression 'public servant', which is sought to be achieved by introducing the definition of 'public duty' in section 2(b) and the definition of 'public servant' in section 2(c) which enlarges the scope of the existing definition of public servant contained in section 21 Indian Penal Code, we do not find any justification for restricting the scope of the wide words used in sub-clause (viii) of section 2(c) in the 1988 Act on the basis of the statement of the Minister so as to exclude Members of Parliament and Members of the State Legislatures. In our opinion the words used in sub-clause (viii) of section 2(c) are clear and unambiguous and they cannot be cut down on the basis of the statement made by the Minister while piloting the Bill in Parliament.

STATEMENT OF MINISTER IN THE COURSE OF DEBATE ON THE PREVENTION OF CORRUPTION BILL, 1988 – IS PROMISSORY ESTOPPEL TO APPLY PC ACT, 1988 TO MPs – SUBMIT APPELLANTS – REJECTED – AGRAWAL, J.

80. Shri D.D. Thakur has invoked the doctrine of promissory estoppel and has submitted that in view of the statement made by the Minister while piloting the Bill in Parliament that Members of Parliament and Members of the State Legislatures do not fall within the ambit of the definition of 'public servant' the State is estopped from taking a contrary stand and to claim that a Member of Parliament is a public servant under section 2(c) of the Act. There is no legal basis for this contention. We are concerned with the provisions of a law made by Parliament. There is no estoppel against the statute.

81. Shri Thakur has also invoked the rule of statutory construction that the legislature does not intend to make a substantial alteration in law beyond what it explicitly declares either in express words or by clear implication and that the general words of the Act are not to be so construed as to alter the previous policy of the law. He has placed reliance on the decision in **M.K. Ranganathan v. Govt. of Madras, AIR 1955 SC 604: (1955) 2 SCR 374.** The said rule can have no application in the present case because the 1988 Act has replaced the 1947 Act. It has been enacted with the specific object of altering the existing anti-corruption laws so as to make them more effective by widening their coverage and by strengthening the provisions and also to widen the scope of the definition of 'public servant'.

MPs OR MLAs PERFORM PUBLIC DUTY WITHIN THE MEANING OF SECTION 2 PC ACT, 1988 – ARE PUBLIC SERVANTS – HELD AGRAWAL, J.

82. Having considered the submissions of the learned counsel on the meaning of the expression 'public servant' contained in section 2(c) of the 1988 Act, we are of the view that a Member of Parliament is a public servant for the purpose of the 1988 Act.

83. In order to show that Members of Parliament are outside the purview of the 1988 Act, the learned counsel for the appellants have referred to section 19 of the 1988 Act which prescribes that no court shall take cognizance of an offence punishable under sections 7, 10, 11, 13 and 15 alleged to have been committed by a public servant except with the previous sanction of the authority specified in clauses (a), (b) or (c) of sub-section (1) of section 19. It is submitted that none of the clauses (a), (b) or (c) of sub-section (1) of section 19 is applicable in respect of a Member of Parliament and that there is no authority who can grant sanction for prosecution of a Member of Parliament which means that a Member of Parliament does not fall within the purview of the 1988 Act. Reliance has been placed on the observations of Shetty, J. and Verma, J. (as the learned Chief Justice then was) in **K. Veeraswami v. Union of India, 1991 (3) SCR 189** and the decision of the Orissa High Court in **Habibulla Khan, 1993 Cr LJ 3604.**

MANY OF THE APPELLANTS HAVE CEASED TO BE MPs – OFFENCES OF 120B, IPC – SECTIONS 7, 13(2), 13 (1)(d), 12 of 1988 ACT ARE NOT COVERED BY SECTION 19(1) OF 1988 ACT – COURT CAN TAKE COGNIZANCE – SUBMITTED ATTORNEY-GENERAL

84. The learned Attorney-General has, on the other hand, urged that the requirement of previous sanction under section 19 of the 1988 Act only imposes a limitation on the power of the court to take cognizance under section 190 Criminal Procedure Code of the offences mentioned in sub-section (1) of section 19 and that if a public servant is not covered by any of the clauses (a), (b) and (c) of section 19(1) and there is no authority who could grant sanction for his prosecution, the limitation imposed by section 19 on the power of the court to take cognizance would not be applicable and it would be open to the competent court to take cognizance of the offences mentioned in section 19(1) without insisting on the requirement of sanction. The submission is that merely because none of the clauses (a), (b) and (c) of section 19(1) is applicable to a Member of Parliament, it cannot be said that he is outside the purview of the 1988 Act. The learned Attorney-General has also urged, in the alternative, that in view of the provisions contained in Articles 102 and 103 the President can be regarded as the authority competent to remove a Member of Parliament and, therefore, he can grant the sanction for his prosecution under section 19(1)(c) and it cannot be said that since there is no authority who can grant sanction for his prosecution a Member of Parliament is outside the purview of the 1988 Act. The learned Attorney-General has also submitted that many of the appellants had ceased to be Members of Parliament on the date of filing of the charge-sheet and that the offence of criminal conspiracy under section 120B, Indian Penal Code read with section 7 and section 13(2) read with section 13(1)(d) of the 1988 Act as well as the offence under section 12 of the 1988 Act are not among the offences mentioned in section 19(1) and that no sanction was required with regard to these offences and that sanction was required only in respect of offences under section 7 and section 13(2) read with section 13(1)(d) of the 1988 Act as against A-4 and A-15 and that in view of sub-section (3) of section 19 the omission of sanction would not have any effect on the trial of the said accused persons.

SECTION 19 PC ACT, 1988 REPRODUCED – AGRAWAL, J.

85. Section 19 of the 1988 Act provides as follows:

"19. Previous sanction necessary for prosecution:—

(1) No court shall take cognizance of an offence punishable under sections 7, 10, 11, 13 and 15 alleged to have been committed by a public servant, except with the previous sanction,

  (a) in the case of a person who is employed in connection with the affairs of the Union and is not removable from his office save by or with the sanction of the Central Government, of that Government;

  (b) in the case of a person who is employed in connection with the affairs of a State and is not removable from his office save by or with the sanction of the State Government, of that Government;

  (c) in the case of any other person, of the authority competent to remove him from his office.

(2) Where for any reason whatsoever any doubt arises as to whether the previous sanction as required under sub-section (1) should be given by the Central Government or the State Government or any other authority, such sanction shall be given by that Government or authority which would have been competent to remove the public servant from his office at the time when the offence was alleged to have been committed.

(3) Notwithstanding anything contained in the Code of Criminal Procedure, 1973 (2 of 1974),—

(a) no finding, sentence or order passed by a Special Judge shall be reversed or altered by a court in appeal, confirmation or revision on the ground of the absence of, or any error, omission or irregularity in, the sanction required under sub-section (1), unless in the opinion of that court, a failure of justice has in fact been occasioned thereby;

(b) no court shall stay the proceedings under this Act on the ground of any error, omission or irregularity in the sanction granted by the authority, unless it is satisfied that such error, omission or irregularity has resulted in a failure of justice;

(c) no court shall stay the proceedings under this Act on any other ground and no court shall exercise the powers of revision in relation to any interlocutory order passed in any inquiry, trial, appeal or other proceedings.

(4) In determining under sub-section (3) whether the absence of, or any error, omission or irregularity in, such sanction has occasioned or resulted in a failure of justice the court shall have regard to the fact whether the objection could and should have been raised at any earlier stage in the proceedings.

Explanation.—For the purposes of this section,—

(a) error includes competency of the authority to grant sanction;

(b) a sanction required for prosecution includes reference to any requirement that the prosecution shall be at the instance of a specified authority or with the sanction of a specified person or any requirement of a similar nature."

DISCUSSION – AGRAWAL, J.

86. The provisions as regards sanction were earlier contained in section 6 of the 1947 Act. Sub-sections (1) and (2) of section 19 substantially reproduce the provisions contained in section 6 of the 1947 Act. Clauses (a), (b) and (c) of sub-section (1) of section 19 are in the same terms as clauses (a), (b) and (c) of sub-section (1) of section 6 of the 1947 Act. Sub-sections (3) and (4) of section 19 of the 1988 Act were not contained in section 6 of the 1947 Act and have been inserted for the first time in section 19 of the 1988 Act.

87. In **Veeraswami** (supra) the question for consideration was whether a Judge of the High Court falls within the ambit of the 1947 Act and in support of the contention that he was not covered by the said Act, it was submitted that for prosecution in respect of an offence under the 1947 Act previous sanction of an authority competent to remove the public servant as provided under section 6 of the 1947 Act is imperative and that the power to remove a Judge of the superior court is not vested in any single individual authority but is vested in the two Houses of

Parliament and the President under Article 124(4) of the Constitution and since there is no authority competent to grant sanction under section 6 of the 1947 Act a Judge of the superior court did not fall within the ambit of the provisions of the 1947 Act. The said contention was rejected by the Court (Verma, J. dissenting). Shetty, J., who delivered the main judgment on behalf of the majority, held that for the purpose of section 6 of the 1947 Act a Judge of the superior court fell in clause (c) of section 6(1) and that the President of India is the authority competent to grant sanction for his prosecution. The learned counsel for the appellants have placed reliance on the following observations in the judgment of Shetty, J. wherein the learned Judge has construed the provisions of section 6 of the 1947 Act: (SCC pp. 694 and 695, paras 29 and 31).

> "Section 6 may now be analysed. Clause (a) of section 6(1) covers public servants employed in connection with the affairs of the Union. The prescribed authority for giving prior sanction for such persons would be the Central Government. Clause (b) of section 6(1) covers public servants in connection with the affairs of the State. The authority competent to give prior sanction for prosecution of such persons would be the State Government. Clauses (a) and (b) would thus cover the cases of public servants who are employed in connection with the affairs of the Union or the State and are not removable from their office save by or with the sanction of the Central Government or the State Government. That is not the end. The section goes further in clause (c) to cover the remaining categories of public servants. Clause (c) states that in the case of any other person the sanction would be of the authority competent to remove him from his office. Section 6 is thus all-embracing bringing within its fold all the categories of public servants as defined under section 21 of the Indian Penal Code.
>
> ***
>
> The provisions of clauses (a) and (b) of section 6(1) of the Act cover certain categories of public servants and the 'other' which means remaining categories are brought within the scope of clause (c)."

It has been pointed out that Verma, J., in his dissenting judgment, has also taken the same view when he said: (SCC p. 737, para 107)

> "107. Clauses (a), (b) and (c) in sub-section (1) of section 6 exhaustively provide for the competent authority to grant sanction for prosecution in case of all the public servants falling within the purview of the Act. Admittedly, such previous sanction is a condition precedent for taking cognizance of an offence punishable under the Act, of a public servant who is prosecuted during his continuance in the office. It follows that the public servant falling within the purview of the Act must invariably fall within one of the three clauses in sub-section (1) of section 6. It follows that the holder of an office, even though a 'public servant' according to the definition in the Act, who does not fall within any of the clauses (a), (b) or (c) of sub-section (1) of section 6 must be held to be outside the purview of the Act since this special enactment was not enacted to cover that category of public servants in spite of the wide definition of 'public servant' in the Act. This is the only manner in which these provisions of the Act can be harmonised and given full effect."

88. The said decision in Veeraswami was given in the context of the definition of 'public servant' as contained in section 21 Indian Penal Code. The various clauses in section 21 Indian Penal Code refer to persons who can be removed from office and keeping in view the criterion of removability from office this Court in Veeraswami has said that clauses (a), (b) and (c) of sub-section (1) of section 6 of the 1947 Act cover all the categories of public servants mentioned in section 21 Indian Penal Code. In the 1988 Act the concept of 'public servant' has been enlarged. A separate provision containing the definition of 'public servant' has been introduced in section 2(c) of the 1988 Act. A comparison of the definition of 'public servant' contained in section 21 Indian Penal Code and that contained in section 2(c) of the 1988 Act would show that section 21 Indian Penal Code did not include persons falling under sub-clauses (ix), (x), (xi) and (xii) of section 2(c). Sub-clause (viii) of section 2(c) is also wider in amplitude than clause (12)(a) of section 21 Indian Penal Code.

89. In Veeraswami while considering whether Parliament is the authority which could grant sanction for prosecution of a Judge of the Supreme Court since under Article 124(4) of the Constitution, the address must be passed by each House of Parliament, Shetty, J. has said: (SCC p. 700, para 40)

> "The grant of sanction requires consideration of material collected by the investigating agency and Parliament cannot properly consider the material. Parliament is wholly unsuitable to that work. It would be reasonable to presume that the legislature while enacting clause (c) of section 6(1) of the Act could not have intended Parliament to be the sanctioning authority."

The enlarged definition of public servant in section 2(c) of the 1988 Act includes persons who are not removable by any single individual authority and can only be removed by a collective body and the aforementioned observation of Shetty, J. made in the context of Parliament would be applicable. Reference, in this context, may be made to sub-clauses (ix) and (xii) of section 2(c). Sub-clause (ix) speaks of a person "who is the President, Secretary or other office-bearer of a registered cooperative society engaged in agriculture, industry, trade or banking, receiving or having received any financial aid from the Central Government or a State Government or from any corporation established by or under a Central, Provincial or State Act, or any authority or body owned or controlled or aided by the Government or a government company as defined in section 617 of the Companies Act, 1956 (1 of 1956).

The President, Secretary and other office-bearers of a cooperative society hold office in accordance with the provisions of the relevant statute governing such society and the rules and bye-laws made thereunder. The said statute and the rules and bye-laws may provide for an elected President, Secretary and other office-bearers who may be removable by a vote of no-confidence by the body which has elected them. Similarly sub-clause (xii) of section 2(c) of the 1988 Act talks of a person "who is an office-bearer or an employee of an educational, scientific, social, cultural or other institution, in whatever manner established, receiving or having received any financial assistance from the Central Government or any State Government, or local or other public authority".

There may be an institution run by a society through an elected Managing Committee. The office-bearer of such an institution would be the elected President or Secretary of the Managing Committee who would be removable only by the body which elected him. The consideration which weighed with this Court in Veeraswami for holding that Parliament could not be intended to be the sanctioning authority under section 6(1)(c) of the 1947 Act would equally apply to the general body of members of a cooperative society under clause (ix) and to the general body of members of a society running an institution referred to in clause (xii) and it can be said that the said bodies could not have been intended by Parliament to be the sanctioning authority for the purpose of section 19(1)(c) of the 1988 Act.

EVEN THOUGH THERE IS NO AUTHORITY TO REMOVE AN MP – OR TO GRANT SANCTION FOR HIS PROSECUTION – STILL AN MP IS 'PUBLIC SERVANT' WITHIN THE SCOPE OF SECTION 2(c)(viii) OF 1988 ACT – HELD AGRAWAL, J.

90. This would mean that the definition of 'public servant' in section 2(c) of the 1988 Act includes persons who are public servants under that provision though the criterion of removability does not apply to them and there is no single individual authority which is competent to grant sanction for their prosecution under section 19 of the 1988 Act. In respect of a Member of Parliament the Constitution does not confer on any particular authority the power to remove him. Clause (1) of Article 103 lays down that if any question arises as to whether a Member of either House of Parliament has become subject to any of the disqualifications mentioned in clause (1) of Article 102, the question shall be referred to the decision of the President and his decision shall be final. The said function of the President is in the nature of an adjudicatory function which is to be exercised in the event of a dispute giving rise to the question whether a Member of either House of Parliament has become subject to any of the disqualifications mentioned in clause (1) of Article 102 being raised.

If the President holds that the Member has become subject to a disqualification mentioned in clause (1) of Article 102, the Member would be treated to have ceased to be a Member on the date when he became subject to such disqualification. If it is not disputed that a Member has incurred a disqualification mentioned in clause (1) of Article 102, the matter does not go to the President and the Member ceases to be a Member on the date when he incurred the disqualification. The power conferred under Article 103(1) cannot, therefore, be regarded as a power of removal of a Member of Parliament. Similarly, under the Tenth Schedule to the Constitution a power has been conferred on the Chairman of the Rajya Sabha/the Speaker of the Lok Sabha to decide the question as to whether a Member of the Rajya Sabha/Lok Sabha has become disqualified for being a Member on the ground of defection. The said decision of the Chairman of the Rajya Sabha and the Speaker of the Lok Sabha that a Member has incurred disqualification on the ground of defection may result in such Member ceasing to be a Member but it would not mean that the Chairman of the Rajya Sabha/Speaker of the Lok Sabha is the authority competent to remove a Member of the Rajya Sabha/Lok Sabha. It is no doubt true that the House in exercise of its power of contempt can pass a resolution for expulsion of a Member who is found guilty of breach of privilege and acceptance of bribe by a Member in connection with the business of the House is regarded as breach of privilege. On that basis it may be possible to say that the House has the power to remove a Member who is found to have indulged in bribery and corruption.

But in view of the decision in Veeraswami wherein Shetty, J. has said that the legislature while enacting clause (c) of section 6 of the 1947 Act could not have intended Parliament to be the sanctioning authority, the House cannot be regarded as the authority competent to grant sanction under section 19(1)(c) of the 1988 Act. On that view of the matter it must be held that there is no authority who can remove a Member of Parliament and who would be competent under clauses (a), (b) or (c) of section 19(1) of the 1988 Act to grant sanction for his prosecution. This does not, however, lead to the conclusion that he cannot be treated as a 'public servant' under section 2(c)(viii) of the 1988 Act if, on a proper interpretation of the said provision he is found to be a public servant. Since on an interpretation of the provisions of section 2(c)(viii) of the 1988 Act we have held that a Member of Parliament is a public servant, a Member of Parliament has to be treated as a public servant for the purpose of the 1988 Act even though there is no authority who can grant sanction for his prosecution under section 19(1) of the 1988 Act.

91. It is then urged that if it is found that there is no authority who is competent to remove a Member of Parliament and to grant sanction for his prosecution under section 19(1) of the 1988 Act then a Member of Parliament would fall outside the purview of the Act because in view of the provisions of section 19 sanction is imperative for prosecution in respect of an offence under the 1988 Act. In support of this contention reliance has been placed on the following observations in the dissenting judgment of Verma, J. in **Veeraswami (SCC p. 737, para 107)**

> "The grant of previous sanction under section 6 being a condition precedent for the prosecution of a public servant covered by the Act, it must follow that the holder of an office who may be a public servant according to the wide definition of the expression in the Act but whose category for the grant of sanction for prosecution is not envisaged by section 6 of the Act, is outside the purview of the Act, not intended to be covered by the Act. This is the only manner in which a harmonious construction of the provisions of the Act can be made for the purpose of achieving the object of that enactment."

92. With due respect we find it difficult to agree with these observations. In taking this view the learned Judge has construed section 6 of the 1947 Act, which like sections 193 and 195 to 197 Criminal Procedure Code was a limitation on the power of the Court to take cognizance and thereby assume jurisdiction over a matter, as a right conferred on a public servant to mean "no public servant shall be prosecuted without previous sanction". This aspect has been considered by this Court in **S.A. Venkataraman v. State, AIR 1958 SC 107: 1958 SCR 1040: (1958) 2 LLJ 1.** In that case the appellant, who was a public servant, had been dismissed after departmental enquiry and thereafter he was charged with having committed the offence of criminal misconduct under section 5(2) of the 1947 Act and he was convicted. No sanction under section 6 was produced before the trial court. It was contended before this Court that the court could not take cognizance of the offence without there being a proper sanction to prosecute. The said contention was rejected on the view that sanction was not necessary for the prosecution of the appellant as he was not a public servant at the time of taking cognizance of the offence. After referring to the provisions contained in section 190 Criminal Procedure Code which confers a general power on a criminal court to take cognizance of offences and after holding that section 6 is in the nature of a limitation on the said power, it was observed:

> "In our opinion, if a general power to take cognizance of an offence is vested in a court, any prohibition to the exercise of that power, by any provision of law, must be confined to the terms of the prohibition. In enacting a law prohibiting the taking of a cognizance of an offence by a court, unless certain conditions were complied with, the legislature did not purport to condone the offence. It was primarily concerned to see that prosecution for offences in cases covered by the prohibition shall not commence without complying with the conditions contained therein, such as a previous sanction of a competent authority in the case of a public servant, and in other cases with the consent of the authority or the party interested in the prosecution or aggrieved by the offence. (pp. 1043, 1044)
>
> ****
>
> When the provisions of section 6 of the Act are examined it is manifest that two conditions must be fulfilled before its provisions become applicable. One is that the offences mentioned therein must be committed by a public servant and the other is that that person is employed in connection with the affairs of the Union or a State and is not removable from his office save by or with the sanction of the Central Government or the State Government or is a public servant who is removable from his office by any other competent authority. Both these conditions must be present to prevent a court from

taking cognizance of an offence mentioned in the section without the previous sanction of the Central Government or the State Government or the authority competent to remove the public servant from his office. If either of these conditions is lacking, the essential requirements of the section are wanting and the provisions of the section do not stand in the way of a court taking cognizance without previous sanction." (p. 1045)

COURT CAN TAKE COGNIZANCE OF AN OFFENCE BY A PUBLIC SERVANT IN CERTAIN CIRCUMSTANCES EVEN WITHOUT SANCTION OR EVEN WHEN THERE IS NO AUTHORITY TO REMOVE HIM – AGRAWAL, J.

This means that when there is an authority competent to remove a public servant and to grant sanction for his prosecution under section 19(1) of the 1988 Act the requirement of sanction precludes a court from taking cognizance of the offences mentioned in section 19(1) against him in the absence of such sanction, but if there is no authority competent to remove a public servant and to grant sanction for his prosecution under section 19(1) there is no limitation on the power of the court to take cognizance under section 190 Criminal Procedure Code of the offences mentioned in section 19(1) of the 1988 Act. The requirement of sanction under section 19(1) is intended as a safeguard against criminal prosecution of a public servant on the basis of malicious or frivolous allegations by the interested persons.

The object underlying the said requirement is not to condone the commission of an offence by a public servant. The inapplicability of the provisions of section 19(1) to a public servant would only mean that the intended safeguard was not intended to be made available to him. The rigour of the prohibition contained in sub-section (1) is now reduced by sub-section (3) of section 19 because under clause (a) of sub-section (3) it is provided that no finding, sentence or order passed by a Special Judge shall be reversed or altered by a court in appeal, confirmation or revision on the ground of absence of, or any error, omission or irregularity in the sanction required under sub-section (1), unless in the opinion of that court, a failure of justice has in fact been occasioned thereby. This would show that the requirement of sanction under sub-section (1) of section 19 is a matter relating to the procedure and the absence of the sanction does not go to the root of the jurisdiction of the court. It must, therefore, be held that merely because there is no authority which is competent to remove a public servant and to grant sanction for his prosecution under section 19(1) it cannot be said that a Member of Parliament is outside the purview of the 1988 Act.

93. In the absence of requirement of previous sanction for initiating proceedings in a court of law against a Member of Parliament in respect of an offence mentioned in section 19(1) of the 1988 Act the possibility of a Member of Parliament being subjected to criminal prosecution on the basis of malicious or frivolous allegations made by interested persons cannot be excluded. It is hoped that Parliament will provide for an adequate safeguard in that regard by making suitable amendment in the 1988 Act. But till such safeguard is provided, it appears appropriate to us that protection from being subjected to criminal prosecution on the basis of malicious or frivolous allegations should be available to Members of Parliament.

94. In Veeraswami this Court, while considering the question regarding the applicability of the provisions of the 1947 Act to Judges of superior courts, has held that Judges of superior courts fall within the purview of the said Act and that the President is the authority competent to grant sanction for their prosecution. But keeping in view the need for preserving the independence of the judiciary and the fact that the Chief Justice of India, being the head of the judiciary, is primarily concerned with the integrity and impartiality of the judiciary, the Court has directed that the Chief Justice of India should be consulted at the stage of examining the question of granting sanction for prosecution. In relation to Members of the Rajya Sabha/Lok Sabha, the Chairman of the Rajya Sabha/Speaker of the Lok Sabha holds a position which is not very different from that held by the Chief Justice of India in relation to members of the superior judiciary. In the United Kingdom, the Speaker of the House of Commons is regarded as the representative of the House itself in its powers, proceedings and dignity and is treated as a symbol of the powers and privileges of the House. (*See*: **May's Parliamentary Practice, 21st Edn., pp. 179, 180.**) The same is the position in India. In the words of Pandit Jawaharlal Nehru: "The Speaker represents the House. He represents the dignity of the House, the freedom of the House...." (*See*: HOP Debate, Vol. IX, (1954), CC 3447-48.) In **Kihoto Hollohan v. Zachillhu, 1992 Supp (2) SCC 651**, this Court has said, "The Speaker/Chairman holds a pivotal position in the scheme of parliamentary democracy and are guardians of the rights and privileges of the House." The Chairman of the Rajya Sabha/Speaker of the Lok Sabha by virtue of the position held by them are entrusted with the task of preserving the independence of the Members of the House. In order that Members of Parliament may not be subjected to criminal prosecution on the basis of frivolous or malicious allegations at the hands of interested persons, the prosecuting agency, before filing a charge-sheet in respect of an offence punishable under sections 7, 10, 11, 13 and 15 of the 1988 Act against a Member of Parliament in a criminal court, shall obtain the permission of the Chairman of the Rajya Sabha/Speaker of the Lok Sabha, as the case may be.

MP DOES NOT ENJOY IMMUNITY UNDER ARTICLE 105 FROM PROSECUTION IF HE HAS OFFER OR ACCEPTANCE OF BRIBE FOR THE PURPOSE OF SPEAKING OR VOTING IN A PARTICULAR WAY IN PARLIAMENT OR COMMITTEE – CAN BE PROSECUTED AS A PUBLIC SERVANT – SHALL OBTAIN PERMISSION OF CHAIRMAN RAJYA SABHA/SPEAKER LOK SABHA AS THE CASE MAY BE – HELD AGRAWAL, J.

95. On the basis of the aforesaid discussion we arrive at the following conclusion:

1. A Member of Parliament does not enjoy immunity under Article 105(2) or under Article 105(3) of the Constitution from being prosecuted before a criminal court for an offence involving offer or acceptance of bribe for the purpose of speaking or by giving his vote in Parliament or in any committees thereof.
2. A Member of Parliament is a public servant under section 2(c) of the Prevention of Corruption Act, 1988.
3. Since there is no authority competent to remove a Member of Parliament and to grant sanction for his prosecution under section 19(1) of the Prevention of Corruption Act, 1988, the court can take cognizance of the offences mentioned in section 19(1) in the absence of sanction but till provision is made by Parliament in that regard by suitable amendment in the law, the prosecuting agency, before filing a charge-sheet in respect of an offence punishable under sections 7, 10, 11, 13 and 15 of the 1988 Act against a Member of Parliament in a Criminal Court, shall obtain the permission of the Chairman of the Rajya Sabha/Speaker of the Lok Sabha, as the case may be.

MP IS A PUBLIC SERVANT UNDER SECTION 2 PC ACT, 1988 – EVEN IF THERE IS NO AUTHORITY TO REMOVE OR SANCTION PROSECUTION OF AN MP STILL HE CAN BE PROSECUTED WITH PERMISSION OF CHAIRMAN OR SPEAKER AS THE CASE MAY BE – ARE CONCURRED – AGREES WITH AGRAWAL, J. – RAY, J.

G.N. RAY, J:—96. I had the privilege of reading both the judgments- one by my learned brother Mr. Justice S.C. Agrawal and the other by learned brother

Mr. Justice S.P. Bharucha. Though I respectfully concur with the findings of Mr Justice Agrawal and agree with the reasoning for such findings that

(1) a Member of Parliament is a public servant under section 2(c) of the Prevention of Corruption Act, 1988 and (2) since there is no authority competent to grant sanction for the prosecution of a Member of Parliament under section 19(1) of the Prevention of Corruption Act, 1988, the court can take cognizance of the offences mentioned in section 19(1) in the absence of sanction but before filing a charge-sheet in respect of an offence punishable under sections 7, 10, 11, 12 and 15 of 1988 Act against a Member of Parliament in a Criminal Court, the prosecuting agency shall obtain the permission of the Chairman of the Rajya Sabha/Speaker of the Lok Sabha, as the case may be.

I have not been able to persuade myself to concur with the reasonings and the finding in the judgment of Mr. Justice Agrawal that a Member of Parliament does not enjoy immunity under Article 105(2) or 105(3) of the Constitution from being prosecuted before a criminal court for an offence involving offer or acceptance of bribe for the purpose of speaking or giving his vote in Parliament or in any committee thereof.

DISAGREE WITH AGRAWAL, J. – MP ENJOYS IMMUNITY UNDER ARTICLE 105 – HELD RAY, J.

97. Article 105 of the Constitution deals with powers, privileges etc. of the Houses of Parliament and the Members and committees thereof. Sub-article (1) of Article 105 makes it evident that subject to the provisions of the Constitution and rules and standing orders regulating the procedure of Parliament, there shall be freedom of speech in Parliament. The provisions of sub-article (1) Article 105 indicate in no uncertain terms that the freedom of speech guaranteed under sub-article (1) of Article 105 is independent of the freedom of speech guaranteed under Article 19 of the Constitution and such freedom of speech under Article 105(1) is not inhibited or circumscribed by the restrictions under Article 19 of the Constitution. In order to ensure effective functioning of parliamentary democracy, there was a felt need that a Member of Parliament will have absolute freedom in expressing his views in the deliberations made on the floor of Parliament. Similarly he must enjoy full freedom in casting his vote in Parliament.

98. The protections to be enjoyed by a Member of Parliament as contained in sub-article (2) of Article 105 essentially flow from the freedom of speech guaranteed under sub-article (1) of Article 105. Both sub-articles (1) and (2) complement each other and indicate the true content of freedom of speech and freedom to exercise the right to vote envisaged in Article 105 of the Constitution. The expression 'in respect of' appearing in several articles of the Constitution and in some other legislative provisions has been noticed in a number of decisions of this Court. The correct interpretation of the expression 'in respect of' cannot be made under any rigid formula but must be appreciated with references to the context in which it has been used and the purpose to be achieved under the provision in question. The context in which the expression 'in respect of' has been used in sub-article (2) of Article 105 and the purpose for which the freedom of speech and freedom to vote have been guaranteed in sub-article (2) of Article 105 do not permit any restriction or curtailment of such right expressly given under sub-article (1) and sub-article (2) of Article 105 of the Constitution. It must, however be made clear that the protection under sub-article (2) of Article 105 of the Constitution must relate to the vote actually given and speech actually made in Parliament by a Member of Parliament.

In my view, the protection against proceedings in court as envisaged under sub-article (2) of Article 105 must necessarily be interpreted broadly and not in a restricted manner. Therefore, an action impugned in a court proceeding which has a nexus with the vote cast or speech made in Parliament must get the protection under sub-article (2) of Article 105. Sub-article (3) of Article 105 provides for other powers, privileges and immunities to be enjoyed by a Member of Parliament. The framers of the Constitution did not catalogue such powers, privileges and immunities but provided in sub-article (3) of Article 105 that until such privileges are defined by Parliament, a Member of Parliament will enjoy such powers, privileges and immunities which had been recognised to be existing for a Member of the House of Commons at the commencement of the Constitution of India.

AGREES WITH BHARUCHA, J. – THAT IN THIS CASE MPs WHO VOTED ARE PROTECTED BY ARTICLE 105(3) – RAY, J.

As I respectfully agree with the reasonings indicated in the judgment of learned brother Mr. Justice S.P. Bharucha that in the facts of the case, protection under Article 105(3) of the Constitution is not attracted but protection under sub-article (2) of Article 105 is available only to those accused, who as Members of Parliament had cast their votes in Parliament, I refrain from indicating separate reasonings in support of such finding.

S.P. Bharucha, J.—(for himself and Rajendra Babu, J.):—99. On 26-7-1993, a motion of no confidence was moved in the Lok Sabha against the minority Government of P.V. Narasimha Rao. The support of 14 Members was needed to have the no-confidence motion defeated. On 28-7-1993, the no-confidence motion was lost, 251 Members having voted in support and 265 against. Suraj Mandal, Shibu Soren, Simon Marandi and Shailendra Mahto, Members of the Lok Sabha owing allegiance to the Jharkhand Mukti Morcha (the JMM), and Ram Lakhan Singh Yadav, Ram Sharan Yadav, Roshan Lal, Anadicharan Das, Abhay Pratap Singh and Haji Gulam Mohammed, Members of the Lok Sabha owing allegiance to the Janata Dal, Ajit Singh group (the JD, AS), voted against the no-confidence motion. Ajit Singh, a Member of the Lok Sabha owing allegiance to the JD, AS, abstained from voting thereon.

APPELLANTS PAID BRIBE TO JMM-JD(A) MPs – ALLEGE RESPONDENTS

100. It is the respondents' case that the above-named Members agreed to and did receive bribes, to the giving of which P.V. Narasimha Rao, MP and Prime Minister, Satish Sharma, MP and Minister, Buta Singh, MP, V. Rajeshwara Rao, MP, N.M. Revanna, Ramalinga Reddy, MLA, M. Veerappa Moily, MLA and Chief Minister, State of Karnataka, D.K. Audi Kesavulu, M. Thimmegowda and Bhajan Lal, MLA and Chief Minister, State of Haryana, were parties, to vote against the no-confidence motion. A prosecution being launched against the aforesaid alleged bribe-givers and bribe-takers subsequent to the vote upon the no-confidence motion, cognizance was taken by the Special Judge, Delhi.

101. The charge framed against P.V. Narasimha Rao reads thus:

> "That you, P.V. Narasimha Rao, between July and August, 1993 at Delhi and Bangalore were party to a criminal conspiracy and agreed to or entered into an agreement with your co-accused Capt. Satish Sharma, Buta Singh, V. Rajeshwara Rao, N.M. Revanna, Ramalinga Reddy, M. Veerappa Moily, D.K. Audi Kesavulu, M. Thimmegowda, Bhajan Lal, JMM (Jharkhand Mukti Morcha) MPs Suraj Mandal, Shibu Soren, Simon Marandi, Shailendra Mahto (approver, since granted pardon on 8-4-1997), Janata Dal (Ajit Group) MPs Ajit Singh, Ram Lakhan Singh Yadav, Ram Sharan Yadav, Roshan Lal, Anadicharan Das, Abhay Pratap Singh, Haji Ghulam Mohammed Khan and late G.C. Munda to defeat the no-confidence motion moved on 26-7-1993 against the then Congress (I) Government headed by you by illegal

means, *viz.*, to offer or cause to offer and pay gratification other than the legal remuneration to your co-accused persons namely JMM and Janata Dal (A) MPs named above as a motive or reward for their helping in defeating the s d no-confidence motion moved by the opposition parties and in pursuance of the said agreement you paid or caused to pay several lakhs of rupees to the above-referred JMM and Janata Dal (A) MPs who obtained or attempted to obtain the same in the manner stated above and thereby you have committed an offence punishable under section 120B Indian Penal Code read with sections 7, 12 and 13(2) read with section 13(i)(d) of the Prevention of Corruption Act, 1988 and within my cognizance.

Secondly, you, P.V. Narasimha Rao in pursuance of the aforesaid criminal conspiracy during the aforesaid period and at the aforesaid places abetted the commission of offence punishable under section 7 of the Prevention of Corruption Act by above-referred JMM and Jaanta Dal (A) MPs and thereby you have committed an offence punishable under section 12 of the Prevention of Corruption Act and within my cognizance."

Similar charges were framed against the other alleged bribe-givers.

102. The charge framed against Suraj Mandal of the JMM reads thus:

"*Firstly*, you between July and August 1993 at Delhi and Bangalore were party to a criminal conspiracy and agreed to or entered into an agreement with your co-accused P.V. Narasimha Rao, Capt. Satish Sharma, Buta Singh, V. Rajeshwara Rao, N.M. Revanna, Ramalinga Reddy, M. Veerappa Moily, D.K. Audi Kesavulu, M. Thimmegowda, Bhajan Lal, JMM (Jharkhand Mukti Morcha) MPs Shibu Soren, Simon Marandi, Shailendra Mahto (approver, since granted pardon on 8-4-1997), Janat Dal (Ajit Group) MPs, Ajit Singh, Ram Lakhan Singh Yadav, Ram Sharan Y dav, Roshan Lal, Anadicharan Das, Abhay Pratap Singh, Haji Gulam Mohammed Khan and late G.C. Munda to defeat the no-confidence motion moved against the then Congress (I) Government headed by accused Shri P.V. Narasimha Rao on 26-7-1993 by illegal means, viz., to obtain or agree to obtain gratification other than legal remunerations from your above-named accused persons other than JMM and Janata Dal (A) MPs as a motive or reward for defeating the no-confidence motion and in pursuance thereof above-named accused persons other than JMM and Janata Dal (A) passed on several lakhs of rupees to you or your other co-accused, namely, JMM and Janata Dal (A) MPs which amounts were accepted by you or your said co-accused persons and thereby you have committed an offence punishable under section 120-B read with sections 7, 12, 13(2) read with section 13(i)(d) of the Prevention of Corruption Act and within my cognizance.

Secondly, that you being a public servant while functioning in your capacity of Member of Parliament (10th Lok Sabha) during the aforesaid period and at the aforesaid places in pursuance of the aforesaid conspiracy demanded and accepted from your co-accused other than JMM and JD (A) MPs mentioned above a sum of Rs 280 lakhs for yourself and other JMM MPs named above other than your legal remuneration as a motive or reward for defeating above-referred no-confidence motion moved against the then Government of Congress (I) headed by your co-accused Shri P.V. Narasimha Rao and thereby you have committed an offence punishable under section 7 of the Prevention of Corruption Act and within my cognizance.

Thirdly, you during the aforesaid peri and at the aforesaid places being a public servant while functioning in your aforesaid capacity of Member of

Parliament by corrupt or illegal means and by abusing your position as a said public servant obtained for yourself or your other co-accused, *i.e.*, JMM MPs named above the pecuniary advantage to the extent of Rs. 280 lakhs and thereby committed an offence punishable under section 13(2) read with section 13(i)(d) of the Prevention of Corruption Act and within my cognizance.

Fourthly, that you during the pendency of investigation of present case while Writ Petition No. 789 of 1996 was pending disposal in the Hon'ble High Court between February to April 1996 at Delhi, Ranchi and other places intentionally caused to bring false evidence into existence by fabricating or causing to fabricate the documents or records, *i.e.*, books of accounts, proceeding books, etc. of JMM Central Office, Ranchi for the purpose of being used in any stage of judicial proceedings and thereby committed an offence under section 193 Indian Penal Code and within my cognizance."

Similar charges were framed against the other alleged bribe-takers of the JMM. Similar charges were also framed against the alleged bribe-takers of the JD, AS, except that there was no charge against them under section 193 of the Indian Penal Code. Shailendra Mahto of the JMM, it may be mentioned, later turned approver and was pardoned.

103. The persons sought to be charged as aforesaid filed petitions in the High Court at Delhi seeking to quash the charges. By the judgment and order which is under challenge, the High Court dismissed the petitions. Hence, these appeals. The appeals were heard by a Bench of three learned Judges and then referred to a Constitution Bench. The argument on behalf of the appellants to be considered by the Constitution Bench, broadly put, is that, by virtue of the provisions of Article 105, they are immune from the prosecution and that, in any event, they cannot be prosecuted under the Prevention of Corruption Act, 1988.

104. Article 105 of the Constitution reads thus:

"105. Powers, privileges, etc., of the Houses of Parliament and of the Members and committees thereof.—

(1) Subject to the provisions of this Constitution and the rules and standing orders regulating the procedure of Parliament, there shall be freedom of speech in Parliament.

(2) No Member of Parliament shall be liable to any proceedings in any court in respect of anything said or any vote given by him in Parliament or any committee thereof, and no person shall be so liable in respect of the publication by or under the authority of either House of Parliament of any report, paper, votes or proceedings.

(3) In other respects, the powers, privileges and immunities of each House of Parliament, and of the Members and the committees of each House, shall be such as may from time to time be defined by Parliament by law, and, until so defined, shall be those of that House and of its Members and committees immediately before the coming into force of section 15 of the Constitution (Forty-fourth Amendment) Act, 1978.

(4) The provisions of clauses (1), (2) and (3) shall apply in relation to persons who by virtue of this Constitution have the right to speak in, and otherwise to take part in the proceedings of, a House of Parliament or any committee thereof as they apply in relation to Members of Parliament."

MPs ENTITLED TO IMMUNITY PROVIDED IN ARTICLE 105(2) – P.V. NARASIMHA RAO ALSO ENTITLED UNDER ARTICLE 105(3) FROM PROSECUTION – SUBMIT APPELLANTS

105. Mr. P.P. Rao addressed us on behalf of P.V. Narasimha Rao, Mr. D.D. Thakur on behalf of Satish Sharma, Mr Kapil Sibal on behalf of Bhajan Lal and Dr. Surat Singh on behalf of some of the JD, AS MPs. All of them relied upon sub-article (2) of Article 105. Only Mr. P.P. Rao, learned counsel for P.V. Narasimha Rao, relied, in addition, upon sub-article (3) thereof.

106. By reason of sub-article (1) of Article 105, Members of Parliament enjoy freedom of speech subject only to the provisions of the Constitution and the rules and standing orders regulating the procedure of Parliament. That express provision is made for freedom of speech in Parliament in sub-article (1) of Article 105 suggests that this freedom is independent of the freedom of speech conferred by Article 19 and unrestricted by the exceptions contained therein. This is recognition of the fact that Members need to be free of all constraints in the matter of what they say in Parliament if they are effectively to represent their constituencies in its deliberations. Sub-article (2) of Article 105 puts negatively what sub-article (1) states affirmatively. Both sub-articles must be read together to determine their content. By reason of the first part of sub-article (2) no Member is answerable in a court of law or any similar tribunal for what he has said in Parliament. This again is recognition of the fact that a Member needs the freedom to say what he thinks is right in Parliament undeterred by the fear of being proceeded against. A vote, whether cast by voice or gesture or the aid of a machine, is treated as an extension of speech or a substitute for speech and is given the protection that the spoken word has.

DISCUSSION – BHARUCHA, J.

Two comments need to be made in regard to the plain language of the first part of sub-article (2). First, what has protection is what has been said and a vote that has been cast, not something that might have been said but was not, or a vote that might have been cast but was not. Secondly, the protection is broad, being "in respect of". It is so given to secure the freedom of speech in Parliament that sub-article (1) provides for. It is necessary, given the role Members of Parliament must perform. The protection is absolute against court proceedings that have a nexus with what has been said, or a vote that has been cast in Parliament. The second part of sub-article (2) provides that no person shall be liable to any proceedings in any court in respect of the publication of any report, papers, votes or proceedings if the publication is by or under the authority of either House of Parliament. A person who publishes a report or papers or votes or proceedings by or under the authority of Parliament is thereby given protection in the same broad terms against liability to proceedings in any court connected with such publication.

The Constitution having dealt with the all-important privilege of Members of Parliament to speak and vote therein as they deem fit, freed of the fear of attracting legal proceedings concerning what they say or how they vote, provides for other powers, privileges and immunities in sub-article (3). Till defined by Parliament by enactment, they are such as were enjoyed before the Constitution came into force, that is to say, they are such as were enjoyed by the House of Commons just before 26-1-1950. For it to be established that any power, privilege or immunity exists under sub-article (3), it must be shown that that power, privilege or immunity had been recognised as inhering in the House of Commons at the commencement of the Constitution. So important was the freedom to speak and vote in Parliament thought to be that it was expressly provided for, not left to be gathered, as other powers, privileges and immunities were, from the House of Commons. Insofar as the immunity that attaches to what is spoken in Parliament and to a vote given therein is concerned, provision is made in sub-article (2); it is only in other respects that sub-article (3) applies. For the sake of completeness, though we are not here concerned with it, we must add that sub-article (4) gives the protection of the sub-articles that preceded it to all who have the right to address the House, for example, the Attorney-General.

107. The provisions of Article 105 and of Article 194, which are in the same terms but deal with the privileges of Legislative Assemblies, have been examined by this Court in the past. In the case of **M.S.M. Sharma v. Sri Krishna Sinha, 1959 Supp (1) SCR 806: AIR 1959 SC 395**, a portion of the speech made by a Member of a Legislative Assembly had been expunged by the orders of the Speaker. Nonetheless, the speech was published in its entirety in a newspaper of which the petitioner was the editor. He was called upon to show cause why action should not be taken against him for breach of privilege of the Legislative Assembly and he challenged the notice by a petition under Article 32. S.R. Das, C.J., speaking for the majority on the Constitution Bench which heard the writ petition, observed that parliamentary privilege in England was defined in May's Parliamentary Practice as "the sum of the peculiar rights enjoyed by each House collectively as a constituent part of the High Court of Parliament, and by Members of each House individually, without which they could not discharge their functions, and which exceed those possessed by other bodies or individuals".

The privileges of the House of Commons, as distinct from those of the House of Lords, were defined as "the sum of the fundamental rights of the House and of its individual Members as against the prerogatives of the Crown, the authority of the ordinary courts of law and the special rights of the House of Lords."

The privileges of the House of Commons included the freedom of speech, which had been claimed in 1554. This comprised the right of the House to provide for the due composition of its own body, the right to regulate its own proceedings, the right to exclude strangers, the right to prohibit publication of its debates and the right to enforce observation of its privileges by fine, imprisonment and expulsion. For deliberative bodies like the Houses of Lords and Commons, this Court said, "freedom of speech is of the utmost importance. A full and free debate is of the essence of parliamentary democracy".

The argument that the whole of Article 194 was subject to Article 19(1)(a) overlooked the provisions of Article 194(2). The right conferred on a citizen under Article 19(1)(a) could be restricted by a law which fell within sub-article (2) of that article and he could be made liable in a court of law for breach of such law but Article 194(2) categorically laid down that no Member of the legislature was to be made liable to any proceedings in any court in respect of anything said or any vote given by him in the legislature or in committees thereof and that no person would be liable in respect of the publication by or under the authority of the House of such a legislature of any report, paper or proceedings. The provisions of Article 194(2), therefore, indicated that the freedom of speech referred to in sub-article (1) thereof was different from the freedom of speech and expression guaranteed under Article 19(1)(a) and could not be cut down in any way by any law contemplated by Article 19(2). A law made by Parliament in pursuance of the earlier part of Article 105(3) or by a State Legislature in pursuance of the earlier part of Article 194(3) was not law made in exercise of constituent power but law made in exercise of ordinary legislative power under Article 246 read with the relevant entries.

Consequently, if such a law took away or abridged any of the fundamental rights, it would contravene the peremptory provisions of Article 13(2) and would be void to the extent of such contravention. It might well be that that was the reason why Parliament and the State Legislatures had not made laws defining their powers, privileges and immunities. It did not, however, follow that if the powers, privileges or immunities conferred by the latter part of Articles 105 and 194 were repugnant to the fundamental rights, they would be void to the extent of such repugnancy. It could not be overlooked that the provisions of Articles 105(3) and 194(3) were constitutional law and not ordinary law made by Parliament or the State Legislatures and that, therefore, they were as supreme as the provisions of Part III of the Constitution. Further, quite conceivably, the Constitution-makers not knowing what powers, privileges and immunities Parliament or the State Legislatures might claim, thought it fit not to take any risk and made such laws subject to the provisions of Article 13; but that, knowing and being satisfied with the reasonableness of the powers, privileges and immunities of the House of Commons at the commencement of the Constitution, they did not, in their wisdom, think it fit to make such powers, privileges and immunities subject to the fundamental right conferred by Article 19(1)(a).

108. The case of **Jatish Chandra Ghosh (Dr.) v. Hari Sadhan Mukherjee, AIR 1961 SC 613: (1961) 3 SCR 486**, dealt with an appellant who was a Member of a Legislative Assembly. He had given notice of his intention to put certain questions in the Assembly. The questions being disallowed by the Speaker, he had published them in a journal in his constituency. The first respondent, whose conduct was the subject-matter of the questions, filed a complaint under the Indian Penal Code against the appellant and the printer and publisher of the journal. The appellant pleaded privilege and immunity under Article 194 of the Constitution as a bar to criminal prosecution. The claim of absolute privilege was disallowed by the Court. It was said with reference to the law in England in respect of the privileges and immunities of the House of Commons, that there was no absolute privilege attaching to the publication of extracts from proceedings in the House. So far as a member of the House of Commons was concerned, he had an absolute privilege in respect of what he had spoken within the four walls of the House, but there was only a qualified privilege in his favour even in respect of what he had himself said in the House if he caused the same to be published in the public press. The legal position, which was undisputed, was that unless the appellant could make out an absolute privilege in his favour in respect of the publication which was the subject-matter of the charge, the prosecution against him could not be quashed. He having no such absolute privilege, it was held that "he must take his trial and enter upon his defence, such as he may have".

109. Special Reference No. 1 of 1964, 1965 (1) SCR 413: AIR 1965 SC 745, known more commonly as **Keshav Singh's** case or the Privileges case, deals extensively with the scope of the privileges of legislative bodies. The Presidential Reference was made in the following circumstances. The Legislative Assembly of the State of Uttar Pradesh committed one Keshav Singh, not one of its Members, to prison for contempt. The warrant it issued was a general warrant, in that it did not set out the facts which had been found to be contumacious. Keshav Singh moved a petition under Article 226 challenging his committal and he prayed for bail. Two learned Judges of the Lucknow Bench of the High Court ordered that Keshav Singh be released on bail pending the decision on the writ petition. The Legislative Assembly passed a resolution requiring the production in custody before it of Keshav Singh, the advocate who had appeared for him and the two Judges who had granted him bail. The Judges and the advocate filed writ petitions before the High Court at Allahabad. A Full Bench of the High Court admitted their petitions and ordered the stay of the execution of the Assembly's resolution. The Legislative Assembly modified its earlier resolution so that the two Judges were now asked to appear before the House and offer an explanation. The President thereupon made the Special Reference.

Briefly put, the questions he asked were: whether the Lucknow Bench could have entertained Keshav Singh's writ petition and released him on bail; whether the Judges who entertained the petition and granted bail and Keshav Singh and his advocate had committed contempt of the Assembly; whether the Assembly was competent to require the production of the Judges and the advocate before it in custody or to call for their explanation; whether the Full Bench of the High Court could have entertained the writ petitions of the two Judges and the advocate and could have stayed the implementation of the resolution of the Assembly; and whether a Judge who entertained or dealt with a petition challenging any order of a legislature imposing penalty or issuing process against the petitioner for its contempt or for infringement of its privileges and immunities committed contempt of the legislature and whether the legislature was competent to take proceedings against the Judge in the exercise of its powers, privileges and immunities. The adjectival clause "regulating the procedure of the legislature" in Article 194(1) governed, it was held, both the preceding clauses relating to "the provisions of the Constitution" and "the rules and standing orders".

Therefore, Article 194(1) conferred on legislators specifically the right of freedom of speech subject to the limitation prescribed by its first part. By making this sub-article subject only to the specified provisions of the Constitution, the Constitution-makers wanted to make it clear that they thought it necessary to confer on the legislators freedom of speech separately and, in a sense, independently of Article 19(1)(a). It was legitimate to conclude that Article 19(1)(a) was not one of the provisions of the Constitution which controlled the first part of Article 194(1). Having conferred freedom of speech on the legislators, Article 194(2) emphasised the fact that the freedom was intended to be absolute and unfettered. Similar freedom was guaranteed to the legislators in respect of the votes they might give in the legislature or any committee thereof. "In other words", this Court said, "even if a legislator exercises his right of freedom of speech in violation, say, of Article 211, he would not be liable for any action in any court. Similarly, if the legislator by his speech or vote, is alleged to have violated any of the fundamental rights guaranteed by Part III of the Constitution in the Legislative Assembly, he would not be answerable for the said contravention in any court. If the impugned speech amounts to libel or becomes actionable or indictable under any other provision of the law, immunity has been conferred on him from any action in any court by this clause. ... It is plain that the Constitution-makers attached so much importance to the necessity of absolute freedom in debates within the legislative chambers that they thought it necessary to confer complete immunity on the legislators from any action in any court in respect of their speeches in the legislative chambers in the wide terms prescribed by clause (2). Thus, clause (1) confers freedom of speech on the legislators within the legislative chambers and clause (2) makes it plain that the freedom is literally absolute and unfettered".

Referring to Article 194(3), this Court said that it was well known that out of a large number of privileges and powers which the House of Commons claimed during the days of its bitter struggle for recognition, some were given up in course of time and some faded out by desuetude. Accordingly, in every case where a power was claimed, it was necessary to enquire whether it was an existing power at the relevant time. It has also to appear that the power was not only claimed by the House of Commons "but was recognised by the English courts. It would obviously be idle to contend that if a particular power which is claimed by the House was claimed by the House of Commons but was not recognised by the English courts, it would still be upheld under the latter part of clause (3) only on the ground that it was in fact claimed by the House of Commons".

In India, this Court said, the dominant characteristic of the British Constitution could not be claimed. The supremacy of the Constitution was protected by an independent judicial body which was the interpreter of the scheme of distribution of powers. It was difficult for this Court to accept the argument that the result of the provisions contained in the latter part of Article 194(3) was intended to be to confer on the State Legislatures in India the status of a superior court of record. It was essential to bear in mind the fact that the status of a superior court of record which was accorded to the House of Commons was based on historical facts. It was a fact of English history that Parliament had been discharging judicial functions and the House of Lords still continued to be the highest court of law in the country. The Legislative Assemblies in India never discharged any judicial functions and their historical and constitutional background did not support the claim that they could be regarded as courts of record in any sense. The very basis on which English courts agreed to treat a general warrant issued by the House of Commons on the footing that it was a warrant issued by a superior court of record was absent in the case of a general warrant issued by a State Legislature in India.

110. In the case of **Tej Kiran Jain v. N. Sanjiva Reddy, 1971 (1) SCR 612: AIR 1970 SC 1573**, it was contended that the immunity granted by Article 105(2) was with reference to the business of Parliament and not in regard to something which was something utterly irrelevant. This Court said: (SCC p. 274, para 8):

> "The article means what it says in language which could not be plainer. The article confers immunity inter alia in respect of 'anything said ... in Parliament'. The word 'anything' is of the widest import and is equivalent to 'everything'. The only limitation arises from the words 'in Parliament' which means during the sitting of Parliament and in the course of the business of Parliament. We are concerned only with speeches in Lok Sabha. Once it was proved that Parliament was sitting and its business was being transacted, anything said during the course of that business was immune from proceedings in any court. This immunity is not only complete but is as it should be. It is of the essence of parliamentary system of Government that people's representatives should be free to express themselves without fear of legal consequences. What they say is only subject to the discipline of the rules of Parliament, the good sense of the Members and the control of proceedings by the Speaker. The courts have no say in the matter and should really have none."

111. The last of the cases to which reference need be made is **State of Karnataka v. Union of India, AIR 1978 SC 68: (1977) 4 SCC 608: (1978) 2 SCR 1.** It was held there that the Constitution vested only legislative power in Parliament and in the State Legislatures. A House of Parliament or State Legislature could not try anyone or any case directly, as a court of justice could. It could proceed *quasi*-judicially in cases of contempt of its authority and take up motions concerning its privileges and immunities because, in doing so, it sought removal of obstructions to the due performance of its legislative functions. If any question of jurisdiction arose, it had to be decided by the courts in appropriate proceedings. Beg, J. added: (SCC p. 656, para 63)

> "For example, the jurisdiction to try a criminal offence, such as murder, committed even within a House vests in ordinary criminal courts and not in a House of Parliament or in a State Legislature."

112. In **Tolaram Relumal v. State of Bombay, 1955 SCR 158: AIR 1954 SC 496** this Court construed the words "in respect of" occurring in section 18(1) of the Bombay Rent Restriction Act, 1947, the relevant portion of which reads thus:

"If any landlord either himself or through any person acting or purporting to act on his behalf ... receives any fine, premium or other like sum or deposit or any consideration, other than the standard rent ... in respect of the grant, renewal or continuance of a lease of any premises ... such landlord or person shall be punished....".

The High Court had observed that the expression 'in respect of' was very comprehensive but this Court took the view that it had laid undue emphasis thereon. This Court said:

"Giving the words 'in respect of' their widest meaning, *viz.*, 'relating to' or 'with reference to', it is plain that this relationship must be predicated of the grant, renewal or continuance of a lease, and unless a lease comes into existence simultaneously or near about the time that the money is received, it cannot be said that the receipt was **'in respect of'** the grant of a lease. ... It is difficult to hold that any relationship of landlord and tenant comes into existence on the execution of an agreement executory in nature or that the expression 'premium' can be appositely used in connection with the receipt of money on the occasion of the execution of such an agreement. It may well be that if a lease actually comes into existence then any receipt of money which has a nexus with that lease may fall within the mischief of section 18(1), but it is unnecessary to express any final opinion on the question as in the present case admittedly no lease ever came into existence and the relationship of the landlord and tenant was never created between the parties."

113. The learned Attorney General submitted that the words 'in respect of' had not always received a broad meaning, and he cited the judgment of this Court in **State of Madras v. Swastik Tobacco Factory** (supra). A provision of the Madras General Sales Tax (Turnover and Assessment) Rules, 1939, which stated that, 'the excise duty, if any, paid by the dealer to the Central Government in respect of the goods sold by him; ...' would be deducted from the gross turnover of a dealer for the purposes of determining the net turnover, was under consideration. The Court noted that the words 'in respect of' had been considered by the House of Lords in **IRC v. Coutts & Co., 1963 (2) All ER 722** and it had observed that 'the phrase denoted some imprecise kind of nexus between the property and the estate duty'. In **Asher v. Seaford Court Estates Ltd., 1950 LR AC 508** the House of Lords had held that the expression 'in respect of' in the Increase of Rent and Mortgage Interest (Restrictions) Act, 1920, must be read as equivalent to 'attributable'. The Privy Council in **Bicber Ltd. v. CIT, 1962 (3) All ER 294**, had observed that these words could mean more than 'consisting of' or 'namely'. This Court said:

"It may be accepted that the said expression received a wide interpretation, having regard to the object of the provisions and the setting in which the said words appeared. On the other hand, Indian tax laws use the expression 'in respect of' as synonymous with the expression 'on'."

In the provision under consideration the expression 'in respect of the goods' was held to mean 'on the goods'.

114. This Court drew a distinction in the above case between the use of the expression 'in respect of' in taxing statutes in India and its use elsewhere. In the context of its use in the Constitution and having regard to the object which is intended to be secured by Article 105(2), we think that the broad interpretation thereof is the most appropriate. It is thus that this Court has already interpreted the provision.

MP HAS TAKEN BRIBE TO VOTE IN A PARTICULAR WAY – NOT ENTITLED TO IMMUNITY FROM PROSECUTION UNDER ARTICLE 105 – SUBMITS ATTORNEY-GENERAL

115. The Attorney-General submitted that a proceeding in court founded on the allegation that a Member of Parliament had received a bribe to vote in a particular way was not a proceeding in respect of a vote that he had given and that, therefore, the Member did not enjoy immunity from the proceeding by reason of Article 105(2). He submitted that the immunity given by Article 105(2) did not cover criminal proceedings. It had been held by the courts of the United States of America, Canada, Australia and, recently, England, he said, that a legislator could be proceeded against for corruption. The Attorney-General relied upon decisions and reports in this behalf to which we shall refer. The Attorney-General submitted that the immunity given by Article 105(2) should be interpreted in the light of the times in which we live and, so interpreting it, should exclude from its coverage corrupt legislators.

* * * * *

ARTICLE 105(2) PROTECTS AN MP FROM PROSECUTION FOR ANYTHING SAID OR VOTE GIVEN BY HIM IN PARLIAMENT – CONTENTION OF ATTORNEY-GENERAL REJECTED – HELD BHARUCHA, J.

131. Broadly interpreted, as we think it should be, Article 105(2) protects a Member of Parliament against proceedings in court that relate to, or concern, or have a connection or nexus with anything said, or a vote given, by him in Parliament.

132. The charge against the alleged bribe-takers is that they "were party to a criminal conspiracy and agreed to or entered into an agreement with" the alleged bribe-givers "to defeat the no-confidence motion ... by illegal means, *viz.*, to obtain or agree to obtain gratification other than legal remunerations" from the alleged bribe-givers "as a motive or reward for defeating the no-confidence motion and in pursuance thereof" the alleged bribe-givers "passed on several lakhs of rupees" to the alleged bribe-takers, "which amounts were accepted" by them. The stated object of the alleged conspiracy and agreement is to defeat the no-confidence motion and the alleged bribe-takers are said to have received monies "as a motive or reward for defeating" it. The nexus between the alleged conspiracy and bribe and the no-confidence motion is explicit. The charge is that the alleged bribe-takers received the bribes to secure the defeat of the no-confidence motion.

133. While it is true that the charge against them does not refer to the votes that the alleged bribe-takers, Ajit Singh excluded, actually cast against the no-confidence motion and that it may be established *de hors* those votes, as the Attorney General argued, we do not think that we can ignore the fact that the votes were cast and, if the facts alleged against the bribe-takers are true, that they were cast pursuant to the alleged conspiracy and agreement. It must then follow, given that the expression "in respect of" must receive a broad meaning, that the alleged conspiracy and agreement had a nexus to and were in respect of those votes and that the proposed inquiry in the criminal proceedings is in regard to the motivation thereof.

134. It is difficult to agree with the learned Attorney-General that though the words "in respect of" must receive a broad meaning, the protection under Article 105(2) is limited to court proceedings that impugn the speech that is given or the vote that is cast or arises thereout or that the object of the protection would be fully satisfied thereby. The object of the protection is to enable Members to speak their mind in Parliament and vote in the same way, freed of the fear of being made answerable on that account in a court of law. It is not enough that Members should be protected against civil action and criminal proceedings, the cause of action of which is their speech or their vote. To enable Members to participate fearlessly in parliamentary debates, Members need the wider protection of immunity against all civil and criminal proceedings that bear a nexus to their speech or vote. It is for that reason that a Member is not 'liable to any proceedings in any court in respect of anything said or any vote given by him'. Article 105(2) does not say, which it would have if the learned Attorney-General were right, that a Member is not liable for what he has said or how he has voted. While imputing no such motive to the present prosecution, it is not difficult to envisage a Member who has made a speech or cast a vote that is not to the liking of the powers that be being troubled by a prosecution alleging that he had been party to an agreement and conspiracy to achieve a certain result in Parliament and had been paid a bribe.

ALLEGED BRIBE-TAKERS HAVE BARTERED AWAY THE SOLEMN TRUST OF THEIR VOTERS – BUT PROTECTED BY ARTICLE 105 OF THE CONSTITUTION – HELD BHARUCHA, J.

135. We are acutely conscious of the seriousness of the offence that the alleged bribe-takers are said to have committed. If true, they bartered a most solemn trust committed to them by those they represented. By reason of the lucre that they received, they enabled a Government to survive. Even so, they are entitled to the protection that the Constitution plainly affords them. Our sense of indignation should not lead us to construe the Constitution narrowly, impairing the guarantee to effective parliamentary participation and debate.

136. We draw support for the view that we take from the decision of the United States Supreme Court in Johnson and from the dissenting judgment of Brennan, J. in Brewster.

137. In Johnson, the United States Supreme Court held that the Speech or Debate Clause extended to prevent the allegation that a Member of the Congress had abused his position by conspiring to give a particular speech in return for remuneration from being the basis of a criminal charge of conspiracy. The essence of such a charge was that the Congressman's conduct was improperly motivated, and that was precisely what the Speech or Debate Clause foreclosed from executive and judicial inquiry. The argument that the Speech or Debate Clause was meant to prevent only prosecutions based upon the content of the speech, such as libel actions, but not those founded on the antecedent unlawful conduct of accepting or agreeing to accept a bribe was repulsed. Also repulsed was the argument that the Speech or Debate Clause was not violated because the gravamen of the charge was the alleged conspiracy, not the speech. The indictment focused upon the motive underlying the making of the speech and a prosecution under a criminal statute dependent on such inquiry contravened the Speech or Debate Clause.

138. Brennan, J., dissenting in Brewster said that Brewster had been charged with a crime whose proof called into question the motives behind his legislative acts. He could not only not be prosecuted or called to answer for his vote in any judicial or executive proceeding but his immunity went beyond the vote itself and precluded "all extra-congressional scrutiny as to how and why he cast, or would have cast, his vote a certain way". Neither the Senator's vote nor his motives for voting, however dishonourable, could be the subject of a civil or criminal proceeding outside the halls of the Senate. The charge of a corrupt promise to vote was repugnant to the Speech or Debate Clause. It might be that only receipt of the bribe and not performance of the bargain was needed to prove the charge, but proof of an agreement to be influenced in the performance of legislative acts was "by definition an inquiry into their motives, whether or not the acts themselves or the circumstances surrounding them are questioned at trial. Furthermore, judicial inquiry into an alleged agreement of this kind carries with it the same dangers to legislative independence that are held to bar accountability for official conduct itself". The Senator's "reprehensible and outrageous conduct", if committed, should not have gone unpunished, but whether a court or only the Senate "might undertake the task is a constitutional issue of portentous significance, which must of course be resolved uninfluenced by the magnitude of the perfidy alleged".

139. We cannot but be impressed by the majority opinion in Brewster but, with respect, are more persuaded by the dissent. The majority opinion stated that the only reasonable reading of the Speech and Debate Clause was "that it does not prohibit inquiry into activities that are casually or incidentally related to legislative affairs but not a part of the legislative process itself". Upon this construction of the Speech or Debate Clause, it came to the conclusion that a court could investigate whether Brewster had taken a bribe to be influenced in the performance of official acts in respect of his action, vote, and decision on postage rate legislation. With respect, we cannot regard the act of taking a bribe to vote in a particular way in the legislature to be merely "casually or incidentally related to legislative affairs". The Library of Congress publication "The Constitution of the United States of America, Analysis and Interpretation" says, and we respectfully agree, "... However, in **United States v. Brewster** (supra) while continuing to assert that the clause 'must be read broadly to effectuate its purpose of protecting the independence of the legislative branch', the Court substantially reduced the scope of the coverage of the clause."

140. For the first time in England Buckley, J. ruled in **R. v. Currie** that a Member of Parliament who accepts a bribe to abuse his trust is guilty of the common law offence of bribery. The innovation in English law needs to be tested in appeal. We say this with respect, having regard to earlier English judgments, and we find support in the Twenty-second Edition of *Erskine May's Treatise on The Law, Privileges, Proceedings and Usage of Parliament,* wherein a footnote (on p. 115) apropos the ruling reads thus:

> "The Court observed: 'that a Member of Parliament against whom there is a *prima facie* case of corruption should be immune from prosecution in the courts of law is to my mind an unacceptable proposition at the present time' [quoted in Committee of Privileges, First Report, HC 351-ii (1994-95) pp. 161-162]. The Court seems to have had in mind, though no attempt was made to define, an area of activity where a Member may act as such, without participating in 'proceedings in Parliament' (where of course Article IX will apply)."

BRIBE-TAKER MPs WHO VOTED – NOT ANSWERABLE TO THE COURT OF LAW – HELD BHARUCHA, J.

141. Our conclusion is that the alleged bribe-takers, other than Ajit Singh, have the protection of Article 105(2) and are not answerable in a court of law for the alleged conspiracy and agreement. The charges against them must fail. Ajit Singh, not having cast a vote on the no-confidence motion, derives no immunity from Article 105(2).

AJIT SINGH HAD NOT VOTED – NOT ENTITLED TO THE BENEFIT OF ARTICLE 105(2) – BRIBE-GIVERS ARE ALSO NOT ENTITLED – HELD BHARUCHA, J.

142. What is the effect of this upon the alleged bribe-givers? In the first place, the prosecution against Ajit Singh would proceed, he not having voted on the no-confidence motion and, therefore, not having the protection of Article 105(2). The charge against the alleged bribe-givers of conspiracy and agreement with Ajit Singh to do an unlawful act would, therefore, proceed.

143. Mr. Rao submitted that since, by reason of the provisions of Article 105(2), the alleged bribe-takers had committed no offence, the alleged bribe-givers had also committed no offence. Article 105(2) does not provide that what is otherwise an offence is not an offence when it is committed by a Member of Parliament and has a connection with his speech or vote therein. What is provided thereby is that a Member of Parliament shall not be answerable in a court of law for something that has a nexus to his speech or vote in Parliament. If a Member of Parliament has, by his speech or vote in Parliament, committed an offence, he enjoys, by reason of Article 105(2), immunity from prosecution therefor. Those who have conspired with the Member of Parliament in the commission of that offence have no such immunity. They can, therefore, be prosecuted for it.

BRIBE-TAKERS ANSWERABLE TO LOK SABHA – BRIBE-GIVERS TO BE TRIED BY COURT – NO CONTRADICTION – HELD BHARUCHA, J.

144. Mr. Rao contended that for the offence that the bribe-takers had allegedly committed they would be answerable to the Lok Sabha. There was a possibility of the Lok Sabha deciding one way upon the prosecution before it of the alleged bribe-takers and the criminal court deciding the other way upon the prosecution of the alleged bribe-givers. A conflict of decisions upon the same set of facts being possible, it had to be avoided. The charge against the alleged bribe-givers had, therefore, to be quashed. There is in the contention a misconception. Article 105(2) does not state that the Member of Parliament who is not liable to civil or criminal proceedings in a court of law is liable to the same civil or criminal proceedings in Parliament. Parliament in India is not a court of record. It may not exercise judicial powers or entertain judicial proceedings. The decisions of this Court so holding have already been referred to. The alleged bribe-takers, except Ajit Singh, who are entitled to the immunity conferred by Article 105(2) are not liable to be tried in the Lok Sabha for the offences set out in the charges against them or any other charges, but the Lok Sabha may proceed against them for breach of privileges or contempt. There is, therefore, no question of two fora coming to different conclusions in respect of the same charges.

145. Mr. Rao submitted that the alleged bribe-givers had breached Parliament's privilege and been guilty of its contempt and it should be left to Parliament to deal with them. By the same sets of acts the alleged bribe-takers and the alleged bribe-givers committed offences under the criminal law and breaches of Parliament's privileges and its contempt. From prosecution for the former, the alleged bribe-takers, Ajit Singh excluded, enjoy immunity. The alleged bribe-givers do not. The criminal prosecution against the alleged bribe-givers must, therefore, go ahead. For breach of Parliament's privileges and its contempt, Parliament may proceed against the alleged bribe-takers and the alleged bribe-givers.

146. Relevant to the submission on Article 105(3) is the judgement in ***Ex Parte* Wason, 1869 LR 4 QBD 573**. Rigby Wason moved the Court of Queen's Bench for a rule to call upon a metropolitan police magistrate to show cause why he should not take on record the complaint of Wason to prosecute Earl Russell, Lord Chelmsford and the Lord Chief Baron for conspiracy. Wason's affidavit in support of the complaint stated that he had given to Earl Russell a petition addressed by him to the House of Lords, which Earl Russell had promised to present. The petition charged the Lord Chief Baron, when a Queen's Counsel, with having told a wilful and deliberate falsehood to a committee of the House of Commons sitting as a judicial tribunal. The petition prayed for an inquiry into the charge and, if the charge was found true, for action against the Lord Chief Baron under the law to remove judges. Earl Russell, Lord Chelmsford and the Lord Chief Baron had, according to the Wason's affidavit, prevented the course of justice by making statements, after conferring together, which they knew were not true in order to prevent the prayer of his petition being granted; Wason alleged that Earl Russell, Lord Chelmsford and the Lord Chief Baron had conspired and agreed together to prevent the course of justice and injure himself.

The alleged conspiracy consisted in the fact that Earl Russell, Lord Chelmsford and the Lord Chief Baron "did agree to deceive the House of Lords by stating that the charge of falsehood contained in my petition was false, and that I was a calumniator; when Earl Russell, Lord Chelmsford, and the Lord Chief Baron well knew that the charge of falsehood committed by the Lord Chief Baron, when Queen's Counsel, was perfectly true". Wason desired "to prefer an indictment against Earl Russell, Lord Chelmsford, and the Lord Chief Baron for conspiracy". The Magistrate had refused to take recognizance of the complaint on the ground that no indictable offence had been disclosed by Wason's information, whereupon Wason moved the Court. Cockburn, C.J. said, "I entirely agree that, supposing the matter brought before the Magistrate had been matter cognizable by the criminal law, and upon which an indictment might have been preferred, the Magistrate would have had no discretion, but would have been bound to proceed......On the other hand, I have no doubt that, supposing the matter brought before the Magistrate does not establish facts upon which an indictment could be preferred and sustained, the Magistrate has a discretion which, if rightly exercised, we ought to uphold; and the question is whether the matter brought by the present applicant before the Magistrate was subject-matter for an indictment....The information then charges that Earl Russell, Lord Chelmsford, and the Lord Chief Baron agreed to deceive the House of Lords by stating that the charge of falsehood brought against the Lord Chief Baron was unfounded and false, whereas they knew it to be true.

Now, inasmuch as these statements were alleged to have been for the purpose of preventing the prayer of the petition and the statements could not have had that effect unless made in the House of Lords, it seems to me that the fair and legitimate inference is that the alleged conspiracy was to make, and that the statements were made, in the House of Lords. I think, therefore, that the Magistrate, looking at this and the rest of the information, was warranted in coming to the conclusion, that Mr. Wason charged and proposed to make the substance of the indictment, that these three persons did conspire to deceive the House of Lords by statements made in the House of Lords for the purpose of frustrating the petition. Such a charge could not be maintained in a court of law. It is clear that statements made by members of either House of Parliament in their places in the House, though they might be untrue to their knowledge, could not be made the foundation of civil or criminal proceedings, however injurious they might be to the interest of a third person.

And a conspiracy to make such statements would not make the persons guilty of it amenable to the criminal law..............". Blackburn, J. was of the same opinion. He said, "When the House is sitting and statements are made in either House of Parliament, the member making them is not amenable to the criminal law. It is quite clear that no indictment will lie for making them, nor for a conspiracy or agreement to make them, even though the statements be false to the knowledge of the persons making them. I entirely concur in thinking that the information did only charge an agreement to make statements in the House of Lords, and therefore did not charge any indictable offence". Lush, J. agreed. He said that he could not doubt that the charge was of "a conspiracy to deceive the House of Lords, and so frustrate the application, by means of making false statements in the House. I am clearly of opinion that we ought not to allow it to be doubted for a moment that the motives or intentions of members of either House cannot be inquired into by criminal proceedings with respect to anything they may do or say in the House".

147. As we read **Ex P Wason** (supra) the Court of Queen's Bench found that Wason desired criminal proceedings to be commenced against three Members of Parliament for conspiring to make, and making statements in Parliament which he alleged were untrue and made to harm his cause. The Court held that criminal proceedings could not be taken in respect of statements made by Members of Parliament in Parliament nor for conspiring to make them. **Ex P Wason** (supra) therefore, does not support Mr. Rao's submission that his client P.V. Narasimha Rao and others of the alleged bribe-givers who were Members of Parliament have "immunity from criminal proceedings in a court of law with respect to the charge of conspiracy in connection with the voting in Parliament on the no-confidence motion". The speech or vote of the alleged bribe-giving Members of Parliament is not in issue nor, therefore, a conspiracy in this behalf. In contrast, all the three alleged conspirators in **Ex P Wason** (supra) were Members of Parliament and what was alleged against them was that they had made false statements to Parliament in consequence of a conspiracy. If what is alleged against Members of Parliament in India is that they had made false statements to, or voted in, Parliament in consequence of a conspiracy, they would be immune from prosecution by reason of Article 105(2) itself and no occasion would arise to look into the privileges enjoyed by the House of Commons under Article 105(3).

LOK SABHA CAN TAKE ACTION ALSO AGAINST BRIBE-GIVER WHETHER THEY ARE THE MEMBERS OF LOK SABHA OR NOT – BUT COURT PROCEEDINGS AGAINST BRIBE-GIVER ARE NOT BARRED – HELD BHARUCHA, J.

148. To repeat what we have said earlier, Mr. Rao is right, subject to two caveats, in saying that Parliament has the power not only to punish its Members for an offence committed by them but also to punish others who had conspired with them to have the offence committed: *first*, the actions that constitute the offence must also constitute a breach of Parliament's privilege or its contempt; *secondly*, the action that Parliament will take and the punishment it will impose is for the breach of privilege or contempt. There is no reason to doubt that the Lok Sabha can take action for breach of privilege or contempt against the alleged bribe-givers and against the alleged bribe-takers, whether or not they were Members of Parliament, but that is not to say that the courts cannot take cognizance of the offence of the alleged bribe-givers under the criminal law.

149. Mr. Rao relied upon observations in the Eighteenth Edition (1971) of *Erskine May's Treatise on The Law, Privileges, Proceedings and Usage of Parliament*. There is before us the Twenty-second Edition. Part of what is contained in the earlier edition is not found in the later edition. That May's treatise is an authoritative statement on its subject has been recognised by this Court (**Keshav Singh case**, Supra). May's earlier edition stated "It is sometimes said that, since the privileges of Parliament do not extend to criminal matters, therefore Members are amenable to the course of criminal justice for offences, committed in speech or action in the House.... It may prove to be true that things said or done in Parliament, or some of them, are not withdrawn from the course of criminal justice....There is more doubt as to whether criminal acts committed in Parliament remain within the exclusive cognizance of the House in which they are committed....". Quoting Mr. Justice Stephen in **Bradlaugh v. Gosset, 1984 (2) QBD 271** where the learned Judge said that he "knew of no authority for the proposition that an ordinary crime committed in the House of Commons would be withdrawn from the ordinary course of criminal justice", May observed that "it must be supposed that what the learned Judge had in mind was a criminal act as distinguished from criminal speech". May went on to state "It is probably true, as a general rule, that a criminal act done in the House is not outside the course of criminal justice. But this rule is not without exception, and both the rule and the exception will be found to depend upon whether the particular act can or cannot be regarded as a proceeding in Parliament ... it would be hard to show that a criminal act committed in the House by an individual Member was part of the proceedings of the House...."

Owing to the lack of precedents there is no means of knowing what view the courts would take of a criminal act committed in Parliament, or whether they would distinguish action from speech in respect of amenability to the criminal law. With regard to a crime committed in Parliament, the House in which it was committed might claim the right to decide whether to exercise its own jurisdiction or to hand the offender over to the criminal courts. In taking this decision, it would no doubt be guided by the nature of the offence, and the adequacy or inadequacy of the penalties, somewhat lacking in flexibility, which it could inflict.... In cases of breach of privilege which are also offences at law, where the punishment which the House has power to inflict would not be adequate to the offence, or where for any other cause the House has thought a proceeding at law necessary, either as a substitute for, or in addition to, its own proceeding, the Attorney General has been directed to prosecute the offender.

150. May's Twenty-second Edition is more succinct, and this is what it says:

> "Moreover, though the Bill of Rights will adequately protect a Member as regards criminal law in respect of anything said as part of proceedings in Parliament, there is more doubt whether criminal acts committed in Parliament remain within the exclusive cognizance of the House in which they are committed. In the judgment of the House of Lords in Elliot case (see pp. 73 and 84n), it was deliberately left an open question whether the assault on the Speaker might have been properly heard and determined in the King's Bench. The possibility that it might legally have been so determined was admitted by one of the managers for the Commons in the conference with the Lords which preceded the writ of error. In **Bradlaugh v. Gosset** (supra) Mr. Justice Stephen said that he 'knew of no authority for the proposition that an ordinary crime committed in the House of Commons would be withdrawn from the ordinary course of criminal justice'. Since he went on immediately to refer to Elliot case and accepted the proposition that nothing said in Parliament by a Member, as such, can be treated as an offence by the ordinary courts', it must be supposed that what the learned Judge had in mind was a criminal act as distinguished from criminal speech.
>
> In such cases, it will be essential to determine where the alleged criminal act stands in relation to the proceedings of the House. An officer carrying out an order of the House is in the same position as the Members who voted the order. In **Bradlaugh v. Erskine**, the Deputy Serjeant-at-Arms was held to be justified in committing the assault with which he was charged, since it was committed in Parliament, in pursuance of the order of the House, to exclude Bradlaugh from the House. As Lord Coleridge observed, 'The Houses cannot act by themselves as a body; they must act by officers.' It would be hard to show how a criminal act committed by a Member, however, could form part of the proceedings of the House. Apart from Elliot's case, 350 years ago, no charge against a Member in respect of an allegedly criminal act in Parliament has been brought before the courts. Were such a situation to arise, it is possible that the House in which the act was committed might claim the right to decide whether to exercise its own jurisdiction. In taking this decision, it would no doubt be guided by the nature of the offence, and the adequacy or inadequacy of the penalties, somewhat lacking in flexibility, which it could inflict."

ARTICLE 105(3) DOES NOT HELP BRIBE-GIVERS – HELD BHARUCHA, J.

151. The learned Attorney-General submitted, and the English judgments and reports dealt with earlier bear out the submission, that the bribery of a Member of the House of Commons, acting in his parliamentary capacity, did not, at the time the Constitution came into effect, constitute an offence under the English criminal law or the common law. Clearly, therefore, no privilege or immunity attached in England to an allegation of such bribery or an agreement or conspiracy in that behalf which could be imported into India at the commencement of the Constitution under the provisions of Article 105(3). Secondly, Article 105(2) provides for the sum total of the privileges and immunity that attach to what is said in Parliament and to votes given therein. Article 105(3) applies only 'in other respects'. To what we are here concerned with the provisions of Article 105(2) apply, to the extent indicated earlier. The provisions of Article 105(3) are, therefore, not attracted and they do not render assistance to the alleged bribe-givers.

PROVISIONS OF PC ACT, 1988 RELEVANT TO THIS CASE REPRODUCED TO FIND OUT IF MPs ARE PUBLIC SERVANTS – BHARUCHA, J.

152. In considering the case on the Prevention of Corruption Act, 1988 (the said Act) we shall not take account of what we have already held and write, as it were, upon a clean slate. Some reference to the provisions of the said Act is necessary at the threshold.

Section 2(b) of the said Act defines 'public duty' thus:

> "2. (b) 'public duty' means a duty in the discharge of which the State, the public or the community at large has an interest."

Section 2(c) of the said Act defines public servant thus:

> "2. (c) 'public servant' means—
>
> (i) any person in the service or pay of the Government or remunerated by the Government by fees or commission for the performance of any public duty;
>
> (ii) any person in the service or pay of a local authority;
>
> (iii) any person in the service or pay of a corporation established by or under a Central, Provincial or State Act, or an authority or a body owned or controlled or aided by the Government or a government company as defined in section 617 of the Companies Act, 1956 (1 of 1956);
>
> (iv) any Judge, including any person empowered by law to discharge, whether by himself or as member of any body of persons, any adjudicatory functions;
>
> (v) any person authorised by a court of justice to perform any duty, in connection with the administration of justice, including a liquidator, receiver or commissioner appointed by such court;
>
> (vi) any arbitrator or other person to whom any cause or matter has been referred for decision or report by a court of justice or by a competent public authority;
>
> (vii) any person who holds an office by virtue of which he is empowered to prepare, publish, maintain or revise an electoral roll or to conduct an election or part of an election;
>
> (viii) any person who holds an office by virtue of which he is authorised or required to perform any public duty;
>
> (ix) any person who is the president, secretary or other office-bearer of a registered cooperative society engaged in agriculture, industry, trade or

banking, receiving or having received any financial aid from the Central Government or a State Government or from any corporation established by or under a Central, Provincial or State Act, or any authority or body owned or controlled or aided by the Government or a government company as defined in section 617 of the Companies Act, 1956 (1 of 1956);

(x) any person who is a chairman, member or employee of any Service Commission or Board, by whatever name called, or a member of any selection committee appointed by such Commission or Board for the conduct of any examination or making any selection on behalf of such Commission or Board;

(xi) any person who is a Vice-Chancellor or member of any governing body, professor, reader, lecturer or any other teacher or employee, by whatever designation called, of any University and any person whose services have been availed of by a University or any other public authority in connection with holding or conducting examinations;

(xii) any person who is an office-bearer or an employee of an educational, scientific, social, cultural or other institution, in whatever manner established, receiving or having received any financial assistance from the Central Government or any State Government, or local or other public authority.

Explanation 1.—Persons falling under any of the above sub-clauses are public servants, whether appointed by the Government or not.

Explanation 2.—Wherever the words 'public servant' occur, they shall be understood of every person who is in actual possession of the situation of a public servant, whatever legal defect there may be in his right to hold that situation.

Section 19 of the said Act deals with the previous sanction that is necessary for prosecution for the offences mentioned therein. It reads thus:

"19. Previous sanction necessary for prosecution.—

(1) No court shall take cognizance of an offence punishable under sections 7, 10, 11, 13 and 15 alleged to have been committed by a public servant, except with the previous sanction,—

(a) in the case of a person who is employed in connection with the affairs of the Union and is not removable from his office save by or with the sanction of the Central Government, of that Government;

(b) in the case of a person who is employed in connection with the affairs of a State and is not removable from his office save by or with the sanction of the State Government, of that Government;

(c) in the case of any other person, of the authority competent to remove him from his office.

(2) Where for any reason whatsoever any doubt arises as to whether the previous sanction as required under sub-section (1) should be given by the Central Government or the State Government or any other authority, such sanction shall be given by that Government or authority which would have been competent to remove the public servant from his office at the time when the offence was alleged to have been committed.

(3) Notwithstanding anything contained in the Code of Criminal Procedure, 1973 (2 of 1974),—

(a) no finding, sentence or order passed by a Special Judge shall be reversed or altered by a court in appeal, confirmation or revision on the ground of the absence of, or any error, omission or irregularity in, the sanction required under sub-section (1), unless in the opinion of that court, a failure of justice has in fact been occasioned thereby;

(b) no court shall stay the proceedings under this Act on the ground of any error, omission or irregularity in the sanction granted by the authority, unless it is satisfied that such error, omission or irregularity has resulted in a failure of justice;

(c) no court shall stay the proceedings under this Act on any other ground and no court shall exercise the powers of revision in relation to any interlocutory order passed in any inquiry, trial, appeal or other proceedings.

(4) In determining under sub-section (3) whether the absence of, or any error, omission or irregularity in, such sanction has occasioned or resulted in a failure of justice the court shall have regard to the fact whether the objection could and should have been raised at any earlier stage in the proceedings.

Explanation.—For the purposes of this section,—

(a) error includes competency of the authority to grant sanction;

(b) a sanction required for prosecution includes reference to any requirement that the prosecution shall be at the instance of a specified authority or with the sanction of a specified person or any requirement of a similar nature."

Section 7, mentioned in section 19, defines the offence of a public servant taking gratification other than legal remuneration in respect of an official act and the penalty therefor. Section 10 sets out the punishment for abetment by a public servant of offences defined in section 8 or 9. Section 11 defines the offence of a public servant obtaining a valuable thing, without consideration, from a person concerned in a proceeding or business transacted by such public servant, and the penalty therefor. Section 13 defines the offence of criminal misconduct by a public servant and the penalty therefor. Section 15 sets out the punishment for an attempt to commit an offence under section 13(1)(c) or (d).

153. The offences with which the appellants are charged are those set out in section 120(B) of the Indian Penal Code read with section 7, section 12, section 13(1)(d) and section 13(2) of the said Act. (We do not here need to deal with the offence under section 293 of the Indian Penal Code with which some of the accused are charged). These provisions read thus:

> ***"Section 120B (of the Indian Penal Code). Punishment of criminal conspiracy.***—(1) Whoever is a party to a criminal conspiracy to commit an offence punishable with death, imprisonment for life or rigorous imprisonment for a term of two years or upwards, shall, where no express provision is made in the Code for the punishment of such a conspiracy, be punished in the same manner as if he had abetted such offence.
>
> (2) Whoever is a party to a criminal conspiracy other than a criminal conspiracy to commit an offence punishable as aforesaid shall be punished with imprisonment of either description for a term not exceeding six months, or with fine or with both.

Section 7 (of the said Act). Public Servant taking gratification other than legal remuneration in respect of an official act. – Whoever, being, or expecting to be a public servant, accepts or obtains or agrees to accept or attempts to obtain from any person, for himself or for any other person, any gratification whatever, other than legal remuneration, as a motive or reward for doing or forbearing to do any official act or for showing or forbearing to show, in the exercise of his official functions, favour or disfavor to any person or for rendering or attempting to render any service or disservice to any person, with the Central Government or any State Government or Parliament or the Legislature of any State or with any local authority, corporation or Government company referred to in clause (c) of section 2, or with any public servant, whether named or otherwise, shall be punishable with imprisonment which shall be not less than six months but which may extend to five years and shall also be liable to fine.

Explanations.—(a) "Expecting to be a public servant." If a person not expecting to be in office obtains a gratification by deceiving others into a belief that he is about to be in office, and that he will then serve them, he may be guilty of cheating, but he is not guilty of the offence defined in this section.

(b) "Gratification". The word "gratification" is not restricted to pecuniary gratifications or to gratifications estimable in money.

(c) "Legal remuneration." The words "legal remuneration" are not restricted to remuneration which a public servant can lawfully demand, but include all remuneration which he is permitted by the Government or the organisation, which he serves, to accept.

(d) "A motive or reward for doing." A person who receives a gratification as a motive or reward for doing what he does not intend or is not in a position to do, or has not done, comes within this expression.

(e) Where a public servant induces a person erroneously to believe that his influence with the Government has obtained a title for that person and thus induces that person to give the public servant, money or any other gratification as a reward for this service, the public servant has committed an offence under this section.

Section 12. Punishment for abetment of offences defined in section 7 or 11. – Whoever abets any offence punishable under section 7 or section 11 whether or not that offence is committed in consequence of that abetment, shall be punishable with imprisonment for a term which shall be not less than six months but which may extend to five years and shall also be liable to fine.

Section 13. Criminal misconduct by a public servant.—(1) A public servant is said to commit the offence of criminal misconduct:—

(a) if he habitually accepts or obtains or agrees to accept or attempts to obtain from any person for himself or for any other person any gratification other than legal remuneration as a motive or reward such as is mentioned in section 7; or

(b) if he habitually accepts or obtains or agrees to accept or attempts to obtain for himself or for any other person, any valuable thing without consideration or for a consideration which he knows to be inadequate from any person whom he knows to have been or to be, or to be likely to be concerned in any proceedings or business transacted or about to be transacted by him, or having any connection with the official functions of himself or of any public servant to whom he is subordinate, or from any person whom he knows to be interested in or related to the person so concerned; or

(c) if he dishonestly or fraudulently misappropriates or otherwise converts for his own use any property entrusted to him or under his control as a public servant or allows any other person so to do; or

(d) if he,—

(i) by corrupt or illegal means, obtains for himself or for any other person any valuable thing or pecuniary advantage; or

(ii) by abusing his position as a public servant, obtains for himself or for any other person any valuable thing or pecuniary advantage; or

(iii) while holding office as a public servant, obtains for any person any valuable thing or pecuniary advantage without any public interest; or

(e) if he or any person on his behalf, is in possession or has, at any time during the period of his office, been in possession for which the public servant cannot satisfactorily account, of pecuniary resources or property disproportionate to his known sources of income.

Explanation.—For the purpose of this section, "known sources of income" means income received from any lawful source and such receipt has been intimated in accordance with the provisions of any law, rules or orders for the time being applicable to a public servant.

(2) Any public servant who commits criminal misconduct shall be punishable with imprisonment for a term which shall be not less than one year but which may extend to seven years and shall also be liable to fine."

154. The said Act replaced the Prevention of Corruption Act, 1947 (the 1947 Act). The said Act was enacted "to consolidate and amend the law relating to the prevention of corruption and for matters connected therewith." Its Statement of Objects and Reasons reads thus:

> "*Statement of Objects and Reasons.*—1. The Bill is intended to make the existing anti-corruption laws more effective by widening their coverage and by strengthening the provisions.
>
> 2. The Prevention of Corruption Act, 1947, was amended in 1964 based on the recommendations of the Santhanam Committee. There are provisions in Chapter IX of the Indian Penal Code to deal with public servants and those who abet them by way of criminal misconduct. There are also provisions in the Criminal Law Amendment Ordinance, 1944, to enable attachment of ill-gotten wealth obtained through corrupt means, including from transferees of such wealth. The Bill seeks to incorporate all these provisions more effective in combating corruption among public servants.
>
> 3. The Bill, *inter alia,* envisages widening the scope of the definition of the expression "public servant", incorporation of offences under sections 161 to 165A of the Indian Penal Code, enhancement of penalties provided for these offences and incorporation of a provision that the order of the trial Court upholding the grant of sanction for prosecution would be final if it has not already been challenged and the trial has commenced. In order to expedite the proceedings, provisions for day-to-day trial of cases and prohibitory provisions with regard to grant of stay and exercise of powers of revision on interlocutory orders have also been included.
>
> 4. Since the provisions of sections 161 to 161A are incorporated in the proposed legislation with an enhanced punishment it is not necessary to retain those sections in the Indian Penal Code. Consequently, it is proposed to delete those sections with the necessary saving provision.
>
> 5. The notes on clause explain in detail the provisions of the Bill."

PROVISION OF SECTION 21, IPC REPRODUCED – BHARUCHA, J.

155. In the 1947 Act the definition of "public servant" in the Indian Penal Code was adopted, section 21 whereof reads as follows:

21. *"Public servant"*. —The words "public servant" denote a person falling under any of the descriptions hereinafter following. namely:—

First.—[Repealed by the Adaptation of Laws Order, 1950.]

Second.—Every Commissioned Officer in the Military, Naval or Air Forces of India;

Third.—Every Judge including any person empowered by law to discharge, whether by himself or as a member of any body of persons, any adjudicatory functions;

Fourth.—Every officer of a Court of Justice (including a liquidator, receiver or commissioner) whose duty it is, as such officer, to investigate or report on any matter of law or fact, or to make authenticate, or keep any document, or to take charge or dispose of any property, or to execute any judicial process, or to administer any oath, or to interpret, or to preserve order in the Court, and every person specially authorised by a Court of Justice to perform any of such duties;

Fifth.—Every juryman, assessor, or member of a panchayat assisting a Court of Justice or public servant;

Sixth.—Every arbitrator or other person to whom any cause or matter has been referred for decision or report by any Court of Justice, or by any other competent authority;

Seventh.—Every person who holds any office by virtue of which he is empowered to place or keep any person in confinement;

Eighth.—Every officer of the Government whose duty it is, as such officer, to prevent offences, to give information of offences, to bring offenders to justice, or to protect the public health, safety or convenience;

Ninth.—Every officer whose duty it is, as such officer, to take, receive, keep or expend any property on behalf of the Government, or to make any survey, assessment or contract on behalf of the Government, or to execute any revenue-process, or to investigate, or to report, on any matter affecting the pecuniary interests of the Government, or to make, authenticate or keep any document relating to the pecuniary interests of the Government, or to prevent the infraction of any law for the protection of the pecuniary interests of the Government;

Tenth.—Every officer whose duty it is, as such officer, to take, receive, keep or expend any property, to make any survey or assessment or to levy any rate or tax for any secular common purpose of any village, town or district, or to make, authenticate or keep any document for the ascertaining of the rights of the people of any village, town or district;

Eleventh.—Every person who holds any office by virtue of which he is empowered to prepare, publish, maintain or revise an electoral roll or to conduct an election or part of an election;

Twelfth.—Every person—

(a) in the service or pay of the Government or remunerated by fees or commission for the performance of any public duty by the Government;

(b) in the service or pay of a local authority, a corporation established by or under a Central, Provincial or State Act or a Government company as defined in section 617 of the Companies Act, 1956 (1 of 1956)."

Section 6 of the 1947 Act dealt with the previous sanction necessary for prosecution. It reads thus:

> "6. Previous sanction necessary for prosecution.—(1) No court shall take cognizance of an offence punishable under section 161 or section 164 or section 165 of the Indian Penal Code, 1860, or under sub-section (2) or sub-section (3A) of section 5 of this Act, alleged to have been committed by a public servant, except with the previous sanction.
>
> (a) in the case of a person who is employed in connection with the affairs of the Union and is not removable from his office save by or with the sanction of the Central Government, of the Central Government;
>
> (b) in the case of a person who is employed in connection with the affairs of a State and is not removable from his office save by or with the sanction of the State Government, of the State Government;
>
> (c) in the case of any other person, of the authority competent to remove him from his office.
>
> (2) Where for any reason whatsoever any doubt arises whether the previous sanction as required under sub-section (1) should be given by the Central or State Government or any other authority, such sanction shall be given by that Government or authority which would have been competent to remove the public servant from his office at the time when the offence was alleged to have been committed."

SANCTION FOR PROSECUTION OF 'ALLEGED BRIBE-GIVERS' HAS NOT BEEN OBTAINED – TRIAL CANNOT PROCEED IN LAW COURT – SUBMITTED APPELLANTS

156. It is not in dispute that the prosecution against all the accused have not received the previous sanction contemplated by section 19 of the said Act.

157. Mr. P.P. Rao submitted that a Constitution Bench had in the case of **R.S. Nayak** (supra), held that a member of a State Legislature was not a public servant, but that the finding therein that he performed a public duty was erroneous and required reconsideration. The expression 'public duty' in section 2(b) of the said Act meant a duty in the context of an interest which could be enforced at law. A mandamus could not issue to a member of Parliament or a member of a State legislature to perform his duty for he could not be compelled to speak or to vote. It was permissible to refer to the speech in Parliament of the Minister who had moved the Bill that became the said Act. He had stated, in response to a question about the position of a member of Parliament or a member of a Legislative Assembly, thus: "......... We have not done anything different or contrary to the law as it stands today. Under the law, as it stands today, the Supreme Court has held in **Antulay's** case that a Member of a Legislative Assembly is not a public servant within the meaning of section 21 of the Indian Penal Code." That this was really the position was supported by the fact that two conditions had to be satisfied for the purposes of bringing someone within the purview of the said Act, namely, that he should be a public servant (section 2) and there should be an authority competent to remove him from his office (section 19). In this behalf, reliance was placed upon the judgment in **K. Veeraswany** (supra). The judgment of the Delhi High Court under appeal noted that it was not disputed that there was no authority competent to remove members of Parliament from their office. This had also been found by the Orissa High Court in **Habibullah Khan v. State of Orissa, 1993 Cr LJ 3604.** A member of Parliament and a member of a State legislature did not hold an office. Section 2(c)(viii) of the said Act postulated the existence of an office independent of the person holding it, and that, by virtue of the office, the holder was authorised or required to perform a public duty. That a member of Parliament did not hold an office was apparent from the Constitution. Whereas the Constitution spoke of other functionaries holding offices, members of Parliament were said to occupy seats.

The conclusion, therefore, was inescapable that the accused could not be prosecuted under the said Act and the charges had to be quashed. Mr. D.D. Thakur echoed these submissions. He added that it was legally permissible, but morally impermissible, for a legislator to vote in exchange for money. The clauses of section 2(c) had to be construed *ejusdem generis* and, so read, could not cover members of Parliament or the State legislatures. Having regard to the fact that the Minister had made a representation to Parliament when the Bill was being moved that it did not cover members of Parliament and the State legislature, it could not be argued on behalf of the Union Government, by reason of the principle of promissory estoppel, that the said Act covered members of Parliament and the State legislatures. The said Act only removed the surplusage in the then existing definition of "public servant" and had to be construed only in that light. The inclusion of members of Parliament in the said Act was not "clearly implicit" nor "irresistibly clear". A member of Parliament had only privileges given to him under the Constitution; his only obligation was to remain present for a given number of days. Mr. Sibal adopted the arguments of Mr. Rao. He added that the Constitution cast no duty or obligation upon a member of Parliament. Consequently, there was no authorisation or requirement to perform a duty under the provisions of section 2(c)(viii) of the said Act. An authority competent to remove a public servant necessarily contemplated an authority competent to appoint him. There was no authority competent to appoint a member of Parliament and, therefore, there was no authority which could remove him.

DISCUSSION – BHARUCHA, J.

158. The Attorney-General submitted that the object behind enacting the said Act was to widen the coverage of the anti-corruption laws, as had been stated in its Statement of Objects and Reasons. 'Public office' had been defined in *Black's Law Dictionary* (Sixth edition, p. 1082) thus: "The right, authority, and duty created and conferred by law, by which for a given period, either fixed by law or enduring at the pleasure of the creating power, an individual is invested with some portion of the sovereign functions of Government for the benefit of the public. An agency for the State, the duties of which involve in their performance the exercise of some portion of sovereign power, either great or small." The *Shorter Oxford Dictionary* (page 1083) defined "Office" thus, "A position to which certain duties are attached, esp. a place of trust, authority or service under constituted authority." In **Antulay's** case it had been held that a member of a legislative assembly "performs public duties cast on him by the Constitution and his electorate". That a member of Parliament occupied an office had been the view taken in the case of Bunting (1884-5 (7) Ontario Reports 524) and Boston 1923 (33) CLR 386 (referred to above). A member of Parliament performed the sovereign function of law making and in regard to the exchequer. He had a fundamental duty to serve. He undertook high public duties which were inseparable from his position. A member of Parliament, therefore, held an office.

The Constitution provided the number of seats for members of Parliament. The tenure of a member of Parliament was fixed. He received a salary and other allowances. It was clear from the Constitution that he performed public duties. The oath that he took referred to his obligation to "faithfully discharge the duty" upon which he was about to enter. The Salary, Allowances and Pension of Members of Parliament Act, 1954, specified that a member of Parliament was entitled to receive a salary *per mensem* "during the whole of his term of office" and an allowance per day "during any period of residence on duty". The accused, other than D.K. Audi Kesavalu and M. Thimmegowda, were, therefore, public servants within the scope of the said Act and could be charged thereunder. Reference to the provisions of section 19 of the said Act and to the Minister's speech on the Bill that became the said Act was, consequently, not called for. The provisions of section 19 were attracted only when a public servant had an authority competent to remove him. Where, as in the case of a member of Parliament or a State legislature, there was no authority which was competent to remove a public servant, the provisions of section 19 were not attracted and a prosecution could be launched and taken cognizance of without previous sanction. Alternatively, the authority to remove a member of Parliament was the President under the provisions of Article 103 of the Constitution.

159. There can be no doubt that the coverage of section 2(c) of the said Act is far wider than that of section 21 of the Indian Penal Code. The two provisions have only to be looked at side by side to be sure that more people can now be called public servants for the purposes of the anti-corruption law. There is, therefore, no reason at all why section 2(c) of the said Act should be construed only in the light of the existing law and not on its own terms. It is for the Court to construe section 2(c). If the Court comes to the conclusion that members of Parliament and the State Legislatures are clearly covered by its terms, it must so hold. There is then no reason to resort to extraneous aids of interpretation such as the speech of the Minister piloting the Bill that became the said Act. The true interpretation of a statute does not depend upon who urges it. The principle of promissory estoppel has no application in this behalf. Further, if the Court comes to the conclusion, based on section 2(c) itself, that members of Parliament and the State legislatures are, clearly, public servants no resort to the provisions of section 19 is required in this regard. The words "public servant" in section 19 must then bear that meaning that is attributed to them on the construction of the definition thereof in section 2(c).

MPs-MLAs HOLD AN OFFICE – DISCHARGE PUBLIC DUTY WITHIN THE MEANING OF SECTION 2(b) OF PC ACT, 1988 – BHARUCHA, J.

160. A public servant is "any person who holds an office by virtue of which he is authorised or required to perform any public duty." Not only, therefore, must the person hold an office but he must be authorised or required by virtue of that office to perform a public duty. Public duty is defined by section 2(b) of the said Act to mean "a duty in the discharge of which the State, the public or that community at large has an interest." In a democratic form of Government it is the member of Parliament or a State legislature who represents the people of his constituency in the highest law making bodies at the Centre and the State respectively. Not only is he the representative of the people in the process of making the laws that will regulate their society, he is their representative in deciding how the funds of the Centre and the States shall be spent and in exercising control over the executive. It is difficult to conceive of a duty more public than this or of a duty in which the State, the Public and the community at large would have greater interest. The submission that this Court was in error in **Antulay's** case (supra) in holding that a member of a State legislature "performs public duties cast on him by the Constitution and his electorate" must be rejected outright. It may be – we express no final opinion – that the duty that a member of Parliament or a State legislature performs cannot be enforced by the issuance of a writ of mandamus but that is not a *sine qua non* for a duty to be a public duty. We reject the submission, in the light of what we have just said, that a member of Parliament has only privilege no duties. Members of Parliament and the State legislatures would do well to remember that if they have privileges it is the better to perform their duty effectively and fearlessly representing their constituencies.

161. In **Antulay's** case (supra) the question relevant for our purpose was whether a member of a Legislative Assembly was a public servant within the meaning of that expression in clauses 12(a), (3) and (7) of section 21 of the Indian Penal Code. These clauses read thus:

> "21. The words 'public servant' denote a person falling under any of the descriptions hereinafter following, namely:—
>
> *Third.*—Every Judge including any person empowered by law to discharge, whether by himself or as a member of, any body of persons, any adjudicatory functions.
>
> *Seventh.*—Every person who holds any office by virtue of which he is empowered to place or keep any person in confinement.
>
> Twelfth.—Every person—
>
> (a) in the service or pay of the Government or remunerated by fees or commission for the performance of any public duty by the Government."

This Court held that a member of a Legislative Assembly did not satisfy the ingredients of these clauses and that, therefore, he was not a public servant within the meaning of that expression in section 21 of the Indian Penal Code. It was in this context that this Court made by the observation that we have already quoted. Having regard to the fact that there was no clause in section 21 of the Indian Penal Code which is comparable to section 2(c)(viii) of the said Act, the decision in **Antulay's** case is of little assistance in this context.

162. The judgment of the Orissa High Court in the case of **Habibulla Khan** (supra) is of assistance because it considered whether a member of a Legislative Assembly was a public servant within the meaning of section 2(c)(viii) of the said Act. Paragraphs 5, 7, 8 and 9 of the principal judgment are relevant. They read thus:

> "5. For the aforesaid clause to be attracted, two requirements must be satisfied: (i) an M.L.A. must hold an office; and (ii) he must perform public duty by virtue of holding that office. The meaning of the word 'office' has been the subject-matter of various decisions of the apex Court and Shri Rath in his written note dated 27.4.1993 has dealt with these decisions in pages 6 to 12, in which reference has been made to what was held in this regard in (1) **Maharaj Shri Govindlal Jee v. C.I.T., Ahmedabad, 34 ITR 92: AIR 1959 Bom 100** (which is a judgment of Bombay High Court rendered by Chagla, C.J.); (2) **Champalal v. State of Madhya Pradesh, AIR 1971 MP 88,** in which the definition of the word "office" given in Corpus Juris Secundum "A position or station in which a person is employed to perform certain duty" was noted; (3) **Statesman v. H.R. Deb** (supra) which is a rendering by a Constitution Bench stating "an office means no more than a position to which certain duties are attached"; (4) **Kanta Kathuria** (supra) in which Hidayatulla, C.J., on behalf of self and J.K. Mitter, J., who were in minority, after referring to the Constitution Bench decision in Statesman's case, referred to the observations of Lord Wright in **McMillan** (supra), that the meaning of the word 'office' covered four columns of the *New English Dictionary,* but the one taken as most relevant was "(a) position or place to which certain duties are attached, especially one of more or less public character"; whereas Sikri, J. speaking for the majority referred to the definition given by Lord Atkin, which was "a subsisting permanent, substantive position, which had an existence independent of the person who filled it, which went on and was filled in succession by successive holders" by further stating that there was no

essential difference between the definitions given by Lord Wright and Lord Atkin; and **Madhukar v. Jaswant, AIR 1976 SC 2283,** in which the definition given in the Statesman's case was quoted with approval.

xxx xxx xxx"

7. Shri Das, learned Government Advocate, does not contest the submission of Shri Rath that the word 'office' should mean, to repeat, "no more than a position to which certain duties are attached, specially of a public character". Let it be seen as to whether the test mentioned by Sikri, J. is satisfied, which as already noted, is that there must be an office which exists independently of the holder of that office. To substantiate this part of his submission, Shri Rath has referred in his written note first to Article 168 of the Constitution which has provided that for every State there shall be a Legislature which shall consist of the Governor, and in case of some States, two Houses and in case of other one House. Article 170 states that the Legislative Assembly of each State shall consist of not more than 500 and not less than 60 members chosen by direct election from the territorial constituencies in the State for which purpose the State is divided into equal number of territorial constituencies. In Article 172, duration of the Legislative Assembly has been specified to be for five years, and Article 173 deals with the conditions of eligibility. Reference is then made to certain provisions of the Representation of the People Act, 1950, which has provided for total number of seats in the Legislative Assembly, and so far as Orissa is concerned, the Second Schedule mentions that the Orissa Legislative Assembly shall consist of 147 members.

8. Relying on the aforesaid provisions, it is contended and rightly, by Shri Rath that the office of the MLA is created by the Constitution read with the Representation of the People Act, 1950, whereas the actual election of MLAs. is supervised, directed and controlled by the provisions contained in Articles 324 to 329 of the Constitution and the provisions of the Representation of the People Act, 1951, which brings home the distinction between "office" and "holder of the office".

9. The aforesaid submission appears to us to be unassailable. We would, therefore, accept the same by stating that an MLA does hold an office, which is one of the two necessary requirements to attract the definition of "public servant", as given in clause (viii) of the Act. Another requirement, as already mentioned, is performance of public duty as holder of such office. This aspect has been dealt with by Shri Rath in paragraph 7 of his written note wherein mention has been made about various duties attached to the office of the MLA as would appear from Chapter III of Part VI of the Constitution – the same being, making of laws, acting conjointly to effectively control the activities of the executive, approval of the finance bill, etc. Indeed, no doubt can be entertained in this regard in view of what was stated in paragraph 59 of **Antulay's** case, which is as below:—

> ".......... it would be rather difficult to accept an unduly wide submission that MLA is not performing any public duty. However, it is unquestionable that he is not performing any public duty either directed by the Government or for the Government. He no doubt performs public duty cast on him by the Constitution and his electorate. He thus discharges constitutional functions..........."

Having held that a member of a Legislative Assembly was a public servant under the said Act, the Orissa High Court went on to consider which authority was competent to give sanction for his prosecution. That is an aspect with which we are not immediately concerned and we shall revert to this judgment later.

MPs AND MLAs ARE PUBLIC SERVANTS WITHIN THE PURVIEW OF 2(c)(viii) OF PC ACT, 1988 – HELD BHARUCHA, J.

163. We think that the view of the Orissa High Court that a member of a Legislative Assembly is a public servant is correct. Judged by the test enunciated by Lord Atkin in **McMillan** (supra) and adopted by Sikri, J. in **Kanta Kathuria's** case the position of a member of Parliament, or of a Legislative Assembly, is subsisting, permanent and substantive; it has an existence independent of the person who fills it and it is filled in succession by successive holders. The seat of each constituency is permanent and substantive. It is filled, ordinarily for the duration of the legislative term, by the successful candidate in the election for the constituency. When the legislative term is over, the seat is filled by the successful candidate at the next election. There is, therefore, no doubt in our minds that a member of Parliament, or of a Legislative Assembly, holds an office and that he is required and authorised thereby to carry out a public duty. In a word, a member of Parliament, or of a Legislative Assembly, is a public servant for the purposes of the said Act.

SANCTION FOR PROSECUTION OF PUBLIC SERVANTS IS REQUIRED ONLY FOR SPECIFIED OFFENCES – NOT ALL – HELD BHARUCHA, J.

164. This brings us to the issue of sanction under the provisions of section 19 of the said Act. The section has been quoted. Sub-section (1) opens with the words "No court shall take cognizance of an offence punishable under sections 7, 10, 11, 13 and 15 alleged to have been committed by a public servant, except with the previous sanction........ " Sanction is not required in respect of all offences covered by the said Act; it is required only in respect of the offences that are punishable under sections 7, 10, 11, 13 and 15. *Secondly*, the person charged must be a public servant at the point of time the court is asked to take cognizance; that is the material time for the purposes of the section. *Thirdly*, the sanction must precede cognizance; it must be prior sanction. *Fourthly*, and this from the point of view of this judgment is most material, the section covers all public servants. In other words, if any public servant is charged with an offence punishable under the aforesaid sections, the court shall not take cognizance in the absence of sanction. That the section applies to all public servants is also clear from the three clauses of sub-section (1). Clause (a) says that the sanction must be of the Central Government in the case of a public servant who is employed in connection with the affairs of the Union and is not removable from his office save by or with the sanction of the Central Government. Clause (b) says that the sanction must be of a State Government in the case of a public servant who is employed in connection with the affairs of that State and is not removable from his office save by or with the consent of the State Government. Clause (c) says that the sanction in the case of any other public servant must be of the authority competent to remove him from his office. Clause (c) is the basket into which all public servants, other than those covered by the terms of clauses (a) and (b), fall.

165. Upon the plain language of sub-section (1) of section 19, analysed above, the argument of the learned Attorney-General that the provisions of section 19 are applicable only to a public servant who is removable from his office by an authority competent to do so must fail.

166. In support of the argument, the learned Attorney-General relied upon the judgment of this Court in **S.A. Venkataraman's** case (supra) in which, with reference to the provisions of section 6 of the 1947 Act, it was observed (at p. 111 of AIR):

> "When the provisions of section 6 of the Act are examined it is manifest that two conditions must be fulfilled before its provisions become applicable. One is that the offences mentioned therein must be committed by a public servant and the other is that that person is employed in connection with the

affairs of the Union or a State and is not removable from his office save by or with the sanction of the Central Government or the State Government or is a public servant who is removable from his office by any other competent authority. Both these conditions must be present to prevent a court from taking cognizance of an offence mentioned in the section without the previous sanction of the Central Government or the State Government or the authority competent to remove the public servant from his office. If either of these conditions is lacking, the essential requirements of the section are wanting and the provisions of the section do not stand in the way of a court taking cognizance without a previous sanction."

The appellant was a public servant who had been dismissed from service consequent upon a departmental inquiry. After his dismissal he was charged with the offence of criminal misconduct under the 1947 Act and convicted. The appellant contended that no court could have taken cognizance of the charge against him because there was no prior sanction under section 6 of the 1947 Act. This Court found, as aforestated, that for the applicability of section 6 two conditions had to be fulfilled, namely, (i) the offence should have been committed by a public servant, and (ii) the public servant is removable from his office by the Central Government or a State Government or a competent authority. This Court held that sanction was not a pre-requisite to the cognizance of the offence with which the appellant was charged and the conditions were not satisfied because, when cognizance of the offence was taken, the appellant had ceased to be a public servant. That the appellant was a public servant was not in dispute; that no sanction had been obtained was also not in dispute. This Court was not concerned with a situation in which there was a public servant but there was no authority competent to remove him from his office. The observations of this Court quoted above were made in the context of the facts of the case and relative thereto. They cannot be examined *de hors* the facts and read as supporting the proposition that the provisions of section 19 are applicable only to a public servant who is removable from his office by an authority competent to do so and, if there is no authority competent to remove a public servant from his office, the embargo arising under section 19 is not attracted and section 19 does not come in the way of a Court taking cognizance. In any event, we cannot, with great respect, agree that the observations fully analyse the provisions of section 19. We have set out above how we read it; as we read it, it applies to all who are public servants for the purposes of the said Act.

167. It is correct to say that section 19 contemplates that for every public servant there must be an authority competent to remove him from his office and that, therefore, the effort must be to identify that authority. But if no authority can be identified in the case of a public servant or a particular category of public servant, it cannot lead to the conclusion that was urged on behalf of the accused, namely, that he is not a public servant or this is not a category of public servant within the meaning of the said Act. We have found, based on the language of section 2(c)(viii) read with section 2(b), that members of Parliament are public servants. That finding, based upon the definition section, must apply to the phrase 'public servant' wherever it occurs in the said Act. It cannot change if it be found that there is no authority competent to remove members of Parliament from office. Members of Parliament would then, not be liable to be prosecuted for offences covered by sections 7, 10, 11, 13 and 15, the condition of prior sanction being incapable of being satisfied, but they would remain liable to prosecution for offences under the said Act other than those covered by sections 7, 10, 11, 13 and 15.

168. The Attorney General drew our attention in this context to the conclusion of the Orissa High Court in the case of **Habibullah Kahn's** case (supra) aforementioned.

The Orissa High Court found that there was no authority which could grant previous sanction, as contemplated by section 19 of the Act, in the case of a member of a Legislative Assembly. Counsel, the High Court recorded, did not contend that even if there be no person competent to give sanction for prosecuting a member of a Legislative Assembly under the said Act, nonetheless sanction for his prosecution had to be obtained because he was a public servant. The High Court was satisfied that although "the MLA would come within the fold of the definition of 'public servant', as given in section 2(c) of the Act, he is not the type of 'public servant' for whose prosecution under the Act, previous sanction as required by section 19 is necessary. We quite realise the anomaly of our conclusion, because though section 19 of the Act makes no distinction between one public servant and another for the purpose of previous sanction, we have made so. But this is a result which we could not have truly and legally avoided."

169. We do not think that the view of the Orissa High Court stated above is correct. Since section 6 of the 1947 Act and section 19 of the said Act make no distinction between one public servant and another for the purpose of previous sanction, the conclusion must be that where the Court finds that there is no authority competent to remove a public servant, the public servant cannot be prosecuted for offences punishable under sections 7, 10, 11, 13 and 15 of the said Act because there is no authority that can sanction such prosecution.

170. This Court in the case of **K. Veeraswami** (supra), considered the applicability of the 1947 Act to a Judge of a High Court or the Supreme Court. A case under the provisions of section 5(2) read with section 5(1)(e) of the 1947 Act had been registered against the appellant, the Chief Justice of a High Court, and on 28th February, 1976, an FIR was filed in the Court of Special Judge. The appellant retired on attaining the age of superannuation on 8th April, 1976. On 15th December, 1977, a charge sheet was filed and process was issued for appearance of the appellant. The appellant moved the High Court to quash the proceedings. The High Court dismissed the application but granted certificate of fitness to appeal. This Court, by a majority, concluded that a Judge of a High Court and the Supreme Court was a public servant within the meaning of section 2 of the 1947 Act. A prosecution against him could be lodged after obtaining the sanction of the competent authority under section 6 of the 1947 Act. For this purpose, the President of India was the authority to give previous sanction.

No criminal case could be registered against a Judge of a High Court or the Supreme Court unless the Chief Justice of India was consulted. Such consultation was necessary also at the stage of examining whether sanction for prosecution should be granted, which should be guided by and in accordance with the advice of the Chief Justice in India. Specifically, the majority view was that a public servant could not be prosecuted for the offences specified in section 6 of the 1947 Act unless there was prior sanction for prosecution from a competent authority. Section 6 was primarily concerned with seeing that a prosecution for the specified offences did not commence without the sanction of the competent authority. A Judge of the superior Courts squarely fell within the purview of the 1947 Act. The second requirement under clause (c) of section 6(1) was that for the purpose of granting sanction for his prosecution there must be an authority and the authority must be competent to remove him. It was, therefore, "now necessary to identify such authority..........."

171. The learned Attorney-General laid stress upon this observation. He submitted that the Court should identify the authority competent to remove a member of Parliament, or a State Legislature, from his office if it found such member to be a public servant within the meaning of section 2(c) and did not accept his contention that the provisions of section 19 did not apply, there being no authority competent to remove such member from his office. In other words, it was the alternative submission of the learned Attorney-General that there was an authority competent to remove such member from his office: in the case of a member of parliament it was the President and in the case of a member of a State Legislature it was the Governor of the State. We shall address ourselves to the submission in a moment.

IF AUTHORITY TO GRANT SANCTION NOT SPECIFIED – PUBLIC SERVANT DOES CEASE TO BE GOVERNED BY PC ACT, 1988 – SUCH AUTHORITY SHOULD BE IDENTIFIED – HELD BHARUCHA, J.

172. The passage in **Veeraswamy's** case (supra) relied upon by learned counsel for the appellants is contained in the dissenting judgment of Verma, J. He said:

> "Clauses (a), (b) and (c) in sub-section (1) of section 6 exhaustively provide for the competent authority to grant sanction for prosecution in case of all the public servants falling within the purview of the Act. Admittedly, such previous sanction is a condition precedent for taking cognizance of an offence punishable under the Act, of a public servant who is prosecuted during his continuance in the office. It follows that the public servant falling within the purview of the Act must invariably fall within one of the three clauses in sub-section (1) of section 6. It follows that the holder of an office, even though a 'public servant' according to the definition in the Act, who does not fall within any of the clauses (a), (b) or (c) of sub-section (1) of section 6 must be held to be outside the purview of the Act since this special enactment was not enacted to cover that category of public servants in spite of the wide definition of 'public servant' in the Act. This is the only manner in which these provisions of the Act can be harmonized and given full effect. The scheme of the Act is that a public servant who commits the offence of criminal misconduct, as defined in the several clauses of sub-section (1) of section 5, can be punished in accordance with sub-section (2) of section 5, after investigation of the offence in the manner prescribed and with the previous sanction of the competent authority obtained under section 6 of the Act, in trial conducted according to the prescribed procedure. The grant of previous sanction under section 6 being a condition precedent for the prosecution of a public servant covered by the Act, it must follow that the holder of an office who may be a public servant according to the wide definition of the expression in the Act but whose category for the grant of sanction for prosecution is not envisaged by section 6 of the Act, is outside the purview of the Act, not intended to be covered by the Act. This is the only manner in which a harmonious construction of the provisions of the Act can be made for the purpose of achieving the object of that enactment."

173. We are unable, with respect, to share this view in the dissenting judgment. It does not appear to take into reckoning the fact that sanction is not a pre-requisite for prosecution for all offences under the statute but is limited to those expressly specified in the sanction provision. Secondly, the question as to whether or not a person is a public servant within the meaning of the statute must be determined having regard to the definition of a public servant contained in the statute. If the person is found to be a public servant within the meaning of the definition, he must be taken to be a public servant for the purposes of all provisions in the statute in which the expression 'public servant' occurs. If, therefore, a person is found to satisfy the requirements of the definition of a public servant, he must be treated as a public servant for the purposes of the sanction provision. In our opinion, it cannot be held as a consequence of the conclusion that there is no authority competent to remove from office a person who falls within the definition of public servant, that he is not a public servant within the meaning of the statute. Where a person is found to satisfy the requirements of the definition of a public servant, the Court must, as was said by the majority in **Veeraswami's** case, attempt to identify the authority competent to remove him from his office. The majority identified that authority in the case of a Judge of a High Court and the Supreme Court and did not need to consider the effect upon the prosecution of not being able to find such authority.

174. It is convenient now to notice a submission made by Mr. Sibal based upon **Veeraswami's** case (supra). He urged that just as this Court had there directed that no criminal prosecution should be launched against a Judge of a High Court or the Supreme Court without first consulting the Chief Justice of India, so we should direct that no criminal prosecution should be launched against a member of Parliament without first consulting the Speaker. As the majority judgment makes clear, this direction was considered necessary to secure the independence of the judiciary and in the light of the "apprehension that the Executive being the largest litigant is likely to abuse the power to prosecute the Judges." Members of Parliament do not stand in a comparable position. They do not have to decide day after day disputes between the citizen and the Executive. They do not need the additional protection that the Judges require to perform their constitutional duty of decision making without fear or favour.

175. Before we move on to consider the alternative submission of the Attorney-General, we must note the judgment in **S.A. Venkataraman's** case (supra), upon which the learned Attorney-General relied for his first proposition, namely, that the provisions of section 19 do not apply to a public servant in respect of whom there is no authority competent to remove him from his office. The appellant Venkataraman was a public servant. After he was dismissed from service consequent upon a departmental inquiry, he was charged with criminal misconduct under the 1947 Act and was convicted. The contention before this Court was that the trial Court could not have taken cognizance of the offence because no sanction for the prosecution had been produced before it. This Court held that no sanction for the prosecution of the appellant was required because he was not a public servant at the time cognizance of the offence was taken. The following passage in this Court's judgment was relied upon (at p. 111 of AIR):

> "It was suggested that clause (c) in section 6(1) refers to persons other than those mentioned in Clause (a) and (b). The words "is employed" are absent in this clause which would, therefore, apply to a person who had ceased to be a public servant though he was so at the time of the commission of the offence. Clause (c) cannot be construed in this way. The expressions "in the case of a person" and "in the case of any other person" must refer to a public servant having regard to the first paragraph of the sub-section. Clauses (a) and (b), therefore, would cover the case of a public servant who is employed in connection with the affairs of the Union or a State and is not removable from his office save by or with the sanction of the Central Government or the State Government and clause (c) would cover the case of any other public servant whom a competent authority could remove from his office. The more important words in clause (c) are "of the authority competent to remove him from his office". A public servant who has ceased to be a public servant is not a person removable from any office by a competent authority. Section 2 of the Act states that a public servant, for the purpose of the Act, means a public servant as defined in section 21 of the Indian Penal Code. Under clause (c), therefore, any one who is a public servant at the time a Court was asked to take cognizance, but does not come within the description of a public servant under clause (a) and (b), is accused of an offence committed by him as a public servant as specified in section 6 would

be entitled to rely on the provisions of that section and object to the taking of cognizance without a previous sanction."

IF PUBLIC SERVANT DOES NOT FALL IN CLAUSE (A) OR (B) OF SECTION 2(C) – HE FALLS IN CLAUSE (C) FOR SANCTION TO PROSECUTION – PRESIDENT OF INDIA IS NOT COMPETENT AUTHORITY FOR MPs – LEFT OPEN – HELD BHARUCHA, J.

We do not find in the passage anything that can assist the Attorney-General's submission rather, it is supportive of the view that we have taken and indicates that the third clause in the sanction provision is a catch-all clause into which all public servants who are not covered by the first two clauses fall. In other words, to prosecute a public servant the prior sanction of the authority competent to remove him is a must.

176. For the purpose of appreciating the argument that the President is the authority competent to remove a member of Parliament from his office, Articles 101, 102 and 103 under the head "Disqualifications of Members" in Chapter II of Part V of the Constitution need to be set out. (Similar provisions in relation to members of State Legislatures are contained in Articles 190, 191 and 192 under the same head in Chapter III of Part VI of the Constitution). Articles 101, 102 and 103 read thus :

"*101. Vacation of Seats.*—(1) No person shall be a member of both Houses of Parliament and provision shall be made by Parliament by law for the vacation by a person who is chosen a member of both Houses of his seat in one House or the other.

(2) No person shall be a member both of Parliament and of a House of the Legislature of a State and if a person is chosen a member both of Parliament and of a House of the Legislature of a State, then, at the expiration of such period as may be specified in rules made by the President, that person's seat in Parliament shall become vacant, unless he has previously resigned his seat in the Legislature of the State.

(3) If a member of either House of Parliament—

(a) becomes subject to any of the disqualifications mentioned in clause (1) or clause (2) of Article 102' or

(b) resigns his seat by writing under his hand addressed to the Chairman or the Speaker as the case may be, and his resignation is accepted by the Chairman or the Speaker, as the case may be, his seat shall thereupon become vacant:

Provided that in the case of any resignation (*sic*) to in sub-clause (b), if from information received or otherwise and after making such inquiry as he thinks fit; the Chairman or the Speaker, as the case may be, is satisfied that such resignation is not voluntary or genuine, he shall not accept such resignation.

(4) If for a period of sixty days a member of either House of Parliament is without permission of the House absent from all meetings thereof, the House may declare his seat vacant:

Provided that in computing the said period of sixty days no account shall be taken of any period during which the House is prorogued or is adjourned for more than four consecutive days.

103. Disqualifications for membership.—(1) A person shall be disqualified for being chosen as and for being a member of either House of Parliament—

(a) if he holds any office of profit under the Government of India or the Government of any State, other than an office declared by Parliament by law not to disqualify its holder;

(b) if he is of unsound mind and stands so declared by a competent Court;

(c) if he is an undischarged insolvent;

(d) if he is not a citizen of India, or has voluntarily acquired the citizenship of a foreign State, or is under any acknowledgment of allegiance or adherence to a foreign State;

(e) if he is disqualified by or under any law made by Parliament.

Explanation.—For the purpose of this clause a person shall not be deemed to hold an office of profit under the Government of India or the Government of any State by reason only that he is a Minister either for the Union or for such State.

(2) A person shall be disqualified for being a member of either House of Parliament if he is so disqualified under the Tenth Schedule.

102. Decision on questions as to disqualifications of members.—(1) If any question arises as to whether a member of either House of Parliament has become subject to any of the disqualifications mentioned in clause (1) of Article 102, the question shall be referred for the decision of the President and his decision shall be final.

(2) Before giving any decision on any such question, the President shall obtain the opinion of the Election Commission and shall act according to such opinion.

177. By reason of Article 101(3)(a), the seat of a member of Parliament becomes vacant if he becomes subject to the disqualifications mentioned in Article 102(1) and (2). Those disqualifications are the holding of an office of profit under the Union or State Government, other than an office declared by Parliament by law not to disqualify the holder; the declaration by a competent Court of unsoundness of mind; undischarged insolvency; the citizenship of a foreign State or acknowledgment of allegiance or adherence thereto; and disqualification under any law made by Parliament or under the Tenth Schedule. Under the provisions of Article 103, it is only if a question arises as to whether a member of Parliament has become subject to any of the disqualifications aforementioned, other than disqualification under the Tenth Schedule, that the question is referred to the President for his decision. The President's decision is final but, before giving it, the President has to obtain the opinion of the Election Commission and has to act according to such opinion.

178. The question for our purposes is whether, having regard to the terms of Articles 101, 102 and 103, the President can be said to be the authority competent to remove a member of Parliament from his office. It is clear from Article 101 that the seat of a member of Parliament becomes vacant immediately upon his becoming subject to the disqualifications mentioned in Article 102, without more. The removal of a member of Parliament is occasioned by operation of law and is self operative. Reference to the President under Article 103 is required only if a question arises as to whether a member of Parliament has earned such disqualification; that is to say, if it is disputed. The President would then have to decide whether the member of Parliament had become subject to the automatic disqualification contemplated by Article 101. His order would not remove the member of Parliament from his seat or office but would declare that he stood disqualified. It would operate not with effect from the date upon which it was made but would relate back to the date upon which the disqualification was earned. Without, therefore, having to go into the connotation of the word "removal" in service law, it seems clear that the President cannot be said to be the authority competent to remove a member of Parliament from his office.

179. The Attorney-General submitted that the scheme of the said Act, as compared to the 1947 Act, had undergone an important change by reason of the introduction of sub-section (3) in section 19. Sanction was no longer a condition precedent. A trial in the absence of sanction was not a trial without inherent jurisdiction or a nullity. A trial without sanction had to be upheld unless there had been a failure of justice. This feature had a material bearing on the present case. The trial Court had taken cognizance of the charges against the accused and the High Court had dismissed the revision petition to quash the charges. In the light of section 19(3), this Court should not interdict the charges, particularly, since a complaint filed today would not require sanction against most of the accused. Having regard to the effect of our findings upon the accused, it is not necessary to consider this submission.

180. We have, as aforestated, reached the conclusion that members of Parliament and the State legislatures are public servants liable to be prosecuted for offences under the said Act but that they cannot be prosecuted for offences under sections 7, 10, 11 and 13 thereof because of want of an authority competent to grant sanction thereto. We entertain the hope that Parliament will address itself to the task of removing this lacuna with due expedition.

QUESTIONS ANSWERED – RETURNED TO THREE JUDGE BENCH – CONSTITUTION BENCH

Conclusions

181. We now set down the effect upon the accused of our findings.

We have held that the alleged bribe takers who voted upon the no-confidence motion, that is, Suraj Mandal, Shibu Soren, Simon Marandi, Shailender Mehto, Ram Lakhan Singh Yadav, Ram Sharan Yadav, Roshan Lal, Anadi Charan Das, Abhay Pratap Singh and Haji Gulam Mohammed (accused Nos. 3, 4, 5, 6, 16, 17, 18, 19, 20 and 21) are entitled to the immunity conferred by Article 105(2).

182. D.K. Audi Keshavalu and M. Thimmegowda (accused Nos. 12 and 13) were at all relevant times private persons. The trial on all charges against them must proceed.

183. When cognizance of the charges against them was taken, Buta Singh and N.M. Revanna (accused Nos. 7 and 9) were not public servants. The question of sanction for their prosecution, does not, therefore, arise and the trial on all charges against them must proceed.

184. P.V. Narasimha Rao, Satish Sharma, V. Rajeswar Rao, Ram Linga Reddy, M. Veerappa Moily and Bhajan Lal (accused Nos. 1, 2, 8, 10, 11 and 14) were public servants, being either members of Parliament or a State legislature, when cognizance of the charges against them was taken. They are charged with substantive offences under section 120B of the Indian Penal Code and section 12 of the said Act. Since no prior sanction is required in respect of the charge under section 12 of the said Act, the trial on all charges against them must proceed.

185. Ajit Singh (accused No. 15) was a public servant, being a member of Parliament, when cognizance of the charges against him was taken. He is charged with substantive offences under section 120B of the Indian Penal Code and sections 7 and 13(2) of the said Act. The trial of the charge against him under section 120B of the Indian Penal Code must proceed.

186. The appeals shall now be placed before a bench of three learned judges for hearing, on any other points that may be involved, and final disposal.

Order accordingly.

Majority view: Member of Parliament holds an office – He is required to perform Public Duties. Hence, Member of Parliament is a public servant under section 2(c) of the Prevention of Corruption Act, 1988.

2. Since there is no authority to remove an MP or to grant sanction for his prosecution under section 19(1) of the Prevention of Corruption Act, 1988 the Court can take cognizance of the offences mentioned in section 19(1) of the Act 1988.

3. Till provision is made by the Parliament by way of suitable amendment, the prosecuting Agency can obtain permission of the Chairman, Rajya Sabha for Members of Rajya Sabha and from the Speaker of the Lok Sabha for Member of the Lok Sabha before filing the challan for offences punishable under section 7, 10, 11, 13 and 15 of the Act 1988 (S.C. Agrawal, J. for himself and on behalf of Dr. A.S. Anand J., G.N. Ray J. concurring).

4. Members of the Lok Sabha who have voted are protected by Article 105(2) of the Constitution of India.

5. Ajit Singh (A-15) had not cast the vote. He is charged for offence punishable under sections 120-B Indian Penal Code read with section 7, 13(2) of the Act, 1988. Trial should proceed against him under section 120B, IPC.

6. D.K. Audi Kesavalu (A-12) and M. Thimmegowda (A-13) are private persons. Hence no sanction is required for their prosection.

7. Buta Singh (A-7) and N.M. Revanna (A-9) were not public servants when cognizance of the charges was taken against them by the Court. The trial can proceed against them.

8. P.V. Narasimha (A-1), Captain Satish Sharma (A-2), V. Rajeshwar Rao (A-8), Rama Linga Reddy (A-10), M. Veerappa Moily (A-11) and Bhajan Lal (A-14) were public servants when cognizance was taken. The Bribe-givers are not protected by any provision of the Constitution of India. However they are charged for offences punishable under section 120B IPC and section 12 of the Act 1988 for which no sanction was required. The trial can proceed against them. (Majority view per S.P. Bharucha, S. Rajendra Babu, JJ. and G.N. Ray, J. concurring).

SUPREME COURT OF INDIA

Review Petition By Ajit Singh Dismissed-Supreme Court

Ajit Singh

v.

State (Delhi), Through C.B.I.

Original Appellate Jurisdiction
Review Petition No. 1023 of 1998 in
Criminal Appeal No. 1219 of 1997

Order

We have read the Review Petition and its Annexures. For the purpose of Review Petition we shall assume that the review Petitioner had voted for the no-confidence motion. The criminal proceedings allege an agreement and bribe to vote against the no-confidence motion. Therefore, the protection of Article 105(2) is not available to the Review Petitioner.

The review petition is dismissed.

Sd/- Justice S.C. Agrawal

Sd/- Justice G.N. Ray

Sd/- Justice A.S. Anand

Sd/- Justice S.P. Barucha

Sd/- Justice S. Rajindra Babu

New Delhi

April 30, 1998

SUPREME COURT OF INDIA

Criminal Appellate Jurisdiction

P.V. Narsimha Rao
v.
State (CBI/SPE)

Criminal Appeal Nos. 1207-1208 of 1997

WITH

(Crl. A. Nos. 1209, 1210-1212, 1213, 1214, 1215, 1216, 1217-1218, 1219, 1220, 1221 1222/1997, 186, 188/1998)

ORDER

All these appeals have been preferred before the trial commenced against the order of the learned Special Judge, indicating the *prima facie* materials exist for framing of charges. The accused persons moved the High Court of Delhi against the said order of the learned Special Judge and, being unsuccessful therein, have moved this court. While the matter was heard before the three-Judge Bench of this Court, it was felt necessary that the matter should be referred to the Constitution Bench for expressing opinion as to whether the Members of Parliament are "public servants" within the ambit of Prevention of Corruption Act and whether privilege under Article 105 of the Constitution of India can at all be claimed. These two questions have now been answered by the Constitution Bench in three different judgments since reported in **[P.V. Narsimha Rao v. State (CBI/SPE), (1998) 4 SCC 626].**

TWO QUESTIONS REFERRED TO THE CONSTITUTION BENCH HAVE BEEN ANSWERED – MATTER REFERRED BACK TO THE THREE-JUDGE BENCH FOR JUDGMENT-HENCE THIS ORDER – THREE JUDGE BENCH

During the pendency of these appeals, as this Court had not granted any stay of further proceeding, the trial has already commenced and is continuing. In view of the questions already answered by the Constitution Bench on the issues posed before their Lordships, it is not necessary for us to go into any other questions raised in these appeals since those questions have to be answered by the Trial Judge bearing in mind the law laid down by the Constitution Bench in the aforesaid case. Needless to mention that any observation that has been made by the High Court on the merits of the proceeding will not weigh with the learned Trial Judge in disposing of the matter and the contentions raised before him. These appeals are accordingly disposed of keeping it open for the parties to raise their contentions before the Trial

Judge as is permissible under the law and the Trial Judge will obviously entertain and dispose them of in accordance with law.

Sd/- Justice G.B. Pattanaik
Sd/- Justic S.P. Kurdukar
Sd/- Justice K.T. Thomas

NEW Delhi
May 05, 1999

IN THE COURT OF SHRI AJIT BHARIHOKE, SPECIAL JUDGE, DELHI

C.B.I.

v.

(1) Shri P.V. Narasimha Rao.
(2) Capt. Satish Sharma.
(3) Shri Buta Singh.
(4) Shri V. Rajeshwar Rao.
(5) Shri H.M. Revanna.
(6) Shri Ramalinga Reddy.
(7) Shri M. Veerappa Moily.
(8) Shri D.K. Audikeshvulu.
(9) Shri M. Thimmegowda.
(10) Shri Bhajan Lal.
(11) Shri Ajit Singh.

R.C. Nos. 1 to 5(A)/96 – C.B.I/A.C.U-VIII/D.L.I.
Under section 120B, IPC read with sections 7, 12, 13(2)
read with 13(1)(d) of P.C. Act, 1988.

C.C. No. 121 of 1996,

C.C. No. 128 of 1996

C.C. No. 11 of 1997

JUDGMENT

That in the general election of 10th Lok Sabha in 1991, Congress (I) emerged as single largest party. It formed the government at the centre under the leadership of accused P.V. Narasimha Rao (A-1). Monsoon Session of 10th Lok Sabha was to commence on 26-7-1993. A "No-Confidence Motion" was moved against the Government by Shri Ajay Mukhopadhya, A C.P.I. (M) M.P. The effective strength of Lok Sabha at that moment was 528 and Congress(I) had 251 members. Thus the government headed by accused P.V. Narasimha Rao (A-1) was short of 14 M.Ps for proving its majority on the floor of house. It is alleged that the opposition parties had made their intention clear to move "No Confidence Motion" against the government well in advance. On 28-7-1993 "No Confidence Motion" was put to vote after the debate and it was defeated with the support of four J.M.M. M.Ps *i.e.* Shri Suraj Mandal (A-3) Shibu Soren (A-4), Shri Simon Marandi (A-5) and Shailender Mahto (A-6) respectively, as well as A-16 to A-21 namely S/Shri Ram Lakhan Singh Yadav, Ram Sharan Yadav, Roshan Lal, Anadi Charan Dass, Abhay Pratap Singh and Haji

Gulam Mohd. Khan respectively and late Shri G.C. Munda, M.P. the break – away group of Janta Dal (A) Party.

COMPLAINT FILED TO CBI – F.I.R. NOT REGISTERED AGAINST NAMED PERSONS – WRIT PETITION FILED BY RAVINDER KUMAR FOR ALLEGED CONSPIRACY AND BRIBING OF MPs – DELHI HIGH COURT DIRECTED CBI TO REGISTER FIR ON COMPLAINT BASIS – CBI REGISTERED F.I.R. – AFTER INVESTIGATION – THREE CHARGE-SHEETS FILED – CBI COURT

2. Complainant Ravinder Kumar, President of Rashtriya Mukti Morcha filed a complaint with C.B.I. alleging that Shri P.V. Narasimha Rao had hatched a criminal conspiracy with Shri V.C. Shukla, Shri R.K. Dhawan, Capt. Satish Sharma, Shri Ajit Singh, Shri Bhajan Lal and Shri Lalit Suri with the object to prove the majority of the Government on the floor of the house by resorting to bribing some of the members of the Parliament to the extent of over Rs. 4 Crores. On the basis of said complaint C.B.I. registered four cases R.C. Nos. 1(A)/96 to R.C. No. 4(A)/96/CBI/ACU-VIII/N.D. against four J.M.M. M,Ps (A3 to A6, since discharged). However, no F.I.R. was registered against A-1, A-2, A-14, A-15 and others named in the complaint. Feeling aggrieved, complainant Ravinder Kumar filed a writ petition in High Court of Delhi for direction to C.B.I. to register a proper F.I.R. as per allegations in the complaint. In the aforesaid writ petition directions were issued by Division Bench of Hon'ble High Court and pursuant to that C.B.I. registered case R.C. No. S(A)/96/ACU-VIII/C.B.I./N.D. against the persons named in the complaint.

3. Pursuant to the investigation conducted in case R.C. Nos. 1 (A)/96 to R.C. Nos. 5(A)/96 – ACU-VIII/C.B.I./N.D., prosecution sought to try Shri P.V. Narasimha Rao (here in after referred to as A-1), Capt. Satish Sharma (hereinafter referred to as A-2), Suraj Mandal (hereinafter referred to as A-3), Shri Shibu Soren (hereinafter referred to as A-4), Shri Simon Marandi (hereinafter referred to as A-5), Shri Shailendra Mahto (approver) (hereinafter referred to as A-6), Shri Buta Singh (hereinafter referred to as A-7), Shri V. Rajeshwar Rao (hereinafter referred to as A-8), Shri H.M. Revanna (hereinafter referred to as A-9), Shri Ramalinga Reddy (hereinafter referred to as A-10), Shri M. Veerappa Moily (hereinafter referred to as A-11), Shri D.K. Audikeshvulu (hereinafter referred to as A-12), Shri M. Thimmegowda (hereinafter referred to as A-13), Shri Bhajan Lal (hereinafter referred to as A-14), Shri Ajit Singh (hereinafter referred to as A-15), Shri Ram Lakhan Singh Yadav (hereinafter referred to as A-16), Shri Ram Sharan Yadav (hereinafter referred to as A-17), Shri Roshan Lal (hereinafter referred to as A-18), Shri Anadi Charan Dass (hereinafter referred to as A-19), Shri Abhay Partap Singh (hereinafter referred to as A-20), and Shri Haji Gulam Mohd. Khan (hereinafter referred to as A-21), *vide* three different charge-sheets filed in the court under section 173 Cr.P.C. First charge-sheet was filled on 30-10-1996. In furtherance of that charge-sheet second and third charge-sheets were filed Under section 173(8) Cr.P.C. on 9.12.1996 and 22.1.1997 respectively.

SHAILENDRA MEHTO BECAME APPROVER – STATEMENT OF APPROVER AND CHARGE-SHEET – DISCLOSED CONSPIRACY BETWEEN A1, A2, A7 TO A14 AS BRIBE-GIVERS AND A3 TO A6 AND A15 TO A21 AND LATE MUNDA AS BRIBE TAKERS – CBI COURT

4. The case of the prosecution as revealed from the respective charge sheets and the statement of the approver Shailender Mahto recorded under section 164, Cr.P.C. is that monsoon session of 10th Lok Sabha was scheduled to commence on 26.7.1993. Much prior to the commencement of monsoon session it was clear that opposition parties intended to bring no confidence motion against the minority government headed by accused P.V. Narasimha Rao (A-1), At that point of time effective strength of Lok Sabha was 528 and strength of Congress (I) members in the Lok Sabha was

251. Thus, there was a real possibility of defeat of the government on the floor of the house. In order to avoid that situation, a conspiracy was hatched between accused Shri Narasimha Rao (A-1) and his supporters namely Captain Satish Sharma (A-2), Shri Buta Singh (A-7), Shri V. Rajeshwar Rao (A-8), Shri H.M. Revanna (A-9), Shri Ramalinga Reddy (A-10), Shri M. Veerappa Moily (A-11), Shri D.K. Audikeshvulu (A-12), Shri M. Thimmegawda (A-13), and Shri Bhajan Lal (A-14) to procure the support of sufficient number of Members of Parliament belonging to the opposition for the government by luring them with the offer of bribe. On the other hand, some members of parliament belonging to the opposition namely 4 JMM, MPs Suraj Mandal (A-3), Shibu Soren (A-4), Simon Marandi (A-5), approver Shailender Mahto and Janta Dal (A) M.Ps namely Shri Ajit Singh (A-15) Shri Ram Lakhan Singh Yadav (A-16), Shri Ram Sharan Yadav (A-17) Shri Roshan Lal (A-18), Shri Anadi Charan Dass (A-19), Abhay Partap Singh (A-20), Shri Hazi Gulam Mohd. Khan (A-21) and late Shri G.C. Munda also smelled the opportunity and started the efforts to extract maximum advantage from the situation. As a result, a multi cornered conspiracy was hatched amongst A-1 to A-21 and late Shri G.C. Munda with the object to defeat the no confidence motion moved by Shri Ajay Mukhopadhaya by illegally securing the votes of some members of parliament namely A-2 to A-6, A-15 to A-21 and late Shri G.C. Munda against the no confidence motion by giving of bribe to those members of parliament and acceptance of bribe by those members of parliament, In order to achieve the object of the conspiracy various participants played different roles at Delhi and Bangalore. Shri P.V. Narasimha Rao was the kingpin of the conspiracy.

BRIBE-GIVERS MOVED IN SUPERSONIC SPEED TO DELIVER MONEY IN LAKHS – TO BRIBE-TAKERS – CBI

5. It is alleged that hectic political activities to save the government started in July, 1993. Capt. Satish Sharma (A-2) took active role in the conspiracy and he mobilised and provided the funds for bribing the opposition members, It is alleged that at the relevant time, Captain Satish Sharma was the Minister of Petroleum in the Government headed by Shri P.V. Narasimha Rao (A-1). Shri B.N. Safaya was his Additional Private Secretary. Shri B.N. Safaya during the period between April, 1993 to May, 1994 received substantial amounts on behalf of Captain Satish Sharma from M/s. Jindal Saw Pipes, M/s Videocon International Limited, M/s. Essar Group of Companies, M/s. Reliance Industries Limited, and M/s. Bindal Agro Industries. After receiving the money from those business houses, Shri B.N. Safaya used to inform Captain Satish Sharma on telephone and then carry the suitcases containing money to Captain Satish Sharma (A-2). It is alleged that on 24-7-1993 one party was hosted by Captain Satish Sharma at his residence. During said party some suitcases supposedly containing money were brought from the farm house of Captain Satish Sharma. On 25.7.1993 in the morning, Captain Satish Sharma visited the residence of Shri P.V. Narashimha Rao. Even accused Buta Singh (A-7) also visited the residence of Shri P.V. Narasimha Rao (A-1) in the morning of 25-7-1993. It is also alleged that around 30th or 31st of July, 1993 Simon Marandi (A-5) visited Shri B.N. Safaya, Additional Private Secretary of Captain Satish Sharma and told that he had come to collect the money which Captain Satish Sharma had promised and after confirming from Captain Satish Sharma, Shri B.N. Safaya brought a sum of Rs. 10 lakhs from the residence of Captain Satish Sharma and delivered it to Simon Marandi in the evening.

JMM MPs ALSO WANTED TO EXPLOIT THIS OPPORTUNITY – CBI

6. It is also alleged that four J.M.M., M.Ps namely Shri Suraj Mandal (A-3), Shibu Soren (A-4), Shri Simon Marandi (A-5) and approver Shri Shailender Mahto

(A-6) did realise the potential of the situation. Thus, they got together in order to extract maximum advantage out of the predicament of Congress (I) Govt. Approver Shailender Mahto approached Shri Ashok Rao Deshmukh, M.P. few days before the voting on no confidence motion and requested him to arrange a direct meeting between him and the Prime Minister Shri P.V. Narasimha Rao (A-1), as he alongwith other three J.M.M. M.Ps namely Suraj Mandal, Shibu Soren and Simon Marandi (A-3 to A-5) wanted to vote against no confidence motion, if some of their demands were met. On 25-7-93 Shri Ashok Rao Deshmukh met accused Shri P.V. Narasimha Rao (A-1) and apprised him about said talks with approver Shailendar Mahto. Shri P.V. Narasimha Rao (A-1) told him to ascertain the demands of J.M.M. M.Ps. Thereafter, Shailender Mahto informed Shri Ashok Rao Deshmukh that they would put their demands directly to the Prime Minister. This information was conveyed by Shri Ashok Rao Deshmukh to Shri P.V. Narasimha Rao (A-1) who then advised Ashok Rao Deshmukh to take J.M.M. M.Ps to Shri V. Rajeshwar Rao (A-8) for further discussion.

7. Shri Ashok Rao Deshmukh contacted Shri V. Rajeshwar Rao (A-8) on 26-7-1993 and fixed a meeting between J.M.M., M.Ps and V. Rajeshwar Rao (A-8) for 11.00 A.M. At the stipulated time, J.M.M. M.Ps arrived at Andhra Bhawan and Shri Ashok Rao Deshmukh took them to the residence of accused V. Rajeshwar Rao (A-8), 7-Swaranamukh Apartments, Andhra Bhavan. V. Rajeshwar Rao (A-8) also confirmed about the message received by him from Shri P.V. Narasimha Rao and thereafter Shri Ashok Rao Deshmukh left the flat. It is alleged that Shri V. Rajeshwar Rao (A-8) had a separate conversation with Suraj Mandal (A-3) and made some offer to him. After said discussion, they came back to the room and thereafter J.M.M. M.Ps left the residence of Shri V. Rajeshwar Rao (A-8). Suraj Mandal (A-3) told other J.M.M. M.Ps (A-4 to A-6) that discussion with V. Rajeshwar Rao (A-8) was not fruitful as he was offering a meagre amount and he suggested a direct meeting with the Prime Minister. In the evening of 26-7-93, all the four J.M.M. M.Ps A-3 to A-6 collected at the residence of Shibu Soren. From there, they went to the residence of Shri Buta Singh and he took those J.M.M. M.Ps to the residence of Shri P.V. Narasimha Rao (A-1). It is further alleged that initially at the residence of Shri P.V. Narasimha Rao, talks regarding creation of Jharkhand Council took place and Shri P.V. Narasimha Rao (A-1) assured that he would call for the file relating to creation of Jharkhand Council from the ministry and do the needful. Thereafter Suraj Mandal (A-3), P.V. Narasimha Rao (A-1) and Buta Singh (A-7) went to a separate room for sometime. After the discussion, they came out from the said room and accused P.V. Narasimha Rao (A-1) told the other J.M.M., M.Ps (A-4 to A-6) that he wanted their help for the moment and in return he would also help them and fulfill the promises made to Suraj Mandal (A-3) in the closed door discussion. While coming back from the residence of Shri P.V. Narasimha Rao (A-1) on the insistence of Shailender Mahto (approver) and Shibu Soren (A-4), Suraj Mandal (A-3) informed that the closed door discussion was to their advantage. He further informed that talks regarding payment of money to them had taken place, but the amount to be paid was not specified.

'NO-CONFIDENCE MOTION' – PUT TO VOTE ON 28.7.1993 – WAS DEFEATED WITH HELP OF JMM MP – JD(A) BREAK-AWAY GROUP – JMM MPs RECEIVED MONEY – CBI

8. On 26-7-1993, no confidence motion moved by Shri Ajay Mukhopadhaya, M.P was put to discussion. After the conclusion of debate, motion was put to vote on 28.7.1993 and it was defeated with the help of votes given by J.M.M. M.Ps (A-3 to A-6) and Janta Dal break away group M.Ps (A-16 to A-21) and late Shri G.C. Munda, M.P.).

8A. It is further alleged that on 29-7-1993 at about 8.00 A.M., 4-5 persons visited the residence of Suraj Mandal at 14 Ferozeshah Road, New Delhi and delivered five suitcases and one bag which were kept locked in a room. It is also alleged that in the same morning in pursuance of the telephone call from Suraj Mandal (A-3), approvar Shailender Mahto (A-6) visited his residence. Accused V. Rajeshwar Rao (A-8) was already present there and in his presence Suraj Mandal (A-3) told the approver Shailender Mahto (A-6) that Rs. 50 lakhs have already been paid and remaining amount would be paid within two days. During said conversation accused V. Rajeshwar Rao (A-8) informed that all the J.M.M. M.Ps (A-3 to A-6) would be paid Rs. 50 lakhs each and the break away group of Ram Lakhan Singh Yadav (A-16) would also be paid Rs. 50 lakhs each besides the allotment of petrol pumps and residential plots of H.U.D.A. in Haryana. Accused V. Rajeshwar Rao (A-8) further informed that the M.Ps who had absented or abstained from voting on no confidence motion would be paid Rs. 30 lakhs each.

9. It is further alleged that on 30-7-1993, 3 boris and 1 suit case supposedly containing money were delivered at the residence of Suraj Mandal (A-3).

JMM MPs DEPOSITED BRIBE MONEY IN PNB NAROJI NAGAR BRANCH NEW DELHI ON 31-7-1993 IN DIFFERENT NAMES – SEPARATELY & JOINTLY – ON DIFFERENT DATES – CBI

10. According to the prosecution, the money delivered at the residence of Suraj Mandal was the bribe money which was distributed by the four J.M.M., M.Ps amongst each other and the said amount was deposited in Punjab National Bank Naroji Nagar, New Delhi with the help of one Sushil Kumar, Chartered Accountant who was maintaining his bank accounts in the said branch. It is alleged that most of the aforesaid bribe money reached Punjab National Bank, Naoroji Nagar Branch by the evening of 31-7-1993, but since it was already late and counting of such a huge cash was impossible on that date, entire cash received in the branch on 31-7-1993 was kept in the strong room. On the next day, *i.e.* 1-8-1993 money was counted and various accounts were opened as per the instructions of J.M.M., M.Ps

11. It is alleged that on the basis of final counting a sum of Rs. 30 lakhs was deposited in the S.F. Account no 17108 of Suraj Mandal (A-3) One Sugam F.D. Account No. 195 was opened in the joint names of all the 4 J.M.M. M.Ps (A-3 to A-6) with Rs. 30 lakhs. One joint S.F. Account in the name of four J.M.M. M.Ps (A-3 to A-6) was also opened with the deposit of Rs. 10,000 in order to facilitate the transfer of interest etc. from the F.D. Account. Similarly, In accordance with the earlier instruction of Shailender Mahto (A-6) one Sugam F.D. Account No. 195 was opened with Rs. 39.80 lakhs in the joint names of Shailender Mahto and his wife Abha Mahto, although his wife did not sign the account opening from. Another F.D. Account no. 194 was opened in the joint names of Shibu Soren (A-4), his wife Smt. Rupi and their two sons, Basant and Hemant with Rs. 30 lakhs. The account opening form was signed by all except Hemant Kumar. One Sugam F.D. Account No. 197 was also opened in the joint names of Simon Marandi (A-8) and his wife Smt. Sushila Hansda with Rs. 12 lakhs. Although account opening form was not signed by Smt. Sushila Hansda.

12. On 2.8.1993 Simon Marandi visited Punjab National Bank Naroji Nagar and deposited another sum of Rs. 21 lakhs in F.D. Account no. 197. After opening of Sugam F.D. Accounts by three J.M.M., M.Ps namely Shibu Soren (A-4), Simon Marandi (A-5) and approver Shailender Mahto (A-6) they also opened Saving Account Nos. 19100, 19307 and 18983 respectively on 8-10-1993, 18-9-1993 and 10-9-1993.

MONEY ARRANGED AT BANGALORE BY A-9 TO A-13 – CBI

13. It is further alleged that accused M.V. Moily (A-11) at the relevant time was Chief Minister of Karnataka. He also played an active role in the conspiracy and he was also one of the leaders who had been assigned the job of organizing funds for bribing J.M.M., M.Ps. It is alleged that Shri M. Veerappa Moily (A-11) came to Delhi on 25-7-93 by morning flight from Bangalore and he camped at Delhi till 29.7.93. During his stay he called on accused P.V. Narasimha Rao (A-1) repeatedly and he also made three attempts to contact Shri V. Rajeshwar Rao (A-8), but he could met him only on one occasion. He further called on Captain Satish Sharma (A-2), Ajit Singh (A-15) and K. Karunakaran.

14. It is also alleged that even before the visit of accused M. Veerappa Moily (A-11) to Delhi, hectic political activities were going on at his official residence at Bangalore. Shri H.M. Revanna (A-9), Shri Ramalinga Reddy (A-10), Shri D.K. Audikeshvulu (A-12) and Shri M. Thimmegowda (A-13) and others had been frequently visiting the official residence of accused M. Veerappa Moily (A-11) and some suitcases supposedly containing money were delivered by them.

15. It is alleged that accused D.K. Audikeshvulu (A-12) was very close to accused V. Rajeshwar Rao (A-8). He (A-12) was also camping at Delhi from 24-7-1993 to 29-7-1993. During said period, he had visited V. Rajeshwar Rao (A-8). Even on 26.7.1993, he was seen at residence of accused V. Rajeshwar Rao (A-8) by Shri Ashok Rao Deshmukh when he had visited said place for introducing four J.M.M. M.Ps to Shri V.Rajeshwar Rao (A-8). Shri D.K. Audikeshvulu (A-12) also left for Bangalore on 29.7.1993 by evening flight of Indian Airlines. It is alleged that Shri D.K. Audikeshvulu is the owner of number of companies/firms under various names and addresses.

16. M/s. Karnataka Breweries and Distilleries (P) Limited (hereinafter referred to M/s. K.B.D.L.) is a major liquor manufacturing company. Shri D.K. Audikeshvulu (A-12) is the Managing Director of the said company. He is also one of the partners of M/s. Sapthagiri Enterprises, which is also engaged in the business of manufacture and bottling of liquor. M/s. KBDL is maintaining Current Account No. 448 with Canara Bank, R.M.V. Extension, Bangalore. M/s. Sapthagiri Enterprises is also maintaining Current Account No. 446 with the same bank. The aforesaid two concerns are also maintaining accounts with Lakshmi Vilas Bank, main branch, Bangalore.

17. It is alleged that Shri D.K. Audikeshvulu issued Cheque Number 348507 dated 29.7.1993 for Rs. 30 lakhs on the account of M/s. Sapthagiri Enterprises drawn on Canara Bank R.M.V. Extension, Bangalore in favour of M/s. Padmavati Enterprises. He also issued cheque No. 372415 and 372414 both dated 30-7-1993 for Rs. 6,17,349 and Rs. 14,78,125 respectively favouring Shri V.P. Ramakrishna an employee of M/s. K.B.D.L.

18. The cheque No. 348507 for Rs. 30 lakhs issued in favour of M/s. Padmavati Enterprises was credited to its Current Account No. 754 held with the aforesaid bank on 30-7-1993. On the same day, the said amount was withdrawn from the current account of M/s. Padmavati Enterprises through cheque dated 30.7.1993 purported to have been signed by Sh. K. Muniraja, proprietor of the said firm. However, the cash payments against the said cheque was received by Shri Dwarka Nath, an employee of M/s K.B.D.L. The funds against other two cheques mentioned above were also withdrawn in cash on 30.7.1993. On the reverse of cheque no. 372415 issued by M/s. K.B.D.L. in favour of Shri V.P. Ramakrishna details of Rs. 50,95,474 have been mentioned which is total of the amount of aforesaid three cheques. This indicates that funds of aforesaid three cheques were received by Shri Dwarka Nath on 30-7-1993. He delivered that amount to Sh. D.K. Audikeshvulu (A-12).

19. It is also alleged that M/s Padmavati Enterprises is a non existent firm. The account opening form relating to the bank account of M/s. Padmavati Enterprises have been filled up by Shri Dwarka Nath who is a close relative of accused D.K. Audikeshvulu (A-12) and employee of M/s. K.B.D.L. That Shri Dwarka Nath filled said account opening form at the instance of accused D.K. Audikeshvulu (A-12) and said account was introduced by M/s Sreevari Enterprises having account No. 732 with Canara Bank, R.M.V. Extension, Bangalore. Said firm has also been found to be non existent.

20. It is further alleged that Shri M. Thimmegowda is the Managing Director of M/s. S.P.R. Group Holding (P) Limited. It is maintaining a Current Account No. 1968 with Canara Bank, Seshadripuram Branch, Bangalore.

21. That on 30.7.1993 Shri M. Thimmegowda approached the branch manager and applied for a temporary over-draft of Rs. 1 crore for 10 days on the pretext of meeting some urgent business commitments. The branch manager then contacted Shri V.A. Prabhu the then General Manager, Circle Office, Canara Bank, Bangalore on telephone and requested for sanction of said temporary over draft. Shri V.A. Prabhu obtained the approval on telephone and conveyed the sanction to Sheshadripuram branch after the banking hours. However, accused M. Thimmegowda insisted for withdrawal of the whole amount on 30-7-1993 itself. Canara Bank, Sheshadripuram branch then arranged the money from cash chest, Canara Bank, R.M.V. Extension. As soon as the cash was received in the branch, Shri M. Thimmegowda (A-13) issued cheques Nos. 959799 and 959798, both dated 30-7-1993 for Rs. 60 lakhs and Rs. 25 lakhs in favour of M/s Ranganatha Group and M/s. Yellamma Enterprises. He also issued a self cheque No. 959800 dated 30-7-1993 for Rs. 15 lakhs on the account of M/s. S.P.R. Group Holdings (P) Limited. The funds against the cheques issued in favour of M/s. Ranganatha Group and M/s. Yellamma Enterprises were credited to the respective accounts by way of transfer. As soon as the said funds were credited to those accounts, Shri M.S. Chelvaraju partner of M/s. Ranganath Groups and Shri T. Shivarama, proprietor of M/s. Yellamma Enterprises issued self cheque dated 30-7-1993 for Rs. 60 lakhs and Rs. 25 lakhs respectively and withdrew the cash. Similarly, Shri M. Thimmegowda also withdrew a sum of Rs. 15 lakhs against above referred self cheques drawn on the account of M/s. S.P.R. Groups Holding (P) Limited. After collecting aforesaid funds, Shri T. Shivarama was asked to leave the bank, whereas Shri M.S. Chelavuraju, accompanied Shri M. Thimmegowda to his residence alongwith said Rs. 1 crore withdrawn from the bank. After sometime, Shri M. Thimmegowda left his residence with 2 big VIP suitcases supposedly containing said Rs. 1 crore. It is further alleged that Shri M. Thimmegowda delivered those two suitcases at the residence of Shri M.V. Moily (A-11) at Banglore in the evening hours of 30-7-93. Accused H.M. Revanna (A-9) and accused Ramalinga Reddy (A-10) also arrived at the residence of accused M.Veerappa Moily (A-11) when the aforesaid suitcases were delivered, It is further alleged that Shri H.M. Revanna (A-9) and Ramalinga Reddy (A-10) remained together at the residence of Shri M. Veerappa Moily for sometime. During said period; Shri M. Veerappa Moily (A-11) asked his household servant to bring one suitcase and one hand bag from the first floor room of his residence which supposedly contained the money. Thereafter Shri H.M. Revanna (A-9) and Ramalinga Reddy (A-10) left the residence of Shri M. Veerappa Moily (A-11) in a car with 3 suitcases and one hand bag including the two suitcases delivered by accused M. Thimmegowda for Bangalore Airport.

MONEY BROUGHT TO DELHI – DELIVERED AT THE RESIDENCE OF A-3 – CBI

22. It is further alleged that accused Shri D.K. Audikeshvulu (A-12) came from Bangalore to Delhi on 30-7-1993 by Indian Airlines evening flight with one V.I.P.

suitcase supposedly containing aforesaid money withdrawn by him from the bank. Shri H.M. Revanna (A-9) and Ramalinga Reddy (A-10) also came to Delhi by the same flight alongwith said 3 suitcases and hand bag supposedly containing money. The flight landed at Delhi Airport at about 10.30 P.M. They were received by Shri Bachan Singh, Roop Ram and one Darmyan Singh attendant of M/s. Mohan Breweries & Distilleries Limited (hereinafter referred to M/s. M.B.D.L.) Guest House, who had also been detailed by Shri K. Narayanan, Care Taker to receive them. They loaded the 3 V.I.P. suitcases and one hand bag in the taxi driven by Shri Rup Ram, whereas V.I.P. suitcases brought by Shri D.K. Audikeshvulu (A-12) was kept in the Maruti Car of M/s M.B.D.L. Thereafter, at the instance of D.K. Audikeshvulu (A-12) they all left for Andhra Bhawan, where D.K. Audikeshvulu (A-12), H.M. Revanna (A-9) and Rama Linga Reddy (A-10) called on Shri V. Rajeshwar Rao (A-8) at Swaranamukhi Apartments Andhra Bhawan, New Delhi. After some discussion, they left for Hotel Claridges. It is further alleged that after making arrangement for the stay of H.M. Revanna (A-9), Ramalinga Reddy (A-10) D.K. Audikeshvulu (A-12) left for M/s M.B.D.L. Guest House. The three V.I.P. suitcases and one handbag brought by H.M. Revanna (A-9), Ramalinga Reddy (A-10) were unloaded by Roop Ram at Hotel Claridges.

23. It is further alleged that accused Buta Singh (A-7) also visited Bangalore at the relevant time. He came back from Bangalore to Delhi on 30-7-1993 by same Indian Airlines Flight I.C. No. 404 in which Shri H.M. Revanna (A-9) Shri Ramalinga Reddy (A-10) and Shri D.K. Audikeshvulu (A-12) travelled.

24. It is further alleged that in the morning of 31-7-93 Roop Ram taxi driver reached Hotel Claridges. Shri Vijay Handa and Shri Harsharan Lal, P.Ws also reached there in the car of Shri Vijay Handa. Accused D.K. Audikeshvulu (A-12) reached Hotel Claridges on 31-7-1993 at about 7.00 A.M. in the Maruti Car of M/s. M.B.D.L. Shri H.M. Revanna (A-9) and Shri Ramalinga Reddy (A-10) came out of the hotel alongwith three V.I.P. suitcases and the hand bag which they had carried from Bangalore. These were loaded in the taxi of Roop Ram and thereafter, they all left for Andhra Bhawan. On arriving at Andhra Bhawan, accused D.K. Audikeshvulu (A-12), H.M. Revanna (A-9), Ramalinga Reddy (A-10), Vijay Handa and Harsharan Lal went up stairs leaving behind the V.I.P. suitcases and hand bags in respective cars. They came down after about one hour alongwith V. Rajeshwar Rao (A-8). Thereafter, at the instance of accused D.K. Audikeshvulu (A-12) the hand bag and one VIP suitcase which were kept in the back-seat of taxi and the VIP suitcase brought by him was shifted to the white Maruti Car of Vijay Kumar Handa, who was a person well known to accused V. Rajeshwar Rao (A8). Shri H.M. Revanna (A9) thereafter sat in the taxi of Roop Ram. The white Maruti Car driven by Vijay Kumar Handa alongwith P.W. Harsharan Lal and P.W. Ganga Singh left for the residence of Suraj Mandal (A-3) at Ferozeshah Road, New Delhi and Roop Ram was asked to follow them. They visited the residence of Suraj Mandal and delivered aforesaid 4 VIP suitcases and hand bags to him. Thus, according to the prosecution, the bribe money was delivered at the residence of accused Suraj Mandal (A-3).

A-14 DELIVERED 3 PACKETS CONTAINING Rs. 1 CRORE EACH TO A-15 – SOUGHT HIS SUPPORT IN NO-CONFIDENCE MOTION – CBI

25. It is alleged that accused Bhajan Lal also played a very important role to achieve the object of the conspiracy. On 24-7-1993, he visited the residence of accused Ajit Singh in the morning. He requested Ajit Singh for supporting Congress (I) Government stating that fate of the government headed by Sh. P.V. Narasimha Rao (A-1) was in his hands. He further delivered three packets containing Rs. 1 Crore each to accused Ajit Singh as a motive or reward for seeking the support of his group for the government. Those packets were unloaded from his car by Capt. Dilawar

Singh. One of those packets, was opened after accused Bhajan Lal left and it was found to contain 200 wads of currency notes of Rs. 500 denomination.

26. It is alleged that accused Ajit Singh (A-15) wanted to gobble up entire money. However, accused Ram Lakhan Singh Yadav (A-16) caught the wind of the matter. He called on accused Ajit Singh (A-15) in the morning of 26-7-1993 and insisted for his share of Rs. 15 lakhs from the amount received by him from Bhajan Lal. Accused Ajit Singh (A-15) denied having received any amount from Bhajan Lal (A-14) and told Ram Lakhan Singh Yadav (A-16) that Bhajan Lal himself was a corrupt person who accused others of corruption. After the aforesaid incident, accused Ajit Singh (A-15) called for a meeting of M.Ps belonging to his party. During said meeting, he expressed his desire to vote in favour of no confidence motion against Congress (I) Government, This led to heated exchanges between Ram Lakhan Singh Yadav (A-16) and Ajit Singh (A-15) and both accused each other for hobnobbing and bargaining with Congress (I) Leaders. Thereafter, Ram Lakhan Singh Yadav (A-15) walked out of the meeting. Shri Ram Sharan Yadav, Roshan Lal, Abhay Partap Singh and Anadi Charan Dass namely (A-18 to A-20) as well as late Shri G.C. Munda also followed him.

RAM LAKHAN SINGH YADAV LED A GROUP OF 7 MPs OF JD(A) AS A BREAK-AWAY GROUP – A-14 PROMISED THEM HUGE MONEY – A-2 ASSURED THEM PETROL PUMPS – A-16 ASSURED A-1 OF THEIR SUPPORT – CBI

27. It is further alleged that 7 M.Ps namely Ram Lakhan Singh Yadav, Ram Sharan Yadav, Roshan Lal, Abhay Partap Singh, Anadi Charan Dass, Hazi Gulam Mohd. Khan and G.C. Munda again assembled at the residence of Ram Lakhan Singh Yadav at 4.00 p.m. During meeting they decided to form a separate entity under the leadership of Ram Lakhan Singh Yadav and vote against no confidence motion. Shri Bhajan Lal visited Ram Lakhan Singh Yadav during said meeting and he also had same secret discussion. Shri Ram Lakhan Singh Yadav spoke telephonically to Shri P.V. Narasimha Rao and assured him that his group would split by evening and Government would survive. He also pleaded that Prime Minister should take care of the rest of the things. Said meeting was also attended by Captain Satish Sharma and during these discussions, accused Bhajan Lal assured these M.Ps substantial sum in cash, Captain Satish Sharma also assured allotment of petrol pumps either to them or their family members.

28. It is further alleged that on 28.7.1993, 6 M.Ps of Janta Dal (A) break away group namely Ram Lakhan Singh Yadav, Ram Sharan Yadav, Roshan Lal, Anadi Charan Dass, Abhay Partap Singh and Late Shri G.C. Munda again assembled at the residence of Ram Lakhan Singh Yadav. On that day, Captain Satish Sharma (A-2), Bhajan Lal (A-14), V.C. Shukla, K. Karunakaran and Jitender Prasad met those M.Ps. Shri Bhajan Lal delivered some suitcases at the residence of Ram Lakhan Singh Yadav on the said day, upon which Parkash Chand Yadav, son of Ram Lakhan Singh, informed the members belonging to break away group that Bhajan Lal has fulfilled the promises which be made.

JD(A) BREAK-AWAY GROUP VOTED AGAINST THE MOTION – IT WAS DEFEATED – MONEY PROMISE FULFILLED – CBI

29. It is alleged that on 28.7.93 Shri V.C. Shukla contacted accused Bhajan Lal (A-14) on telephone and informed him that Hazi Gulam Mohd. Khan was present in his parliament house office. Accused Bhajan Lal then went to parliament house and returned after half an hour with Hazi Gulam Mohd. Khan. It is further alleged that Bhajan Lal and Captain Satish Sharma then assured that Rs. 20 lakhs would be paid to every member of Janta Dal break away group led by Ram Lakhan Singh Yadav before the voting and another sum of Rs. 20 lakhs each would be paid after the voting of no confidence motion. Besides that, they also promised the allotment of petrol pumps to these M.Ps or their family members. From the residence of Ram Lakhan Singh Yadav, all those 7 M.Ps proceeded to parliament house alongwith Bhajan Lal and they received their respective shares of Rs. 20 lakhs each before leaving for parliament on 28.7.1993. It is further alleged that subsequently on 28.7.1993 above referred 7 M.Ps led by Ram Lakhan Singh Yadav voted against no confidence motion and motion was defeated.

30. According to the prosecution, accused Ajit Singh sent Captain Dilawar Singh Sangwan to meet Hazi Gulam Mohd. Khan and Ram Sharan Yadav to persuade them to rejoin the Janta Dal (A). Both Haji Gulam Mohd. Khan and Ram Sharan Yadav admitted before Captain Dilawar Singh Sangwan about receiving a payment of Rs. 20 lakhs in cash from Bhajan Lal. They also told him about promise of allotment of petrol pumps.

A-14 MANAGED MONEY – CAMPED AT DELHI – PROCLAIMED HAVING MANAGED 7 MPs – CBI

31. It is alleged that Bhajan Lal was camping at Delhi to pursue the object of conspiracy from 23-7-1993 to 2-8-1993, except on 26-7-1993. During this period, he was in constant touch with P.V. Narasimha Rao (A-1), Captain Satish Sharma (A-2) and other accused persons. He also actively mobilized the funds before voting on no confidence motion and obtained Rs. 30/Rs.40 lakhs from the office bearers of Saraswati Kunj House Building Society for granting license to the society for colonization. It is also alleged that Bhajan Lal extended hospitality to Hazi Gulam Mohd. Khan and G.C. Munda at Hotel Rajhans from 1.8.1993 to 3.8.1993 and paid the bill for Rs. 40,000. He also provided a taxi to Hazi Gulam Mohd. Khan for a period of one month and paid the bill of Rs. 17,000. It is further alleged that accused Bhajan Lal in a public meeting at Hissar on 11.8.1993 admitted to have engineered the defection of 7 M.Ps of Janta Dal (A) within 48 hours which led to survival of Congress (I) Government.

A-16 INDUCTED AS A UNION MINISTER LATER ON – HUDA PLOTS – PETROL PUMPS ALLOTTED TO SOME MPs OF JD(A) BREAKAWAY GROUP – CBI

32. It is further alleged that as a reward, accused Ram Lakhan Singh Yadav was inducted as a union minister in the cabinet of Shri P.V. Narasimha Rao (A-1) in February, 1994. He was also allotted a plot of land in HUDA from the discretionary quote of Chief Minister *i.e.*, Bhajan Lal. Besides that Ram Sharam Yadav acquired a plot of land in Mohan Garden, Uttam Nagar, New Delhi for Rs. 2.75 lakhs during October, 1993 and constructed a palatial house costing more than Rs. 20 lakhs on the said plot. It is further alleged that son of Ram Sharan Yadav namely Ajay Akela has also been allotted a petrol pump at Khagaria District in Bihar in September, 1994 for which he applied on 10.3.1993.

SOME OF JD(A) BREAK-AWAY GROUP MPs INVESTED MONEY IN PROPERTY – BANKS – FLATS ETC. – CBI

33. According to the prosecution, Parkash Chand Yadav called one Shri Anil Sanghi, Chartered Accountant in August, 1993 and sought his advice for laundering some money received by his father. Accordingly, on the advice of Anil Sanghi, a company in the name of M/s. Patliputra Credit and Securities Limited was registered with the Registrar of companies. Account of the said company was opened with State Bank of India Main Branch, New Delhi, Thereafter, Parkash Chand Yadav started delivering cash to Sh. Anil Sanghi for arranging cheques for crediting the amount to the account of the said company. Sh. Anil Sanghi opened two current accounts in the names of M/s. Anil Sanghi and Associates and M/s. Ganpati Investment Consultants with Jammu & Kashmir Bank, NOIDA branch on 1.3.1994. It is alleged that during the period w.e.f. 5-3-1994 to 31-7-1994, Shri Anil Sanghi deposited Rs. 1.5 crores in the said accounts in cash as provided by Parkash Chand Yadav. Against those cash deposits Anil Sanghi then issued cheques from the said bank accounts in favour of M/s. Patliputra Credit and Securities Limited. Thus, as per prosecution, the amount received as bribe by Parkash Chand Yadav was laundered through said device.

34. It is also alleged that after the defeat of no confidence motion, accused Roshan Lal has deposited a sum of Rs.12.80 lakhs during July to November, 1993 in South Indian Bank and State Bank of India, Delhi and Punjab and Sindh Bank and Central Bank of India in Dehradun. He has also acquired a flat on 6-9-1993 for a sum of Rs. 9 lakhs, out of which, he paid a sum of Rs. 5,51,000 approximately till date.

JMM MPs FORGED DONATION SLIPS, PROCEEDING BOOKS ETC. LATER ON – CBI

35. It is further alleged that during the investigation of this case, in order to avoid detection, accused Suraj Mandal, Shibu Soren, Simon Marandi and Shailender Mahto, all J.M.M., M.Ps (A-3 to A-6) in pursuance of criminal conspiracy have fabricated false documents *i.e.*, donation coupons, proceeding book and books of accounts with the intention to use those documents during the judicial proceedings or in any other proceedings initiated in accordance with law before a public servant, so as to suggest that above referred amounts deposited in the bank accounts were the proceeds of donation received in favour of J.M.M. Party.

CBI FILED 3 CHARGE-SHEETS – ALLEGING COMMISSION OF OFFENCES – CBI COURT

36. On the aforesaid allegations, prosecution has filed three charge sheets seeking to try above referred accused persons for having committed offences punishable Under sections 120B, I.P.C. read with section 193, I.P.C. and sections 7, 12, 13(2) read with 13(1)(d) of P.C. Act, 1988 and the substantive offences therein.

COPIES SUPPLIED TO ACCUSED – DEFENCE PLEAS TAKEN BY THEM – REJECTED – CBI COURT

37. On appearance, accused persons were supplied with the requisite copies of the charge sheets. During the course of arguments on charge accused persons contended that no case for framing of charges against them was made out. Besides that they claimed immunity from trial in view of Article 105 of Constitution of India on the ground that trial of the case would amount to an enquiry into the motives of the members of Parliament for voting on no confidence motion. They also took a plea that a member of parliament is not a public servant within the ambit of the P.C. Act, 1988 and as such no case under P.C. Act, 1988 is made out. All the pleas of accused persons were rejected and they were directed to be charged for having committed the offence of conspiracy punishable under sections 120B, I.P.C. read with sections 7, 12 and 13(2) read with 13(1)(d) of P.C. Act, 1988 and 193 I.P.C. and substantive offences committed by respective accused persons.

DELHI HIGH COURT DISMISSED REVISION PETITIONS – SUPREME COURT GRANTED RELIEF TO MPs WHO VOTED – CBI COURT

38. Feeling aggrieved, accused persons went in revision. Hon'ble High Court dismissed the revision petition and rejected legal pleas of accused persons as well as their contentions on merits of the case. Accused persons then preferred to file Special Leave Petition in Hon'ble Supreme Court. Matter was initially heard by three Judges Bench of the Apex Court. Since important constitutional questions were involved, the case was referred to the constitution bench by the Appellate Bench. Constitution Bench disposed of the reference *vide* three different judgments. As per majority view, it was held that member of parliament is a public servant within the scope of P.C. Act, 1988.

39. The claim of alleged bribe taking MPs except Ajit Singh (A-15) seeking immunity from prosecution under Article 105 of the Constitution of India was accepted by majority judgment of the Constitution Bench of the Apex Court, However, majority view held that since accused Ajit Singh (A-15) did not vote on no confidence motion in the Lok Sabha, he could not claim immunity under Article 105 of the Constitution of India. Regarding remaining accused persons *i.e.,* alleged bribe givers, it was held that no immunity under Article 105 of the Constitution was available to them.

A3 TO A5, A16 TO A21 DISCHARGED – CHARGES AMENDED SUITABLY *QUA* ACCUSED UNDER TRIAL – CBI COURT

40. In view of the finding of the Constitution Bench of the Apex Court, accused Ram Lakhan Singh Yadav (A-16), Ram Sharan Yadav (A-17), Roshan Lal (A-18), Anadi Charan Dass (A-19), Abhay Partap Singh (A-20) and Hazi Gulam Mohd. Khan (A-21) were discharged. Charges under section 120B, I.P.C. read with sections 7, 12, 13(2) read with 13(1)(d) P.C. Act, 1988 and substantive offences under sections 7 and 13(2) read with 13(1)(d) of P.C. Act, 1988 against accused Suraj Mandal (A-3), Shibu Soren (A-4) and Simon Marandi (A-5) were dropped. Since the offence punishable under section 193, I.P.C. is a magisterial trial and it was allegedly committed much after the alleged transaction of bribing of M.Ps in furtherance of conspiracy, it was directed that separate charge sheet for offence punishable under section 193, I.P.C. be filed in the court of competent jurisdiction.

ACCUSED PLEADED NOT GUILTY – WENT ON TRIAL – PROSECUTION EXAMINED 117 WITNESSES – DOCUMENTARY EVIDENCE ALSO PRODUCED – CBI COURT

41. Charges against accused persons namely Shri P.V. Narasimha (A-1), Captain Satish Sharma (A-2), Shri Buta Singh (A-7) Shri V. Rajeshwar Rao (A-8), Shri H.M. Revanna (A-9), Shri Ramalinga Reddy (A-10), Shri M. Veerappa Moily (A-11) Shri D.K. Audikeshvulu (A-12), Shri M. Thimmegowda (A-13), and Shri Bhajan Lal (A-14) were amended suitably and they all were charged for offence punishable under section 120B, I.P.C. read with sections 7 and 12, 13(1)(d) of P.C. Act, 1988 as well as substantive offence punishable under section 12 of the P.C. Act, 1988. They all pleaded not guilty to the charge and claimed trial.

42. Accused Ajit Singh (A-15) was charged for having committed offences punishable under sections 120B, I.P.C. read with sections 7, 12, 13(2) read with 13(1)(d) of P.C. Act, 1988 as well as substantive offences punishable under section 7 and 13(2) read with sections 13(1)(d) of P.C. Act, 1988. He also pleaded not guilty to the charge and claimed trial.

43. In order to establish the existence of criminal conspiracy and the roles played by respective accused persons to achieve the object of the conspiracy, prosecution has examined 117 witnesses in all. For the sake of brevity, I am now detailing gist of the statement of witnesses relevant to the charge.

44. P.W. 102 is the complainant Ravinder Kumar. P.W. 14 Ajay Mukhopadhaya and P.W. 15 Manoranjam Bhakt are the witnesses to establish the motive and the background of the case. P.W. 104 Shri D.N. Chaudhary, DSP, P.W. 105 Inspector V.K. Pandey, P.W. 106 Shri R. Shivaji, DSP, P.W. 107 Shri Rajesh Kumar, Inspector, P.W. 108 Shri Hari Kesh, Inspector, P.W. 109 Shri M.C. Sawhney, DSP, P.W. 111,

Shri Harish Chander Sharma, Inspector, P.W. 112, Shri Parveen Kumar, Inspector, O.N.G.C. Dehradun, P.W. 114 Shri G.N. Gupta, DSP, P.W. 115 Shri Arun Kumar Sinha, DIG and P.W. 116 Shri Vivek Johri, DIG are the Investigating Officers who conducted the investigation of the case at one stage or the other.

45. In order to establish the motive of the conspiracy, existence of conspiracy as well as role played by accused Shri P.V. Narasimha Rao (A-1) main witnesses examined by prosecution are P.W. 1 to P.W. 8, P.W. 10, P.W. 13 to P.W. 15, P.W. 51 to 54, P.W. 62, P.W. 64 and P.W. 68. Out of aforesaid witnesses, P.W. 14, P.W. 3, P.W. 4, P.W. 51 to P.W. 54 and P.W. 64 are hostile witnesses and they have not supported the case of prosecution.

46. In order to establish the role played by accused Captain Satish Sharma (A-2) main witnesses examined by prosecution are P.W. 1, P.W. 3, P.W. 11, P.W. 12, P.W. 69 to P.W. 77, P.W. 86, P.W. 88 and P.W. 90. Out of said witnesses P.W. 3, P.W. 69, P.W. 70, P.W. 74, P.W. 77, P.W. 86, P.W. 88 and P.W. 90 are hostile witnesses.

47. In order to establish the role played by accused Buta Singh (A-7), main witnesses examined by prosecution are P.W. 1, P.W. 9, P.W. 13, P.W. 20, P.W. 50, P.W. 96, P.W. 100 and P.W. 101.

48. In order to establish the role played by accused V. Rajeshwar Rao in the conspiracy, main witnesses examined by prosecution are P.W. 1, P.W. 46 to P.W. 48, P.W. 64, P.W. 87, P.W. 89 and P.W. 93, Out of these witnesses P.W. 46 to P.W. 48, P.W. 64, P.W. 87, P.W. 89 and P.W. 93 are hostile witnesses.

49. In order to establish the role played by accused H.M. Revanna and accused Ramalinga Reddy in the conspiracy, main witnesses examined by prosecution are P.W. 9, P.W. 31, P.W. 32, P.W. 46 to P.W. 49, P.W. 51 to P.W. 54. Out of these witnesses P.W. 46 to P.W. 49 and P.W. 51 are hostile witnesses.

50. In order to establish the role played by accused M. Veerappa Moily in the conspiracy, main witnesses examined by prosecution are P.W. 9, P.W. 43, to P.W. 45, P.W. 51 to P.W. 54 and P.W. 58. Out of these witnesses, P.W. 51 to P.W. 53 are hostile witnesses and they have not supported the case of prosecution.

51. In order to throw light upon the role played by accused D.K. Audikeshvulu in the conspiracy, main witnesses examined by prosecution are P.W. 30, P.W. 31, P.W. 33, P.W. 34, P.W. 46 to P.W. 48, P.W. 52, P.W. 53, P.W. 56 to P.W. 59, P.W. 87 and P.W. 93. Out of these witnesses, P.Ws 46 to P.W. 48, P.W. 52, P.W. 53, P.W. 56 to P.W. 59, P.W. 87 and P.W. 93. are hostile witnesses. They have not supported the prosecution cases.

52. In order to throw light upon the role played by accused M. Thimmegowda in the conspiracy, main witnesses examined by prosecution are P.W. 24 to P.W. 28, P.W. 51, P.W. 52, P.W. 53, P.W. 58, P.W. 60, P.W. 61, P.W. 63, P.W. 65 to P.W. 67 and P.W. 84. Out of these witnesses, P.W. 51 to P.W. 53, P.W. 61, P.W. 66, P.W. 67 and P.W. 84 are hostile witnesses and they have not supported the case of the prosecution.

53. In order to establish the role played by accused Bhajan Lal in the conspiracy, main witnesses examined by prosecution are P.W. 3, P.W. 4, P.W. 20, to P.W. 23, P.W. 35, to P.W. 39, P.W. 40 to P.W. 42, P.W. 75, P.W. 76, P.W. 78 to P.W. 80, P.W. 85, P.W. 86, P.W. 88, P.W. 90, P.W. 91, P.W. 110. Out of aforesaid witnesses, P.W. 3, P.W. 4, P.W. 23, P.W. 36, to P.W. 39, P.W. 76, P.W. 78 to P.W. 80, P.W. 85, P.W. 86, P.W. 88, P.W. 90, P.W. 91, P.W. 110 are hostile witnesses and they have not supported the case of prosecution.

54. In order to establish the role played by accused Ajit Singh, main witnesses examined by prosecution are P.W. 1, P.W. 4, P.W. 82, P.W. 88, P.W. 92 and P.W. 102. Out of these witnesses, P.W. 4, P.W. 83, P.W. 88 and P.W. 92 are hostile witnesses.

PROSECUTION CLOSED EVIDENCE – STATEMENTS OF ACCUSED RECORDED – ACCUSED EXPLAINED THEIR STORY – PLEADED FALSE IMPLICATION – CBI COURT

55. Statements of respective accused persons were recorded under section 313 Cr.PC. In the said statements, accused persons have not disputed that after the election of 10th Lok Sabha, Congress (I) formed a minority government at the centre under the leadership of Shri P.V. Narasimha Rao. It is also not disputed that in July, 1993 total strength of Congress (I) M.Ps in the 10th Lok Sabha was 251 as per the list Ex. P.W. 15/B and that a no confidence motion was moved against the Congress (I) Government on 26-7-93 by P.W. 14 Shri Ajay Mukhopadhaya the then member of Lok Sabha. It is also not disputed that on 28-7-1993, no confidence motion was put to vote and it was defeated despite of the fact that Congress (I) M.Ps were in the minority in the Lok Sabha. However all the accused have denied having any association with any conspiracy to manage the defeat of no confidence motion by illegal means *i.e.* giving of bribe to the members of parliament belonging to the opposition and taking of bribe by them.

56. Shri P.V. Narasimha Rao has taken the defence that he has been falsely implicated in this case because of political reasons. He has explained that during his tenure as Prime Minister his Government faced one confidence motion, two no confidence motions and it piloted six budgets with large number of cut motions. In all those trials of strength, the government won the vote comfortably. According to him, his government survived solely on the basis of over-all good-will based on its performance. There was no effort whatsoever to mobilise strength by any monetary inducement to the members of parliament at any time.

57. Captain Satish Sharma while denying the allegations against him has come out with the explanation that case against him is false and it is result of witch-hunt against him and his family members.

58. Accused Buta Singh has also denied the prosecution version in toto. According to him, only approver Shailender Mahto has deposed against him and his version is incorrect. He has further submitted that even during the debate in parliament on 28-2-1996, he gave his explanation to the parliament denying the allegations.

59. Accused M. Veerappa Moily has denied the prosecution version in toto. In answer to question No. 132, he has stated that case against him is politically motivated false case. He has explained that he was asked to give statement against accused Shri P.V. Narasimha Rao. He refused to oblige, therefore, he has been falsely implicated. Besides that, he has submitted a written explanation Ex. DX, wherein he has explained that during the year 1992, his predecessor government had granted licences for a period of five year ending in the 1997 to various parties to manufacture and bottle arrack in the State of Karnataka. Several companies owned by accused D.K. Audikeshvulu held such licenses and accused M. Thimmegowda was also beneficiary of such licence. He has stated that his government decided to prohibit bottling and manufacture of liquor by the private parties and to grant such licence only in favour of fully owned government companies. In order to give effect to the said decision, Karnataka Ordinance No. 6 of 1993 was promulgated on 10-5-1993, which was challenged by various parties including D.K. Audikeshvulu and M. Thimmegowda in High Court of Karnataka and these writ petitions were dismissed vide judgment dated 30-6-1993. Thereafter, Special Leave Petitions were filled against the judgment of Karnataka High Court by the companies owned by Shri D.K. Audikeshvulu in Supreme Court of India and some of the effected parties also filed independent writ petitions under Article 32 of Constitution of India before the Supreme Court of India. Even in these petitions, Hon'ble Supreme Court declined to grant stay of the above referred ordinance *vide* order dated 26-7-93. Accused

M. Veerappa Moily has explained that all through Shri D.K. Audikeshvulu and M. Thimme Gowda were hostile to him and his government on account of stringent measures taken by him in favour of the public, which act has resulted in financial loss to accused D.K. Audikeshvulu's and accused M. Thimmegowda's companies. Therefore, it is most uncharitable to claim that they would have provided any funds to him or at his instance. Shri M. Veerappa Moily denied the allegations that D.K. Audikeshvulu and M. Thimmegowda were close to him and were visiting his house frequently. He denied that at his instance they provided funds for bribing the members of parliament in order to procure their votes against no confidence motion. He has denied any role in the defeat of no confidence motion in the parliament. He has explained that he was present in New Delhi between 25th to 29th of July, 1993 in connection with the above referred petitions pending before Hon'ble Supreme Court and also other official engagements in various ministries of the Union of India. According to him, he has no role in the conspiracy in question or mobilizing as well as routing of the funds to J.M.M., M.Ps.

60. Accused V. Rajeshwar Rao has denied the prosecution version in toto. He has denied any association with the alleged conspiracy or the winning over of opposition M.Ps by offering them bribe or organizing the delivery of bribe amount to the JMM MPs. He has explained that he has been falsely implicated because of political consideration.

61. Accused H.M. Revanna and accused Ramalinga Reddy have also denied the prosecution case. They have explained that they have been falsely implicated in this case because C.B.I. wanted them to give statement against P.V. Narasimha Rao and M. Veerappa Moily. Since they declined to oblige, they have been falsely implicated in this case. Both of them have submitted written explanations Ex. DY and Ex. DZ. According to their written explanations, in connection with the work of Karnataka State Unit of the Party, they both had come to Delhi to hold discussions with Congress (I) M.Ps. For that purpose, they travelled to New Delhi in the evening of 30-7-2000 by Indian Airlines flight. They stayed at the residence of Shri Hari Prasad M.P. for the night and on 31.7.1993 they held discussions with Shri Hari Prasad and other Congress M.Ps from Karnataka. Thereafter, they returned to Bangalore on 31-7-1993. They have denied having any association with the conspiracy to defeat the no confidence by bribing the Members of Parliament.

62. Accused D.K. Audikeshvulu has denied having any association with the alleged conspiracy to bribe the members of parliament. According to him, no witness has deposed against him. He has admitted that he was Managing Director of M/s. Karnataka Breweries & Distillery Limited (M/s. K.B.D.L.) and M/s. Saptha Giri Enterprises was sister concern of M/s. K.B.D.L. He has further admitted that M/s K.B.D.L. had a Current Account No. 448 and M/s. Saptha Giri Enterprises had current account no. 446 in Canara Bank, R.M.V. Extension Branch, Bangalore and that he was authorized signatory of both the accounts. He has denied that M/s. Padmavati Enterprises was sister concern of M/s. K.B.D.L. According to him, said firm was a bottle suppliers of M/s. K.B.D.L. He has admitted that on 30-7-1993 he issued one cheque no 348507 dated 29.7.1993 for Rs. 30 lakhs Ex. P.W. 30/A favouring M/s. Padmavati Enterprises and the amount of said cheque was credited to the current account no. 754 of M/s. Padmavati Enterprises. He has also admitted that he issued one cheque Ex. P.W. 29/C for Rs. 14,78,125 and another cheque of Rs. 6,17,349 Ex. P.W. 29/B, both favouring one V.P. Rama Krishna. It is submitted that both cheques were for payment of Govt. Excise duty to be remitted in Government Treasury. He has denied that after the credit of Rs. 30 lakhs in the account of M/s. Padmavati Enterprises, said company issued a self drawn cheque Ex. P.W. 29/A for Rs. 30 lakhs and the amounts pertaining to above said cheque was also collected by

Shri V.P. Rama Krishna an employe of M/s. K.B.D.L. He has denied that he brought the amounts withdrawn by cheques Ex. P.W. 29/A to Ex. P.W.29/C in a briefcase to Delhi or the said amount ultimately found way to the residence of Suraj Mandal via accused V. Rajeshwar Rao.

63. Accused M. Thimmegowda has also denied the prosecution version. According to him on 30-7-1993, he in his capacity as the Managing Director, S.P.R. Gourp Holding (P) Limited applied for a temporary over draft facility in a sum of Rs. 1 crore and the same was granted. Out of this sum, a sum of Rs. 60 lakhs was paid to the firm M/s. Ranganatha Group by means of cheque and a sum of Rs. Twenty Five Lakhs was paid to the firm M/s. Yellamma Enterprises also by means of cheque on the same day. A sum of Rs Fifteen Lakhs was withdrawn by him to meet urgent business commitments. The Mg. Partners of the two firms *i.e,,* M/s. Ranganatha Group and M/s. Yellamma Enterprises have utilized the amounts drawn by them in connection with their business. The payment of Rs, 60.00 lakhs and Rs. 25.00 lakhs to the two firms was given by way of temporary loans and the said firms have repaid the loans in question in the course of subsequent 2 or 3 months. All these transactions are reflected in the books of accounts of his company maintained in the regular course of business. The Income Tax Authorities have also accepted this position. The officials of the C.B.I. have questioned him in the course of investigation and he has supplied them relevant material. However, they put pressure on him to make false statements to suit their case and as he refused to accede to it, they have falsely implicated him in this case. He is not aware of any conspiracy as alleged by the prosecution nor he is a party to any such conspiracy. He has absolutely no role to play in the defeat of the No Confidence Motion against the Government. He is innocent.

64. Accused Ajit Singh has denied having any association with alleged conspiracy to bribe the M.Ps. He denied that he received three packets containing Rs. 1 crore each from accused Bhajan Lal as a motive or reward for ensuring the support of his group of M.Ps against no confidence motion. According to him, he consistently supported the no confindence motion and voted for no confidence motion. He claims himself to be innocent.

65. Accused Bhajan Lal has denied having any association with the alleged conspiracy. According to him, this is a politically motivated false case and he is a victim of witch-hunt. He denied that he gave bribe of Rs. 3 crore to accused Ajit Singh as a motive or reward for getting the support of the members of parliament belonging to the group of Ajit Singh against no confidence motion. He has also denied that he ever lured any member of parliament with bribe either in cash or kind in order to ensure the defeat of no confidence motion.

NO DEFENCE WITNESS EXAMINED – CBI COURT

66. No witness in defence has examined by either of the accused persons.

ACCUSED FILED WRITTEN SUBMISSIONS – MADE ORAL SUBMISSIONS – EVIDENCE PERUSED – SUBMISSIONS CONSIDERED – CBI COURT

67. I have heard the oral submissions made by Id. Special prosecutor as well as respective counsels appearing on behalf of accused persons. Ld. Prosecutor as well as accused Captain Satish Sharma, Bhajan Lal, V. Rajeshwar Rao, M. Veerappa Moily, H.M. Revanna, Ramalinga Reddy, D.K. Audikeshvulu and M. Thimmegowda have opted to file written submissions. I have carefully considered the written arguments as well as oral submissions made on behalf of the prosecution as well as accused persons and perused the material on record. I intend to discuss the relevant arguments of parties at appropriate stages in the judgment.

68. Charge against the accused persons is that they all were party to a criminal conspiracy having the object to defeat the no confidence motion moved against the government headed by accused P.V. Narasimha Rao by resorting to the illegal means *i.e.*, offering or causing to offer or giving illegal gratification to certain members of parliament belonging to the opposition namely Suraj Mandal (A-3), Shibu Soren (A-4), Simon Marandi (A-5), Shailender Mahto (Approvar A-6), Ajit Singh (A-15), Ram Lakhan Singh Yadav (A-16), Ram Sharan Yadav (A-17), Roshan Lal (A-18), Anadi Charan Dass (A-19), Abhay Partap Singh (A-20), Hazi Gulam Mohd. Khan (A-21) and late Sh.G.C.Munda, as a motive or reward for securing their votes in favour of the government.

69. Prosecution has examined 116 witnesses to prove the charge of existence of criminal conspiracy amongst the accused persons and to establish the active roles played by various accused persons in order to achieve the object of the conspiracy.

LAW ON CONSPIRACY AND MANNER OF ITS PROOF DISCUSSED – CBI COURT

70. Before appreciating the evidence led by the prosecution, I deem it necessary to have a look upon the law relating to conspiracy and the manner in which criminal conspiracy can be proved in a court of law. Section 120A of Indian Penal Code defines conspiracy as an agreement between two or more persons to do an illegal act or a legal act by illegal means. The law relating to criminal conspiracy is well settled. Apex Court while interpreting the law of conspiracy has time and again held that a conspiracy is an agreement between two or more persons to commit an offence or to do a legal act by illegal means. It is not necessary that all the participants of conspiracy must enter into an agreement for achieving the common object at one and the same time. Some of the participants of conspiracy may join it at a later stage before the achievement of the object of the conspiracy.It has also been consistently held by the apex court that conspiracy by its very nature is generally hatched in secrecy. Thus it is very rare to have direct evidence to prove a conspiracy. Thus, the conspiracy can be inferred from circumstantial evidence relating to the roles played by various participants of the conspiracy in order to achieve its object.

Reference may be made to:

(i) 1970 SCC (Cri) 274 **(Noor Mohd. Mohd. Yusuf Mobin v. State of Maharashtra).**

(ii) (1988) 3 SCC 609 **(Kehar Singh v. Delhi Administration)**

(iii) (1973) 3 SCC 805 **(Ram Narain v. State of Rajasthan)**

(iv) 1978 Cr LJ 189 **(Yash Pal Mittal v. State of Punjab)**

(v) 1995 Suppl (1) SCC 80 **(Suresh Chand Bahri v. State of Bihar)**

(vi) (1999) 5 SCC 253 **(State v. Nalini)**

71. In the latest pronouncement on law relating to conspiracy Hon'ble Justice D.P. Wadhwa of the Apex Court in the matter of **State v. Nalini, reported in (1999) 5 SCC 253** has enumerated the broad principles relating to law of conspiracy as follows:

> "Some of the broad principles governing the law of conspiracy may be summarized though, as the name implies, a summary cannot be exhaustive of the principles.
>
> 1. Under section 120A, I.P.C. offence of criminal conspiracy is committed when two or more persons agree to do or cause to be done an illegal act or legal act by illegal means. When it is a legal act by illegal means

overt act is necessary. Offence of criminal conspiracy is an exception to the general law where intent alone does not constitute crime. It is intention to commit crime and joining hands with persons having the same intention. Not only the intention but there has to be agreement to carry out the object of the intention, which is an offence. The question for consideration in a case is did all the accused have the intention and did they agree that the crime be committed. It would not be enough for the offence of conspiracy when some of the accused merely entertained a wish, howsoever horrendous it may be, that offence be committed.

2. Acts subsequent to the achieving of the object of conspiracy may tend to prove that a particular accused was party to the conspiracy. Once the object of conspiracy has been achieved, any subsequent act, which may be unlawful, would not make the accused a part of the conspiracy like giving shelter to an absconder.
3. Conspiracy is hatched in private or in secrecy. It is rarely possible to establish a conspiracy by direct evidence. Usually, both the existence of the conspiracy and its objects have to be inferred from the circumstances and the conduct of the accused.
4. Conspirators may, for example, be enrolled in a chain – *A* enrolling *B*. *B* enrolling *C*. and so on; and all will be members of a single conspiracy if they so intend and agree, even though each member nows only the person who enrolled him and the person whom he enrolls. There may be a kind of umbrella-spoke enrolment, where a single person at the centre does the enrolling and all the other members are unknown to each other, though they know that there are to be other members. These are theories and in practice it may be difficult to tell which conspiracy in a particular case falls into which category. It may however, even overlap. But then there has to be present mutual interest. Persons may be members of single conspiracy even though each is ignorant of the identity of many others who may have diverse roles to play. It is not a part of the crime of conspiracy that all the conspirators need to agree to play the same or an active role.
5. When two or more persons agree to commit a crime of conspiracy, then regardless of making or considering any plans for its commission, and despite the fact that no step is taken by any such person to carry out their common purpose, a crime is committed by each and every one who joins in the agreement. There has thus to be two conspirators and there may be more than that. To prove the charge of conspiracy it is not necessary that intended crime was committed or not. If committed it may further help prosecution to prove the charge of conspiracy.
6. It is not necessary that all conspirators should agree to the common purpose at the same time. They may join with other conspirators at any time before the consummation of the intended objective, and all are equally responsible. What party each conspirator is to play may not be known to everyone or the fact as to when a conspirator joined the conspiracy and when he left.
7. A charge of conspiracy may prejudice the accused because it forces them into a joint trial and the court may consider the entire mass of evidence against every accused. Prosecution has to produce evidence not only to show that each of the accused has knowledge of the object of conspiracy but also of the agreement. In the charge of conspiracy the

court has to guard itself against the danger of unfairness to the accused. Introduction of evidence against some may result in the conviction of all, which is to be avoided. By means of evidence in conspiracy, which is otherwise inadmissible in the trial of any other substantive offence, prosecution tries to implicate the accused not only in the conspiracy itself but also in the substantive crime of the alleged conspirators. There is always difficulty in tracing the precise contribution of each member of the conspiracy but then there has to be cogent and convincing evidence against each one of the accused charged with the offence of conspiracy. As observed by Judge Learned Hand "this distinction is important today when many prosecutors seek to sweep within the dragnet of conspiracy all those who have been associated in any degree whatever with the main offenders."

8. It is the unlawful agreement and not its accomplishment, which is the gist or essence of the crime of conspiracy. Offence of criminal conspiracy is complete even though there is no agreement as to the means by which the purpose is to be accomplished. It is the unlawful agreement which is the gravemen of the crime of conspiracy. The unlawful agreement which amounts to a conspiracy need not be formal or express, but may be inherent in and inferred from the circumstances, especially declarations, acts and conduct of the conspirators. The agreement need not be entered into by all the parties to it at the same time, but may be reached by successive actions evidencing their joining of the conspiracy.
9. It has been said that a criminal conspiracy is a partnership in crime, and that there is in each conspiracy a joint or mutual agency for the prosecution of a common plan. Thus, if two or more persons enter into a conspiracy, any act done by any of them pursuant to the agreement is, in contemplation of law, the act of each of them and they are jointly responsible therefor. This means that everything said, written or done by any of the conspirators in execution or furtherance of the common purpose is deemed to have been said, done or written by each of them. And this joint responsibility extends not only to what is done by any of the conspirators pursuant to the original agreement but also to collateral acts incidental to and growing out of the original purpose. A conspirator is not responsible, however, for acts done by a co-conspirator after termination of the conspiracy. The joinder of a conspiracy by a new member does not create a new conspiracy nor does it change the status of the other conspirators, and the mere fact that conspirators individually or in groups perform different tasks to a common end does not split up a conspiracy into several different conspiracies.
10. A man may join a conspiracy by word or by deed. However, criminal responsibility for a conspiracy requires more than a merely passive attitude towards an existing conspiracy. One who commits an overt act with knowledge of the conspiracy is guilty. And one who tacitly consents to the object of a conspiracy and goes along with other conspirators, actually standing by while the others put the conspiracy into effect, is guilty though he intends to take no active part in the crime.

KEEPING IN VIEW THESE PRINCIPLES OF LAW ON CONSPIRACY EVIDENCE EXAMINED – MOTIVE EXISTED – HELD CBI COURT

72. Keeping in view the above referred principle of law, I now proceed to analyse the evidence of the prosecution.

73. In the present case, prosecution is seeking to establish the conspiracy on the basis of evidence relating to roles played by different participants in furtherance of the object of the conspiracy *i.e.*, to defeat the no confidence motion by luring the members of parliament belonging to opposition with the offers of bribe and giving of bribe to them. Since, there is no direct evidence regarding the common agreement constituting criminal conspiracy amongst all the accused persons, the motive assumes significance. In my opinion, motive is an important factor for arriving at the conclusion regarding the existence of criminal conspiracy. It has to be looked into whether or not there was any occasion or need to bribe the members of parliament belonging to the opposition for securing their votes against no confidence motion.

74. In order to establish the motive, prosecution has examined P.W. 14 Ajay Mukhopadhaya, P.W. 15 Manoranjan Bhakt and P.W. 1 Approver Shailender Mahto. Prosecution is also relying upon document No. 3 in the list of documents namely *Lok Sabha Debates* (English Version) Tenth Series, Vol. XXII, No. 3. Wednesday, July, 28 1993 published by the Lok Sabha Secretariat, New Delhi. Although this document has not been proved by anyone, but in my opinion, the document being a public document published by Lok Sabha Secretariat containing record of proceedings of parliament is admissible in evidence and judicial notice of the contents of this document under section 57 of the Indian Evidence Act can be taken.

75. P.W. 14 Shri Ajay Mukhopadhaya has stated that he moved no confidence motion against the government of Congress (I) led by Shri P.V. Narasimha Rao (A-1) on the first day of commencement of the monsoon session 1993 *i.e.*, 26-7-1993. His aforesaid version is corroborated by the above referred Lok Sabha Debates detailed in document No. 3 which shows that no confidence motion moved by Shri Ajay Mukhopadhaya was put to vote after the debate on 28-7-1993. P.W. 15 Shri Manoranjan Bhakt was Secretary of Congress (I) parliamentary Party at the relevant time. He has stated that on 18-5-1993 he was elected as Secretary Congress (I) Parliamentary Party. In October, 1996 he handed over to CBI the list of Congress (I) members of Lok Sabha as on 1-7-1993. He has proved said list detailing the names and addresses of 251 members of parliament belonging to Congress (I) as on 1.7.1993 as Ex. P.W. 15/B, From the aforesaid evidence, it is obvious that in July, 1993 total strength of Congress (I) members in Lok Sabha was 251. Perusal of the aforesaid Lok Sabha Debate (English Version) Tenth Series, Vol. XXII, No. 3, Wednesday, July 28, 1993 published by Lok Sabha Secretariat would reveal that no confidence motion was put to vote on 28-7-1993 and it was defeated by following split:

Ayes	-	251
Noes	-	265

This imply that 516 Members of Lok Sabha voted on the no confidence motion. Since the strength of Congress (I) members in the Lok Sabha at that time was 251, it is obvious that Congress (I) party was in minority in the Lok Sabha when the no confidence motion was moved by Shri Ajay Mukhopadhaya on 26-7-1993. P.W. 1 Approver Shailender Mahto has categorically stated on oath that much before the commencement of monsoon session of 1993 opposition parties had made it clear that they would be presenting a no confidence motion against the government in the monsoon session. His version is not seriously controverted by accused persons during his cross examination or in their statements under section 313, Cr.P.C. Thus, from the aforesaid evidence, it can be safely concluded that sometimes prior to 26-7-1993 it was known in the political circles that no confidence motion would come against the government in the monsoon session and it was actually moved by P.W. Ajay Mukhopadhaya on 26-7-1993 and at that juncture Congress (I) Party was in minority in the Lok Sabha. Thus, I have no hesitation in holding that there was a real risk of the fall of government on the floor of parliament which means that there existed situation conducive to the origin of the conspiracy to win over the members of parliament belonging to opposition by luring them with the offer of illegal gratification. Thus, the motive in this case is established.

EXISTENCE OF CONSPIRACY DISCUSSED – CBI COURT

76. The motive by itself is not a proof of conspiracy. It is only a circumstance, leading to a presumption of possibility that motive might have culminated into an agreement between the accused persons resulting in a criminal conspiracy. Thus, prosecution in order to bring home the charge of criminal conspiracy is required to establish beyond doubt that above referred motive actually culminated into an agreement between the accused persons to defeat the no confidence motion by resorting to an illegal act *i.e.*, offering or causing to offer and giving of bribe to the members of parliament belonging to the opposition, resulting in a criminal conspiracy punishable under section 120B, I.P.C. read with sections 7 and 13(2) read with 13(1)(d) of P.C. Act, 1988.

77. In order to establish criminal conspiracy amongst the accused persons, prosecution is relying upon the evidence relating to the respective roles played by different accused persons to achieve the main object of the conspiracy *i.e.* to defeat the no confidence motion. As per the prosecution version, narrated in the respective charge sheets, there are three main limbs of the conspiracy in question:

78. First limb relates to the role played by accused Bhajan Lal in offering and giving of bribe (allegedly 3 crores) to accused Ajit Singh and the role played by him.

79. Second limb of the conspiracy relates to the offering as well as giving of bribe by the accused Bhajan Lal, Captain Satish Sharma as well as Shri P.V. Narasimha Rao to the members of parliament belonging to Janta Dal (A) break away group namely Ram Lakhan Singh Yadav (A-16) Ram Sharan Yadav (A-17), Roshan Lal (A-18), Anadi Charan Dass (A-19), Raja Abhay Partap Singh (A-20), Hazi Gulam Mohd. Khan (A-21) and late Shri G.C. Munda.

80. Third limb of the conspiracy relates to offering and giving of bribe by accused V. Rajeshwar Rao, accused P.V. Narasimha Rao and accused Buta Singh with the help of accused M. Veerappa Moily accused D.K. Audikeshvulu, accused M. Thimmegowda, accused H.M. Revanna and accused Ramalinga Reddy to the J.M.M., M.Ps Suraj Mandal, Shibu Soren, Simon Marandi and approver Shailender Mahto and acceptance of bribe by them.

81. For the sake of convenience, I propose to deal with the evidence of prosecution relating above said three arms of conspiracy one by one.

82. So far as this limb of conspiracy is concerned, allegations of the prosecution are that in the morning of 24-7-1993 accused Bhajan Lal visited the residence of accused Ajit Singh in furtherance of the conspiracy with a view to solicit the support of his group of M.Ps against the no confidence motion and he also delivered three packets supposedly containing Rs. 1 crore each to accused Ajit Singh as a motive or reward for his bailing out the government. It is also the case of the prosecution that when accused Bhajan Lal left, Ajit Singh opened one of those packets in presence of Captain Dilawar Singh and it was found to contain 200 wads of G.C. notes of Rs. 500 denomination each.

83. In order to prove the above said role of accused Bhajan Lal and accused Ajit Singh and subsequent conduct of accused Ajit Singh, prosecution is mainly relying upon the testimonies of P.W. 1 Shailender Mahto (approver), P.W. 4 Captain Dilawar Singh, P.W. 82 Shri Sunil Shastri, then Member of Parliament, P.W. 83 Attar Singh, driver of accused Ajit Singh and P.W. 92 Constable Onkar Prasad, the Personal Security Officer to accused Ajit Singh.

84. P.W. 82 Shri Sunil Shastri has stated on oath that he does not remember whether or not accused Bhajan Lal and Captain Satish Sharma visited accused Ajit Singh during the relevant time/period. Therefore, his testimony is of no avail to the prosecution.

85. P.W. 4 Captain Dilawar Singh, P.W. 83 Attar Singh, driver and P.W. 92 Constable Onkar Prasad were examined to establish the giving of bribe by Bhajan Lal to the accused Ajit Singh. They have not supported the prosecution case regarding the giving of bribe *i.e.* aforesaid there packets by accused Bhajan Lal to accused Ajit Singh. During their respective cross examination, they have denied the suggestions given to them in this regard by the learned prosecutor.

86. Though in his written arguments dated 29-8-2000, learned prosecutor has more or less conceded that prosecution has failed to prove this limb of the conspiracy, but he has orally submitted that Captain Dilawar Singh, P.W. 4 deposed about following facts which establish the involvement of accused Bhajan Lal and accused Ajit Singh in this limb of conspiracy.

87. According to ld. Prosecutor, P.W. 4 Captain Dilawar Singh has deposed that on 24.7.1993 accused Bhajan Lal visited the residence of accused Ajit Singh and discussed "no confidence motion" with him. He also sought support of accused Ajit Singh for the government by saying "CHAUDHARY SAHEB SAARI JIMMEWARI APKE KANDHO PAR HAI. AAP UNKI KISHTI DUBO SAKTE HAIN AUR BACHA BHI SAKTE HAIN AUR BACHANE KE LIYE MAIN AAPKE PAAS AYA HUN AAP HAMARI MADAD KARO. And, thereafter, he looked at him (Capt. Dilawar Singh) and stopped talking.

88. Capt. Dilawar Singh, P.W.4 has also deposed that one and half hour after said meeting with accused Bhajan Lal, accused Ajit Singh had a meeting with Suraj Mandal and Shibu Soren at his residence and during said meeting they discussed about having a joint strategy in relation to "no confidence motion". Similar version is given by approver Shailender Mahto, who has stated that on 24/25-7-1993, he alongwith Suraj Mandal and Shibu Soren went to the residence of accused Ajit Singh. They talked about the respective strategies to be followed on no confidence motion and accused Ajit Singh suggested that they should form a joint strategy. Thus, it is established that accused Ajit Singh also met JMM MPs on 24-7-1993 after the visit of Bhajan Lal and discussed the strategy to be adopted for "no confidence motion".

89. That P.W.64 Capt. Dilawar Singh has also deposed that Sh. Ram Lakhan Singh Yadav visited accused Ajit Singh on 26-7-1993 and protested as to why he had assured Bhajan Lal that his party would either support the government or abstain from voting, without consulting other members of the party, subsequently a meeting of Janta Dal (A) Parliamentary Party was called on 27-7-1993 at the behest of accused Ajit Singh in which Sh. Rashid Masood expressed his view to vote in favour of no confidence motion and Ram Lakhan Singh Yadav took a stand that party should either vote against the motion or abstain from voting as the accused Ajit Singh has promised to Bhajan Lal.

90. Learned prosecutor has contended that though Capt. Dilawar Singh, P.W. 4 has turned hostile on the point of passing of bribe from accused Bhajan Lal to accused Ajit Singh, above referred circumstances established from his testimony are sufficient to raise an inference of involvement of the accused Bhajan Lal and accused Ajit Singh in the criminal conspiracy. He has contended that if no money had passed from accused Bhajan Lal to accused Ajit Singh, he would not have met J.M.M., M.Ps on the same day within one and half hour to discuss the strategy on no confidence motion and accused Ajit Singh would not have suggested that his group and J.M.M., M.Ps should form a joint strategy on no confidence motion. He has also contended that the conduct of accused Ram Lakhan Singh Yadav suggests that he came to know about the aforesaid transaction of bribe between Bhajan Lal and Ajit Singh and, therefore, he insisted for his pound of flesh while protesting as to why accused Ajit Singh had cut a deal with Bhajan Lal without consulting him or other party colleagues. Learned prosecutor has contended that if no transaction of money had taken place on 24-7-1993 there was no occasion for the aforesaid conduct of Shri Ram Lakhan Singh Yadav (A-16) Janta Dal (A) M.P.

PAYMENT OF MONEY BY BHAJAN LAL TO AJIT SINGH ON 24 JULY, 1993 IN THE LATER'S HOUSE IS PROVED – CONSPIRACY IS NOT PROVED – SUPPORT OF MOTION BY A-15 ALSO RULES OUT RECEIPT OF MONEY BY HIM FROM A-14 – HOLDS CBI COURT

91. I have carefully considered the submissions of learned prosecutor. In my opinion, above referred circumstances, pointed out by learned prosecutor are not sufficient to conclusively infer participation of accused Bhajan Lal and accused Ajit Singh in the criminal conspiracy so far as this limb of conspiracy is concerned. There is no evidence on record to establish the passing of bribe money from accused Bhajan Lal to accused Ajit Singh. Perusal of the content of request made by accused Bhajan Lal to accused Ajit Singh would reveal that in the aforesaid request, there is no direct or indirect suggestion of offer of bribe or giving of bribe. Similarly, regarding the meeting with J.M.M., M.Ps version of prosecution witnesses is that during said meeting only the strategy to be followed on no confidence motion was discussed and accused Ajit Singh suggested that they should form common strategy. There is no hint in the evidence of prosecution to suggest that during said meeting with J.M.M. M.Ps, accused Ajit Singh either informed them about the visit of accused Bhajan Lal or he mentioned any illegal gratification or monetary benefit in the event of forming of joint strategy between Janta Dal (A) Group and aforesaid J.M.M., M.Ps namely Suraj Mandal (A-3), Shibu Soren (A-4), Simon Marandi (A-5) and Shailender Mahto (approver A-6) Those meetings between accused Ajit Singh and accused Bhajan Lal as well as accused Ajit Singh and J.M.M. M.Ps fall within the definition of political parleys. Admittedly, political situation in the country at the relevant time was volatile. Therefore, there is nothing unnatural in various political personalities meeting each other and discussing their strategy on no confidence motion and persuading each other. Even the conduct of Ram Lakhan Singh Yadav (A-16) by itself do not suggest that visit of accused Bhajan Lal dated 24-7-93 to the residence of accused Ajit Singh was in furtherance of criminal conspiracy unless there is some evidence on record to suggest that illegal gratification was either offered to accused Ajit Singh or was given to him by accused Bhajan Lal. On the aforesaid aspect of the matter, none of the prosecution witnesses have supported the prosecution.

92. Learned prosecutor has further contended that P.W. 4 Captain Dilwar Singh is not a truthful witness. He admittedly wrote letter Ex. P.W. 4/A to the Director of C.B.I. and alongwith said letter he enclosed his signed statement, Mark-B-3 detailing the facts within his knowledge. He has contended that perusal of Mark-B-3 would reveal that in that statement, Captain Dilawar Singh Sangwan has categorically mentioned that accused Bhajan Lal actually delivered three packets to accused Ajit Singh and one of those packets when opened in his presence was found to contain 200 wads of G.C. notes of Rs. 500 denomination each. Ld. Prosecutor had argued that Captain Dilawar Singh had falsely denied that Mark-B-3 is not the enclosure which was sent alongwith Ex.P.W. 4/A. In support of this contention, he has drawn my attention to the effect that Mark-B-3 bears the signatures of Captain Dilawar Singh Sangwan at page No. 10.

93. Captain Dilawar Singh has explained in his cross examination that he sent a four page handwritten enclosure detailing the facts within his knowledge alongwith letter Ex.P.W. 4/A. He has further explained that during the investigation his signatures were obtained by the C.B.I. officials on blank papers implying thereby that aforesaid blank signed papers have been converted into typed statement Mark-B-3.

94. Aforesaid explanation of P.W. 4 Captain Dilawar Singh is apparently false. Admittedly, he sent his written statement to the C.B.I. alongwith letter Ex. P.W./4/A. Perusal of the said letter would reveal that at the bottom there is an endorsement "encl. as above 10 pages". This imply that Captain Dilawar Singh sent a 10 page written statement to C.B.I. alongwith this letter and not a four page hand-written statement as explained by the witness. Perusal of the statement Mark-B-3 would reveal that this statement is a 10 page typed statement and it bears the signatures of Captain Dilawar Singh Sangwan at Page No. 10. Therefore, I have no hesitation in concluding that Mark-B-3 is the actual enclosure to the letter Ex. P.W. 4/A.

95. Perusal of letter Ex. P.W. 4/A would reveal that the above referred written statement Mark-B3 was sent by Captain Dilawar Singh to Director, C.B.I. in furtherance of the investigation of the case. Therefore, at the most, aforesaid statement is a statement of witness under section 161, Cr.P.C. Thus, in view of section 162, Cr.P.C. aforesaid statement is inadmissible in evidence and at the most, it can be used by the prosecution to contradict the witness in the manner provided by section 145 of the Indian Evidence Act. Thus, it is obvious that Mark-B3 cannot be used as substantive evidence to infer or conclude the guilt of the accused person.

96. However, from the aforesaid discussion, it is apparent that Captain Dilawar Singh is not a wholly truthful witness and he is concealing certain facts relating to the meeting dated 24-7-1994 between accused Bhajan Lal and accused Ajit Singh, The aforesaid suspicion however strong cannot be made basis to conclude that the meeting dated 24-7-1993 between accused Bhajan Lal and accused Ajit Singh had some criminal overtones or they are involved – any criminal conspiracy so far as this limb of conspiracy is concerned, more so, because of the fact that there is no evidence on record to prove the allegations of passing of bribe from accused Bhajan Lal to accused Ajit Singh.

97. It may not be out of place to mention that subsequent conduct of accused Ajit Singh in voting in favour of no confidence motion also belies the theory of the prosecution that he received a bribe of Rs. 3 crore from the accused Bhajan Lal for voting against the motion. Further, if the allegations of the prosecution were true then the question arises where such a huge amount of money has vanished. Investigating Agency has not been able to locate the traces of alleged bribe money either in cash or in the form of investments in property or some deposits in banks etc. This circumstance, also dilutes the above referred suspicion raised by concealment of fact by hostile witness P.W. 4 Capt. Dilawar Singh.

NO PROOF IF CAPT. SATISH SHARMA ENTERED INTO ANY CONSPIRACY WITH AJIT SINGH – HOLDS CBI COURT

98. Although, in the narrative of respective charge-sheets filed in this case, there is no allegation of giving of any money by Captain Satish Sharma to accused Ajit Singh, the prosecution has tried to establish from the testimony of P.W. 74 Shri B.N. Safaya that in the year 1993 a sum of Rs. 20 lakhs was paid by Captain Satish Sharma through his Additional Private Secretary, Shri B.N. Safaya to Sat Pal Singh, Additional Private Secretary of accused Ajit Singh on behalf of accused Ajit Singh. Aforesaid suggestion of learned prosecutor has been denied by P.W. 74 Shri B.N. Safaya in his cross examination. Therefore, said allegation is not established.

99. There is no evidence to show that accused Bhajan Lal, Ajit Singh and Captain Satish Sharma actually entered into an agreement constituting criminal conspiracy with anyone.

100. In view of my discussion above, I am constrained to hold that prosecution has failed to establish this limb of conspiracy beyond reasonable doubts.

101. Coming to the second limb of conspiracy Case of the prosecution is that Captain Satish Sharma had been receiving financial contributions from various industrial houses. Thus, he was having a capacity to provide money for bribing the members of parliament. Accused Bhajan Lal also played a role in mobilizing the fund and at the relevant time he received a sum of Rs. 30 to 40 lakhs from the office bearers of Saraswati Kunj House Building Society as a motive or reward for granting them licence for colonization. It is alleged that Captain Satish Sharma and Bhajan Lal played an active role in soliciting the support of members of parliament belonging to Janta Dal (A) break away group by luring them with the offer of cash bribe as well as allotment of petrol pumps and HUDA residential plots in Haryana to those MPs or their family members and also paying the bribe to them. It is also the case of the prosecution that accused P.V. Narasimha Rao was also in touch with those developments and during one such meeting between Janta Dal (A) break away group and Bhajan Lal, Shri P.V. Narasimha Rao had a telephonic conversation with Ram Lakhan Singh Yadav (A-16), leader of Janta Dal break away group.

MATERIAL WITNESSES WENT HOSTILE – ALLEGED BRIBING OF MPs BY CAPT. SATISH SHARMA NOT PROVED – CBI COURT

102. In order to establish the allegations that accused Captain Satish Sharma had been receiving financial contributions from various industrial houses, through his Additional Private Secretary Shri B.N. Safaya, prosecution has examined P.W. 70 Shri Kuldip Dravu, Chartered Accountant-cum Advisor to M/s. Videocon Groups of Industries, P.W. 71 Shri Sandeep Bhargava of M/s. Essar Group of Industrial P.W. 72 Shri V.N. Dhoot, Chairman of M/s. Videocon International Limited, P.W. 73 Shri Rajiv Wadhwa, Accounts Executive, M/s. Videocon International Limited, and P.W. 77 Shri Shashi Ruiya, Chairman of M/s. Essar Groups of Industries.

103. Above referred witnesses have not supported the case of prosecution regarding receiving of financial contribution by Captain Satish Sharma from various industrial houses.

104. P.W. 74 Shri B.N. Safaya during his cross examination has stated that he does not know if Prithvi Raj Jindal of M/s. Jindal Saw Pipes, Shri V.N. Dhoot owner of M/s. Videocon International Limited, Shri Shashi Ruiya of M/s. Essar Groups, Shri Dhiru Bhai Ambani and Shri Mukesh Ambani of M/s. Reliance Groups and Shri Oswal of M/s. Bindal Agro, Ludhiana used to visit Captain Satish Sharma at his official residence. He has stated that however he has knowledge that some of them have visited Captain Satish Sharma in the office of ministry. This witness had denied the suggestion of learned prosecutor to the effect that from January, 1993 onwards above referred industrial houses used to send money to Captain Satish Sharma either at his official residence or at his (B.N. Safaya) residence bearing No. 129 Pandara Road, New Delhi. The witness has also denied the suggestion to the effect that on the instructions of Captain Satish Sharma he used to receive the financial contribution from the owners/representatives of those industrial houses and thereafter he used to forward said money to Captain Satish Sharma. He has denied the specific suggestion that in April/May, 1993 a sum of Rs. 50 lakhs was brought by Shri Prithvi Raj Jindal of Jindal Saw Pipes, Hissar or that in July, 1993 and October, 1993 payments at Rs. 1 Crores each were brought by Shri Wadhwa of Videocon, Aurangabad. He has also denied that a sum of Rs. 3 crores and Rs. 2 crores respectively were sent by Essar Groups through Shri Aggarwal or Sandeep Bhargava respectively in November, 1993. He has further denied the suggestion that M/s. Reliance Industries sent a payment of Rs. 1 crore in June, 1993, Rs. 1 crore in October, 1993 and Rs. 2 crores in December, 1993 through Shri Setu Raman. He has further denied the suggestion that Bindal Agro, Ludhiana sent payments of Rs. 1.5 crores during the period w.e.f. April to May, 1993 through Anil Bhalla.

105. P.W. 70 Shri Kuldip Dravu, P.W. 72 Shri V.N. Dhoot and P.W. 73 Shri Rajiv Wadhwa have been examined by the prosecution to prove the financial contributions made by M/s. Videocon Group of Industries to Captain Satish Sharma through his Additional private Secretary P.W. 74 Shri B.N. Safaya. Aforesaid three witnesses are also hostile to the case of prosecution and they have denied having paid any amount whatsoever on behalf of M/s. Videocon Group of Industries to Captain Satish Sharma through Shri B.N. Safaya.

106. P.W. 71 Shri Sandeep Bhargava and P.W. 77 Shri Shashi Ruiya have been examined to establish that M/s. Essar Groups also made financial contributions to Captain Satish Sharma. They are also hostile to the case of prosecution. They have denied the specific suggestion put to them during cross examination by learned special prosecutor.

107. P.W. 69 Constable Rakesh Kumar was P.S.O. provided to Captain Satish Sharma, from July, 1992 till April, 1995, He is also a hostile witness and he has not supported the prosecution case.

108. Thus considering the above referred testimony of witnesses, I am of the view that prosecution has failed to establish that Captain Satish Sharma used to receive financial contributions from various industrial houses and he was in a position to finance the bribery of members of parliament in furtherance of the conspiracy.

SINCE MATERIAL WITNESSES WENT HOSTILE – ALLEGED AVAILABILITY OF FUNDS FOR BRIBING OF JD(A) BREAK AWAY GROUP BY BHAJAN LAL CM HARYANA IS NOT PROVED – HOLDS CBI COURT

109. Regarding the financial capability of accused Bhajan Lal and the role played by him in mobilizing the funds, allegations of the prosecution are that one Saraswati Kunj Cooperative Group Housing Society had applied for the licence for colonization of 150.6 acres of agricultural land in 1992-93 to the Director, Town & Country Planning, Haryana at Chandigarh. For that purpose, they contacted Shri Kuldip Singh, son of accused Bhajan Lal with the help of one architect of Preet Vihar. Shri Kuldip Singh demanded illegal gratification of Rs. 3 crores per acre for helping the society in getting the license for colonization and in furtherance of said deal aforesaid society had paid a sum of Rs. 3.3 crores to Shri Kuldip Singh. It is also the case of prosecution that aforesaid amount was paid from time to time and in the end of July, 1993 a demand was made through Shri Subhash with specific instructions to make payment in currency notes of Rs. 500 denomination. Accordingly, in furtherance of said demand approximately Rs. 30 lakhs were paid to Shri Kuldip Singh in the end of July, 1993.Thus, from the aforesaid allegations, prosecution is trying to establish that accused Bhajan Lal was flushed with money which be used for bribing the M.Ps and in July, 1993 he hurriedly arranged a sum of Rs. 30 lakhs through Saraswati Kunj Cooperative Group Housing Society in the form of currency notes of Rs. 500 denomination each for the purpose of bribing the M.Ps.

110. To prove aforesaid allegations, prosecution has examined P.W. 79 Shri Ram Gopal Sharma, treasurer of the aforesaid society and P.W. 80 Iftekhar Hassan, besides P.W. 78 Shri Parveen Bhutani, Chartered Accountant and Shri Dinesh Chand Aggarwal, Commissioner of Income Tax.

111. P.W. 78 Shri Parveen Bhutani, P.W. 79 Shri Ram Gopal Sharma and P.W. 80 Shri Iftekhar Hassan are hostile witnesses and they have not supported the case of the prosecution. They were cross examined at length by learned prosecutor, but in vain. All of them have denied the suggestion of learned prosecutor regarding the meeting of P.W. Iftekhar Hassan and Ram Gopal Sharma with Kuldip Singh, son of accused Bhajan Lal with the help of one Subhash. They have also denied the suggestion regarding any deal pertaining to above referred licence of colonization to Saraswati Kunj Cooperative Group Housing Society with Kuldip Singh. They have also denied the suggestion that Saraswati Kunj Cooperative Group Housing Society or its office bearers have paid any amount whatsoever to Kuldip Singh, son of Bhajan Lal in furtherance of said deal.

112. Learned prosecutor has submitted that though Iftekhar Hassan and Ram Gopal Sharma have turned hostile, but it has come in the statement of P.W. 95 Shri Dinesh Chand Aggarwal, Commissioner Income Tax that their statements were recorded by him on oath under section 131 of Income Tax Act in question answer form. Learned prosecutor has submitted that aforesaid statement of Iftekhar Hassan and Ram Gopal Sharma are proved on record as Ex. P.W. 95/A (P.W. 80/Mark-A) and Ex. P.W. 95/B (P.W. 79/Mark-B). It is argued by learned prosecutor that perusal of aforesaid statements Ex. P.W. 95/A and Ex. P.W. 95/B would show that Iftekhar Hassan and Ram Gopal Sharma in their statement on oath made during income tax proceedings have admitted the factum of their deal with Kuldip Singh, son of Bhajan Lal and they have also admitted that in furtherance of said deal they have paid an amount of Rs. 3.3 crores to accused Bhajan Lal through his son Kuldip Singh. He has further contended that above referred statement also established that in the end of July, 1993 a sum of Rs. 30 lakhs was paid by Saraswati Kunj Cooperative Group Housing Society to Kuldip Singh, son of Bhajan Lal in the form of G.C. notes of Rs. 500 denomination each. Thus, it is contended that from the above referred statements Ex. P.W. 95/A and Ex. P.W. 95/B the financial capabilities and role of accused Bhajan Lal in mobilizing the fund on urgent basis is established.

113. I do not agree with the above referred contentions of learned prosecutor. Statements Ex. P.W. 95/A and Ex. P.W. 95/B made before income tax authorities at the most amounts to either admission of the witnesses Iftekhar Hassan and Ram Gopal Sharma or their extra judicial confession regarding their involvement in a deal which amounts to commission of offence punishable under Prevention of Corruption Act, 1988. If those statements are taken as admissions relating to transaction made by the witnesses, then as per the law of admissions enumerated in sections 17 to 23 Indian Evidence Act, those admissions can be used in a trial against the said witnesses as a relevant fact. However, said admissions cannot be used as a proof of transaction against a third person *i.e.* accused Bhajan Lal. Since the witnesses Iftekhar Hassan and Ram Gopal Sharma have not supported the case of prosecution in relation to the deals mentioned in Ex. P.W. 95/A and Ex. P.W. 95/B, said previous statements cannot be used in the present proceedings as substantive evidence against accused persons under trial. If the above referred statement are taken as extra judicial confession, made by the said two witnesses before income tax authorities, then also their aforesaid extra judicial confession is of no avail to the prosecution. Said extra judicial confession *per se* is not admissible against accused Bhajan Lal because as per section 30 of the Indian Evidence Act, confession of a person is admissible against a co-accused, if they are being tried jointly for the same offence. In the present case, neither P.W. Iftekhar Hassan nor P.W. Ram Gopal Sharma are undergoing trial alongwith accused Bhajan Lal, therefore, section 30 of the Indian Evidence Act is not attracted and above referred statements *per-se* cannot be used against accused Bhajan Lal as substantive evidence. Thus, in my view, above referred statement Ex. P.W. 95/A and Ex. P.W. 95/B can only be used as previous statements made by the witnesses for contradicting them cast a doubt against the credibility. Aforesaid contradictory version in the statements Ex. P.W. 95/A and Ex.P.W. 95/B at the most raise a suspicion against the correctness of version of P.W. 79 Ram Gopal Sharma and P.W. 80 Iftekhar Hassan and it cannot be substitute for proof. Thus, under the circumstances, I am of the view that prosecution has failed to establish that accused Bhajan Lal actually had financial capability to provide funds for bribing the M.Ps or actually he played a role in mobilizing the funds.

ROLE OF BHAJAN LAL – CAPT. SATISH SHARMA IN PAYMENT OF BRIBE TO MPs OF JANATA DAL (A) BREAK-AWAY GROUP – DISCUSSED – CBI COURT

114. To establish this limb of conspiracy and the actual role played by main players namely accused P.V. Narasimha Rao (A-1), Captain Satish Sharma (A-2), and accused Bhajan Lal (A-14) prosecution is mainly relying upon the oral testimonies of P.W. 3 Devender Mukhiya, P.W. 4 Captain Dilawar Singh, P.W. 86 Raj Kumar Jain, P.W. 90 Gopi Krishan Yadav and P.W. 110 Parduman Kumar.

115. As per the allegations of the prosecution above referred persons are witnesses to various acts of accused Bhajan Lal, Captain Satish Sharma and Ram Lakhan Singh Yadav which throw light upon the relevant roles played by accused Bhajan Lal Captain Satish Sharma and P.V. Narasimha Rao to achieve the object of this limb of conspiracy.

116. P.W. 3 Devender Mukhiya is a journalist. He is a hostile witness. According to him, he does not have any knowledge regarding the facts and circumstances which led to the defeat of no confidence motion on 28-7-1993. He was cross examined at length by the learned prosecutor, but nothing incriminating against either the accused Bhajan Lal or Captain Satish Sharma or any other accused has come out in his testimony. He has denied all the material suggestions put by learned prosecutor relating to the prosecution case pertaining to the roles played by accused Bhajan Lal and Captain Satish Sharma in luring J.M.M., M.Ps or Janta Dal (A) break away M.Ps to vote in favour of government by offering and giving them illegal gratification. He has denied the suggestion that accused Bhajan Lal told him that he was keen to save government of P.V. Narasimha Rao or that Shri Bhajan Lal deputed him to stay at Delhi and keep an eye on the developments and keep Shri Bhajan Lal informed about the developments at Delhi. He has denied the suggestion of learned prosecutor that on 22.7.1993 during a meeting conducted at the Ashram of Chandraswamy, Captain Satish Sharma in presence of Ram Lakhan Singh Yadav, MP, Roshan Lal, MP, Hazi Gulam Mohd. Khan, MP, G.C. Munda, MP and Simon Marandi, MP offered illegal gratification of Rs. 50 lakhs each to the members of parliament who would vote in favour of the government besides the allotment of petrol pumps and gas agencies.

117. P.W. 3 Devender Mukhiya was further cross examined by learned special prosecutor on 22-10-1999 after seeking permission from the court. During said cross examination, witness admitted that he filed an affidavit Ex. P.W. 3/X1 in High Court of Delhi in Civil Writ Petition No. 789 of 1996 filed by Rashtriya Mukti Morcha. Certified copy of said affidavit is Ex. P.W. 3/X-1. The facts narrated in Para Nos. 1 to 3 of the affidavit narrate a different story. Those paragraphs are reproduced as follows:

> "1. I say I am correspondent by profession. In March, 1993 I came into contact with the then Chief Minister of Haryana Shri Bhajan Lal Ji. I came very close to him. In June, 1993 when Harshad Mehta levelled charge against P.V. Narasimha Rao for taking 1 crore, the entire opposition started bringing No Confidence Motion against the Government.
>
> 2. I say I was called at Chandigarh and Shri Bhajan Lal said that you somehow help to save the Government and I came back to Delhi. I contacted

many MPs and MPs of Jharkand Mukti Morcha. I introduce many MPs to Capt. Satish Sharma and his P.A. Safya Ji and got the deal settled.

3. I say, in the meanwhile, a meeting was arranged for those persons in the Ashram of Tantrik Chandra Swami. Swami Ji was abroad. Many of them – Ram Lakhan Yadav, Roshan Lal, Hazi Gulam Mohd. and V.C. Shukla and Satish Sharma and others talked with Chandra Swami over telephone. After sometime, Swami Ji called back and said that he had just talked with Prime Minister and everything would be all-right and every one would receive as settled. Next day a meeting was held in Hotel Holiday Inn and as such Rao Government was saved in July, 1993."

118. Learned prosecutor has contended that witness P.W. 3 Devender Mukhiya has been pressurized and won over by accused, that is why, he has given false version. He has contended that his aforesaid contention finds support from the allegations in the affidavit of Devender Mukhiya Ex. P.W. 3/X-1 which was filed in Hon'ble High Court of Delhi. It is argued that contents of aforesaid affidavit are sufficient to establish the active role played by Bhajan Lal and Captain Satish Sharma in furtherance of the conspiracy to win over the support of Janta Dal (A) break away group M.Ps as well as J.M.M. M.Ps by luring them with offers of bribe and giving them bribe.

119. I do not agree with this contention of learned prosecutor. In my opinion, affidavit of Devender Mukhiya Ex. P.W. 3/X-1 at the most can be termed as his previous statement relating to the facts and circumstances which led to the defeat of no confidence motion. That statement cannot be substitute for the testimony of Devender Mukhiya during trial. At the most, prosecution can use said affidavit in order to contradict the witness and shake his veracity. It may not be out of place to mention that during his further cross examination by learned prosecutor dated 12-10-1999 witness has stated that complainant Ravinder Kumar, Shri P.N. Lekhi and two others obtained his signatures on blank papers on the pretext that they were applying for security for him. He further testified that it appears that said papers have been converted into his affidavit, copy of which is Ex. P.W. 3/X-1. If aforesaid explanation of P.W. 3 Devender Mukhiya is true, then affidavit Ex. P.W. 3/X-1 loose significance. Further perusal of the averments made in para no.3 of the affidavit of P.W. 3 Devender Mukhiya Ex. P.W. 3/ X-1 would reveal that those are not consistent with the version allegedly given by witness P.W. 3 Devender Mukhiya in his statement under section 161 Cr. P.C. *i.e.,* Mark A-1. The case suggested by learned Special Prosecutor to P.W. 3 Devender Mukhiya on the basis of his statement Mark A-1 is that during the meeting conducted at the ashram of Chandraswamy, Captain Satish Sharma accused also offered a bribe of Rs. 50 lakhs to members of parliament for voting in favour of the government besides the offer of allotment of petrol pumps and gas agencies to them. On the other hand, in the averments made in Ex. P.W. 3/X-1 it is no where mentioned that during the meeting at the ashram of Chandraswamy, Captain Satish Sharma offered bribe either in cash or kind to the members of parliament. It only speaks of meeting arranged in the ashram of Chandraswamy who at that time was abroad. Above referred contradictions in the version of P.W. 3 Devender Mukhiya alleged statement Mark A-1 and in his purported affidavit Ex. P.W. 3/ X-1 casts doubt on the correctness of averments made in the affidavit Ex. P.W. 3/ X-1. Therefore, reliance cannot be placed upon the aforesaid affidavit Ex. P.W. 3/ X-1 of P.W. 3 Devender Mukhiya. Otherwise also, above referred affidavit Ex. P.W. 3/ X-1 can be termed only as a previous statement made by the witness in Hon'ble High Court and it cannot be taken as substitute for the substantive evidence *i.e.* testimony on oath of P.W. 3 Devender Mukhiya during the trial. Thus in my view, the evidence given by P.W. 3 Devender Mukhiya is of no avail to the prosecution.

120. P.W. 86 Shri R.K. Jain at the relevant time was Personal Assitant to Sh. G.C. Munda, M.P. He is also a hostile witness, According to him, accused Bhajan Lal and accused Capt. Satish Sharma had played no role in defeating the no confidence motion. During his cross examination, though he has admitted that on a day prior to voting on no confidence motion, a meeting of Janta Dal (A) break away group was held at the residence of Ram Lakhan Singh Yadav. However, he has neither admitted nor denied that said meeting was also attended by accused Bhajan Lal and Captain Satish Sharma. According to him, he was not present inside the meeting hall, therefore, he does not know who else except G.C. Munda attended said meeting. He has denied the suggestion of learned prosecutor that during his meeting accused Bhajan Lal assured the payment of huge amounts to the M.Ps belonging to Janta Dal (A) break away group for supporting the government. He has further denied the suggestion that Captain Satish Sharma also assured allotment of petrol pumps or gas agencies to those M.Ps or their family members. He has also denied the suggestion that on 28-7-1993 at the residence of Ram Lakhan Singh Yadav, Shri V.C. Shukla told Shri G.C. Munda that Prime Minister had agreed to make him Deputy Minister. He has further denied the suggestion that in the after-noon of 28-7-1993 he noticed Shri Karunakaran, Shri Jitender Prasad, Shri Bhajan Lal and Captain Satish Sharma visited the residence of Ram Lakhan Singh Yadav and joined the meeting of Janta Dal (A) break away group M.Ps. He has further denied the suggestion that on the same day, he saw men of accused Bhajan Lal carrying suit-cases in their hands to the residence of Ram Lakhan Singh Yadav. He has also denied the suggestion that on 28.7.1993 Capt. Satish Sharma reiterated his promise of allotment of petrol pump to the son of late Shri G.C. Munda or that Bhajan Lal said that petrol pumps shall be allotted to all the 7 M.Ps. He has further denied the suggestion that he over-heard personal staff of Ram Lakhan Singh Yadav saying that Bhajan Lal has brought huge cash for Ram Lakhan Singh Yadav. This witness had further denied the suggestion of learned prosecutor that in the evening of 28.7.1993 while starting for parliament house, Shri G.C. Munda told him that he would be made a Deputy Minister and petrol pump would be allotted to his son. He has also denied the suggestion that in first week of August, 1993, he accompanied Shri G.C. Munda and his family to Suraj Kund and stayed at Hotel Rajhans or that expenses for boarding and lodging of the aforesaid stay of the family of G.C. Munda were borne by Bhajan Lal. He has also denied the suggestion that before going to Suraj Kund, late Shri G.C. Munda told him that he had been paid Rs. 5 lakhs for voting against the no confidence motion, though he had been promised an amount far more than Rs. 5 lakhs. He has also denied that about a week later he alongwith G.C. Munda went to the office of Captain Satish Sharma in Shastri Bhawan and there they were made to wait for 15 minutes by Shri B.N. Safaya, Additional Private Secretary to Captain Satish Sharma or that thereafter Shri G.C. Munda starting shouting at Shri B.N. Safaya that he had been cheated by all of them as no petrol pump had been allotted to his unemployed son. He has further denied the suggestion that Captain Satish Sharma then called them to his chamber where Shri G.C. Munda reminded Captain Satish Sharma of promise and Captain Satish Sharma assured that he will do the needful in due course of time. He has denied that few days later he accompanied G.C. Munda to the residence of Ram Lakhan Singh Yadav and in his presence G.C. Munda accused Ram Lakhan Singh Yadav of having grabbed all the money for voting against no confidence motion or that he threatened to report the matter to Bhajan Lal and other politicians. He has further denied the suggestion that after some days Shri G.C. Munda visited the residence of accused Bhajan Lal at Chandigarh and protested against non-fulfilment of promises made to him and on this Shri Bhajan Lal consoled him by saying that he would talk to the prime minister to do something for him. He denied the suggestion of learned prosecutor that thereafter Shri Bhajan

Lal gave Rs 10,000 to meet his exigencies and out of the said amount Shri Munda gave him Rs. 1000. From the aforesaid version it is obvious that witness R.K. Jain, P.W. 86 has not supported the case of prosecution.

121. P.W. 90 Shri Gopi Krishan Yadav was Personal Assistant to Shri Ram Sharan Yadav in 1993. He is a hostile witness and has not supported the case of prosecution. He has denied knowledge of any meeting of Janta Dal (A) break away group namely Ram Lakhan Singh Yadav, Ram Sharan Yadav, Roshan Lal, Raja Abhay Partap Singh, late Shri G.C. Munda and Hazi Gulam Mohd. Khan which took place in the evening of 27-7-1993. He has denied the suggestion of learned prosecutor that aforesaid meeting of those M.Ps was attended by Shri Bhajan Lal and Captain Satish Sharma within his knowledge. He has also denied the suggestion that on 28.7.1993 all the M.Ps of Janta Dal (A) break away Group except Hazi Gulam Mohd. Khan gathered at the residence of Ram Lakhan Singh Yadav. He has further denied the suggestion that said meeting was joined by various congress leaders including Bhajan Lal and Captain Satish Sharma. He has also denied that when Bhajan Lal arrived at the residence of Ram Lakhan Singh Yadav on 28-7-1993 he was accompanied by some persons carrying suitcases which were kept in a room. He has denied the suggestion that thereafter he overheard Parkash Chand Yadav, son of Ram Lakhan Singh Yadav saying in presence of above referred members of parliament that Bhajan Lal has fulfilled his promise and now there was no cause for them to worry. He has also denied the suggestion that Bhajan Lal left that meeting for half an hour and returned back with Hazi Gulam Mohd. Khan. He has also denied the suggestion that he over- heard personal assistants and security persons saying that Bhajan Lal has paid a huge amount to Ram Lakhan Singh Yadav for voting against no confidence motion. He has also denied the suggestion that few days after the voting, he further heard Ram Lakhan Singh Yadav and Ram Sharan Yadav arguing on distribution of money and Ram Sharan Yadav accused Ram Lakhan Singh Yadav of having kept his share of money. He has further denied that similar allegations were made by Shri G.C. Munda. Thus, it is obvious that testimony of this witness is of no avail to the prosecution case.

122. P.W. 110 Parduman Kumar has also been examined by the prosecution to establish the role played by accused Bhajan Lal and Captain Satish Sharma in winning over the Janta Dal (A) break away group of M.Ps. He has not supported the prosecution. He was cross examined at length by learned special prosecutor, but nothing important throwing light upon the incriminating role played by Captain Satish Sharma and Bhajan Lal have come on record. He has denied all the material suggestions relating to role played by Bhajan Lal or Captain Satish Sharma during his cross examination. He has denied that on 27-7-1993 a phone call was received by him from the Prime Minister's house and he handed over the phone to Shri Ram Sharan Yadav. He has denied that he over-heard Ram Sharan Yadav saying on phone "MAIN APKE SAATH HUN AUR AAP KI SARKAR KO BACHAUNGA MAI UMEED KARTA HUN KI AAP BHI APNA WADA PURA KARENGE." He has further denied the suggestion that on 28-7-1993 at around noon time, he accompanied Ram Sharan Yadav and his son Ajay Kumar Akela to the residence of Ram Lakhan Singh Yadav, where Ram Lakhan Singh Yadav, Abhay Partap Singh, Roshan Lal, Anadi Charan Dass and Shri G.C. Munda were already present. He has also denied the suggestion that during said meeting Bhajan Lal, K. Karunakaran, V.C. Shukla, Jitendar Prasad and Captain Satish Sharma also arrived. He has also denied the suggestion that when Shri Bhajan Lal arrived, he noticed that men of Bhajan Lal carrying suitcases in their hands which were taken to a separate room in the house of Ram Lakhan Singh Yadav. He has further denied that on 28-7-93 while the meeting of those M.Ps was going on phone call came and Parkash Chand Yadav gave cordless phone to Bhajan Lal, who after a brief talk on phone left the residence of Shri Ram Lakhan Singh Yadav. He further denied the suggestion that Bhajan Lal came back within half an hour accompanied by Shri Haji Gulam Mohd. Khan. He also denied the suggestion that on 28-7-1993 at about 5.00 p.m. all the 7 M.Ps belonging to Janta Dal (A) break away group and some Congress leaders left together in different cars for Parliament House. He has further denied the suggestion that before leaving for Parliament House above referred members of parliament of Janta Dal (A) break away group except Ram Lakhan Singh Yadav made arrangement for dispatch of one suitcase each through their personal staff or sons. He has further denied the suggestion that after the voting on no confidence motion Shri Ram Sharan Singh Yadav told him that Bhajan Lal and Captain Satish Sharma have made a commitment to pay Rs. 40 lakhs each to all the defecting members of Janta Dal (A) and as per settlement Rs. 20 lakhs each was to be paid to every member of parliament of their group before their voting and balance was to be paid after voting. He has further denied the suggestion that Ram Sharan Yadav admitted having received payment of Rs. 20 lakhs. He has also denied the suggestion that few days after the vote on no confidence motion arguments took place between Ram Lakhan Singh Yadav and Ram Sharan Yadav and during said argument Ram Sharan Yadav accused Ram Lakhan Singh Yadav of having grabbed his share of money for voting against no confidence motion. He has also denied the suggestion that one and half months later Ram Sharan Yadav had altercation with Ram Lakhan Singh Yadav in the lobby of parliament house because of aforesaid reasons. However, this witness has admitted that Shri Ram Sharan Yadav has purchased a plot measuring 500 sq. yards for Rs. 2,75,000 after the voting on no confidence motion and raised construction thereon. He neither admitted nor denied the suggestion that if a sum of Rs. 20 lakhs was spent on the said construction by Ram Sharan Yadav. He has admitted that he filed a complaint Ex. P.W. 110/B at police post South on 30.7.93 alleging that Shri Ram Sharan Yadav, his son Ajay Akela and one Rajesh Kumar visited him at 42 Staff quarters, South Avenue and threatened him for giving a statement to CBI against Ram Sharan Yadav.

123. Learned prosecutor has contended that witness P.W. 110 Parduman Kumar has been pressurized and won over by the accused persons. In support of his contention, he has drawn my attention to copy of the complaint Ex. P.W. 110/B filed by P.W. 110 Parduman Kumar against Ram Sharan Yadav, his son Ajay Akela and one Rajesh at Police Post South Avenue. Allegations in the said complaint are that Ram Sharan Yadav, his son Ajay Akela and Rajesh Kumar visited the witness at 42 Staff Ouarters South Avenue on 30-7-1997 and threatened him for his having given a statement against Ram Sharan Yadav to C.B.I. There is nothing in the evidence to suggest what is the outcome of investigation of said complaint, if at all it was investigated. Therefore, in my opinion, the allegations in the complaint against Ram Sharan Yadav are not established. Even if for the sake of arguments, it is assumed that such a threat was actually extended to the witness on behalf of Ram Sharan Yadav, then aforesaid allegations could only be relevant under section 8 of the Indian Evidence Act as subsequent conduct of Ram Sharan Yadav provided he was on trial in this case. Aforesaid evidence of conduct of Ram Sharan Yadav cannot be used against the accused persons under trial to infer their involvement in any conspiracy to bribe the members of parliament for seeking their support against the no confidence motion. Thus, aforesaid complaint Ex. P.W. 110/B is not of much help to the prosecution. Since P.W. 110 Parduman Kumar is a hostile witness and he has not stated anything against any of the accused persons, his testimony is of no avail to the prosecution case.

MATERIAL WITNESSES GONE HOSTILE – CONSPIRACY OF OFFER OF BRIBE OR GIVING OF BRIBE BY BHAJAN LAL – CAPTAIN SATISH SHARMA TO JD (A) BREAK-AWAY GROUP NOT PROVED – HOLDS CBI COURT

124. P.W. 88 Om Parkash is a friend of Ajay Kumar, son of Ram Sharan Yadav, M.P. He has not supported the prosecution case. He has been cross examined at length by learned prosecutor, but nothing incriminating against the accused have come out on record. He has denied the suggestion that he was telephonically called by Shri Ram Sharan Yadav to 9 Pandit Pant Marg, New Delhi alongwith Manoj. According to him about five and half years prior to the date of his testimony *i.e.,* 29-7-1999 he alongwith Manoj and Ram Sharan Yadav went to the residence of Ram Lakhan Singh Yadav. He has denied the suggestion of ld. Prosecutor that there he was introduced to Parkash Chand Yadav, son of Ram Lakhan Singh Yadav. He has further denied the suggestion of learned prosecutor that he was informed that a group of members of parliament present at the residence of Ram Lakhan Singh Yadav wanted to save Congress (I) Government and supporters of accused Ajit Singh wanted to abduct the members of parliament of their group and as such it was enquired from him, if some musclemen could be arranged. He has also denied the suggestion of learned prosecutor that he and Manoj assured that any number of people could be arranged as and when required. He has also denied the suggestion of learned prosecutor that in the house of Ram Lakhan Singh Yadav, Anadi Charan Dass, G.C. Munda, Raja Abhay Partap Singh, Roshan Lal, Captain Satish Sharma, Jitender Prasad and Bhajan Lal were present. He has further denied the suggestion that in his presence Parkash Chand Yadav received a telephone call on cordless and he called Shri Bhajan Lal outside the room or that Parkash Chand Yadav informed Bhajan Lal that it was a call from V.C. Shukla who has informed that Mulla Ji had reached at his office at Parliament House. He has also denied the suggestion that thereafter Bhajan Lal spoke to Shri V.C. Shukla on phone and immediately after the telephone, he left the place and at that moment Parkash Chand Yadav exclaimed. "AB HAMARE AADMI PURE HO GAYE HAIN". This witness has denied the suggestion of ld. Prosecutor that after half an hour accused Bhajan Lal returned to the residence of Ram Lakhan Singh Yadav alongwith Haji Gulam Mohd. M.P. of Janta Dal (A). He has further denied the suggestion that when those members of parliament left the residence of Ram Lakhan Singh Yadav, Shri Parduman Kumar, P.A. to Shri Ram Sharan Yadav informed them that Ram Sharan Yadav would be taken as minister in the government, as a reward for saving Congress (I) Government. He has also denied the suggestion of learned prosecutor that on his enquiry Shri Ram Sharan Yadav informed him that he would be taken as Deputy Minister in the government as promised by Congress (I) leaders. He has further denied the suggestion that accused Bhajan Lal called up Shri Ram Sharan Yadav and after said conversation Shri Yadav told him that accused Bhajan Lal wanted him to inform the Prime Minister about the role played by accused Bhajan Lal for ensuring the defeat of no confidence motion. From the aforesaid testimony, it is obvious that this witness has not supported the prosecution case at all.

CAPTAIN DILAWAR SINGH ONLY – OVERHEARD RAM LAKHAN SINGH YADAV ASSURING PM ON PHONE THAT HE WILL NOT ALLOW HIS GOVERNMENT TO FALL – BRIBE MATTER NOT PROVED – HELD CBI COURT

125. P.W. 4 Captain Dilawar Singh is also a hostile witness, but he has admitted certain facts in his testimony on oath. During his cross examination by learned prosecutor, he has stated that on 27-7-1993 at about 4.00 p.m. on the directions of accused Ajit Singh he went to the residence of Ram Lakhan Singh Yadav. Shri Roshan Lal, Abhay Partap Singh, Anadi Charan Dass and Ram Sharan Yadav, M.Ps were already sitting in his drawing room. Personal Assistant of Ram Lakhan Singh Yadav took him to the bed room. There, he noticed Ram Lakhan Singh Yadav assuring someone on telephone that he would not allow the government to fall and if need be he would split the party. Captain Dilawar Singh has reproduced the words of Ram Lakhan Singh Yadav on telephone as follows:

> "SIR NISCHINT RAHIYEGA: SHAAM TAK SPLIT HO JEYEGI: CHAAR AA GAYE HAI: MUNDA ABHI AANE WALA HAI: YEH MERA VADA HAI SIR, AAPKI SARKAR NAHI JANE DOONGA: BAAKI AAP DEKH LENA: ACHCHA SIR NAMASKAR: SIR, VEH DONI BHI AA GAYA HAI: NAMASKAR SIR....... ACCHA HUA PM SAHIB SE BHI BAAT HO GAYEE".

126. He has also stated that Shri Bhajan Lal and Subramaniam Swamy were sitting in the bed room. He requested Ram Lakhan Singh Yadav to give him two minutes in private, but Ram Lakhan Singh Yadav refused. He has admitted the suggestion of learned prosecutor that he requested Ram Lakhan Singh Yadav and Shri Bhajan Lal to talk with accused Ajit Singh on telephone and remove the misunderstanding. Both of them refused to talk with accused Ajit Singh and Bhajan Lal said "tell Ajit Singh to surrender, one day he will have to come to the Congress fold". However, he has denied the suggestion of learned prosecutor that Shri Bhajan Lal also said "ISKO EK C.M. SE BAAT KARNE KI TAMIJ TO HONI CHAHIYE: AAKHIR MAIN US SAE UMAR ME BHI BARA HOON: PAISE KI KAMI THI AUR MAANG LETA, GAALI-GALOCH AUR DHAMKI SE BOLNA KAUN BARDAST KAREGA: PAISE USNE LIYE THE, MAINE NAHI". According to this witness when he was leaving the residence of Shri Ram Lakhan Yadav, he noticed G.C. Munda, M.P. also getting down from his car alongwith P.A. Shri Jain

127. From the above referred testimony of P.W. 4 Captain Dilawar Singh relating to episode dated 27-7-1993 one fact is established that Ram Lakhan Singh Yadav was assuring someone on telephone that he would not allow the government to fall and if need be he shall split the party and at that time Bhajan Lal and Subramaniam Swamy were sitting in the same bed room. Careful perusal of the words uttered by Ram Lakhan Singh Yadav while giving assurance on telephone would reveal that Ram Lakhan Singh Yadav was actually talking to the Prime Minister *i.e.*, accused P.V. Narasimha Rao, (A-1) otherwise there was no occasion for him to say "ACHA HUA PM SAHIB SE BHI BAAT HO GAYEE", However, aforesaid utterances of Ram Lakhan Singh Yadav, MP only establish that Ram Lakhan Singh Yadav had given assurance to the Prime Minister that he would not let the government fall and he also informed him that he would manage the split in Janta Dal (A) Party by the evening and he also informed the Prime Minister that 4 M.Ps had already reached at his residence and G.C. Munda was about to come. This conversation do not establish that it was in response to some offer of bribe given by either accused P.V. Narasimha Rao (A-1) or Bhajan Lal (A-14) or Subramaniam Swamy to Ram Lakhan Singh Yadav. Perusal of the case of the prosecution would reveal that Ram Lakhan Singh Yadav as per prosecution was also offered ministry in the cabinet of accused P.V. Narasimha Rao (A-1) and admittedly after the defeat of no confidence motion he was inducted in the ministry. Therefore, it cannot be ruled out that above referred response of Ram Lakhan Singh Yadav on telephone was a result of offer of ministry and not the lurement of bribe. Presence of accused Bhajan Lal at the time of said conversation by itself will not lead to an inference of existence of any criminal conspiracy to bribe Ram Lakhan Singh Yadav or his associate M.Ps unless there is some evidence on record to suggest that some offer of bribe was given or suggested to the Janta Dal (A) break away group of M.Ps including Ram Lakhan Singh Yadav or some bribe was actually given. Neither Captain Dilawar Singh nor the other witnesses examined by prosecution to prove the allegations of offer or giving of bribe to Janta Dal (A) break away group of M.Ps have deposed to support the allegations, therefore, aforesaid circumstance by itself cannot be made basis for concluding the existence of conspiracy in relation to this limb of conspiracy.

128. P.W. 4 Captain Dilawar Singh has also stated that on 28-7-1993 he went to the residence of Ram Lakhan Singh Yadav, but he was not permitted to meet him by Shri Parkash Yadav. He has also stated that at that moment he noticed Bhajan Lal coming out of the residence of Shri Ram Lakhan Yadav in his car, but he did not see Haji Gulam Mohd. Khan in his car. He has denied the suggestion of learned prosecutor that Bhajan Lal again came back in his car alongwith Haji Gulam Mohd. Khan. He has stated that on 31-7-1993 he went to find out if Haji Gulam Mohd. Khan was ready to come back to the fold of Ajit Singh Group of Janta Dal Party. He has denied the suggestion that when he persuaded Haji Saheb, he agreed to join the group of Ajit Singh provided Ajit Singh first pay him Rs. 10 lakhs which was balance from the payment received at the time of his previous defection from Janta Dal in August, 1992. He has also denied the suggestion of learned prosecutor that Hazi Gulam Mohd. Khan further imposed a condition that Ajit Singh should fulfill the commitments given to all the 7 defecting M.Ps by Shri Bhajan Lal and other Congress leaders at the residence of Shri Ram Lakhan Singh Yadav on 28-7-1993, when they resolved to split from Janta Dal (A). He has further denied the suggestion that Hazi Gulam Mohd. Khan told him that commitment made by Congress leaders in the meeting dated 28-7-1993 was to pay Rs. 40 lakhs in cash to each of the defecting M.P. alongwith the allotment of petrol pump. He has further denied the suggestion of learned prosecutor that on 31-7-1993 he also had similar discussions with Ram Sharan Yadav or that Ram Sharan Yadav confirmed having received Rs. 20 lakhs as part payment and told that balance amount was to be paid by 5-8-1993 besides the commitment of allotment of petrol pump. Aforesaid version of Captain Dilawar Singh clearly shows that he had not supported the case of prosecution in respect of the allegations regarding the offer or giving of bribe by accused Bhajan Lal, accused Captain Satish Sharma or accused P.V. Narasimha Rao to Janta Dal (A) break away group of M.Ps nor he has supported the allegations regarding the circumstances suggestive of offer or giving of bribe to those members of parliament by the accused persons. Thus, his testimony is also of no avail to the prosecution to prove the allegations relating to this limb of conspiracy. So far as his previous statement Mark-B-3 sent alongwith letter Ex. P.W. 4/A to Director, C.B.I. is concerned, I have already discussed the evidentiary value of the said previous statement and held that it can only be used for contradicting the witness in order to challenge his veracity and it is not a substitute for substantive evidence to prove the allegation.

R.K. DAYAL PROVED ARRIVAL OF CAPT. SATISH SHARMA, BHAJAN LAL, IN THE HOUSE OF RAM LAKHAN SINGH YADAV ON 28 JULY 1993 – TAKING OF SUITCASES OR BRIBE STORY NOT PROVED – HELD CBI COURT

129. Besides aforesaid star witnesses, prosecution has also examined P.W. 75 Shri R.K. Dayal who took photographs of the visitors to the residence of Ram Lakhan Singh Yadav on the day of no confidence motion. Said photographs are Ex. P.W. 75/A to Ex. P.W. 75/C. Witness has stated that those photographs were published in Indian Express dated 29-7-1993. And has proved the copy of relevant newspaper Ex. P.W. 75/B. Perusal of those photographs clearly shows that Captain Satish Sharma and accused Bhajan Lal had visited Ram Lakhan Singh Yadav. Witness R.K. Dayal also deposed that he reached at the residence of Ram Lakhan Singh Yadav on the said day at around 8.00 or 8.30 A.M. He talked with Ram Lakhan Singh Yadav who after sometime told him to leave as he was to go to parliament. He has further stated that thereafter he came out and stood at the entrance gate of the residence of Ram Lakhan Singh Yadav. However, security staff did not allow him to stand there and even threatened to break his camera, if he failed to leave. He has further deposed that thereafter he went across the road and stood at the bus stop to keep a watch for the visitors. He noticed Shri Karunakaran, Captain Satish Sharma, Bhajan Lal and Jitender Prasad visiting the house of Ram Lakhan Singh Yadav and he managed to take the photographs.

130. From the above said testimony of P.W. 75 R.K. Dayal supported by photograph Ex. P.W. 75/C and the newspaper report Ex. P.W. 75/D, it is obvious that Captain Satish Sharma and Bhajan Lal actually visited the residence of Ram Lakhan Singh Yadav, MP on the relevant day. It is also established from the testimony of P.W. 75 Shri R.K. Dayal that in the morning of 28-7-1993 there was some anxiety on the part of Ram Lakhan Singh Yadav to keep away the press reporters. This circumstance may raise a suspicion of existence of something secret, but by itself it cannot be taken as a proof of existence of conspiracy to bribe Janta Dal (A) break away group of M.Ps.

131. It may not be out of place to mention that the case suggested by learned prosecutor to the other material witnesses relating to this limb of conspiracy is that when accused Bhajan Lal arrived at the residence of Ram Lakhan Singh Yadav, his men were seen carrying certain suitcases which were taken to a room in the house of Ram Lakhan Singh Yadav. If that allegation was true, then photographer P.W. 75 Shri R.K. Dayal would have noticed and photographed those persons carrying suitcases when he took photograph of Bhajan Lal getting out of his car. However, there is no photograph to support said allegations of prosecution which of-course have been denied by the witnesses P.W. 86 Shri R.K. Jain, P.W. 90 Shri Gopi Krishan Yadav and P.W. 110 Shri Parduman Kumar.

132. Thus, in my opinion, testimony of P.W. 75 Shri R.K. Dayal and the photograph Ex. P.W. 75/C as well as newspaper report Ex. P.W. 75/D are of no avail to the prosecution.

BHAJAN LAL PROVIDED CAR TO HAZI MOHD. KHAN MP OF JD(A) BREAK-AWAY GROUP FROM 4.8.1993 TO 30.8.1993 – BRIBED BY BHAJAN LAL FOR DEFEAT OF NO CONFIDENCE MOTION NOT PROVED – HELD CBI COURT

133. In order to establish the role of accused Bhajan Lal in the conspiracy to bribe the Janta Dal (A) break Away Group of M.Ps, prosecution is also relying upon testimony of P.W. 35 Shri Naresh Arora, Counter Incharge, Haryana Tourism Office, Chanderlok Building, Janpath, New Delhi, P.W. 36 Shri K.L. Nijhawan Project Officer of Haryana Tourism Department, Chanderlok Building, Jarpath, New Delhi, P.W. 37 Ashok Kumar, driver, Haryana Tourism, Chanderlok Building, Janpath, New Delhi, P.W. 38 Constable Nizamuddin, P.S.O. to Hazi Gulam Mohd. Khan, M.P., P.W. 39 Shri Vinod Kumar, constable to Hazi Gulam Mohd. Khan, MP and P.W. 91 Shri Ashok Jolly, the then P.A. to Chief Minister, Haryana *i.e.,* accused Bhajan Lal. Aforesaid witnesses have been examined to establish that immediately after the defeat of no confidence motion, a car No. HR-37-T-0118 was hired for Hazi Gulam Mohd. Khan at the instance of accused Bhajan Lal. Said car was used by Hazi Gulam Mohd. Khan for the period w.e.f. 4-8-1993 to 30-8-1993 and the total bill after 20 per cent discount was paid by accused Bhajan Lal.

134. P.W. 36 Shri K.L. Nijhawan, Project Officer of Haryana Tourism Department, Chanderlok Building, Janpath, New Delhi though a hostile witness has stated that on 3-8-93 Shri Ashok Jolly, P.A. to Chief Minister, Haryana telephoned him and instructed him to send a taxi at the residence of Shri Gulam Mohd. Khan, M.P.

In pursuance of said phone call, he detailed Ashok Kumar, driver alongwith Car No. HR-37-T-0118 for duty at the residence of Shri Haji Gulam Mohd. Khan, MP. According to him the car was initially booked for one day, but lateron on the request of Hazi Gulam Mohd. Khan, booking was extended till 30-8-1993. In support of this contention, he has proved the log book of the car Ex. P.W. 36/B besides the bills issued for the hire of the car Ex. P.W. 36/C1 to Ex. P.W. 36/C-12. Perusal of the log book Ex. P.W. 36/B would reveal that it contains entries Ex. P.W. 36/A and Ex. P.W. 37/A-1 to Ex. P.W. 37/A-23 pertaining to the user of the car by Shri Gulam Mohd. Khan, M.P. w.e.f. 4-8-1993 till 30-8-1993. In the entry dated 4-8-1993, in colum No. 7, it is specifically mentioned "C.M. guest M.P. G.M. Khan", P.W. 37 Shri Ashok Kumar, driver has also corroborated the above referred version. He has stated that he was the driver of Ambassador Car No. HR-37-T-0118 which was used by Shri Gulam Mohd. Khan, M.P. from 4-8-1993 to 30-8-1993. He has proved the log book entries Ex. P.W. 36/A and Ex. P.W. 37/A1 to Ex. P.W. 37/A-23. This witness has stated in his cross examination by learned prosecutor that Shri K.L. Nijhawan, Project Officer had instructed him to work properly while on duty with Shri G.M. Khan as he was the guest of C.M. P.W. 38 Constable Nizamuddin and P.W. 39 Constable Vinod Kumar were the P.S.Os attached to Shri Gulam Mohd. Khan at the relevant period. Both of them have admitted that one Ambassador Car was available with Shri Hazi Gulam Mohd. Khan during said period. Though they neither admitted nor denied that aforesaid car was provided by Haryana Tourism. From the above discussed testimony of Shri K.L. Nijhawan, Project Officer and the driver Ashok Kumar of the car coupled with the log book entries Ex. P.W. 36/A and Ex. P.W. 37/A1 to Ex. P.W. 37/A-23, it is established on record that above referred Ambassador Car No. HR-37-T-0118 was provided to Shri G.M. Khan, M.P. as guest of C.M. by Haryana Tourism from 4-8-1993 to 30-8-1993.

135. P.W. 36 Shri K.L. Nijhawan had stated that 12 bills pertaining to aforesaid hire of car Ex. P.W. 36/C-1 to Ex. P.W. 36/C-12 were raised the payment of those bills was deposited by him in the State Bank of India, Chanderlok Building, Janpath, New Delhi vide pay in slip Ex. P.W. 35/D. Though, he has denied the suggestion that payments of those bills was made by P.W. 91 Shri Ashok Jolly, Resident P.A. to Chief Minister, Haryana Bhawan, He has admitted that he had gone to Haryana Bhawan to collect the payment because he had received a message that party was sitting in the canteen of Haryana Bhawan and he should collect the payment. After collecting the cash payment pertaining to those bill, he deposited said amount in State Bank of India. Similarly, P.W. 37 Ashok Kumar, driver of said car has stated that he had taken Shri K.L. Nijhawan to Haryana Bhawan for collecting the payment of those bills because party was sitting there. He has also denied the suggestion that aforesaid payment was made by Shri Jolly, resident P.A, to C.M. Haryana Bhawan.

136. P.W. 91 Shri Ashok Jolly has been examined by prosecution. Learned prosecutor has not put him any question to find out whether or not Shri K.L. Nijhawan collected the payment for the user of the said car from him at Haryana Bhawan. Ld, prosecutor has also failed to seek clarification from P.W. 36 K.L. Nijhawan or driver Ashok Kumar, P.W. 37 about the identity of the party who made the payment. Thus the evidence of the prosecution is inconclusive though it raises a strong suspicious that the payment pertaining to hire of said car on behalf of Gulam Mohd. Khan, M.P. have been made by someone at Haryana Bhawan probably at the instance of accused Bhajan Lal. Even if this fact is taken to be proved, then also this circumstance, in absence of any other evidence regarding the giving of offer or paying of bribe by accused Bhajan Lal to the Janta Dal (A) break away group of M.Ps is not sufficient to conclude beyond doubt that aforesaid facility was provided to Shri G.M. Khan, M.P. in furtherance of the conspiracy.

IDENTITY OF GUESTS WHO ENJOYED HOSPITALITY IN HARYANA GUEST HOUSES NOT PROVED – NOR ANY LINK WITH BHAJAN LAL CM – HOLDS CBI COURT

137. Prosecution has further examined P.W. 40 Shri Rajiv Sabharwal, the then Assistant P&B Manger, Hotel Rajhans, Surajkund, Faridabad, P.W. 41 Shri Uma Shankar Bhardwaj, Front Office Manager, Hotel Rajhans, Surajkund, Faridabad, P.W. 42 Shri Parveen Kohli, Deputy General Manager, Haryana Tourism Corporation posted at Hotel Rajhans and P.W. 91 Shri Ashok Jolly to establish that after the defeat of no confidence motion, Shri Bhajan Lal extended hospitality to Shri G.M. Khan and Shri G.C. Munda, M.Ps at Haryana Tourism Hotel Rajhans, Surajkund from 1-8-1993 to 3-8-1993 and the bill for boarding and lodging of aforesaid members of parliament was borne by him.

138. P.W. 42 Shri Parveen Kohli, Deputy General Manager, Hotel Rajhans has stated that some guests stayed at Kurukshetra and Pinjore suites at Hotel Rajhans during the period 1-8-1993 to 3-8-1993. Entry of the stay of those guest was not made in the guest register of the hotel as the hotel staff was not aware of the identity of those guests. He has further stated that he received instructions from the Managing Director, Shri Ashok Lavasa that those guests were V.V.I.Ps and hotel staff should not make any entry regarding the stay of those guests and they should also not raise any bill for stay or consumption of foods and beverages. He has also stated that subsequent to the departure of those guests, they received the message from the head office at Chandigarh and also from Haryana Bhawan that payment of those guest as well as bill for consumption of food and beverages be collected from Ashok Jolly, P.A. to C.M., Haryana. On this, he directed P.W. 40 Shri Rajiv Sabharwal to go to Haryana Bhawan and collect the payments.

139. P.W. 40 Shri Rajiv Sabharwal was working as Food & Beverages Manager, Hotel Rajhans, Surajkund, Faridabad. He has proved the relevant detail of consumption of food and beverages by the guests of Kurukshetra suite and Pinjore suite as Ex. P.W. 40/B. He has also proved the bill in relation to above referred consumption Ex. P.W. 40/A. He has further stated that payment of the said bill was made in his presence by Shri Ashok Jolly at Haryana Bhawan. He has proved carbon copy of the receipt of payment Ex. P.W. 40/C. According to this witness, Shri Parveen Kohli had given them instruction that those guests were V.I.Ps guests of Deputy Commissioner, Faridabad and they should not insist for the payment of individual bills and that the final bill shall be cleared as and when the guests leave or as per the instructions from Managing Director Shri Ashok Lavasa, I.A.S. P.W. 41 Shri Uma Shankar Bhardwaj has also deposed to similar effect and he has stated he was instructed by Shri Parveen Kohli, Deputy General Manager that aforesaid guests were complementary guest, therefore no entry in respect of their stay should be made in the register.

140. Above referred evidence only proves that some V.I.P. guests stayed at Kurukshetra and Pinjore suites of Hotel Rajhans Faridabad, during the period w.e.f. 1-8-1993 to 3-8-1993. However, from the aforesaid evidence, the identity of those guests is not established, as none of these witnesses have named those guests. Testimony of P.W. 91 Shri Ashok Jolly, Resident P.A. to C.M., Haryana Bhawan *i.e.* Bhajan Lal, accused has also failed to throw light upon the identity of those V.I.P. guests, whose bills were cleared by Haryana Bhawan. He has denied the suggestion that accused Bhajan Lal has entertained Hazi Gulam Mohd. Khan and G.C. Munda at Hotel Rajhans, Suraj Kund or that their bill amounting to Rs. 40,000 was paid by him under the instructions of accused Bhajan Lal. Thus, in my opinion, above referred evidence is insufficient to conclude that Hazi Gulam Mohd. Khan and G.C. Munda were entertained by accused Bhajan Lal at Hotel Rajhans, Faridabad immediately after the defeat of no confidence motion.

BHAJAN LAL'S SPEECH SHOWS THAT WITHIN 48 HOURS HE HAD WON OVER 7 MPs – DOES NOT PROVE IF HE HAD BRIBED THEM – HELD CBI COURT

141. Ld. Special Prosecutor has pointed out that prosecution has proved one video cassette Ex. P1 containing video recording of speech given by accused Bhajan Lal at Hissar on 11-8-1993. According to him, the video recording of the speech establishes the role of accused Bhajan Lal in the conspiracy. Video recording of aforesaid cassette Ex.P1 reproduced as follows:—

> "MAIN TEESRI BAR AAPKI SEWA MEIN MUKHYA MANTRI KE ROOP MAIN KHARA HUN. AB TARIF BHARAT SARKAR KI, KHULE AAM KAHTE THE BAHUT. MAINE UNSE BAAT KI, KAL RAJYA TOOT JAYEGA. KAYA BJP KE RAJYA MEIN LANA HAI, TAB UNKE KUCH SAMAJH MEIN AYI BAAT. TO UNONE AAP JANTE HAIN KI SAT MP KO ARTALIS GHANTE KE ANDAR, SAAT MP IZZAT SE TORE HUMNE OR PHARAK ITNA THA, CHAUDAN KA MATLAB SAAT AUR WOH SAAT NA TOOTTE TO AUR VOTE UDHAR DE JATE TO BARABAR HO JAATE. TO PM KO ISTIFA DENA PARTA KYON KI BAHUMAT SIDH KARNA CM YA PM KA KAAM HOTA HAI. HOUSE MEIN PARDHAN MANTRI KA KAAM HOTA SIDH KARNA."

142. Perusal of aforesaid speech of accused Bhajan Lal would show that in the above referred speech though accused Shri Bhajan Lal has talked of winning over seven Members of Parliament, but it by no mean suggests that those Members of Parliament were won over by offering or giving bribe to them, In the speech, he has said "SAAT MPs IZZAT SE TORE HAMNE " which only mean that he persuaded seven Members of Parliament to vote for the government and nothing more. Therefore, this video cassette Ex. P1 is also of no avail to the prosecution.

RAM SHARAN YADAV PURCHASED PLOT – CONSTRUCTED HOUSE OVER DOES NOT PROVE IF IT WAS BRIBE MONEY – HOLDS CBI COURT

143. Ld. Prosecutor has submitted that though material witnesses examined by prosecution to establish this limb of conspiracy have turned hostile, P.W. 110 Parduman Kumar has deposed that Shri Ram Sharan Yadav purchased a plot measuring 500 square yards for Rs. 2,75,000 sometimes before October, 1993 and he constructed a house thereon. Ld. Prosecutor has contended that this circumstance clearly shows that accused Ram Sharan Yadav have made substantial investments in the above referred plots and its construction which factor clearly suggest that he was actually bribed and that is why he came into possession of money to purchase the plot and raise construction thereon.

144. This contention of learned prosecutor is baseless because investment in acquisition of plot and construction by itself is not a circumstance to conclude that Shri Ram Sharan Yadav has taken the bribe or he was bribed. This could be an incriminating circumstance provided there is no reasonable explanation coming forth as to from where said person managed the funds. There is no evidence on record to suggest that Shri Ram Sharan Yadav has not been able to explain the above referred investments. Therefore, said circumstance is of no consequence to establish this limb of conspiracy.

CIRCUMSTANCES PROVED – NO EVIDENCE OF BRIBING JD(A) BREAK-AWAY GROUP – HOLDS CBI COURT

145. On overall consideration of discussed evidence relating to this limb of conspiracy, the prosecution has been able to establish following circumstances:

(i) on 27-7-1993, Ram Lakhan Singh Yadav, M.P. had a telephonic conversation with accused P.V. Narasimha Rao and he assured that he would not allow the government to fall and bring about the split in Janta Dal (A) party, if required:

(ii) that on 27-7-1993 at the time of said telephonic call accused Bhajan Lal and Subramaniam Swamy were also present in the bed room of Shri Ram Lakhan Singh Yadav, M.P. and accused Bhajan Lal met the break away group of M.Ps of Janta Dal (A) on the said day at the residence of Ram Lakhan Singh Yadav:

(iii) that on 28-7-1993 *i.e.*, day of voting on no confidence motion, Captain Satish Sharma as well as accused Bhajan Lal visited the residence of Ram Lakhan Singh Yadav and on the said day, all the M.Ps belonging to Janta Dal (A) break away group also collected at the residence of Ram Lakhan Singh Yadav and from there they proceeded for parliament house.

146. Aforesaid circumstances in absence of any evidence to show that accused persons or anyone of them offered or gave illegal gratification to the members of parliament belonging to Janta Dal (A) break away group are not sufficient to conclude that accused P.V. Narasimha Rao, Bhajan Lal and Captain Satish Sharma or anyone else was party to a criminal conspiracy to bribe those Janta Dal (A) break away group of M.Ps with the object to muster their support against no confidence motion by luring them with offers of bribe and giving them bribe. Since the witnesses have turned hostile, prosecution has not been able to establish this limb of conspiracy.

147. Coming to third limb of conspiracy. Case of the prosecution as per respective charge sheets is that accused P.V. Narasimha Rao, V. Rajeshwar Rao, Buta Singh, Captain Satish Sharma, Ajit Singh, Bhajan Lal, M. Veerappa Moily, Ramalinga Reddy. H.M. Revanna, D.K. Audikeshvulu and M. Thimmegowda are the party to the conspiracy relating to the giving of bribe to the J.M.M., M.Ps Suraj Mandal, Shibu Soren, Simon Marandi and Shailender Mahto (approver) as a motive or reward for their voting against the no confidence motion in order to save the government.

148. There is no direct evidence to establish a common agreement amongst all the above referred accused persons constituting a criminal conspiracy.

149. It is well-settled position of law that it is not necessary that all the conspirators should agree to the common purpose at the same time. They may join with other conspirators at any time before the intended objective of the conspiracy is achieved. What part each conspirator is to play may not be known to every one or the fact as to when a conspirator joined the conspiracy and when he left. (**Reference made to (1999) 5 SCC 253, State v. Nalini and others)**. It is also a settled position of law that criminal conspiracy is normally hatched behind the curtain in privacy, therefore, it is rarely possible to establish a criminal conspiracy by direct evidence. Usually, both the existence of conspiracy or its object have to be inferred from the circumstances and conduct of the accused or accused persons.

150. In the earlier part of my discussion, I have already concluded that there existed a motive on the part of accused P.V. Narasimha Rao and his supporters to win the support of opposition M.Ps by offering or causing to offer and giving illegal gratification to them as a motive or reward for their voting against the no confidence motion. Document No. 3 is the Lok Sabha debate (English Version) pertaining to the proceedings of Tenth Lok Sabha dated Wednesday, July 28, 1993 published by Lok Sabha Secretariat, New Delhi. Perusal of this document would reveal that J.M.M. M.Ps Shailender Mahto, Suraj Mandal, Simon Marandi and Shibu Soren had voted against the no confidence motion. Though said Lok Sabha debate has not been proved in evidence, in my opinion, those can be taken into consideration because said document is a public document published by Lok Sabha Secretariat containing the record of proceedings of parliament, as such it is admissible in evidence and judicial notice of the content of this document can be taken in view of section 57 of the Indian Evidence.

TENDER OF PARDON TO SHALENDER MAHTO IS ILLEGAL – CONTEND ACCUSED – REJECTED – OFFER OF PARDON TO SHAILENDER MAHTO WAS VALID – HOLDS CBI COURT

151. P.W. 1 Shailender Mahto is the star witness of the prosecution to establish the criminal conspiracy relating to the bribing of JMM MPs belonging to Soren Group and also to establish the respective roles played by various accused persons to achieve the end of conspiracy.

152. Learned counsel for accused P.V. Narasimha Rao has contended that tender of pardon to approver Shailender Mahto has resulted in a material irregularity, which cannot be cured by applying section 465 of the Code of Criminal Procedure, thus, his testimony cannot be read as legal evidence against the accused persons. He has argued that tender of pardon granted to an accused by a Special Judge under section 5(2) of the P.C. Act, 1988 for the purpose of section 308 Cr.P.C. is deemed to be a pardon tendered under section 307, Cr.P.C. He has pointed out that section 308(1) of the Code of Criminal Procedure, 1973 provides that if a person who has accepted tender of pardon fails to abide by conditions of pardon either by wilfully concealing anything material or by giving false evidence, he may be tried for the offence in respect of which the pardon was so granted to him or any other offence of which he appears to have been guilty in connection with the same matter and also for the offence of giving false evidence. Ld. Counsel for accused P.V. Narasimha Rao has argued that conjoint reading of section 5(2) of P.C. Act, 1988 and section 308 of the Code of Criminal Procedure clearly show that a pardon can be tendered only to a person who is a co-participant in the crime for which he can be tried and punished. Any other interpretation according to ld. defence counsel would make section 308(1) redundant.

153. Ld. defence counsel has further argued that in the present case as per the majority decision of the Constitution Bench of the Apex Court, approver Shailender Mahto being a member of parliament has an immunity from prosecution for the offence in question in view of Article 105 of the Constitution in India. That being a case in the event of his failing to make full and true disclosure of fact within his knowledge, he cannot be tried and punished for the offence. Thus, learned counsel for accused P.V. Narasimha Rao (A-1) has submitted that in the present case, pardon has been granted to Shailender Mahto ignoring the constitutional immunity available to him and section 308 (1) of the Code of Criminal Procedure, 1973. This has resulted in a material irregularity which cannot be cured, thus, it is argued that testimony of approver cannot be read in evidence against the accused persons.

154. I do not agree with the above contentions of learned defence counsel. Section 5(2) of the P.C. Act, 1988 is reproduced as follows:—

> "A special judge may with a view to obtaining the evidence of any person supposed to have been directly or indirectly concerned, in or privy to, an offence, tender a pardon to such person on condition of his making full and true disclosure of the whole circumstances within his knowledge relating to offence and to every other person concerned, whether as principal or abettor, in the commission thereof and any pardon so tendered shall, for the purpose of sub-section (1) to (5) of section 308 of the Code of Criminal Procedure, 1973 (2) of 1974 be deemed to have been tendered under section 307 of that Code."

155. Bare perusal of section 5(2) of P.C. Act, 1988 would reveal that tender of pardon can be granted by a Special Judge to any person who is supposed to be directly or indirectly concerned or privy to commission of offence.

156. In the present case, as per the evidence collected during investigation and the statement of the approver recorded under section 164, Cr.P.C. the approver has implicated himself in the criminal conspiracy under trial. He has confessed having accepted illegal gratification as a motive or reward for voting against no confidence motion. Thus, it is obvious that P.W. 1, Shri Shailender Mahto, approver has been directly concerned in the commission of offence in question. Merely because approver P.W. 1 Shailender Mahto has a constitutional immunity under Article 105 of the Constitution of India, being a Member of Parliament, it cannot be said that he is not an accomplice or co-participant in the offence or that since he cannot be tried for the aforesaid offence in view of the constitutional immunity, he could not have been granted pardon in this case.

157. In my opinion, section 5(2) of the P.C. Act, 1988, which confers upon a Special Judge power to grant pardon to an approver is independent provision of law. It is not subject to section 308 of the Code of Criminal Procedure, 1973. Section 308(1) of the Code of Criminal Procedure, 1973 comes into operation only if the approver who has been tendered pardon fails to make full and true disclosure of whole circumstances within his knowledge or gives false evidence. In that eventuality such a person may be tried for the offence in question or any other related offence provided the prosecutor certifies that the approver has either testified falsely or has wilfully concealed anything material to the trial.

158. The idea of conferring power upon a Special Judge to tender pardon to an accomplice is motivated with the object to ensure production of evidence to establish the commission of offence and role played by various accused persons in the cases in which sufficient evidence cannot be obtained by ordinary method. If the interpretation of Ld. defence counsel is accepted, aforesaid object which is the basis of section 5(2) of P.C. Act, 1988 shall be frustrated.

159. In the matter of **Suresh Chand Bahri v. State of Bihar, 1995 Supp (1) SCC 80**, apex court has held that:

> "...... the basis of the tender of pardon is not the extent of the culpability of the person to whom pardon is granted but the principle is to prevent the escape of the offenders from punishment in heinous offences for lack of evidence. There can therefore be no objection against tender of pardon to an accomplice simply because of his confession, he does not implicate himself to the same extent as the other accused because all that section 306 requires is that pardon may be tendered to any person believed to be involved directly or indirectly in or privy to an offence......."

160. Above referred judgment of the Apex Court clearly shows that culpability of an accused has not much bearing on the grant of pardon to him. Only requirement of law is that he should be directly or indirectly involved in or privy to the offence.

161. Even if for the sake of argument, it is assumed that an accused cannot be tendered pardon unless the court is assured that he can be tried and punished for the offence in respect of which pardon was so tendered if he fails to make true disclosure of the fact that, then also, I do not find any defect in the tender of pardon because approver as per the charge sheet is alleged to be guilty of related offence, *i.e.*, the forgery of donation coupons and the minutes books relating to the meeting of the Executive Body of JMM, MPs. If after the trial, it is found that Shailender Mahto, approver has failed to make true disclosure of all the essential facts relating to the offence under section 193, IPC to which the immunity under Article 105 of the Constitution of India does not extend.

162. Thus, I do not find any defect in the tender of pardon to the approver.

SHAILENDER MAHTO APPROVER P.W. 1 IS THE STAR WITNESS – GIST OF HIS VERSION NARRATED – CBI COURT

163. Prosecution case is mainly based upon the testimony of approver Shailender Mahto, therefore, I deem it proper to detail the gist of his version at the outset.

164. P.W. 1 Shailender Mahto, approver has stated that there were newspaper reports prior to the beginning of monsoon session of parliament in 1993 that opposition parties would be moving no confidence motion against the Government. He has also stated that on 24th or 25th July, 1993 he alongwith Suraj Mandal, Shibu Soren and Simon Marandi met accused Ajit Singh in his office. In the said meeting, they discussed the respective plans of their parties regarding no confidence motion and accused Ajit Singh suggested that their group should form a joint strategy on the no confidence motion with his party.

165. Approver has also stated that at that time Simon Marandi informed him that talks with accused Satish Sharma in respect of no confidence motion were going on and if they supported the Government, they would be paid cash besides the allotment of Petrol Pumps and Plots of HUDA in Haryana.

166. Approver has further deposed that on 25.7.1993 P.W. 2 Ashok Rao Anand Rao Deshmukh, a Congress M.P. asked him in the presence of Shibu Soren and Suraj Mandal if they would help the Congress Government. He showed his inclination to consider supporting the Government provided the Prime Minister was ready to take some decision to constitute Jharkhand Council. On this, Sh. Deshmukh replied that he would talk to the Prime Minister and get back to them. On the same day at about 5.00 PM., P.W. Deshmukh informed them that they were to visit V. Rajeshwar Rao on the same day. Approver has further stated that on 26.7.1993 at 10.00 A.M. they visited the residence of accused V. Rajeshwar Rao at Andhra Bhawan. P.W. Ashok Rao Anand Rao Deshmukh was already present there and he left them after introducing with the accused V. Rajeshwar Rao. He has stated that during said meeting V. Rajeshwar Rao and Suraj Mandal went towards the verandah and had a separate conversation for about 10 or 15 minutes. While they were coming back from the residence of V. Rajeshwar Rao, Suraj Mandal told them that V. Rajeshwar Rao was offering a meagre amount and suggested that they should have a direct talk with the Prime Minister.

167. Approver Shailender Mahto, P.W.1 has also deposed that in the evening of 26.7.1993 at about 7.00 P.M., J.M.M., M.Ps. proceeded to the residence of accused Buta Singh from the house of Suraj Mandal. M.P. While they were having tea, accused Buta Singh remarked that the Prime Minister has remembered them. On this, Suraj Mandal protested that what was the use of Prime Minister remembering them as the matter of Jharkhand Council was still unresolved. On this, accused Buta Singh suggested that they should have a direct conversation with the Prime Minister.

DEAL WAS STRUCK AT THE RESIDENCE OF PM BETWEEN SURAJ MANDAL, BUTA SINGH AND PM – DEPOSED APPROVER – CBI COURT

168. Approver has further stated that they all went to the residence of the accused P.V. Narasimha Rao and had a meeting with him. During said meeting, accused Buta Singh initiated the conversation by saying that the matter of Jharkhand Council was still unresolved. Suraj Mandal. M.P. intervened and told the Prime Minister that he has not resolved the matter of Jharkhand Council, therefore, how could they support the Government. On this, accused P.V. Narasimha Rao assured that he would summon the file of Jharkhand matter and resolve the same. He further requested that for the moment J.M.M. M.Ps should help him. P.W. Shailender Mahto has further stated that thereafter accused P.V. Narasimha Rao and accused Buta Singh went to other room and after some time Suraj Mandal, M.P. was called to that room. Five or six minutes later they came back and accused P.V. Narasimha Rao said, "AT PRESENT YOU SHOULD HELP ME AND IN RETURN I WILL ALSO HELP YOU." He further added "WHATEVER CONVERSATION HAS TAKEN PLACE WITH SURAJ MANDAL, THOSE PROMISES SHALL BE FULFILLED."

169. Approver Shailender Mahto has further stated that on their way back, he asked Suraj Mandal about the details of conversation which had taken place with Buta Singh and the Prime Minister. On this, Suraj Mandal said " PHAIDE KI BAAT HAI". Thereafter, Simon Marandi insisted for specific details of the said conversation saying "SURAJ TUM SPASHT BATAO, NAHIN TO HUM VOTE NAHIN DENGE." On this, Suraj Mandal told "PAISE KI BHI BAAT HUI HAI, KITNA PAISE MILEGA ABHI TAI NAHIN HUA."

170. P.W. 1 Shailender Mahto has also stated that on 28.7.1993 after the debate, no confidence motion was put to vote and it was defeated. Approver Shailender Mahto has further stated that on 29.7.1993 at around 8 or 9.00 a.m., he visited the residence of Suraj Mandal in response to his telephone call. Accused V. Rajeshwar was also present there. Suraj Mandal told him that Rupee Fifty Lakhs have been sent for them and the remaining would reach them within a day or two. He has also deposed that V. Rajeshwar informed them that J.M.M. M.Ps would be paid Rupees Fifty Lakhs and the group of Ram Lakhan Singh Yadav was joining the Congress, therefore, they would be paid Rupees Fifty Lakhs each besides the allotment of Petrol Pumps and Huda Plots in Haryana. He further informed that those M.Ps who have absented or abstained from voting to help the Government, shall be paid Rupees Thirty Lakhs each.

ON 30.7.1993 SURAJ MANDAL INFORMED JMM MPs THAT MONEY HAS BEEN RECEIVED – INFORMED APPROVER – CBI COURT

171. P.W. 1 Shailender Mahto has also stated that on 30.7.1993, Suraj Mandal, M.P. told him "PAISA AA GAYA HAI, TUMHARA CHALEES LAKH RUPIYA YE PAISA HAI." Suraj Mandal explained that out of Rupees Fifty Lakhs offered to him, Rupees Forty Lakhs was being given as his share and remaining Ten Lakhs would be deposited in the bank in the joint names of Suraj Mandal, Shailender Mahto, Shibu Soren and Simon Marandi. Approver has deposed that since he was not having any vehicle, he left the residence of Suraj Mandal saying that he would collect that later.

STOOD CONCLUSIVEY PROVED THAT JMM MPs RECEIVED RS. 1,62,80,000 – DEPOSITED IN DIFFERENT NAMES IN DIFFERENT ACCOUNTS ON 1/2.8.1993 IN PNB NAOROJI BRANCH NEW DELHI – HOLDS CBI COURT

172. P.W. Shailender Mahto has also stated that Simon Marandi, M.P. visited his residence in the morning of 30.7.1993 alongwith the money and informed him that it consisted of his share of Rupees Forty Lakhs. Simon Marandi suggested that they should go to Punjab National Bank and deposit said money with the help of one Sushil Kumar, Chartered Accountant who would meet them there. Thereafter, they went to the Bank but could not deposit the amount as Sushil Kumar, Chartered Accountant was not available. From the Bank, they went to the residence of one R.K. Jaitley at Mandakini Enclave. R.K. Jaitley was out of station but his wife and children were present. The driver of Simon Marandi as well as the driver of R.K. Jaitley got the said cash stuffed in two gunny bags and a big bag at the residence of R.K. Jaitley. Thereafter, money stuffed in gunny bags was shifted into suitcases, fetched from the Market. Simon Marandi left alongwith the bag containing cash leaving behind the approver and two suitcases containing cash.

173. P.W. 1 approver Shailender Mahto has further deposed that in the next morning Simon Marandi visited the residence of R.K. Jaitley. From there, he accompanied Simon Marandi to the residence of Shibu Soren alongwith those suitcases containing cash. Simon Marandi left after dropping him at the residence of Shibu Soren.

174. In the afternoon, Manager of Punjab National Bank, Nauroji, New Delhi alongwith Sushil Kumar, Chartered Accountant came to the residence of Shibu Soren to collect the cash. The aforesaid suitcases were loaded in the Car of Sushil Kumar and they all went to Punjab National Bank. Approver has deposed that he opened a Sugam Account in the joint names of self and his wife Abha Mahto by depositing Rs. 39,80,000 and kept Rs. 20,000 in cash with himself. He has proved the Account Opening Form Ex. P.W. 1/C and corresponding specimen Signatures Card Ex. P.W. 1/D. He has stated that he signed the Account Opening Form for his wife also.

175. Approver has further deposed that on 1.8.1993 a joint account in the names of all the four J.M.M. M.Ps. was opened by depositing Rupees Thirty Lakhs which included his share of Rs. 7,50,000. The balance Rs. 2,50,000 pertaining to his share was kept by Suraj Mandal for party fund. He has proved the relevant Account Opening Form Ex. P.W. 1/B. Approver has further proved the photo copy of Constitution of Jharkhand Mukti Morcha Ex. P.W. 1/A. He has stated that till 1993, coupons for collecting donations on behalf of Jharkhand Mukti Morcha Party were not printed and no books of accounts of Jharkhand Mukti Morcha were maintained during his tenure as General Secretary. According to him, the resolutions of the Executive Committee of Jharkhand Mukti Morcha Ex. P.W. 1/H1 to Ex. P.W. H3, which are purported to have been signed on 11-1-1993, 4-7-1993 and 10-7-1994, were actually signed by him at Ranchi Airport in April, 1996.

176. Section 133 and section 114 *illustration (b)* of the Indian Evidence Act deals with the law relating to the evidence of the approver. Section 133 of the Act provides that approver is a competent witness and conviction of the accused can be based upon his testimony, though uncorroborated. However, section 114, illustration (b) of the Act introduce a rule of caution. It provides that court may presume that an accomplice is unworthy of credit, unless his testimony is corroborated in material particulars of the case. With the passage of time, aforesaid rule of caution has more or less become a rule of law and the Courts while appreciating the testimony with suspicion and are reluctant to act upon it unless said testimony is corroborated on material aspects of the case by some independent evidence either direct or circumstantial. Reference be made to 1963 (2) Cr LJ 671: 1970 Cr LJ 1994: 1994 Supp. (2) SC 73: (1979) 4 SCC 145: (1994) 4 478: AIR 1988 SC 139: AIR 1957 SC 637: AIR 1988 SC 599: (1996) 10 SC 330: 1952 Cr LJ 549: (1996) 10 SCC 310: 1952 Cr LJ 839 and 1970 Cr LJ 1994.

177. A close look at the testimony of P.W.1 approver Shailender Mahto would reveal that according to him, J.M.M. M.Ps were soliciting bargain in connection of their voting in favour of the Government against the no confidence motion. In the process, they were offered illegal gratification by accused V. Rajeshwar Rao as well as accused P.V. Narasimha Rao and Buta Singh. That on 28-7-1993, no confidence motion was put to vote and defeated. Thereafter the amount of illegal gratification was delivered at the residence of Suraj Mandal. Said amount was distributed amongst JMM MPs namely Suraj Mandal, Simon Marandi, Shibu Soren and the approver Shailender Mahto and ultimately it found way to Punjab National Bank, Naoroji Nagar, New Delhi in the form of various deposits.

178. At the moment, without going into the question who offered bribe to JMM, MPs and how the offer was given, I propose to analyse the prosecution evidence regarding the receipt of money by the J.M.M., M.Ps.

179. Relevant testimony of approver P.W. 1 Shailender Mahto is that on 30-7-1993, Suraj Mandal informed him on telephone that money has been received and his share would be Rs. 40 lakhs. P.W. 1 Shailender Mahto has further stated that Suraj Mandal also told him that out of his promised share of Rs. 50 lakhs, Rs. 40 lakhs would be given to him and remaining Rs. 10 lakhs would be deposited in the joint names of all the four J.M.M., M.Ps.

180. P.W. 1 Shailender Mahto has further stated that on 30-7-1993 at around 10.00 or 11.00 A.M. Simon Marandi visited his residence alongwith cash contained in two gunny bags and a big bag. He informed the approver that said money also consisted of his share of Rs. 40 lakhs and suggested that they should go to Punjab National Bank, Naoroji Nagar, New Delhi where an acquaintance of Suraj Mandal namely Sushil Kumar, Chartered Accountant would meet them and help them in the depositing of amount in their accounts. Thereafter, they went to the bank alongwith cash. Since Sushil Kumar, Chartered Accountant was not available there, they went to the residence of an acquaintance Shri R.K. Jaitley at Mandakini Enclave, New Delhi without depositing the cash. Shri R.K. Jaitley was not present at his residence, but the wife and children were present at home. Approver Shailender Mahto, P.W. 1 and Simon Marandi sent their deliver as well as driver of Shri R.K. Jaitley to the market for bringing three or four suitcases. Thereafter, the money contained in the gunny bags was transferred into the suitcases. Simon Marandi left alongwith bag containing cash and the approver Shialender Mahto stayed at the residence of R.K. Jaitley over-night.

181. Approver P.W. 1 Shailender Mahto has also deposed that in the next morning Simon Marandi collected him from the residence of R.K. Jaitley. They went to the residence of Shibu Soren alongwith the cash. Simon Marandi left for his residence after leaving him (approver) at the residence of Shibu Soren. On the same day in the afternoon, the manager of Punjab National Bank, Naoroji Nagar, New Delhi and Sushil Kumar, Chartered Accountant visited the residence of Shibu Soren. Shibu Soren and approver Shialender Mahto then accompanied them to Punjab National Bank, Naoroji Nagar, New Delhi along with cash.

182. Approver Shailender Mahto has further stated that he opened a Sugam Deposit Account in the joint names of self and his wife Abha Mahto with Rs. 39.80 lakhs and kept Rs. 20,000 with him. He has further deposed that on 1-8-1993 one joint account in the names of Shailender Mahto, Suraj Mandal, Simon Marandi and Shibu Soren was opened in Punjab National Bank with a sum of Rs. 30 lakhs. Approver has further deposed that Suraj Mandal explained to him that Rs. 7.50 lakhs out of his balance share was deposited in the said joint account and balance Rs. 2.50 lakhs was kept for the party fund.

183. Prosecution has examined P.W. 94 Neeta Jaitley and P.W. 97 Bal Kishan, the driver of Shri R.K. Jaitley to corroborate the version of the approver Shailender Mahto, P.W. 1 that on 30-7-1993 he visited the residence of R.K. Jaitley alongwith Simon Marandi and there they transferred the cash from gunny bags into two suitcases. Said witnesses have turned hostile and they have not supported the version of the approver that they carried cash to the residence of R.K. Jaitley and there they transferred said cash from gunny bags into two suitcases. However, P.W. Neeta Jaitley and P.W. Bal Kishan have partly corroborated the version of the approver regarding his visit dated 30-7-1993 to the residence of R.K. Jaitley alongwith Simon Marandi.

184. The version of approver Shailender Mahto finds very strong corroboration from the testimony of various officials of Punjab National Bank, Naoroji Nagar, New Delhi as well as the corresponding record of the bank.

185. Ex. P.W. 18/DA is the account opening form pertaining to Sugam Fixed Deposit Account No. 194 Punjab National Bank, Naoroji Nagar in the joint names of Shibu Soren, Mrs. Roopi Devi, Hemant Kumar and Shri Basant Kumar. This account opening form is dated 1-8-1993. Ex. P.W. 18/A is the statement of account pertaining to aforesaid Sugam Account No. 194 which revealed that on 1-8-1993 this account was opened with the deposit of Rs. 30 lakhs.

186. Ex. P.W. 1/B is the account opening form pertaining to Special Fixed Deposit Account No. 195 Punjab National Bank, Naoroji Nagar, New Delhi in the joint name of Shibu Soren (MP) Suraj Mandal, Simon Marandi and Shailender Mahto. This account opening form is also dated 1-8-1993. Ledger sheet of the aforesaid account is Ex. P.W. 18/B which reveals that on 1-8-1993, this account was opened with a sum of Rs. 30 lakhs.

187. Ex. P.W. 1/C is the account opening form pertaining to Sugam Account No. 196 in Punjab National Bank, Naoroji Nagar, New Delhi in the joint names of approver Shailender Mahto and his wife Abha Mahto. Its corresponding ledger sheet as Ex. P.W. 18/C which reveals that on 1-8-1993 said account was opened with the deposit of Rs. 39.80 lakhs.

188. Ex. P.W. 18/DB is the account opening form pertaining to opening of account number Sugam 197 in Punjab National Bank, Naoroji Nagar, New Delhi in the joint names of Simon Marandi and Sushila Hansda. This form is dated. Ex. P.W. 18/D is the ledger sheet pertaining to the said account. According to this ledger sheet, above referred account was opened with a sum of Rs 12 lakhs on 1-8-1993. The ledger sheet further reveals that on 2-8-1993 a sum of Rs. 21 lakhs was further deposited in the above referred account.

189. P.W. 16 Shri Balraj Suri, Senior Manager, Punjab National Bank, has categorically stated that he worked as Senior Manager in Punjab National Bank Naoroji Nagar Branch from December 1990 till June, 1992. During his tenure, one S.B. Account No. 17108 was opened in the name of Suraj Mandal with his permission without prior submission of the account opening form. He has proved the original ledger sheet pertaining to above referred account Ex. P.W. 16/B. As per said ledger sheet in the aforesaid Saving Account of Suraj Mandal a sum of Rs. 30 lakhs cash was deposited on 1-8-1993. The corresponding deposit slip for Rs. 30 lakhs is Ex. P.W. 10/C-1 and debit voucher is Ex. P.W. 103/E. Said deposit slip, debit voucher and the ledger sheet clearly show that on 1-8-1993, a sum of Rs. 30 lakhs received in cash was credited in the S.B. Account of Suraj Mandal.

190. Above referred record of the Bank conclusively establish that a sum of Rs. 1,41,80,000 was deposited in Punjab National Bank, Naoroji Nagar, New Delhi in above mentioned accounts of J.M.M., M.Ps on 1-8-1993. Above said evidence further establish that a sum of Rs. 21 lakhs was further deposited in Sugam Account No. 197 in the joint names of Simon Marandi and his wife on 2-8-1993. Thus, it is established that on 1st and 2nd of August, 1993, a total sum of Rs. 1,62,80,000 was deposited by J.M.M., MPs in above referred accounts.

191. P.W. 103 Satish Kumar Sharma, Manager, Punjab National Bank has thrown light upon the manner in which aforesaid cash was collected and deposited in Punjab National Bank, Naoroji Nagar, New Delhi in the above referred accounts of J.M.M., M.Ps. He has stated that one Sushil Kumar, Chartered Accountant was a customer of the Bank. Said witness informed him a day or two before 31-7-1993 that he would bring huge deposits to the Bank on 31-7-1993. Sushil Kumar. Chartered Accountant telephonically requested him to reach at the residence of Suraj Mandal, J.M.M. M.P to collect the money for depositing in various accounts in Punjab National Bank, Naoroji Nagar, New Delhi. On this, he requested Sushil Kumar, Chartered Accountant to reach at Punjab National Bank, Naoroji Nagar, New Delhi. He has further stated that he took permission from his Senior Manager P.W. 18 Shri B.L. Verma and accompanied Sushil Kumar, Chartered Accountant, Cashier Mohan Chand (since expired) and peon Jawahar Lal, P.W. 98 to the residence of Suraj Mandal, at Ferozeshah Road, New Delhi. He also carried some account opening forms, pay in slips as well as round stamps of the bank. He has deposed that there Shri Suraj Mandal produced two suitcases and informed that those suitcases contained Rs. 60.10 lakhs. He instructed that out of that money Rs. 30 lakhs were to be deposited in Account No. 17108 and sum of Rs. 30 lakhs was to be deposited in the shape of fixed deposit in the joint names of Suraj Mandal, Shibhu Soren, Simon Marandi and Shailender Mahto and balance Rs. 10,000 was to be deposited in the S.B. Account to the joint names of said four persons. The witness has further deposed that suitcases were opened which were found to contain GC notes of assorted denominations which were mixed lot of new and old currency notes. Since the money could not be counted, he checked the number of packets of GC notes and on the basis of the same, money appeared to be Rs. 60.10 lakhs, therefore, he gave a kacha receipt to Suraj Mandal.

192. P.W. 103 Satish Kumar has further stated that Suraj Mandal told him that some more money was to be collected from the residence of Shibu Soren. Therefore, he directed the cashier and peon to carry the cash collected from the residence of Suraj Mandal to the bank and he proceeded to the residence of Shibu Soren at Gurdwara Raqab Ganj Road alongwith Sushil Kumar. They reached there at around 4.00 P.M. Shri Shibu Soren took them to his bed room and produced one big suitcase, one small suitcase and plastic cloth bag

193. Shibu Soren informed that big suit case contained Rs. 39.80 lakhs belonging to Shailender Mahto, small suitcase contained Rs. 12 lakhs belonging to Simon Marandi and plastic cloth bag containing Rs. 30 lakhs belonged to him. P.W. Satish Kumar has further deposed that Shibu Soren instructed that out of the aforesaid money, Rs. 39.80 lakhs was to be deposited in the fixed deposit account in the joint names of Shailender Mahto and Abha Mahto. Rs. 12 lakhs was to be deposited in the joint names of Simon Marandi and his wife Sushila Hansda and Rs. 30 lakhs were to be deposited in the joint names of Shibu Soren, his wife Rupi and sons Hemant Kumar and Basant Kumar. Witness has deposed that he obtained the signatures of Shibu Soren, his wife Rupi and son Basant Kumar on the account opening form for the joint fixed deposit of Rs. 30 lakhs, but signatures of Hemant Kumar could not be obtained as he was not available. Thereafter said two suitcases and plastic cloth bag were loaded in maruti car of Sushil Kumar, and brought to the bank. Shibu Soren also followed the maruti car. According to this witness, since it was very late, he called for two steel trunks. The money contained in suitcases and plastic cloth bag brought from the residence of Shibu Soren was counted bundlewise and denomination wise but actual counting was not done. Thereafter, said money was kept in one steel trunk. Similarly, the money contained in suit cases brought from the residence of Suraj Mandal was transferred into the second steel trunk. Both the trunks were locked and kept in the strong room. Shibu Soren was requested to come again in the next morning, so that money could be counted in his presence. According to this witness, on 1-8-1993 steel trunks were taken out from the strong room. The money contained therein was counted in presence of Shibu Soren, Simon Marandi and Sushil Kumar, who was representing Suraj Mandal. After counting, it was confirmed that money collected from the residence of Suraj Mandal was

Rs. 60.10 lakhs and money brought from the residence of Shibu Soren was Rs. 81.80 lakhs as detailed by him.

194. The witness has further stated that above said money was deposited in various accounts as per the instructions of the parties. He has proved the account opening form pertaining to joint account in the names of Shibu Soren, Suraj Mandal and Shailender Mahto as Ex. P.W. 1/B, He has also proved the corresponding pay in slip for Rs. 30 lakhs deposit as Ex. P.W. 103/A. He has further proved account opening form Ex. P.W. 1/C. regarding Sugam Fixed deposit account in the joint names of Shailender Mahto and Abha Mahto. He has proved the corresponding deposit vouchers for Rs. 39.80 lakhs Ex. P.W. 103/B. This witness has further proved account opening form pertaining to Sugam Fixed Deposit Account No. 197 in the joint names of Simon Marandi and Sushila Hansda Ex. P.W. 18/DB. He has also proved corresponding deposit voucher for Rs. 12 lakhs Ex. P.W. 103/C. Witness has further proved the account opening form relating to Sugam Account No. 194 in the names of Shibu Soren, Mrs. Roopi, Hemant and Basant Kumar Ex. P.W. 18/DA. He has stated that a sum of Rs. 30 lakhs was deposited in the said account. Witness has further stated that balance Rs. 30 lakhs was deposited in existing saving bank account of Suraj Mandal vide voucher Ex. P.W. 103/E. He has also proved the kachha receipt given by him at the residence of Suraj Mandal Ex. P.W. 1/C1 and Ex. P.W. 1/C2. Version of this witness is fully corroborated by P.W. 98 Shri Jawahar Lal, Peon of Punjab National Bank, Naoroji Nagar, New Delhi as well as P.W. 18 Shri B.L. Verma, Senior Manager, Punjab National Bank.

195. From the above referred testimony of P.W. 103 Satish Kumar, which is also corroborated by P.W. 98 Jawahar Lal, peon and P.W. 18 B.L. Verma Senior Manager, Punjab National Bank, Naoroji Nagar, New Delhi, it is established beyond doubt on the record that on 31-7-1993 P.W. Satish Kumar accompanied by the cashier and peon Jawhar Lal of the bank as well as Sushil Kumar, Chartered Accountant visited the residence of Suraj Mandal, MP at Ferozeshah Road, New Delhi and from there he collected a sum of Rs. 60.10 lakhs contained in two suitcases. Thereafter, on the information given by Suraj Mandal, P.W. Satish Kumar accompanied Sushil Kumar, Chartered Accountant visited the residence of Shibu Soren and from there he collected a sum of Rs. 81.80 lakhs contained in two suitcases and a plastic cloth bag and brought the cash to the bank. Since it was very late, the cash was counted bundlewise and denomination wise and it was kept in the strong room without actual counting. On the next date, *i.e.*, 1-8-1993 aforesaid cash was actually counted and it was found to be Rs. 1,41,90,000 in all. Said amount as per the instructions received from Suraj Mandal and Shibu Soren was deposited in various accounts namely Sugam Account No. 194 with the deposit of Rs. 30 lakhs in the joint names of Shibu Soren, his wife Smt. Rupi and his two sons Hemant Kumar and Basant Kumar, fixed deposit account no.195 in the joint names of Suraj Mandal, Shibu Soren, Simon Marandi and Shailender Mahto worth Rs. 30 lakhs, Sugam Account No. 196 in the joint names of Shailender Mahto of Rs. 29.80 lakhs, Sugam Account No. 197 of Rs. 12 lakhs in the joint names of Simon Marandi and Sushila Hansda and balance Rs. 30 lakhs was deposited in already existing S.B. Account No. 17108 of Suraj Mandal. It is also clear from the perusal of the ledger account Ex. P.W. 18/D relating to Sugam Account No. 197 belonging to Simon Marandi and his wife that on 2-8-1993 a further sum of Rs. 29 lakhs was deposited in the said account. Thus, I have no hesitation in holding that during the period 31-7-1993 to 2-8-1993 a total sum amounting to Rs. 1,62,80,000 was deposited in the above referred accounts relating to JMM, MPs and the said amount was channelized from the residence of Suraj Mandal and Shibu Soren.

196. The above referred testimony of the bank officials as well as the record of Punjab National Bank, Naoroji Nagar, New Delhi provides sufficient, corroboration to the testimony of Shailender Mahto that the amount in question came to be delivered at the residence of Suraj Mandal and from there it found way to various accounts in the names of JMM, MPs formally opened on 1-8-1993 at Punjab National Bank, Naoroji Nagar and the previously existing S.B. Account No. 17108 in the name of Suraj Mandal in the said bank.

P.V. NARASIMHA RAO AND HIS SUPPORTERS WON OVER 4 JMM, MPs – THEY VOTED AGAINST THE NO CONFIDENCE MOTION – GOVT. WAS SAVED – JMM MPs GOT RS. 1,62,80,000-DEPOSITED IN PNB NEW DELHI – CONCLUSIVELY PROVES THAT JMM MPs RECEIVED ILLEGAL GRATIFICATION AS A REWARD FROM A1 AND OTHERS – HOLDS CBI COURT

197. So far I have concluded that there existed a motive on the part of accused P.V. Narasimha Rao (A-1) and his supporters to win over the members of parliament belonging to opposition in order to save the government. That on 28-7-1993, no confidence motion was put to vote and JMM, MPs voted against the no confidence motion. From the evidence discussed above, it is also established that during the period w.e.f. 31-7-1993 to 3-8-1993 a huge sum of Rs. 1,62,80,000 was deposited in respective accounts of 4 JMM, MPs/their family members and a joint account in the name of those 4 JMM, MPs. A close proximity of the date of voting on no confidence motion and the dates on which the above referred amount was deposited in the respective bank accounts of J.M.M., M.Ps in Punjab National Bank, Naoroji Nagar, New Delhi, when viewed in the aforesaid back ground leads me to the conclusion that there is a direct relation between the voting of J.M.M., M.Ps against no confidence motion and the money which came to be deposited in the bank accounts. Thus, I have no hesitation in holding that the aforesaid money was received by JMM, MPs as an illegal gratification as a motive or reward for their saving the government by voting against no confidence motion.

JMM, MPs CLAIMED THIS AMOUNT WAS PARTY FUND COLLECTION – RESOLUTIONS WERE PROVED- IF IT HAD BEEN PARTY FUND – WOULD NOT HAVE BEEN DEPOSITED IN INDIVIDUAL NAMES OF JMM, MPs AND THEIR FAMILIES – THESE RESOLUTIONS WERE FORGED – INTERPOLATIONS WERE MADE STILL AFTER TO JUSTIFY NAMES OF FAMILY MEMBERS – CLEARLY IT WAS AMOUNT OF ILLEGAL GRATIFICATION AS A REWARD – PROVED CONCLUSIVELY – HELD CBI COURT

198. Perusal of the charge sheet would reveal that during investigation of this case, J.M.M., M.Ps tried to explain that above referred amount which came to be deposited in their respective accounts in Punjab National Bank, Naoroji Nagar, New Delhi as donation received by J.M.M. Party.

199. Explanation apparently appears to be false because had the aforesaid money been party fund, it would not have been deposited in personal account of J.M.M., M.Ps and their family members. Further said explanation is negatived by the version of the approver P.W. 1 Shri Shailender Mahto, who has deposed that on 30-7-1993, P.W. 1 approver Shailender Mahto while informing him about the receipt of money also told him that out of promised Rs. 50 lakhs, Rs. 40 lakhs were being given to him as his share and remaining Rs. 10 lakhs would be deposited in the joint names of all the four J.M.M., M.Ps including the approver. He has also deposed that on 1-8-1993 a sum of Rs. 39.80 lakhs was deposited in his joint account with his wife Smt. Abha Mahto and he kept Rs. 20 thousand in cash with him. He has further deposed that out of balance Rs. 10 lakhs, his share of Rs. 7.50 lakhs deposited in the joint account alongwith other JMM, MPs and Rs. 2.50 lakhs were kept by Suraj Mandal for the party fund. Said version finds corroboration from the testimony of the officials of Punjab National Bank, Naoroji Nagar, New Delhi as well as account opening form Ex. P.W. 1/B pertaining to the joint account of J.M.M., M.Ps and corresponding pay-in-slip for deposit of Rs. 30 lakhs Ex. P.W. 103/A. Similarly the version regarding deposit of Rs. 39.80 lakhs in joint account of self and Smt. Abha Mahto, his wife is also corroborated by account opening form Ex. P.W. 1/C and corresponding deposit voucher Ex. P.W. 103/A.

200. Above said version of P.W. 1 approver Shailender Mahto clearly shows that account in question was the bribe money out of which the share of the approver was Rs. 50 lakhs and Rs. 2.50 lakhs out of the same was kept by Suraj Mandal as party fund. If Rs. 2.50 lakhs was retained by Suraj Mandal as a party fund, then the explanation to the effect that entire money was political donations received by J.M.M. Party is obviously incorrect.

201. Approver Shailender Mahto has also deposed that on or around 2-4-1996 at Ranchi Airport, his anti dated signatures were obtained on three resolutions Ex. P.W. 1/H1 to Ex. P.W. 1/H3. The resolution relevant to the explanation given by JMM, MPs Ex. P.W. 1/H1 is purported to be passed on 11-7-1993. Perusal of resolution Ex. P.W. 1/H1 would reveal that it was to authorize the deposit of donation received by the party in Punjab National Bank, Naoroji Nagar, New Delhi in the names of office bearers of the party namely Shibu Soren, Shailender Mahto (approver), Simon Marandi and Suraj Mandal. If the aforesaid resolution is genuine, then the said money, if it was party fund, should have been deposited in the account of JMM Party or in the joint names of said four JMM, MPs. But it is not the case. Actually, the money in question as per above discussed evidence has been deposited in five different accounts. In three such accounts, family members of Shailender Mahto, Shibu Soren and Simon Marandi are respective joint account holders. This fact by itself leads me to the conclusion that money in question was not the party fund, but it was meant for use and consumption of JMM, MPs. Further perusal of resolution Ex. P.W. 1/H1 would reveal that in this resolution the words "TATHA SURAKSHA KI DRISHTI SE APNE PARIVAR KE SADASYON KE NAAM BHI JOR SAKTE HAIN" have been added subsequently with a different ink. It is apparent that those words have been added in the aforesaid resolution on an after-thought in order to justify the opening of accounts in the joint names of respective JMM MPs and their family members. This circumstance clearly shows that Ex. P.W. 1/H1 is not a genuine resolution. It appears that after the forgery of this resolution, on an after thought, JMM, MPs realised that aforesaid resolution would not help them, therefore, in order to create more plausible explanation for joint accounts in the names of JMM, MPs and their family members, above referred words were added subsequently in the resolution. Thus, considering that resolution Ex. P.W. 1/H1 is not a genuine document and it has been fabricated to create an explanation for the aforesaid huge deposits in the accounts of JMM, MPs. This subsequent conduct of JMM, MPs clearly shows their guilty conscious. If the amount which was deposited in various accounts of JMM MPs was not the bribe amount, there was no occasion for JMM, MPs to fabricate the proceedings of the Executive Committee of JMM Party in order to create an explanation that those deposits were actually the politically donations received by JMM, MPs. In view of my above discussion, I conclude that aforesaid amount of Rs. 1,62,80,000 which was deposited in various accounts of JMM, MPs and their respective family members was illegal gratification received by them as a motive or reward for voting against no confidence motion.

CRIMINAL CONSPIRACY UNDER SECTION 120B, IPC OF ILLEGAL AGREEMENT OF GIVING BRIBE FOR VOTING AGAINST NO CONFIDENCE MOTION AND TAKING OF BRIBE BY JMM MPs FOR DOING SO – CLEARLY PROVED – HOLDS CBI COURT

202. If JMM, MPs were recipients of the bribe then there necessarily have to be one or more bribe givers, who have abeted the taking of bribe by those JMM, MPs. This imply that there must be some agreement between those abettors *i.e.* bribe givers and JMM, MPs regarding the giving of bribe and taking of bribe by JMM, MPs as a motive or reward for their casting votes against no confidence motion. Thus, it is apparent that there was an agreement amongst JMM, MPs as well as the bribe givers to defeat the no confidence motion by illegal act *i.e.*, offering or causing to offer and giving bribe to the members of parliament. Thus the offence of criminal conspiracy as defined under section 120A, I.P.C. is established.

203. Now, it is to be seen from where the above mentioned huge amount came into the hands of JMM, MPs Suraj Mandal, Simon Marandi, Shibu Soren and approver Shailender Mahto. And who are the persons responsible for bribing those MPs.

ROLE OF BHAJAN LAL IN BRIBING JMM, MPs NOT PROVED BEYOND DOUBT – HOLDS CBI COURT

204. Ex. P.W.2/A is the complaints of Ravinder Kumar, which set investigating agency into motion. Allegations in the complaint are that in July, 1993 a criminal conspiracy was hatched by accused P.V. Narasimha Rao. V.C. Shukla, R.K. Dhawan, Ajit Singh, Bhajan Lal and Lalit Suri to prove the majority of the government on the floor of the house on 28.7.1993 by bribing MPs of different political parties, individuals and groups by paying an amount of over Rs. 3 crores. In furtherance of the said criminal conspiracy, Rs. 1.10 crores was handed over by aforesentioned persons except Ajit Singh to Suraj Mandal in Hotel Holiday Inn, Barakhamba Road, New Delhi.

205. Though in the summary of facts revealed during investigation detailed in respective three reports under section 173, Cr.P.C., there is no allegation that accused Bhajan Lal was involved in offering or payment of bribe to the JMM, MPs. Prosecution has examined P.W. 3 Devender Mukhiya to establish his involvement in the bribe of JMM, MPs. P.W. 3 Devender Mukhiya is hostile witness and he has not supported the prosecution case in this regard. During his cross examination by learned prosecutor, he has denied the suggestion that in the night of 23-7-1993 at Holiday Inn, a meeting was held with the JMM, MPs which was also attended by accused Bhajan Lal or that after the meeting accused Bhajan Lal and JMM, MPs went to some unknown place. He has also denied the suggestion that accused Bhajan Lal made an extra-judicial confession before him at Haryana Bhawan that the matter has been settled with the JMM MPs and half of the amount settled has been paid to them in the morning of 27-7-1993 and remaining half amount would be delivered to them on 29-7-1993. He has further denied that accused Bhajan Lal told him that some personal friends of Captain Satish Sharma have helped in delivery of said money. There is no other evidence on record to suggest the involvement of accused Bhajan Lal in the bribing of JMM, MPs either directly or indirectly. Thus, I am of the view that prosecution has failed to establish his role in the bribing of JMM MPs beyond doubt.

MATERIAL WITNESSES WENT HOSTILE – STATEMENT OF APPROVER NOT CORROBORATED – ROLE OF CAPT. SATISH SHARMA IN BRIBING JMM MPs NOT PROVED – HOLDS CBI COURT

206. Coming to the role played by Captain Satish Sharma in bribing the JMM, MPs. First allegation of the prosecution against him is that he had been receiving financial contributions from various business houses around the period of conspiracy. Thus, he was having a capacity to finance the bribery of JMM, MPs. I have already discussed the evidence regarding all these allegations and concluded that prosecution has failed to establish the allegations.

207. Prosecution by examining P.W. 3 Devender Mukhiya has tried to establish that said witness arranged a meeting between Simon Marandi and Shri Braham Dev Paswan with Captain Satish Sharma. During said meeting, Captain Satish Sharma requested them to vote for the government and promised to ensure payment of money as well as allotment of petrol pumps or gas agencies to them. Prosecution has also tried to establish through testimony of P.W. 3 Devender Mukhiya that in the evening of 22.7.1993 one meeting was held at the Ashram of Chandraswamy which was attended by various persons including Captain Satish Sharma, Ram Lakhan Singh Yadav, Roshan Lal, Haji Gulam Mohd. Khan, G.C. Munda and Simon Marandi and in the aforesaid meeting Captain Satish Sharma offered the bribe of Rs. 50 lakhs each besides allotment of petrol pumps and HUDA residential plots to the MPs voting in favour of the government. However, P.W. 3 Devender Mukhiya turned hostile and he has not supported the above-said case of the prosecution. He has denied the above-said case suggested to him during his cross examination by learned prosecutor. Thus the aforesaid role of Captain Satish Sharma is not established on record. P.W. 3 Devender Mukhiya has also denied the suggestions that Shri B.N. Safaya, Additional Private Secretary of accused Capt. Satish Sharma at his instance paid a sum of Rs. 50,000 to Shri Braham Dev Paswan to arrange a meeting with him and Simon Marandi or that Shri B.N. Safaya also paid money to Simon Marandi. Thus, prosecution has failed to establish this allegation.

208. Other circumstance against accused Capt. Satish Sharma as per charge sheet No. 1 is that at the instance of Captain Satish Sharma his Additional Private Secretary P.W. 74 Shri B.N. Safaya paid a sum of Rs. 10 lakhs to Simon Marandi, a J.M.M., M.P. P.W. 74 Shri B.N. Safaya has not supported this allegation. He was cross examined at length by learned prosecutor, but nothing worth while in this regard has come out from his cross examination. Thus, prosecution has failed to prove this allegation also.

209. Lastly P.W. 1 approver Shailender Mahto has stated that on 24th or 25th of July, 1993, he alongwith Suraj Mandal, Simon Marandi and Shibu Soren visited the residence of accused Ajít Singh and met him in his residential office. There they discussed the strategy of their group as well as the party of Ajit Singh on no confidence motion. During said meeting, Simon Marandi told him that talks with Captain Satish Sharma in respect of no confidence motion were going on. He further informed that if they would support the government, they would be paid cash and petrol pumps shall be allotted to them.

210. Ld. Prosecutor has contended that above referred version of P.W. 1 Shilender Mahto, approver clearly establish the role played by accused Captain Satish Sharma in offering the bribe to JMM, MPs. Thus, he is guilty participant in the conspiracy.

211. On the other hand, learned defence counsel for accused Captain Satish Sharma has submitted that above referred version of approver Shailender Mahto cannot be accepted because there is no independent direct or indirect corroboration to the version of approver Shailender Mahto. He has argued that it is settled law that before accepting the testimony of an approver, the court must seek some independent corroboration not only qua the commission of offence, but also *qua* the complicity of the concerned accused person in the commission of said offence. Since said corroboration is not forth coming, the testimony of approver in this regard should be rejected. He has cited "**Shankar v. State of Tamil Nadu, (1994) 4 SCC**

478, A. Devendran v. State of Tamil Nadu, (1997) 11 SCC 720, in support of his arguments.

212. Perusal of above cited judgments would show that it is settled law that while appreciating the testimony of an approver, the court must seek corroboration on material aspects of the case not only qua the commission of offence, but also *qua* the complicity of the accused concerned in the commission of said offence.

213. P.W. 4 Captain Dilawar Singh, is the another witness pertaining to the meeting dated 24-7-1993 which took place between accused Ajit Singh and JMM, MPs. In his cross examination by learned prosecutor, he has admitted that in the morning of 24-7-1993, 1½ hours after the visit of accused Bhajan Lal, Shibu Soren and Suraj Mandal had a meeting with accused Ajit Singh. It is to be borne in the mind that it was not suggested by learned prosecutor to the witness Captain Dilawar Singh that Simon Marandi was present in that meeting. Further, this witness has stated that during said meeting, aforesaid JMM, MPs and accused Ajit Singh discussed about having a joint strategy in relation to the no confidence motion. This imply that above referred meeting took place in presence of Captain Dilawar Singh. However, this witness nowhere states that Simon Marandi was present in the meeting or he disclosed in that meeting that some talks were going on with accused Captain Satish Sharma or that he told in that meeting that if JMM, MPs would support the government, they would be paid cash and petrol pumps or plots of HUDA would be allotted to them. Thus, testimony of P.W. 4 instead of providing corroboration to the version of approver P.W. 1 Shailender Mahto suggests that aforesaid version of the approver relating to the role of Captain Satish Sharma is an improvement.

214. Thus, under the circumstances, I am of the view that the test of corroboration is not satisfied so far as the aforesaid role of offering of bribe by accused Captain Satish Sharma to Simon Marandi is concerned. My aforesaid view is further strengthened of the fact that prosecution has not led any evidence to suggest that after the defeat of no confidence motion, any petrol pump or HUDA plot was allotted to the JMM, MPs or their, relatives. In view of my aforesaid discussion, I am of the opinion, that prosecution has not been able to establish the role played by accused Captain Satish Sharma in the bribing of JMM, MPs.

NAMES MENTIONED IN CHARGE-SHEET NO. 2 – CBI COURT

215. Charge-sheet No. 2 filed in this case relates to the role played by accused V. Rajeshwar Rao, M. Veerappa Moily, H.M. Revanna, Ramalinga Reddy, M. Thimmegowda, D.K. Audikeshvulu and Buta Singh in mobilizing the funds for bribing the JMM, MPs at Bangalore, bringing it to Delhi and delivery of said amount to accused Suraj Mandal, MP on 31-7-1993. The allegations of the prosecution relating to Bangalore angle of conspiracy have been detailed in the narration of facts in the earlier part of the judgment.

M. THIMMEGOWDA IS PROVED TO HAVE WITHDRAWN RS. 1 CRORE ON 30.7.1993 AFTER BANK HOURS AS OVER DRAFT ON TEMPORARY BASIS AND URGENTLY – HOLDS CBI COURT

216. As per allegations in charge-sheet No. 2 accused Thimmegowda (A-9) is one of the main players in the Bangalore and of the conspiracy. It is contended that he in his capacity as Managing Director of M/s. S.P.R. Groups Holdings (P) Limited, on 30-7-1993 withdraw a sum of Rs. 1 crore from the account of said company and after the said withdrawal, he passed on said money to accused No. 11 M. Veerappa Moily. Thereafter, said amount reached Delhi for being paid to the JMM, MPs.

217. To prove the withdrawal of money, prosecution has examined P.W. 24 Shri P.S. Rasamani, Senior Manager, Canara Bank, Bangalore, P.W. 25 Shri M. Sridhar,

Senior Manager, Canara Bank, Bangalore, P.W. 26 Shri A.V. Krishnamurthy, Senior Manager, Canara Bank, Bangalore, P.W. 27 Shri Mohd. Anwar, Senior Manager, Canara Bank, Bangalore, P.W. 28 Shri B.S. Mahle, Senior Manager, Canara Bank, Bangalore, and P.W. 60 Shri Padmanabha Rao, Chief Manager, Canara Bank, Bangalore.

218. Certain undisputed facts which can be gathered from the evidence placed on the record are:

(i) that accused M. Thimmegowda at the relevant was the Managing Director of M/s. S.P.R. Groups Holdings (P) Limited:

(ii) that M/s. S.P.R. Groups Holdings (P) Limited during the said period was maintaining Current Account no. 1968 in Canara Bank, Sheshadripuram Branch, Bangalore,

(iii) that accused M. Thimmegowda was authorized to operate said account in the capacity of Managing Director of the company,

(iv) that on 30-7-1993 accused M. Thimmegowsa applied for temporary over-draft of Rs. 1 Crore for 10 days vide application Ex. P.W. 25/J1 in the account of M/s. S.P.R. Groups Holdings (P) Limited

(v) that on 30-7-93 M/s. S.P.R. Groups Holdings (P) Limited withdrew from the account, a sum of Rs. 1 crore in following manner:

  (a) Rs. 15 lakhs through self cheque Ex. P.W. 25/A issued under the signatures of accused Sh. M. Thimmegowda.

  (b) Rs. 60 lakhs by way of credit (transfer entry) to the account of M/s. Ranganatha Groups against cheque Ex.P.W. 25/D issued under the signatures of Shri M. Thimmegowda, accused

  (c) Rs. 25 lakhs by way of credit (transfer entry) to the account of M/s. Yellamma Enterprises against the cheque Ex. P.W. 25/E issued under the signatures of accused M. Thimmegowda.

219. Case of the prosecution is that M/s. Ranganatha Groups and M/s. Yellamma Enterprises were benami concerns of accused M. Thimmegowda and their affairs were being controlled by Shri M. Thimmogowda. (A-9). It is further the case of the prosecution that under a well thought scheme, P.W. 61 M.S. Chelvaraju and P.W. 67 Shri T. Shivarama who were employees and relatives of accused M. Thimmegowda, issued cheques Ex. P.W. 25/B and Ex. P.W. 25/C for Rs. 60 lakhs and Rs. 25 lakhs respectively against the Current Accounts of M/s. Ranganath Groups and M/s. Yellamma Enterprises maintained in Canara Bank, Sheshadripuram Branch, Bangalore. They after withdrawing the amount on 30-7-1993 handed over the cash to accused M. Thimmegowda, who ultimately delivered it at the residence of accused M. Veerappa Moily.

220. Ld. prosecutor has contended that aforesaid cheque transactions between M/s. S.P.R. Groups Holdings (P) Limited and M/s. Ranganath Groups as well as M/s. Yellamma Enterprises were done with a view to ensure that withdrawal of money at a later stage may not be connected with the accused M. Thimmegowda.

221. To prove the aforesaid allegations, prosecution has examined P.W. 61 M.S. Chelvaraju and P.W. 67 T. Shivarama who actually withdrew the amount of Rs. 60 lakhs and Rs. 25 lakhs from the respective accounts of M/s. Ranganatha Groups and M/s. Yellamma Enterprises. Both of them have failed to support the case of the prosecutions.

222. P.W. 61 M.S. Chelvaraju have stated that the transaction of Rs. 60 lakhs from the account of M/s. S.P.R. Groups Holdings (P) Limited to the account of

M/s. Ranganath Groups vide cheque Ex. P.W. 25/D was a borrowing made on behalf of M/s. Ranganatha Groups. He has stated that on 30-7-1993, he withdrew from the account of M/s. Ranganath Group a sum of Rs. 60 lakhs under cheque Ex. P.W. 25/B and utilized the money for the payment of excise as well as other business commitments.

223. P.W. 67 Shri T. Shivarama of M/s. Yellamma Enterprises has also stated that on 30-7-1993 his concern borrowed a sum of Rs. 25 lakhs from M/s. S.P.R. Groups Holdings (P) Limited as the money was required for payment of excise and the other business commitments. He has also stated that in his capacity as partners of M/s. Yellamma Enterprises, he withdraw from the bank sum of Rs. 25 lakhs *vide* cheque Ex. P.W. 25/c and utilized the money for the benefit of his establishment. These two witnesses have not stated that after collection the payments of cheque Ex. P.W. 25/B and Ex. P.W. 25/C they respectively passed on the money to the accused M. Thimmegowda on 30-7-1993. Witnesses were treated hostile by the prosecution They were cross examined at length, but nothing worth while of prosecution case has been elected in their cross examination. They have denied the relevant suggestions relating to the prosecution case put to them during their cross examination. Thus, from the testimony of P.W. 61 Shri M.S. Chelvaraju and P.W. 67 Shri T. Shivarama it cannot be concluded that sums of Rs. 60 lakhs and Rs. 25 lakhs withdrawn by M.S. Chalvaraju and T. Shivarama under cheques Ex. P.W. 25/B and Ex .P.W. 25/C came into the hands of accused M. Thimmegowda.

224. Prosecution has examined P.W. 66 Manohar who was working as an Assistant in M/s. S.P.R. Groups Holdings (P) Limited and P.W. 84 Shri Gopal to establish that M/s. Ranganatha Groups and M/s. Yellamma Enterprises were benami concerns of accused M. Thimmegowda or that he was controlling the affairs of the said concerns. Both these witnesses are hostile to the case of prosecution and their testimony also is of no avail to the prosecution. It may not be out of place to mention that photocopy of partnership deed of M/s. Ranganatha Groups is proved on record as Ex. P.W. 61/DA. As per said partnership deed, besides M.S. chelvaraju, Shri Anne Gowda, Smt. Jaya Lakshmamma and Shri Chikka Thimmamma are the partners of M/s. Ranganatha Groups. There is no evidence on record to link any of the partners with accused M. Thimmegowda.

225. Prosecution has examined P.W. 65 Shri Radhakrishna, Assistant Commissioner of Income Tax, Central Circle-III, Bangalore. He incidentally was the Assessing Officer pertaining to the income tax returns filed by M/s. S.P.R. Groups Holdings (P) Limited, M/s. Ranganath Groups and M/s. Yellamma Enterprises. In his examination in chief he has stated that above referred three business concerns have not shown the above referred loan transactions of Rs. 60 lakhs and Rs. 25 lakhs in their respective income tax returns Ex. P.W. 65/A to Ex. P.W. 65/C. However in the cross examination witness has admitted that on 23-12-1993 a raid was at the business premises of M/s. S.P.R. Groups Holdings (P) Limited. In that raid, all the books of accounts including ledger book and cash book etc. were seized and those are still in the custody of Shri Lucas Peter, Deputy Commissioner of Income Tax, Central Circle-III, Bangalore. Ex. P.W. 65/D1 is a letter written by Shri Lucas Peter to the Director M/s. S.P.R. Groups Holdings (P) Limited. Ex. P.W. 65/D2, Ex. P.W. 65/D3 and Ex. P.W. 65/ D4 are the annexures to the aforesaid letters. P.W. 65 Shri Radha Krishna has admitted in his cross examination that Ex. P.W. 65/D2 to Ex.P.W. 65/D4 are true extracts of the ledger book and cash book of M/s S.P.R. Groups Holding (P) Limited. And these are certified to be true extracts of the documents seized by the income tax authorities in the search proceedings dated 13-12-1993 by Shri Lucas Peter, Deputy Commissioner of Income Tax. Perusal of Ex. P.W. 65/D2 and Ex. P.W. 65/D3 would reveal that these are supposed to be true extracts of the ledger book of M/s. S.P.R. Groups pages 108 and 109. According to these extracts, the borrowing of Rs. 25 lakhs and Rs. 60 lakhs by M/s. Yallamma Enterprises and M/s. Ranganath Groups *vide* cheques dated 30-7-1993 are reflected in the ledger books maintained by M/s. S.P.R. Groups Holdings (P) Limited, Ex. P.W. 65/D4 is the copy of the cash book of M/s. S.P.R. Groups Holding (P) Limited. In this cash book, on page 249 the above referred borrowings of Rs. 25 lakhs and Rs. 60 lakhs to the said concerns are mentioned. Therefore, the testimony of P.W. 65 Shri Radhakrishna do not establish that the above referred transactions were not reflected as loan transactions in the account book.

226. Further, P.W. 65 Shri Radhakrishna has stated that in his assessment order, he has accepted the payments of Rs. 60 lakhs and Rs. 25 lakhs made by M/s. S.P.R. Groups Holding (P) Limited on 30-7-1993 to M/s. Ranganath Groups and M/s. Yellamma Enterprises. However, he did not accept the information furnished by M/s. Ranganath Groups and M/s. Yellamma Enterprises regarding the source of repayment of above referred amounts to M/s. S.P.R. Groups Holdings (P) Limited. Thus, he took those amounts as income of the respective firms. This imply that even as per this witness, income-tax authorities have accepted that sums of Rs. 60 lakhs and Rs. 25 lakhs were paid *vide* cheques by M/s. S.P.R. Groups Holidags (P) Limited to M/s Ranganatha Groups and M/s. Yellamma Enterprises respectively.

227. Ex. P.W. 25/JI is admittedly the application submitted by accused M. Thimmegowda, Managing Director of M/s. S.P.R. Groups Holding (P) Limited seeking temporary over-draft of Rs. 1 crore in the current account no. 1968 of M/s. S.P.R. Groups Holdings (P) Limited. As per P.W. 60 Shri Padmanabha Rao, Chief Manager, this application was moved on 30-7-1993. P.W. 60 Shri Padmanabha Rao has stated that he telephonically obtained the sanction for temporary over-draft from Circle Office, Canara Bank, Bangalore. The sanction was received on telephone. Ex. P.W. 25/J2 is the confirmation letter regarding the receipt of sanction of temporary over draft which was signed by this witness. According to P.W. 60 Shri Padmanabha Rao after the receipt of confirmation and indent for Rs. 1 crore was sent to currency chest R.M.V. Extension, Bangalore. The indent is proved on record by P.W. 24 Shri P.S. Rasamani, who at that time was posted as Senior Manager in the currency chest, R.M.V. Extension, Bangalore. P.W. 24 Sh. P.S. Rasamani has stated that on the basis of indent, he prepared debit slip Ex. P.W. 24/B and in pursuance of the indent Rs. 95 lakhs was released to the representative of Sheshadripuram Branch of Canara Bank after obtaining his signature in token of the receipt of cash at the back of debit slip.

228. P.W. 25 Shri M. Sridhar, Senior Manager who was posted in Sheshadaripuram Branch of Canara Bank has proved his signature on indent Ex. P.W. 24/A and he has also admitted that he received the cash after signing at the back of debit slip Ex. P.W. 24/B. According to P.W. 25 Shri M. Shridhar, he had gone to collect the cash alongwith Shri C.K. Rao, Shri B.S. Mahle and Shri G.N. Sridhar, Managers. His version is supported by P.W. 28 Shri B.S. Mahle.

229. P.W. 60 Shri Padmanabha Rao has further stated that the cheque Ex. P.W. 25/A, Ex. P.W. 25/D and Ex. P.W. 25/E for Rs.15 lakhs, Rs. 60 lakhs and Rs. 25 lakhs respectivedy were passed on the same day. Cash payment of Rs. 15 lakhs was made against the cheque Ex. P.W. 25/A and the amounts of Rs. 60 lakhs and Rs. 25 lakhs relating to the cheque Ex. P.W. 25/D and Ex. P.W. 25/E were credited in the accounts of M/s. Ranganatha Groups and M/s. Yellamma Enterprises. He has also stated that on the same day Shri M.S. Chelvaraju of M/s Ranganatha Group issued a cheque of Rs. 60 lakhs Ex. P.W. 25/B and Shri T. Shivarama of M/s. Yellamma Enterprises issued a cheque of Rs. 25 lakhs Ex. P.W. 25/C. Both those cheques were passed and payments were made.

230. Perusal of the cheques Ex. P.W. 25/A, Ex. P.W. 25/B and Ex. P.W. 25/C would show that as per the stamp of the bank, it appears that payment against those cheques have been made on 31-7-1993. Whereas P.W. 60 Shri Padmanabha Rao and P.W. 29 Shri B.S. Mahle, Managers, Canara Bank have stated that payments against those cheques were made on 30-7-1993. This fact gets explained from the letter Ex. P.W. 25/K1 written by Sheshadripuram Branch to Circle Office, Bangalore, wherein it is clearly mentioned that the payment was made later on 30-7-1993 and the branch concerned has noted to collect T.O.D. interest from 30-7-1993 also. This imply that since the payment was made on 30-7-1993 after banking hours, the transaction has been reflected to have been conducted on 31-7-1993.

231. From the aforesaid evidence, one thing is obvious that the sum of Rs. 1 crore was withdrawn from Canara Bank Sheshadripuram Branch, Bangalore on urgent basis. This is evident from the fact that on 30-7-1993 accused M. Thimmegowda applied for temporary over-draft of Rs. 1 crore. The sanction for said over-draft was obtained telephonically by the manager, which was received after banking hours. Despite of that, cash was fetched from the currency chest R.M.V. Extension, Bangalore against an indent Ex. P.W. 25/A and the payments were made against the cheque Ex. P.W. 25/A, Ex. P.W. 25/B and Ex. P.W. 25/C on 30-7-1993. Though the transactions as per stamp of the bank on cheque have been reflected to be conducted on 31-7-1993.

232. The urgency to withdraw the amount is also evident from the letter of Canara Bank, Sheshadripuram Branch, Bangalore Ex. P.W. 25/K1 to LBA section, Circle Office, Bangalore. This letter is dated 4-8-1993. *Vide* this letter, Senior Manager, Sheshadripuram Branch has informed the Circle Office:

> "As the party urgently required cash on 30-7-93 and our cash transactions closes at 1. p.m. we have indented cash from Currency Chest, RMV Extension, Bangalore and accounted same as late cash and made payments of Rs. 1 Crore as late payment on 30-7-1993. We have noted to collect T.O.D. interest for 30.7.1993 also. This has concurrence of our Chief Manager."

233. The contents of this letter clearly show that payment was made against the cheques Ex. P.W. 25/A to Ex.P.W. 25/C on the request of the party at late hour.

SUSPICION ABOUT THE ROLE OF M. THIMMEGOWDA – MATERIAL WITNESSES WENT HOSTILE – NOT PROVED IF MONEY WITHDRAWN BY HIM WAS USED FOR BRIBING JMM MPs – HOLDS CBI COURT

234. On over-all view of above discussed evidence produced against accused M. Thimmegowda, I am of the opinion that prosecution has failed to establish beyond doubt that the money withdrawn from Canara bank, Sheshadripuram Branch on 30-7-1993 against the cheque Ex. P.W. 25/A to Ex. P.W. 25/C actually came into the hands of accused M. Thimmegowda. Only fact conclusively proved by this evidence is that on 30.7.1993 accused M. Thimmegowda sought temporary over draft of Rs. 1 Crore against the account of M/s. S.P.R. Groups Holdings (P) Limited out of which he withdraw Rs. 15 lakhs in cash. Remaining amount was transferred pursuant to the cheques Ex. P.W. 25/D and Ex. P.W. 25/E in the accounts of M/s. Ranganatha Groups and M/s. Yellamma Enterprises.

235. From the evidence of the bank officials and the relevant documents proved on record, following chain of events is established:

(1) Accused M. Thimmegowda (A-9) on 30-7-1993 applied for temporary over-draft of Rs. 1 Crore in the account of M/s. S.P.R. Groups Holdings (P) Limited;

(2) that sanction for temporary over draft was obtained telephonically and the party insisted for cash payment on the same date.

(3) that accused M. Thimmegowda issued cheque Ex. P.W. 25/D for Rs. 60 lakhs dated 30-7-1993 favouring M/s. Ranganatha Groups. The cheque was passed on the same day and thereafter P.W. M.S. Chelvaraju withdrew exact amount of Rs. 60 lakhs *vide* cheque Ex. P.W. 25/B;

(4) that accused M. Thimmegowda issued cheque Ex. P.W. 25/E dated 30-7-1993 for Rs. 25 lakhs favouring M/s. Yellamma Enterprises. It was passed on 30-7-1993. On the same day P.W. T. Shivarama of M/s. Yellamma Enterprises withdrew the exact amount of Rs. 25 lakhs *vide* cheque Ex. P.W. 25/E.

236. Above referred circumstances raise suspicion that the aforesaid banking transactions dated 30-7-1993 between M. Thimmgowda of M/s. S.P.R. Groups Holding (P) Limited, M.S. Chelvaraju of M/s. Ranganatha Groups and Shri T. Shivarama are not that innocent as those are projected to be. The urgency shown by the accused M. Thimmegowda in applying for temporary over-draft of Rs. 1 crore against the account of M/s. S.P.R. Groups Holding (P) Limited on 30-7-1993, his insistence for clearance of the cheques Ex. P.W. 25/A, Ex. P.W. 25/D and Ex. P.W. 25/E on the same day, and the fact that on 30-7-1993 itself after the amounts of cheques Ex. P.W. 25/D and Ex. P.W. 25/E were credited in respective account of M/s. Ranganatha Groups and M/s. Yellemma Enterprises, the amounts of Rs. 60 lakhs and Rs. 25 lakhs were withdrawn by M.S. Chelvaraju of M/s. Ranganatha and T. Shivarama of M/s. Yellamma Enterprises *vide* cheques Ex. P.W. 25/B and Ex. P.W. 25/C raised some suspicion that the amount in question may have come into the hands of accused M. Thimmegowda. But suspicion under law is no substitute for the proof. In the matter of **Sarwan Singh Rattan Singh v. State of Punjab, AIR 1957 SC 637,** Hon'ble Supreme Court has observed:—

> "It is no doubt a matter of regret that a foul cold-blooded and cruel murder should go unpunished. There may also be an element of truth in the prosecution story against the accused. Considered as a whole, the prosecution story may be true: but between 'may be true' and 'must be true' there is inevitably a long distance to travel and the whole of this distance must be covered by the prosecution by legal, reliable and unimpeachable evidence before and accused can be convicted."

237. From the aforesaid judgment of the Apex Court, it is obvious that in order to bring home the guilt of the accused, prosecution cannot take help of suspicious circumstances only. It is required to discharge a legal onus to prove the incriminating circumstances against the accused by legal, reliable and unimpeachable evidence before an accused can be convicted.

238. Even if, for the sake of prosecution, it is assumed that on 30-7-1993, Rs. 1 crore withdrawn under the cheques Ex. P.W. 25/A to C came into the hands of accused M. Thimmegowda, then also in order to establish his role in the conspiracy, prosecution is required to establish other link in the chain of circumstances that he delivered said money at the residence of accused M. Veerappa Moily.

239. To prove said allegations, prosecution has examined P.W. 51 Shri T.R. Suresh, the then telephone operator posted at the home office of accused M. Veerappa Moily. P.W. 52 Sh. Parmesh, the then cook posted at the official residence of accused M. Veerappa Moily. P.W. 53 Shri Negraj C. Dalayat (assistant cook) posted at the residence of accused M. Veerappa Moily and P.W. 54 Shri B. Harish Chander Bhatt, P.R.O. posted in the office of accused M. Veerappa Moily. Above referred witnesses have not supported the case of prosecution. They were declared hostile by learned prosecutor and cross examined at length. However, nothing worth while could be elicited from their cross examination. There is nothing in the testimony of said witnesses to suggest that accused M. Thimmegowda delivered two suitcases at the residence of accused M. Veerappa Moily on 30-7-1993 Thus, this link in the chain of events is also not established.

EVIDENCE PERUSED – SUBMISSIONS CONSIDERED ABOUT ROLE OF AUDIKESHVULU IN THIS CONSPIRACY – CBI COURT

240. Coming to the role of accused D.K. Audikeshvulu. According to the prosecution, he is also a source of money which originated at Bangalore and came into the hands of JMM, MPs as illegal gratification. He is alleged to have played role, in arranging the money and also carrying it into Delhi and delivering it at Andhra Bhawan from where it was allegedly taken to the residence of Suraj Mandal.

241. There is no direct evidence against accused D.K. Audikeshvulu to establish his involvement in the conspiracy. Prosecution has sought to establish the complicity of accused D.K. Audikeshvulu in the conspiracy to bribe JMM, MPs or other members of parliament by circumstantial evidence.

242. First allegation against accused D.K. Audikeshvulu (A-12) is that he was very close to accused V. Rajeshwar Rao (A-8). He was at Delhi from 24-7-1993 to 29-7-1993 in connection with some writ petition filed by him in Supreme Court of India. That on 26-7-1993, he was seen at the residence of accused V. Rajeshwar Rao by P.W. 64 Shri Ashok Rao Anand Rao Deshmukh when he had gone there to introduce four JMM, MPs with accused V. Rajeshwar Rao.

243. Prosecution has not led any evidence to prove close association between V. Rajeshwar Rao, accused and D.K. Audikeshvulu, accused or to prove that accused D.K. Audikeshvulu was present at the residence of accused V. Rajeshwar Rao on 26-7-1993 when four J.M.M., M.Ps have allegedly gone there to meet him. P.W. 64 Ashok Rao Deshmukh could be the witness to prove said fact. He is a hostile witness. He was cross examined at length by learned prosecutor. However, even a suggestion was not put to P.W. 64 Ashok Rao Anand Rao Deshmukh that he saw accused D.K. Audikeshvulu at the residence of accused V. Rajeshwar Rao on 26-7-1993. Thus, allegation No. 1 is not established.

244. Second allegation of the prosecution against accused D.K. Audikeshvulu is that during the relevant period besides others he was in constant touch with accused M. Veerappa Moily, the then Chief Minister of Karnataka. P.W. 51 Shri Suresh, P.W. 52 Shri Parmesh, P.W. 53 Shri Nagraj. C and P.W. 54 Shri Harish Chandara Bhatt, are the four witnesses who were attached to the then Chief Minister of Karnataka, accused M. Veerappa Moily in one capacity or the other. Those witnesses have been examined by the prosecution to establish the above referred allegations. They have not supported the case of the prosecution. They do not say anything about their having seen accused D.K. Audikeshvulu at the residence of accused M. Veerappa Moily or his home office during their tenure in the establishment of accused M. Veerappa Moily. Those witnesses were treated hostile by the prosecution. Nothing worth while has been elicited by learned prosecutor during their cross examinations.

245. The basic allegation against accused D.K. Audikeshvulu is that he was Managing Director of M/s. Karnataka Breweries & Distilleries Limited. M/s. Karnataka Breweries & Distilleries Limited, (M/s. K.B.D.L.) and Managing Partner of M/s. Sapthagiri Enterprises, a sister concern of M/s. K.B.D.L. Both the establishments were having current account in R.M.V. Extension, Bangalore Branch of Canara Bank. According to learned prosecutor, one Padmavati Enterprises was also having a Saving Account in Canara Bank, R.M.V. Extension, Bangalore. Shri K. Muniraja was shown to be the proprietor of said firm. M/s. Padmavati Enterprises as per prosecution was a fictitious firm and actually accused D.K. Audikeshvulu was the benami owner of the said firm. It is alleged that on 29-7-1993 accused

D.K. Audikeshvulu issued a cheque. Ex. P.W. 30/A for Rs. 30 lakhs in favour of M/s. Padmavati Enterprises from the account of M/s. Sapthagiri Enterprises. The said amount of Rs. 30 lakhs was withdrawn on 30-7-1993 by a cheque Ex. P.W. 29/A purported to have been issued under the signature of Sh. K. Muniraja proprietor of M/s. Padmavati Enterprises, but the payment of the said cheque was received by P.W. 33 Dwarka Nath, an employee of accused D.K. Audikeshvulu. On 30-7-1993 two other cheques Ex. P.W. 29/B and Ex. P.W. 29/C for Rs. 7,17,349 and Rs. 14,78,125 were issued from the account of M/s K.B.D.L. in favour of one Shri V.P. Ramakrishna. According to the prosecution, the amount withdrawn *vide* three cheques ultimately came into the hands of accused D.K. Audikeshvulu and he carried it to Delhi on 30-7-1993 by evening flight of Indian Airlines from Bangalore.

246. To prove aforesaid allegations, prosecution has examined P.W. 29 Smt. Vijay Parkash, Clerk, Canara Bank, RMV Extension, Bangalore, P.W. 30 Manager Shri H.S. Parbhakar, Canara Bank, RMV Extension, Bangalore and P.W. 33 Shri Dwarka Nath, an employee of M/s. K.B.D.L. Certain undisputed facts established from the evidence on record and the admissions made by the accused D.K. Audikeshvulu in his statement under section 313, Cr.P.C. are:

(i) that accused D.K. Audikeshvulu was the Managing Director of M/s. K.B.D.L;

(ii) that M/s. K.B.D.L. was maintaining Current Account no. 448 in Canara Bank, R.M.V. Extension Branch, Bangalore and accused D.K. Audikeshvulu was the authorized signatory of the said account;

(iii) that M/s. Sapthagiri Enterprises was the sister concern of M/s. K.B.D.L. and accused D.K. Audikeshvulu was the Managing Partner of the said firm;

(iv) that M/s. Sapthagiri Enterprises was maintaining Current Account No. 446 in Canara Bank, R.M.V. Extension Branch, Bangalore and accused D.K. Audikeshvulu was the authorised signatory of the said account;

(v) that a cheque dated 29-7-1993, Ex. P.W. 30/A for Rs. 30 lakhs favouring M/s. Padmavati Enterprises was issued under the signature of accused D.K. Audikeshvulu and the amount of said cheque was credited to the account of M/s. Padamavati Enterprises namely C.A. No. 754 maintained in Canara Bank, R.M.V. Extension Branch;

(vi) that accused D.K. Audikeshvulu also issued two cheques Ex. P.W. 29/B and Ex. P.W. 29/C, both dated 30-7-1993 for Rs. 6,17,349 and Rs. 14,78,125 favouring V.P. Ramakrishna from the account of M/s. K.B.D.L. which were honoured.

247. P.W. 30 Shri H.S. Parbhakar, Manager, Canara Bank, R.M.V. Extension Branch, Bangalore has stated that on 30-7-1993 self cheque Ex. P.W. 29/A for Rs. 30 lakhs issued by M/s. Padmavati Enterprises purported to have been signed by Shri K. Muniraja, was presented in the branch.

248. P.W. 29 Smt. Vijaya Parkash was the clerk Canara Bank, R.M.V. Extension Branch, Bangalore and she has made the payments against the three cheque Ex. P.W. 29/A to Ex. P.W. 29/C. She has stated on oath that she made payments of cheque Ex. P.W. 29/A for Rs.30 lakhs favouring self issued by M/s. Padmavati Enterprises, cheque Ex. P.W. 29/B and Ex.P.W. 29/C for Rs. 6,17,349 and Rs. 14,78,125 favouring V.P. Ramakrishna issued under the signature of accused D.K. Audikeshvulu on behalf of M/s. K.B.D.L. According to her, she made payment of all the three cheques to Shri V.P. Ramakrishna because M/s. K.B.D.L. and M/s. Padmawati Enterprises were sister concerns and V.P. Ramakrishna used to bring the cheques of both the concerns for payment. She has also stated that she made endorsement Ex. P.W. 29/D at the back of cheque Ex. P.W. 29/B while making said payment.

249. Perusal of endorsement Ex. P.W. 29/D at the back of cheque Ex. P.W. 29/B would reveal that aforesaid endorsement contains the details of the denomination of currency notes *vide* which the payment has been made to the party. Said detail is for the payment of Rs. 50,95,474. If we add up the amounts of cheques Ex. P.W. 29/A to Ex. P.W. 29/C, the amounts come to Rs. 50,95,474. This circumstance clearly shows that witness Smt. Vijay Parkash is telling the truth.

250. If V.P. Ramakrishna took payment of Rs. 50,95,474 against the said three cheques, he alone could be the best witness to tell whether or not said money reached into the hands of accused D.K. Audikeshvulu on 30-7-1993 or how the money was utilized by him. Prosecution has not cared to examine V.P. Ramakrishna as a witness nor he has been cited as a witness. Therefore, it cannot be conclusively said that aforesaid amount was delivered by V.P. Ramakrishna to accused D.K. Ausikeshvulu.

251. P.W. 33 Dwarka Nath, Accounts Officers, M/s. K.B.D.L. is the witness examined by the prosecution to establish that the amount of those cheques after encashment came into the hands of accused D.K. Audikeshvulu. P.W. 33 Dwarka Nath is a hostile witness. He was cross examined at length by learned prosecutor, but nothing worth while has come in evidence. This witness has denied the suggestion that on 30-7-1993 he alongwith V.P. Ramakrishna had gone to Canara Bank, RMV Extension, Bangalore for collection of money against cheques Ex. P.W. 29/A to Ex. P.W. 29/C and they together collected the sum of Rs. 50,95,474. He has also denied the suggestion that he brought Rs. 30 lakhs paid against cheque Ex.P.W. 29/A to the office on 30-7-1993 and handed over said money to accused D.K. Audikeshvulu. If the aforesaid suggestions put to the witness during cross examination by the prosecutor is any indication, the case of prosecution appears to be that only the sum of Rs. 30 lakhs received against cheque Ex. P.W. 29/A was brought by P.W. 33 Dwarka Nath to the office of M/s. K.B.D.L. on 30-7-1993 and delivered to accused D.K. Audikeshvulu. However, Dwarka Nath has not supported this version. Therefore, reaching of money withdrawn either against cheque Ex. P.W. 29/A or cheque Ex. 29/B and Ex. P.W. 29/C in the hands of accused D.K. Audikeshvulu is not established.

252. Learned prosecutor has submitted that M/s. Padmavati Enterprises was a fictitious concern and it was a benami firm controlled by accused D.K. Audkeshvulu. In support of his contention, he has submitted that P.W. Dwarka Nath has admitted in his cross examination that account opening form pertaining to Current Account No. 754 of M/s. Padmavati Enterprises Ex. P.W. 20/DA is filled in the handwriting of P.W. Dwarka Nath. He has further pointed out that P.W. Dwarka Nath has also admitted that cheque Ex. P.W. 29/A is filled in his handwriting. According to learned prosecutor if M/s. Padmavati Enterprises had no concern with M/s. K.B.D.L., then there was no occasion for P.W. Dwarka Nath an employee M/s. K.B.D.L. either to fill up account opening form for M/s. Padmavati Enterprises or to fill in the cheque Ex. P.W. 29/A for Rs. 30 lakhs on behalf of said firm. Ld. prosecutor has contended that aforesaid two circumstances clearly show that M/s. Padmavati Enterprises was a fictitious firm of accused D.K. Audikeshvulu and the amount of cheque Ex. P.W. 29/A was withdrawn by P.W. Dwarka Nath on behalf of M/s. Padmavati Enterprises and delivered to accused D.K. Audkikeshvulu. He has also argued that the deposit of money *i.e.,* Rs. 30 lakhs *vide* Ex. P.W. 30/A in the account of M/s. Padmavati Enterprises and subsequent withdrawal from the account of M/s.Padmavati Enterprises was done only with a view to ensure that the withdrawal of money vide cheques Ex. P.W.2/A to Ex. P.W. 2/C may not be linked with the accused D.K. Auskeshvulu at a later stage.

BANK TRANSACTIONS CONDUCTED WITH UNDUE HASTE ON 30.7.1993 BY D.K. AUDIKESHVULU BY HIS FIRM – BY HIS MEN – DO CREATE A SUSPICION ABOUT HIS CONNECTION WITH THIS CONSPIRACY – AND BRIBING OF JMM, MPs – HOLDS CBI COURT

253. The above referred circumstances pointed out by learned prosecutor raise a suspicion that the banking transactions conducted *vide* cheques Ex. P.W. 30/A and Ex. P.W. 29/A to Ex. P.W. 29/C are not that innocent as the same are projected to be. There is a possibility that the prosecution story may be true, but suspicion however strong is no substitute for the proof. Considering the fact that V.P. Ramakrishna, who as per the testimony of P.W. 29 Smt. Vijay Parkash, cashier/clerk, Canara bank, RMV Extension, Bangalore collected the sum of Rs. 50,95,474 against those three cheques, has not been cited nor examined by the prosecution and that P.W. 33 Dwarka Nath has not supported the case of the prosecution that he delivered Rs. 30 lakhs to accused D.K. Audikeshvulu, it cannot be concluded beyond doubt that the amount in question actually reached in the hands of accused D.K. Audikeshvulu.

254. In order to establish that M/s. Padmavati Enterprises, Proprietor K. Muniraja was a fictitious firm, prosecution has examined P.W. 34 Smt. Ammne Thomas, beat postwoman.

255. Ex. P.W. 29/DA is the account opening form relating to Current Account No. 754 Shri Padmavati Enterprises, Proprietor K. Muniraja. This account was opened on 19-5-1992. In this account opening form there are two addresses one Muniraja, s/o K.B. Krishaniah,203, 6th Cross, Victoria Layout and other 6-311, Gandhi Street, Sri Kalahasthi, Chittoor, District, 517644 (A.P).

256. P.W. 34 Smt. Ammne Thomas, has stated that she was beat post-woman relating to Victoria Layout within the jurisdiction of Vivek Nagar District Post Office. According to her, there was no house No. 203, 6th Cross, Victoria Layout Bangalore in the year 1992.

257. From this testimony also, prosecution is trying to establish that the address of Sri Padmavati Enterprises given in the account opening form Ex. P.W. 29/DA was a fictitious address, implying thereby that firm was a fictitious concern. In my opinion, above referred testimony of P.W. Ammne Thomas is not sufficient to conclude that M/s. Padmavati Enterprises was a fictitious concern, firstly because P.W. 34 Smt. Ammne Thomas in her cross examination done on behalf of accused D.K. Audikeshvulu has stated that pin code of Vivek Nagar was 560047. She has also stated that she does not know the pin code of Victoria Layout of Raj Mahal Vilas Post Office, Bangalore. This answer given by P.W. Ammne Thomas, though not very clear, imply that possibly there was another Victoria Layout in Bangalore located within the area of Raj Mahal Vilas Post Office. There is nothing on the record to suggest that CBI officers have done personal investigation to check whether or not there were more than one Victoria Layout and if so whether or not 203, 6th Cross, existed in some other Victoria Layout at the relevant time. Further, as per the account opening form Ex. P.W. 29/DA, one other address of Sri Padmavati Enterprises, 6-311, Gandhi Street, Sri Kalahasthi, Chittoor, District 517644 (A.P.) is mentioned. No attempt has been made by investigating agency to verify whether or not Sri Padmavati Enterprises existed at the aforesaid address of Sri Kalahasthi, Chittoor, AP.

258. P.W. 116 Shri Vivek Johri, DIG, the Chief Investigating Officer has admitted in his cross examination that in the Indian Express dated 16-7-1996 Ex. P.W. 33/B a news report was published mentioning that M/s. Padmavati Enterprises was a non existent firm. He has also admitted that consequent to the said news report one K. Muniraja wrote a letter dated 4-1-1997 to the Director, C.B.I. alongwith copies to S.P. C.B.I. as well as the Investigating Officer refuting the correctness of said news report. He has proved photo copy of the said letter Ex. P.W. 116/B1 and its annexures Ex. P.W. 116/B2 to Ex. P.W. 116/B-23.

259. Perusal of the letter Ex. P.W. 116/B-1 would show that *vide* this letter K. Muniraja insisted that M/s. Padmavati Enterprises was an existing concern and it was conducting business from premises 6.311 Gandhi Street, Sri Kalahasthi, Chitoor District 517644 (A.P).

260. Ex. P.W. 116/B-2 to Ex. P.W. 116/B-23 are photo copies of certain assessment orders of Commercial Tax Department, Certificates of Registration of M/s. Sri Padmavati Enterprises, Income Tax Returns of K. Muniraja, his ration card and the voters list etc. suggesting that M/s. Padamavati Enterprises was a genuine concern based at the address of Sri Kalahasthi and K. Muniraja was a genuine person.

261. Despite of receiving said information furnished by K. Muniraja admittedly Shri Vivek Johri did not care to send any investigating team to Sri Kalahasthi in order to verify the correctness of the information. In his cross examination, he has given an explanation that he did not consider it necessary to verify that averment in letter Ex. P.W. 116/B-1 because charge sheet relating to Bangalore angle of conspiracy was already submitted in the court.

262. In my opinion, explanation of the Investigating Officer Shri Vivek Johri is not satisfactory because admittedly further investigation of the case was going and final charge sheet was filled subsequently on 22-1-1997.

263. P.W. Vivek Johri in his further cross examination has stated that he is not aware as to how many Victoria Lay outs are there in Bangalore. That being the case, it is obvious that a serious investigation to verify the correctness of the address mentioned in account opening form Ex. P.W. 29/DA has not been done. Therefore, it cannot be concluded that M/s. Padmavati Enterprises was a fictitious firm or K. Muniraja was no existent person.

264. In view of above discussion, though there is some cause for suspecting that prosecution story may be true, yet the evidence adduced by the prosecution to establish that the funds of cheque Ex. P.W. 30/A reached in the hands of accused D.K. Audikeshvulu falls short of actual proof.

265. Even if, for the sake of arguments, it is assumed that the amounts withdrawn *vide* cheques Ex. P.W. 29/A to Ex. P.W. 29/C reached in the hands of accused D.K. Audikeshvulu, then also in order to establish his complicity in the conspiracy, prosecution has to establish a link between aforesaid money withdrawn from Canara Bank, R.M.V. Extension on 30-7-1993 with the money delivered at the residence of Suraj Mandal.

TRAVEL BY INDIAN AIRLINES BY AUDIKESHVULU ON 30.7.1993 FROM BANGALORE TO DELHI AFTER CONDUCTING BANK TRANSACTIONS IN HASTE – WITH CO-ACCUSED – ALSO CREATE SUSPICION ABOUT HIS CONNECTION WITH THIS CONSPIRACY – AND BRIBING OF JMM MPs – HOLDS CBI COURT

266. It is admitted that on 30-7-1993 accused D.K. Audikeshvulu travelled from Bangalore to Delhi by evening flight of Indian Airlines. Accused H.M. Revanna and Ramalinga Reddy and Buta Singh also travelled from Bangalore to Delhi in the same flight.

267. Prosecution has examined P.W. 46 Bachan Singh, driver of the staff car of M/s. M.B.D.L. guest House, P.W. 47 Darmyan Singh, an employee of guest house and P.W. 48 Roop Ram, taxi driver to establish that on 30-7-1993 accused

D.K. Audikeshvulu arrived at Delhi Airport alongwith H.M. Revanna and Ramalinge Reddy. They were carrying suitcases and handbag. Their suitcases and hand bag were loaded in the car of Bachan Singh and Roop Ram and thereafter they all went to Andhra Bhawan, where accused H.M. Revanna, accused Ramalinga Reddy and accused D.K. Audikeshvulu went upstairs to meet accused V. Rajeshwar Rao. After sometime, they came back and went to Hotel Claridges. Accused Ramalinga Reddy and accused H.M. Revanna checked in hotel on the night of 30-7-1993 alongwith suitcases and hand bag and accused D.K. Audikeshvulu went and stayed at M.B.D.L. Guest House. He also carried a suitcase brought from Bangalore.

268. P.W. 46 Bachan Singh, P.W. 47 Darmyan Singh and P.W. 48 Roop Ram are hostile witnesses and they have not supported the above referred allegations of the prosecution. They were cross examined at length by learned prosecutor, but nothing worth while against either accused D.K. Audikeshvulu, accused H.M. Revenue or accused Ramalinga Reddy has come on record. A close perusal of the testimony of these witnesses would show that to most of the suggestions put to them by learned special prosecutor they have taken shelter of memory by stating that they do not remember in respect of suggestions put to them. This raise a slight suspicion that these witnesses may be concealing the truth, but a possibility cannot be ruled out that they actually may not be remembering about those facts because alleged incident took place on 30-7-1993, whereas the witnesses were examined 6 years later in the year 1999.

269. Further, case of the prosecution is that on 31-7-1993, morning accused D.K. Audikeshvulu went to Hotel Claridges in the car of M.B.D.L. alongwith driver Bachan Singh. He carried suitcase brought from Bangalore alongwith him. At the hotel he was joined by accused H.M. Revanna and accused Ramalinga Reddy. Suitcases and hand bag brought by them were loaded in the taxi of Roop Ram, who had also arrived there. P.W. Vijay Handa and P.W. Harsharan Lal also reached at Hotel Claridges at that time. Thereafter, they all went to Andhra Bhawan and from there after having a talk with accused V. Rajeshwar Rao the money brought from Bangalore by D.K. Audikeshvulu, accused H.M. Revanna and accused Ramalinga Reddy in respective VIP Suitcases and hand bag was sent to the residence of Suraj Mandal and delivered there. According to, the prosecution, money was carried to the residence of Suraj Mandal in the Maruti Car of Vijay Handa in which Harsharan Lal and Ganga Singh travelled and also in the taxi of Roop Ram in which accused H.M. Revanna travelled.

270. To prove aforesaid allegations, prosecution has examined P.W. 48 Roop Ram, P.W. 87 Harsharan Lal P.W. 89, Ganga Singh and P.W. 93 Vijay Handa. Above referred witnesses have not supported the prosecution story. They were declared hostile and cross examined at length, but nothing worth while has come out from their cross examination.

271. Ld. Prosecutor has contended that despite of the fact that witnesses examined by the prosecution regarding the chain of events to establish D.K. Audikeshvulu, H.M. Revanna and Ramalinga Reddy from Bangalore to Delhi and from Delhi Airport to Hotel Claridges and lastly to the residence of Suraj Mandal in the morning of 31-7-1993 *via* Andhra Bhawan have not supported the case of prosecution, the testimony of P.W. 100 Shri Dara Ravani, the cook of Suraj Mandal, M.P. coupled with the evidence pertaining to the presence of accused H.M. Revanna, Ramalinga Reddy and D.K. Audikeshvulu at Delhi in the night of 30-7-1993 and also in the morning of 31-7-1993 establish the Bangalore angle of conspiracy.

272. P.W. 100 Dara Rawani was the cook of Suraj Mandal at the relevant time. He has stated that around six years prior to his testimony in the Court one morning during rainy season 3/4 persons visited the residence of Suraj Mandal, M.P. in two cars. They delivered three suitcases and two packets which were kept in a room. He has also stated that on the same day P.W. 101 Kamal Yadav brought Sushil Kumar accompanied by two persons to the residence of Suraj Mandal at around 12.00 noon or 1.00 p.m. He served them tea in the room where said suitcases and bags were lying and he noticed that one of those suitcases was open and it contained G.C. Notes of Rs. 100 denomination, each. According to this witness, 2/3 hours later Sushil Kumar and said persons left alongwith said suitcases and bags containing money. If this version is analysed in the background of testimony of P.W. 103 Satish Chand Sharma, Manager, Punjab National Bank, Naoroji Nagar, New Delhi who had collected money from the residence of Suraj Mandal, then it appears that money was delivered at the residence of Suraj Mandal on 31.7.1993 However, the version of Dara Ravani is contradicted by P.W. 101 Kamal Yadav who has, without specifying the date, stated that he was told by Dara Ravani that Suraj Mandal has kept three or four suitcases in a room and locked it. He has further stated that on the day, after Dara Ravani told him about those suitcases, he was sent by Suraj Mandal to call Sushil Kumar from his residence. On the same day at around 1.30 or 2.00 p.m. Sushil Kumar arrived at the residence of Suraj Mandal alongwith two or three persons and they carried two suitcases in a Maruti Gipsy. As per the version of Kamal Yadav, the suitcases must have been delivered at the residence of Suraj Mandal on 30.7.1993 because according to P.W. 103 Satish Chand Sharma, he collected the money from the residence of Suraj Mandal alongwith Sushil Kumar on 31.7.1993. Dara Ravani in his cross-examination by Counsel for accused M. Veerappa Moily has stated that Sushil Kumar visited the residence of Suraj Mandal one or two days after the delivery of those suitcases and bags at his residence and thereafter he has added that on the next day of delivery, Sushil Kumar took away those bags and packets in the vehicle of Suraj Mandal. This version coupled with the testimony of Kamal Yadav imply that money referred to by Dara Ravani was delivered on 30.7.1993. Thus, by no stretch of imagination it can be linked with the money allegedly brought by accused H.M. Revanna, Ramalinga Reddy and D.K. Audikeshvulu from Bangalore in the night of 30-7-1993. Further, even if it is assumed that the money referred to by P.W. 100 Dara Ravani was delivered at the residence of Suraj Mandal in the morning of 31-7-1993, then also, his testimony do not throw any light on the identity of person or persons who had delivered the money at the residence of Suraj Mandal. Therefore, it cannot be concluded that the persons who delivered money at the residence of Suraj Mandal as per the version of P.W. 100 Dara Ravani were P.Ws Harsharan Lal, Vijay Kumar Handa, Ganga Singh, Roop Ram driver and accused H.M. Revanna. Thus, I do not find much force in the contention of learned prosecutor.

273. Next allegation of the prosecution against the accused D.K. Audikeshvulu is that while the present case was being investigated, accused D.K. Audikeshvulu approached Shri K. Narayanan, Resident Manager of M/s. M.B.D.L. to destroy the occupancy register of M/s. M.B.D.L. Guest House for the year 1993 as well as relevant log book of Maruti Car of the guest house. It is also the case of prosecution that on 29.10.1996 he again approached Shri K. Narayanan and asked him about the enquiries made from him by CBI. Thereafter, he gave Rs. 49,000 to Sh. K. Narayanan with the directions that he should ensure that Bachan Singh should make himself unavailable for sometime.

274. P.W. 55 Rais Ahmed P.W. 56 Dildar Ahmed, P.W. 57 Gurdial Singh and P.W. 59 K. Narayanan have been examined to prove said allegation. They have not supported the prosecution case. They have been cross examined by learned prosecutor, but in vain. They have denied the material suggestions put by learned prosecutor.

SUSPICION ABOUT THE ROLE OF AUDIKESHVULU IN THIS CONSPIRACY IS MADE OUT – MATERIAL WITNESSES WENT HOSTILE – NOT CITED – NOT EXAMINED – REMAIN SHORT OF PROOF OF HIS COMPLICITY – HOLDS CBI COURT

275. From the circumstances discussed above, I am of the view that though the prosecution evidence raise slight suspicion suggesting that prosecution story may be true, but it falls short of the actual proof. Therefore, I am of the view that prosecution has not been able to establish complicity of accused D.K. Audikeshvulu in the conspiracy beyond reasonable doubt.

EVIDENCE PERUSED – SUBMISSIONS CONSIDERED ABOUT THE ROLE OF REVANNA – RAMALINGA REDDY – M. VEERAPPA MOILY, CM, KARNATAKA IN THIS CONSPIRACY – CBI COURT

276. Coming to the role of accused H.M. Revanna, Ramalinga Reddy and M. Veerappa Moily. Basic allegations against them are that accused M. Veerappa Moily came from Delhi to Bangalore on 29-7-1993 with the object to mobilize and send the funds for bribing JMM, MPs. At his instance, accused D.K. Audikeshvulu and accused M. Thimmegowda mobilized the funds. Accused M. Thimmegowda delivered two suitcases containing Rs. 1 Crore at the residence of accused M. Veerappa Moily. From there, accused H.M. Revanna and accused Ramalinga Reddy carried said two suit-cases plus one other suit-case and a hand bag containing money to Bangalore Airport. They came to Delhi by evening flight of Indian Airlines. Accused D.K. Audikeshvulu and accused Buta Singh also travelled to Delhi by same flight. At Delhi, said money was ultimately delivered at the residence of Suraj Mandal with the help of P.Ws Harsharan Lal, Vijay Kumar Handa, Ganga Singh and taxi driver Roop Ram.

277. In my earlier discussion, I have already concluded that prosecution has failed to establish beyond doubt that accused M. Thimmegowda on 30-7-1993 delivered Rs. 1 Crore contained in two suitcases at the residence of accused M. Veerappa Moily. Though prosecution has been able to establish that accused D.K. Audikeshvulu, Buta Singh, H.M. Revanna and Ramalinga Reddy travelled by evening flight of Indian Airlines on 30-7-1993 from Bangalore to Delhi, but it failed to establish that any money was brought by accused D.K. Audikeshvulu, H.M. Revanna and Ramalinga Reddy. In suitcases from Bangalore to Delhi or said money was ultimately delivered at the residence of Suraj Mandal at the instance of accused V. Rajeshwar Rao.

278. Only other circumstance alleged against accused M. Veerappa Moily, accused H.M. Revanna and accused Ramalinga Reddy is that on 30.7.1993 from the residence of accused M. Veerappa Moily, accused H.M. Revanna and accused Ramalinga Reddy carried three V.I.P. suitcases and hand bag containing money to Bangalore Airport which ultimately reached Delhi and was delivered to Suraj Mandal. In order to prove carrying of said three V.I.P. suit-cases and a hand bag by accused H.M. Revanna and accused Ramalinga Reddy from the residence of accused M. Veerappa Moily, prosecution has examined P.W. 51 R.R. Suresh P.W. 52 Smt, Parmesh, P.W. 53 Shri Nagraj. C and P.W. 54 Shri B. Harish Chander Bhatt. Those witnesses were in the personal staff of accused M. Veerappa Moily at the relevant time. They have not supported above referred story of prosecution. They were declared hostile and cross examined at length by learned prosecutor, but nothing worth-while to implicate accused H.M. Revanna, accused Ramalinga Reddy or accused M. Veerappa Moily has come out on the record.

MATERIAL WITNESSES WENT HOSTILE – PROSECUTION FAILED TO PROVE CASE OF COLLECTING – BRINGING MONEY FROM BANGALORE TO DELHI – PASSING ON TO JMM, MPs AGAINST H.M. REVANNA – RAMALINGA REDDY – M. VEERAPPA MOILY, CM, KARNATAKA – HOLDS CBI COURT

279. In view of aforesaid circumstances, I am of the opinion that prosecution has failed to establish the role played by accused H.M. Revanna, accused Ramalinga Reddy and accused M. Veerappa Moily in the conspiracy.

280. The allegations against accused Buta Singh in relation to Bangalore end of conspiracy is based upon the assumption that he visited Bangalore on 30-7-1993 in order to supervise the mobilizing of the funds and bring it back to Delhi under his supervision. In view of my discussion above, prosecution has failed to establish beyond doubt that any money was brought from Bangalore or got delivered at the residence of Suraj Mandal, M.P. Thus, complicity of accused Buta Singh so far as Bangalore end of conspiracy is concerned cannot be concluded.

AJIT SINGH HAD NO ROLE IN THE BRIBING CASE OF JMM OR ANY OTHER MPs – HOLDS CBI COURT

281. Coming to the role of accused Ajit Singh in the conspiracy to bribe J.M.M., M.Ps only circumstance against him is the statement of P.W. 1 Shailender Mahto approver and the statement of P.W. 4 Captain Dilawar Singh. According to said two witnesses on 24-7-1993 J.M.M., M.Ps Suraj Mandal, Shibu Soren, Simon Marandi and Shailender Mahto had a meeting with accused Ajit Singh, in which they discussed the respective strategies of J.M.M. Party and the group of Ajit Singh for no confidence motion. They have also stated that during said conversation accused Ajit Singh suggested to J.M.M., M.Ps that their group should form a joint strategy with his group on the no confidence motion.

282. In my opinion, aforesaid conduct of accused Ajit Singh by itself cannot be termed as incriminating unless there is something more to show the complicity of accused Ajit Singh in the conspiracy to bribe the J.M.M., M.Ps There is nothing in the evidence to suggest that during the above referred meeting dated 24-7-1993 with JMM, MPs, Ajit Singh or JMM, MPs suggested bribe or illegal gratification. Therefore, it cannot be assumed that meeting in question was in relation to the conspiracy. Admittedly, political situation in the country in July, 1993 was volatile. There was a possibility of defeat of Congress Government on the floor of Lok Sabha. Under said circumstances, it is not un-natural that political personalities of various political groups were meeting each other to finalise their approach towards the no confidence motion which was to be moved in the monsoon session. Thus, under the circumstances, only on the basis of above-said evidence, it cannot be concluded beyond doubt that accused Ajit Singh was a party to the bribing of JMM, MPs or any other MP.

P.V. NARASIMHA RAO – BUTA SINGH AND V. RAJESHWAR RAO – SUBMITTED COMPLAINT WAS FILED FALSELY BY RAVINDER KUMAR WITH ULTERIOR MOTIVE – CONSIDERED – NOT ACCEPTED – CBI COURT

283. So far as the allegations of prosecution pertaining to participation of Shri P.V. Narasimha Rao (A-1), Shri Buta Singh (A-7) and Shri V. Rajeshwar Rao (A-8) in the conspiracy is concerned, prosecution case is mainly based upon the testimony of the approver P.W. 1 Shailender Mahto. Before looking into the prosecution evidence concerning individual role played by said three accused persons in the conspiracy, I propose to deal with some arguments raised by respective defence counsels which are common to all the three accused persons.

284. First contention put forth by learned defence counsels appearing on behalf of respective accused persons is that the present trial is basically based upon a falsehood *i.e.,* the complaint Ex. P.W. 102/A filed by the complainant Ravinder Kumar who is not a truthful witness. To prove this point, learned counsel for accused Shri P.V. Narasimha Rao has taken me through the cross examination of complainant P.W. 102 Ravinder Kumar and contended that perusal of cross examination of P.W. 102 Ravinder Kumar would reveal that he is not a truthful witness and since filing of the complaint all through, it has been his endeavour to fix the accused persons particularly accused P.V. Narasimha Rao. According to learned defence counsel motive behind aforesaid action of the complainant is that he was in connivance with the leaders of B.J.P. to tarnish the image of Congress party and the image of the government run by accused P.V. Narasimha Rao with a view to cause consequential political advantage to B.J.P. in coming general elections of 1996. He has further argued that since complainant Ravinder Kumar is not a truthful witness, his complaint is obviously false. Therefore, the prosecution case which is built upon said falsehood shall be rejected.

285. I find myself unable to accept the arguments because the complainant Ravinder Kumar as per the allegations in the complaint and his testimony has a limited role to play in this trial. He has only set the investigating agency into motion by filing the complaint. He is not an eye witness to prove the roles played by either of the accused persons in the alleged conspiracy or the circumstances leading to the conclusion of existence of conspiracy. Allegations in his complaint are based upon the information derived by him from the newspaper reports, other sources and Punjab National Bank, Naoroji Nagar, New Delhi. Since his complaint Ex P.W. 102/A disclosed commission of cognizable offence, the case on the basis of complaint was registered and investigated. The fate of this case is dependent upon the evidence collected by the C.B.I. during investigation and produced during trial. The version of the complainant Ravinder Kumar has nothing to do with the said evidence and it cannot be used as a piece of substantive evidence to prove the criminality or otherwise. Therefore, the contention of learned defence counsel based upon certain contradictory versions of P.W. 102 complainant Ravinder Kumar in relation to his complaint and the proceedings in Civil Writ Petition No. 789 of 1996 filed before Hon'ble High Court of Delhi by itself cannot be taken as a circumstance to discard the prosecution case without the appreciation of the evidence. The fact of the case, in my opinion, shall depend upon the material evidence relating to facts and circumstances of the case produced by the prosecution during-trial. However, the circumstance pointed out by learned defence counsel though not fatal to the case of prosecution calls for extra care and caution at the time of appreciation of the evidence against the accused persons.

286. Second contention of learned counsels appearing on behalf of Accused Shri P.V. Narasimha Rao (A-1), Shri Buta Singh (A-7) and Shri V. Rajeshwar Rao (A-8) is that this is a false case foisted upon them because of political considerations. It is argued that charge-sheet was filed in **Hawala** case against Sh. L.K. Advani, a Senior B.J.P. Leader on 23-1-1996 and this case appears to be a counter blast to the aforesaid charge-sheet. It is further contended that the term of 10th Lok Sabha was coming to an end in the year 1996 and in fact, elections for the 11th Lok Sabha as per the version of complainant Ravinder Kumar took place in May, 1996. Admittedly, the approver Shailender Mahto joined BJP on 7.1.1996. The complaint Ex. P.W. 102/A is dated 1-2-1996. As per the version of Ravinder Kumar, complainant, it was despatched to C.B.I. on 7-2-1996. He filed Writ Petition on behalf of Rashtriya Mukti Morcha in Delhi High Court on 22.2.1996. Admittedly, the approver Shailender Mahto issued press release Ex. P.W. 1/DP in the press conference arranged by B.J.P. at Parliament Annexe and that press release as per approver was drafted after discussions with

Shri Ram Jethmalani, a Senior Criminal Lawyer of India. The learned defence counsel has contended that the above referred sequence of events clearly show a political design of senior B.J.P. leaders in connivance with the complainant Ravinder Kumar and the approver Shialender Mahto who also had a desire to contest the ensuing elections for the 10th Lok Sabha on B.J.P. ticket. It is also contended that the presence of top lawyer Shri Ram Jethmalani in the picture clearly indicates that there was a desire to nail the Congress Government as Shri Ram Jethmalani had all the time opposed the Congress.

287. While appreciating the contention put forth by the learned defence counsel, it is to be borne in mind that the present trial is the result of a political situation *i.e.,* the "No Confidence Motion" moved against Congress (I) Government led by the accused P.V. Narasimha Rao in July, 1993. Therefore, the main players of this case namely the accused persons and the witnesses are bound to be politicians. A possibility cannot be ruled out that some opposition parties might have tried to take political mileage out of the situation. This does not necessarily mean that a fake case has been foisted upon the accused persons or that the evidence produced during trial is not reliable. Fate of the prosecution case basically depends upon the reliability of the evidence which has to be examined in the light of various accompanying circumstances in order to assess whether or not the witnesses concerned are truthful. The circumstances pointed out by learned defence counsel by itself do not provide any reason for outright rejection of the testimony of the witnesses who otherwise may appear to be truthful. However, the above referred sequence of events pointed out on behalf of the accused persons do call for a very careful appreciation of the evidence of the prosecution in order to avoid miscarriage of justice.

APPROVER SHAILENDER MAHTO HAD ADDRESSED PRESS CONFERENCE CALLED BY BJP – JOINED BJP WITH A VIEW TO CONTEST 1996 ELECTIONS – RESIGNED – WANTED TO JOIN CONGRESS – NOT ALLOWED – REJOINED JMM – CONTRADICTORY STATEMENTS – HENCE UNRELIABLE – HIS TESTIMONY BE REJECTED – SUBMIT ACCUSED A1-A7-A8

288. Next contention of the Learned Counsel appearing on behalf of accused P.V. Narasimha Rao (A-1), Buta Singh (A-7) and V. Rajeshwar Rao (A-8) is that the approver Shailender Mahto is a political opportunist and his conduct all through since the beginning of the year 1996 suggests that he can do anything without any pangs of conscience to promote his political ambitions. Thus, his testimony is liable to outright rejection. In support of this contention Learned Counsel for accused P.V. Narasimha Rao has pointed out certain sequence of events suggesting the conduct of the approver P.W. 1 Shailender Mahto. He has argued that 10th Lok Sabha came into existence in the year 1991 and its term was to come to an end in the year 1996. In fact, the elections for the next Lok Sabha were held in May, 1996. Knowing this fact, P.W. 1 Shailender Mahto, approver joined B.J.P. on 7-1-1996 admittedly with the intention to contest coming Lok Sabha Elections on B.J.P. ticket. According to Learned Defence Counsels, in order to achieve that end, he became a tool in the hands of B.J.P. and gave press statement Ex. P.W. 1/DF on 26.2.1996 in the press conference arranged by B.J.P. Admittedly, the approver resigned from B.J.P. on 18.3.1996 *vide* his resignation letters Ex. P.W. 1/DC and Ex. P.W. 1/DD respectively in Hindi and English, wherein he criticised B.J.P. for exploiting him with the object to malign congress relating to the episode of defeat of no confidence motion in July, 1993. Learned Defence Counsels have contended that aforesaid resignation of Shailender Mahto from B.J.P. was obviously because of the reason that he was not offered the B.J.P. ticket. Thereafter, he admittedly applied for Congress Membership *vide* his application Ex. P.W. 1/DH dated 25.3.1996 and when Congress Party did not oblige him he rejoined his old friends in Jharkhand Mukti Morcha on the last date of filling the nomination for Lok Sabha elections and contested the Lok Sabha Election of 1996 on J.M.M. ticket. Thus, it is contended that aforesaid sequence of events calls for outright rejection of testimony of the approver.

289. It is further contended by respective defence counsels appearing on behalf of accused P.V. Narasimha Rao (A-1), Buta Singh (A-7) and V. Rajeshwar Rao (A-8) that approver P.W. 1 Shailender Mahto is not a reliable witness because during his testimony in the court, he has made marked improvement relating to the roles played by accused P.V. Narasimha Rao, Buta Singh and V. Rajeshwar Rao in offering and giving of bribe to JMM, MPs. In support of this contention, they have drawn my attention to following previous statements of the approver relating to the episode. Ex. P.W. 1/DP is the press release dated 26-2-1996 admittedly issued by Shailender Mahto in the press conference held at Parliament Annexe. Ex. P.W. 1/DP1 to Ex. P.W. 1/DP3 are the previous statements of approver Shailender Mahto recorded by C.B.I. during investigation on 28-6-1996, 20-6-1996, 22-6-1996. Ex. P.W. 1/DB is the further statement of approver recorded by C.B.I. on 22-6-1996 and Ex. P.W. 1/DP4 is the statement of approver P.W. 1 Shailender Mahto recorded by C.B.I. on 12-9-1996. Ex. P.W. 1/DC and Ex. P.W. 1/DD are the resignation letters dated 28-3-1997 of approver resigning from the membership of B.J.P. Ex. P.W. 1/DG is the copy of the Lok Sabha Debates dated 29-2-96 during which P.W. 1 Shailender Mahto made a statement in the Lok Sabha denying the bribery of JMM, MPs in relation to no confidence motion dated 28-7-1993. Ex. P.W. 1/DL is the bail application dated 15-10-1996. Ex. P.W. 1/DO is the bail application dated 25-9-1996 moved by P.W. 1 approver Shailender Mahto in the court after his arrest. Ex. P.W. 1/DM is the copy of the petition made by Shailender Mahto to Human Rights Commission alleging his maltreatment by C.B.I. during the period of his police custody remand and also about the inducements given to him by C.B.I. to implicate various persons including accused P.V. Narasimha Rao in the matter of bribery of M.Ps.

290. It is contended on behalf of respective counsels for accused P.V. Narasimha Rao, Buta Singh and V. Rajeshwar Rao that aforesaid previous statements relating to the facts and circumstances of the case made by approver Shailender Mahto do not disclose about the alleged meeting between accused V. Rajeshwar Rao and J.M.M., M.Ps at Andhra Bhawan in the morning of 26-7-1993 nor those statements mention about offer of bribe given by accused V. Rajeshwar Rao to Suraj Mandal, M.P. during said meeting by taking him aside in the verandah. It is also pointed out that previous statements of the approver Shailender Mahto Ex.P.W. 1/DP as well as Ex. P.W. 1/DP1, to Ex. P.W. 1/DP4 and Ex. P.W. 1/DB do not disclose about the alleged closed door meeting between accused P.V. Narasimha Rao, Buta Singh and Suraj Mandal at the residence of accused P.V. Narasimha Rao in the evening of 26-7-1993 or about any offer or bribe given by accused P.V. Narasimha Rao to Suraj Mandal during said meeting. Thus, it is contended that the approver has obviously improved upon his aforesaid previous statements and as such, his testimony is bound to be rejected as not reliable.

ENTIRE EVIDENCE HAS TO BE ANALYSED TOGETHER – NOT ISOLATED STATEMENTS – EVEN EVIDENCE OF ONE WITNESS HAS TO BE READ AS A WHOLE – PLACED RELIANCE ON SC JUDGMENT – HENCE SUBMISSIONS OF ACCUSED REJECTED – CBI COURT

291. I do not agree with above contentions put forth by Learned Defence Counsels. In my opinion, the credibility of a witness cannot be assessed on the basis of one or more isolated circumstances. While assessing the evidence of a witness, the Court in my view, is supposed to appreciate it in the background of all the accompanying circumstances in order to arrive at a conclusion whether or not any credence can be attached to the testimony of the witness or any part thereof.

292. Learned Defence Counsels by challenging the reliability of the testimony of the approver on the basis of above referred instances, in my view are trying to seek a compartmentalized analysis of the evidence of the approver based upon isolated circumstances. In fact, Learned Counsel for accused V. Rajeshwar Rao has cited the Judgement of Hon'ble Supreme Court **"AIR 1957 SC 637, Sarwan Singh v. State of Punjab"** and contended that Hon'ble Supreme Court in the above referred case has observed as follows:—

> "Approver is undoubtedly a competent witness under the Evidence Act, but appreciation of his evidence has to satisfy a double test. His evidence must show that he is a reliable witness and that is a test which is common to all the witnesses. If this test is satisfied, then second test which still remains to be applied is that the approver's evidence must receive sufficient corroboration."
>
> "Every person who is a competent witness is not a reliable witness and the test of reliability has to be satisfied by an approver all the more before the question of corroboration of his evidence is considered by criminal courts."

293. Ld. Defence counsel has contended that in view of aforesaid ratio of judgment in **Sarwan Singh's** case, there is no need for the court to look into the question of corroboration of the testimony of the approver and the testimony of approver should be rejected out-rightly because he happens to be a political opportunist having no scruples and admittedly his testimony against accused V. Rajeshwar Rao as well as P.V. Narasimha Rao and Buta Singh is a bunch of improvements on material aspects of the case upon his previous statements.

294. I do not agree with the aforesaid contention raised by Ld. Defence counsel. The law relating to appreciation of evidence of a witness in order to conclude whether or not it is reliable and credit worthy is well settled. While appreciating the testimony of the witness, the trial court is expected to make a sincere endeavour to arrive at the truth by looking into all the accompanying circumstances of the case as well as corroborating evidence. A witness cannot be dubbed as unreliable or unworthy of credit on the basis of one or more isolated circumstances ignoring the other circumstances which may point towards the truthfulness of the version of the witness. So far as **Sarwan Singh's** case is concerned, it was considered by Hon'ble Supreme Court in the matter of '**State of Andhra Pradesh v. Ganeshwara, 1968 (2) Cr LJ 671**' wherein the Apex Court has held that:—

> "While it must be shown that an approver is a witness of truth, the evidence adduced in a case cannot be considered in compartments and even for judging the credibility of the approver the evidence led to corroborate him in material particulars would be relevant for consideration. The Court should bear this in mind for deciding whether the evidence of the approver should be acted upon or not."

295. The ratio of the aforesaid Judgement clearly shows that on the basis of isolated circumstances, testimony of a witness cannot be outrightly rejected. It has to be assessed in totality of circumstances.

296. The reliability of the witness can be tested from various circumstances, such as the character and the status of the witness in the society, whether the version of the witness is consistent or otherwise, the demeanour of the witness, whether the testimony of witness suffers from material contradictions or material omissions vis-à-vis his previous statements made in respect of the facts and circumstances of the case and the corroboration from some independent evidence either direct or circumstantial. Sometimes, it may be so that there may be some infirmities in the testimony of a witness, but his testimony may find a strong corroboration from some independent evidence giving assurance of credibility. In that event, those infirmities such as some omissions or contradictions pale into insignificance. On some occasions, there may be some cogent explanation for previous contradictory statements made by the witness. Thus, in my opinion, while judging the credibility of the version of a witness no set rules can be applied and testimony of a witness is required to be appreciated in the context of totality of accompanying circumstances with due care and caution, so as to eliminate any possibility of miscarriage of justice.

ROLE OF V. RAJESHWAR RAO IN THIS CONSPIRACY CONSIDERED – CBI COURT

297. Coming to the role played by accused V. Rajeshwar Rao (A-8) in the conspiracy to bribe the members of parliament. There is no direct evidence on the record to establish that accused V. Rajeshwar Rao was a party to the conspiracy. Prosecution is seeking to establish the complicity of accused V. Rajeshwar Rao on the basis of following alleged circumstances:

(I) that in the morning of 26-7-1993, accused V. Rajeshwar Rao met J.M.M., M.Ps namely Suraj Mandal, Shibu Soren, Simon Marandi and Shailender Mahto, approver at his residence. He took Suraj Mandal, M.P. aside in the verandah and offered him illegal gratification as a motive or reward for those J.M.M., M.Ps voting against no confidence motion;

(II) that in the morning of 29-7-1993 accused V. Rajeshwar Rao visited the residence of Suraj Mandal, M.P. In his presence, Suraj Mandal told approver Shailender Mahto that Rs. 50 lakhs have already been paid and remaining amount would be paid within two days. During said conversation, accused V. Rajeshwar Rao (A-8) informed that all the J.M.M., M.Ps would be paid Rs. 50 lakhs each and the break away group of Ram Lakhan Singh Yadav would also be paid Rs. 50 lakhs each besides the allotment of petrol pumps and residential plots of HUDA in Haryana. He further informed that the M.Ps who have absented or abstained from voting on no confidence motion would be paid Rs. 30 lakhs each;

(III) that he was a party to the mobilising of funds (for payment of bribe to M.Ps) at Bangalore, and delivery of said money brought from Bangalore by accused Ramalinga Reddy, H.M. Revanna and D.K. Audikeshvulu, to the residence of Suraj Mandal in the morning of 31-7-1993.

V. RAJESHWAR RAO IS NOT A PARTY TO BANGALORE END OF CONSPIRACY – THAT ASPECT ITSELF NOT PROVED – HOLDS CBI COURT

298. So far as, circumstance No. III relating to the complicity of accused V. Rajeshwar Rao (A-8) in the Bangalore end of conspiracy is concerned, I have already concluded that prosecution has failed to establish beyond doubt the Bangalore end of conspiracy *i.e.*, mobilising of the funds at Bangalore, bringing of said money to Delhi on 30-7-1993 or delivery of said money at the residence of Suraj Mandal in the morning of 31-7-1993 *via* the residence of accused V. Rajeshwar Rao (A-8). Thus, Circumstance no. III against accused V. Rajeshwar Rao (A-8) is not established.

ROLE OF V. RAJESHWAR RAO(A8) IN THE DEAL WITH JMM MPs CONSIDERED – CBI COURT

299. So far as circumstance No. I and II are concerned, prosecution is depending upon sole testimony of the approver P.W. 1 Shailender Mahto. Regarding the role played by accused V. Rajeshwar Rao (A-8) approver P.W. 1 Shailender Mahto has stated that on 25-7-1993, P.W. 64 Shri Ashok Rao Anand Rao Deshmukh, a Congress M.P. enquired from him in the presence of Shibu Soren and Suraj Mandal, if they would help the Congress Government (?). He showed his inclination to consider supporting the government provided some decision to constitute Jharkhand council was taken. On this P.W. 64 Shri Ashok Rao Anand Rao Deshmukh replied that he would have a talk with the prime minister and inform them later. Approver Shailender Mahto has further deposed that on 25-7-1993 at about 7.00 p.m. Shri Ashok Rao Anand Rao Deshmukh told him that they (JMM, MPs) were required to meet accused V. Rajeshwar Rao (A-8) on the next day. Thus, on 26-7-1993 at about 10.00 a.m. he alongwith Shibu Soren, Suraj Mandal and Simon Marandi visited the residence of accused V. Rajeshwar Rao (A-8) at Andhra Bhawan. P.W. 64 Ashok Rao Anand Rao Deshmukh was already present there and he left after introducing them (JMM, MPs) to accused V. Rajeshwar Rao (A-8). According to this witness, accused V. Rajeshwar Rao (A-8) and Suraj Mandal went towards the verandah leaving remaining three JMM, MPs including the approver in the room. They had some conversation and came back after 10-15 minutes. Approver has further stated that while they were coming back from the residence of accused V. Rajeshwar Rao (A-8), Suraj Mandal told them that accused V. Rajeshwar Rao (A-8) had offered a meagre amount. Thereafter, Suraj Mandal suggested that they should have a direct talk with the prime minister.

300. In respect of Circumstance No. II, approver Shailender Mahto has stated that in the morning of 29-7-1993 he visited the residence of Suraj Mandal between 8.00 a.m. to 9.00 a.m. Accused V. Rajeshwar Rao (A-8) was already present there. Suraj Mandal, MP told in presence of accused V. Rajeshwar Rao (A-8) that Rs. 50 lakhs have been sent for them (JMM, MPs) and remaining money would reach within a day or two. He has also stated that accused V. Rajeshwar Rao (A-8) told that they would be paid Rs. 50 lakhs each. The group of Ram Lakhan Singh Yadav was joining Congress. Therefore, they would be paid Rs. 50 lakhs each, besides the allotment of petrol pumps and HUDA Plots in Haryana. According to him, **Accused v. Rajeshwar Rao** also informed that the members of parliament who had abstained from voting in order to save the government would be paid Rs. 30 lakhs each.

301. Ld. Prosecutor has submitted that above referred version of approver Shailender Mahto clearly establish the complicity of accused V. Rajeshwar Rao (A-8) in the conspiracy to bribe the JMM, MPs. He has contended that version of the approver that they were offered and paid bribe stands corroborated from the testimony of the various officials of Punjab National Bank, Naoroji Nagar, New Delhi namely P.W. 16 Balraj Suri Senior Manager, P.W. 17 O.P. Aneja, Senior Manager, P.W. 18 B.L. Verma, Senior Manager, P.W. 19 M.S. Jayant, Assistant Manager, P.W. 98 Jawahar Lal, peon and P.W. 103 Satish Kumar Sharma, Manager as well as the record of the bank relating to the deposits made in the bank accounts of respective J.M.M., M.Ps and their family members.

302. First challenge of learned defence counsel to the testimony of approver P.W. 1 Shailender Mahto relating to the role played by accused V. Rajeshwar Rao (A-8) is that aforesaid version is not reliable being an improvement upon various previous statements made by the approver prior to deposing in the court.

303. Ld. counsel for accused V. Rajeshwar Rao has contended that perusal of Ex. P.W. 1/DF (press statement released by approver Shailender Mahto on 26-2-1996), Ex. P.W. 1/DG (statement made by the approver in the parliament on 29.2.1996) and Ex. P.W. 1/DP1 to Ex. P.W. 1/DP4 (the statements made by the approver Shailender Mahto to C.B.I. during the investigation on 18-6-1996, 20-6-1996, 22-6-1996 and 12-9-1996 respectively) would show that in none of those previous statements approver has referred to the accused V. Rajeshwar Rao (A-8) or the meeting of J.M.M., MPs with him on 26-7-1993. He has contended that in those statements, he has not even mentioned the name of Shri V. Rajeshwar Rao (A-8). According to learned defence counsel, during cross examination, when the approver was confronted with this fact, he came out with an explanation that while making his previous statements, he did not disclose all the facts because of pressure and threat of his J.M.M. colleagues and the Congress party. Aforesaid explanation as per Ld. Defence counsel is not acceptable because approver Shailender Mahto has admitted that when he released his press statement Ex. P.W. 1/DF at that time, he was not under any pressure. If that was the case, then under natural course of circumstances, there should have been reference of the role played by accused V. Rajeshwar Rao in the conspiracy in Ex. P.W. 1/DF if the allegation were true. Thus, it is argued that version of approver Shailender Mahto pertaining to the role played by accused V. Rajeshwar Rao in offering bribe to J.M.M., M.Ps on 26-7-1993 (29.7.1993 ?) morning through Suraj Mandal, M.P. should be discarded.

304. While appreciating above contention of Ld. Counsel for accused V. Rajeshwar Rao, one cannot loose sight of the fact that approver Shailender Mahto alongwith other J.M.M., M.Ps had accepted bribe for voting against no confidence motion. Therefore, under the normal course of circumstance, he was not expected to admit the offer of bribe given by various persons including accused V. Rajeshwar Rao and the acceptance of bribe in furtherance of the said offer in the exact term. Such an admission would also have lowered the prestige and image of the approver, who is a politician, in the eyes of public. This circumstance, in my opinion explains as to why in the previous press statement Ex. P.W. 1/DP, approver Shailender Mahto has not narrated the true facts relating to the bribery of JMM, MPs. Perusal of press release Ex. P.W. 1/DP would reveal that this is a self exculpatory statement made by approver Shailender Mahto. In this press statement, while speaking about the meeting dated 26-7-93 with accused Buta Singh (A-7) and P.V. Narasimha Rao (A-1) at the residence of the Prime Minister, witness has mentioned "UNOHNE AAGE KAHA KI BUTA SINGH JI AUR SURAJ MANDAL JI SE JO BAAT HUI HAI WOH PURI KI JAYEGI. US SAMAY MAIN IN BAATON KA BHAV NAHIN SAMAJH PAYA".

305. In the last but one paragraph of the press release, approver P.W. 1 Shailender Mahto has mentioned that 3-4 days after the said incident, Suraj Mandal gave him Rs. 40 lakhs saying that the Prime Minister has sent the said money. It is also mentioned in the said paragraph that Suraj Mandal told him to use said money for party work in his District. In the last paragraph of said statement, approver Shailender Mahto has mentioned that at that time, it did not occur to him that he was doing something wrong. He has also explained in the last paragraph of Ex. P.W. 1/DF that he used money out of that amount for political work and intended to use balance Rs. 20 lakhs (approximately) for political work only.

306. Aforesaid contents of said previous statement Ex. P.W. 1/DP would reveal that said statement has been released with due care and caution to steer clear of making a confession for admission of accepting the illegal gratification. If that was the state of mind of the approver at the time of release of press statement Ex. P.W. 1/DF, then it is obvious that aforesaid statement was not expected to give full details of the episode, as such much significance cannot be attached to omission of the role played by accused V. Rajeshwar Rao in giving offer of bribe to J.M.M., M.Ps through Suraj Mandal. Same argument also applies to the previous statements made by approver during investigation of the case because at that time approver Shailender Mahto was under the fear of prosecution and as such he was not expected to admit his guilt during investigation conducted by C.B.I. However, aforesaid circumstance calls for extra care and caution while appreciating the version of the approver against V. Rajeshwar Rao so as to exclude any possibility of miscarriage of justice.

307. Ld. Counsel for accused V. Rajeshwar Rao has contended that in order to be acceptable the testimony of the approver qua accused V. Rajeshwar Rao needs to be corroborated from some independent evidence either direct or circumstantial. He has contended that in this case, there is no corroboration to the evidence of the approver relating to the meeting allegedly held between JMM, MPs and the approver P.W. 1 Shailender Mahto, wherein he offered illegal gratification for JMM, MPs to Suraj Mandal, MP as a motive or reward for voting against no confidence motion.

308. It is well-settled principle of law that testimony of approver should be approached by the court with due care and caution. In order to be acceptable evidence, the testimony of approver must pass the twin test of reliability and corroboration. Meaning thereby that testimony of an approver can be accepted only if it is corroborated on material aspects by independent evidence either direct or circumstantial not only qua the prosecution story but also *qua* the role played by concerned accused in the crime.

309. Since in the previous statements of the approver namely Ex. P.W. 1/DF and Ex. P.W. 1/DP1 to Ex. P.W. 1/DP4 as well as Ex. P.W. 1/DG, there is no mention of role played by accused V. Rajeshwar Rao in the conspiracy. It becomes necessary to find out if the version of the approver *qua* accused V. Rajeshwar Rao is corroborated by some independent evidence either direct or circumstantial.

310. According to the approver, the meeting dated 26-7-1993 between J.M.M., MPs and accused V. Rajeshwar Rao (A-8) was arranged by P.W. 64 Shri Ashok Rao Anand Rao Deshmukh, who left the residence of accused V. Rajeshwar Rao after introducing JMM, MPs with him. But Shri Ashok Rao Anand Rao Deshmukh, P.W. 64 is a hostile witness and he has not corroborated the above referred version of the approver.

311. Admittedly, Suraj Mandal, M.P. was having a police security during July, 1993. He was provided round the clock personal security officers. Ex. P.W. 5/B is the daily diary register maintained at his residence by those personal security officers. In order to cross check the version of the approver Shailender Mahto regarding the visit of JMM, MPs to the residence of accused Shri V. Rajeshwar Rao (A-8) in the morning of 26-7-1993 aforesaid daily diary register can be of help.

312. P.W. 13 Shri Davender Kumar, Head Constable has deposed that he was posted as personal security officer with Suraj Mandal, MP from August,1992 till September,1993. He has proved daily diary Entries Nos. 2 and 4 to 10 Ex. P.W. 13/D1 to Ex. P.W. 13/DB, all dated 26-7-1993 in the daily diary register Ex. P.W. 5/B, as the entries made by him. According to him, the aforesaid entries are correct.

313. Perusal of diary Entry No. 2 dated 26-7-1993 Ex. P.W. 13/D1 would reveal that as per this entry Shri Davender Kumar, Head Constable of Delhi Armed Police reported for P.S.O. duty at the residence of Protected Person Suraj Mandal on 26-7-1993 at 8.10 a.m. and he took charge of the fire arm from Constable Mahesh Kumar.

314. Daily diary Entry No. 4 dated 26-7-1993 is proved as Ex. P.W. 13/D2. This entry in my opinion is very relevant for the appreciation of the version of approver P.W. 1 Shailender Mahto relating to the role played by accused V. Rajeshwar Rao (A-8) on 26-7-1993. It is reproduced as follows:-

> "SAMAY 10.10 BAJE DIN CONSTABLE MAJKURA MAN HAMRAH CONSTABLE ANOOP SINGH NO. 9740/DAP MAI P.P. SAHEB PARLIAMENT KO RAVANA HOTA HUN."

This entry implies that on 26-7-1993 at about 10.10 a.m. Suraj Mandal, M.P. left his residence for parliament alongwith Constable Davender Kumar and Constable Anoop Singh. This means that till 10.10 a.m. Suraj Mandal was present at his residence.

315. Perusal of testimony of approver P.W. 1 Shailender Mahto would reveal that according to his version he, Shibu Soren and Simon Marandi collected at the residence of Suraj Mandal, M.P. on 26-7-1993 at 10.00 a.m. and from there they all alongwith Suraj Mandal, M.P. proceeded to Andhra Bhawan to meet accused V. Rajeshwar Rao (A-8). Thereafter, this witness goes on to narrate about their introduction with accused V. Rajeshwar Rao (A-8) and the offer given by accused V. Rajehswar Rao (A-8) to Suraj Mandal. M.P. after taking him aside towards the verandah. If the aforesaid version of the approver is to be believed. Then Suraj Mandal, MP left with other three JMM MPs for the residence of accused V. Rajeshwar Rao (A-8) on 26-7-1993 sometime around 10.00 a.m. They must have consumed sometime in travelling from the residence of Suraj Mandal at Ferozshah Road to Andhra Bhawan. As per the version of approver, after they were introduced to accused V. Rajeshwar Rao, he and Suraj Mandal went towards the verandah and had some conversation. Approver Shailender Mahto has stated that they returned back after 10-15 minutes and thereafter they all (JMM, MPs) left the residence of accused V. Rajeshwar Rao.

ROLE OF V. RAJESHWAR IN THIS CONSPIRACY NOT PROVED BEYOND DOUBT – HOLDS CBI COURT

316. Aforesaid version suggests that JMM, MPs must have stayed at the residence of accused V. Rajeshwar Rao for about 30 minutes w.e.f. 10.00 a.m. onwards. If that is the case then by no stretch of imagination Suraj Mandal could have left his residence on 26-7-1993 at 10.10 a.m. alongwith his P.S.O., P.W. Constable Devender Kumar and Constable Anoop Singh for the Parliament House. Thus, the fact narrated in Daily Diary Ex. P.W. 13/D2 cannot be re-conciled with the version of the approver. If the version of the approver is true then the daily diary entry surely would have-reflected that Suraj Mandal, M.P. left his residence for Andhra Bhawan at around 10.00 a.m. Since the version of approver Shailender Mahto cannot be reconciled with daily diary entry Ex. P.W. 13/D2 maintained in due course of business, I am of the view that instead of being corroborated by the daily diary entry Ex. P.W. 14/D4 the testimony of the approver relating to the role played by accused V. Rajeshwar Rao in giving offer of bribe to JMM, MPs through Suraj Mandal on 26-7-1993 is contradicted. Thus, under the circumstances, I do not deem it safe to accept the testimony of approver relating to aforesaid role played by accused V. Rajeshwar Rao (A-8) in offering illegal gratification to JMM, MPs, more so because of the improvements in his testimony pointed out by learned defence counsel for accused V. Rajeshwar Rao (A-8).

317. Approver P.W. 1 Shailender Mahto has also stated that on 29-7-1993 he visited the residence of Suraj Mandal, MP between 8.00 a.m. or 9.00 a.m. Accused, Rajeshwar Rao was present there and in his presence, Shailender Mahto told that Rs. 50 lakhs have been sent for them and remaining money would reach within a day or two. Thereafter, witness goes on to narrate that accused V. Rajeshwar Rao told them that they would be paid Rs. 50 lakhs each. He also informed that group of Ram Lakhan Singh Yadav, MP would also be paid Rs. 50 lakhs each besides the allotment of petrol pumps and plots of HUDA in Haryana and the M.Ps who have absented or abstained from vote to save the government would be paid Rs. 30 lakhs.

318. I find it very difficult to accept above referred version of approver Shailender Mahto relating to the episode dated 29-7-1993, firstly because his version regarding offer dated 26-7-1993 given by accused V. Rajeshwar Rao (A-8) to JMM, MPs is not acceptable. Secondly prosecution case relating to this aspect of the matter is highly confused. Ld. prosecutor while cross examining P.W. 87 Harsharan Lal put certain suggestions relating to the case of prosecution which were denied. One of those suggestions was that Harsharan Lal visited the residence of Shailender Mahto in the evening of 29-7-1993 and from there he came to know that Shailender Mahto had gone to the residence of Shibu Soren at 17, Gurdwara Rakabganj Road, New Delhi. As such he went there. Other suggestion put to P.W. Harsharan Lal was that approver Shailender Mahto was present at the residence of Shibu Soren and on seeing witness Harsharan Lal, Shailender Mahto as well as other persons started shouting on him that while they have done their job on 28-7-1993, Shri Rajeshwar Rao still has not met their requirement. This suggestion imply that case of the prosecution is that in the evening of 29-7-1993 approver P.W. 1 Shailender Mahto protested to Harsharan Lal, P.W. that accused Shri V. Rajeshwar Rao (A-8) have not fulfilled his promise despite of the fact that J.M.M., M.Ps have voted in favour of the government on 28-7-1993. If that is the case of the prosecution, then it cannot be reconciled with the version of the approver to the effect that in the morning of 29-7-1993, Rs. 50 lakhs has already been received at the residence of Suraj Mandal with the promise to pay the balance amount within a day or two. Therefore, under the circumstances, I do not deem it safe to rely upon the aforesaid sole version of the approver to base the conviction of accused V. Rajeshwar Rao (A-8).

ROLE OF P.V. NARASIMHA RAO, BUTA SINGH IN THIS CONSPIRACY – CONSIDERED – CBI COURT

319. As per the prosecution case, the role played by accused P.V. Narasimha Rao (A-1) and Buta Singh (A-7) in the conspiracy to bribe JMM, MPs is based upon common evidence.

320. Relevant version of the approver against P.V. Narasimha Rao (A-1) and Buta Singh (A-7) is that in the evening of 26-7-1993 sometime around 7.00 p.m., JMM, MPs Suraj Mandal, Simon Marandi and Shibu Soren visited the residence of accused Buta Singh (A-7). While they were having tea there, accused Buta Singh remarked that Prime Minister has remembered them. On this Suraj Mandal reacted that what was the use of the Prime Minister remembering them as the matter of creation of Jharkhand Council was still unresolved. On this accused Buta Singh suggested that they should have a direct meeting with the Prime Minister. Thereafter, said JMM, MPs alongwith accused Buta Singh visited the residence of accused P.V. Narasimha Rao (A-1) and had a meeting with him. During said meeting, accused Buta Singh initiated the conversation by bringing up the issue of creation of Jharkhand Council. Suraj Mandal told accused P.V. Narasimha Rao that he has not resolved the matter of Jharkhand, as such how could they support his government. On this, accused P.V. Narasimha Rao (A-1) assured that he would summon the file of Jharkhand matter from the Home Ministry and resolve the matter. He further requested J.M.M., M.Ps to help him for the moment.

321. Approver Shailender Mahto has also deposed that thereafter accused P.V. Narasimha Rao (A-1) and Buta Singh (A-7) went to the other room. After sometime Suraj Mandal, MP was also called to that room. 5-6 minutes later, they came out and accused P.V. Narasimha Rao asked for the help of JMM, MPs and said that whatever conversation has taken place with Suraj Mandal, those promises shall be fulfilled.

322. Approver Shailender Mahto has also deposed that on their way back from the residence of P.V. Narasimha Rao (A-1), he enquired from Suraj Mandal, MP about the details of his conversation with the accused P.V. Narasimha Rao (A-1) and Buta Singh (A-7). Suraj Mandal gave cryptic reply "PHAYEDE KI BAAT HAI" On this Simon Marandi insisted for the details of conversation, failing which he threatened that they would not vote against the no confidence motion. Thereafter Suraj Mandal disclosed "PAISE KI BHI BAAT HUI HAI. KITNA PAISE MILEGA, ABHI TAI NAHI HAI."

323. Accused P.V. Narasimha Rao (A-1) in their respective statements recorded under section 313, Cr.P.C. have not disputed that JMM, MPs initially visited the residence of accused Buta Singh (A-7) in the evening of 26-7-1993. From there, they alongwith accused Buta Singh (A-7) came to the residence of accused P.V. Narasimha Rao (A-1) and had a meeting with him. It is also not disputed that during said meeting talks regarding creation of Jharkhand council took place. However, both the accused have denied that any closed door meeting between them and Suraj Mandal, MPs took place or in that meeting accused P.V. Narasimha Rao (A-1) offered illegal gratification or reward for JMM, MPs supporting the government by voting against no confidence motion. They have also denied that after such closed door meeting, accused P.V. Narasimha Rao (A-1) sought help of JMM, MPs and promised that whatever conversation has taken place with Suraj Mandal, it shall be honoured and promises shall be fulfilled.

324. The reliability of the testimony of the approver is challenged by respective defence counsels appearing on behalf of accused P.V. Narasimha Rao (A-1) and Buta Singh (A-7) on the ground that during his testimony in the court he has improved upon his previous statements Ex.P.W.1/DF dated 26-2-1996 as well as statements Ex. P.W. /DP1 to Ex. P.W.1/DP4 made to CBI during investigation on 18-6-1996, 20-6-1996, 22-6-1996 and 12-9-1996 respectively. It is contended that comparison of those previous statements, with the testimony of the approver in court would reveal that the version of the approver in court regarding the closed door meeting between accused P.V. Narasimha Rao (A-1), Buta Singh (A-7) and Suraj Mandal, MP and the offer of bribe given by accused P.V. Narasimha Rao to Suraj Mandal during said meeting, is a material improvement upon his previous statement. According to defence counsels, if the version of the approver relating to the closed door meeting was true then he would not have failed to mention such an important fact in his previous statement. Thus, it is contended that his aforesaid version is liable to be rejected as unreliable. In support of this contention, they have referred to number of judgments. To name the few are **1994 Supp (2) SCC 73, Ram Pal Pithura Rahi Dass v. State of Maharashtra; (1979) 4 SCC 145, Baldev Singh v. State of Maharashtra; (1979) 4 SCC 105, Baldev Singh v. State of Punjab; (1974) 1 SCC 722, Kali Ram v. State of Himachal Pradesh; (1996) 5 SCC 369, Alil Mollah v. State of West Bengal; AIR 1975 SC 216, R. Kondia v. State of Andhra Pradesh; AIR 1957 SC 637, Sarwan Singh v. State of Punjab; 1980 Cr LJ 1397, Randhir Singh v. State.**"

325. I have gone through the above referred judgments cited on behalf of accused persons. All those judgments related to the appreciation of evidence. The ratio which culls out of those judgments is that if a witness is found to have made previous statements, relating to the facts and circumstances of the case which are either contradictory to his testimony in the court on material particulars or which suffers from some material omissions, then the testimony of the witness becomes suspect provided there is no explanation for aforesaid contradictions or material omissions in the previous statements.

326. In the matter of **Sarwan Singh v. State of Punjab, AIR 1957 SC 637,** Hon'ble Supreme Court has made following observations relating to the appreciation of the testimony of an approver:

> "It seems to us that if it was found that the approver's account against one of the accused persons was wholly discrepant, this finding itself should inevitably have led the Court to scrutinize his evidence in respect of the other accused persons with greater caution."
>
> "If this was a case where the statements made by the approver on subsequent occasions merely added details which were not included in the first statement, it may perhaps have been a different matter. It is true that omissions have not always the same significance as contradictions, but in the present case it is patent that the two sets of statements are wholly inconsistent

and irreconcilable and that obviously leads to a very serious infirmity in the character of the witness."

327. Cumulative effect of the above referred observations of Hon'ble Supreme Court is that at the time of appreciation of evidence of the approver Shailender Mahto, his testimony in the court and his previous statements made in relation to the facts and circumstances of the offence or the role played by an accused are to be read side by side. If the statement of the approver during trial merely add some detail which was not included in the previous statement and if such details are not inconsistent with the facts mentioned in the previous statement of the witness, then such improvements may not be of much significance to impeach the credit of the witness. However, if the discrepancy in two sets of statements are wholly inconsistent and irreconcilable, then it would definitely affect the reliability of the witness.

328. Ex. P.W. 1/DF is the initial statement made by approver Shailender Mahto relating to the facts of the case. It is a signed press release dated 26-2-1996 issued by approver Shailender Mahto. Perusal of this press release would show that the approver in this statement has alleged that two days prior to the voting on no confidence motion, JMM, MPs visited the residence of accused Buta Singh (A-7). From there they alongwith accused Buta Singh (A-7) came to the residence of accused P.V. Narasimha Rao (A-1). In that meeting, accused Buta Singh (A-7) raised the issue of Jharkhand Council and during that discussion, the Prime Minister said that he would summon the file from the Home Ministry and resolve the matter, but it would take some time. It is also mentioned in the statement that Prime Minister told that he would do something for J.M.M., M.Ps in the meanwhile and promised that whatever talks have taken place with accused Buta Singh (A-7) and Suraj Mandal, those promises shall be fulfilled. Version of the approver in his statement Ex. P.W. 1/DP4 dated 12.9.1996 made to C.B.I. during investigation is more or less similar.

329. If we compare the above referred previous statements in Ex. P.W. 1/DF and Ex. P.W. 1/DP4 with the testimony of the approver in the Court, I do not find much difference in two sets of statements, but for the version of the approver during trial that after talking about Jharkhand Council, accused P.V. Narasimha Rao (A-1), Buta Singh (A-7) and Suraj Mandal, M.P. had a closed door meeting in the next room and after coming out from the room accused P.V. Narasimha Rao (A-1) sought support of JMM, MPs and assured them that whatever talks have taken place with Suraj Mandal, those promises shall be fulfilled. According to respective defence counsels, the closed door meeting is a very important detail. If the version of the approver Shailender Mahto was truthful, he would not have missed mention about it in his press release Ex. P.W. 1/DF. In my opinion, the aforesaid reference to the closed door meeting is in the nature of the details relating to the above referred meeting. The important factors are that JMM, MPs had a meeting with accused P.V. Narasimha Rao (A-1) and Buta Singh (A-7) at the residence of Prime Minister on 26-7-1993. In that meeting Shri P.V. Narasimha Rao sought help of JMM, MPs in relation to the no confidence motion and he told them that promises made to Suraj Mandal, MP shall be fulfilled. All these important facts are there in the previous statements Ex. P.W. 1/DF and Ex. P.W. 1/DP4. Thereafter, the testimony of the approver cannot be termed as wholly inconsistent or irreconcilable with his previous statements Ex. P.W. 1/DF and Ex. P.W. 1/DP4. Thus, I am not impressed with the arguments advanced on behalf of accused P.V. Narasimha Rao and accused Buta Singh.

330. Further Ex. P.W. 1/DF is admittedly a press release. The document being a statement issued in the form of hand note in the press conference was expected to be brief. Therefore, non mention of minor details like closed door meeting between the Prime Minister, Buta Singh and Suraj Mandal in the said press note cannot be termed as material omission, which may be termed as a contradiction in the version of the approver. Further, it is to be kept in mind that Shailender Mahto alongwith other JMM, MPs had accepted illegal gratification for voting against no confidence motion, which under law is an offence punishable under P.C. Act, 1988, therefore, obviously, under the natural course of circumstances, he must have taken due precautions to release only those facts in his press statement which may not implicate him or call for his prosecution. It is evident from the text of Ex. P.W. 1/DF discussed earlier that there has been a clear attempt to stear clear of making any confession of the guilt by the approver in the press release. If that was the state of mind of the approver, he was not expected under the natural course of circumstances, to mention all the details in the press statement Ex. P.W. 1/DF as it would have amounted to a confession of guilt. In the press release Ex. P.W. 1/DF while disclosing about the role played by accused P.V. Narasimha Rao (A-1) and Buta Singh (A-7), approver Shailender Mahto has tried to pass himself as an innocent victim of circumstances, who at the relevant time could not understand the import of the assurance given by accused P.V. Narasimha Rao (A-1) that the talks which had taken place with Suraj Mandal, MP shall be honoured. Thus, in my opinion, there is a clear attempt to exculpate himself in Ex. P.W. 1/DF. This explains why all the details are not mentioned in Ex. P.W. 1/DF. As such, the inconsistency pointed out on behalf of accused P.V. Narasimha Rao (A-1) Buta Singh (A-7) *qua* previous statement of the approver Shailender Mahto is not significant. Same argument applies to the statements made by approver Shailender Mahto during investigation of the case.

331. It is further contended by respective counsels for accused persons that admittedly the press release dated 26-2-1996 was drafted by eminent criminal lawyer Shri Ram Jethmalani after the approver has disclosed all the facts to him. They have argued if that was the case, then there is no reason as to why the fact of separate meeting is not mentioned in the press release. This circumstance, therefore, adversely effect the credibility of the approver so far as testimony in relation to closed door meeting is concerned. It is also argued that very drafting of the press release Ex. P.W. 1/DF by Shri Ram Jethamlani at the instance of approver Shailender Mahto is motivated with the intention of foisting a false criminal case against the leaders of Congress.

332. I am not much impressed with this argument. Approver Shailender Mahto has stated that he contacted Shri Ram Jethmalani as a lawyer. It is obvious that Ex. P.W. 1/DF is a political statement. As per my earlier discussion, it is also apparent that while releasing such statement, approver Shailender Mahto has tried to ensure that he may not make any confession of his guilt. This circumstance explains as to why the approver Shailender Mahto consulted Shri Ram Jethmalani and why the closed door meeting between accused R.V. Narasimha Rao (A-1), Buta Singh (A-7) and Suraj Mandal, MP do not find mention in Ex. P.W. 1/DF.

333. It is also argued that testimony of the approver Shailender Mahto is not reliable because he admittedly made a statement Ex. P.W. 1/DG in the parliament denying the allegations of acceptance of bribe by JMM, MPs., Ld. Defence counsels have argued that the witness has stated that he made a false statement in the parliament. If the witness can make a false statement in the parliament, he is not expected to tell the truth in the court. Thus, there is a serious doubt about his truthfulness and reliability.

334. I do not find any merit in the aforesaid contention, because at the time of making statement Ex. P.W. 1/DG dated 29-2-1996 in the Parliament, approver Shailender Mahto had a reason for the same. If he has disclosed the truth in the aforesaid proceedings it would have invited proceedings against him before the Privilege Committee of the Parliament as well as the prosecution for acceptance of bribe. Thus, no significance can be attached to this factor.

335. Ld. counsel for accused P.V. Narasimha Rao has contended that the application of approver Ex. P.W. 1/DV dated 16-3-1997 moved in this court seeking tender of pardon, as well as his confessional statement made before the Court of Shri Harish Dudani, Metropolitan Magistrate, Delhi and the consequent version of the approver Shailender Mahto in this court relevant to the role played by accused P.V. Narasimha Rao (A-1) and Buta Singh (A-7) is the result of threat and inducement on the part of C.B.I.

336. Elaborating on the arguments, he has pointed out that on 13-9-1996, Shri G.N. Gupta D.S.P., C.B.I. an Investigating Officer of this case moved an application in the court of Learned Chief Metropolitan Magistrate, Delhi requesting for recording of confessional statement of approver Shailender Mahto on the ground that he has expressed desire to confess his guilt. Pursuant to that application Shri Rajinder Kumar, Metropolitan Magistrate, Delhi, to whom the application was marked, gave time to the approver to re-consider whether or not he wanted to make a confessional statement. Ultimately on 23-9-1996 approver Shailender Mahto *vide* his statement Ex. P.W. 1/DN declined to make a confession and explained that during his police custody remand, Shri Arun Kumar Sinha, S.P., C.B.I. used to threat him and persuade him to take the name of accused P.V. Narasimha Rao (A-1) as the person who has sent bribe to JMM, MPs. It is contended that in view of the said statement of the approver, it is doubtful that the present statement made by the approver during trial is without any inducement or threat. It is also pointed out that on 13-9-1996 accused Shailender Mahto was produced for extension of judicial custody remand in the court of Special Judge, but at that time Shri G.N. Gupta, D.S.P. did not disclose to the Special Judge that Shailender Mahto has expressed his desire to make a confession. However, after seeking the remand he went to the Court of Ld. Chief Metropolitan Magistrate and moved an application for recording of confession of Shailender Mahto. This circumstance clearly shows that Investigating Officer because of some ulterior motive did not want the Court of Special Judge, Delhi to know that the approver wanted to make a confession.

337. I do not find much merit in the contention of Ld. Defence Counsels, because had the Investigation Officer moved an application for recording of confession of approver Shailender Mahto at the time of taking of judicial remand before the Court of Special Judge, then also the application would have been marked to some Metropolitan Magistrate. Thus, moving of application before Chief Metropolitan Magistrate cannot be attached much significance. Further, approver during his cross examination has explained that he did not make confession before Shri Rajinder Kumar. Metropolitan Magistrate because at that time he was under threat and pressure from Congress and his J.M.M. colleagues and also because his counsel Shri Ajay Burman, advocate had advised him that if he became an approver while he was in custody, he would not be released on bail till the conclusion of trial. Aforesaid explanation in my opinion is satisfactory. Therefore, the refusal of the approver to make confessional statement before Shri Rajinder Kumar Metropolitan Magistrate, Delhi vide statement Ex. P.W. 1/DN is of no consequence. Moreover, the application Ex. P.W. 1/DV was moved by the approver Shailender Mahto during trial on his own. There is no evidence on record to suggest that said application was moved by him under any threat or pressure from any corner. Therefore, in absence of any evidence in this regard, it cannot be said that the application Ex. P.W. 1/DV was moved by approver under some threat or inducement or his confessional statement pursuant to said application and his testimony in the court is the result of some inducement or threat given to the approver.

338. It is also contended on behalf of accused P.V. Narasimha Rao and Buta Singh that Mrs. Abha Mahto, wife of the approver Shailender Mahto contested the election of Lok Sabha shortly after Shailender Mahto became an approver and appeared as a witness in this case. This circumstance according to the accused persons indicates that Shailender Mahto became an approver and deposed against accused P.V. Narasimha Rao and other as a part of bargains that his wife would be given a B.J.P. ticket for the Lok Sabha Election. Thus, his testimony is not worthy of any credit.

339. The argument put forth by learned defence counsels in my opinion is far fetched. There is no evidence on record to suggest that there was any bargain between approver Shailender Mahto and B.J.P. that Abha Mahto would be given a B.J.P. ticket for Lok Sabha Elections as a quid-pro-quo for his deposing against accused P.V. Narasimha Rao and others. Thus, I do not find any merit in this contention.

340. Ld. Counsel for accused P.V. Narasimha Rao has also challenged the credibility of approver Shailender Mahto on the ground that during his testimony in the court, he has given false facts and contradicted himself time and again. Some of the instances pointed out by him are as under:

(i) that the approver Shailender Mahto during his cross examination has stated again and again that he was called by Shri Atal Bahari Vajpayee on 25-2-1996 in pursuance of newspaper report in The Statesman relating to bribing of JMM, MPs. Whereas said newspaper report appeared only on 26-2-1996;

(ii) that the approver initially denied having applied to any political party for a ticket for contesting elections of 11th Lok Sabha. When he was confronted with his letter Ex. P.W. 1/DH dated 25-3-1996, he admitted having applied for the Congress ticket and came out with an explanation that he wrote that letter at the instance of Shri Gyan Ranjan a Congress M.P. from Rajya Sabha;

(iii) that Shailender Mahto has deposed that he decided to become an approver while he was in judicial custody, which is not true because of the fact that he had confessed everything before C.B.I. during his police custody remand as it is apparent from the application dated 13-9-1996 moved by Shri G.N. Gupta, D.S.P., C.B.I. in the Court of Learned Chief Metropolitan Magistrate, Delhi for recording of his confession under section 164, Cr.P.C.;

(iv) that initially the approver has stated that he did not know complainant Ravinder Kumar, but later on when he was confronted with his own letter, he admitted that he knew him;

(v) though the witness has stated that he did not make confessional statement before Shri Rajinder Kumar, Metropolitan Magistrate, Delhi, because he was under threat and pressure from his JMM colleagues and Congress Party, yet when his statement was recorded in the chamber of learned Magistrate, he did not mention about any threat which was allegedly communicated to him by the brother of his wife;

(vi) that the approver has admitted that he did not protest against the incomplete facts mentioned in his press note Ex. P.W. 1/DF., which according to him was drafted in consultation with Shri Ram Jethmalani;

(vii) though this witness admits that he sent resignation letters Ex. P.W. 1/DC and Ex. P.W. 1/DD (Hindi and English version) resigning from the membership of BJP stating that he has been exploited by BJP and used against Shri P.V. Narasimha Rao and also stating that reason for JMM, MPs voting against no confidence motion was that the government has assured that it would resolve the matter of creation of Jharkhand Council, yet he did not disown the statements made in those resignation letters prior to appearing as a witness in the court.

341. Above referred infirmities pointed out by learned defence counsels in my opinion are insignificant and no weight can be assigned to those infirmities. The testimony of the witness in my opinion has to be tested in the background of accompanying circumstances and also on the anvil of independent corroboration.

342. Challenging the veracity of the approver it is contended on behalf of accused persons that approver Shailender Mahto as per his own admissions have made false statements relating to the facts of the case in the parliament and also before C.B.I. during investigation as well as before learned Shri Rajinder Kumar, Metropolitan Magistrate, Delhi while declining to confess his guilt. The explanation given by him for making said false statement is that at the relevant time, he was under fear and pressure. It is argued that aforesaid circumstance clearly show that either the approver Shailender Mahto has no regards for the truth or that he is not a man of character and he can succumb to pressure and tell a lie. Thus, a possibility cannot be ruled out that he is not making truth in the court because of some pressure or inducement.

343. In my opinion, above referred circumstances pointed out by itself are not sufficient for outright rejection of the testimony of the approver. In view of my earlier discussion, it is obvious that the testimony of the approver relating to the receipt of illegal gratification in relation to voting on no confidence motion has been fully corroborated by the evidence of the officials of Punjab National Bank, Naoroji Nagar, New Delhi as well as the record of the bank. Therefore, approver Shailender Mahto cannot be termed as a wholly unreliable witness. While deposing in the court, approver Shailender Mahto has given a self-inculpatory version, which itself is an assurance that some part of his version, if not the entire version, is true. Therefore, under the circumstances, it becomes a duty of the court to carefully scrutinize and evaluate his testimony on all aspects of the case in order to arrive at the truth. Thus, his version, in my opinion, irrespective of the infirmities pointed out by learned respective defence counsels has to be carefully scrutinised in the background of accompanying circumstance in order to find out if his version relating to the roles played by accused P.V. Narasimha Rao (A-1), Buta Singh (A-7) and others in achieving the end of the conspiracy as true. It has to be tested on the anvil of corroboration by independent source of evidence either direct or circumstantial.

344. Before embarking upon the scrutiny of testimony of the approver, it is necessary to deal with one more argument advanced on behalf of accused P.V. Narasimha Rao (A-1) and Buta Singh (A-7). It is contended on their behalf that testimony of the approver so for as it relates to the conversation which allegedly took place during that closed door meeting between P.V. Narasimha Rao (A-1), Buta Singh (A-7) and Suraj Mandal MP is a hear-say evidence as it is in the nature of narration of the facts pertaining to said conversation disclosed by Suraj Mandal to him. Therefore, said testimony being hear-say evidence is not admissible in evidence and liable to be rejected.

345. Section 10 of the Indian Evidence Act, 1872 provides for an exception to the hear-say evidence rule in certain cases. It is reproduced as follows:

> "Things said or done by conspirator in reference to common design – Where there is reasonable ground to believe that two or more persons have conspired together to commit an offence or an actionable wrong, anything said, done or written by any one of such persons in reference to their common intention, after the time when such intention was first entertained by anyone of them, is a relevant fact as against each of the persons believed to be so conspiring, as well for the purpose of proving the existence of the conspiracy as for the purpose of showing that any such person was a party to it."

346. This section lays down that in prosecutions for conspiracy when concert and connection between the persons charged have been sufficiently established, the statements, acts or declarations of each conspirator, in reference to their common intention are admissible as evidence against the others, provided such statements or acts or declarations were made after the time when such intention was entertained by anyone of them and before the accomplishment of the object of the conspiracy.

347. In my earlier discussion, I have already concluded that there was a conspiracy amongst J.M.M., M.Ps and the bribe givers with the object to defeat the no confidence motion by offering and giving of bribe to JMM, MPs and acceptance of the same by them. Thus, section 10 comes into operation and anything said or done by any of the co-conspirators with reference to their common intention till the accomplishment of the object of the conspiracy is admissible in evidence. The reference made by the approver in his testimony that Suraj Mandal after the closed door meeting disclosed to them that his conversation with accused P.V. Narasimha Rao (A-1) and Buta Singh (A-7) was to their benefit and that the talks regarding money had also taken place though the amount to be paid has not been specified, is admissible in evidence under section 10 of the Evidence Act, because from the sequence of evidence, it is obvious that if the aforesaid conversation had taken place, it was during the currency of conspiracy before its object was achieved.

348. It is also contended by respective counsels appearing on behalf of accused P.V. Narasimha Rao (A-1) and Buta Singh (A-7) that if at all any closed door meeting took place between Suraj Mandal, M.P., Buta Singh (A-7) and P.V. Narasimha Rao (A-1), he alone could be the best witness to narrate said conversation. Though he was initially arrayed as an accused in this case, but later on after the judgment of Constitution Bench of the Apex Court upholding the immunity under section 105 of the Constitution of India to the bribe taking M.Ps he was discharged from the case. It is contended that after his discharge, he did not remain as an accused and as such he was competent to depose as a witness in this case. Despite of that, prosecution has not cared to examine said best witness to establish the role played by P.V. Narasimha Rao (A-1) and Buta Singh (A-7) in the conspiracy, as such an adverse presumption should be drawn against the prosecution that if Suraj Mandal had appeared in the witness box he would not have supported the case of the prosecution.

349. In order to appreciate above contention, it is necessary to have a feel of background facts of this case. Suraj Mandal is one of the accused named in the FIR. During investigation, his stand was that he was not a party to any conspiracy to bribe members of parliament including himself. He was charge sheeted as one of the co-accused. He argued against the framing of charges, which arguments were not accepted and he was formally charged for the offence punishable under section 120B IPC read with section 7, 12 and 13(2) read with 13(1)(d) of P.C. Act, 1988 as well as substantive offences. Suraj Mandal pleaded not guilty to the charge and claimed trial. He even cross examined the approver Shailender Mahto and suggested to him that there was no conspiracy as narrated by him. From the aforesaid circumstances, it is obvious that Suraj Mandal even if produced as a witness was not going to support the prosecution case. Given that background, prosecution was expected to call Suraj Mandal in support of its case. Therefore, in my opinion, there is no question of drawing an adverse presumption due to non production of Suraj Mandal in the witness box. It may not be out of place to mention that having the knowledge of aforesaid stand of Suraj Mandal, accused P.V. Narasimha Rao (A-1) and Buta Singh (A-7) have not cared to summon him as a defence witness. If accused P.V. Narasimha Rao (A-1) and Buta Singh (A-7) were sure of their defence, they could easily have summoned Suraj Mandal in defence, to disprove the version of Shailender Mahto. They have not opted to do so. Therefore, under the circumstances, now they cannot be allowed to take advantage of non-production of Suraj Mandal as a witness by the prosecution.

APPROVER SHAILENDER MAHTO DEPOSED THAT ON 26.7.1993 AROUND 7 P.M. BUTA SINGH (A7) HAD TAKEN JMM MPs TO A1 – DEAL FOR SUPPORTING THE GOVERNMENT WAS STRUCK – CBI COURT HELD

350. Having concluded that the discrepancies pointed out on behalf of accused P.V. Narasimha Rao and Buta Singh are not sufficient for outright rejection of the testimony of the approver. Now, I proceed to analyse the evidence to find out if there is sufficient corroboration to the testimony of the approver from independent evidence either direct or circumstantial to lend it assurance of credibility despite of aforesaid discrepancies.

351. Learned Counsels for the accused P.V. Narasimha Rao and Buta Singh have contended that it is settled proposition of law that the testimony of an approver is to be viewed with suspicion and the Courts should be slow in acting upon said testimony. As a matter of prudence and caution, the Courts before acting upon the testimony of the approver must seek corroboration to the testimony of the approver on material aspects of the prosecution case not only *qua* the commission of offence, but also *qua* the role of the accused which links him with the offence. In support of their contention, they have relied upon "**Sarwan Singh v. State of Punjab, AIR 1957 SC 637; Chanden v. State of Rajasthan, AIR 1958 SC 599; Sera Singh v. State of Punjab, (1996) 10 SCC 330; State of Tamil Nadu v. Suresh, (1988) SCC 372; Ram Narain v. State of Rajasthan, (1973) 3 SCC 805 and Lal Chand v. State of Haryana, (1984) 1 SCC 686.**"

352. It is further argued on behalf of accused P.V. Narasimha Rao (A-1) and Buta Singh (A-7) that there is no corroboration to the testimony of approver regarding the alleged closed door meeting between accused P.V. Narasimha Rao (A-1), Buta Singh (A-7) and Suraj Mandal, M.P. at the residence of P.V. Narasimha Rao on 26.7.1993 nor there is any corroboration relating to any offer of bribe given to Suraj Mandal during said closed door meeting or the assurance given by accused P.V. Narasimha Rao to the J.M.M., M.Ps after said closed door meeting that promises made to Suraj Mandal shall be fulfilled. It is thus contended that in absence of such corroboration no reliance can be placed upon the testimony of the approver particularly in the light of the discrepancies pointed out earlier and the fact that approver has come out with the version regarding closed door meeting for the first time only during trial of the case.

353. Learned Counsel for accused P.V. Narasimha Rao has further added that the reliability of the version of the approver is suspect because as per his version, some part of the money was received at the residence of Suraj Mandal on 29.7.1993, while the remaining part was received in the early morning of 30.7.1993. He has further specified that this money was deposited in the Bank on 31-7-93 and that on 30-7-1993 approver alongwith Simon Marandi also went to Punjab National Bank, Naoroji Nagar. This shows that the case of the approver is that the money was available with JMM, MPs on 30-7-1993. In the circumstances, the facts disclosed by the approver cannot stand in the face of allegations made in the charge sheet relating to withdrawal of money at Bangalore on 30-7-1993 and was delivered at the residence of Suraj Mandal, MP on 31-7-1993. The aforesaid inconsistency between the case put up by C.B.I. in the second charge sheet and the testimony of the approver as well as C.B.I. case is motivated and not reliable.

354. In **Sarwan Singh v. State of Punjab, AIR 1957 SC 637** while dealing with the question relating to the approver's evidence and the extent of corroboration required, Hon'ble Supreme Court has held:

"Courts are naturally reluctant to act on the tainted evidence of an approver unless it is corroborated in material particulars by other independent evidence. But it would not be right to expect that such independent corroboration should cover the whole of the prosecution story or even all the material particulars. If such a view is adopted it would render the evidence of the accomplice wholly superfluous. On the other hand, it would not be safe to act upon such evidence merely because it is corroborated in minor particulars or incidental details because in such a case, corroboration does not afford the necessary assurance that the main story disclosed by the approver can be reasonably and safely accepted as true."

355. In the matter of **A. Devendran v. State of Tamil Nadu, (1997) 11 SCC 720,** Hon'ble Supreme Court while dealing with the question of extent of corroboration required for the testimony of approver has observed as follows:—

"Ordinarily an approver's statement has to be corroborated in material particulars. Certain clinching features of involvement disclosed directly to an accused by an approver must be tested *qua* each accused from independent credible evidence and on being satisfied the evidence of an approver can be accepted. What is the extent of corroboration that is required before the acceptance of the evidence of the approver would depend upon the facts and circumstances of the case. The corroboration required, however, must be in material particulars connecting each of the accused with the offence. In other words the evidence of the approver implicating several accused persons in commission of the offence could not only be corroborated generally but also *qua* each accused. But that does not mean that there should be independent corroboration of every particular circumstance from an independent source. All that is required is that there must be some additional evidence rendering it probable that the story of the accomplice is true. Corroboration also could be both by direct or circumstantial evidence."

356. Similarly in the matter of **Sevaka Perumal v. State of Tamil Nadu, (1991) 3 SCC 471** Hon'ble Court has held as follows:—

"An approver is a competent witness against the accused person. But the Court, to satisfy its conscience, insists as caution and prudence to seek, as a rule, corroboration to the evidence of the approver, a *particips criminis* from independent evidence ocular or circumstantial, of general particulars regarding the story spoken of by the approver of the commission of the crime and the part played by the accused therein to find whether it is true and worthy of acceptance. The reliability of the evidence of an approver should be considered from totality of the facts and circumstances. In the present case the canopy of the material evidence from independent sources sufficiently corroborates the approver's evidence."

357. From the aforesaid judgments, it is apparent that the law relating to the extent of corroboration required for the testimony of approver is that his version should be corroborated by other independent evidence on material aspects of the case not only to establish the commission of offence, but also qua the role played by the accused. However, it is not necessary that the independent corroboration must cover the whole of the prosecution story or all the material aspects of the prosecution case or should be sufficient to prove the offence or the guilt of the accused. It is also well settled that the corroboration required to lend assurance to the testimony of the approver should not necessarily be from the direct evidence. Said assurance and corroboration can be sought even from the circumstantial evidence.

MEETING OF JMM MPs WITH PM AND BUTA SINGH ON 26.7.1993 IS ADMITTED – VOTING OF JMM MPs IN FAVOUR OF GOVERNMENT ON 28.7.1993 IS PROVED – RECEIPT OF RS. 1,62,80,000 BY JMM, MPs IS PROVED BY PNB RECORD OF 1-2 AUGUST, 1993 – AMOUNTS TO CORROBORATION OF APPROVER'S STATEMENT BY UNIMPEACHABLE CIRCUMSTANTIAL EVIDENCE – HOLDS CBI COURT

358. In the present case, as per the story narrated by approver in his testimony none other than the conspirators *i.e.* four J.M.M., M.Ps., including the approver, P.V. Narasimha Rao (A-1) and Buta Singh (A-7) were present during the meeting dated 26-7-1993 which took place at the residence of Shri P.V. Narasimha Rao. Other participants of the meeting being the co-conspirators are not expected to support the prosecution case by admitting the guilt. Therefore, only corroboration to the testimony of the approver can come from circumstantial evidence.

359. As per my earlier discussion, prosecution has been able to establish from the evidence independent of testimony of approver following circumstances:—

(i) that on 26.7.1993, no confidence motion was moved against the Government led by accused P.V. Narasimha Rao;

(ii) that at the relevant time, the strength of Congress (I) members in the Lok Sabha was less than 50 per cent of total strength of Lok Sabha as such there existed motive on the part of accused P.V. Narasimha Rao and his supporters to win over the opposition M.Ps.;

(iii) that on 28-7-1993, no confidence motion was put to vote and defeated. As per the parliamentary proceedings dated 28-7-1993 published by Lok Sabha Secretariat, J.M.M., M.Ps voted against the no confidence motion;

(iv) that from the admissions of accused Buta Singh and P.V. Narasimha Rao, it is established that on 26-7-1993, JMM, MPs including the approver Shailender Mahto initially visited the residence of accused Buta Singh and from there they accompanied them to the residence of accused P.V. Narasimha Rao (A-1);

(v) that it is also admitted by accused Buta Singh and P.V. Narasimha Rao that on 26-7-1993 they had a meeting with JMM, MPs at the residence of accused P.V. Narasimha Rao,

(vi) that from the testimony of the officials of Punjab National Bank, Naoroji Nagar, New Delhi and the record of said bank, it is established that on 1st and 2nd of August, 1993, a huge sum of Rs. 1,62,80,000 was deposited in various accounts of JMM, MPs/their family members as well as a joint account of all the four JMM, MPs. From the testimony of P.W. 103 Satish Kumar Sharma and P.W. 98 Jawahar Lal, it is established that aforesaid money was collected by him from the residence of Suraj Mandal and Shibu Soren;

(vii) that in my earlier discussion, I have also concluded that aforesaid amount which came to be deposited in respective accounts of JMM, MPs was illegal gratification.

360. In view of my above referred circumstances, established on record by independent evidence provides sufficient corroboration to the self-inculpatory version of the approver Shailender Mahto that JMM, MPs were offered and given bribe in consideration of their saving the government of accused P.V. Narasimha Rao by voting against the no confidence motion. The visit of JMM, MPs including approver Shailender Mahto to the residence of Buta Singh (A-7) and from there, their visit alongwith accused Buta Singh to the residence of accused P.V. Narasimha Rao (A-1) is also not disputed. This provides an assurance that whatever the approver is stating about the incident dated 26-7-1993 at the residence of accused P.V. Narasimha Rao is correct. Version of the approver further finds corroboration from the proximity between the aforesaid meeting of JMM MPs with accused P.V. Narasimha Rao (A-1) and Buta Singh (A-7), the date of voting on no confidence motion, the voting pattern of J.M.M., M.Ps and the fact that substantial amounts totaling Rs. 1,62,80,000 came to be deposited in various accounts of JMM, MPs at Punjab National Bank, Naoroji Nagar, New Delhi within few days of the defeat of no confidence motion *i.e.,* by 2-8-1993. The version of the approver also finds assurance of credibility from the fact that main beneficiary from the defeat of no confidence motion was the accused P.V. Narasimha Rao (A-1) because it was his government which was saved.

361. If the J.M.M., M.Ps have been bribed, then there must be someone who has paid or caused to be paid bribe to them. It does not appeal to the reason that anyone else except the main beneficiary might have paid or caused to be paid aforesaid bribe amount to JMM, MPs unless he was asked to do so by the main beneficiary *i.e.* accused P.V. Narasimha Rao (A-1) and unless he was given an assurance that he would be awarded or compensated subsequently.

362. Considering the aforesaid circumstances, I am of the view that there is sufficient circumstantial evidence on record to lend assurance of credibility to the testimony of the approver Shailender Mahto irrespective of the infirmities pointed out on behalf of accused persons and the fact that prosecution unfortunately have not been able to establish on record the identity of actual source from where the money came and the person or the persons who delivered said money to Suraj Mandal, M.P.

363. Approver has categorically stated that in the evening of 26-7-1993, JMM, MPs visited accused Buta Singh (A-7) and it was accused Buta Singh who suggested a direct meeting with accused P.V. Narasimha Rao. When this evidence was put to accused Buta Singh (A-7) for his explanation he denied that he gave such suggestion to J.M.M., M.Ps. However, he did not come out with the name of anyone who suggested that he should accompany them to meet the Prime Minister. Admittedly, accused Buta Singh had accompanied JMM, MPs in the evening of 26-7-1993 from his residence to the residence of accused P.V. Narasimha Rao. This must have been on the suggestion of someone, if not Buta Singh (A-7). But accused Buta Singh (A-7) in his explanation has not told as to who suggested that he should accompany them to the residence of accused P.V. Narasimha Rao. Therefore, I am not inclined to accept his explanation. One wonders as to why accused Buta Singh (A-7) has denied having suggested that JMM, MPs should have a direct meeting with the prime minister.

364. Approver Shailender Mahto has also stated that initially at the residence of P.V. Narasimha Rao, creation of Jharkhand council was discussed. Thereafter, accused P.V. Narasimha Rao and Buta Singh went to another room. After sometime, they called Suraj Mandal, MP to that room and 5-6 minutes later they all came out of that room and accused P.V. Narasimha Rao sought the support of JMM, MPs for his government and promised that whatever conversation has taken place with Suraj Mandal, those promises shall be fulfilled. Approver has also stated that on their way back from the residence of accused P.V. Narasimha Rao (A-1) Suraj Mandal disclosed that the conversation in the aforesaid room was to the benefit of JMM, MPs and he also disclosed on the insistence of Simon Marandi that talks regarding payment of money have also taken place, but the amount to be paid has not been specified.

365. If the assurance given by the Prime Minister to the JMM, MPs, that the promise to Suraj Mandal shall be fulfilled, is considered in the background of the gist of conversation disclosed by the Suraj Mandal to JMM, MPs, then it is obvious that accused P.V. Narasimha Rao (A-1) and Buta Singh (A-7) have actually offered illegal gratification to accused Suraj Mandal, who was acting on behalf of

JMM, MPs during said closed door meeting dated 26-7-1993, which offer of bribe amounts to the abetment of commission of offence punishable under section 7 and 13(2) read with section 13(1)(d) of P.C. Act, 1988 by the JMM, MPs.

CHARGES AGAINST P.V. NARASIMHA RAO AND BUTA SINGH PROVED – HOLDS CBI COURT

366. Overall view of the version of the approver and the other evidence of the prosecution conclusively establish that there was actually a conspiracy to defeat the no confidence motion by illegal act *i.e.,* offering or causing to offer or giving illegal gratification to the members of parliament (JMM, MPs) and acceptance of bribe by them. Thus in my view, the prosecution has bring home the charges against accused P.V. Narasimha Rao and accused Buta Singh beyond reasonable doubt.

367. Ld. Counsel for accused Buta Singh (A-7) has contended that accused Buta Singh (A-7) have played no role in the conspiracy to bribe the JMM, MPs. He has pointed out that during the tenure of accused Buta Singh as Home Minister, one committee was formed for Jharkhand matters and said committee had submitted a report. This was the reason, as per ld. Defence counsel, that J.M.M., M.Ps had approached accused Buta Singh in the evening of 26-7-1993 and took him to the residence of accused P.V. Narasimha Rao in order to use his good offices for achieving their end of creation of Jharkhand State. He has contended that there is no evidence that accused Buta Singh either offered or suggested any bribe to JMM, MPs, therefore, he cannot be termed as a conspirator who has agreed with anyone to commit an illegal act *i.e.* to offer or cause to offer illegal gratification to the members of parliament.

368. I do not find merit in the contention put forth on behalf of accused Buta Singh (A-7). Testimony of the approver establish that after having initial conversation regarding creation of Jharkhand council, accused P.V. Narasimha Rao and Buta Singh went to the other room. After sometime, they called Suraj Mandal in the said room and 5-6 minutes later they all came out of the room and accused P.V. Narasimha Rao sought help of JMM, MPs and assured that promises made to Suraj Mandal Shall be fulfilled. The closed door meeting between Shri P.V. Narasimha Rao and Buta Singh before calling Suraj Mandal to the aforesaid room and thereafter the offer of bribe given to Suraj Mandal in presence of accused Buta Singh clearly established his complicity in the conspiracy.

369. In over-all view of above discussed evidence, I conclude as follows:—

(i) that prosecution has been able to prove the existence of conspiracy amongst the JMM, MPs, accused P.V. Narasimha Rao, accused Buta Singh and other unknown persons with the object to defeat the no confidence motion by illegal means *i.e.,* offering or causing to offer and giving illegal gratification to the members of parliament and acceptance of illegal gratification by them as a motive or reward for using their franchise against the no confidence motion;

(ii) that prosecution has also been able to prove beyond doubt on record that in furtherance of said conspiracy accused P.V. Narasimha Rao (A-1) and accused Buta Singh (A-7) played an active role and abetted the commission of offence of taking bribe by the public servants *i.e.,* members of parliament belonging to JMM Party namely Suraj Mandal, Shibu Soren, Simon Marandi and Shailender Mahto. Thus, I hold that prosecution has been able to prove the charges against accused P.V. Narasimha Rao (A-1) and Buta Singh (A-7) for the offences punishable under section 120B IPC read with sections 7, 12 and 13(2) read with 13(1)(d) of PC Act, 1988 as well as the substantive offence punishable under section 12 of the P.C. Act, 1988. So far as other accused persons namely accused Capt. Satish Sharma, Bhajan Lal, M. Veerappa Moily, Ajit Singh, V. Rajeshwar Rao and H.M. Revanna are concerned, prosecution has failed to establish the charges against them beyond reasonable doubt.

ACCUSED P.V. NARASIMHA RAO (A1) AND BUTA SINGH (A7) CONVICTED FOR OFFENCES PUNISHABLE UNDER SECTIONS 120B, IPC READ WITH SECTIONS 7, 12, AND 13(2) READ WITH SECTION 13(1)(d) OF PC ACT, 1988 – HOLDS CBI COURT

370. In view of the aforesaid conclusions, I convict accused P.V. Narasimha Rao (A-1) as well as accused Buta Singh (A-7) for having committed offences punishable under section 120B IPC read with sections 7, 12 and 13(2) read with 13(1)(d) of P.C. Act, 1988 as well as substantive offence punishable under section 12 of the P.C. Act, 1988.

ACCUSED CAPT. SATISH SHARMA, BHAJAN LAL, M. VEERAPPA MOILY, AJIT SINGH, D.K. AUDIKESHVULU, M. THIMMEGOWDA, RAMALINGA REDDY, V. RAJESHWAR RAO AND H.M. REVANNA GIVEN BENEFIT OF DOUBT & ACQUITTED – HOLDS CBI COURT

371. I, acquit accused persons namely Capt. Satish Sharma, Bhajan Lal, M. Veerappa Moily, Ajit Singh, D.K. Audikeshvulu, M. Thimmegowda, Ramalinga Reddy, V. Rajeshwar Rao and H.M. Revanna of the charges under sections 120B, IPC read with sections 7, 12 and 13(2) read with 13(1)(d) of P.C. Act, 1988 as well as the substantive offence punishable under section 12 of the P.C. Act, 1988, giving them benefit of doubt.

Announced in open court. (AJIT BHARIHOKE)

Dated:- 29-9-2000 SPECIAL JUDGE: DELHI

IN THE COURT OF SHRI AJIT BHARIHOKE SPECIAL JUDGE, DELHI

INTERIM ORDER DATED 29.9.2000

29.9.2000 Present: Shri R.M. Tewari, Special P.P. alongwith

Shri A.K. Dutt, Special P.P. for C.B.I.

Accused P.V. Narasimha Rao in person with Shri R.K. Anand, Senior Advocate assisted by Shri Arun Birbal, advocate.

Accused Captain Satish Sharma on bail with Shri H.R. Bhardwaj, Senior Advocate assisted by Shri Arun Bhardwaj, advocate.

Accused Buta Singh on bail with Sh. Satish Tamta, advocate.

Accused V. Rajeshwar Rao on bail with Shri IU Khan, advocate.

Accused HM Revenna, Ramalinga Reddy, M. Veerappa Moily, M. Thimmegowda on bail with Shri Chandershekhara, advocate.

Accused D.K. Audikeshvulu on bail with Shri C.V. Nagesh, advocate and Shri R.K. Singh, advocate.

Accused Bhajan Lal on bail with Shri Mohit Mathur, advocate.

Accused Ajit Singh on bail with Sh. Rajiv Naseem, advocate.

Judgment is announced in open court separate detailed judgment

Accused P.V. Narasimha Rao and Buta Singh are convicted for having committed offences punishable under sections 120B, IPC read with sections 7, 12, 13(2) read with section 13(1)(d) of the PC Act, 1988 as well as substantive offence punishable under section 12 of the PC Act, 1988.

So far as other accused namely Capt. Satish Sharma, Bhajan Lal, Ajit Singh, V. Rajeshwar Rao, D.K. Audikeshvulu, Ramalinga Reddy, M. Thimmegowda and H.M. Revenna are concerned they are acquitted of the charges punishable under section 120B, IPC read with sections 7, 12, 13(2) read with 13(1)(d) of the PC Act, 1988 as well as substantive offences punished under section 12 of the PC Act. Bail cun surety bonds of the accused persons who are acquitted, stand discharged.

Put on 11-10-2000 for order on sentence. Notice to approver Shailender Mahto be issued for the date fixed.

Special Judge
Delhi 29.9.2000

IN THE COURT OF SHRI AJIT BHARIHOKE, SPECIAL JUDGE, DELHI

C.B.I.
v.
Shri P.V. Narasimha Rao

RC Nos. 1 to 5(A)/96/CBI/ACU-VIII/DLI

Order on the Point of Sentence on 12.10.2000

1. Shri P.V. Narasimha Rao and Shri Buta Singh have been respectively convicted for having committed offences punishable under section 120B, IPC read with sections 7, 12 and 13 (2) read with 13(1)(d) of P.C. Act, 1988 and also for having committed substantive offence punishable under section 12 of the P.C. Act, 1988 *vide* my detailed judgement dated 29.9.2000.

2. I have heard learned Special Prosecutor as well as learned Counsels appearing on behalf of Shri P.V. Narasimha Rao and Shri Buta Singh on the point of sentence.

3. Learned Counsel for convict P.V. Narasimha Rao has claimed benefit of probation under section 360, Cr.PC for his client on the ground that he is a senior citizen aged 79 years and has serious medical problems detailed below:—

(i) Non-insulin dependent diabetes mellitus: Controlled presently on oral hypoglycemic drugs.

(ii) Coronary artery disease: He underwent coronary artery bypass surgery for unstable angina and triple vessel disease in July, 1990. He has been periodically screened with exercise thallium studies. The latest was performed in October, 1995 which revealed normal exercise tolerance and abnormal thallium-201 image consistent with exercise induced ischemia in the inferior wall region. There was no significant change in this finding as compared to the previous study of February, 1992.

His left ventricular function has been assessed periodically (echocardiography/radionuclide studies) and the last Muga study was done in August, 1996 which revealed an ejection fraction of 56%

(iii) Essential hypertension: Detected in 1990 and initially controlled on nifedipine and atenolol. Presently controlled on atenolol tablets.

(iv) Cerebrovascular Disease: Had transient ischemic attacks (sensory) during February-April, 1994. Suffered a sensory stroke with right sided dysesthesiae in April 1994. Evaluation with magnetic resonance imaging and magnetic resonance angiography revealed a left thalamic infarct in May 1994. Subsequent sensory symptoms (thalamic syndrome) treated with amitryptaline.

(v) Suffers from Carotid Artery Occlusive Disease which has resulted in a thalamic Stroke in 1994. Again had recurrent Transient Ischaemic Attacks in 1998 when investigations revealed tight narrowing of left internal carotid artery. Underwent Carotid endarterectomy in December, 1998. He also has 50% narrowing of right carotid artery and is maintained on antiplatelet agents for the same.

(vi) Has mild renal impairment with elevated urea and creatinine levels, in all probability due to long standing diabetes.es. He is maintained on diuretics for the same.

(vii) The applicant has significant peripheral vascular disease involving both lower limbs, abdominal aorta and left renal artery.

(viii) The applicant has a history of upper gastrointestinal bleeding (June 1999) requiring hospitalization. Upper GI endoscopy was done which showed severe gastritis. This was controlled and there has been no recurrence.

(ix) The applicant also suffers from mild benign hypertrophy of prostate. The applicant had surgeries for cataract in both his eyes.

4. In support of this contention, he has drawn my attention to photo copies of medical certificates issued from All India Institute of Medical Sciences as well as other medical record.

5. In support of the claim for probation and lenient view, learned Counsel for accused Shri P.V. Narasimha Rao has further pointed out that he has been prominent politician having meritorious record. He has been the Prime Minister of India for a period of five years between 1991-1996. When he became the Prime Minister of India, this country was facing many crisis at political and economic, fronts and under his leadership because of his efforts, the country made recovery on the economic as well as on political front. Many political problems such as Punjab crisis and Assam crisis were solved during his tenure. Besides that it is submitted that Shri P.V. Narasimha Rao is not a previous convict. Learned Defence Counsel in support of his plea for lenient view has taken me through the evidence and submitted that the conviction of the accused is based upon scanty circumstantial evidence and because of this circumstance also, he is entitled to the benefit of probation or minimal punishment. He has further argued that as per the case of prosecution, bribe was given to JMM, MPs in order to save the Government and not in respect of some governmental function, therefore, the gravity of the offence is much lesser.

6. Ld. Counsel for accused Buta Singh has submitted that as per the prosecution case, role played by him in the present conspiracy is minor one. His conviction is based upon only circumstantial evidence and it is not clear what precise role he actually played in the conspiracy. Therefore, he is entitled to a lenient view. He has further contended that as per the prosecution case, Shri P.V. Narasimha Rao was running a minority government. When it was facing no confidence motion in July, 1993 the JMM, MPs were running around to extract monetary benefit from the situation in which Congress Government was placed and according to the prosecution case, the accused persons were confronted with a Hebson's choice either to pay the JMM, MPs or allow the Government to fell and lead the country to a fresh general elections, which is obviously a very expensive process. If they opted for the second choice, it was surely under compulsion and threat, therefore, the offence committed by the accused cannot be termed as grave, more so because of the fact the bribe takers because of the constitutional immunity under Article 105(2) of the Constitution of India are enjoying the money received by them. Thus, he has contended that this is a fit case in which accused Buta Singh is entitled to benefit of probation under section 360, Cr. P.C. because he has a past meritorious career as a politician and he is not a previous convict.

7. Ld. Special Prosecutor has submitted that circumstances pointed out by respective counsels for accused persons do not call for a lenient view. He has contended that the offence committed by Shri P.V. Narasimha Rao and Shri Buta Singh is of grave nature. They have indulged in corrupting the legislature by offering illegal gratification to them and if such acts are allowed to go unpunished, it would send wrong signals to the society and encourage corruption amongst public servants. In support of this contention, he has drawn my attention to the observations of Hon'ble Supreme Court in the matter of **State of Madhya Pradesh v. Ram Singh, (2000) 5 SCC 88** and pressed for exemplary punishment.

8. In support of his contention, learned Counsel for convict P.V. Narasimha Rao has relied upon **(1992) 2 SCC 198 and (1980) 1 SCC 74.**

9. In support of his contention, ld. Counsel for convict Buta Singh has relied upon **(2000) 6 SCC 168.**

10. I have carefully considered the submissions made on behalf of Shri P.V. Narasimha Rao and Shri Buta Singh as well as the contention of the ld. Special Prosecutor. I have also gone through the respective judgements cited by the parties.

11. In my opinion, the circumstances pointed out as mitigating on behalf of convict shri P.V. Narasimha Rao and Shri Buta Singh do not call for a lenient view.

12. While deliberating upon the quantum of sentence to be awarded to the convicts, it is necessary to take into consideration the gravity and the nature of offence committed by them. Accused Shri P.V. Narasimha Rao and Shri Buta Singh have been convicted for the charge of abetting the acceptance of illegal gratification by the JMM, MPs as a motive or reward for voting against the no confidence motion in furtherance of a conspiracy. Aforesaid act of theirs in my view is a crime of grave nature, because by bribing JMM, MPs accused Shri P.V. Narasimha Rao with the help of Shri Buta Singh have tried to purchase the right to remain in power and rule the country. Said act by its very nature amounts to cutting at the roots of democratic system provided by the Constitution of India. To some extent, it may even be termed as subversion of Constitution.

13. Hon'ble Justice K.T. Thomas in the matter of **State of Madhya Pradesh v. Ram Singh, (2000) 5 SCC 88,** have explained the characteristics and effects of corruption as follows:—

> "Corruption in a civilized society is a disease like cancer which if not detected in time, is sure to maliganise (*sic*) the polity of the country leading to disastrous consequences. It is termed as a plague which is not only contagious but if not controlled spreads like a fire in a jungle. Its virus is compared with HIV leading to AIDS, being incurable. It has also been termed as royal thievery. The socio-political system exposed to such a dreaded communicable disease is likely to crumble under its own weight. Corruption is opposed to democracy and social order, being not only anti-people, but aimed and targeted against them. It affects the economy and destroys that cultural heritage. Unless nipped in the bud at the earliest, it is likely to cause turbulence shaking of the socio-economic-political system in an otherwise healthy, wealthy, effective and vibrating society."

14. In the above referred paragraph of Judgment Hon'ble Justice K.T. Thomas has highlighted the need for nipping the corruption in the bud at the earliest as it is likely to cause turbulence/shaking of the socio-economic-political system in an otherwise healthy, wealthy, effective and vibrating society. The best way to discourage corruption in the public life particularly in the high places is to award exemplary punishment to the high ranking servants in order to send a message to the society that corruption is not a low return high risk business but it is really a high risk business.

15. Thus, keeping in view the circumstances pointed out by accused Shri P.V. Narasimha Rao and Shri Buta Singh and the nature of offence, committed by them, I am of the view that they are not entitled to the benefit of probation or lenient view.

P.V. NARASIMHA RAO AND BUTA SINGH SENTENCED TO RI FOR 3 YEARS AND TO THE FINE AMOUNT OF RS. 1 LAKH EACH FOR OFFENCES PUNISHABLE UNDER SECTION 120B, IPC READ WITH SECTIONS 7, 12, 13(2) READ WITH SECTION 13(1)(d), PC ACT, 1988-CBI COURT

16. Keeping in view the facts and circumstances of the case and gravity of offence and the mitigating circumstances pointed out on behalf of accused Shri P.V. Narasimha Rao and Shri Buta Singh for the offence punishable under section 120B, IPC read with sections 7, 12, 13(2) read with 13(1)(d) of PC Act, 1988, I hereby sentence convict Shri P.V. Narasimha Rao and Shri Buta Singh to undergo R.I. for the period of 3 years. They are further sentenced to pay a fine of Rs. 1 lakh respectively. In the event of any of the accused failing to pay the fine imposed, he shall undergo R.I for further period of 6 months. For the offence punishable under section 12 of the PC Act, 1988, both the convicts are further sentenced to undergo R.I. for the period of 3 years and also to pay fine of Rs. 1 lakhs each. In the event of any of the accused failing to pay the fine imposed, he shall undergo R.I. for further period of 6 months.

17. Substantive sentences awarded to both the convict persons for respective offences shall run concurrently.

* * * * *

File be consigned to record room.

Announced in the Open Court (AJIT BHARIHOKE)

Dated 12.10.2000 SPECIAL JUDGE: DELHI

NOTE: IN THE REMAINING PART OF THIS ORDER OF SENTENCE SOME OBSERVATIONS WERE MADE ON MPs PART OF THE ORDER OF THE SUPREME COURT WAS REPRODUCED. CBI WAS DIRECTED TO INVESTIGATE THE CASE AGAINST MPs IN TERMS OF THE ORDER OF SUPREME COURT.

ORDER ON THE STAY APPLICATION

IN THE COURT OF SH. AJIT BHARIHOKE, SPECIAL JUDGE, DELHI

CBI
v.
P.V. Narasimha Rao

R.C. No. 1 to 5(A) 96 CBI-ACU-VIII/DLI

ORDER ON THE STAY APPLICATION ON 12.10.2000

Present: Shri R.M. Tewari, Special P.P. for CBI

Convict P.V. Narasimha Rao with Shri R.K. Anand, Sr. Advocate assisted by Shri Arun Birbal, Advocate AND Shri Sri Bhagwan Advocate.

Convict Buta Singh with Shri Sri Satish Tamta, Advocate.

Order on sentence is announced vide separate detailed order. Accused P.V. Narasimha Rao and Buta Singh are sentenced under sections 120-B-IPC read with sections 7, 12, 13(2) read with 13(1)(d) of P.C. Act, 1988 to undergo RI for the period of 3 years. They are further sentenced to pay a fine of Rs. 1 lakh respectively. In the event of any of the accused failing to pay the fine imposed, he shall undergo RI for further period of 6 months.

For the offence punishable under section 12 of the P.C. Act, 1988 both the accused/convicts are further sentenced to undergo R.I. for the period of 3 years each and also to pay a fine of Rs. 1 lakh each. In the event of any of the convict failing to pay the fine imposed, he shall undergo R.I. for further period of 6 months.

Substantive sentences awarded to both the convict persons for respective offences shall run concurrently.

THE CONVICTS INTEND TO FILE APPEAL – ADMITTED TO BAIL TILL 8.11.2000 – CBI COURT

Both the accused/convicts have moved applications for grant of bail and suspension of execution of sentence under section 389, Cr. P.C. mentioning that they intend to go in appeal against the order of conviction and sentence.

Heard. In order to enable the convicts to file appeal against the order as desired by them, they are directed to be released on bail till 8-11-2000 on their furnishing bail bound in the sum of Rs. 2 lakhs with one surety each respectively. In the event of acceptance of bail-cum-surety bond, the sentence awarded to them shall remain suspended till 8-11-2000. File be consigned to record room.

12-10-2000 Sd/- Special Judge, Delhi

DELHI HIGH COURT

P.V. Narasimha Rao
v.
State

2002 CR LJ 2401

Coram: R.S. SODHI, J. (Single Bench)

Cri. A. No. 638 With 621 of 2000 and 33 of 2001 Decided on 15-3-2002

JUDGMENT

R.S. SODHI, J.:—1. Shri P.V. Narasimha Rao and Shri Buta Singh have filed Criminal Appeal Nos. 638 of 2000 and 621 of 2000 respectively challenging the findings of the Special Judge holding them guilty of the charges framed against them while the Rashtriya Mukti Morcha has filed Criminal Revision No. 33 of 2001 challenging the acquittal of Capt. Satish Sharma, Shri V. Rajeshwar Rao, Shri H.M. Revenna, Shri Ramalinga Reddy, Shri M. Veerappa Moily, Shri D.K. Audikeshavulu, Shri M. Thimme Gowda, Shri Bhajan Lal and Shri Ajit Singh, charged and tried along with the appellants.

2. The relevant facts of the case, as noted by the trial court are:

> "**1.** That in the General Election of 10th Lok Sabha in 1991, Congress (I) emerged as single largest party. It formed the Government at the centre under the leadership of accused, P.V. Narasimha Rao (A-1). Monsoon Session of 10th Lok Sabha was to commence on 26-7-1993. A "No Confidence Motion" was moved against the Govt. by Shri Ajay Mukhopadhya, a C.P.I. (M) M.P. The effective strength of Lok Sabha at that moment was 528 and Congress (I) had 251 members. Thus, the Government headed by accused P.V. Narasimha Rao (A-1) was short of 14 M.Ps. for proving its majority on the floor of house. It is alleged that the opposition parties had made their intention clear to move "No Confidence Motion" against the Government well in advance. On 28-7-93 "No Confidence Motion" was put to vote after the debate and it was defeated with the support of four J.M.M., M.Ps. *i.e.,* Shri Suraj Mandal (A-3), Shibu Soren (A-4), Shri Simon Marandi (A-5) and Shailender Mahto (A-6) respectively as well as A-16 to A-21 namely S/Shri Ram Lakhan Singh Yadav, Ram Sharan Yadav, Roshan Lal, Anadi Charan Dass, Abhey Pratap Singh and Haji Gulam Mohd. Khan respectively and late Shri G.C. Munda, M.P. the break-away group of Janta Dal (A) Party.

2. Complainant, Ravinder Kumar, President of Rashtriya Mukti Morcha filed a complaint with C.B.I. alleging that Shri P.V. Narasimha Rao had hatched a criminal conspiracy with Shri V.C. Shukla, Shri R.K. Dhawan, Capt. Satish Sharma, Shri Ajit Singh, Shri Bhajan Lal and Shri Lalit Suri with the object to prove the majority of the

Government on the floor of the house by resorting to bribing some of the members of the Parliament to the extent of over Rs. 4 crores. On the basis of said complaint, C.B.I. registered four cases R.C. Nos. 1(A)/96 to R.C. No. 4(A)/96/CBI/ACU-VIII/N.D. against four J.M.M., M.Ps. (A3 to A6) since discharged. However, no FIR was registered against A-1, A-2, A-14, A-15 and others named in the complaint. Feeling aggrieved, complainant Ravinder Kumar filed a writ petition in High Court of Delhi for direction to C.B.I. to register a proper FIR as per allegations in the complaint. In the aforesaid writ petition directions were issued by Division Bench of the Hon'ble High Court and pursuant to that C.B.I. registered case R.C. No. 5(A)/96/ACU/VIII/C.B.I./N.D. against the persons named in the complaint.

3. Pursuant to the investigation conducted in Case R.C. Nos. 1(A)/96 to R.C. Nos. 5(A)/96-ACU-VIII/C.B.I./N.D., prosecution sought to try Shri P.V. Narasimha Rao (hereinafter referred to as A.1), Capt. Satish Sharma (hereinafter referred to as A.2), Suraj Mandal (hereinafter referred to as A.3), Shri Shibu Soren (hereinafter referred to as A.4), Shri Simon Marandi (hereinafter referred to as A.5), Shri Shailender Mahto (approver) (hereinafter referred to as A.6), Shri Buta Singh (hereinafter referred to as A.7), Shri V. Rajeshwar Rao (hereinafter referred to as A.8), Shri H.M. Revenna (hereinafter referred to as A.9), Shri Ramalinga Reddy (hereinafter referred to as A.10), Shri M. Veerappa Moily (hereinafter referred to as A.11), Shri D.K. Audikeshvulu (hereinafter referred to as A.12), Shri M. Thimme Gowda (hereinafter referred to as A.13), Shri Bhajan Lal (hereinafter referred to as A. 14), Shri Ajit Singh (hereinafter referred to as A.15), Shri Ram Lakhan Singh Yadav (hereinafter referred to as A.16), Shri Ram Sharan Yadav (hereinafter referred to as A. 17), Shri Roshan Lal (hereinafter referred to as A.18), Shri Anadi Charan Dass (hereinafter referred to as A.19), Shri Abhay Partap Singh (hereinafter referred to as A.20) and Shri Haji Gulam Mohd. Khan (hereinafter referred to as A.21), vide three different charge-sheets filed in the Court under section 173, Cr.P.C. First charge-sheet was filed on 30-10-1996. In furtherance of that charge-sheet second and third charge-sheets were filed under section 173(8), Cr.P.C. on 9-12-1996 and 22-1-1997 respectively.

4. The case of the prosecution as revealed from the respective charge-sheets and the statement of the approver Shailender Mahto recorded under section 164, Cr.P.C. is that monsoon session of 10th Lok Sabha was scheduled to commence on 26-7-1993. Much prior to the commencement of monsoon session it was clear that opposition parties intended to bring no confidence motion against the minority Government headed by accused P.V. Narasimha Rao (A-1). At that point of time effective strength of Lok Sabha was 528 and strength of Congress (I) members in the Lok Sabha was 251. Thus, there was a real possibility of defeat of the Government on the floor of the house. In order to avoid the situation, a conspiracy was hatched between accused P.V. Narasimha Rao (A-1) and his supporters namely Capt. Satish Sharma (A-2), Shri Buta Singh (A-7), Shri V. Rajeshwar Rao (A-8), Shri H.M. Revenna (A-9), Shri Ramalinga Reddy (A-10), Shri M. Veerappa Moily (A-11), Shri D.K. Audikeshvulu (A-12), Shri M. Thimme Gowda (A-13) and Shri Bhajan Lal A-14) to procure the support of sufficient number of Members of Parliament belonging to the opposition for the Government by luring them with the offer of bribe. On the other hand, some members of Parliament belonging to the opposition namely 4 JMM, M.Ps., Suraj Mandal (A-3), Shibu Soren (A-4), Simon Marandi (A-5), approver Shailender Mahto and Janta Dal (A) M.Ps. namely Shri Ajit Singh (A-15), Shri Ram Lakhan Singh Yadav (A-16), Shri Ram Sharan Yadav (A-17), Shri Roshan Lal (A-18), Shri Anadi Charan Dass (A-19), Abhay Partap Singh (A-20), Shri Hazi Gulam Mohd. Khan (A-21) and late Shri G.C. Munda also smelled the opportunity and started the efforts to extract maximum advantage from the situation. As a result, a multi cornered conspiracy was hatched amongst A-1 to A-21 and late Shri G.C. Munda against the no confidence motion by giving of bribe to those members of Parliament and acceptance of bribe by those Members of Parliament. In order to achieve the object of the conspiracy various participants played different roles at Delhi and Bangalore. Shri P.V. Narasimha Rao was the kingpin of the conspiracy.

5. It is alleged that hectic political activities to save the Government started in July, 1993. Capt. Satish Sharma (A-2) took active role in the conspiracy and he mobilized and provided the funds for bribing the opposition members. It is alleged that at the relevant time, Capt. Satish Sharma was the Minister of Petroleum in the Government headed by Shri P.V. Narasimha Rao (A-1). Shri B.N. Safaya was his Additional Private Secretary. Shri B.N. Safaya during the period between April 1993 to May 1994 received substantial amounts on behalf of Capt. Satish Sharma from M/s. Jindal Saw Pipes, M/s. Videocon International Limited, M/s. Essar Group of Companies, M/s. Reliance Industries Limited and M/s. Bindal Agro Industries. After receiving the money from those business houses, Shri B.N. Safaya used to inform Capt. Satish Sharma on telephone and then carry the suit-cases containing money to Capt. Satish Sharma (A-2). It is alleged that on 24-7-1993 one party was hosted by Capt. Satish Sharma at his residence. During said party, some suit- cases supposedly containing money were brought from the farm house of Capt. Satish Sharma. On 25-7-1993 in the morning, Capt. Satish Sharma visited the residence of Shri P.V. Narasimha Rao. Even accused Buta Singh (A-7) also visited the residence of Shri P.V. Narasimha Rao (A-1) in the morning of 25-7-1993. It is also alleged that around 30th or 31st of July, 1993 Simon Marandi (A-5) visited Shri B.N. Safaya, Additional Private Secretary of Capt. Satish Sharma and told that he had come to collect the money which Capt. Satish Sharma had promised and after confirming from Capt. Satish Sharma, Shri B.N. Safaya brought a sum of Rs. 10 lakhs from the residence of Capt. Satish Sharma and delivered it to Simon Marandi in the evening.

6. It is also alleged that four J.M.M., M.Ps. namely, Shri Suraj Mandal (A-3), Shibu Soren (A-4), Shri Simon Marandi (A-5) and approver Shri Shailender Mahto (A-6) did realise the potential of the situation. Thus, they got together in order to extract maximum advantage out of the predicament of Congress (I) Govt. Approver Shailender Mahto approached Shri Ashok Rao Deshmukh, M.P. few days before the voting of no confidence motion and requested him to arrange a direct meeting between him and the Prime Minister Shri P.V. Narasimha Rao (A-1), as he along with other three J.M.M., M.Ps. namely Suraj Mandal, Shibu Soren and Simon Marandi (A-3 to A-5) wanted to vote against no confidence motion, if some of their demands were met. On 25-7-93 Shri Ashok Rao Deshmukh met accused Shri P.V. Narasimha Rao (A-1) and apprised him about the said talks with approver Shailender Mahto. Shri P.V. Narasimha Rao (A-1) told him to ascertain the demands of J.M.M., M.Ps. Thereafter, Sailender Mahto informed to Ashok Rao Deshmukh that they would put their demands directly to the Prime Minister. This information was conveyed by Shri Ashok Rao Deshmukh to Shri P.V. Narasimha Rao (A-1), who then advised Ashok Rao Deshmukh to take J.M.M., M.Ps. to Shri V. Rajeshwar Rao (A-8) for further discussion.

7. Shri Ashok Rao Deshmukh contacted Shri V. Rajeshwar Rao (A-8) on 26-7-1993 and fixed a meeting between J.M.M., M.Ps. and V. Rajeshwar Rao (A-8) for 11.00 a.m. At the stipulated time, J.M.M., M.Ps. arrived at Andhra Bhawan and Shri Ashok Rao Deshmukh took them to the residence of accused V. Rajeshwar Rao (A-8), 7, Swaranamukh Apartments, Andhra Bhavan. V. Rajeshwar Rao (A-8) also confirmed about the message received by him from Shri P.V. Narasimha Rao and thereafter Shri Ashok Rao Deshmukh left the flat. It is alleged that Shri V. Rajeshwar Rao (A-8) had a separate conversation with Suraj Mandal (A-3) and made some offer to him. After said discussion, they came back to the room and thereafter J.M.M., M.Ps. left the residence of Shri V. Rajeshwar Rao (A-8). Suraj Mandal (A-3) told other J.M.M., M.Ps. (A-4 to A-6) that discussion with V. Rajeshwar Rao (A-8) was not fruitful as he was offering a meagre amount and he suggested a direct meeting with the Prime Minister. In the evening of 26-7-93, all the four J.M.M., M.Ps., A-3 to A-6, collected at the residence of Shibu Soren (A-4). From there, they went to the residence of Shri Buta Singh and he took those J.M.M., M.Ps. to the residence of Shri P.V. Narasimha Rao (A-1). It is further alleged that initially at the residence of Shri P.V. Narasimha Rao, talks regarding creation of Jharkhand Council took place and Shri P.V. Narasimha Rao (A-1) assured that he would call for the file relating to creation of Jharkhand Council from the Ministry and do the needful. Thereafter, Suraj Mandal A-3), P.V. Narasimha Rao (A-1) and Buta Singh (A-7) went to a separate room for some time. After the discussion, they came out from the said room and accused P.V. Narasimha Rao (A-1) told the other J.M.M., M.Ps. (A-4 to A-6) that he wanted their help for the moment and in return he would also help them and fulfill the promises made to Suraj Mandal (A-3) in the closed door discussion. While coming back from the residence of Shri P.V. Narasima Rao (A-1) on the insistence of Shailender Mahto (approver) and Shibu Soren (A-4), Suraj Mandal (A-3) informed that the closed door discussion was to their advantage. He further informed that talks regarding payment of money to them had taken place, but the amount to be paid was not specified.

8. On 26-7-1993, no confidence motion moved by Shri Ajay Mukhopadhaya, M.P. was put to discussion. After the conclusion of debate, motion was put to vote on 28-7-93 and it was defeated by the help of votes given by JMM, MPs (A-3 to A-6) and Janta Dal break-away group MPs (A-16 to A-21) and late Shri G.C. Munda, MP.

8A. It is further alleged that on 29-7-1993 at about 8.00 a.m. 4-5 persons visited the residence of Suraj Mandal at 14, Ferozeshah Road, New Delhi and delivered five suit cases and one bag which were kept locked in a room. It is also alleged that in the same morning in pursuance of the telephone call from Suraj Mandal (A-3), approver Shailender Mahto (A-6) visited his residence. Accused V. Rajeshwar Rao (A-8) was already present there and in his presence Suraj Mandal (A-3) told the approver Shailender Mahto (A-6) that Rs. 50 lakhs have already been paid and remaining amount would be paid within two days. During said conversation accused V. Rajeshwar Rao (A-8) informed that all the 4 JMM, MPs (A-3 to A-6) would be paid Rs. 50 lakhs each and the break away group of Ram Lakhan Singh Yadav (A-16) would also be paid Rs. 50 lakhs each besides the allotment of petrol pumps and residential plots of H.U.D.A. in Haryana. Accused V. Rajeshwar Rao (A-8) further informed that the M.Ps. who had absented or abstained from voting on no confidence motion would be paid Rs. 30 lakhs each.

9. It is further alleged that on 30-7-1993, 3 boris and 1 suit case supposedly containing money were delivered at the residence of Suraj Mandal (A-3).

10. According to the prosecution, the money delivered at the residence of Suraj Mandal was the bribe money which was distributed by the four JMM, MPs amongst each other and the said amount was deposited in Punjab National Bank, Naroji Nagar, New Delhi with the help of one Sushil Kumar, Chartered Accountant who was maintaining his bank accounts in the said branch. It is alleged that most of the aforesaid bribe money reached Punjab National Bank, Naroji Nagar Branch by the evening of 31-7-1993, but since it was already late and counting of such a huge cash was impossible on that date, entire cash received in the branch on 31-7-1993 was kept in the strong room. On the next day, *i.e.* 1-8-1993 money was counted and various accounts were opened as per the instructions of JMM, MPs.

11. It is alleged that on the basis of final counting a sum of Rs. 30 lakhs was deposited in the S.F. Account No. 17108 of Suraj Mandal(A-3), one Sugam F.D. Account No. 195 was opened in the joint names of all the 4 JMM, MPs (A-3 to A-6) with Rs. 30 lakhs. One joint S.F. Account in the name of four JMM, MPs. (A-3 to A-6) was also opened with the deposit of Rs. 10,000/- in order to facilitate the transfer of interest etc. from the F.D. Account. Similarly, in accordance with the earlier instructions of Shailender Mahto (A-6) one Sugam F.D. Account No. 196 was opened with Rs. 39.80 lakhs in the joint names of Shailender Mahto and his wife Abha Mahto, although his wife did not sign the account opening form. Another F.D. Account No. 194 was opened in the joint names of Shibu Soren (A-4), his wife Smt. Rupi and their two sons, Basant and Hemant with Rs. 30 lakhs. The account opening form was signed by all except Hemant Kumar. One Sugam F.D. Account No. 197 was also opened in the joint names of Simon Marandi (A-5) and his wife Smt. Sushila Hansda with Rs. 12 lakhs although account opening form was not signed by Smt. Sushila Hansda.

12. On 2-8-93 Simon Marandi visited Punjab National Bank, Naroji Nagar and deposited another sum of Rs. 21 lakhs in F.D. A/c. No. 197. After opening of Sugam F.D. Accounts by three JMM, M.Ps. namely Shibu Soren (A-4), Simon Marandi (A-5) and approver Shailender Mahto (A-6) they also opened Saving Account Nos. 19100, 19307 and 18983 respectively on 8-10-93, 18-9-93 and 10-9-93.

13. It is further alleged that accused M. V. Moily (A-11) at the relevant time was Chief Minister of Karnataka. He also played an active role in the conspiracy and he was also one of the leaders who had been assigned the job of organising funds for bribing JMM, MPS. It is alleged that Shri M. Veerappa Moily (A-11) came to Delhi on 25-7-1993 by morning flight from Bangalore and he camped at Delhi till 29-7-1993. During his stay, he called on accused P.V. Narasimha Rao (A-1) repeatedly and he also made three attempts to contact Shri V. Rajeshwar Rao (A-8) but he could meet him only on one occasion. He further called on Capt. Satish Sharma (A-2), Ajit Singh (A-15) and K. Karunakaran.

14. It is also alleged that even before the visit of accused M. Veerappa Moily (A-11) to Delhi, hectic political activities were going on at his official residence at Bangalore. Shri H.M. Revenna (A-9), Shri Ramalinga Reddy (A-10), Shri D.K. Audikeshvulu (A-12) and Shri M. Thimmegowda (A-13) and others had been frequently visiting the official residence of accused M. Veerappa Moily (A-11) and some suit cases supposedly containing money were delivered by them.

15. It is alleged that accused D.K. Audikeshvulu (A-12) was very close to accused V. Rajeshwar Rao (A-8). He (A-12) was also camping at Delhi from 24-7-93 to 29-7-1993. During said period, he had visited V. Rajeshwar Rao (A-8). Even on 26-7-93, he was seen at the residence of accused V. Rajeshwar Rao (A-8) by Shri Ashok Rao Deshmukh when he had visited said place for introducing four JMM, MPs to Shri V. Rajeshwar Rao (A-8). Shri D.K. Audikeshvulu (A-12) also left for Bangalore on 29-7-1993 by evening flight of Indian Airlines. It is alleged that Shri D.K. Adikeshvulu is the owner of number of companies/firms under various names and address.

16. M/s. Karnataka Breweries and Distilleries (P) Limited (hereinafter referred to M/s. K.B.D.L.) is a major liquor manufacturing company. Shri D.K. Audikeshvulu A-12) is the Managing Director of the said company. He is also one of the partners of M/s. Sapthagiri Enterprises, which is also engaged in the business of manufacture and bottling of liquor. M/s. KBDL is maintaining Current Account No. 448 with Canara Bank, R.M.V. Extension, Bangalore. M/s. Sapthagiri Enterprises is also maintaining Current Account No. 446 with the same bank. The aforesaid two concerns are also maintaining accounts with Lakshmi Vilas Bank, main branch, Bangalore.

17. It is alleged that Shri D.K. Audikeshvulu issued Cheque Number 348507 dated 29-7-1993 for Rs. 30 lakhs on the account of M/s. Sapthagiri Enterprises drawn on Canara Bank, R.M.V. Extension, Bangalore in favour of M/s. Padmavati Enterprises. He also issued Cheque No. 372415 and 372414 both dated 30-7-1993 for Rs. 6,17,349 and Rs. 14,78,125 respectively favouring Shri V.P. Ramakrishna, an employee of M/s. K.B.D.L.

18. The cheque No. 348507 for Rs. 30 lakhs issued in favour of M/s. Padmavati Enterprises was credited to its Current Account No.754 held with the aforesaid bank on 30-7-1993. On the same day, the said amount was withdrawn from the current account of M/s. Padmavati Enterprises through cheque dated 30-7-93 purported to have been signed by Sh. K. Muniraja, proprietor of the said firm. However, the cash payments against the said cheque was received by Shri Dwarka Nath, an employee of M/s. K.B.D.L. The funds against other two cheques mentioned above were also withdrawn in cash on 30-7-1993. On the reverse of cheque No. 372415 issued by M/s. K.B.D.L. in favour of Shri V.P. Ramakrishna details of Rs. 50, 95, 474 have been mentioned which is total of the amount of aforesaid three cheques. This indicates that funds of aforesaid three cheques were received by Shri Dwarka Nath on 30-7-1993. He delivered that amount to Sh. D.K. Audikeshvulu (A-12).

19. It is also alleged that M/s. Padmavati Enterprises is a non-existent firm. The account opening form relating to the bank account of M/s. Padmavati Enterprises have been filled up by Shri Dwarka Nath who is a close relative of accused D.K. Audikeshvulu (A-12) and employee of M/s. K.B.D.L. That Shri Dwarka Nath filled said account opening form at the instance of accused D.K. Audikeshvulu (A-12) and said account was introduced by M/s. Sreevari Enterprises having account No. 732 with Canara Bank, R.M.V. Extension, Bangalore. Said firm has also been found to be non-existent.

20. It is further alleged that Shri M. Thimmegowda is the Managing Director of M/s. S.P.R. Group Holding (P) Limited. It is maintaining a Current Account No. 1968 with Canara Bank, Seshadripuram Branch, Bangalore.

21. That on 30-7-1993 Shri M. Thimmegowda approached the Branch Manager and applied for a temporary over-draft of Rs. 1 Crore for 10 days on the pretext of meeting some urgent business commitments. The Branch Manager then contacted Shri V.A. Prabhu the then General Manager, Circle Office, Canara Bank, Bangalore on telephone and requested for sanction of said temporary over-draft. Shri V.A. Prabhu obtained the approval on telephone and conveyed the sanction to Sheshadripuram Branch after the banking hours. However, accused M. Thimmegowda insisted for withdrawal of the whole amount on 30-7-1993 itself. Canara Bank, Sheshadripuram Branch, then arranged the money from cash chest, Canara Bank, R.M.V. Extension. As soon as the cash was received in the branch, Shri M. Thimmegowda (A-13) issued cheques Nos. 959799 and 959798, both dated 30-7-1993 for Rs. 60 lakhs and Rs. 25 lakhs in favour of M/s. Ranganatha Group and M/s. Yellamma Enterprises. He also issued a self cheque No. 959800 dated 30-7-1993 for Rs. 15 lakhs on the account of M/s. S.P.R. Group Holdings (P) Limited. The funds against the cheques issued in favour of M/s. Ranganatha Group and M/s. Yellamma Enterprises were credited to the respective accounts by way of transfer. As soon as the said funds were credited to those accounts, Shri M.S. Chelvaraju, partner of M/s. Ranganatha Groups and Shri T. Sivarama, proprietor of M/s. Yellamma Enterprises issued self cheque dated 30-7-1993 for Rs. 60 lakhs and Rs. 25 lakhs respectively and withdrew the cash. Similarly, Shri M. Thimmegowda also withdrew a sum of Rs. 15 lakhs against above referred self cheques drawn on the account of M/s. S.P.R. Groups Holding (P) Limited. After collecting aforesaid funds, Shri T. Sivarama was asked to leave the bank, whereas Shri M.S. Chelavuraju, accompanied Shri M. Themmegowda to his residence along with said Rs. 1 Crore withdrawn from the bank. After sometime, Shri M. Thimmegowda left his residence with 2 big VIP suitcases supposedly containing said Rs. 1 Crore. It is further alleged that Shri M. Thimmegowda delivered those two suitcases at the residence of Shri M.V. Moily (A.11) at Bangalore in the evening hours of 30-7-1993. Accused H.M. Revenna (A.9) and accused Ramalinga Reddy (A.10) also arrived at the residence of accused M. Verappa Moily (A.11) when the aforesaid suitcases were delivered. It is further alleged that Shri M. Verappa Moily (A.11), Shri H.M. Revenna (A.9) and Rammalinga Reddy (A.10) remained together at the residence of Shri M. Veerappa Moily for sometime. During said period, Shri M. Veerappa Moily (A.11) asked his household servant to bring one suitcase and one hand bag from the first floor room of his residence which supposedly contained the money. Thereafter, Shri H.M. Revenna (A.9) and Ramalinga Reddy (A.10) left the residence of Shri M. Veerappa Moily (A.11) in a car with 3 suitcases and one hand bag including the two suitcases delivered by accused M. Thimmegowda for Bangalore Airport.

22. It is further alleged that accused Shri D.K. Audikeshvulu (A.12) came from Bangalore to Delhi on 30-7-93 by Indian Airlines evening flight with one V.I.P. suitcase supposedly containing aforesaid money withdrawn by him from the bank. Shri H.M. Revenna (A.9) and Ramalinga Reddy (A.10) also came to Delhi by the same flight along with said 3 suitcases and hand bag supposedly containing money. The flight landed at Delhi Airport at about 10.30 p.m. They were received by Shri Bachan Singh, Roop Ram and one Darmyan Singh attendant of M/s. Mohan Breweries and Distilleries Limited (hereinafter referred to M/s. M.B.D.L.) Guest House, who had also been detailed by Shri K. Narayanan, Care Taker to receive them. They loaded the 3 V.I.P. suticases and one hand bag in the taxi driven by Shri Roop Ram, whereas V.I.P. suitcases brought by Shri D.K. Audikeshvulu (A.12) they all left for Andhra Bhawan, where D.K. Audikeshvulu (A.12), H.M. Revenna (A.9) and Rama Linga Reddy (A.10) called on Shri V. Rajeshwar Rao (A.8) at Swaranamukhi Apartments, Andhra Bhawan, New Delhi. After some discussion, they left for Hotel Claridges. It is further alleged that after making arrangement for the stay of H.M. Revenna (A.9), Ramalinga Reddy (A.10), D.K. Audikeshvulu (A.12) left for M/s. M.B.D.L. Guest House. The three V.I.P. suitcases and one hand bag brought by H.M. Revenna (A.9), Ramalinga Reddy (A.10) were unloaded by Roop Ram at Hotel Claridges.

23. It is further alleged that accused Buta Singh (A-7) also visited Bangalore at the relevant time. He came back from Bangalore to Delhi on 30-7-1993 by same Indian Airlines Flight I.C. No. 404 in which Shri H.M. Revenna A-9), Shri Ramalinga Reddy (A-10) and Shri D.K. Audikeshvulu (A-12) travelled.

24. It is further alleged that in the morning of 31-7-1993 Roop Ram taxi driver reached Hotel Claridges. Shri Vijay Handa and Shri Harsharan Lal, PWs also reached there in the car of Shri Vijay Handa. Accused D.K. Audikeshvulu (A-12) reached Hotel Claridges on 31-7-1993 at about 7.00 a.m. in the Maruti Car of M/s. M.B.D.L. Shri H.M. Revenna A-9) and Shri Ramalinga Reddy (A-10) came out of the hotel along with three V.I.P. suitcases and the hand bag, which they had carried from Bangalore. Those were loaded in the taxi of Roop Ram and thereafter, they all left for Andhra Bhawan. On arriving at Andhra Bhawan, accused D.K. Audikeshvulu (A-12), H.M. Revenna (A-9), Ramalinga Reddy (A-10), Vijay Handa and Harsharan Lal went upstairs leaving behind the V.I.P. suitcases and hand bags in respective cars. They came down after about one hour along with V. Rajeshwar Rao (A-8). Thereafter, at the instance of accused D.K. Audikeshvulu A-12) the hand bag and one V.I.P. suitcase which were kept in the back-seat of taxi and the VIP suitcase brought by him was shifted to the white Maruti Car of Vijay Kumar Handa, who was a person well known to accused V. Rajeshwar Rao (A-8). Shri H.M. Revenna (A-9) thereafter sat in the taxi of Roop Ram. The white Maruti Car driven by Vijay Kumar Handa along with P.W. Harsharan Lal and P.W. Ganga Singh left for the residence of Suraj Mandal (A-3) at Ferozeshah Road, New Delhi and Roop Ram was asked to follow them. They visited the residence of Suraj Mandal and delivered aforesaid 4 VIP suitcases and hand bags to him. Thus, according to the prosecution, the bribe money was delivered at the residence of accused Suraj Mandal (A-3).

25. It is alleged that accused Bhajan Lal also played a very important role to achieve the object of the conspiracy. On 24-7-1993, he visited the residence of accused Ajit Singh in the morning. He requested Ajit Singh for supporting Congress (I) Government stating that fate of the Government headed by Sh. P.V. Narasimha Rao (A-1) was in his hands. He further delivered three packets containing Rs. 1 Crore each to accused Ajit Singh as a motive or reward for seeking the support of his group for the Government. Those packets were unloaded from his car by Capt. Dilawar Singh. One of those packets, was opened after accused Bhajan Lal left and it was found to contain 200 wads of currency notes of Rs. 500 denomination.

26. It is also alleged that accused Ajit Singh (A-15) wanted to gobble up entire money. However, accused Ram Lakhan Singh Yadav (A-16) caught the wind of the matter. He called on accused Ajit Singh (A-15) in the morning of 26-7-93 and insisted for his share of Rs. 15 lakhs from the amount received by him from Bhajan Lal. Accused Ajit Singh (A-15) denied having received any amount from Bhajan Lal (A-14) and told Ram Lakhan Singh Yadav (A-16) that Bhajan Lal himself was a corrupt person who accused others of corruption. After the aforesaid incident, accused Ajit Singh (A-15) called for a meeting of MPs belonging to his party. During said meeting, he expressed his desire to vote in favour of no confidence motion against Congress (I) Government. This led to heated exchanges between Ram Lakhan Singh Yadav (A-16) and Ajit Singh (A-15) and both accused each other for hobnobbing and bargaining with Congress (I) Leaders. Thereafter, Ram Lakhan Singh Yadav (A.15) walked out of the meeting. Shri Ram Sharan Yadav, Roshan Lal, Abhay Pratap Singh and Anadi Charan Dass namely (A-18 to A.20) as well as late Shri G.C. Munda also followed him.

27. It is further alleged that 7 M.Ps. namely Ram Lakhan Singh Yadav, Ram Sharan Yadav, Roshan Lal, Abhay Pratap Singh, Anadi Charan Dass, Hazi Gulam Mohd. Khan and G.C. Munda again assembled at the residence of Ram Lakhan Singh Yadav at 4.00 p.m. During meeting, they decided to form a separate entity under the leadership of Ram Lakhan Singh Yadav and vote against no confidence motion. Shri Bhajan Lal visisted Ram Lakhan Singh Yadav during said meeting and he also had some secret discussion. Shri Ram Lakhan Singh Yadav spoke telephonically to Shri P.V. Narasimha Rao and assured him that his group would split by evening and Government would survive. He also pleaded that Prime Minister should take care of the rest of the things. Said meeting was also attended by Captain Satish Sharma and during those discussion, accused Bhajan Lal assured those M.Ps. substantial sum in cash. Captain Satish Sharma also assured allotment of petrol pumps either to them or their family members.

28. It is further alleged that on 28-7-1993 6 M.Ps. of Janta Dal (A) break away group namely Ram Lakhan Singh Yadav, Ram Sharan Yadav, Roshan Lal, Anadi Charan Dass, Abhay Partap Singh and late Shri G.C. Munda again assembled at the residence of Ram Lakhan Singh Yadav. On that day, Captain Satish Sharma (A.2), Bhajan Lal (A.14), V.C. Shukla, K. Karunakaran and Jitender Prasad met those M.Ps. Shri Bhajan Lal delivered some suitcases at the residence of Ram Lakhan Yadav on the said day, upon which Parkash Chand Yadav, son of Ram Lakhan Singh, informed the members belonging to break away group that Bhajan Lal has fulfilled the promises which he made.

29. It is alleged that on 28-7-1993 Shri V.C. Shukla contacted accused Bhajan Lal A-14) on telephone and informed him that Hazi Gulam Mohd. Khan was present in his Parliament House office. Accused Bhajan Lal then went to Parliament House and returned after half an hour with Hazi Gulam Mohd. Khan. It is further alleged that Bhajan Lal and Captain Satish Sharma then assured that Rs. 20 lakhs would be paid to every member of Janta Dal break away group led by Ram Lakhan Singh Yadav before the voting and another sum of Rs. 20 lakhs each would be paid after the voting of no confidence motion. Besides that, they also promised the allotment of petrol pumps to those M.Ps. or their family members. From the residence of Ram Lakhan Singh Yadav, all those 7 M.Ps. proceeded to Parliament House along with Bhajan Lal and they received their respective shares of Rs. 20 lakhs each before leaving for Parliament on 28-7-1993. It is further alleged that subsequently on 28-7-1993 abovereferred 7 M.Ps. led by Ram Lakhan Singh Yadav voted against no confidence motion and motion was defeated.

30. According to the prosecution, accused Ajit Singh sent Captain Dilawar Singh Sangwan to meet Hazi Gulam Mohd. Khan and Ram Sharan Yadav to persuade them to rejoin the Janta Dal (A). Both Haji Gulam Mohd. Khan and Ram Sharan Yadav admitted before Captain Dilawar Singh Sangawan about receiving a payment of Rs. 20 lakhs in cash from Bhajan Lal. They also told him about promise of allotment of petrol pumps.

31. It is alleged that Bhajan Lal was camping at Delhi to pursue the object of conspiracy from 23-7-1993 to 2-8-1993, except on 26-7-1993. During this period, he was in constant touch with P.V. Narasimha Rao (A-1), Captain Satish Sharma (A-2) and other accused persons. He also actively mobilized the funds before voting on no confidence motion and obtained Rs. 30/Rs. 40 lakhs from the office bearers of Saraswati Kunj House Building society for granting licence to the society for colonization. It is also alleged that Bhajan Lal extended hospitality to Hazi Gulam Mohd. Khan and G.C. Munda at Hotel Rajhans from 1-8-1993 to 3-8-1993 and paid the bill for Rs. 40,000. He also provided a taxi to Hazi Gulam Mohd. Khan for a period of one month and paid the bill of Rs. 17,000. It is further alleged that accused Bhajan Lal in a public meeting at Hissar on 11-8-1993 admitted to have engineered the defection of 7 M.Ps. of Janta Dal (A) within 48 hours which led to survival of Congress (I) Government.

32. It is further alleged that as a reward, accused Ram Lakhan Singh Yadav was inducted as a Union Minister in the cabinet of Shri P.V. Narasimha Rao (A-1) in February, 1994. He was also allotted a plot of land in HUDA from the discretionary quota of Chief Minister *i.e.* Bhajan Lal. Besides that Ram Sharan Yadav acquired a plot of land in Mohan Garden, Uttam Nagar, New Delhi for Rs. 2.25 lakhs during October, 1993 and constructed a palatial house costing more than Rs. 20 lakhs on the said plot. It is further alleged that son of Ram Sharan Yadav namely Ajay Akela has also been allotted a petrol pump at Khagaria District in Bihar in September, 1994 for which he applied for 10-3-1993.

33. According to the prosecution, Prakash Chand Yadav called one Shri Anil Sanghi, Chartered Accountant in August, 1993 and sought his advice for laundering some money received by his father. Accordingly, on the advice of Anil Sanghi, a company in the name of M/s. Patliputra Credit and Securities Limited was registered with the Registrar of Companies. Account of the said company was opened with State Bank of India, Main Branch, New Delhi. Thereafter, Parkash Chand Yadav started delivering cash to Shri Anil Sanghi for arranging cheques for crediting the amount to the account of the said company. Sh. Anil Sanghi opened two current accounts in the names of M/s. Anil Sanghi and Associates and M/s. Ganpati Investment Consultants with Jammu and Kashmir Bank, NOIDA branch on 1-3-1994. It is alleged that during the period w.e.f. 5-3-1994 to 31-7-1994, Shri Anil Sanghi deposited Rs. 1.5 Crores in the said accounts in cash as provided by Parkash Chand Yadav. Against those cash deposits, Anil Sanghi then issued cheques from the said bank accounts in favour of M/s. Patliputra Credit and Securities Limited. Thus, as per prosecution, the amount received as bribe by Parkash Chand Yadav was laundered through said device.

34. It is also alleged that after the defeat of no confidence motion, accused Roshan Lal has deposited a sum of Rs. 12.80 lakhs during July to November, 1993 in South Indian Bank and State Bank of India, Delhi and Punjab and Sindh Bank and Central Bank of India in Dehradun. He has also acquired a flat on 6-9-1993 for a sum of Rs. 9 lakhs, out of which, he paid a sum of Rs. 5,51,000 approximately till date.

35. It is further alleged that during the investigation of this case, in order to avoid detection, accused Suraj Mandal, Shibu Soren, Simon Marandi and Shailender Mahto, all JMM, MPs (A-3 to A-6) in pursuance of criminal conspiracy have fabricated false document *i.e.* donation coupons, proceeding book and books of accounts with the intention to use those documents during the judicial proceedings or any other proceedings initiated in accordance with law before a public servant, so as to suggest that above referred amounts deposited in the bank accounts were the proceeds of donation received in favour of JMM Party.

36. On the aforesaid allegations, prosecution has filed three charge-sheets seeking to try above referred accused persons for having committed offences punishable under sections 120B, IPC read with 193, IPC and sections 7, 12, 13(2) read with 13(1)(d) of P.C. Act, 1988 and the substantive offences therein.

COPIES OF DOCUMENTS SUPPLIED TO ALL ACCUSED – SUBMISSIONS HEARD – DOCUMENT PERUSED – FRAMING OF CHARGES ORDERED BY TRIAL COURT – DELHI HIGH COURT

37. On appearance, accused persons were supplied with the requisite copies of the charge-sheets. During the course of arguments on charge accused persons contended that no case for framing of charge against them was made out. Besides that, they claimed immunity from trial in view of Article 105 of Constitution of India on the ground that trial of the case would amount to an enquiry into the motives of the members of Parliament for voting on no confidence motion. They also took a plea that a Member of Parliament is not a public servant within the ambit of the P.C. Act, 1988 and as such no case under P.C. Act, 1988 is made out. All the pleas of accused persons were rejected and they were directed to be charged for having committed the offence of conspiracy punishable under sections 120B, IPC read with sections 7, 12 and 13(2) read with 13(1)(d) of P.C. Act, 1988 and 193, IPC and substantive offences committed by respective accused persons.

DELHI HIGH COURT DISMISSED REVISION PETITION FILED BY ACCUSED – SLP FILED – CONSTITUTION BENCH BY MAJORITY HELD MPs PUBLIC SERVANTS UNDER PC ACT, 1988 – BRIBE TAKING MPS WHO VOTED – ENTITLED TO PROTECTION OF ARTICLE 105 – DELHI HIGH COURT

38. Feeling aggrieved, accused persons went in revision. Hon'ble High Court dismissed the revision petition and rejected legal pleas of accused persons as well as their contentions on merits of the case. Accused persons then preferred to file Special Leave Petition in Hon'ble Supreme Court. Matter was initially heard by three-Judges Bench of the Apex Court. Since important constitutional questions were involved, the case was referred to the Constitution Bench of the Appellate Bench. Constitution Bench disposed of the reference vide three different judgments. As per majority view, it was held that Member of Parliament is a public servant within the scope of P.C. Act, 1988.

39. The claim of alleged bribe taking MPs except Ajit Singh (A-15) seeking immunity from prosecution under Article 105 of the Constitution of India was accepted by majority judgment of the Constitution Bench of the Apex Court. However, majority view held that since accused Ajit Singh (A-15) did not vote on no confidence motion in the Lok Sabha, he could not claim immunity under Article 105 of the Constitution of India. Regarding remaining accused persons *i.e.* alleged bribe givers, it was held that no immunity under Article 105 of the Constitution was available to them.

40. In view of the finding of the Constitution Bench of the Apex Court, accused Ram Lakhan Singh Yadav (A-16), Ram Sharan Yadav (A-17), Roshan Lal (A-18), Anadi Charan Dass (A-19), Abhay Partap Singh (A-20) and Hazi Gulam Mohd. Khan (A-21) were discharged. Charges under section 120B, IPC read with sections 7, 12, 13(2) read with 13(1)(d) of P.C. Act, 1988 and substantive offences under sections 7 and 13(2) read with 13(1)(d) of P.C. Act, 1988 against accused Suraj Mandal (A-3), Shibu Soren (A-4) and Simon Marandi (A-5) were dropped. Since the offence punishable under section 193, IPC is a magisterial trial and it was allegedly committed much after the alleged transaction of bribing of MPs in furtherance of conspiracy, it was directed that separate charge-sheet for offence punishable under section 193, IPC be filed in the Court of competent jurisdiction.

41. Charges against accused persons, namely, Shri P.V. Narasimha Rao (A-1), Captain Satish Sharma A-2), Shri Buta Singh (A-7), Shri V. Rajeshwar Rao (A-8), Shri H.M. Revenna (A-9), Shri Ramalinga Reddy (A-10), Shri M. Veerappa Moily (A-11), Shri D.K. Audikeshvulu (A-12), Shri M. Themmegowda (A-13) and Shri Bhajan Lal (A-14) were amended suitably and they all were charged for offence punishable under section 120B, IPC read with sections 7, 12 and 13(1)(d) of P.C. Act, 1988 as well as substantive offence punishable under section 12 of the P.C. Act, 1988. They all pleaded not guilty to the charge and claimed trial.

42. Accused Ajit Singh (A-15) was charged for having committed offences punishable under sections 120B read with sections 7, 12, 13(2) read with section 13(1)(d) of P.C. Act, 1988. He also pleaded not guilty to the charge and claimed trial."

AFTER APPRECIATION OF EVIDENCE AND CONSIDERING OF SUBMISSIONS – TRIAL COURT ACQUITTED ALL OTHERS EXCEPT BUTA SINGH AND P.V. NARSIMHA RAO – CONVICTED AND SENTENCED THEM TO 3 YEARS R.I. AND FINE OF RS. 1 LAKH EACH – DELHI HIGH COURT

3. The learned Judge, on appreciation of evidence placed before him, found that charges against Shri Buta Singh and Shri P.V. Narsimha Rao had been substantiated by the prosecution while against the other accused they stood not proved, consequently, went on to hold the appellants guilty and further by his order dated 12-10-2000 imposed the following sentence:

> "Keeping in view the facts and circumstances of the case and gravity of offence and the mitigating circumstances pointed out on behalf of accused Shri P.V. Narasimha Rao and Shri Buta Singh for the offence punishable under section 120B, IPC read with sections 7, 12, 13(2) read with section 13(1)(d) of P.C. Act, 1988, I hereby sentence convict Shri P.V. Narasimha Rao and Shri Buta Singh to undergo R.I. for the period of 3 years. They are further sentenced to pay a fine of Rs. 1 lakh respectively. In the event of any of the accused failing to pay the fine imposed, he shall undergo R.I. for further period of 6 months. For the offence punishable under section 12 of the P.C. Act, 1988, both the convicts are further sentenced to undergo R.I. for the period of 3 years and also to pay fine of Rs. 1 lakh each. In the event of

any of the accused failing to pay the fine imposed, he shall undergo R.I. for further period of 6 months.

Substantive sentences awarded to both the convict persons for respective offences shall run concurrently."

COUNSEL FOR APPELLANTS SUBMITTED ABOUT DECISION OF SUPREME COURT – DELHI HIGH COURT

4. Shri R.K. Anand, learned Senior Counsel appearing for Shri P.V. Narasimha Rao, submitted that the Constitution Bench of the Supreme Court adjudicated upon question of law that arose for consideration before it, namely:

(i) Whether Article 105 of the Constitution of India confers immunity on a Member of Parliament from being prosecuted in a criminal Court for an offence involving offer or acceptance of bribe?

(ii) Whether a Member of Parliament is excluded from the ambit of Prevention of Corruption Act, 1988 for the reason that – he is not a public servant as defined under section 2(c) of the Prevention of Corruption Act, 1988; and he is not a person under clauses (a), (b) and (c) of sub-section (1) of section 19 of the Prevention of Corruption Act, 1988.

SUPREME COURT HAD HELD THAT WHEN COGNIZANCE WAS TAKEN BY THE TRIAL COURT BUTA SINGH AND H.M. RAVANNA WERE NOT PUBLIC SERVANTS – A1, A2, A8, A10, A11, A14, A15 WERE PUBLIC SERVANTS – DELHI HIGH COURT

5. The Constitution Bench of the Supreme Court *vide* its judgment dated 17-4-1998, (1998) 4 SCC 626: (1998 Cri LJ 2930) held that (Paras 181-186):

> "We now set down the effect upon the accused of our finding.
>
> We have held that the alleged bribe-takers who voted upon the No Confidence Motion, that is Suraj Mandal, Shibu Soren, Simon Marandi, Shailendra Mahto, Ram Lakhan Singh Yadav, Ram Sharan Yadav, Roshan Lal, Anadicharan Das, Abhay Pratap Singh and Haji Gulam Mohammed (Accused 3, 4, 5, 6, 16, 17, 18, 19, 20 and 21) are entitled to the immunity conferred by Article 105(2).
>
> D.K. Audikesavulu and M. Thimmegowda (Accused 12 and 13) were at all relevant times private persons. The trial on all charges against them must proceed.
>
> When cognizance of the charges against them was taken, Buta Singh and H.M. Revanna (Accused 7 and 9) were not public servants. The question of sanction for their prosecution does not, therefore, arise and the trial on all charges against them must proceed.
>
> P.V. Narasimha Rao, Satish Sharma, V. Rajeshwara Rao, Ramalinga Reddy, M. Veerappa Moily and Bhajan Lal (Accused 1, 2, 8, 10, 11 and 14) were public servants, being either Members of Parliament or a State Legislature, when cognizance of the charges against them was taken. They are charged with substantive offences under section 120B of the Indian Penal Code and section 12 of the said Act. Since no prior sanction is required in respect of the charge under section 12 of the said Act, the trial on all charges against them must proceed.
>
> Ajit Singh (Accused 15) was a public servant, being a Member of Parliament, when cognizance of the charges against him was taken. He is charged with substantive offences under section 120-B of the Indian Penal

Code and sections 7 and 13(2) of the said Act. The trial of the charge against him under section 120B of the Indian Penal Code must proceed.

The appeals shall now be placed before a Bench of three learned Judges for hearing on any other points that may be involved and for final disposal."

REVIEW PETITION FILED BY CBI WAS DISMISSED BY SUPREME COURT – SLP DECIDED BY THREE JUDGE BENCH OF SUPREME COURT – DELHI HIGH COURT

6. The CBI filed a review petition dated 12-11-1998 against the judgment dated 17-4-1998 which was dismissed on 16-12-1998. The Supreme Court further *vide* order dated 5-5-1999 disposed of the Special Leave Petitions with the following order:

"..........While the matter was heard before a three-Judge Bench of this Court, it was felt necessary that the matter should be referred to the Constitution Bench for expressing opinion as to whether the Members of Parliament are "public servants" within the ambit of Prevention of Corruption Act and whether privilege under Article 105 of the Constitution of India can at all be claimed. These two questions have now been answered by the Constitution Bench in three different judgments since reported in **(1998) 4 SCC 626: (1998 Cr LJ 2930) [P.V. Narasimha Rao v. State (CBI/SPE)] ....** it is not necessary for us to go into any other questions raised in these appeals since those questions have to be answered by the learned Trial Judge bearing in mind the law laid down by the Constitution Bench in the aforesaid case. Needless to mention that any observation that has been made by the High Court on the merits of the proceeding will not weigh with the learned trial Judge in disposing of the matter and the contentions raised before him............."

AS PER SUPREME COURT JUDGMENT A16 TO A21 DISCHARGED – A3 TO A5 DISCHARGED FROM ALL OTHER OFFENCES EXCEPT UNDER SECTION 193, IPC – HELD LIABLE TO BE TRIED BY MAGISTERIAL COURT – DELHI HIGH COURT

7. In view of the law enunciated by the Supreme Court, the learned trial Judge vide order dated 4-6-1999 dropped proceedings and charges under section 120B, IPC read with sections 7, 12, 13(2) read with section 13(1)(d) of the Prevention of Corruption Act, 1988 framed against Shri Suraj Mandal, Shri Shibu Soren, Shri Simon Marandi, Shri Shailender Mahto, Shri Ram Lakhan Singh Yadav, Shri Ram Saran Yadav, Shri Roshan Lal, Shri Anadi Charan Das, Shri Abhay Pratap Singh and Shri Haji Gulam Mohd. Khan although the learned trial Judge ruled that charge under section 193, IPC against Shri Suraj Mandal, Shri Shibu Soren and Shri Simon Marandi shall proceed. The trial for charges under section 193, IPC against the aforesaid accused persons was separated and directed to be tried by a separate Court.

AMENDED CHARGE SHEET FRAMED AGAINST REMAINING ACCUSED BY TRIAL COURT AS PER SUPREME COURT JUDGMENT – PLEADED NOT GUILTY – DELHI HIGH COURT

8. Also following the Supreme Court judgment, an amended charge was framed on 20-7-1999 against the remaining accused. The charges framed were under section 120B, IPC read with sections 7, 12, 13(2) read with section 13(1)(d) of the Prevention of Corruption Act.

COUNSEL FOR APPELLANTS QUESTIONED LEGALITY AND VALIDITY OF PARDON GIVEN TO SHAILENDER MAHTO APPROVER AMONG OTHER SUBMISSIONS – DELHI HIGH COURT

9. Learned counsel submitted that, *inter alia,* the question that needs to be adjudicated in this appeal is whether Shri Shailender Mahto could have been made an Approver, granted pardon and his testimony used as that of an accomplice protected by the pardon.

10. Shri Rajinder Singh, learned Senior Counsel for Shri Buta Singh, contended that the entire case of the conspiracy theory is based on the solitary testimony of PW-1, Shri Shailender Mahto. He submitted, while adopting the argument of Shri R.K. Anand that Shri Shailender Mahto cannot be made an Approver for reasons that even before Shri Shailender Mahto's testimony can be considered, the Approver must first satisfy the test of reliability. He submitted that from the contradictions and improvements made during deposition in Court by Shri Shailender Mahto there can only be one conclusion, namely, that PW-1 is a dishonest witness. Therefore, his testimony cannot be relied upon and ought to be thrown out lock, stock and barrel in which case the prosecution has miserably failed to establish the charge framed against his client.

11. Shri Rajinder Singh, *inter alia,* submitted that the only evidence to connect his client with the offence is the alleged "close door" meeting between Shri P.V. Narasimha Rao, Shri Buta Singh and Shri Suraj Mandal on 26-7-1993 at the residence of Shri P.V. Narasimha Rao and this has been introduced for the first time in the statement dated 22-3-1997 under section 164, Cr.P.C. after it was known to the Prosecution, during the arguments on framing of charge, that the material put up for examination by the Prosecution did not establish, the much harped off, conspiracy and, therefore, in the statement dated 22-3-1997 under section 164, Cr.P.C., the Prosecution got PW-1 to introduce "a close door meeting" between Shri P.V. Narasimha Rao, Shri Buta Singh and Shri Suraj Mandal to be the conspiracy to give bribe to JMM, MPs in consideration of their vote against the Motion in Parliament. He submitted that Shri Shailender Mahto was extensively interrogated and examined by senior CBI officers on at least four different dates and four different statements were recorded under section 161, Cr.P.C. but in none of the statements is there any mention of the so-called "close door meeting" which is the crux of the Prosecution's case to establish conspiracy. He further submitted that a self-confessed liar like PW-1 cannot pass the first test of reliability that is essential for a witness before his statement can be considered.

12. Shri R.K. Anand, learned Senior Counsel appearing on behalf of the appellant, Shri P.V. Narasimha Rao, submitted that Shri Shailender Mahto, PW-1, could not have been made as an Approver and granted pardon as for the offence charged he could not have been prosecuted and punished in view of the immunity enjoyed under Article 105(2) of the Constitution nor statement of this accomplice be treated to be that of an ordinary witness as the same would be hit by section 163, Cr.P.C. and section 24 of the Evidence Act. He submitted that if this witness is discarded, the Prosecution has no other material on which it can base its claim that a conspiracy was hatched by Shri P.V. Narasimha Rao, Shri Buta Singh and Shri Suraj Mandal to bribe JMM, MPs to exercise their vote against the Motion in Parliament.

13. It was argued by learned counsel that the learned Special Judge has, in his judgment dated 29-9-2000, after recording the facts of the case, divided the entire case into three compartments. The first limb relates to the role played by Shri Bhajan Lal in offering and giving bribe to accused, Ajit Singh and the role played by him. The second limb of the conspiracy relates to the offering and giving of bribe by Shri Bhajan Lal, Capt. Satish Sharma as also Shri P.V. Narasimha Rao to the MPs of

Janata Dal (Ajit) break-away group, Shri Ram Lakhan Singh Yadav, Shri Ram Saran Yadav, Shri Roshan Lal, Shri Anadi Charan Das, Shri Abhay Pratap Singh, Shri Haji Gulam Mohd. Khan and Shri G.C. Munda. The third limb of the conspiracy relates to offering and giving of bribe by Shri V. Rajeshwara Rao, Shri P.V. Narasimha Rao and Shri Buta Singh with the help of accused Shri M. Veerappa Moily, Shri D.K. Audi Kesavalu, Shri M. Thimmegowda, Shri H.M. Revenna and Shri Ramalinga Reddy to the JMM, MPs , Shri Suraj Mandal, Shri Shibu Soren, Shri Simon Marandi and the Approver, Shri Shailender Mahto, and accepting of bribe by them.

TRIAL COURT ACCEPTED STATEMENT OF APPROVER *QUA* A1, A7 BUT NOT *QUA* OTHERS – CBI HAS NOT FILED APPEAL AGAINST ACQUITTAL OF OTHERS – FINDINGS OF TRIAL COURT *QUA* A1 AND A7 ARE WRONG – SUBMITTED APPELLANTS

14-15. The trial Court did not accept the statement of PW-1, Shri Shailender Mahto, in reference to all the other accused except in the case of Shri P.V. Narasimha Rao and Shri Buta Singh which findings have not been challenged by the Prosecution as no appeal was filed by them. According to the trial Court, the Prosecution's case dealing with the role of Shri P.V. Narasimha Rao and Shri Buta Singh in the conspiracy to bribe the JMM, MPs is based on common evidence the key stone of which is the statement of PW-1, Shri Shailender Mahto.

16. According to the learned counsel the trial Court has wrongly held that PW-1's statement connects Shri P.V. Narasimha Rao and Shri Buta Singh with the conspiracy.

17. It was contended by learned counsel for the appellants that the reasoning of the trial Court in holding that the Approver is a trustworthy witness inspite of contradictions and improvements and further by corroborating him with his own previous statement was bad. In other words, it was contended by learned counsel that firstly the reasoning of the trial Court in coming to the conclusion that the Approver is a trustworthy witness, is not correct and secondly the grant of pardon is also bad.

PARDON GRANTED TO SHAILENDER MAHTO WAS LEGAL AND VALID – SUBMITTED THE STATE – RELIED ON SUPREME COURT JUDGMENTS – DELHI HIGH COURT

18. It was argued on behalf of the State that the pardon granted to the Approver, PW-1, is valid and his statement pursuant to that pardon can be taken into consideration as statement of an Approver. Mr. Sud, learned Additional Solicitor General, argued that it is not necessary that the Approver must be an accused but can be any person supposed to have been directly or indirectly concerned in or a privy to an offence. He drew my attention to the fact that PW-1, Shri Shailender Mahto, filed an application dated 16-3-1997 under section 306, Cr.P.C. before the trial Court on 17-3-1997. At that stage arguments on framing of charge were being addressed by counsel for the accused including that of the Approver. Earlier to moving the application on 17-3-1997, PW-1 had moved an application while he was in custody but when he was produced before the learned Metropolitan Magistrate, he declined to make such statement giving his reasons that he was being pressurized to do so. At the time when the Approver made a second application for grant of pardon dated 16-3-1997, he was being prosecuted for the offence under the Prevention of Corruption Act before the Special Judge. The application for grant of pardon was dealt with under section 5(2) of the Prevention of Corruption Act which application was supported by the Prosecution. Consequently, the learned Special Judge allowed recording of statement under section 164, Cr.P.C. which was recorded by the learned Metropolitan Magistrate, Shri Harish Dudani, on 22-3-1997 after due compliance with provisions of law. On 8-4-1997, the learned Special Judge granted conditional pardon and accused, Shri Shailender Mahto, became the prosecution witness as Approver.

19. It was contended by learned Additional Solicitor General that even if Shri Shailender Mahto was not an accused, yet pardon could have been tendered to him in view of section 5(2) of the Prevention of Corruption Act under which section it is not necessary for a person to be an accused so long as the Court is satisfied that the person to whom pardon is to be granted, directly or indirectly be involved in the offence and that on condition of his making full and true disclosure of circumstances within his knowledge, the Court can grant the pardon. The grant of pardon is a pact between the person and the State to the effect that if a full and true disclosure is made, prosecution against him in respect of the offence *qua* which the person has deposed will not be launched against him. Therefore, according to the learned Additional Solicitor General, the evidence obtained by the State after grant of pardon cannot be termed as "illegal". The pardon so tendered under section 5(2) of the Prevention of Corruption Act shall, for the purposes of sub-sections (1) to (5) of section 308, Cr.P.C. be deemed to have been tendered under section 307, Cr.P.C. which, in turn, gives power to the Court of Session to grant pardon on the case being committed to Sessions. The learned Special Judge, while exercising power under section 5(2) of the Prevention of Corruption Act, combines in it the power of a Magistrate to commit and the power of the Sessions to try. Therefore, when power is exercised by a Special Judge under section 5(2) of the Prevention of Corruption Act, he is deemed to have the powers of the Magistrate as also that of the Sessions Judge. Section 308, Cr.P.C. does not provide any safeguard or pre-condition for granting pardon. Therefore, Article 105(2) of the Constitution does not reflect on the competency of such person making a statement as an Approver. The mere fact that Shri Shailender Mahto, PW-1, has deposed before the trial Court and has been cross-examined by the defence, can be of no prejudice nor can the evidence adduced on record be washed away.

20. On immunity under Article 105(2) of the Constitution conferred upon PW-1, learned Additional Solicitor General submitted that the Constitution bench judgment of the Supreme Court provided immunity from prosecution to alleged bribe takers who voted on 28-7-1993. It does not wash off or efface the crime, rather immunity pre-supposes the guilt or being concerned or being privy to the crime. He referred to the judgment of the Supreme Court in **Jasbir Singh v. Vipin Kumar Jaggi, 2001 Cr LJ 3993** under the NDPS Act, the relevant portion thereof is as under:

> "The underlying rationale of section 64 is that the Government which is vitally interested in getting hold of the culprits, must be allowed to assess the strength of the evidence available to it and, if necessary, bolster its case with evidence of an accomplice. Therefore, the section serves the same purpose as the grant of pardon to approvers under section 307, Cr.P.C. The object of section 64 being the same as section 307, it should logically follow that it may be exercised at any time during the course of the trial. It is true that the words 'immunity from prosecution' have been used, but the phrase does not mean anything more than the power to withdraw from prosecution. That can be exercised at any time in the course of trial but before judgment is delivered." (para 28).

21. The learned Additional Solicitor General submitted that grant of immunity means that they were not liable for either being punished or prosecuted but by no stretch of imagination it can mean that they are not the accused who allegedly committed the offence for which they were charged. The judgment nowhere says that after the grant of immunity they cease to be an accused of the offence charged nor does immunity mean this. On the other hand, the very basis of granting immunity to the person is that the person has done something which is an offence, hence an accused in the eyes of law, but for that act/offence he will not be prosecuted in the Court of law, meaning thereby that the grant of immunity only bars the prosecution of the person but it does not wash away the character of the person as an accused nor his complicity/knowledge of the offence committed. He submitted that it is not at all necessary that the person to whom pardon is tendered should be an accused in the common sense as used or understood strictly. A person who had actually been involved in commission of an offence but has not been charged by the prosecution can also approach the Court and pray for pardon and can be examined as an Approver and if he answers fully the character of an Approver witness and his competence to depose as a witness is not impaired or whittled down. Learned Additional Solicitor General relied upon the decision of the Privy Council as reported in **Balraj Kunwar v. Jagat Pal Singh, (1904) ILR 26 All 393 (PC)** and submitted that the meaning of the words "any person" in section 337(i), Cr.P.C. (old Code), which corresponds to section 306 of the new Code appears to be abundantly clear being subject to the qualification expressly laid down in the said provision *viz.* "supposed to have been directly or indirectly concerned in or privy to the offence" and not in any way otherwise circumscribed to denote a person who has actually been made an accused. The only condition is that he would make "a full and true disclosure of the circumstances etc."

22. Learned Additional Solicitor General further relied upon the decisions in **Kashiram v. Emperor, AIR 1923 Nag 248: 1923 (24) Cr LJ 566; Santosh Saha v. State, 1973 Cr LJ 968 (Cal); Rabi Das v. State, 1976 Cut LR 25: (1976 Cr LJ 2004) and Lt. Commander Pascal Fernandes v. State of Maharashtra, AIR 1968 SC 594: (1968 Cr LJ 550).** He submitted that there can be no doubt that the section is enabling and its terms are wide enough to enable the Special Judge to tender a pardon to any person who is supposed to have been directly or indirectly concerned in or privy to an offence. This must necessarily include a person arraigned before him. But it may be possible to tender pardon to a person not so arraigned. The power so conferred can also be exercised at any time after the case is received for trial and before its conclusion. Learned Additional Solicitor General further submitted that pardon is not only granted to a person already charged for an offence but also to a person not charged for an offence just to remove the fear from his mind that the disclosure made by him before the Court will not make him liable to be tried for the offence even henceforth. This is the raison *detre* of the pardon *i.e.* to remove even the remotest fear psychosis while making clean breast of guilt or conduct of unworthy nature.

23. An Approver need not inculpate himself in the offence. The words "concerned to the offence" does not mean that he must be a party to the offence. It shows that contours of Approver's being concerned and yet being a competent witness. The learned Special Judge has all the powers to tender the pardon and no committal proceedings are required because the Special Judge himself has powers of a Magistrate as well as of the Sessions Judge for the purpose of sections 337 and 338, Cr.P.C. (old Code). The legal position under the new code is also unaltered.

24. Learned Additional Solicitor General submitted that in this case the approver Shri Shailendra Mahto was amongst the accused persons who were charged-sheeted for the offences, hence he was a person directly concerned or privy to the offence. He was a person falling within the scope of section 5(2) of the Prevention of Corruption Act. There can be no dispute whatsoever about the powers and jurisdiction of the Court to tender conditional pardon. The law is settled that the pardon may be tendered at any stage of the proceedings before pronouncement of the judgment.

25. Moreover, the appellants and others in their criminal revision petitions before this Hon'ble Court for quashing of the order dated 8-5-1997 of the trial Court directing framing of charges against them had also questioned legality and propriety of order dated 9-4-1997 granting pardon to PW-1. The above petitions were dismissed on 12-9-1997 and the order granting pardon was not interfered with. The above judgment is reported as **1997 (5) AD (Del) 265, P.V. Narasimha Rao v. Central Bureau of Investigation.**

26. While dismissing the petition, the Court observed that there is nothing under section 164, Cr.P.C. which warrants the proposition that if a statement or confession is recorded during trial, the same becomes inadmissible and, in any case, it is not a defect of substance. The Court also held that the powers of Special Judge are not circumscribed by any condition excepting that the person must be one who is supposed to have been directly or indirectly concerned in or privy to an offence. The power so conferred can be exercised at any time after the case is received and before its conclusion. But, then before the Special Judge acts or tenders pardon, he must know the nature of the evidence the person seeking conditional pardon is likely to give, the nature of complicity and the degree of his culpability in relation to the offence and in relation to co-accused. After all it is duty of the Special Judge to be very cautious as to whom he admits to give evidence as an Approver and should carefully inquire to what extent this Approver, if mixed up with the transaction and if he be an accomplice, into the extent of guilt. This Court, in ultimate result held that the statement so recorded shall be admissible in evidence.

27. The appellants along with others also filed Special Leave Petitions in the Supreme Court impugning the order dated 12-9-1997 of this Court. The Special Leave Petitions were finally disposed of on 5-5-1999 after the constitution bench judgment dated 17-4-1998. It is important to note that the order dated 8-4-1997 of the trial Court granting pardon to PW-1 was not interfered with by the Supreme Court and met the approval of the Supreme Court and it is not open to agitate the same at this stage once again.

28. While disposing of the Special Leave Petitions, the Supreme Court left it for the trial Court to deal with other accused persons (other than the persons entitled for immunity under Article 105(2) of the Constitution) in accordance with law and so has allowed the trial to proceed ahead. Neither was any objection raised nor any clarification sought on the status of Approver by the appellants. The evidence already adduced by him during trial is hence admissible. The appellants cannot be allowed to question the legality or propriety of the order tendering pardon to PW-1 on this ground also.

29. Even if the statement recorded before the trial Court is by a person who could not have been made an Approver, his evidence will still be admissible and cannot be discarded as such once having been adduced. If the evidence is relevant, the Court is not concerned with the method by which it was obtained, as has been held in **Pushpadevi M. Jatia v. M.L. Wadhawan, Additional Secretary Govt. of India, (1987) 3 SCC 367: (1987 Cr LJ 1888).**

30. According to the learned Additional Solicitor General, the logic behind the scheme of grant of pardon as provided under section 5(2) of the Prevention of Corruption Act, in return for a full and true account of the offence, is to allay the fear of being prosecuted from the mind of the person making such disclosure. When PW-1 made the application for grant of pardon before the trial Court, he was an accused. Even if we take the contention of the appellants to be correct, for the sake of this argument, it would mean that the mind of the Approver is free from fear of prosecution and it will mean that the Approver is more trustworthy because he will not be liable for prosecution even if he deviated during the deposition as PW-1 from the facts stated by him in his statement under section 164, Cr.P.C.

STATEMENT OF APPROVER – CORROBORATED BY OTHER EVIDENCE – SUBMITTED – ADDITIONAL SOLICITOR-GENERAL

31. The learned Additional Solicitor General further submitted that even till today, the approver has not appeared before any competent authority or Court retracting from the facts stated by him in his deposition as PW-1. Thus the evidence adduced by the Approver has a high degree of reliability.

32. To establish the veracity of the statement of the Approver, the learned Additional Solicitor General submitted that the statement of the Approver stands substantially corroborated by independent evidence in all material particulars. The nature of corroboration is to be found in the judgment of the Supreme Court in **Rameshwar v. State of Rajasthan, AIR 1952 SC 54: (1952 Cr LJ 547)**, was contended that it is not necessary that there should be independent confirmation of every material substance but the corroboration from an independent source must be substantial rendering it probable that the story of the accomplice is true and that it is reasonably safe to act upon it. The nature of corroboration in this case, according to the learned Additional Solicitor General that has been brought on record is that in the monsoon session of 10th Lok Sabha in 1993, a No Confidence Motion against the Govt. headed by the appellant, Shri P.V. Narasimha Rao was moved. The appellant's Government was short by 14 votes to win the No Confidence Motion and required the support of MPs of other parties. It is also undisputed that at the relevant point of time, appellant, Shri Buta Singh, was the person competent to deal with the bribe-takers being in a position of the Home Minister in the Government. There was a meeting of JMM, MPs with appellant, Shri Buta Singh, and subsequently with the appellant, Shri Narasimha Rao. Discussions/bargaining took place for the purpose of buying over the votes of bribe-takers. The main aspect being the passing of money. Appellant, Buta Singh's trip to Bangalore and return to Delhi on the same day along with the other accused. Withdrawal of money from the Banks in Bangalore after the banking hours. Deposit of money in the bank accounts of 4 JMM, MPs immediately after opening fresh accounts. Efforts to fabricate the evidence regarding the receipt of money of coupons at a subsequent stage showing back dated receipt of money by JMM leaders by way of donation. Another chart submitted by the learned Additional Solicitor General in his written submissions shows a comparison between the statement under section 161 Cr.P.C., statement under section 164, Cr.P.C. and the deposition in Court as PW-1.

STATEMENT OF APPROVER – QUALIFIES ALL TESTS – SUBMITS ADDITIONAL SOLICITOR-GENERAL

33. It was submitted that while appreciating the evidence of an approver the Hon'ble Supreme Court in **Lachhi Ram v. State of Punjab, 1967 Cr LJ 671** held in para 9 that first test to be applied is that the Court should find that there is nothing inherent or improbable in the evidence given by the approver, and that there is no finding that the approver has given false evidence, the second test which thereafter still remains to be applied in the case of an approver, and which is not always necessary when judging the evidence of other witness, is that his evidence must receive sufficient corroboration.

34. Discrepancies and contradictions in the evidence of some witness, does not mean that the entire evidence of the prosecution is to be discarded. It is only after exercising caution and care and sifting the evidence to separate the truth from untruth, exaggeration, embellishments and improvements, the Court comes to the conclusion what can be accepted. Supreme Court has held that *"falsus in uno, falsus in omnibus"* is not a sound rule for the reason that one hardly comes across a witness whose evidence does not contain a grain of untruth or at any rate exaggeration, embroideries or embellishments; **AIR 1972 SC 2020: 1972 Cr LJ 1302 Sohrab v. State of Madhya Pradesh.**

35. The contradiction on ancillary or incidental matters of details or omissions of irrelevant details not going to the root of prosecution case in cases of nature at hand need not be given importance and do not detract the evidentiary nature of the statement of the approver.

36. Efforts should be made to find the truth, this is the very object for which Courts are created. One has to comprehend the totality of the facts and the circumstances as spelled out through the evidence, depending on the facts of each case, **[JT 1999 (1) SC 149: (1999 Cr LJ 1334) Mohan Singh v. State of Madhya Pradesh]** *"Falsus in Uno, Falsus in Omnibus"* does not apply to criminal trials and it is the duty of the Court to disengage the truth from falsehood, **Chand Khan v. State of Uttar Pradesh, (1995) 5 SCC 448**. The maxim *"Falsus in Uno, Falsus in Omnibus"*, is not a sound rule to be applied in India, **AIR 1973 SC 1409: (1973 Cr LJ 1120), Ranbir Singh v. State of Punjab).**

37. Inconsistencies here and discrepancies there, but that is a shortcoming from which no criminal case is free. The main thing to be seen is whether those inconsistencies etc. go to the Root of the matter, **AIR 1981 SC 1237: (1981 Cr LJ 743), Krishna Pillai Sree Kumar v. State of Kerala)**. Exaggeration and falsehood in prosecution evidence on points which do not touch the core of the prosecution story are not be given undue importance, **Dharam Das v. State of Uttar Pradesh, 1973 SCC (Cri) 765: (1973 Cr LJ 1181.**

38. Learned Additional Solicitor General also relied on a number of judgments of the Supreme Court in **Inder Singh v. The State (Delhi Administration), (1978) 4 SCC 161: 1978 Cr LJ 766; State of Punjab v. Jagir Singh, Baljit Singh and Karam Singh, (1974) 3 SCC 277: 1973 Cr LJ 1589; State of Himachal Pradesh v. Lekh Raj, JT 1999 (9) SC 43: 2000 Cr LJ 44; M. Narsinga Rao v. State of Andhra Pradesh, (2001) 1 SCC 691: 2001 Cr LJ 515; State of West Bengal v. Mir Mohammad Omar, 2000 (2) SCC (Cri) 1516: 2000 Cr LJ 4047; Pawan Kumar v. State of Haryana, (2001) 3 SCC 628: 2001 Cr LJ 1679; Yash Pal Mittal v. State of Punjab, (1977) 4 SCC 540: 1978 Cr LJ 189; Firozuddin Basheeruddin v. State of Kerala, JT 2001 (6) SC 547: (2001 Cr LJ 4215).**

GUILT OF THE APPELLANTS ESTABLISHED BEYOND DOUBT – SUBMITS – ADDITIONAL SOLICITOR-GENERAL

39. He submitted that once PW-1, Shri Shailender Mahto, the Approver, is a reliable witness, consequently both the appellants, namely, Shri P.V. Narasimha Rao and Shri Buta Singh would be guilty of charge under section 120B, IPC read with sections 12, 5(2) read with section 15(1)(d) of the Prevention of Corruption Act, 1988 as well as section 12 of the Act. In support of this contention learned Additional Solicitor General relied upon the following decisions of the Supreme Court in: **Girja Shanker v. State of Madhya Pradesh, 1989 Cr LJ 242 (MP); Jamuna Singh v. State of Bihar, AIR 1967 SC 553: 1967 Cr LJ 541; Faguna Kanta Nath v. State of Assam, AIR 1959 SC 673; Gallu Shah v. State of Bihar, 1958 Cr LJ 1352.**

40. Further he submitted that with the aid of section 10 of the Evidence Act, the Prosecution has been able to bring home the guilt of the accused beyond reasonable doubt. The accused persons were, well-informed, powerful and influential persons and the Prosecution painstakingly, with great professionalism, investigated and collected all possible material available which squarely points at the guilt of the appellants.

AFTER PERUSAL OF EVIDENCE AND CONSIDERATION OF SUBMISSIONS – DISCUSSION – HIGH COURT

41. The question that has arisen for my attention is whether PW-1, Shri Shailender Mahto, is a reliable witness and, if so, is the grant of pardon, in view of the judgment of the Supreme Court holding that he was shielded from prosecution on account of Article 105(2) of the Constitution, appropriate?

42. It is the admitted case of the parties that in the charge-sheet filed before the Special Court, PW-1, Shri Shailender Mahto, was an accused facing a charge framed against him. During the course of trial, the Supreme Court, *vide* its judgment dated 17-4-1998, held that he was protected from prosecution for his acts in Parliament under Article 105(2) of the Constitution.

43. Consequently, the status of Shri Shailender Mahto became clear and charges against him were dropped, but before this stage, his deposition had already been recorded by the Court as an accomplice/Approver. There is no gainsaying that the judgment of the Supreme Court declared the law, as was at the advent of the Constitution. In other words, Shri Shailender Mahto, enjoyed an immunity and could never have been prosecuted for the charge for which he was arrayed as an accused. The law on pardon is well-settled. It is a contract between the State and the individual in which the State bargains for a full and true disclosure within his knowledge relating to the offence and to every other individual person whether principal or an abettor in the commission of the crime. It is a surrender of the right of the State to prosecute the individual in the event of his being implicated in the crime by granting a pardon. The Supreme Court in **The State v. Hiralal Girdhari Lal Kothari, AIR 1960 SC 360: (1960 Cr LJ 524)** has held that "protection granted under section 337 of the Code of Criminal Procedure (now section 306/307, Cr.P.C. and section 5(2) of the Prevention of Corruption Act), is a protection from prosecution, failure to comply with the condition on which the pardon is granted, removes that protection". In other words, the grant of pardon carries an imputation of guilt and an acceptance thereof. A pardon is an act of grace which exempts the individual, on whom it is bestowed, from prosecution/punishment that the law may inflict for the act. A person to be entitled to pardon under section 5(2) of the Prevention of Corruption Act, must be directly or indirectly concerned with or privy to the offence. Such persons should then make a full and true disclosure of the circumstances within his knowledge relating to the offence as also identify other persons concerned with the commission of the crime be they principal or abettors. The person, if does not make a complete and full disclosure of circumstances within his knowledge, the pardon granted can be withdrawn. The pardon under section 5(2) of the Prevention of Corruption Act is deemed to be one under section 307 of the Code of Criminal Procedure.

44. The argument of learned counsel for the appellant that Shri Shailender Mahto, who enjoyed the immunity under Article 105(2) of the Constitution being a Member of Parliament alleged to have accepted bribe in connection with the voting in Parliament cannot be a person envisaged under section 5(2) of the Prevention of Corruption Act, would mean that the grant of pardon under section 5(2) of the Prevention of Corruption Act is bad in law. In other words, the Court granting pardon had no jurisdiction to do so. Undoubtedly, if the grant of pardon is without jurisdiction, the testimony of PW-1 cannot be used as an Approver nor can it be used as if he were an ordinary witness.

45. Having heard learned counsel for the parties and having bestowed my careful attention to the argument addressed before me, I deem it appropriate to reflect even at the cost of repetition on the conditions under which this case seen the light of the day. It is admitted case between parties that in the General Elections of the 10th Lok Sabha held in 1991, Congress (I) Party emerged as a single largest party and was called upon to form Government at the Center with Shri P.V. Narasimha Rao as Prime Minister. In 1993, during the monsoon session of Lok Sabha commencing on 26-7-1993, a No Confidence Motion had been moved against the Government by PW-14, Shri Ajay Mukhopadhayay. At that time the effective strength of the Lok Sabha was 528 of which Congress (I) Party had 251 Members. The Congress (I) Party needed 14 votes to avert the No Confidence Motion. The Congress Party, as a whole, including the Prime Minister was busy garnishing strength to infuse the much needed life blood. The Government did succeed in defeating the Motion by a slender margin. On the defeat of the Motion, there was hue and cry about the methods used to obtain the result. The question of use of money to buy support was serious enough to warrant a discussion in Parliament. The Nation watched against their Representatives discussing the state of affairs. It took three years for PW-1 to spill the beans before Shri Atal Bihari Vajpayee who, in turn, referred him to Shri Ram Jethmalani who heard PW-1 at length and dictated a Press Note which was released at a Press Conference. The revelation shocked the conscience of every right thinking person while the wheels of criminal justice stood jammed. Even Shri Jethmalani, a Senior Advocate, except for deriving political mileage and media coverage showed no inclination to set into motion the investigative machinery. In any event, the powers that controlled the system at the highest level were themselves allegedly responsible for flouting the rule of law, public morality and parliamentary discipline. It took Shri Ravinder Kumar, an Advocate, to move the High Court by way of a writ petition to get an FIR registered.

46. Being seized of the matter, it fell to the lot of the judiciary to goad the unwilling investigative agency, (the CBI), to investigate the complaint of Shri Ravinder Kumar. Finally, a report under section 173 Code of Criminal Procedure was placed before the trial Court forming the basis of a charge against 21 persons who were arrayed as accused. At the stage of arguments on charge, PW-1, Shri Shailender Mahto, turned Approver. The standard of investigation and the material placed before the Court can be gaged from the fact, that both parties have argued before me, that but for the statement of the Approver, PW-1, Shri Shailender Mahto, no case is made out against the accused persons. After the deposition of PW-1 was recorded, the legal mind went into top gear. Challenge was made to the framing of charge on the ground, *inter alia,* that accused being Members of Parliament were protected from prosecution under Article 105(2) of the Constitution. This controversy was finally put to rest by the Supreme Court which, by a majority judgment, reported in **(1998) 4 SCC 626: (1998 Cr LJ 2930),** held that some of the alleged bribe-takers were protected under Article 105(2) of the Constitution. Charge was amended against those accused who fell in the judicial drag-net. At the end of the trial only the appellants herein, namely, Shri P.V. Narasimha Rao and Shri Buta Singh were convicted while the others were acquitted.

STATEMENT OF APPROVER IS VALID AND ADMISSIBLE – HIGH COURT HELD

47. Coming to the question whether PW-1 could have been made an Approver, it would be proper to note that at the time of grant of pardon, there was no procedural or jurisdictional error and PW-1, who was an accused, could very well be granted pardon. The Supreme Court interpretation of law in respect of Article 105(2) of the Constitution, does set at naught a valid proceedings taken by a Court of competent jurisdiction. What was correctly admitted into evidence could not be wished away.

48. The effect of the law declared by the Supreme Court while interpreting Article 105(2) of the Constitution is, that those Members of Parliament who allegedly accepted illegal gratification and cast their vote in the proceedings of the No Confidence Motion were protected. This does not mean that a person envisaged under section 5(2) of the Prevention of Corruption Act could not be a person protected from prosecution within the narrow ambit of the judgment of the Supreme Court. The grant of pardon implies immunity from prosecution not only from the offence for which charge has been framed, but also allied offences which may arise consequent to the disclosure implicating the Approver. Therefore, it is legitimate for the Court to accept the grant of pardon to a person who is not an accused. A person who is not an accused but fears that he may be prosecuted on his disclosures can ask for pardon and the State in order to get information relevant to the case within his special knowledge may bargain, in the interest of the case, to secure conviction. Merely because a limited protection is granted under Article 105(2) of the Constitution is no ground to disentitle a person from turning Approver. There may be other offences for which he may be prosecuted.

49. In this view of the matter, the testimony of PW-1 is admissible and can be relied upon as that of an Approver. In **A. Devedran v. State of Tamil Nadu, (1997) 11 SCC 720: (1998 Cr LJ 814),** the question was of jurisdiction and, therefore, the Supreme court held that the individual who could not be made an Approver for want of jurisdiction, stood discarded, his testimony cannot be used at all for any purpose. Such a statement cannot be treated as that of an ordinary witness as the same would be hit by section 163 of the Code of Criminal Procedure and section 24 of the Indian Evidence Act. This is not the case here. The statement of the Approver is admissible.

APPROVER MADE STATEMENTS ON DIFFERENT DATES – TRIAL COURT BELIEVED HIS STATEMENT *QUA* APPELLANTS – BUT NOT *QUA* OTHERS – HELD HIGH COURT

50. Now, coming to the question of reliability of PW-1, the Approver. His statement has been attacked on various grounds by learned counsel for the appellants, namely, his competence as a witness on account of contradictions, improvements, omissions and confessed lies. To appreciate the challenge of learned counsel for the appellants, it is necessary to examine at length the material on record *qua* the various statements made by PW-1 at various times/occasions. The material which could legitimately be referred to, is the press statement dated 26-2-1996, confession application dated 16-3-1997, confession statement dated 22-3-1997 and deposition in Court dated 14-11-1997 to 28-11-1997.

51. There is no doubt that this witness has changed his stand from time to time. The trial Court, while appreciating his evidence, has chosen to disregard his statement qua the co-accused by taking recourse to the non-availability of material to corroborate the statement. However, while dealing with the case of Shri Buta Singh and Shri Narasimha Rao, the trial Court has found corroboration which corroboration was common to all the accused.

52. Coming to the relevant portion of the deposition of this witness regarding meeting of Shri Buta Singh, Shri Narasimha Rao and the JMM MPs on 26-7-1993, which is the cornerstone of the Prosecution's case, it would be relevant to extract the various statements made by the Approver.

In the Press release dated 26-2-1996, he has stated as under:

"In July 1993, *i.e.* two days before the voting on the No Confidence Motion, Shri Suraj Mandal, MP, telephoned me. I was told to come to the house of Shibu Soren, MP, at 51, Gurdwara Rakab Ganj Road. The time was of the evening. When I reached the house of Shibu Soren, there I found Simon Marandi, MP, and Suraj Mandal.

Suraj Mandal told us that we have to meet Shri Buta Singh and thereafter we have to go to meet the Prime Minister. We were further told that the Central Government is ready to accept our demand of formation of the Jharkhand Council provided we support the Government during the vote on the No Confidence Motion. All of us, at about 8 p.m., went to the house of Shri Buta Singh. From there, we went to the house of the Prime Minister at 7, Race Course road, with him. There, we along with Shri Buta Singh went inside and found the Prime Minister waiting for us. I clearly remember that Pradhan Mantri was sitting in a very pensive mood and posture. The Prime Minister requested us to take a seat.

Thereafter, Shri Buta Singh raised the issue of Jharkhand Council. He told the Prime Minister that he should resolve this issue at his personal level.

Shri Buta Singh further said that JMM should vote in favour of the Government during the No confidence Motion. The Prime Minister said that he would personally call for the file from the Home Minister and would resolve the issue. However, this may take some time. However, till then, I would also do something for you. He said that whatever has been talked between Shri Buta Singh and Suraj Mandal, shall also be fulfilled. At that time, I could not understand the exact context of above.

Thereafter, Suraj Mandal said that against our previous inclination to vote against, now we would vote against the No Confidence Motion. We all acted accordingly and voted against the No Confidence Motion. This saved the Government by two votes. In fact, Shri Buta Singh contacted us only after Shri Ajit Singh disappointed the Prime Minister."

53. In his confession application dated 16-3-1997, he states as under:

"On 26 July, 1993, the monsoon Session of the Parliament started. On the same day, the opposition parties moved a No Confidence Motion against the Government of Shri P.V. Narasimha Rao.

Same evening, on the invitation of Shri Buta Singh, we all the 4 MPs namely Shibu Soren, Suraj Mandal, Simon Marandi and Myself reached at his Government accommodation. While taking tea, Shri Buta Singh asked for our support in favour of the Congress Party and told us that the Prime Minister is remembering us. Thereafter, all 4 of us accompanied Shri Buta Singh to the residence of the Prime Minister at 7, Race Course Road, where we met the Prime Minister".

54. In his statement dated 22-3-1997, he has stated as under:

"At about 7 PM on 26-7-1993, Suraj Mandal telephoned me and informed that I should reach the house of Guruji (Shibu Soren) from where we have to proceed to the house of Shri Buta Singh. I reached at the house of Shibu Soren at 17, Gurdwara Rakab Ganj Road. From there, all of us went to the house of Buta Singh in a car. Buta Singh was waiting for us.

There, we sat in his drawing room and were offered tea. During the tea, he told us that the Prime Minister is remembering us. On this, Suraj Mandal replied that what is the use of the Prime Minister remembering us now as our matter of Jharkhand Council is still hanging fire and he has not found any solution for the same. On this, Buta Singh stated that if it is so, then we should directly talk to the Prime Minister on this issue. After having tea, we and Buta Singh proceeded to the house of the Prime Minister at 7, Race Course Road, in our respective vehicles. From the gate, we walked on foot and then sat in the waiting room. After sometime, we were called to the room of the Prime Minister. There, he was sitting alone in a pensive posture. Buta Singh started the talk by saying that when he was the Home Minister, the talks of formation of Jharkhand Council was initiated and a Committee was formed, and the said Committee gave its report as well.

Further, no decision has been taken on the said report. On this, Suraj Mandal also said that you have not taken any decision on the Jharkhand matter till date and therefore how can we support you. The Prime Minister told us that he would call for the file and would ensure personally that the work is completed. Thereafter, the Prime Minister, Buta Singh and Suraj Mandal went to a separate room. They talked for some time and then came out. The Prime Minister told all 3 of us waiting MPs that we should help him and he would also help us. The Prime Minister also stated that whatever has been talked with Suraj Mandal separately shall also be fulfilled. Thereafter we walked on foot upto the gate and from there Buta Singh went to his residence and we 4 MPs also came back."

On the way back, I asked Suraj Mandal that what was talked separately between 3 of you. Then, Suraj Mandal told that talks for our benefit have taken place. On this, Simon Marandi intervened and said that Suraj you should state more elaborately as to what was talked, otherwise we will not vote. On this, Mandal said that be patient as talks of money have also taken place. However, how much money would be paid, is still not clear. I was dropped at 51, South Avenue."

55. In his statement before the Court as PW-1, this witness deposed as under:

"On the evening of 26-7-1993 at 7.00 P.M. accused Suraj Mandal rang me up on telephone and told me to come to the house of accused Shibu Soren. I went to the house of accused Shibu Soren at 17, Gurdwara Rakab Ganj Road. We all four members of JMM (Soren Party) had collected at the house of Shibu Soren. Suraj Mandal told us that we were required to go to the house of Shri Buta Singh. From the house of Shibu Soren, myself, Shibu Soren, Suraj Mandal and Simon Marandi went to the residence of Shri Buta Singh in Ambassador Car. Shri Buta Singh was waiting for us. He made us sit in drawing room and served us with the tea. While we were having tea, accused Buta Singh present in the Court told us that Prime Minister had remembered us. Suraj Mandal replied "what would be there by Prime Minister remembering us as the matter of Jharkhand Council will still unresolved". On this accused Buta Singh suggested us to have direct conversation with the Prime Minister. Thereafter, we all went to the residence of Prime Minister, 7, Race Course Road. Buta Singh traveled in his own car with his security guards and we four went in our Ambassador car. We left the cars at the entrance gate and went inside the residence on foot. We sat in the waiting room for some time. After some time one security official came and accused Buta Singh went inside with him. After some time accused Buta Singh returned back and took us to meet the Prime Minister. Accused Shri P.V. Narasimha Rao was sitting in the room and we also sat there. Shri Buta Singh initiated the conversation by saying that the matter of Jharkhand Council was still unresolved. He further told the Prime Minister that during his tenure as Home Minister one committee was formed about Jharkhand matters and the said committee had already submitted its report. Despite of that matter of Jharkhand Council was unresolved. Accused Suraj Mandal intervened and said "you have not resolved the matter of Jharkhand and as such how can we support your Government". Accused Shri P.V. Narasimha Rao replied that he would summon the file of Jharkhand matter from Home Ministry and look into the matter and resolve it. He said at present you should help me. Thereafter, accused P.V. Narasimha Rao and Buta Singh went to the other room. After some time Suraj Mandal accused was also called to that room. We remained waiting in the first room. 5/6 minutes later, Shri P.V. Narasimha Rao, Buta Singh and Suraj Mandal came back to our room. Shri P.V. Narasimha Rao said "at present you should help me and in return I will also help you". He also said that "whatever conversation has taken place with Suraj Mandal, those promises shall be fulfilled. Thereafter, we all came on foot till main gate of the residence of Shri P.V. Narasimha Rao. Accused Buta Singh went away on his car and we returned back on our car and I was dropped at my residence. In the way I asked Suraj Mandal about the conversation which has taken place between him, Buta Singh and the Prime Minister. Suraj Mandal replied "Phayde ki baat hai". On this Simon Marandi said "Suraj tum spasht batao nahi to hum vote nahin denge". On this Suraj Mandal told "paise ke bhi baat hui hai, kitna paise milega abhi tai nahin hua".

No conversation regarding payment of money, took place in my presence at the residence of Prime Minister in the aforesaid meeting at the residence of Prime Minister. We had a conversation with the Prime Minister and we told him that if he was ready to accept our demand for creation of Jharkhand Autonomous council we would support the government.

It is correct that on 26-7-1993 Suraj Mandal rang me up. He told me on telephone to reach at the residence of Shibu Soren. Probably I might have stated to CBI during investigation that on 26-7-1993 Suraj Mandal came to my residence. In the evening of 26-7-1993 in pursuance of the message of Suraj Mandal, I visited the house of Shibu Soren. Perhaps I went to the residence of Shibu Soren on 26-7-1993 at 7.00 P.M. in an auto rickshaw. At that time, I did not have a car. From the residence of Shibu Soren on the same day we went to the house of Shri Buta Singh, in the car of Shibu Soren. I do not remember the make of said car. It is correct that in my examination dated 4-11-1997 I stated that we went to the house of Shri Buta Singh in Ambassador car. I do not remember, if I had previously stated somewhere that we went to the house of Shri Buta Singh in a Maruti Gypsy. I must have stated this to CBI on 20-6-1996. We met Shri Buta Singh at his residence on 26-7-1993. On the same day from the residence of Shri Buta Singh we went to the residence of Shri P.V. Narasimha Rao. At the house of Shri P.V. Narasimha Rao I did not have any direct conversation regarding money with him."

THREE STATEMENTS OF APPROVER MADE AT DIFFERENT TIME – SUFFER FROM MATERIAL CONTRADICTIONS – IMPROVEMENTS – HELD HIGH COURT

56. Analysing the three statements, it is evident that there are material contradiction/improvements made by this witness from stage to stage. In the Press release there is no invitation by Shri Buta Singh to the JMM, MPs. While in the confession application, the Approver has invited the element of invitation by Shri Buta Singh but there is no mention of going to the house of the Prime Minister. In the confession statement dated 22-3-1997, there is an omission of invitation and also going to the house of the Prime Minister. From further comparison between the Press release and the confession statement it is evident that there is a contradiction in the manner of meeting between the JMM, MPs, Shri Buta Singh and the Prime Minister. In one version he says JMM, MPs along with Shri Buta Singh together went inside and met the Prime Minister while in the later statement he says that initially only Mr. Buta Singh was called inside first and they were called inside later on. In the Press release dated 26-2-1996, which was admittedly prepared at the behest of Shri Ram Jethmalani, he does not speak of the close-door meeting between Shri Suraj Mandal, Shri Buta Singh and the Prime Minister, while in his confession statement dated 22-3-1997 this fact has been introduced for the first time, namely, "thereafter the Prime Minister, Shri Buta Singh and Shri Suraj Mandal went to a separate room. They talked for some time and then came out. The Prime Minister told all 3 of us waiting MPs that we should help him and he would help us. The Prime Minister also stated that whatever has been talked with Suraj Mandal separately shall also be fulfilled". Interestingly, in the Press statement, there is no separate "close door meeting" and the words attributed to the Prime Minister are – "he said that whatever has been talked between Shri Buta Singh and Shri Suraj Mandal, shall also be fulfilled" implying thereby that a meeting had taken place between Shri Buta Singh and Shri Suraj Mandal in the absence of the Prime Minister. This meeting obviously was not at the house of the Prime Minister and from the evidence it appears that the meeting between Shri Buta Singh, Shri Suraj Mandal and the JMM, MPs was regarding formation of the Jharkhand Council; money did not figure anywhere.

57. The confession statement dated 22-3-1997 is a clear improvement on his past statements where he has deliberately introduced two more elements *i.e.* separate meeting in separate room and also supports the separate meeting by saying that the Prime Minister said that whatever he has talked with Shri Suraj Mandal separately shall also be fulfilled. This is a material contradiction and gives an impression that these statements were made at the behest of the Prosecution as a bargain for this witness being treated as an Approver.

58. Coming to the statement of PW-1 as Prosecution witness, there are material contradictions with his earlier statements. In his confession statement dated 26-7-1993, the Approver states that the Prime Minister, Shri Buta Singh and Shri Suraj Mandal went to a separate room while in the statement in Court he says that initially Shri Narasimha Rao and Shri Buta Singh went to the other room and later on they called Shri Suraj Mandal. He further states that after the Prime Minister, Shri Buta Singh and Shri Suraj Mandal came out of the meeting, the Prime Minister told the Approver and other MPs that they should help him and he would help them while in his statement in Court he says that the Prime Minister, while discussing the matter with the other MPs, said that they should help him and he would help them. In his Press Conference he states that the Prime Minister said that whatever was talked between him, Shri Buta Singh and Shri Suraj Mandal, shall be fulfilled while in the confession statement he states that the Prime Minister told that whatever has been talked between Shri Suraj Mandal, shall be fulfilled. Again he omits to mention Mr. Buta Singh. This shows that in the so-called separate meeting, Shri Buta Singh was not present and, therefore, not a party to any understanding between the Prime Minister and Shri Suraj Mandal. These contradictions are material.

59. From an analysis of the material in the statements made by the Approver it appears that the question of money was never an item for discussion. Even as per the settled law, to make the statement of a co-conspirator relevant under section 10 of the Evidence Act, the accomplice should be the agent of any other co-conspirators to make him an accomplice. Here it is clear that even if Shri Suraj Mandal went in the separate room to talk to the Prime Minister and Shri Buta Singh, he had no authority or agency of the other JMM, MPs to talk about money and the only issue which could have been discussed by him was formation of Jharkhand Council as that was the only issue on which JMM, MPs were working from the beginning when they contacted Mr. Buta Singh and also the Prime Minister. Therefore, even if it is assumed that a separate meeting took place in the separate room, then at the best it was an independent conspiracy between the Prime Minister, Shri Buta Singh and Shri Suraj Mandal and since no other person was present, only one out of the three could be a relevant witness under section 10 of the Evidence Act. In so far as the Approver is concerned, since he was admittedly not there in the meeting, he is not a co-conspirator in respect thereof and accordingly his statement is neither relevant nor admissible under section 10 of the Evidence Act. In fact, the same is barred under section 60 of the Evidence Act as it is only hearsay. Accordingly, the testimony of the Approver is liable to be rejected on this score. Reference may be had to **(1998) 3 SCC 410: 1998 Cr LJ 1905, CBI v. V.C. Shukla; (1998) 4 SCC 351: 1998 Cr LJ 2251, State of Gujarat v. Mohammed Atik; (1999) 5 SCC 253: 1999 Cr LJ 3124, State v. Nalini.**

STATEMENT OF APPROVER BEING FULL OF CONTRADICTIONS MAKE HIM UNRELIABLE – CANNOT BECOME BASIS OF CONVICTION – HELD HIGH COURT

60. It is the law of evidence that the story of a person especially of the Approver must be consistent and logical. Therefore, omissions and contradictions cannot be overlooked and statement of the Approver could be hit by section 155 of the Indian Evidence Act as the testimony stands impeached and discredited. There are material contradictions, improvements and omissions regarding the meeting on 24/25-7-1993 between the JMM, MPs and Shri Ajit Singh. There are material contradictions and improvements regarding the talks between Captain Satish Sharma and Shri Simon Marandi, also regarding meeting between the JMM, MPs and Shri Ashok Rao Deshmukh on 25-7-1993 as well as regarding meeting with Shri Rajeshwar Rao on 26-7-1993. There are contradictions, improvements and omissions regarding meeting of the JMM MPs with Shri Sita Ram Kesari on 26-7-1993 in Parliament House; regarding event leading to payment of money on 29-7-1993; regarding payment to Shri Ram Lakhan Singh Yadav Group; regarding events of payment of money on 30-7-1993, 31-7-1993 and 1-8-1993; regarding Press Conference dated 26-2-1996; regarding his statement made in Parliament on 29-2-1996; regarding the details of meeting with Shri Ram Jethmalani and Shri Atal Bihari Vajpayee; regarding signing of Resolution dated 11-7-1993; regarding the bail application before the trial Court; regarding threats extended to the Approver and his family and also regarding contradictions and improvements with respect to statement under section 161 Code of Criminal Procedure which was put to the witness. He is blatant enough to state that his statement in Parliament on the subject of his taking money pursuant to the Press Conference was a lie. It is difficult to place reliance, for the purpose of conviction, on such a witness. His statement is riddled with material contradictions/ improvements making it unreliable, therefore, ought to be discarded.

61. If there was an substance in the conspiracy theory propounded by the Prosecution by introducing a "close door meeting" between the Prime Minister, Shri Buta Singh and Shri Suraj Mandal, there is no reason why this important facet was not got corroborated by independent evidence. PW-1 relating the entire story to Shri Atal Bihari Vajpayee, who then sent him to Shri Ram Jethmalani. There too this witness narrated the entire incidence. On the basis of the information supplied to Shri Ram Jethmalani, a press Note was prepared where this important aspect of a close door meeting is missing. It is not possible that Shri Ram Jethmalani, a Senior Advocate, having extensive practice on criminal side could have overlooked this important facet of "close door meeting" had it been told to him. Even otherwise, the

Prosecution knew very well that the cornerstone of their case lies in the statement of the Approver insofar as he has introduced the "close door meeting" with the Prime Minister, Shri Buta Singh and Shri Suraj Mandal. There was nothing stopping them from corroborating this important fact by calling Shri Ram Jethmalani and of Shri Atal Bihari Vajpayee into the witness box.

The very fact that the prosecution, knowing its case fully well did not deliberately examine Shri Atal Bihari Vajpayee or Shri Jethmalani as prosecution witnesses, shows that this introduction by the Approver of the "close door meeting" was merely a "red herring". To give further instances of the unreliability of PW-1, he is also a self-confessed liar admittedly making false statements. He states "my statement to CBI during investigation as well as statement dated 29-2-1996 in the Parliament had no relation with truth". He further admits "I did not tell the CBI about meeting with Shri Narasimha Rao and Shri Suraj Mandal in the separate room. I must have concealed this fact from CBI before recording my aforesaid statement. I was advised by CBI Officers to narrate the truth. It is correct that some other CBI officer recorded my statement on 20-6-1996. He thoroughly examined me for about three hours. I do not remember if on 20-6-1996, I did not tell the Investigating Officer about separate meeting between PM, Buta Singh and Suraj Mandal in a separate room. Further, he admits that "I do not remember if during my interrogation dated 12-9-1996 I was asked about the details of meeting which took place at the residence of Shri P.V. Narasimha Rao. I do not remember if in the said statement, I did not mention about meeting between PM, Suraj Mandal and Buta Singh in a separate room".

It is admitted by the witness that "it is correct that Shri Buta Singh did not talk about money with me. It is also correct that in my presence the talks which took place with Shri Buta Singh were only in relation to creation of Jharkhand Council. It is correct that it was the agenda of JMM to ensure creation of separate Jharkhand State since 1971-72. It is correct that during his tenure as Home Minister Shri Buta Singh had taken interest in the issue of creation of Jharkhand and his Ministry recommended creation of separate Jharkhand Council. It is correct that when the issue of No Confidence Motion came up, we four JMM, MPs discussed and decided to exploit the situation for obtaining creation of Jharkhand. When we met Shri Buta Singh we told him that our demand for creation of Jharkhand Council was not fulfilled and on this he suggested a meeting with Shri P.V. Narasimha Rao and told "let's go and resolve this issue with the Prime Minister". It is admitted by the witness that "no conversation regarding payment of money took place in his presence at the residence of Prime Minister".

It is further admitted by this witness that "it is correct that prior to my statement dated 22-3-1997, I did not disclose it in my earlier statement about the fact that while coming from the residence of Shri P.V. Narasimha Rao I asked Suraj Mandal the nature of conversation which took place between him, Shri Buta Singh and Shri P.V. Narasimha Rao and on this Suraj Mandal replied that it was of our benefit and thereafter Simon Marandi intervened and told Suraj Mandal to clearly specify the conversation failing which he threatened that he would not vote in favour of the Govt. and on this Mandal replied that talks regarding money has taken place but quantum has not been settled".

62. The law regarding appreciation of evidence of an Approver is quite clear. Firstly, he must be a reliable witness and, if found to be reliable, then his statement must be corroborated by independent witness in material particulars. Reference may be had to **AIR 1957 SC 637: (1957 Cr LJ 1014), Sarwan Singh Rattan Singh v. State of Punjab,** where the Supreme Court has held (Para 7):

> "In other words, the appreciation of an approver's evidence has to satisfy a double test. His evidence must show that he is a reliable witness and that

is a test, which is common to all witnesses. If this test is satisfied the second test which still remains to be applied is that the approver's evidence must receive sufficient corroborations. This test is special in the cases of weak or tainted evidence like that of the approver".

63. Reference may also be had to **(1996) 5 SCC 368: 1996 Cr LJ 3842, Alil Mollah v. State of West Bengal,** where the Court has held that (Para 6):

"Conviction can be based on the testimony of a single eye-witness provided the Court finds from the scrutiny of his evidence that if he is wholly reliable witness. Where, however, the Court is of the opinion that the single eye-witness is only partly reliable, prudence requires that corroborations of his testimony in material particulars should be sought before recording conviction."

CORROBORATION OF APPROVER'S STATEMENT SHOULD BE BY AN INDEPENDENT EVIDENCE – NOT BY HIS OWN STATEMENT – TAINTED EVIDENCE DOES NOT LOSE TAINT BY REPETITION – NOT BELIEVABLE – HELD HIGH COURT

64. The statement of PW-1 is being sought to be corroborated by his statement under section 164, Code of Criminal Procedure. Such corroboration is impermissible. The statement under section 164, Code of Criminal Procedure cannot be used to corroborate the testimony of a witness who needs to be corroborated by material particulars by independent evidence. The corroboration must necessarily come from source de hors, the Approver or an accomplish. There is no such material in the entire case and the only corroboration is the statement under section 164, Code of Criminal Procedure cannot be used to corroborate the testimony of a witness who needs to be corroborated by material particulars by independent evidence.

The corroboration must necessarily come from source de hors, the Approver or an accomplish. There is no such material in the entire case and the only corroboration is the statement under section 164 Code of Criminal Procedure of the Approver. It is well settled that a witness who needs corroboration cannot corroborate himself by any statement made earlier or later. His evidence needs to be corroborated by independent evidence and his own previous statement cannot be said to be independent evidence. **AIR 1952 SC 54: (1952 Cr LJ 547), Rameshwar s/o Kalyan Singh v. The State of Rajasthan,** deals with evidence of an accomplish. It lays down that there must be an additional evidence rendering it probable that the story of the accomplish is true and it is reasonably safe to act upon it. The independent evidence must not only make it safe to believe that crime was committed but, must in some way, reasonably connect or tend to connect the accused with it by confirming in some material particulars the testimony of the accomplice or complainant that the accused committed the crime. The corroboration must come from independent source and thus ordinarily the testimony of one accomplice would not be sufficient to corroborate that of another.

In the present case, the material particulars is the "close door meeting" for which the only additional evidence is the money lying in the bank which has not been connected with the appellants herein. Moreover, this has been disbelieved by the trial Court and there is no appeal against this finding. In the present case, the total evidence against Shri Buta Singh and Shri P.V. Narasimha Rao is the separate meeting between them and Shri Suraj Mandal for about 5-6 minutes where, according to the Prosecution, the money deal was settled. Therefore, the only incriminating act of Shri Buta Singh is coming to another room with Shri P.V. Narasimha Rao and Shri Suraj Mandal and their deciding about money deal. It was incumbent upon the Prosecution to lead evidence to corroborate this incidence which is woefully absent.

On the contrary, the fact of the matter is that is no previous statement other than under section 164, Code of Criminal Procedure this meeting is highlighted.

It is settled law that where important evidence or allegations are not disclosed by witness at the earliest occasion or when it would have been natural for him to disclose, does amount to contradiction (section 162, Cr.P.C. Explanation). In **Mohd. Hussain Umar Kochra v. K.S. Dalipsinghji, AIR 1970 SC 45,** the Supreme Court has held "that combined effect of sections 133 and 144, Illustration B, is that though a conviction based upon accomplice evidence is legal, the Court will not accept such evidence unless it is corroborated in material particulars, the corroboration must connect the accused with the crime. It may be direct or circumstantial. It is not necessary that corroboration should confirm all the circumstances of the crime. It is sufficient if the corroboration is in material particulars. Corroboration must be from an independent source. One accomplice cannot corroborate the other". **AIR 1949 PC 257: (1949 (50) Cr LJ 872), Bhuboni Sahu v. The King,** lays down "the statement made by an Approver under section 164, Code of Criminal Procedure plainly does not amount to corroboration in material particulars which the Courts require in relation to evidence of an accomplice. An accomplice cannot corroborate himself. Tainted evidence does not lose its taint by repetition."

Criminal Revision Petition No. 33 of 2001

REVISION FILED AGAINST THE ACQUITTAL OF OTHERS – SUBMISSIONS BY THE CBI

65. Coming to the revision petition, this revision petition seeks to challenge the acquittal of Capt. Satish Sharma, Shri V. Rajeshwar Rao, Shri H.M. Revenna, Shri Ramalinga Reddy, Shri M. Veerappa Moily, Shri D.K. Audikesavulu, Shri M. Thimma Gowda, Shri Bhajan Lal and Shri Ajit Singh. It was argued by learned Senior Counsel, Shri P.N. Lekhi, that while deciding the revision petition, the Courts need to have a creative legal approach and that such an approach was necessitated for reasons that the law makers themselves have chosen to trample the Rule of Law. Creative criminology is the need of the 21st Century because of mounting political and other corruptions. He relied upon the judgments of the Supreme Court to advance his arguments on this score. The following judgments were referred to:

66. Sunil Batra v. Delhi Administration, AIR 1978 SC 1675: 1978 Cr LJ 1741; The State of Karnataka v. Ranganatha Reddy, AIR 1978 SC 215; R. v. Lambert, (2001) 3 All ER 577; Rajendra Prasad v. State of Uttar Pradesh, AIR 1979 SC 916: (1979 Cr LJ 792); Nidamarti Maheshkumar v. State of Maharashtra, AIR 1986 SC 1362; Candler v. Crane Christmas and Co., (1951) 1 All ER 426; State of Uttar Pradesh v. Kishori Lal Minocha, AIR 1980 SC 680; Warehousing and Forwarding Company of East Africa Ltd. v. Jafferali and Sons, Ltd., (1963) 3 All ER 571; Midland Bank Trust Co. Ltd. v. Hett, Stubbs and Kemp, (1978) 3 All ER 571; Henderson v. Merrett Syndicates Ltd., Hallam-Eames v. Merrett Syndicate Ltd., Hughes v. Merrett Syndicate Ltd., Arbuthnott v. Feltrim Underwriting Agencies Ltd., Deeny v. Gooda Walker Ltd., (1994) 3 All ER 506 and Dalbir Singh v. State of Punjab, AIR 1979 SC 1384: (1979 Cr LJ 1058).

67. He submitted that by order dated 8-4-1997 the trial Court granted pardon to PW-1, Shri Shailender Mahto. In his deposition, PW-1 has referred to special events which were to take place in Parliament. He has referred to Capt. Satish Sharma, Shri Ajit Singh, Shri Ashok Rao Deshmukh and Shri V. Rajeshwar Rao and has pointed out that Shri Suraj Mandal told them that Shri Rajeshwar Rao had offered a meagre amount and, therefore, it was suggested that they meet Shri P.V. Narasimha Rao. He has also mentioned about Shri Buta Singh waiting for the JMM, MPs to take them to a meeting with Shri P.V. Narasimha Rao. This witness has also referred to the meeting with Shri Sita Ram Kesri and his appeal to the JMM, MPs to save the Government with the assurance that whatever Shri P.V. Narasimha Rao had promised shall be fulfilled. PW-1 has also deposed to the effect that Shri Rajeshwar Rao told them that they would be paid rupees fifty lakhs each, a petrol pump and a plot in HUDA. He has also stated that Shri Ram Lakhan Singh Yadav was going to join Congress. This witness has also deposed receiving of bribe money and the manner in which it was deposited in the Punjab National Bank. He has described the happenings of 2-4-1996 at Ranchi Airport when his signature was obtained in the Minute Book of the JMM Party on a back-dated document, the purpose being to create evidence regarding printing of party coupons for collecting party funds although in 1993 when he was the General Secretary of his party no books of accounts were maintained. In fact, no meeting of the Executive of the Central Committee of JMM ever took place in Delhi.

68. Learned counsel further submitted that PW-4, Capt. Dilwar Singh, who was cross-examined by the Public Prosecutor, has referred, amongst others, to Capt. Satish Sharma, Shri Ajit Singh, Shri Bhajan Lal, Shri Shibu Soren, Shri Suraj Mandal, Shri Ram Lakhan Singh Yadav, Shri Anadi Charan Das, Shri Abhay Pratap Singh and Shri Ram Sharan Yadav and has given a graphic description of the activities in the residence of Shri Ajit Singh, Shri Ram Lakhan Singh Yadav etc. and also overheard the telephonic conversation. He has admitted sending of Ex.PW-4/A which, in fact, in his written admission of all the facts that were recorded in his statement under section 161 of the Code of Criminal Procedure. Learned counsel submitted that a hostile witness could very well be relied upon and in this case, PW-4, Capt. Dilawar Singh has corroborated the testimony of PW-1. Devender Mukhia, PW-2 filed an affidavit before the High Court regarding his meeting with Shri Bhajan Lal, Capt. Satish Sharma, Shri Simon Marandi, Shri Shailender Mahto, Shri Ram Lakhan Singh Yadav, Shri Vidya Charan Shukla and Shri B.N. Safaya and has admitted doing so in his cross-examination. The facts contained in the affidavit were denied by him before the trial Court but the Court can always, while appreciating evidence, remove the chaff from the grain. PW-74, B.N. Safaya has denied knowing anybody of the name of Shri Simon Marandi. He has also denied having made a statement to the CBI indicating the receipt of funds though in his statement under section 161 of the Code of Criminal Procedure, he has given a detailed account of the amounts received from various sources and also the role he played in disbursing it to various accused persons. His pretended ignorance and his resiling from the statement under section 161, Cr.P.C. is an act to cover up.

69. PW-75, R.K. Dayal, according to the learned counsel, was directed by the Editor of his paper to go to the residence of Shri Ram Lakhan Singh Yadav. He was hounded out of that place but he could see many people entering the house of Shri Ram Lakhan Singh Yadav on the day when No Confidence Motion was to be debated and the photographs he took are Ex. PW-75/D published in the newspaper issue dated 29-7-1993. These photographs show, amongst others, Capt. Satish Sharma, Shri Bhajan Lal, Shri Jitender Prasad and Shri Karunakaran visiting the house of Shri Ram Lakhan Singh Yadav. Except for Shri Ram Lakhan Singh Yadav, all the abovenamed were on 28-7-1993 members of the political party to Shri P.V. Narasimha Rao. Shri Karunakaran was the Chief Minister of Kerala, Shri Bhajan Lal was the Chief Minister of Haryana and Shri Veerappa Moily was the Chief Minister of Karnataka. It is clear that all these Chief Ministers were put on the job to muster sufficient number of MPs to defeat the No Confidence Motion. PW-86, Raj Kumar Jain, has supported the testimony of PW-1, Shri Shailender Mahto since he neither admitted nor denied the questions put to him. The statement of PW-77, Shashi Ruia, tallies with the statement of PW-74, B.N. Safaya, which he gave to the CBI. The conspiracy to collect money is proved by the fact that money was available with Shri P.V. Narasimha Rao to keep his Government in power and all the accused persons were part of that conspiracy. The trial Court erred in not noticing that circumstantial evidence existed.

70. Learned counsel submitted that PW-60, Padmanabha Rao, Chief Manager of Canara Bank, Bangalore, proved withdrawal of rupees one crore on an application signed by Shri M. Thimme Gowda. This amount was paid in cash against the cheques. Shri Thimme Gowda did not lead evidence to show how the cash withdrawal was utilized by him or his firm. Learned counsel, therefore, submitted that benefit of doubt given in the case of acquitted accused is fanciful. He submitted that exaggerated devotion to the Rule of benefit of doubt must not nurture fanciful doubts. Letting guilty escape is not doing justice according to law, as held in, **Gurbachan Singh v. Satpal Singh, (1990) 1 SCC 445: (1990 Cr LJ 562).** Learned counsel further submitted that it is the duty of the Court to make genuine effort to unearth the realities, as held in **Mohan Singh v. State of Madhya Pradesh, (1999) 2 SCC 428: (1999 Cr LJ 1334).** He further submitted that giving of benefit of doubt was an act of vacillating mind, the Court should have looked into the matter from the balance of probabilities.

SUBMISSIONS OF THE RESPONDENTS IN THE REVISION PETITION – AND THE LAW RELIED UPON BY THEM – HIGH COURT

71. Learned counsel appearing on behalf of the respondents in the revision petition have primarily confined their arguments to the parameters set down by the Supreme Court while dealing with the cases of acquittal and revisions at the instance of the complainant.

72. In **D. Stephens v. Nosibolla, AIR 1951 SC 196: 1951 Cr LJ 510,** the Supreme Court held that in cases of revision against acquittal, the Court ought not to interfere with orders of acquittal. It should do so only on exceptional grounds. It further held as under:

> "10. The revisional jurisdiction conferred on the H.C. under section 439, Criminal P.C., is not to be lightly exercised, when it is invoked by a private complainant against an order of acquittal against which the Government has a right of appeal under section 417. It could be exercised only in exceptional cases where the interests of public justice require interference for the correction of a manifest illegality, or the prevention of a gross miscarriage of justice. This jurisdiction is not ordinarily invoked or used merely because the lower Ct. has taken a wrong view of the law or misappreciated the evidence on record."

73. In **Harihar Chakravarty v. State of West Bengal, AIR 1954 SC 266: 1954 Cr LJ 724** the Supreme Court has reiterated what was stated in **D. Stephens'** (supra) case at para 11. In **K. Chinnaswamy Reddy v. State of Andhra Pradesh, AIR 1962 SC 1788: 1963 (1) Cr LJ 8,** the Supreme Court has held that:

> "(7) It is true that it is open to a High Court in revision to set aside an order of acquittal even at the instance of private parties, though, the State may not have thought fit to appeal, but this jurisdiction should in our opinion be exercised by the High Court only in exceptional cases, when there is some glaring defect in the procedure or there is a manifest error on a point of law and consequently there has been a flagrant miscarriage of justice. Sub-section (4) of section 439 forbids a High Court from converting a finding of acquittal into one of conviction and that makes it all the more incumbent on the High Court to see that it does not convert the finding of acquittal into one of conviction by the indirect method of ordering retrial, when it cannot

itself directly convert a finding of acquittal into one of conviction. This places limitation on the power of High Court to set aside a finding of acquittal in revision and it is only in exceptional cases that this power should be exercised. It is not possible to lay down the criteria for determining such exceptional cases which would cover all contingencies. We may however would indicate some cases of this kind, which would in our opinion justify the High Court in interfering with a finding of acquittal in revision. These cases may be; where the trial Court has no jurisdiction to try the case but has still acquitted the accused or where the trial Court has wrongly shut out evidence which the prosecution wished to produce or where the appeal Court has wrongly held evidence which was admitted by the trial Court to be inadmissible, or where material evidence has been overlooked either by the trial Court or by the appeal Court, or where the acquittal is based on a compounding of the offence, which is invalid under the law. These and other cases of similar nature can properly be held to be cases of exceptional nature, where the High Court can justifiably interfere with an order of acquittal; and in such a case it is obvious that it cannot be said that the High Court was doing indirectly what it could not do directly in view of the provisions of section 439(4). We have therefore to see whether the order of the High Court setting aside the order of acquittal in this case can be upheld on these principles."

74. In **Mahendra Pratap Singh v. Sarju Singh, AIR 1968 SC 707: (1968 Cr LJ 665)** the Supreme Court held that:

"8. The practice on the subject has been stated by this Court on more than one occasion. In **D. Stephens v. Nosibolla, 1951 SCR 254: AIR 1951 SC 196: 1951 Cr LJ 510,** only two grounds are mentioned by this Court as entitling the High Court to set aside an acquittal in a revision and to order a retrial. They are that there must exist a manifest illegality in the judgment of the Court of Session ordering the acquittal or there must be a gross miscarriage of justice. In explaining these two propositions, this Court further states that the High Court is not entitled to interfere even if a wrong view of law is taken by the Court of Sessions or if even there is misappreciation of evidence. Again, in **Logendranath Jha v. Polailal Biswas, 1951 SCR 676: AIR 1951 SC 316,** this Court points out that the High Court is entitled in revision to set aside an acquittal if there is an error on a point of law or no appraisal of the evidence at all. This Court observes that it is not sufficient to say that the judgment under revision is "perverse" or "lacking in true correct perspective." It is pointed out further that by ordering a retrial, the dice is loaded against the accused, because however much the High Court may caution the Subordinate Court, it is always difficult to re-weigh the evidence ignoring the opinion of the High Court. Again in **K. Chinnaswamy Reddy v. State of Andhra Pradesh, 1963 (3) SCR 412: AIR 1962 SC 1788: (1963) 1 Cr LJ 8,** it is pointed out that an interference in revision with an order of acquittal can only take place if there is a glaring defect of procedure such as that the Court had no jurisdiction to try the case or the Court had shut out some material evidence which was admissible or attempted to take into account evidence which was not admissible or had overlooked some evidence. Although the list given by this Court is not exhaustive of all the circumstances in which the High Court may interfere with an acquittal in revision it is obvious that the defect in the judgment under revision must be analogous to those actually indicated by this Court. As stated not one of these points which have been laid down by this Court was covered in the present case. In fact on reading the judgment of the High Court it is apparent to us that the learned Judge has reweighed the evidence from his own point of view and reached inferences contrary to those of the Sessions Judge on almost every point. This we do not conceive to be his duty in dealing in revision with an acquittal when Government has not chosen to file an appeal against it. In other words, the learned Judge in the High Court has not attended to the rules laid down by this Court and has acted in breach of them."

AFTER PERUSAL OF EVIDENCE AND CONSIDERATION OF SUBMISSIONS – DISCUSSION – HIGH COURT

75. In the present revision petition, none of these points, which have been laid down by the Supreme Court, arise. The Supreme Court has further held in **Khetra Basi Samal v. State of Orissa, AIR 1970 SC 272: 1970 Cr LJ 369,** that:

"10. This Court has had to examine the jurisdiction of the High Court under this section on several occasions. In **D. Stephens v. Nosibolla, 1951 SCR 284: AIR 1951 SC 196: 1951 Cr LJ 510,** it was pointed out (*see* at p. 291 of SCR): (at p. 199 of AIR) that:

"The revisional jurisdiction conferred on the High Court under section 439 of Code of Criminal Procedure is not to be lightly exercised, when it is invoked by a private complaint against an order of acquittal, against which the Government has a right of appeal under section 417. It could be exercised only in exceptional cases where the interests of public justice require interference for the correction of a manifest illegality, or the prevention of a gross miscarriage of justice. This jurisdiction is not ordinarily invoked or used merely because the lower Court has taken a wrong view of the law or misappreciated the evidence on record."

Again in **Logendranath Jha v. Polailal Biswas, 1951 SCR 676: AIR 1951 SC 316** where the High Court had set aside an order of acquittal of the appellant by the Sessions Judge and directed their re-trial, this Court, (see at p. 681 of SCR – at p. 318 of AIR) said:

"Though sub-section (1) of section 439 authorises the High Court to exercise, in its discretion, any of the powers conferred on a Court of appeal by section 423, sub-section (4) specifically excludes the power to convert a finding of acquittal into one of conviction." This does not mean that in dealing with a revision petition by a private party against an order of acquittal, the High Court could in the absence of any error on a point of law re-appraise the evidence and reverse the findings of facts on which the acquittal was based, provided only it stopped short of finding the accused guilty and passing sentence on him. By merely characterizing the judgment of the trial Court as "perverse" and lacking in perspective, the High Court cannot reverse pure findings of fact based on the trial Court's appreciation of the evidence in the case."

11. In **K. Chinnaswamy Reddy v. State of Andhra Pradesh, 1963 (3) SCR 412 (418): AIR 1962 SC 1788 (1791),** the Court proceeded to define the limits of the jurisdiction of the High Court under section 439 of the Criminal Procedure Code while setting aside an order of acquittal. It was said:

"..................... This jurisdiction should in our opinion be exercised by the High Court only in exceptional cases when there is some glaring defect in the procedure and there is a manifest error on a point of law and consequently there has been a flagrant miscarriage of justice................ It is not possible to lay down the criteria for determining such exceptional cases which would cover all contingencies. We may however indicate some cases of this kind, which would in our opinion justify the High Court in interfering with a finding of acquittal in revision. These cases may be: where the trial Court has no jurisdiction to try the case but has still acquitted the accused, or where the trial Court has wrongly shut out evidence which the prosecution wished to produce or where the appeal Court has wrongly held evidence which was admitted by the trial Court to be inadmissible, or where material evidence has been overlooked either by the trial Court or by the appeal Court or where the acquittal is based on a compounding of the offence, which is invalid under the law."

12. It may be that a case not covered by any of the contingencies mentioned above may still arise. But, where, as here, the appeal Court (the High Court in this case) has set aside the order of acquittal almost entirely on the ground that the Magistrate should not have disbelieved the three eye-witnesses, viz. P.Ws. 1, 2, and 5, the case clearly falls within the contingencies mentioned in the above decision of this Court. The High Court judgment does not show that the trial Court shut out any evidence which the prosecution wanted to produce or admitted any inadmissible evidence or overlooked any material evidence. The Magistrate examined the evidence produced by the prosecution.................................. The High Court proceeded to re-appraise the evidence of the witnesses and upset the finding of the Magistrate thereon on the ground that he "had not taken the trouble of sifting the grain from the chaff." Clearly such a course is not permissible under section 439 of the Criminal Procedure Code."

76. Further, the Supreme Court has in, **Chaganti Kotaiah v. Gogneni Vankateshwara Rao, AIR 1973 SC 1274: 1973 Cr LJ 978)** held that:

"19. We are of the opinion that the entire approach made by the High Court in dealing with the Criminal Revision filed against acquittal by the private party is contrary to the principles laid down in the decisions referred to above. Notwithstanding the fact that sub-section (4) of section 439 does not authorize the High Court to convert a finding of acquittal into one of conviction, it has in fact contravened this provision by recording a finding of guilt against the accused and directing the trial Court to convict them after a retrial. There is no question of lack of jurisdiction in the trial Court to try the case; nor was any attack made that any evidence has been shut out at the trial. Whether the dying declaration, Ex. P. 15, by Ratnababu can be taken into account regarding the attack on Koteswara Rao, is a matter which the trial Court was entitled to decide one way or the other. If its view was wrong, the High Court could have gone into that aspect and differed from this opinion of the Sessions Court if the State had filed an appeal against acquittal. Further the mere fact that the learned trial Judge held that this piece of evidence is not relevant, while considering the attack on Koteswara Rao, does not amount to shutting out of evidence at the trial. In fact that evidence has already come on record. Therefore, in this case there has been no shutting out at the trial of any evidence which the prosecution wanted to adduce or the defence wanted to lead. All available evidence has been let in by both the prosecution and the accused.

20. Nor can it be stated that there has been any glaring defect in the procedure or a manifest error on a point of law and consequently leading to a flagrant miscarriage of justice. As mentioned earlier, sub-section (4) of section 439 forbids a High Court from converting a finding of acquittal into one of conviction by an indirect method of ordering retrial when the High Court itself cannot directly convert a finding of acquittal into a finding of

conviction. The High Court, in our opinion, has missed these very important limitations on its power to set aside the findings of acquittal in revision which could be done only in very exceptional circumstances. In the case on hand, the High Court was not justified in considering the evidence in such detail if it was really going to order a retrial. Such a detailed consideration of evidence and an expression of opinion about the guilt of the accused, in our opinion, has really loaded the dice against the accused when the case goes back for retrial. Much stress has been laid by the High Court that though substantive charges had been framed against the accused read with section 34 or alternatively with section 149, IPC, the trial Court has not recorded any finding in this regard. Here again, the High Court's view is erroneous. We have already referred to the finding recorded by the trial Court that in view of the definite case of the prosecution and the nature of the evidence, none of the accused can be held constructively liable. It is on that ground that the Trial Court has not found the accused constructively guilty.

21. We have indicated the reasons, which promoted the High Court to order a retrial. The consequence of this will be to put considerable, strain on the accused who have already gone through a trial at considerable stress and expenses. After going through the judgment of the learned Sessions Judge, we cannot certainly say, particularly in view of the evidence on record that either the acquittal of the twenty-two accused or the acquittal of the eight convicted accused of the rest of the charges was not justified. At any rate, it may be safely stated that the learned Sessions Judge has taken into account all the relevant circumstances. It may be that there are slight mistakes in some of the reasons given by him but the judgment as a whole shows that he has really applied his mind to the various pieces of evidence before passing the order of acquittal in the manner he has done. In the particular circumstances of this case, the interference in revision by the High Court at the instance of the private party was not justified. The two appeals filed by the convicted accused, namely, Criminal Appeals Nos. 201 and 202 of 1969 have not been dealt with by the High Court on merits. The appellants therein have a right to have those appeals heard and disposed of by the High Court according to law."

77. To the same effect is the judgment of the Supreme Court in **Pakalapati Narayana Gajapathi Raju v. Bonapalli Peda Appadu, AIR 1975 SC 1854: (1975 Cr LJ 1646) (at para 3)**. Similarly, recourse may be had to the decision of the Supreme Court in **Bansi Lal v. Laxman Singh, AIR 1986 SC 1721: 1986 Cr LJ 1603 and Vimal Singh v. Khuman Singh, (1998) 7 SCC 223: (1998 AIR SCW 3326.**

SUPREME COURT HAS LAID DOWN LIMITS IN WHICH HIGH COURT CAN EXERCISE REVISIONAL JURISDICTION – CONSIDERATION OF THIS REVISION PETITION FALLS OUTSIDE ITS SCOPE – HELD HIGH COURT

78. In view of the law on the subject clearly defining the limits in which the High Court can exercise its powers, what has to be seen is, therefore, whether the trial Court has committed any of these errors which would justify this Court from exercising its revisional jurisdiction. Learned counsel has not brought to my notice any evidence which has been wrongly admitted or not considered or, if admitted, not considered and/or any other defect or illegality which may necessitate an interference by this Court. Bound by the law laid down by the Supreme Court, judicial propriety and discipline, I have no option but to hold that where the trial Court has appreciated the evidence and there is no illegality by admitting inadmissible material or any perversity, it would not be open for this Court to set aside its order merely because another opinion is possible on the same evidence.

79. Before parting, I must express my appreciation for the labour put in by learned counsel for the parties and for rendering great assistance in this case; a special mention is due in the case of learned Additional Solicitor General, Shri K.K. Sud, who has conducted the case with great fairness and professionalism.

CRIMINAL APPEAL FILED BY P.V. NARSIMHA RAO AND BUTA SINGH ACCEPTED – JUDGMENT OF THEIR CONVICTION AND SENTENCE SET ASIDE – REVISION PETITION FILED BY STATE (CBI) AGAINST ACQUITTED PERSONS DISMISSED – HIGH COURT

80. In view of the above discussion, I allow Cri. A. 638 of 2000 and Cri. A. 621 of 2000, set aside the judgment of conviction and sentence of the Special Judge dated 29-9-2000 and 12-10-2000 and acquit the appellants of all charges. I also dismiss Criminal Revision Petition No. 33 of 2001.

Order accordingly.

THE TRIBUNE

116TH YEAR OF PUBLICATION

Chandigarh: Thursday, May 16, 1996

Vajpayee invited to form govt

To prove majority by May 31

From K. Sriram

Tribune News Service

NEW DELHI, May 15 – President Shankar Dayal Sharma today named the Bharatiya Janata Party leader, Mr Atal Behari Vajpayee, as the new Prime Minister and invited him to be sworn in along with his team at noon tomorrow. Mr Vajpayee was further asked to prove his party's majority on the floor of the House by May 31.

The President did not lose any time in inviting the BJP to form its first government at the Centre after the Election Commission formally conveyed to him that the eleventh Lok Sabha had been duly constituted with the elections for 534 seats having been completed.

Within moments of the formal presentation to him by the Chief Election Commissioner, Mr T.N. Seshan, and the Election Commissioners, Mr G.V.G. Krishnamurthy and Mr M.S. Gill, the President called Mr Vajpayee in for what most newspersons gathered in the forecourt of Rashtrapati Bhavan thought was a consultation meeting.

After his 15-minute meeting with the President, Mr Vajpayee came towards the waiting newspersons and announced with a deadpan expression that he had been appointed Prime Minister by the President and asked to prove his majority in the House by May 31.

Mr Vajpayee, drove straight to the Pandara Road house of the BJP President, Mr L.K. Advani, to personally convey the happy tidings to him. The two leaders readily posed before another battery of photographers even as boxes of sweets were opened with much gaiety.

THE TRIBUNE

CHANDIGARH, THURSDAY, MAY 16, 1996

VAJPAYEE INVITED TO FORM GOVERNMENT

To prove majority by May 31

From K. Sriram, Tribune News Service:

NEW DELHI, MAY 15.—President Shankar Dayal Sharma today named the Bharatiya Janata Party leader, Mr. Atal Behari Vajpayee, as the new Prime Minister and invited him to be sworn in along with his team at noon tomorrow. Mr. Vajpayee was further asked to prove his party's majority on the floor of the House by May 31.

The President did not lose any time in inviting the BJP to form its first Government at the Centre after the Election Commission formally conveyed to him that the eleventh Lok Sabha has been duly constituted with the elections for the 534 seats having been completed.

Within moments of the formal presentation to him by the Chief Election Commissioner, Mr. T.N. Seshan and the Election Commissioners, Mr. G.V.G. Krishnamurthy and Mr. M.S. Gill, the President called Mr. Vajpayee in for what most newspersons gathered in the fore-court of Rashtrapati Bhavan thought was a consultation meeting.

After his 15-minutes meeting with the President, Mr. Vajpayee came towards the waiting newspersons and announced with a deadpan expression that he had been appointed Prime Minister by the President and asked to prove his majority in the House by May 31.

Mr. Vajpayee drove straight to the Pandara Road House of the BJP President, Mr. L.K. Advani, to personally convey the happy tidings to him. The two leaders readily posed before another battery of photographers even as boxes of sweets were opened with much gaiety.

THE TRIBUNE

116TH YEAR OF PUBLICATION

Chandigarh: Thursday, May 16, 1996

Rao accepts verdict

NEW DELHI, May 15 (PTI) – The outgoing Prime Minister, Mr P. V. Narasimha Rao, today said that the Congress accepted the people's verdict in the Lok Sabha elections with "humility" and pledged to continue with the twin objective of ending

poverty and sustaining a rapid rate of growth.

"You had given me and my party the privilege and the honour of serving this country for the past five years. You have now given a different verdict. We accept your decision with humility," he said in a farewell broadcast over AIR and Doordarshan.

Asserting that his government had steadfastly pursued the national goals of unity, integrity, secularism and stability, Mr Rao said: "We pledge ourselves afresh at this juncture to continue the pursuit of these goals."

Page 16

THE TRIBUNE

Chandigarh, Thursday, MAY 16, 1996

RAO ACCEPTS VERDICT

NEW DELHI, May 15 (PTI)—The outgoing Prime Minister, Mr. P.V. Narasimha Rao, today said that the Congress accepted the people's verdict in the Lok Sabha elections with "humility" and pledged to continue with the twin object of ending poverty and maintain a rapid rate of growth.

"You had given me and my Party the privilege and honour of serving this country for the past five years. You have now given a different verdict. We accept your decision with humility," he said in a farewell broadcast over AIR and Doordarshan.

THE TRIBUNE

116TH YEAR OF PUBLICATION

Chandigarh: Friday, May 17, 1996

Vajpayee sworn in Prime Minister

Tribune News Service

NEW DELHI, May 16 — Mr Atal Behari Vajpayee was today sworn in as the country's 11th Prime Minister by President Shanker Dayal Sharma at a simple, 20-minute ceremony at the Rashtrapati Bhawan here.

An 11-member Council-of-Ministers, comprising Mr Sikandar Bakht, Mr Suraj Bhan, Mr Ram Jethmalani, Mr Murli Manohar Joshi, Mr V. Dhananjay Kumar, Mr Pramod Mahajan, Mr Karia Munda, Mr Suresh Prabhakar Prabhu, Mr Sartaj Singh, Mr Jaswant Singh and Mrs Sushma Swaraj, was also sworn-in along with him as part of the first-ever BJP-led government at the Centre.

"We will give an honest and sensitive government to the people," Mr Vajpayee declared shortly after the swearing-in ceremony.

Sitting by the side of outgoing Prime Minister P.V. Narasimha Rao, the 71-year-old BJP leader told enquiring newspersons that he would be able to demonstrate a support of majority of the MPs on the floor of the House by May 31. Asked as to whether he would seek the support of the Congress, Mr Vajpayee said, "Ask Mr Rao."

Mr Narasimha Rao declined to answer queries from newsmen saying that as Mr Vajpayee was the groom today, the press should direct its queries to him.

THE TRIBUNE

Chandigarh, Friday, May 17, 1996

VAJPAYEE SWORN-IN PRIME MINISTER

NEW DELHI, MAY 16—Mr. Atal Behari Vajpayee was today sworn-in as the country's 11th Prime Minister by President Shankar Dayal Sharma at a simple, 20-minute ceremony at the Rashtrapati Bhawan here.

An 11-member Council-of-Ministers, comprising Mr. Sikandar Bakht, Mr. Suraj Bhan, Mr. Ram Jethmalani, Mr. Murli Manohar Joshi, Mr. V. Dhananjay Kumar, Mr. Pramod Mahajan, Mr. Karia Munda, Mr. Suresh Prabhakar Prabhu, Mr. Sartaj Singh, Mr. Jaswant Singh and Mrs. Sushma Swaraj, was also sworn-in along with him as part of the first-ever BJP-led government at the Centre.

"We will give an honest and sensitive government to the people," Mr. Vajpayee declared shortly after the swearing-in ceremony.

Sitting by the side of outgoing Prime Minister P.V. Narasimha Rao, the 71-year-old BJP leader told enquiring newspersons that he would be able to demonstrate a support of majority of the MPs on the floor of the House by May 31. Asked as to whether he would seek the support of the Congress, Mr. Vajpayee said, "Ask Mr. Rao"

Mr. Narasimha Rao declined to answer queries from newsmen saying that as Mr. Vajpayee was the groom today, the press should direct its queries to him.

Vajpayee Government could not last long. It could not succeed in getting the vote of confidence on the floor of the House. VAJPAYEE REMAINED AS PRIME MINISTER TILL 1 JUNE, 1996.

Then the coalition led by Janata Party supported by Congress came in power. H.D. Deve Gowda being the leader of the Janata Party took over as Prime Minister on 1 June 1996 who remained as Prime Minister till 21 April, 1997. Then another combination of Janata Party coalition, supported by Congress came into power and Shri I.K. Gujral took over as Prime Minister on 21 April, 1997 and remained in power till 19 March 1998.

Lok Sabha was dissolved and fresh elections were ordered. In the fresh elections for 12th Lok Sabha NDA(BJP and its allies) emerged as the largest group. Shri Atal Behari Vajpayee as leader of the NDA took over as Prime Minister on 19 March, 1998. He lost the Trust vote on 17 April, 1999 on the floor of the Lok Sabha by the narrowest margin-one vote. His resignation was accepted by the President of India and he continued as caretaker Prime Minister till 13 October, 1999.

12th LOK SABHA SABHA WAS DISSOLVED AND fresh elections were ordered. In the fresh elections to the 13th Lok Sabha, NDA (BJP and its allies) got absolute majority and the leader of the BJP, MR. ATAL BEHARI VAJPAYEE WAS SWORN IN AS PRIME MINISTER FOR A THIRD TERM on 13 October, 1999, A DISTINCTION HE SHARED WITH TWO OF HIS PREDECESSORS, JAWAHARLAL NEHRU AND INDIRA GANDHI. Shri Atal Behari Vajpayee completed full term upto 22nd May, 2004 as his Government had ordered the fresh elections about 6 months earlier than its due date. Then the Congress party came in power and Dr. Manmohan Singh took over as Prime Minister on 22nd May, 2004. This Government won two parliamentary elections and Dr. Manmohan Singh continued as Prime Minister upto 26th May, 2014.

In the elections held in April-May 2014, BJP got absolute majority and allies separately. Shri Narinder Modi took over as Prime Minister on 26th May, 2014.

SUBJECT INDEX

D

T

U

NAME INDEX

S

T

U

V

•••